Scented Flora of the World

Roy Genders spent a lifetime in horticulture, and his gardening books have been read in all parts of the world. Many of his articles have appeared in *Countryman*, *Country Fair*, *Lady*, *Farmers' Weekly*, *Popular Gardening* and other magazines.

Scented Flora of the World

ROY GENDERS

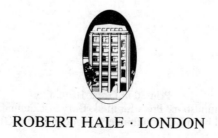

ROBERT HALE · LONDON

© *Roy Genders 1977 and 1994*
First published in Great Britain 1977
This paperback edition 1994

ISBN 0 7090 5440 8

Robert Hale Limited
Clerkenwell House
Clerkenwell Green
London EC1R 0HT

2 4 6 8 10 9 7 5 3 1

Printed in Great Britain by
St Edmundsbury Press Limited, Bury St Edmunds, Suffolk
Bound by WBC Bookbinders, Bridgend, Mid-Glamorgan

This book is dedicated
with gratitude and in honour
of the late
James Verner Claypool
and to his wife and family
Irma Hartley Claypool
James Hartley Claypool
David Woodward Claypool
Caroline Claypool Chisholm
Elisabeth Claypool Dudley
Ann Claypool Stiles
Judith Claypool Bowman

Contents

II ALPHABETICAL GUIDE

Appendices

Classified Lists

Acknowledgements

I wish to thank Miss Anne Bonar for revising and correcting the nomenclature of the plants to Kew standards. She is well qualified to do so and I am most grateful to her. My thanks are also due to Margaret Ness for so patiently sorting out my copious notes made over many years and for making them readable and to Doris Gatling for preparing and typing the Index.

Wherever appropriate, the culture of the plants described in this book is given, either for indoors or in the open, so that it will be a practical guide to growing scented plants.

I have tried to describe the many different scents as accurately as possible but these vary slightly between one person and another.

March 1977   R.G.

PART I

HISTORY, CLASSIFICATION AND EXTRACTION OF SCENTS

1

Scented Flowers and Leaves in History

The Garden of Eden—The early spice traders—Temples of the Nile—
The Holy Anointing Oil—Perfumes of the East—Scented flowers in
medieval Britain—Plants for strewing—Scented waters and powders—
The early gardening—The new gardening

The Garden of Eden. The first book of Moses called Genesis, written some 4,000
years before the birth of Christ—at about the time the Temple of the Sphinx
and the great pyramid of Cheops were built—tells how 'the Lord God planted
a garden eastward in Eden and out of the ground made the Lord God grow
every tree that is pleasant to the sight and good for food . . . and a river went
out of Eden to water the garden'. We do not know whether the trees were
fragrant, nor is there any mention of flowers in Genesis, for trees and ferns were
the first plants to cover the earth's surface, providing food and shade from the
heat of the sun.

The river which watered the Garden of Eden 'became four heads', one of
which, named Pison, irrigated the land called Havilah where gold was to be
found, and bdellium and onyx. There have been various translations of
'bdellium', one being 'crystal', but the Greek word of the same spelling was the
name given to the *Balsamodendron* from which an aromatic gum is obtained and
which the Scriptures call myrrh. If such a derivation is correct, this is the first
mention of a scented plant that we have.

Myrrh was from earliest times recognized as the most valuable possession of
civilized man, for the use of alcohol in which to dissolve the essential oils of
flowers was unknown, and myrrh was the only substance which could provide
a powerful and lasting scent. It is a yellow gum-resin secreted by the prickly
shrub *Balsamodendron myrrha*, found in Arabia and in that region irrigated by
the Tigris and Euphrates which was known as Babylonia at the time of Moses.
Here, at the junction of the two mighty rivers, was supposedly situated the
earthly paradise, the Garden of Eden.

Sir William Willcocks, who surveyed the entire region at the beginning of the
twentieth century, concluded that the Babylonian Tablets of the Creation were
correct in naming this vast low-lying land Eden, which in the language of the
inhabitants signified 'a plain'. It was, in the time of Moses, approximately at the

centre of the civilized world which extended from the Nile in the west to India in the east, and from the southernmost tip of Arabia to the Black and Caspian Seas in the north. It is an area of intense heat and aridity and from earliest times was the centre of the perfume trade. Here were to be found the most potent of the scented woods and leaves from which resinous gums were obtained.

Early man must surely have been aware of the preservative properties of spices and gums as well as their value for flavouring food and drink. The cooling properties of trees and shrubs with scented foliage were also appreciated by those who inhabited the warmer parts. Not only did they provide shade but brought about a reduction in the air temperature around them. They were also appreciated for their powers of refreshment and recuperation from the production of ozone formed by the oxidization of the volatile oils. Newton in the *Herbal of the Bible* (1597) said that it was the custom for the peoples of Palestine at that time to stick branches of fresh green leaves over their beds because of their cooling properties; and for the same reason they would bedeck their living-rooms with fragrant foliage.

The ancient Egyptians were the first people to show an appreciation of perfume, using them for religious rites and funeral honours, and also for their toilet, massaging their bodies with fragrant oils to give elasticity to their sun-baked skin.

The Early Spice Traders. The Egyptians first began to import aromatics about 2000 B.C., and according to Genesis they were carried to Egypt by Ishmaelite traders who went 'from Gilead, with their camels, bearing spices and balm and myrrh'. Ancient Ishmaelia, situated in the most southerly part of Palestine, was then the hub of the important caravan routes which traded spices and aromatics. It later became the kingdoms of Edom and Moab, territory now under Jordanian sovereignty.

The 'balm' mentioned in Genesis was not, however, the celebrated Balm of Gilead which was later cultivated around Jericho in the mountainous country of Gilead, situated between the Sea of Galilee and the Dead Sea; this plant, *Commiphora opobalsam*, grew only in the southernmost part of Arabia, called *Felix Arabia*, until introduced into Palestine during the time of Solomon—it formed one of the gifts brought to him by the Queen of Sheba whose country occupied that part of Arabia now known as Yemen.

The 'balm' carried by the traders was most likely the exudation of *Pistacia lentiscus*, a fragrant terebinthine obtained by making incisions in the stem and which appears as pale-yellow transparent drops. Known in commerce as 'Mastic', it was used by the Egyptians for burning as incense and by the children of Palestine to chew, for it was believed to strengthen the teeth and gums. At a later date the Greeks flavoured a liquor with the gum.

In Joseph's time, Jericho was the principal trading post for aromatics and spices, many of which arrived by camel and donkey train from Babylon on the Euphrates. One of the most highly prized aromatics brought by the traders was spikenard, whose scented roots were obtained from the valleys of the Himalayas. From Babylon, the caravans would follow the Euphrates in a northerly direction, stopping first at the royal city of Mari, the most important city in the East until overrun by the Babylonians in 1700 B.C. From Mari, the caravan would turn westwards, crossing the inhospitable Syrian Desert by way of the oasis at Palmyra, still a watering stop for tribesmen, then southwards to Damascus. From here, the traders would follow the green valley of the Jordan as far south as Jericho on the northerly shores of the Dead Sea, and there unload their precious cargo for the Ishmaelite traders to collect.

Their next destination was Canaan, the strip of land extending from Hamath to Gaza, along the Mediterranean coastline. It was also the central market for the purple dye, famed throughout Egypt and used by the royal household for colouring their robes. This dye was obtained from the shellfish murex which took on its deep-purple colouring only when out of the water and directly exposed to the heat of the sun. It was so precious a commodity that Canaan was known as the 'Land of Purple' and no caravan train would make the journey into Egypt without taking with it at least a small amount. From this time, purple became the symbolic colour of royalty throughout the world for it was so costly that no other people could afford to use it. In the Greek language, the dye was called *Phoenicia* and those who collected it were the Phoenicians, a people who occupied that part of Canaan to the north of the Sea of Galilee extending to the Mediterranean. Here too grew the dense cedar forests of Mount Lebanon, indigenous only to that area. The cedar is one of nature's most handsome creations, growing to a great height and spreading out its branches horizontally for a considerable distance, the evergreen leaves appearing in small tufts like those of the larch. The Egyptians believed that the wood of the cedar was imperishable and that it had the property of preserving for ever anyone it enclosed. It was therefore much in demand by the Pharaohs for the building of ships and for making the doors of their temples. It was also used for coffins, and the fragrant wood was burnt as incense as an offering to the gods. Cedarwood oil was used to rub over the body after bathing and was included in the most expensive cosmetics and unguents.

Ishmaelia was also the terminus of another important spice route taken by the caravans bringing frankincense and myrrh from Yemen, and known as the Incense Road. Frankincense exudes from the smooth-barked tree or shrub *Boswellia serrata,* all parts of which are fragrant. After myrrh, its fragrant gum was the most prized substance of the East and was the one most widely used as incense. Like myrrh it was found only at the southernmost tip of Arabia and on the coast of Somaliland where it grows on rocky hillsides and in desert ravines, and its collection and transportation presented the utmost difficulty. Here 'in fortunate Arabia', wrote Dionysius, 'you can always smell the sweet perfume of marvellous spices, whether it be incense or myrrh', for both grew plentifully in the spice kingdoms of Minaea and Sheba. Here, gardens of unprecedented beauty were washed by a great natural dam which collected the waters of the River Adhanat. The lush vegetation resembled that of Eden when it was watered by the Tigris and Euphrates, and the kings and queens of southern Arabia were able to exploit the favourable situation to the advantage of their country. Almost daily, the spice caravans travelled along the tortuous coastal road of the Red Sea; they had to cover 1,200 miles and frequently came under attack from marauding tribesmen.

For 2,000 years, this distant corner of Arabia continued to supply the civilized world with frankincense. Then, in about 1000 B.C., the empire of Solomon, which extended from Jerusalem to Damascus and as far south as the flourishing port of Ezion-Geber on the Gulf of Aqaba, caused serious difficulties for those using the Incense Road. For the first time, it was necessary to pass through Israeli territory before continuing the journey into Egypt, and Israel, now a prosperous empire, showed no friendliness at all towards its neighbours in the south. At this time, however, Sheba was ruled by a queen who, besides her fabulous beauty, was an astute businesswoman and a superlative diplomat. Realizing that a hostile Israel could terminate the lucrative trade with Egypt on which her country's economy depended, she lost no time in dispatching her agent to Jerusalem to arrange an immediate interview with Solomon. Chronicles tell how 'she came to prove Solomon with hard questions at Jerusalem, with a great company, and with camels that bare spices, and gold in abundance, and precious stones'. It was no easy task for a woman to undertake a journey of more than 2,000 miles across some of the most desolate country in the world, and it proves Sheba's queen to have been a woman of considerable daring. Solomon must have been greatly impressed by the courage and business acumen of his guest; 'and when she was come to Solomon she communed with him of all that was in her heart'.

Temples of the Nile. On the walls of the magnificent temple at Der-al-Bahari in Upper Egypt, built in 1500 B.C., by Queen Hatshepsut, there is a relief painted in the most brilliant colours which depicts the traffic in the precious resins and gums. It describes in great detail the expedition which set out from Ezion-Geber on the queen's behalf to far-away Punt, a legendary place in Somaliland, situated at the easternmost tip of Africa. Five barges left the chief port of the Red Sea laden with copper and turquoise to be exchanged for thirty-one incense trees, together with a cargo of ebony, sandalwood, ivory and apes. The relief shows how the incense trees were brought back, with roots in deep boxes and probably covered with soil to prevent them from drying out. According to Pliny these trees were so sacred that, when removing the gum for use in the temples, the men were to be kept free from pollution.

There are numerous reliefs which tell of the extensive use of incense and perfumes in ancient Egypt. Fragrant woods were first used as offerings to the gods and burnt on altars in temples, the daily ritual being performed by the priests who lived in compounds attached to the temple. They were provided with food and wine and with linen for their clothes whilst large quantities of incense were stored in rooms specially set aside for the purpose.

The word perfume, from the Latin *per*, 'through', and *fumum,* 'smoke', shows that the origin of the word lay in the burning of incense, both to 'offer up' the gratitude of the people to the gods for favours received, and to ask for their blessing in time of trouble. The Egyptians believed that their prayers would reach the gods more quickly, wafted by the blue smoke which slowly ascended to heaven, and the belief persisted. Since the heavy intoxicating smoke also brought on religious ecstasies, the burning of incense was employed in all forms of primitive worship.

Every temple at Luxor and at Memphis smoked with the fragrant woods of Arabia at the more important festive occasions, whilst offerings were made in the streets and in the homes of the people. Karnak, situated on the left bank of the Nile, near Thebes, was the largest and greatest Egyptian temple. Here an inscription and a relief show the commanding figure of Ramses III exhorting Amun to bring him victory in battle and reminding him that he has already sacrificed 30,000 oxen to him and 'sweet smelling herbs and the finest perfumes'.

At Heliopolis, where the sun was worshipped under the name of Re, incense was burnt thrice daily. Resinous gums were offered with the rising of the deity; myrrh when in the meridian; and a concoction of sixteen fragrant herbs and resins at the setting. This was the most expensive offering made and was known as *Kyphi* or *Khepri*. It was described by Plutarch and Dioscorides, and was adopted by the Greeks and Romans at a later date. According to the French chemist Loret, its chief constituents were *Acorus calamus, Andropogon, Schoenanthus,* cassia, cinnamon, peppermint, *Pistacia* and *Convolvulus scoparius,* which were dried and powdered and then mixed together. Equal quantities of juniper, acacia, henna and *Cyperus longus* were macerated in wine and added to honey, resin, myrrh and raisins steeped in wine. The whole concoction was beaten up, made into a paste and allowed to solidify. It was then ready to be placed in the burner as an offering to Re who reigned supreme at Heliopolis until the founding of the royal house at Thebes and the inauguration of the new god Amun. From the days of Chephren, builder of the Sphinx, the kings took the title 'Son of Re', and retained it until the time of Cleopatra.

Plutarch said that the aromatic substances included in the perfume *Kyphi* 'lulled one to sleep, allayed anxieties and brightened dreams', that the perfume was 'made of those things that delight most in the night', from which it would appear that the incense was burnt at night in the homes of those who could afford to buy it as well as for an offering to Re.

Democrates said that spikenard, crocus (saffron) and bdellium were also included in the recipe, and this is confirmed by Plutarch. Myrrh was also mixed into the perfume *Mendesium,* the other ingredients being oil of ben and cinnamon, which was found in Nepal and Sikkim and is the *Kayu-gadis* of Malaya. The fragrant bark may have found its way into Persia and Babylonia from the valleys of the Himalayas, together with the hairy roots of *Nardostachys jatamansi,* the spikenard of the Scriptures. They were the most prized of aromatics for, although obtained under extremely difficult conditions, they never deteriorated during transportation, their fragrance actually increasing the drier they became.

Cinnamon was also used in the perfume known as *Metopium,* which contained honey, wine, resinous gums (including myrrh) and almonds. It was rubbed on the feet and legs and, like most of the concoctions made in the temples which contained only wine and honey and natural herbs, was also taken internally to sweeten the breath.

At the opening of the tomb of Tutankhamen in 1922 a large number of exquisitely made vases were discovered, some of them containing unguents which, when opened, released a faint but quite distinctive perfume. The vases which were of calcite had been sealed by the crystallization of salts in the unguent, and the contents, though solidified, released the smell of spikenard when melted by the warmth of the hand.

At a meeting of the British Association held at Oxford in 1926, Chapman and Plenderleith described the detailed analysis they had made of the substance, concluding that about 90 per cent of it consisted of animal fat, and that its scent was due mostly to the presence of olibanum or gum-resins of local origin, together with some matter resembling Indian spikenard. The substance was described by those who made the discovery as being somewhat sticky, 'consisting of yellow nodules, together with a chocolate coloured body'. Dating from 1350 B.C., it had retained its scent for more than 3,000 years and confirmed the opinions of Herodotus and Democrates who, on visiting Egypt during the Hellenistic period, declared that the people were masters of the art of perfumery.

It was during this period that the Egyptians became familiar with the art of floral extraction as depicted on the walls of the great temple of Edfu, sixty miles south of Luxor and begun by Ptolemy III in 237 B.C. This relief shows perfume being distilled from the flowers of the white Madonna lily, *Lilium candidum*, one of the oldest plants still to be found in cottage gardens everywhere. A floral perfume, green in colour, was also obtained from the flowers of the Henna, every part of which is fragrant; known as *Cyprinum*, it was heavy and lasting, and is believed to have been used to drench the sails of the royal barges during the Hellenistic period.

Their belief in the transmigration of souls led the Egyptians to take great care in embalming the bodies of the dead. After the intestines were removed, oil of cedar was injected and other perfumes such as myrrh and cassia. The body was then kept in natron solution for 70 days to dry out the flesh, and afterwards it was wrapped in linen smeared with scented gums before being placed in a case made of cedar wood.

The use of perfumes for sacred rites was gradually adapted to private use, for the Egyptians were the first people of refined tastes and habits. Perfumes and unguents for anointing the body were manufactured in the laboratories of the temples. One such room can be identified in the temple at Edfu: on the walls are numerous inscriptions which clearly reveal the manner in which unguents and perfumes and ritual oils were made, the most subtle scents taking as long as six months to mature. The priests alone were in charge of perfumery and in the temples was stored the greater part of all the aromatics brought into the country. They were kept in pots and vases made of onyx, alabaster and glass and in beautifully carved boxes of wood or ivory.

Both men and women of high rank considered perfume an essential accessory. Though the men only used them for festive occasions, the women, during the Late Period, improved their appearance with all manner of cosmetics. Indeed, the women of Thebes, who had a reputation for beauty, used a number of paints and powders for beautifying the face and body, including henna (*Lawsonia inermis*) leaves to rub on the cheeks and hands for creating a rosy tint, kohl, made from antimony, to accentuate the beauty of the eyes, and scented oils to pour over the body.

In the beautiful temple of Hatshepsut at Thebes, carved out of the mountain face, there is a painting in the most brilliant colours which shows a lady of the court going through the daily routine of her toilet. She is attended by four maidens, two of whom pour fragrant oil over her body whilst a third massages her shoulder with one hand and, with the other, holds up a lotus flower for her to smell. The fourth maiden holds a polished copper mirror before her, that metal having been introduced into Egypt by Ammenemes III in about 1800 B.C. Later, when the copper mines of Sinai became exhausted, mirrors and em-balming tools were made of bronze. Censers and wine bottles were also made of copper or bronze, though a material known to the Egyptians as 'brilliant' soon became fashionable. This was a type of quartz which was given an enamel-like finish after being dyed with the brilliant blue and green compounds of copper. But alabaster was most commonly used to store unguents on account of its density and coolness which prevented rapid evaporation.

With each dynasty the use of perfumes increased and with the advent of the Macedonian princess Cleopatra, who governed Egypt from the city founded by her countryman Alexander the Great in 336 B.C., they were used in abundance. Cleopatra, who ruled from 40 to 30 B.C. when the kingdoms conquered by Alexander had already fallen to the Romans, seduced Mark Antony by her lavish use of perfume in the hope of recovering her lost territories. At her first meeting with the Roman the purple sails of her barge were saturated with perfume, for Nile barges, dyed with the symbolic purple of royalty, were washed with scented waters for all state occasions. Perfume bottles, made of glass or terracotta, were prominent amongst the gifts presented to important visitors. In the British Museum there is a scent bottle of Egyptian design, made of richly coloured glass and dating from the fifth century B.C. It was discovered on the island of Rhodes and dates from the time of the domination of the country by Alexander the Great. It was probably given to a person of high rank when on a visit to Egypt.

Herodotus, the Greek historian who visited Egypt on several occasions during the Hellenistic period, and described the country, its people and customs, saw slaves at festive banquets anointing the heads of the guests whose wigs of human hair gave protection from the heat of the sun. Each guest was also crowned with a chaplet of scented flowers, white Madonna lilies, the saffron crocus, and that sacred and most fragrant of all flowers, the lotus. Wreaths of fragrant leaves hung from the walls to cool the atmosphere, and incense burners on which aromatic woods were thrown were placed at intervals about the room.

The lotus was the most noticeable of the flowers of ancient Egypt and grew wherever the water was still. The Egyptians believed that the creator had sprung from a lotus flower so that from an early date it became a symbol of reincar-nation. The blue-flowered lotus or water-lily, *Nymphaea coerulea,* was held to be sacred on account of its soft delicate perfume. It is depicted in a painting on the walls of the tomb of Menkheper at Thebes, dating from about 1500 B.C.: four men seated at a funeral banquet are each holding and smelling a lotus flower. Another painting in Thebes depicts both living and dead inhaling the delicious scent, here shown as a symbol of immortality.

The death of Cleopatra brought to an end the grandeur of Egypt with its then unparalleled appreciation of beauty and good living. For more than 4,000 years perfumes had been used on a gigantic scale and almost all had been obtained from Palestine, Persia, India and Arabia in ever-increasing quantities. The Jews were to continue this practice begun by the Egyptians, both in their religious rites and for their personal enjoyment.

The Holy Anointing Oil. It would seem that they brought with them from Egypt the art of making floral perfumes, ointments and oils. Returning to their own country, they were able to bring into cultivation, with their newly acquired knowledge, the fragrant trees and shrubs which abound in the Holy Land. Most plentiful was the amyris (*Commiphora*), a shrub found in the mountains of Gilead which yields the famous Balm of Gilead.

In Exodus there are directions given to Moses upon his return from the land of captivity for erecting an altar of incense and for making the holy anointing oil: 'Thou shalt take unto thee principal spices, of pure myrrh five hundred shekels; and of sweet cinnamon half so much, two hundred and fifty shekels; and of sweet calamus two hundred and fifty shekels; and of cassia five hundred shekels; and of olive oil, an hin [a gallon]. And thou shalt make an oil of holy ointment; an ointment compound after the art of the apothecary [or perfumer] and it shall be a holy anointing oil.' The ceremony was performed only by the high priest, who poured the oil on the head in sufficient quantity for it to run down the beard and on to the clothes. Eusebius contended that the practice continued until the time of Christ.

The instructions given to Moses for compounding the holy incense were: 'Take unto thee sweet spices, stacte and onycha and galbanum; with pure frankincense; of each shall there be a like weight; and thou shalt make it a perfume, a confection after the art of the apothecary, tempered together pure and holy.' Belazeel and Aholiab were entrusted with the task of preparing the holy oil and it was forbidden to use it for any other but sacred purposes. In Exodus it says that: 'Whosoever shall make like unto that to smell thereto, shall even be cut off from his people', and only the priests could offer up incense in the temples. The penalties decreed by Moses against the private use of fragrant oils and incense would seem to be proof that the Jews, like the Egyptians, were beginning to use perfumes for their own purposes, chiefly for means of seduction.

In the Canticles there are numerous references to aromatics used by the Jewish people:

> Thy plants are an orchard of pomegranates, with pleasant fruits; camphire with spikenard, spikenard and saffron; calamus [sweet rush] and cinnamon, with all trees of frankincense; myrrh and aloes, with all the chief spices.

These were the principal aromatics of the Near East and they are used in perfumery to this day. Myrrh, by far the most prized possession of the civilized world, and used by Nicodemus to anoint Christ's body when taken from the Cross, is used in the making of modern perfumed soaps of the highest quality, and has valuable medicinal qualities. *Commiphora opobalsamum* produces the gum known as Balm of Gilead.

Another of the ancient bases for perfume was labdanum or ladanum, obtained from the Cretan Rock rose, *Cistus villosus,* and *C. ladaniferus,* to be found in Macedonia and Greece and on most islands of the eastern Mediterranean. Labdanum is a black exudation secreted by the stems and from the glandular hairs on the undersides of the leaves, particularly of *C. villosus.* The resinous gum is collected by shepherds who comb it from the fleeces of their sheep exactly as they did in biblical days. In Crete, to collect the resin from the plants, a special instrument is used, called a *ladanisterion,* a type of hand rake with leather thongs instead of metal teeth. The resin is scraped off the thongs or straps with a knife and moulded into cakes. It is laborious work and an efficient worker will collect only 2 to 3 lb a day during the summer months when the secretions are most active. Dioscorides, living at the time of Christ, described in detail the method by which the resinous substance was obtained from the beards of goats. The purest labdanum is almost black in colour and readily softened by the heat of the hand. It has a most agreeable balsamic perfume, like that of ambergris when diluted. It gives off a delicious scent when applied to a flame, but when dissolved in rectified spirit, the vapour of the golden oil has a narcotic quality.

Spikenard is *Nardostachys jatamansi,* a dwarf member of the valerian family, with an aromatic root, found only in certain valleys of the Himalayas, though Dioscorides knew of a species growing in the Ganges valley, *N. grandiflora*; a form of inferior quality (*Valeriana celtica*) was later discovered in the European Alps. The portion of the plant which is fragrant is the hairy stem, immediately above the root, grey in colour and of finger thickness. The plant derived its name *jatamansi* from the Hindu meaning 'locks of hair' because of the peculiar hairy rootstock. Spikenard was one of the ingredients of the ointment in the alabaster box used by Mary to anoint the feet of Jesus. The name given to the ointment by the old apothecaries was *Unguerentum nardinum,* and its other ingredients are believed to have been costus, the root of *Aplotaxis lappa, Juncus, Amomum,* myrrh, balm, omphacium, the oil of unripe olives, belamium and malabathrum, the leaf of the cinnamon. Anointing the feet was a custom of the time, and both Horace and Pliny, living in the same period, make mention of anointing the feet of guests at important functions.

Cinnamon is the dried back of *Cinnamomum zeylanicum* and was used to perfume clothes and beds as mentioned in Proverbs, 'I have perfumed my bed with myrrh, aloes and cinnamon'.

Theophrastus, who wrote a treatise on perfumes, said that some were 'made from stalks and some from roots', and since earliest times plants with aromatic roots were considered to be the most precious of all in the manufacture of perfumes, perhaps because of the ease with which the roots could be dried and transported from Asia to all parts of the Middle East and from thence into Europe.

Ginger, for example, was imported from the Arabian peninsula and had been a favourite flavour with the Romans long before they introduced it into Britain when it later became a common ingredient in Anglo-Saxon recipes. Russell, in his *Boke of Nurture,* mentions several kinds, for it was readily grown in Britain if given hot-bed cultivation; Gerard attempted to grow it as a hardy plant, but without success. In Shakespeare's time, the rhizome-like roots were known as a racine or race, and its peppery smell and hot taste were much appreciated.

Perfumes of the East. The Koran describes Paradise as being filled with nymphs created out of musk, and so fond of musk were the followers of Mohammed that it was mixed with the mortar used for building their temples so as to give off a lasting scent which is noticeable to this day. The gardens of the East were used by the wealthy for repose, and for this reason the plants were either aromatic or bore scented flowers. Here would be found the myrtle, rose, hyacinth and jonquil, flowers of the Garden of Eden. It is said that the Hanging Gardens of Babylon, made by King Nebuchadnezzar for his wife Amytes, daughter of the King of the Medes, contained only the most powerfully scented plants; and the terraces, where bloomed the rose and the lily, were the most favoured by the Queen for her walks. According to Herodotus, Arabia alone had to provide a thousand talents of frankincense to the temples of Babylon, and on the golden altar in the great temple erected in honour of Baal, a thousand talents of incense were burned each year.

The countries of the Middle East abound with fragrant plants, and it is from Palestine and Asia Minor that so many of them reached Britain. 'The gardens that surround the city of Damascus', wrote Buckingham, 'glow with dazzling beauty, forming a delightful retreat in the cool of the evening for recreation and listening to the warblings of the nightingale, and to breathe an air impregnated with the odour of flowers'. The Damask rose (hence Damascus) grew in almost every garden in Syria, and the country takes its name from the word *suri*, meaning 'land of roses'.

The most beautiful poem in the Persian language was written by Sadi in praise of the red rose. Rose sellers in the streets of modern Persia make their cry: 'Buy my roses. The rose was a thorn; from the sweat of the Prophet it blossomed.' This refers to the miracle recorded by Mohammed: that when he was taken up to Heaven, his sweat fell upon the earth and from it sprang the rose. 'Whosoever would smell my scent would smell the rose', he said. And, in northern Persia to this day, apartments are fumigated as of old, by burning aromatic gums and fragrant woods; and each Friday, after bathing, the body is purified with sweetly smelling unguents. To perfume the beard civet is used and musk to give fragrance to various parts of the body.

The Persians have brought the preservation of flowers to a fine art. To enjoy roses out of season, the buds are gathered and placed in earthenware jars sealed with clay. The jars are then buried in the garden, to be lifted when the flowers are required for some special occasion, when they are removed and placed in water in the sun or in a warm room. Red rose petals, dried and mixed with eastern spices, are also placed about the home in open bowls and will remain fragrant for many weeks.

The Greeks ascribed a divine origin to scented flowers and leaves. Homer classified the fragrant oils under the name *elaion*, though the general name for perfumes was *myron*, possibly derived from myrrh which was the best known of all the aromatics. In his *Treatise on Perfumes*, Apollonius of Herophila described at length those he considered best and from where they should be obtained. 'The iris is best in Elis and Cyzious; whilst the perfume made from Roses is most excellent at Phaselis, and that made at Naples and at Capua is also fine. That made from Saffron is in highest perfection at Soli in Cilicia and at Rhodes. The essence of spikenard is best at Tarsus, and the extract of vine leaves is made best at Cyprus. The best perfume from marjoram comes from Cos ... cyperus from Egypt ...' Apollonius said that the best of all perfume was made at Ephesus, whilst the most deliciously perfumed wines came from Byblos in Phoenicia.

The most wealthy Greeks applied a different perfume to each part of the body. In Antiphanes we read that:

> He bathes
> In a large gilded tub, and steeps his feet
> And legs in rich Egyptian unguents;
> His jaws and breasts he rubs with thick palm oil
> And both his arms with extract sweet, of mint;
> His eyebrows and his hair with marjoram,
> His knees and neck with essence of ground thyme.

It was the custom to offer guests a bath followed by sweet oils to rub on themselves before sitting to table; later garlands of scented flowers were brought in to crown the guests. The furniture and hangings of the banquet room were sprinkled with scented waters. Fragrant oils were rubbed on the head, for the Greeks thought that the best recipe for health was to apply sweet scents to the brain. Anacreon also recommended that both men and women anoint their breasts with scented unguents, as being the seat of the heart, for he believed it to be soothed by perfumes.

From earliest times, perfumes were used by the Greeks in their funeral rites, and it was also the custom to strew fragrant flowers and sweet perfumes over the tombs of the dead.

According to Ovid, the spices of the East were almost unknown to the Romans during earlier times. It was not until the influence of the Greeks was recognized, bringing with them all the refinements of luxury, that perfumes came to be used by the Romans in their religious ceremonies and for their personal use. A bronze incense-burning censer found at Pompeii clearly shows Greek influence in its design. The early Romans buried their dead, but when Greek traditions came to be adopted, the dead were cremated amidst a pile of scented woods.

Julius Caesar, believing the use of scented oils and powders to be effeminate, published a decree forbidding their sale. Caligula, however, spent enormous sums on perfumes for his bath, whilst Nero had concealed, beneath ivory plates, silver pipes which would spray the guests at meal times with scented waters whenever the plates were moved.

The Romans used three kinds of perfumes known as *hedysmata,* or solid unguents; *stymmata,* or liquid unguents; and *diapasmata,* or powdered perfumes. The simple unguents were flavoured with perhaps a single odour, such as *rhodium* from roses, or *malobathrum,* made from a tree thought to be *Cinnamomum cassia.* The compound unguents contained several ingredients. Most popular was *susinum,* made of oil of ben, lily, calamus, honey, cinnamon, saffron and myrrh, whilst Pliny praised most highly *nardinum,* made from oil of ben, calamus, costus, spikenard, amomum, myrrh and balm; and the regal unguent, prepared originally for the king of the Parthians at great cost and which contained 27 ingredients.

Saffron was one of the most cherished of all perfumes, for. the Romans had their apartments and banqueting halls strewn with the flowers, and the most prized essences were made from it. Saffron is the product of the dried stigmata of *Crocus sativus* which grows in profusion in parts of southern Europe and as far east as Kashmir. It is the Karkon of the Song of Solomon, and is *Kirkum* in the Indian language. From this, it became 'Crocum' to western Europeans. Linnaeus used the name *Crocus* for those corm-bearing plants which he grouped under this genus.

The stigmata of *Crocus sativus* ripen only in hot, dry regions, although in the fourteenth century it was cultivated in England, in that part of Essex now known as Saffron Walden, where it had been introduced by Sir Thomas Smith, Secretary of State to Edward III, in 1330. His idea was to initiate a new industry for the villagers and there it continued to be grown until the beginning of the seventeenth century. Once open, the reddish-purple blooms seem unable to close up again, so that only in a hot, dry season is it possible to preserve the product, for, if allowed to become damp, the stigmata will be spoiled by mildew. As recently as a century ago, almost 50,000 lb of saffron was imported into England from Spain alone, its value being estimated at nearly £100,000.

Saffron takes its name from the Arabic *sahafarn,* meaning 'a thread', because of the thread-like stigmata. In an early English vocabulary the name appears: 'Hic crocus, a safarroun', and it is mentioned in a tenth-century Leechbook: 'When he bathes, let him smear himself with oil mingled with saffron'. This was how it was used by the Romans who may have introduced it into Britain. Later, it was valued as a dye in the making of Church vestments as an alternative to gold thread. It coloured the garments worn by Henry VIII's knights at the Field of the Cloth of Gold and it was used by the monks instead of gold leaf in the illumination of missals. Saffron was also an important ingredient of cooking, being used to flavour bread and cakes and to give pastry a richer appearance.

At the time of Alexander the Great saffron was distributed by merchants to all parts of the Macedonian Empire for it filled so many needs. Above all, it was renowned for its medicinal powers, and was used in perfumery. From it unguents and essences were made and prized above all others except perhaps for spikenard. In the Koran, the ground of the Garden of Paradise is composed of pure wheaten flour mixed with saffron and musk. But saffron also had more commercial uses than any plant with the possible exception of flax and, as 70,000 blooms were needed to produce a single pound of the product, it was extremely costly. Only the wealthiest could afford to use it for strewing over the floor of banqueting halls and apartments. Horace has told of its being placed in fountains, to be sprayed into the air during banquets in the halcyon days of the Roman Emperors. And during the games, it was sprinkled from the valerium which formed the roof of the amphitheatre. The Romans did things lavishly or not at all.

In the East, scented flowers and perfumes are used in Hindu worship, and incense is burned on all ceremonial occasions, whilst freshly gathered fragrant flowers adorn the temples. In Tibet, where fragrant gums are scarce, scented wood is burned in the temples, usually the wood of juniper, which is fired in a large burner resembling a kiln. At Hindu marriages of the wealthy, a canopy is erected over the bride and groom beneath which burns the sacred fire, kept alight by placing on it sandalwood, scented oils and aromatic gums. Scented woods are also used in funeral pyres.

In India and Burma, as in the Near East, roses abound in the north, whilst in equal favour are the jasmines which Hindu poets call 'Moonlight of the Groves'. Sambac, a perfume made from the blossom of *J. sambac,* is still the most popular of all Hindu perfumes, though Pandang, made from the flowers of *Pandanus tectorius* (syn. *P. odoratissimus*), and Champac, the product of *Michelia champaca,* are still widely used.

To facilitate the extraction of the otto, sandalwood shavings are placed with flowers, so that Hindu perfumes usually carry the heavy scent of the wood, from which the perfumes of the Orient may be recognized. Other flowers used for perfume-making include *Mimusops elengi* (Bookool) and *Lawsonia inermis*. The essences are distilled around Ghazepore, situated on the north bank of the Ganges, above Benares. The petals are placed in stills with twice their weight of water, the produce being exposed to the air. Next day the otto is present on the surface and is collected by skimming. Perfumed oil is also made by placing gingelly oil seeds in alternating layers with fresh flowers, in a covered container. After several weeks, during which time the flowers are renewed, the seeds are pressed, when the oil will be impregnated with the fragrance of the flowers.

Amongst other perfumes used by the women of India, foremost is *Abir*, a scented talcum powder which is also sprinkled on clothes and linen. It is made from sandalwood, aloes, turmeric, rose petals, camphor and civet. A sweet ointment known as *urgujja,* made of sandalwood, aloes, otto of roses, and essence of jasmine, is also much used for applying to the body.

In China, Confucius recorded that scented flowers were scattered about on all festive occasions, and on New Year's Day houseboats and temples alike were hung with the fragrant blossoms of the peach and magnolia, the jasmine and jonquil. Indeed, so enormous was the consumption of incense burned in the temples that at one time, in the province of Canton alone, there were said to be more than 10,000 makes of incense sticks for use in the temple and in the home, where the incense burner was, and still is, an indispensable item of furniture.

The earliest treatise to be written on flowering plants was by Chi Han, of the Tsin dynasty in the third century A.D., who recorded the names of plants growing in southern China in a work called *Nam Fang Ts'ao Mu Chang*. In it he mentions the jasmine which is also mentioned in a book of the ninth century, *Yu Yang Ts'a Tsu,* which states that the plant is a native of Persia. Also mentioned in both works is the Sambac jasmine which was at one time cultivated from Peking to Canton for its use in perfumery. There were gardens devoted solely to the cultivation of the various jasmines. On each day of summer, the unopened buds were gathered to be sold for decorating the hair of Chinese girls, and to perfume tea. At Foochow in Fukien Province, it was estimated that more than 3,000,000 lb of jasmine buds were produced each summer to flavour tea. Jasmine growing in China reached its peak of popularity about four centuries ago, in the province of Kwangtung, where the jasmine gardens extended for miles along the banks of the Pearl River.

The unopened buds would be collected before dawn and placed in a wet cloth in which they would be taken to city flower sellers who would string them into garlands and bracelets for the ladies to wear in the evening. The flowers were also in great demand to make fragrant oils and perfumes to rub on the body, and also to scent wines and tea, whilst jasmine 'balls' were given to people who had attended dances and banquets to inhale, to clear the head. The ability of jasmine flowers to 'cleanse' an oppressive atmosphere made them much in demand in China to drape around the bed at night.

Scented Flowers in Medieval Britain. Though a number of scented flowers are native to Britain, many reached this island first with the Romans and later with the Norman Invasion. The old roses are examples of these, in particular the red rose, *Rosa rubra* or *R. gallica officinalis,* also the Apothecary's rose, so called because its dried petals would retain their perfume longer than that of any other rose, so it was extensively used in medicine; this was introduced by the Romans by way of Gaul, hence its alternative botanical name. It is the rose which from earliest times has been grown for its petals at Provins, near Paris; indeed, as early as 1160, a charter was granted to the French perfume makers of Provins.

The Damask rose is also believed to have been introduced at an early date, possibly with the Crusaders. This is the rose mentioned by Herodotus as having 'a scent surpassing all others', and the late Miss Sinclair Rohde, a specialist in the culture of ancient herbs and flowers who planned the original herb garden at Lullingstone Castle, Kent, described it as being 'one of the loveliest flowers in the world'. *Rosa damascena* is pale pink with a delicious, sweet perfume, and is mentioned in a 'Bill of Medicines furnished for the use of Edward I' in 1307, the year of his death. Edward I was the first monarch to use the rose as his emblem.

Dianthus caryophyllus, a parent of the modern carnation, was introduced by the monks of Normandy immediately following the invasion of England in 1066. It is to be found growing to this day about the ruined walls of many Norman castles and monastic foundations. The flowers, with their pronounced clove perfume, were much used for flavouring wine and ale, hence the ancient name for Pinks of 'sops-in-wine'.

Roses and clove-scented gilliflowers were in great demand for garlands, and it is recorded by Wharton in his *Historie de Episcopis et Dicanis* that when Roger de Walden was made Bishop of St Paul's in 1405, he was crowned with a garland of red roses. Indeed, frequent use was made of garlands of scented flowers during the Middle Ages, not only for religious occasions but also for wearing by ladies, to attract their lovers with the perfume. White and red roses, *Rosa alba and R. gallica,* were the most popular of all flowers for garlands, for they were the most fragrant.

Much use was made of scented flowers in the church, to decorate statues and shrines and to garland priests. The monastic gardens were in the care of the sacristan whose duty it was to provide these flowers on feast days throughout the year. In the accounts of St Mary Hill, London, for the year 1483, there is an item 'for Garlandes on Corpus Christi Day—10d. And a dozen and a half Rose Garlandes on St Barnebe's Day—8½d.'

Of the milkwort, Gerard writing of the various plants in his garden in Holborn said: 'it doth flourish in Rogation Week; of which flower, the maidens which walke the procession do make themselves garlands and nosegays. In English we call it Cross Flower or Rogation Flower'.

During the Crusades a number of fragrant plants reached England from the Near East, which besides the Damask rose included lilies and irises. 'A lily pale with Damask dye to grace her', wrote Shakespeare, and from the time of its introduction the rivalry between the lily and the rose as to which is the rightful 'queen of flowers' has persisted to this day. 'Their silent war of lilies and of roses', wrote Shakespeare, his reference being to *Lilium candidum,* the Madonna lily, which grows wild in Palestine and was dedicated to the Virgin on account of the purity of its bloom. Together with the Damask rose, its flowers were more widely used by medieval artists than any others, particularly in paintings of the Annunciation.

Plants for Strewing. During medieval and Tudor times scented flowers and herbs were used for strewing on the pews and floors of church and manor to combat the unpleasant mustiness caused by damp earthen floors and lack of window space. In Pegge's *Curalia* it is said that 'at the Court of King Stephen ... and in houses of inferior rank upon occasions of feasting, the floor was to be strewn with flowers', and that, 'Thomas à Becket ordered his hall to be strewed every day, in the spring with fresh May blossom, and in summer with Sweet-scented Rushes fresh gathered ... that such knights as the benches could not contain, might sit on the floor without dirtying their clothes.'

The scented rush, *Acorus calamus,* was much in demand for strewing. Also known as the Cinnamon iris, for when crushed it gives off the same aromatic scent as cinnamon, it was difficult to obtain as it grew only in East Anglia, and was accordingly expensive. One of the charges of extravagance brought against Cardinal Wolsey was that he ordered the floors of his palace of Hampton Court to be covered much too often with rushes. *A. calamus* has flag-like leaves, and its flowers appear in a cylindrical spike on stems 1.8 m (6 ft) tall. From the leaves, which resemble those of the water iris, a volatile oil is distilled which is an ingredient of perfumery and is used for making aromatic vinegars; whilst the root, dried and powdered, yields a refreshing talcum powder which the ancient Greeks sprinkled over their beds and clothes. At one time the root was much in demand for imparting its flavour to wine, beer and gin.

The root, dried and powdered, is also an ingredient of one of the most popular modern perfumes, Chypre. It was widely used at the French court during the reign of Henry IV, and more recently it was the favourite essence of the last Tsarina of Russia. The powder was composed of benzoin, storax, calamint, coriander seed and calamus root in about equal quantities. The modern Chypre also includes musk and civet which give it a more powerful and lasting quality.

Herbs, too, were widely grown for strewing, especially those which released their aromatic fragrance when trodden upon, such as germander and hyssop, which Parkinson said were much used for the purpose, 'being pretty and sweet'. In his *Five Hundred Points of Good Husbandry,* published in 1573, Thomas Tusser recommended twenty plants for strewing, among them basil and balm, camomile and costmary, lavender and hyssop, sage and thyme. Surprisingly he made no mention of meadowsweet, which Queen Elizabeth most enjoyed to have on the floor of her apartments. It is said that her nasal organs were finely developed and she hated unpleasant smells. So desirous was she of having a regular supply of flowers and herbs for strewing, that a woman was appointed to the Queen's Household with a fixed salary for the sole purpose of having suitable flowers always in readiness. Of meadowsweet, Gerard said: 'The leaves and flowers far excell all other strewing herbs to deck up houses, to strew in chambers, halls and banqueting houses in summer time, for the smell thereof makes the heart merry and joyful, and delighteth the senses.' Parkinson, who dedicated his *Paradisus* to Queen Henrietta Maria, enjoyed its 'pretty, sharp scent'. Both the flowers and the leaves are scented, but the aromatic perfume released by the leaves and stems when trodden upon is more pleasing than the scent given off by the flowers.

In his *Description of England,* Harrison mentioned that a Dr Leminius when on a visit to this country in 1560 had this to say of an English home he visited: '... The neat cleanliness, the exquisite fineness, the pleasant and delightful furniture ... wonderfully rejoiced me; their chambers and parlours strewed over with sweet herbs, refreshed me'. And he also made mention of the 'sundry sorts of fragrant flowers' used about the house, including pots of rosemary, and lavender hung on the wall.

Though the practice of strewing diminished in the early seventeenth century, it continued on special occasions. At the time of the accession of James II, one Mary Cowle, was 'Strewer of Herbs in Ordinary to His Majesty' and before the coronation ceremony had instructions to 'spread two breadths of Blue Broadcloth' in the aisle, '... which cloth is strewed with nine baskets full of sweet herbs and flowers'. For the coronation of William and Mary there is an order for 'a gown of scarlet cloth with a badge of Her Majesty's cypher on it for the Strewer of Herbs to Her Majesty, as was provided at the last coronation'.

At the coronation of George III, the King's groom of the vestry appeared dressed in scarlet and holding a perfuming pan, burning aromatic perfumes, as at previous coronations. Yet shortly after the king's accession, an Act was put through Parliament: 'That all women of whatever rank, age, profession or decree, whether virgins, maids, or widows, that shalt from such Act, impose upon, seduce, or betray into matrimony, any of His Majesty's subjects by the use of scents, paints, cosmetic washes, artificial teeth, false hair, iron stays, hoops, high-heeled shoes, bolstered hips, shall incur the penalty of the law now in force against witchcraft ... and that the marriage be null and void.'

But the use of fumigants and of strewing continued, and in Huish's *History of the Coronation of George IV* there is a detailed account of the Herb Strewer and her functions. We are told that the King chose Miss Fellowes, sister of the Secretary to the Lord Great Chamberlain, and that six young ladies assisted her, 'dressed in white muslin with flower ornaments', who walked in front of the procession. A colour print depicts Miss Fellowes holding a basket in one hand and strewing blossom over the ground from the other.

Green rushes formed a cool and pleasant 'carpet' in church and home, but had the fault of attracting fleas and other insects, and it was necessary to burn Fleabane (*Erigeron acris*) at regular intervals. Rue was also in demand to keep away fleas and bugs which were commonly supposed to be the cause of so many diseases. It was one of a number of herbs, rich in essential oil, which the disease-carrying bugs would not go near, used to combat the Black Death and later the Plague. In 1750, rue was used to strew the dock of the Central Criminal Court at the Old Bailey as a guard against jail fever which at that time was raging in Newgate Prison, and the custom continued until the present century.

Scented Waters and Powders. The distillation of flowers and leaves was one of the chores in all large houses from the beginning of the sixteenth century. The household books (1502) of the 5th Earl of Northumberland contain the names of 'herbes to stylle', to make sweet waters to use for personal cleanliness, in cooking, and for medicine. Balm and sage, marigold and tansy were amongst the most widely grown plants for distillation, and every garden had its rosemary and lavender bushes. All large houses possessed a room for the drying of herbs and another for their distillation where the ladies took lessons in the art of making sweet waters. These were given as presents at Christmas or for birthdays.

A hand water for use at table was one of the refinements of a more enlightened age, and in all wealthy men's houses, silver bowls filled with rose-water were kept in the bedrooms to be used for washing the hands and face. Sir Hugh Platt gives a recipe for making a scented water consisting of lavender, a few cloves, orris-powder, together with four ounces of benjamin, 'a little of which will sweeten a basin of fair water for your table'. Sir Walter Raleigh had a cordial water made from wild strawberry leaves and enjoyed having his rooms filled with the scent of a dry pot-pourri made with Damask roses and orris-powder.

The Eastern fashion of sprinkling rose-water over one's clothes was prevalent. In Marston's play *Antonio and Mallida,* a gallant enters carrying a casting bottle of rose-water which he sprinkles on himself. Sir Hugh Platt, in his *Delights,* gives instructions for a 'casting bottle': to rose-water he suggests adding three drams of spikenard oil; one dram each of oil of thyme, lemon and cloves, together with a grain of civet, which must be shaken well together before being placed in the bottle.

It was also common practice to sprinkle rose and other fragrant waters on the floors of apartments whenever necessary. In Marlow's *Doctor Faustus,* Pride complains, 'Fye, what a smell is here, I'll not speak another word for a king's ransome, unless the ground is perfumed'. And in *A Winter's Tale,* the beggar Autolycus sings out a list of the wares he carries around the countryside to earn a few pence:

> Bugle-bracelet, necklace amber,
> Perfume for a lady's chamber.

This would be a cheap scented water to sprinkle over the floor, possibly made from the roots of native plants which were readily available about the countryside. One of these was *Sedum rhodiola,* known as Roseroot since its roots yield the fragrance of the rose. It grew in every cottage garden and on old walls and cliffs.

Tinkers included amongst their wares bracelets and necklaces made of scented gums which, after setting hard, were threaded on to lengths of twine. In a manuscript in the British Museum, Mary Doggett says that the 'beads' should be made as large as nutmegs and coloured with lamp-black. As the 'beads' were being fashioned, oil of jasmine was poured on to the hands and this gave the 'beads' a brilliant gloss and pleasant perfume.

Pomanders were also carried by the tinkers during Shakespeare's time. They first came to be used in France, possibly as a protection against the plague. Henry V, victor of Agincourt, carried with him 'a musk ball of gold' which he may have obtained during his French campaign. This was a ball of musk-smelling amber (*pomme d'ambre*), which was later replaced by dried oranges stuck with cloves, like the one which Cardinal Wolsey carried with him on his visiting days, tied to his belt. George Cavendish, usher to the Cardinal, has left a graphic description of Wolsey and his pomander which, near the end of his term of office, was filled with a sponge soaked in scented vinegar. This was to give protection 'against the pestilent airs, the which he most commonly smelt unto, passing among the press, or else he was pestered with many suitors'.

Elizabeth I usually carried with her a pomander made in the shape of a ball composed of ambergris and benzoin, and showed her obvious delight when once presented with 'a faire gyrdle of pomanders' (this was really a number of small pomanders, strung together and worn around the neck). Later, pomanders were made of silver or gold and worn as a pendant to a lady's girdle. They were constructed with a central core around which were grouped six orange-shaped segments held in place by a ring fastened to the top of the column. When the ring was lifted, the segments opened, each being attached to the base of the column by a hinge. Along the top edges of the segments were slides which opened to allow each one to be filled with a different perfume.

An earlier type of pomander, shown in an illustration for the 'Boat of Foolish Women', one of a series of five caricatures published in 1502 by Jodocus Badius, was perforated with small holes. It was similar both in size and shape to the pomanders of glazed porcelain and those made in the traditional blue jasper-ware of Wedgwood design which are obtainable today.

The cassolette or printanier was a popular device for diffusing perfumes and was introduced towards the end of the sixteenth century. In the British Museum there is a manuscript containing a recipe for 'a paste for a cassolette' made to the requirements of the Duchess of Braganza. It suggests mixing together two drachms each of ambergris, musk and civet, to which is added a little oil of cloves and three drachms of essence of citron. The whole should be made into a paste with rose-water and placed in the cassolette, a small box made of ivory, silver or gold, its lid being perforated with holes through which the scent of the paste could be inhaled.

Perfumes were also burnt in rooms. Perfumers travelled around, calling at the houses of the rich to fumigate musty apartments with fragrant woods. During the brief reign of Edward VI, his apartments were always kept pleasantly scented. First the foul air was cleared away by burning juniper or cypress wood; then the room was made to smell as though it were filled with roses by burning over hot embers 'twelve spoonsful of red rose water into which is added the weight of a sixpence of fine sugar'.

In his *Herbal,* Dr Turner gives instructions for scenting a house in Tudor times. If Southernwood is burnt in a room, it will not only make the room fragrant with its pungent smoke, but will 'drive away serpents' lurking in corners. This may be taken to mean frogs and toads and other unsavoury creatures which often sought shelter from the heat of the day within the damp, dark walls of castle and cottage.

Sweet-smelling woods or roots, when dry, were thrown on a low fire to scent a room. Most of these fumigants were obtained from the countryside, and even the cottager could scent his humble abode. A plant which was a particular favourite was *Inula conyza.* Both its flowers and leaves emit a refreshing perfume, but it was for the burning of its roots that it was most esteemed, and because of their scent the plant came to be known as Ploughman's Spikenard. In Scotland where the Scots pine grew everywhere, the Highlanders cut the roots into thick 'candles' which, when lighted, burnt with a low flame, providing both light and a sweet aromatic fragrance.

Seeds of several plants readily obtainable from hedgerow and field were also used for burning. In his *Calendar for Gardening* (1661), Stevenson suggests that one should 'be sure every morning to perfume the house with angelica seeds, burnt in a fire-pan or chafing dish on coales'. This handsome herb, *Angelica officinalis*, native of the Northern Hemisphere, has purple stems covered in a grape-like 'bloom' and, if cut when young, they will impart a musky flavour to stewed apples or rhubarb. From the seeds, an essential oil is obtained which has a similar musk-like smell and is used by the monks of La Grande-Chartreuse in making their celebrated liqueur. 'The whole plant, leaf, roots and seed is of an excellent comfortable scent, savor and taste,' wrote Parkinson.

Fragrant woods and roots were also used to impart their perfume to clothes and linen. 'Now are the lawn sheets fumed with violets,' says Marston in *What You Will*, and hence the reference is surely to burning elecampane roots. The elecampane is a handsome native plant which bears a bloom like that of a sunflower and has orris-scented roots. When dry and burned, they do indeed release a violet-like perfume.

Clothes were kept in coffers made of fragrant wood such as juniper, cedar or sandalwood which impregnated the clothes.

Perfumes did not come into general use until the reign of Elizabeth I when Edward de Vere, Earl of Oxford, brought from Italy 'perfumed gloves, sweet bags, and other pleasant things'. From that time onwards, the use of perfumes became fashionable, with civet and musk the basis of most costly preparations.

The gloves presented to Elizabeth would be scented with frangipani, one of the most famous of all perfumes which owes its origin to a prominent Roman family, several members of whom served in the Papal army at the time of the Italian Renaissance. It was distilled from the flowers of *Plumeria alba*, which grows on several of the West Indian islands, and its scent was first brought to the attention of Europeans by Mercutio Frangipani, a botanist of renown who accompanied Columbus on his voyage to the New World in 1492. As they approached Antigua, they noticed a delicious scent in the air which Mercutio said came from some sweet-smelling flower. On landing, they found the island filled with small trees bearing white flowers which became known as the Frangipani, to commemorate the man who had first recognized the perfume. The plant was later named *Plumeria alba*, by Tournefort, to honour the French botanist and Franciscan monk, Fr Charles Plumier, who died in 1706. The White frangipani grows 4.5 m (15 ft) tall and has long brittle leaves which curl inwards at the margins. The flowers are of purest white with a long in-curving tube, and the scent they diffuse is similar to that of white jasmine.

Later, in the seventeenth century, a Marquis de Frangipani, of the same family, created the perfume bearing his name from the flowers of *Plumeria rubra* which grows mostly on the islands of Jamaica and Martinique and is known there as Red jasmine; the native women adorn their hair with the crimson-red flowers and place them amongst clothes for, like those of the Red rose, the petals retain their perfume for several months after drying. One of the ingredients of the scent was the bark of *Cascarilla gratissima*—*Cascarilla* is Spanish for 'little bark' and alludes to the short curled pieces of bark which are stripped from the branches and burnt to fumigate apartments. The plant was re-named *Croton eleutheria* after Eleuthera, the island in the Bahamas where it was found. It is a member of the Euphorbia family and releases a thick balsam-scented juice when the stems are broken. The bark, which is known to the natives as 'sweet-wood', has been shipped to the perfumers of Europe since the sixteenth century. The leaves also are scented and are used by the islanders for placing amongst clothes.

The idea of scented gloves was quickly taken up by the fashionable of the time. A grease or pomade was prepared which was then rubbed into the gloves and thus absorbed by the hands. Scented gloves came to be made in England by milliners who lived and worked alongside the herbalists in that part of London known as Bucklersbury, situated between the Mansion House and Cheapside. It also became the fashion to wear clothes perfumed with expensive powders. Amongst other pleasant things brought from Italy by the Earl of Oxford was a perfumed jerkin made of suede which he presented to Queen Elizabeth. Even her shoes were scented, and she was very fond of a cloak made of Spanish perfumed leather, imported just before the Armada, which she wore on all special occasions. Some idea of its cost may be obtained from Charles Piesse's book *The Art of Perfumery,* published in 1880, in which he mentions that *peau d'Espagne* was then sold by the Bond Street perfumers at a shilling a square inch.

The skins were first steeped in an otto made up of the oils of neroli rose, sandalwood, lavender and verbena, to which was added a small quantity of the oils of clove and cinnamon. All this was added to a half pint of spirit in which four ounces of gum benzoin were dissolved. The skins were left in this mixture for a day or so and were then dried by exposure to the sun and air. Next, a paste was made by rubbing together in a mortar one drachma of civet and one of musk, with gum tragacantha to give a spreading consistency, and into this was mixed the residue of the otto in which the skins had been soaked. It was spread on the skins which were then placed together, one above another like a sandwich, and over them were placed several sheets of paper. The skins were then pressed with weights for several days, during which time they became so saturated with the perfume that they retained it permanently. The strips of leather, known as *peau d'Espagne,* were used as book marks and for bindings as well as for numerous objects of clothing.

One of Queen Elizabeth's perfumers was Ralph Rabbards who edited Ripley's *Compound of Alchemy,* and who concocted a number of perfumes for the Queen's use, made to his own secret formula. In a letter to the Queen, Rabbards said that he had many 'rare inventions, as I have for long studied and with practice found out', and he extols the virtues of a number of his perfumes 'of odours most sweete and delicate'. He suggested for the Queen's use his renowned 'water of violets' and his gillyflower water which would not 'retain their own proper odours, except they be distilled very cunningly'. She spent large sums on perfumes and cosmetics and her annual expenses for the year 1584, according to Peck's *Desiderata,* included the sum of £40 (a considerable amount in those days) for the services of John Kraunckwell and his wife as 'stillers of sweet waters'.

The Elizabethans kept their scented waters in small bottles of chastened silver, one of the finest examples of which, dating from about 1565, is to be seen in the Victoria and Albert Museum. It may have been made by Robert Danby (or Danbe) whose speciality was making communion cups and who was a member of the select and powerful silversmiths' guild which up to that time had provided the city of London with seventeen lord mayors. This charming piece of Tudor refinery is only four inches tall and is fitted with a silver base which enables it to stand upright when not in use. A silver chain fastened to the shoulders allows the bottle to be suspended from the girdle.

Towards the end of Elizabeth's reign, the first glass scent bottles were made in England. Their manufacture was in the hands of Huguenots who had fled from France after the Massacre of St Bartholomew and who had set up in business at Crutched Friars in London. One of them, named Jean Caré, following protests by English glass-makers resentful of the competition, was compelled to move his business to Stourbridge. Shortly after, a Venetian, Jacopo Verzellini, began making glass wine and scent bottles in the Venetian style and persuaded Elizabeth to prohibit the importation of all foreign glass.

But it was not for another two hundred years that scent bottles came to be manufactured on any considerable scale, when the exquisite blue bottles with golden floral sprays began to be made at Bristol, by William Lowdin and his successors at their works known as Redcliffe Backs. The bottles, which were only three inches high, were also produced in green and amethyst, though the most handsome of all were those made in opaque-white with paintings of flowers by Michael Edkins. Several of these delightful bottles have survived and are eagerly sought after by collectors.

Originally, the pouncet-box which came to be used for containing snuff was for keeping pumice-stone used in the preparation of parchment for writing. Later, during Elizabethan times, a pouncet was the name given to any type of box usually of scented wood which held scented powder for placing between linen, blowing about a room or on to a lady's hair with bellows, or which contained leaves and roots to be taken as snuff.

Sachet powders were popular with Elizabethan housekeepers, to place amongst clothes and to keep away moths. The violet scent of orris-root was much in demand, also the dried leaves of mint and thyme, rosemary and lavender. Few actual flowers retain their perfume when dry, and only Red and Damask roses were used, the petals being powdered in a mortar and afterwards sifted. Sir Hugh Platt made a sweetly scented powder by pounding and mixing together orris, calamus, cloves, storax and rose petals, and it would retain its perfume for a year or more.

Snuff, in the form of powdered leaves of fragrant plants, had been taken by countrymen since earliest times to clear the head of a cold or of melancholia, but it was not until the reign of Charles II that snuff-taking became fashionable at Court, although during Shakespeare's day aromatic powders made of orris and the dried leaves of camomile and White pellitory were passed round after banquets. The principal ingredients of Elizabethan snuffs were camomile leaves and those of alehoof and pellitory, the latter being known as the Sneezewort, for according to Turner, 'the flowers make one sneeze exceedingly'. The leaves had a similar effect and from them a tea was brewed. Peppermint, woodruff and thyme were also used in snuffs after they had been dried and ground to a powder, likewise the dried roots of the Sweet flag.

It is possible, too, that tobacco snuff reached England during Shakespeare's lifetime, for the herb had been introduced into Europe in 1560 by Jean Nicot, French Ambassador to Portugal, who planted it in the garden of the Embassy in Lisbon; the first cigars were made about the same time, by Demetrio Pela, a Spaniard. It is believed that the word cigar was originally derived from the Spanish *cigarral*, little garden, for most gardens in the Iberian Peninsula had plants of *Nicotiana tabacum*. Certainly by the late Elizabethan era, the tobacconist was as firmly established in the city of London as the herbalist. Gerard, writing in 1597, said: 'The dry leaves are used to be taken in a pipe and set on fire and sucked into the stomach and sucked forth again from the nostrils'.

In France, tobacco snuff had been taken since the time of Catherine de' Medici who, after receiving a quantity from Jean Nicot, started the fashion at Court. The habit quickly achieved such popularity that, in 1624, Pope Urban VIII issued an order banning its use from places of worship and excommunicating those who did not conform. But snuff-taking did not become really popular in England until the Great Plague, when it was thought to have valuable antiseptic properties. Snuff is essentially powdered tobacco, fermented in salt, then ground and scented. There are two forms: dry, which is made from tobacco stems; and moist, from the leaves. But the skill in its manufacture lies in the blending and in its flavouring with various attars for which cinnamon, cloves, lavender and bergamot were the most popular scents. Some snuffs were prepared from orris-root to impart its violet-like perfume; others from fennel, sage and rosemary. Tobaccos were also compounded with cascarilla bark or with the Tonka bean, which has the smell of newly mown hay and was often placed in snuff-boxes for its flavour.

The distillation of lavender, which began early in the seventeenth century, was the first attempt at any form of commercial scent production in the British Isles. Mitcham in Surrey was the home of lavender growing, and its climate and soil produced the world's finest lavender-water. Later, lavender was grown and distilled at Hitchin in Hertfordshire, in Norfolk, and at Market Deeping in Lincolnshire where a number of ancient distilling plants can still be seen; but it is at Mitcham that most of the lavender-water is manufactured today. It is estimated that half a hundredweight of lavender flowers will yield about sixteen ounces of essential oil. It is, however, not from the actual flowers that the oil is obtained but from the tiny green bracts which enclose them, for the flowers of lavender and all the labiates are entirely devoid of perfume. In the finest ottos, the stems are excluded because, though useful for burning indoors, they yield little essential oil.

To plant an acre of ground, 3,500 plants are required and, at their fourth or fifth year, these yield about six quarts of otto. After six years, the plants are taken up and burnt and the delicious scent spreads for miles around. The lavender is harvested in August and September, when it is cut with a sickle and placed on mats for conveying to the still-house. The otto is grouped into 'firsts' and 'seconds', the latter being the end of the distillation and used for perfuming soaps. The finest lavender-water is made by the distillation of the essential oil with rectified spirit and rose-water, the final product being pure white.

The earliest recipe for English lavender-water is from a manuscript of 1615 which directs that the flowers be distilled with canella bark, wallflowers and grains of paradise; and the distillate could be taken internally as well as being used as a perfume and toilet water. Lavender-water was the favourite scent of Queen Henrietta Maria. In the garden of her manor of Wimbledon grew large borders of 'rosemary, rue and white lavender', which is believed to yield the most pleasing lavender water.

The Early Gardening. Almost all the fragrant flowers and leaf-bearing plants grown for their medicinal value, for strewing and for other purposes during medieval times, were mostly of dwarf habit so that they were suitable for growing in small beds which were situated inside the castle walls or within the walls of the fortified manor houses where there was only a limited amount of space available for a garden. The garden would usually be divided into small squares surrounded by stone paths or by paths planted with those fragrant herbs which emit their scent when trodden upon; these were planted also because they spread out and so made the ground clean to walk upon between the beds during wet weather. It was Falstaff who said of camomile, most frequently used for planting in walks, with thyme and burnet:

> The more it is trodden on,
> The faster it grows

Each square plot of ground would usually be planted with but one variety of plant. There would be violets whose flowers were eaten raw in salads; likewise roses which were also used in salads and to make into garlands. There would be cowslips and primroses, used for making wine, and also gillyflowers, the old name for clove-scented stocks and pinks, and derived from 'July-flowers', for they were in bloom at that time.

'In July come gilliflowers of all varieties,' said Bacon and Michael Drayton wrote, 'The July-flower declares his gentleness'. They were the 'sops-in-wine' of Chaucer and Shakespeare. Culpeper said that 'It is vain to describe a herb so well known as the pink'.

Plants of *Dianthus caryophyllus* would be most suitable for small beds, and carnations too. There would be daffodils, and lily of the valley, Chaucer's 'Heven's Lilie'; *Crocus sativus,* the saffron; and Herb Robert *(Geranium rober-tianum).* There would be beds of wallflowers and marigolds; of sage and thyme; of lavender and rosemary, kept dwarf by clipping; of marjoram and hyssop; mint and germander, all of which were used for strewing as well as for flavouring and in medicine. Every plant had to make its contribution to the requirements of the times. The beds would usually be surrounded by parsley, an excellent way of growing it, or maybe by thrift, whilst later the small-leaf box was used; by Tudor times it was popular for making 'knotted' beds, often in the most complicated designs. Hampton Court was said to be 'so enknotted it cannot be expressed'. In the accounts of the Duke of Northumberland for the year 1502, there is mention of a gardener being employed 'to attend hourly for setting of erbis (herbs) and clypping of knottes, and sweeping the said garden cleaner'. At Hampton Court and elsewhere, low wooden rails painted green and white, the Tudor colours, surrounded the beds, and later honeysuckle and wild roses were allowed to climb up them.

Gardens not surrounded by a wall were protected by thick hedges, and Elizabethan gardeners had some delightful ideas for making a hedge. Thomas Hill, in *The Profitable Art of Gardening,* suggested planting together whitethorn or hawthorn, with its fragrant flowers, and sweet-briar, 'interlaced together and roses one, two or more sorts placed here and there amongst them'. In the book there are two woodcuts of designs for mazes, one a circle in a square, the other a square, to be formed of 'Issop and Thyme or Lavender Cotton . . . in the middle, a proper herber decked with roses or else with some fayre tree of rosemary . . .'

Of the cypress Parkinson wrote, ' . . . they give a pleasant and sweet shadow', the word 'sweet' being used here to describe the pungent, refreshing smell of the foliage. Rosemary was also planted for a hedge, being allowed to grow thick and tall without being trimmed. 'You must take such things as are green all winter,' wrote Bacon.

But the first attempt to deal with the laying out of gardens was made by Gervase Markham in a treatise called *The Country Farm* compiled in 1615. In it he gave a plan of a garden for a Kentish yeoman's house and farm in which he separated the kitchen garden from the pleasure garden. Each garden was to be divided into quarters comprising knots or interlacing figures, each to be planted differently with the scented flowers and leaves already named. For the first time those plants for long grown in cottage gardens for their many virtues were to be planted to an ordered design. In the *New Orchard and Garden* by William Lawson, published three years later, the author makes similar suggestions. He lists all the scented flowering plants of the time to be 'comely and orderly placed in your borders and squares', and he wrote that 'of all flowers, pinks are the most pleasant to see and to smell'. The new gardening by design, expressed by Markham and Lawson, remained unaltered for at least a hundred years.

It was also Gervase Markham who was the first to describe the making of a grass lawn, for until the early seventeenth century lawns were made of scented plants such as camomile and thyme.

Each garden had its bower where one could sit and talk in private and which was covered with plants bearing sweet-smelling flowers, especially jasmine, honeysuckle and eglantine. Ben Jonson, friend and contemporary of Shakespeare, describes the pleasures to be enjoyed from scented climbing plants in the *Vision of Delight:*

> So, the blue bindweed doth itself enfold
> With honeysuckle; and both these entwine
> Themselves with briony and jessamine,
> To cast a kind and odoriferous shade.

But the earliest description is of the garden bower at Woodstock wherein Henry II spent all too fleeting hours in the company of his mistress, fair Rosamond Clifford. The bower may have been clothed with the native honeysuckle or with the vine, a popular plant to enclose a bower and which had been introduced to Britain during the Roman occupation; or maybe with the clematis known as Traveller's Joy, a native plant.

During Elizabethan times, the honeysuckle took pride of place for the arbour, and Shakespeare often mentions it. Writing shortly afterwards, Parkinson suggests 'the jasmine, white and yellow [the summer and the winter-flowering], the double honey-suckle, the Ladies' Bower, white and red and purple, single and double' as being suitable plants.

To give protection from strong sunshine and wet weather, walks and paths about the garden were covered with arches made of intertwining climbing plants 'beneath which one may walk in shade'. 'He who will set roses to run about his arbour ... must set them in February', wrote Thomas Hill in *The Profitable Art of Gardening* (1563), 'and in the like manner, if you will sow that sweet tree or flower named Jacemine, Rosemary or Pomegranate seed, unless you had rather deck your arbours comelier with vines'.

Usually, the arbour or bower would be cut into the alley or walk and with the seats made of wood or stone there would be a table where guests were able to partake of food during summer, and to enjoy the fragrance of the flowers and herbs for, indeed, the word arbour was derived from the word *herber*, a place where grew fragrant plants: 'With arbors and alleys so pleasant and so dulse, the pestilent ayres with flavors to repulse'.

The delightful idea of the garden bower in this age seems to be neglected and yet may be simply constructed of trellis in some sunny corner about which several of the fragrant climbers could be grown. The fragrant Virgin's bower, *Clematis flammula,* which was introduced to Britain before Parkinson had completed the writing of his *Paradisus,* could be grown where the soil is of a chalky nature. It blooms in the autumn and no other plant at the time can equal its perfume. With it, *C. montana* could be planted, to drape its scented flowers about the trellis in early summer.

Where the soil is of an acid nature, the Chinese gooseberry has a beauty rarely exceeded. It is known botanically as *Actinidia chinensis,* and throughout summer bears handsome buff-coloured flowers which are sweetly scented and which are followed by edible fruits, as large and as delicious as 'Leveller' gooseberries. And to accompany it, the Carolina jasmine, *Gelsemium sempervirens,* with its honey-scented flowers would be most suitable.

The appreciation of sweet-smelling flowers and leaves continued until nearly the end of the seventeenth century when, immediately after London's Great Fire of 1666, Sir Christopher Wren put forward plans for the provision of a Green Belt when the City of London was rebuilt. John Evelyn carried the idea further, suggesting to Charles II that large areas, 30 to 40 acres in extent, should be filled with all manner of scented plants, 'such shrubs as yield the most fragrant and odiferous flowers, and are aptist to tinge the air upon every gentle emission at a great distance'. The beds and borders should be filled 'with pinks, carnations, stocks, gillyflowers, primroses, avunculas (auriculas), violets, etc.'.

A delightful idea but one which Charles, due to the large sums to be found for his costly wars and pleasures, was unable to carry out.

Charles and his courtiers were great lovers of perfumes, indeed the appreciation of perfumes and cosmetics reached its peak during his reign. It had gathered momentum from the time of Elizabeth I and the first Stuarts, fanned by the appearance in 1610 of Gervase Markham's famous skin lotion distilled from rosemary, featherfew, fennel, violets and nettles.

The chief reason for the appreciation of perfumes during Stuart times was that personal and public hygiene was at a low ebb, due in no small measure to the tax on soap introduced during the time of Charles I. This, more than anything, may have contributed to the Plague of 1665. The subsequent use of antiseptics in medicine, and the realization that aromatic herbs were of value in combating pest and disease brought about the greater use of perfumes during the time of Charles II.

Yet, for all this, the appreciation of scent in flowers began to deteriorate in the latter years of the seventeenth century.

The New Gardening. The New England discoveries of John Tradescant jun., made towards the mid-seventeenth century, brought about the first appreciation of scentless flowers, and by a remarkable coincidence, Tradescant himself had no sense of smell.

His voyage to Virginia in 1637 resulted in the introduction to Britain of the Michaelmas daisy, the tradescantia and the North American golden-rod, amongst other plants, all of which were scentless. 'These North American composites in borders', wrote the Victorian authority, William Robinson, 'exterminate valuable plants, and give a coarse ragged appearance to the garden'. Yet they became widely planted, for they were extremely hardy and free-flowering, and moreover they mostly bloomed during late summer and throughout autumn when, until their introduction, gardens had been devoid of colour. The more dainty, scented flowering plants could not compete against their vigorous, rampant habit and they quickly lost popularity in the quest for something 'new'.

With the Restoration of Charles II, who was on intimate relations with the Court of Louis XIV for whom Le Nôtre was covering some 200 acres with gardens at Versailles, a new concept of gardening was taking place. Le Nôtre's influence was soon felt by Vanbrugh who, having built the great houses at Castle Howard and Blenheim, demanded that the gardens be laid out to the same proportions as the houses: thus long avenues of trees replaced the small 'knot' and walled gardens of earlier times. These were the days of William Kent, and of 'Capability' Brown, who had little interest in flowers as a means of beautifying the garden. Tradescant's recent robust introductions from America were highly suitable for this style of gardening, whilst the tulip had now replaced the pink and the wallflower for early summer display. In *The Dutch Gardener* by Henry van Oosten published in 1703 we read, 'Those that place the July-flowers above the tulips, because of their pleasant smell, long lasting qualities and bearing of more flowers, ought to consider that the sight of flowers ought to have the pre-eminence, and that smell gives them no beauty . . .'. And so, for the first time perhaps, the old, sweetly scented, cottage garden flowers had to make way for the 'new' flowers, many of them better suited to the gardening of the times. It should be said however, that there are a number of modern tulips which possess a rich, sweet, honey-like perfume to augment their brilliance of colour.

There followed the era of Joseph Paxton, who became head gardener to the 6th Duke of Devonshire at Chatsworth in 1826, a year which coincided with the introduction to Britain of orchids, begonias and other exotic plants, obtained from the tropical forests of South America and the Far East. To keep these plants alive in our cold winter climate, it was necessary to provide them with similar conditions to those in which they grew in their native lands. Cast iron was just about to come into use for the construction of buildings and, in conjunction with glass, produced a structure which was light and airy and enabled most of the exotic plants to be accommodated under the warm, humid conditions they most enjoyed. It was Paxton who modelled the Crystal Palace on the great glasshouse specially constructed at Chatsworth in 1850 to accommodate the scented, giant Amazon water-lily. The use of glass to house the more tender plants during winter opened up a new era in gardening, for the plants of the tropics could be housed in heated greenhouses during winter, and used for bedding out in summer, and were of such exotic colourings that all gardeners had a wish to grow them. That they possessed no perfume, depending entirely upon brilliance of colour to draw humming-birds for their pollination, and demanded considerable attention with their lifting after flowering and replanting each year, and that they required to be kept warm for at least six months of the year, presented few problems, for labour and fuel were readily and inexpensively available. For almost a hundred years, begonias and pelargoniums and other exotic plants from the tropics were used to the almost complete exclusion of the simple cottage garden plants.

And yet, the people had not entirely lost the sense of smell and the pleasures to be obtained from it. With the gardens now almost entirely devoid of scented flowers and leaves, and confronted by the ugliness of new buildings brought about by the Industrial Revolution, the people retained a desire to inhale the sweet perfumes of a former age. And so the potters of Staffordshire devised a method by which fragrance in flowers could be replaced by synthetic perfumes in the home. Pastilles of scented resin were burnt in dainty model cottages made of bone china, which were able to withstand considerable heat. As the pastilles smouldered, the smoke arose through the tiny chimney to give its fragrance to the room. The most popular scents were rose, orange and vanilla, the separate ingredients being made into a paste and shaped into a cone which, when dry, was set alight. To lend additional atmosphere to the perfumes, the cottages were decorated with the leaves and flowers of those scented plants now regrettably displaced. But not entirely, for in the Paisley district near Glasgow, the weavers kept alive the clove-scented Laced pinks, and around the woollen towns of Yorkshire, sheltered beneath the Pennines, the deliciously scented auriculas and the gold-laced polyanthus were taken up by those who could not see these delightful flowers become lost for all time.

The pastille burners of the nineteenth century were only a slight modification of those of medieval times, which were known as osselets of Cyprus. They were made of gum resins, obtained on the island, and were first introduced to England when Richard I, at the time of the Crusades, proclaimed himself king of Cyprus. The cakes of aromatic gums were placed upon glowing embers and produced a vapour which filled the room with fragrance.

The pastilles of more recent date were made by mixing together ground sandalwood, gum benzoin and Tolu with otto of cassia, clove and santal. Potassium nitrate was then dissolved in mucilage of tragacanth and added to the mixture which was then beaten in a mortar, made into tiny cakes and allowed to dry.

Chinese joss sticks were also burnt indoors in European homes, as they were in the temples of Buddha, likewise scented spills. These were made by steeping a sheet of light paper in a saltpetre solution, made by dissolving two ounces in a pint of water. The paper was then dried and on to it was rubbed a solution made by dissolving olibanum or myrrh in rectified spirit. This was applied to both sides of the paper, which was then hung up to dry. Strips of the paper were cut and rolled into spills for lighting. They burnt slowly, releasing their fragrance about the home, and can still be used today.

2

What is Scent?

The music of scents—The olfactory system—The reactions to scents—The appreciation of scent—The constituents of scent—The functions of scent in flowers and leaves.

The Music of Scents. At first aromatic plants had been most in demand for purifying the air and for placing amongst clothes, and it was not until later that they were used to revive the spirits. In his *Essay on Health and Long Life* (1690), Sir William Temple wrote, '. . . the use of scents is not practised in modern physic but might be carried out with advantage, seeing that some smells are so depressing and others so inspiring and reviving'. Ralph Austen said that 'sweet perfumes work immediately upon the spirits, for their refreshing, sweet and healthful ayres are special preservatives,to health', and William Coles wrote in 1656,

Herbes . . . comfort the wearied braine with fragrant smells which yielde a certaine kind of nourishment

Again, in his essay *Of Gardens,* Francis Bacon wrote that a garden 'is the greatest refreshment of the spirits of man', and went on to compare the smell of flowers to musical notes: 'And because the breath of flowers is far sweeter in the air (where it comes and goes, like the warbling of music) . . .' Miss Sinclair Rohde has also written that 'the fragrance of flowers may be described as their music, none the less beautiful because it is silent. In every scented flower and leaf, the perfume is exhaled by substances so perfectly blended as to give the impression of a single scent, just as different notes make a chord.' Yehudi Menuhin, the famous violinist, has said that he considers scent even more elusive than music, stirring in one unconscious thoughts and emotions difficult to analyse.

In the oil of the rose are at least eight substances so exquisitely blended and 'in tune' with each other as to produce a perfect chord of scent. 'The melodies of the flowers', said Miss Rohde, 'cannot be heard by mortal ears', but they reach our senses by other means and are no less enjoyable.

Charles Piesse, the famous French perfumer of the late nineteenth century, pointed out that perfumes should correspond with a scale, like notes of music, and that one false scent or note will ruin the harmony.

Scents, like sounds, influence the sense of smell, the olfactory nerve, in certain degrees. There is an octave of odours as well as an octave of notes in music. Certain odours coincide or blend, like the keys of an instrument. For example, almond, heliotrope and vanilla blend together. The citrons and verbena also blend, forming a higher octave of scent, as it were, and this is taken to a higher note by a combination of rose, pettitgrain and neroli (orange-blossom). Patchouli, sandalwood and cedar blend to perfection, and so on throughout the whole of the floral kingdom. It is said that the perfumer has over 4,000 raw materials from which to work, the most famous perfumes being likened to the world's great symphonies.

The Olfactory System. Olfaction is usually considered to be the lowest and most animal of all our senses. It is the most primitive, and in man no evolutionary change has taken place since the beginning of time, for olfactory development is linked with the habits of the different species. Quadrupeds have a more highly developed sense of smell than man who relies almost entirely on his vision for survival and thus neglects his sense of smell. In the insect world, too, survival depends more on the sense of smell than upon vision.

Our sense of smell has been maintained more by the mouth than through the nose, for we have come to appreciate the sensation of flavour in food and drink more than those things which merely have a pleasant perfume. That which we understand as flavour in food is really its odour, transmitted from the sensory cells present in the lining of the nasal cavity.

The apparatus which allows us to distinguish between various smells is contained in the epithelium linings situated at the top of the nose. They are like tiny rods, from which protoplasmic filaments known as the olfactory 'hairs' project into the mucous membrane. The end olfactory cells taper into a nerve fibre which is in direct contact with the central nervous system, and their function is to pass the scent from the nose to it. The same thing happens when we eat and drink: when we open the mouth, the aroma is taken up through the nose, the molecules of the odorous substance come into contact with the olfactory cells, and are transmitted to the nervous system. It is this which determines whether we appreciate a particular perfume (or food) or not. It has been estimated that whereas the reactionary time for auditory sensation is about .15 of a second, that for smell is .5 of a second; pain, takes .9 of a second to register. And whilst the gas chromatograph can detect a thousandth of a millionth of a gramme of certain substances, the human nose can detect a hundredth of that.

The Reactions to Scents. The nerve endings of the olfactory cells may become oppressed by a too powerful perfume, as when used in a too concentrated form or experienced at close range; the nerves are then unable to appreciate the scent. An example of this is the extremely powerful fragrance emitted by flowers of the Austrian brier, *Rosa foetida* (syn. *R. lutea*), which has been widely used by rose breeders to impart its brilliant-yellow colouring to modern roses. If its fragrance is inhaled at a distance it is quite pleasant, but inhaled close to it is most unpleasant: it is a fetid smell (hence its botanical name) similar to that of decaying fish, owing to the presence of indole. A similar experience may be had when inhaling narcissus blooms in a warm room. On the other hand, the fragrance of the violet rapidly tires the sense of smell. At first the scent is sweet and pleasing, but the olfactory nerves quickly become fatigued, and the longer it is inhaled, the more completely the scent fades, leaving only a faint smell of damp moss or cut cucumber. Professor Zwaordemaker has shown that when the olfactory nerve endings have become fatigued by a certain smell, they are also insensitive to other scents which may resemble it, though differing in chemical composition.

Towards the end of the nineteenth century, Parville, a French scientist, stated that the scent of the violet had an injurious effect on the voice, and there is on record the experience of the celebrated singer, Marie Sass, who was unable to sing a note after smelling a bunch of Parma violets presented to her. This was due to the perfume acting upon the nerves, and bringing about a tumefaction of the vocal chords. For this reason, teachers of singing forbid the use of perfume made from violets. A concentration of musk, used as a perfume, has a similar effect.

Dr F. A. Hampton, an authority on scented plants, has described the effect a field of beans in bloom had on an acquaintance: the girl, who was in her teens, would become greatly excited, with rapid beats of the heart and quickening breathing. A bed of hyacinths or of the night-scented stock, has been known to cause the same reaction when inhaled in the stillness of evening, producing a form of intoxication. Because of this property, the bean was considered a sacred plant both to the Greeks and to the Romans; until modern times, the flowers were widely used for love charms on account of their heady perfume, and there is an old Leicestershire superstition that to sleep in a bean field all night will send a person crazy.

On the other hand, it has been reported that a person suffering from severe headaches found relief almost immediately when sitting near a gorse bush in full bloom, perhaps owing to its refreshing fruity perfume which has been likened to that of orange or pineapple.

The subject of emotional floral responses is so great that some seventy-four aspects have been covered extensively, and from earliest times have formed the basis of folk medicine, herbalism and homoeopathic flower healing. For example, the clove and lavender scents have a powerful attraction for the male; a young Greek girl is said to have been transformed into a nymphomaniac after inhaling the flowers of *Jasminum officinale*.

The famous painter Pietro Annigoni uses perfume to create atmosphere between himself and his sitter, and is himself exhilarated by the aroma of burning wood and by the smell of old books.

Appreciation of Scent. The leaves of fragrant plants never become oppressive as do certain flowers; indeed, the more highly aromatic the perfume, the more pleasing it becomes. It is the excessive sweetness of certain flowers which causes them to become overpowering and unpleasant. This is due to the substance indole, which is present in the putrefaction of animal tissue, and is also present in the flowers of the narcissus and jonquil and of the lily. In excessive amounts it produces an almost identical perfume to that of the substance (skatol) obtained from the sex glands of the civet, which is widely used in the perfumery trade. It is a primitive, heady scent which can be most unpleasant when inhaled in quantity.

Dr Hampton has stated that, as flowers die, the sweet-scented compounds are broken down into simpler substances which have either a pleasant or unpleasant smell as the case may be. As the same kind of decomposition occurs in animal (and human) tissue, this may give rise to the pleasantly sweet scent observed by those in attendance at the death of loved ones, and of the unpleasant smell which occurs later.

It is reported that when St Mark's tomb was opened at Alexandria for the conveying of his body to Venice in A.D. 827 'so sweet an odour spread through the city, that all the spiceries of Alexandria could not have caused the like'. When St Alban's grave was opened, in obedience to a sign from heaven, people were amazed at the fragrance of his remains, and the same was said of St Thomas Becket's remains when they were removed from his shrine at Canterbury.

In April 1965, it was reported that a group of scientists at the Illinois Institute of Technology were carrying out the experiment of 'bottling' people to discover whether the odour given off by their bodies could be accurately recorded; volunteers were placed in large bottles of purified air, the outgoing air being trapped in containers and analysed. According to the scientists, the odours given off by humans can be used to determine sex, attire, crimes and, in particular, diseases.

Sexual attraction between humans may depend on odours generated by male and female, which are so delicate as to be imperceptible to others. Experiments carried out at the Primate Research Centre at Beckenham, in England, showed that the sexual desires of male monkeys depended entirely upon the hormones given to the females. When the females were given oestrogen hormones (which naturally reach their maximum concentration in the body at the time of ovulation), the males responded vigorously. Dr Weiner of the Pfizer Laboratories in New York suggested that the male monkeys were attracted by the smell of the particular hormone, and the same reaction may take place between human beings. Similarly, there are butterflies which attract their mates by secreting a perfumed substance on to their wings. It is said that the male silkworm can detect a female from six miles away by her smell.

According to Dr Louis Leakey, the Kenya-born anthropologist, man survived the first twenty million years on earth because of his distinctive body odour which was so offensive that it 'turned' the stomach of animals and they left him alone. Dr Leakey estimated that man's natural 'smell' began to disappear some two million years ago when he had learned the use of weapons for his own protection.

So sensitive is the nervous system to temperament that scent worn on the skin of a woman will change entirely during emotional stress. For the same reason, a dog may attack a person when it can detect a certain smell given off by fear.

Perfumes do not smell the same to different people. To some, a perfume may possess a pleasant smell, whilst to others it may have no fragrance at all or be decidedly unpleasant. This is because the olfactory mucous membrane is covered with pigment which differentiates the degree of perfume. A dark-haired

person has a far keener sense of smell than one who is fair-haired, whilst albinos
have no sense of smell at all, hence the difficulty in classifying scents.

To a particular person, a certain flower will always smell the same if inhaled
from a similar distance, but it may act upon our feelings in a very different way.
The smell of fish, attractively presented on the table, may be satisfying to those
who enjoy fish as a food, but a flower with a similar fishy smell, will be anything
but pleasant to the same person. The almost overpowering fragrance of the lily
may not be appreciated by one who is suffering from fatigue, but may give quite
a different feeling if inhaled when refreshed by sleep.

Fragrance in a flower may be likened to that of expensive artificial perfume
in that it has three distinct 'notes', to use a metaphor of music once again. The
first is the impact or top note, which usually takes one by surprise. This is
followed by the middle note, the 'life' of the fragrance which, once it has
established itself, is the true, lasting scent. Then comes the bottom or final note,
as the perfume begins to disappear (in the case of the violet) or when one moves
away to inhale another flower or scent. As with most pleasing things, it is
possible to have too much at any one time, and then olfactory fatigue sets in,
making it difficult to appreciate the true scent of a flower or perfume. After
inhaling any particular flower allow a little time to elapse before moving on to
another.

The scents of flowers are usually more pronounced on a warm, calm day,
especially plants growing in the semi-shade of valleys (even in the Himalayas)
and woodlands; they frequently have a more powerful perfume than those
which are common to higher regions. This is because in the more shaded places
the flowers rely almost entirely upon their perfume to attract pollinating insects;
also, the perfume seems more powerful because it is not so readily diffused as
it is on higher ground swept by wind.

Gardeners of earlier times relied upon walls and thick hedges to retain the
perfumes of the flowers, and when planting a scented garden some form of
enclosure should be provided, possibly evergreen hedge plants bearing scented
flowers which will provide year-round protection. One such plant is *Viburnum
tinus* (*laurustinus*), or the escallonias which, with their resinous foliage, are
tolerant of salt-laden winds, and several of which bear scented flowers. For the
same reasons, scented plants growing against a wall will give a more pronounced
perfume than elsewhere in the garden.

The Constituents of Scent. Few plants yield simple (pure) odours as Jacques
Passy pointed out in a report to the French Academy of Sciences in 1892, and
even pure substances do not necessarily possess simple odours.

At the end of the nineteenth century, Professor Mesnaud conducted
experiments at the Sorbonne which confirmed Passy's opinion, and also revealed
the manner in which the perfume of flowers is generated. Mesnaud took the
orange-blossom as an example, placing a section on a drop of glycerine beneath
a bell-jar. The reagent employed was pure hydrochloric acid, the acid vapours
given off being absorbed by the glycerine. In this way complete hydration of
sections of the flower in the presence of an acid was obtained, and after a few
moments of exposure to the presence of the reagent, the essential oil appeared
in the form of transparent golden-yellow drops.

The experiment disclosed the presence of several distinctive essential oils. One is contained in the secretory glands on the lower surface of the petals or sepals, and when these same glands were eliminated in an unopened bud, the 'orange' perfume was in no way harmed. Indeed, it was found that the finest neroli is produced solely on the upper surface of the petals, thus proving that the odour of orange-blossom is compound, the scent of the upper petal surface being more agreeable than that of the underside.

To show how the perfume of a flower is generated, Mesnaud took the jasmine flower. Its essential oil, which is the most pure and difficult to imitate, is situated in the row of epidermal cells on the upper side of sepals and petals, also in the corresponding layer on the under surface where the sepals are coloured by a violet pigment. If the evolution of the cell contents in flowers at different stages of development is followed, at first nothing but chlorophyll is found in the tissue. Next to appear is tannin (intermediate glucoside) or pigment. In Mesnaud's experiment, the acid vapours furnished a means of distinguishing all the tannoid compounds intermediate between the chlorophyll and tannin on the one hand, and between the chlorophyll and essential oil on the other. On the lower surface which in the bud was exposed to the action of light and the oxygen of the air, the tannoid compounds were only slowly oxidized, thereby generating tannin. The upper surface, on the contrary, was hidden inside the bud and the parts were not exposed, so that these agencies were inoperative, and the same compounds were converted into essential oil. This oxidizes when in contact with air and produces the sensation of perfume.

The essential oils are secreted into cells from which the protoplasm has disappeared, and there stored as a glucoside (combined with sugar), which can be released only by the action of a ferment found in the living cells.

It is possible that the decomposition of the glucoside is a reversible action, stopping altogether if the essential oil accumulates. Thus the essential oil is not oxidized when the flower closes and gives off no scent.

The strength of any perfume when inhaled will play a large part in determining its pleasantness. Most perfumes are pleasant when inhaled in small amounts, but can be most disagreeable in large doses. A flower may contain several different odours, as Passy suggested, presenting an agreeable perfume which is not intense and which alone may be perceived when the quantity is minute; and an odour which is intense but unpleasant and which quite overpowers the pleasant scent when inhaled in larger quantity. Indeed, attar of roses in quantity is most unpleasant because it is so overpowering, but it does not represent the true rose perfume which is dependent on a number of other substances for its delicacy. The same feeling may also be experienced with the tuberose, the intense odour of which is revealed in concentrated form when the oil forms into small drops under the influence of a hydrochloric acid reagent.

To revert to the jasmine, its attar is composed of benzyl acetate, shaded off with traces of benzyl formate and toned with methyl anthranilate and indole, and with various fruit-scented substances to give the perfume 'lightness'.

Towards the end of the nineteenth century, Dr Piesse undertook a series of experiments to measure the intensity of an odour, for he had observed that when alcoholic solutions of essences were allowed to evaporate they underwent a natural analysis. The most volatile were the first to evaporate. This he called the 'velocity of odours' and suggested that odours affect the olfactory nerves in direct proportion to their volatility. Thus bodies possessing a very low degree of volatility are known as strong odours, e.g. patchouli, cedar; those with a high degree of volatility are known as feeble odours, e.g. citron, English lavender. The most powerful odours are produced by the most slowly released odorous waves. Dr Piesse formulated a table showing the volatility or strength of odours in comparison with water taken as a single unit.

Acorus calamus	0.007
Bergamot	0.055
Cedarwood	0.002
Citron	0.248
Clove	0.003
Geranium (Spanish)	0.010
Lavender (English)	0.062
Lemon-grass	0.017
Lemon-thyme	0.006
Neroli	0.033
Opoponax	0.003
Otto of roses (Bulgarian)	0.005
Patchouli	0.001
Thyme (ordinary)	0.022

The Functions of Scent in Flowers and Leaves. Plants use their essential oils as protection against insects, such as ants which may attack the leaves and stems. Plants with scented leaves are rarely attacked by pests, and are rarely in need of protecting sprays as are scented flowering plants. They also offer protection against animals, as an alternative to the formation of thorns for, with but one or two exceptions, plants with thorns rarely have scented foliage. Again, as most of the highly aromatic plants grow in hot, arid parts, they protect themselves from desiccation by releasing an oily vapour from the leaves which acts as a barrier against the hot sunshine, as it does against animals and insects. A number of plants carry their protective powers a step further in that their leaves are covered with downy hairs, the peppermint-scented pelargonium, *P. tomentosum*, being a striking example; the leaves of this plant are so thick and velvet-like that Miss Gertrude Jekyll described them as being like 'a fairy's blanket'.

Originally, scent in plants was of antiseptic or protective value to the plant. For example, the first plants to cover the earth's surface, the conifers, the balsam poplars, the walnut and the birch, which are wind-pollinated plants (for there were few insects), produced an antiseptic, gum-like substance wherever the bark was punctured. This was used by primitive man for treating his own wounds, and Friar's Balsam is still used for treating cuts and soothing a sore throat. The aromatic foliage of these plants also protected them from browsing animals.

Oils extracted from plants which have fragrant leaves have a greater antiseptic value than those obtained by extraction from petals. Attar of roses is the exception to this, its antiseptic qualities being the most potent of all flowers, and having seven times the antiseptic strength of carbolic acid; but the oil from the leaves of thyme is even more powerful for it has twelve times the antiseptic strength of carbolic acid. Those who may smile at the use of sprigs of rue and rosemary, when worn by members of the jury at the Old Bailey as protection against fever, should realize that both these herbs have many times the antiseptic value of carbolic acid in which today there is so much faith. These plants also possessed an additional value in their ability to keep away pests which carried diseases, and many of the aromatic oils were used to soak into clothes worn by soldiers and prisoners at a time when they were not housed under the best of conditions.

In experiments on the germicidal power of essential oils over the typhoid bacillus, Professor Chamberlain found that oil of cinnamon completely killed the germs in 12 minutes, oil of cloves within 25 minutes, and oil of thyme, verbena (Indian) and geranium in less than 50 minutes. Professor Riedlin reported that, from his own experiments conducted over a long period, the essential oils which had the most antiseptic value were those of lavender, rosemary and clove. Not only are these herbs of great value in combating germs, but unlike many modern chemical preparations, they are completely safe and are most pleasant to use. Yet they are so rarely used today, and often only as a symbol as, for example, when the boys of Christ's Hospital walk before members of the Skinner's Company, carrying bouquets of flowers and herbs to 'ward off the plague'.

In the early twentieth century, Professor Tyndale made a number of experiments to ascertain the precise cooling effects of certain fragrant plants obtained by discovering their powers of absorption of heat. He found that rosemary had 74 times the cooling effect of fresh air, thyme 68 times, and lavender 60 times, so that the old gardeners knew exactly what they were about when covering brick walls, which would become exceedingly hot during summer, with rosemary, a custom which Thomas Hill said was 'exceedingly common in England'. In the *Herbal of the Bible* (1587), Newton says that it was the custom for the peoples of Palestine to 'stick fresh green leaves over and about their beds for coolness', and Tusser suggested 'herbs and branches' for growing in pots indoors for summer coolness in addition to 21 herbs he named for strewing, which would give the same effect.

3

Flower Scents and Pollination

Lepidoptera and pollination—Night-scented flowers—Hymenoptera and pollination—Pollination by birds—Self-pollinating flowers—Evil-smelling flowers

Lepidoptera and Pollination. Survival of plant and insect are inter-related, and whereas flower scents are given by nature for the plant's fertilization, they are of equal importance for the survival of the fertilizator. Flowers where the nectar is deeply secreted in long tubes are usually heavily scented to attract the long-tongued Lepidoptera, the butterflies and moths, which are drawn by scent rather than by sight.

The butterfly is known as the 'flower of the air' not so much because of its beauty but because of its fragrance. The German naturalist Dr Hermann Müller first drew attention to this characteristic: he found that scent varies in different species, some smelling like jasmine, others like bean flowers, but mostly they carried the scent of honey. Indeed, some butterflies may visit only flowers emitting a similar scent to that carried by themselves, so confining their visits mostly to honey-scented flowers much as honeysuckle, buddleia and *Sedum spectabile* on which they settle in numbers during August and September, especially the Red Admiral, Peacock and Small Tortoiseshell.

The scent of butterflies is due to an oil secreted at the base of a tuft of hairs which are folded along the inner edge of the wings. During mating, the fragrant oil is secreted along the hairs which the male brushes against the female, covering her with the perfume. As with flowers, the scent is retained by a greasy substance with which the hairs are covered. In some species of moth, the scent hairs are found on the front legs, in others it is on the abdomen, but it is used in exactly the same way.

The function of the scent of butterflies was confirmed by Dr Carpenter in 1914. He reported on his observations of the courting and mating of several African species when he witnessed the male hovering above the female and protruding his scented hairs on to her.

The French naturalist Fabre has written of the attractions a female Great Peacock moth had for some 40 males of the same species, from which it would appear that the female also has scented attractions. The female had entered a room in his home and that same night, which was dark and stormy, he was amazed to observe as many as 40 male moths enter in some way in search of a mate. Fabre noticed that the males did not make straight for the female, a characteristic movement when directed by sight, but first went into other rooms as if trying to discover the source of her scent. Fabre observed that when he placed the female moth beneath gauze or muslin the males always found her, yet when she was placed beneath a glass container they were unable to follow her scent. He noted that moths of no other species sought her out.

Night-scented Flowers. Flowers which are fertilized by butterflies and moths are the most strongly scented, guiding the pollinating insects to them by their perfume. Especially fragrant are the night-scented flowers, and those which grow in shade and are evanescent, being mostly white or pale yellow. So great is the economy of nature that the night-scented flowers open only in the lower temperatures of shady places and at night, when they give off their perfume, relying almost entirely for their pollination upon the night hawk-moths.

The Evening primrose, for example, is prevented from opening its clear yellow flowers during the day by the hooks of the tapering sepals clasping each other. Then, as twilight descends and the air becomes cooler, the flower discards its protective hood and opens in all its fragrant loveliness.

Most of the night-flowering blossoms open only for a single night and, after fertilization, die. The scent tends to be more powerful when released in the dampness of night-time than is the case with flowers which release their scent by day. This factor, together with their evanescent colouring, enables the moths to pollinate as rapidly as possible whenever conditions permit.

Papilionaceous flowers offer many different and fascinating adaptations for their pollination. The case of the night-flowering *Posoqueria fragrans* (Rubiaceae) has been described by Fritz Müller: the flower has stamens which are irritable, so that when a moth visits a flower the anthers explode, covering the moth with pollen. Then one of the filaments, broader than the others, moves and closes the flower for about 12 hours, after which it will resume its original form. Thus the stigma cannot be pollinated by the same flower, only with pollen brought by a moth from another flower.

Most of the flowers pollinated by night-flying Lepidoptera are tubular, hence the insects are able to reach the deeply concealed nectar with their elongated tongues, and the flower makes quite sure that both anther and stigma are touched by the insect's long proboscis. Examples are *crinum, pancratium* and *cyrtanthus,* which are amongst the most powerfully scented of all flowers.

The only crucifer adapted for pollination by Lepidoptera is *Hesperis matronalis* which blooms at night and secretes its honey in a deep tube.

The night-scented *Lonicera caprifolium,* the honeysuckle of southern Europe, has a tube so long that its honey is available only to Lepidoptera with a proboscis 3 cm. (over 1 in) long, which abound in the area. *Lonicera periclymenum,* on the other hand, which is native to the British Isles and northern Europe, is scented both by day and by night for, in the cooler, moister climate, night-flying Lepidoptera are less numerous, and during adverse weather may not visit the flowers. The flowers have a tube only 2 cm ($\frac{3}{4}$ in) long, and so the honey is accessible also to bees and butterflies. In contrast, the shade-loving orchid of Madagascar, *Angrasecum aesquipedale,* with a spur no less than 22.5 cm (9 in) long, is pollinated by a hawk-moth found on the island which, as foretold by Darwin, has an even longer proboscis.

The tongue of all Lepidoptera has replaced the rest of the mouth organs; the upper lip and mandibles are aborted, and the mouth is simplified into two long hollow filaments. These have grooves on the inner surface and are so close together as to form a tube through which nectar can be sucked in. When not in use, they are kept coiled in a spring-like spiral which is tucked away in a small space. It is uncurled in a moment as the insect alights on a flower. At the end of the proboscis are minute hairs, varying in size according to the different species, and at the ends of these are minute rods resembling olfactory hairs which may be the means of conveying scent to the nervous system.

Apart from insects which enter flowers for warmth and protection from adverse weather, the night-flying Lepidoptera are the only insects which visit flowers for their nectar at night, moving from one to another in rapid movements. Rapidity is essential if the flowers are to be fertilized when ready, which will ensure the continuity of the species, and it is of equal importance for its survival that the moths are able to obtain as much nectar as possible whilst the flowers remain open.

As a general rule, flowers fertilized by night-flying Lepidoptera grow within woodlands or wooded valleys, or in tropical areas, the plants being protected from cold winds by the terrain and by trees, and the calm, humid conditions being enjoyed by the pollinators. Of the rhododendrons of the Himalayas and the mountainous regions of Burma and China, those which bear fragrant flowers grow deep down in sheltered valleys whilst those growing in the rarefied atmosphere of the mountains are entirely devoid of perfume. For the same reason, few plants of Canada, New Zealand, Scandinavia, the European alpine regions and the Caucasus bear scented flowers, for Lepidoptera are unable to tolerate the cold climatic conditions, though there are a number of migrating species which visit the more sheltered parts in summer.

It would appear that colour also plays a part in attracting butterflies in the same way that the paler colours attract the nocturnal Lepidoptera, for the flowers mostly visited by butterflies, e.g. buddleia and dianthus, bear flowers of pink colouring. I have observed that red-coloured dianthus are neglected by the butterflies, though they will make use of them in the absence of pink blooms. It should be noted that the flowers of *Lonicera periclymenum* have a pink rather than a yellow appearance when observed from above, hence the particular attraction of this species for the butterfly as well as the moth.

Flowers which emit a 'fruity' perfume appear to rely on beetles for their pollination. In flowers where the honey is exposed in a shallow disc, e.g. those of the Umbelliferae and Compositae, Coleoptera lick the disc, whilst in Ranunculaceae and Plantaginaceae beetles often feed upon the pollen. Almost all bear scentless flowers. Flowers of the tree peony, magnolia and illicium are, however, fertilized entirely by Cetonia (beetles) which enter the buds before the flowers open; whilst Cryptocephalus appear to be the sole pollinators of ulex, genista and *Nuphar lutea,* each of which bear flowers scented of ripe fruit, an association of the larvae of beetles and their feeding upon apples and other fruits.

Almost all the large plant families, such as Umbelliferae and Compositae, are pollinated by Diptera (flies), for the flowers are conspicuous by their appearance in umbels or heads, and present a flat and easily traversed surface. The flies can pollinate rapidly whilst obtaining the honey which is readily accessible to their short tongues. In Umbelliferae, the honey lies fully exposed upon the fleshy disc, whilst in Compositae the honey is secreted by a ring surrounding the style at the base of the narrow corolla tube where it accumulates. As it does so, it rises into the wider part of the corolla where the anthers shelter it from rain and where it is readily accessible to the short-tongued Diptera as well as to bees and butterflies.

Both Compositae and Umbelliferae are occasionally visited by field bugs (Hemiptera) in search of honey but no flower seems especially adapted to them.

The Diptera, being the less intelligent of insects, only feed where the least ingenuity is needed to do so, i.e. where the pollen and nectar are readily available and where little or no effort is needed. Flowers of Compositae and Umbelliferae are noted for their unpleasant smell whilst those visited by bees have no scent. In passing, it is of interest that flowers which have deeply secreted nectar also have their pollen deeply situated. The most highly scented flowers attract the most intelligent insects, and on the whole are provided with a tube so long and narrow that only Lepidoptera are able to reach the honey. Though not readily observed, the dianthus has such a tube so that the honey is available only to the longest-tongued butterflies and Humming-bird hawk-moths.

Hymenoptera and Pollination. Flowers beloved by bees, which use their sight rather than their sense of smell, have a different function to play for they attract the bees by means of distinguishing marks, like the rays of a pansy bloom or the bright-yellow eye of the forget-me-not. Mostly they are coloured blue, and Sprengel maintained that the distinguishing marks served as guides to the nectary. The order of Hymenoptera is of the highest rank in its adaptations concerning fertilization.

That the distinguishing marks of flowers have been developed in correlation with the nectary is borne out by Darwin who observed that the two upper petals of the common pelargonium have marks near their base. These marks disappear when the nectary aborts, thus confirming that the marking and the nectary have been developed together, to guide the pollinating insects to the nectar in the quickest possible time. Thus the quality of the pollen brought from distant plants is preserved so that the chances of fertilization may not be impaired. In the same way, the shape of the nectary and adjoining parts are related to the particular insects which visit the flowers.

One of the most primitive species of Hymenoptera is Prosopis which is almost hairless, except for the first tarsal joint upon which pollen adheres. They possess a peculiar odour and confine their activities to flowers of similar odour, e.g. *Matricaria, Achillea,* or *Ruta,* in which both honey and pollen are readily accessible. This is necessary, for the insects are provided with only a short tongue. In Andrana and Haliotus, the tongue is more elongated and is hairy, whilst in the most specialized species, Bombus (the humble-bee), and Apis (the hive-bee), the tongue is longer still and more densely hairy. They fly from flower to flower with the proboscis extended, introducing it into the tube of the flower upon alighting, though the tongue is concealed within a sheath to protect the hairs. Able to withstand adverse weather, the humble-bee and hive-bee are considered to be the most important of all insects in the pollination of the flora of the British Isles.

Though bees can readily distinguish most colours, they are unable to distinguish red from green, both of which appear to them as grey, and so they normally concentrate their energies on blue and, to a lesser degree, yellow flowers. Many of the flowers visited by bees possess little or no perfume, for it is not necessary for the survival of either plant or insect. Of a large number of blue-flowering plants which have no scent, almost all are of perennial habit and are mostly members of the Campanulaceae, Boraginaceae and Labiatae families, bearing bell-shaped flowers which allow the bees to probe the wide base in search of the nectar, whilst in the case of borage the bee is able to hang below the drooping flowers which protect the pollen and nectar from moisture and rain.

Hermann Müller has written of the acute powers of vision possessed by bees, also confirmed by Darwin and described in his *Cross- and Self-fertilization of Plants.* Darwin showed how bees will single out flowers of the same species (especially if blue) for visiting in search of pollen, flying from one to another and entirely neglecting other flowers. 'On one occasion', he relates, 'I observed humble-bees flying in a straight line from a tall blue-flowered larkspur (*Delphinium consolida*) which was in full flower to another plant of the same species at a distance of 15 yards which had not a single flower open and on which the buds showed only a faint tinge of blue'. As the flowers of the larkspur are scentless, it means that the bees were able to distinguish the flowers and buds by their keen powers of discrimination.

More than 2,000 years ago, Aristotle observed that bees and certain insects usually visit flowers of the same species for as long as possible before going on to another species. The reason why they do so is possibly that, knowing the exact arrangement of the parts of a flower of a certain species, they are able to work faster than if they moved from one species to another.

For the same reason, it has been observed that where there are large numbers of flowers of a species growing in close proximity, bees will bore through the side of the flowers at the point where the nectar is secreted in order to save the time of entering and leaving the flowers. The bees seem to be stimulated into working at a faster rate by the rivalry of large numbers working together in search of nectar from a concentration of flowers of a single species.

That bees work entirely by sight was confirmed by Darwin when, on a warm day, he observed them visiting the blue flowers of *Lobelia erinus*; he removed the petals of a number of flowers and noted that the bees did not again visit them. He also observed that, if the sun ceased to shine for only half an hour, the visits of the bees to *L. erinus* slackened and finally stopped completely, from which it would appear that a certain degree of warmth is necessary for the secretion of nectar.

That blue flowers do perhaps possess some degree of scent or distinguishing matter was confirmed by von Frisch, who found that when a worker returns to the hive with nectar, the other workers probe her with their antennae and fly off to the same plants which have provided the nectar. The bee with the 'scented' nectar communicates to the others that nectar is to be obtained from a certain nearby plant. In insects, the olfactory organ is situated at the end of the antennae.

Blue-flowering plants visited by bees

Botanical name	Family
Aconitum napellus	Ranunculaceae
Amsonia salicifolia	Apocynaceae
Anchusa azurea	Boraginaceae
Aster novi-belgii	Compositae
Baptisia australis	Leguminosae
Borago longifolia	Boraginaceae
Borago officinalis	Boraginaceae
Brunnera macrophylla	Boraginaceae
Campanula latifolia	Campanulaceae
Codonopsis ovata	Campanulaceae
Commelina caelistis	Commelinaceae
Cyanthus lobatus	Campanulaceae
Cynoglossum nervosum	Boraginaceae
Delphinium consolida	Ranunculaceae
Downingia pulchella	Campanulaceae
Erigeron speciosus	Compositae
Gentiana purpurea	Gentianaceae
Geranium pratense	Geraniaceae
Jasione perennis	Campanulaceae
Lithospermum gastonii	Boraginaceae
Lobelia erinus	Campanulaceae
Mertensia virginica	Boraginaceae
Moltkia caerulea	Boraginaceae
Myosotis sylvatica	Boraginaceae
Ostrowskia magnifica	Campanulaceae
Platycodon grandiflorus	Campanulaceae
Polemonium coeruleum	Polemoniaceae
Pulmonaria angustifolia	Boraginaceae
Scabiosa caucasica	Dipsaceae
Stokesia cyanea	Compositae
Trachelium caeruleum	Campanulaceae
Trachystemon orientalis	Boraginaceae
Tradescantia virginiana	Commelinaceae
Vernonia noveboracensis	Compositae
Wahlenbergia gracilis	Campanulaceae

The only scented species of the mainly blue campanula family is the yellow-flowered *C. thyrsoides,* and whilst the pink and yellow columbines possess a soft, clove-like perfume, no scent is apparent in those bearing blue (or crimson) flowers. Again, in the predominantly blue borage family, only the species bearing white or pale-yellow flowers have any degree of perfume. Scent is lost where pigment (colour) is intensified. The only scented gentians are the yellow *Gentiana lutea,* the purple *G. purpurea* and, to a lesser degree, *G. verna;* the only really powerfully scented aquilegias are those bearing white flowers, native of the Himalayas and Siberia and pollinated by night-flying insects. Thus the non-blue flowers (usually yellow, white or purple) which tend to be neglected by bees, have been endowed by nature with perfume to attract other long-tongued insects, usually Lepidoptera.

Flowers which rely to a large extent upon insects for their pollination are frequently proterandrous, that is to say that their pollen in released before the stigma is ready to receive it. In the case of *Dianthus caryophyllus,* the pollen is shed long before the stigmas are ready to be fertilized, and so the plant relies upon the ability of its flowers to entice insects from the flowers whose pollen is available, just when its own stigmas are most ready to receive it. Hence the flowers possess outstanding perfume, to attract the insects from a considerable distance. Darwin discovered that some plants of *Reseda odorata* (mignonette) were quite sterile without the aid of insects, and to attract them its flowers have outstanding perfume rather than an outstanding colour.

Not all flowers of the same order have the same pollinators. An example is the salvia. *Salvia patens* which bears a blue flower is attractive to the bee; its lower lip which protects the stamens and stigmas forms a landing-stage upon which the bee alights before it enters the flower. The red-flowered *S. splendens* is of quite a different construction. It is native to South America and bears brilliant-scarlet flowers. There, it is visited by humming-birds, themselves not much larger than a moth or bee and, because the bloom has no lip to conceal its reproductive organs, and on which a bee may land, it is pollinated by the long tongues of the birds which hover in front of it almost without movement whilst they obtain the nectar.

Pollination by Birds. Birds are unable to distinguish blue from green and so are always to be found near flowers of scarlet or gold which are common in the tropics wheareas blue flowers are rare. The flowers attract by colour and not by their fragrance, which is usually totally absent since, in any case, birds make no use of their olfactory organs.

A number of unrelated families may be classed as nectar-feeding. They are the humming-birds and honey-creepers of the New World, the sunbirds of Africa and southern Asia, and the honey-eaters of Australia where there are few scented flowers. All inhabit the tropical or sub-tropical regions and visit flowers which are of similar colouring to their plumage. They take their name from the humming sound caused by the vibrations of their wings which is noticeable when hovering in front of a flower, the tongue being thrust in and out with great rapidity.

The beaks of humming-birds are adapted to the various flowers which they visit. In Brazil, the birds fertilize the long tubular flowers of *Manettia* and species of *Abutilon* and *Hibiscus* (Malvaceae) which are sterile without their aid, whilst a sunbird with an especially long beak fertilizes the flowers of the *Datura* in Madagascar though it mostly frequents open spaces and mountainous areas where scented flowers are rare. Likewise the honey-eaters of Australia and New Guinea, areas almost devoid of scented flowers.

Almost all members of the mostly tropical Malvaceae family bear scentless flowers, as well as *Malva neglecta* (syn. *M. rotundifolia*), the most northerly species whose anthers remain extended so that they are touched by the sides of the curling stigmas. It comes early into bloom when there are few pollinating insects about and so has been endowed by nature in such a way that it can pollinate itself. *Lavatera* and *Althaea rosea* (hollyhock) are also self-pollinating, likewise *Plagianthus*, the most southerly member of the family, and all are completely devoid of perfume.

Of interest is the family Oxalidaceae, closely related to Geraniaceae. Where the corolla of the flower is funnel-shaped, pollination is by bees and the flowers are scentless, but where it is of narrow tubular formation, pollination is by butterflies and moths, and the flowers have a pronounced perfume, for example *Oxalis enneaphylla*.

In South America, humming-birds frequent the red flowers of *Impatiens*, and Darwin reported that in Chile he often saw the yellow head of a Mimus covered with cassia pollen. In New Zealand, the red flowers of *Knightia excelsa* are visited by bell-birds which push their beaks into the narrow tubes as they open, and receive the pollen on the front of the head. In this way it is transferred to other flowers.

Where certain insects are scarce, the flowers have been provided with characteristics to attract those insects which are most prevalent. In New Zealand, where bees are few, blue flowers are rare whilst white and pale-yellow flowers, the most primitive forms, predominate. There is no blue-flowered clematis, violets are white, and the bluest of all flowering plants, the gentian, bears white flowers. They are pollinated by night moths, and many are fragrant only by night. *Clematis afoliata* is an example, its leafless stems bearing small greenish-yellow flowers which are highly scented after dusk.

Thomson and Cheeseman, who observed the pollination of the orchids of New Zealand at the beginning of the twentieth century, found that the species of *Cypripedium* which were self-pollinating had no perfume, and that scent was most pronounced in the white-flowering *Earina* and *Dendrobium* species, which rely upon pollination by Lepidoptera. In *Earina suaveolens*, whose powerfully scented flowers are only of $\frac{1}{8}$-in diameter, the position of the sexual parts is so arranged as to make self-pollination impossible, but an insect, on visiting the flowers, would insert its proboscis into the aperture between the labellum and column, and upon withdrawing would come into contact with the rostellum and bring away the pollinia. Upon withdrawal, the cap of the anther would pull them down so that they could readily be placed on the stigma of another flower.

When, of flowers of the same plant family, some open at night and others by day, it is noticeable that those which open in the evening (usually white or pale yellow) are scented, whilst those opening by day have no perfume. The white-flowered *Morea odorata*, opening by night, is powerfully scented, whilst *M. plumaria*, bearing bright-blue flowers and opening by day, is entirely devoid of scent. The one is adapted for pollination by night-flying Lepidoptera, the other, by bees. Again, *Satyrium candidum* bears richly scented white flowers opening by night, whilst *S. corriifolium*, opening by day, bears bright-yellow flowers which are entirely devoid of perfume.

Autumn-flowering plants are usually highly coloured, pigment (tannin) having replaced perfume, even at the expense of the reproductive organs. In none of these plants, mostly members of the Compositae family, is there the slightest trace of scent, though a number have aromatic foliage. The colours of the autumn flowers are similar to those of the leaves of deciduous trees which, at this time, take on colours of gold, crimson, scarlet and brown before they die. Like the autumn-flowering perennials with which we are familiar, deciduous trees which are natives of the same regions of North America take on richer autumnal colourings than the foliage of other trees. The maples are perhaps the obvious example, chlorophyll, the green colouring matter of the leaves, disappearing as the sun loses strength to reveal highly coloured pigments such as carotin and xanthophyll.

Self-pollinating Flowers. Few self-pollinating flowers are scented. For example, the edible pea, *Pisum sativum,* which has flowers adapted for self-fertilization, though it secretes nectar and bears much pollen is rarely, if ever, visited by pollinating insects, either in Britain or (as observed by H. Müller) in Europe. Again, the plants of the family Scrophulariaceae are scentless for the same reason, and though they may be visited by many forms of insect life, this is not necessary for their survival. The calceolaria, for instance, bears flowers adapted to cross-fertilization, and great care is necessary to exclude insects if the plant is to breed true, for the flowers are self-fertile if insects are excluded.

Darwin experimented with flowers of *Verbascum thapsus,* of the same family, and found that covered flowers were as thickly loaded with seed capsules of good quality as flowers which were frequented by insects, thus proving they are able to pollinate themselves.

In the order Ranales, which is closely connected to the conifers and in which oil-containing cells are present in the wood and leaves, and whose plants must be amongst the most primitive of those to bear scented flowers, pollination is mostly by Coleoptera (beetles) which enter the buds as they are unfolding. Amongst the most primitive of insects, the beetles would act as pollinators when few other insects had evolved.

Experiments made with the common red poppy, *Papaver rhoeas,* of British cornfields, and closely related to Ranales with its hypogynous flowers with free sepals, petals and stamens, revealed that the anthers shed their pollen on the radiating stigmas so that self-pollination does take place, though beetles occasionally visit the flowers, attracted by the brilliance of their colour. It is interesting that few members of Papaveraceae which grow in the warmer parts of south-eastern Europe and Asia, bear scented flowers, each of the species being self-fertile, yet members of the family which are native to the cooler climatic regions, e.g. *Papaver nudicaule* of Siberia and *Romneya coulteri* of western America, are endowed with some scent, for they must attract with every possible means the few insects to assist with their pollination. They are the sole exceptions to this predominantly scentless family which includes the *meconopsis, macleaya, eschscholtzia* and *sanguinaria,* each of which is self-fertile.

Evil-smelling Flowers. Not all scented flowers have been endowed with a pleasing perfume and, indeed, a number have a scent which is most unpleasant. Some plants of the rose family (Rosaceae), including the hawthorn and rowan, the cotoneaster and pyracantha, are members of the aminoid group each possessing the same unpleasant sweet-fishy perfume when inhaled at close range. They do, in fact, contain the substance trimethylamine, which is also present in fish brine and occurs in the early stages of putrefaction. The scent attracts dung and flesh-flies to the plants as decaying animal matter does. Likewise flowers of the stapeliad group, which includes the *stapelia, duvalia* and *caralluma,* give off a fetid smell which to *Sarcophaga carnaria* flies represents the smell of decaying flesh. The repulsive smell of the brown and yellow-spotted flowers of *Stapelia variegata* has earned for it the name of Carrion-plant. It is a member of the indoloid group, all of which are pollinated solely by dung-flies, for the nectar is available in shallow cups of easy access to the short proboscis of the flies. The petals also have the thick, velvet-like texture of meat, and *S. hirsuta* bears a bloom covered in 'fur' which gives it the appearance of flesh in an advanced condition of decay. Flies lay their eggs on the petals.

Several members of the large Araceae family, consisting of more than 2,000 species, bear evil-smelling flowers. Amongst these is the Monarch-of-the-east or Voodoo lily *Sauromatum guttatum,* so named because of the evil smell of its beautiful flowers. It will come into bloom if the flat tuber is placed in a bowl of water in a warm room but, as the spathe begins to open, a nauseating odour is emitted, so strong and unpleasant that it is usually necessary to remove the plant without delay. Like the flowers of *Stapelia variegata,* its flowers have the smell of well-decayed meat, and dull, reddish-brown, meat-like markings on the spathe. This is the time when pollination by bluebottles, which swarm about the plant, takes place.

Similar is the largest member of the group, *Amorphophallus titanum,* native to Sumatra. The tubers may measure up to 60 cm (2 ft) across, and the spadix is often 1.8 m (6 ft) tall. It is protected by a mottled spathe to attract flies, and the spadix gives off an abominable stench of decayed flesh. About two days after pollination has taken place, the smell disappears.

Of the same group is the Cuckoo-pint, *Arum maculatum,* the Parson-in-the-pulpit or Priest's hood of the countryside. Its pale-green sheath, like a hood, encloses a purple spadix which actually becomes warm as the flower unfolds in spring, sometimes reaching a temperature of more than $11°C$ ($20°F$) above the surrounding air. When touched, the spadix releases a smell like stale urine which will persist on the fingers even after washing. The smell is attractive to a species of midge, *Psychoda phaloenoides,* which pollinates the plant. The foul smell is present only for a day or so whilst pollination takes place, and disappears immediately afterwards, the spadix losing heat at the same time.

Trillium erectum, native of the damp woodlands of North America is another plant to bear evil-smelling flowers. They appear in May, are the colour of decayed meat, and are pollinated by flies. The variety *album* which bears flowers of ivory-white emits no unpleasant smell, neither do any of the other numerous species which bear white or pink-tinted flowers.

Ferraria undulenta, native of Cape Province, also bears a flower with the smell and appearance of decayed meat. The blooms are of plum-purple colouring, spotted and marked at the centre with brown, and attract flies for their pollination.

4

Classification of Scents in Flowers and Leaves

Flower perfume groups—Leaf perfume groups—The scent of wood, bark and roots—The scent of fungi

NO recognized classification of scent has ever been made because there is so great a variation in perfume. A scent which may be placed in one category by one person may be considered by another to possess quite a different quality, possibly owing to the type of pigment present in the olfactory mucous membrane. Again, perfumes change with dilution, and may be pleasing at a distance, but most unpleasant at close range or in greater concentration. Association also plays a part, and those who do not like the raspberry as a food afford it an unpleasant perfume, whilst those who do will appreciate the raspberry perfume in flowers, as in certain roses.

Flower Perfume Groups. It was not until 1893 that the first attempt was made to classify flower perfumes by Count von Marilaun who arranged them into six main groups according to the chemical substance that predominated in their essential oil: indoloid, aminoid, benzoloid, terpenoid, paraffinoid and the honey group. Several, however, were unsatisfactory: in the terpenoid group which comprised the lemon-scented flowers, it became apparent that the scentless terpenes make no contribution to the perfume and it was later changed to the lemon group. It was also considered necessary to divide the benzoloids into three main groups, heavy, aromatic and violet-scented, so that there are now ten groups of classified flower scents, though they have never been given official recognition. They are however, useful in the study of scented plants.

Indoloid Group. Indole is present in quantity in the flowers of this group which are usually of a pale-brown or chrome colour, often blotched with purple to resemble carrion in appearance. With but one or two exceptions the plants are of the following families and genera: *Amorphophallus,* mostly natives of South Africa and South-east Asia; Araceae. in particular *Arum maculatum* (Cuckoo-pint); *Aristolochia; Caralluma europaea;* the skunk-cabbage of North America (*Lysichitum americanum*); *Stapelia,* especially *S. variegata,* and *Trillium erectum,* as well as a number of fritillaries and *Ferraria undulenta.* The flowers all possess the fetid smell of decayed meat, or of fish. They are visited by Diptera (dung-flies, midges and bluebottles) for pollination, for their nectar is contained in shallow cups and is readily accessible to the short tongues of these insects.

Aminoid Group. Here, the flowers are dingy white or cream-coloured, the plants relying on their unpleasant, ammonia-like fragrance to attract dung-flies and other insects. The individual flowers are small and are borne in dense inflorescences or clusters, their nectar being readily available. They have a powerful scent which, if inhaled at close range, is most unpleasant, with a stale, fishy aroma (and an undertone of ammonia) due to the presence of trimethylamine which occurs in the early stages of putrefaction and is also present in herring brine. Included in this group is *Amelanchier, Cotoneaster frigida* (to the author, the most disagreeable of flower scents, resembling a mixture of decaying fish and stale perspiration), *Crataegus* (the hawthorn, not so unpleasant as the others, for anisic-aldehyde is also present), *Pyracantha, Rhaphiolepsis, Sorbus,* and *Stranvaesia,* all of them tree-like and members of Rosaceae, flowering in June. Privet, too, may be considered in this group. Likewise, the flowers of many of the Umbelliferae have a similarly unpleasant smell and are of similar colouring, also being pollinated by flies. The plants are mostly natives of the Northern Hemisphere. Examples are the giant fennel and the hemlock, the flowers smelling heavily of garlic or of decaying fish, a smell which is present in the leaves of *Oxytropis foetida* and which remains long on the fingers after touching.

Trees bearing flowers of unpleasant smell should be grown away from the house, where the scent will be more pleasant inhaled from a distance, especially whilst the flowers are in a fresh condition. Their scent becomes distinctly more unpleasant after pollination and as the flowers die.

Heavy Group. Flowers of this group, which are amongst the oldest known to man, have a scent like those of the aminoid group, though it is sweeter and usually without any unpleasantness. Indole is present in the essential oil but in less concentrated form than in the indoloid group, together with benzylacetate and methyl anthranilate. Nevertheless, it gives rise to the unmistakable smell of putrefaction when the flowers are inhaled in quantity. Here again, the flowers are mostly white or pale cream, and include the Pheasant's eye narcissus, James Thomson's jonquil 'of potent fragrance', *Lilium candidum,* the tuberose (*Polianthes tuberosa*), and plants of the lilac and olive family, the syringas and several species of *Osmanthus* and *Ligustrum*. The *philadelphus* (mock orange-blossom) and *viburnum* may also be included in this group, also *Hemerocallis lutea* and *Eucharis grandiflora,* all of which are more heavily scented in the evening. The unpleasant undertones disappear when the flowers are inhaled at a distance, for then the animal quality closely related to methyl indol (scatol), the active principle of civet, becomes sweet and flower-like. Many of the plants grow in the warm sub-tropical, heavily wooded regions of South America and central China, relying on their powerful scent for pollination by moths. To a less degree may be included *Daphne laureola,* the lily of the valley, *Moneses uniflora,* and the honeysuckle, woodland plants of the British Isles and northern Europe which may be said to have a 'tropical' quality necessary to draw the moths into the depths of the woodlands, but are also pollinated by other insects.

Aromatic Group. The flowers in this group are amongst the most pleasingly scented of all and contain those essential oils found in the leaves of such attractively aromatic plants as the cinnamon and clove (eugenol). Also included here are the delicious vanilla and balsam scents. The spicy clove scent due to eugenol is found in double stocks; in pinks and carnations; in the night-scented catchfly of the same family; in *Viburnum carlesii* and its hybrids; in *Gladiolus caryophyllus* and *G. tristis*; in *Cyclamen creticum,* and in peonies. The scent of aniseed (without the unpleasant amines as in the aminoid group) is to be detected in cowslips and primroses, and in several members of the magnolia family e.g. *Illicium anisatum,* the bark of which is burnt as incense by the Japanese; *Drimys winteri,* and the magnolias themselves. Again, all bear flowers of purest white, pale yellow or palest pink. The balsam scent is present in the Oriental hyacinth and in the bluebell, also in the night-scented stock, though some would list these plants under the heavy group, for their powerful fragrance can have quite a disturbing effect (like the flowers of the field bean) when inhaled in quantity.

The vanilla scent with an undertone of spice or lemon is present in several of the evergreen *Lonicera,* in *Hamamelis mollis* (witch hazel), *Berberis darwinii, Clematis montana* and *C. flammula*; *Laburnum vossii,* the lupin (tree), acacia, bean and the sweet pea, the last five all members of the Leguminosae family in which the flowers have the same delicious perfume. It is the most pleasing of all flower perfumes, sweet yet unobtrusive and may be enjoyed from a distance for vanillin is perceptible when its presence amounts to only 0.000000005g to a litre of air. It is equally pleasing when inhaled close to, with an undertone of cloves when in concentrated form and warmed by the sun.

The almond fragrance may also be included in this group, being most pronounced in the heliotrope. It is a bitter-sweet scent similar to that of *Convolvulus arvensis* and the flowering rush, pleasant to some but not to those who prefer a sweeter or more refreshing fragrance. The same bitter-sweet perfume is present in the Hybrid tea rose Francine, which is plum-coloured with a white reverse, though some can detect the violet perfume in it; to the author, it has the distinctive smell of red ink. In this group may be included the Mexican orange-blossom, *Choisya ternata,* though to some its white flowers have a more aromatic scent. Many of the flowers in this group are pink and rely on butterflies for their pollination.

Violet Group. The violet is unusual amongst flowers in that it is pollinated by self-fertilizing 'flowers' which require no help from insects, and so it does not rely upon its scent to attract. This is just as well, for its fragrance quickly tires the nerves, and it is possible that insects experience this effect. The same scent is found in *Iris reticulata, Crinum powellii,* several of the mimosas (*Acacia*), mignonette, *Gladiolus recurvus, Leucojum vernum, Asparagus tenuifolius,* and in the flower of the vine.

As the perfume fades it takes on the refreshing smell of damp woodland moss. To some, it is likened to the smell of freshly cut cucumber. The particular scent is due to a ketone, ionone, in flowers; to irone in violet-scented roots.

An interesting letter concerning the perfume of the violet appeared in the magazine *Country Life,* on 6 January 1966. Lt.-Col. Goodden, of Falmouth, wrote that many years ago, his father had been sent from California some yellow violets which had no trace of the scent of our purple violets, but instead a rich apricot scent, like that of gorse in sunshine. It is indeed true that flowers of *Viola odorata sulphurea* have quite a different smell from the purple violet, but it may to a certain extent be a play upon the imagination, for it should be noted that the perfume was likened to that of gorse, another yellow flower whose perfume is thought by some to resemble the aroma of the apricot or pineapple. In the same way flowers of *Clethra arborea* look and smell to some exactly like the lily of the valley, but have quite a different scent when inhaled without being seen.

To some people all white (and all yellow) flowers smell exactly the same (like lilies), but whilst it may be true to say that in general white flowers are the most powerfully scented of all (e.g. jasmine, the Madonna lily, narcissus and white violet, which has a far more pronounced scent than the purple violet), all white flowers do not have the same scent, though indole is present in most and may be detected as common to each. It is possible that the variation in strength of perfume between white, yellow and purple flowers may be accounted for by the likening of the different perfumes to the scent of other flowers of the same colouring, e.g. the yellow violet with gorse, the white jasmine with the jonquil. But not all white or yellow flowers of every genus are more powerfully scented than other colours of the same genus; purple flowers are equally strongly scented. For example, whereas the double white and double yellow primrose are entirely without perfume, the double mauve Marie Crousse and Arthur du Moulin smell exactly like honeysuckle ripened by the sun, a luscious, sweet perfume which is present in several of the Asiatic species and those other members of the family, the auriculas. Again, several of the purple tulips have a richer honey scent than those in other colours.

The perfume of the apricot-coloured Hybrid tea roses Chantré and André le Troquer has been likened to the aroma of ripe apricots which, again, may be the work of the imagination; likewise roses which are thought to smell of raspberries are always of similar cerise-red colouring.

Rose Group. This is often considered the most pleasing of all perfumes, for it is not heavy and though sweet is usually combined with a fruity scent so that it is refreshing even in a concentrated form, a quality on which Theophrastus commented more than 3,000 years ago. Parkinson wrote of the Damask rose as being 'neither heady nor too strong, nor stuffing nor unpleasantly sweet'.

The essential oil contains geraniol, an alcohol which also occurs in a number of fragrant-leaf plants and is especially pronounced in the Rose-leaf geranium, *Pelargonium capitatum*, and in the leaves of the Australian pine from which it is more easily extracted. The rose scent is also present in *Iris hoogiana* and in several of the peonies, but is purer in leaves than in flowers which contain substances similar in fragrance to the essential oil but which are not exactly the same. Thus we get the rose perfume with overtones of spice or fruit, or maybe of violet or heliotrope which is more complex. At the same time it is more delicate than the pure rose perfume obtained from the Rose-leaf geranium and which is incorrectly sold in the markets of the East as attar of roses, when the true attar is obtained only from the flowers.

The finest attar of roses is obtained from Bulgaria and from the valley of Kasanlik in Persia where the most highly fragrant of the Damask roses are grown, double blooms being more fragrant and so providing most attar. The plants attain their full vigour and the blooms yield the most attar between the third and twelfth year, after which they begin to decline and are replaced. As with most flowers of fruity perfume, e.g. magnolia and *Paeonia suffruticosa,* roses secrete no nectar and are visited by beetles.

Lemon Group. The refreshing scent of lemons is found in few flowers, though often in leaves. It could almost be classed as a subsection of the rose group for its main component, citral, is the first product of geraniol by oxidation. It is most pronounced in the flowers of *Rosa bracteata,* the Macartney rose of China, a shrubby climber suitable for planting against a warm wall, which brings out the fragrance of its flowers to the full. The large, single blooms, with their golden stamens, smell strongly of lemons, and the same refreshing perfume is present in the evening primrose, *Oenothera odorata.* The flowers of the water-lily, *Nymphaea odorata,* and those of the verbena (though sweeter) and of *Abronia latifolia,* the Sand verbena, possess a more delicate lemon perfume, and the scent is present in the flowers of *Magnolia soulangeana* with sweeter undertones. Most of these flowers are visited by beetles for their pollination.

Fruit-scented Group. Here may be included all the fruit-scented flowers which are not of the lemon group. The flowers of several species of the philadelphus, and the rambler roses The Garland and Wedding Day carry the distinctive perfume of the orange, whilst *Cytisus battandieri* and the gorse smell of pineapple, a clean invigorating fragrance. Freesias have the scent of ripe plums, likewise the flowers of *Muscari racemosum* and *Leucocoryne ixioides. Rosa wichuraiana,* the Japanese rambler rose, has the fragrance of green apples which is also present in the hybrid Silver Moon. *R. dupontii* and *R. soulieana* bear flowers with the scent of ripe bananas. The flowers of *Iris graminea* have the delicious smell of apricots.

Animal-scented Group. This group is joined to the fruit-scented one by the esters (compounds formed by the combination of an acid and alcohol) of fatty acids, some producing a fruity scent, others the scent of animals. In certain flowers, such as the early purple orchis, the blooms as they open have a pleasant vanilla scent from a distance, but smell unpleasantly of tom cats after pollination and as the flowers age. Perhaps a more obvious example is *Hypericum* which gives off the unmistakable smell of goats and also of ripe apples from the pellucid glands in its leaves.

When the fruity scent is entirely absent, the plant emits a more objectionable smell, likened to that of animal fur, of cats, foxes or dogs, examples being the Crown imperial, (*Fritillaria imperialis*), the Lizard orchid and *Codonopsis,* the former having a fox-like smell, the latter smelling of ferrets.

There are also objectionably smelling plants, notably the Valerian and the Ox-eye daisy, which cannot be conveniently placed in the indoloid, aminoid or heavy groups. They contain valeric acid and smell of human perspiration in which valeric acid is also present. There is certainly an animal link but these plants do not have the animal-like character of *Codonopsis* or the Lizard orchid.

In this group could be included the musk scent which is the connecting link between the animal-scented group and the honey group.

The original musk-plant, with its trailing habit, had no scent and only when it 'sported' to take on hairy characteristics did the rich, animal, musk-like scent appear. Then for some unknown reason the plants, which for long had been grown in small pots in cottage windows, completely lost their perfume. This happened in about 1913. The cause may lie in the glandular hairs with which the old musk 'sport' was covered in the same way that the hairs of the Moss rose (*Rosa muscosa*) have a musk-like scent which remains on the fingers after touching. In certain parts of the world, the musk not only loses its hairs but also its perfume. Similarly when the hairs of the Sweet-briar are removed by scraping, the sweet refreshing scent is entirely lost.

The musk scent has not been entirely lost in flowers, for it is present in the flowers of the Musk-hyacinth, *Muscari moschatum*, from which the *Muscari* genus takes its name. To some, the white flowers of the Musk rose of the Himalayas, *Rosa moschata*, have the smell of musk. Miss Sinclair Rohde describes the blush-white form as being definitely musk-scented and this may have been the form loved by Shakespeare and by Bacon, '. . . the sweetest smell in the air is the violet, next to that is the Musk Rose', though it is probable that it was *R. arvensis,* the native field rose, whose flowers have a less pronounced musk scent. The foliage of *Delphinium brunonianum* is also musk-scented. Native to the Himalayas, it grows less that 30 cm (1 ft) tall and bears purple-blue flowers which are heavily veined and hooded and carry the musk perfume of the foliage but in less pronounced form.

The musk-scented flowers are closely allied to the honey group, and the flowers of the witch hazel carry a musk-like perfume to some and to others a honey scent. Almost all the musk-scented flowers are native of the mountainous regions stretching from Afghanistan to western China where the musk-deer is to be found, and it may possibly feed upon these plants.

Honey Group. This group could be a sub-section of the animal group which includes flowers with the musk perfume, but as the honey-like perfume in flowers is unmistakably sweeter, it is given a class to itself. One of the most pronounced honey scents is present in the flowers of the Buddleia family which are so attractive to butterflies. The same may be said of *Sedum spectabile*; the scent of the blooms changes to a slight, musk-like fragrance as they begin to fade. Flowers of the meadowsweet (with a fishy undertone), the sweet scabious, and the sweet sultan have the honey fragrance, and those of several of the evergreen escallonias have a similar delicate scent. Pink clover and honeysuckle come into this category and all are visited by butterflies.

There are flowers which cannot be included in any of these groups, such as the sweet alyssum (*Lobularia maritima*), which has the refreshing smell of newly mown hay, like the sweet vernal grass, *Anthoxanthum odoratum,* and woodruff which releases its scent as it becomes dry, owing to the presence of coumarin, but most may be classified into one of the ten main groups.

A number of flowers appear to give a different scent by day and by night, though it would seem that this is the same perfume in more concentrated form. The orchid *Dendrobium glumaceum* which has the strong almond scent of the heliotrope by day, is thought by some to smell of lilac at nightfall, but some consider the lilac perfume merely a less concentrated form of the heliotrope.

Few plants have both scented leaves and flowers, for nature is not wasteful and it is not necessary for pollination or protection. There are exceptions. Both the leaves and flowers of the French marigold have the same characteristic pungent smell, and both flowers and leaves of *Chimonanthus fragrans* and

Drimys aromatica have the same pleasing perfume. In each case the scent of the flowers is similar to the smell of the leaves but less concentrated. In *Rosa setipoda,* the flowers, stems and leaves are scented, and in the allspice, *Calycanthus floridus,* the flowers smell deliciously of apples whilst the wood and roots have a powerful camphor-like scent.

Leaf Perfume Groups. The essential oil is stored in cells, often as pellucid dots, and is clearly visible in many leaves. Though many of the flower oils occur in leaves, the composition of the essential oil is more straightforward, in some cases being no more than a single substance such as methylsalicylate, the principal constituent of wintergreen (*Gaultheria procumbens*). Many fragrant leaves contain substances not present in flowers, and it is these that give the refreshing, pungent quality. Borneol acetate, with its pine scent, is found in the needle-like leaves of conifers and in rosemary, whilst eucalyptol is present in wormwood (*Artemisia*) and Cotton lavender (*Santolina*). Citral is present in lemon-thyme, and in the leaves of the lemon-verbena, *Lippia citriodora,* and *Pelargonium crispum.* Geraniol, the chief substance of attar of roses, is found in the Rose-leaf geranium, *Pelargonium capitatum,* together with phenyl ethyl alcohol, also present in attar of roses. Leaf odours are more persistent than those of flowers for, whereas the scents of leaves increase in strength as the leaves age and even when dried, the opposite (with but one or two exceptions) occurs in the case of flowers. The increased fragrance of leaves is due to evaporation of moisture from the leaf cells as the plant ages, leaving behind the essential oils in concentrated form. The scent is released from its glucoside form by the action of a specific ferment, amygdalose, which does not come into contact with the glucoside until the plant cells are broken, usually when the leaf is bruised (pressed).

The leaf scents fall into four main groups.

Turpentine Group. Here the essential oil is borneol acetate, present in rosemary.

Camphor and Eucalyptus Group. The essential oil here is camphor and eucalyptol, present in sage, wormwood, camomile, catmint and Cotton lavender. It is present in all parts of the Carolina allspice (*Calycanthus floridus*) and in the leaves of *Lindera benzoin*; also in the Bay laurel (*Laurus nobilis*), where it is combined with a rose perfume and with the spicy aromatic scent of cloves. The leaves of *Pelargonium clorinda* smell strongly of eucalyptol which is also present in the eucalyptus trees of Australasia, as well as in the leaves of lavender, rosemary, thyme and myrtle.

Mint Group. The essential oil is menthol, present in all forms of mint as well as in eucalyptus leaves and certain of the scented-leaved pelargoniums.

Sulphur Group. Compounds of sulphur, with their unpleasant smell, occur only in leaves and roots, and are present in mustard, onions, garlic and watercress, all of which may be pleasant to eat and health-giving but would not be included in the garden for their fragrance.

In addition, a number of plants with scented leaves may be included under the ten flower scent groups.

The Indoloid Group is represented here by the Stinkwood, *Celtis reticulata.*

The Aminoid Group includes the Dog's mercury (*Mercurialis perennis*), and the Stinking Goosefoot (*Chenopodium vulvaria*) for their leaves contain tri-methylamine, also present in flowers of the hawthorn and cotoneaster.

The Heavy Group includes the scented-leaf geranium, *Pelargonium* Pretty Polly, whose leaves have a strong, heady perfume almost like jonquil.

The Aromatic Group, as with flowers, is the most attractive group of all, for the leaves have a most refreshing smell. It includes the Carolina allspice and *Humea elegans*, the incense plant; *Liquidambar orientalis* and *Illicium anisatum*, whose leaves have the smell of incense, though to some it is closer to aniseed; the bay, which is sweetened with the rose perfume; the wintergreen and meadowsweet, whose leaves have quite a different scent from the flowers; *Pelargonium fragrans*, with its strong pine scent, and *P.* Prince of Orange with its attractive orange perfume; rue, with its undertones of orange, may be included here or in the fruit group.

In the Violet Group, the rhizomes of *Iris florentina* and *I. pallida* provide the violet-perfumed orris-powder when dried. After rain, the leaves of *Veronica cupressoides* smell distinctly of the violet, a scent not unlike cedarwood. The wood of *Juniper virginiana* has the unmistakable violet perfume, also present in the Indian violet grass, *Andropogon muricatus*.

The Rose Group is most widely represented in the Rose-leaf geranium where it is purer than in most rose flowers. The leaves of *Pelargonium capitum, P. denticulatum, P. graveolens, P. radula* and *P.* Attar of Roses all have a strong rose perfume.

The Lemon Group scent is present in the leaves of balm, lemon-verbena, southernwood (*Artemisia abrotanum*) and lemon-thyme, and in those of numerous pelargoniums including *P. crispum variegatum*, a delightful house-plant, *P. c. major* and *P. citriodorum*. It is also present in *Micromeria corsica* which the late Clarence Elliott said was like 'a mixture of oysters and lemon juice'.

The Fruit Group includes the leaves of *Pelargonium odoratissimum*, the apple-mint and the sweet-briar, *Rosa eglanteria*, each of which smells strongly of apples; the pineapple-scented *Salvia nutilans*; the bergamot (also included in the heavy group) with its pungent, fruity aroma, rue and all members of the family with similar orange undertones.

In the Animal Group, the leaves of the Burning bush, *Dictamnus alba*, and of hyssop, both resinous plants, have a fur-like smell, pungent but not unpleasant, and likewise the leaves of *Canella winteriana*, a native of Florida and Cuba. The animal smell is present in wild strawberry leaves when dying, in walnut leaves, which have a sweet resinous undertone, and in the leaves of *Olearia moschata*, which gives off a musk-like smell. Clary leaves have a cat-like smell when bruised which becomes musk-like as they dry.

The Honey Group: there are few leaves which have the honey perfume, though in the case of the olearias both flowers and leaves have a honey-like fragrance which is closely allied to the musk.

The Scent of Wood, Bark and Roots. Trees and shrubs with fragrant wood and bark, usually native of the sub-tropical areas, may be divided into two main groups:

1. *The Aromatic Group.* It includes plants whose wood and bark exude a

gum-like substance of resinous quality, often with the odour of aniseed, balsam or cinnamon, and usually differing from that of leaves and flowers, though of greater purity.

In an experiment carried out to determine the various amounts of essential oil to be obtained from all parts of the shrub *Lindera benzoin,* a deciduous North American shrub inhabiting damp lands and shady localities, the following amounts of oil were obtained:

	Percentage	*Odour*
From the bark	0.43	Wintergreen
From the berries	5.00	Allspice
From the twigs	0.30	Camphor
From the leaves	0.35	Lavender

It is of interest that each part of the plant yielded an oil with a different perfume, and each of these perfumes may be detected in the appropriate parts of the plant when growing.

Bark which is used commercially is usually removed by beating. The cinnamon bark of the tree *Canella winteriana,* an evergreen tree of the southern United States, Bahamas and Jamaica, is removed by beating the tree with a stout stick. The outer layer readily comes away, and a second beating is then performed to loosen the inner bark, which is comprised of two under-layers. This is slowly dried in the shade before it is packed for exporting. The bark reaches Europe in the form of long quills, rolled up like cinnamon, and silver-grey in colour, the large yellow oil cells being clearly visible. The volatile oil supplies the odorous constituent, the oil being composed of four distinct oils, one of which is eugenol, another being closely allied to the oil of cajuput.

Trees and shrubs with aromatic bark have a commercial value above all other plants for use in both perfumery and medicine. From the bark of *Cusparia officinalis,* found about the Gulf of Santa Fe, angostura is obtained which is both a stimulant and a tonic, and is used to flavour drinks. From the bark and wood of the tree *Cinnamomum camphora* which grows in great abundance around the districts of Kiushiu and Shikoka in Japan, commercial camphor is extracted, the roots also yielding their quota of high-grade camphor. The bark of a number of sub-tropical trees which may be grown in sheltered gardens of the British Isles emits most agreeable perfumes, none being more delicious than that of the magnolia family, namely Winter's bark, *Drimys winteri,* and *Magnolia soulangeana,* the latter having a refreshing lemony scent similar to that of the flowers. One of the most handsome trees of the garden is the Carolina allspice, for the flowers have a distinctive spicy fragrance reminiscent of cinnamon, as do all other parts of the plant, including the roots. The same may be said of the sassafras, which Linnaeus named *Laurus sassafras* (now *Sassafras albidum*) and which, though common in Canada and the United States, is today rarely seen in European gardens. Yet it is quite hardy and is a most interesting plant, with its deeply furrowed greyish-brown bark which is pleasantly perfumed, more so than the wood beneath. With a similar perfume is the Swamp sassafras of the southern United States, *Magnolia virginiana,* a low-growing deciduous tree.

Almost every country has its own 'sassafras'. The Brazilian sassafras is

Nectandra cymbarum, native of the tropical forests of Rio Negro, whose bark smells of rosemary and orange, whilst the Australian sassafras is *Atherosperma moschatum.* Safrol is present in each of these trees, giving the bark its unique perfume, a combination of bergamot and cinnamon. It is identical with the body called Shikomol, present in the bark of *Illicium floridanum,* the Star anise of western Florida, and of *Amyris punctata* whose leaves are marked with glandular dots which when bruised release a similar perfume. In *Illicium anisatum,* the odour is of incense, as in *Boswellia olibanum.*

Almost all the aromatic barks are thick and rough, in some cases more than half an inch in thickness, with tissues rich in long, thin fibres, and with the oil ducts most freely scattered over the outer layer. The odour of barks varies with the age of the tree, being most pronounced as the tree reaches maturity, and thereafter losing strength. Warmth and constitution also play a part, strong sunlight bringing the fragrance nearer the surface, and a plant growing under ideal conditions will have the most pronounced fragrance.

In the Aromatic Group may also be included *Betula lenta* of the eastern United States, its bark smelling powerfully of wintergreen; *Dicypellium caryophyllatum* of Guyana, its bark yielding a delicious clove-like perfume; and *Mespilodaphne pretiosa* which smells refreshingly of bergamot.

2. *The Turpentine Group.* The outstanding example is the bark of *Pistacia lentiscus* and *P. terebinthus,* from which turpentine is obtained. The plants bear through their bark and leaves the essential oil, borneol acetate; also included in this group are conifers which exude an aroma like that of turpentine, such as the evergreen cypress and the fir, the Scots pine, and the deciduous larch.

Ovid wrote of 'trees in tears of amber run', for an amber-like resin exudes from the bark of the conifers, most of which (but not all) are resinous, for example the Deodar cedar with its graceful, curving branches forming a pale-green pyramid; the Italian cedar which makes a spire-like tree of olive-green; and the Blue cedar with its glaucous foliage as if brushed with silver. Perhaps more fragrant than any of the conifers are the Balsam and Blue spruces of America, for all parts of these trees give off a pungent, balsam-like perfume.

In addition to the two main groups, the rose perfume is represented in the wood of *Convolvulus scoparius* of the Canary Islands, and in *Asarum canadense.* It is also present in the roots of *Sedum rhodiola,* the rose-root of old cottage gardens from which an exquisitely scented rose-water was prepared.

The violet scent is present in the dried roots of *Iris florentina* and *I. pallida* which, when crumbled, are known as orris-powder. The scent becomes more pronounced as the root ages. The same scent is also present in the wood of several junipers, the most obvious example being *Juniperus virginiana.*

Not all bark smells are pleasant. That of the common elder smells of stale perspiration, owing to the presence of valeric acid, also present in the flowers of the common valerian.

The Scent of Fungi. The fungi have similar smells to those found in flowers and leaves; they may likewise be divided into several groups, though it should be stressed that there is a tendency for the scents to change as the fungus matures.

Indoloid Group: represented by the Wood-witch or Stinkhorn, *Phallus impudicus,* whose fetid stench may be detected from a considerable distance.

Bluebottles feed on its filthy slime and disseminate the spores. *Amanita virosa* and *Marasmius perforans* have a similar stench.

Aminoid Group: Omphalina ericetorum, found growing in damp mossy ground, has a powerful fishy smell, like that of Dog's mercury, as do *Lactarius volemus* and *Russula virescens* of deciduous woodlands.

Sulphur Group: represented by *Tricholoma sulphureum* and *Marasmius scorodonius* which is found about the stumps of trees. Both have a powerful smell of garlic or sulphuretted hydrogen. *Russula consobrina* is similar.

Aromatic Group: Tricholoma nudum, the familiar blue-cap, found in woodlands where it grows in fairy-rings, has a pleasant aromatic smell and is good to eat. The Fairy-ring champignon, *Marasmius oreades*, a familiar fungus of fields and lawns, has an aromatic clove-like smell and is also pleasant to eat. Several of the Clitocybe, which smell pleasantly of anise, may be included here.

Rose Group: represented by *Russula masculata*.

Violet Group: Russula badia, a poisonous fungus of pine woods, has a pleasant violet-like scent similar to juniper and cedarwood.

Fruit Group: the delicious chanterelle, *Cantharellus cibarius*, of deciduous woodlands, has a distinct apricot smell, whilst *Craterllus lutescens* and *Hebeloma sinuosum*, which grow in pine woods, have a refreshing pear-like smell. *Pholiota aurea* smells of ripe apples.

Animal Group: Hygrophorus russocariaceus smells of Russian leather and *H. cossus* has a distinct hypericum smell, like that of goats.

Honey Group: Russula melliolens smells distinctly of honey whilst *Lactarius helvus* has a musk-like smell.

5

Composition and Extraction of Scent

Colour and perfume—Essential oil—The first perfumes—The perfume industry—Methods of obtaining essential oil—Home extraction of scent—Harvesting and drying scented leaves and herbs

---

SCENT is the oxidization of the essential oils of flowers and leaves. In flowers, the essential oil is in the epidermal cells of the petals, or in the sepals or bracts, which may be there as petal replacements. The oil is usually present on the upper surface of the petals, but is found on both surfaces while the petals are concealed in the bud. Essential oil is not found on the anthers though they may absorb some of the perfume from the petals just as the leaves of the auricula, or those of the Princess of Wales violet, absorb the perfume from the flowers. The stamens of the rose, if removed, have a moss-like perfume which may add to the scent of some varieties. The most powerfully scented flowers, e.g. lily of the valley, tuberose, orange-blossom and others most used for extraction, have thick velvet-like petals which retain their perfume and prevent much of the essential oil from evaporating until the flower has perished. Few flowers with large, thin petals possess any pronounced fragrance.

The essential oil is present in the petals in an inert form, being stored in 'containers', as a mixture of oil and sugar known as a glucoside, and the perfume cannot be released until a state of fermentation has begun to take place. If a flower bud is opened it will give off no scent. The essential oil is not lost when the flower is closed, only when open, which explains why flowers which open at night are most fragrant.

The production of the essential oil continues only whilst the flower remains alive, for as soon as a drop of oil has been released, another begins to form. Some flowers, such as the Apothecary's rose, jasmine, orange-blossom and the tuberose, continue to give off their essential oils after being gathered fresh. Scent is a waste or excretory product of a plant, and for this reason is stored in special cells or containers away from the living cells, in the same way that an animal secretes its smell into the cavity formed round the lanoline glands. Methyl indole (skatol), the active principle of civet, is a well-known example. In its original and concentrated form it has a most unpleasant smell, owing to the presence of indole.

It is the chlorophyll, the first substance to appear in the evolution of the flower, which produces the essential oil in inverse ratio to the amount of pigment in the flower. The essential oil is the result of a transformation of the chlorophyll into tannoid compounds or pigments, and this process can be more readily understood if it is admitted that the floral organs of a plant are but leaves modified for the performance of a new function. This is why green-petalled flowers have no perfume, and white flowers are the most fragrant, e.g. *Lilium candidum*, white jasmine, *Rosa* McGredy's Ivory and *R. alba*; also the lily of the valley and the tuberose, the white violet, white carnations and pinks, white heliotrope, the jonquil and pheasant-eye narcissus, orange-blossom and white peonies, all of which have petals of the same thick velvet-like quality.

Colour and Perfume. It is estimated that there are 4 to 5,000 species of plants utilized for various purposes and, of these, no more than one-tenth have a pleasing perfume, the rest either being scentless or having an unpleasant smell. Of just over 4,000 plants examined by a French authority on scented flowers at the end of the nineteenth century, white and yellow flowers (and especially those which are pale yellow in colour) accounted for more than 60 per cent of all fragrant flowers; the rest with but one or two exceptions, bearing flowers of pale-pink or purple colouring.

The order of strength of perfume released by flowers in respect of their colouring is as follows: white, blush-white, pale pink, mauve-pink, pale yellow, yellow and purple; plants bearing blue, orange, red or brown flowers have a high degree of pigmentation and generate little or no scent.

As colour (pigment) is bred into flowers, scent is usually lost. The white flowers of the sweet alyssum smell of new-mown hay, yet in the variety Rosie O'Day, which has rosy-purple flowers, the smell has almost entirely disappeared, though this is unusual in flowers of purple colouring. The scarlet Sweet William has little or no perfume, whilst Pink Beauty has more but is much less fragrant than the white form. *Clematis montana* Alexander which bears large flowers of purest white is powerfully scented, yet in the crimson form, *rubens,* most of the scent is lost. The almost winter-flowering *C. rehderiana* bears pale-yellow flowers which smell of cowslips, whilst one of the very few scented varieties of the large-flowered garden hybrids, Duchess of Edinburgh, bears double blooms of purest white with thick velvety petals. Few other clematis hybrids have developed perfume to any appreciable degree. In almost all flowers, scent is usually present as a substitute for colour, and where colour is intensified, scent is diminished.

Scents of the various genera which comprise a plant family are usually similar throughout that family. All members of the Leguminosae family possess the same refreshing vanilla-like perfume, with a slight but piercing undertone of lemon, as in the sweet pea and laburnum; plants of the Caprifoliaceae family all have the same sweet honeysuckle scent. The leaves of the rue give off an unmistakable orange scent when bruised, and, indeed, both the rue and the orange are of the Rutaceae family. A number of plant orders are almost entirely devoid of perfume, perhaps the most striking example being the Scrophulariaceae family, which includes the foxglove, antirrhinum (there are now one or two slightly scented varieties), calceolaria and celsia, alonsoa and nemesia, phygellius and pentstemon. They are mostly native of Mexico and

South America, bearing long tubular flowers of brilliant colouring, and are pollinated by humming-birds. The now scentless mimulus (musk) is also of this family.

The high degree of pigmentation which is apparent in autumn flowers (and leaves) accounts for so many of them possessing little or no perfume—for instance the chrysanthemum (though its leaves have an attractive pungency), Michaelmas daisy, helenium (orange, brown or yellow), rudbeckia, heliopsis and helianthus. All are members of the Compositae family and are native of North America. They are pollinated by short-tongued insects, mostly Diptera, and are amongst the least scented of all flowering plants.

Essential Oil. The essential oil is secreted in minute droplets which evaporate when exposed to the air, to give off a sweet (or unpleasant) vapour, depending upon the chemical composition of the flower, which is most noticeable on a warm, calm day. Essential oils are insoluble in water and it only became known at the end of the fourteenth century that alcohol was a suitable solvent for them. The alcoholic solution is known as an 'essence' and the essential oil of flowers is called its attar (or otto), from a Persian word meaning 'smell' or 'scent'.

The essential oil in leaves acts as a protection for the plant. Plants with scented leaves are amongst the most primitive and are usually free of thorns; they grow in warm climatic regions, especially near the shores of the Mediterranean, and the oxidized oil provides an invisible cloud which protects the plant from scorching and undue loss of moisture.

In leaves, the oil is stored in numerous ways. In the bay leaf (and *Hypericum*), which does not easily release its fragrance, the oil is stored in capsules. In the myrtle, the oil is embedded deep inside the leaf tissue, and the scent is released only after considerable pressure. In the Balsam poplar, the oil is secreted on to the bud where it is fixed with a sticky wax-like substance to prevent rapid evaporation. If held over a low flame, the balsam-like fragrance is immediately released, owing to the melting of the wax. In rosemary and southernwood, the oil is stored on the leaf surface, in oblong cells which are broken down when the leaves are pressed and the aromatic perfume is released. With thyme, the cells are nearer the surface so that the scent is released by the sun when the foliage is dry. In *Cistus*, the rock rose, the scent is produced by glandular hairs on the underside of the leaves, as with the Moss rose.

The essential oil of a flower is composed of numerous chemical compounds. The most common are known as esters, formed by the combination of an acid and an alcohol. Thus, in the magnolia, acetic acid has combined with ethyl alcohol to produce ethyl acetate which has a sweet, lemon-like smell, far more pleasant than that of acetic acid itself. Methyl anthranilate which smells strongly of oranges is found in attar of orange-blossom and, in association with indole, in most heavily scented flowers.

There are a number of alcohols in essential oil, their names all ending in -ol. Borneol is the chief alcohol of leaves. Geraniol, which is present in greatest concentration in the Rose-leaf geranium, gives the rose its pleasant sweet scent, but the particular perfume of an individual variety depends upon eight other substances.

Another alcohol, menthol, is found in the mints, whereas the rich scent of the clove is due to methyl eugenol. Indole is the principal substance of the jonquil. Eucalyptol (or cineol) is present in the essential oil of a number of plants, and the more it is purified, the more it loses the characteristic odour of the plant from which the sample was obtained. It is present in:

> *Alpinia galanga* as Oil of Galanga
> *Artemisia cana* as Oil of Wormseed
> *Canella winteriana* as Oil of Cinnamon
> *Curcuma zedoaria* as Oil of Zedoary
> *Cinnamomum camphora* as Oil of Camphor
> *Laurus communis* as Oil of Laurel
> *Lavandula stoechas* as Oil of Lavender
> *Melaleuca leucodendron* as Oil of Cajuput
> *Myrtus communis* as Oil of Myrtle
> *Rosmarinus officinalis* as Oil of Rosemary
> *Salvia officinalis* as Oil of Sage

Linalol, another alcohol, is also present in lavender. When combined with acetic acid, it produces the bergamot-scented linalyl acetate which, in turn, by evaporation, becomes geraniol. By polymerization, this eventually becomes nerol which, with acetic acid, again changes to geranyl acetate, adding softness to the scent.

Aldehydes are present as citral in many leaves, in the lemon-scented verbena and in lemon-grass. Anisic aldehyde is found in the hawthorn flower, in which the unpleasant fishy undertone is given by the amine, trimethylamine, a compound of ammonia, also found in the leaves of the Stinking goosegrass.

Acids are also present in flowers: acetic acid in magnolia blossom and lavender, valeric acid (smelling of perspiration) in the valerian, the moon-daisy and many other flowers of the Composite family, caprioc acid (smelling of wet goat fur) in the leaves of *Hypericum hircinum*.

The scent of the violet is due to a ketone, ionone, in the violet flower, and irone in orris-root. The same compound is present in animal musk. Ionone dulls the sense of smell within a very short time, and so it is not the flower which loses its fragrance when cut, but our own powers of smell which are lost. If the flower is smelled again after several minutes, the perfume returns, only to disappear once more as it begins to tire the senses. This elusive quality has endeared the flower to all for it is impossible to enjoy an excess of its perfume.

The chemical principle which causes the odour of orris-root was isolated in 1893 by Tiemann and Kruger who, in a memoir presented to the French Academy of Sciences, stated that it was a ketone which they named irone. This they obtained by exhausting the orris-root with ether. The extract was distilled in a strong current of steam and dilute sulphuric acid was added to the oily substance remaining in the retort. The pure irone then passes over on distillation. The substance is freely soluble in alcohol, ether and chloroform.

Experimenting further with a view to obtaining irone synthetically, Tiemann and Kruger discovered that an isomeric ketone, ionone, which has the odour of violets, may be obtained from the aldehyde citral. By the action of alkalines with acetone, citral is converted into the ketone pseudo-ionone, which, by the action of dilute acids, is then converted into the isomeric ketone, ionone. The structure of irone was finally established in 1947 following Ruzicka's years of experimentation.

Irone, which has a delightful violet odour, costs more than £12 an ounce and, though a synthetic, is more expensive than most natural oils.

Odourless terpenes are found in essential oils and are present in attar of orange-blossom; whilst benzene compounds are present in attars of all strongly scented flowers. Benzyl acetate is prominent in attar of jasmine which also contains indole, though less than in the jonquil, owing to the presence of balsamic compounds. Compounds of sulphur are present in a number of Cruciferae.

The First Perfumes. It was the Arabian doctor, Avicenna, in the late tenth century, who first rendered the volatile aroma of flowers permanent by means of distillation; until his discoveries, the famed 'perfumes of Araby' existed only in scented gums. The first of his experiments was made with Damask rose petals, and his formula for his deliciously scented rose-water soon spread around the Eastern world.

Alcoholic perfumes do not appear to have been known until 1370, when Hungary Water, obtained from a distillation of rosemary, was first prepared by Queen Elizabeth of Hungary from a recipe given to her by a hermit. It is the first recorded act of seduction by the use of an alcoholic scent for the queen retained her beauty by its use until late in years, and at the age of 72 she married the King of Poland.

One hundredweight of rosemary will yield about twenty-four ounces of otto, and it is the most refreshing of all perfumes. It is used in Eau de Colognes which are of more complex blending, whereas the ingredients of Hungary Water, with the exception of otto of lemon peel, are obtained from ordinary garden plants. It consists of a gallon of grape spirit, two ounces of otto of rosemary, one ounce each of otto of balm and lemon peel, a half drachm of otto of mint, and one pint each of extract of rose and orange-flower. Should the orange-flower extract prove difficult to obtain, it can be omitted and the *esprit de rose* increased to two pints. Hungary Water may be applied to the handkerchief and will refresh a tired mind, but its primary use is as a face wash or to add to bath water, when it will act as an invigorating tonic.

A toilet-water possessing similar qualities was prepared by the nuns of the Carmelite abbey of Saint-Just. So renowned did the water become that the nuns were requested to send samples to all parts of Europe. The distillation became known as Carmelite Water and was an important addition to the toilet preparations of cultured men and women of medieval Europe. Its principal ingredient is balm, *Melissa officinalis,* which grows wild in central and southern Europe and which has become naturalized in the hedgerows. It was grown in every cottage garden in Elizabethan times, as its lemon-scented leaves were used for strewing and released their refreshing perfume when walked on, whilst the stems were woven into chaplets.

Carmelite Water is made by taking two pounds of fresh balm leaves, a quarter of a pound of lemon peel, two ounces each of nutmeg, cloves, coriander seed, some cinnamon and angelica root. These are placed in a still with half a gallon of orange-flower water and a gallon of alcohol and slowly distilled until a gallon of the water is obtained.

Growing naturally in profusion all over Corsica, rosemary was the favourite scent of Napoleon and was the main ingredient of Eau de Cologne which he used extravagantly all his life. It consists of the otto of neroli and other orange ottos, mixed with otto of rosemary and bergamot and dissolved in spirit. Bergamot was produced in Lombardy, from plantations of the Bergamo orange which grew near the city bearing that name. During Napoleon's lifetime, demand was such that the perfumers of Paris could never obtain enough. The greenish-tinted otto has a refreshing smell, like that of rosemary, and is obtained from the rind of the pear-shaped fruit. Mixed with rectified spirit, it forms 'extract of bergamot', which was once widely used on handkerchiefs.

The finest French product, like the best Cognac, is made with grape spirit, which gives the true Eau de Cologne its own particular scent (due to the oenanthic ether it contains). It is essentially a man's perfume, used in modern 'after-shave' lotions.

Eau de Cologne began as *'Aqua Admirabilis'* at the beginning of the eighteenth century when the brothers Johann Maria and Johann Baptiste Farina moved from Santa Maria Maggiore in Italy to open a fancy-goods business in Cologne. The cordial water they made achieved considerable popularity during the Seven Years War, the troops quartered in Cologne taking away supplies for their families at home when peace was eventually declared. By the middle of the century, the Farina brothers' elixir had become world-famous and was known as Eau de Cologne after the city of its origin. It has retained its popularity ever since.

The Perfume Industry. The history of perfumery really began in France at the time of Philip-Augustus who in 1190 granted a charter to the perfumers of Paris. By patents granted in 1426 by Henry VI of England who, during the troubles of Charles VII of France, styled himself King of France, the arms of the perfumers were registered in the Armorial General of France as 'Argent, three gloves (scented) gules, chief azure, charged with an antique scent-box of gold'. When Catherine de'Medici married Henry II, the use of perfumes was considered so important that the queen brought with her her own perfumer, a Florentine named René who set up in business on the Pont au Change, and soon afterwards perfumery came into general use amongst the wealthy. In 1582, Nicolas de Montaut in his *Miroir des François* reproaches the ladies of his time for using 'all sorts of perfumes, waters, civet, musk, ambergris, and other precious aromatics to perfume their clothes and linen and even their bodies'. Indeed, under the House of Valois, the use of perfumes and pomades was carried to excess.

The perfume industry now is concentrated around the small town of Grasse, situated at the foot of the Maritime Alps, some ten miles from the Mediterranean coast in the valley of the Var. Here are to be found plantations of the Damask, *alba* and *centifolia* roses; of violets, jasmine, tuberose, mimosa, narcissus (jonquil) and orange-blossom, these being the most suitable flowers for extracting the essential oil for making into perfume. From Turkey and Bulgaria comes the far-famed attar of roses, whilst Italy produces essences of bergamot, and of members of the citrus family. The only two perfumery ingredients in which England excels are lavender and peppermint.

Several of the newly established African states have begun to experiment with the cultivation of a number of perfumer's flowers. In the valley of the Limpopo, and in the Shire valley of southern Malawi, marjoram, lavender and thyme are being grown commercially, and in Tanzania, eucalyptus, rosemary, coriander and dill.

In France, the harvesting of flowers continues almost throughout the year, beginning with the rose, jonquil and mimosa in January and continuing until the end of April when (until early June) the orange-blossom is ready. From July until early October the violets are harvested, also the jasmine and tuberose. The land is densely planted, as many as a hundred thousand jasmine plants occupying a single acre of ground from which, over an entire season, they may be expected to yield about 7,000 lb of flowers, the perfume being obtained by *enfleurage* or maceration.

The orange tree requires a deep well-prepared soil to be long-living, and it may be expected to attain at least a hundred years of age. It begins to bear bloom and fruit when six years old and reaches maturity at about eighteen years when each tree will yield in a single season, which lasts for about a month, 25 lb of blossom. A hundred orange trees occupying an acre of ground will produce, during the season, about 2,500 lb of blossom which will yield by distillation about 2 lb of neriol worth more than £500.

The mimosa or acacia tree requires rather less room for its development and an acre will accommodate about 300 trees which, upon maturity, will attain a height of about 3.6 m (12 ft) and a width of about 1.8 m (6 ft). Like all flower perfumes, with the possible exception of the rose and orange, the acacia flower has its scent extracted by *enfleurage* and, as the fluffy yellow ball-shaped flowers open in succession, the manufacturer can make repeated changes of blossom. In this way the fat used for extraction is fully charged with the perfume, and consequently flowers which open over several weeks are the most valuable for scent extraction. About 10 lb of acacia flowers make 1 oz of attar.

Of roses, Henry Phillips in the *Sylva Florifera*, Vol. II (1823), tells of a perfumer in Paris who made attar for the Court of Louis XVI and who said that it needed two tons or about 100 m. petals to yield 1 lb of oil which, today, is worth over £300. To put it more simply, 2,000 roses will yield 1 gramme of attar. The rose is one of the few flowers whose essential oil is unharmed by the process of distillation, mostly used for the extraction of the odorous principle from leaves, barks and woods. Though in the South of France large areas are down to rose growing to supply the manufacturers with blossom, it is in the Rose Valley of northern Bulgaria that the finest attar is produced. Here, at Kazanluk and for miles around, the fields are carpeted with the pink Damask rose and its perfume is overwhelming at the height of the season. It takes about 250 lb of rose petals to produce 1 oz of the attar and June is the busiest month for collecting the flowers. As many as ten thousand pickers are employed at the height of the season, and they make their way to the fields shortly after daybreak, before the rising sun causes evaporation of the essential oil from the petals. In a vintage year, the crop will yield as much as two tons of attar of such outstanding quality that imitators cannot hope to match it by a chemical process.

The amount of essential oil (attar) which is yielded by various plants (per 10lb) is as follows:

Acorus calamus	1–2 oz
Aniseed	1 oz
Balm	$\frac{1}{4}-\frac{1}{2}$ oz
Caraway seed	6–8 oz
Cassia	1–2 oz
Cedarwood	1–2 oz
Cinnamon	1–2 oz
Clove	20–30 oz
Geranium (leaf)	trace
Lavender	3–4 oz
Marjoram	1–2 oz
Orange peel	1 oz
Origanum	2–3 oz
Patchouli	2–3 oz
Peppermint (black)	1–2 oz
Peppermint (white)	1 oz
Rose-wood	$\frac{1}{8}-\frac{1}{4}$ oz
Sandalwood	3 oz
Thyme	$\frac{1}{2}-1$ oz
Vetivert	1–2 oz
Violet	1 oz

The attar of orange-blossom does not smell much like oranges but it is possible to bring out the perfume when it is mixed with other substances. The art of the perfumer is both skilful and complex: he works at an 'organ' where, once again using a metaphor of music, the various ingredients are arranged around him in scales of scent. There may be as many as 10 tiers, each accommodating more than 100 bottles, carefully marked and arranged on three sides so that each one of the thousand or so bottles may easily be reached. The perfumer relies on his trained sense of smell to create a symphony of fragrance which he 'composes' over many days, adding a touch of one ingredient, then another, using maybe a hundred or more until he is satisfied that he has obtained the right blend. This is known as the 'chord'. The 'bass notes' are those which last longest whilst the 'top' notes have the most immediate effect upon the sense of smell. He has to adjust the balance of the scent, replacing those which may have been lost in the extraction, or toning down a scent which may be too pronounced, and all the time he must guard against creating artificial scents which do not resemble the true flower perfumes. Besides the attars, there are the 'woody' perfumes, of oil of sandalwood from India, of cinnamon from Ceylon, of cypress and bergamot (used in colognes) from Italy, rosemary from Spain, oil of cloves from Zanzibar, labdanum from Crete, and many more which provide the subtle undertones to a perfume.

If the perfumer wishes to make a bouquet from primitive odours, he must take such odours as chord together, to give a harmonious perfume. In the same way that an artist blends his colours, the perfumer must blend his scents. In making a 'bouquet' each primitive odour must be brought to a standard of strength or 'power of odour'. For example, Dr Piesse suggested using the otto of the following together to form a bouquet of chord C: sandalwood, geranium, acacia, orange-blossom and camphor; and to form a bouquet of chord F, musk, rose, tuberose, tonquin bean, camphor, and jonquil.

The wax or resin, which prevents the rapid evaporation of the essential oil in the plant, must be replaced by a fixative to hold the scent. The best fixatives are animal secretions which are first treated with alcohol to dilute their strong scent. The most widely used is ambergris, a grey wax-like substance (grey amber) obtained from the intestines of the large-headed sperm whale which feeds upon the cuttle-fish, though in tropical seas ambergris may be found floating on the water. It is the result of a diseased state of the whale, and is the most expensive of all the fixatives, used only in the most exotic perfumes. It is found chiefly on the coasts of Greenland, India and Japan, but has been known on the coast of Kerry and Sligo and of the Isles of Aran. It has a smell similar to that of labdanum and the resin of the Balsam poplar. There is an account of a piece found on the coast of Sligo in 1691 weighing over 50 lb, which was sold in London for £100. Ambergris releases its odour only when dissolved in spirit.

Civet, a sex gland secretion of the civet cat of Ethiopia, Burma and Thailand, has for long been used as a fixative. It is of butter-like appearance and is usually exported in the horn of an ox. At one time, civet cats were kept by Dutch merchants at Amsterdam where the substance was obtained from them twice weekly. Civet was in general use in the perfumery trade in Shakespeare's time, usually mixed with other ingredients to rub on the body, and the poet makes numerous references to it.

Extract of civet is prepared by rubbing together in a mortar 1 oz of civet with 1 oz of powdered orris-root. This is placed in a gallon of rectified spirit. After macerating for a month it is strained and is ready for mixing with attars. At one time it was mixed with attar of roses and rubbed into the leather of a writing-desk. This would impregnate writing-paper with a delightful odour which it retained when sent through the post.

Castor, the secretion of the beaver, is now less commonly used in perfumery, but tarquin musk, a secretion found in a 'pod' beneath the belly of the male musk-deer, an ounce of which the animal takes four years to produce, is still used as a fixative. It is a reddish substance which turns black on exposure to air and has a honey-like smell. This is why flowers smelling of musk are often classified with those of honey perfume.

When adulterated, musk has a sweet smell but according to Chardin, it is so powerful that when removed from the animal, hunters cover their mouth and nose with linen for it is capable of bringing about haemorrhage and death. Musk is the most powerful and durable of all perfumes and is found in less degree in the musk-ox and musk-rat. The musk-deer is believed to derive its odour from feeding on musk-smelling herbs of the mountain ranges of China, Tibet and Assam which it inhabits. The substance, obtained only from the male animal, is known to the Chinese as *shay leang,* animal perfume.

The Empress Josephine was fond of musk and her dressing-room was filled with it daily. It is said that fifty years after her death, the walls of her room at Malmaison which, in the meantime had been frequently washed and painted, still smelled strongly of musk.

Sweet gums and resins, which harmonize with the perfume, are also used as fixatives. Oils of cedarwood and of sandalwood are amongst them and are less expensive than the animal fixatives, contributing 'warmth' besides staying power to a perfume.

So important is it when introducing a modern commercial product to be quite certain its fragrance has 'appeal', that firms have been set up to concoct suitable scents for almost every saleable item, from detergents to aerosols, from printer's inks to plastics. In the United States there is at least one firm experimenting with perfumes in petrol so that the smell of exhaust fumes is replaced by a pleasing fragrance.

Synthetic odours in perfumes took a leap forward in 1868 when Sir William Perkin discovered the chemical manufacture of coumarin, with its scent of new-mown hay. By the turn of the century, the use of chemical compounds in the creation of new perfumes ran complementary to the use of natural flower oils, though almost always synthetics lack the 'warmth' of natural substances. Yet one of the great perfumes of the world, Chanel No. 5, created by Ernst Beaux in 1923, was one of the first to contain synthetic odours. Coty's *L'Aimant* and Lanvin's *Arpège* followed in their use of synthetics and, with Chanel No. 5, became three of the most popular perfumes, a position they have retained ever since.

L'Aimant, which means 'magnet', and was introduced in 1927 by François Coty after he had spent five years perfecting it, may be described as a subtly balanced floral 'bouquet' based on jasmine but with the top note a vibrant and lasting synthetic, blended with natural citrus and floral oils including Bulgarian rose, Italian bergamot, Algerian geranium and, of course, jasmine. The middle or body-note includes vanilla from tropical South America and vetivert from the Orient, whilst the base note has the animal warmth of Himalayan musk and of civet from Ethiopia. One of the all-time classic perfumes, it is blended from materials obtained from all parts of the world.

At exactly the time Coty was introducing his *L'Aimant* perfume, Jeanne Lanvin was crowning her creative ability as a *couturier* with the introduction of *Arpège* which was also to become a star creation in the world of fragrance. Like Coty's *L'Aimant*, it was an immediate success. It is an 'arpeggio' of the most delicately scented flowers, including the attars of jasmine, Bulgarian rose, camellia and lily of the valley. It is said that the volume of flowers used each year to make Lanvin perfumes would be equal in bulk to those needed for a building of the size of the Arc de Triomphe. As an alternative to the famed attar of rose from Bulgaria which costs over £20 an ounce, a new synthetic rose oil recently introduced as Attarose ABR 5000 is now being used. But Bulgarian attar, though the most expensive and desirable of all rose attars, is by no means the dearest of attars. That of jasmine costs twice as much whilst the essential oil of the tuberose is priced at £2,500 a pound and is used only in the most expensive perfumes.

The use of synthetic perfumery in the future must be on an ever-increasing scale for the chemist now has a number of new devices to help him to discover nature's secrets. Ultra-violet spectroscopy, gas-liquid chromatography and NMR spectrometry enable him to identify essential oils and even trace elements which may be present in the most minute quantities. New synthetic preparations continue to appear each year.

Discoveries this century have included terpined, a product of turpentine which reproduces the odour of purple lilac, and a styrolyl acetate which has an odour resembling gardenia flowers. Further developments of synthetic perfumery included the synthesis of phenylethyl alcohol by Radziszewski, and the manufacture of hydroxycitronellal in 1905. This enabled the lily-of-the-valley fragrance to be added to the list of synthetic perfumes. Shortly afterwards, Blanc discovered how to manufacture cyclamen aldehyde.

A synthetic heliotrope perfume was first obtained in the U.S.A. by Schimmel and Co. of New York, following the distillation of oil of sassafras, obtained from the bark of the *Laurus sassafras*. Crude oil of sassafras contains about 90 per cent safrol which has a pleasant aromatic odour. By treating it with permanganate of potash, safrol yields piperonylic acid known in perfumery as heliotropin, which has a scent resembling the sweet cherry-pie smell of wild heliotrope.

The synthetic perfume of citrus is provided by linalyl acetate, a product of linalol present in oil of lavender. It was the Frenchman Bouchardat who found that acetic anhydride reacted with linalol at ordinary temperatures to form linalyl acetate, which has a sharp lemon-like smell; and he took his experiment a stage further when he saponified linalyl acetate with alcoholic potash which, when heated to 92°C (230°F) and combined with four equivalents of bromine, forms an alcohol which has the identical rose scent of geraniol.

From earliest times, man has sought to imitate nature by reproducing the scents of flowers and leaves, and when it is realized that the chief soap-flake and detergent manufacturers each use as much as a hundred tons of perfume each year, it is understandable that only a small proportion of their requirements can be provided by natural oils. Today, more than two-thirds of the materials used in perfumery and in manufacturing processes are man-made, but, try as he may, man cannot reproduce in the laboratory exactly the scent of many flowers, though he can create aromatic chemicals which give off an odour greatly resembling those flowers.

These aromatic chemicals resemble in smell various flowers:

Anisic aldehyde	Hawthorn (Aniseed)
Benzophenone	Rose
Benzyl acetate	Jasmine
Bornyl acetate	Pine
Citral	Lemon
Coumarin	Hay
Cyclamen aldehyde	Cyclamen
Diphenyl oxide	Geranium
Ethyl acetate	Lemon
Farnesol	Cedarwood
Geraniol	Rose
Heliotropin	Heliotrope
Hydroxycitronellal	Lily of the valley

Ionone	Violet
Linalol	Lavender
Linalyl acetate	Citrus
Methyl anthranilate	Orange
Methyl chavicol	Aniseed
Methyl cinnamic aldehyde	Cinnamon
Methyl eugenol	Clove-carnation
Nerol	Lemon
Phenylacetaldehyde	Hyacinth
Phenyl ethyl alcohol	Rose
Phenyl methyl carbinyl acetate	Gardenia
Perpineol	Lilac
Vanillin	Vanilla

Why perfume and not scent? In England the word 'scent' has always been used to denote the manufactured product, but the Americans have followed the French in their use of the older word 'perfume', used by Shakespeare and the Bible, which seems a more appropriate name for the sophisticated product, whilst scent is more suited to describe the sweet smell of a flower or leaf.

To find if a perfume is suitable for one's personality, it is necessary to 'wear' it. Sniffing from a bottle is only the first step in its appreciation: it must be applied to one's skin, where in a few seconds the warmth of the body will release its subtle qualities.

Methods of Obtaining Essential Oil. The four most widely used methods of obtaining the essential oils are distillation, extraction, *enfleurage* or absorption, and expression.

Distillation. The method of obtaining essential oil by distillation is suitable only for flowers whose attar will withstand considerable heat (e.g. boiling water) without suffering change. In addition, the flowers must contain a large amount of attar for the method to be profitable, and so distillation is confined almost exclusively to orange-blossom and the rose, and to the woods and barks of trees. At the height of the season, distillation continues throughout the night.

The blooms are gathered early morning and are taken indoors as quickly as possible and placed in a large tank. When almost filled, a steam jet is started at the base and the steam makes its way through the flowers so that when finally driven off and collected, it is laden with the volatile oil. It is then allowed to cool and the oil, being insoluble in water, is obtained by drawing off with the mouth into a glass container. A more simple method is to suspend a wire basket over a steam jet.

Extraction. The second and more gentle method of extraction, whereby the scent is washed from the flowers by a solution of petroleum-ether, results in the most concentrated form of all essences. The flowers are placed on perforated plates in a hermetically sealed vat where they are washed repeatedly, until the solvent is highly charged with the scent. It is then distilled at a low pressure, and the solid and wax-like substance left behind is known as a 'floral concrete'. Before being used it is washed with alcohol which dissolves the essential oil from the solid. The alcohol is then removed by distillation to leave behind the pure essential oil, known as a 'floral absolute'. This is the most concentrated form of floral scent known, and when diluted will give the identical perfume of the flower. Jasmine will yield about 0.25 per cent of 'floral concrete' and sometimes the petals are put under pressure to release more essential oil. About 1 ton of jasmine petals will be required to extract 1 lb of 'floral absolute'.

Enfleurage. The third method, known as *enfleurage*, is even more expensive for it is carried out entirely by hand. Some flowers are killed by treating with a solvent such as petroleum-ether, or by heat, but *enfleurage* ensures that the perfume is obtained directly from the living flowers. As they continue to give off their essential oils long after being gathered, the scent of the lily of the valley, jasmine, tuberose and violet is best captured by *enfleurage*, for these flowers will be killed by heat.

The flowers are spread out on large sheets of clean glass, each of which is enclosed in a wooden frame. The glass is covered with animal fat over which the flowers are placed. Another frame is put into position above the flowers and the same procedure continues until about twenty frames are stacked one above another, where they are allowed to remain for 24 hours; then the flowers are replaced with others. As much as a month may elapse before the fat is saturated with the perfume, the flowers being changed every day, while they remain in bloom. The fat is then scraped off the glass and the perfume extracted with alcohol, when the resulting scent will be found to be the most delicate and delicious of all perfumes.

Extract of jasmine is prepared by pouring alcohol on to the pomade and allowing them to remain together for two weeks. Two pounds of pomade should be used to every quart of spirit, the pomade being cut up before the alcohol is added. With mignonette, a pint of alcohol is used to extract the scent from every pound of pomade. After the essence has been filtered, it is usual to add an ounce of extract of tolu to give it greater permanence.

The oils of the same flowers may be made to yield their perfume by first saturating muslin cloths in olive oil and placing them over the frames which have had the glass removed. The cloths rest on the wire supports and over them the flowers are spread out, to be removed and replaced by others as previously described. Again, after about a month, the oil is saturated with their scent and it is then removed from the cloths under considerable pressure and the scent extracted by an alcoholic solvent.

One of the greatest difficulties when using fat is to ensure that it is entirely free from any odorous principle, and when it is to be used for pomade, it must be prevented from becoming rancid. A century ago, Dr Charles Redwood, writing in the *Pharmaceutical Journal* (Vol. XIV, No. 5), suggested that a small quantity of gum benzoin added to the fat would prevent this. The finest fat oil is known as oil of Ben which is colourless, tasteless and inodorous and never becomes rancid. The Behen tree is *Hyperanthera moringa*, an Eastern tree now naturalized in the West Indies, the seeds of which yield 25 per cent of oil. Benzoic acid, prepared from the resinous gum of *Styrax benzoin* by the humid process, is also odourless.

Expression. Expression is the method used to extract the essential oil from the rind of citrus fruits. As the fruits are being crushed between rollers, a heavy jet of water is sprayed on them so as to separate the juice from the solids. The oil is then separated from the juice by the method of extraction.

Home Extraction of Scent. A successful method of making perfume at home may be carried out by a simple method of *enfleurage*. Three-quarters of a pound of animal fat, such as that obtained from beef or pork, and a quarter of lard should be boiled with one quart of water to which has been added a teaspoonful of alum. When completely dissolved, it is strained through muslin and allowed to cool. It is then separated from the liquid and re-heated, and finally poured into two shallow pans or dishes.

The flowers, which should be in perfect condition when harvested, must first have the stems removed and are then placed on top of the fat in one dish, to a depth of several inches. The other dish, lined with the fat, is then placed over the flowers, pressing them down so that the rims of the dishes are in contact with each other. They are left for 24 hours, then the flowers are removed and replaced by others. Each day they are changed for as long as the flowers are available, by which time the fat will have absorbed the perfume. The fat is then scraped into a bottle and covered with equal parts of spirits of wine. The stopper is put on and sealed with wax, and the jar placed in a dark cupboard for several months, being shaken up each day to extract the scent. After three or four months, the liquid is removed and will have become strongly perfumed. It should be given a fixative such as a drop of sandalwood and will then be ready to use.

Another method is to gather the flowers when dry and in perfect condition, and place them in a jar filled with olive oil. After 24 hours, remove the blossoms to a muslin bag. Squeeze them, allowing the oil to run back into the jar. This procedure should be repeated until the soil is saturated with the perfume. An equal quantity of pure alcohol should then be added and the mixture should be shaken up each day for at least two weeks. The alcohol is then poured off and will be strongly fragrant.

Violet perfume may be readily obtained by shaking 2 oz of alcohol with $\frac{1}{2}$ oz of dried orris-root, finely cut up. After a week, if the bottle has been tightly stoppered, the alcohol will have the perfume of the violet.

Harvesting and Drying Scented Leaves and Herbs. The harvesting and drying of herbs and scented leaves calls for almost as great attention to detail as for flowers. First, it is necessary for the foliage to have reached as perfect a condition as possible before removal, for only then is its full fragrance or flavour released and retained for any length of time. Much depends upon the weather, for most herbs are harvested, whether for their leaves or seeds, towards the end of summer or early in autumn, when the weather should be dry and sunny. A dry soil and a dry climate will ensure that the foliage (or seed) is rich in essential oil but whatever the conditions, there is a period in the life of each plant when it reaches full maturity; afterwards it begins to die back. The plant must, therefore, be harvested before this happens and the correct time can be ascertained only by constant attention.

When the plants are growing under the conditions they enjoy, it is generally possible to make two harvestings, one in midsummer, the other in autumn, but here again, much depends upon the weather. May and June, however, are often dry, sunny months and it may be advisable to harvest some foliage towards the end of June to make sure of at least one good crop. The shrubby thymes and the sages usually bear two crops.

Select a dry day for harvesting, before the flowers or leaves begin to die back, when the valuable oils return to the roots or base of the plant. Should a dry period be enjoyed immediately before the herbs reach their most potent condition, it is advisable to cut without delay, for if the plants are cut when damp, mildew may set in before they can be correctly dried, and the crop will rapidly deteriorate. Dryness from beginning to end is the secret of successful herb growing and harvesting.

The shrubby herbs, e.g. sage, savory and thyme, should be cut with a large and sharp knife, the stems being removed about 3 in above the base to prevent an excess of old wood from forming. When cutting savory and thyme, the whole plant may be held with one hand, while the cutting is done with the other hand, the sprigs being placed over sacking laid on the soil. Very hard-wooded plants such as southernwood or sage which have become 'leggy', are best cut with a pair of secateurs to prevent undue pulling of the plant, which could loosen the roots. Soft-wooded plants may be cut with a pair of strong scissors. Into this category come the mints, woodruff and parsley. Others, such as the mullein and tarragon, die down completely after flowering, and where it is required that the plants seed themselves the leaves should be removed from drying at the appropriate time and the flowers left to form seed. The stems should then be cut back, whilst annual and biennial plants are removed altogether. Plants grown for the value of their stems, such as the angelica, should be cut at regular intervals throughout summer, for it is the young stems which are used for candying and for stewing with rhubarb, to which they impart a unique flavour.

Care must be exercised with the harvesting of plants grown for their seeds, such as cumin, dill and coriander. The seed should be fully ripe before harvesting, but if the seed-pods are allowed to open the seed will be scattered and lost. As they reach maturity, the pods or seed-heads should be inspected daily and removed at the first signs of any seed shedding. The seed of annual plants to be used for propagating should receive similar attention, for unripened seed will not keep or germinate satisfactorily.

The seed-heads should be removed only when quite dry, or mildew may occur. The heads should be cut and dropped into a cardboard box and removed at once to a dry room. There they should be placed in fine muslin bags and hung up to become thoroughly dry, after which the seed is separated by opening the pods over a fine riddle.

Drying. To dry leaves and herbs if cut on a calm, warm day, the foliage should be left for an hour or so to become as dry as possible. Over-exposure to the hot rays of the sun, however, should not be allowed or the scent will lose strength. If drying on a large scale either for commercial sale or for home use, a small especially constructed drying room is a decided acquisition. This should be built of wood with suitable ventilation in or near the roof to permit the escape of moisture given off by the drying foliage. A small aperture at either end of the shed or a cowl fixed in the roof is efficient but if excess moisture cannot escape, efficient drying will not take place and the leaves will become mildewed and musty. Shelves should be placed around the shed and should be made of laths with a 1-in space between each. When small leaves are being dried, lengths of muslin or hessian should be placed over the laths. Roof windows may be used or windows let into the sides of the shed to enable the dryer to carry out the operation with ease, and to provide a circulation of fresh air. Vents made just above ground level will also ensure an intake of fresh air which will pass through the leaves and leave the house by the top vents.

Herbs may be dried in the home either by tying into bunches and suspending from the roof of a dry shed or room (an attic is an ideal place), or they may be spread out on shelves or on trays away from the direct rays of the sun. Wherever they are drying, they should be turned daily so that fresh air reaches all parts of the leaves. The drying should be completed as quickly as possible for only in this way will the herbs retain their full colour and maximum fragrance. Especially is rapid drying necessary with thick-leaved herbs which contain a large amount of moisture, for mildew sets in if drying proceeds slowly. An attic or shed should be selected if possible, for the heat of the sun on the roof will enable quite high temperatures to be maintained, a temperature of $39^{\circ}C$ ($100^{\circ}F$) not being excessive when drying mint and parsley.

A rack for drying herbs may be made by using a number of trays about 4 ft square, using 1-in timber. To each tray is tacked a square of hessian canvas and the finished trays are held in position one above another by means of four lengths of 2 by 2-in timber fixed to the corners of the frames. About 12 in should be allowed between each tray to enable the herbs to be turned and a free circulation of fresh air to reach them. A rack just over 6 ft may be inexpensively made and will contain six trays, thus enabling a large number of herbs to be dried.

Where space is limited and only a small number of herbs are to be dried, trays of similar construction should be made to the measurements of shelves. These should stand on pieces of 2-in timber fastened at each corner of the tray. This will keep the hessian 2 in above the shelving and permit fresh air to circulate around the herbs. This is vitally important for rapid drying. The drying room should not be made of stone nor of corrugated iron, for both materials tend to form condensation which will greatly hamper the drying. Where there is neither attic nor shed available, an airing cupboard is suitable, especially if there is an immersion heater to maintain warmth. The door of the room or cupboard should be left open to allow any moisture to escape.

Storing. Where there is sufficient heat, most herbs will have dried within a week, whilst those having thick leaves will take several days longer. If the herbs have to depend upon the natural warmth of the atmosphere, they may take up to three weeks to become thoroughly dry, at which point they should 'crackle' and snap to the touch. The leaves (or flowers) may then be rubbed from the stems between the palms of the hands, after which all unwanted material is removed. The dried leaves are then placed in a fine-meshed riddle so that soil, dust and chaff may be removed, the remaining leaves then being placed in containers for storing. Screw-topped air-tight glass jars may be used where small quantities of herbs are grown for home use, each jar being carefully labelled and placed on a shelf away from the sun. When storing larger quantities, possibly for sale, a large container will be necessary. Wooden drums are ideal for the purpose, for wood will not absorb moisture from the atmosphere. For this reason tins of any description should never be used, for they may cause the herbs to become damp. The herbs should be kept in a dry room, away from the direct rays of the sun and they may be mixed as required for use in many ways in the home.

No mention has yet been made about harvesting the root herbs. These reach maturity and their maximum flavour as soon as the leaves begin to die back. Where required for drying, to be grated down when needed, this is the time to lift. Select a day when the soil is reasonably dry, probably following a dry week which may often be experienced in autumn and lift the roots carefully with a garden fork. They should be allowed to remain on the ground for several hours to become partially dry when as much soil as possible should be shaken off. The roots should then be placed in rows on strips of canvas where they are removed to a dry room, a cellar being suitable. All foliage is cut off and after a few days the roots should be rubbed with the canvas to clean off as much soil as possible before being placed in a warm, open oven to bake. They may then be stored in jars until required for grating.

PART II

ALPHABETICAL GUIDE

A

ABELIA (Caprifoliaceae—Honeysuckle Family)

A genus of 12 or so evergreen or deciduous shrubs, mostly native of China or Mexico and valued for their freedom of flowering during late summer. They require a warm sheltered position in full sun where they will bloom intermittently throughout winter and spring, and a well-drained loamy soil with a high chalk content. Propagation is by layering the young shoots or by cuttings of the half-ripened wood which should be removed in August and inserted in sandy soil in a cold frame.

Species. *Abelia chinensis.* A deciduous hairy shrub, discovered in China in 1816 by Robert Abel after whom the genus is named. It grows 1.2 to 1.5 m (4 to 5 ft) tall with small oblong leaves and is in bloom during August and September and, if the weather is mild, until the end of autumn. It bears its rose-tinted flowers, like miniature foxgloves, in pairs at the ends of the stems, and they are sweetly scented.

A. floribunda. It is only half hardy in northern Europe and should be confined to sheltered gardens of the south and western coastline where it will retain its leaves through winter. It is a native of Mexico and makes a compact evergreen shrub 0.9 to 1.2 m (3 to 4 ft) tall. In a mild winter it blooms towards the end of February, bearing delicately scented tubular flowers of rosy-mauve in drooping clusters.

A. serrata. A beautiful Chinese evergreen shrub 0.9 to 1.2 m (3 to 4 ft) in height with oblong serrated leaves; in mild weather it blooms towards the end of February. One of the few shrubs to bear brightly coloured flowers which are fragrant, as the flowers have a rich spicy scent. The white or blush-pink blooms are splashed with orange.

A. triflora. An erect and graceful Himalayan shrub which grows 1.5 m (5 ft) in height and flowers earlier than the other species, blooming before the end of June. The flowers are borne in terminal clusters and are white, flushed with yellow on the inside whilst the tube is tinted with pink or purple; they appear from the axils of the leaves and the tips of the branches, and have the fragrance of vanilla.

ABELIOPHYLLUM (Oleaceae—Olive Family)

A genus of a single species.

Species. *Abeliophyllum distichum.* It is a slow-growing winter-flowering shrub, native of Korea, which grows 2.7 to 3 m (9 to 10 ft) high and almost as wide. At its best trained against a sunny wall where it will bloom when young and with the warmth of the February sunshine, bearing its bell-shaped blooms of blush-white with an attractive orange centre, along the stems. The flowers, borne in short racemes on the previous year's wood, have a sweet penetrating perfume which, if the plant is growing against an open window, will scent the largest of rooms, and a few sprigs taken indoors with Winter Jasmine will be appreciated at this time of the year. The flowers bloom early in January and continue until April, followed by flat fruits.

ABIES (Pinaceae—Pine Tree Family)

A genus of 50 species, known as the spruce or fir, and mostly native of the Northern Hemisphere. They make tall, handsome trees and several are resinous.

They prefer a soil containing more moisture than other conifers and should not be planted too close together or they will lose their lower branches as they grow large.

Species. *Abies amorika.* The Serbian spruce, it makes a tall, narrow tree with flat grey-green leaves, like *Thuya occidentalis* rather than the Norway spruce. It is an excellent tree for the back of a plantation for it makes rapid growth.

A. balsamea. The Balsam fir, it is a slender, elegant tree, the blunt dark-green leaves being silvery white on the underside, whilst the 10-cm (4-in) cones are round and violet-coloured. A resin is extracted from incisions made in the bark which yields a substitute for Balm of Gilead from which Friar's Balsam is obtained, still the best curative for a sore throat. The leaves and buds also yield a balsam-like fragrance.

A. bracteata. (syn. *A. venusta*). Native of the Santa Lucia Mountains of California where the trees reach a height of 60 m (200 ft), clothed in graceful branches of brightest green. The slender cones are borne singly and when ripe are covered in globules of balsamic resin.

A. grandis. Native to Canada and the northern United States, where it is known as the Western white fir or the Lowland balsam, for it is found in the valleys and lower hillsides, growing 60 to 90 m (200 to 300 ft) tall. It exudes a pungent, balsamic fragrance over the countryside. The gum which exudes from the bark has a similar scent, and is used (mixed with lard) as an ointment.

ABOBRA (Cucurbitaceae—Gourd Family)

A genus of a single species native of South America which climbs by means of tendrils, rapidly covering a trellis.

Species. *Abobra tenuifolia.* It is a tuberous root perennial with glossy leaves of palest green, and bears powerfully scented flowers of greenish-white. The female flowers are followed by large oval scarlet fruits in autumn before the stems and foliage die down. Except in warmer parts of the British Isles and Europe, the roots are lifted and stored during winter like dahlias, to be replanted in the open in May. It does best in a sunny position and

light soil, and is propagated by seed sown in spring in a frame. Planting out should be when frosts have finished.

ABRONIA (Nyctaginaceae—Jalap Family)

A genus of about 12 species of trailing downy herbs all native of California and, though really of perennial habit, usually treated as half-hardy annuals in northern Europe on account of their tenderness.

Like the Verbena, the abronias are of semi-trailing habit, bearing their flowers in verbena-like clusters and diffusing a rich honey perfume. The plants require a light, well-drained soil and an open, sunny situation. With their trailing habit, they are suitable for hanging baskets.

Germination of the seed is slow unless the husk is first peeled off or the seed is soaked in warm water for several hours previous to sowing. The plants may also be propagated from cuttings.

Species. *Abronia arenaria.* The Sand verbena which grows to 30 to 37 cm (12 to 15 in) tall with kidney-shaped leaves and is in bloom during late summer. The lemon-yellow flowers are borne in dense clusters and diffuse a delicious honeysuckle perfume most noticeable at nightfall.

A. fragrans. The Californian verbena which forms an erect plant of branching habit and eventually attains a height of 60 cm (2 ft) or more. It is in bloom during July and August, bearing its pure-white flowers in terminal clusters, and they open only in the coolness of evening, diffusing a vanilla-like perfume.

A. umbellata. A dwarf trailing plant growing only 15 cm (6 in) high with oval elliptic leaves, and one of the few plants bearing rose-pink flowers which are powerfully scented. At one time much in demand for hanging baskets in conservatories, it blooms during late summer and autumn.

ACACIA (Mimosa) (Leguminosae— Laburnum Family)

The genus *Acacia* is widely distributed throughout Australia and Tasmania, South Africa, and along the shores of the Mediterranean where it was most likely introduced. Of the 400 or more species, only one or two are sufficiently hardy for outdoor planting in the British Isles and northern America for they bear their golden sprays of violet-like perfume during February and March. The stamens of acacia flowers are 'free', whilst those of the closely related Albizzia are joined at the base.

The acacias abound in Australia and are known as Wattles. They are able to withstand extreme drought. Several species are armed with spines. In colder climes they are best given the protection of a warm greenhouse or walled garden.

Species. *Acacia armata.* Known as the Kangaroo Thorn, it makes a small spiny shrub and bears its rich golden flowers along the whole length of the upright stems. The flowers are delicately scented.

A. baileyana. One of the species from which the florists' 'mimosa' is obtained: a tree in full bloom, growing against a background of evergreens, presents one of the most beautiful sights in an early spring garden. A native of the more temperate parts of Australia (where it is known as the Cootamandra wattle) and New Zealand, in Britain its planting should be confined to the Falmouth area and in the United States to the south. The tree attains a height of 9 m (30 ft) and blooms in January. Its tiny golden fluffy balls, which are really bunches of numerous golden stamens, appear in sprays of a dozen or more and are violet-scented: its drooping branches are covered in sea-green feathery leaves.

A. dealbata. In Australia, it is known as the Silver wattle and is one of the species supplying the 'mimosa' of European flower-shops. It grows to a height of 12 m (40 ft) or more along the Cornish Riviera and the Mediterranean shores where it blooms about mid-January: its violet-like perfume can be quite intoxicating on a calm day where growing in quantity. It forms a spreading tree and has attractive fern-like foliage.

A. drummondii. For a small greenhouse, it is a compact plant which can be grown in a 22-cm (9-in) pot. It has small bipinnate leaves, and early in the year bears cylindrical spikes of fragrant fluffy yellow flowers.

A. farnesiana. The only wattle found in both the Northern and Southern Hemispheres, named after the Farnese Palace in Rome. It is the acacia most cultivated at the flower farms along the Mediterranean for the production of cassia oil. It grows to a height of about 1.8 m (6 ft) and during October and November is covered in tiny golden violet-scented blooms visible through the emerald foliage. The oil is used to fortify the violet perfume.

The plant requires a dry soil and an open, sunny situation where a fully grown tree 10 years old will yield up to 9 kg (20 lb) of blossom each season.

A. longifolia. The Sydney Golden Wattle, common to the sandy coastline of New South Wales and Victoria. It has narrow lance-shaped leaves and bears its bright-yellow violet-scented flowers in elegant cylindrical spikes, usually from August until November.

A. melanosoylon. A hard-wooded tree which is used for furniture. The flowers are borne in globular heads of as many as 50 and they are palest yellow with a penetrating scent. They are followed by an oblong pod containing black seeds.

A. mollissima. Known as the Black wattle of South Africa, it makes a large tree with deep-green foliage and with the young shoots slightly tomentose. The leaves are bipinnate, and the flower-heads globular, composed of about 50 pale-yellow 'balls' which emit a powerful sweet scent.

A. podalyriifolia. The Silver wattle of Queensland which makes a tall shrub covered all over with fine hairs. The fluffy golden-yellow balls are produced in dense heads and emit a delicate sweet perfume.

A. suaveolens. It makes a neat, slender shrub and bears its powerfully scented flowers of palest yellow in axillary racemes. Known as the Sweet-scented wattle, it is common about the barren coastline of Queensland and Tasmania and has handsome glaucous foliage.

ACERAS (Orchidaceae—Orchid Family)
A genus of a single species

Species. *Aceras anthropophorum.* Like the closely related Lizard orchid, it is distributed across northern Europe from South-east England, through Holland and

Belgium to the Soviet Union. It is unusual amongst hardy orchids in that its leaves when dry give off the scent of newly mown hay, owing to the presence of coumarin (as in woodruff).

The 'Man orchid', as it is known to countrymen, is one of the earliest orchids and bears its flowers in May and June on a columnar spike to a height of about 37 cm (15 in). The hooded flowers are greenish yellow and have a long slender lower lip with 2 lateral and 2 terminal lobes which give the impression of a man's arms and legs. The nectar is found in a shallow spur which is readily accessible to hover-flies drawn to it by the unpleasant smell.

ACHILLEA (Yarrow) (Compositae— Daisy Family)

A large genus of herbaceous and alpine plants renowned for the beauty of their foliage. They grow best in a well-drained sandy soil and a position of full sun which will bring out the silver of the foliage and the pungent aroma. The plants are increased by root division in spring or autumn, or cuttings of the young shoots may be removed late in summer and inserted in sandy soil in a frame to root. They will be ready to plant out the following spring.

Species and Varieties. *Achillea ageratum.* A native of Greece, it is believed to have reached England in 1573 and is known as Sweet maudlin. It is an alpine plant, growing 15 to 17 cm (6 to 7 in) tall, its narrow leaves being crisped at the edges and arranged in dense silvered rosettes, and richly pungent when pressed. It blooms in summer, bearing large solitary white flowers well above the foliage.

A. argentea. It forms its foliage in neat rosettes and is heavily silvered; this is accentuated by the flowers of purest white.

A. clypeolata. A plant of rapid growth, its feathery grey leaves quickly hiding the soil around it, and having a pleasant aromatic scent.

A. eupatorium. Native of the Caucasus, it grows 1.5 m (5 ft) tall, its hairy pinnate leaves being lobed and serrated. Besides its attractive foliage, it is one of the longest flowering of all plants, bearing its flat, plate-like heads of rich yellow from June

until October. The variety Gold Plate is finer still, with large flower-heads of brilliant gold; the dried leaves have a pungency similar to that of featherfew and are excellent to use in pot-pourris.

Coronation Gold is a dwarf edition of Gold Plate, growing only 60 cm (2 ft) tall with attractively cut foliage and bearing flowers of golden yellow.

A. King Edward. A hybrid which grows only 15 cm (6 in) tall and is suitable for planting at the front of a border. Its fern-like leaves are beautifully silvered and emit a powerful aromatic scent when pressed, and the tiny cream flower-heads are borne from June until October.

A. millefolium. A plant native to the British Isles, at one time used to heal wounds made by carpenter's tools; in France, it is the *herbe aux charpentiers.* Its name comes from Achilles, who it is said was told of the qualities of the plant by the centaur Chiron.

It is a common plant of pastures and hedgerows where it grows to a height of 60 cm (2 ft) and bears its tiny blush-white flowers in large corymbs from mid-June until September. The flowers have a peculiar musky scent about them, whilst the handsome fern-like leaves have the refreshing pungent smell of featherfew. For this reason it was used for bridal wreaths and was known as Venus's-tree to countrymen. It has for long been a popular border plant, the varieties Cerise Queen and the crimson-flowered Fire King being most colourful in the garden and long lasting when cut.

A. Moonshine. A hybrid of exceptional beauty. It grows 60 cm (2 ft) tall and has finely cut leaves like those of a fern, of bright silvery grey. In summer the pungent leaves are as if covered with hoarfrost, and the yellow flower-heads are borne from July until September.

A. rupestris. A plant for the alpine garden or for edging for it grows only 15 cm (6 in) tall and blooms in May, bearing umbels of purest white above compact tufts of scented grey-green foliage.

A. taygetea. It grows 45 cm (18 in) tall with pungent leaves which are beautifully serrated and bears large flat heads of glistening yellow.

A. Weston. A hybrid growing 30 cm (12 in) tall, its silvery-white leaves appearing, like those of *A. argentea*, in compact rosettes. Of rapid growth, it makes a valuable edging plant.

ACHIMENES (Gesneraceae—Gloxinia Family)

A genus of tuberous rooted plants, the flowers, which appear at the leaf joints, resembling those of the gloxinia. They are native of tropical South America and are plants for a warm greenhouse or garden room, reaching a height of 37 cm (15 in) and making such bushy growth that they require minimum support.

Indoors, they bloom from early June until October and should be started into growth towards the end of March, the most suitable time for their propagation by division of the tubers. Of semi-trailing habit, the tuberous plants may be started in pots, and in early May may be planted into indoor hanging baskets; they will bear their tubular flowers all summer and diffuse a subtle fragrance about the garden room. The plants require ample supplies of moisture as they come into growth. After flowering, they should be dried off by turning the pots on their side and keeping them away from frost. They may be brought into bloom again in the same pots in spring.

The most fragrant varieties are the pure-white *gloxiniflora* and *longiflora*, with its contrasting trumpets of deepest royal purple. The scarlet *coccinea* has no perfume.

ACIDANTHERA (Iridaceae—Iris Family)

A small genus of gladiolus-like plants of which only one species *A. bicolor* and its variety, *murielae*, and the hybrid *A. tubergenii*, is in general cultivation. It is hardy only in the more favourable climatic areas of Britain and America, elsewhere the corms should be lifted and stored each year as for gladioli and most other African plants.

Species. *Acidanthera bicolor*. It is native of the highlands of western Abyssinia and requires a well-drained soil and shelter from cold winds. The corms should be planted 7 to 10 cm (3 to 4 in) deep late in spring for they will not come into bloom until early autumn. As many as 6 creamy-white flowers blotched with maroon at the base appear to each 90-cm (3-ft) stem from a sheath of narrow gladiolus-like leaves. The blooms have a sweet, penetrating perfume which is even more pronounced in the variety *murielae*.

A. candida. Native of the steppes of the Altai Plains of East Africa, it has narrow pointed leaves and bears its violet-scented pure-white flowers with their long cylindrical tube on 45-cm (18-in) stems. It requires warm climatic conditions to bloom outdoors.

A. tubergenii. A beautiful hybrid of *A. bicolor* and its variety *murielae* which comes into bloom fully 3 weeks before either parent. The richly scented white flowers measure 10 cm (4 in) across and have a maroon blotch at the base like *murielae*. Outdoors it should have a warm corner.

ACOKANTHERA (Apocynaceae— Periwinkle Family)

A small genus of shrubby stove plants, native of South Africa where they grow into small trees. The leaves are pale green, tough and leathery, and the 5-lobed flowers are tubular in shape like those of the bouvardia. They are produced in corymbs at the leaf axils and -at the extremities of the shoots, so freely as to form sprays of inflorescences, and they diffuse the exotic lily-like fragrance of many tropical plants.

Species. *Acokanthera thunbergii* (syn. *Toxicophaea thundergii*). In cooler climes, it is a valuable pot-plant and will bloom when quite small though the plants have a tendency to grow stiff and erect; to persuade them to develop a bushy habit, it is necessary to pinch back the shoots regularly and especially when young for they are difficult to correct afterwards. Plant in a 25-cm (10-in) pot and water sparingly in winter.

ACORUS (Sweet flag) (Araceae—Arum Lily Family)

A small genus of semi-aquatic herbaceous plants, closely related to the Arums and native to many parts of the world. It is not a flag but a rush with a creeping rootstock and flag-like leaves, found by streams and ponds. It is increased by division of the rootstock in spring.

Species. *Acorus calamus.* Both the leaves and the roots have the refreshing scent of cinnamon, hence the great esteem in which the plant was held during the Middle Ages: the bright-green leaves were used for strewing.

It is also found in low-lying ground in North America, and in India and Burma where a drug known as Vaka is obtained from the root, but it must not be confused with the Indian lemon-grass, *Calamus aromaticus* (*Andropogon schoenanthus*).

From the leaves which resemble those of the iris, a volatile oil is distilled and is used in perfumery and for making aromatic vinegars. The roots, dried and powdered, were in demand for scenting snuffs, and at one time the plant was used to flavour beer and give it a clear appearance. From the rootstock is obtained the drug Calamus. In Canada and the United States, the roots are sliced and boiled in maple syrup, and when dried provide a delicious candied sweetmeat.

The volatile oil is contained in the outer skin of the rhizome and to peel the rhizome, as is done in Europe, before it is used is most wasteful for the most potent part is lost. The root is yellowish-brown when lifted but after peeling is greyish-white. The oil from the root is more powerful than from the leaves and is likened to that of camphor. From the root, Faust in 1867 extracted the bitter principle Acorin from which Thomas later obtained a neutral resin, Acoretin, which when reduced from alkaline solution gives essential oil and sugar as final products. After shaking out the Acorin with ether, calamine solution is obtained.

The flowers possess a sombre beauty, in appearance resembling the spire of a church, being greenish-brown in colour with the surface covered in a golden mosaic. They appear in June, on stems up to 1.8 m (6 ft) in length, and like the leaves are fragrant when bruised.

The plant is propagated by lifting the rhizomes in November when they are divided and re-planted 20 to 22 cm (8 to 9 in) deep by the waterside. When growing in gardens, it will not usually bloom.

ACRADENIA (Rutaceae—Rue Family)

A genus of a single species, native of Tasmania.

Species. *Acradenia frankliniae.* It forms a low shrub and has thick leathery leaves which emit a pungent orange-like smell when handled. It is not a hardy plant and requires greenhouse protection, except in the most sheltered parts. Height in its natural habitat is about 3 m (10 ft), somewhat less in cultivation. The white flowers have no scent.

ACROLOPHIA (Orchidaceae—Orchid Family)

A small genus of branched herbs with fleshy cylindrical roots. The erect leathery leaves clasp the stem at the base and the flowers are borne in loose racemes. The plant is native to South Africa where it is found on sandy flats and mountainous slopes.

Species. *Acrolophia bolusii.* It forms a tall-branched plant, and in its native haunts, bears in November-December, loose racemes of yellowish-brown flowers which have a soft sweet perfume.

ACTINIDIA (Actinidiaceae—Actinidia Family)

A small genus of mostly deciduous Asiatic twining plants closely related to the Camellias and thriving in a rich loamy soil. They give a better account of themselves in the more favourably situated gardens of the south and should be given a southerly aspect. The stems are covered in a soft silky down and the scented flowers are followed by edible fruits.

Like *Clematis montana*, several of the species show great vigour and will lift themselves up through the branches of tall trees or hedges which become beautified with the masses of fragrant blossoms during summer. Or they may be planted against a warm wall.

Propagation is by layering the shoots in autumn or by cuttings of the half ripened wood, removed and inserted under glass in August.

Species and Varieties. *Actinidia arguta.* Native of Japan it is a vigorous species for a sheltered garden. It has broad green, glossy foliage and from early June until August is covered in small white flowers tinted with green and having attractive purple anthers. The sweetly scented flowers are followed by greenish-yellow edible fruits, like the gooseberry.

The form *cordifolia* has heart-shaped leaves and striki.·g purple stems.

A. chinensis. Known as the Chinese gooseberry, its handsome leaves are often 20 cm (8 in) wide and are heart-shaped, downy on the underside. It will reach a height of 4.5 m (15 ft) or more and bears its scented buff-coloured flowers throughout summer on the previous year's wood so should be pruned but little, cutting out only the dead wood. The flowers are followed by edible fruits.

A. coriacea. One of the few evergreen species, it is native of Japan and has leathery lanceolate leaves. It bears its softly scented flowers of clear rose-pink during May and June.

A. kolomikta. Native of northern China, its large oblong leaves taper to a point and have white and pink variegation which is especially pronounced when growing against a warm wall. The stems are covered with white down and the solitary flowers which appear from the leaf axils during summer have a soft, sweet perfume.

A. melanandra. One of the most attractive species, the dark lanceolate leaves having bright crimson stems. The lemon-yellow flowers are produced in masses and have unusual grey anthers and a soft aromatic perfume.

A. polygama. A native of Japan, it is an outstanding wall plant growing 3 to 3.6 m (10 to 12 ft) in height; the handsome heart-shaped leaves have red stems and are bronzy-green at first. The fragrant white flowers open in June and are followed by sweet yellow fruits.

ADENANDRA (Rutaceae—Rue Family)

A small genus of compact evergreen shrubs, native of Cape Province where they grow on warm rocky slopes near the coast, flowering from April until December. Both the flowers and the foliage have an aromatic scent.

Species. *Adenandra umbellata.* A slender but vigorous shrub found on the summit of Table Mountain with alternate leaves, narrow and pointed and covered with highly scented oil glands. The white flowers, produced almost throughout the year, appear in small clusters at the end of the branchlets.

A. uniflora. A compact shrub 0.9 to 1.2m (3 to 4 ft) tall with hairy oblong leaves, it bears solitary white flowers at the end of the branchlets. The flowers are usually tinted with crimson on the underside, and the hairy sepals are glandular like the leaves.

ADENOCARPUS (Leguminosae—Laburnum Family)

A genus of some eight species of hairy or downy shrubs which require a warm sheltered garden and a soil containing a mixture of loam, sand and peat. It does well near the sea.

Species. *Adenocarpus decorticans.* Native of the Spanish Mediterranean coast and resembling the Common furze, though it is spineless. Its branches are densely covered with dark-green leaves cut into 2- to 3-foliate leaflets against which the masses of sweetly scented pea-like flowers of golden yellow are most showy.

A. viscosus. It grows to a height of 1.8 to 2.4 m (6 to 8 ft), its dark-green stems covered in tiny leaves, and throughout summer it bears yellow almond-scented broom-like flowers in long racemes.

ADENOPHORA (Campanulaceae—Campanula Family)

A genus of about 12 hardy plants, mostly native of northern Asia and similar to the campanulas. They have the thick fleshy roots characteristic of plants of that region, e.g. Peony The Bride (*P. albiflora*) and *Hemerocallis dumartieri*. They resent disturbance and require a well-drained soil and an open position. One species only bears scented flowers, *A. fischeri*, and it is one of the few plants of the family to do so.

Species. *Adenophora fischeri* (syn *A. lilifolia*). Native of Siberia and northern China, it makes a compact plant 45 to 50 cm (18 to 20 in) tall and grows bushy but in no way coarse. The heart-shaped leaves are toothed and it blooms in August, remaining colourful until the end of September. The pale-blue flowers are borne in loose pyramids and they have a sweet but refreshing perfume.

ADIANTUM (Adiantaceae—Adiantum Family)

The sole genus of the family with about 200 species, mostly native of tropical America.

Species. *Adiantum amabile.* It is native of Brazil and has a perceptible fragrance. Known as the Scented maidenhair, the gracefully curved fronds are noticeably scented when young. It requires stove conditions in northern Europe, i.e. a winter temperature of 15 to 18°C (60 to 65°F) and ample supplies of moisture at its roots.

ADOXA (Adoxaceae—Adoxa Family)

A genus of a single species closely allied to Caprifoliaceae.

Species. *Adoxa moschatellina.* It is a small glabrous herb with a creeping rhizomatous rootstock. Widely distributed over the northern temperate zone, it is perennial and is found in a few places of the British Isles, usually in hedgerows. It is a delightful little plant, growing 15 cm (6 in) tall with long-stalked radical leaves, ternately divided into triangular leaflets. The two-leaved stem ends in a cluster of 5 to 7 tiny greenish-yellow flowers arranged symmetrically and appearing during April and May. The whole plant diffuses a delicious musk-like perfume similar to elder blossom before fertilization has occurred. Cross-pollination is effected by small insects, attracted to the musky smell and the nectar secreted at the base of the stamens.

AESCULUS (Sapindaceae—Horse-Chestnut Family

A genus of about 14 species of trees or shrubs with compound leaves which are deciduous. They are mostly native of North America or south-eastern Europe and are amongst the most handsome of ornamental trees. Included amongst them is the Horse-chestnut which reached England in the middle of the sixteenth century; Gerard, the first writer to mention it, spoke of it as a 'rare foreign tree', but Evelyn wrote in 1663 that 'it bears a most glorious flower, even in our cold country'. Sir Christopher Wren had William III plant the mile-wide avenue at Bushey Park with the tree and many of them still stand.

Species. *Aesculus californica.* A handsome native of California, attaining a height of 12 m (40 ft) or more with smooth oblong lanceolate leaves and bearing in May hyacinth-like spires of white- or blush-coloured flowers which are the most highly scented of the species.

A. flava. The Sweet buck-eye of North America so called because the blooms yield a sweet nectar which is delicious when sucked out. It is a beautiful tree of compact habit and in May bears tubular primrose-yellow flowers, enhanced by the downy leaves. The flowers have a slight perfume.

A. hippocastanum. The Common horse-chestnut, a noble tree of southern Europe, its huge leaves divided into 8 lobes. In May, it bears white or pink flowers, sometimes speckled with red, possibly to guide the bees which pollinate them, in tall hyacinth-like racemes and they have a delicate honey-like perfume. The flowers are followed in autumn by polished brown fruits encased in spiny capsules.

The form *flore plena* bears double flowers which are slightly scented but does not bear fruit.

A. parviflora. Native of southern Europe, it is a delightful small garden tree, introduced into Britain in 1785 and not exceeding a height of 3 m (10 ft). The leaves are downy and grey-green; the erect flower spikes, often 30 cm (12 in) long, are white with long thread-like filaments, pink in colour and with a red anther. The flowers, which do not appear until August, have a delicate honey perfume. The leaves turn yellow before they fall.

AETHUSA (Umbelliferae—Parsley Family)

A genus of a single species.

Species. *Aethusa cynapium.* It is a smooth, leafy annual, native of the British Isles and northern Europe, and known as Fool's parsley. It is named from the Greek *aitho*, to burn, from its acrid qualities. It grows 30 to 60 cm (1 to 2 ft) tall, with deep-green, 2-pinnate leaves, and bears white flowers in terminal umbels during July. All parts have the evil smell of hemlock, and it is equally poisonous; it is sometimes known as the Lesser hemlock. Differentiation from the true Wild parsley lies in the unpleasant smell and white, rather than yellow, flowers.

AFZELIA (Leguminosae—Laburnum Family)

A genus of 14 species of small trees, native of tropical and South Africa and South-east Asia.

Species. *Afzelia quanzensis.* It is found from the Transvaal northwards to Rhodesia and is known as the Mahogany bean. The purple-pink flowers, like those of the fuchsia, have the sweet-pea scent of the family and are followed by long dark-brown pods which are 5 cm (2 in) wide. Inside is a row of 6 to 9 brownish-black seeds of acorn shape, polished like mahogany, but with their surface covered by a vermilion cup.

AGANOSMA (Apocynaceae—Periwinkle Family)

A genus of 10 species, inhabiting the tropical forests of south-eastern China and Indonesia, and climbing plants of vigorous habit. They bear large panicles of pure-white flowers with a powerful scent, and the leaves of several species are fragrant.

Species. *Aganosma caryophyllata.* A climbing plant of giant proportions, it has large leathery leaves which release a powerful clove-like perfume when handled.

AGATHOSMA (Rutaceae—Rue Family)

A genus of heath-like shrubs, native of Cape Province and taking its name from the Greek words *agathos*, good, and *osme*, smell, for the leaves have an aromatic scent when pressed. The flowers are borne in a terminal umbel of as many as 25 and are creamy-white or palest mauve-pink with a pleasing perfume. They are mostly found on sandstone ridges near Cape Point and on the western slopes of Table Mountain.

Species. *Agathosma bifida* (syn. *A umbellata*). It grows 90 cm (3 ft) tall with erect linear leaves, hairy on the underside. The peduncles are glabrous, as long as the surrounding leaves. The flowers are creamy-white, with staminodes as long as the petals and spreading.

A. capensis. Common in shallow gravelly soils, it makes a dense shrublet about 30 cm (12 in) tall, the leaves acute and slightly incurved at the apex. The flowers are either white or lilac and are borne in dense heads, the petals being twice as long as the sepals.

A. hookeri. It is low-growing and spreading, its oblong leaves having stiff white hairs on the underside. The flowers are borne in dense heads and are creamy-white, the petals being almost twice as long as the sepals, with the staminodes erect.

A. lanceolata. It makes a small spreading shrub with ovate-lanceolate leaves and bears flowers of palest lilac with petals twice as long as the sepals. The whole plant has a very strong smell of liquorice.

AGLAIA (Meliaceae—Mahogany Family)

A genus of about 250 species of trees or shrubs, native of China, Malaya and the Pacific Islands, and distributed also throughout India and Siam.

Species. *Aglaia odorata.* An elegant, leafy tree, called by the Chinese *Yu-chu-lan*, its flowers being in demand for flavouring tea, for the composition of joss-sticks, and for making necklaces. The flowers, which are extremely small, are borne on slender pedicles in lax panicles, and are said to be the most exquisitely scented of all flowers, like vanilla but with spicy undertones. They retain the same sweet, spicy perfume when dry, and indefinitely, so that they are widely used in pot-pourris.

It will grow well in a stove house, with a compost containing plenty of peat or similar material, and semi-ripened short cuttings will root in heat and a very sandy compost.

AGRIMONIA (Rosaceae—Rose Family)

A small genus of stately herbaceous plants with fern-like leaves and bearing golden-yellow flowers in corymbose cymes.

Species. *Agrimonia eupatoria.* The Common agrimony, a perennial plant native to the British Isles and northern Europe, grows along banks and hedgerows, bearing its golden-yellow spikes on 60-cm (2-ft) stems during July and August. The attractive leaves are composed of 7- or 9-toothed leaflets. Both the flowers and the roots have a delicate fruity perfume similar to that of ripe apricots. A concoction of the leaves and roots was used in Culpeper's time for alleviating kidney troubles.

A. odorata. The Scented agrimony, a species closely allied to the Common agrimony, but the leaves and flowers have a delicious resinous quality, like that given off by the leaves of the walnut tree. It is a perennial plant native to the British Isles and was held in much esteem during the Middle Ages for the tonic brew made from its leaves.

It is a plant of more branched habit than the Common agrimony with large yellow flowers held more closely together on the spike and they are almost as powerfully scented as the leaves. Both flowers and leaves retain their refreshing scent when dried and so may be used to stuff pillows or in pot-pourris.

AILANTHUS (Simarubaceae—Simaruba Family)

A small genus of rapid-growing soot-tolerant trees, native of northern China and Mongolia.

Species. *Ailanthus glandulosa.* (syn. *A. altissima*). Known in its native China and Manchuria as the Tree of Heaven, it is a hardy fast-growing tree, closely related to the Phellodendrons, its branches resembling a stag's horns. It is an excellent town tree and has been widely planted in New York City where it attains a height of 15 m (50 ft). It is also used for park bedding schemes, cut back each year to almost ground level so that new shoots arise in spring.

The blooms are insignificant but the large pinnate leaves have glandular teeth near the base which release a pungent aroma when pressed.

A. sinensis (syn. *Cedrela sinensis*). The Chinese Mahogany tree, also known as the 'Father tree' on account of its longevity, and as the Incense tree because its wood is burnt as incense in the temples. Its long panicles of pure-white blossoms diffuse a powerfully sweet scent. It is a deciduous tree growing 15 m (50 ft) tall with large handsome leaves.

AJUGA (Labiatae—Lavender Family)

A genus of about 30 species.

Species. *Ajuga chamaepitys.* The Ground-pine or Yellow bugle, which differs from all other British species of the family in its appearance and fragrance. It is an annual of prostrate habit with hairy stems and leaves, reddish-brown in colour and releasing the turpentine smell when pressed or trodden upon; they are divided almost to the base into 3-linear segments. The yellow bugle-shaped flowers are borne in axillary pairs and have red spots on the lower lip of the corolla; they bloom from May until August. The plant frequents damp woodlands.

Culpeper said it smells 'somewhat strong like unto resin', though to some the whole plant gives off an unpleasant smell, unlike that of any of the aromatic labiates. A decoction of the leaves is used for kidney complaints and as a gentle laxative, mixed with the pulp of figs and made into pills. It was also taken as a remedy for a cough.

AKEBIA (Lardizabalaceae—Lardizabala Family)

A genus of only two species which are evergreen in warm, sheltered districts of the British Isles. Natives of China and Japan, they are plants of twining habit and bloom early in spring. When growing against a sunny wall the first flowers appear before the end of March, and are sweetly scented. They have long, cylindrical fruits, but these are seldom seen in cultivation. Propagation is by cuttings of half-ripened wood with a little heat; they can also be layered in early spring.

Species. *Akebia lobata.* It has trifoliate leaves and is native of China, growing to a height of 4.5 to 6 m (15 to 20 ft). The deep-purple flowers appear in drooping racemes at the end of March and are scented, though not so powerfully as those of *A. quinata.*

A. quinata. A fast-growing climber with bright-green leaves made up of 5 leaflets.

Well-grown plants reach a height of 9 m (30 ft) or more, retaining their foliage almost throughout the year; in spring and early summer they bear their deliciously scented flowers of chocolate-purple in long racemes.

ALANGIUM (Thymeleaceae—Mezereon Family)
A genus of a single species.

Species. *Alangium chinense.* It is native of south-western China and makes a shrub 1.8 m (6 ft) tall with handsome maple-like leaves. It blooms during June and July; the white flowers, like tiny lilies, are sweetly scented and have recurved petals. They are borne in elegant cymes.

Though the plant is tender and in European and North American gardens may be cut down by frosts in winter, new shoots will form in spring from the older basal wood. Pruning is not necessary.

ALBIZZIA (Leguminosae—Laburnum Family)
A small genus of deciduous trees native of South Africa, Rhodesia and Western Australia, and famed for their beautiful fern-like foliage. They bear either pale-yellow or pink flowers which diffuse the delicious sweet-pea scent of the family.

Species. *Albizzia gummifera.* Native of the coastal forests of South Africa where it attains a height of 15 cm (50 ft) or more with low-spreading branches. The small funnel-shaped flowers, borne several to a head, are yellow with crimson anthers, and like the laburnum carry the vanilla scent far and wide.

A. lophantha. Native of Western Australia, it makes a small tender tree with attractive mimosa-like dark-green foliage divided into 8 or 10 pairs of leaves. In northern Europe it is suitable only for greenhouse culture where it blooms in spring. The flowers are of pale sulphur-yellow, borne in bottle-brush-like racemes and have a soft sweet-pea fragrance.

ALBUCA (Liliaceae—Lily Family)
A small genus of bulbous plants native to tropical and South Africa which in all but the warmest parts of Britain and the United States require warm greenhouse

treatment. They are closely related to *Galtonia candicans* and are of similar appearance. When growing indoors, the albucas require potting in October and should be kept at about 15°C (60°F). They will need more moisture as they come into bloom in April or May.

Species. *Albuca fragrans.* Native of Cape Province, it forms a small globose bulb from which arises a raceme of scented golden-yellow flowers with a green stripe down the centre of each petal.

A. nelsonii. A native of Natal, it bears its nodding white bell-shaped flowers on 1.5-m (5-ft) stems and each petal has a red candy-stripe down the middle. It is sweetly scented.

ALHAGI (Leguminosae—Laburnum Family)
A genus of five species of thorny sub-shrubs, native of the Sahara regions, the coastline of the Mediterranean and the Near East.

Species. *Alhagi camelorum.* Probably the aspalathus of the Apocrypha, it is a much-branched shrub, its stems covered with sharp axillary spines, and known as Camel's Thorn. Like those of the gorse and spartium, to which it is closely related, the pea-like flowers are pineapple-scented.

ALLIUM (Liliaceae—Lily Family)
A large genus which includes the onion, garlic and shallot. The ornamental species and varieties are known as the 'ornamental onions' or 'flowering garlics'. They were widely grown in Elizabethan gardens and were known as 'mollies', a name derived from *Allium moly*, the Golden garlic, said by Pliny to be amongst the most precious of all plants.

The ornamental onions are perhaps interesting rather than beautiful but are valuable plants to naturalize in a dry soil, whilst those of daintier habit are most suitable for the rock garden. The roots and foliage have a garlic aroma about them, but the flower-heads of several species are sweetly scented and in some instances the plants are free of any garlic smell. Here is an example of white and yellow flowers having most perfume, for the blue-flowering species have none. Almost all are extremely hardy and their flowering period covers the whole of summer. Where naturalized, they will seed themselves or they may be increased by the small offsets as for the garlic or onion. Plant the bulbs in autumn, 7 cm (3 in) deep and 15 cm (6 in) apart.

Species. *Allium moly.* The golden-yellow star-like flowers are borne in dense globes resembling *Primula denticulata*, and on 30-cm (12-in) stems. A native of southern Europe, it blooms during midsummer and the flower is softly scented.

A. neapolitanum. The first to bloom, in a sheltered corner in full sun, opening its loose umbels of purest white during early spring. A native of Italy, it blooms on 30-cm (12-in) stems above dark-green strap-like leaves, but in the British Isles is not hardy away from the South-west. The sun brings out the sweet scent of the flowers, the plant being free of any onion smell.

A. narcissiflorum. Native of the lower slopes of the Italian alpine regions, it is at its best in the rock garden for it is of neat, compact habit and is slow to increase. It blooms during June and July, forming a pair of strap-like leaves and a pendulous flower of ruby-red held on a 22-cm (9-in) stem. It enjoys scree conditions and an open situation. Its flowers have a pleasant sweet scent, similar to that of *A. neapolitanum.*

A. triquetrum. Like *A. neapolitanum*, it is native to Italy and parts of southern Europe, forming at the end of each 30-cm (12-in) stem umbels of up to 12 dangling bell-shaped blooms of purest white and sweetly scented. In Britain it blooms during early summer and spreads so rapidly that it should be confined to the wild garden.

A. ursinum. The broad-leaf garlic, to the countryman known as Ramsons, a plant which is common in damp woodlands and hedgerows throughout the Northern Hemisphere, bearing lance-shaped leaves and large umbels of pure-white flowers. The whole plant, including the root, gives off the sulphurous smell of the garlic, but the leaves are used by West Countrymen to flavour pilchards and stews, for the garlic flavour is less pronounced than in the bulbous roots of the culinary garlic.

ALOCASIA (Araceae—Arum Family)

A genus of eight species of tuberous rooted herbs or dwarf shrubs, native of South-east Asia and the islands of the Pacific. The roots are boiled and used as food by the natives.

Species. *Alocasia odorata.* Native of south-east Asia, it was once a popular greenhouse plant, grown for the fragrance of its flowers which are greenish-yellow and diffuse the scent of mignonette with undertones of clove. It is the most pleasantly scented of all the Arum family.

ALOYSIA (Verbenaceae—Verbena Family)

A genus of 30 or more species native of the warmer parts of South America, only one of which will survive an average winter in the British Isles and northern Europe.

Species. *Aloysia citriodora.* The Lemon verbena. Its leaves, with their powerful lemon smell are valuable to include in pot-pourris. It forms a shrub 1.2 to 1.5 m (4 to 5 ft) tall but needs the protection of a warm wall and shelter from cold winds if it is not to be cut down by frost. It will usually form new shoots with the beginning of warmer weather.

ALPINIA (Zingiberaceae—Ginger Family)

A genus of tropical plants, mostly native of South-east Asia and Japan with one species native to New South Wales. They are perennial herbs with a rhizomatous rootstock and bear a terminal inflorescence on a leafy shoot.

Species. *Alpinia aromaticum.* Native of the valleys of eastern Bengal where it blooms before the rains commence. The flower stems are enclosed by the leaf sheaths, the lanceolate leaves being about 30 cm (12 in) long and 7 cm (3 in) wide. The flower spikes are borne at a height of about 90 cm (3 ft) and are composed of pale-yellow blossoms, each emerging from the axil of a concave bract, the corolla being a long slender tube of 3 segments.

The fruit ripens in September and is sold to the druggists as *Morung elachi*, the seeds having a spicy cardamom smell. The Bengal cardamom, as it is called, is ovoid, about 2.5 cm (1 in) long, triangular and conical. Its three valves open to reveal about 80 seeds agglutinated together by a sticky sweet pulp. They have a camphoraceous odour.

A. officinarum. From the thick tuberous roots (rhizomes), a product is obtained which has the same peppery aromatic taste as ginger. *A. officinarum* is a native of China where from the early fifteenth century, the product galingale was in common use. The plant grows to a height of 0.9 to 1.2 m (3 to 4 ft), with leaves borne in long, smooth sheaths of brightest green. The flowers are white with red veinings and are borne in terminal spikes. The roots are cut into 7-cm (3-in) lengths whilst fresh, the external surface being reddish-brown in colour with the parenchyme cells filled with resin and essential oil, the whole root giving off a pungent odour. In Russia the root was at one time in great demand for flavouring a liqueur called *Nastoika* and also for flavouring tea. The commercial oil Galangal is used in remedies for indigestion and in the manufacture of vinegar and pickles as well as in flavouring liqueurs.

A. sessilis. The roots do not yield galingale but are most agreeably fragrant; they are dried and powdered and used by Hindu women as a talcum powder.

The plant is common in Bengal where the dried roots are marketed under the name of *Kamala*, and is most handsome bearing its flowers in the sheaths of the leaves. The flowers are pure white except for a purple dot at each of the petal edges.

ALSTROEMERIA (Amaryllidaceae— Narcissus Family)

Though of the narcissus family this genus has no bulb but produces a mass of tuberous roots. It is usually sold by the bushel and is one of the most popular and profitable of all cut flowers. Though also known as the Peruvian lily, amongst market growers it is always referred to by its botanical name, which it was given in honour of the Swedish botanist, Baron Alströemer. Though hardy, it is not sufficiently so in Britain to survive the winter unless the roots are 30 cm (12 in) below soil level. Great success may be enjoyed with the plant if it is grown in a well-drained loam and receives a regular mulch of decayed manure, peat or litter

when it dies down in autumn. It is delightful grown in beds for it provides brilliant colour in the garden and weeks of cut blooms for the home; no flower remains longer in a fresh condition in water.

When planting, the roots are spread out like the fingers of a hand and should have a mixture of peat and sand packed about them before covering with soil. They require an open sunny position but should have protection from prevailing winds. Spring planting is advisable.

Species. *Alstroemeria caryophyllea.* Native of ·tropical Brazil, it requires warm greenhouse culture in the Northern Hemisphere and produces its scarlet-red flowers during February and March. It grows only 22.5 cm (9 in) tall and makes an admirable pot-plant for the flowers fill the ·greenhouse with their clove perfume. The plant should be rested during late autumn and early winter, and given only sufficient moisture to keep it alive. Then at the year end, increase waterings and bring into bloom in a temperature of 15°C (60°F). The plants may be moved outdoors for the summer when fear of frost has vanished.

A. ligtu. A native of Chile and Peru growing 60 to 90 cm (2 to 3 ft) tall with narrow lance-shaped leaves, it bears small lily-like blooms of white and yellow which diffuse the sweet fragrance of mignonette. The ligtu hybrids bloom during July and August and come in shades of cream, buff, pink and salmon, all of which have the same delicious perfume. *A. ligtu* is quite hardy.

ALTERNANTHUS (Amaranthaceae— Amaranthus Family)

A genus of glabrous desert plants which appear leafless for the leaves have been reduced to sheaths. The plants are native of all the deserts of the Near East and bear hairy, ovoid fruits which are extremely aromatic when handled.

Species. *Alternanthus tortuosus* (syn. *Pityranthus tortuosus*).
A plant of bushy habit with numerous twisting stems, blue-green in colour and bearing a few umbels of white flowers followed by aromatic seeds.

A. triradiatus. It forms a bushy plant

with pale-yellow stems and bears large umbels of white flowers and pungently scented seeds.

ALYSSUM (Cruciferae—Wallflower Family)

A genus of 150 species distributed across Europe to Siberia.

Species. *Alyssum maritimum* (syn. *Lobularia maritima*). Though really perennial, Sweet alyssum is almost always treated as a half-hardy annual, the seed being sown in gentle heat early in the new year and the plants set out with geraniums, begonias and salvias with which it is used as an edging to a bed. No plant is more satisfactory used in this way, the pure-white form providing a suitable contrast to the brilliant colours of the other plants. The flowers have the refreshing scent of newly mown hay, hence its country name of Sweet Alyson. The more recently introduced American varieties, Rosie O'Day and Pink Heather, have lost much of the fragrance of the white alyssums, neither do they make such valuable spreading plants as Little Dorrit which grows only 10 cm (4 in) tall but is covered in a mass of tiny white clusters from June until November.

Even more compact and spreading is Snow Cloth which for many weeks of summer is studded with tiny white sweet-scented flowers. The perfume is entirely lost in the purple-flowered Violet Queen and Royal Carpet.

AMARYLLIS (Amaryllidaceae—Narcissus Family)

A genus restricted to a single species.

Species. *Amaryllis belladonna.* A beautiful South African autumn-flowering plant which is at its best following a dry summer. For this reason, it gives greater satisfaction in California and Australasia than in Britain. The bulbs need copious amounts of moisture just before they come into growth, usually in July, but if growing outdoors they require a well-drained soil and a sunny, sheltered situation. There, like most of the family, the bulbs should be left undisturbed and given only a top dressing of decayed manure each winter.

Seven or eight strap-like leaves appear in May and at the end of a solid 45-cm (18-in) scape 8 or 9 drooping funnel-shaped pink flowers appear in August and emit a powerful sweet perfume. It is also known as the Belladonna Lily.

AMBROSIA (Compositae—Daisy Family)

A genus of about 40 species of annual plants mostly native of Mexico and central North America which takes its name from the refreshing scent of its bright-green foliage, containing coumarin and resembling newly-made hay as it dries. The flowers, which are borne on long spiral stems, are like large yellow daisies and are similarly scented.

Species. *Ambrosia mexicana.* Native of Mexico and Central America, it has bright-green foliage and bears large yellow daisy-like flowers which smell of newly made hay; the scent becomes especially pronounced as the flowers age.

AMOMUM (Zingiberaceae—Ginger Family)

A genus once comprising 150 species of tropical plants with aromatic seeds, but now reduced to one, the rest being mostly transferred to *Afromomum.* This is *Amomum kepulago* (syn. *A. cardamon*), which furnishes the 'round' cardamom described by Dioscorides and by Pliny: the fruits are round like a black cherry, and the seeds when dry have a powerful camphoraceous smell. The seed is usually bleached before commercial use.

The plant reaches a height of about 90 cm (3 ft) and produces rather small, yellow flowers in August. Stove house conditions are required and increase is by division in spring, when growth has just started.

AMOORA (Meliaceae—Mahogany Family)

A genus of 15 species, closely related to *Aglaia*, and native of Nepal, Sikkim and the Malayan Archipelago where they grow at altitudes of 600 to 1,200 m (2,000 to 4,000 ft), making large spreading trees with thick trunks.

Species. *Amoora decandra.* It makes a tall tree with leaves long and narrow, and the white 5-petalled flowers are borne on long slender panicles and possess outstanding perfume.

AMORPHA (Leguminosae—Laburnum Family)

A small genus of shrubs which flourish in a dry soil in an open, sunny situation, bearing racemes of purple, laburnum-like flowers which have a similar fragrance.

Species. *Amorpha fruticosa.* It grows 1.8 to 2.1 m (6 to 7 ft) tall and is known as the 'False indigo'. It has small pinnate leaves and in July bears slender racemes of small bluish-purple pea-like flowers which have the vanilla perfume.

AMORPHOPHALLUS (Araceae—Arum Lily Family)

A genus of about 100 species of tropical plants native of Africa and Asia with a large corm-like rhizomatous root.

Species. *Amorphophallus campanulatus.* Native of South-east Asia and the Fiji Islands, it forms a large corm from which develops a single, segmented leaf. When dying, a conical purple-brown flower appears, and when ripe for pollination develops a fetid smell to attract carrion flies and midges.

A. titanum. The largest member of the Aroid family and a native of Sumatra where the tubers attain an enormous size, as much as 1.5 m (5 ft) in diameter. The spathe-like inflorescence, too, is the largest of any known plant, with the browny-red spadix up to 1.8 m (6 ft), in length and backed by leaves 3 to 3.6 m (10 to 12 ft) high. The spadix when ripe for pollination emits a most disagreeable smell, more repulsive even than that of the Monarch of the East. Immediately after pollination, the spadix withers and loses its stench.

AMYRIS (Lauraceae—Bay Tree Family)

Small trees or shrubs, native of Palestine, Arabia and parts of India and Ceylon. The leaves are alternate and pinnate, the flowers borne in terminal panicles.

Species. *Amyris punctata.* A deciduous arboreous shrub, native of the Middle East and of Chittagong, which grows about 3.6 m (12 ft) tall with smooth rust-coloured bark, slightly fragrant. The branches are thin and spreading, the lower ones touching the ground. The pinnate leaves are as much as 45 cm (18 in) long and appear after the flowers in March; they are covered with glandular dots, and when handled give off the odour of sassafras. From them an essential oil, similar in colour and in odour to sassafras oil, is obtained. The numerous white flowers are formed in terminal panicles and are scented.

ANACAMPTIS (Orchidaceae—Orchid Family)

Species. *Anacamptis pyramidalis.* Unlike the Gymnadenis which frequents the cooler parts of Britain and Europe, the Pyramid orchid enjoys the warmth of southern England and Europe, being especially common near the Mediterranean coast of North Africa. The stem arises from 2 egg-shaped tubers and may reach a height of 45 cm (18 in) with the flower-spike some 7 cm (3 in) long, packed with bright-pink flowers in pyramidal form. The blooms, which are at their best during July, have a long spur and are mostly pollinated by butterflies attracted to the pronounced day-time scent resembling vanilla. Few night moths visit the flowers for they emit a goat-like aroma when damp with dew and this acts as a repellent.

ANAGYRIS (Leguminosae—Laburnum Family)

A small genus of plants of shrubby habit present in the British Isles only south of the Thames and in southern Europe.

Species. *Anagyris foetida.* The Bean trefoil, one of the few plants of this large family with a disagreeable odour. A rancid smell is emitted when the leaves are bruised, though the yellow laburnum-like flowers produced in June in short racemes emit the exquisite vanilla-like perfume of the family.

It is native of southern Europe and will flourish in any well-drained soil, reaching a height of 2.1 to 2.4 m (7 to 8 ft). It has hairy flowers, and leaves which are composed of three widely spreading lance-shaped leaflets, but care should be taken not to rub against them for all parts of the plant are poisonous.

ANCHUSA (Boraginaceae—Forget-me -not Family)

A genus of 50 species native of Europe and North Africa. The flowers are not scented but the leaves of one species are scented when dry.

Species. *Anchusa officinalis.* Known as Common alkanet, it is a rare soft hairy plant of the British Isles with an angular stem and long lanceolate leaves. A biennial, growing 60 cm (2 ft) tall, the flowers are borne during June and July in one-sided racemes and are deep violet in colour. Evelyn described the plant as being 'much like Borage' and recommended the flowers to be used as a conserve for they were thought to have great restorative powers. It may have been more common in Evelyn's time. The leaves are covered with short hairs and when dry emit a rich musky fragrance, like wild strawberry leaves drying. The plant is readily raised from seed sown in July in shallow drills. Transplant in October 60 cm (2 ft) apart.

ANDROSACE (Rock Jasmine) (Primulaceae—Primrose Family)

A genus of more than 40 species of small tufted alpine plants of intense hardiness, found at high altitudes where they grow in chinks and fissures of large rocks. Here, the androsaces are usually happier than in the garden for like all members of the family they enjoy cool conditions and ample moisture at the roots, requiring a well-drained loam containing peat or leaf-mould and an open situation. Young plants are propagated by division in spring. Of a large number of species and varieties only one or two bear scented flowers.

Species. *Androsace pubescens.* It is found at high altitude in the Savoy Alps, tucked away in the crevices of overhanging cliffs so that it is well-nigh inaccessible; it sends out its roots through layers of shale. It loves the cold air and to have its roots in moisture. It should therefore be planted in a deep crevice filled with gritty compost and, unlike *A. villosa*, requires more shade than sunshine.

The plant forms a tiny hummock of deep-green rosettes from which arise, on stems no more than 2.5 cm (1 in) long, solitary round white flowers which diffuse an extravagant scent of honey. Like *A. villosa*, it makes an admirable subject for pan culture and comes later into bloom, being at its best outdoors during June and July.

A. villosa. A native of the Pyrenees, it requires scree conditions and lime in the soil. It is a plant for a cold greenhouse or frame, and several growing in a pan containing a sharp compost to which limestone chippings have been added will scent the still air during April and May with a honey-like perfume.

The plants form neat leafy rosettes covered in silky hairs from which arise dainty heads of blush-white. Outdoors, the plants will bloom in May, an established plant bearing multitudes of blossom which will send out its perfume for a greater distance than any other plant of its size.

ANGELICA (Umbelliferae—Parsley Family)

A large family of 150 genera and more than 1,500 species bearing white flowers in umbels which are pollinated by flies.

Species. *Angelica officinalis.* This handsome herb grows in all parts of northern Europe, from Lapland to Sweden and Norway, and the British Isles. It is perennial but is usually treated as a biennial, the seed being sown in August where the plant is to mature, though the seedlings will transplant if necessary. It may be kept growing almost indefinitely if one or two plants are cut down in June each year, for they will send out strong side growths which may be allowed to grow to maturity the following year. It grows up to 1.8 m (6 ft) tall and should be kept at the back of the border where it will appreciate the shade given to its roots by other plants. There, in a moist soil, it will seed itself and may even become a nuisance.

It is a handsome plant with purple-tinted stems appearing as if polished, and covered with a plum-like 'bloom'. The stems are cut in June, when young, to candy and are used in confectionery, also to flavour apple tarts, tomato chutney and rhubarb, for they have a musky smell. The wild form *A. sylvestris*, however, is almost flavourless.

From its aromatic seeds an essential oil

is obtained, also from the scented roots. The seeds yield 1.15 per cent of essential oil, which has a musk-like smell and is used to flavour liqueurs, especially Chartreuse. In his *Callender for Gardening* for July, written in 1661, Stevenson suggests that one should 'be sure every morning to perfume your house with angelica seeds, burnt in a fire-pan or chafing dish of coales'; it does indeed send a delicious aromatic scent to all parts of the house.

Bees visit the white flowers. The leaves and roots are used in the making of Vermouth, and according to Parkinson the dried roots powdered and taken in water 'will abate the rage of lust in young persons'.

ANGRAECUM (Orchidaceae—Orchid Family)

A genus of about 220 species, distributed chiefly throughout tropical Africa and Madagascar. They are epiphytic herbs, the flowering shoots arising from the axils of the older leaves. Darwin wrote of *A. sesquipedale*, native of Madagascar, with a spur 45 cm (1½ ft) long. Several plants bear attractively scented flowers. They should be given the same cultural treatment as *Vanda*.

Species. *Angraecum fastuosum.* The white flowers are more than 2 cm (1 in) across, borne 2 to 4 in a spike, and smell strongly of tuberose. It is rather a rare species, unfortunately, from Madagascar, and reaches only a few inches in height.

A. fragrans. The 5-cm (2-in) white flowers are produced on stems about 15 cm (6 in) tall, and are scented; the spur is green. The leaves are also fragrant when bruised, and were once imported from Mauritius for their vanilla scent. They have also been used as tea after crushing and drying.

ANISE: see PIMPINELLA

ANONA (Anonaceae—Anona Family)

A genus of about 120 species found in tropical America, with laurel-like, evergreen leaves containing resinous glands, and edible fruit. They require stove house conditions and a rich compost; increase is by seed sown in heat, or by ripened cuttings sown in sandy compost.

Species. *Anona cherimolia.* From Peru, the Cherimoya tree grows to about 6 m (20 ft), less in cultivation, with somewhat velvety petals produced in July. The roundish fruit with its white flesh is about 10 cm (4 in) long and edible.

A. glabra (syn. *A. palustris*). Native of the Fiji Islands where it is known as the Pond apple, for it is found in the swamplands of the coastal strip between Reiva and Deuba; also found in Peru and Florida. It makes a tree 6 m (20 ft) tall, with glossy laurel-like leaves containing aromatic oil cells. From the axils of the leaves appear the flower buds, like small walnuts, which open to creamy-white flowers of spicy perfume in July. The flowers are followed by large, oblong, inedible fruits of yellow, shaded with red.

A. muricata. This West Indian tree grows about 4.5 m (15 ft) tall, with large handsome shining leaves, and very fragrant, rather fleshy flowers, green and yellow. The fruit is very large, the outer skin smelling unpleasant, but the flesh is good to eat.

A. squamosa (syn. *A. cinerea, A. biflora*). A common tree of the Fiji Islands, and also found in tropical America, it grows 4.5 to 6 m (15 to 20 ft) tall with spreading branches. It has oblong-lanceolate, leaves and bears creamy-white, wax-like flowers which are sweetly scented. The fruit, which measures about 7 to 8 cm (3 in) across, is greenish-yellow and edible.

ANTHEMIS (Compositae—Daisy Family)

A genus of 80 or more species of herbs with scented bipinnate leaves and with flowers, composed of a single row of ray-florets, borne in solitary heads. It is distributed across Europe, N. Africa and temperate Asia.

Species. *Anthemis cotula.* The Stinking camomile, it is native of the British Isles and an annual of upright growth. The leaves are cut into hair-like segments and dotted with glands which release a most disagreeable odour when handled, causing blisters to appear. The ray-florets are white with a yellow disc and have the unpleasant smell associated with flowers of the family.

A. cupaniana. The Rock camomile of the Caucasus and central Europe, a slow-growing plant which will eventually reach a height of 35 cm (14 in). It has finely serrated grey foliage which is pungent, and bears small white daisy-like flowers which, unusual in this family, are pleasantly scented. The flowers may be dried and used as a tobacco substitute. They also make a better tea than *A. nobilis,* being less bitter, and it is delicious mixed with lemon juice. Plants are readily raised from seed sown in drills in the open.

A. nobilis. The camomile, a creeping much-branched perennial, the pungent leaves cut into pointed segments and flowers with white ray petals. It is indigenous to southern England and as far north as Derbyshire and to Ireland. It is less common in northern England and is absent from Scotland. In bloom from June to August, it is found in pastureland and on waste ground. It was used in Elizabethan times to make a fragrant 'lawn'. Sow the seed thinly in April and broadcast, thinning the plants to 10 cm (4 in) apart. By October, Evelyn said 'it will now be good to beat, roll and mow, carpet walks of camomile'. But rather than mow it, clip it with shears and the following summer the 'lawn' may then be freely walked upon.

A diffusion of the flowers (1 oz to a pint of boiling water) makes a soothing tea, and when cold may be rubbed on the scalp to improve the hair. From the fruity scent of the leaves, it derives its name *anthemis* from the Greek meaning 'earth apple'. Before the introduction of tobacco its leaves were dried and smoked.

ANTHERICUM (Liliaceae—Lily Family)

A genus of about 40 species distributed about tropical and South Africa, South America and central Europe, and forming tuberous roots. The flowers are white, sometimes hairy, and are borne in elongated racemes.

Species. *Anthericum chamydophyllum.* Native of South Africa where it is a rare plant of lower mountainous slopes, flowering in October. Its blooms open exactly at 5 p.m. The plant forms a dense tuft of hollow glabrous leaves and from the side arises an almost horizontal raceme, shorter than the leaves, of pearly-white flowers which are sweetly scented.

A. liliago. Closely related to the asphodel, it is the St Bernard's lily of the European Alps and has white fleshy roots, like those of the alstroemeria, from which arises a 60-cm (2-ft) stem carrying funnel-shaped flowers of sophisticated beauty. The pure-white blooms are more than 5 cm (2 in) across, each segment being tipped with green and with striking golden anthers. They appear in May, diffusing their sweet lily-like perfume over the alpine meadows.

ANTHOXANTHUM (Graminaceae—Grass Family)

The huge grass family numbers at least 4,000 species and includes wheat, oats and barley as well as the West Indian sugarcane. The genus *Anthoxanthum* bears grass with the scent of new-mown hay, owing to the compound coumarin, also present in woodruff and melilot and in the flowers of the Sweet alyssum.

Species. *Anthoxanthum odoratum.* Known as Sweet vernal grass, it is found in pastureland, displaying its tiny green flower spikes during May and June. It has a shiny stem and grows 45 cm (18 in) tall. Only as it dries after cutting does it release its fragrance which persists long after it has been baled or made into a stack; so powerful is its aroma that a small quantity will scent a large stack. It is a refreshing smell, somewhat pungent but difficult to describe.

A. puelii. A smaller species with multi-branched stems and with lax panicles. It is an annual, in flower during July and August, and is occasionally found about sandy land. Its sweet scent is not so pronounced as that of *A. odoratum.*

A. drogeanum. Native of South Africa where it is found on grassy flats around Kenilworth, it grows about 30 cm (12 in), tall with thin hairy leaves and bears its flowers in a spike-like inflorescence composed of numerous branched spikelets. In its native land it flowers during September and October when the whole plant gives off a penetrating perfume.

ANTHRISCUS (Umbelliferae—Parsley Family)

A genus of 20 species, native of southeastern Europe and northern Asia, one of which has pleasantly scented leaves and is present in hedgerows in the British Isles though is not common.

Species. *Anthriscus cerefolium* (Chervil). A hardy annual, native of central Europe and Asia with handsome fern-like leaves, 'deeply cut or jagged', wrote Gerard, 'of a very good and pleasant smell ... which hath caused us to call it sweet chervil'. The leaves were used in salads to which they imparted a taste of aniseed.

The plant grows 60 cm (2 ft) tall, and to provide a regular supply of leaves throughout summer seed is sown where it is to mature, every fortnight in shallow drills from mid-March until the end of August. There is also a plain-leaved form which is equally aromatic. The herb greatly resents transplanting.

ANTHYLLIS (Leguminosae—Laburnum Family)

A genus of some 20 species with pinnate leaves and bearing flowers in clusters at the ends of the branches. Several species are suitable to plant on a wall or between paving-stones.

Species. *Anthyllis montana.* Known as the Mountain Vetch, it is native of the Alps and grows 7 to 10 cm (3 to 4 in) high, forming a dense mat of silky leaves which are divided into numerous tiny leaflets. It is native mostly of the French alpine regions and grows well in poor sandy soil. It blooms during June and July, bearing dense heads of small clover-like flowers which are pink or purple and which emit the soft vanilla scent common to the order, and most pronounced after rain. The form *rubra* bears crimson-red flowers which are not so fragrant.

ANTIRRHINUM (Scrophulariaceae— Foxglove Family)

A genus of about 25 species, it is of the same family as *Linaria, Penstemon, Nemesia, Alonsoa* and *Calceolaria*, a family which is almost entirely devoid of perfume. Only recently did scent make its appearance in the Antirrhinum to permit its inclusion here.

Species. *Antirrhinum majus.* It is a plant so long established in Britain that it is now included amongst British wild flowers. Henry Phillips in his *Flora Historica* says that it 'is found on the cliffs of Dover and is now classed as one of the native plants of England . . . '. He tells us that 'on pressing the sides of the flower, it opens like a gaping mouth, the stigma appearing to represent the tongue and on removing the pressure the lips of the corolla snap together; hence it has been named Snapdragon'.

Like the wallflower, it grows on exposed cliffs and high towers where its reproductive parts are guarded against adverse weather by its unusually-shaped corolla. Self-pollinating, it defies anything to gain entry until pollination has taken place when the mask falls away to allow the seed-vessel free access to the air. Like the other plants of the family, as the antirrhinum does not require insects for its fertilization it does not need perfume to attract them.

The antirrhinum became scented only in 1963 when appeared a trio of hybrid varieties of outstanding beauty. The tall, graceful spikes are furnished with as many as 40 or more flowers of great size, with ruffled petals and fully double, and diffusing a pleasant sweet perfume. Growing to a height of nearly 90 cm (3 ft), they branch near the base and produce as many as 10 to 12 spikes in bloom at one time.

SUPER JET. One of the most beautiful plants of the garden, bearing its frilly-petalled flowers of deep apricot-yellow on long graceful stems, and delicately perfumed.

VANGUARD. Of the scented trio, this is the most fragrant, being almost clove-scented when warmed by the July sun, and the fully double flowers are a lovely shade of deep rosy-cerise.

VENUS. The blooms are semi-double and frilled, and of an attractive combination of peach and pink, with a soft sweet perfume.

The plant requires an open sunny situation and a rich loamy soil. Though perennial, the antirrhinum is usually treated as a half-hardy annual: the hardened plants are set out after an early sowing made in gentle heat.

APHYLLANTHES (Liliaceae—Lily Family)

A genus of a single species, native of the western Mediterranean coastal areas, though it grows only in peaty soils.

Species. *Aphyllanthes monspeliensis.* The slender erect stems arise from a branched rhizome to a height of about 22 cm (9 in), each stem having a brown sheath at the base. The tubular flowers with their 6 spreading petals are purple-blue and are surrounded by coloured bracts. They have a sweet perfume. A valuable border plant for a peaty soil, the plants require copious amounts of moisture during the growing season. They remain in bloom from June until September. Where grown out of doors, they do best in a sunny position and need winter protection, otherwise they can be grown in a cool, sunny well-ventilated greenhouse. Seed is sown when ripe, or propagation is made by division.

APIOS (Leguminosae—Laburnum Family)

A genus of three species of tuberous-rooted climbing perennials which are natives of North America where at one time the fleshy roots were eaten as a substitute for potatoes.

Species. *Apios tuberosa.* It is annual in growth, the shoots dying back in winter, to arise again the following year when it will quickly cover an arbour or trellis. In appearance, it is almost like wistaria for it bears its purple pea-like flowers in dense axillary racemes, and they are violet-scented. In a warm, dry situation and a well-drained sandy soil it will be long-lived, the tuberous roots increasing in size and number each year.

APIUM (Celery) (Umbelliferae—Parsley Family)

A genus of a single species, present in Europe and India, northern and southern Africa.

Species. *Apium graveolens.* A biennial found throughout the British Isles, but in the wild state the stems are too bitter to be palatable, though when broken they release the pungent aromatic smell characteristic of the plant. The seeds, which have the same smell, are used for flavouring soups and sauces and are valuable for kidney complaints. The blanched stems of the cultivated forms make a delicious vegetable braised or served with white sauce.

APLOTAXIS (Compositae—Daisy Family)

A genus of a single species, present in eastern Asia, and by some botanists, now classed with *Saussurea.*

Species. *Aplotaxis lappa.* From the dried root, costus, a favourite perfume of the East is obtained, It has something of the mossy smell of the violet when fresh but tends to develop a fur-like aroma with age, becoming even goat-like and unpleasant. Like the Valerian, it is a plant of the higher Himalayas.

APONOGETON (Aponogetonaceae— Pondweed Family)

A genus of South African plants with creeping roots and floating or submerged leaves, several of which are hardy in the warmer regions of Europe and the British Isles, and are invaluable for ponds. From the scent of their flowers which contain anisic aldehyde they are known as the Water hawthorns, though the fishy undertone is absent.

The genus is the only member of the pondweed family to bear its flowers above water and to be pollinated by insects, hence its scent; *Potamogeton,* which also bears its flowers above water, is wind-pollinated and scentless.

Species. *Aponogeton angustifolius.* Native of Cape Province, it is one of the less hardy species, and may be grown in tubs or pans of water in a greenhouse, though it will survive the winter outdoors in the warmer localities. It has narrow, lanceolate leaves and is a miniature form of *A. distachyus.* It will grow in shallow water, where the purity of its snow-white flowers is enhanced by the absence of black anthers; its almond fragrance is even more pleasant than the hawthorn-like perfume of *A. distachyus.*

AQUILARIA (Thymeleaceae—Mezereon Family)

A genus of 15 species, native of China and South-east Asia, being evergreen plants with thick leathery leaves.

Species. *Aquilaria agallocha.* A large evergreen tree 30 m (100 ft) tall found in the forests of Malaysia and western China. It has alternate lance-shaped leaves and bears its snow-white bell-shaped flowers which are sweetly scented at the leaf axils and at the ends of the shoots. Mature trees become saturated with resin and the fragrant wood is burnt as incense in the temples and the bark used to make joss-sticks; from it is distilled an essential oil used in Eastern perfumery.

Known as Eagle-wood, it may also be the Aloes-wood of the Old Testament which today is called 'lign-aloes'. Proverbs says: 'I have perfumed my bed with myrrh, aloes and cinnamon', for Aloes-wood and cinnamon were dried and powdered and sprinkled about the bed clothes. The fragrance is more pronounced when the wood is decaying.

Dr Theodor in his *Medicinal Counsels* tells that Louis XIV of France had his shirts washed in rose-water with which had been boiled previously aloes-wood, nut-megs, cloves, storax benzoin, jasmine, orange-flower water and a few grains of musk.

AQUILEGIA (Ranunculaceae—Buttercup Family)

A genus of 100 species of hardy peren-nial plants, native of north temperate regions. The flowers have a long spur at the bottom of which honey is secreted, and are visited by bees. The flowers of only a few species are scented.

Species. *A. fragrans.* The branched columbine of the Himalayas, a plant with downy leaves which requires a warm, sheltered corner and a well-drained sandy soil. The blooms are white or purple and appear in May, with long slender stems, and they have a rich, clove-like perfume.

A. glauca. A Himalayan plant which like *A. fragrans* grows about 60 cm (2 ft) tall and requires similar conditions. It also blooms in May, bearing 3 or 4 sweetly scented flowers to each stem, and they are white, shaded with purple.

A. viridiflora. The Green columbine of eastern Siberia which grows 45 cm (18 in) tall and in May bears bell-shaped flowers of darkest green which diffuse an exquisite perfume, suggesting *Daphne mezereon*; it is the most powerfully scented of all the aquilegias.

A. vulgaris. Widespread throughout the northern temperate regions of the world,

especially on chalk or limestone forma-tions. A perennial, it bears its purple, crimson-brown or white flowers during May and June on 60-cm (2-ft) stems. Those bearing purple-blue flowers pollinated by Hymenoptera have no per-fume but those with white flowers have a soft clove scent. This is most pronounced in the sub-species *pyrenaica*, present from the Pyrenees to northern Asia and par-ticularly in the temperature western Himalayas where it bears mostly blush-white flowers with a long slender spur and egg-shaped sepals.

ARAUJIA (Asclepiadaceae—Stephanotis Family)

A genus of six species of twining hairy plants, native of tropical Brazil, where they pull themselves up trees to a considerable height. They require stove treatment in the British Isles and are best grown as a flowering pot-plant; the shoot tips should be picked out to encourage bushy growth. Requiring a winter temperature of at least 16°C. (60°F.), they are rarely grown but are delightful plants, in bloom throughout late summer, their funnel-shaped flowers diffusing a powerful odour which is almost lily-like; they are indeed the most highly scented of forest plants. They require a 25-cm (10-in) pot when fully grown and a compost composed of fibrous turf and peat in equal parts. They should be kept thoroughly moist at the roots during summer.

Species. *Araujia albens* (syn. *Physianthus albens*). A native of the Argentine, it is known as the Cruel Plant for its handsome bell-shaped flowers which resemble those of the tuberose entrap the pollinating moths. They are purest white with a powerful, almost unpleasant perfume when closely inhaled, and they appear during summer. It is also known as the Silk tree for inside the green nuts which are 15 cm (12 in) long are strands of silvery silk wrapped round the fruit.

A. grandiflora. This species bears umbels of pure-white flowers resembling those of the stephanotis in appearance and in fragrance.

A. graveolens. It covers itself in umbels of large, sweetly scented, funnel-shaped flowers, which are a delicate shade of yellow and which feel fleshy to the touch, like those of the stephanotis, lily and tuberose which it resembles in perfume.

ARBUTUS (Ericaceae—Heather Family)

A genus of about 12 species found in the United States, southern Ireland, Greece and Italy. With the possible exception of *A. menziesii*, none may be considered hardy in the British Isles though they do well near the coast and, surprisingly for members of the Heath family, do well in a limestone soil.

The plants have been renowned for their delicious fruit since earliest times. It is known as the Strawberry tree for its fruits resemble the strawberry, and in Rome, in Pliny's day, the fruit was known as *unedo* (*unum edo*) which meant that so delicious was it that a person should eat only one. This same tree, *Arbutus unedo*, is still grown in gardens wherever the climate is favourable to the ripening of the fruit, and is one of the most interesting of trees. For the more exposed garden *A menziesii* should be grown instead; it is hardy and a tree of exceptional beauty, ideal for a small garden for it grows upright and remains neat and compact, retaining its leafy branches close to the ground so that it casts shade for only a small radius.

What is more, the trees are evergreen, with handsome leaves like those of the rhododendron, and the flowers diffuse the sweet musky fragrance of honey, similar to the scent of the buddleias.

Propagation is either from seed of the ripened fruit sown in a closed frame, or from cuttings of the half-ripened wood inserted in a sandy compost under glass.

Species. *Arbutus andrachne.* A native of Greece and Crete, it grows 3 to 3.6 m (10 to 12 ft) tall with smooth blunt-ended leaves and blooms early in spring. Its greenish-white flowers are sweetly scented and held in erect terminal panicles.

A. hybrida. A hybrid of *A. andrachne* and *A. unedo*, it possesses the tenderness of both species. It should be confined to a sheltered garden where it will bear its scented flowers of purest white in drooping clusters from the tips of the shoots. It is a handsome plant growing 3 m (10 ft) in height, with laurel-like leaves which

enhance the snow-white bottle-shaped blossoms during January and February. The reproductive parts are protected against the winter weather and the pendent position throws off the dews and keeps the anthers dry, thus enabling pollination to take place even in winter.

A. menziesii. The Californian Strawberry tree which will attain a height of 15 m (50 ft) in the British Isles where it is completely hardy. It is one of the finest of all trees with terracotta bark, most pronounced during winter when the old bark has peeled off to leave a smooth under-surface which takes on a warm, glowing appearance. The leaves are similar to those of the rhododendron, being glossy and dark green in colour with a leathery appearance. It blooms in April, its waxy-white pitcher-shaped flowers held in upright panicles, and when the air is calm their honey-like fragrance wafts across the garden. Of neat, upright habit, it makes a delightful tree for a lawn, remaining in bloom for at least two months.

A. unedo. The Strawberry tree of southern Ireland and the eastern Mediterranean which grows to a height of 3 to 3.6 m (10 to 12 ft) with oblong lance-shaped leaves, smooth and glossy and of deepest green, and with the same cinnamon-coloured bark as *A. menziesii*. The flowers are like those of the heather creamy-white, borne in dense clusters, and have a soft honey scent, though not so pronounced as in *A. menziesii*. To obtain fruit, two or three should be planted together for pollination. The fruits ripen in 12 months and there will always be some fruit on the trees.

Though the trees will flourish on limestone, they do require some humus, preferably peat, about the roots if they are to fruit well.

ARISTOLOCHIA (Aristolochiaceae—Birthwort Family)

A genus of about 180 species of evergreen and deciduous herbaceous and climbing plants scattered throughout the world. The plants have a tuberous rootstock and bear strangely curved tubular flowers of various shades of yellow, brown and crimson, like those of the stapelias and with the same fetid smell of decaying flesh,

hence their attraction for flies which ensure their pollination.

Species. *Aristolochia clematitis.* A
European perennial now naturalized in the
British Isles. Growing 60 cm (2 ft) in
height, it has heart-shaped leaves and
bears its unpleasant-smelling yellow
flowers during August and September, in
clusters of 6 to 8 and with a slender curved
tube.

A. elegans. A Brazilian climbing plant
with heart-shaped leaves and, though
usually given greenhouse culture,
specimens do flower outdoors in the more
favourable parts. It blooms during August
and September; the pale-yellow flowers
have green tubes blotched with purple and
brown and a crimson band around the
throat. They are amongst the most beautiful of flowers but emit a horrible smell of
decaying flesh.

A. sipho. A hardy North American
climber which attains a height of 9 m (30
ft) and is useful to trail over a dead tree
stump. The heart-shaped leaves have long
footstalks and it blooms during May and
June, its yellowish-brown flowers having a
long curved tube, hence its name of
Dutchman's pipe, though its smell is more
like rotten manure than tobacco.

ARNEBIA (Boraginaceae—Forget-me-not Family)

A genus of six species, native of south-
eastern Europe, the Near East and the
western Himalayas, only one of which is
regularly cultivated, *Arnebia echioides,* the
Prophet flower.

Species. *Arnebia cephalotes* (syn. *Macro-
tonia cephalotes*). Now rarely seen in gardens. According to Clarence Elliott, the
plant was discovered in the Taurus
Mountains by E. K. Balls during a plant
collecting expedition in 1934, and the
finder considered it to be the most beautiful plant he had ever seen.

It makes a spreading plant of perennial
habit, about 30 cm (1ft) tall, and bears
throughout summer large flower-heads of
deep golden-yellow which emit a sweet
honey-like perfume, like that of *onosma*.
The leaves are silvery. It is not easily
grown, preferring a warm, sunny, very
sharply drained position in the rock gar-

den, but it is well worth trying. Increase by
seed, or by heeled cuttings in autumn, in
sand, placed in a greenhouse.

AROMADENDRON (Magnoliaceae—Magnolia Family)

A genus of three species of exotic trees,
native to Malaya, Borneo and Java, and
differing from *Magnolia* by the number of
petals.

Species. *Aromadendron elegans.* An exotic
tree distinguished from the magnolia and
talauma by its petals, which number about
28. It is indigenous only to the mountainous regions of Java where in the rain-
drenched atmosphere it attains a height of
more than 45m (150 ft). It has oblong-
lanceolate leaves and bears large white
solitary flowers with narrow petals
arranged in quarters like the old Bourbon
rose Boule de Neige, and diffusing the
exotic sweet-clove fragrance of the spice
islands. The bark is also aromatic.

ARTABOTRYS (Anonaceae—Anona Family)

A genus of about 100 species, mostly
native of tropical Africa and India, which
climb by means of recurved hooks.

Species. *Artabotrys odoratissima.* Native of
India and Java, it is a plant of shrubby
climbing habit with handsome elliptical
leaves. It bears fragrant pale-yellow
flowers followed by small golden pear-
shaped fruits which are most ornamental.
From the flowers, which smell of ripe
apples and are almost hidden by the
leaves, an Eastern perfume is made.

ARTEMISIA (Compositae—Daisy Family)

A genus of 200 species of the northern
temperate zone, of hairy herbs or sub-
shrubs with alternate pinnately dissected
leaves and bearing flowers in drooping
racemes. Since earliest times they have
been held in great esteem for the highly
scented leaves had many uses. The plants
prefer an open, sunny situation and a
well-drained soil. They will tolerate a poor
dry soil, and the scent of the leaves will
then be more pronounced.

Species. *Artemisia abrotanum.* The Lad's
Love or southernwood, so called to distinguish it from other artemisias because it is

native of southern Europe, though it will survive the winter in the British Isles. The pinnate leaves are grey-green with a refreshing lemon-like perfume so were much used in pot-pourris and to place amongst clothes for it is said that the clothes-moth will keep away from it hence its French name of *Garde-robe*.

As a help against sleeplessness, the dried leaves may be placed in muslin bags beneath the pillowcase, and one writer of old suggests pounding the fresh leaves with sugar in a mortar until it is like a paste and 'three times a day take the bigness of a nutmeg of this . . . it is a composer and always disposes persons to sleep'.

In a shady situation, it makes a plant 1.2 m (4 ft) tall and grows to a similar width, so should be given plenty of room. Both the stems and leaves are covered with silvery hairs which give it a most attractive appearance and the yellow flowers, the size of buttons, are produced in close panicles.

The form Lambrook Silver is more heavily silvered, the foliage enhanced by cascading flowers of the colour and appearance of mimosa.

A. argentea. Native of Madeira, it grows 30 cm (12 in) tall. Its finely divided leaves, which are pleasantly aromatic, are densely covered in white hairs, giving the appearance of filigree lace dusted with silver. The flowers are borne in July.

A. borealis. It has pleasing grey foliage with the same pungent aroma as that of southernwood.

A chamaemelifolia. A hardy perennial, its country name is Lady's maid. It has attractive feathery foliage which is refreshingly aromatic, and the plants may be clipped to form a dwarf hedge to surround a bed of herbs.

A. dracunculus. Commonly known as tarragon and a native of Asia. Like southernwood it loses its leaves during winter but is perennial in a dry, rather poor, sandy soil. Seed is both difficult to obtain and to germinate, so propagation is usually by cuttings which will readily root in sandy soil. The leaves possess a hot, rather bitter flavour, and no more than two or three should be shredded and mixed with a salad. Steeped in vinegar they provide a condiment to use with fried fish, and the best *sauce tartare* is made from tarragon leaves.

The odour and taste of its essential oil is like that of anise bark, both containing methyl-chavicol which yields anisic acid on oxidation.

A. maritima. The Sea wormwood, found on cliffs and coastal areas in South-east England. It is a perennial plant resembling *A. absinthinum* but smaller, with twice-pinnatifid leaves with numerous blunt segments and covered in down. The bright-orange flowers are borne in heads and may be erect or drooping. They are borne from July until September. The whole plant has a sweet aromatic scent.

A. odoratissimum. Native of southern Europe, it grows 60 cm (2 ft) tall and has beautiful fern-like leaves of grey-green, covered in silvery hairs, giving the plant a whitish hue from a distance. It blooms during the late summer, bearing its milk-white flowers in crowded heads, and they diffuse a delicious fruity scent for some distance around.

ARUM (Araceae—Arum Family)

A genus of about 12 erect or dwarf perennials with thick rhizome-like rootstocks and bearing flowers in the form of a spadix enclosed by a protective sheath. Most are native of tropical south-eastern Asia and are evil-smelling, though to the same family belongs the Sweet flag, *Acorus calamus.*

Species. *Arum crititum.* A native of Corsica, it is an evil-smelling plant known as Dragon's mouth from the grotesque shape of its flowers which when open reveal a gaping cavern from which protrudes the spadix.

The leaves overlap on the 30 cm (12 in) stem, and in May the spathe appears, speckled with purple on the outside, furry on the inside; it has the appearance of decaying meat to attract the blow-fly, and emits a nauseating smell. From the open flowers protrudes a cylindrical spadix which is also hairy and dark purple-brown. Yet, in spite of its unpleasant qualities, it is an interesting plant. Only half hardy in the British Isles, it should be confined to a warm border or shrubbery. It is propagated by division of the tuberous roots in spring.

A. maculatum. It has been given more quaint country names than any other native plant, among them Cuckoo-pint, Wild arum, Lords and ladies, Jack-in-the-pulpit and Priest's hood. The plant grows about woodlands and hedgerows and in dry ditches; its dark-green arrow-shaped leaves with their long stalks are spotted with black or purple, and they have attractively waved margins and net-like veins.

The flowers appear early in April and from earliest times have excited great interest for they are one of the wonders of nature. As the spathe opens, the purple-brown spadix (sometimes browny-yellow) begins a rise in temperature of as much as 11°C. (20°F.) and begins to emit a foul and urinous smell. This is part of the flower's elaborate mechanism of pollination for the odour is attractive only to a species of midge (*Psychoda*) which climbs down the spadix beyond a bunch of 'hairs' situated near the base, above the male flowers. Beyond are more hairs which turn downwards, so trapping the midges whilst pollination of the female flowers takes place. After fertilization, the hairs wither enabling the midges to crawl back up the spadix and to move on to other flowers with the ripened pollen. The spadix immediately loses heat and soon dies away to be replaced by a bunch of scarlet berries which are poisonous.

ARUNCUS (Rosaceae—Rose Family)

A genus of about 50 species of herbaceous or shrubby plants. Most are native to the Northern Hemisphere and only a few bear scented flowers. They may be planted either in the herbaceous border or in the shrubbery, towards the back, where their feathery plumes will bring a welcome softness amongst plants of stiffer habit. The herbaceous forms die back during winter but those of shrubby habit lose only their leaves. The plants require a cool, moist soil, and those of herbaceous habit are especially suitable for planting near water. The flowers are either rose-pink or creamy-white but only the latter are scented.

Species. *Aruncus sylvester.* Native of northern Europe, Asia and America, it is known as Goat's beard for it bears its white flowers in slender beard-like spikes during June and July. The thrice-pinnate leaves with their serrated leaflets are most handsome, a setting for the stately plumes which attain a height of 1.2 to 1.5 m (4 to 5 ft) and have a similar scent to the flowers of the meadowsweet.

ASARUM (Aristolochiaceae—Birthwort Family)

A genus of some 60 species of perennial herbs, mostly native of the tropics, with creeping rootstocks and long-stalked heart-shaped leaves. The roots of all the American and European species have a pungent, aromatic smell, described by Miss Gertrude Jekyll in *Wood and Garden* as being like 'mild pepper and ginger mixed, but more strongly aromatic', The description most accurately describes the penetrating smell when plants of *A. canadense* are being divided in autumn.

Species. *Asarum canadense.* The Canadian Snake-root which grows 30 cm (12 in) high with kidney-shaped leaves borne in pairs. In May, it bears brownish-purple bell-shaped flowers which have an unpleasant smell, but the roots, especially when quite dry, smell strongly of ginger.

A. candatum. Native of California with downy heart-shaped leaves and bearing its reddish-brown flowers of unpleasant smell in July and August. The roots have an aromatic fragrance when lifted.

A. mairanthum. A Chinese species with marbled foliage which is pleasantly aromatic when handled.

ASCLEPIAS (Asclepiadaceae—Stephanotis Family)

A genus of about 60 species of erect perennial herbs with opposite leaves, usually with distinct transverse veins, and bearing flowers in simple, terminal or axillary umbels. They flourish in a peaty soil in the herbaceous border and are increased by root division in spring. Almost all are native of the western side of North America and though many are unsuitable for garden culture and do not bear scented flowers, several are plants of outstanding beauty, suitable for the semi-wild garden, and bear flowers of sweetest perfume.

Species. *Asclepias douglasii.* A handsome plant growing 90 cm (3 ft) tall with thick woolly stems and short-stalked heart-shaped leaves, smooth above, downy on the underside. The large wax-like flowers are produced in many-flowered umbels during summer and are rich purple-lilac and sweet-scented.

A. quadrifolia. Native of the State of New York, it is a perennial growing 12 in tall and is distinguished from other species by its pointed leaves arranged 4 in a whorl. It bears its pale-lilac flowers in July and they are small, sweetly scented and with red nectaries.

A. syriaca. One of the most vigorous species growing to a height of 1.2 to 1.5 m (4 to 5 ft), with oval, lance-shaped leaves up to 15 cm (6 in) long, downy on the underside. It bears its pale-purple flowers in July and August and they appear in loose drooping umbels, diffusing a delicious scent about the garden.

A. verticillata. A native of New Jersey, it grows 45 cm (18 in) tall with erect, branching stems which have a downy line on one side. The very narrow linear leaves are borne in whorls and the sweet-scented yellowish-green flowers are borne in umbels during July and August.

ASPALATHUS (Leguminosae— Laburnum Family)

A large genus of shrubs confined to South Africa and named from the Greek *aspalathos*, a scented shrub. The leaves, without stipules, are arranged in tufts on the stem, called the leaf tubercle, the outer being trifoliate, the inner being reduced to a single leaflet. The flowers, like those of the laburnum, are mostly yellow and have the vanilla-like scent of the family. The plants grow about sandy hills and on mountainsides.

Species. *Aspalathus callosus.* An erect, compact plant with ascending branches, the trifoliate leaves having prominent petioles with a tuft of hair in the axils. The bright-yellow flowers are borne in dense terminal spikes.

A. linearifolius. It forms a tall, erect shrub covered in long silky hairs. The oblong leaflets are silvery-grey because of the hairs, against which the pale-yellow flowers, borne in long leafy spikes, look striking. The petals are also silky.

A. suffruticosus. It grows on the hillsides of Cape Point and is a shrublet of almost

prostrate habit with trailing branches thinly covered in hairs. The leaflets are small and narrow, usually spine-tipped, and the pale-yellow flowers are borne in short axillary branchlets.

A. thymifolius (syn. *A. comosa*). An erect shrub with spreading pubescent branches and tufted leaves. The flowers are large and borne in long loose spikes and have a pronounced fragrance.

ASPARAGUS (Liliaceae—Lily Family)

A genus of tuberous-rooted perennials which form new stems annually. The stems are usually woody and erect or climbing, the leaves often produced as basal spines. The flowers are small and borne in axillary racemes, and in several species are sweetly scented.

Species. *Asparagus capensis.* Native of South Africa where it grows about flats and lower mountainous slopes, it forms a dense bushy shrub with spines at the tips of the branches. The flowers are greenish-white with narrow segments and yellow anthers and diffuse a sweet scent. They are followed by small scarlet berries.

A. stipulapis. An erect grey-green shrub with spine-tipped branches· which flourishes where the ground has suffered from fire. It is native of the hillsides of Cape Province where it blooms during July and August, scenting the air with its tiny greenish-white flowers.

ASPERULA (Rubiaceae—Bedstraw Family)

A genus of about 80 species closely related to the exotic Gardenia, of the same family. It is native of northern Europe extending from the British Isles to the Caucasus. The tiny woodruffs bear their leaves in whorls and are amongst the loveliest plants for a crazy-paving path where they may be planted with the thymes to give fragrance all the year. They are also suitable for the rock-garden.

Species. *Asperula gussoni.* It forms a tuft only 5 to 7 cm (2 to 3 in) high and is studded throughout summer with tiny pink 'bugles'. The foliage is fragrant and becomes more so as it dries.

A. lilaciflora caespitosa. Of carpeting habit, it forms a mat of emerald green covered in summer in deep-pink flowers, the whole plant being sweetly scented.

A. odorata. Containing coumarin and giving off its sweet scent of newly-mown hay as the leaves begin to dry, it is native of the British Isles and one of the daintiest of plants, its tiny leaves being borne in whorls like ruffs. Tusser advised using the leaves to make 'sweet water' for bathing the face, and it was known as Sweet grass. The leaves were hung up to dry in houses to keep the rooms cool and fragrant during summertime. It is better known as wood-ruff.

The plants are best raised from seed sown as soon as it is ripe, and if sown where the plants are to grow the seedlings should be thinned to 30 cm (12 in) apart. They grow only 15 cm (6 in) tall and so may be sown alongside a path. In May they bear multitudes of tiny white flowers.

A. orientalis. A handsome Caucasian annual growing 30 cm (12 in) tall, bearing 8 lance-shaped bristly leaves in a whorl. It bears a profusion of lovely sky-blue flowers throughout summer and they are sweetly scented.

A. suberosa. Its fragrant grey-green tufts are in direct contrast to the emerald green of *A. lilaciflora* and are enhanced by the shell-pink flowers which are scented.

ASPHODELINE (Liliaceae—Lily Family)

A genus of a single species distinguished from *Asphodelus* by its erect leafy stems and clusters of linear leaves.

Species. *Asphodeline lutea.* The sweetly scented yellow flower spikes are produced on 60- to 90-cm (2- to 3-ft) stems, in a dense raceme, each flower arising from the axils of a buff-coloured bract. There is also a double variety of great beauty which is as sweetly scented as the single form. The plant blooms in July and from the appearance of its elegant spike is known as Kings' spear.

ASPHODELUS (Liliaceae—Lily Famiiy)

A genus of 12 species found from the eastern Mediterranean to the Himalayas with narrow strap-like leaves from which arise flower spikes varying in height from 0.3 to 1.5 m (1 to 5 ft). Several are sweetly scented.

Species. *Asphodelus cerasiferus.* Previously known as *A. ramosus,* it grew in Tudor gardens. Its tall white spikes, often reaching a height of 1.5 m (5 ft) and in bloom in June, carry a soft, sweet perfume.

A. fistulosus. The most compact of the border Asphodels growing only 45 cm (18 in) tall and readily distinguished by its upright leaves. It blooms later than the others, showing colour about mid-July, its white flowers having a brown line down the centre of each petal.

ASPLENIUM (Aspleniaceae—Asplenium Family)

A cosmopolitan family of about 650 species which includes *A. nidus,* the Bird's-nest fern, a common epiphyte of the tropics of the Old World. One species has outstanding fragrance.

Species. *Asplenium fragrans.* A wild fern of North America, it emits a pleasant sweet scent when handled. At one time the fronds were carefully dried and used for filling pillows and mattresses which would remain fragrant for a considerable time.

ASTRALAGUS (Leguminosae— Laburnum Family)

A genus of about 1,600 species of herbs or sub-shrubs, common throughout the world except for Australia, mostly bearing purple-blue flowers and pollinated by bees. Few have any scent but *A. glycyphyllos,* native of the British Isles, has scented foliage and *A. gummifera* may have been the 'bed of spices' referred to in the Song of Solomon.

Species. *Astralagus glycyphyllos.* Known as the Milk-vetch or Wild liquorice, it is a glabrous prostrate perennial and is usually found on grassy banks. Its flowers are greenish-yellow and are borne in June. They are scentless though the large pinnate leaves emit a sweet, aromatic scent when handled.

A. gummifera. The line in the Song of Solomon, 'My beloved is gone down into his garden, to the beds of spices ...' may refer to it for it is native of dry mountainous regions and is a dwarf shrubby plant growing 60 cm (2 ft) tall, its woolly branches armed with spikes and bearing yellow pea-like flowers from the leaf axils.

From the branches, a gum is exuded which is used as incense. It has no scent until it burns.

ASTROPHYTUM (Cactaceae—Cactus Family)

A genus of six species of strikingly beautiful Mexican plants which grow at an altitude of about 2,400 m (8,000 ft). The plants have 4 to 8 ribs and sit on the soil like a tea-cosy with a single flower, mostly white or pale yellow, borne at the top. From above, it has a star-like appearance, hence its name of Star cactus. It grows well in a sunny window.

Species. *Astrophytum myriostigma.* It is divided into 8 ribs, like segments of an orange, and is covered with much smaller white marks than most species whilst it has brown areoles. From its shape it is known as the Bishop's Cap cactus and its yellow flowers have a distinctive perfume resembling the violet.

ATHEROSPERMA (Atherospermataceae —Atherosperma Family)

A genus of one species.

Species. *Atherosperma moschata.* It makes a small tree and is indigenous to Australia and Tasmania where it is known as the Australian Sassafras. It has 4-cornered branches and all parts of the tree are aromatic. It bears solitary, axillary flowers of palest greenish-white which diffuse a sweet perfume and they are followed by nuts which have a musk-like fragrance similar to that of the nutmeg and are known as 'Plume nutmegs'.

AZALEA: *see* RHODODENDRON

AZARA (Flacourtiaceae—Flacourtia Family)

A genus of 11 species of evergreens native of Chile and the Argentine, most of which are too tender for gardens of northern Europe. Several of the hardier species may be grown in favourable districts where they should be given protection from prevailing winds. They grow better near the coast where severe frost is rare, and they require a sandy soil containing some leaf-mould and a little decayed manure. Most species bloom late in autumn and when the weather is mild in winter will continue to bloom until springtime.

Species. *Azara dentata.* This species from the Chilean Andes blooms during July and August and is a highly attractive plant for a sheltered garden, with large oval dentate leaves and bearing a profusion of sweetly scented orange-yellow flowers. It is especially suited for growing against a sunny wall.

*A. gilliesi (*syn. *A. petiolaris).* It attains a height of 4.5 m (15 ft) and is one of the most striking of all shrubs with its reddish coloured wood and large pale-green leaves which are toothed like those of the holly. It begins to bloom late in autumn, its tiny bright-yellow flowers appearing in dense clusters and with the refreshing fragrance of orange peel. Possibly the hardiest species for it has been known to withstand 27 degrees of frost without harm.

A. integrifolia. It grows 5.4 m (18 ft) tall where it is happy, being especially so against a wall. It has smooth oblong leaves and like all the Azaras it blooms early in autumn, its golden-yellow flowers with their orange anthers appearing in short spikes and having a delicious vanilla scent. The form *variegata* has leaves which are attractively marked with creamy-yellow and pink.

A. lanceolata. The most recent of the species to arrive in Europe, it grows 2.4 to 2.7 m (8 to 9 ft) tall with bright-green leaves and in February, if the weather is mild, covers itself in a mass of tiny mustard-coloured flowers which have a delicious vanilla fragrance.

A. microphylla. Growing 12 m (40 ft) tall in its native habitat, it forms a dainty tree with glossy evergreen box-like leaves. In autumn and again in spring, and intermittently throughout a mild winter, it bears tiny flowers composed of greenish-yellow stamens and yellow anthers and with a powerful vanilla-like perfume. The flowers, which are borne at the axils of the leaves, are followed by tiny orange berries.

With *A. gilliesii* it is the hardiest species and may be grown with success in most sheltered gardens, doing especially well on a warm wall.

B

BABIANA (Iridaceae—Iris Family)

A genus of South African plants distributed in Transvaal and the central districts, with fibrous-coated corms and plaited leaves like those of the gladioli. The flowers are funnel-shaped and are usually blue or violet with, in several species, a sweet carnation or freesia-like perfume. They may be treated like freesias, grown outdoors in a sunny position in the more favourable parts of the British Isles and North America and given a winter covering of bracken or heather, or they may be grown in pots in a cool greenhouse or in a frame. If grown outdoors, the corms should be planted 15 cm (6 in) deep in a well-drained soil. *Babiana ringens* (syn. *Antholyza ringens*) which is fertilized by sugar-birds, bears scarlet flowers which are scentless.

Species. *Babiana bainsii* (syn. *B. hypogea*). A beautiful plant of the Cape which has the rare distinction in the British Isles of flowering in autumn. Like most of the babianas, which take their name from the Dutch for little baboon, it is a valuable alpine garden plant, bearing its sweetly scented sky-blue flowers on 15-cm (6-in) stems.

B. disticha. Known as the Hyacinth-scented babiana for its pale-blue flowers, with the 2 lower lobes marked with yellow or red, and borne in June on 22-cm (9-in) stems, emit a pleasingly sweet balsamic perfume.

B. plicata. Similar to *B. disticha* but with flowers of soft lilac-mauve which carry a delightful carnation-like perfume. The flowers appear in May or earlier when grown under glass, during August and September in their native haunts where they are found on mountainous slopes.

B. sambucina. So named because its handsome purple flowers carry the rich muscat-like fragrance of the flowers of the Elder. Several flowers appear on the 15-cm (6-in) stem.

B. stricta. The finest of the species, it has erect spreading leaves and sends up its flower stem to a height of 25 cm (10 in). The flowers, pale blue or violet, are borne in a lax spike and have a sweet perfume.

B. tubiflora. Native of Cape Province where it grows in sandy flats near the coast, it has leaves 30 cm (12 in) long with the flower stem shorter. The flowers which appear in autumn, are creamy white with a slender perianth tube and are sweetly scented.

BAECKEA (Myrtaceae—Myrtle Family)

A genus of 67 species, native of northern and Western Australia and New Caledonia. They are small trees or shrubs, known for the camphor-like smell of their leaves.

Species. *Baeckea camphorosma* (syn. *Babingtonia camphorosma*). Native of the Swan River district of Western Australia, it is an evergreen, its leaves emitting a powerful camphor-like scent when handled, and it bears pale-pink flowers in autumn. In the British Isles and northern Europe, the plants require the protection of a greenhouse and prove more satisfactory if heat is available to extend the growing season. They are, however, happy if provided with a night temperature of 9 to 10°C (48 to 50°F) in winter.

B. gunniana. It is abundant in sub-alpine habitats in Tasmania and Victoria and is of prostrate habit, pulling itself over the boulders. The glossy blunt-ended leaves are covered with large glandular dots and release a powerful aromatic scent when handled.

B. leptocaulis. A slender, erect shrub with narrow linear leaves in which the scent glands cannot be seen with the naked eye, but they release a highly pungent smell when crushed. It is found only in Tasmania, growing on damp heathlands on the western side of the island.

BAILLONIA (Verbenaceae—Vervain Family)

A genus of three species, native of South America.

Species. *Baillonia juncea* (syn. *Diostea juncea*). It is a slender-growing shrub of rush-like habit and will attain a height of 3.6 to 4.5 m (12 to 15 ft) in a sheltered garden. From June until September it bears small sweetly scented flowers of palest mauve with yellow throats.

BALANITES (Balanitaceae—Balanites Family)

A genus of 25 plants native of Africa, the Near East, India and Burma, one of which may have provided the Balm of Gilead of the Scriptures.

Species. *Balanites aegyptiaca.* It makes a tree 3 m (10 ft) tall and is present in North Africa, Egypt and Palestine. With its healing properties it may have been the balm referred to in several places in Genesis and Jeremiah.

It is a tree with thorny branches and woolly leaves from the axils of which appear clusters of greenish-white flowers. From the fruit, an intoxicating drink is made and, when boiled, oil is extracted which has healing properties. Hasselquist, whose early death was lamented by Linnaeus, described the gum of the plant as being 'yellow in colour, resinous, balsamic and very agreeable. It is very tenacious, sticking to the fingers and may be drawn into long threads'. 'I have seen it in a Turkish surgeon's, who had it from Mecca', he wrote, '. . . and described it as being the best stomachic they know and a most excellent remedy for curing wounds, for if a few drops are applied to a fresh wound, it cures in a short time'.

BALLOTA (Labiatae—Lavender Family)

A genus of 35 species, mostly native of Europe and the Mediterranean regions.

Species. *Ballota nigra.* Known as the Black or Fetid horehound it is the only British species. Though its flowers, borne in whorls during July and August, are an attractive reddish-purple colour, its leaves emit a most unpleasant smell when bruised like stale perspiration and bearing little resemblance to the fragrant White horehound (*Marrubium vulgare*) from whose flowers a delicious beer is brewed. The Black horehound is perennial and grows 90 cm (3 ft) tall with downy, wrinkled leaves. It is usually found growing on waste ground where its presence may be detected from afar by its obnoxious smell.

BALM: *see* MELISSA

BAPTISIA (Leguminosae—Laburnum Family)

A genus of about 14 species of herbaceous perennials native of North America of which only the white-flowered *B. alba* and *B. leucophaea* bear slightly scented flowers. The plants require a rich loamy soil, well drained, and an open situation. The leaves are digitately 3-foliolate: the flowers with their bell-shaped calyx are borne in terminal racemes during June and July.

Species. *Baptisia alba.* It grows 60 cm (2 ft) tall with smooth-stalked leaves divided into oblong blunt leaflets and it bears ivory-white flowers in terminal racemes.

B. leucophaea. A perennial growing 30 cm (12 in) tall, it has hairy leaves and comes into bloom in July, its creamy-white flowers leaning to one side.

BAROSMA (Rutaceae—Rue Family)

A genus of six or more evergreen species native to South Africa, particularly the Cape of Good Hope. The leaves possess a penetrating odour and are used by the natives as an ingredient of perfume and as a stimulant and tonic. The leaves are smooth and serrated at the margins and are pale grey beneath with glands filled with essential oil. Several species were introduced into Britain early in the nineteenth century and proved quite hardy in sheltered gardens, but owing to difficulty with their propagation have been allowed to die out almost entirely.

Species. *Barosma crenulata.* A familiar tree about the stony hills around Cape Town where it forms a low shrubby plant with handsome oblong leaves which are strongly scented.

B. serratifolia. Found on the mountainous slopes to the east of Cape Town where it forms a small shrubby tree. The leaves are long with the sides running parallel with each other and terminating with an oil gland at the apex. In commerce, the leaves are known as 'long' Buchu to distinguish them from those of *B. crenulata.*

BARTHOLINA (Orchidaceae—Orchid Family)

A small genus named in honour of the Dutch botanist, Bartholin. The plants are native to South Africa, where they are known as the Spider orchids and are present on flats and mountainous slopes. The scented flowers are borne on long, slender stems with a solitary basal leaf; the root is tuberous. Cool greenhouse cultivation is required, and increase is by division.

Species. *Bartholina burmanniana.* The creamy-white flowers, flushed with mauve, appear in June-July, and are borne solitary. The erect sepals are joined at the base, and long, narrow, thread-like petals and a short spur give the flowers a spider-like appearance. The flowers are delicately scented.

B. etheliae. This species follows *B. burmanniana* in bloom in August, being at its loveliest during November-December. The petals are mauve above, greenish-brown beneath, on a 10-cm (4-in) stem, and are especially fragrant at eventide.

BASIL: see OCYMUM

BAUHINIA (Leguminosae—Laburnum Family)

A small genus of deciduous winter-flowering trees or shrubs distributed from Assam eastwards to Burma and into China where it is planted for ornamental purposes. The genus was named after the sixteenth-century herbalists, Jean and Caspar Bauhin, Linnaeus remarking that 'the two lobed leaves recalled the noble pair of brothers'.

Species. *Bauhinia purpurea.* It is a medium-sized tree, met with only occasionally throughout India, Burma and western China though it is indigenous to all parts of those lands. It has ash-grey bark and two-lobed leaves which are as broad as they are long and are covered with minute hairs on the underside. The tree begins to lose its leaves when the flowers appear in September, the large lilac-purple flowers appearing in terminal racemes and emitting the vanilla-like perfume of the family. The flower stalks and calyces are covered with a powdery brown substance. The flower has petals about 5 cm (2 in) long and 3 fertile stamens and numerous antherless filaments. They are followed by long laburnum-like pods, often 30 cm (12 in) in length and of greenish-purple colouring, and as they begin to form whilst the tree is in bloom present a striking picture along with the purple flowers which continue until the year end.

Known as the Purple bauhinia, the tree yields a resinous gum and from the bark a valuable wash for skin ulcers is made. The rather bitter flowers are made into pickles and may be eaten raw as a laxative.

B. variegata. It grows about 6 m (20 ft) tall and is used for ornamental planting though it is tender away from the warmest parts of India and Burma.

The bark is dark brown whilst the young shoots are covered in greyish-brown pubescence. It loses its broad 2-lobed leaves in November with the new leaves appearing in May, and it bears its flowers from January until the appearance of the new leaves. The flowers are formed in small racemes at the ends of the branches and at the leaf axils. The calyx tube is long whilst the claw-like petals measure 5 cm (2 in) in length. Usually four petals are of pale lilac-mauve with the fifth petal heavily veined with darker purple and with five fertile stamens. Like *B. purpurea,* the vanilla-scented flowers are pollinated by bees. There is also a white-flowering variety, Candida, which has the fifth petal splashed with yellow.

From the bark a sticky exudation is obtained, whilst the slightly aromatic leaves are used by the natives to roll cigarettes, and together with the flowers are used in salads.

The tree is considered sacred to Buddhists and is usually seen in temple gardens. For this reason it is known as the Buddhist bauhinia.

BEAUMONTIA (Apocynaceae— Periwinkle Family)

A genus of climbing shrubs, native of the tropical forests of Burma and western China, and famous for the lily-like scent of their flowers. In the British Isles and northern Europe, the plants require the protection of a warm greenhouse, and a minimum winter temperature of 16°C (60°F), with as much light as can be supplied, and a rich compost. Pruning is carried out after flowering, and cuttings are used for propagation, with gentle heat, inserted in March.

Species. *Beaumontia fragrans.* This most fragrant species has white, rather flat bell-shaped flowers in summer, and is a native of Cochin China.

B. grandiflora. A plant of vigorous twining habit which throughout summer bears waxy, white, trumpet-shaped flowers, similar to those of the Datura, and emitting the powerful scent of the Madonna lily.

BEGONIA (Begoniaceae—Begonia Family)

A genus of tender plants of tropical regions numbering more than 1,000 species with fibrous, rhizomatous or tuberous rootstocks. Few species are scented. The first species to be found was the scentless *B. rotundiflora,* discovered in the West Indies in 1690 by a Franciscan monk named Fr. Charles Plumier for his patron, Michel Begon, the French governor of Santo Domingo, after whom the genus is named. From the West Indies too came the first species, *B. macrophylla,* to reach England, introduced in 1793 by Captain William Bligh of the Bounty fame, but the first truly scented variety was *B. rosaeflora.* This was perhaps the most important of all

the tuberous-rooted begonias in the raising of those wonderful large-flowered hybrids made famous by Woolmans, Blackmore and Langdon and others. But it was James Veitch of Exeter, and later of Chelsea, who laid the foundations for the success of others when in 1862 he sent Richard Pearce to look for new begonias in Bolivia and Peru. One of Pearce's discoveries was a begonia bearing rose-scented flowers which he named *B. rosaeflora* and which was taken up by Veitch's foreman, John Seden, and crossed with *B. boliviensis.* The result was *B. sedeni* which appeared in 1868 and which, when crossed with *B. dregei,* produced the first white-flowered tuberous hybrid called White Queen. Alas, like all the ensuing hybrids, it had no perfume. It was not until *B. baumannii* was introduced into the breeding of tuberous begonias by Benary in 1916, that the new race of *B. narcissiflora* hybrids bearing slightly scented flowers of daffodil form appeared but without achieving much popularity. *B. baumannii* was, however, taken up by Mr Leslie Woodriff of Oregon in the raising of a new race of basket or weeping begonias to which it has passed on its sweet perfume.

Species and Varieties

TUBEROUS. *Begonia baumannii.* It was discovered in the Peruvian Andes by Dr Sace, resident physician of Cochabamba in Bolivia, and it was introduced by the famous French hybridizer, Victor Lemoine of Nancy, in 1890. In its native land it is said to form a tuber as large as a watermelon. It is a short-stemmed species bearing large rose-pink flowers which emit a noticeably sweet perfume. It is the only tuberous begonia to pass on its fragrance to others; it has recently given it to a new race of pendulous hybrids known as the 'weeping' begonias, originally raised in France and introduced into the U.S.A. by the late Frank Lloyd. One, John White, bearing double blooms of palest pink, has the same sweet scent as *B. baumannii,* and more recently Mr Leslie Woodriff of the Fairyland Gardens, Oregon, has succeeded in raising Yellow Sweetie and Orange Sweetie.

B. micranthera fimbriata. It was discovered in the Argentine in 1937 by Dr Goodspeed of the University of California.

It is tuberous rooted with short succulent stems and hairy leaves. toothed at the margins. The single flowers borne in pairs, are brilliant scarlet-orange with masses of yellow stamens and are sweetly scented.

A hybrid of this species and *B. baumannii*, raised and introduced by Mr Leslie Woodriff in 1940, is a delightful plant which he named *B.* Wild Rose. The single pale-pink flowers, like the wild rose of the English hedgerow, have a soft sweet perfume.

FIBROUS ROOTED. *Begonia odorata alba.* A popular American species of unknown parentage and introduction. It has a most floriferous habit with small glossy leaves. The pistillate flowers have two conspicuous bracts at the base of the ovary. The flowers are borne in clusters like those of *B. semperflorens* and are white or blush-white with a sweet spicy scent.

A hybrid of *B. odorata* and *B.* Byoude Jardin, raised by Mr Woodriff and called Pet, bears scented flowers of palest pink in short inflorescences, and another he raised at the same time (1938) named Tea Rose, grows 60 cm (2 ft) tall and has bright-pink flowers with the unmistakable fragrance of the early tea roses.

B. roxburghii. It was discovered in the lower Himalayan regions in 1864 by Dr Roxburgh. Its numerous stems which arise from the base attain a height of 60 cm (2 ft) with large glossy bright-green leaves toothed at the margins. The large pure-white single flowers are borne close to the stems and are delicately scented.

B. venosa. Discovered in Brazil at the end of the nineteenth century by Professor Lofgren, it bears a flower of icy white which emits a spicy, clove-like scent. It is the most richly scented of all begonias and is in all respects a most unusual plant with thick erect stems and kidney-shaped leaves, strikingly frosted on the upper side. The flowers appear in long-stalked inflorescences.

BEILSCHMIEDIA (Lauraceae—Bay Tree Family)

A small genus of lofty Australasian trees, described by Bentham under *Nesodaphne* but now named *Beilschmiedia.* The alternate leaves are oblong, entire; the flowers are borne in terminal or axillary panicles.

Species. *Beilschmiedia obtusifolia.* A large handsome tree growing in the scrub-lands of Queensland, north of Brisbane, also on the banks of the Clarence river of New South Wales. It has alternate aromatic leaves and rough grey bark half an inch thick and brown internally, with a delicious aromatic odour though the oil ducts are neither numerous nor large. At one time it was used by the bushmen to flavour tea. Safrol is present in the bark.

B. tarairi. Native of the North Island of New Zealand, around the Auckland district where it blooms in November. It is a handsome tree growing up to 24 m (80 ft) tall with large aromatic glossy leaves, the stalks clothed in rusty down. The inconspicuous flowers are borne in branched panicles.

B. tawa. A tree 21 m (70 ft) tall with slender branches and with pale-green narrow leaves 4 in long and aromatic. Native of North and South Island of New Zealand and known to the Maori as *Tawa.* The flowers are borne in slender panicles. the fruit being damson-like and edible.

BEJARIA (Ericaceae—Heather Family)

A genus of 30 species of tropical shrubs. native of South America where they are the counterpart of the rhododendron of the Old World, mostly growing in the valleys of the Andes, as does the rhododendron in the valleys of the Himalayas, hence their heavy perfume.

Species. *Bejaria racemosa.* An evergreen shrub, 1 to 1.5 m (3 to 5 ft) tall, it bears its funnel-shaped flowers, like those of the azalea, at the end of the branches and they are delicate mauve-pink with a delicious perfume. They appear in July. The plant is known to the people of South America as the Sweet-scented bejaria.

A sandy, acid loam containing peat is required and cool house temperatures. Unripened cuttings will root in a sandy compost with a little heat.

BERBERIS (Berberidaceae—Barberry Family)

A genus of about 450 species of hard woody shrubs, evergreen or deciduous, native of North and South America, Europe and Asia, often with spiny stems or leaves. The plants grow well in most types of soil and in full sun or semi-shade. Most are spring-flowering and are followed by conspicuous berries in autumn. The plants have many uses as shelter for game birds and as hedges. They are also tolerant of salt-laden breezes.

Species. *Berberis verruculosa.* One of the best of all garden shrubs, growing 1.5 m (5 ft) tall and almost as wide. It is evergreen, the glossy leaves being white on the underside. The arching stems are thickly set in early summer with sweetly scented pendent flowers of lemon-yellow, followed in autumn by large black fruits which have a grape-like 'bloom'.

BERGAMOT: *see* **MONARDA**

BETULA (Birch) (Betulaceae—Birch Tree Family)

An important family of graceful ornamental trees or shrubs, flourishing in damp woodlands. *Betula lenta*, the Sweet Cherry birch of North America, provides not only timber but a valuable oil, and an agreeable tea is made from its aromatic leaves. The oil of *Betula lenta* has the same aromatic fragrance as Wintergreen and when decolourized is a more satisfactory substitute for the true Wintergreen.

Species. *Betula alba.* The Silver or White birch, native of the British Isles and growing 18 m (60 ft) tall. The flaky white bark when tapped yields a resinous substance from which beer was made in early times, and from the distillation of the bark the once much-admired perfume known as Russian Leather was obtained. This was done by dressing leather with the birch bark oil, which is dark brown in colour and has a penetrating musky odour. At one time the oil was used in medicated soaps for the treatment of eczema.

B. glandulosa. A handsome Canadian shrub growing 90 cm (3 ft) tall and valuable for ground cover or on hilly ground. The branches are covered with aromatic glands, and the stalkless serrated leaves are pleasantly fragrant when crushed.

B. lenta. A deciduous tree of North America, inhabiting the woodlands which stretch from New England to Illinois where it grows to a height of 24 m (80 ft). All parts are used for distillation—the wood, the bark and the branches. After the tree has been cut near the base, new growths arise which in 5 years attain a height of 3 m (10 ft), and they may then be removed for distillation.

The greatest yield is obtained from wood cut during summer. It is chopped into small pieces and placed in a vat for distilling by the steam process in the same way as sassafras. Of the three layers of bark, the outer paper-like layer contains no oil, neither does the secondary layer; the oil is contained entirely in the inner layer. The oil of *B. lenta* is considered to be superior to that of the more common source of Wintergreen, *Gaultheria procumbens*, for the latter has also the somewhat irritating smell of black pepper.

B. lenta is a most attractive garden tree with sharply serrated heart-shaped leaves which when pressed emit a pleasant aromatic scent.

BIGNONIA (Bignoniaceae—Bignonia Family)

A family of almost scentless plants, represented also by the Jacaranda tree and the Tecoma, and taking its name from the Abbé Bignon, librarian to Louis XIV of France. They are all tropical, mostly climbing plants of India and tropical South America though they are hardier than most plants growing in those parts. With their long trumpet-shaped flowers, they are pollinated mostly by humming-birds, also by bees.

Species. *Bignonia chelonoides* (syn. *B. tereospermum chelonoides*). In Hindustani, it is *Padri* and is native to India and the islands of the Indian Ocean where all parts, including the root, are used medicinally. The tree attains enormous proportions with thick, scabrous brown bark, slightly scented and from which, as well as from the fragrant flowers, a cooling sweet drink is made and used in fevers. It blooms during the hot and rainy seasons, the pale-yellow flowers having a pronounced fragrance.

B. quadrilocularis. Native of the Circar Mountains where it forms a large straight trunk of considerable height, its grey bark having a few scabrous spots. The branches spread out widely to form a large head, with pinnate leaves up to 60 cm (2 ft) long. The flowers, which appear at the beginning of the hot season, are borne in large erect terminal panicles and are an attractive rose-pink with a delicious sweet perfume.

B. suaveolens. Native of the moister parts of central and eastern India where it is known as *Madonna-Kama-pu*. It is the *Patala* (meaning rose-coloured) of Sanskrit writers and its flowers are said to intoxicate the bees. It blooms early in spring, before the leaves appear, and in India is known as the 'Messenger of Spring'. The flowers are large and dull purple, described by Sir William Jones in his *Asiatic Researches* as 'light purple above, brownish purple below ... exquisitely fragrant ... The whole plant except the root, being very downy and viscid'. The fruit, which is not ripe until the winter, is white and is sweet and delicious.

B. suberosa. Also known as *Millingtonia hortensis* under which name it figures in Hooker's *Flora of British India*. It makes a thin straight tree, growing up to 24 m (80 ft) tall, and is distributed throughout Burma and the Malayan Archipelago and also parts of central India. It is known as the Indian Cork tree for from its thick yellow bark cork is obtained, whilst its wood is used to make furniture. The leaves are 45 cm (18 in) long and are bipinnate, with lance-shaped leaflets. It is almost evergreen but usually sheds some of its leaves in March which are immediately renewed.

The tree blooms from September until the year end and is as if covered in snow with the flowers growing in large panicles at the end of the branches and filling the air with a delicious perfume, so that it is also known as the Tree jasmine. The bloom is composed of a tube 7 cm (3 in) long which expands into 4 wax-like petals, flushed with pink, the larger or lower petal having a deep groove. The 4 stamens are crowned with yellow anthers with the style protruding beyond the petals.

B. xylocarpa. A tall elegant tree of the forests of western India, first observed and introduced to the Botanical Gardens at Calcutta towards the end of the eighteenth century by Dr Andrew Berry. In six years the young trees reach a height of 7.5 m (25ft), with a straight trunk. The bark is ash-coloured, spongy and cracked. The leaves may be as much as 1.2 m (4 ft) long and are deciduous, appearing with the flowers in spring. The flowers are large and white with a tinge of yellow about them and appear in large terminal panicles. They are deliciously scented. The natives extract from the wood a resinous substance which they use to treat skin eruptions.

BILLARDIERA (Pittosporaceae— Pittosporum Family)

A genus of one species.

Species. *Billardiera longiflora*. It is a native of Tasmania where it is known as the Climbing blueberry. It requires the protection of a sheltered garden in the British Isles and northern Europe when it will grow 2.4 to 2.7 m. (8 to 9 ft) in height. It is useful to cover a low wall for it is evergreen with narrow lance-shaped leaves and bears, during June and July, deliciously scented tubular flowers of yellowish-green. These are followed by edible dark-blue fruits 2 cm ($\frac{3}{4}$ in) long which are most decorative.

BILLBERGIA (Bromeliaceae—Bromelia Family)

A genus of epiphytic winter-flowering plants, native of the tropical forests of Brazil and central South America where they mostly live on trees, requiring no contact with the soil. Several, however, will flourish in light shade in a compost composed of sand, peat and loam in equal parts. The plants should be re-potted immediately after flowering, towards the end of winter, and as the new shoots arise the old flowered shoots must be removed. In Brazil, the plants are hung from balconies where the beauty and fragrance of their flowers are much appreciated.

Species. *Billbergia chantinii*. It is known as the Queen's Tear Drops for the yellow and red flowers sheathed in their scarlet bracts resemble tear drops and emit a soft sweet perfume.

BIRCH: see BETULA

BLUMEA (Compositae—Daisy Family)

A genus of about 50 species of annual or

perennial weeds, native of South America and Madagascar, South-east Asia and islands of the Pacific, mostly with camphor-smelling leaves. They are dwarf shrubs with yellow flowers.

Species. *Blumea balsamifera*. It grows 60 cm (2 ft) tall and has leaves which when bruised smell strongly of camphor. From them a camphor is distilled.

B. lacera. Native of South Africa, it bears golden-yellow daisies and has brilliant green leaves smelling of turpentine.

BOLDOA (Nyctaginaceae—Four O'Clock Family)

A genus of one species.

Species. *Boldoa fragrans*. It is a native of Chile and has been found nowhere else in the world. It grows in isolation on the hills around Valparaiso and Santiago and is a most handsome evergreen, all parts being strongly aromatic. What is more, it is almost perpetually in bloom and even at Kew its deliciously fragrant flowers appear outdoors in winter when the weather is mild.

It reaches a height of 6 m (20 ft) and has cylindrical branches covered in smooth grey-brown bark which is highly aromatic. The thick dark-green leaves, paler on the underside where hairy, are covered on the surface with tiny resinous glands. When dried, the leaves become reddish-brown and yield a sweet resinous scent like that of the Sweet Gale. The dry leaves are known as Boldo leaves. The essential oil they yield is deliciously fragrant, and an infusion of the young fresh leaves possesses valuable tonic qualities.

The fruits, little more than pea-size and greenish-yellow in colour, are also fragrant. They are dried and made into necklaces by the natives, and when warmed by the body or the sun they release the scent of cinnamon; the leaves when dried and powdered are scattered amongst clothes to sweeten them and keep away moths.

BORAGO (Boraginaceae—Forget-me-not Family)

A genus of hairy annuals or perennials bearing drooping blue flowers in loose cymes.

Species. *Borago officinalis*. A native of the British Isles growing 45 cm (18 in) tall. Its leaves and flowers possess a cool cucumber-like flavour and smell and are used in claret-cup and cider. The leaves may also be chopped and used in salads, and before the introduction of lettuce were in great demand for this purpose. It should be treated as an annual or biennial, and in favourable districts a sowing should be made in August to produce flowers and leaves for use early in summer, with another sowing made in April to continue the supply of leaves until well into autumn for the leaves also make an effective winter cordial. The plant prefers a dry, well-drained soil and a sunny position. It may be sown about the flower border, for its drooping sky-blue flowers, with their striking black anthers and hairy sepals held on 5-cm (2-in) stems, are most colourful. It is also valuable for bees, supplying them with large quantities of nectar which is secreted at the base of the ovary. The plant seeds itself with freedom. At one time, its flowers were candied like those of the violet and rose, and used in confectionery, whilst a concoction made from its leaves was considered an excellent tonic. Dr Fernie in *Herbal Simples* (1895) said that its reputed powers of invigoration could be substantiated for 'the fresh juice contains 30% nitrate of potash'.

BORONIA (Rutaceae—Rue Family)

A genus of heath-like shrubs indigenous to parts of Australia, especially New South Wales, and which in cooler climes are cultivated as house or greenhouse plants. Though the flowers look insignificant, they scent the air with a lemon-like fragrance, whilst the leaves have the orange scent of the rue. Indoors, the plants bloom profusely from early February until midsummer, and they are devoid of that stiffness of habit possessed by most hardwooded plants. They are also less liable than most pot plants to be beset by trouble, and so remain fresh and attractively scented for many years. A minimum night temperature of 7°C (45°F) is sufficient to keep the plants healthy during winter.

Species. *Boronia ledifolia*. It grows to such profusion in the sandstone of Sydney that it has become known as the Sydney boronia. It is the first of the species to bloom in Australia and is the most handsome, the larger than usual blooms opening star-like and being a lovely strawberry-pink. The leaves, trifoliate or pinnate, are glossy green and highly aromatic.

B. megastigma. It is the Brown boronia, native only of the Perth district of Western Australia but grown in the perfume-making districts of southern Europe for an essence which is obtained from its flowers. The blossom impregnates the air for miles around with a lingering verbena-like scent. The small four-petalled shell-like flowers are purple-brown on the outside, yellow within and appear in great profusion.

B. pinnata. This is the Pink boronia of New South Wales where it makes a small tree. It is one of the best of all pot plants, remaining healthy and free-flowering in a 37-cm (15-in) pot for 10 or more years, and bearing at the top of the stems a mass of dull purple-pink flowers which emit a powerful balsamic perfume.

B. serrulata. It grows wild in the countryside near Sydney in New South Wales and is the most compact of the species. It bears its flowers at the joints and tips of the shoots and blooms from April until June. The purple-pink flowers possess so powerful a scent that a single plant, when displayed, will perfume a large exhibition hall. The leaves are also scented, containing an aromatic oil. It is the native rose of the Australian bush and it is distinctive with its rhomboid saw-edged leaves and aromatic scent.

BOSWELLIA (Burseraceae—Frankincense Family)

A genus of 24 aromatic trees or shrubs all parts of which are fragrant and which furnished the frankincense of the ancients. They are native of Africa, Arabia and tropical Asia.

Species. *Boswellia serrata* (syn. *B. thurifera*). Native of the southern end of the Red Sea, the Yemen, parts of northwestern Pakistan, India and the Malayan Archipelago. It is a smooth-barked tree yielding the sweet-smelling gum olibanum which is dried and burnt as incense in holy places. The leaves, when bruised, and wood emit an aromatic citrus-like odour.

To the ancient world it was the most prized commodity of all and was the chief source of wealth of that part of Southern Arabia ruled over by the Queen of Sheba. It supplied the temples of Egypt with incense and was as much in demand in Imperial Rome.

The flowers are star-like and greenish-white, the leaves resembling those of Mountain ash. The gum exudes from the branches as bright oblong drops and is brittle. It is yellow or pale red in colour and has a bitter taste, but when warmed or burnt gives off a pleasant balsamic odour. It is collected by making incisions in the bark.

BOUGAINVILLEA (Nyctaginaceae—Four O'Clock Family)

A genus of 18 species, native only of South America, though *B. glabra* is now prominent in southern Europe and Africa.

Species. *Bougainvillea glabra.* Native of Brazil, it reached the African continent and the countries of the Mediterranean in 1829. It is a plant of climbing habit making rapid growth, and in the warmer climes is grown to provide shade and shelter to a garden bower or to cover a sunny wall. It is spiny, with small oval leaves produced in whorls and with vividly coloured bracts (its flowers) which are deliciously scented. In the British Isles, it may be grown indoors in pots and kept neat and bushy by continually pinching out the shoots. The best form is *B. glabra* Alexander which is covered in masses of fragrant magenta bracts almost the whole year.

BOUVARDIA (Rubiaceae—Bedstraw Family)

A genus of 30 species of woody plants which rank amongst the most free-flowering of all evergreens, being almost continuously in bloom; also, they bloom when quite small. But in order to bloom continuously it is necessary for the plants to form a continuous supply of new wood, and this they will only do in a winter temperature of 18 to 21°C (65 to 70°F).

The plant was found in Mexico by Baron Humboldt who gave his name to the white-flowered species *Bouvardia humboldtii corymbiflora*, its large blossoms smelling deliciously of jasmine. The bouvardia is an outstanding example of scent diminishing in proportion to the amount of pigment (colour) present in the flower, for those bearing pure-white and pale-yellow blooms are jasmine-scented, whilst those bearing scarlet flowers (e.g. *B. ternifolia*) are scentless.

Plants bloom within 12 months from the time the shoots of the half ripened wood are removed in October. They should be planted in a sandy compost around the side of a pot, and kept in a temperature of 18°C (65°F). They root within a month and should then be moved singly to small pots and later to larger ones. Early in June, they may be encouraged to make bushy growth by pinching out the ends of the shoots, and from this time they should be given plenty of moisture, and may be stood out of doors in a frame. In winter the temperature should not fall below 13°C (55°F). Pruning time is in February, cutting back the previous year's growths hard. Any repotting is carried out in March.

Species. *Bouvardia candissima.* The flowers are snowy white and are sweetly scented.

B. flava. Extremely free-flowering, the blooms are primrose yellow in colour with the soft, delicate perfume of woodland primroses.

B. humboldtii corymbiflora. With dark-green leaves and large, white, fragrant flowers, this is a particularly good species, flowering in late autumn and winter.

B. jasminiflora. A species of robust habit: the flowers resemble the white jasmine and have a powerful fragrance.

BRABEIUM (Proteaceae—Protea Family)

A small genus of shrubs or trees, present in South Africa and Australia and bearing lanceolate leaves in whorls of 6, toothed at the margins. The flowers are borne in axillary racemes and, unusual in this family, are white and emit a sweet perfume; they are pollinated by butterflies, whereas birds are the usual pollinators of the family.

Species. *Brabeium stellatifolium.* It is native only of South Africa where it grows on the eastern slopes of Table Mountain. It has large lanceolate leaves and bears its flowers in racemes in the axils of the upper leaves. The flowers are white and sweetly scented and have earned for the plant the name of Cape Almond Blossom.

BRACHYGLOTTIS (Compositae—Daisy Family)

A small genus of trees or shrubs native, like so many composites, to New Zealand. The leaves are dull green above, white with tomentum on the underside, and the flowers are borne in drooping panicles.

Species. *Brachyglottis rangiora.* The Maoris have named it Rangiora and use the leaves, which exude a balsamic juice when bruised, to apply to wounds. The flowers are also heavily scented and borne in large plumes. They are much visited by bees.

B. repanda. A dwarf New Zealand shrub which is known as the Wavy-leaved Rangiora. It has large sage-green leaves, white on the underside, and throughout summer bears panicles of white flowers which emit the sweet scent of mignonette, especially pronounced at eventide.

BRACHYSTEGIA (Leguminosae—Laburnum Family)

A genus of trees native to South Africa and Rhodesia where they are found grouped about the hilltops, growing amongst boulders of granite. They have attractive foliage.

Species. *Brachystegia tamarindioides.* It makes a small flat-topped tree with attractive feathery foliage and in spring bears sprays of greenish-white flowers with a perfume described by Livingstone as 'ravishing'. The young leaves appear in September when they are of brilliant golden colouring.

BRAMBLE: *see* RUBUS

BRASSICA (Cruciferae—Cabbage Family)

A large cosmopolitan genus which includes many of the world's most valuable edible crops including the cabbage, turnip and mustard. In abundance the rich-yellow flowers of *Brassica nigra* emit a pleasing perfume which is perceptible only if several flowers are inhaled together.

Species. *Brassica nigra.* It provides the mustard of commerce, a valuable condiment in England since Tudor times. It takes its name from *mustum,* must—newly-fermented grape juice, with which it was originally mixed—and *ardens,* burning, a reference to its 'hot' taste. The Black mustard is a crop of rich alluvial soils. Sown thickly, a mustard field in bloom can be seen from afar and on a warm day its fragrance is almost as powerful as a bean field in bloom. After harvesting, the seed is crushed and releases a penetrating odour which causes the eyes to run. Hot water poured on Black mustard seed will help to clear a heavy cold if the feet are immersed for ten minutes, and mustard flour is an antiseptic and sterilizing agent. It is also an efficient deodorizer and if rubbed onto the hands will take away any offensive smell; it will also deodorize utensils and has the property of dispelling the powerful odours of musk and camphor.

The best continental mustard is made at Dijon, in France, as it has been since 1382 when Philip the Bold made a grant of armorial bearings to the town in recognition of its mustard industry.

BRUCKENTHALIA (Ericaceae—Heath Family)

A genus of a single species, native of south-eastern Europe and Asia Minor.

Species. *Bruckenthalia spiculifolia.* It is a small, heath-like shrublet growing only 30 cm (1 ft) tall with dark-green, needle-like foliage, white on the underside. The rose-pink flowers appear at the ends of the shoots early in June and have a soft honey-like fragrance which is especially noticeable after rain. The plant requires the same cultural conditions as the heaths, and is increased mainly by cuttings, or division in spring. It likes a sunny position.

BRUNFELSIA (Solanaceae—Nightshade Family)

A genus of 30 species of dainty evergreen shrubs, native of the West Indies and tropical South America, which in the British Isles and northern Europe require the warmth of a stove greenhouse. There they bear pretty, salver-shaped flowers in white, yellow or palest blue, which diffuse a soft, sweet perfume as they open. Like

Tabernaemontana coronaria, the plants require an acid soil, and quantities of peat should be incorporated into the potting compost. When in bloom in 15-cm (6-in) pots in summer, the plants will require a daily syringe and copious amounts of moisture at the roots, together with liquid fertilizer, but supplies must be reduced when the plants are wintering. Some pruning is required after flowering. Cuttings are taken between February and August of young growths inserted in sandy compost with bottom heat.

Species. *Brunfelsia americana.* A shrub 1.2 to 1.8 m (4 to 6 ft) high, its flowers appear early in summer and are palest yellow fading to white; they emit a somewhat spicy fragrance when opening.

B. calycina. The flowers are a delicate sky blue but have only the minimum of perfume; it is a small, 60-cm (2-ft) shrub, with large leaves.

B. undulata. A native of Jamaica, the flowers are pure white and are borne in late summer and autumn, emitting a soft sweet perfume. This reaches a similar height to *B. americana.*

BUDDLEIA (Buddleiaceae—Buddleia Family)

A genus of some 70 species named in honour of Rev. Adam Buddle and native of sub-tropical America and Asia, though most are hardy in the British Isles. The tiny blooms are borne in dense cymes and during late summer are usually littered with butterflies, hence the plant has come to be known as the Butterfly bush. Growing well in a sandy loam, the buddleia is at its best growing close to the sea where it makes as much as 1.8 m (6 ft) of new wood in a single season. To maintain its shape and vigour, the plant should be cut hard back each year early in spring, or in a mild district immediately after flowering; it will send out new cane-like growth in the spring and early summer and come into bloom during July and August, though several species are winter- and spring-flowering.

The buddleias make a most attractive scented hedge planted 1.2 m (4 ft) apart. They require a sunny position and may be trained along wires, with the old wood cut back each spring to maintain the shape.

Several species flowering at different times may be planted together, or several varieties of *B. davidii* such as Royal Red, White Bouquet and Black Night, will provide a pleasing display with their contrasting colours.

If planted 90 cm (3 ft) from a window, the buddleias will give hours of pleasure when in bloom to those confined indoors, for the heavy fragrance of the flower spikes—often 30 cm (1 ft) in length—is delicious when warmed by the late summer sun and Red Admirals and other butterflies and bees alight on the flowers in such numbers as to weigh down the spikes on occasion.

Though mostly deciduous, the hardy buddleias retain their foliage during a mild winter, at least until the new year, which adds to their value as a windbreak.

Like the chalk-loving *B. globosa*, *B. davidii* in particular, appreciates a soil containing plenty of lime, and where this is lacking a quantity of lime rubble should be spread about its roots at planting time.

Species and Varieties. *Buddleia alternifolia.* It grows 2.4 to 3 m (8 to 10 ft) tall and is like a weeping willow; its leaves are also willow-like whilst during July and August its arching branches are clothed with pale-lilac flowers which have the delicious scent of heliotrope, almost almond-like. The variety *argentea* has foliage densely covered in minute hairs, which gives it a silvery appearance.

B. auriculata. A native of South Africa, it will withstand up to 12 degrees of frost and in all but the most sheltered of gardens should be grown against a sunny wall. It is a most valuable plant in that it blooms early in October and continues until Christmas. It makes a loose shrub with drooping branches, the green lance-shaped leaves being grey beneath; the flower spikes borne from the leaf joints are made up of multitudes of tiny blossoms of an attractive flesh-pink which diffuse a sweet honey scent.

B. caryopteridifolia. It blooms during May and June, earlier if the spring is warm, and has usually finished flowering before the late summer-flowering species come into bloom. It should be pruned but little for its honey-scented flowers of palest lilac are borne on the previous year's

wood. The wood and foliage are densely covered in white hairs.

B. crispa (syn. *B. paniculata*). Native of the Himalayas and Afghanistan and growing nearly 3,000 m (10,000 ft) above sea-level, which accounts for its hardiness. It begins to bloom in February when *B. auriculata* has finished and continues until mid-May, its heavily laden spikes of lilac-pink with their golden 'eye' scenting the air to a considerable distance. It requires a deep, moist loam and is happiest where given the protection of a warm wall.

The form *farreri* is taller-growing and should be given a sunny wall. The large handsome leaves are white on the under-side and are covered in short hairs. The fragrant flowers of rosy mauve appear in March.

B. davidii. Native of China and Tibet, this is the buddleia we know best, a most elegant shrub growing to 3 m (10 ft) in height and the same across, with grey-green willow-like leaves often 9 in long. From early July until mid-September it bears masses of tiny flowers crowded together in long terminal sprays and they emit the musk-like fragrance of heather honey. A number of lovely varieties have been introduced during the past sixty years:

BLACK NIGHT. Introduced in 1960, it bears elegant cymes of deepest violet-purple with a pronounced perfume.

CHARMING. The flowers are the nearest to true pink of all the buddleias and they carry a soft honey perfume.

DUBONNET. The most vigorous variety bearing huge cymes of rich royal purple.

ELSTEAD. The blooms are a delightful apple-blossom combination of pink and white with a pronounced perfume.

WHITE CLOUD. The pure-white spikes present an arresting sight when covered with Red Admiral butterflies.

B. fallowiana. Always at its best in a sandy soil and in a coastal garden, it is a native of western China and its foliage is so densely covered with hairs as to appear silvered. The pale lavender-blue flowers are borne in large panicles and are the most richly scented of all the buddleias. The white form, *alba*, is especially lovely and with its silvered foliage appears to be covered in snow.

B. forrestii. Native of southern China, it requires a sheltered garden in the South-west to be hardy in Britain. It grows 1.8 to 2.4 m (6 to 8 ft) tall, its young leaves being covered in brown 'felt' beneath, whilst its flowers, borne in cylindrical inflorescences, are lilac with maroon shadings and are very heavily scented.

B. globosa. Though a native of Chile, it is hardy in the British Isles, withstanding many degrees of frost. It is evergreen in all but the severest of winters, with beautifully netted foliage though it grows 3.6 m (12 ft) high and has sparse foliage. It blooms in May, bearing a profusion of small orange flower-heads, held erect like orange golf balls, which scent the air for a considerable distance with a sweet honey-like fragrance.

BULBOPHYLLUM (Orchidaceae— Orchid Family)

A large genus of epiphytic plants, native of the warmer parts of the Old and New Worlds, particularly of the islands of South-east Asia and Polynesia. Many have small, hollow bulbs of coffee bean form, others longer fleshy roots from which arise solitary or twin leaves. The flowers are mostly borne in small spikes.

Species. *Bulbophyllum beccari.* A most remarkable orchid with a very thick rhizome, often growing to a considerable length and sometimes as much as 20 cm (8 in) in diameter. The flowers are pale brown with a purple flush, produced in the autumn, and have an unbearably unpleasant smell, out of all proportion to their size. The leaves may grow 60 cm (2 ft) long and are the largest of any known orchid.

B. coccinum. A small orchid with small white flowers, flushed with pink, set closely on an arching flower stem. They are strongly scented of coconut, and appear in winter.

B. comosum. From Burma, this pleione-like species bears tiny white flowers in a raceme in winter; they are long-lasting and smell of hay, as do the leaves.

B. odoratissimum. A very fragrant species from Burma, it has considerable charm with its small, creamy-white flowers, 12 or more in a cluster. It is a tiny plant not much more than 5 cm (2 in) high.

B. suavissimum. A summer-flowering plant, it bears yellow flowers in a raceme about 25 cm (10 in) long. Its sweet scent is very pronounced.

Bulbophyllums require a warm, moist atmosphere, and a compost of 3 parts osmunda fibre, and about 3 parts sphagnum moss. Suspended pans are best, and propagation is by division of plants in spring. Cultural requirements are varied, owing to their extremely wide range of habitat.

BUPLEURUM (Umbelliferae—Parsley Family)

A genus of 60 species of shrubs and annual or perennial herbs with simple entire leaves. They are native of the northern temperate regions (four are British) and sub-tropical areas, but are represented mostly in southern Europe, where the plants are of shrub-like form. The flowers are borne in dense umbels, the petals being flat and incurved at the apex.

Species. *Bupleurum fruticosum.* A native of Spain, it makes a dense, evergreen bush 1.5 to 1.8 m (5 to 6 ft) tall with attractive purple branches along which it bears narrow, pointed leaves of rich sea-green, paler on the underside, which when bruised release a pungent smell. Its pale greenish-yellow flowers, borne from July to September, have long bracts and appear in umbels at the end of the stems. It is not completely hardy, and does best by the sea. There are no particular soil requirements; planting is in autumn or spring, and increase is by cuttings planted in a frame in September.

BURKEA (Leguminosae—Laburnum Family)

A genus of only two species, native of West and South Africa, also Rhodesia. It is to be found from the Orange River northwards to Rhodesia and is prevalent in the Matopos where it makes a tree about 6 m (20 ft) in height. It is known as the Rhodesian Ash for it has deciduous ash-like leaves, silvery-grey in colour, and bears small white flowers in long drooping racemes which have the familiar sweet-pea perfume of this plant family. The flowers are followed by clusters of tiny hairy pods containing a single seed.

BURSARIA (Pittosporaceae—Pittosporum Family)

A genus of four species of trees or shrubs, evergreen and native to Australia and Tasmania, where the common name is the Christmas Bush, as it is at its loveliest at that time of year.

Species. *Bursaria spinosa.* The most common species, found in most parts of Australia and Tasmania. It is a glabrous, thorny shrub, growing to about 4.5 m (15 ft), with alternate leaves which are evergreen, and it bears numerous, tiny white flowers in terminal panicles, in July and August. They are deliciously scented. The petals are small and spread out from the base, and because of their sweet perfume, the plant is called in Victoria the Sweet bursaria. The brown seeds are shaped like a purse, hence its botanical name from the Latin *bursa,* a purse. Hardy in very sheltered parts only, it needs a cool greenhouse otherwise, and is increased by cuttings which root with the help of a little bottom heat.

BURNET: see POTERIUM

BUTOMUS (Alismataceae—Water-plantain Family)

A genus of a single species.

Species. *Butomus umbellatus.* It is native of the British Isles and Europe and takes its name from the Greek words *bous,* an ox, and *temno,* to cut, for grazing cattle were apt to cut their mouths on the sharp leaves.

It grows in low-lying meadows and by slow-running streams, and is a perennial plant with sword-shaped leaves 0.9 to 1.2 m (3 to 4 ft) long which arise from a creeping rootstock. The rose-coloured flowers have a smell of bitter almond and are 2.5 cm (1 in) across. They are borne in a terminal umbel and are enhanced by their red anthers.

BUXUS (Buxaceae—Box Tree Family)

A genus of 70 species present in the British Isles and northern Europe, in tropical and South Africa and South-east Asia, with several showing exceptional hardiness.

The evergreen foliage is pungently scented, especially when wet. To some, the pungent scent of the box is most pleasing, to others quite the opposite. In *Adventures in my Garden,* the American writer Louise Wilder has written, 'the pungent smell of the leaves is to me highly refreshing and stimulating, but all do not like it. Near me is a cottage half surrounded by a fine Boxwood hedge but of it the woman who dwells therein . . . said, "It's gloomy and I don't like the smell all through the day and night".' Louise Wilder mentions the hypnotic effect the smell has on some people, like the flowers of the field bean, and mentions a Dr Holmes who called its scent 'that of eternity, one of the odours that carries us out of time into the abyss of the unbeginning past'.

The dwarf form used for hedging is readily propagated by division, whilst the taller-growing box may be increased from cuttings taken in late summer and inserted in sandy soil in a frame or around the side of a pot.

Box grows best in a chalky soil. Its close-grained pale yellow wood is heavier than any other English wood, and will sink in water. It is much used for making furniture and musical instruments, and a century ago was used to make printers' blocks.

Species and Varieties. *Buxus elegantissima.* One of the neatest of all evergreens, it makes a small rounded tree, its silvery foliage being edged with white.

B. sempervirens. This is the tall-growing box of the woodlands with stout leaves of shining green and of leathery texture. There is also an attractive golden-leaf form, *aurea.*

B. suffruticosa. The dwarf or Dutch box, which is very slow-growing and valuable for a dwarf hedge.

C

CACALIA (Compositae—Daisy Family)

A genus of 50 or more mostly scentless plants, native of eastern Asia with one present in North America.

Species. *Cacalia septentrionalis*. It is a low-growing perennial, native of Indonesia, with small yellow daisy-like flowers which release a soft pleasant perfume only when the sun's rays shine upon them. If the rays are intercepted by a cloth or sheet of cardboard, the scent is lost at once but is noticeable again as soon as the shield is removed.

CAESALPINIA (Leguminosae—Laburnum Family)

A genus of tropical evergreen trees, shrubs and climbing plants, native of South America, where they festoon the forest trees with their dark, glossy pinnate leaves and orange-fragrant blossoms.

Species. *Caesalpinia paniculata* (syn. *C. nuga*). A vigorous climber with dark-green pinnate leaves and bearing in summer its white, orange–scented blossom in dense axillary racemes. It requires a warm greenhouse and a compost containing plenty of peat or leaf-mould. Soft, young cuttings are the best for rooting, in a very sandy compost and heat.

CALAMINTHA (Labiatae—Lavender Family)

A small genus of downland plants closely related to the thymes and differing chiefly in having a tubular, 2-lipped calyx and a larger 2-lipped corolla protruding from it. They are mostly perennial plants of low-growing habit, useful for the rock garden, and for planting between paving-stones. They require a well-drained, sandy soil and are propagated by division in spring or from cuttings removed in July and rooted in a sandy compost. Five or six species are natives of the British Isles.

Species. *Calamintha acinos*. Known as Basil thyme, it makes a neat bushy plant 15 cm (6 in) tall, with hairy leaves, and in August bears violet-purple flowers in whorls of 5 or 6, the corolla being spotted with white.

C. glabella. A delightful little plant for paving, for it is of almost prostrate habit, with small, lance-shaped leaves, and in late summer covers itself in a profusion of tubular, purple flowers which are deliciously scented.

C. grandiflora. A species of southern Europe growing 22 cm (9 in) tall with coarsely toothed leaves and bearing, in June and July, scented flowers of lilac-purple in loose racemes. The flowers are nearly 5 cm (2 in) long, inflated at the throat, and carry a delicious minty scent.

C. nepeta. The Lesser calamint, a British plant which frequents dry banks, mostly south of the Thames. It grows 37 cm (15 in) tall with erect stems and oval, serrate, shortly stalked leaves. The pale-purple flowers are borne in forked cymes. The whole plant has a refreshing, thyme-like scent. It is perennial.

C. officinalis. Known as the Common calamint or Mountain balm, it is a perennial plant of low, prostrate habit, occasionally found by the side of fields, but always happiest under dry, hilly conditions. The stems are downy, and it bears its blue and purple flowers late in summer and in loose racemes, whilst the leaves are broad and blunt-ended. If trodden upon, the whole plant emits a sweet and refreshing mint-like smell.

C. sylvatica. Closely related to the Common calamint, it is perennial, in bloom during August and September, and is occasionally found on dry downlands from the South Downs westwards through Hampshire and Dorset to the Devon borders. It has large, deeply serrated leaves and bears large flowers with the upper calyx teeth reflexed. In all respects the largest of the calamints.

C. vulgare. The Wild basil, which makes a straggling plant 20 to 25 cm (8 to 10 in) high with hairy stems and slightly toothed leaves. From July until September it bears whorls of rosy-red flowers in stool-shaped involucres, and the whole plant has a delicious fragrance, like that of mint and equally refreshing, hence its name from the Greeek words *kolos* and *minta,* 'beautiful mint'.

CALENDULA (Marigold) (Compositae—Daisy Family

A genus of about 20 species of annual plants, mostly native of southern Europe and North Africa, of which *C. officinalis* with its pungent scent is the best known. It has been grown throughout Europe since earliest times for flavouring soups and stews; its almost evergreen leaves made it a most valuable culinary plant. The plant received its botanical name *Calendula* because it was believed to be in bloom on the first day (the calends) of each month. It is dedicated to Our Lady for a similar reason, being in bloom at the time of all the festivals of the Virgin. Its old country name was 'mary-buds'.

Turner mentions that the flowers of the marigold were used to turn the hair yellow, but of greater importance was its use in the American Civil War when doctors collected the leaves for treating open wounds.

Species and Varieties. *Calendula officinalis.* An annual which in spite of being native to the warmer climes is so hardy that it will remain green and bear flowers almost throughout the coldest winter. It seeds itself so readily that from an original planting will follow a never-ending supply.

The plants grow 30 to 37 cm (12 to 15 in) tall and have succulent stems covered with fine hairs. The oblong sessile leaves are bright green and pungent to the touch, and impart their flavour to salads and soups. The flowers are 5 to 7 cm (2 to 3 in), in diameter, often with fluted petals which radiate from a central boss, and they possess a similar pungency.

From a sowing made in the open in March, the plants begin to bloom in June, producing a never-ending supply for the rest of the year. Allow 30 cm (12 in) between the plants and they will grow well in all soils, in full sun or partial shade.

Probably the best variety is Radio, pure orange with quilled petals, and its yellow counterpart, Golden Beam. Cream Beauty completes a delightful trio which will provide flowers for house and garden for almost the whole year.

CALLISTEMON (Myrtaceae—Myrtle Family)

A genus of tall shrubs with alternate, narrow leaves, and bearing their flowers in cylindrical spikes 7 to 10 cm (3 to 4 in) long. The genus is native of Australia and Tasmania, mostly of Victoria and New South Wales where they are known as Bottle-brushes. Several species have aromatic foliage.

Species. *Callistemon citrinus* (syn. *C. lanceolatus).* It grows 1.5 to 1.8 m (5 to 6 ft) in height with thick lance-shaped leaves which when pressed emit a refreshing scent of lemon. It blooms from spring through summer, bearing spikes of deep crimson, conspicuous by their deeper crimson anthers.

C. pinifolius. A rare plant found only in sandy dunes near Sydney where it makes a loose bush some 90 cm (3 ft) tall, the flowers being composed of green filaments. The pine-like foliage has also the aromatic scent of pine woods.

C. salignus. It makes a tree 6 to 9 m (20 to 30 ft) tall and is common to the swamplands of Queensland and New South Wales. It is one of the most handsome of trees, with white papery bark, whilst the young foliage appears as brilliant rose-red. It is known as the Willow Bottle-brush with leaves 7 cm (3 in) long and flowers of a similar length. It blooms from October until December, the loose spikes being composed of yellow filaments. It has aromatic foliage.

CALLITRIS (Cupressaceae—Cypress Tree Family)

A genus of 16 species native of Tasmania and New Caledonia, one being found along the northern coastline of Africa. Known as the Cypress pines, they bear their leaves in whorls.

Species. *Callitris quadrivalvis.* It abounds along the northern coast of Africa where it reaches a height of 6 m (20 ft) with drooping branches of flattened leaves and globular cones. It is known as the Arar tree and grows well in a sandy soil. Its wood is scented, like cedar wood, and is readily worked by hand. For this reason it was used in the construction of the ninth-century cathedral of Cordova in Spain.

CALOCHORTUS (Liliaceae—Lily Family)

A genus of hardy plants known as the Maripose lilies, and which in their native haunts grow all along the Pacific Coast of North America from British Columbia to Mexico. They require warm, dry conditions after flowering, but plenty of moisture before, and so are difficult to establish away from their natural home. Only two species have any degree of perfume, *C. pulchellus* and *C. uniflorus*, from the woodlands of northern California and Oregon, which are more readily established outdoors in the British Isles and northern Europe than other species. Bulbs are planted in November 10 cm (4 in) deep, and protected from frost. Well-drained soil is essential. Increase by offsets, or seeds sown in spring in sandy soil.

Species. *Calochortus pulchellus.* A beautiful plant, known as the Golden Lantern, forming numerous branches and growing 30 cm (1 ft) high. From each stem hangs a group of 3 or 4 golden bells, which are sweetly scented. It is at its loveliest during June, and is in all respects a most attractive plant.

C. uniflorus. A small species reaching only about 15 cm (6 in) at the most, but with a group of 5 or 6 pale-purple flowers hanging by long pedicels from a short main stalk. It is summer-flowering.

CALODENDRUM (Rutaceae—Rue Family)

A genus of two species, native of tropical Africa.

Species. *Calodendrum capense.* Known as the Cape Chestnut, it is a semi-tropical, evergreen tree which grows in the forests of Natal and the Transvaal, also in Kenya. It has been widely planted in gardens throughout South Africa and, more recently, India for the rich perfume diffused by its pale-pink flowers and the orange scent of its leaves when handled. It is a valuable timber tree growing 15 m (50 ft) tall, with smooth grey bark and spreading branches. The flowers are borne in bunches at the ends of the branches, with about 8 blooms to each bunch. They each have 5 curling petals and in the middle are 5 upright stamens, spotted with crimson. The tree has opposite, oblong leaves, whilst the fruit is two shining black seeds enclosed in a round shell covered in spines, hence its local name.

In a warm greenhouse it will reach about 3 m (10 ft). It requires a sunny position and a compost containing plenty of peat and loam. Propagation is by young cuttings taken in June and placed in a closed frame with gentle heat.

CALONYCTION (Convolvulaceae—Bindweed Family)

A large genus of mostly climbing plants numbering about 500 species, mostly native of tropical North and South America.

Species. *Calonyction aculeatum.* A native of Greece, it has long been grown in the British Isles, but to modern gardeners is almost unknown. Until recently it was called *Ipomaea bona-nox* (Beauty of the Night), for its large, trumpet-shaped flowers resemble those of the convolvulus, having a waxy-white appearance at eventide, hence the common name of Moonflower.

It is a plant of climbing habit, and in a warm summer will attain a height of nearly 6 m (20 ft) in a single season, bearing its large trumpets in succession from July until October. The blooms often measure nearly 15 cm (6 in) across and diffuse a powerful scent at night. A warm greenhouse suits it, and it is grown from seed sown in spring.

CALOPHACA (Leguminosae—Laburnum Family)

A genus of 10 species of woolly (hairy) sub-shrubs, native of Russia, Siberia and northern China, only one of which has any garden value.

Species. *Calophaca volgarica.* Present along the banks of the Volga River, its foliage is divided into 6 to 8 pairs of tiny leaflets, and in May and June from the leaf axils it bears racemes of small yellow laburnum-like flowers which have a soft vanilla-like fragrance.

CALOPHYLLUM (Guttiferae—St John's Wort Family)

A genus of more than 100 species of trees, distributed throughout tropical South-east Asia, Australia and the Fiji Islands, and yielding a valuable sweet resinous compound. Stove-house conditions are required in this country, and half-ripened cuttings are used for propagation.

Species. *Calophyllum inophyllum.* Native mostly of the Fiji Isles and the East Indies, where it is usually found in coastal areas, growing to a height of 12 m (40 ft) or more. The evergreen, opposite leaves are thick and shiny; the small flowers of 6 petals, formed in inflorescences, are creamy-white, unusual in this family, and have a soft, sweet perfume. The flowers are followed by globular fruits of the size of a horse-chestnut, and from them an aromatic resinous oil is obtained which is used as a liniment. The wood is also resinous.

CALYCANTHUS (Calycanthaceae—Allspice Family)

A genus of several species of small trees or shrubs native of eastern Australia and the United States which require a well-drained peaty soil, and in the British Isles a sheltered situation, protected from cold winds. They are delightful when grown against a wall for they bloom longer than any tree.

Species. *Calycanthus floridus.* The Carolina Allspice, native of North America, where it is known as the Sweet-Scented Shrub. It is small and deciduous, 1.8 to 2.4 m (6 to 8 ft) in height with spreading branches and ovate leaves, downy on the underside. The flowers, which appear in June, are made up of a large number of narrow sepals and petals of purple and dull red, and have the refreshing scent of ripe apples. The leaves, wood and roots smell powerfully of camphor, whilst in the U.S.A. the bark smells like cinnamon and is used as a substitute, hence the plant's name of All-spice.

C. glaucus (syn. *C. fertilis*). It grows 1.5 to 1.8 m (5 to 6 ft) in height with lance-shaped leaves which are downy and glaucous beneath and smell strongly of cinnamon. The lurid purple flowers have only slight perfume.

C. laevigatus. Native of the mountainous regions of Carolina and Virginia, its leaves are rough and wrinkled, glaucous and downy beneath with the smell of camphor. The brilliant-purple flowers have little scent.

C. occidentalis (syn. *C. macrophyllus*). It grows to a height of 3 to 3.6 m (10 to 12 ft) and has heart-shaped leaves which, like the wood, are pleasantly aromatic though the handsome red flowers, 10 cm (4 in) across and appearing from June until the end of autumn, are devoid of perfume. This is one of the longest in bloom of all trees, distinguished from the others by its long flower stalk.

C. praecox. Now known as *Chimonanthus fragrans*, it bears sweetly scented flowers in winter and is described under that species.

CALYPTRANTHES (Myrtaceae—Myrtle Family)

A genus of 100 or more species of small trees or shrubs, native of tropical America and the West Indies.

Species. *Calyptranthes aromaticus.* The flower buds are used as a substitute for cloves and the leaves have a similar clove-like fragrance.

CAMELLIA (Theaceae—Tea Family)

Named after the Jesuit priest, Fr. Camellus, who found *Camellia japonica* on the island of Luzon in the Philippines two centuries ago, the genus is amongst the most beautiful of all and is hardier than generally believed. Camellias grow well in a deep, peaty loam where lime is excluded, and they require protection from cold winds. They also need a continuous supply of moisture at the roots in summer. Low-growing shrubs planted about the roots provide protection from wind and also prevent the soil from drying out too rapidly, for camellias are copious drinkers and appreciate a daily syringeing of the foliage during dry weather. Like all peat-loving plants, they enjoy a position of partial shade provided by trees and shrubs requiring similar conditions.

Camellias are usually grown in pots and should be planted late in July when the weather is often showery so that they do not suffer from evaporation of moisture from the foliage. If conditions are dry and warm, a twice-daily syringeing of the foliage is advisable.

The evergreen C. japonica is the best-known species and the parent of many lovely hybrids but none have scented flowers. A fragrant species is C. sasanqua, which is native to Japan. As it often flowers in mid-winter, it may be included with the fragrant winter-flowering plants.

Species and Varieties. Camellia sasanqua. Like C. japonica it is evergreen, with shiny somewhat smaller dark-green leaves. The small, flat white flowers are single and, in a sheltered position, appear as soon as the sun loses its strength in November or earlier, continuing in a mild winter until the first days of spring. But it is a less hardy plant than C. japonica and requires all the protection it can be given. The blooms have a delicate sweet perfume. The plants attain a height of 3 m (10 ft) where happily situated.

The variety Azuma Nishiki is a more vigorous grower with larger flowers of white flushed with pink and they have a richer perfume. The buds have a crimson flush on the outside before opening, making it extremely lovely when in bud. The form rubra has flowers of deep ruby-red which are not so fragrant.

Mini-no-yuki has deliciously scented cream-coloured flowers which are fully double, whilst Momozono bears semi-double flowers of soft pink which are equally fragrant. There is a form variegata

which is also pink-flowering and which has pretty variegated leaves.

C. sinensis. An evergreen shrub, native of the hillsides of tropical India, Ceylon, Malaya, China and Indonesia, its dried leaves with the familiar aroma providing the tea of commerce which is drunk in all parts of the world. The alternate leaves are leathery to the touch and are borne on short stalks. The leaves are used for drying when the plant is 4 years old and under good cultivation prove economical for almost half a century. The flowers are white or blush-white, measuring about 2.5 cm (1 in) across and borne at the axils of the leaves; they are deliciously scented. A fragrant essential oil is obtained from the seeds but has no commercial use.

CAMPHOR: see **DRYOBALANOPS**

CAMPHOROSMA (Chenopodiaceae—Beetroot Family)

A genus of 10 or 11 species, native of Europe, the Near East and central Asia.

Species. Camphorosma monspeliaca. It is found in southern Europe growing along the coast stretching from the French Riviera to Italy. An evergreen shrub, it rarely exceeds a height of 60 cm (2 ft) and has small grey leaves and flowers in June. It is a plant which commands little attention but the tiny linear leaves when bruised, and the wood, give off the powerful smell of camphor. In the British Isles it does best in a sandy soil near the coast but requires a warm garden on the western side of the country.

CANANGA (Anonaceae—Anona Family)

A genus of one or possibly two species, native of tropical Asia and Australia, and cultivated for their highly scented flowers.

Species. Cananga odorata. A native of Burma, the Malayan Archipelago and the Philippines where it is known as the Ylang-ylang tree. It makes a small twiggy tree and bears masses of inconspicuous dull-yellow flowers which have the fragrance of jasmine. From them cananga perfume (ylang-ylang) is obtained and also Macassar oil. As the odour has little force, it takes a considerable quantity of otto to provide any lasting fragrance, and so it is usually mixed with otto of pimento to intensify the clove-like undertones.

CANARIUM (Burseraceae—Frankincense Family)

A genus of trees or shrubs which yield the Elemi of perfumery, a resinous exudation. The plants are mostly native of the Philippine Islands and the gum they exude is more correctly known as 'Manilla elemi'. The plants are also found in Penang and the Moluccas and in Queensland. Dr A. W. Bennett, one-time lecturer in botany at St Thomas's Hospital and author of the *Flora of India*, stated that there were 30 species, mostly distributed throughout tropical Asia and the Philippines, of which *C. commune* is the most important commercially.

Species. *Canarium commune.* It makes a tree 12 m (40 ft) tall with hard wood which exudes from cuts made in the bark a white gum known to the natives as Brea. The gum is soft and tacky to the touch and has a sharp lemon perfume, likened by some to that of fennel from which a similar substance, phallandrene, is obtained. It is also present in the roots of *Angelicia archangelica* and in Black Pepper. The leaves are 30 cm (12 in) or more in length and it bears its fragrant greenish-white flowers in panicles during May and June.

C. edule. It is described in Maloney's *Forestry of West Africa* as 'having under the bark, large masses of (verbena) scented gum which is carried by the natives to fumigate themselves and their cloths'.

C. muelleri. It grows in Queensland, in the region of Johnstone River where it was discovered towards the end of the nineteenth century. The scent of the gum was described by J. H. Maiden, then curator of the Technological Museum, Sydney: 'Upon cutting a long incision, Dr Bancroft observed a flow of honey-like liquid which had a delicious turpentine smell, mixed with lemon, a very different smell from that of the official elemi. When digested in cold alcohol, its lemon odour is so strongly brought out as to almost bring the substance into the category of a perfume'. It is entirely without the fennel odour.

CANDYTUFT: see IBERIS

CANELLA (Canellaceae—Canella Family)

A small genus of trees, native of Florida, the Bahamas and the West Indies.

Species. *Canella alba* (syn. *Canella winteriana*). An evergreen tree growing to a height of 6 to 9 m (20 to 30 ft) and branched only at the top. The bark is silvery-white, its beauty being accentuated by the smooth glossy leaves. At the end of the branches are clusters of violet-coloured flowers which, though rarely fully opening, scent the whole neighbourhood with their musk-like perfume. When the flower sprays are dried and kept for a considerable time and are then placed in warm water, they emit the same scent as when on the tree. The leaves and the black seeds are also fragrant, whilst its bark, known in the Bahamas as 'Cinnamon bark', has the aromatic smell of the true cinnamon. The bark is sold in long quills roiled up like cinnamon. It is removed by beating the tree with stakes, a second beating often being necessary to loosen the inner bark. When Meyer and Von Reiche discovered the odorous principle it was found to contain eugenol, the chief principle of oil of cloves.

CANNABIS (Cannabinaceae—Hemp Family)

A genus of a single species.

Species. *Cannabis satira.* Hemp is an annual plant, native of India and central Asia where it grows to a height of 2.4 m (8 ft) or more and is cultivated for the valuable fibrous content of its stems. It has alternate leaves, divided into 5 to 11 lance-shaped segments, and they emit a resinous compound. The flowers appear in June, the males in short panicles, the females clustered between the sessile bracts.

CARANGA (Leguminosae—Laburnum Family)

A genus of spiny shrubs and trees, native of the vast land area stretching north from Tibet to northern Siberia and eastwards to the China coast. They are hardy anywhere and grow best in a dry, sandy soil.

Species. *Caranga aurantiaca.* From Siberia, it attains a height of 90 cm (3 ft) with pointed linear leaflets and in May and June the deep orange-coloured flowers are suspended from the branches in great profusion, having a refreshing sweet scent.

C. boisii. A native of Tibet it grows 1.2 m (4 ft) tall and is the most heavily spined of all the species and bears its leaves in small tufts at the end of the stems, together with small yellow laburnum-like flowers which have a peculiar sweetish scent.

C. chamlagu. From northern China, probably the best form for a sea-coast garden, making a rounded bush some 1.2 m (4 ft) tall with dark-green leaves. At the ends of the stems it bears broom-like flowers of yellow and red during April and May when it emits a treacle-like smell.

CARAWAY: see CARUM

CARDIOCRINUM (Liliaceae—Lily Family)

A genus of only three species, until recently classed with the genus *Lilium* but differing in that the leaves are broad and cordate and the seed capsules toothed. Growing to 1.8 m (6 ft) or more in height, the cardiocrinums are amongst the most stately of all garden plants with a beauty apparent only in plants of the Far East. The plants are native of the woodlands of south-western China and northern Burma and require a position of partial shade and a well-drained soil containing some humus in the form of peat or leaf-mould and a little decayed manure.

Species. *Cardiocrinum cathayarum.* It was discovered growing by mountain streams in western China by E. H. Wilson, bearing at the top of a 1.2 m (4 ft) stem a cluster of funnel-shaped flowers of creamy white spotted with brown, which are pleasantly fragrant. It is rarely seen in gardens, though it responds to culture as given to *C. gigantium.*

C. cordatum. It was first discovered in Japan in 1778 but was not established at Kew until a century later. The heart-shaped leaves are coppery-red whilst the sweetly scented flowers are greeny-white with yellow in the throat and spotted with purple. The bulbs die back after flowering but the newly-formed bulblets bear bloom the following year.

C. giganteum. It was discovered by Dr

Wallich in Nepal and it also grows in Assam and Sikkim, usually in woodland clearings at an altitude of between 1,500 to 2,400 m (5,000 to 8,000 ft) though in the hills of Simla it grows as high as 3,600 m (12,000 ft), scenting the air around with its rich sweet perfume.

The plant likes a well-drained soil containing some grit and plenty of humus for it is a heavy feeder, sending up its stems to a height of 3 m (10 ft) and bearing up to 18 or more long narrow trumpets of glistening white striped red on the inside, green without. The dark-green bulbs should not be planted with more than 2.5 to 5 cm (1 to 2 in) of soil above them, and the plants benefit from top dressing each year in summer.

The variety Yunnanense grows to only half the height and has bronzy-green leaves and stems which enhance the long white tubes devoid of any red markings.

CARDUUS (Thistle) (Compositae—Daisy Family)

A genus of perennial or biennial plants with spinous-toothed leaves and bracts to the tubular flower-heads, with the pappus consisting of many rows of bristles. The Musk or Scottish thistle (*C. nutans*), which grows from the British Isles across Europe, into northern Asia and as far south as North Africa, is scented, and so is *C. arvense.*

Species. *Carduus arvense.* The Creeping or Corn thistle of fields and downland. It is a perennial plant, creeping by underground stems and growing less than 60 cm (2 ft) high with an erect angular stem and wavy pinnatifid leaves, extremely spinous. The small purple-pink flower-heads and the entire plant diffuse a warm musky aroma.

C. nutans. An attractive plant though an obnoxious weed in the garden. A biennial, it usually grows on chalky headlands or on waste ground by the sea-shore and is prominent in North-east and South-east England and in Scotland. It is easily recognizable by the manner in which the crimson-purple flowers hang their heads. The flowers, and indeed the whole plant, give off a pleasing musk-like perfume, hence its name. It grows 60 cm (2 ft) in height with a furrowed stem and blooms from June until September, being the largest of all the thistles and drawing from afar the butterflies and bees. The deeply lobed grey-green foliage and stems are covered with hairs and sharp spines.

CARMICHAELIA (Leguminosae— Laburnum Family)

A genus of 40 evergreen species, natives of New Zealand and resembling the Caranga in that the tiny leaflets are borne so close to the singularly flattened stems as to give them an almost leafless appearance. Like most members of the family, the plants are happiest in a sandy soil and are hardy in coastal districts of the warmer parts of Europe.

Species. *Carmichaelia australis.* Of upright habit, it has strangely flattened stems, as if they have been crushed, whilst its leaves are tiny protrusions along the stems. Growing to a height of 1.8 m (6 ft), it bears in July clusters of mauve flowers, like those of the Brooms and with a rich orange scent, this being especially pronounced towards evening. It is a rare plant of Lord Howe's Island.

C. petriei. A plant of erect growth, it has rounded twiggy stems and it grows 1.2 to 1.5 m (4 to 5 ft) tall. In July it bears racemes of small purple broom-like flowers which have the sweet fragrance of the laburnum.

CARPENTERIA (Saxifragaceae— Rockfoil Family)

A genus of but a single species, closely related to the Mock Orange and bearing flowers of similar form but with a more delicate sweet perfume.

Species. *Carpenteria californica.* Native of the western United States, especially of the Sierra Nevada, it is a handsome shrub which grows 1.8 to 2.4 m (6 to 8 ft) in height with lanceolate leaves. Its large, single, glistening white flowers are borne in June and resemble those of *Anemone japonica,* with golden anthers and a sweet perfume. The plant requires a well-drained sandy soil and a warm, sheltered garden.

CARPODETUS (Saxifragaceae—Rockfoil Family)

A genus of eight species, native to New Zealand and New Guinea, which form trees or shrubs with alternate leaves and bear their small white flowers in axillary panicles. Unfortunately it is the home of the Maori Devil, the *weta,* a large insect of the genus *Deinacrida* which bores holes in the stems and lays its eggs in them.

Species. *Carpodetus serratys.* A flat-topped tree 6 m (20 ft) tall with hairy branches spreading out fan-wise. The leaves are serrated and are attractively veined and marbled whilst the tiny white flowers, borne in broad cymes, are hidden amongst the leaves. Unusual in this family, they possess a powerful daphne-like perfume and are followed by black pea-like fruits. Native only of New Zealand, it is found from North Cape to Stewart Island and is in bloom from November until March.

CARRUTHERSIA (Apocynaceae— Perwinkle Family)

A genus of six or seven species, native of the Philippines, the Solomon Islands and Fiji, being climbing plants with opposite leaves 12 to 15 cm (5 to 6 in) long and 7 cm (3 in) wide and bearing scented flowers.

Species. *Carruthersia latifolia.* A common vine-like plant, climbing by tendrils to a considerable height with broad ovate leaves and long tubular white flowers, like those of jasmine and with a powerful vanilla-like perfume. They are followed by large round fruits resembling small oranges.

CARUM (Umbelliferae—Parsley Family)

Its name is derived from the Arabic, *Karawya* (the name of the seed), and it is a plant indigenous to all parts of Europe and the Near East, found from Iceland to the Western Himalayas, especially around the Mediterranean.

Species. *Carum carvi.* It is now almost entirely grown for its seed, and for this to ripen in time it should be treated as biennial, the seed being sown in August the previous year. The plant grows 90 cm (3 ft) tall. Oil extracted from the seed is used to make the liqueur Kümmel, while the seeds are used in Ireland to flavour bread and on the Continent to flavour cakes. In

Shakespeare's time they were used for flavouring apples, and it is said that they were taken with fruit to relieve indigestion. An excellent old remedy for flatulence is to crush some caraway seed and add to half a pint of boiling water; allow to get cold and take a teaspoonful whenever necessary. It is excellent for children suffering from wind and is known as gripe-water.

The roots are also fragrant and in earlier times were used as a substitute for parsnips to which they have a superior flavour, whilst the leaves were used to impart their aromatic flavour to soups and sauces.

The essential oil distilled from the seed contains carvol and carvene, the latter being a by-product which does not possess the delicate odour of carvol and is used in perfuming soaps of inferior quality.

CARYA (Juglandaceae—Walnut Tree Family)

A small genus of handsome deciduous walnut-like trees, the pinnate leaves having serrated leaflets; like those of the walnut, they are resinous. The drupe is ovoid and 4-valved. They are plants of the eastern United States and of Canada.

Species. *Carya alba.* The Shell-bark hickory of the eastern United States and Canada where it grows up to 21 m (70 ft) tall. Its aromatic compound leaves are divided into 5 serrated leaflets. It bears greenish catkins in May and these are followed by globular fruits containing a white thinly shelled nut.

C. amara. The Swamp hickory, native of the eastern United States and Canada where it reaches a height of 15 m (50 ft) or more. The resinous compound leaves are composed of 11 or more lance-shaped leaflets, downy when young, and in spring it bears greenish catkins in pairs. The nut is round and sharply pointed.

C. microcarpa. The most handsome of all the hickories for its large broad leaves, divided into 5 leaflets, are richly aromatic and turn a soft primrose-yellow colour in autumn. It makes a tall, spreading tree up to 24 m (80 ft) tall.

CARYOPTERIS (Verbenaceae—Vervain Family)

A genus of handsome, deciduous, herbaceous plants of shrubby habit, native of northern China and Japan, and hardy in the British Isles and northern Europe in all but the most exposed gardens. They bear almost scentless flowers, but have handsome indented leaves which emit a powerful, incense-like scent when handled. They may be increased by division or by cuttings.

Species. *Caryopteris mastacanthus* (syn. *C. incana*). A Chinese shrub growing 60 to 90 cm (2 to 3 ft) tall and a most exotic plant, known as the Blue Spiraea. It has rich grey, felt-like leaves, downy on the underside which, when bruised, give off a strong aromatic fragrance, likened by some to that of spearmint. The flowers, which are produced in autumn, are lavender-blue and are borne in clusters at the end of the shoots and from the leaf axils, and they too are slightly pungent. It is a hardy plant except in the most exposed gardens, but it requires a rich loamy soil and should never be allowed to dry out at the roots during summer.

A natural hybrid, *C. clandonensis*, which is derived from *C. mastacanthus*, grows to a similar height and has narrow, grey-green leaves, which are also aromatic though not so pronounced as the parent. The flowers, of periwinkle-blue, are borne in September and October, when two or three plants growing together will present a picture of great beauty.

CASSIA (Leguminosae—Laburnum Family)

A genus of 500 or more species of ornamental trees or shrubs which like a well-drained sandy soil containing peat. With but one or two exceptions, they are trees of the East, famed for the sweet vanilla scent of their blossom and, in some cases, their aromatic bark.

Species. *Cassia corymbosa.* A native of South America where it is found in the neighbourhood of Buenos Aires growing to a height of 3 m (10 ft). It has lance-shaped pointed leaflets and throughout summer bears its vanilla-scented racemes of golden-yellow flowers in profusion.

C. fistulosa. It makes a tree about 7.5 m (25 ft) tall and is widely planted on roads. The bark is ash-coloured and the compound leaves, often 37 cm (15 in) long, are deep green. Each leaf is divided into 4 to 8 pairs of opposite leaflets about 10 cm (4 in) in length. The erect branches of the tree distinguish it from the other species of Cassia which have drooping branches. The flowers are borne in drooping racemes up to 45 cm (18 in) long, each flower being held on a 5-cm (2-in) stalk. The flowers are golden-yellow with a calyx of 5 sepals folding back, whilst the 5 petals are oval in shape and are veined with green. The 10 thread-like stamens are crowned with brown anthers but 3 stamens are about twice the length of the others and curl back in a most attractive manner. They diffuse the delicious laburnum perfume.

The flowers are followed by pods as straight as a reed pipe which may be 90 cm (3 ft) in length. Each pod contains up to 100 seeds covered by a sweet brown pulp which in Bengal is used to flavour tobacco. The pods hang on the tree until the leaves begin to fall.

The tree is leafless only during March when the leaves fall, to be almost immediately replaced by new ones with which the flowers appear and last until the end of June or later.

CASTANOPSIS (Fagaceae—Beech Tree Family)

A genus of 120 species of evergreen trees or shrubs, closely allied to the Sweet chestnut (*Castanea*) and distributed throughout tropical Asia, with one species in north-western America. The catkins are borne upright and, as in *Pasania,* have an unpleasant hawthorn-like smell to attract Diptera (midges) for their pollination.

Species. *Castanopsis chrysophylla.* This forms a leafy bush in cultivation although in its native habitat it may reach 30 m (100 ft) as a tree. It is found in north-western America, where it grows on acid soils. The fruit is a nut, covered with a prickly coat.

C. delavayi. An extremely attractive evergreen tree reaching 15 m (50 ft), with silvery-grey or whitish under-surfaces to the leaves. The male flowers are in yellow spikes, the females in catkins, both up to 12 cm (5 in) long.

CATALPA (Bignoniaceae—Bignonia Family)

Valuable in that they provide fragrant blossom in late summer are the Catalpas, of which the hardiest is *C. bignonioides,* native of North America though it is known as the Indian Bean tree. They are trees of noble stature but in northern Europe require the partial shelter afforded by other, more hardy trees, when they will attain a height of 15 m (50 ft). A rich loamy soil suits them best. The flowers are borne in forked panicles at the end of the branches and they appear towards the end of July or early in August.

Species. *Catalpa bignonioides.* It bears white tubular flowers, speckled with purple and gold in the throat, and they are followed by long cylindrical seed-pods, hence its name of Cigar tree. The blooms have a sweet perfume. The broad heart-shaped leaves, hairy on the underside, are attractively scented when bruised.

C. kaempferi. Most fragrant are the small, clear-yellow flowers, spotted with brown. It is a Japanese species, hardy in Britain only in the South-west. In its native country, the flowers are considered the most valuable of all as honey producers.

Once established in a rich loamy soil, the trees soon attain a height of 9 m (30 ft) and more, their attractive heart-shaped leaves being downy on the underside and giving them a striking appearance even when not in bloom. They have an aromatic fragrance when pressed.

CATASETUM (Orchidaceae—Orchid Family)

A genus of epiphytic orchids with large pseudo-bulbs native to tropical America and the West Indies. An interesting characteristic is that the male and female flowers are borne separately and are often completely different within each species; they may also be produced at different times of the year. Little is known about them, although they are some of the most attractive orchids. They are easily grown in well-drained pots of osmunda fibre, and a warm humid atmosphere. After flowering they require a long rest.

Species. *Catasetum warscewiczii* (syn. *C. scurra*). A low-growing species, this has whitish or greenish-white flowers in summer and autumn on a drooping spike, long-lived and with a strong lemon fragrance. A pretty orchid, it comes from Panama and Brazil and is well worth growing.

CATTLEYA (Orchidaceae—Orchid Family)

A genus of 65 species, native to Mexico, tropical America and the West Indies. They are epiphytic plants, closely related to *Laelia,* and in cultivation require a temperature of about 16°C (60°F). When planting, over-potting must be guarded against for the roots must be able to utilize excess moisture. Half fill the pots with crocks, over which is placed a layer of sphagnum moss, raising the plants just above the rim. Around the plants work in a mixture of peat and moss, pressing it firmly. Planting should be done when the plants begin to make new growth. Take care not to over-water, and give moisture only when necessary; when resting, give only sufficient to prevent the bulbs from shrivelling.

Species. *Cattleya citrina.* As it grows downwards, it is best suspended in a basket from the roof of a greenhouse. It forms 2 glaucous leaves from which arise the golden-yellow flowers, white at the margin of the lip in autumn and spring, and they have the unusual scent of lime fruits.

C. quadricolor (syn. *C. chocoensis*). Sometimes considered a variety of *C. labiata,* this is a white, purple and yellow orchid, with a frilled lip, smelling strongly of ripe plums. Flowering time is December to February, and the flowers, although quite large, never open completely; they are bell-shaped.

C. schroederae. Spring-flowering, with a strong fragrance of almonds, this is a large-flowered species with light-rose sepals and petals and an orange throat. It grows to a height of about 30 cm (1 ft).

C. walkeriana (syn. *C. bulbosa*). A species with short stems but large flowers of purple-rose, with a yellowish lip. Flowering time is February to May. The vanilla fragrance is very strong and lasting.

C. warscewiczii (syn. *C. gigas*). The rosy-mauve to crimson flowers of this species are most handsome particularly with the yellow markings on the throat. Flowering time is summer. It has the fragrance of violets.

CEANOTHUS (Rhamnaceae—Buckthorn Family)

A genus of about 30 species of beautiful, mostly evergreen but also deciduous, shrubs. Mostly natives of California, they have become known as the Californian lilacs for they bear their flowers in dense sprays like smaller editions of the Common lilac. Unfortunately, few bear scented flowers.

Not quite hardy in the British Isles, the plants are usually grown against a sunny wall and are grouped with climbing plants. In the open, however, they form densely rounded bushes and are happy in almost all soil types, especially so in a limestone or chalky soil which accentuates the vivid blue colouring of the flowers of many species. They are propagated by layering the flexible young shoots or by cuttings of the half-ripened wood.

Species. *Ceanothus* Gloire de Versailles. One of a number of gorgeous deciduous hybrids of *C. americanus* and *C. azureus* but the only one bearing fragrant flowers. Against a wall it grows up to 6 m (20 ft) high, but only about half that height in the open, and throughout late summer and autumn, it bears large powder-blue panicles which have a soft sweet perfume.

C. incanus. An evergreen growing 1.2 m (4 ft) in height with thorny branches which are an unusual whitish-grey colour. It blooms in April, bearing small trusses of creamy-white flowers which are sweetly scented.

CEDRELA (Meliaceae—Mahogany Family)

A small genus of trees, native of tropical Africa, China and the West Indies, which are valuable for the timber they yield. In the family is the true Mahogany, *Swietenia mahagoni,* and the cedarwoods of commerce which have an incense-like perfume.

Species. *Cedrela sinensis.* The Chinese Mahogany tree, the 'father' tree on account of its longevity. It is also the Chinese Incense tree for its wood is burnt as incense in the temples whilst its long panicles of pure-white blossoms diffuse a powerfully sweet scent. It is a tree growing 15 m (50 ft) tall with large handsome leaves which are deciduous.

C. odorata. Native of the West Indies where it makes a tall tree and yields the cedarwood of commerce, used in the manufacture of cigar boxes.

CEDRONELLA (Labiatae—Lavender Family)

Closely related to *Dracocephalum*, this is a small genus of the northern temperate regions. They may be hardy or not quite hardy in the British Isles, but in the most favourable districts some survive all but the most severe winters if given the protection of a warm wall. The plants require a rich sandy loam, to which some peat or leaf-mould has been added, and they are happiest in partial shade.

Species. *Cedronella cana.* This is an erect evergreen growing to 90 cm (3 ft) tall, which also has fragrant leaves, and very bright purple or dark-red flowers in spikes during July. It is quite hardy and can be increased by division.

C. triphylla. This is better known, though incorrectly, as the Balm of Gilead, and is a shrubby perennial growing 0.9 to 1.2 m (3 to 4 ft) high, with lance-shaped, ternate leaves which emit a powerful odour when bruised, likened by some to lemon, to others camphor. It blooms in July, its white or pale-mauve flowers being borne in loose terminal whorls. It is also known as *Dracocephalum canariense*, and is a delightful plant for a warm greenhouse.

CEDRUS (Pinaceae—Pine Tree Family)

A genus of four species, native of North Africa, Lebanon and the western Himalayas, being amongst the most noble of all evergreens and reaching enormous proportions. Indeed, the name is derived from an Arabic word denoting strength.

Species and Varieties. *Cedrus atlantica.* The Atlas cedar, native of the Atlas Mountains of North Africa, with cones resembling those of the Cedar of Lebanon. It makes a dense, closely branched tree of pyramidal form. *C. glauca* is even finer

and, with its blue foliage, is known as the Blue cedar.

C. deodara. The Indian cedar, native to the western Himalayas, which did not reach Britain until 1731. In its native haunts it always grows in almost soil-less rocky formations, and on the cold northerly side of mountains, which will give some idea of its hardiness. It is perhaps the most beautiful of all coniferous trees, with gracefully drooping branches almost to the ground, and forming an elegant pyramid of soft grey-green. It was completely hardy in my north-east coastal garden of England and grows at the rate of about 45 cm (1½ ft) a year.

C. libani. It is native of the Lebanon and attains a height of 36 m (120 ft). To the ancients it was one of the most precious commodities for its wood is extremely durable and its fragrance transcends that of all other woods. The Temple of Solomon, begun by David, was made entirely of it, and over a quarter of a million men were used to plunder the great forests of the Lebanon to satisfy the needs of the builders. It was used to make the cases for Egyptian mummies, and objects found in Egyptian tombs and made of cedar still retain the delicious fragrance after 3,000 years.

Cedars prefer a well-drained rich soil and are not quick growers. Cones are not produced until the trees are at least 40 years old. Seed is sown in spring from two-year-old cones, and the seedlings transplanted a year later.

CELERY: *see* APIUM

CELSIA (Scrophulariaceae—Foxglove Family)

A genus of about 30 species of tall-growing biennial plants which are closely allied to the mulleins, the flowers being borne in short spikes at the ends of the shoots. They are native to southern Europe and in Britain require a warm garden. They are best treated as biennials, sown in a cold frame in August and planted in their flowering quarters in May. Only one species has pronounced fragrance.

Species. *Celsia cretica.* A native of the southern Mediterranean it is a most handsome plant for the back of a border where it attains a height of 1.5 m (5 ft). The lower leaves are downy and oblong, the upper leaves serrated, and it blooms during July and August. The flowers, which measure more than 5 cm (2 in) across, are bright yellow with a maroon blotch at the base of the petals and they diffuse the delicious scent of ripe pine-apple.

CENTAUREA (Gentianaceae—Gentian Family)

A genus of more than 600 species, few of which are plants of garden merit whilst fewer still have any degree of perfume. Of the several annual (or biennial) species, only *Centaurea moschata* (syn. *C. odorata*) has perfumed flowers. This is the plant we know as the Sweet Sultan, a native of the Middle East which reached England early in the seventeenth century by way of Turkey (hence its country name) and the overland route to Paris. It was known to Parkinson who said that 'it was a stranger of much beauty . . . and of so exceeding a sweet scent that it surpasseth the finest civet there is . . .'.

Species and Varieties. *Centaurea moschata.* The Sweet Sultan, named in honour of the Sultan of Constantinople, bears thistle-like flowers in shades of purple, lilac, yellow and white. The plants grow about 60 cm (2 ft) tall and are raised by sowing seed where they are to bloom, early in spring. The plants bloom from July until October and diffuse the musk-like perfume of the East.

The Giant Sweet Sultans are amongst the most conspicuous plants of the garden. These are varieties of *C. imperialis*, said to be obtained from *C. moschata* and the vigorous form *C. margaritae* whose large white flowers are the most richly perfumed of all and which has passed on its size and much of its scent to the varieties of *C. imperialis*.

There is another form of *C. moschata*, now known as *C. suaveolens*, native of the Near East, which grows 45 cm (18 in) tall and bears powerfully scented flowers of citron-yellow. It is the Yellow Sweet Sultan, known in earlier times as *Amberboa odorata*, the blooms being enhanced by the brilliant-green foliage.

C. minus (syn. *Erythraea centaurium*).

The Common centaury which is widespread in the British Isles and northern Europe, usually present on sand-dunes. It is a hairless annual growing 25 cm (10 in) tall, the pale-pink flowers borne in terminal clusters. The plant is entirely scentless but if the stems are cut and immersed in warm water for 24 hours, a most penetrating odour will be observed upon distillation, and will yield a thin oil which is greenish in colour and agreeably scented.

CENTRANTHUS (Valerianaceae— Valerian Family)

A genus of 10 species of ornamental plants which flourish in ordinary soil and often grow on the walls of old buildings, where they have their roots in the mortar.

Species. *Centranthus ruber*, the Red valerian, a native of Europe and naturalized in Britain. It grows 60 to 90 cm (2 to 3 ft) tall and has lance-shaped leaves. It blooms from July until September, bearing its crimson or white flowers in dense corymbs, delightful to behold but with an unpleasant smell of perspiration.

CENTROSEMA (Leguminosae— Laburnum Family)

A genus of 45 species of climbing plants, native to North and South America.

Species. *Centrosema grandiflora.* A half-hardy perennial climber, native of central South America, which should be given greenhouse protection in northern Europe and the British Isles. It blooms in June, covering itself with delightful inverted pea-shaped flowers of about 5-cm (2-in) diameter which have the appearance of small butterflies, hence its name of the Butterfly Pea. The colour is rosy-mauve with a broad feathered white marking through the centre, whilst the back of the flower is pure white. They have the vanilla-like odour of the family and when in water remain fresh for almost a week.

CEPHALANTHUS (Rubiaceae—Bedstraw Family)

A genus of 17 species, native of the warmer parts of America and Asia.

Species. *Cephalanthus occidentalis.* The

North American Button bush, it is a hardy shrub, requiring the same soil conditions as the azaleas and other peat-loving plants. It attains a height of 1.5 to 1.8 m (5 to 6 ft) and has shining oval leaves which are deciduous. The creamy-yellow flowers appear in August, in small round heads at the end of the shoots, and they possess a soft sweet fragrance like newly mown hay, as do the leaves when dry.

CERADIA (Compositae—Daisy Family)

A genus of about 150 species of low-growing shrubs, native of South Africa and tropical Asia. Most species have tuberous roots and thick, fleshy lobed leaves. The flowers are white or yellow.

Species. *Ceradia furcata* (syn. *Othonna furcata*). A low-growing South African shrub bearing yellow flowers. From its leaves and stems, an oily resinous substance is exuded which smells like myrrh. When the lower leaves and branches are walked upon, the fragrance released scents the air around and is especially pronounced at nightfall.

CERASTIUM (Caryophyllaceae—Pink Family)

A genus of about 65 species distributed throughout the temperate world and mostly perennial plants with narrow downy or hairy leaves and bearing their flowers in terminal forked cymes. The plants are hardy and grow almost anywhere, on the rockery, on grassy banks and as an edging to a border, for they are not particular as to soil and, being in most cases evergreen, are most valuable. They are propagated by division in spring or by cuttings taken and inserted into shady beds of sandy soil early in June when they will root by the end of July.

Species. *Cerastium tomentosum.* Native of southern Europe, it is sufficiently hardy to be planted in the most exposed gardens of the British Isles where it will spread rapidly. The small leaves, in shape like a mouse's ear, are densely covered in white down and the flowers are borne in cymes on erect 15-cm (6-in) stems. They appear during June and July and are white, with grey-green lines down the inside of the petals, possibly as a guide for pollinating insects. The whole plant has a greyish-white appearance, hence its name of Snow-in-summer. Contrary to popular belief the flowers emit a pleasant mossy scent, like that of the primrose.

CERATOPETALUM (Cunoniaceae— Cunona Family)

A genus of four species, confined entirely to Australia and represented mostly in Queensland. They are small trees or shrubs with opposite trifoliate leaves, serrated at the edges, and small white flowers which turn red after pollination.

Species. *Ceratopetalum gummiferum.* In its native Australia it is known as Christmas Bush, a name given to *Bursaria spinosa* in Tasmania. It is almost entirely confined to coastal inlets and to the Dividing Range where, during December, the plants are a mass of bloom borne in dense cymes. After pollination, the calyx lobes enlarge and turn pinky-red, and in a short time the plant is one mass of brilliant red against the glossy dark-green leaves which are pleasantly aromatic.

CERINTHE (Honeywort) (Boraginaceae—Forget-me-not Family)

A genus of 10 species of annual (or perennial) plants which are natives of south-eastern Europe. The plants are readily raised from seed sown in April where they are to bloom.

Species. *Cerinthe minor.* Known as the Honeywort, it is a wild flower of the fields of south-eastern Europe, the honey juice contained in the flower tubes being a great attraction to bees. The plant grows 30 cm (12 in) tall, the heart-shaped leaves being covered in tiny white warts, whilst the tubular flowers are pale yellow and have purple-brown markings on the tube. They carry a rich honey-like perfume.

CEROPEGIA (Asclepiadaceae— Stephanotis Family)

A genus of 160 species, native of tropical and South Africa; South-east Asia, and Queensland, which are of trailing habit. They have a tuberous rootstock and, usually, fleshy stems. They may be grown in a warm greenhouse and trained over the roof; their leafless stems and strikingly beautiful lantern- or funnel-shaped blooms are of interest, but they give off an unpleasant smell, their means of attracting flies for pollination. The insects are trapped upon entering, unable to leave because of the downward-pointing hairs. Though the plant is not classed as carnivorous, the flies rarely go free after pollination for they have to wait a considerable time before the hairs wither to permit their escape.

Species. *Ceropegia sandersoni.* It is native of Natal and the coastal regions of West Africa and Madagascar, and is a plant of erect, twining habit with leafless stems. The flowers are purplish-green and are funnel-shaped, about 7 cm (3 in) long with 5 points which arch over the tube to give protection from rain or to prevent the escape of pollinating insects. They emit a disagreeable smell, like decaying meat.

CESTRUM (Solanaceae—Nightshade Family)

A genus of about 150 species, native of tropical America, the West Indies and the South Pacific Islands, where they may have been introduced. They are herbs or shrubs with simple, alternate leaves, and some have scented flowers.

Species. *Cestrum parqui.* A half-hardy Chilean shrub suitable for growing against a warm wall in the most favourably situated gardens of Europe and the British Isles where it will attain a height of 2.4 m (8 ft). It is deciduous, flowering during June and July, its tubular blossoms of greenish-yellow appearing in terminal panicles; they are fragrant at night, the perfume becoming more pronounced with the fall in temperature.

CHAMAECYPARIS (Pinaceae—Pine Tree Family)

Members of the Pine Tree family which have flat branches and small cones have been grouped together to distinguish them from the Cypress which has rounded branches and larger cones. The foliage of several species is noticeable for its pungent, resinous scent.

Species and Varieties. *Chamaecyparis lawsoniana.* Lawson's Cypress, though native to California, was so called because it was first grown from seed in Britain by Lawson of Edinburgh. The dark-green glossy foliage with its pungent smell is glaucous and appears in drooping branchlets, whilst the cones, no larger than peas, are borne in profusion. The yellow variety *lutea*, is extremely beautiful. The following are amongst the best of many lovely varieties:

C.l. allumii. One of the strongest and hardiest of all the cypress family, growing to a point and with blue-green foliage.

C.l. erecta viridis. Of neat, erect habit with vivid foliage, it is kept in shape by shortening the branches each spring.

C.l. fletcheri. It makes a spire-like tree with moss-like foliage of silvery-green. A most excellent variety, but it will become bare at the base if not protected from cold winds.

C.l. fraseri. It makes a tall spire with blue-green foliage and is of rapid growth.

GOLDEN KING. Of deeper colour than *C.l. stewartii,* which is also golden, the branch tips droop whilst those of *C.l. stewartii* are upright. The foliage is most resinous to the touch.

C.l. pottenii. Of pyramidal habit, its feathery foliage is a lovely sea-green.

C.l. SOMERSET. A beautiful cypress of unusual form raised at the Royal Nurseries of John Scott at Merriott. It forms a narrow column of great height, the pale-green foliage having the appearance of being tinged with gold-leaf.

C.l. stewartii. The most richly golden of all the *cupressus,* it forms a pyramid of closely set side-shoots.

C.l. TRIOMPHE DE BOSKOOP. One of the best of the family, it makes a dense pyramid of silvery-green with the tips of its branches drooping gracefully.

C. leylandii. Raised from *Chamaecyparis nootkatensis* × *Cupressus macrocarpa,* it is the most popular of all the coniferous evergreens, making a specimen tree of almost columnar habit which is valuable for a hedge or screen. As it is tolerant of a calcareous soil and a salt-laden atmosphere, it is the best form for coastal planting, being hardier than *C. macrocarpa.* Its feathery foliage of palest green has the same sweet, resinous scent as that of its parents.

Use pot-grown plants and for a hedge, set them 60 to 90 cm (2 to 3 ft) apart. If kept watered during dry weather, they will grow 1.2 m (4 ft) tall in two to three years. To encourage bushy growth, trim back 15 cm (6 in) in April each year.

C. nootkatensis. The Nootka or Yellow Cypress of Alaska and Oregon. It makes a tall tree of large girth and is distinguished from Lawson's Cypress by its more drooping branchlets. *Argenteo-variegata* has foliage splashed with cream whilst that of *lutea* is suffused with yellow. The variety *pendula* with its long pendant branches is one of the most graceful of all evergreens, whilst the hybrid (from a cross with Lawson's Cypress) *nidifera* makes a low blue-green bush with its branches radiating horizontally. All release a smell of turpentine when the foliage is pressed.

C. obtusa. The Hinoki Tree of Japan, with very dark-green foliage, much slower in growth than *C. lawsoniana.* Most of the numerous forms are miniature in habit and best grown in the rock garden or in pots.

C. pisifera. The Japanese Sarawa Cypress, it resembles Lawson's Cypress, but has a more open habit. *Aurea* is a beautiful golden-leaf form.

CHAMAEDAPHNE (Ericaceae—Heather Family)

A small genus of evergreen shrubs with alternate, shortly stalked leaves, which bear their flowers in the axils of the upper leaves. They do best in a porous soil, and preferably not in a position which catches the midday sun. Layers, cuttings or seed are used for increase.

Species. *Chamaedaphne calyculata* (syn. *Andromeda calyculata*). A swamp shrub of the State of Virginia and of eastern Canada, growing 30 to 60 cm (2 to 3 ft) tall, with leathery, oblong leaves which are as if rusted on the underside. The flowers are produced early in spring, appearing at the axils of the upper leaves and are white, tinted with pink, in form like those of lily of the valley, and they carry a similar delicate and refreshing scent. *Angustifolia,* with its waved leaves, closely resembles *C.*

calyculata and may be a variety. It has similar, scented flowers.

CHEILANTHES (Sinopteridaceae— Sinopteris Family)

A genus of about 180 species, native of tropical and warm temperate regions.

Species. *Cheilanthes fragrans* (syn. *Polypodium fragrans*). A little gem of a fern, native of southern Europe where it grows amongst stones. It is suitable for greenhouse culture, requiring a minimum winter temperature of 10°C (50°F). The deep-green fronds are tinted with orange, and when handled emit a scent of newly-mown hay, owing to the presence of coumarin, which becomes more pronounced as the fronds become dry. *C. odora,* native of Madeira, has similar attractions.

CHEIRANTHUS (Wallflower) (Cruciferae—Wallflower Family)

A small genus of perennial or biennial herbs, amongst which is *Cheiranthus cheiri,* the wallflower which, though perennial, is usually treated as a biennial, the seed being sown in May each year for the plants to bloom in the early summer of the following year.

Species. *Cheiranthus cheiri.* The wallflower is a member of the same 4-petalled family as the Stock and Sweet rocket whose flowers are amongst the most powerfully scented of all, though most plants of the family are scentless. The scent of the wallflower, similar to that of the pink and carnation, earned for it the name of (Wall) Gillyflower, a name used also for the Stock and Sweet rocket. Indeed, the scent of the stock and wallflower are so similar that the wallflower was known to Gerard as the Yellow Stock-gillyflower, though Parkinson and William Lawson, writing about the same time, referred to it as the 'Wall-gilloflower'. Parkinson described seven kinds, including the double red and double yellow. He said that 'the sweetness of the flowers causeth them to be used in nosegays and to deck up houses'. So common was the wallflower for use as a nosegay that it was given its botanical name *Cheiranthus*, which means 'hand-flower'.

It is native to central Europe and not to the British Isles, though it has long been nationalized there and no plant is more representative of an English cottage garden. It was well known to Elizabethan gardeners who on account of its sweet perfume called it the chevisaunce, an old English word meaning 'comforter'.

Robert Ingram, gardener to the Duke of Rutland, would raise his seedlings over a slate bed so as to prevent their forming a large tap-root. To encourage the plants to build up a fibrous rooting system he would sow the seed in a bed of prepared soil in April, transplant in June and again in August, each time pinching out any tap-roots and the growing point to encourage bushy growth. The plants were in their flowering quarters, planted 22 cm (9 in) apart, by early October so that they would become established before the first hard frosts In growing wallflowers, we cannot improve upon the methods of this famous Scottish gardener. A common cause of failure with wallflowers is to sow the seed too late.

There are today many lovely varieties and strains, all bearing powerfully scented flowers, the double-flowered being even more pronounced in scent whilst the flowers are very long-lasting in the garden. *See also* **ERYSIMUM.**

CHENOPODIUM (Chenopodiaceae—Beetroot Family)

A genus of about 50 species of mostly annual herbs, native of sub-tropical regions, with alternate flat leaves which in several species emit a most disagreeable odour. They usually grow on the banks of rivers and canals and are a maritime order.

Species. *Chenopodium ambrodioides.* It has yellow-green leaves which when pressed yield an unpleasant fetid odour.

C. botrys. The deeply cut leaves emit an agreeable aromatic smell when handled.

C. vulvularia. A low-growing plant which bears its flowers in axillary clusters. Its rhomboid leaves of pale green have the smell of decaying fish, hence its name of Stinking goosegrass.

CHERVIL: *see* ANTHRISCUS

CHIAPASIA (Cactaceae—Cactus Family)

A genus of a single species, native of Mexico and closely related to *Epiphyllum.*

Species. *Chiapasia nelsonii.* It is without spines and bears its flowers on the upper areoles. They are funnel-shaped and are carmine-red with carmine stamens and emit the fragrance of violets, remaining open for several days. It requires the same culture as *Epiphyllum.*

CHIMAPHILA (Ericaceae—Heather Family)

A genus of four species of smooth stolon-bearing perennial herbs, by some authorities included in the Pyrolaceae family, closely related to the wintergreen and bearing their fleshy leaves in whorls. The flowers are borne in terminal corymbs and are fragrant. The plants are native to the Northern Hemisphere and are evergreen; with their dwarf, spreading habit this makes them valuable for ground-cover. They are tolerant of shade, but are not, on the whole, easily grown, doing best in a lime-free soil which is fairly damp but well-drained. They can be increased from seed, or by division.

Species. *Chimaphila maculata.* A procumbent North American species, with leathery, lance-shaped leaves striped with white and borne 4 in a whorl. The white-flowers appear in June on downy stalks, and are attractively drooping. They are deliciously scented.

C. umbellata. It makes a spreading plant less than 15 cm (6 in) tall with lance-shaped serrated leaves borne 4 or 5 in a whorl. The flowers appear in June and are greenish-white tinted with red and ‚have a sweet but refreshing perfume.

CHIMONANTHUS (Calycanthaceae—Allspice Family)

A genus of only three species.

Species. *Chimonanthus fragrans.* It was introduced into Britain in 1766 and is closely related to the Carolina Allspice, *Calycanthus floridus.* It was formely known as *Calycanthus praecox,* under which name it was described in *Curtis Botanical Magazine* (1800). It attains a height of 3 m (10 ft) or more, and from mid-December until Easter its leafless twigs are covered with blossoms which have the smell of jonquil and violet. They are borne at the axils of the old leaves. The flowers have 6 middle petals of crimson-brown, backed by 8 petals of ivory-yellow, and their fragrance may be noticed 50 yards away. The leaves, too, are fragrant; pale-green and pointed, they appear when flowering has ended, in April. When the flowers are inhaled close to for any length of time, like the violet, they appear to lose their fragrance.

The plant, which is a native of China, requires a moist, rich soil and a sunny position, away from cold winds. The form *grandiflorus* has larger flowers, 5 cm (2 in) in diameter, of a deeper colour and composed of 20 segments, but is not so fragrant, whilst *luteus* has sepals and petals of clearest yellow and comes later into bloom.

The most satisfactory way to grow the plant is against a wall (like *Camellia sasanqua*), training and tying in the shoots, and it will eventually cover a wall to a height of 3.5 m (12 ft). Increase is by layering, in early spring.

CHIONANTHUS (Oleaceae—Olive Family)

A genus of two species of smooth or downy deciduous shrubs or small trees which bear scented flowers and because of the narrow fringe-like petals, have become known as the Fringe trees. Hardy in almost all parts, they are most handsome when in flower but do not bear blossom until well established.

Species. *Chionanthus retusus.* A low-growing Chinese shrub with long-stalked retuse leaves, hairy on the underside. It bears panicles of white flowers during May and June and they are more powerfully scented than those of *C. virginicus.*

C. virginicus. The Fringe tree of the eastern United States and the Snow-flower tree of Texas where it grows 9 m (30 ft) tall but less than half the height in northern European gardens. It has smooth lance-shaped leaves of deep green which turn golden-yellow in autumn, and in June and July bears pure white flowers in drooping racemes. The flowers have a purple spot at the base of each petal and are conspicuous

by their 4 or 5 narrow fringed petals. They have a delicate sweet perfume and are followed by egg-shaped fruits of purple-blue.

In its native lands it is pollinated by the bee, *Samia adunca,* which sweeps the pollen dust into its densly tufted abdomen bristles where it stores it. In other species, this collecting dust is usually in the legs. In Britain and northern Europe, few bees are about when the plants are in bloom.

CHLIDANTHUS (Amaryllidaceae— Narcissus Family)

A genus of a single species.

Species. *Chlidanthus fragrans.* It is a half-hardy plant which in the British Isles flourishes in the open only in the most favourable districts. Elsewhere it should either be grown in pots indoors or the bulbs should be lifted in the autumn after flowering and stored in a frost-free room. Native of the Peruvian Andes, it has a large ovoid bulb and grey-green linear leaves. It blooms in June, before the leaves appear, bearing tubular flowers 7 to 10 cm (3 to 4 in) long in small umbels on a 30-cm (12-in) stem. The blooms are pale yellow, like miniature daffodils, and are powerfully scented, especially when warmed by the sun. The plant received an Award of Merit in 1948 but is comparatively rare in cultivation.

If planted in the open, the bulbs are put in 7 cm (3 in) deep in April, and lifted in October to be stored in a frost-free place. When grown in pots they should be planted singly, 5 cm (2 in) deep in a 12-cm (5-in) pot, in a cool greenhouse. No water should be given after September until repotting.

CHLORANTHUS (Chloranthaceae— Chloranthus Family)

A genus of tropical evergreen under-shrubs or herbaceous plants having jointed stems and opposite simple leaves which are aromatic when handled. The flowers, called *Chu-han* by the Chinese, are also fragrant and are disposed in loose, slender terminal spikes.

Species. *Chloranthus elatior.* Native of China and Korea where it makes a dense shrub 1.8 m (6 ft) tall with scandent branches and oblong-lanceolate leaves. The flowers are yellow and borne in long, slender terminal spikes. All parts of the plant are scented.

C. inconspicuus (syn. *Nigrina spicata*). It grows less than 30 cm (12in) tall and is native of China and Japan, with serrated oblong leaves which have an aromatic perfume whilst the scented flowers are borne in axillary spikes.

C. monostachys. In its native China it makes a shrub 45 cm (18 in) tall with serrated, elliptic leaves. The flowers are yellow and crowded together on the spikes and like the leaves are sweetly scented.

C. officinalis. Native of the higher mountainous regions of Java where it grows 0.9 to 1.2 m (3 to 4 ft) tall with lanceolate leaves whilst the flower spikes are borne in branched terminal spikes. The whole plant is deliciously aromatic and scented.

C. serratus (syn. *Nigrina serratus*). Native of the Japanese mountainous interior where it grows 30 cm (12 in) tall, its oblong leaves are doubly serrated. Its flowers are borne in axillary spikes and are spice-scented.

CHOISYA (Rutaceae—Rue Family)

A genus of six species of small trees or shrubs distributed throughout Mexico, one of which is found in gardens of the British Isles and northern Europe.

Species. *Choisya ternata*. It is known as the Mexican Orange and forms a shrub 1.5 to 3 m (5 to 10 ft) tall with opposite leaves, smooth and glossy and filled with pellucid oil glands which upon pressing release the unmistakable pungent orange scent of the family. In the British Isles and northern Europe it should be confined outside to warm gardens, or it makes a pleasing pot plant for a warm greenhouse, filling the air with the heavy orange-blossom perfume from its large white flowers, produced near the ends of the branches.

CHRYSANTHEMUM (Compositae— Daisy Family)

A genus of about 200 species of annual or perennial plants, usually woody at the base and with alternate leaves, lobed and toothed. The flowers are borne solitary or in loose corymbs.

Species. *Chrysanthemum balsamita*. The Costmary, an Asian plant introduced to the British Isles early in history and known to cottagers as Alecost for it was used to clarify and flavour ale. A perennial, it grows 90 cm (3 ft) tall with entire leaves which have a balsamic scent when pressed, and it bears clusters of bright-yellow flowers in August. It is propagated by root division in spring.

C. haradjanii. A miniature of great beauty, growing less than 15 cm (6 in) tall with silver leaves similar to the feathers of a bird and deliciously pungent when pressed.

C. indicum. The leaves possess the same pungent fragrance, refreshing and lemon-like, similar to that given off by the foliage of the artemisias and camomile of the same family. It is one of the oldest cultivated plants and is native to China and Japan. Confucius mentioned it as long ago as 797. It was taken by the Emperor of Japan, as his emblem, and is represented in the national flag of the country. It was not however, introduced into Britain until the beginning of the nineteenth century, the first plants being cultivated at Kew Gardens in 1790. The Stoke Newington Society, later to become the National Chrysanthemum Society, was founded in 1846.

It was not until 1890 that the first of the large-flowering Japanese varieties reached Britain, by way of Boston, U.S.A., having been sent there by a Japanese boy to a Mrs Hardie, wife of a naval captain who had befriended him as an orphan. Mrs Alpheus Hardie was the first named variety: it was white and was exhibited by Mrs Hardie at the Boston Show in 1888.

C. leucanthenum. Known as the Moon daisy or Ox-Eye daisy, it is one of a genus of annual or perennial plants native of the British Isles with woody stems and attractively toothed leaves. It grows 60 cm (2 ft) in height and frequents meadows and waste ground. It has beautifully cut leaves and blooms from June until September, its pure-white flowers with long-rayed petals and a central boss of gold. Unfortunately, like so many of the 'daisies' which are pollinated by small flies, the flowers have a smell of stale perspiration when inhaled.

C. parthenium. The Giant Featherfew, native of northern Europe which makes a bushy plant 60 cm (2 ft) tall and has refreshing aromatic foliage which is deeply cut and lobed. According to Parkinson, an infusion was taken once a month by women. Today, the leaves are dried and placed amongst clothes in muslin bags to keep away moths. The small flowers are white, those of the double form, *flore pleno*, being like small white buttons. The plants are generally raised from seed sown in spring and at one time were widely grown for the cut-flower trade and for summer bedding.

C. poterifolium. A delightful plant for edging for it grows only 15 cm (6 in) tall, its leaves reminiscent of leaves of the date-palm and profusely silvered. It is one of the most exquisite of silver-leaf plants and emits a lemon-like fragrance when handled.

CIMICIFUGA (Bugwort)
(Ranunculaceae—Buttercup Family)

A genus of ornamental herbaceous plants, mostly native of America and northern Europe, which, with one exception, bear white flowers in racemes and have a most unpleasant smell.

The plants prefer a moist soil and a semi-shaded situation. In medieval times, the leaves were used to drive away bugs from buildings, hence the name bugwort.

Species. *Cimicifuga americana.* This species is the only one to bear sweetly scented flowers, though some species are less unpleasant than others. It grows 0.9 to 1.2 m (3 to 4 ft) in height with tripinnate leaves and blooms later than other species, bearing its handsome, feathery panicles of creamy-white flowers during August and September, and they have a pleasant sweet perfume.

C. elata. Native of North America and Siberia, it grows 66 cm (2 ft) tall with ternate or biternate leaves which give off an evil smell. The panicled racemes of white flowers which appear in June also have an unpleasant smell, resembling that of skunk.

C. foetida. Native of northern Europe, it grows 90 cm (3 ft) tall with tripinnate leaves, and in July bears panicles of white flowers which emit the obnoxious smell of decaying fish; the green seed-pods have a similar smell. From a distance it is a most

handsome plant yet is amongst the most evil smelling of all.

CINNAMODENDRON (Canellaceae—Canella Family)

A genus of sub-tropical trees grown for the commercial value of their bark and closely related to *Canella*. They are native of Brazil and Jamaica.

Species. *Cinnamodendron axillare.* Native of Brazil it yields a bark with similar properties to *Canella alba.* It grows 6 m (20 ft) tall with smooth white bark which cracks transversely. The leaves are elliptic, smooth and leathery. The flowers are axillary, nodding, and have 3 bracts and 5 petals.

C. corticosum. Found only on the island of Jamaica where it makes a tree of massive stature, growing some 30 m (100 ft) tall and flourishing in the mountainous woods of St John. It was first named and described by Miers in 1838 who allied it to the genus *Canella* from which it differs only in that its flowers are axillary whilst those of *Canella alba* are terminal. Its bark does, however, contain tannin which is absent in *C. alba,* and though not so pure it has a similar fragrance.

CINNAMOMUM (Lauraceae—Bay Tree Family)

A genus of 250 or so aromatic trees of economic importance, mostly evergreen and native of the damp forests of northern India and Ceylon and South-east Asia, with alternate leaves, simple and entire and containing aromatic oil glands. The flowers are borne in terminal or axillary inflorescences and are pollinated by Diptera.

Species. *Cinnamomum camphora.* Native to southern India, Japan and the islands of the Malayan Archipelago, it makes a tall tree with alternate, glossy leaves and from its wood, cut into chips and boiled, it yields on cooling a white crystalline substance which is the finest form of camphor. The wood was also burnt during epidemics.

In 1885, Messrs Schimmel & Co. of Leipzig discovered the safrol was present in oil of *C. camphora* and that it could be separated in a state of purity. It is this that gives the pleasant smell to many barks, with its undertones of orange and bergamot.

C. cassia. An evergreen growing 6 m (20 ft) high, it yielded the 'cassia' of the Scriptures. All parts of the tree are fragrant. The plant is present in Afghanistan, northern India and western China and yields the cassia oil of commerce. The best oil is obtained from the young bud-stalks but the leaves also yield a brightly coloured distillate with the smell and taste of cinnamon.

The oil was (and in some parts still is) obtained by stripping the trees of bark and boiling it, and from the aromatic juice oil of cassia was obtained by distillation. It is amber-coloured and mostly comes from the Chinese provinces of Kwang-Si and Kwang-Tung. In Palestine and the East, it is mixed with olive oil to rub into the skin and to massage into the scalp.

C. glanduliferum. In its native northern India and western China it makes a tall tree and is evergreen, with broad leathery leaves, pale green above, white beneath and covered in pellucid dots. They are pleasantly aromatic when crushed. The bark, known as the Sassafras of Nepal, has the refreshing scent which we associate with cinnamon. It is dark brown and is readily removed from the tree without causing it to die. As the tree becomes older, the strength of the bark's aroma diminishes. Pieces of bark are rolled one inside another and they quickly dry to enable it to be finely ground and mixed with frankincense and myrrh. In the Near East, the bark was used to flavour wines whilst the oil extracted from it was used as a bactericide.

Though requiring a warm climate, the plant may be grown in the British Isles in sheltered gardens of the West and in the southern United States.

C. parthenoxylon. Native of the tropical forests of Sumatra and Java, its bark yields the 'Oriental Sassafras' which has a refreshing lemon-like quality.

C. pedatinervum. It grows 9 m (30 ft) tall with ovate leaves 15 cm (6 in) long of palest green, glossy on the upper surface. It is native of Fiji and the Polynesian Islands where the bark was used for scenting coconut oil.

C. zeylanicum. This is the species which provides most of the commercial product, the bark in powdered form being much used in cookery whilst the essential oil is a powerful bactericide. A native of Ceylon, where the tree grows to a height of 9 to 12 m (30 to 40 ft), it is evergreen, with aromatic leaves.

The bark is smooth and ash coloured whilst the leaves, bright green above and white on the underside, are 22.5 cm (9 in) long; the flowers white. Strips of bark are removed when the trees are about 6 years old, the best grade coming from young branches. Incisions are made lengthwise on both sides of a branch then the bark is removed as a hollow cylinder. It is tied into bundles weighing about 450 g (1 lb). The very finest is obtained from Ceylon where the tree is known as *Korunda guahah*.

Oil of cinnamon is obtained from the fruit or by soaking the bark and then distilling it. It was one of the principal ingredients for the holy oil which Moses was commanded to use in the Tabernacle. In Biblical times, it was imported into Judea by the Phoenicians from India by way of Persia, the caravans meeting at Babylon on their way westwards to Palestine and the Mediterranean.

CINNAMOSMA (Magnoliaceae—Magnolia Family)

A genus of three species, native of Madagascar where *C. odorata* is grown for its aromatic leaves. They are small trees or shrubs found near the coast.

Species. *Cinnamosma odorata.* A small tree with extipulate leaves which when pressed emit the aromatic smell of cinnamon. The flowers are also scented and are borne from the axils of the leaves. The calyx is made up of three sepals and the corolla increases in length as the flower ages.

CISTUS (Cistaceae—Rock Rose Family)

They are amongst the most beautiful of shrubs, being evergreen and mostly with resinous leaves. They are native of the Mediterranean regions, and more especially of Cyprus and the lofty mountains near the town of Baphos. In Britain they need the shelter of a warm garden and in a dry, sandy soil they will be unharmed in all but the severest weather. They are especially happy in a coastal garden where plants may be set on a sunny bank and will scent the air to a considerable distance with their incense perfume. From the glandular hairs of the leaves, a gum is collected which is used in the East as a perfume.

The blooms are single, similar to those of the Wild rose, and though lacking perfume enhance the grey-green foliage.

Plants are readily increased from cuttings of half-ripened wood taken in August and inserted in sandy soil when they will readily root. After rooting, they should be grown on in small pots, as they resent disturbance.

Species. *Cistus aquilari.* The tallest growing of all the cistus, attaining a height of 2.4 m (8 ft) with strongly resinous foliage and bearing large white flowers with a golden eye.

C. cyprius. It abounds in Cyprus, and is a vigorous shrub with leaves of dull grey-green, sticky to the touch. From this species it is said that the purest labdanum is obtained. It grows 1.8 m (6 ft) in height and blooms during May and June, bearing its clear-white flowers in clusters; at the base of each petal is a scarlet spot.

C. elma. A hybrid of extreme hardiness, raised by Captain Collingwood Ingram. It makes a spreading bush with grey-green foliage which is most aromatic and bears large white flowers which have a small yellow centre.

C. ladaniferus. The Gum cistus and a native of Portugal and Spain. It grows 1.2 m (4 ft) in height and has long, narrow leaves, dark green in colour, which are gummy to the touch, especially when young. The leaves release their sweet balsam-like fragrance during the summer, especially early in the morning.

The flowers possess extreme beauty. Opening to 10 cm (4 in) across they are pure white with a crimson blotch at the base of each petal. The variety *Immaculatus,* which also bears pure-white flowers which last well when cut, gained an Award of Merit from the Royal Horticultural Society in 1925.

C. laurifolius. It grows 1.8 m (6 ft) tall and has laurel-like lance-shaped leaves, hairy beneath, and throughout the year they give off an aromatic sweetness. The flowers are white and are borne in clusters during June and July, their pale-green bracts being most ornamental before the buds open.

C. skanbergii. A most beautiful plant with grey, downy foliage which releases a distinct spicy fragrance when rubbed against, whilst its stems smell strongly of cedarwood. It makes a low, spreading bush, its grey foliage enhanced by the flowers of 2.5-cm (1-in) diameter, which are bright rose-pink and, though they retain their beauty only for a day, are quickly replaced by others.

C. villosus. C. creticus, the most prolific source of labdanum, is a mauve-flowered variety of this species of southern Europe which bears flowers of rosy-purple and has leaves which exude balsamic resin, so fragrant during the warm days of summer.

CITRUS (Rutaceae—Rue Family)

A genus of 12 species of small trees or shrubs, often spiny, with alternate leaves in certain species joined to the stem with a winged footstalk. The flowers are extremely fragrant and are white, appearing in never-ending succession at the same time as the fruit.

Native of China and Japan, several species reached the Mediterranean regions at an early date when plantations were established in Palestine, Spain and northern Africa. The plants may be made to fruit in a heated greenhouse in the British Isles, whilst several species will survive a mild winter outdoors in districts enjoying mild climatic conditions.

The blossom most used in perfumery is that obtained from *C. bigarradia,* the Bitter orange, from which the essential oil known as neroli is obtained, one of the chief ingredients of Eau de Cologne. There are several oils present in orange-blossom. The one contained in the secretory glands which occur on the lower surface of the petals or sepals is not pure neroli but is an oil analogous to that of petit-grain; by eliminating these glands in an unopened bud, the orange-like scent of the flower as it expands is in no way diluted. Essential oil is also present in the epidermis of both surfaces of the petals, and even upon the periphery of the petaloid filaments of the stamens. By preventing the liberation of the perfume in the different parts of the flower it has been ascertained that the odour corresponding to that of neroli is produced only on the upper surface of the petals, and that the odour of the flowers is compound. All parts of the tree yield a fragrant oil, that obtained from the leaves being known as petit-grain and from the rind of the fruit, oil of bigarrade.

The largest plantations of *C. bigarradia* are in Spain, France and Sicily where a fully grown tree will yield 22.5 to 27 kg (50 to 60 lb) of blossom in a season. A grove of matured orange trees scents the air for miles around with its rich, spicy perfume.

Though Virgil and Palladius described a plant that may be taken to be the orange, it is believed that this native of the East Indies reached Europe only in the eleventh century, introduced by the Portuguese when orange cultivation became established in the Iberian Peninsula.

The first orange to be grown in Italy was said to have been planted in Rome by St Dominic in the year 1200. In France, the oldest known tree was that which grew in the orangery at Versailles until a century ago, raised from seed obtained in 1421 by the Queen of Navarre. But it was not until 1595 that the orange came to be planted in England, in the garden of Sir Thomas Carew at Beddington, from seed obtained in Spain by Carew and Raleigh some years before. According to Philip Miller, the orange trees at Beddington 'always bore fruit in great plenty and perfection; they grew on the south side of a wall, not nailed against it but at full liberty to spread . . . and there they lived until entirely killed by the great frost of 1740'.

With the orange, use is made of its scent in the dissemination of the seeds, the fruit having only a faint scent until the seeds are ripe when its essential oil develops a sweet, aromatic quality which, though attractive to the nose, has a burning taste. This acts as a deterrent to insects but not to birds which tear apart the fruits, thereby scattering the bitter seeds.

Species. *Citrus aurantium.* The Seville orange of Spain and Portugal which grows 1.2 to 1.3 m (4 to 5 ft) tall, its oblong leaves having a winged stalk. The flowers are white and sweetly scented and are followed by small sour fruits with a reddish-orange skin, used to make Oil of Portugal.

C. bigarradia. Its blossoms are those most used in the making of perfume, its essential oil being one of the chief ingredients of Eau de Cologne. It makes a small bushy tree with large creamy-white flowers which drench the surrounding air with a delicious perfume.

Neroli derives its name from Flavio Orsini, Prince of Nerola, who was of a wealthy Roman family in the sixteenth century, and whose second wilfe found the distillate greatly to her liking.

Eau de Cologne consists of otto of neroli mixed with otto of rosemary and bergamot, this being obtained from the Bergamo orange which grew around the town of that name. The otto is obtained from the rind of the pear-shaped fruit and mixed with rectified spirit to form 'extract of bergamot'. The finest Eau de Cologne is made, like the best Cognac, with grape spirit.

C. ichangense. Native of the highlands of south-western China, it grows about 90 cm (3 ft) tall, its narrow leaves having winged stalks. The heavily scented flowers are white and are followed by lemon-shaped fruits of excellent flavour.

C. limon. The lemon of commerce which makes a neat spiny tree with small toothed leaves. It bears its tiny white flowers, shaded with pink on the outside, in clusters and these are followed by bright-yellow fruits, mentioned by Shakespeare, which are extremely sour.

C. limonia mayeri. It is known as the Chinese lemon and makes an ideal and easily manageable pot plant, never exceeding a height of 50 cm (20 in) and growing dense and bushy. It blooms in profusion, the white blossom being attractively tinted with pink and it gives off a heavy, jonquil-like perfume. The blossom is followed by tiny lemon-like fruits which have the full lemon flavour. It is known as Meyer's lemon and is possibly the hardiest of all the citrus species.

C. maxima. The Grapefruit, bearing the largest of all the citrus fruits and making a tree 1.8 m (6 ft) tall with large glossy leaves. The small white flowers are not as heavily scented as those of the other citrus species but are sweet and pleasant and are followed by large pale-yellow fruits of between 15 to 20 cm (6 to 8 in) diameter, flattened at one end.

C. medica. A small spiny tree with a stalk that is not 'winged'. The flowers are large, some being 7.5 to 10 cm (3 to 4 in) across and are shaded with purple on the underside. Extremely fragrant, the flowers are followed by long, narrow fruits which have a lemon-coloured skin, used in candying. This fruit is known as the Citron lemon.

C. nobilis. The Tangerine orange of China which makes a small spineless tree, the oblong leaves having a narrow winged stalk. The white flowers are small but powerfully scented and are followed by sweet, aromatic fruits of brilliant orange with a loose skin.

C. taitensis. Known as the Otaheite orange, it makes a small bushy plant after the style of Meyer's lemon, covered in an abundance of white blooms of outstanding perfume. The flowers are followed by small oranges which begin to colour in October, reaching perfection by the year end, thus making it a most decorative winter glasshouse plant.

C. trifoliata. Native of Japan, it makes a woody shrub 1.2 m (4 ft) tall and has trifoliate leaves. The fragrant white flowers, which appear before the leaves, are produced during April and May and are followed by small orange-yellow fruits. It has proved capable of surviving a mild winter in the British Isles.

This species has given rise to a hybrid, *C. americana*, from a crossing with *C. auranticum*.

CLADANTHUS (Compositae—Daisy Family)

A genus of four species of annual plants, native of southern Spain and north-western Africa and closely related to *Tagetes* with the same degree of hardiness. The plants should be treated as half hardy in northern Europe and North America, the seed being sown under glass in February and the young plants moved to the open ground during May when hardened. They bear masses of bright golden-yellow flowers from mid-June until the end of October.

Species. *Cladanthus arabicus.* Though rarely seen in gardens, it is one of the longest-flowering of all summer annuals and makes a colourful display, planted in groups in the border or in beds to themselves. It grows 60 cm (2 ft) tall with masses of feathery brilliant-green foliage and bears golden-yellow flowers about 5 cm (2 in) across, like yellow pyrethrums. Both the foliage and the flowers have a refreshingly aromatic scent. It requires a light sandy soil and an open sunny situation.

CLADRASTIS (Leguminosae—Laburnum Family)

A genus of four species of small ornamental trees with flowers emitting the soft vanilla perfume of the family. The plants grow well in a sandy loam, and are propagated from imported seeds, or by root cuttings.

Species. *Cladrastis amurensis* (syn. *Maackia amurensis*). The Chinese 'Yellow Wood', native of the Amur Valley, is not so hardy as *C. lutea* and should be confined to a warm, sheltered garden where it will grow to a height of 2.4 to 3 m (8 to 10 ft). Its leaves are composed of 4 pairs of oblong leaflets and it blooms during August, the small greenish-white flowers with their soft vanilla scent being borne in long erect racemes.

C. lutea (syn. *Virgilia lutea*). Native of North America where it is known as the Yellow Wood, it makes a small tree, the smooth pinnate leaves having 7 to 11 ovate leaflets. It blooms in May, bearing its scented, white flowers in drooping racemes.

CLAUSENA (Rutaceae—Rue Family)

A genus of 30 species of small trees or shrubs, native of South-east Asia and Africa. Closely related to *Citrus*, all parts of the plant are scented.

Species. *Clausena anistata.* It is present about the savannah country of Kenya and East Africa and is armed with spines for its protection. Growing up to 1.8 m (6 ft) tall, it has leaves and twigs which smell strongly of aniseed when crushed. The natives make use of the twigs to pull through their teeth to clean them. As with other members of the family, the leaves contain a volatile oil which is contained in tiny glands on the surface. The white flowers, borne in clusters, are also scented.

CLEMATIS (Ranunculaceae—Buttercup Family)

A genus of shrubby plants which climb by means of their leaf stalks and have opposite leaves without stipules. The calyx consists of 4 or more petal-like sepals with no corolla. Fruit is a head of sessile or stalked achenes with long awns or styles which adds to the winter beauty of several species. One species, *Clematis vitalba*, Traveller's Joy or Virgin's Bower, is native to the British Isles, particularly to the chalky South-east. Gerard mentions that it was common in every hedgerow from Gravesend to Canterbury 'making a goodly shadow' beneath which travellers could rest, 'thereupon have I named it Traveller's Joy'. In an Anglo-Saxon vocabulary of the eleventh century it is called 'Viticella-woodebinde'.

The word clematis is derived from the Greek *klema*, meaning 'vine branch', probably because it resembles the vine in climbing by means of tendrils. The plants are always happiest in the company of other plants to which they look for support and possibly for protection from cold winds. They love to have their roots in lime rubble and appreciate an annual mulch of decayed manure.

Unfortunately, few of the many beautiful garden hybrids have scented flowers yet *C. fortunei*, introduced by Robert Fortune early in the nineteenth century, which was widely used in raising the early large-flowered hybrids, had a delicious perfume. The past tense is intentionally used as *C. fortunei* now seems to have disappeared from European gardens and there is no opportunity of using it again in an attempt to breed in its scent.

Species and Varieties. *Clematis afoliata.* Native of New Zealand, it is a most unusual species with leafless stems, and it bears yellow flowers which emit a powerful daphne scent. It is mostly present in South Island, in the country around Christchurch, where it twines up trees and shrubs, with its rush-like stems. The flowers (composed of sepals rather than petals) are tubular and open star-like, with splayed anthers. They are especially scented at night.

In the British Isles, the plant requires a warm wall facing south and should be given the protection of other wall plants. Flowering time is May.

C. armandii. Native of western China, it is an evergreen climber, attaining a height of 7.5 m (25 ft). It is best in a sunny, sheltered situation, in the company of other plants. It has attractive, tripinnate leaves and it blooms during April and May, bearing clusters of three pure-white flowers of sweet perfume. The flowers turn pink with age.

C. cirrhosa. It is evergreen and is said to have been discovered in Spain by the botanist Clusius and to have reached England during Elizabethan times. It grows to a height of 2.4 to 2.7 m (8 to 9 ft) and in a mild area will bloom early in the year and continue until April or May, its bell-shaped flowers of greenish-white having a soft sweet perfume. Gertrude Jekyll tells of seeing this clematis growing near Algiers and of the 'groves of Prickly Pear, wreathed and festooned with the graceful tufts of bell-shaped flowers and polished leaves of *Clematis cirrhosa*'.

C. coerulea odorata. At one time called *C. aromatica* on account of its powerful aromatic perfume. It is a semi-herbaceous species growing 1.2 m (4 ft) in height and throughout summer bears violet-purple flowers about 5 cm (2 in) across with prominent white stamens and with the powerful scent of hawthorn blossoms.

C. crispa. It is a hardy North American evergreen growing 1.2 m (4 ft) tall and it has hard purple wood. It blooms from June to September, its pale lilac-white flowers having a delicate vanilla perfume.

C. davidiana. Known as the Abbé David's Clematis, like *C. coerulea* it is a herbaceous species, native of China, with large leaves and growing 1.2 m (4 ft) tall. It also blooms from August to October, when it bears clusters of sweetly scented flowers of bright hyacinth-blue, being one of the few plants of its colour to bear scented flowers. Each year after flowering it should be cut back almost to the ground.

C. eriostemon. Raised at the St John's Wood Nursery of Mr Henderson in 1835, it is possibly a *C. viticella* hybrid to which it has passed on its purple colouring. It reaches a height of 3 m (10 ft) and throughout summer bears nodding violet-purple flowers some 5 cm (2 in) across which have a soft sweet perfume.

C. flammula. Called the Fragrant Virgin's Bower, it reached Britain from Spain early in the seventeenth century. It is one of the beauties of autumn when it bears masses of small creamy-white flowers with the pronounced scent of meadowsweet, almost too powerful to be enjoyable if inhaled near to. It is a vigorous climber, retaining its leaves almost until the year end, and its flowers are followed by fluffy silvery seed-heads. The form rubra-marginata (a hybrid of C. flammula and C. viticella), also bears fragrant flowers of a soft port-wine colour. It should be pruned hard in February each year.

C. fortunei. Native of Japan it now seems to have disappeared from British gardens, but it was a beautiful climber with leathery trifoliate leaves and produced its small fragrant double flowers of creamy-white right through summer.

DUCHESS OF EDINBURGH. A large-flowered hybrid, it is the only variety which has been given the fragrance of C. fortunei, from which it may have been raised. It bears white flowers which like those of C. fortunei are fully double and it blooms during May and June on the old wood.

C. grata. A tall, woody climber, pulling itself up by its leaf stalks which wrap around the stems of other plants. It is a plant of sub-tropical India, Afghanistan, Africa and China, found at elevations of nearly 2,400 m (8,000 ft). It resembles the British species, C. vitalba, with its pinnate leaves, sharply toothed and hairy, whilst its creamy-white flowers, produced in autumn, are borne at the ends of the branches and at the leaf axils, petals being absent. The flowers are delicately scented.

C. jouiniana. A shrubby climber with large leaves and like most of the shrubby semi-herbaceous species, it is autumn-flowering, bearing a profusion of small lilac tubular flowers like those of the hyacinth. They have a soft sweet perfume which is more pronounced in the erect shrubby form, campanile, its azure-blue flowers having the scent of honeysuckle.

C. montana. The climbing Mountain clematis of the Himalayas and the most vigorous of all the species, climbing up trees or against an old wall to a height of 6 m (20 ft) or more, a well-established plant forming a thick gnarled trunk which is almost indestructible. Early in May it begins to bloom, its fragrant flowers of ivory-white almost completely hiding the foliage for several weeks to form a shimmering cascade. The form Alexander bears larger flowers of purest white with a powerful vanilla scent, whilst wilsonii also bears white flowers which are powerfully scented but does not bloom until the others have almost finished. It has attractively twisted sepals (petals). Elizabeth bears masses of fragrant flowers of softest pink, whilst rubens bears flowers of rosy-pink which have some scent though not so pronounced as the others. It is compensated by its beautiful purple-bronze foliage.

C. orientalis. A native of India, it is a plant of slender upright growth but eventually reaches a height of 3 to 3.6 m (10 to 12 ft). In Britain, it needs the protection of a sheltered garden and a wall preferably facing west where, during autumn, it bears masses of greenish-yellow flowers tinted with rust which have a delicate cowslip perfume.

C. paniculata. A Japanese species which against a warm wall attains a height of 9 m (30 ft). It blooms from August till October, bearing panicles of small white flowers which have the powerful aromatic perfume of the daphnes. The flowers are followed by masses of feathery seed-heads.

C. pavoliniana. A native of China, it is evergreen and requires a warm sheltered garden in the British Isles. It blooms in June, bearing its small white flowers in axillary clusters and they have a delicious sweet scent.

C. rehderiana (syn. C. nutans). A most beautiful autumn-flowering Chinese species of vigorous habit which bears its attractive little recurving flowers in large panicles. The flowers are bell-shaped, of a soft primrose-yellow with a distinctive cowslip perfume.

C. uncinata. A most attractive Chinese species which is evergreen and requires a sheltered garden in the British Isles. The tiny leaves are glaucous beneath, and the fragrant white flowers, no more than 2.5 cm (1 in) across, are borne throughout midsummer in elegant panicles.

C. verdariensis rosea. Similar to *C. montana* with the same vigorous habit, it may also be grown against a bleak northerly wall. Like *C. montana,* it blooms in May and June, its attractive shell-pink flowers having a delicious vanilla perfume.

CLEMATOCLETHRA (Actinidiaceae— Actinidia Family)

A small genus of rare deciduous climbing plants related to *Actinidia* and flowering in midsummer.

Species. *Clematoclethra integrifolia.* A native of western China with ovate toothed leaves. It attains a height of 6 m (20 ft) or more against a warm wall where it will bear multitudes of snow-white flowers with a spicy perfume.

CLERODENDRON (Verbenaceae— Vervain Family)

A genus of about 400 species of deciduous or evergreen plants of shrubby or twining habit, several of which are scented, and which make delightful plants to twine around a pillar or against a trellis in a garden room. They are mostly native to the equatorial forests of South America, central Africa and the Far East, and all but the hardy *Clerodendron trichotomum* require winter protection in northern Europe. Those growing in pots may be given early help with their twining by inserting a small cane before it is planted against a wire or wooden screen. Where grown indoors, a minimum night temperature in winter of 13°C (55°F) is required.

Species. *Clerodendron bungei* (syn. *C. foetidum*). It is a shrub growing 1.5 to 1.8 m (5 to 6 ft) in height and, though its flowers are deliciously scented, the foliage leaves behind a most unpleasant smell on the hands when touched. Each year it sends up new wood from the base until it becomes a dense mass of shoots. The leaves are heart-shaped and covered in purple hairs, and the stems too are purple. During August and September it bears scented, rosy-mauve flowers in dense terminal corymbs with the stamens protruding to form a landing place for insect pollinators.

C. fargesii. It makes a dense shrub 3 m (10 ft) in height with leaves almost 15 cm (6 in) long, which are purple when young but turn dark green as they age. Known as the Star Tree, it blooms in July, its sweetly scented, star-like flowers borne in dense clusters; these are followed by small black fruits.

C. fragrans. Native of China where it is a common garden plant but in Europe requires protection. It will quickly cover a screen in the garden room, blooming from early July until late autumn. It bears clusters of double blooms of creamy white, like tiny rambler roses, which emit a sweet clove-like perfume greatly resembling the scent of the pink, Mrs Sinkins.

C. inerme. Native of India, Ceylon and Java, it makes a straggling bush 1.8 m (6 ft) tall, its name in Hindustani being *Sangkupi.* It usually grows close to the sea. Its shoots when young are grey-pubescent, and are slightly scented of apple. The same refreshing smell is given off by the leaves when broken or dry; they are also grey-pubescent when young. The flowers are white, tipped with red, and are slightly scented.

C. myricoides. Native of South Africa and Abyssinia, where it was at one time appreciated for the exotic fragrance of its flowers with their attractive greenish-white petals, like butterfly wings.

CLETHRA (Clethraceae—Clethra Family)

A genus of about 24 species of trees and shrubs, valuable in that they are autumn-flowering and flourish in a moist peaty soil. They should be confined to gardens of southern England and Ireland enjoying a favourable winter climate. They are increased from suckers and by layering the stems or from cuttings of the ripe wood removed in August and inserted in a sandy soil in a frame. The plant takes its name from the Greek *Klethra,* alder tree, which its leaves resemble. It was at one time included with the Ericaceae but having free (separate) petals it is now placed in its own family.

Species and Varieties. *Clethra acuminata.* Native of Carolina, it makes a shrub (or tree) 3.6 m (12 ft) tall, its oval serrated leaves being glaucous beneath and particularly hairy along the veins. It produces its powerfully fragrant white flowers in downy racemes from early July until October when the leaves turn to a rich golden-yellow. In its native land, it usually grows on cliffs and mountainsides.

C. alnifolia paniculata. The Sweet Pepper bush or Mignonette tree of the eastern United States, introduced into Britain in 1731. It is a handsome shrub growing 2.4 m (8 ft) tall and bearing during August and September long, densely packed racemes with sweetly scented creamy-white flowers. The hardiest of the Clethras, it makes a dense-growing shrub with dark-green leaves which also emit a powerful scent when bruised. The variety *paniculata* bears larger flowers than the type and is quite as sweetly scented, but the flowers of *rosea* have not such a powerful perfume. The plants withstand clipping and make an attractive informal hedge.

C. arborea. Native of Madeira where it attains a height of nearly 6 m (20 ft), it is hardy in Britain only in southern England and Ireland where it will grow to a height of 3.6 to 4.5 m (12 to 15 ft). It has narrow, shining dark-green leaves and in autumn bears sprays of urn-shaped flowers of purest white, like those of the lily of the valley and with a similar pervading perfume hence its name of Lily of the Valley tree. Like other members of the species, it requires a peat-laden soil and does better in sight of the sea where severe frost is rarely experienced.

C. canescens. Also *C. barbinervis*, it is a pretty Chinese shrub with serrated leaves and in July bears fragrant white hawthorn-like blossom in long racemes.

C. delavayi. Native of China, it is a beautiful deciduous tree-like shrub, its large hairy leaves deeply veined and dark green, providing a striking foil for the horizontal sprays of pure-white urn-shaped flowers which resemble the Lily of the Valley in appearance and have a similar perfume. It was discovered in the mountains of Talifu in 1884 by Abbé Delavay and introduced into Britain in 1913 by George Forrest.

C. fargesii. Native of central China, it grows 2.4 to 3 m (8 to 10 ft) tall and bears in July and August fragrant flowers of purest white in dense drooping racemes

almost 30 cm (12 in) in length. It is one of the most decorative of late-summer flowering plants but it must be protected from cold winds. A deciduous plant, its dark-green leaves have serrated margins.

C. tomentosa. It is a native of the eastern United States, closely allied to *C. alnifolia* and making a dense shrub some 1.8 to 2.1 m (6 to 7 ft) in height. The young shoots and the flower stalks and calyx are covered with down which, with its pure-white flowers, gives it a cool grey appearance.

C. phlomoides. Of climbing habit, this Indian species has clusters of yellowish-white flowers, having a rich sweet scent with clove undertones.

C. trichotomum. Known as the Glory Tree, it is native of China and Japan, and makes a handsome small tree or shrub growing up to 6 m (20 ft) high with bold, dark evergreen leaves which taper at both ends. The white star-shaped flowers are produced in 3-branched corymbs, and they have a crimson-purple, inflated calyx. They appear towards the end of August, and emit a delicious balsam-like perfume; the leaves are also balsam-scented. The flowers are followed by china-blue berries, surmounted by the crimson calyces. This plant will grow well in a sheltered garden in the British Isles, but should be given a westerly situation where the early morning frost has time to clear before the sun's rays reach it.

CLIFFORTIA (Rosaceae—Rose Family)

A large genus of erect or procumbent shrubs named in honour of George Cliffort of Amsterdam, a patron of Linnaeus. They are mostly native of the mountainous regions of South Africa and have stems clothed in long hairs. Pollinated by wind, the flowers are not scented but the foliage of *C. odorata* has the refreshing scent of eglantine.

Species. *Cliffortia odorata.* It is a shrub of bramble-like habit, of which the stems and sharply toothed leaves are covered in hairs. The plant gives off a pleasantly sweet scent which is more pronounced after rain.

CODONOPSIS (Campanulaceae— Harebell Family)

A genus of 12 or more species of annual or perennial plants with a tuberous rootstock and flourishing in ordinary soil. Native of the Himalayas, they are hardy in the British Isles and in North America but are difficult to propagate by root division and are best raised from seed.

Species. *Codonopsis ovata.* Native of the western Himalayas, it forms a multi-branched plant 45 cm (18 in) tall with ovate leaves and it bears its nodding bells in June. The blooms are palest blue, veined with purple, and inhaled near to have the unpleasant odour of fur, likened by some to the smell of ferrets.

COFFEA (Rubiaceae—Bedstraw Family)
A small genus of evergreen plants, native to the sub-tropical regions of Asia and West Africa, South America and Indonesia.

Species. *Coffea arabica.* The Arabian coffee plant of commerce, it is a slender evergreen with glossy dark-green leaves which do not fall under warm greenhouse conditions. It makes an admirable pot plant, bearing clusters of fragrant white flowers at the axils of the leaves, and these are followed by brilliant scarlet berries which contain two coffee beans. The plant requires a minimum night temperature of 13°C (56°F) which may be raised to 18°C (65°F) during spring and summer.

The aromatic smell of the roasted coffee-bean is considered by many to be the most appetizing of all aromas. The alkaloid caffeine, the aromatic principle of coffee given off when the berries are roasted, may be isolated by distilling roasted coffee in water, agitating the distillate with ether and afterwards evaporating the ether. The product is a brown oil, heavier than water and possessing the delicious coffee aroma to a powerful degree.

C. liberica. The Liberian coffee chiefly grown in Brazil, which country exports more than half the world's coffee requirements. A small evergreen, it has glossy leaves and scented white flowers, followed by a 2-seeded cherry-like drupe, the seed or coffee-bean having a groove on the ventral side.

COLEONEMA (Rutaceae—Rue Family)
A small genus of dainty heath-like shrubs, native of South Africa, and found on rocky formations near the coast.

Species. *Coleonema alba.* It bears, in the axils of the leaves, small white flowers and makes an excellent winter pot plant. The foliage gives off the pungent orange-like fragrance of the family, and the flowers are sweetly scented.

COLLETIA (Rhamnaceae—Buckthorn Family)
A genus consisting of 17 species of curious shrubs producing little or no foliage but instead forming thick, fleshy, cactus-like branches armed with triangular spines up to 2 cm (1 in) long. These are formed at the axils of the leaves, a secondary bud forming the flowers. Natives of Uruguay, they flourish under arid conditions, requiring a hot, dry soil, and will not survive otherwise. Cuttings of half-ripened shoots are used for propagation.

Species. *Colletia armata.* So named because it is armed with angry-looking thorns and it takes on a most ferocious appearance when it has attained its full height of 2.4 to 2.7 m (8 to 9 ft). But it is worthy of a place in a seaside garden where it may be expected to do well, if only for the exotic almond fragrance of its pure-white, bell-shaped flowers, like those of the lily of the valley, which appear in September and October.

C. cruciata. It grows 3 m (10 ft) tall, its stems being composed of triangular spines which appear in pairs, each being at right angles to the next pair to give a cross-like appearance. The small, creamy-white flowers appear early in autumn and are without petals but are extremely beautiful; they are sweetly scented.

COMBRETUM (Combretaceae— Combretum Family)
A genus of about 250 attractively flowering plants, native of the South African Veld and sub-tropical Africa, also India and South-east Asia, which vary in size from small bushes to large trees, most having winged fruits. They are evergreen and several are scented. Stove-house conditions are required, and they do best if pruned hard after flowering. Increase is by cuttings taken in summer.

Species. *Combretum apiculatum.* It is a pretty species, common in Rhodesia, and is an evergreen tree. It bears yellow, catkin-like flowers, like those of the willow, which appear in October before the leaves and they diffuse a rich perfume, almost like lily of the valley.

C. oatesii. It is a common low-growing shrub of the African Veld bearing catkin-like flowers of softest perfume.

COMMIPHORA (Burseraceae—Frankincense Family)

A genus of about 180 species of highly aromatic trees or shrubs, mostly native of the Arabian Peninsula and western India, of which *C. myrrha* furnished the most valuable of all perfumes known to the ancients; gum myrrh was used in the manufacture of pastils and fumigating spirits. The Arabs feed it to their horses to prevent fatigue.

Species. *Commiphora myrrha* (syn. *C. opobalsamum, Balsamodendron myrrha*). A small thorny shrub found in Arabia and on the Abyssinian coast of the Red Sea where it is known as *Kurbeta.* It yielded to the ancients the only substance that provided a strong and lasting perfume. There are two forms, one a dwarf shrub with dull-green serrated leaves; the other a small tree growing 3 m (10 ft) tall, yielding a substance more like balm than myrrh. This is *C. kataf.* The yellow gum exudes from the bark and the Arab people collected it from the beards of goats which browsed amongst the shrubs, also where it exuded from the bark and from the glandular hairs on the underside of the leaves. The drops quickly solidify and fall to the ground. It was an ingredient of the ointment of the alabaster box used to anoint the feet of Jesus, and as mentioned in Proverbs it was placed amongst clothes and linen to impart its rich resinous perfume. Because of its lasting fragrance, it was used by the Egyptians for embalming the dead.

It is a small twiggy evergreen with white flowers borne in small clusters. The gum ('balm') is collected from incisions made in the bark and it quickly solidifies in contact with the air. It was one of the 'gift of spices' made by the Queen of Sheba to King Solomon, and from the seeds arose plantations or orchards which were in commercial use at the time of the subjugation of the Jews by Titus Vespasian in A.D 70. Yet, by the time of the Crusades, there was no trace of the trees in Palestine.

COMPTONIA (Myricaceae—Sweet Gale Family)

It was at one time classed with *Myrica* but is now known as *Comptonia,* named in honour of Henry Compton, Bishop of London in the reign of James II. They are plants for growing in a moist, peaty soil and partial shade, and so may accompany azaleas and rhododendrons and other plants enjoying similar conditions.

Species. *Comptonia asplenifolia.* The North American Sweet Fern bush, a deciduous shrub growing 1.2 m (4 ft) tall with handsome dark-green lance-shaped leaves pinnately cut and covered with golden resinous spots. The leaves resemble those of the Ceterach Fern, and at the least touch give off a rich spicy fragrance, likened to that of cinnamon and cassia and released by a gentle breeze, so near the surface are the resinous glands; the scent increases when the leaves are dried. It is readily increased by suckers. It bears small white flowers in catkins early in spring, both male and female flowers appearing on the same plant.

C. paniculata. A native of Carolina growing 0.9 to 1.2 m (3 to 4 ft) tall with pointed lance-shaped leaves. It bears its white flowers, which are extremely fragrant, in long hoary panicles, from July until the end of autumn.

C. tomentosa. Native of Virginia, its grey-green leaves are so densely covered in hairs as to give them a chalky-white appearance beneath. It bears snow-white flowers in woolly racemes from July until October, and they have a powerful fragrance.

CONIUM (Umbelliferae—Parsley Family)

A genus of four species of poisonous plants, native of northern Europe.

Species. *Conium maculatum.* The Common hemlock, an annual plant native to the British Isles and Europe. It was a draught of hemlock which caused the death of Socrates for it is extremely poisonous. All parts of the plant when bruised, emit a nauseating smell, 'much offending the senses' in Culpeper's words and sufficient to warn one of its poisonous qualities.

It grows about waste places and is readily distinguishable for it is the only member of the family which has smooth stems entirely devoid of hairs; they are deeply marked with reddish-purple spots. It grows to a height of 1.2 m (4 ft) and blooms in July, the tiny white flowers borne in densely packed umbels.

CONOPHYTUM (Aizoaceae—Aizoon Family)

A large genus of more than 270 species, native of Cape Province and closely related to Lithops, the 'living stones'. New plants are formed within the old ones and are protected from grazing animals by the dead appearance of the dry skin of the old plant. The flowers appear from a cleft at the top of the stone-like plant and in one or more species they are scented.

Species. *Conophytum obcordellum.* It eventually forms a cushion of numerous flowering bodies formed by the uniting of twin leaves which produce a flat, stone-like surface about 1 cm ($\frac{1}{2}$ in) long. They are bluish-green, dotted with red, and from the cleft appears a pale-yellow flower which is scented like vanilla.

They require a very sharply drained compost with a little rich loam in it, and well-drained pots in a sunny position. Potting is carried out in August, and only a little water is given from October to April. In May, June and July, they should not be watered at all. A minimum winter temperature of 13°C (55°F) is required.

CONVALLARIA (Lily of the Valley) (Liliaceae—Lily Family)

A genus of a single species, native of the deciduous woodlands of the British Isles, northern Europe and the Allegheny Mountains of North America.

Species. *Convallaria majalis.* It is a perennial with a creeping rootstock, and between a pair of bright-green lance-shaped root leaves it bears a one-sided spike of dangling bells of purest white and with a sweet spicy perfume.

Henry Lyte in his *New Herbal* (1578)

calls it the Lilly Convall with flowers 'as white as snow and of a pleasant strong savour. The water of the flowers comforteth the heart ... and doth strengthen the memorie'. In *The Flower Garden* (1726) John Lawrence said 'the conval-lily is esteemed to have, of all others, the sweetest and most agreeable perfume; not offensive nor overbearing, even to those who are made uneasy with the perfumes of other sweet scented flowers'.

Gerard tells us that the plant grew plentifully on Hampstead Heath, four miles from London (where in Kenwood it still grows plentifully) and also at Lee in Essex. There is a double form, *flore plena*, and also one bearing pink flowers, *rosea*.

CONVOLVULUS (Convolvulaceae—Bindweed Family)

About 200 species are comprised in the genus which is distributed throughout the world mainly in the tropics, but only a few bear fragrant flowers. Of the Greater bindweed, *Calystegia sepium*, incorrectly called Convolvulus, which twines about the hedgerows, handsome with its lance-shaped leaves, and bearing in July and August trumpets of dazzling white, Pliny in the *Historia Naturalis*, wrote: 'There is a herb named in Latin *Convolvulus* growing among shrubs and bushes, which carrieth a flower not unlike to the lily, save that it yieldeth no smell ... (it was) as if Nature in making this flower, were learning and trying her skill how to frame the lily.'

Pliny was right in saying that 'it is without perfume', though Gerard, confusing it with *C. arvensis*, described it as 'sweet of smell'. The species which is scented is *Convolvulus arvensis*, the Lesser or Smaller bindweed, also the Field bindweed, an obnoxious but attractive weed of countryside and garden, its underground roots being difficult to eradicate wherever it takes hold. It is often found about sand pits and quarries and is Wordsworth's 'Cumbrous bind-weed, with its wreaths and bells'. It is the only British member of the family, distinguished from *Calystegia* by the bracteoles which envelop the calyx.

Species. *Convolvulus arvensis.* It is usually found about hedgerows or cornfields, rambling over the ground and over nearby plants rather than twining with the vigour of the Greater bindweed. It has arrow-shaped leaves and its flowers are white, suffused with pink and often striped with green. They are usually in pairs and are much smaller than those of *C. sepium,* no more than 2.5 cm (1 in) across. They appear during July and August and often into autumn, spreading a scent of heliotrope far and wide but only when the sun shines upon them for in dull weather they refuse to open.

COOPERIA (Amaryllidaceae—Narcissus Family)

A genus of 9 or 10 species of bulbous plants, native of Central America and Mexico and resembling *Zephyranthes* in habit but distinguished from it by its stamens and long cylindrical tube. The flowers are funnel-shaped with spreading segments whilst the linear leaves appear with the flowers. The genus was named after Joseph Cooper, head gardener at Wentworth Woodhouse, Yorkshire.

Species. *Cooperia drummondii.* Known as the Evening Star flower for its long tubular white flowers diffuse a delicate primrose-like perfume only at night. From the round, short-necked bulbs appear the narrow leaves 30 cm (12 in) long, and the flowers are borne on slender stems of similar length. The flowers, tinted red on the outside, appear throughout summer. In the northern temperate regions, the plants are hardy only in the most favourably situated gardens where the bulbs should be planted 7.5 cm (3 in) deep and 15 cm (6 in) apart. They require a well-drained gritty soil.

COPERNICIA (Palmaceae—Palm Tree Family)

A genus of 30 species, native of tropical South America and the West Indies.

Species. *Copernicia cerifera.* The Wax Palm of Brazil where it grows to a height of nearly 30 m (100 ft) with a trunk of about 30-cm (12-in) diameter. The leaves arise at the top of the trunk and are brilliant green, terminating at the apex in a sharp point. The solitary flowers along the spadix are small and externally are green, internally brown. The terminal

leaf-bud called the 'palm cabbage' is sweet and nutritious. From scales situated at the axils of the leaves, a wax is secreted which falls to the ground when the tree is shaken.

The Brazilian or Carnuba wax, as it is known commercially, is collected by removing the young leaf buds and scales which are dried and powdered. It is then melted and run into 'cakes' which set hard and brittle and are of an ashen colour with an odour resembling new-mown hay. A mature tree will yield about 2.250 kg (5 lb) of wax.

C. cerifera is the most extensively planted species for it remains luxuriant in the most prolonged drought. In Brazil, its timber is used in construction, whilst its roots possess the same medical properties as sarsaparilla. Wine is made from the 'palmetto top', which is also a sweetening product, whilst a nutritious flour is made from the trunk. Cork is obtained from the pith, and the nut is used as a substitute for coffee.

CORDYLINE (Liliaceae—Lily Family)

A small genus of palm-like trees, native of all parts of New Zealand where they are a familiar part of the landscape, found from the coast to an altitude of 700 m (2,500 ft). Pioneers named it the 'Cabbage tree' for the young shoots make a tasty and nourishing vegetable.

Species. *Cordyline australis.* The hardiest member of the genus which attains a height of 9 to 12 m (30 to 40 ft) in a sheltered situation. A native of New Zealand, it forms a single stem at the top of which are formed the large sword-like leaves, each up to 90 cm (3 ft) in length and with parallel veins. The creamy-white lily-like flowers are produced in enormous panicles 90 cm (3 ft) in length and their delicious sweet scent pervades the air to a considerable distance.

It is a beautiful specimen tree for a lawn and does well in ordinary loamy soil but usually survives a severe winter only when growing near the coast. In Britain it should be confined to favourably situated gardens in south-western England and Ireland and the western coast of Scotland.

During Victorian times, young plants were in demand for bedding out early in summer in the more favourable parts of

Britain when their presence gave a 'tropical' effect.

In their native land, the trees are almost indestructible and when cut almost to ground level send up fresh shoots.

The roots were at one time used by the Maoris as food, having a ginger-like smell and taste.

CORIANDRUM (Umbelliferae—Parsley Family)

A genus of a single species.

Species. *Coriandrum sativum.* It is an annual, forming an attractive plant nearly 90 cm (3 ft) tall, with glossy dark-green leaves and bearing small pale mauve-pink flowers. Whilst its leaves are useful for flavouring soups, stews, curries and other Eastern dishes, it is the small round seeds that are most in demand, to flavour pickles and to cover with sugar in making 'sweets'. The seeds, which have a most unpleasant smell at first, should be removed on the point of ripening, usually early in September, and dried in a warm room where they will emit a highly attractive scent as they become dry, and the longer they are kept the more fragrant they become. In the Book of Numbers, manna is likened unto coriander seed. Native of the Levant, the plant was introduced to England by the Romans. Its popular name is coriander.

In Britain, to allow the seeds time to ripen, the plant is best treated as a biennial, sowing the seed in September in a light, well-drained soil and in spring thinning the seedlings to 15 cm (6 in) apart.

The whole plant has a smell which has been likened to that of bugs. The seeds, however, when dry give off an orange scent which is intensified in the essential oil of the ripened seeds.

CORNUS (Dogwood) (Cornaceae— Dogwood Family)

A genus of about 50 species native to the Northern Hemisphere of small trees or shrubs with crimson-purple stems which are most colourful during winter. Most bloom before the leaves appear, the creamy-white flowers having a soft delicate sweet perfume. They are followed by olive-like drupes which may be made into a conserve.

Species. *Cornus alba.* The White-fruited dogwood, native of Siberia and northern Asia and making a slender bush 3 m (10 ft) high. The scent of the cream-coloured flowers, which are borne in flat umbels, is more pronounced than in other species, in order to attract the few insects available when it blooms. It is a most attractive plant with bronzy-green leaves, and bearing white fruit, whilst its young wood is brilliant red. For a continuous supply of young wood, cut down the old wood to the base each year.

C. circinata. Native of North America, it grows 2.4 m (8 ft) tall with purple stems and with large oval leaves, abruptly pointed and covered on the underside with down. It blooms in June, bearing its delicately scented snow-white flowers in flat cymes, and these are followed by brilliant blue berries of pea size.

C. macrophylla. A handsome Japanese species, it is known as the Large-leaf dogwood, its large green leaves having crimson stalks. The leaves are rose-tinted in autumn. The flowers are borne in greenish-yellow clusters during July and August and have a soft sweet perfume.

CORONILLA (Leguminosae—Laburnum Family)

A genus of about 20 species native of southern Europe which grow 1.8 m (6 ft) in height. They require a well-drained soil and a warm situation when they will survive all but winters of extreme severity. By planting several species, their fragrant flowers, borne on long-stalked umbels, may be enjoyed throughout the year, though only a single species is winter-flowering.

Species. *Coronilla glauca.* It has fleshy, glaucous grey leaves and makes a dense bush. It usually blooms from early July till the year end, bearing bright-yellow laburnum-like flowers in attractive crown-like clusters. But, if the weather continues mild, it will remain in bloom until early spring, requiring only a short rest period before blooming again, and it will retain its leaves throughout if protected from cold winds. It is best grown at the foot of a warm wall, in sandy compost, and pot-grown plants should always be obtained.

C. emerus. It is taller-growing than *C*

glauca, the winter-flowering species, attaining a height of 2.4 m (8 ft) where sheltered from cold winds, though it is of a hardier constitution than the others. Its bright-green pinnate leaves provide a delightful contrast for the pale-yellow flowers of broom-like form which appear in April, 4 or 5 to each stem. The sweetly scented flowers continue until June, then after a short rest, they appear again in September and continue until the colder weather.

CORYLOPSIS (Hamamelidaceae—Witch Hazel Family)

A genus of 20 species of deciduous Hazel-like shrubs, native of the Himalayas and eastern Asia.

Species and Varieties. *Corylopsis himalayana.* Like all members of the family, it is a dainty, attractive shrub, sufficiently hardy to bloom well in the shelter of a wall or of other shrubs, in gardens situated south of the Thames. It attains a height of 1.8 m (6 ft), its round leaves being covered with silky down on the underside. Its pale-yellow flowers appear towards the end of February, held in drooping racemes. They are enhanced by the brown anthers at the centre and have a sweet, delicate scent, like primroses.

C. pauciflora. It forms a neat shrub about 1.2 m (4 ft) in height and the same across and should be given a sunny position, protected from cold winds. It will then bloom from about mid-February until the end of April. The flowers are produced in pairs, and arise from the nodes where the leaves have fallen the previous year. They appear at intervals of 5 to 7.5 cm (2 to 3 in) along the stems and consist of 5 spreading petals of golden tinsel enhanced by orange anthers, and they emit a delicious almond perfume. A plant in full bloom has the appearance of being covered in golden snow.

C. spicata. A native of Japan and one of the garden's most attractive plants. It makes an open shrub 1.5 m (5 ft) in height and blooms in February; from its hoary stems appear long drooping racemes of primrose-yellow starry flowers held together by string-like stems. At the base is a pale-yellow leaf bract, which greatly enhances the display. Each of the 5 petalled flowers measures nearly 2.5 cm (1 in) across and at the centre is a bunch of pretty red anthers. The fragrance of the flowers is sweet and refreshing, like that of cowslips.

C. willmottiae. A native of western China and the hardiest species, it resembles *C. spicata* though it is more vigorous and grows to a height of 2.7 to 3 m (9 to 10 ft). It blooms towards the end of February, bearing its pale-yellow flowers in drooping racemes but held closer to the stem than those of *C. spicata.* They have the same refreshing sweet cowslip fragrance. Like all the species, it is best propagated from layers in autumn.

C. wilsonii. Native of China, it grows 3 m (10 ft) tall with wide oval leaves and in March bears its racemes of primrose-yellow flowers before the leaves appear. The flowers possess the woodland fragrance of the primrose, the smell of damp moss.

CORYPHA (Palmaceae—Palm Tree Family)

A genus of eight species, native of Ceylon and South-east Asia and growing to a considerable height. The enormous flower-heads are so powerfully scented that they have to be removed before they fully open if growing near houses, and they also terminate the life of the tree.

Species. *Corypha umbraculifera.* The Fan or Umbrella palm, native of Ceylon where the large leaves are used to give protection from the hot sun and are also used by the natives to thatch their dwellings. The flowers are deep yellow and appear in huge trusses with a scent so powerful as to be nauseating.

COTONEASTER (Rosaceae—Rose Family)

A genus of about 20 species of erect or trailing trees and shrubs, evergreen or deciduous, the white flowers being borne in terminal cymes in May and June, followed by round bright-red fruit. It is closely related to the Hawthorn, Spiraea and Mountain ash of the same family, and they are like each other in the scent of the blossom. The Cotoneasters make excellent

trees for a town garden and for a thin
chalk-laden soil, but the scent of the white
flowers is anything but pleasant when
inhaled near to, similar to decaying fish.
Like the Hawthorn and Mountain ash, the
flowers contain trimethylamine which is
present in large quantities in herring brine,
though the undertone of sweetness present
in the Hawthorn is lacking in the
Cotoneasters. The flowers rely upon flies
and midges for their pollination.

Species and Varieties. *Cotoneaster
acuminata.* A deciduous Himalayan species
growing 3 to 3.6 m (10 to 12 ft) tall with
long tapering leaves, its pinky-white
flowers followed by scarlet fruit. The
flowers have the fetid smell of those of *C.
frigida.*
    C. bacillaris. From Nepal and the most
vigorous of all the Cotoneasters, attaining
a height of 6 m (20 ft) with long, narrow
leaves, its clusters of white flowers being
followed by black fruits. But, like all the
family, its flowers are evil-smelling.
    C. cornubia. A hybrid, not so vigorous as
C. frigida, but with its multi-branched
head making an excellent windbreak. Like
C. frigida it retains its foliage until almost
the end of winter, and its rather sickly-
smelling white flowers are followed by
clusters of scarlet berries.
    C. frigida. A native of Nepal and
resembling *C. acuminata,* growing 3.6 m
(12 ft) high with lance-shaped leaves. Its
white flowers appear in May and June, in
woolly cymes. Like those of *C. acuminata,*
they have a most unpleasant fishy smell. It
is, however, a most attractive tree,
especially in the standard form in which it
makes a large 'head' and is semi-
evergreen, its long pointed leaves being
glossy green on the surface and pale green
beneath, most beautiful against the
bunches of brilliant-scarlet berries which
are retained almost through winter.
    C. watereri. Similar in habit and in ap-
pearance to *C. frigida* but with longer
leaves, in size and shape resembling those
of the laurel, its fishy-smelling white
flowers being followed by clusters of
brilliant-crimson berries. A variety, St
Monica, has greater vigour and is best
confined to the large garden but is a most
handsome tree where the space is available.

COTULA (Compositae—Daisy Family)
A small genus of glabrous and creeping
annuals, a single species of which is to be
found on low-lying ground in the Wirral
Peninsula.

Species. *Cotula coronopifolia.* A hairless
prostrate annual with small flat unrayed
flowers borne solitary and resembling
buttons, hence its name of Buttonweed.
The alternate pinnatifid leaves are
yellowish-green and the whole plant
releases an aromatic pungent smell when
handled.

COTTON LAVENDER: *see* SANTOLINA

CRAMBE (Cruciferae—Wallflower Family)
A genus of 16 species of mostly maritime plants, one of which, *C. cordifolia,*
bears flowers with the fragrance of the
wallflower. The herbaceous forms are
vigorous, coarse-growing plants, suitable
for the wild garden and border. They grow
well in partial shade.

Species. *Crambe cordifolia.* A deep-rooting
perennial, native of the Caucasus and
forming generous tufts of heart-shaped
leaves, lobed and wrinkled and nearly 45
cm (18 in) wide. The white cross-shaped
flowers are produced in branched panicles
some 1.2 to 1.5 m (4 to 5 ft) above the
foliage and they emit a delicious wallflower scent when warmed by the June
sunshine. The flowers are an admirable
foil for blue delphiniums which bloom at
the same time.

CRASSULA (Crassulaceae—Stonecrop Family)
Also known as *Kalosanthes,* this is a
genus of shrubby succulent plants native of
South Africa, particularly of Cape
Province. Several bear scented flowers and
are suited to greenhouse cultivation in the
British Isles, mostly flowering through
summer. Of compact branching habit, the
plants carry their flowers in large trusses
on the extremities of the shoots, those
bearing scarlet flowers making a brilliant
display against the bright-green fleshy
foliage.
    They are amongst the easiest of all
plants to propagate, every piece sending

forth roots if placed on a damp surface. Spring is the most suitable time, for the plants will then become hard before winter. The shoots will root in three weeks when they should be moved to small pots containing a compost made up of fibrous turf loam, sharp sand and decayed manure in equal parts. They require a minimum winter temperature of 5°C (42°F) and should be watered sparingly.

Species. *Crassula arborescens.* Found in the Karroo of South Africa, it is almost impossible to detect amongst the stones. It flowers only once, bearing a large white, sweetly scented bloom, which lasts a month before it dies.

C. coccinea. Of perennial form, it bears its pretty heads of glabrous magenta-red blooms for a month or more and they emit a peculiar scent, likened to that of pear-drop sweets.

C. jasminea. A dainty species, so named for the resemblance of its flowers to those of the summer jasmine, being white with a soft jasmine-like perfume.

C. lactea. The pointed oval leaves of this species are dotted with white, and it bears its slightly scented flowers of creamy-white in terminal racemes throughout winter.

CRATAEGUS (Rosaceae—Rose Family)

A genus of about 200 species of deciduous, mostly spiny trees, distributed around the northern temperate regions of the world, with handsome pinnate leaves and bearing its flowers in terminal cymes. Pollination is by midges, attracted to the flowers by their unpleasant fishy smell, due to the presence of trimethylamine, a substance which occurs in putrefaction. When freshly open, the flowers have more pleasant balsamic undertones.

The best forms for the garden are the double-flowered forms in white, red and pink; the latter is a lovely shade of strawberry pink with just a little perfume, but the red has none—an instance of colour in a flower displacing scent.

Species and Varieties. *Crataegus carierei.* Its leaves are glossy green and attractively serrated, its haws being bright orange, whilst its silver-coloured stems are quite thornless. The blooms are larger than usual with a more pleasant smell.

C. crus-galli. The Cockspur Thorn of North America, remarkable for its long thorns, which bears edible scarlet haws amidst brilliantly coloured autumnal foliage. Its white flowers are tinted red.

C. flava. Like so many of the Thorns, it is native of North America and is unusual in that its pear-shaped fruit is yellow and edible. It makes a small compact tree.

C. orientalis. Of compact habit, it is almost thornless, with hoary branches and grey foliage, its sweetly scented white flowers followed by attractive orange fruit. Native of the Levant, it is a good small garden tree.

C. oxyacantha. The Common hawthorn or May, native to the British Isles, with shining, wedge-shaped leaves, pinnately cut. Its white flowers, sometimes tinted with pink, are produced in May and June and are pleasantly scented only at a distance. The variety Paul's Double Scarlet is most colourful but, like so many red flowers, is completely without scent.

C. tanacetifolia. Native of the Black Sea regions, it grows 3 m (10 ft) or more in height, with downy leaves which are deeply cut and serrated. It blooms later than the other species, during June, and the flowers, like those of *C. orientalis,* are more sweetly scented than all other Thorns, free from fishy undertones. It is known as the Sweet-scented Azarole. The fruit is yellow, similar in size to a cherry.

CRINUM (Amaryllidaceae—Narcissus Family)

A large genus of bulbous plants native of the southern United States, South Africa and South-east Asia, producing large bulbs with long necks and bearing several large funnel-shaped flowers on stems 90 cm (3 ft) in length. Though most are better suited to cool greenhouse culture, several may be brought into bloom outdoors in favourable parts of the British Isles and northern Europe if given the backing of a sunny wall. Plant the bulbs in May, 30 cm (12 in) apart with the neck at soil level.

Species. *Crinum americanum.* Native of the southern United States, it has bulbs of 10-cm (4-in) diameter and has arching leaves 90 cm (3 ft) long. It bears 4 to 6 pure-white flowers on a 60-cm (2-ft) stem, the richly scented blooms being cylindrical, with narrow segments.

C. asiaticum. It forms a huge rounded bulb from which arises a stout stem some 90 cm (3 ft) tall at the end of which appear 40 to 50 flowers in an almost circular umbel. The lily-like blooms recurve considerably and are white shading off to palest pink. They emit a sweet, lily-like perfume which is especially pronounced at night to attract night-flying Lepidoptera for their pollination.

C. bracteatum (syn. *C. brevifolium*). Native of the Seychelles, with ovoid bulbs and leaves 45 cm (18 in) long, waved at the margins. The sweetly scented white flowers are borne 12 to 20 on a 30-cm (12-in) stem, the slender tubes being 7.5 cm (3 in) long.

C. bulbispurmum (syn. *C. capense* and *C. longifolium*). It is native of the Transvaal and Natal where it blooms in October, but in Britain it blooms in a sunny border in June when 12 or more bell-shaped blooms appear on a 60-cm (2-ft) stem. They are pale pink with deeper pink veins and they emit a sweet, somewhat spicy odour which is especially pronounced at nightfall.

C. moorei. A parent of the more common *C. powellii*, it is native of Natal and is hardy in parts of Britain enjoying a favourable winter climate. From the large bulbs arise 12 or more dark-green straplike leaves 10 cm (4 in) broad and 60 cm (2 ft) long. As many as 8 to 10 bell-shaped blooms appear on a 60-cm (2-ft) scape and are a lovely shell pink. The flowers emit a rich spicy odour.

C. pedunculatum. It is a plant mostly of the swampy coastal areas of Queensland and New South Wales and is particularly common along the banks of the Murray River, hence its name of Murray Lily. From the axils of the lower leaves appear the flower stems some 60 cm (2 ft) tall, at the end of which appear 12 or 15 pure-white flowers with long thin petals and sepals. They are sweetly scented.

C. × *powellii.* A hybrid and the best for gardens of Britain and North America, where it blooms during August and September. The bulbs are of 15-cm (6-in) diameter and they bear lily-like flowers of rose-pink in umbels of 6 to 10, held on a 60-cm (2-ft) stem. They are sweetly scented.

CROCOSMIA (Montbretia)
(Iridaceae—Iris Family)

A genus of six species, native of Natal and the Cape and closely allied to Tritonia. They take their name from *crocus,* saffron, and *osme,* smell, for although the flowers when fresh are entirely without perfume, when dried and immersed in warm water they release a scent like that of the Saffron crocus.

Species. *Crocosmia aurea.* It has fibrous-coated corms and narrow grass-like leaves 30 cm (12 in) long. The flowers, borne from July to September, are of rich golden-orange with a cylindrical perianth tube and prominent stamens. The flowers are borne in an elegant panicle on 60-cm (2-ft) stems. Working with this species and *C. pottsii,* Lemoine in France raised a number of almost hardy garden hybrids known as the Garden montbretias.

CROCUS (Iridaceae—Iris Family)

A genus of 75 species, native of southern Europe and the Mediterranean regions. The flowers are visited by bees and butterflies and close up at night. By day, many species are scented and by planting for a succession of bloom throughout autumn, winter and spring, the flowers will provide perfume when few other flowers will do so.

The crocus is a plant that does well in town and country gardens, growing well in short grass or beneath trees, and it is an ideal subject for the alpine garden. All that it asks for is a well-drained soil. The spring-flowering species should be planted in October and November, whilst those that bloom in autumn and early winter are planted in June.

Species. *Crocus chrysanthus.* It was found in Bulgaria and is also present in Greece and Asia Minor. The most variable species known as regards colour, it comes into bloom before the end of January and continues through March. The blooms are globular and a rich golden-yellow but with little perfume. A number of varieties raised in the 1920s by the late E. A. Bowles are, however, sweetly scented though this quality is not mentioned by him in his writings. The one most scented is Snow

Bunting, the white flowers being stippled with palest blue on the outside. The fragrance is most noticeable indoors, and in the open the flowers are a great attraction for bees during the early days of spring.

C. *graveolens.* George Maw in his *Monograph of the Genus Crocus* (1886) treated it as a variety of *C. vitellinus* with which it is to be found growing in the wild. It differs, however, in several respects, having narrow leaves which spread over the soil whilst its flowers are smaller, more heavily marked with brown on the exterior, and emit a most unpleasant smell like that of Elder bark, a smell of stale perspiration 'added to which' wrote E. A. Bowles, 'is a whiff of black beetles'. He added that the dried flowers retain the smell for many years and will even impregnate with it the paper between which the flowers are pressed. It blooms in February and March.

C. *imperati.* It is valuable in that it ensures continuation of the fragrance given off by the blooms of *C. laevigatus,* for it blooms early in February, when *C. laevigatus* is ending. It is found around the Bay of Naples and southwards to Calabria whilst north of Naples and south of Rome grows the equally fragrant *C. suaveolens,* a closely related species.

C. *imperati,* named after the sixteenth-century Italian botanist, Ferrante Imperato, is the largest-flowered of the Italian species, the blooms measuring 10 cm (4 in) across. The segments are violet-coloured, tinted with buff on the outside and with orange-scarlet anthers. It emits a sweet honeysuckle perfume, pronounced when indoors. Roman women would dry the petals and use them to fill pillows and cushions, and they washed in toilet water made from the fresh flowers.

C. *laevigatus.* It is native of Greece and Bulgaria, and though rare in gardens it is a hardy species, in bloom during the coldest days of winter, from November until early in March, brightening the dull days with its tubes of white, veined and feathered with richest violet, whilst the exterior is feathered with brown. Its sweet scent is almost as powerful as that of *C. longiflorus* and in pots it will scent a large room or greenhouse. An added attraction is its pure-white anthers.

C. *leichtlinii.* Collected in Asia Minor, it was first distributed by Max Leichtlin as a variety of *C. biflorus* but it is distinct from it in several ways, the corm tunic being free of basal rings whilst the basal spathe is absent. The flowers are small and an unusual pale greenish-yellow, the anthers being of similar colouring. The flowers appear early in February and emit the sweet mossy scent of primroses.

C. *longiflorus* (syn. *C. odorus*). It bears the most richly scented flowers of all the crocus species, being so powerful that two or three blooms growing in a pot will scent a large room for several weeks. A native of southern Italy, Sicily and Malta, it blooms during October and November, at the same time as its leaves appear. The tube is long and elegant, and the deep-violet segments open to display brilliant-orange anthers and orange shading in the throat. The scent resembles that of *Iris unguicularis,* being likened to ripe plums or to the double primrose Marie Crousse which smells of honeysuckle.

C. *sativus.* The Saffron crocus, one of the oldest plants in cultivation, believed to be the *Karkom* of the Song of Solomon which gave the name Crocus to the genus. It is now rare in Britain but is still cultivated commercially from Spain to Kashmir, its native lands, and is now only used in Britain to flavour and colour saffron cakes. The blooms give off a delicate perfume when inhaled near to, and it is more pronounced in the dried saffron collected from the stigmata which hang out of the flowers in a most peculiar manner. Another peculiarity is that its flowers remain open during dull weather and at night-time, for once having opened they seem unable to close again. The blooms are produced only following a hot, dry summer and are extremely beautiful, being reddish-purple with deeper veining of violet.

C. *suaveolens.* The Roman crocus, it follows *C. imperati* into bloom, flowering late in February and until the end of March, its star-like blooms having the sweet scent of honeysuckle, almost as powerful as the Border auricula. The tube is 10 cm (4 in) long with narrow lilac segments, shaded with buff on the outside, but as E. A. Bowles so rightly said, it 'is a poor relation of *C. imperati*' being smaller and less conspicuous, but its perfume is if anything more pronounced.

C. versicolor. In its native haunts of the rocky seaboard of the French Riviera, Farrer tells us that 'a hundred forms of it may be found' for it is as variable as *C. chrysanthus.* It is the last of the scented species to bloom, being at its best in March and into April. Closely related to *C. suaveolens* and *C. imperati,* it is the only spring-flowering crocus to be feathered on the inside of the segments. Originally *C. fragrans,* it may have been given its present name by Parkinson for it was first illustrated in the *Paradisus.* It is also Philip Miller's 'Party-coloured Crocus', and by the end of the nineteenth century there were as many as 18 named varieties. The blooms have a soft, sweet mossy perfume, like that of woodland primroses.

C. vitellinus. It is one of the yellow-flowered *aureus* group, native of Syria and the Lebanon and is winter-flowering, the blooms appearing early in December and continuing until the end of February. They are a deep golden-yellow with narrow pointed segments, the outer petals being feathered with bronze. The blooms are sweetly scented.

CROTON (Cascarilla) (Euphorbiaceae—Spurgewort Family)

A genus of annual or perennial trees or shrubs numbering some 1,000 species which release a milky, acrid juice when the stems are broken. They are native of tropical Africa, South America, the South Sea Islands and the Bahamas, and most are grown for the exotic colourings of their leaves, often measuring 60 cm (2 ft) long or more, Several species have attractively scented bark.

Species. *Croton eleutheria.* It is native of the Bahamas and makes a small tree seldom more than 6 m (20 ft) in height. At the top it forms numerous brittle branches which, when broken, exude a thick balsamic-scented juice. The greyish-brown bark, usually covered with a white crustaceous lichen will, when dried and burnt, give off a powerful balsamic perfume which is most refreshing when used indoors. Tromsdorff found that this balsamic perfume was due to a resin in the bark which yields upon distillation by steam a volatile oil with the same powerfully penetrating balsamic odour. The bitter principle contained in the bark is known as cascarillin.

The bark arrives on the market as short curled pieces, usually the product of the younger branches from which it is readily detached. To the taste it is bitter and aromatic and is known to the natives as 'Sweet-wood'.

C. malombo. It is native of the South American state of Colombia where it grows to tree-like proportions with browny-red bark which has the scent of *Acorus calamus,* the scent being more pronounced as the bark becomes dry.

CUMINUM (Umbelliferae—Parsley Family)

A genus of a single species.

Species. *Cuminum cyminum.* It is a native of Egypt and Ethiopia but will ripen its seed as far north as England and the Baltic countries. It is an annual requiring half-hardy culture, the seeds, which are aromatic when dry, being sown under glass in February. The seedlings should be planted out early in May, and spaced 37.5 cm (15 in) apart. The plant grows 45 cm (18 in) high with fern-like leaves which have a pungent aroma when bruised. During midsummer it bears umbels of rose-pink flowers. 'Cummin good for eyes', wrote Spenser, for in his time an infusion of the leaves was often used for bathing the eyes. In Germany, the seeds are used to flavour bread but not since Elizabethan times has the plant been in demand in Britain, though in Cornwall it was traditional to offer the monarch a pound of cumin seed at his coronation, and this continued up to the coronation of George VI.

CUNNINGHAMIA (Taxodiaceae—Yew Tree Family)

A genus of three species, native of China and Formosa.

Species. *Cunninghamia lanceolata.* It is known as the Chinese Fir and in the British Isles should be confined to sheltered gardens of western coastal areas where it will grow into a tall handsome tree with emerald-green foliage which turns bronze in the autumn. It is deliciously resinous when rubbed against.

CUPHEA (Lythraceae—Loosestrife Family)

A large family of more than 250 species of trees, shrubs and annual plants which, being native of Mexico, require half-hardy treatment. They should be given a warm, sheltered border and a sunny aspect. The annual forms may be raised in gentle heat and planted in masses in sunny beds, after hardening, in June.

Species. *Cuphea lanceolata.* It grows about 60 cm (2 ft) tall with downy, lance-shaped leaves and it bears curiously-shaped flowers which appear on long stems and have 2 large upper petals and 4 small ones. The colour varies from deep purple to maroon and carmine, and the flowers emit an exotic incense-like fragrance. It is in bloom from July to September.

CUPIA (Chinchonaceae—Chinchona Family)

Native of Malabar, Ceylon and the hills of northern China, it is so closely allied to *Webera* as to be sometimes classified with them. The Cupias are evergreen shrubs found about rocky hillsides at altitudes of 900 to 1,500 m (3 to 5,000 ft).

Species. *Cupia corymbosa.* It makes a dense shrub some 1.8 m (6 ft) tall with lanceolate-oblong leaves 15 cm (6 in) long, glossy and with hairy glands in the axils of the large veins which gives them a resinous scent. The flowers are borne in terminal corymbs and are small, white at first, turning pale yellow and fragrant. The extremities of the young shoots are covered with a white resinous substance which is powerfully scented.

C. cymosa. A native of Borneo, it is an arborescent shrub with pubescent branches and ovate-acute shining leaves. The axillary cymes are composed of numerous white flowers of exquisite fragrance.

C. scandens. Native only of Silhet where it is called *Gujer-Kota.* It is a small scandent shrub with glossy acuminated leaves 15 cm (6 in) long. The large funnel-shaped flowers are borne in axillary cymes and are

white at first, turning pale yellow, and powerfully scented.

C. thyrsoides. A small tree or shrub found only about the hills of the Deccan Peninsula. It has woody branches covered with scented brown pubescence whilst the flowers are dingy-white and richly scented.

C. truncata. Native of Penang, it is a twining plant with ovate leaves 10 cm (4 in) long, dark and glossy on the upper side, whilst the flowers which are white are borne in short terminal panicles and have a potent scent, like that of jonquils.

CURCUMA (Zingiberaceae—Ginger Family)

A small genus of semi-tropical plants with perennial tuberous rootstocks and annual stems. The roots are highly fragrant and, when dried and powdered, form an ingredient (Zedoary) together with cloves, deodar and other aromatics, of a compound known to the Hindus as *Abir.* The same substance may also be mixed with the powdered roots of *Hedychium spicatum* and sandalwood. From the roots of *Curcuma aromatica,* native women extract a substance which, when applied to the body, imparts a delicious fragrance. The word Curcuma is from the Persian, *Kurkum,* referring to the saffron colouring of the rhizome-like roots. The plants can be grown in a warm greenhouse and a very peaty compost. Propagate by dividing the tubers in spring.

Species. *Curcuma longa.* Native to South-east Asia and the East Indies, with Malabar, Java and Haiti the main centres of its cultivation, it is a perennial plant with a rhizomatous rootstock known in commerce as turmeric. The rhizomes vary in size from 2 to 7 cm (1 to 3 in) long and are cylindrical, tapering at both ends and with a rough appearance. When dry, they have an aromatic, peppery odour, and when finely ground the powder is used in the kitchen for meat and egg dishes and is an ingredient of most curry powders. The seed contains about 5 per cent of essential oil which also has a pungent, peppery smell.

C. rubescens. A native of Bengal, it is a beautiful species, its bright-yellow flowers being deliciously fragrant, whilst the leaves (when bruised) and the roots give off a pleasant aromatic scent. The root consists of several pearl-coloured bulbs, strongly aromatic, which provide support for the previous year's foliage and which die back when the scapes of the new season arise from the newly-formed tubers.

C. viridiflora. The yellow, tuberous roots of this species are used by the people of Sumatra as a dye, and they have a bitter, camphorous taste and smell.

All the Curcumas flower during the warm April-May period, soon after the leaves appear. The plants require a rich soil, usually that occupied by sugar cane the previous year. Planting is done along the top of ridges, using small pieces of root and setting them 60 cm (2 ft) apart. The plants are lifted at the end of the season when the roots are dried and marketed.

C. zedoaria. This is native, not only of Bengal where it is common in gardens around Calcutta, but also of Malaya, China and of several islands of South-east Asia. The roots are deep yellow, whilst the flower stem consists only of the sheath of the leaves which are covered with down. From the sheath the flower spike arises, the tubes being pink with a fleshy yellow interior, and they have a powerful aromatic perfume; the roots emit a powerful camphor-like smell.

C. zerumbet. It is a native of Chittagong and, like *C. zedoaria,* the roots have a camphor-like smell. In the Bombay markets, the root is known as *Kachoora,* with an odour described by Dr Dymock as being 'analogous with that of ginger until the rhizome is powdered, when it develops a powerful aromatic odour similar to that of cardamoms'.

According to Bucholtz, the essential oil consists of two oils, one being lighter, the other heavier than water, with a camphoric smell and taste. From the roots a colouring matter, curcumin, is obtained after the essential oil has been distilled.

CUSCUTA (Dodder) (Convolvulaceae— Bindweed Family)

A genus of slender, twining leafless parasitic plants, mostly annuals. The flowers are white and rose and borne in dense clusters.

Species. *Cuscuta epithymum.* It is an annual, known as the Lesser Dodder, and is a parasitic plant of the British Isles, found on gorse and ling and other heathland plants. It twines around its host with a thread-like stem to which it clings by means of suckers and which extract the necessary nutrition for its support. The tiny clusters of pinky-white flowers (the reddish calyx being shorter than the white corolla) appear from June until September and emit a remarkably sweet perfume, especially pronounced towards evening. After flowering, the stems turn brown and disappear.

C. nitida. Native of South Africa where it grows on open hillsides and blooms during December and January. It has long slender stems and bears sweetly scented flowers of rosy-red, the corolla having broad lanceolate lobes as long as the tube.

CYANELLA (Amaryllidaceae—Narcissus Family)

A genus of seven species, native of South Africa; as their botanical characteristics come somewhere between Liliaceae and Iridaceae, they are often included in the family Tecophileaceae. They are perennial herbs with a white, corm-shaped rhizome covered in a fibrous tunic. The name comes from the Greek *kyanos,* blue, though the flowers are lilac-mauve rather than blue. It has lance-shaped leaves and bears its flowers in loose racemes. The perianth is 6-lobed with the 3 outer segments drooping.

Species. *Cyanella capensis.* Common on flats and hillsides of the Cape Peninsula, where it blooms from October until April, it has sword-like leaves, and bears scented lilac flowers in a racemose inflorescence on 30 cm (12 in) stems. The blooms are enhanced by the yellow stamens. In the British Isles and northern Europe, it blooms during July and August, and the corms should be lifted and dried off when the leaves have died down. Planting is in November in a really sunny sheltered position. Cover with bracken or similar material through the winter. Propagation is by seed or offsets.

C. odoratissima. It has lance-shaped leaves and bears its flowers on branched stems 30 cm (12 in) tall. The flowers are deep rose-pink and possess a powerful lily-like scent, appearing in July and August.

CYATHODES (Epacridaceae—Epacris Family)

A genus of 15 species, native of Tasmania, New Zealand and Hawaii. They are small, spreading heath-like shrubs which bear their flowers in axillary clusters. One species bears flowers with pronounced scent.

Species. *Cyathodes colensii.* A native of New Zealand, it grows less than 30 cm (12 in) tall with blue-grey leaves which are evergreen, and like so many of the peat-loving plants it blooms in autumn. The tiny creamy-white flowers are produced in axillary clusters and are sweetly scented. They are followed by scarlet berries.

CYCLAMEN (Primulaceae—Primrose Family)

A genus of 15 species of plants with fleshy corm-like tubers and suitable for naturalizing beneath mature trees or for growing in the alpine house or garden. By planting several fragrant species, the blooms may be enjoyed almost throughout the year, with the exception of mid-summer.

The plant reached England early in her history. The first to be grown in gardens was *C. coum*, a winter-flowering species, but its carmine-pink flowers carry no perfume. It is possible that both *C. hederaefolium* and *C. europeum,* the Common Sowbread, native to most European countries, were also native British plants for Gerard tells that *C. hederaefolium* 'groweth upon the mountains of Wales and on the hills of Lincolnshire and Somerset', whilst *C. europeum* is to be found to this day naturalized in parts of Kent and Sussex, on limestone formations.

When planting the corms, they should have the upper surface exposed, merely pressing them into the ground which should first have been shallowly enriched with leaf-mould and some decayed manure and with mortar or limestone chippings. A well-drained friable soil is necessary otherwise the corms may decay during periods of root inactivity when excessive rainfall is often experienced. *C. europeum* is the exception to the need for shallow planting for it requires to be set 15 cm (6 in) deep where the soil is light and friable. This species is also the exception to the rule of planting the hardy early-flowering cyclamen in July for it is then coming into bloom and is best planted in spring; the round or smooth side should be placed downwards and the corms kept moist until established. Most of the species do not bloom during their first season owing to the breaking off of the woody 'arms' on the upper surface but more than compensate by their beautifully mottled foliage, especially of *C. europeum* which is evergreen and acts as a foil for the blue-flowering squills.

These species requiring shallow planting should be given a top dressing each year as they tend to push themselves out of the ground whilst they form their roots from around the upper surface. Leaf-mould and a little decayed manure should be pressed around the corms after flowering, and they benefit from an occasional dressing with mortar or lime rubble.

Species. *Cyclamen africanum.* Native of the deciduous woodlands of North Africa, it forms a large black tuber 15 to 20 cm (6 to 8 in) across, and the leaves are of similar breadth. Toothed at the margins, the leaves are marbled with white and are purple on the underside. The flowers are sweetly scented and appear in October. They are deep rosy-red with a purple spot at the base of each petal.

C. cilicium. It should be planted in July and blooms early in September, continuing to produce its pretty pink flowers with their attractively twisted petals until mid-November if the weather is mild. Like all the hardy cyclamen, the dainty flowers hover above the foliage like moths and they have a delicious vanilla-like perfume. *C. cilicium* is a native of the pine forests of the Lebanon and grows only 7.5 to 10 cm (3 to 4 in) tall. Its rounded leaves have a pretty heart-shaped zone of silver. In exposed gardens, the plant should be confined to the shelter of trees or shrubs, and it is also suitable for the alpine garden or a trough.

C. creticum. Native of the mountains of Crete where it shelters between the rocks, it requires a position of almost complete shade. It is late into bloom, the small white flowers with their carnation-like perfume appearing towards the end of April. The dark-green ivy-shaped leaves are toothed and are mottled with silver. Like the other species native of the southern Mediterranean regions, it should be grown under glass in the cooler parts of the British Isles and northern Europe.

C. cyprium. Native only of Cyprus, it is closely related to *C. neapolitanum,* differing in its unlobed leaves and narrower flower petals. The leaves are dark velvety-green with pale-green markings and shaded crimson on the underside. The flowers are small and are white or pinkish-white, each petal being spotted with crimson at the base. They appear in October and are heavily scented. The plant is less hardy than other species and should be grown in a cold greenhouse or frame in the cooler parts.

C. europeum (syn. *C. odoratum*). It may be said to be a native plant and was grown in Elizabethan knot gardens. It bears the most sweetly scented flowers of all the hardy cyclamen, and it is summer-flowering, remaining in bloom from mid-July until the beginning of winter. It is native of limestone mountainous regions in all parts of Europe and during Parkinson's time had become naturalized in South-east England. From the heavy perfume of its flowers, it was also known as *C. odoratum.* The heart-shaped leaves are marbled with white and are purple on the underside whilst the flowers are purple-red, shaded darker at the base.

The plant is a lover of shade and appreciates some moisture about its roots, and under the right conditions an established corm will bear upwards of a hundred fragrant blooms during a season.

C. neapolitanum. Native of southern Italy, the leaves are strikingly marbled with white and as they appear early in autumn and remain until spring, they provide valuable and attractive cover for the early spring bulbs.

The corms are flat and increase in size for 50 years or more until they are more than 30 cm (12 in) across. Above them in autumn hover multitudes of slightly fragrant flowers of clear rose-pink. There is also an attractive white form, *album,* which as would be expected is more sweetly scented.

The corms appreciate a mulch of decayed manure each year after flowering as they tend to exhaust the soil.

C. persicum (syn. *C. latifolium*). In spite of its name it is not a native of Persia but of the Lebanon, Crete and Rhodes. It is unique amongst cyclamen in that its flower stem is not coiled but when the seed is ripe bends over and deposits the seed on the surface of the soil. The ovate leaves are toothed at the margins, the upper surface being marbled with white. The flowers appear in March and are white with a purple spot at the base of each petal. They are slightly scented, a quality not passed on to the large-flowered florists' varieties derived from the species.

C. repandum. It grows in mountainous regions of central and southern Italy, at altitudes of 1,500 to 1,800 m (5 to 6,000 ft) and though the corms are small, it is the most free-flowering of all the species, an established plant bearing as many as 200 blooms of rosy-white, spotted with purple at the base. They are sweetly scented and appear during April and May, a few weeks later than *C. libanoticum* but before those of *C. europeum.* There is an attractive pure-white form, *album.*

CYMBIDIUM (Orchidaceae—Orchid Family)

A genus of some 50 species, found chiefly in the river valleys of central and southern China. Few bear scented flowers, though *Cymbidium virescens* is one of the most beautifully scented of all flowers, and is one of the longest-lasting orchids, remaining fresh for several weeks.

The Cymbidiums require warm house cultivation, but do not tolerate excessive heat. A constant temperature of around 13°C (65°F) is ideal. Their large fleshy roots need plenty of pot room and good drainage. The compost should be composed of turf loam, peat or leaf-mould and sphagnum moss in equal parts. After planting, the compost should be just below the rim of the pot to make for easier watering. The plants may remain undisturbed for several years.

When in bloom, shade from strong sunlight. Increase is by division of large old plants.

Species. *Cymbidium cyperifolium.* Pale green and yellow with red streaks, the fragrant flowers of this species appear in winter 4 to 7. on a stem. It is a Himalayan orchid, with leaves up to 60 cm (2 ft) long.

C. eburneum. The ice-white, waxy flowers have a strong fragrance and are long-lasting, being produced in spring in inflorescences about 30 cm (1 ft) long.

C. kanran. This bright-green to yellowish-green orchid has purple spots and markings on the petals and lip. Its sweet fragrance adds to its attraction. The flowering season is variable.

C. mastersii. An Indian orchid, strongly scented of almonds, which has ice-white flowers with pink markings on the lip. The flowers are produced 3 to 10 in a raceme in winter.

C. sinense. A very fragrant Cymbidium with brown and purple petals, and green-yellow lip. It flowers in autumn on a tall, erect stem carrying many flowers.

C. suave. From Australia the fleshy greenish, or yellowish-green flowers are powerfully fragrant, and borne on drooping stems; at most seasons of the year.

C. tracyanum. A very attractive and fragrant orchid, but not often seen. It has large greenish-yellow flowers with crimson stripes and creamy-white lip, 12 to 20 of them being produced on the arching stems. Flowering-time is late autumn for this Burmese species.

C. virescens. The spring-flowering orchid of the Yangtze River Valley which has been grown in China (and also Japan) since ancient times, for the delicate sweet fragrance of its flowers has been called 'the scent of the kings'.

With its graceful, grass-like foliage the plant has been widely depicted in Chinese paintings, though the colour of its flowers is of secondary importance to its sweet perfume. It was described in works of the Sung dynasty (960-1279) by Chao Shih-keng and others, and in modern times the flowers are widely cultivated in the silk town of Soochow.

The plant bears a single flower shaded green and yellow with a red-blotched lip, and it appears early in spring, heralding the new-born vitality of nature in the same way as the primrose of the Western world.

CYMBOPOGON (Gramineae—Grass Family)

A genus of perennial aromatic grasses, closely allied to *Andropogon* and distributed about dry, stony places in North and South Africa, in India and South-east Asia, which are valued for their aromatic principles. They form densely tufted plants with the inflorescences crowded at the end of naked stems with the spikes borne in pairs.

Species. *Cymbopogon citratus.* Present in southern India, Ceylon, and in the Moluccas where it inhabits barren land. It grows 30 cm (1 ft) tall with thin, grass-like leaves and is known as Lemon-grass. From the leaves, an oil smelling of verbena is obtained which is used to perfume soaps. The Lemon-grass otto, as its essence is called, is extremely potent and has great purity of scent.

C. martinii. From this is obtained the *palma rosa* or rose-geranium oil of India, used in soaps and perfumery.

C. nardus (syn. *Andropogon nardus*). Present in South Africa where it is known as Tambatie grass, and in Ceylon, Malaya and Java. All parts are highly aromatic, especially the dried roots which smell of spikenard, hence its earlier name, *Andropogon nardus*. It grows 30 to 37 cm (12 to 15 in) tall with flat leaves with a prominent midrib, the spikelets crowded together in a dense inflorescence. It is the source of oil of citronella.

C. proximus. Found in several parts of North Africa, Egypt and the Near East, it is a densely tufted grass with thin leaves. It bears a reddish-brown panicle and below, numerous branched spikelets in dense clusters. When handled, it releases a lemon scent with rose undertones.

C. schoenanthus. By the oil distillers of Khandesh it is called 'Motiya' when the inflorescence is young and bluish-white in colour, and 'Sonfiya' after ripening to a crimson-red colour, for the oil obtained from the young grass has a more delicate odour. It grows freely on open hillsides in West Khandesh and is cut and harvested late in September, after the rains. It is sold to distillers who stock it and set up stills by the side of streams. The product which has a powerful rose perfume is packed in skins for transportation to Bombay and the Middle East where it is sold to adulterate otto of roses.

It must not be confused with *Acorus*

calamus, though to add to the confusion it is the 'sweet calamus' of Exodus which was used in making the holy anointing oil.

CYPERUS (Galingale) (Cyperaceae— Sedge Family)

An order of some 2,000 or more grass-like plants usually found growing by the banks of ponds and streams and in wet copses and marshland. The name *Souchet* is used by French perfumers for the fragrant tuberous roots of *Cyperus longus* and other species which when dried and powdered, or by distillation, yield an aromatic perfume used for making cosmetics.

Species. *Cyperus aromaticus.* It grows in damp pastures and about marshland in central India, Burma and in certain islands of the Pacific, being a serious weed in several of the Fiji Islands where it is known as the Navua sedge. It grows 60 to 90 cm (2 to 3 ft) tall, but has been known to reach a height of 1.8 m (6 ft), its linear lanceolate leaves mostly borne from the base of the stem. They are usually 15 cm (6 in) long and 4 mm (1/8 in) wide, and are aromatic when bruised or trodden upon. It spreads rapidly by means of a tuberous underground stem and once established is difficult to eradicate.

C. longus. The Sweet sedge or Galingale, a plant native of the British Isles, where it grows in marshland and by the side of lakes. Like all the sedges, it increases by a creeping rootstock from which arise 3-angled stems 60 to 90 cm (2 to 3 ft) high. During August and September, it bears its reddish-coloured flower spikes in elegant umbel-like cymes from the base of which arise gracefully recurving leaves. From the stems and roots (but not from the flowers or leaves) is emitted a sweet moss-like perfume, resembling that of the violet but not so pure. It is in fact, a compound odour which Gerard described as 'a most sweet and pleasant smell when (the stem is) broken'. Its essence, obtained both from the stems and roots, is used to mix with lavender-water. Like the orris, the roots become more fragrant with age and emit a similar perfume. The elegant flower sprays are most ornamental during August.

C. odoratus. Native of South Africa

where it is occasionally found about damp low-lying ground, it is a perennial with 3-angled stems and sheathing basal leaves. The greenish-yellow spikelets are borne in an umbel, surrounded by leafy bracts. The stems have a more pronounced perfume than in any species.

C. rotundus. It is a common Eastern species, especially in India about Lahore and Madras where the dried and powdered roots are used by Indian women as talcum powder. It was the *radix junci* of the Romans, and Herodotus mentions that it was used by the Scythians for embalming. It is mentioned in the *Iliad* and in the *Odyssey,* and Pliny calls it *Juncus angulosus* for the stems are triangular, attaining a height of 60 cm (2 ft); they are naked and smooth, and the base is sheathed by the leaves which are smooth and glossy.

The plants grow from rhizomes which become long and sausage-like. Externally they are dark brown turning black when dried, but white within. They have the aromatic smell of *Acorus calamus.*

On examination by microscope, it is found that the outer layer is composed of bundles of reddish-brown cells containing essential oil, starch granules and resinous matter.

C. scariosus. In Sanskrit it is *Nagar moostaka,* in Arabic, *Soade-Kufi,* and like *C. rotundus* it is tuberous-rooted with numerous dark-brown fibres which when bruised emit a powerful fragrance. Its slender delicate form distinguishes it from other species. It grows 0.9 to 1.2 m (3 to 4 ft) tall, its flowers appearing in compound umbels. The roots yield a perfume for the hair, which is also used in the dyeing and preparing of fabrics. It grows about damp ground in Bengal and Rajputana and is sold on the Bombay market as *surat.*

CYPRIPEDIUM (Orchidaceae—Orchid Family)

A genus which includes several of the most beautiful plants of the world's flora distributed throughout the tropics and in a few places of the Northern Hemisphere where they are known as Slipper orchids from the appearance of the flower with its inflated lower lip. The flowers are pollinated by small bees attracted to the nectar, which, as with the labiates, use the lip as a landing stage.

Species. *Cypripedium calceolus.* The Lady's Slipper orchid, a rare plant of the limestone cliffs of North Yorkshire though it is more common in parts of the Swiss Alps. It has a creeping rhizomatous rootstock and forms a downy stem 30 cm (12 in) high at the end of which it bears 1 or 2 large flowers with broad reddish-brown sepals and petals, with a large inflated lower lip or pouch of pale yellow. It blooms in May, the flowers having a soft rose-like perfume.

C. montanum. It is native only of Oregon and is a rare gem, bearing on a 30 cm (12 in) stem chocolate-coloured flowers with an inflated white lower lip, and exhaling a delicate vanilla-like perfume.

C. spectabile (syn. *C. hirsutum*). It is the Showy Lady's Slipper orchid, growing in the eastern provinces of Canada and in Newfoundland. It grows to a height of nearly 60 cm (2 ft) with pale-green leaves covered in downy hairs. The bloom measures 5 cm (2 in) across and is purest white, the pouched lip which forms the slipper having crimson veins.

CYRTANTHUS (Amaryllidaceae— Narcissus Family)

A genus of 48 species, closely related to *Vallota* and native of South Africa where they frequent the Drakensberg Mountains. They have large, tunicated bulbs and bear funnel-shaped flowers, usually 5 or 6 to a 30-cm (1-ft) stem with hollow peduncles, which nod and dance in the warm breezes. They are mostly of brilliant-scarlet colouring and at the Cape bloom in March and April, elsewhere in the autumn. They are called Fire Lilies and several have perfume, scent being most pronounced in the yellow-flowered *Cyrtanthus ochroleucus.* They are excellent plants for a cool greenhouse, to be planted in March in a compost made up of loam, leaf-mould and coarse sand in equal parts.

Species. *Cyrtanthus cooperi.* Possibly a species, or a variety, of *C. mackenii.* The flowers appear 5 to 7 on a thin wiry stem

before the leaves and are smaller than those of most species; they are pale primrose-yellow with a soft sweet perfume.

C. ochroleucus. The flowers appear 6 to 7 on a thin wiry stem before the leaves and are smaller than most forms, borne 2 to 3 on a slender stem. They are pale primrose-yellow with a soft sweet perfume.

C. odorus. It has ovoid bulbs of 5-cm (2-in) diameter from which arise 2 to 3 liner leaves about 30 cm (1 ft) long, and narrow, bell-shaped flowers of brilliant scarlet which are unusual for the richness of their perfume in flowers of this colour. They bloom during July and August.

CYTISUS (Leguminosae—Laburnum Family)

A genus of about 40 species native of Europe and the Mediterranean shores, most of which are without spines and which distinguishes them from the closely related gorse (*Ulex*).

Species. *Cytisus battandieri.* It is native of the coastline of Morocco and is thus more tender than other species but it is one of nature's most beautiful plants. It is tall-growing, attaining a height of 4.5 m (15 ft), and so may be planted against a warm wall where it receives protection from cold winds. It has silvery clover-like foliage and in June bears densely furnished spikes of lupin-like flowers which are golden-yellow and emit the fragrance of ripe pineapples. The flowers persist until the very end of summer, and where growing against an open window will scent the largest of rooms when the weather is calm and warm. The plant may be kept under control by cutting back the flowering shoots at the end of summer.

C. supranubius (syn. *C. fragrans, Genista fragrans*). Though one of the most tender of the brooms, the Teneriffe broom is one of the most beautiful, covered in emerald-green foliage throughout the year, and bearing in May and June deliciously scented pinkish-white blossom on its drooping branches. It should be grown only in a sheltered garden and in a position of full sun, where it will reach a height of about 2.4 m (8 ft).

D

DACTYLANTHUS (Balanophoraceae—Balanophora Family)

A genus of a single species.

Species. *Dactylanthus taylori.* It is a parasitic plant, native of New Zealand where it was discovered in 1857 by the Rev R. Taylor, growing near the head waters of the Wanganui River. In his *New Zealand and its Inhabitants*, Taylor described it as having an earthy smell like a mushroom, though its scent has also been likened to that of a ripe melon.

It attaches itself to the roots of Pittosporum and forms a tubercle. The parasite sends out cells which penetrate between the vascular bundles of the host's roots, the tissues of the two plants forming an intermediate zone, like the grafting of two plants. The tubercle then grows to about 15-cm (6-in) diameter and from it appear fleshy shoots. These are covered in scales and enclose the flowers which resemble fungoid growths. They mimic fungi in all respects being of dingy-cream colouring, tinged with pink, like the mushroom. The Maoris call it *Pua-o-te-reinga*, Flower of Hades.

DAMNACANTHUS (Rubiaceae—Bedstraw Family)

A genus of six spiny plants, native of the Himalayas, central China and Japan, which in all but the mildest parts of the British Isles and North America require the protection of a greenhouse during winter.

Species. *Damnacanthus indicus.* It makes a dainty pot plant growing less than 45 cm (18 in) tall, its woody stems being covered with spines. Its small white flowers are borne at the axils of the leaves and are sweetly scented. They are followed by attractive red berries. The leaves, when dry, smell of new-mown hay.

DAPHNE (Thymeleaceae—Mezereon Family)

A genus of about 400 evergreen or deciduous shrubs or sub-shrubs, famed for the powerful exotic fragrance of their blossom, which are suitable for the shrubbery or alpine garden according to the habit of their growth. Most are very slow-growing, making only an inch or so of new growth in a year, and they require little or no pruning. They are increased by layering the lower branches or by cuttings of the half-ripened wood, inserted in a sandy compost beneath a handlight or frame. Almost all the daphnes grow well in a chalky soil. Several bear their scented blossom on leafless stems during winter.

Species and Varieties. *Daphne alpina.* A deciduous plant native of the European Alps where it grows 45 cm (18 in) tall and blooms from May until July. Growing naturally only on limestone formations, it requires a well-drained gritty soil with some lime rubble incorporated, but unless raised from seed and grown on in small pots until ready for planting out, it is a most difficult plant to establish. The leaves are lance-shaped, woolly on the underside, whilst the white flowers are borne in terminal clusters and have a sweet perfume, with a spicy undertone of clove.

D. arbuscula. In its native Hungary it makes a tiny rounded shrublet about 30 cm (12 in) in height, crowded with narrow leaves which are evergreen and appear as if polished. It blooms in May and June, bearing clusters of rose-pink flowers which have a rich aromatic perfume.

D. aurantiaca. One of the most beautiful of the daphnes, it is native of central China, growing about 90 cm (3 ft) in height with oblong leaves which are evergreen. It comes into bloom in March, its flowers being golden-yellow like the Winter jasmine and having a delicate sweet perfume.

D. blagayana. Native of the mountainous regions of Eastern Europe, it grows only 37.5 cm (15 in) tall, and where it can be given a sheltered corner of the alpine garden, it will begin to bloom towards the end of a warm February. It is evergreen, of spreading, almost trailing habit, the leaves being formed only at the end of the reddish-brown stems and resembling rhododendron leaves. The deliciously fragrant milky-white blooms are borne in dense terminal clusters with the leaves acting as a ruff. Propagation is by layering the shoots in autumn, holding them in position with a large stone. The plants require a humus-laden soil preferably with some lime rubble about the roots.

D. caucasica. A deciduous shrub from the Caucasus, clothed with narrow leaves of palest green, which in May and June bears sweetly scented flowers of purest white in terminal clusters.

D. cneorum. Known as the Garland daphne or Garland flower, it is native of southern Europe and is one of the outstanding alpine plants, trailing about the limestone rocks and sending out its shoots to a distance of several feet. It forms tufts of lance-shaped leaves 1 cm ($\frac{1}{2}$ in) long and bears its intensely sweet-scented flowers of rose-pink in terminal clusters. It blooms throughout May and again in August and as it is evergreen remains attractive even when not in bloom. There is also a white-flowered form, *alba*, with pale-green leaves and equally fragrant.

The form Exima is of almost prostrate habit, the crimson buds opening to bright rose-pink, whilst *album* bears attractive white flowers which contrast beautifully with those of the type.

Using *D. cneorum* as one parent and *D. caucasica* as the other, the late Mr Albert Burkwood raised two magnificent sister hybrids which he named *D. burkwoodii* and *D.* Somerset, the latter being the

superior plant. It is faster-growing than any of the daphnes, making nearly 1.2 m (4 ft) of growth in 5 to 6 years. In fact, it grows so rapidly once established that the new shoots should be pinched back towards the end of the summer to maintain a bushy habit. It also flowers at an early age, every shoot being covered in clusters of pinky-white during June; they are so powerfully scented that a single plant when 5 years old will scent a large garden. It retains its leaves through winter only in a sheltered garden.

D. collina. The Neapolitan daphne, native of the hills of southern Italy and of Crete, also *D. sericea.* It makes a compact plant 30 to 3 7.5 cm (12 to 15 in) tall and is evergreen, the dark-green leaves being covered in brown hairs. In a mild winter and in a sunny sheltered garden it will bloom before Christmas, but usually begins about the first day of spring and continues until June, its purple-pink jasmine-like flowers making a most attractive display against the dark leaves and black stems, and having a rich sweet perfume.

The variety *neapolitana* does not flower until early May and grows to almost twice the height, covering itself in clusters of fragrant lilac-pink flowers.

D. gnidium. The Flax-leaf daphne, native of southern Europe and northern Africa where it attains a height of about 60 cm (2 ft). It is evergreen but in a cold garden needs the shelter of a warm wall to survive an average winter. It is the latest of all the daphnes to bloom, flowering late in June and continuing until the end of August, its sweetly scented blush-white flowers appearing in terminal clusters.

D. laureola. The British Spurge laurel which is always found growing in dense shade and is a handsome evergreen 0.9 to 1.2 m (3 to 4 ft) tall, with bare silvery-green stems at the top of which are tufts of laurel-like leaves which when young are tinted with red. The greenish-white flowers are borne in clusters of 5 or 6 and are surrounded by a collar of lance-shaped leaves, glossy and almost stalkless. It blooms from the early New Year until April and, like almost all the daphnes, the flowers are sweetly scented. The large flat flower-heads of the blooms, which have no petals, are followed by extremely poisonous oval black fruits. A hybrid when crossed with *D. mezereum*, named *D. houtteana*, has purple leaves and dark-red flowers.

D. mezereum. Native to the woodlands of southern Europe, it is completely hardy. Gerard wrote of it as the Mezereon and it was cultivated as a garden plant as early as the sixteenth century. It makes an upright bush and is slow-growing, adding less than 30 cm (12 in) to its stature in about as many years. For this reason it was widely grown in cottage gardens where it appreciated the company of other plants providing cool conditions for its roots. No winter-flowering plant is more colourful for from the early New Year until the end of March, its naked branches are wreathed in tiny flowers of purple-pink. The flowers have thick petals and curl back to reveal their bright-orange stamens, and emit a delicious sweet perfume.

There is a deeper-coloured form, *rubrum*, and a white form, *alba*, its beauty accentuated when growing with the purple-flowering varieties. Its snow-white blooms appear in June and are followed by amber-yellow berries whilst those of the type are crimson-red in colour. The form *grandiflora* blooms in October and bears larger flowers than the type whilst *alpinium*, from the Swiss Alpine regions, makes a tiny scented shrublet 37.5 cm (15 in) tall. The berries are all poisonous.

The secret of success with *D. mezereum* is to provide it with a cool soil, one which is deeply worked and enriched with leaf-mould. The best plants are those raised from seed which, however, take more than two years to germinate, and it will be another decade before the plants reach 30 cm (12 in) in height. It is unwise to cut the flower spikes to enjoy indoors however tempting it may be to do so, for *Daphne mezereum* resents cutting in any way, especially when in bloom. It should be left to beautify the winter garden.

D. odora. This half-hardy Chinese shrub growing 90 cm (3 ft) tall should, in gardens of northern Europe, be confined to a sheltered position and, during periods of low temperatures, be given some protection. It is an evergreen which, when the weather is mild, blooms from October until spring, the purple-pink flowers backed by a collar of leaves, appearing on terminal shoots, and they are more powerfully fragrant than all the daphnes, with a spicy undertone. There is a white-flowered form, *alba*, and one with shiny evergreen leaves edged with gold, *aurea-marginata*, which is hardier than the type and bears pale-pink flowers.

D. odora (also *D. indica* and wrongly-named) makes a round compact bush and like *D. mezereum* must be given a deep, moist soil.

The plant was originally called *Shui Hsiang* (Sleeping Scent) in its native China for there is a legend that a monk of Lu Shan discovered the plant growing high on a cliff, upon awakening from a nap and inhaling its spicy fragrance. It was brought into cultivation during the Sung dynasty (960-1279).

D. oleodes. So called because it makes a small twisted tree resembling the olive, and is distributed about the mountainous regions of south-eastern Europe, to Tibet and northern China. It grows about 60 cm (2 ft) in height and is evergreen. It blooms in April and May, bearing its creamy-white flowers in terminal clusters surrounded by the rosette of leaves, and they have a clove-like perfume.

D. petraea. Also *D. rupestris*, it is the Rock daphne, a slow-growing evergreen which rarely exceeds 10 to 12.5 cm (4 to 5 in) in height and is only found naturally about the limestone cliffs above Lake Garda, hanging in shrubby mats from the crevices well out of each of most plant-lovers. The roots run deep into the rocks and are most difficult to dig out for they readily break under the slightest pressure. Usually it is propagated by grafting on to roots of *Daphne mezereum*, which is best done early in spring.

Plants on their own roots enjoy the company of tufa stone into which their long roots can penetrate, and where this cannot be provided they should be given liberal quantities of mortar about the roots at planting time.

A plant in full bloom in May presents a magnificent spectacle with its dark-green leathery leaves formed in rosettes and bearing large flowers of rose-pink which have a wax-like appearance and emit an almost intoxicating perfume. An established plant covers an area of several feet and is smothered in blossom for at least six weeks.

The form *grandiflora* has larger flowers which, if anything, are produced with even greater freedom.

D. pontica. An evergreen from eastern Europe growing 1.5 to 1.8 m (5 to 6 ft) in height and resembling *D. laureola.* In March it begins to bear fragrant flowers of greenish-yellow in upright clusters and these are backed by a collar of glossy, lance-shaped leaves, like those of the Spurge laurel. This is a most valuable plant in that it flourishes in dense shade and in a heavy, poorly drained soil.

D. retusa. Native of western China, it is one of the supreme beauties of the genus. It grows about 45 cm (18 in) tall, making a neat rounded head from a single stem with dark-green fleshy evergreen leaves, and unlike the others it seems to do best in a soil where lime is absent. The purple-pink buds open to waxy-white tubular blooms which have a heavy exotic perfume.

D. striata. It is a native of the Italian Alps and is a plant of vigorous trailing habit with spoon-shaped leaves which are deciduous and stalkless. Again, it does better when grafted on to the roots of *D. mezereum* to give it a start, but should be encouraged to form its own roots by deep planting.

The flowers, which are borne in June and July, are a delightful lilac-rose and have a rich penetrating scent with a touch of clove which makes it less sickly-sweet than the perfume of the other daphnes. There is also a white form, *alba*, a beautiful variety which is unfortunately rare. It has the same clove-like fragrance of the type.

D. tangutica. It blooms from March until the end of May and is a hardy and vigorous plant growing 90 cm (3 ft) tall and almost as wide, with thick evergreen diamond-shaped leaves. It bears pinkish flowers in terminal clusters.

DATURA (Solanaceae—Nightshade Family)

A genus of sub-tropical plants, native of Peru and of other parts of South America, which in the British Isles and northern Europe require warm greenhouse culture. They are plants of shrubby, tree-like habit, and where growing in a greenhouse may be restricted by confining them to pots or tubs. They bear large funnel-shaped flowers varying in colour from the delicate whiteness of *D. suaveolens* and *D. knightii* to the intense red of *D. bicolor.* The most fragrant are the white-flowering varieties whilst *D. bicolor* has little or no perfume. Outdoors in their native land where their wood is well ripened by the sun, the trees present a sight of great beauty, covered in hundreds of large tubular flowers, each emitting the powerful exotic perfume associated with the Madonna lily and Narcissus (for indole is present) and other flowers of similar petal texture. Indoors, they bloom almost the whole year.

The annual Daturas are readily raised from seed but are of tender habit. Seed is sown in gentle heat early in the year and the plants set out in June after hardening. They lend an exotic appearance when used with summer bedding plants.

Species. *Datura ceratocaula.* A Cuban annual growing 60 to 90 cm (2 to 3 ft) high, its purple stems covered with grey down or powder, whilst the large lance-shaped leaves are hairy on the underside. The large white trumpets are tinted with purple and open late afternoon, and as the temperature falls the blooms emit a powerful, almost oppressive perfume. In sheltered gardens of south-western England and Ireland, it will seed itself.

D. chlorantha. Also *D. flava* and really a variety of *D. metei*, it is an Indian plant growing 60 cm (2 ft) in height with large leaves of darkest green. It is valuable in that it blooms during September and October until cut down by frost, its drooping yellow trumpets being double, formed one inside another, and they have a delicious sweet perfume as they open at night.

D. fastuosa. The Egyptian Thorn-apple, its toothed leaves emitting a most unpleasant smell when bruised, though its large white trumpets, borne in July and August and shaded violet on the outside, have a pleasant fragrance at eventide. There is also a double-flowered form and both are varieties of *D. metei*.

D. metei. A native of the tropics, it is a hairy (downy) annual of which there are several forms or varieties. When bruised, its heart-shaped leaves have an unpleasant smell but its large white trumpet-shaped flowers have an exotic fragrance and are followed by fruits the size of an apple.

D. meteloides. It is a tuberous-rooted perennial and a native of Texas and Mexico, growing 0.9 to 1.2 m (3 to 4 ft) high and distinguished from *D. metel* by its looser habit. In Britain, it should be grown as a half-hardy annual when it will bloom from July until late October, its funnel-shaped flowers, often 15 cm (6 in) across, being of pearly white with a delicious perfume.

D. stramonium. The Thorn-apple, is an annual, occasionally found on waste ground about the English countryside. It grows about 60 cm (2 ft) in height with branched stems and ovate, dentate leaves, and bears white or mauve funnel-shaped flowers in the forks of the branching stems. The whole plant gives off a nauseating stench, similar to that of the closely related Henbane. The oval fruits are spinous and 4-valved, resembling those of the horse-chestnut.

D. suaveolens. It is a Mexican species of the Thorn-apple and is not sufficiently hardy to withstand a winter outdoors in the British Isles unless given the protection of a walled garden in the South-west. The plants are most attractive grown in large pots as standard trees for the centre piece of half-hardy summer bedding plants, to be lifted under glass in October where the plants remain until the end of May, wintering them in gentle heat.

D. suaveolens attains a height of 3 to 3.6 m (10 to 12 ft) and has elliptic oblong leaves, smooth above, downy beneath, and during July and August bears large white trumpet-shaped flowers which have a powerful lily-like scent. It is especially pronounced at night, diffusing its sweet perfume far and wide.

DAUCUS (Umbelliferae—Parsley Family)

A genus of hairy annual or biennial plants, mostly native to the Mediterranean countries, with pinnately compound leaves and flowers borne in many-rayed umbels.

Species. *Daucus carota*. Native to the British Isles and northern Europe with elegant fern-like leaves, the Wild carrot is usually found in pastureland. The root is reddish-orange owing to the presence of the colouring matter' carotene. The aniseed-like smell of the wild form resembles that of the cultivated carrot.

DAVIDIA (Davidiaceae—Davidia Family)

A genus of a single species which bears brilliant-green leaves like those of the lime and emitting a pungent incense-like smell when handled.

Species. *Davidia involucrata*. A native of China, it is known as the Chinese Dove tree or Handkerchief tree, also the Ghost tree, for in May it is draped with large white drooping bracts, like white handkerchiefs, which are produced in pairs and surround the inflorescences. The fruit is like that of the walnut. Not completely hardy in the more exposed parts of the British Isles and North America, it should be given a mild locality where, in a moist rich soil, it will attain a height of 12 m (40 ft) or more.

DECASPERMUM (Myrtaceae—Myrtle Family)

A genus of about 100 species, native of Indonesia and islands of the South Pacific and closely related to the Clove tree. They are mostly trees or shrubs with simple, opposite leaves and bear their flowers in terminal cymes.

Species. *Decaspermum fruticosum* (syn. *Nelitris fruticosa*). Known in the Fiji islands as *Nuqanuqa*, it is a handsome small tree or shrub of the drier parts which covers itself in snow-white flowers emitting a powerful perfume.

DECUMARIA (Hydrangeaceae—Hydrangea Family)

A genus of only two species of self-clinging climbers closely related to the Clinging hydrangea, *H. petiolaris,* which has no scent. *Decumaria barbara* is the hardier species of the two and may be grown against a north wall or allowed to climb up tree trunks, and is hardy in almost all parts of Britain and America. The Decumarias grow well in any ordinary loam and enjoy a winter mulch of decayed manure.

Species. *Decumaria barbara*. Native of the eastern United States, it attains a height of 9 m (30 ft) or more and where not too exposed to cold winds is evergreen. It has slightly toothed leaves and during June and July bears its pure-white flowers in corymbs, and they are sweetly scented.

D. sinensis. Possibly not quite as hardy as *D. barbara* but will prove so in a sheltered garden. It is a plant of great beauty bearing its corymbs of green and white in profusion right through summer and they are deliciously honey-scented.

DELPHINIUM (Ranunculaceae— Buttercup Family)

A genus of about 40 species of annual or perennial herbs with alternate cut or lobed leaves of which only *D. brunonianum* and *D. leroyi* bear fragrant flowers.

Species. *Delphinium brunonianum.* It is a native of the lower Himalaya regions, and like so many plants of that part has leaves which are covered in silky hairs. They are kidney-shaped and deeply divided. The plant grows only 30 cm (12 in) tall and blooms in June. The flowers are large and hooded and of pale-blue colouring with purple margins and a jet-black centre. Several appear on each stem and have an almost transparent appearance. They emit a powerful musk-like scent until they begin to fade. The plant requires a light, well-drained soil and an open situation, and should be protected during winter with a covering of straw or bracken. Spring planting is desirable. It has been said, perhaps erroneously, that the Musk-deer obtains its musk-scented characteristics by feeding on this plant.

D. leroyi. Native of central Africa, this handsome species was rediscovered in 1961 and is being used by Dr Legro at Wageningen University in Holland to breed in its exotic perfume to the large-flowered delphiniums.

Its home is Mount Kilimanjaro where it grows at about 1,500 m (5,000 ft) above sea-level and is covered in snow for more than half the year. It is a plant of vigorous branching habit, growing 60 cm (2 ft) tall, and throughout summer bears deliciously scented flowers of palest blue.

DENDROBIUM (Orchidaceae—Orchid Family)

A genus of nearly 1,000 species, native of tropical Asia, Australia and Polynesia.

They are epiphytic herbs of rigid habit with narrow leaves, thick and leathery, and bear large flowers, usually in racemes. The name is taken from two Greek words signifying 'tree-life', denoting the epiphytic quality. Clasping the bark of trees and rocks by their roots, they produce in addition filamentous roots, the outer surface of which is spongy and enables the plant to obtain any available moisture.

Under cultivation, they require a minimum temperature of 21°C (70°F) and plenty of sunlight. When in full growth, they require plenty of moisture at the roots, but it is essential that the new growth be thoroughly ripened. This is achieved by placing the plants in a temperature of 16°C (60°F) and giving the minimum of moisture. A buoyant atmosphere is required. After this rest or ripening period, the plants will show their flower buds. Immediately after flowering is the time to repot. Use a pot which will allow no more than 2 to 5 cm (1 to 2 in) of soil around the plants. The compost should consist of equal parts of peat and sphagnum moss, made as firm as possible.

Species. *Dendrobium aemulum.* Found in open country, only on Iron-barks, or growing on the Brush Box. It has short, swollen, jointed stems and at the end appear twin leaves. From the axils arise an inflorescence of up to 20 white flowers of exotic perfume.

D. aureum. From India and Burma, this bright, deep-yellow orchid has a velvety appearance to the petals and is strongly scented with violets. The 7-cm (3-in) flowers are produced in twos and threes in February.

D. linguiforme. Known as the Tongued orchid, for its thick, fleshy leaves take the shape of a tongue. From the leaf axils appear the inflorescences of fragrant, snow-white flowers, the sepals and petals being so narrow as to give them a thread-like appearance.

D. moschatum. The strong musk scent of the flowers would make this species more popular, but the height of its stems, as much as 1.8 m (6 ft), prevents this. The yellowish and rose-tinged flowers appear in June, with a reddish-purple blotch in the throat.

D. nobilis. Its flowers have the scent of

musk by day and of new-mown hay at night. Grown, and popular, for more than 100 years in Great Britain, this species has white and rose-purple flowers in spring and early summer. They last well when cut. There are a great number of varieties.

DESFONTAINEA (Loganiaceae— Strychnine Family)

A genus of but a single species which delights in partial shade and a well-drained sandy soil containing peat, which soil also suits the closely related buddleias. And it is from plants of this same family that the deadly *Nux Vomica* or strychnine of commerce is obtained.

Species. *Desfontainea spinosa.* Named after Louis Desfontaines, the French botanist, it is one of the most beautiful plants in cultivation. It is native of the Chilean Andes and in Britain and North America requires a warm sheltered garden and a position where the roots are in cool shade but where the sun's rays may reach its branching stems.

It has attractive shining evergreen leaves of palest green, like those of the holly, being about 5 cm (2 in) long and spiny. Growing to a height of 1.2 to 1.5 m (4 to 5 ft), it comes into bloom towards the end of June and continues whilst the weather remains mild. The flowers are most exciting, being tubular and about 4 cm ($1\frac{1}{2}$ in) long, and are scarlet tipped with yellow, and softly honey-scented.

DEUTZIA (Saxifragaceae—Rockfoil Family)

It is one of the few exceptions to the family which includes the saxifrage, heuchera, and astilbe, none of which bear flowers with any pronounced fragrance. All are tolerant of light shade and flourish in ordinary well-drained soils which contain some humus and decayed manure. They are deciduous plants and bloom from mid-May until the end of July. Propagation is by layering or from shoots of the half-ripened wood which will readily root in a sandy compost under glass.

Species. *Deutzia campanulata.* It is a most valuable shrub for a small garden for it grows only 90 cm (3 ft) tall and the same

across, making a dense bush with its many branches which are dark green and polished, like the leaves. Towards mid-May the pure-white flowers appear and waft their fragrance about the garden.

D. compacta. A native of central China, it forms a neat bush 60 to 90 cm (2 to 3 ft) in height and it bears its blush-white flowers in corymbs 7.5 to 10 cm (3 to 4 in) wide. They resemble those of the hawthorn in appearance but have a rich, sweet perfume.

D. corymbosa. A most beautiful Himalayan shrub growing to a height of about 1.5 m (5 ft) with lance-shaped leaves. Towards the end of May it bears forked panicles of snow-white flowers which have the scent of hawthorn but without the fishy undertone.

D. elegantissima. It makes a most graceful shrub, 1.2 m (4 ft) in height and almost as wide, with small glossy leaves. Along the whole length of the branches appear scented star-like flowers of palest pink.

D. magnifica. A hybrid of *D. scabra* and *D. vilmorinae*, it reaches a height of 1.8 to 2.1 m (6 to 7ft), its graceful arching spikes being crowded with double flowers of purest white and delicately scented, reminding one of white lilac blossom.

D. parviflora. A Chinese species which grows 1.5 m (5 ft) tall with lance-shaped leaves which are toothed and wrinkled. It is the first of the deutzias to bloom, opening its tiny creamy-white flowers before April has ended. They are borne all along the stems and have a delicious honey fragrance.

D. sieboldiana. A delightful Japanese shrub growing 1.2 to 1.5 (4 to 5 ft) in height and having attractive heart-shaped leaves. It blooms in June, its vanilla-scented flowers of purest white appearing in loose clusters.

D. staminea. A Himalayan shrub growing 0.9 to 1.2 m (3 to 4 ft) in height with lance-shaped leaves, downy on the underside against which the fragrant pure-white flowers, borne in June, present a delightful cool appearance in woodland shade.

D. vilmoreana. A Chinese species which requires a warm, sheltered garden where it will attain a height of 3 m (10 ft) or more with long lance-shaped leaves. It blooms in June, bearing strikingly beautiful sprays of large white flowers, resembling orange-blossom and with golden anthers. The flowers have a delightful sweet honey fragrance.

DIANTHUS (Caryophyllaceae—Pink Family)

A genus of about 80 species of annual, biennial or perennial plants with glaucous grass-like foliage and bearing their flowers either solitary or in terminal clusters. They are mostly plants of the northern temperate zone, able to survive intense cold. A number of species bear clove-scented flowers. The Athenians afforded it the highest honour, naming the plant *Dianthos*, Flower of Jove, and it was the chief flower used in the making of garlands and coronets; hence its name 'coronation' from which the name carnation is derived.

Dianthus caryophyllus, the clove-scented pink, is believed to have reached England from Normandy at the time of William the Conqueror. The plant was called 'giloflier' by the Normans, denoting its clove perfume, a name later given to all plants bearing clove-scented flowers. The flowers were used to flavour wine, hence their name 'sops-in-wine', By Tudor times, there were two distinct groups; those with single flowers, known as pinks and descended chiefly from *D. plumarius*, and those bearing double (or semi-double) flowers, offspring of *D. caryophyllus*.

With their pink or rose-red flowers and long narrow passage in which the honey is secreted, the flowers are visited by butterflies, though the protruding anthers are taken advantage of by insects which act as secondary pollinators.

Species and Varieties. *Dianthus arenarius.* Native of northern Europe, it is one of the few pinks to prefer semi-shade rather than full sun, and a cool, moist soil. It forms a mat of small leaves, and blooms in mid-summer, bearing its flowers on 15-cm (6-in) stems. They are white or pale pink, with purple hairs at the base of the deeply fringed petals, and are sweetly scented.

D. arvernensis. Found wild only in the Auvergne Mountains of France, it enjoys the same conditions as the Cheddar pink and is also a splendid wall plant, forming dense hummocks of grey-green leaves, above which it bears, on 10-cm (4-in) stems, toothed flowers of rose-pink which are sweetly scented.

D. barbatus. The Sweet-william, a native of central and eastern Europe, is a perennial plant though it is usually treated as a biennial, with the seed sown early in summer for the plants to bloom the following year. It is believed that the plant is indigenous to southern Germany, from whence it reached most parts of Europe; the first writer to mention the plant, a Flemish. doctor, Rembertus Dodeons, physician to the Emperor Charles V, wrote in his *Historie of Plants* published in 1554 and later translated and enlarged upon by Lyte as the *New Herbal,* that it grew in exposed, hilly places in Germany. He also mentioned that the plant grew wild in Flanders and about the hills of Normandy, yet it did not come with the Conqueror and, contrary to popular belief, does not bear his name; it was not to be found in English gardens until the middle of the sixteenth century. Possibly the earliest mention of its planting was in the accounts of the additions made by Henry VIII to Wolsey's Hampton Court gardens, for which Sweet-williams were purchased at 3*d.* a bushel, each bloom resembling a pink. It was not mentioned by an English writer until the appearance of Lyte's *New Herbal* in 1578, and later of Gerard's *Herball* in 1597.

Linnaeus named the plant *D. barbatus* from the pointed scales of the calyx, but towards the end of the Tudor era it was known as 'London Tufties'. Gerard was the first to call it Sweet William in honour, it has been said, of William Shakespeare, though it is more likely the name is derived from the French *oeillet*. Alice Coats, in her book *Flowers and their Histories,* suggests the flower was named after St. William of Aquitaine.

The early Sweet-williams grew less than 10 cm (4 in) tall, almost like the modern Wee Willie strain, bearing zoned or edged clusters in combinations of crimson, rose-pink and white. Gerard said that 'the flowers at the top of the stalks are very like to the small Pinks, many joined together in one tuft . . . of a deep red colour'. And he added, 'the plants are kept and maintained in gardens more to please the eye, than either the nose or belly . . . (They) are not used either in meat or medicine but are esteemed for their beauty to deck up gardens, the bosoms of the beautiful, garlands and crowns for pleasure'. The plants were easily raised from seed and with their compact habit, freedom of flowering, hardiness and clove perfume, were ideal for planting in small beds near to the house. By the beginning of the seventeenth century, the Sweet-william was found in almost every garden.

Parkinson describes the single red Sweet-william, the Velvet William with 'flowers thicker, closer and more in number in the head or tuft' than the Sweet John; 'the colour is of a deep red without any mixture at all', a colour found today in the Scarlet Beauty strain. He also describes the double form known as King William, still found in cottage gardens.

By the early nineteenth century, the Sweet-william had joined the flaked carnation and the laced pink as a florist's flower. Mrs Loudon says the finest were grown by the Clyde, whilst it is said that in the garden of a Mr Hunt of High Wycombe there grew 100 varieties bearing flower-heads with 30 or more florets of all colours and variations, many of which are to be found to this day. Not least in beauty are the old auricula-eyed strains, in which the clove perfume is most pronounced.

AURICULA-EYED VARIETIES. These are depicted in Parkinson's *Paradisus* and have been with us ever since. Each bloom, about 2 cm ($\frac{3}{4}$ in) across, has a clear white centre which is surrounded by crimson or red colouring with an edging of white in varying widths. Each truss is composed of between 20 to 30 blooms which make up a rounded head of great beauty, held on a 37-cm (15-in) stem and diffusing a rich clove perfume. If the dead flower stems are removed without delay, the plants will remain healthy and vigorous for several years.

Outstanding Varieties

DOBIES ALLDOUBLE. Raised by Dobies of Chester, this is an outstanding plant for cut-flower and garden display, bearing large clusters of double flowers on 45-cm (18-in) stems, which are crimson,

salmon and pink with a clove perfume.

DUNNETT'S CRIMSON. An old variety bearing large refined heads of brilliant velvety crimson whilst the foliage is also tinted with crimson.

DWARF RED MONARCH. A 1966 introduction by Messrs Hurst & Son. It is a plant of ideal bedding habit, growing 22 cm (9 in) tall and being bushy and branching. It bears glowing crimson-red flowers during June and July which are scented.

GIANT WHITE. Should be planted with Scarlet Beauty or Dunnett's Crimson as contrast, for its enormous clove-scented heads are of glistening white.

INDIAN CARPET. The plants grow only 20 to 22 cm (8 to 9 in) tall and cover themselves in small, neat flower-heads of all the familiar Sweet-william colourings.

PINK BEAUTY. The blooms, with their attractively toothed petals, are a lovely bright salmon-pink.

SCARLET BEAUTY. The large flower-heads are of brightest crimson-scarlet, held aloft on 60 cm (2 ft) stems.

In 1920, Montague Allwood made his famous cross between the Sweet-william and *Dianthus allwoodii*. The result was the Sweet Wivelsfield and it was the first fertile hybrid raised from the Sweet-william, for previously the carnation had been used as the male parent and had raised the 'Mule' pinks. The plants have a sturdy, compact habit, growing 30 cm (1 ft) tall and are available in all the Sweet-william colours, some having picotee edges. They are produced from June until October, and have the Sweet-william perfume.

The finest of the Sweet Wivelsfields is undoubtedly Red Bedder, a double-flowering form, possessing only slight perfume but bearing trusses of glowing scarlet over many weeks. Of this plant the BBC's most famous garden broadcaster of the 1930s, the late C. H. Middleton, said that it was the best of all red-flowering plants for summer bedding.

D. carthusianorum. Native of central Europe, it is closely related to the Sweet-william and is believed to have been introduced into England by Carthusian monks. It was in cultivation in England in 1573 and is interesting rather than beautiful, one of those old cottage-garden flowers which must never be allowed to pass from cultivation. The plant may reach a height of 60 to 90 cm (2 to 3 ft) but usually bears its flowers on 45-cm (1½-ft) stems. They are bright magenta-purple, the colour of the early Hybrid Perpetual roses, with a sweet perfume.

D. caryophyllus. A native of southern Europe from Spain to the Balkans and also of many islands of the Mediterranean. Like all dianthus, the plant grows amongst rocky limestone formations and is a much-branched perennial growing up to 60 cm (2 ft) tall, with linear, awl-shaped, glaucous leaves 10 to 12 cm (4 to 5 in) long. It comes into bloom towards the end of June, its flesh-pink flowers measuring 3 cm (1½ in) across with broad petals, slightly toothed. From this plant have been raised over the years many varieties of hardy garden habit which are known as Hardy Border Carnations, a number of which carry the rich clove perfume of the parent. Amongst these may be included the old Crimson Clove, of which Parkinson said, 'none will give so gallant a tincture to syrup'. Almost no perfume is present in the orange and yellow-flowering varieties. This species is also the parent of the Perpetual-flowering carnation.

HARDY BORDER CARNATIONS WITH CLOVE PERFUME

CORAL CLOVE. The blooms are an unusual coral-red, of outstanding substance and shape and with the clove perfume developed to a marked degree.

CRYSTAL CLOVE. A delightful companion for Scarlet Fragrance, and equally free-flowering. The medium-sized blooms are of clearest white with pronounced clove perfume.

DONN'S CLOVE. It bears a profusion of medium-sized blooms of perfect form and with outstanding clove perfume.

EGLANTINE CLOVE. A lovely old variety, still growing strong and healthy, and bearing flowers of a unique shade of salmon-rose. Also known as Rose Eglantine.

EDENSIDE CLOVE. It has long been a premier winner on the show bench, the white blooms, edged and striped with maroon, having exquisite form and pronounced scent.

FENBOW'S NUTMEG CLOVE. This is one of the oldest garden plants still in cultivation, dating from the fourteenth century, and may well be Chaucer's Sops-in-Wine. It was rediscovered in 1960, by Mr Sanderson of Leeds, growing in the garden of Colonel Fenbow, in whose family are preserved records which say that the nutmeg clove was growing in the same garden in 1652, planted there by a certain Julian Fenbow, to provide its powerful nutmeg scent to flavour wines. It bears a small, but fully double, flower of crimson-maroon with slightly feathered petals and measures little more than 2.5 cm (1 in) across. The leaves are blue-green and upright.

IMPERIAL CLOVE. An outstanding border plant in any company, bearing enormous flowers of clearest violet and with a rich perfume.

KING OF CLOVES. Of dwarf, upright habit, the large wine-red blooms are powerfully spice-scented.

LAVENDER CLOVE. The large, full-centred blooms are held on erect stems, and do not burst their calyx. The colour is rich heliotrope, enhanced by the glaucous foliage.

LESLIE RENNISON. The large orchid-pink flowers are 'shot' with cerise, and the sheen gives a delightful shot-silk effect.

MERLIN. A fine old exhibition 'fancy', the large white blooms being edged and flecked with purple.

MRS A. BROTHERSTONE. A most unusual variety, the white blooms being suffused and spotted with crimson.

NEYRON CLOVE. A charming variety bearing a profusion of medium-sized blooms which remain fresh when cut longer than any other variety, and which are a lovely shade of rose-neyron.

OAKFIELD CLOVE. An old variety, still the finest crimson border carnation, exceptional in the rich glowing colour and the pronounced clove scent of its bloom.

PINK CLOVE. The late Montague Allwood, who did so much for the dianthus, considered this to be the most fragrant of all his border varieties, and the large blooms are a lovely soft powder pink.

ROBIN THAIN. A superb variety, the

white blooms being striped with crimson; they are deliciously scented.

ROYAL CLOVE. Probably the most free-flowering pink, bearing flowers of exhibition form on long stems and of deep cardinal pink.

SALMON CLOVE. It blooms in profusion, the large flowers being deep salmon-pink with the rich clove fragrance.

SCARLET FRAGRANCE. One of the most fragrant of all scarlet flowers, it bears large refined blooms of clearest signal-red.

SIDNEY CROWHURST. A purple self of exquisite form and of vigorous habit.

SNOW CLOVE. A variety of short, sturdy habit, bearing a large, fully-built bloom of perfect form and with outstanding perfume.

STEERFORTH. Winner of numerous awards on the show bench, it bears a large bloom of pure white, edged and splashed with crimson.

YELLOW CLOVE. The first yellow carnation or pink to bear a clove-scented flower. The medium-sized blooms are pale yellow and freely produced.

A number of strains of hardy border carnations which may be raised from seed, bear clove-scented flowers and bloom from July until September:

EARLY DWARF VIENNA. An excellent bedding strain, growing less than 45 cm (1½ ft) tall and coming into bloom early in June. The medium-sized blooms appear in the well-known carnation colours and have the rich clove perfume.

GRENADIN. The clove-scented blooms are borne in profusion on stems 60 cm (2 ft) long and embrace shades of pink, salmon, crimson, white and flesh.

COTTAGE CARNATIONS WITH THE CLOVE PERFUME.
Developed by Montague Allwood, they have a shorter habit than many of the old border kinds and a longer flowering season, blooming from June until well into September. The following have especially pronounced scent:

COTTAGE CORAL. The blooms are of perfect form and a lovely coral salmon with a sweet scent.

COTTAGE CRIMSON. The blooms are deepest crimson like the old Crimson Clove and they have a rich clove perfume.

COTTAGE WHITE. The white blooms are of most attractive form, with a strong cinnamon scent.

PERPETUAL-FLOWERING CARNATIONS.
Also known as Tree carnations, they are the aristocrats of the dianthus family, requiring winter protection. They are grown commercially in large numbers to supply the trade, the blooms being especially in demand during the winter months. The blooms are rather larger than those of the hardy border carnation and several carry the clove perfume. The plants require good light and ventilation and are usually grown in specially constructed greenhouses, where the temperature does not fall below 5°C (42°F) during winter.

ALLWOOD'S CREAM. The beautifully formed blooms are of great size and are a lovely pale creamy-yellow.

CLAYTON WHITE. The blooms are neat and of exquisite form, ideal for a button-hole, and are pure white with outstanding perfume.

EDWARD ALLWOOD. Of vigorous habit, it forms a bloom of large proportions and a most attractive bright cerise-pink, like the colour of the rose Zephirine Drouhin, and with outstanding clove perfume.

FRAGRANT ANN. It has the freedom of flowering of Clayton White with the quality of George Allwood, and the intense clove perfume of both.

GEORGE ALLWOOD. With Robert Allwood (scarlet), possibly the finest Perpetual ever raised. The massive fringed blooms are of glistening white with the most powerful clove scent of all the family.

MONTY'S PALE ROSE. Montague Allwood's finest pink, perfect in form and of palest rose-pink colouring. The sweet perfume has undertones of clove.

ROYAL CRIMSON. Like the old Crimson Clove, the bloom is large, of perfect form and of deepest crimson colouring, with the same intense clove perfume.

D. gratianopolitanus. The Cheddar pink, native of the limestone rocks of the

Cheddar Gorge in Somerset, and also found in limestone rocky formations of western Europe. It is Francis Bacon's 'matted pink', and is increased by root division. It also sets and ripens seed freely and is readily raised from it. The plant forms a prostrate mass of greeny-blue leaves which are linear and blunt, and from June until late summer covers itself in daintily fringed, single flowers about 2 cm (1 in) across, deep rose-pink and deliciously scented. It is at its best growing from a wall, in pockets of lime-rubble or between crazy-paving, and is a long-lived plant. There is also a double form, *flore plena*, more beautiful and more powerfully scented.

D. libanotis. Native of the mountainous regions of Syria and the Lebanon, it requires protection from an excess of winter moisture. It has blue-green foliage and bears its flowers in loose sprays 30 cm (1 ft) long. The white flowers, flushed with mauve, have a delicious perfume, and appear in early summer.

D. minutiflorus. Like *D. noëanus*, it is a plant for the trough garden for it grows less than 15 cm. (6 in) tall, forming a tiny clump of narrow, needle-like leaves above which it bears its dainty, pure-white flowers of sweetest perfume from early June until September.

D. monspessulanus. This is the Montpelier pink which was introduced into England in 1764. A native of central and eastern Europe, it is a plant of spreading habit, bearing on 22-cm (9-in) stems deeply fringed flowers of rose-pink which have a rich sweet perfume, between May and August.

D. noëanus. Native of Turkey and the Balkans, it is named after a chemist of Istanbul called Noë. It is a delightful plant for a trough garden, readily seeding itself and forming a tiny hummock of stiff spiny leaves, grey-green in colour, above which it bears in summer, on graceful arching stems, tiny pure-white flowers with a sweet perfume.

D. plumarius. Distributed throughout southern Europe as far east as the Caucasus, it has glaucous, linear, rough-edged leaves which it forms into compact hummocks, and bears rich-pink flowers on 22-cm (9-in) stems. The petals are bearded and jagged, whilst the flower diffuses a powerful clove scent. It received its name *plumarius* from Gerard, on account of its feathered petals, and in his *Herball* he lists and illustrates twelve varieties which he calls 'Wild Gilloflowers'. They all bear single flowers as did almost all pinks up to the beginning of the eighteenth century. Those that have survived from the sixteenth or early seventeenth century all bear single flowers with deeply serrated petals, and all are deliciously scented. They bloom in June and early July.

Fourteenth-century Pinks: 'SOPS-IN-WINE'. A plant of this name still survives and may well be the original of Chaucer's time, for it is believed to have reached England during the early fourteenth century, from a monastery garden situated near Orleans. It flourishes in cottage gardens in Buckinghamshire and Berkshire, where it is called by its ancient name. The white flower is extremely fringed and has a black central zone, whilst its perfume resembles that of the old Nutmeg Clove carnation which may have reached England at about the same time.

Fifteenth-century Pinks: CAESAR'S MANTLE. It is the Bloody Pink of early Tudor and Elizabethan times and may well date from the end of the fifteenth century. It bears a flower more than 2.5 cm (1 in) across, of a dark blood-red colour, covered in a grape-like 'bloom'. The crimson-red becomes almost black at the centre, and the petals are deeply toothed. It has a powerful clove scent.

Sixteenth-century Pinks: FOUNTAINS ABBEY. It resembles the equally old Queen of Sheba in appearance, the flowers being less than 2.5 cm (1 in) in diameter but semi-double. The petals are beautifully fringed and the black lacing on a white ground is the equal of the old Scottish pinks.

NONSUCH. It is of the Painted Lady type, and is believed to have been discovered in the gardens of Henry VIII's palace of Nonsuch, though it may have received its name from its great beauty. The petals are more deeply fringed than others of this type, and the ground colour is pink, with ruby-red flashes.

OLD MAN'S HEAD. Dating from the early seventeenth or late sixteenth century, and re-discovered in a north Yorkshire garden. It is a sturdy grower bearing white, semi-double flowers, curiously spotted and splashed with purple, and with a powerful clove perfume.

PAINTED LADY. It was re-discovered in 1950, growing in a Monmouthshire garden, and resembles in all characteristics an illustration of 'Ye Gallant's Fayre Ladye' pink which appears in a 1603 book of garden flowers. It forms a bloom only 2.5 cm (1 in) across and is semi-double with fringed petals which are white, flashed with purple. In his book *Old Carnations and Pinks,* the Rev. Oscar Moreton writes that it grows in his garden at Chipping Norton and has the 'strongest and sweetest clove scent of all'.

QUEEN OF SHEBA. A pink of the Painted Lady type, bearing single flowers 2½ cm (1 in) across, with neat serrated petals which are laced with magenta-purple on a white ground. Of the late Elizabethan era, either late sixteenth or early seventeenth century.

UNIQUE. Of the same age as surviving members of the Painted Lady type. The flowers are single and of outstanding beauty, the ground colour being red and covered all over with flashes of black and pink.

Seventeenth-century Pinks: BAT'S DOUBLE RED. It is a pink which has been growing in the Botanic Garden at Oxford since the end of the seventeenth century and is thought to be that raised by a Thomas Bat in London, and until 1950 believed to be lost. It has blue-green foliage, and bears flowers with bluntly toothed petals of rich ruby-red over a long period.

BRIDAL VEIL. One of the old fringed pinks, possibly of the late seventeenth century, the double blooms of ice-white having a crimson patch at the base of each petal. They are heavily scented.

FIMBRIATA. Its origin is lost in antiquity but it is most likely a late-Elizabethan pink, the creamy-white flowers with their fringed petals having pronounced perfume.

GREEN EYE. Also Charles Musgrave or Musgrave's Pink, named by the late Mr George Allwood after the owner of the cottage garden where it was re-discovered. It is said to be identical with plants which have been growing in the Palace garden at Wells since the end of the seventeenth century. The blooms are single, of 3-cm (1½-in) diameter and of purest white, with slightly fringed petals which overlap and with a conspicuous green eye or zone. The blooms have outstanding fragrance.

OLD FRINGED. It is one of the oldest pinks in cultivation, most likely grown in gardens of the late Elizabethan period. It is a delightful plant of dwarf, compact habit, and bearing semi-double flowers of purest white with extremely fringed petals, and of exquisite clove perfume. It is the seed-bearing parent of the first *allwoodii* pink.

PHEASANT EYE. One of several pinks surviving from the early seventeenth century, though each of them may be older. It is found in both the single and semi-double form with the petals deeply fringed, whilst the ground colour is white or blush, with a conspicuous purple-brown 'eye' at the centre. Occasionally the flowers have lacing of the same colour.

Eighteenth-century Pinks: BEVERLEY PINK. Found in the cottage garden of a Mr Williams at Beverley, where it had grown since at least early in the century. The small, semi-double blooms of crimson-red are flaked with white and yellow, and have the true clove perfume. It was re-discovered by Miss Gladwin who described it in the Journal of the Royal Horticultural Society.

CHELSEA PINK. Also Little Old Lady. It was to be found in Chelsea gardens early in the century. It is like a Painted Lady, with glorious perfume, the small double flowers of crimson-red being edged and splashed with white.

GLORIOSA. An old Scottish pink, possibly having a carnation for one parent, for the flowers are a beautiful shape and fully double, being of pale-pink colouring with a crimson eye, and having outstanding fragrance.

INCHMERY. This variety makes a neat compact plant and bears a profusion of double flowers which open flat without splitting their calyces, and are an attractive bright clear pink, a pleasing foil for the silvery foliage. It has outstanding perfume, 'as heady as that of Mrs Sinkins but not so cloying', wrote Mr Ingwersen.

MONTROSE PINK. Also the Cockenzie Pink for it was discovered in the Scottish fishing village of that name and was also found growing in the garden of Montrose House where it had been since early in the century. It is still listed by Forbes of Hawick and is a beauty, growing 22 cm (9 in) tall and bearing on stiff stems, fully double blooms of brilliant carmine-pink.

PADDINGTON COB. Raised by a Mr Richard Cob in his garden at Paddington and not 'to be confused with Hogg's Paddington. It is a small edition of Pheasant Eye.

PRINCE OF CARRICK. An Irish pink of great antiquity bearing large single blooms of salmon-pink with zones of scarlet and grey, and with deeply toothed petals.

THE IRISH PINK. This was discovered in 1937 in a garden in Cork where it had been growing for at least two centuries. The semi-double blooms are about 3 cm (1½ in) across and are of rich crimson, striped with white, and of rich clove perfume.

Nineteenth-century Pinks: AVOCA PURPLE. This may be very much older, for it is to be found in many Co. Wicklow cottage gardens. It bears a small purple flower, streaked with lines of darker purple; it is sweetly scented.

BLACK PRINCE. An old Irish variety now rarely seen and somewhat resembling Sops-in-wine, its semi-double flowers being white with a large black centre, or eye, and with similar nutmeg scent.

EARL OF ESSEX. One of these much-loved garden pinks which splits its calyx, but is always welcome in the garden. The clear rose-pink blooms with their fringed petals have a small dark zone, and sweet perfume.

EMILE PARÉ. One of the truly outstanding pinks, raised in 1840 in Orleans, France, by André Paré, probably having the Sweet-william for one parent, for it bears its double salmon-pink flowers in clusters and survives only a few years so that it should be constantly renewed from slips.

FETTES MOUNT. An old Scottish pink now seldom seen and bearing large heads of double salmon-pink flowers, the petals having jagged edges. Possibly of Sweet-william parentage which would account for its short life, but the perfume is remarkably sweet.

LINCOLNSHIRE LASS. It has been known since the beginning of the century and may be much older. The flowers are an uninteresting flesh colour but the delicious scent makes it worthy of cultivation.

MRS SINKINS. It was raised by a Mr Sinkins, Master of Slough Workhouse, and named after his wife. The plant, which has the distinction of being incorporated in the Arms of the Borough of Slough, was introduced by the Slough nurseryman, Charles Turner, one of the great florists of the time and who had introduced the Cox's Orange Pippin apple to commerce. It is a pink of great character, its large, white, cabbage-like blooms, borne on 30-cm (1-ft) stems above a mat of silvery-green foliage, possessing an almost overpowering perfume.

NAPOLEON III. Raised by André Paré in Orleans in 1840 from a Sweet-William crossing and, like Emile Paré, flowers itself to death in two years. It bears on 25-cm (10-in) stems large heads of double clove-scented flowers of a striking scarlet-cerise.

PADDINGTON. It was raised about 1820 by Thomas Hogg, a nurseryman of the Paddington area of London. Of dwarf habit, its double pink blooms have serrated edges and are richly scented.

ROSE DE MAI. It may be traced back to the beginning of the century and it is a beauty, the double blooms being a lovely creamy-mauve with fringed petals and glorious perfume.

RUTH FISCHER. Dating from the end of the century, it is a most attractive variety of compact habit and bearing small, fully double flowers of purest white with a rich, sweet perfume.

SAM BARLOW. At one time it grew in every cottage garden, though it is now rarely seen. Like Mrs Sinkins and so many of the old double pinks, it splits its calyx, but blooms in profusion, its white flowers having a maroon blotch at the centre, and a penetrating clove perfume.

WHITE LADIES. To the grower of cut flowers, it is with *Scabiosa* Clive Greaves the most profitable of all plants, bearing its sweetly scented blooms of purest white throughout the summer; moreover, they do not split their calyces. Obviously a variety of *D. plumarius*, for it has the same fringed petals, it is a plant of neat habit and is tolerant of all conditions.

Twentieth-century Pinks: DUSKY. The result of back crossing the old fringed pink with an *Allwoodii* seedling; it is free and perpetual flowering. The blooms have fringed petals and are a lovely dusky pink.

ENID ANDERSON. A most striking pink, its semi-double, clove-scented flowers of glowing crimson being enhanced by the silver-grey leaves.

FRECKLES. An Imperial pink, it bears a double bloom of unusual colouring, being dull salmon-pink flecked with red, and with a penetrating spicy scent.

GUSFORD. An outstanding pink, bearing large double blooms of rosy-pink on 30-cm (1-ft) stems, which are deliciously scented.

HASLEMERE. Raised at the Ipswich nurseries of Thompson and Morgan, the large, fragrant, double flowers have a deep-chocolate centre and fringed petals.

ICE QUEEN. A 'sport' from Dusky, it bears a highly scented double bloom of icy-white, which does not burst its calyx, and which has fringed petals.

LILAC TIME. Raised by Mr C. H. Fielder of the Lindabruce Nurseries, Lancing, it is an Imperial pink and bears fully double blooms of a lovely lilac-pink, with a powerful scent.

MISS CORRY. Raised in Holland, it bears large, double blooms of richest wine-red, with the true clove perfume.

PINK BOUQUET. This makes a tidy, compact plant and bears candy-pink flowers on 25-cm (10-in) stems.

SWANLAKE. An Imperial pink of exquisite form, with rounded petals of purest white, whilst the bloom has the clove perfume.

WINSOME. It forms a neat, compact plant and bears large double blooms of pure deep pink with a crimson eye, which are sweetly scented.

LACED PINKS. The laced pinks are those with a band of dark colour near the margin of the petal, on a light-coloured ground. Several are thought to have survived from the time of their greatest glory in Scotland and from them, possibly renamed, a number of scented, laced pinks were raised by the Allwood Brothers between the two world wars. They have the habit of the *allwoodii* pinks and from them Mr F. R. McQuown continued the programme in raising a number of laced pinks to which he gave the 'London' prefix. They had as parents the laced *allwoodii*, the *herbertii* pinks and perpetual-flowering carnations.

CHARITY. The habit is short and tufted, and the plant is free-flowering. The semi-double blooms have a white ground with a clearly defined lacing of bright crimson.

FAITH. The first of the laced *allwoodii* varieties (1946). The blooms are small but fully double, with the petals broad and fringed. The ground colour is rosy-mauve with a lacing of cardinal red.

GLORY. The large, double blooms of rose-pink are laced and zoned with maroon.

HOPE. Raised with Faith it has semi-double blooms heavily laced with crimson over a white ground. Deliciously scented.

JOHN BALL. Raised and introduced by Turner of Slough, about 1880. The bloom is large and double, with a white ground, and lacing and zoning of velvet-purple.

LONDON SUPERB. The large, double blooms have a pale-pink ground, and are laced with purple. The fringed petals and perfume give it the old world charm.

VICTORIAN. A laced pink of early Victorian times, bearing huge blooms which often burst their calyx, but it is still a most attractive variety. The white ground is zoned and laced with chocolate.

WILLIAM BROWNHILL. It dates from about 1780 and is one of the best of the laced pinks, the beautifully formed blooms being white, laced and zoned with maroon and they do not burst their calyces.

SCENTED ALLWOODII. The result of crossing the old fringed pink *D. plumarius*, with the Perpetual-flowering carnation. Several varieties have a pronounced perfume, and the plants are perpetual-flowering, remaining in bloom from early June until September.

ANNE. The blooms, are held above the foliage on 30-cm (1-ft) stems, are double, and a lovely salmon-pink, zoned with scarlet.

BLANCHE. Very free-flowering, the double blooms are of purest white with deeply fringed petals.

DORIS. The double blooms of salmon-pink with a darker eye are sweetly scented and are of ideal exhibition form.

MARY. The first *allwoodii*, bearing double blooms of lavender-pink, zoned with maroon, and with a delicate sweet perfume.

MONTY. The blooms are of 3-cm (1¼-in) diameter, and are of solferino-purple, zoned with chocolate.

WILLIAM. One of the best of all white pinks, with broad petals and outstanding clove perfume.

WINSTON. The large double blooms are of bright crimson, borne in profusion, and with outstanding clove perfume.

SCENTED SHOW PINKS. The result of a cross between the *allwoodii* and *herbertii* pinks. The plants have a habit more vigorous than either parent and bear a refined bloom, like a border carnation.

SHOW ARISTOCRAT. The plant has beautiful silver foliage and bears sweetly scented double blooms of flesh pink with a deeper pink eye.

SHOW CLOVE. The rose-pink bloom is smaller than usual in this group but it carries the true clove perfume.

SHOW EXQUISITE. The bloom is almost as large as a Malmaison carnation and a lovely soft pink, with a sweet perfume and spicy undertones.

HYBRID ALPINE PINKS (Scented). These have been evolved through the years by crossing *D. allwoodii* with *D. alpinus* and *D. arenarius*, and with *D. gratianopolitanus* and *D. squarrosus*, all of which bear scented flowers. They range in height from 7 to 15 cm (3 to 6 in), and are delightful plants for the trough or alpine garden.

ELIZABETH. A treasure for the alpine garden, with erect, silvery-green foliage and bearing, on a 10-cm (4-in) stem, a tiny double bloom of dusky pink with a brown centre. The scent diffused by so tiny a flower is truly remarkable.

ERNEST BALLARD. Raised at the Old Court Nurseries, Malvern, this forms a dense prostrate mat of grey foliage above which are borne, on stiff stems, double flowers of crimson-red with the old clove perfume.

GRACE MATHER. A real gem for the trough garden forming a prostrate mat of neat blue-green foliage and bearing, on 12-cm (5-in) stems, large double blooms of deep salmon-pimk.

MARS. One of the 'great' plants of the alpine garden, forming a dense tuft of silvery-grey above which it bears bright crimson-red flowers with the true clove perfume.

MISS SINKINS. A tiny replica of the more robust Mrs Sinkins, and found in a garden at Henfield, Sussex, The heavily fringed blooms of purest white have a delicious perfume.

NYEWOODS CREAM. A delightful plant forming a hummock of grey-green above which it bears scented flowers of Jersey cream colour.

D. squarrosus. Native of eastern Russia and Siberia, it has narrow, awl-shaped leaves which become quite spiny as they age. The plant forms a dense hummock, grey-green in colour which provides a pleasing foil for the pure-white flowers, finely jagged at the edges. They diffuse the powerful sweet perfume that is usual with flowers of the region.

D. superbus. The fringed pink of central eastern Europe and Asia, it is a sub-alpine species of somewhat lax habit, inhabiting the lower alpine meadows. It has broader leaves than most and they are borne in tufts, above which it displays, on 30-cm (1-ft) stems, huge flowers with jagged petals of soft lilac colouring with a green centre, which have a soft sweet perfume. It was one of the favourite plants of Linnaeus who gave it a special name. It has an additional value in that it is at its loveliest in autumn and will remain so right into winter, in a sheltered place.

Dianthus superbus was introduced into England towards the end of the sixteenth century and was well established by the time Parkinson wrote his *Paradisus*, in which it is attractively illustrated. It was called the Sweet John, possibly to distinguish it from the Sweet william, introduced at about the same time. 'The Sweet John', wrote Parkinson, 'hath his leaves broader, shorter and greater than former gillyflowers but narrower than Sweet Williams . . . and with stems about a foot and a half high . . . '. It was considered one of the most popular garden flowers of the time.

From this plant, Montague Allwood raised *Dianthus* Loveliness, also known as Rainbow Loveliness, from a crossing made with Sweet Wivelsfield. In his address to the members of the Royal Horticultural Society given on 12 July 1955, he said that the hybrid 'is exceedingly hardy and flowers from May until winter and is perhaps, the most fragrant of all flowers'. The plants grow 45 cm (1½ ft) tall and have the same jagged-petalled flowers (like love-in-a-mist) as *D. superbus*; they appear in crimson, lavender and white, with a green eye.

From a crossing of *D.* Loveliness with Sweet Wivelsfield again, Allwood raised *D.* Sweetness, a plant of similar habit, with the powerfully scented blooms appearing in large trusses. They have fringed petals and appear in every dianthus colour with the exception of yellow.

Again using *D.* Loveliness for a parent, Allwood crossed this with the Blue dianthus, a hybrid Sweet william. It has the same long flowering season, the same deeply lacinated petals and the same perfume. The plant was named Blue Peter and is a lovely lavender-blue.

DIAPENSIA (Diapensiaceae—Diapensia Family)

A genus of only two species, both native of Lapland and the Arctic Regions. They form plants of spreading habit and are valuable for ground-cover in cold, shady gardens. They require a moist peaty soil.

Species. *Diapensia lapponica.* It is a vigorous evergreen of almost prostrate habit with shining leathery leaves which are spoon-shaped and it blooms during July and August. The small solitary flowers are held on short stems above the foliage and possess a soft, delicate perfume. Propagation is by division in spring.

DICENTRA (Papaveraceae—Poppy Family)

A genus of 20 species of hardy, erect or climbing plants, native of North America and of China and Formosa, amongst which is the Bleeding Heart, which does not bear scented flowers. Dicentra is of the sub-family Fumarioideae, distinguished from Papaveraceae by the spur-formation at the base of the outer petals, as in the scentless Fumitory *(Fumaria)*. The rhizome of several species resembles a bulb. They are easily grown in a light, well-fed soil, and will stand light shade. Division in early spring is the easiest method of increase.

Species. *Dicentra chrysantha* (syn. *Dielytra chrysantha*). A native of California, it is an herbaceous perennial with stiff stems like the Golden Rod, and growing 1.2 m (4 ft) tall. The branching racemes of brilliant golden-yellow flowers appear in August and September and remain colourful until late autumn, the flowers having an unusual but agreeable scent.

DICYPELLIUM (Lauraceae—Bay Tree Family)

A genus of a single species, it is native of Brazil and Guiana where it is known as *Licari Kanali*. It has alternate oblong leaves, tapering to a point, which are smooth above, netted on the underside. The small, white flowers are followed by a drupe, ovate and depressed at the apex. The bark has the spicy scent of cloves, a concoction of which is hot and aromatic to the taste, with valuable tonic properties. The bark is known as Cayenne Sassafras.

DIERVILLA: *see* WEIGELA

DILL: *see* PEUCEDANUM

DILLENIA (Dilleniaceae—Dillenia Family)

A genus of about 55 species of which *D. indica* is the best known. All are tropical trees, *D. indica* being distributed throughout the forests of Assam and Burma, and throughout Indo-China and Indonesia where it grows alongside streams and rivers, with its roots in damp soil. The genus was named by Linnaeus in honour of the German botanist, Johann Dillenius (1684-1747), Professor of Botany at Oxford University.

Species. *Dillenia indica.* An evergreen tree reaching a height of about 9 m (30 ft), in its growth resembling the Holm-oak, the spreading branches forming an attractive head of brilliant green, the leaves growing at the ends of the branches. The leaves measure 22.5 to 30 cm (9 to 12 in) long and are 10 cm (4 in) wide and lance-shaped, ending in a point, and with their nerves running parallel to the serrated edges, a beautiful fluted appearance is produced.

The flowers appear in June and, as Linnaeus said, 'Dillenia has of all plants the showiest flower and fruits'. The flowers appear at the end of the branches and may exceed a 15-cm (6-in) diameter. The calyx is composed of 5 fleshy sepals, and the pure-white petals are beautifully waved. The stamens form a crown of gold around the ray-like stigmas and the whole is sweetly scented.

The fruits quickly grow to the size of a horse-chestnut 'conker' and later reach the size of a tennis ball; they are fleshy, with the seeds surrounded by a glutinous pulp.

DIMOPOTHECA (Compositae—Daisy Family)

A genus of about 20 species of smooth or downy annual or perennial plants, native of South Africa. They are only half-hardy in the British Isles and should be grown only in areas which enjoy a favourable climate. Several perennial species are valuable for the shrubbery and none more so than *D. barberiae*. The plants require a well-drained sandy soil and a position where they receive as much sunlight as possible.

Species. *Dimopotheca barberiae.* It is a handsome plant with hairy stems and lance-shaped leaves, like those of the Moon-daisy and they bear a flower of similar type, the bright-pink daisy-like flowers appearing throughout the summer. The flowers are scentless but the foliage is pleasantly aromatic. The plant grows 60 cm (2 ft) in height.

The form *compacta* grows less than half the height and is similar in all respects to the type, but it tends to be hardier and may be grown under less favourable conditions.

DIOSMA (Rutaceae—Rue Family)

A small genus of evergreen shrubs with heath-like foliage; in their natural state they grow about rocks and ledges around the coast of the Cape Peninsula. The plant takes its name from the Greek words *dios*, divine, and *osme*, odour, for the leaves when bruised emit the orange-like fragrance of the rue. A sandy, peaty soil is required, and soft cuttings in sand are used for propagation.

Species. *Diosma ericoides.* Only half-hardy in Britain and northern Europe, the plant should be confined to the most sheltered gardens and a position of full sun. It is a shrub 30 to 60 cm (1 to 2 ft) tall, and the white flowers are borne on the terminal shoots; the foliage is strongly pungent with undertones of orange.

D. oppositifolia (syn. *D. succulenta*). Usually found on sandy flats and mountainous slopes, this grows 60 cm (2 ft) with opposite leaves, thick and narrow and grooved on the upper surface. They emit a powerful pungent scent when handled. The flowers, borne in cymose clusters, are white.

D. pulchella. A small shrublet which in northern Europe should be confined to a warm greenhouse where, in a small pot, it will grow 30 cm (1 ft) tall and bushy and bear masses of tiny mauve flowers in spring. The foliage is highly aromatic.

D. vulgaris (syn. *D. hirsuta*). Common on flats and mountainous slopes, there are two forms, one bearing white flowers and growing erect, which is glabrous; the other with red flowers, which grows low and spreading, the foliage being covered in hairs. Both emit the scent of rue when bruised.

DIPELTA (Caprifoliaceae—Honeysuckle Family)

A genus of about 12 species, closely related to *Weigela* and *Lonicera,* with bell-shaped flowers borne in clusters. The plants enjoy a moist loamy soil and partial shade to provide the necessary protection from the cold winds of springtime when the plants are in bloom. Propagation is from cuttings of the new season's wood which will root readily in a sandy compost.

Species. *Dipelta floribunda.* It is one of the most beautiful of all Chinese shrubs, of upright habit and reaching a height of 3 m (10 ft) where it is happy. It blooms early in May or in April if the weather is kind, its finely arched stems being clothed in deliciously fragrant pink flowers with yellow shading in the throat, and these are followed by strange brown fruit bracts.

D. yunnanensis. From Yunnan, it is a suitable subject for a small garden for it grows less than 1.8 m (6 ft) tall, making a compact bush of upright habit. In May, it bears pinkish-white bell-shaped flowers, shaded with orange in the throat and with a rich, sweet perfume.

DIPTERIX (Leguminosae—Laburnum Family)

A small genus of large trees, native of the tropical forests of South America, especially of the Brazilian Amazon, remarkable for this family in that it has single-seeded, indehiscent pods.

Species. *Dipterix odorata.* Native of Brazil, Guiana and Martinique, the flowers are borne in racemes, like those of the laburnum, and are powerfully scented. They are followed by oval fruits of a thick fleshy substance enclosing a shiny black seed known as the Tonquin bean, containing coumarin and releasing the scent of new-mown hay. At one time the beans were ground and used in sachet powders and were placed amongst clothes and linen. They were also used to impart their perfume to snuff. As in Sweet Vernal grass and Woodruff, the scent of sweet hay is only released when the bean is removed from the plant and begins to dry. The scent, like that of orris, continues to increase as the beans age. The bean has depreciated in value since Sir William Perkin made the synthetic discovery of coumarin in 1868.

DIRCA (Thymeleaceae—Mezereon Family)

A genus of two species, related to the daphnes and which grow in peaty swamps of North America. They are also valuable for growing in shade. Increase is easy, from seed, or by layers.

Species. *Dirca palustris.* This makes a multibranched shrub 0.9 to 1.8 m (3 to 6 ft) tall, with the branches arising from a central stem to give it the appearance of a small tree. The long dark-green leaves are deciduous, and the flowers appear early in March before the leaves. They are borne in terminal clusters and are tubular in shape, of pale-yellow colouring with protruding yellow stamens and they have a soft sweet perfume. The plant is sometimes known as the Leather-wood, the shoots being very tough but flexible, and useful in basket-making.

DISA (Orchidaceae—Orchid Family)

A genus of 130 species native to tropical and South Africa, and Madagascar, usually found in rocky clefts. The tubers are small, the basal leaves often reduced to sheaths, and the flowers appear solitary or in loose racemes. Where solitary, they are blue or pinky-red and are pollinated by bees, being scentless. Those with scent are purple. The petals are thick, with incurved tips and with a spur or pouch.

Species. *Disa cooperi.* A species from Natal, the blooms have a white hood flushed with pink, and a greenish-yellow lip. They are strongly clove-scented, and are produced in February on stems about 30 to 60 cm (1 to 2 ft) high.

D. cornuta. Found in barren or sandy wastes, it grows 45 cm (1½ ft) tall with a stout leafy stem, the lower leaves having magenta markings. The flowers are produced in December, in a dense spike and they have a refreshing spicy scent, the hood being dullish purple, the lip yellow and blackish-purple.

D. cylindrica. It grows about 15 cm (6 in) tall, the stem being enclosed by the erect basal leaves. The flowers are borne in a dense spike and are yellowish-green with a soft, sweet perfume.

D. maculata. Present about Kalk Bay in South Africa, where it grows 15 cm (6 in) tall, with 4 to 8 lanceolate basal leaves, and partly sheathing cauline leaves. Its flowers are borne solitary and are mauve, with the hood striped with green. They are clove-scented. Usually found in damp, shaded rock clefts, the plants requiring partial shade and a moisture-holding soil.

D. obtusa. Common in valleys and mountainous slopes, it grows 37 cm (15 in) tall and forms a dense spike of sweetly scented creamy-white flowers, the lip being spotted with purple.

D. tenella. It is a rare orchid, recorded on the eastern side of Table Mountain. It forms a dense spike of purple-mauve sweetly scented flowers which arise from a wide sheath.

DISCARIA (Rhamnaceae—Buckthorn Family)

A genus of 10 species, closely related to *Colletia* and native of New Zealand and Chile. They are much-branched shrubs, the twiggy branches often armed with spines. They require to be grown under warm, sheltered conditions and in a light well-drained soil.

Species. *Discaria serratifolia.* Native of Chile, it is a plant of graceful habit growing 3 m (10 ft) tall with slender drooping branches clothed with glossy dark-green serrated leaves and furnished with a pair of stout spines at each joint. The small greenish-white flowers are borne in July in dense clusters at the axils of the leaves and emit a powerful but pleasingly sweet perfume.

DOLICHOLOBIUM (Rubiacceae—Bedstraw Family)

A genus of 20 species of small trees or shrubs, native of the Philippines, New Guinea and Fiji, with opposite leaves and bearing white tubular jasmine-like flowers followed by long cylindrical fruits.

Species. *Dolicholobium knollysii.* It makes a small tree with handsome evergreen leaves 15 cm (6 in) long and 7.5 cm (3 in) wide, from the axils of which it bears 2 to 3 large white heavily scented flowers.

D. macgregori. Called *Na Ura* in the Fiji Islands where it makes a tree about 6 m (20 ft) tall, it has large glossy leaves and bears large white tubular flowers in axillary racemes; they have a powerful scent and are followed by the longest seed capsule in all the plant world, often measuring 45 to 50 cm (18 to 20 in) long and nearly 1 cm ($\frac{1}{2}$ in) across.

DOLICHOTHELE (Cactaceae—Cactus Family)

A genus of a single species, closely related to *Mammillaria.*

Species. *Dolichothele camptotricha.* It is native of Mexico and has a brilliant-green body of about 5-cm (2-in) diameter, covered in long slender tubercles. At the axils white hairs are present and also at the tips of the tubercles. The tiny white flowers are formed in the axils of the tubercles and are powerfully scented.

DORYCNIUM (Leguminosae—Laburnum Family)

A genus of 15 species, native of southern Europe, being deciduous sub-shrubs with downy leaves. They require an open, sunny situation and a sandy soil, and can be propagated from seed. They are closely related to the trefoils (*Trifolium*).

Species. *Dorycnium hirsutum* (syn. *Cytisus lotus*). This semi-herbaceous species grows 60 cm (2 ft) high and has leaves like the clover, covered in hairs. The white flowers, sometimes pink, are borne from June to September in many-flowered heads, and are scented.

D. suffruticosum. A sub-shrub growing 60 to 90 cm (2 to 3 ft) high, it has lance-shaped leaflets, and in June bears flowers like those of the pea, white with a red keel; they carry a faint perfume.

DORYPHORA (Atherospermataceae—Atherosperma Family)

A genus of a single species.

Species. *Doryphora sassafras.* Native of New South Wales where its bark is known as New South Wales Sassafras. It makes a pyramidal tree 24 to 30 m (80 to 100 ft) in height with a trunk 0.6 to 0.9 m (2 to 3 ft) in diameter. It is furnished with smooth toothed leaves which like the bark and wood emit an agreeable balsamic odour.

DRACEANA (Liliaceae—Lily Family)

A large genus native of the East Indies, the South Sea Islands, and central Africa, and grown in the British Isles as foliage house plants for many species require a minimum winter temperature of 13°C (56°F). The plants have been known to bloom in the open in a sheltered garden in the south-west; a writer in *The Field* towards the end of the nineteenth century referred to their doing so in April when 'their perfume was most powerful in the air for a long distance', and added that 'the seed ripened perfectly'. Probably the finest form is *D. fragrans,* a native of New Guinea, which may have been the species referred to in *The Field.* It is a plant of tree-like habit.

Species. *Draceana fragrans.* It requires a 37.5-cm (15-in) pot when grown indoors and attains a height of 0.9 to 1.2 m (3 to 4 ft) with lance-shaped leaves 0.9 m (3 ft) in length and of glossy green which are gracefully waved and twisted along their entire length. The flowers, borne in sprays, emit a powerful scent. When young, this is an easily managed house plant, flourishing in a window which receives little sunlight.

DRACOCEPHALUM (Labiatae—Lavender Family)

A genus of some 30 annual or perennial plants usually with toothed lance-shaped leaves and bearing blue or purple flowers in spiked whorls. The plants take their name of Dragon's Head from Greek words denoting the strangely shaped flowers. They are delightful plants which like all members of the family, enjoy an open sunny situation and a well-drained sandy soil.

Species. *Dracocephalum moldavica.* It is a native of Siberia and is an annual plant of extreme hardiness being of erect bushy habit and with attractive grey-green foliage. From seed sown outdoors in early April, the plants will commence to bloom in July. The flowers are lavender-blue, borne in long racemes, and like the foliage emit a most refreshing smell of lemon, like that of balm. The flowers have great attractions for bees, and they remain fragrant and fresh for several weeks.

DRACUNCULUS (Araceae—Arum Family)

A genus of a single species, native to the Mediterranean coastal regions, its flowers being fertilized in the same way as *Arum maculatum,* which it resembles.

Species. *Dracunculus vulgaris.* It is known as the Dragon or Snake Plant from the appearance of its fleshy stems and leaves which are green, mottled with black. It has a stem 60 cm (2 ft) tall arising from a large tuber and in July appears the chocolate-brown spathe, red on the inside, from which protrudes the reddish-brown spadix, giving off a most unpleasant odour.

If growing outdoors, plant beneath a warm wall where it will bloom in June. Indoors, plant one tuber to a 15-cm (6-in) pot containing a compost made up of 2 parts turf loam, 1 part peat and 1 part sand, and as it comes into growth early in the year, water copiously. Indoors it will bloom in April. It reaches a height of about 60 to 90 cm (2 to 3 ft) and is propagated by dividing the tubers in October or March.

DRAGEA (Asclepiadaceae—Stephanotis Family)

A genus of six species of climbing plants, native of the tropics of the Old World.

Species. *Dragea sinensis.* It is a deciduous Chinese climbing plant of considerable hardiness and will survive all but the most exposed situations in the British Isles and northern Europe. It reaches a height of 4.5 m (15 ft), its dark-green leaves being downy on the underside, whilst its deliciously hop-scented flowers are white with a zone of crimson spots and are borne in umbels during June and July.

DRIMYS (Magnoliaceae—Magnolia Family)

A genus of evergreen trees and shrubs native to sub-tropical climes of South America and Australasia, with aromatic bark and foliage and scented flowers. It takes its name from the Greek meaning pungent.

Species. *Drimys aromatica.* It is a native of Tasmania and grows 3 m (10 ft) high with tapering leaves of palest green. In June, it bears small pinkish-white flowers, females on one plant, males on another. More tender than *D. winteri*, it requires protection in the British Isles and northern Europe.

D. axillaris. The axil-flowering drimys of New Zealand. It is an evergreen tree with simple, alternate leaves and almost black bark, the scented flowers appearing in the leaf axils or in the scars of fallen leaves. The leaves are covered with pellucid oil cells.

D. colorata. Native to the South Island of New Zealand, it is called by the Maoris 'Pepper' tree, for all parts have the pungent smell of pepper. It is a small evergreen tree with red wood, almost like cedarwood both in its smell and appearance, and is used for inlaid work. The same red pigment is present also in the leaves which are blotched with red whilst the underside is covered with a reddish-purple 'bloom'. The leaves are highly pungent when handled and a decoction of the leaves and bark is a valuable tonic and astringent.

D. winteri. In its native South America, it is known as Winter's bark for it was discovered there by Captain Winter in 1578, when in command of one of Drake's ships near the Straits of Magellan, though it is found on high ground throughout South America. Its bark, reddish-brown when young, has a powerful aromatic smell whilst its creamy-white flowers, like those of the hawthorn, have the delicate fragrance of the jasmine. In the British Isles, it flourishes only in the most sheltered gardens of the South-west. In a well-drained, sandy loam enriched with peat or leaf-mould, it will attain a height of 6 m (20 ft) and flowers early in summer.

The tree has knotty branches whilst the bark is thick and has a pungent aroma. It is ash-grey in colour and contains resinous matter and 0.64 per cent of aromatic essential oil.

Commercial Winter's bark reaches Britain in short quills or channelled sections, the inner part being characterized by small cracks which form when the bark is dried.

DRYOBALANOPS (Dipterocarpaceae—Dipterocarpus Family)

A genus of about 50 species, of tree found in the tropical forests of India, Malaya, China and Indonesia, with alternate leathery leaves and bearing the flowers in axillary panicles.

Species. *Dryobalanops aromatica.* Native of the tropical forests of Borneo and China, where the scented wood is in demand for making boxes to contain documents and other valuables for it is the only wood capable of resisting the white ant. It makes a large tree, and from the branches and roots Borneo Camphor is obtained after boiling the wood and purifying the deposits by sublimation. An average of 450 g (1 lb) of crude camphor is obtained from 4.5 kg (10 lb) of wood and roots. From incisions in the bark, a clear yellow gum is obtained which is an excellent inhalant.

DRYOPTERIS (Aspidiaceae—Aspidium Family)

A cosmopolitan genus of about 150 species of ferns with divided leaves, folded in the bud and arising from a creeping rootstock. They increase by means of spores, grouped together in raised brown 'warts' which occur on the back or edges of the leaves. They inhabit leafy woodlands and hedgerows and also grow from between limestone rocks where the roots enjoy the damp, shady conditions. Several species are native to the British Isles.

Species. *Dryopteris aemula.* Known as the Hay-scented Buckler fern for its leaves contain coumarin, the hay-like scent being released as the leaves turn brown and dry in autumn. It grows 60 cm (2 ft) tall with 3-pinnate triangular leaves of brilliant green, whilst the stalks are dark brown in colour and covered with brown scales. It inhabits limestone rocks mostly in north-western England and Ireland.

D. villarsii. It has blue-green fleshy leaves, 2-pinnate with pointed secondary leaflets and is known as the Rigid Buckler fern. It is common in north-western England and Wales and is readily distinguished by the heavy balsamic smell of its leaves.

DYSOXYLUM (Meliaceae—Mahogany Family)

A genus of about 200 species, native of warmest Australia, Indonesia and islands of the South Pacific, noted for their hard, fragrant wood. *D. fraseranum* is the Australian mahogany.

Species. *Dysoxylum hornei*, var. *glabratum*.

A small upright tree, common in most of the Fiji Islands with 5- to 7-pinnate leaves and pale yellowish-green sweetly scented flowers followed by globular fruits.

E

EARINA (Orchidaceae—Orchid Family)

A genus of seven species, native to New Zealand and Polynesia. They are epiphytic herbs with narrow, leathery leaves which prevent excessive transpiration. This is necessary for the plants fix themselves to the trunks of trees and stones so that no moisture can be obtained from the ground. Their roots, too, produce additional membranous roots covered with spongy tissues that absorb moisture from the atmosphere. The flowers are white and borne in terminal spikes. They are powerfully scented for they rely on insects for their pollination.

Species. *Earina mucronata.* Present in New Zealand and Polynesia, it has long, pointed strap-like leaves and bears its flowers during November and December, in slender panicles.

E. suaveolens. It has alternate, linear leaves and bears its flowers in short racemes. The petals are ovate, the lip broad and 3-lobed, marked with two orange spots. It blooms from April until June, the scent being excessively pronounced.

ECHINOCEREUS (Cactaceae—Cactus Family)

A genus of about 80 species formerly included with *Cereus.* Native of the southern United States and Mexico, they have oval or elongated stems, branching at the base and form large, spreading plants. An unusual characteristic is that the new stems frequently burst through the tissue. The flowers, opening by day and mostly scarlet, are scentless but several species bearing yellow or purple flowers have a powerful scent.

Of easy culture, the plants require full sunshine and should be kept dry in winter, and in a frost-free room. Provide them with a compost made up of leaf-mould, decayed manure, grit and lime rubble in equal parts.

Species. *Echinocereus luteus.* Native of western Mexico, it makes a single oval stem, rarely branching at the base and with 8 to 9 ribs with small spines. The flowers with their long strap-like petals are borne in May and June and are yellow, the outer petals being splashed with red. They are sweetly scented.

E. scopulorum. Native of Mexico, it resembles *E. luteus* in its habit, forming a single stem with 14 ribs clothed in short spines. The flowers, borne at the top, are large and funnel-shaped; they are purple-pink, paler at the outside, and are sweetly scented.

ECHINOPS (Globe-Thistle) (Compositae—Daisy Family)

A genus of 70 or more species of thistle-like annuals or perennials, the pinnately-cut leaves having spiny lobes, the l-flowered capitules borne in terminal globose clusters, usually blue. Pollination is mostly by bees.

Species. *Echinops sphaerocephalus.* This handsome member of the genus, most of which are lacking in perfume, is possibly the sole exception. A clove-like smell is noticeable in the pale grey-blue flower-heads, and this was confirmed by Mr Christopher Lloyd in an article in *Country Life* (2 September 1965); he mentioned that in a friend's garden the flower scent was 'strongly reminiscent of carnations', but added 'it has never given off the same scent since I have had it'.

It grows to a height of about 1.8 m (6 ft) with spiny waved leaves of grey-green, woolly on the underside.

ECHINOPSIS (Cactaceae—Cactus Family)

A genus of large cylindrical plants with the areoles arranged on the sharp mid-ribs, closely resembling the Hedgehog cacti. Native of Central America, they are of easy culture and bear large pale funnel-shaped flowers with the perianth tube covered in overlapping scales and bearing bundles of hairs in the axils. In several species the flowers are scented. It can be planted out in summer for all it needs is a minimum night temperature of 7°C (45°F).

Species. *Echinopsis campylacantha.* Native of western Argentina it forms 12 to 14 ribs. The areoles bear 8 radical spines and brown central spines 5 cm (2 in) long. The flowers, pure white on the inside, brown on the outside, are violet-scented.

E. eyriesii. Native of southern Brazil and Uruguay, it forms a plant of 15-cm (6-in) diameter with 12 ribs and has tiny dark-brown spines. It blooms when only a small plant, the large white flowers having a vanilla-like perfume.

E. kratock viliana. It is most free-flowering with large white tubular flowers, shaped like a funnel and power-fully scented. Several blooms together will scent a large room with their heavy jonquil-like odour.

E. leucantha. Native of Argentina, it makes a globular plant with 14 prominent ribs with long spines. The flowers which appear on a long woolly tube have green lanceolate outer petals and inner petals of pure white, and they emit the scent of violets.

E. leucorhodantha. It is present in the most northerly part of Argentina and makes a globular plant of darkest green with 20 acute ribs. The flowers, borne on a long hairy tube have brown outer petals and pink inner petals and are deliciously scented.

E. multiplex. Native of Brazil, it forms a globular plant of pale green with 12 to 14 ribs and awl-shaped spines. The flowers, produced on a long woolly tube, are palest

pink with a mass of central stamens and have the scent of the tuberose.

E. polyancistra. It is a rare native of the northernmost part of Argentina and forms a small globe, like a golf ball in size and with as many as 20 or more ribs. The flowers, with their long slender tube are white and have the scent of freesias.

E. turbinata. Native of Brazil, it forms a cylindrical dark-green stem with 14 ribs covered in long needle-like spines. The handsome flowers are borne on a long hairy green tube and have green outer petals and pure-white inner petals. They emit the delicious scent of jasmine.

EDGEWORTHIA (Thymeleaceae— Mezereon Family)

A genus of a single species.

Species. *Edgeworthia papyrifera* (syn. *E. chrysantha*). It is native of western China and the eastern Himalayas, and is closely related to the Daphnes. At one time it was called *Daphne chrysantha*, and was re-named *Edgeworthia* in honour of Maria Edgeworth of Edgeworthstown, Co. Long-ford, in Ireland. It is a most interesting plant though suitable only for the more favourable parts of the British Isles and northern Europe. Since earliest times it has been used in China for making high-quality paper, but apart from its commer-cial value it has a beauty all its own. It grows 90 cm (3 ft) tall and is deciduous, with narrow dark-green leaves, From the ends of the stems are borne in clusters small bright golden-yellow flowers covered with silky white hairs and carrying a pronounced clove perfume, as spicy as the most fragrant clove pink or carnation. The blooms appear before the leaves, in February if the weather is mild or in March, and on a calm day scent the air with their aromatic perfume. Propagation is best done by layering the pliable shoots in autumn. So pliable are the shoots that they may be tied into knots without inter-fering with their growth.

EHRETIA (Boraginaceae—Forget-me-not Family)

A genus of two species of small trees, native of south-eastern China, Formosa and Korea, which in the British Isles will survive the winter in the more sheltered gardens of the South-west. They grow well in ordinary loam and are tolerant of a small quantity of lime in the soil.

Species. *Ehretia dicksonii.* It makes a small sturdy tree with large glossy leaves often 30 cm (12 in) long and in June, on the ripened wood of the previous season, bears handsome panicles of creamy-white flowers which emit a powerful spicy fragrance.

E. thyriflora. Not so readily established as *E. dicksonii,* it blooms during August, bearing panicles of dainty white flowers which have a soft sweet perfume.

ELAEAGNUS (Elaeagnaceae—Oleaster Family)

A genus of 45 species, native of Europe, Asia and America. They are shrubs or small trees able to survive in barren land and tolerant of sea winds. The shrubby species are natives of China and Japan with a single exception, the Silverberry of North America, and they make dense bushy plants with attractive foliage and fruit. They also make an excellent hedge, planted 90 cm (3 ft) apart, especially for a seaside garden, being tolerant of salt-laden winds.

The flowers which are produced at the leaf axils are mostly hidden by the foliage and at a distance cannot be seen, but as one approaches the bush a powerful sweet scent is observed, almost as strong as orange-blossom when the day is calm. It is remarkable that so tiny a flower is able to diffuse so redolent a perfume.

Species and Varieties. *Elaeagnus angustifolia.* A narrow-leaved, stiff-branched tree, prominent in Palestine about Mt Tabor and Samaria. The leaves are blue-green, silver on the underside, and the small white tubular flowers are extremely fragrant. The wood is hard and of fine grain and is much used in carving. The flowers are followed by grey fruits which have a pleasant sugary taste.

E. argentea. A native of North America, where it is known as the Missouri Silver tree or Silver-berry, it is a beautiful shrub growing 2.4 m (8 ft) tall and is readily recognized by its wavy silver-grey leaves 5 cm (2 in) long. Unfortunately, its leaves fall with the first hard frost, usually in December. The small pale-yellow flowers appear in June and July and are deliciously scented, and are followed by bright-silver berries.

E. glabra. It is evergreen, with smooth stems and leaves which are long and tapering and covered with rust-coloured scales beneath. The tiny white flowers are produced at the leaf axils late in autumn, and they have a pungent scent. The plant makes rapid growth in sandy soil and makes a most efficient hedge.

E. longipes (syn. *E. multiflora, E. odorata edulis).* It is a Japanese shrub growing 1.8 to 2.4 m (6 to 8 ft) tall with attractive reddish stems and it is deciduous, the dark-green leaves being silvery beneath. It blooms during early summer, the inconspicuous white flowers having the sweet fragrance of lilac and the flowers are followed by juicy, orange-red berries, pungent and delicious.

E. macrophylla. A Chinese species which grows 1.8 m (6 ft) tall and very bushy. It has shining grey-green leaves covered with silvery scales and silvered on the underside which gives the plant an attractive cool, grey appearance. The white flowers, like those of *E. glabra,* are produced late in autumn and persist until almost the year-end and have a daphne-like perfume.

E. pungens. Native of Japan, it is evergreen, its long wavy leaves being bright green above, silver beneath with a prominent mid-rib whilst the wood is covered in brown scales. The tiny white flowers appear in August and have a sweet but pungent perfume.

There is a most decorative form, *aureovariegata,* with bright-golden leaves, whilst *variegata* has leaves of deep green splashed with cream.

E. umbellata (syn. *E. parvifolia).* It is found from Afghanistan to the China coast, growing 2.4 to 3 m (8 to 10 ft) in height, its branches being covered in brown scales. The narrow leaves, grey-green above and silver beneath, take on darker shades with age whilst the flowers, which appear early in summer and are borne in clusters, have the same heavy scent as all the species.

ELDER: *see* **SAMBUCUS**

ELETTARI (Zingiberaceae—Ginger Family)

A tropical genus of large perennial herbs, similar in appearance to *Amomum* but distinguished from it by the elongated form of the corolla and by the filaments not being prolonged beyond the anther. They are native only to tropical India, the best known being *E. cardamomum* whose fruit is known as the Malabar cardamom.

Species. *Elettari cardamomum*. It grows in abundance on the mountainous coast of Malabar to an altitude of about 1,500 m (5,000 ft) but for commercial purposes is cultivated in clearings by inducing spontaneous germination. This is achieved by felling trees and shaking the soil; in about a month, seedlings appear and produce a crop four years later.

The plant forms a thick rhizome-like rootstock, ringed with the scars of previous leaves. From the rootstock arises a stem about 2.4 m (8 ft) tall, enveloped in the spongy sheath of the leaves which grow 60 cm (2 ft) in length and terminate in a point. They are silky on the underside. The flowers and branches alternate, one from each joint of the scape. The flowers are borne solitary at each joint of the racemes and are short-stalked. The calyx is funnel-shaped with the corolla long and slender. The plant requires an annual rainfall of over 250 cm (100 in) to succeed. The fruit begins to ripen in October, the ripe and unripe fruit being removed on the one stalk. They are left for a few days on mats to dry. They are then detached from the stalks and allowed to complete their drying either in the sun or over a fire, suspended in shallow baskets.

Cardamoms differ in size and shape, colour and aroma. The Malabar 'shorts', as they are called in the trade, are shortly ovoid or almost globular. The capsule is triangular, grey or yellowish-brown, opening by 3 valves, each compartment containing about 16 seeds, reddish-brown, wrinkled and wedge-shaped. They have a pleasant aromatic odour and taste.

In the Ceylon variety, *major*, the seeds are larger and more numerous and are yellow, tinted with red. They have their own peculiar odour and taste which is more ginger-like than the camphor-like odour of the Malabar form.

ELSHOLTZIA (Labiatae—Lavender Family)

A genus of 35 species, native of Asia and Ethiopia, and named in honour of the German botanist, Elsholtz.

Species. *Elsholtzia stanptarii*. It is a native of China, making a loosely-growing shrub 1.8 m (6 ft) tall. The long, oval leaves are dark green above, pale green beneath, and when bruised release a refreshing minty fragrance. The plant bears its spikes of violet-pink flowers in September and October, and is extremely showy at this time of year. It is hardy and deciduous and grows well in a sunny position, and although it may die back in winter, it will produce plenty of new growth the following year. Increase by semi-ripe cuttings in August in sandy compost under glass.

EMBOTHRIUM (Proteaceae—Protea Family)

A genus of eight species, native of eastern Australia and the Chilean Andes, few of which are fragrant.

Species. *Embothrium coccineum*. Native of the Andes where it is known as the Fire Bush for the brilliant colouring of its tubular flowers. In Britain and North America, it is able to survive the winter only in sheltered gardens of the south where it will attain a height of 4.5 (15 ft) or more. In May, it bears long drooping racemes of honeysuckle-like flowers of brilliant scarlet, with a soft honey fragrance unusual in flowers of this colouring which are visited by hummingbirds for their pollination.

ENDIANDRA (Lauraceae—Bay Tree Family)

A small genus of sub-tropical trees, native of the rain forests of the Indian Archipelago and of Australia, chiefly Queensland and New South Wales. They have alternate leaves and bear small white scented flowers in compound cymes, followed by a large berry or drupe.

Species. *Endiandra sieberi*. It makes a small glabrous tree with glossy oblong leaves, prominently veined, and bearing tiny greenish-white flowers followed by oval black drupes about 2.5 cm (1 in) long which have the aromatic scent of the nutmeg.

ENDYMION (Liliaceae—Lily Family)

A genus of 10 species, native of western Europe, several of which bear scented flowers.

Species. *Endymion non-scriptus* (syn. *Scilla non-scripta, Hyacinthoides non-scripta*). The English bluebell, not to be confused with the bluebell of Scotland which is the harebell of the English moorlands. It is also known as the Wild hyacinth, the solitary scapes 37 cm (15 in) long, arising from a pear-shaped bulb of about 2-cm (1-in) diameter. At the end of the stem appear 8 to 12 dangling bells of richest purple-blue, which diffuse a balsam-like scent in the sunshine.

From the bulbs, the Elizabethans obtained a starch to stiffen their ruffs and glued their books with the same sticky substance. Parkinson tells us that Dodonaeus called it *Hyacinthus non-scriptus* 'because it is not written of by any author before himself'.

ENKIANTHUS (Ericaceae—Heather Family)

A genus of 10 species of partially evergreen shrubs growing 1.8 m (6 ft) tall and native of the Himalayas and Japan. The leaves take on rich autumn colourings which they retain well into winter, The plants require a moist peaty soil and they are successfully propagated by layering the young shoots.

Species. *Enkianthus campanulatus.* It grows 2.4 m (8 ft) tall with dull green finely toothed leaves and in May bears drooping racemes of greenish-white bells, like lily-of-the-valley flowers, and which to some have a sweet perfume. The flowers may sometimes be edged with crimson.

The form *albiflorus* bears flowers of ivory-white and is a plant of more compact habit with the additional virtue that its leaves change to a clear golden-yellow which they retain into winter.

E. perulatus. Also *E. japonicus,* it makes a slender shrub 1.8 to 2.4 m (6 to 8 ft) tall and early in spring bears its scented white bell-shaped flowers in drooping clusters from the tips of the shoots. The leaves turn a rich golden colour and then scarlet before they fall.

EPACRIS (Epacridaceae—Epacris Family)

A genus of 40 species of evergreen plants, native of New South Wales, Tasmania and New Zealand, one of which, *E. pulchella,* bears such attractively scented flowers that it is known as the Sweet-scented Epacris. They usually bear flowers of blush-white or pale pink which hang in graceful plumes from the slender shoots, giving the plant an elegant appearance surpassed by few others.

They bloom towards the end of winter, or early in spring where growing under glass, and retain their blossom for several weeks. The flowers also remain fresh when the sprigs are removed and placed in damp sand, diffusing their scent about the home, like *Chimonanthus fragrans* treated in the same way.

The epacris grows best in a fibrous peat to which some sand has been added. They require a winter temperature of no more than 5°C (42°F) at night and 10°C (50°F) by day. For best effect, the side growths should be fastened to short canes fixed around the pot. After flowering, if the shoots are cut hard back they will 'break' again and so maintain the bushy habit of the plant.

Species. *Epacris hyacinthina candidissima.* The pure-white tubular flowers are produced in profusion early in spring and diffuse a delicious hyacinth-like fragrance about the greenhouse.

E. pulchella. Its masses of pale-pink tubular flowers look delightful against the neat dark-green foliage and are the most sweetly scented of the whole family.

EPIDENDRUM (Orchidaceae—Orchid Family)

A genus of more than 1,000 species, native to tropical America and the West Indies, and bearing their flowers in a terminal spike. Tall-growing plants, they require a light, well-ventilated house and a temperature of 16°C (60°F) when they will open their flowers in succession over three to four months. They grow well in a compost composed of 3 parts sphagnum moss and 1 of peat, and whilst growing must be well watered.

Species. *Epidendrum inversum.* A very heavily scented species, smelling of cloves so as to be almost cloying. The flowers are borne in a crowded inflorescence and are white with a rose flush, or a dull pale yellow, in both cases streaked and spotted with purple.

E. radiatum. The creamy-white flowers of this orchid, with their bright-purple streaks, appear in spring and summer. It is Mexican, and the whole plant may grow to about 15 cm (6 in) high. The fragrance is of lilac, and in some cases may be strong enough to be unpleasant.

EPIGAEA (Ericaceae—Heather Family)

Its name is derived from two Greek words meaning 'upon the earth' which gives some idea of its habit. It is native of the eastern United States and Canada and was named Mayflower by the Pilgrim Fathers for it blooms in May. It is also known as the Ground Laurel on account of its evergreen laurel-like leaves. The genus is characterized by 3 leaflets on the outside of the 5-part calyx. It grows in shade and in a peaty soil and is valuable to plant around rhododendrons and other peat-loving plants enjoying shade. It is propagated either by layering or root division in autumn.

Species. *Epigaea asiatica.* It is a native of Japan and is of creeping habit with leathery bronze-green leaves. It bears its tubular sweetly scented rosy-white flowers in clusters in May and they are attractively surrounded by small bracts.

E. repens. Ground laurel once grew on every rockery but is now rarely found, possibly rightly so for it is so much better in the wild garden. It is a pretty and completely hardy evergreen with heart-shaped leaves and blooms early in May, bearing dense clusters of pinky-white tubes which give off a rich spicy perfume. It is a valuable plant to use about the base of pine trees for it revels in the acid soil formed by the pine needles.

EPILOBIUM (Onagraceae—Evening Primrose Family)

A genus of about 160 species distributed over the temperate and alpine regions of both hemispheres. They are known as the Willow-herbs and are erect or creeping herbs or undershrubs with alternate or opposite entire or toothed leaves and 4-petalled flowers with a long slender calyx tube. Many species have only nuisance value in the garden but several have great beauty and are excellent plants to use by the side of a stream or pond, keeping company with the willows though they take their name from their willow-like foliage. One, *E. hirsutum,* is delightfully fragrant.

Species. *Epilobium hirsutum.* Known as 'Codlins and Cream' to the countryman, for the plants have the refreshing scent of ripe apples. It is not the flowers that are scented (though they have some perfume) but the stems and leaves are covered with a soft down which emits the smell of the Moss rose and the Eglantine. It is native of the British Isles and northern Europe where its graceful arching stems attain a height of 1.2 m to 1.8 m (4 to 6 ft) and in July it bears flowers of reddish-mauve, similar in colour and appearance to the Purple loosestrife.

Dr Hamilton and Dr Thakur of Durham University have succeeded in raising a number of new hybrids by crossing *E. hirsutum* with *E. luteum* (native of Oregon), and they bear flowers of a unique shade of dog purple with a contrasting white stigma. The fragrance of the blooms is very much more pronounced than in the parents though the plants are free of down and with its loss, the apple scent is also absent. However, by crossing back to *E. hirsutum,* this returns and is also present on the purple-black flowers with the return of the refreshing apple perfume.

EPIPACTIS (Orchidaceae—Orchid Family)

A genus of 24 species, native of north temperate regions, tropical Africa and Mexico, one of which, *E. atrorubens,* is present in the British Isles.

Species. *Epipactis atrorubens.* It grows in woodland clearings in north-western Yorkshire and the Lake District and in the Burren Mountains of Co. Clare, in Ireland. From its spreading mint-like roots, the flower stems arise to a height of 30 cm (12 in), each with as many as 20 or more purple-red flowers which have a sweet vanilla-like fragrance. It is known as the Red helleborine.

EPIPHYLLUM (Cactaceae—Cactus Family)

A genus of 17 species, native to Mexico, tropical South America and the West Indies. They are not parasitic plants but root on host plants, and are usually found high above ground in the forks of trees, their roots growing in hollows which have become filled with sand or soil and decayed vegetable matter. They are common plants of the tropical forests of Paraguay, their smooth, flat, succulent stems providing them with moisture to tide them over periods of drought. The stems replace leaves and are produced both as side shoots and from the base, often measuring up to 50 cm (20 in) long. From the ends appear the flowers. The plants were named by Rudolph Hermann, Professor of Botany at Leiden University in 1689, from the Greek *epi*, upon, and *phyllos*, a leaf, for the flowers appear at the end of the leaf-like stems.

The plants require a humus-laden soil containing a high proportion of sand to promote good drainage, though they should not be dried off like cacti. They require a minimum winter temperature of 5°C (42°F) and sufficient moisture to keep them alive, increasing supplies in summer. Give them a sunny window in winter and partial shade in summer with frequent spraying.

Though the colours of the blooms range from scarlet and bright pink to pale yellow and white, it is only the latter which have perfume, and it is most pronounced in the glistening white flowered *Epiphyllum cooperi*, especially at night. Propagation is by cuttings taken from the ends of the stems. They should be allowed to become partly callous for several days before inserting in a sandy compost. Shade from the sun and keep them moist.

Species. *Epiphyllum anguliger.* It bears its strangely notched stems up to 45 cm (1½ ft) long at the end of which appear large tubular flowers, the outer petals being pale yellow, the inner ones white, and they are sweetly scented both by day and night. It blooms in October.

E. cooperi. The slowest-growing species

and possibly a natural hybrid, it bears most of its flowers on basal shoots. The flowers are pure white and tubular, but open almost flat, like camellias. They remain fresh for about three days, scenting the air by day and by night with an exotic, lily-like perfume which is most pronounced when first open.

A number of hybrids of the *cooperi* type are of great beauty but only London Sunshine, palest yellow, bears scented flowers.

E. darrahii. Prominent in southern Mexico, it forms long, straggling branches, deeply notched at the sides, and alternate to each other. The flowers, which have a long, greenish-yellow tube and outer petals of lemon yellow have inner petals of pure white with a powerful, lily-like scent.

E. oxypetalum. This species opens its flowers by night; larger than most, they are ivory white, tinted with rosy-red on the outside, and powerfully scented.

EPIPOGIUM (Orchidaceae—Orchid Family)

A genus of two species, one inhabiting the cooler regions of the Northern Hemisphere, the other tropical South-east Asia. The plants form a strange coral-like rhizome covered with hairs upon which adheres a fungus which supplies the plant with nourishment.

Species. *Epipogium aphyllum.* Its habitat extends from central Europe to the arctic north and across Europe and Asia. Though it has been seen in southern England during this century, it may now be extinct in the British Isles. It blooms in May or June, the large flowers being pink and said to smell of ripe bananas.

ERANTHIS (Ranunculaceae—Buttercup Family)

A small genus of five or six species, native of western and south-eastern Europe, of Siberia and Japan. They are perennial plants of extreme hardiness and are tuberous-rooted, like the ranunculus. They bloom from early in the year in Britain and North America and continue, depending upon species, until May, bearing their golden chalices as the snow melts from them. They are suitable for planting beneath mature trees, where the summer shade prevents the grass from growing high and where against the brown earth the golden bowls, borne on 5-cm (2-in) stems, present a delightful picture in the depth of winter. The flowers are backed by an attractive green ruff.

The name *Eranthis* means 'flowers of the earth'. It is also known as the Winter aconite, Thomas Noel's 'gloom-gliding aconite' of which Gerard wrote, 'it groweth upon the mountains in Germany; we have great quantities of it in our London gardens. It bloweth in January . . . yea, the colder the weather is and deeper the snow, the fairer and larger is the flower'. Though none of the species bear flowers having any real perfume, a hybrid of *E. hyemalis*, Guinea Gold, bears fragrant blossoms. It is more beautiful than its parents for it bears large globes of shining rich yellow tinted with bronze which diffuse a delicious sweet perfume in spring. The flowers remain fresh for several weeks. Plant the tubers 5 cm (2 in) apart and 5 cm deep.

ERCILLA (Phytolaccaceae—Poke-Weed Family)

A genus of two species, native of Chile and Peru, and climbing by adhesive discs.

Species. *Ercilla volubilis.* It may be planted against a warm wall and is an evergreen but should be confined to a sheltered garden where it will grow to a height of 6 m (20 ft). It has thick leathery leaves and blooms early in March, bearing from the axils spikes of small purple-white flowers which have a delicate sweet perfume.

EREMOPOGON (Graminaceae—Grass Family)

A genus of four species of grass, native of Africa, tropical Asia and India.

Species. *Eremopogon faveolatus.* It is a slender, much-branched grass growing in tufts on stony ground in Egypt, mostly near the coast. The leaves are narrow and are blue-green while the flowers appear in spire-like terminal racemes. It is pleasantly aromatic.

EREMURUS (Liliaceae—Lily Family)

A genus of about 30 species of fleshy rooted plants which attain noble proportions and should mostly be confined to the

back of the border. They are native of central Asia, from Persia and Afghanistan across northern India to central China and Japan, and only the pale-pink, white and yellow species are scented. Given the protection of a little bracken or litter during winter, the plants are hardy in the British Isles and North America but the Eremurus is a gross feeder and appreciates a forkful of decayed manure placed about the roots in winter.

The plants like an open position and a well-drained soil, and though deep planting would give protection from frost the Eremurus will resent it. Plant in March or October, spreading out the roots over a layer of sand or peat and if the soil is of a heavy nature, leave the crown slightly exposed. Otherwise just cover them. The roots are brittle and should be handled with care. Propagation is by division of the crowns but the plants do not take kindly to disturbance and should be left undisturbed for at least six years. By that time they will bear up to a dozen flower-thick spikes about which the individual florets are clustered, hence its name of the Foxtail lily. Several species carry the rich perfume of the lily.

Species and Varieties. *Eremurus elwesii.* It has striking grey-green sword-like leaves and bears its enormous spikes to a height of 1.8 m (6 ft), blooming early in June. The flowers are flesh-coloured with a sweet scent even more pronounced in the lovely white form, *albus*, which received an Award of Merit in 1905.

E. kaufmannianus. From the regions of the Black Sea, it attains a height of 1.2 m (4 ft) and bears a large cylindrical spike of pale primrose-yellow which is powerfully fragrant.

E. olgae. From the Black Sea regions, it comes into bloom late in May and remains in bloom for about two months, producing its lilac-pink spikes to a height of 1.5m (5 ft) with the spikes at least 0.9 m (3 ft) in length. The individual bell-shaped florets are clustered together about the spike so that no stem can be seen, whilst down each petal is a central brown stripe.

ERICA (Heather) (Ericaceae—Heather Family)

A widely dispersed genus of more than

500 species of evergreen bushes and shrubs which has given its name to the family. Though most of the species require an acid soil, *Erica carnea*, the Winter-flowering heather, discovered in the Italian Alps, tolerates lime in the soil as does *E. vagans*, the Cornish heath. Though the foliage of all the heathers has that invigorating musky tang which scents the moorland air for miles around, only one or two species bear scented flowers. They are plants requiring an acid soil and unfortunately do not possess the extreme hardiness of the others, being native of southern Europe. The fragrant heathers are mostly spring and early summer flowering.

The heathers should be given an open, sunny situation though the tree heathers require warmth and shelter. The heaths are readily increased by taking cuttings of the ripened wood in August and inserting them in a peat and sand compost, whilst most may be propagated by root division in November.

Species and Varieties. *Erica arborea*. This most graceful of all heaths is found along the shores of the Mediterranean and as far south as the Canary Islands where it attains almost tree-like proportions, 3 m (10 ft) or more, with hairy stems and grey-green leaves. Unusually for heathers, it flowers in March and April, bearing its pure-white flowers in large clusters, and the warm spring sunshine brings out their sweet, honey fragrance. Unfortunately the plant is tender in the British Isles away from the warmer parts of S.W. England and Scotland though the dwarf form, *alpina*, a conical shrub growing less than half the height, is more hardy. It blooms in April/May when the fragrant white flowers are enhanced by the dark-green foliage. From the roots, briar pipes are made on the Continent, 'briar' being derived from the French *bruyère*, heath. The roots have a pleasant sweet aroma.

E. bowieana. Bowie's heather, it is almost winter flowering in a mild climate, bearing its beautiful greyish-white flowers from August until the end of November, and diffusing a delicate sweet scent.

E. fragrans. It grows 25 to 30 cm (10 to 12 in) in height and from April until June bears spikes of purple which have a honey-like perfume.

E. mediterranea. The Irish heath, native of the heathlands and bogs of Co. Mayo as well as of the countries bordering the Mediterranean where it grows 1.2 m (4 ft) or more in height. It blooms in April, the bell-shaped flowers with their broad lobes, and a lovely rich pink, appearing in dense racemes, and they are sweetly scented. The variety *Superba* is an improvement on the type, bearing deep rose-pink flowers of delicious honey perfume, which are enhanced by the dark-green foliage.

E. denticulata. The Sweet-scented heath of South Africa which bears in August pure-white tubular blossoms with a perfume like that of honeysuckle. It is one of the few white heathers amongst some 500 species bearing flowers of flaming scarlet or gold but it is the only one of the South African heaths that is fragrant.

E. lusitanica. Native of south-western Europe where it attains a height of 1.5 m (5 ft) or more and is one of the tree heaths. It is somewhat tender but in a sheltered garden blooms during March and April, bearing its tapering spires of pink-tipped white flowers amidst pale-green leaves. The flowers have a soft sweet perfume, beautifully described by Miss Sinclair Rohde as being 'the quintessence of the scent of wild open spaces in springtime'.

E. odorata. One of the spring-flowering heathers, it was seen by the author in a sheltered garden in the West Country in 1950 but never since, and now seems to have disappeared from British gardens and those of northern Europe. It bears dainty upright spikes of purest white and the bells have the heavy fragrance of honeysuckle, especially pronounced at eventide. It blooms during May and June.

E. veitchii. A hybrid of *E. ciliaris* (the Dorset heath) and *E. tetralix* and though neither parent has fragrant flowers, *E. veitchii* bears sweetly scented flowers of pinkish-white. It makes a small tuft less than 30 cm (12 in) high and blooms during August and September.

ERIGERON (Compositae—Daisy Family)

It comprises a large genus of 100 or more species several of which, under the correct climatic conditions, yield a resinous substance resembling labdanum. The erigerons grow in all well-drained soils and are increased by root division.

Species. *Erigeron glaucum.* It is native of North America where it grows little more than 22.5 cm (9 in) high. It is an evergreen with oblong leaves which are glaucous and clammy to the touch, leaving on the fingers a balsamic perfume. It bears its lilac-mauve daisies throughout summer and autumn.

ERINACEA (Leguminosae—Laburnum Family)
A genus of a single species.

Species. *Erinacea pungens.* It is native of North Africa and of Spain and is known as the Hedgehog broom for it grows about 60 cm (2 ft) tall and is densely covered in spines, like the gorse (*Ulex*). It requires a well-drained soil and an open situation where it will be baked by the sun and bear masses of violet-coloured flowers during May and June. The whole plant emits a pleasant pungent smell.

ERINUS (Scrophulariaceae—Foxglove Family)
A genus of a single species.

Species. *Erinus selaginoides.* It is a half-hardy annual bearing its flowers in dense terminal spikes. The plant has long-stalked, spoon-shaped leaves and it comes into bloom before the end of May. Its flowers are borne in terminal spikes and are white with a yellow centre and with hairs in the throat. At night they emit a delicious, heavy perfume which, if the plants are set out in beds, will reach to all parts of the garden when the air is calm and warm.

The seed should be sown under glass in March, one to a 6-cm (2½-in) pot, for the plants resent root disturbance. When growing in their flowering quarters, the shoots should be trained over wires stretched across the walls and roof of a greenhouse or verandah. The blooms will remain open until the sun gathers strength towards noon, when they close up, and open again in the evening.

ERIOBOTRYA (Rosaceae—Rose Family)
A genus of 40 species, native of the Mediterranean regions and southern Asia, and valued by the local people for their edible fruit.

Species. *Eriobotrya japonica.* The Japanese medlar or loquat, though it will not produce fruit in the British Isles. Native of China and Japan, it makes a small tree or shrub 6 to 9 m (20 to 30 ft) tall, and is evergreen, with handsome, long wrinkled leaves, downy on the underside, which often measure up to 30 cm (1 ft) long. It comes into bloom in November in a sheltered garden, bearing its white, hawthorn-like flowers in drooping clusters, and they emit a most potent oriental perfume. Well-drained soil suits it best, and cuttings of ripe wood in sandy soil in a cold frame provide a method of propagation. They should be taken in August.

ERIOSTEMON (Rutaceae—Rue Family)
A genus of 32 species of evergreen plants, native mostly of New South Wales and which in Britain, under glass, may be brought into bloom almost throughout the year. They also bloom at an early age and, like the epacris, tolerate a temperature which is just sufficiently high to keep the plants from frost damage. They are also very long-living when confined to pots and in a compost which is also suitable for the epacris. Like all evergreens under glass, they appreciate a daily syringeing during periods of warm weather.

Species. *Eriostemon buxifolius.* The Box-leaf eriostemon whose foliage has a similar resinous scent when handled whilst its white flowers are most attractive against the dark-green foliage.

E. myoporeoides. It is an erect-growing plant with medium-sized glossy leaves which are fragrant when handled and it bears its pure-white flowers in bunches of five or six at every leaf joint.

E. neriifolius. It has leaves like the oleander which are pungently fragrant and it is most free-flowering, the individual flowers being larger than any of the order.

ERITRICHIUM (Boraginaceae—Forget-me-not Family)
A genus of 70 or more species of tufted, spreading habit, of which only one or two have garden value and only one, *E. nothofulvum*, bears scented flowers.

Species. *Eritrichium nothofulvum.* It is a pretty annual growing 30 cm (12 in) tall and very similar to the Forget-me-not, but pure white and emitting a powerful honeysuckle perfume. Treated as a biennial and massed as a carpet for summer-flowering annuals, it will cover the ground with its racemes of purest white and when so used, its perfume is outstanding.

ERODIUM (Geraniaceae—Geranium Family)

A genus of herbs with swollen nodes and attractive fern-like leaves, toothed, lobed or pinnately dissected, and growing on waste ground, usually near the sea. Several species are native to the British Isles and southern Europe and are known as the Storksbills. Several emit a peculiar (to some, unpleasant) smell when bruised, whilst a number have pleasantly scented foliage.

Species. *Erodium glandulosum*. Known as Heron's-bill, it is closely related to the Cranesbill or Wild geranium and is a charming plant growing 15 to 22.5 cm (6 to 9 in) tall, and so may be grown at the front of a border or on a rockery, where its balsam-scented foliage will be much appreciated. It requires a position of full sun, and being native to the Pyrenees loves to have its roots beneath stones with its head in the sun. The blooms are grey, tinted and veined with purple-rose, the lower petals being larger than the upper ones. The twice divided leaves are covered in glandular down and are pleasantly aromatic.

The plants are interesting in that they sow their own seed. The 'beak' which accompanies the seed is hygroscopic, becoming twisted when dry but when damp it straightens itself out and at the same time ejects the seed.

E. moschatum. The Musk storksbill which makes a larger, more robust plant than the Common storksbill and is chiefly found in Britain, inhabiting rocky ground near the coast in the South-west and in the Channel Islands. An annual, it grows to a height of 30 to 37.5 cm (12 to 15 in) with attractive fern-like leaves which are covered in hairs and are clammy to the touch. They carry a strong scent of musk when bruised. During July and August it bears magenta-pink flowers in small umbels and is altogether a delightful plant.

ERYNGIUM (Sea Holly) (Umbelliferae—Parsley Family)

A genus of more than 100 species of thistle-like herbs with spiny leaves and flower heads surrounded by a whorl of spiny bracts. The eryngiums are perennial border plants of great beauty, delighting in a sandy soil for they are plants of the seaside, *E. maritimum*, the Common Sea holly, being native to the British Isles. It is this species which has fragrant roots resembling those of the parsnip, of the same family.

Species. *Eryngium maritimum*. The Common Sea holly which grows to a height of 0.9 m (2 ft), its glaucous leaves having a whitish hue whilst they are extremely spiny, resembling those of the holly. The ball-shaped flower-heads are bluish-white and, if cut and placed indoors without water, retain their beauty for several weeks.

In Elizabethan times, the fleshy roots were much in demand as a vegetable, cooked and eaten like parsnips which they resemble in their sweet smell and taste. The candied roots of the Sea holly were known as eringoes, to which Shakespeare refers in *The Merry Wives of Windsor*.

ERYSIMUM (Cheiranthus) (Cruciferae—Wallflower Family)

A genus of more than 100 biennial or perennial plants, mostly native of north temperate regions, from North America to the Caucasus, though several species grow in the Pyrenees and in northern India and western China. The leaves are usually covered with down to give the plant a hoary appearance and they bloom almost the whole year. They are of dainty habit, forming tiny tufts and grow well in the crevice of a dry wall in full sun as they do in the alpine or trough garden. The flowers of several species diffuse a scent which resembles the clove-like sweetness of the stock of the same family. It is a spicy fragrance, as refreshing in winter as it is during spring and summer. Several are of unpleasant smell, due to compounds of sulphur.

The plants possess extreme hardiness and being evergreen may also be used for a window-box garden or to plant in small beds with the fragrant purple or blue winter-flowering pansies; in the rock garden they are completely at home, flowering whenever the winter sun shines down upon them and continuing until the end of summer.

Species. *Erysimum alliaria.* The Garlic mustard or Jack-by-the-hedge is a common plant in copses and ditches, and on a calm day emits a strong smell of garlic which is especially pronounced when the leaves are bruised. In medieval times, the leaves were used to flavour stews and sauces (hence its name, Sauce-alone) and were also placed upon ulcers and sores.

The heart-shaped leaves are scalloped and veined and are attached to the main stem by small footstalks. The brilliant green of the leaves in spring and early summer make the Wild garlic one of the most handsome plants of the hedgerow but its garlic smell is not to everyone's taste. It grows to a height of 0.9 m (3 ft) and bears its tiny white flowers in clusters at the end of the stems.

The roots also have a garlic smell and are used to make up an ointment (heating the chopped roots with vaseline) to rub onto the chest to bring relief to bronchitis.

E. alpinum. A native of the rocky formations which arise above the Norwegian fiords, it is a charming little plant growing 15 cm (6 in) tall, with lance-shaped leaves covered with down. It blooms most profusely during summer, its sulphur-yellow flowers having a pronounced cinnamon perfume. The variety Moonlight bears flowers of a paler yellow, also scented.

E. linifolium. It is like a miniature wallflower and was introduced into Britain by the late Mr Clarence Elliott in 1913. In his book *Rock Garden Plants*, he describes how he obtained seed from Vigo in Spain, which was virtually thrown into a seed-pan and left to take care of itself. 'In September,' he writes, 'I planted out the starved weaklings in a little colony in my own garden ... They grew at once into hearty little bushes and produced a mass of delicious scented lilac flowers which persisted right through the dirtiest weather of that autumn and winter.' This is in fact the best way to grow it, from seed sown in a starved soil. The plants will be quite long-lasting and will bear their scented flowers in short racemes, like a tiny wallflower, at a height of only 12.5 cm (5 in).

E. odoratum. Native of northern Asia, it is an erect robust herb with oblong or lance-shaped leaves, covered in hairs and it bears pale-yellow flowers which are powerfully scented. It is closely allied to *E. melicentae*, endemic in Kashmir, but which has deep-orange flowers entirely devoid of scent, an example of pigment replacing perfume. *E. odoratum* grows in the Himalayas up to almost 3,000 m (10,000 ft).

E. pulchellum. One of the few Eastern species, native of the rocky formations of China and Japan, over which the plants grow like an aubrietia, making a tufted mass of foliage and bearing, from early spring until the end of summer, racemes of softly scented flowers of sulphur-yellow.

E. pumilum. A treasure of the Pyrenees and Swiss Alps, it is evergreen, making a tiny branched shrub 7.5 cm (3 in) tall and in width, and being so densely furnished with pale-green foliage that its bare woody parts are hidden. The flowers are produced in terminal racemes and are less than 1 cm ($\frac{1}{2}$ in) across, cruciform like the wallflower and stock, greenish-yellow in colour and deliciously scented. Like all the erysimums it loves a dry, sun-baked situation and may be planted in a rock crevice or wall where it will soon cover a large area, the shoots taking root in the mortar.

E. suffruticosum. Really a perennial though usually given annual or biennial treatment. Seed is sown in July for the plants to bloom in spring, whilst from a spring sowing, the display will be enjoyed almost the whole year round. The sweetly scented yellow flowers are produced on 30-cm (12-in) stems.

ESCALLONIA (Saxifragaceae—Rockfoil Family)

A genus of about 40 species of evergreen shrubs, native of Chile and named in honour of Prof. Escallon, a Spanish botanist. They flourish in the sandy soil of a coastal garden and with their resinous foliage are tolerant of salt-laden sea breezes. For a hedge, they are amongst the finest of all shrubs for a coastal garden for they make rapid growth and if carefully clipped never become 'leggy', being clothed from top to bottom with small glossy leaves, serrated at the edges and sticky to the touch, leaving on the hands a resinous smell similar to that of the walnut tree foliage. Several bear flowers which have a sweet fragrance.

Species and Varieties. *Escallonia illinita.* It is as if the leaves have been varnished over, so resinous and glossy are they, and they are thought by some to possess an unpleasant foxy or animal smell. This smell is noticeable in nearly all resinous scents though it is usually counteracted by a sweetness, most pronounced in the pine and walnut foliage and somewhat similar in the escallonias. *E. illinita* is a vigorous plant, growing 3 m (10 ft) in height, its pungent flowers of purest white providing a striking display against the almost black-green foliage.

E. macrantha. It grows to a height of 1.8 to 2.4 m (6 to 8 ft) and makes a splendid hedge or wall shrub, bearing clusters of brilliant-red flowers from July until October, the leaves and flower having a pungent smell.

E. pterocladon. A native of Patagonia, famed for its winged branches and tiny leaves. It is best grown against a wall, and during July and August bears resinous-scented flowers of creamy-white.

E. virgata. It may not be fully evergreen in the most exposed gardens but it is a delightful plant, and its appearance of brittle frailty belies its ruggedness. It grows no more than 1.5 m (5 ft) in height and from June until September its branches are covered in sweetly scented flowers of starry whiteness.

E. viscosa (syn. *E. glutinosa*). It is so named because its foliage is more sticky than in any other species and has a more 'foxy' odour. It is, however, hardier than most species and bears its white flowers from June until September.

A number of beautiful hybrids have been introduced by the Slieve Donard Nurseries of Northern Ireland, mostly having either *E. macrantha* or *E. virgata* for a parent, and several bear sweetly scented flowers.

DONARD GEM. In growth, it is neat and compact, growing 1.2 m (4 ft) tall and the same across and bearing in May and June, very sweetly scented flowers of clearest pink. It blooms again in autumn.

IVEYANA. It grows to a height of 1.8 m (6 ft) and from June until October bears its tubular flowers of white flushed with pink, in large clusters. It has the scented variety Exonensis as one parent. Also a plant of great vigour, its flowers are of similar colouring.

EUCALYPTUS (Gum tree)
(Myrtaceae—Myrtle Family)

A genus of about 150 species of trees and shrubs mostly native of Australia and New Zealand. Until recent years the Eucalyptus tree or Blue gum tree of Australia was hardy in only the most sheltered gardens of Britain and North America. Now, however, Messrs John Scott & Co. have raised plants from seed of *C. coccifera* sent over from the Forestry Commission of Tasmania which may be successfully grown in protected gardens in the Cotswolds, along the western coast of Scotland and in parts of Northern Ireland and Eire. This Mountain blue gum is evergreen, with glossy glaucous foliage whilst the bark is smooth and grey in colour. In Australasia the eucalyptus is planted in unhealthy low-lying districts for its foliage has valuable antiseptic properties, its oil being extracted for medicinal use (it was made official in the *British Pharmacopoeia* in 1885). Seed may be obtained from the Forestry Department, Perth, Western Australia, and should be sown in John Innes compost; the young plants are grown on in pots.

The gums are shallow-rooting and should be supported during their first year, and planted only where they may receive protection from prevailing winds.

Species and Varieties. *Eucalyptus cneorifolia.* It yields the purest of all the eucalyptus oils with a smell of caraway and lemon. It is a shrub rather than a tree, found only on Kangaroo Island along the banks of the Cygnet River where it grows 3.6 m (12 ft) in height, and it is much branched at the base. Known as the Narrow-leaf eucalyptus, its leaves are extremely pungent.

E. coccifera. The Blue gum of Australasia which makes a small tree of blue appearance. Its lance-shaped leaves taper to a point and are extremely aromatic.

E. dumosa. It abounds in the Murray Desert of Australia where it forms a dense bush and yields an oil of more than usual purity with a strong camphor smell. It is of too tender habit for British gardens.

E. globosus. It was discovered in Tasmania by Labillardière and introduced into Europe in 1856 by Ramel who had noticed its beneficial effects in malaria-ridden districts by taking up moisture in marshy land. By absorbing vast quantities of moisture in its tissues, the tree rapidly reaches amazing proportions, and its salubrious effect is increased by the balsamic emanations from its leaves. Though of rapid growth, the tree has great durability under water whilst its immunity to White ant attack makes it the most valuable of all Australasian trees. It is known as the Victoria Blue gum, 'blue' referring to its glaucous blue foliage, 'gum' to the balsamic gum which exudes from the trunk. But it is from the leaves and twigs that oil of eucalyptus is obtained. It is used in the treatment of lung diseases, and in its unadulterated form is so powerful as to almost numb the senses.

Only in the most favourable areas does the tree survive the winters of the Northern Hemisphere, and so it is usually cultivated under glass to be used for decorative summer bedding. It is a graceful plant with beautiful glaucous leaves which wave attractively in the wind.

E. gunnii. Native of Tasmania, it is the hardiest and fastest-growing species, reaching a height of 9 m (30 ft) in the British Isles and southern Europe. It has ovate lance-shaped blue-grey leaves which are very aromatic. The bark is deciduous though it is persistent at the base of young trees.

EUCHARIS (Amaryllidaceae—Narcissus Family)

A genus of eight species, all native of the Colombian Andes. The bulbous plants need a minimum temperature of 15°C (60°F) in northern Europe and tolerate a higher temperature when in full growth. The bulbs measure 7.5 cm (3 in) across and need a large pot to contain their considerable rooting system. From the large strap-like leaves arises the 60-cm (2-ft) scape with 6 to 8 drooping tubular flowers, snow-white and possessing a powerful narcissus-like scent.

Species. *Eucharis candida.* On a 60-cm (2 ft) stem it bears up to 12 drooping white flowers, almost 7.5 cm (3 in) across and powerfully scented.

E. grandiflora. (syn. *E. amazonica).* On a 60-cm (2-ft) stem it bears about 6 large flowers almost 15 cm (6 in) across with the corona tinted with green and emitting the almost overpowering scent of *Lilium regale.*

EUCOMIS (Liliaceae—Lily Family)

A small genus of South African perennials having large truncated bulbs and oblong leaves. The flowers are borne in dense racemes and are surmounted by a rosette of leafy bracts. They like a rich, moist soil and an open, sunny situation. Coming into bloom late in July, they provide colour in the border when the early summer flowering plants are ending and they remain fresh for several weeks. The star-like flowers are similar to the ornithogalum to which the genus is related and several of the species bear sweetly scented flowers. Plant 15 cm (6 in) deep and give winter protection by covering with bracken or peat.

Species. *Eucomis autumnalis.* Also *E. undulata,* it is native of Natal and it is at its best during August. It bears its greenish-yellow flowers, about 2.5 cm (1 in) across in a dense spike on a stem 30 to 37.5 cm (12 to 15 in) long and they emit a faint perfume. The sweet scent is more pronounced in the white-flowered variety Regia, the bloom being enhanced by the tuft of leaves at the top of the stem.

E. comosa (syn. *E. punctata).* Also a native of Natal, it is the hardiest and best species for English gardens. It has handsome glossy deep-green leaves, spotted with purple on the underside and it bears its flowers on a 60-cm (2-ft) scape from mid-July until the end of September. The starry white blooms appear in a cylindrical truss and diffuse their sweet perfume over a considerable distance.

EUCRYPHIA (Eucryphiaceae—Eucryphia Family)

Native of Chile, Australia and Tasmania, the eucryphias enjoy a moist peaty soil and some shade and shelter from cold winds. For this reason they should be confined to gardens of the south-west and the west coast of Scotland, though splendid examples are to be found inland in gardens in the southern counties of England; William Robinson reported that *E. glutinosa* had withstood severe winters near London.

Species and Varieties. *Eucryphia glutinosa* (syn. *E. pinnatifolia*). It is native of Chile and makes a small well-branched tree or shrub eventually attaining a height of 3 m (10 ft). The flowers are amongst the most attractive of all shrubs, opening to 7.5 cm (3 in) across, like large single white roses with crimson anthers, and they have a delicate perfume. The flowers appear during August and September near the end of the shoots and the leaves take on brilliant tints in autumn. Propagation is by layering.

E. nymansay is a hybrid of *E. glutinosa* and is evergreen. It quickly grows into a columnar tree 6 m (20 ft) tall and in autumn bears its large scented white flowers.

E. lucida (syn. *E. billardieri*). It is native of Tasmania and less hardy than *E. glutinosa* and its hybrids. But it is a glorious dwarf tree, growing 3 m (10 ft) in height with shining evergreen leaves and in autumn bears cup-shaped flowers of purest white with pink anthers. It is the most strongly scented of all the eucryphias, its honey-like perfume pervading the air for a considerable distance.

The variety *Milligani* is equally fragrant but is much slower growing and perhaps more tender.

EUGENIA (Myrtaceae—Myrtle Family)

A genus of evergreen trees or shrubs, native of the sub-tropical West Indian Islands, the islands of Madagascar and South-east Asia; one species is native of New Zealand. The leaves are oblong, lanceolate, pointed at the tip, while the flowers are borne in axillary or terminal corymbs. Like the myrtle, all parts of the plant have an aromatic fragrance, the essential oil of the leaves and seeds being widely used in commerce. They are easily grown in a warm greenhouse or in stove conditions, being potted in February or March, and increased by cuttings taken in summer and placed in sandy soil, with heat, under a handlight.

Species. *Eugenia aromatica.* The species of evergreen tree which provides the cloves of commerce is native only of the Moluccas, from where it was introduced to the island of Mauritius by the French in 1770. From there the clove reached Zanzibar, flourishing in the yellow clay subsoil, and bringing great wealth to the island. But long before, cloves were imported from the East to be used for flavouring. The Swahili word for clove is *garafa*, from the French *giroflier*, from which is also derived the ancient word 'gillyflower', used during Elizabethan times to represent all those plants whose flowers had the spicy fragrance of the clove. Shakespeare mentions the custom of sticking cloves into dried oranges and lemons which were usually stuffed with spices. The spiced fruits were known as pomanders, probably derived from the ancient custom of sticking cloves into apples used for baking.

E. caryophyllus. The harvesting of the cloves commences when the tree is six years old and continues until it approaches 100 years. It is evergreen, attaining a height of 18 m (60 ft), with smooth grey bark. The opposite leaves are lance-shaped, about 15 cm (6 in) long, and covered with oil glands which release a clove-like aroma when pressed. The crimson-purple flowers are also fragrant and are borne in cymes at the end of the branchlets.

It is the dried flower buds that yield the cloves. These are picked off by hand and dried, the season being from August to November when each tree is picked over once each month. The buds are yellow at first, turning pink then red as they mature. The drying takes about seven days, during which they lose 50 per cent of their weight. The finest cloves are crimson when dried and are considered to have a superior flavour to black cloves. Best Zanzibar cloves are known as 'red-heads'.

Cloves are used whole or powdered, the world's annual consumption being about

10 million pounds. The essential oil made from distillation of the flower buds and stems is used as an antiseptic and in medicine and perfumery.

E. brachyandra. It is the Red Apple of Queensland and New South Wales, bearing globular red fruits about 2 cm (1 in) in diameter. It makes a tree 9 m (30 ft) high with oblong leaves about 15 cm (6 in) long, which are aromatic when bruised. It blooms in spring, bearing clusters of tiny red scentless flowers.

E. chequen (syn. *M. chekan*). Native of Chile, it is a small evergreen tree, to be found growing on the banks of most small rivers. Under the name of Chekan, an infusion of the leaves has for long been used as an aromatic astringent whilst the essential oil has the powerful smell of eucalyptus to which it is closely related. Plants were introduced into Britain in 1862 by Messrs Veitch & Son.

E. citrifolia. The Lemon-scented eugenia, so called from the pungent, lemon-like smell released when the leaves are bruised. It is to be found in most islands of the Caribbean where it grows 6 m (20 ft) tall, the leaves, flower-buds and berries possessing a 'hot', pungent taste and smell.

E. maire. Native only of New Zealand where it makes a tree 15 m (50 ft) tall, its evergreen leaves being dotted with resinous glands. It blooms during June, bearing its flowers in axillary or terminal corymbs, and these are followed by bright-red berries of aromatic fragrance. The tree is enhanced by its attractive white bark.

E. smithii. A glabrous small tree of northern Australia where it is known as Lilly-Pilly. The glossy, dark-green leaves are scented when bruised and are pink when opening whilst the scented white flowers are followed by pale-mauve fruits of gooseberry size.

EUPATORIUM (Hemp Agrimony) (Compositae—Daisy Family)

A large genus of some 1,200 species of herbs or undershrubs, bearing their flowers with tubular florets in corymbose cymes. The styles are longer than the florets. The Common hemp agrimony is the only species native to the British Isles for most belong to the American continent.

Species. *Eupatorium cannabinum.* The Hemp or Water agrimony, one of the most handsome native plants of the British Isles. It grows some 60 cm (2 ft) in height along the banks of streams and in damp woodlands. Both stems and leaves are covered with down and, if pulled through the hands, leave behind a strong resinous smell which Culpeper likened to 'cedar when it is burnt'. The flowers have a similar resinous smell when handled and are bright pink, borne in inflorescences and well supplied with nectar. They are much visited by butterflies. The bracts surrounding the flowers also release a resinous smell when handled.

E. odoratum. A herbaceous perennial, native of central North America, which bears panicles of rose-pink flowers with a sweet resinous perfume. They are visited by butterflies.

E. weinmannianum (syn. *E. micranthum*). It is a native of Chile and Mexico and may be included with the winter-flowering shrubs for it comes into bloom in September and given mild weather continues until the year end. It grows 2.4 to 2.7 m (8 to 9 ft) tall with evergreen leaves, oblong and toothed, and at the ends of the shoots bears large flat heads of creamy-white which are strongly fragrant.

EUPHORBIA (Euphorbiaceae— Spurgewort Family)

A genus of more than 600 species amongst which is included the Castor oil plant. The leaves are smooth and undivided whilst the flowers with involucres are arranged in terminal cymes or borne from the axils of the leaves. They are native of South Africa and the Canary Islands and in a cool climate should be kept quite dry when wintering indoors.

Species. *Euphorbia cereiformis.* It forms a thick stem, containing numerous small nipples from the centre of which protrudes an angry-looking spine an inch or more in length. At the top of the stem, clusters of small greenish flowers are formed which emit a refreshing lemon-like (verbena) perfume in the evening.

E. mellifera. It is the most robust of the genus, attaining a height of 1.8 m (6 ft) or more and making a dense bush with brilliant-green foliage about which it bears in May multitudes of pinkish-brown flowers which emit a delicious honey perfume.

E. obesa. It makes a compact globular plant like an orange divided into segments with purple leaves. The flowers are formed in rings at the top and those of the female plant only are sweetly scented.

EVODIA (Rutaceae—Rue Family)

A genus of small trees or shrubs, mostly native of the Indian Archipelago, the leaves being full of pellucid dots which when bruised release a resinous orange-like fragrance associated with the family. The flowers are minute and disposed in oblong axillary panicles and they have much the same sweet citrus-like smell of the leaves.

Species. *Evodia drupaceae.* Native of New Caledonia where it grows 1.8 m (6 ft) tall with smooth oblong leaves, aromatic when handled, and it bears its flowers in axillary corymbs.

E. hortensis. Native of the Friendly Isles where it makes a shrub 1.5 to 1.8 m (5 to 6 ft) tall with trifoliate leaves covered in pubescence like the wood. The whole of the plant is scented and used by the natives to flavour cocoa-nut oil.

EVOTA (Orchidaceae—Orchid Family)

A small genus of tuberous-rooted plants, native of South Africa and growing in damp places about Table Mountain. The flowers are borne solitary or in a short raceme and have the smell of sweet-scented toilet soap.

Species. *Evota bicolor.* It grows about 15 cm (6 in) tall with erect leaves whilst its flowers are borne in small racemes of usually 3 to 5. They are bright yellow, with brown stripes down the lip, the appendage of the lip having two long horns.

It requires a position of semi-shade and a moisture-retentive soil containing peat or leaf-mould to grow successfully away from its native haunts.

EXACUM (Gentianaceae—Gentian Family)

A genus closely related to the scentless gentians of which only one member is in general cultivation.

Species. *Exacum affine.* It is a biennial, native to the Island of Socotra, and is a tropical plant, in Britain and northern Europe hardy only in the most favourable parts where it should be planted out in June. Elsewhere it should be grown under glass; from a sowing made indoors in September, with the seedlings grown in small pots, the plants will bloom early the following summer. It likes a peaty compost and should be shaded from strong sunlight.

E. affine makes a bushy plant 30 cm (12 in) tall and is one of the few plants bearing light-blue flowers with any degree of perfume.

EXOHEBEA (Iridaceae—Iris Family)

A small genus of South African plants formerly and incorrectly named *Hebea*. The plants are prominent about mountainous slopes of Cape Province where they bear clove-scented flowers during December and January. The flowers are spirally arranged around the tall leafless stem and resemble the gladiolus in their form.

Species. *Exohebea parviflora.* The most common and attractive species bearing numerous yellow and crimson flowers on each stem; their spicy scent is most pronounced. The perianth tube is short and curved, widening at the top with the lobes longer than the tube. The leaves appear at the base.

F

FAGOPHYRUM (Buckwheat)
(Polygonaceae—Dock Family)

A genus of annual plants, closely allied to *Polygonum* but differing in the position of the embryo.

Species. *Fagophyrum esculentum.* It is the Common buckwheat, much in demand in central Asia and in Europe for the flour obtained from its seed whilst it is also grown to feed pheasants. It is also a valuable plant for bee-keepers who sow it around the hives. It grows 45 cm (18 in) tall and, from an early spring sowing, will bloom from June until September; its pretty pink and white flowers appear in clusters and have a pleasant sweet honey scent. It is pollinated by bees and short-tongued insects in search of the nectar secreted at the base of the stamens and made accessible by the shallow perianth. Hermann Müller has recorded more than 40 insect visitors to the flowers during the course of one summer.

FENNEL: *see* FOENICULUM

FERULA (Umbelliferae—Parsley Family)

A genus of about 130 species of annual and perennial plants. In deep, rich soil they are most handsome, growing 2.4 to 3.6 m (8 to 12 ft) tall with fern-like leaves, deep green in colour, which appear early in spring. The plants however are quite without the pleasant sweet, hay-like smell of the fennel and instead have a fetid smell of stale fish.

Species. *Ferula assafoetida.* The drug as-safoetida, used in Persia as a condiment, is obtained by notching the stem just above soil level. It has a most unpleasant smell and is used in medicine as a stimulant.

F. communis. The Giant fennel of southern Europe which in a sheltered garden may reach a height of 3 m (10 ft), making a most handsome plant with its finely cut needle-like foliage. Its flowers are yellow and appear in June in large umbels and have a most unpleasant rancid smell, depending upon flies for their pollination.

F. galbaniflua (syn. *F. persica*). In Exodus it says, 'Take unto thee sweet spices, stacte, onycha and galbanum'. Galbanus was obtained from the strong-rooted perennial which forms umbels of unpleasant-smelling yellowish-white flowers and produces a milky juice from incisions in the stem which solidifies in the air. When collected it has a pleasing pungent, balsamic smell and is used medicinally and to make varnishes.

F. glauca. It is native of southern Europe and grows 2.1 to 2.4 m (7 to 8 ft) tall with deeply toothed glaucous leaves. It bears yellow flowers in June, in large umbels, and they have a stale fetid smell.

FILIPENDULA (Rosaceae—Rose Family)

A genus of some 50 species of perennial plants which include the lovely Meadow-sweet and several other species bearing scented flowers. The spiraeas, which they were previously called, are moisture-loving plants with lobed leaves and bear their flowers in clustered panicles which produces a foam-like appearance from a distance. They grow well in ordinary loam but require ample supplies of moisture during summer.

Species. *Filipendula hexapetala, flore pleno.* The double form of our native Dropwort which comes into bloom in June. It has attractive fern-like foliage and at a height of 50 cm (20 in) bears flat heads of creamy-white flowers which carry much of the perfume of meadowsweet.

F. kamtschatica. An Asiatic species but one which is completely hardy even if the water about its roots becomes frozen solid. It grows to a height 1.8 to 2.4 m (6 to 8 ft) with lobed leaves borne along the whole length of stem. In June it bears corymbose heads of creamy-white flowers which have a powerful sweet scent from a distance but have the fishy undertone when inhaled near to. It is a suitable plant for the wild garden and also for the back of a border, but only when its roots are in moisture does it attain its full height and beauty.

F. pubescens. It is a native of Mongolia, growing 60 cm (2 ft) in height, its 3-lobed leaves being wrinkled and deeply serrated. It blooms towards the end of February or early March, bearing its pure-white flowers in rounded heads, and they have a soft sweet perfume.

F. ulmaria. Ben Jonson called it Meadow's Queen and no plant was held in greater esteem during Elizabethan times. It was Elizabeth I's favourite strewing plant, for although the creamy-white flowers have a sickly scent, the leaves are pleasantly aromatic when trodden upon. This is due to the presence of oil of Wintergreen. Gerard, writing in about 1600, said that 'the smell (of the leaves) makes the heart merry and delighteth the senses; neither doth it cause headache as some other sweet smelling herbs do'.

A glabrous perennial growing 0.9 to 1.2 m (3 to 4 ft) tall with furrowed stems and pinnate leaves, dark green above, grey on the underside, owing to being covered with hairs which release the aromatic oil when pressed. In bloom from June to September, the flowers are found in crowded racemes. It frequents damp woodlands, marshland and meadows throughout the British Isles.

FOENICULUM (Fennel)
(Umbelliferae—Parsley Family)

A small genus of perennial, annual or biennial herbs, native of Mediterranean countries and of central Asia, and grown commercially for the flavouring power of the seeds.

The seeds are described in the *British Pharmacopoeia* as 'About 3 lines long and one broad; elliptical, curved, beaked, with 8 pale brown longitudinal ribs, the two lateral being double; taste and odour aromatic'. They are pale grey-green in colour and sweetly fragrant but only when correctly dried, Likewise, the seeds should be fully mature and dry before distillation otherwise the essential oil will have a most unpleasant smell.

Species. *Foeniculum vulgare.* Because of its pronounced hay-like smell, the Romans gave it the name of *foeniculum* and it is one of the oldest of cultivated plants, steeped in history. The seed, which has an aromatic smell like that of aniseed, is used to flavour gin. The leaves were much used in Shakespeare's day as an accompaniment for fish.

Fennel grows nearly 1.8 m (6 ft) tall and bears yellow flowers in June and July, whilst later, its feathery leaves take on a bronze tint. It grows in any soil but requires a sunny position to ripen its seed. The pungent leaves are used as required whilst the roots may be eaten braised like celery. The aromatic water in which the seed has been steeped is good for stomach disorders.

FORSYTHIA (Oleaceae—Olive Tree Family)

A genus of hardy and easily grown deciduous shrubs which, like the jasmine, may be grown against a wall, where their deep golden-yellow bells provide colour when the winter jasmine is coming to an end. The plants grow well in a chalky soil though they are just as happy in a sandy loam. Propagation is by layering or from cuttings of the half-ripened wood. The plant was named after William Forsyth, the celebrated botanist who was at one time superintendent of the Royal Gardens. They are amongst the finest of the early-flowering shrubs, their branches being wreathed in golden bells with the first warmth of the February sunshine. Unfortunately only the winter-flowering *F. ovata* and *F. giraldiana* bear scented flowers, the former being equally successful in an acid soil.

Species. *Forsythia giraldiana*. Native of Yunnan, it grows 2.4 to 3 m (8 to 10 ft) tall and blooms early in February, bearing hanging bells of palest yellow which have a most pleasing vanilla perfume. The leaves appear when the flowers are over and are rich bronzy-green.

F. ovata. Native of Korea, it is slow-growing and rarely exceeds 1.5 m (5 ft) in height. But what it loses in vigour it makes up by its daintiness, bearing in February deliciously scented bells of purest gold.

FORTUNELLA (Rutaceae—Rue Family)

A genus of six species, native of the Malay Peninsula and eastern Asia, the fruits of several species making for delicious eating.

Species. *Fortunella japonica*. Known in the East as the Kumquat, it makes a small tree 1.8 m (6 ft) tall with sweetly scented pure-white flowers followed by round bright-yellow fruits of rich flavour.

FOTHERGILLA (Hamamelidaceae— Witch Hazel Family)

A genus of but two species, native of North America and deciduous, which bloom before the last days of winter. They enjoy a lime-free peat-laden soil and a position of partial shade, and also grow well by the coast, in a sandy soil enriched with peat or leaf-mould. Apart from their conspicuous flower spikes, the plants have brilliant autumnal foliage and are uninteresting only during the mid-winter months.

Species. *Fothergilla gardenii* (syn. *F. alnifolia*). It has toothed leaves and makes a compact bush no more than 60 cm (3 ft) in height. It begins to bloom just before the end of March, its white sweetly scented flowers appearing before the leaves in dense upright spikes, each being composed of clusters of white stamens. Its leaves, like those of the Witch hazel take on brilliant autumnal tints.

F. monticola. Though like the other species it is slow growing, it attains a height of 2.4 m (8 ft) or more, bearing at the end of winter spikes of fragrant creamy-white flowers. The leaves take on every imaginable autumnal tint.

FRAGARIA (Rosaceae—Rose Family)

A genus of 15 species, native of North and South America, the British Isles and southern Europe. They are perennial plants which increase by runners or by division.

Species. *Fragaria vesca*. A perennial herb with ternate sessile leaves and propagated by division or from its runners. It is the Wild strawberry, native of the British Isles and northern Europe, and in addition to the aroma of its ripened fruits (berries), its leaves release a musky scent when dying, a scent which may be extracted, when it takes on an undertone of Russian leather. It is one of Francis Bacon's 'best of all scents'. The fruits are yellow flushed with red and are held on drooping stems. In their native haunts, the plants flourish in the partial shade of nearby weeds.

The wild and alpine strawberries grow best in partial shade and in a humus-laden soil, moisture being necessary to increase the size of fruit. The commercial strawberry has been obtained from *F. chiloensis*, native of Chile. Its fruit is fragrant but not the foliage.

FRANKLINIA (Theaceae—Tea Family)

A genus of a single species.

Species. *Franklinia alatamaha*. Closely related to the Magnolia and Gardenia, it is one of the world's rarest trees and one of the most beautiful. It was discovered on the banks of the Alatamaha River in Georgia in 1765 by America's first great botanist, John Bartram who named the tree after Benjamin Franklin. Bartram planted a young tree in his garden at Kingsessing on the banks of the Schuyllkil River which was soon to become the only known specimen for shortly after the Alatamaha River banks were cleared of timber and the species has never again been seen in the wild. Bartram's tree still stands where he planted it, whilst specimens in the Arnold Arboretum in Massachusetts are recorded as having survived more than 50 degrees of frost. It is therefore quite hardy in the British Isles where the tree will flourish in a moist, deeply worked soil, and eventually attain a height of more than 6 m (20 ft).

F. alatamaha is an elegant deciduous

tree with a slender trunk and tan-coloured bark and it comes into bloom late in autumn, after its handsome polished leaves have turned crimson and have fallen. Its chalice-like flowers of purest white, 7.5 cm (3 in) across, diffuse their exquisite vanilla-like perfume in autumn until almost the year end.

FRAXINUS (Ash) (Oleaceae—Olive Tree Family)

Of this large genus of deciduous ornamental trees, only the Manna ash bears scented flowers and from it a honey-tasting liquid is obtained by making incisions in the bark. This may be the 'manna' of Exodus. for the tree is native of the Lebanon and Turkey and of southern Italy where it grows over rocky limestone formations. It was introduced into England by the Duchess of Bedford in 1697.

Species. *Fraxinus ornus.* The Flowering or Manna ash which grows 9 m (30 ft) tall in its native land but only half that height in the British Isles. When young, its branches are purple, dotted with yellow and have lance-shaped leaflets. With the leaves, the tiny white sweetly scented flowers appear in large hanging clusters from the side of the branches. There is a form, *violacea*, which bears greyish-mauve flowers, also scented. It is a handsome tree with smooth bark and it flourishes in a limestone soil.

FREESIA (Iridaceae—Iris Family)

A genus of very few species, each of which may be a variety of *F. refracta,* corms of which first reached Britain about 1860. It is native of the Cape of Good Hope and is one of the few native flowers to possess rich perfume. The cream-coloured funnel-shaped flowers with a throat of deep orange carry a sweet, refreshing perfume, to the author one of the most exquisite of all flower scents.

The freesia for long remained sadly neglected in spite of its perfume, until at the end of the nineteenth century a certain Mr Armstrong brought back to Kew from his travels in South Africa the first pink form. It was closely related to *F. refracta* but was classed as a separate species and named *F. armstrongii.* F. H. Chapman was the first to cross it with *F. refracta* and, later, crossings were made by Rev. Jacob

and Mr G. H. Dalrymple with the result that a number of lovely hybrids appeared bearing flowers in soft pink, lilac, orange, gold and red, Here again, as pigment appeared in the flowers, they lost much of their scent and only those bearing white or pale-yellow flowers possess the true 'freesia' scent which is almost entirely absent in the red and deep-orange flowers.

Freesias are readily raised from seed which will germinate like mustard and cress, but as the seedlings do not readily transplant they should be sown about 1 May where they are to bloom, either in prepared beds or in deep boxes in a slightly heated greenhouse. They grow best in a sterilized loam to which peat is added, but no manure otherwise the plants will grow tall and lanky. Only just cover the seed with a sprinkling of peat and sand and place the boxes in a frame, shaded by whitening, until germination takes place. Surprisingly for natives of South Africa, freesias require cool conditions, a greenhouse temperature of only 10°C (50°F), to bring them into bloom and they require to be grown almost dry from the time the seed is sown, until ready to open their buds, and given only enough moisture to prevent them from flagging.

Freesias may be flowered to perfection in a sunny window of the living-room if seed is sown in pots early in May. As the seedlings make growth, they should be supported by placing short cones around the pot side about which is looped green twine or raffia. They will come into bloom early in the new year and continue for several weeks, scenting the room with their delicate fragrance.

If it is not practical to raise plants from seed, corms may be planted in August and the pots (or boxes) placed in a frame until growth commences when they may be transferred to a warm room. Freesias must never be kept in the dark, and after flowering allow them to die down completely before removing the pots to a shed or garage where they remain until started into growth again in August.

In the dry climate of south-east England, freesias may be grown outdoors, planting the corms 7.5 cm (3 in) deep on a bed of peat and sand about 1 May. They grow to perfection if planted between clumps of dwarf heathers, in an open situation. The heathers will provide support for the growth and also keep the roots shaded from the midday sun and give protection from heavy rain.

Planted beneath dwarf shrubby plants in this way, the corms may be expected to survive all but the severest of winters, otherwise the corms should be lifted and stored when the foliage has died down in autumn.

Species and Varieties. *Freesia refracta.* It grows 60 cm (2 ft) tall with grass-like foliage and bears its cream-coloured funnel-shaped flowers 5 or 6 to a stem. The stems bend over at the end so that the flowers open upright to reveal their full beauty.

The variety *alba* bears flowers of purest white whilst *leichtlinii* bears primrose-yellow with a throat of deeper yellow. All are deliciously scented:

The following hybrids are also sweetly scented:

ALISON JOHNSON. One of Mr Dalrymple's Bartley strain, bearing on short sturdy stems 6 or 7 large trumpets of glistening white.

GOLD COAST. A superb variety, bearing large trumpets of rich golden-yellow deliciously scented.

RYNVELD'S GOLDEN YELLOW. It bears its handsome buttercup-yellow flowers in large sprays and is long-lasting in water.

TREASURE. Its large pale-yellow blooms are shaded in the throat with lilac and gold.

WHITE GIANT. The broad-petalled flowers, which are borne on stiff stems, are of exquisite texture and as white as frozen snow with a powerful perfume.

WHITE SWAN. Probably the finest freesia ever raised, it received an Award of Merit from the R.H.S.; the flowers open like lilies, and are of purest white throughout with a heavenly scent.

FRITILLARIA (Liliaceae—Lily Family)

A genus of 50 or so species which include *F. meleagris,* the Snake's head fritillary, only few of which bear scented flowers though *F. imperialis,* the Crown imperial, is noted for its foxy smell.

All the fritillaries have drooping lily-like flowers of bell shape and consisting of six petals, at the base of each being a nectar-bearing hollow. The species are mostly distributed on the western seaboard of North America, in Britain and southern France, along the northern shores of the Mediterranean and in Asia Minor, Afghanistan and the Himalayas. The plants require a soil retentive of summer moisture but one which is well-drained in winter.

Species. *Fritillaria camchaticensis.* It is to be found throughout Alaska, Siberia and about the high mountains of British Columbia. It grows 10 cm (4 in) tall and bears sweetly-scented flowers of crimson-black, hence its name of Black lily.

F. citrina (syn. *F. bithynica*). A native of Asia Minor, in Britain it blooms in May, bearing its nodding bells of lemon yellow on 15-cm (6-in) stems. Inside the bloom are green markings, and the whole flower has a beautiful silvery sheen and a scent similar to that of the box tree. The plant is enhanced by the glaucous leaves.

F. imperialis. Introduced into Europe in 1576 by Clusius, it reached England in 1580; Gerard in his *Herbal* said that 'the plant hath been brought from Constantinople, amongst other bulbous roots, and made denizans in our London gardens, whereof I have great plenty'. Since then it has not changed in any way, there being just two varieties, the yellow (*lutea*) and the red (*rubra*) as in Gerard's day.

The flowers smell of wet fur and garlic and should be left to enhance the garden with their great beauty. Plant the bulbs in early autumn 22.5 cm (9 in) apart with the base of the large bulbs 15 cm (6 in) deep so that about 7.5 cm (3 in) of soil covers them. To encourage drainage, set the bulbs on their side on a layer of sand or peat and pack peat around them before covering with soil. After flowering, allow the foliage to die down before it is removed in autumn.

The blooms are produced at the end of a 60-cm (2-ft) stem, at the end of which is a circle of corollas which turn downwards with the stigmas protruding. The organs of reproduction are thus protected from adverse weather. The flower-head is crowned by a tuft of bright-green leaves. Hence its name of Crown imperial.

G

GALANTHUS (Amaryllidaceae—Narcissus Family)

A genus of about 12 species, one of which, *G. nivalis,* may be indigenous to the British Isles but may have become naturalized at an early date in our history for it grows in deciduous woodlands throughout central Europe from northern France to the Caspian Sea. It is a plant of extreme hardiness, pushing up through the melting snow and often blooming before the end of January. Because of this, the French call it *perce-neige,* though in Italy it is called the Milkflower from the Greek words *gala* and *anthos.*

Snowdrops should be lifted, divided and replanted as soon after flowering as possible, when the clumps are still green, or like the primrose they may be moved when in bloom. If planting bulbs, the 3-cm size should be used for anything smaller will not bear bloom for several years.

Species. *Galanthus latifolius.* Known as the Caucasian snowdrop, it is to be found about the mountains of southern Russia. The blooms are free of any green segment markings which gives them a milk-white appearance. The form *ikariae,* found naturally only on the Island of Nikaria in the eastern Mediterranean, may be distinguished by the long outer segments. It grows only 12.5 cm (5 in) tall and bears a bloom which has a more pronounced perfume than any other snowdrop.

G. nivalis. It comes into bloom during January, depending upon the weather, and is often found in bloom during April. From the bulb springs two glaucous leaves 15 cm (6 in) long between which appears a solitary drooping flower on a stem 15 cm (6 in) long. The form *viride-spice* has at-tractively green-tipped petals whilst there is also a double-flowered form, *flore pleno.* The variety *flavescens* has pale-yellow markings whilst Colesbourne, which received an Award of Merit from the R.H.S. in 1951, grows only 10 cm (4 in) tall and bears flowers of great substance which carry a pronounced mossy perfume.

GALINGALE: *see* **CYPERUS**

GALIPEA (Angostura) (Rutaceae—Rue Family)

A small genus of evergreen trees or shrubs, native of Cuba, Guyana and Venezuela, all parts of which are fragrant.

Species. *Galipea aromatica.* It is a native of Guyana where it grows to a height of 0.9 to 1.2 m (3 to 4 ft) and is evergreen with smooth trifoliate leaves and it bears its scented greenish-white flowers in racemes. Like *G. cusparia,* the bark is extremely aromatic and resinous but it does not appear to have any commercial use. The plant requires tropical conditions for its survival.

G. cusparia (syn. *Galipea officinalis*). The trees yielding this important bark grows naturally only in Venezuela, especially around the Gulf of Santa Fe, and it takes its name from the district where first discovered, where it grows to a height of about 15 m (50 ft). Seen from a distance, it has the appearance of a palm tree for its fragrant leaves of palest green are produced in a tuft at the top. The leaves are bright green, full of glandular dots and release an aromatic orange-like odour when bruised. The flowers are white, tinted with pink and are also scented.

The outer ᐧsurface of the bark is

yellowish in colour and is soft so that it may be removed by a finger nail to expose the more aromatic (resinous) blackish-brown under-surface. The peculiar resinous order is due to an essential oil first discovered by Hertzog, whilst the bitter principle was discovered by Saladin and named Cusparine. The bark also contains resin.

The bark is a stimulant and a tonic and at one time was used to combat fevers but is today used only to make the aromatic Angostura Bitters which acts as a tonic and an appetizer when added to sherry or gin.

G. odoratissima. A native of the hillsides around Rio de Janeiro, in Europe it requires hothouse conditions and will attain a height of 60 to 90 cm (2 to 3 ft), covered from top to bottom in broad deep-green leaves. When it is in bloom, the hothouse is perfumed as if by jasmine. The bark too is pleasantly aromatic.

G. ossana. It grows about the countryside in Cuba, making a shrub 1.8 m (6 ft) tall with smooth trifoliate leaves, aromatic when bruised, the stalks being longer than the leaves. The small greenish-white flowers are borne in panicles and diffuse an orange-like perfume.

GALIUM (Rubiaceae—Bedstraw Family)

Widely dispersed throughout the British Isles, it takes its name from the Greek gala, milk, for the leaves were used to curdle milk. Annual or (mostly) perennial, the plants have elliptic leaves borne 4 in a whorl and flowers with a rotate 4-lobed corolla.

Species. Galium cruciata. Known as the Crosswort, it grows about grassy mountainous slopes and downlands of a chalk or limestone nature. It is a hairy perennial of almost prostrate habit, growing 30 cm (12 in) long with soft downy elliptic leaves. Its pale-yellow flowers are borne during May and June, 6 to 8 in axillary cymes, and they have a sweet powerful perfume.

G. saxatile. A slender matted perennial of heathlands, hence its name of Heath bedstraw, bearing in a whorl 4 to 6 small obovate leaves fringed with a few prickles. The flowers are white, borne in small opposite groups along the stems, and they have an almost overpowering sickly perfume.

GALTONIA (Liliaceae—Lily Family)

A genus of only two species of South African bulbous plants known as the Cape hyacinths, which are most effective when massed in the border. Known also as the Spire lilies, they attain a height of 1.2 to 1.5 m (4 to 5 ft), bearing their drooping bell-shaped flowers in racemes on leafless scapes. The bulbs may be planted in rough grass or in the shrubbery and will not need disturbing for a number of years provided they are given an occasional top dressing of decayed manure or hop manure.

Closely allied to the hyacinth, the plant was named after Francis Galton, an authority on the flora of South Africa. In Britain and most of Europe it is completely hardy.

Species. Galtonia candicans. The large round bulbs should be planted in spring 7.5 to 10 cm (3 to 4 in) deep in a sandy, well-drained soil. From the strap-like leaves which are about 60 cm (2 ft) in length, arises the glaucous stem at the end of which the drooping bells of purest white appear in June, diffusing a sweet soft perfume about the garden.

G. princeps. It attains a height of about 60 cm (2 ft) at the end of which appear greenish-white bells with spreading segments. They have a gentle fragrance which is not so pronounced as that of G. candicans but is more noticeable when the flowers are cut and taken indoors.

GARDENIA (Rubiaceae—Bedstraw Family)

A large genus of mostly evergreen trees and shrubs, named by Linnaeus in honour of Dr Garden, a botanist of Charleston, U.S.A. They are native of tropical Asia and Africa, Japan, China and the East Indian islands, and in the British Isles and northern Europe require stove conditions. They will come into bloom in early spring and continue throughout summer. They are deservedly prized for the exquisite fragrance of their blossom which is produced in great freedom though usually solitary, borne at the leaf axils and at the extremities of the shoots. With their soft milky-whiteness, the flowers, especially those of *G. citriodoram,* are often used in bouquets as a substitute for orange-blossom, being remarkably similar both in appearance and in perfume.

When growing in pots under glass they require a minimum winter temperature of 13 to 15°C (55 to 60°F), increasing to 18°C (65°F), and giving copious amounts of moisture as the early spring sunshine gathers strength. The potting compost should be composed of turf loam, decayed manure, peat and sand in equal amounts.

Species. *Gardenia arborea.* Native of the East Indies where it grows 6 to 9 m (20 to 30 ft) tall and is deciduous and unarmed. It is one of the most fragrant of all trees, the bark when cut and also the leaves yielding a resinous gum, clear yellow in colour with a balsam-like scent; the flowers, for their beauty, size, fragrance and number excel those of all other species. The native people eat the aromatic fruit when ripe.

G. calyculata. A small shrubby plant, native of the mountainous parts of southern India. It is unarmed and bears its solitary white flowers at the ends of the shoots. They are large and pure white, with the anthers enclosed within the swollen tube of the corolla.

G. carinata. It is to be found in the hills of Penang where it grows 3 m (10 ft) tall. Its bark is resinous with the leaves elliptic, ribbed and villous beneath. The flowers are small and open white at first, gradually turning pale yellow and later to deep orange. They are powerfully scented.

G. citriodora. Native of Natal, it is of very dwarf habit and makes a valuable pot plant with its small glossy leaves and small white flowers of delicious orange perfume.

G. clusloefolia. A native of the Bahamas where it makes a shrub 1.5 m (5 ft) tall and bears its flowers on long pedicels. They are white with a green tube and salva-shaped corolla and diffuse a scent like that of the hyacinth.

G. coronaria (syn. *G. costata).* It was introduced to the Calcutta Botanical Gardens from the mountainous regions of Chittagong where it makes a tree 6 m (20 ft) tall with leaves up to 30 cm (12 in) long and it is without spines. The large white flowers are terminal, with a tube at least 7.5 cm (3 in) long and of 10 cm (4 in)

diameter, its 5 anthers enclosed within the mouth of the tube. It has a balsamic perfume.

G. devoniana. Found only in Sierra Leone, it makes a small twiggy tree and bears flowers of enormous size, like water-lilies, pure white at first but changing to straw colour, and with exquisite scent which can be detected from a great distance.

G. grandiflora. Native of Indo-China where it makes a small, unarmed tree growing on river banks. The leaves are lanceolate and shining whilst the flowers are large, pure white and very fragrant.

G. gummifera. Native of Ceylon, it makes a low shrub 60 cm (2 ft) tall and, like *G. arborea,* exudes a balsamic gum from its bark; the buds are also resinous. The flowers are axillary, short-peduncled and are pure white with a balsamic fragrance.

G. jasminoides (syn. *C. floride).* It is native of Florida and of central China where it is called *Pak-sema-Liva* and is used to flàvour tea. It is an erect shrub 0.9 to 1.2 m (3 to 4 ft) tall, unarmed and much branched with the leaves elliptic. The salver-shaped flowers, like those of the jasmine, are borne at the end of the shoots and are of purest white and with the scent of white jasmine. There is a double-flowered form, *flore pleno,* described in Miller's *Gardener's Dictionary,* which bears flowers 10 cm (4 in) across and of remarkable perfume.

G. latifolia. Native of the East Indies, it makes an unarmed tree 3 to 3.6 m (10 to 12 ft) tall, bearing its leaves 3 in a whorl. They are resinous and in the axils of the veins beneath are hollow glands with hairy margins. The flowers are of great size and open white but change to pale yellow before the day has ended. They are amongst the most richly scented of all species.

G. lillii. It makes a small tree 4.5 m (15 ft) tall with glossy dark-green leaves 10 cm (4 in) long and 2.5 cm (1 in) wide. Its creamy-white flowers, powerfully scented, are borne solitary from the axils of the leaves.

G. lucida. Native of the Philippine island of Luzon, it is a deciduous tree growing 4.5 m (15 ft) tall. From its bark a fragrant gum is exuded and, as with *G. gummifera,* the buds are also resinous. The glossy oblong leaves measure up to 22.5 cm (9 in) long whilst the terminal, solitary flowers are large and though opening white soon turn pale yellow. They have a rich lily-like perfume.

G. montana. A spiny tree-like shrub of the East Indies, with the bark white and spongy and the spines short, acute and stiff. The deciduous leaves are smooth and shining above, downy on the underside. Three to five flowers appear from the buds, on short pedicels and are large, opening white and changing to yellow. They have a spicy perfume.

G. radicans. A native of China, Japan and the East Indies and making a plant only 37.5 to 45 cm (15 to 18 in) tall, of dense shrubby habit but free of thorns, with radicant stems and small lanceolate leaves. The flowers are solitary, with the length of the calyx equal to the tube of the corolla, purest white at first, turning pale yellow later and scented of jonquil.

G. rothmannia (syn. Rothmannia capensis). Native of Cape Province, it makes a shrub 2.4 to 3 m (8 to 10 ft) tall, its oblong leaves having glandular hairs on the axils of the veins and they are aromatic. The terminal flowers with their campanulate throat and spreading segments are white, spotted with red, and diffuse a sweet exotic perfume.

G. stanleyana. Native of Sierra Leone, it is remarkable in that its branches grow horizontal, attaining a considerable size whilst its flat purple-spotted white flowers are produced on the upper sides of the shoots, above the leaves. It has a jonquil-like perfume.

G. thunbergii (syn. Thunbergia capensis). It is native of Cape Province and of Manila in the Philippines, where it is a mountainous shrub 0.9 to 1.2 m (3 to 4 ft) tall with the leaves borne 3 or 4 in a whorl. The flowers are as white as driven snow and are amongst the largest of the species with pronounced scent.

G. tomentosa. A small tree which is native of Java, its branches, leaves and flower calyces being covered in velvety tomentum which leaves a resinous smell on the hands when touched. The tube of the flowers is only as long as the calyx and they are white with a sweet perfume.

G. vitiensis. Native of South-east Asia and Pacific islands, it makes a small dense shrub with large leaves 12.5 to 15 cm (5 to 6 in) long and 5 cm (2 in) wide, and bearing its sweetly scented white flowers in a terminal inflorescence.

GASTRODIA (Orchidaceae—Orchid Family)

A genus of 20 species, native of Southeast Asia and New Zealand. They are leafless terrestrial herbs with twisted fleshy roots whilst the stems are clothed in brown scales.

Species. Gastrodia cunninghamii. It is present on both islands of New Zealand where its thick, starchy rootstock was used for food by the natives. It is present in damp undergrowth where it grows up to 60 cm (2 ft) in height and bears its dingy brownish-green flowers, 10 to 20 to a spike during December and January. As they open, the flowers have a refreshingly aromatic scent which becomes fetid and unpleasant as the flowers fade.

GAULTHERIA (Ericaceae—Heather Family)

A genus of nearly 100 mostly trailing shrubs to be found growing in the Northern Hemisphere. They like an acid soil but one that is well-drained, and are happiest in a mixture of sand and peat and in semi-shade. They are excellent plants to carpet a woodland garden or to grow amongst other peat-loving plants for they help to retain moisture about the roots and also suppress weeds. Several have foliage which is very aromatic and being evergreen, this quality is especially valuable. The gaultherias are valuable plants to give ground cover in pine woods and other conifer plantations.

Gaultherias are propagated by layering of the ripened shoots in autumn or by division in spring which should be done before the new bright-green leaves appear and provide a striking contrast to the older dark-green leaves. In Canada and in the Himalayas, the new leaves were at one time used to make a delicious tea, known as Canada or Mountain tea and possessing a pleasing aroma. The flowers of the gaultherias have the same aromatic perfume as the foliage.

Species. *Gaultheria cuneata.* It makes a low, spreading bush 25 to 30 cm (10 to 12 in) tall and hides the soil as it grows in an outwards direction. Its handsome dark evergreen leaves are enhanced by pure-white fragrant flowers which are followed by ivory-white fruits in autumn.

G. forrestii. It is a highly attractive Chinese species of spreading habit and bearing, on white stems, waxy white flowers of richest perfume, followed by bright-blue berries.

G. fragrantissima. It grows 1.8 m (6 ft) tall and is a native of India and Ceylon. Its oblong leaves of darkest green, rolled back at the edges, have a powerful camphor perfume when rubbed, and from the axils it bears throughout summer sprays of pale-red bells, with a scent like lily of the valley, and followed by bright-blue berries.

G. miqueliana. It grows 30 cm (12 in) tall and makes a spreading plant of dark evergreen leaves. In May and June, it bears scented nodding white flowers followed by white fruits, flushed with pink.

G. nummulariodes. A trailing Himalayan species, its deep-green aromatic leaves turn to a rich crimson colour in autumn and they possess a distinct cedar-like aroma. The flowers are white, like those of the lily of the valley, and they too have an aromatic scent.

G. procumbens. Known as the Creeping wintergreen or Checkerberry, it is a native of Canada and the northern United States being especially abundant in the pine forests of New Jersey. It has finely toothed leaves which have the penetrating aroma of wintergreen in the manufacture of which its essential oil is used, and they take on rich autumnal tints. The drooping white waxy flowers, borne on red stalks and in summer, are also aromatic. They are followed by large edible crimson berries which persist through winter. William Robinson considered it 'one of the brightest plants in the rock garden' though it is happier in the shade of woodlands. All parts of the plant are aromatic.

G. serpyllifolia. The Thyme-leaved snowberry, abounding where conifers are present, from Lake Michigan to Pennsylvania. It is a small, creeping plant with oval leaves covered in pellucid dots and which, like the white berries, have the odour of wintergreen.

G. shallon. It is a procumbent North American plant with hairy stems and heart-shaped leaves of darkest green. The pinkish-white flowers are followed by aromatic purple berries which are appetizing to pheasants.

G. trichophylla. From the Himalayas, it makes a dwarf mat of bright-green leaves covered in minute hairs, which release a hot, aromatic fragrance when pressed. The white flowers are followed by berries which are first grey-white, then pink and finally taking on a purple-blue colour.

GAYLUSSACIA (Vacciniaceae— Cranberry Family)

A genus of about 40 species closely related to the Vacciniums and named in honour of the French scientist Gaylussac. In America they are known as the Huckleberries and are best suited to a peaty soil and some shade. Like the Gaultherias, they flourish in pine woods and may be planted in the wild garden about rhododendrons, though they are tall growing and unsuited for ground cover.

Species. *Gaylussacia baccata* (syn. *G. resinosa, Vaccinia resinosa*). It is native to the Great Lakes area of Canada and Pennsylvania. It is one of the best of all the species, growing 45 cm (18 in) tall, its small oval leaves covered with globules on the underside from which a resinous gum is exuded. The cylindrical flowers appear in June are pinky-red and are followed by deliciously sweet blue-black berries.

GEITONOPLESIUM (Philesiaceae— Philesia Family)

A genus of a single species, native of eastern Australia, the Philippines and South Pacific islands.

Species. *Geitonoplesium cymosum.* It is a common climbing plant, its alternate leaves having prominent parallel nerves, like those of *dakua,* hence its name *Wadakua.* Its numerous creamy-white flowers are borne in a terminal cyme and they are sweetly scented.

GELSEMIUM (Loganiaceae—Strychnine Family)

A small genus of climbing plants native

to the southern United States where it is known as the Carolina jasmine but it is hardy in the British Isles only in the South-west. A single species appears to be successful in Britain and northern Europe.

Species. *Gelsemium sempervirens.* It reaches a height of 2.4 to 2.7 m (8 to 9 ft) with slender downy stems and broad pointed leaves 15 cm (6 in) long which are evergreen. It comes into bloom before the end of March, its pale-yellow flowers having peculiarly twisted lobes and a long cylindrical tube covered with down; they emit a honey-like perfume.

GENISTA (Leguminosae—Laburnum Family)

A genus of 70 or more deciduous species, many armed with spines and only a few bearing flowers with pronounced perfume.

Species. *Genista aetnensis.* The Mount Etna broom, making a slender bush 2.7 to 3 m (9 to 10 ft) tall, its thin green leafless branches smothered in golden flowers during July and August. They have a delicious vanilla fragrance.

G. hispanica. The Spanish gorse which grows 0.6 m (2 ft) high and makes a dense rounded shrub with hairy, lance-shaped leaves and has branched spines. It flowers during May and June, bearing its golden blossoms in crowded racemes and they have a sweet, refreshing perfume, like ripe apples or pineapples.

GENTIANA (Gentianaceae—Gentian Family)

A family of about 400 species of annual or perennial herbs, distributed throughout all climes from the snow-capped mountains of North America, Scotland and the Himalayas to the warm sands of South America and India where the flower colour is predominantly red; blue elsewhere. All members of the family have bitter properties and are used to make tonic medicines but, as with most blue and red flowers, scented attractions are rare.

Species. *Gentiana pannonica.* An alpine species of central Europe growing about 45 cm (1½ ft) tall, the stem leaves being ovate and lance-shaped. It blooms in June, the

deep-purple bell-shaped flowers having a yellow tube, and they are borne in clusters at the axils and at the end of the shoots. They have the scent of the old tea rose. Increase is by seed sown when ripe, in a well-drained compost, in a frame. Established plants also require a very well-drained but moist soil, and some sun.

GEONOMA (Palmaceae—Palm Tree Family)

A genus of handsome palms, 4 to 18 m (15 to 60 ft) tall, native of Brazil and the surrounding countries, but which in the British Isles require a brisk heat to maintain their growth, a rich peaty soil, and ample space to develop. Specimens of any size are therefore little seen outside botanical gardens where they can be grown under the tropical conditions of their native lands, but when young they are ornamental, and can be grown for a short time as house plants. Increase is by seed or suckers.

Species. *Geonoma pumila.* A plant of slender habit with graceful drooping leaves which, when young, carry the sweet fragrance of violets.

GERANIUM (Geraniaceae—Geranium Family)

A genus of about 100 species of hardy herbs or sub-shrubs, usually with palmately lobed leaves and 5-petalled flowers with 10 stamens and 5 carpels, separating below and curling upwards when ripe around a central column, like a crane's bill, hence its name and that of the family from the Greek *geranos*, a crane. The true geraniums are plants of the Northern Hemisphere and are amongst the longest-flowering of all plants. Several are native to the British Isles, amongst them Herb Robert.

Species. *Geranium robertianum.* Herb Robert, named after the French abbot who in the eleventh century founded the Cistercian Order, is one of the prettiest plants of the English countryside with its dainty frond-like leaves and wiry red stems, covered in small hairs. Like all the wild geraniums, it blooms over a long period, from May until September, its tiny pink flowers, beautifully veined, appearing in succession. The plant is of straggling habit and grows in hedgerows and on old walls. Though so charming, it gives off a peculiar odour, particularly pronounced after rain when the smell is foxy. Yet Miss Sinclair Rohde considered it to be 'the most sweetly scented of the wild geraniums', so perhaps its scent strikes a different note with those who most appreciate its charms. It has since earliest times been appreciated for its healing powers and is described in glowing language in *The Feast of Gardening* by Master John, gardener, the earliest work on gardening in the English language.

GEUM (Rosaceae—Rose Family)

A genus of some 30 species of perennial plants bearing tufts of pinnate leaves. The species having aromatic roots are those which are native to the British Isles, *Geum urbanum* and *G. rivale*, to be found growing on shady banks and in ditches, both enjoying damp conditions.

Species. *Geum rivale.* The Water Avens, found in moist ditches and by the banks of streams where it grows 60 to 90 cm (2 to 3 ft) in height. It blooms during May and June and has drooping flowers of orange-red 2.5 cm (1 in) across and greatly toothed leaves. The roots are purple-brown in colour and in U.S.A. are known as 'chocolate root' for at one time they were used as a substitute for cocoa. In Britain, the roots were used to make a tonic beer, and to quote Culpeper 'the root in the spring-time steeped in wine, doth give it a delicate taste . . . and is a good preservative against the plague'.

G. urbanum. Its country names are Herb Bennet, Blessed herb, and Holy herb, so called on account of its valuable medicinal properties whilst the roots were used as a charm against superstitions, being considered an antidote against serpents' bites. To the countryman, the five petals of the golden-yellow flowers, which appear during July and August, represented the five wounds of Christ.

The roots, dried and tied in small bundles, can be used as a substitute for cloves in an apple tart for they impart a delicious aromatic flavour. In the Middle Ages, they were used to flavour beer. The foliage, too, has a delicate clove fragrance,

and as Culpeper says 'was used to expel crude and raw humours from the belly by its warm savour and warming quality'.

GILIA (Polemoniaceae—Phlox Family)

A genus of about 120 species of pretty annuals all of which are native of California and Oregon and of other parts of temperate America. The plants require a light well-drained soil and a sunny situation and are most successful if sown where the plants are to bloom. The plants are completely hardy and seed may be sown in April to bloom from June until early autumn. They grow from 30 to 60 cm (1 to 2 ft) in height depending upon the species but the one which bears scented flowers is *G. androsaceus.*

Species. *Gilia androsaceus* (syn. *Leptosiphon androsaceus*). It grows 37.5 cm (15 in) tall with star-like flowers which vary in colour from purple, to lilac, rose-red and white and they are especially scented in the morning, when washed with dew.

G. elegans (syn. *Layia elegans*). Possibly the best form, it grows 37.5 to 45 cm (15 to 18 in) tall and blooms over a long period. It is a most attractive plant, its stems and leaves being covered in soft downy hairs which give it a glaucous appearance. The flowers are 5 cm (2 in) across and are of golden yellow, tipped with white, hence its popular name of Tidy Tips. To complete a charming ensemble, the flowers have a pleasant sweet perfume.

GLADIOLUS (Iridaceae—Iris Family)

A genus of more than 150 species, all of which with but one or two exceptions are native of South Africa. Like so many plants of that country, very few of the Sword lilies, or Corn flags as they are called, possess perfume. One species, *G. illyricus*, is native of the British Isles, where it grows only in parts of the New Forest and in the Isle of Wight. A beautiful plant, bearing 4 to 8 magenta-red bell-shaped flowers on a 60-cm (2-ft) stem, it is scentless. Other scentless European species are *G. communis, G. segetum* and *G. byzantinus* which grow in the cornfields of southern Europe and are similar to *G. illyricus* in form and colour. They were known to Gerard, and to Parkinson who held the former in scant respect saying that in a garden, 'it will choke and pester it'. It would appear that none of the European species have been used in the raising of the modern large-flowered gladioli, nor until recently have the few that bear scented flowers. Mr T. Barnard has sought to correct this lack of scent by raising a group numbering several varieties from the five or six most fragrant species, though not without difficulty in raising a strain which will be hardy in Britain and Europe.

The first of the scented species to reach Britain was *G. tristis*, bearing pale-yellow flowers which open at night and emit a clove-like perfume. The scented gladioli may be divided into two main categories, those carrying a clove scent and those scented like violets. Almost all bloom in spring or early summer and should be given the protection of a warm wall in a sheltered garden or of a greenhouse. It is for this reason that the scented species have been neglected in the British Isles and North America.

The corms should be planted in autumn 10 to 12.5 cm (4 to 5 in) deep in the open with a protective covering of peat or leaf-mould or with glass cloches.

Species. *Gladiolus alatus.* This is the only red gladiolus to bear scented flowers. A native of Cape Province, where it is found on hilly slopes, it grows 30 cm (12 in) tall and makes a 4- or 5-flowered spike. In northern Europe where it blooms early in summer, it is best confined to a warm greenhouse. The fragrance is unusual in that it resembles that of the Sweetbriar and is almost refreshing.

G. carinatus. It is found throughout Cape Province, bearing its attractive little flowers of pale lilac-mauve, with a yellow throat. The flowers are borne 2 to 8 on a 60-cm (2-ft) stem and emit a powerful violet-like perfume.

G. caryophilaceus. The clove-scented gladiolus of South Africa where it is known as the Pink Afrikander lily. It is also *G. hirsutus* from its handsome hairy red-margined leaves. It blooms early in summer, bearing its large rose-pink flowers on a 60-cm (2-ft) stem and they emit a delicious stock-like perfume.

G. gracilis. Native of Cape Province, it is a charming species, in bloom in northern Europe in May and June and bearing 4 to 6 pinky-mauve flowers on a thin wiry stem which arises to a height of 45 cm (18 in) from narrow, grass-like leaves. The blooms smell deliciously of violets.

G. grandis. It is one of the so-called Brown Afrikanders which blooms during winter. The flowers measure 10 cm (4 in) across and number about 4 to each 60-cm (2-ft) stem. In colour they are a combination of brown and yellow, and though open by day diffuse a powerful clove-like scent only at night, hence its name of Evening Flower. It is pollinated by night-flying moths.

G. hirsutus. Known in South Africa as the Large Pink Afrikander, the leaves and stem are covered in silky hairs. It grows 45 cm (18 in) tall and bears bright-pink tubular flowers with markings of white and with a pronounced clove perfume.

G. maculatus. It is native of Cape Province where it is known as the Small Brown Afrikander, its pinky-brown funnel-shaped flowers being delicately veined with purple. It frequents lower mountain slopes where it blooms during May and June and is one of the most fragrant of all gladioli.

G. orchidiflorus. Also *G. viperatus*, the Viper's cornflag, which blooms in the British Isles late in summer though only in the most favourable parts does it survive the winter and is best grown indoors. The flowers are greenish-white with brown throat markings and scented of violets.

G. recurvus (syn. *G. odorus*). It is found throughout South Africa where it is known as the Blue Afrikander for it bears violet scented flowers in shades of grey-blue, pale and dark blue and purple. There are attractive gold markings on the three lower lips, and one of the leaves shielding the stem is also covered with spots.

G. tristis. A native of Natal where it is known as the Yellow Marsh Afrikander, it bears its sulphur-yellow funnel-shaped flowers spotted with red on a slender stem 15 cm (18 in) tall. Though open by day, the flowers diffuse their clove-like perfume only at night, the reason for this being unknown.

The variety *concolor*, which bears a bloom without any red markings, has the same carnation-like perfume.

The plant was grown in the Chelsea Physic Garden as long ago as 1745 and when crossed with *G. cardinalis* produced *G. colvillei* which has no perfume.

GLEDITSCHIA (Leguminosae—Laburnum Family)

A genus of four or five low-growing deciduous trees, armed with spines and best suited to coastal planting in favourable areas.

Species. *Gleditschia macrantha.* A Chinese tree, hardy only in southern England and Ireland. Like all members of the family, it is deciduous and armed with spines, its fleshy oblong leaves having serrated edges. In midsummer, it bears greenish-white flowers in clustered cymes and they have the delightful vanilla fragrance of the family.

G. sinensis. A Chinese species, reaching a height of 9 m (50 ft) and armed with angry spines. It bears small blunt-ended leaves and throughout summer bears greenish-white flowers in clustered racemes.

G. triacanthos. The Honey locust of the U.S.A. where it forms a robust tree 15 m (50 ft) tall, its greenish-white flowers, borne in midsummer, having a pleasing scent.

GLOTTIPHYLLUM (Aizoaceae—Aizoon Family)

A small genus of tender succulents, native of South Africa, which in the British Isles require the protection of a warm greenhouse and a position of full sunshine. The plants require almost no moisture when resting in winter.

Species. *Glottiphyllum fragrans.* A most pleasing succulent on account of the delicious vanilla-like perfume of its large golden-yellow flowers measuring 10 cm (4 in) across and which appear in July. The brilliant-green leaves appear in pairs and are arranged in two rows.

GLYCYRRHIZA (Leguminosae—Laburnum Family)

A genus of 18 species of sub-tropical and temperate regions of the world, most important being *G. glabra*, the liquorice.

Species. *Glycyrrhiza glabra.* It is an interesting plant, grown commercially around the Pontefract district of England to which it was introduced by the Black Friars about the mid-sixteenth century. Stowe, in his *History of London*, mentions that the plant was introduced in the first year of Elizabeth's reign, possibly from Spain, where it was grown in large quantities. By the end of her reign, home-grown liquorice had become a popular commodity for Parkinson in the *Paradisus* wrote that 'it is more pleasing to us than that brought from beyond the sea'.

It is grown in deep loam for the extraction of its root juices which are used to make the celebrated Pontefract cakes and liquorice all-sorts. It was also used with horehound to make a cough syrup and with the juice of figs to relieve constipation, and there is still no finer remedy. According to Culpeper, the juice distilled in rose-water is an excellent medicine for hoarseness and wheezing. It was also used to brew a beer to be taken during spasms of coughing; John Josselyn gives the recipe in his *New England's Rarities Discovered,* and he used to give it to the Indians suffering from chest complaints.

The plant is perennial but the roots are lifted annually in October when a portion is cut into small pieces, each with an 'eye' or two and replanted, in the manner of rhubarb which is grown on a commercial scale in the same district. The roots, which reach down to a depth of 1.2 m (4 ft) have the characteristic sweet, pungent smell when broken.

GOODYERA (Orchidaceae—Orchid Family)

A genus of 40 species, native of temperate Asia, North America, the British Isles and Europe. It is distinguished from *Spiranthes* by its creeping stem, the flowers borne in one-sided spiral racemes.

Species. *Goodyera repens.* The Creeping Ladies' Tresses orchis, distributed in pine woods throughout Scotland and the Orkneys, in bloom during July and August. Growing only 10 to 12.5 cm (4 to 5 in) tall, it does not bloom until its eighth year. The white flowers, borne in a slender twisted row, are sweetly scented by day and by night, to attract the maximum number of Lepidoptera which are scarce in northern pine woods.

GORDONIA (Theaceae—Tea Family)

A genus of ten or so species of deciduous and evergreen trees and shrubs with leathery shining green leaves, oblong and serrated. They require similar conditions to the Camellia, a peaty soil free from lime, and shelter from cold winds. As they are natives of the swamps of southern United States, they require ample supplies of moisture at the roots during summer. They may be propagated from layers of the ripened shoots in August or from cuttings inserted in a mixture of peat, leaf-mould and sand, and kept in gentle heat.

Species. *Gordonia alatamaha.* See *Franklinia alatamaha.*

G. chrysandra. Native of south-eastern China and Formosa, it grows 3.6 to 4.2 m (12 to 14 ft) in height and it blooms throughout summer, bearing masses of flat camellia-shaped flowers 7.5 cm (3 in) across, creamy-white and with a powerful perfume.

G. lasianthus. From the swamplands of the southern United States, it is an evergreen growing 2.4 to 3 m (8 to 10 ft) tall with smooth serrated oblong leaves, and from the axils are produced white camellia-like flowers 10 cm (4 in) across which are sweetly scented. It blooms from July until September.

GUAIACUM (Zygophyllaceae—Lignum Vitae Family)

A genus of about ten species of trees or shrubs, indigenous to tropical America and the islands of the West Indies, the most common being *G. officinale,* the Lignum Vitae which grows on the desert plains which stretch south from Florida to Venezuela. Since its introduction, it is now common in southern India, especially in Madras.

Species. *Guaiacum officinale.* It makes a crooked tree 12 m (40 ft) tall with deeply grooved bark. Its branches grow closely together to make a neat rounded head composed of multitudes of tiny stalkless leaflets half an inch long. The tiny blue flowers, like forget-me-nots, grow in clusters at the ends of the branches and are scentless but most striking with their ten stamens bearing golden anthers. The ex-tremely durable wood is used to make pulleys and bowls for the game made famous by Drake. When heated it gives off an aromatic scent whilst the bark and wood shavings are used in medicine. The resin from the wood is green in colour with a pungent, aromatic smell.

GUAREA (Meliaceae—Mahogany Family)

A genus of about 170 species, distributed throughout tropical America and Africa, and used for their timber. The cultural conditions required are similar to those needed for *Guaiacum.*

Species. *Guarea grandifolia.* Native of Guyana and the Caribbean, where it is known as Alligator or Musk-wood, for all parts of the tree, especially the bark, smell strongly of musk. It grows 9 m (30 ft) tall, with wood so bitter as to render it of no use in making staves for rum hogsheads. Instead, the wood and bark are used to give their musk-like smell to liquors. The leaves, which are large and divided into pairs of oblong leaflets 22 cm (9 in) long, also smell strongly of musk. The flowers, appearing in February, are borne in long racemes, the petals being silky on the outside, whilst the stamen tube is entire, not toothed at the apex, as in *Melia.*

G. trichilioides. Native of the islands of the Caribbean, it grows about 6 m (20 ft) tall with leaves smaller than those of *G. grandifolia* and with reddish bark which is musk-smelling. The flowers are white and appear in June–July.

GYMADENIA (Orchidaceae—Orchid Family)

A genus of 10 species of leafy plants native of Canada, the British Isles, and northern Europe, with the flowers sessile and spurred.

Species. *Gymnadenia albida* (syn. *Leuconchis albida*). It is common to the grassy hills of the lowlands of Scotland and is also found in parts of Derbyshire and Yorkshire but is rare further south. It is prevalent across northern Europe to Siberia and Japan and also grows in North America from Alaska to Newfoundland. It rarely exceeds a height of 15 cm (6 in) with a 7.5-cm (3-in) flower spike composed of

30 or more blooms of white, tinted with green. They emit a powerfully sweet perfume, most pronounced at night to attract the night moths for pollination.

G. canopsea. Known as the Sweet-scented or Common Fragrant orchid, it is native to the British Isles, found about hilly pastures usually with a chalky subsoil and often in sight of the sea. It also grows across Siberia and northern China and in Japan and further south in Asia Minor. It forms a slender stem 30 to 37.5 cm (12 to 15 in) tall, and bears in July and August flowers with long slender spurs (twice as long as the ovary), half-filled with nectar and pale-lilac in colour, with a delicious perfume which is especially pronounced at night. This is interesting for the flowers are pollinated by Night Hawk-moths which have a longer proboscis than the bees. Pollination is carried out by the moth's proboscis coming into contact with the viscidia, the pollen being carried to the stigma of another bloom.

The form *densiflora*, the Marsh Fragrant orchid, is as its name implies found in wet, low-lying land and bears a larger, more densely flowered spike which is if anything more powerfully scented. The flowers have a greater depth of colour whilst the leaves are broader. It blooms during July and August.

G. odoratissima. It grows in limestone localities of central Europe and in Scandinavia but has been seen in only one place in the British Isles, in Co. Durham. It resembles the Common Fragrant orchid though it bears a slightly smaller bloom and has narrower leaves. If anything, the scent is more pronounced and at night becomes so overpowering that it may be detected from a distance.

H

HAAGEOCEREUS (Cactaceae—Cactus Family)

A genus of about 50 species, native only of the Peruvian Andes and capable of existing under dry conditions. Night-flowering, the blooms have long slender tubes whilst the fruits are an unusual pinkish-grey.

The plants require a calcareous soil, one made up of sterilized loam, grit, decayed manure and lime rubble in equal parts. They prefer partial shade and require an abundance of moisture at the roots in summer but only sufficient in winter to keep the plants alive.

Species. *Haageocereus decumbens.* A plant of semi-prostrate habit, branching from the base, the areoles with short white radical spines. The nocturnal flowers are white and are sweetly scented. They are followed by large smooth pink fruits.

HAEMANTHUS (Amaryllidaceae—Narcissus Family)

A genus of 50 species, native of tropical Africa, South Africa and Socotra. It takes its name from the Greek *aima*, blood, and *anthos*, flower, denoting the colour of the lily-like flowers of most species which appear before the twin tongue-shaped leaves measuring up to 60 cm (2 ft) in length. They are mostly pollinated by honey birds, and one species only has scented flowers.

Species. *Haemanthus moschatus.* Though (wrongly) known as the Blood-flower, its blooms, borne in dense heads and surrounded by deep-pink bracts, are of coral-red tipped with white and with white filaments. The flowers have a musk-like scent which they retain for a considerable time.

Indoors, it blooms in early autumn, before the leaves. Plant one 10-cm (4-in) bulb to a pot of a size which allows 2.5 cm (1 in) all round the bulb. Plant in July after the leaves die back and give a long period of baking in the sun with minimum moisture before bringing them into bloom. When they show colour, place them in a cool room. Keep the compost moist until the leaves have died back about mid-summer. They require a compost made up of turf loam, leaf-mould and decayed manure in equal parts.

HALESIA (Styraceae—Storax Family)

The Snowdrop trees of the United States, a genus of small deciduous trees with finely toothed leaves and bearing drooping white flowers in clusters. They enjoy best a sandy soil enriched with leaf-mould and a little decayed manure. They are quite hardy in all except the most exposed parts of the British Isles.

Species. *Halesia carolina.* A native of North America, it makes a low spreading tree with pendulous branches and in May bears in profusion snowdrop-like flowers with a delicate sweet perfume.

H. hispida. Native of Japan, it grows to a height of 3 to 3.6 m (10 to 12 ft) with large heart-shaped leaves and in May and June bears its pure-white 'snowdrops' in corymbose racemes. The slightly scented flowers are followed by fruits which are covered in hairs.

H. monticola. In the United States it attains a height of nearly 24 m (80 ft) and has large leaves with serrated edges. In early summer it bears large snowdrop-like flowers in dense racemes and they have a soft sweet fragrance.

H. tetraptera. The true Snowdrop tree of North America, growing to a height of 6 m (20 ft) with lance-shaped leaves, pointed and toothed. It comes into flower in May, bearing as many as 8 or 9 faintly perfumed milk-white blooms in a drooping cluster. It makes a most attractive specimen tree for a lawn for which purpose it should be more widely planted.

HALIMODENDRON (Leguminosae—Laburnum Family)

A genus of a single species.

Species. *Halimodendron argenteum.* It is the Salt tree of Siberia, which is able to tolerate a dry, sandy soil and a position close to the sea for the salt-laden winds seem to cause it no harm. But it will not thrive in a soil containing any lime. It is closely allied to the *Robinea* and possesses extreme hardiness.

It makes a dainty shrub 1.5 to 1.8 m (5 to 6 ft) tall with silky silvery leaves, the leaf stalks ending in a spine, and it blooms during May and June. The flowers are quite large, like those of the Everlasting pea of the same family, and are pale mauve-pink with a delicate sweet almond perfume. Borne in drooping clusters, the flowers are a pleasing contrast to the silver-grey foliage.

It is especially attractive grown as a standard by grafting onto a laburnum but is difficult to obtain in this form. It is readily increased by layering the young shoots or from cuttings, taken in August and rooted in a sandy compost.

HAMAMELIS (Hamamelidaceae—Witch Hazel Family)

A genus of about 30 species of trees or shrubs, several of which bear richly scented flowers in winter. The curiously shaped flowers with their twisted petals are able to withstand the bleakest weather, and the foliage takes on rich autumnal colourings.

Species and Varieties. *Hamamelis japonica.* Native of Japan, it makes a neat, bushy plant and may be grown as a pot plant to bloom under glass at Christmas. Outdoors, it blooms during February and March, its lemon-yellow flowers being borne in dense clusters on leafless stems. The variety *zuccariniana* is more lime-tolerant than the other forms and is the hardiest of all the Witch Hazels, with attractively twisted flowers of pale citron-yellow, borne in March and pungently scented; its glossy leaves turn orange-scarlet before they fall in autumn.

Jelena or Copper Beauty is another fine form, the result of a cross with *H. mollis,* bearing large flowers of a distinctive coppery-orange and with a powerful fragrance.

Moonlight is another beautiful form, making a large shrub with ascending branches; the leaves turn yellow in autumn. The quite large flowers have crimpled petals of sulphur-yellow with a red mark at the base and emit a powerful sweet perfume.

The variety *arborea* (tree-like) was introduced from Japan where the plants grow to a height of 6 m (20 ft) and more, though less than half that height in Britain. The flowers appear in the new year on leafless grey-green branches and are primrose-yellow with narrow twisted petals and a hairy calyx of claret-red. They are sweetly but not strongly scented.

H. mollis. The Chinese Witch Hazel, introduced to garden culture by Professor Maries in 1879. It makes a large shrub with rounded leaves, and from December until April bears clusters of golden-yellow flowers with broad petals along the whole length of the stem. The variety *brevipetala* bears shorter-petalled flowers with a heavy incense-like perfume, whilst *pallida* bears heavily scented pale-yellow flowers clustered along the naked stems.

H. vernalis. The Ozark Witch Hazel of America, a plant of upright habit and bearing coppery-orange flowers in January and February with a scent that is heavy and pungent.

H. virginiana. The source of the witch hazel of commerce, used in beauty parlours everywhere. Native of the eastern United States, it is a large tree-like shrub, and from September until November bears multitudes of small yellow flowers with a soft sweet perfume.

HAMILTONIA (Rubiaceae—Bedstraw Family)

A genus of a single species, native to sub-tropical India.

Species. *Hamiltonia suaveolens.* It is an evergreen shrubby plant growing 1.2 to 1.8 m (4 to 6 ft) tall, found about rocky hillsides, and it bears plume-like heads of creamy-white tubular flowers which emit a sweet, jonquil-like perfume. Flowering is in October.

It requires stove-house cultivation and a peaty compost, and can be increased by planting half-ripe cuttings in sand, with bottom heat.

HARNUNGIA (Cruciferae—Wallflower Family)

A small genus of scree plants growing about the rock face of the Cheddar and Avon Gorges in England.

Species. *Harnungia petraea.* From the peppery smell of its leaves it is known as the Rock pepperwort. The tiny flowers appear in spring and have narrow white petals whilst the stems and leaves are covered in minute hairs. The leaves have the peculiar peppery odour of watercress to which it is closely related.

HAWORTHIA (Liliaceae—Lily Family)

There are two types of this succulent member of the lily family: those with hard leaves which have toothed edges and are covered in tubercles, and those having soft leaves which are heavily veined. To the latter group belongs *H. tessellata*, a native of Mexico.

Species. *Haworthia tessellata.* It sends up a stem several feet tall at the end of which are borne insignificant greenish-white flowers which diffuse a soft lily-like perfume.

HEATHER: *see* **ERICA**

HEBE: *see* **VERONICA**

HEBENSTREITIA (Scrophulariaceae— Snapdragon Family)

A genus of 40 species of annual or perennial herbs or shrubs with linear leaves, toothed in the upper part. The flowers are borne in spikes, the bracts being longer than the calyx. The genus was named in honour of J. E. Hebenstreit, a professor of botany at Leipzig University.

Species. *Hebenstreitia comosa.* A native of South Africa where it is a plant of perennial habit, though in Britain it should be given half-hardy annual treatment, sowing the seed under glass in February and retaining for only a single season. Or in a warm, sheltered garden, the seed may be sown where the plants are to bloom, in April. The small white or pale-yellow flowers are spotted with orange and are borne in dense spikes. At night they diffuse a delicious lily-like perfume. The plant grows 37.5 cm (15 in) tall and blooms from June until September.

HEDYCARYA (Monimiaceae— Hedycarya Family)

A genus of 25 species of trees, native to Australia and New Zealand and the Solomon Islands, with opposite leaves covered in resinous glands and bearing flowers in axillary panicles.

Species. *Hedycarya arborea.* Native of both islands of New Zealand where it flowers in December. It grows 9 m (30 ft) tall and has aromatic bark dark brown in colour, and coarsely-toothed leaves 5 to 7.5 cm (2 to 3 in) long which are hairy. The flower panicles are also hairy, and are pale yellow with the fruit orange-red and oblong. The flowers are sweetly scented.

HEDYCHIUM (Zingiberaceae—Ginger Family)

A genus of eastern Indian herbaceous plants amongst the most beautiful and sweetly scented known throughout the entire world. They grow between 0.9 to 1.5 m (3 to 5 ft) tall, and when grown indoors require an ample amount of pot room. The blooms are produced in the form of large erect spikes at the apex of the shoots and are mostly either purest white or pale yellow, their scent being particularly pronounced towards evening. Several species, namely *H. gardnerianum,* survive all but the most severe winters in the South-west of England, but mostly they are grown indoors where their blossom renders the atmosphere extremely pleasant. They require a winter temperature of not less than 11°C (52°F), and when coming into growth in early summer enjoy a buoyant atmosphere and plenty of moisture at the roots. They are propagated by division early in spring.

From its roots, a product known as Kapur-Kadri is obtained which is used in perfumery in the East, whilst from the dried root of *H. spicatum* an incense is obtained which is used in Hindu worship.

Species. *Hedychium angustifolium.* Native of the eastern parts of Bengal where it flowers at the beginning of June. Indoors, it attains a height of 1.5 m (5 ft) and in early summer bears handsome purple-red flowers which are scented, though of a different scent to *H. coronarium.*

H. spicatum. It takes its name from two Greek words meaning 'sweet snow' from the snow-whiteness of its sweetly smelling flowers. The dried roots are used by the Hindus to burn as incense, and the plant is native of the Punjab Himalayas where the roots form a considerable article of commerce. The root is reddish-brown and marked with white rings. Internally it is starchy in substance with a fragrant, somewhat pungent smell and bitter to the taste. Dr Dymock, in his *Notes on Indian Drugs* has described the scent as similar to that of orris-root but more powerful. There is a Chinese form which is rather less strongly scented.

A chemical examination of the root was made by Dr Thresh in 1880 which proved that the odorous principle exists in minute amounts in cells which contain resin and an essential oil. So powerful is this oil that one drop upon the clothes renders them highly perfumed for a considerable time. Indoors, where the fragrance is most appreciated, it may be said to resemble the perfume of hyacinths.

H. coronarium. It is known in the East as the Indian Garland flower and is a stately plant with handsome foliage and bearing pure-white flowers of delicious perfume over a long period. There is also a pale-yellow variety.

H. flavum. Its pale-yellow flowers diffuse such exquisite perfume that it is almost sacred to Hindu worshippers. Dr Wallich in his *Flora Indica* says that the flowers are about one-third smaller than those of *H. coronarium* and possess the rare scent of *Michelia champaca.*

H. gardnerianum. It attains a height of 1.8 m (6 ft) where given plenty of root room and it bears large handsome spikes of palest yellow flowers scented like jasmine.

H. gracile. It is a native of Brazil where the sweetly scented creamy-white blossoms are used by the women to decorate their hair. It is a slender species growing 0.9 m (3 ft) tall.

H. villosum. Native of the mountains of north-eastern Bengal, it differs from *H. gracile* in the length of its spikes and size of bloom. It grows less than 90 cm (3 ft) tall and, like all the family, has long sheath-like leaves which wrap themselves around the stems. The flower spike may be as much as 30 cm (12 in) long, all parts being covered in down and densely packed with pale-yellow flowers which retain their powerful fragrance even when dry.

HEDYOSMOS (Labiatae—Lavender Family)

A genus of 14 species, native to eastern North America, from New York State to the Mexican border. The plants grow on dry hillsides and are short and bushy with small ovate leaves which are pleasantly aromatic.

Species. *Hedyosmos mariana* (syn. *Cunila mariana*). It is known in the U.S.A. as the Common dittany and is especially prolific in the hills around New York where it grows about 30 cm (12 in) tall and has small narrow thyme-like leaves. Like the thyme, the plant bears small tubular lilac flowers whilst the leaves smell of thyme.

HEDYOSMUM (Chloranthaceae—Chloranthus Family)

A genus of 41 species, all but one being native of the sub-tropical areas of the New World, especially the West Indian islands.

Species. *Hedyosmum nutans.* Native of Jamaica where it grows on the hills above Port Royal and about the Blue Mountains to a height of about 1,800 m (6,000 ft). It is known in Jamaica as the Tobacco bush for the leaves, borne opposite and 10 to 12.5 cm (4 to 5 in) long with serrated edges, emit an odour which resembles tobacco leaf, and to some resembles the smell of Brown Windsor soup. The tobacco aroma is more pronounced in the essential oil which has a smell likened to that of fine 'honeydew' cake.

HEDYSARUM (Leguminosae—Laburnum Family)

A genus of about 50 silky-haired perennial plants and shrubs, native of central Europe and Asia, one, the French Honeysuckle *(H. coronarium),* being especially fragrant and suitable for planting in the border. Like the laburnum, the flowers are borne in axillary racemes and appear throughout summer.

Parkinson tells us that the plant, a native of southern Italy, was first grown in Britain in the garden of a Master William Coys (who introduced the artichoke into Britain) at North Okenden, and he describes it as 'being of an excellent shining red or crimson, like unto stain of that colour'. Francis Bacon includes it with the plants which are of 'the greatest refreshment to the spirits of man'.

Species. *Hedysarum coronarium.* It grows 1.2 m (4 ft) tall and requires an open, sunny position. It is happy in any well-drained soil. The flowers are borne in crowded racemes throughout summer and are enhanced by the rounded leaflets which are hairy on the underside. It has a scent similar to that of clover, and from its flowers the children of Italy, where it is used as a forage crop, suck the sweet nectar.

H. multijugum. Native of Mongolia, it grows to a height of 1.2 to 1.5 m (4 to 5 ft), with twisting stems which are covered in silky hairs. The leaves are composed of 20 to 30 oblong leaflets with soft hairs on the underside, and from the axils are borne during July and August short racemes of delicately scented mauve-pink flowers.

HELENIUM (Compositae—Daisy Family)

A genus of about 40 species from which have been raised many outstanding border plants, though unfortunately almost all are lacking in perfume. They are autumn-flowering with a high pigment content which has displaced scent. This is present only in *H. nudiflorum* and in the annual *H. setigera.* The plants are native of North America, especially Texas, and are hardy. They are tolerant of most soil conditions, even a cold clay soil.

Species. *Helenium nudiflorum atropurpureum.* Native of Texas, it is perennial and grows 90 cm (3 ft) tall with lance-shaped leaves. It bears flowers which measure about 5 cm (2 in) across, the rayed florets of purple-brown being grouped around a central cone. The flowers, which are long-lasting both in the garden and when cut and placed in water, emit a soft sweet perfume.

H. setigera. An annual, it is native of Texas and bears bright-yellow flowers on 45 cm (18 in) stems. The flowers may be dried like everlasting flowers and will retain their fragrance for several years.

HELIANTHUS (Compositae—Daisy Family)

A genus of about 50 species, mostly native of North and South America, one of which, *Helianthus annuus*, the Sunflower of Peru, has aromatic properties.

Species. *Helianthus annuus.* A native of Peru where it was the emblem of the Sun God, it is to be found carved on the walls of Inca temples. It was first described by Dr Nicholas Monardes (of Monarda fame) and it possibly reached England from Spain during Elizabethan times for Gerard is the first to describe it in detail. The plant sends up a stem 2.4 to 3 m (8 to 10 ft) in height and has large heart-shaped leaves. At the end of the stem appears a flower of brilliant golden-yellow some 30 cm (12 in) across, the centre of which is, in Gerard's words, 'like some curious cloth wrought with the needle . . . from which sweats forth excellent fine and clear turpentine'. Parkinson added to this by saying that in warm weather both the flowers and leaf joints 'sweat out a fine thin and clear rossin or turpentine, so like clear Venice turpentine that it cannot be known from it'.

HELICHRYSUM (Compositae—Daisy Family)

A genus of more than 100 annual or perennial herbs mostly native of Australasia with tubular flowers and having several rows of involucral bracts. Almost all bear golden flowers hence its name *helios,* sun, and *chrysos,* gold. The fragrant ones bear white flowers, depending upon the scent for pollination.

Species. *Helichrysum angustifolium.* A native of South Africa, it is fully perennial and proves quite hardy in sheltered European gardens in a well-drained sandy soil. In a position of full sun its attractive silvery foliage scents the evening air with a strong smell of curry. Its leaves may be used either fresh or dry in stews or soups to impart a curry-like flavour. During late summer it bears clusters of bright-yellow 'everlasting' flowers on 30- to 35-cm (12- to 14-in) stems. The plants bloom the first year from a sowing of seed made in heat early in January. It is known as the Curry plant.

H. antennarium. Native of Australia it is an evergreen shrub growing 1.8 m (6 ft) tall and it flowers in June, bearing white daisy-like flowers which have the scent of hawthorn but without the fishy undertone.

H. elatum. A perennial species of New South Wales where it is known as the Love flower. It may reach a height of 1.8 m (6 ft) with woolly leaves which taper to a point, and it bears flower-heads usually 2 or 3 to a stem. The bracts are white and like paper to the touch and diffuse a delicate sweet perfume, also noticeable when the flowers have been dried for indoor decoration.

H. italicum. The Miniature Curry plant, altogether a delightful plant. Of shrubby habit, it grows upright and does not exceed a height of 30 cm (12 in), but as it withstands clipping it may be kept much lower. Its bright silvery-grey foliage, which it retains in winter, has a powerful curry-like pungency.

H. rosmarinifolius (syn. *Ozothamnus rosmarinifolius*). It is native of Tasmania where it attains a height of 3 m (10 ft). In the British Isles and in northern Europe it should be given the protection of a warm garden and a well-drained, sandy soil. The blunt-linear leaves are like those of the Rosemary and possess a similar aromatic fragrance. In July and August it bears small white flower-heads in dense clusters; they are also fragrant, smelling of vanilla and, it is said by some, with an undertone of wet bran!

It is propagated by removing the half-ripened flowerless shoots in August and inserting in sandy soil under a cloche or bell-jar.

HELIOTROPIUM (Boraginaceae— Borage Family)

It is a genus of 100 or more species and one of the few members of this mostly blue-flowered family to bear scented flowers. The flowers have a most unusual perfume, like that of cherries baked in a pie hence its country name, Cherry Pie, though perhaps a more apt description of its fragrance is that of sweet almonds. Not all the species are fragrant. *H. anchusaefolium* bears flowers entirely without scent; likewise *H. europeum* which bears tight clusters of white or pale-lilac flowers. Most popular is the Peruvian heliotrope which was at one time widely used for summer bedding and for indoor pot culture for it produces its flowers all through the winter. It is a half-hardy perennial which may be treated as an annual for it blooms the first summer if the seed is sown in gentle heat early in the year.

Species. *Heliotropium convolvulaceum.* A half-hardy annual growing 60 cm (2 ft) tall, it is native of New Mexico and is a plant similar in habit to the better known Peruvian form. It flowers throughout summer if seed is sown in heat in January, but it opens its pure-white flowers only in the cool of the evening when its delicious perfume with spicy undertones blends to perfection with the scent of *Hesperis matronalis* and the Evening primrose.

H. peruvianum. Native of Peru, it is a plant of dwarf shrubby habit, in the garden reaching a height of about 60 cm (2 ft). It is of branching habit with hairy, lance-shaped leaves which have a grey appearance and so provide a pleasing foil for geraniums and other brilliant summer bedding flowers. It produces its feathery flowers of (usually) purple or white throughout summer and autumn.

Of a number of varieties, outstanding is Marguerite which makes a bushy plant less than 45 cm (18 in) tall and bears large fragrant umbels of dark-blue flowers, The lilac-flowered Lemoine's Giant is also fine and for contrast plant White Lady which bears flowers of purest white. All were grown a century ago.

In its native land and in parts of southern Ireland, *H. peruvianum* is widely planted as a hedge, growing up to 1.5 m (5 ft) tall and diffusing its fragrance about the countryside.

HELLEBORUS (Ranunculaceae—Buttercup Family)

A genus of 12 species of perennial plants which bloom during winter and early spring. They have leathery leaves and bear flowers which are either white, green or purple. One species, however, *H. odorus*, bears sweetly scented flowers. The more familiar *H. niger*, the Christmas rose, has been known to British gardeners since Roman times, indeed it was used by the physician Melampus, who practised at Pyles in Greece about 1500 B.C. (at the time of Moses or thereabouts), to cure the daughters of Proetus, King of Argos, of insanity. It is thus one of the oldest medicinal plants in history, all parts possessing cathartic qualities. The hellebore figures in the frontispiece to Burton's *Anatomy of Melancholy*:

> *Borage and Hellebor fill two scenes,*
> *Sovereign plants to purge the veins*
> *of melancholy, and cheer the heart*
> *of those black fumes which make it*
> *smart.*

At that time, the powdered roots were used as snuff. *H. odorus* is, however, a plant of more recent introduction, reaching Britain early in the nineteenth century from Hungary, and is now rarely found.

Species. *Helleborus foetidus.* It is native of the British Isles and is evergreen, its deep-green glossy leaves being divided into 5 or 7 linear, toothed leaflets from which it takes its name of Bear's-foot. It is native of chalky pasturelands where it grows 60 to 90 cm (2 to 3 ft) in height and is a most handsome plant in winter, forming a luxuriant tuft from which arise the flower stems. The cup-shaped blooms, about 2.5 cm (1 in) across, are green with purple markings at the petal tips. They appear in February in drooping cymes and are amongst the most beautiful of all native flowers. The whole plant, however, gives off a most unpleasant smell like that of decaying meat, perhaps to warn of its poisonous properties. It is the Stinking Hellebore.

H. odorus. It is known as the Sweet-scented hellebore. It enjoys a position of partial shade, such as at the base of a wall facing north, and it requires a rich loamy soil, if possible enriched with a little decayed manure. It blooms from February until April, the flowers being greenish-white and drooping and about 5 cm (2 in) across, with a most powerful sweet perfume. They are borne on 45-cm (18-in) stems above pale-green leaves streaked with white and are propagated by division of the roots after flowering.

HEMEROCALLIS (Liliaceae—Lily Family)

Though of the lily family, it has thick fleshy roots and is increased by division of the roots in autumn; they should be treated in the same way as for the alstroemeria. The plants require a deeply dug soil and flourish either in full sun or partial shade. They bloom during July and August, lasting only for a day, hence its name, Day lily, but others take their place in one long succession over many weeks. The funnel-shaped flowers are borne in clusters on 60- to 90-cm (2 to 3-ft) stems above a clump of strap-like leaves. Those of yellow colour usually carry the sweet perfume of the sweetly scented *H. flava*, a native of central Europe which grows in pastureland like the cowslip of the English Midlands, scenting the air for a distance when warmed by the summer sunshine. Many strikingly lovely hybrids have been raised during the past decade varying in colour from blackish-red to orchid pink, all of them descended from *H. flava* and *H. fulva*, the latter a scentless species bearing orange flowers. They grew in Gerard's Holborn garden and may have been familiar to Shakespeare. They were then known as Asphodel lilies for they have the roots of the asphodel and bear a flower of lily form.

Henry Phillips wrote that the flowers of *H. flava* 'give out their agreeable fragrance . . . more particularly when planted in a moist soil and in a shady place'. He also mentions that the Yellow Day lily is readily raised from seed sown in the autumn when it will bloom in the second year.

Species and Varieties. *Hemerocallis citrina.* Native of northern Japan, it forms a clump of strap-like leaves above which it bears on 90-cm (3-ft) stems, creamy-yellow flowers of pronounced honeysuckle fragrance.

H. dumartieri. It is native of north-eastern Siberia and China and grows 45 cm (18 in) tall bearing on each stem 3 or 4 large golden flowers flushed with orange and it is sweetly scented.

H. flava. Native of northern Europe and westwards across Siberia to Japan, it is the most sweetly scented of all the species and is a delightful subject for indoor decoration. Growing 90 cm (3 ft) tall, it bears its golden-yellow flowers, scented like honeysuckle, in large clusters and remains in bloom over a long period.

Scented hybrids of *H. flava:*

BAGETTE. It received an Award of Merit in 1955 and is a wide-petalled bicolour of lemon-yellow with old rose shadings.

GOLDEN SCEPTRE. It grows 90 cm (3 ft) tall and bears large clusters of blooms of a unique bright Empire yellow.

GOLDEN WEST. Taller-growing than most, reaching a height of 1.05 m (3½ ft), it bears large flowers of deep golden-yellow.

HONEYSUCKLE. Like all the yellows it is tall-growing, the deep golden-yellow blooms having a rich honeysuckle perfume.

HYPERION. It grows 60 cm (2 ft) tall and bears large blooms of pale citron-yellow with a delicious sweet perfume.

IRIS, LADY LAWRENCE. It grows only 45 cm (18 in) tall and bears large flowers a lovely soft creamy-apricot which are sweetly scented.

JAS. KELSEY. It bears sparkling clusters of medium-sized flowers of soft buttery yellow.

MARY RANDALL. It grows 75 cm (2½ ft) tall and bears flowers a soft lemon-yellow with a deeper yellow line down each petal.

RADIANT. It received an Award of Merit for its bright golden-apricot flowers possess exceptional perfume and are borne in profusion.

H. minor (syn. *H. graminea*). Native of Siberia and northern China, it is a subject for the alpine garden for it grows only 15 cm (6 in) tall and from a clump of pale-green grass-like leaves bears large sulphur-yellow flowers tinted with green, which have the powerful scent of honeysuckle.

HEMIZONIA (Compositae—Daisy Family)

A genus of 30 species of mostly annual plants, all of which are native of California, weeds of hillside and highway.

Species. *Hemizonia luzulaefolia*, var. *lutescens.* It covers the hillsides and the verges to highways, being particularly noticeable north of San Francisco. It is a low-growing plant bearing in spring, summer and autumn, masses of bright-yellow daisy-like flowers whilst from its leaves, stems and buds, is exuded a sticky golden liquid which smells of balsamic resin. On a warm, calm day the smell is noticeable from a distance, scenting the air with its aromatic odour. It is known as the Hayfield tarweed though the smell more greatly resembles juniper or the Balsam poplar, being greatly refreshing during the heat of summer.

HERACLEUM (Umbelliferae—Parsley Family)

A genus of 70 species distributed throughout the northern temperate regions of the world and named after Heracles, hero of Greek mythology. They are weeds of waste ground and few are scented, though in the Giant hogweed scent glands can be seen through the outer case of the seed capsules.

Species. *Heracleum persicum* (syn. *H. mantigazizanum*). Introduced into Europe and Britain at an early date, possibly by the Romans, it is now naturalized and grows in moist places, attaining a height of 3 m (10 ft) or more with leaves 90 cm (3 ft) long whilst the flowers are borne in umbels often more than 3 ft across. In bloom June and July, the flowers are followed by large flat seed-heads, like those of Honesty, and on either side of a central division which separates the seed receptacles can be seen a long red moon-shaped gland which releases, upon pressing, a pleasantly scented aromatic oil. The plant may be used to effect near a lake or pond where it will contrast in height with the flat surface of the water. It may also be grown in the wild garden.

HERMANNIA (Sterculiaceae—Streculia Family)

A large genus of sub-tropical plants

native of Africa, America and Australia, and named after the Dutch botanist Hermann. The plants require winter protection in the British Isles and North America. The flowers have the petals, sepals, stamens and styles arranged in fives. Those bearing orange and scarlet flowers have no scent. They require cool greenhouse treatment and are increased by tip cuttings.

Species. *Hermannia fragrans.* It is evergreen, forming a low sub-shrub, and it requires an open, sunny situation and a soil well enriched with peat. It blooms early in summer bearing small nodding flowers of golden-yellow which are deliciously scented. The flowers, which appear in clusters, are enhanced by the dark-green leaves whilst the stems are covered in long hairs.

HERMINIUM (Orchidaceae—Orchid Family)

A genus of leafy plants with ovoid tubers, so named from the Greek *hermin*, a bed-post, from the shape of the tubers. The plants have few leaves and sessile flowers with the lip, 3-lobed and pouched.

Species. *Herminium monorchis.* The Musk orchid of the South Downs and Cotswolds of England which also grows across northern Europe to Leningrad and in Asia, from Mongolia and northern China to Tibet and Korea in the south but enjoying the coldness of high altitudes. It is a tiny plant, never growing more than 15 cm (6 in) tall and always found in short grass, its slender stem arising from two glossy leaves. It bears its minute green flowers during June and July and they smell of fur (not of musk), a scent likened by some to the foliage of currants and which attracts beetles for pollination.

HERNIARIA (Caryophyllaceae—Pink Family)

A genus of about 35 species of matted perennials, native to Europe, the Near East and South Africa. The leaves are alternate, with the flowers borne in small clusters along the stems.

Species. *Herniaria glabra.* A rare plant of the hedgerows of England, it is hairless with the flowers borne in short racemes.

Though the flowers have no perfume, the leaves emit a musky smell when handled.

HERRERIA (Liliaceae—Lily Family)

A genus of eight species, native of South America, and named after the fifteenth-century Spanish botanist Gabriel Herrera. They are tuberous-rooted plants of climbing habit, their lance-shaped leaves being produced in whorls, and they bear their small, heavily scented flowers in axillary racemes.

Species. *Herreria salsaparilla* (syn. *H. parviflora*). Native of the valleys of the Brazilian Amazon, and requiring stove conditions away from the warmer parts, they climb to a height of 2.4 to 2.7 m (8 to 9 ft), and from the axils of the leaves bear greenish-yellow flowers during the summer months.

Indoors, they should be grown in a compost composed of 2 parts peat, 1 part sterilized loam and 1 part sand (parts by bulk), and a minimum temperature of 16°C (60°F) should be maintained.

HESPERANTHA (Iridaceae—Iris Family)

A small genus of South African bulbous plants closely related to the Tigridia, the Tiger flower, which has no perfume. Requiring a warm, sheltered garden in the British Isles, the blooms open in the early evening as the Tiger flowers begin to close, and when the night air is warm and dry their sweet clove-like perfume is diffused about the garden throughout the night. The plants require a well-drained sandy soil and a position of full sun to ripen the bulbs. They should be given the same treatment as the better-known ixias.

Species. *Hesperantha buchrii.* It grows 45 cm (18 in) tall and bears its night-scented flowers in dainty racemes. The blooms are pale pink on the outside, white within and are borne in profusion during July and August.

H. stanfordiae. A beautiful plant which attains a height of nearly 60 cm (2 ft) and blooms early in June. The blooms are of bright clear yellow, not quite so richly scented as those of *H. buchrii,* and they begin to unfold as the afternoon sun moves into the west. The scent becomes more pronounced as the sun goes down, until in the evening they diffuse a lily-like perfume.

HESPERIS (Cruciferae—Wallflower Family)

A genus of some 20 species of biennial or occasionally perennial herbs, mostly native of southern Europe, Russia and Siberia, and scented in the cool of evening.

Species. *Hesperis fragrans.* A native of Siberia, it is scented only by night, the flowers being of a dull mauve colour and smelling of cloves. It grows 22.5 to 25 cm (9 to 10 in) tall, the upper leaves being coarsely toothed at the base.

H. matronalis. The Damask violet or Dame's violet, it is of the same family as the stock and wallflower, which possess a similar clove-like fragrance. Probably native to the British Isles as well as to central and southern Europe, it grows to a height of 60 to 90 cm (2 to 3 ft) with ovate lance-shaped leaves, and bears early in summer flowers of white or palest lilac, arranged in the manner of double stocks and smelling strongly of violets by day but more especially in the evening when they take on an undertone of clove. The double form, *flore pleno,* known as the Double White rocket, is more strongly perfumed, the flowers having the heavy scent of the double stock and wallflower. It grows well in a dry soil and especially between the stones of old walls, where it may be sown with wallflowers for it blooms shortly afterwards. The double form should be propagated from cuttings (which readily root in sandy soil) or by root division in October.

Gerard describes the Dame's violet as having 'great large leaves of a dark green colour, snipt about the edges; ... the flowers come forth at the top of the branches, like those of the Stock gilloflower, of a very sweete smell'. Hence their name of Queen's gillyflower for they were considered superior in perfume to all other clove-scented flowers.

H. odoratissima. Native of the Caucasus and about Tiflis on the Black Sea, it is an erect shrub growing 45 cm (18 in) tall with toothed leaves covered with down. It is also found in Afghanistan and in western Tibet, growing in rocky formations at a height of 3,000 to 3,600 m (10 to 12,000 ft).

The flowers are large, of a dingy cream colour, turning purple-brown with age but diffusing at night a delicious clove-like perfume.

H. tristis. One of the night-scented flowers, it is native of central Europe, southern Russia and of the Naples district of Italy where it inhabits the edge of fields and woods. It grows 45 cm (18 in) tall and is much branched at the top, the leaves being covered with hairs. The flowers are of dirty cream or purple-brown colour and smell like violets at night. By close proximity of the sepals and claws of the petals, all insects are excluded from its nectar apart from nocturnal Lepidoptera which is also the case in *H. odoratissima.*

H. violacea. A native of Asia Minor, it grows 30 to 37.5 cm (12 to 15 in) tall with tufts of hairy (or downy) leaves, its sweetly scented violet flowers, with deeper veinings, appearing during May and June on stems held well above the foliage. The plant may be treated as a biennial and sown in July to bloom the following year.

HESPEROCALLIS (Liliaceae—Lily Family)

A genus of a single species, native of the desertlands of California and south-western America. It takes its name from the Greek *hesperos,* evening, and *kallos,* beauty, for it opens its white, tubular flowers in early evening when they scent the air around.

Species. *Hesperocallis undulata.* The bulbs are large and are said to be edible, and bury themselves in the sand to a depth of up to 50 cm (20 in). The linear leaves are attractively edged with white. It is rarely found in cultivation away from its native lane. Flowering is in early spring, and it requires a cool greenhouse for cultivation, though it may be grown in very sheltered, warm parts of the south-west of Britain in the open. Increase is by offsets or suckers in spring.

HETEROMELES (Rosaceae—Rose Family)

A genus of a single species, native only to California.

Species. *Heteromeles arbutifolia.* It is an evergreen tree growing to 9 m (30 ft) with foliage similar to that of the arbutus, whilst it bears panicles of white flowers which have a scent similar to that of *Crataegus* (hawthorn) and other members of the family, and is pleasant only from a distance.

It is very similar also to *Photinia* and was formerly placed in that genus; it is a handsome tree flowering in August, and is really only hardy in the south and west of Britain.

HEXAGLOTTIS (Iridaceae—Iris Family)

A small genus of corm-bearing plants, growing in the Newlands district of Cape Town, usually on dry mountainous slopes. They bear dingy brownish-yellow flowers which are pollinated by midges and emit an unpleasant smell.

Species. *Hexaglottis longifolia.* The lower leaves are long and narrow and prominently veined with the upper short and sheathing. The flowers are produced in loose clusters on the branched stems and die immediately after pollination.

HIBISCUS (Malvaceae—Mallow Family)

A genus of more than 300 species of herbs, trees or shrubs, growing in the marshlands of North America and in France, also in tropical Indonesia, Martinique, and South America. The flowers are not scented for they are visited by humming-birds, but seeds of *H. moschatus* yield 0.25 per cent of essential oil of musk-like odour and known in perfumery as ambrette. Farnesol, smelling of cedar wood, is also present in the seeds.

Species. *Hibiscus moschatus.* Its name is derived from ibis, a stork, for the bird is said to feed upon the plant. It makes a dense shrub 1.8 to 2.1 m (6 to 7 ft) tall and is native of South America, Indonesia and Martinique. It has angled, serrated leaves and bears sulphur-brown flowers, dark blue at the centre and borne singly at the end of the stems. The fruit capsules are conical and covered with bristles whilst the large seeds emit a pronounced musk-like scent when ripe.

When hair powder was the fashion, perfumers would scent the starch-like powder with ground ambrette and it was also used to make powders for sachets.

HIEROCHLOE (Graminaceae—Grass Family)

A genus of 30 species native to the northern temperate regions and to high ground in the warmer parts, e.g. Tasmania. It takes its name from two Greek words *hieros,* holy, and *chloe,* grass.

Species. *Hierochloe borealis* (syn. *H. odorata).* It is a grass of the northern temperate zones growing across North America (where it is used for making table mats and baskets) and throughout northern Europe where it is known as the Holy or Sacred-grass for in medieval times it was used to strew over the floors of churches. It emits a powerful scent of hay when drying. It grows 30 cm (12 in) tall and from its creeping rootstock arise tufted stems at the end of which is a 3-flowered spikelet. In Britain, it is found mostly in Scotland, on wet banks.

H. horsfeldii (syn. *Ataxia horsfeldii).* A native of Java and the Straits Settlements, it frequents coastal areas. When bruised it emits an odour similar to that given off by Sweet vernal grass.

H. redolens. Native of higher mountainous slopes of Tasmania, it grows 60 cm (2 ft) tall and is densely tufted, with the panicle 22.5 cm (9 in) long. It is very sweetly scented when drying.

HIMANTOGLOSSUM (Orchidaceae—Orchid Family)

A genus of tuberous orchids of robust proportions, native of south-east England and of the Mediterranean coast. The flowers have bracts which are larger than the flowers themselves and have a short spur.

Species. *Himantoglossum hircina.* The Lizard orchid, growing in deciduous woodlands of Kent and Suffolk where it blooms in June. The large flowers are borne in a loose spike on a stem 60 to 90 cm (2 to 3 ft) long and are green, spotted with red, whilst the lip is more than 2.5 cm (1 in) long and is white, spotted with purple-red. As the flower spike appears, the leaves begin to wither. The blooms emit a most unpleasant fur-like smell, especially when wet, and are pollinated by beetles and other insects.

H. longibracteatum. A large orchid

growing 60 cm (2 ft) tall with oval glossy leaves and bearing its flowers in a densely packed spike. The flowers have narrow bracts of greenish-purple whilst the upper segment of the flower is purple with the lip crimson-purple. The flower spike appears in April and diffuses a lily-like odour, especially pronounced at nightfall.

HOHERIA (Malvaceae—Mallow Family)

A genus of about five species of small trees, native of New Zealand. One is deciduous, the rest evergreen. They are not completely hardy in northern Europe, and in the British Isles only survive outdoors if the winters are mild, or they are grown in a sheltered position in the South-west. Increase is by cuttings or layers.

Species. *Hoheria lyallii* (syn. *Plagianthus lyallii*). A beautiful and interesting shrub which grows to a height of 6 m (20 ft), and in New Zealand is deciduous above an altitude of 900 m (3,000 ft), evergreen below. The leaves are heart-shaped and in June, on the previous year's wood, it bears drooping clusters of sweetly scented flowers of purest white which have a bunch of yellow anthers at the centre. Frequently, the branches bend under the weight of bloom and scent the countryside far and wide. From its bark, the Maoris make a soothing drink.

HOLBOELLIA (Lardizabalaceae—Lardizabala Family)

A genus of handsome twining evergreens, closely related to *Akebia* and *Stauntonia*. Both male and female flowers are borne on the same plant and emit a powerful sweet perfume. The flowers differ from *Stauntonia hexaphylla* in that their six stamens are free instead of being united.

Species. *Holboellia latifolia*. This attractive twining evergreen is a native of the higher Himalayas and is hardy in Britain south of the Thames and in the western coastal districts where its stems reach a height of 6 m (20 ft) or more. The plant is covered in glossy deep-green leaves, each being divided into 3 or 5 leathery leaflets, and early in spring appear the flowers, greenish-purple females and white males which are produced in axillary clusters.

The flowers have the exotic perfume of the East.

HOLODISCUS (Rosaceae—Rose Family)

A genus of eight species native to western North America and closely related to *Spiraea*.

Species. *Holodiscus discolor*. An elegant shrub attaining a height of 3.6 m (12 ft) it has handsome leaves which are covered with tomentum on the underside. In July it bears long drooping panicles of creamy-white flowers like those of Meadowsweet and with a similar perfume. It is a hardy plant, well able to withstand the bleak climate of a European winter.

HOLOTHRIX (Orchidaceae—Orchid Family)

A small genus of South African plants with small globose tubers and bearing several small flowers in a dainty spike. Found in damp, shady crevices on mountainous slopes, the flowers of several species have a powerful scent.

Species. *Holothrix candensata*. It grows 15 to 20 cm (6 to 8 in) tall with a slightly curved stem which arises from 2 fleshy, hairy leaves. The flowers are greenish-yellow with long narrow petals and a short straight spur.

H. villosa. It grows 30 cm (12 in) tall with 2 cordate leaves and all parts of the plant except the flowers are covered in long silky hairs. The flowers are pale yellow with a lip divided into 3 lobes and a short curved spur.

HOMERIA (Iridaceae—Iris Family)

A genus of 37 species, native to South Africa where they grow on sandy flats and lower mountainous slopes. The corms are globose, covered with coarse tunics and with 1 to 3 lower leaves which are long and narrow, the others being sheathing. The flowers are borne in terminal clusters and are bell-shaped with 6 erect or spreading segments with the filaments uniting in the tube. The flowers emit a powerful scent which is unpleasant near to, though flowers of *H. miniata* and *H. simulans* have a soft, sweet perfume. They require the same treatment as Ixia and Tigridia. In South Africa they bloom from

August until the year end, in the British Isles and northern Europe during May and June.

Species. *Homeria miniata.* The loveliest species, growing 60 cm (2 ft) tall and bearing bulbils in the axils of the lower leaves. The salmon-pink flowers have a yellow star at the centre and are deliciously scented.

H. ochroleuca. It is the most vigorous species, attaining a height of 90 cm (3 ft) and it is the hardiest in northern European gardens. The yellow flowers are shaded with pink but have an excessively sweet cloying perfume.

H. simulans. It forms a branched stem 37.5 cm (15 in) tall which arises from the fold of the 2 lower leaves and it bears pleasantly scented star-like flowers of pale yellow. The perianth segments form a small cup or bell.

HONEYSUCKLE: *see* **LONICERA**

HOP: *see* **HUMULUS**

HOPEA (Dipterocarpaceae—Dipterocarpus Family)
A genus of large resin-bearing trees, native of India, Malaya and the East Indies, and differing from *Shorea* only in the number and disposition of the stamens.

Species. *Hopea odorata.* It is native of Chittagong where it reaches a height of 24 m (80 ft) and has shining leaves of bottle-green with a large single resin gland at the axils of the veins. The small yellow flowers are borne in drooping terminal panicles and appear from the exterior axils. They possess extreme fragrance.

HOSTA (Liliaceae—Lily Family)
A genus of nine species of ornamental herbaceous plants which are suitable for waterside planting and for tub culture. The leaves are heart-shaped with parallel veins, whilst the funnel-shaped flowers are borne on naked scapes 45 cm (18 in) tall. They require a moist well-nourished soil.

Species. *Hosta plantaginea.* Native of China, it is the only species to bear scented flowers and it is the best, with handsome heart-shaped leaves 15 cm (6 in) across

and held on stalks 15 cm long. The drooping snow-white flowers are borne on slender stems and appear during August and September, emitting a delicious lily-like perfume.

The variety Royal Standard which blooms at the same time is also scented. The flowers are of purest white, borne at the end of 45-cm (18-in) stems above brilliant-green leaves. It will withstand a temperature of 10°F below zero without harm.

HOTTONIA (Water Violet) (Primulaceae—Primrose Family)
A genus of two species of aquatic plants known as the Water violets and named in honour of Peter Hotton, Professor of Botany at Leiden University.

Species. *Hottonia palustris.* It is a rare British plant, also growing in northern Europe and Asia where it is occasionally to be found in mud by the margins of lakes and ponds. It bears its flowers in whorls in May and June around a leafless stem and they are of deep violet-pink with a striking golden eye. They have the delicate mossy scent of the primrose or the fading perfume of the violet. Like all members of the family, the blooms may be either pin-eyed or thrum-eyed.

Shallow, still water suits them best, and they are good oxygenating plants: increase is by seed or division in spring.

HOUMIRI (Houmiriaceae—Houmiri Family)
A genus of three or four trees or shrubs, native of tropical South America and noted for their pleasantly smelling bark.

Species. *Houmiri floribunda.* It makes a small tree which, from incisions in the bark, secretes a resinous liquid. In his *Travels up the Amazon and Rio Negro,* A. R. Wallace tells of a native perfume called 'Umari' which is used to rub over the body; the natives insert pieces of wool under the bark and leave them a week until saturated by the secretion. They then intertwine the scented wool into their long hair plaits and leave it there until the perfume has evaporated, which takes several weeks.

HOUTTUYNIA (Piperaceae—Pepper Family)

Closely related to *Piper nigrum,* the pepper of commerce, it is a genus of two species native of central China. One, *Houttuynia cordata,* bears clusters of pure-white flowers which have a delicate perfume and leaves which smell powerfully of lemons. The plants should be treated as bog plants for they require a peaty soil and ample moisture about their roots during flowering time. They are propagated by division of the roots in March.

Species. *Houttuynia cordata.* It is a plant of erect habit growing less than 30 cm (12 in) tall with broad heart-shaped leaves of deepest bottle-green which turn purple with age and are heavily nerved beneath. When pressed, the leaves emit a refreshing lemon perfume, mint to some.

The flowers are borne in July, in erect cylindrical spikes at the tips of the branches, and are composed of 4 ivory-white petal-like bracts. The double form, *flore plena,* is extremely lovely when in full flower, with its white conical heads measuring 5 cm (2 in) across; it received an Award of Merit at the Royal Horticultural Society Show in July 1965, when exhibited by the Sunningdale Nurseries.

HOVENIA (Rhamnaceae—Buckthorn Family)

A small genus of plants, closely related to *Ceanothus.*

Species. *Hovenia dulcis.* Though native of western China and the Himalayas, it is also widely cultivated in Japan for its sweet, fleshy peduncles which in taste resemble the Bergamot pear. It makes a small, deciduous tree 6 m (20 ft) tall, with glossy heart-shaped leaves, deeply serrated, and it bears small, scented white flowers in terminal cymes. Reasonably hardy, it does best in a well-drained soil containing some sand, and can be increased from hardwood cuttings placed in sand under a hand light.

HOYA (Asclepiadaceae—Stephanotis Family)

A genus of 200 species of tropical plants, mostly of India, China and Borneo which are either of neatly twining habit or are bushy with slender branching stems. The honey-like scent of the flowers is remarkable. Sir John Hooker called *Hoya bella* 'the first gem of the air' and likened its flower 'to an amethyst set in frosted silver'. From the thick glistening appearance of the flowers they are known as the 'wax plants'.

The plants may be used to clothe a slender post or pillar of the garden room, and eventually trained over the rafters, but they require a minimum winter temperature of 14°C (58°F). The flowers which are very long-lasting are borne in bunches from spurs which arise from the base of the leaf stalks as the young shoots are formed. It is therefore important that these spurs should not be removed if the flowers are cut, otherwise the plants will cease to bear bloom. They grow well in a fibrous turf loam into which coarse sand has been incorporated to assist drainage.

Species. *Hoya australis.* Native of the warmer parts of Australia and South-east Asia, it is known as *Wa Tabua* in the South Pacific islands where it climbs to a great height over other vegetation. The leaves are fleshy and broadly elliptic whilst the creamy-white flowers are borne 20 to 30 to each umbel and are powerfully scented.

H. bella. Native of Malacca, it is a plant of shrubby half-procumbent habit, in pots requiring short canes to support its stems. It has small thick deep-green leaves and bears its flowers in clusters. They have a waxy appearance, glistening in the sunlight and are of blush-white with an amethyst centre.

H. carnosa. Of climbing habit it has thick fleshy leaves and bears wax-like flowers of pinkish-white which are carried in pendent umbels, diffusing an incense-like perfume. The form *variegata exotica* has leaves which vary in colour from golden-yellow to palest cream.

H. globulosa. A native of northern India, it is of climbing habit with the familiar thick leathery leaves and bears heavily scented straw-coloured flowers of great beauty.

HUMEA (Compositae—Daisy Family)

A genus of seven species, native of South Australia and Madagascar.

Species. *Humea elegans.* Native of South Australia, it is a half-hardy biennial, growing from 1.2 to 2.4 m (4 to 8 ft) in height yet retaining a compact symmetry. In the British Isles and northern Europe it may be grown outside only during the summer months when it adds character to any garden with its drooping pyramids of crimson grass-like florets. The whole plant gives off the rich smell of dry Virginia tobacco leaf which is specially pronounced after a shower during warm weather.

Seed is sown in July in a frame, the young plants being potted in September and kept in the frame over winter, with very little water. Plant outside during June.

HUMULUS (Hop) (Cannbinaceae—Hemp Family)

A genus of two species of twining perennial herbs with heart-shaped serrated leaves and bearing drooping flowers, the males in panicles, the females in the axils of the pointed bracts to form a short rounded spike. The hop is a handsome plant to cover a trellis or arbour over which its flowers will cast a pleasing scent whilst the leaves are refreshingly aromatic.

Species. *Humulus japonicus.* Native of China and Japan, it is hardy in northern Europe only in the more sheltered places where it will attain a height of nearly 6 m (20 ft) in a single season. The leaves are paler green and more rounded than those of the Common hop whilst the stem is covered with hairs.

H. lupulus. The Common hop, native of the British Isles and grown for centuries for brewing beer. It is a vigorous climbing plant with alternate heart-shaped leaves and it bears greenish-yellow flowers, the females in the axils of the bracts to form a rounded spike. The bracteoles bear glandular hairs to yield lupulin which is the requisite ingredient in brewing.

HYACINTHUS (Liliaceae—Lily Family)

A genus of 30 species, native of the south-eastern Mediterranean regions and closely related to the Scilla. The flowers of most species have a delicious balsamic perfume which is most appreciated indoors.

Top-size bulbs should be used for Christmas flowering, planting three or four in a bowl in September and keeping them in a cool dark place for 8 to 9 weeks when they may be introduced to room temperature. They may also be grown entirely without soil by placing them in the neck of glass jars filled with rain water to the base of the bulb. They should then be placed in a dark room until they have formed shoots about 5 to 7.5 cm (2 to 3 in) high when they may be introduced to the light and warmth.

When planting in beds outdoors, second-size bulbs may be used and should be planted in a rich soil in October, 10 to 12.5 cm (4 to 5 in) deep and spaced 15 to 20 cm (6 to 8 in) apart. They will bloom in May. When the glossy strap-like leaves begin to wither towards the month-end the bulbs may be taken up to make way for summer bedding plants, and dried off to be replanted in October.

The Roman hyacinths, really a French form (*albulus*) of *H. orientalis*, have the same delicious perfume but a more graceful branching habit. The so-called Fairy or miniature hyacinths are similar. They may be massed outdoors beneath ornamental trees (the blue-flowered Borah is delightful beneath early-flowering cherries) or in the shrub border and left undisturbed, or prepared bulbs may be planted in pots in September and forced into flower by early December.

Species and Varieties. *H. orientalis.* Native of the Near East, especially of Persia and Turkey, it is a charming plant in its own right, bearing a dozen or more nodding bells of palest mauve on stems 25 cm (10 in) long. The bells open like stars and diffuse about them a perfume equalled only by that of the stock. From this lovely plant, the enormous spikes of the Dutch or florists' hyacinths have been evolved, and from the variety *albulus* with its blooms of virginal whiteness, a native of southern France, has been raised the early-flowering Roman hyacinths.

Varieties of *H. orientalis* include:

ANN MARY. The huge thick spikes, arising from upright strap-like leaves are of clearest pink with perfect placement of the bells around the stem.

BEN NEVIS. The finest of all the whites with a powerful balsam-like perfume whilst the large bells of ivory-white are fully double.

BISMARCK. Long in commerce, it has never been surpassed in its colour which is light porcelain-blue with a delicious perfume.

CITY OF HAARLEM. Later-flowering than most, which will prolong the season, it forms a flower spike of great substance and a lovely creamy-yellow with a soft sweet perfume.

JAN BOS. It forms a magnificent spike of ox-blood red which does not fade as the spike ages.

KING OF THE BLUES. A magnificent late-flowering variety with a powerful scent and bearing an enormous spike of deep indigo, flushed with purple.

LADY DERBY. It forms a beautiful broad spike of a most attractive bright salmon-pink.

LA VICTOIRE. Excellent for forcing, it forms a truss of perfect proportions with its bells of rosy-crimson beautifully placed.

L'INNOCENCE. Probably more widely grown indoors than any variety, it forms the largest spike of all, bearing enormous bells of purest white with a ravishing perfume.

MYOSOTIS. The finest of all the light-blue hyacinths, exactly of forget-me-not colour, the bells having a silver centre and delicious perfume.

ORANGE CHARM. It bears a large compact truss of exquisite colouring being an unusual buff-yellow with orange shading.

OSTARA. The finest in its colour, bearing a spike of exhibition form, its large fleshy bells being of clear dark blue and free of any purple shading.

PRINCESS IRENE. A variety of uncommon beauty, bearing a handsome spike of soft silvery-pink.

SCARLET PERFECTION. A fully double form of Tubergen's Scarlet, bearing a spike of perfect symmetry and of deepest scarlet-red.

WINSTON CHURCHILL. It is worthy of the name it carries, being a spike of perfect form with large fleshy bells of richest sky-blue.

YELLOW HAMMER. It forms a compact spike of a lovely deep creamy-yellow with a pronounced scent.

H. romanus. This is the true Roman hyacinth which is widely distributed throughout southern Europe. It may be said to resemble the Musk Grape hyacinth in its inconspicuous flower and its delicious scent for it bears bells of dingy greenish-yellow with a rich incense-like perfume.

The Multiflora or miniature hyacinths are derivatives of H. samapus, and varieties include:

BORAH. It is known as a Multiflora or Fairy hyacinth, its numerous flower spikes which arise from a small bulb more nearly resembling H. amethystinus in form, and they are a lovely lavender-blue. Indoors, prepared bulbs (subjected to retarding) may be made to bloom for Christmas, whilst outside the bulbs are suitable for naturalizing.

ROSALIE. A most elegant pink-flowered form of Borah, its bright-pink flowers being held on dainty stems.

SNOW PRINCESS. In habit it is similar to Borah and is a delightful companion, bearing flowers of purest white.

VANGUARD. Very early flowering indoors, it forms sweetly scented heads of loosely formed bells a brilliant sky-blue.

HYDNORA (Hydnoraceae—Hydnora Family)

A genus of eight species to be found on sand dunes of Cape Province and the Malagasy Islands, of which the most common is *Hydnora africana.*

Species. *Hydnora africana.* It is a rootless and leafless parasite without green matter, which attaches itself to the root of its host plant, *Euphorbia caput-medusae.* The fleshy solitary flowers appear above ground from a branched rhizome and consist of 3 or 4 perianth leaves. They are externally brown with red anthers and a red stigma and emit a most unpleasant smell. They are visited by dung-flies which act as pollinators. Though the flowers are so unpleasant, the underground fruit with its leathery outer skin and gelatinous interior is edible.

HYDRANGEA (Hydrangeaceae—Hydrangea Family)

A genus of about 80 species, native to

eastern North America, Japan and the Philippine Islands. Small trees or shrubs, deciduous or evergreen, occasionally climbing with opposite or alternate leaves; simple, dentate, exstipulate. Flowers borne in a cymose inflorescence, the outer often sterile, those of eastern North America having scented attractions.

Species. *Hydrangea arborescens.* Native of North America, it is distributed in deciduous woodlands from Nova Scotia south to Virginia and was the first species to be introduced into Britain. It makes a dense rounded shrub 1.5 to 1.8 m (5 to 6 ft) tall with coarsely toothed heart-shaped leaves, downy on the underside, and late in summer bears sweetly scented white flowers in flat corymbs. Though not a showy plant it is hardy and usually grows in shade, hence its flowers have been endowed by nature with scent to attract pollinators.

H. quercifolia. A handsome native of Virginia and Florida and partially tender in the British Isles north of the Thames, it is a handsome species growing 1.5 to 1.8 m (5 to 6 ft) tall with large leaves like those of the Plane, hairy on the underside, likewise the stalks. It blooms in June and July, bearing its flowers in flat corymbs. They are white changing to an unusual greenish-purple colour as they age, and when first appearing the snowy panicles emit a soft sweet scent for several days. It was one of the first hydrangeas to be planted in George Washington's garden at Mount Vernon, Virginia, where it grows wild in deciduous woodlands.

HYLOCEREUS (Cactaceae—Cactus Family)

A genus of about 18 species of epiphytic plants with stems climbing by means of aerial roots and with short spines. The flowers are nocturnal and are white with red or purple sepals. The plants require semi-shade and a compost rich in humus, made up of peat or leaf-mould, sand or grit, and decayed manure in equal parts. But no lime rubble. Keep the plants dry during winter, increasing moisture as the sun gathers in strength and the plant makes growth.

Species. *Hylocereus extensus.* Native of Trinidad, it has long triangular stems and areoles with short, thick spines. The flowers remain open both by day and by night, the outer petals being greenish-purple, the inner white, flushed with rose. They are sweetly scented.

H. guatemalensis. It has glaucous stems with angular ribs and brown conical spines. The very large, heavily scented flowers have outer petals of pink, inner petals white. The large red fruits are edible.

H. polyrhizus. The stems are 4- to 5-angled and with aerial roots descending to the ground. The long richly scented flowers have red outer petals, white within.

H. venezuelensis. It has triangular stems and black spines and flowers which resemble those of *H. polyrhizus* in colour and with the same powerful scent.

HYMENOCALLIS (Amaryllidaceae— Narcissus Family)

A large genus of exotic-looking flowering plants, closely allied to *Pancratium* with which at one time they were grouped. The Hymenocallis is native to South America, particularly to Peru, and as to be expected, is not able to survive a cold winter outdoors in Britain unless growing in the most favourable districts. The bulbs are best lifted after summer flowering has ended. The plant is known as the Spider lily for the blooms have elongated perianth segments which give them a spider-like appearance. The blooms have the rich exotic perfume of the jonquil and similar strap-like foliage. The bulbs, too, resemble those of the jonquil, being globular with a long neck. If planted in April 15 cm (6 in) deep they will bloom before the end of June. Where the bulbs can be left undisturbed for several years, they will bear their flowers in great profusion. *H. narcissiflora* is the hardiest species and has the most powerfully scented flowers.

Species. *Hymenocallis amancaes.* It bears its flowers on 45-cm (18-in) stems and they are bright yellow, streaked with green at the base. Usually three or five blooms appear to each stem with the outer segments of the flowers as much as 7.5 cm (3 in) long. It is a native of Peru and not quite so fragrant as the white-flowered forms but is a plant of exquisite beauty.

H. harrisiana. It is native of Mexico, the pure-white powerfully scented flowers having a perianth tube nearly 15 cm (6 in) long. Usually two or three flowers appear on a stem 30 cm (12 in) long. After flowering the plant dies back completely, and growing in a pot should be placed on its side and given no water until growth recommences in spring.

H. narcissiflora (syn. *H. calathina*). The finest of all the species, .it was in ancient times known as the Sea daffodil, though under natural conditions it grows only in the Peruvian Andes. The long perianth tube is surrounded by long outer segments 7.5 cm (3 in) long whilst the flowers are white, striped green in the throat, with a powerful scent and borne four or five to a stem. It is hardy in the more favourable parts of the British Isles.

H. rotata (syn. *H. lacera*). It is a native of Florida and South Carolina, making a large bulb and bearing umbels of pure-white chalice-shaped flowers on 37.5 cm (15-in) stems. The flowers have a jonquil-like perfume.

H. speciosa. It was discovered in the mountainous regions of the West Indies in 1759 and is best given greenhouse culture for it blooms in April and where growing outdoors in the British Isles may be damaged by adverse weather.

The large white, sweetly-scented flowers are borne in umbels of five or more on 30-cm (12-in) stems.

HYMENAEA (Leguminosae—Laburnum Family)

A genus of 25 species of evergreen trees from tropical America which are very ornamental, with large white or yellow flowers and handsome foliage. They require stove-house cultivation, with a rich peaty compost, and can be increased from ripened shoot cuttings taken in spring and rooted in heat.

Species. *Hymenaea courbarli.* The Locust tree, 15 m (50 ft) in its native country, it has pale yellowish flowers with purple streaks. The bark produces a fragrant resin.

HYOSCYAMUS (Solanaceae—Nightshade Family)

A genus of 20 species of narcotic plants, native of northern Africa and Europe.

Species. *Hyoscyamus niger.* The Stinking henbane it is called by the countryman and it is a shrubby plant growing 60 cm (2 ft) high with deeply toothed leaves which, like the stems, are covered in hairs. The flowers are borne at the axils of the leaves and are bright yellow, veined with mauve, most attractive to behold but emitting a sickly fishy smell similar to the flowers of *Cotoneaster frigida.* 'The whole plant', wrote Culpeper, 'hath a very ill, sodoriferous smell'.

The plant is a product of waste ground and is a narcotic. From the seeds and leaves, the drug hyoscyamine is obtained which when used under medical super-vision is a valuable sedative, but causes paralysis if the dose is exceeded. This may have been the plant, the juice of which killed Hamlet's father.

HYPARRHENIA (Graminaceae—Grass Family)

A genus of 75 species, native of Africa and Arabia.

Species. *Hyparrhenia pista.* It is found amongst stones at the southern end of the Red Sea and along the eastern coast of Africa to Cape Province. It is a perennial grass of tufted habit, the stems terminating in spire-like racemes, each raceme surrounded by a spathaceous sheath. The spikelets are hairy and diffuse a pronounced perfume when handled.

HYPERICUM (Guttiferae—St John's Family)

The genus contains about 160 species of deciduous and (mostly) evergreen under-shrubs most of which are hardy in the British Isles. Included amongst the species is the native Common tutsan or Sweet amber with its scented flowers and leaves; also the beautiful but scentless Rose of Sharon (*H. calycinum*) which is naturalized in parts of Britain if not a native plant. Altogether, there are about 12 species native to the British Isles where they grow in woodlands and thickets. All bear brilliant-yellow flowers and have evergreen foliage. Plant them for ground cover.

Several species give off a most unpleasant musty goat-like smell when approached. This is due to minute oil glands in the leaves, which may be observed by holding a leaf to the light and which contain caproic acid. But of all herbs, the hypericum has most medicinal value. An infusion of the leaves is valuable for a bad cough and was at one time used to prevent children from bed-wetting. Gerard tells us that the oil obtained from the leaves is the best remedy for deep wounds of the flesh 'made by a venomed weapon', whilst modern medical practitioners recommend its use to treat bed sores, an ointment being prepared from the flowers and olive oil.

The plant takes its country name from John the Baptist and its association with the mystic rites of Midsummer's Eve, a celebration which goes back to pre-Christian days. The plant was also hung above the entrance to a dwelling to prevent the entry of evil spirits.

Species. *Hypericum androsaemum.* The Common tutsan or Sweet amber frequenting woodlands and shady places usually about the western side of England and Scotland. It is a most handsome plant, growing 0.9 to 1.2 m (3 to 4 ft) in height with a woody stem and leaves 7.5 cm (3 in) long. These are covered in pellucid dots which release a resinous smell when bruised. The golden flowers of five petals are most attractive, with radiating stamens formed in bunches of five. They appear in July and are followed by crimson-black fruits. It takes its old English name from the French *Tout-saine*, All-heal, for the leaves contained antiseptic properties and were used to cover open wounds.

H. elegans. A native of Siberia growing 30 cm (12 in) high, with stems which are covered with black oil glands. The blunt, lance-shaped leaves are also dotted, the whole plant emitting a powerful goat-like smell, most pronounced when wet.

Said to be named in honour of St John owing to the many uses the plant enjoyed in ancient medicine, the hypericums have red sap in their leaves and stems which was thought to be the blood of the saint.

H. hircinum. It smells so strongly of goats that it has been named the Goat-smelling St John's wort. It is native of southern Europe and forms a multi-branched shrub 1.2 m (4 ft) in height with ovate lance-shaped leaves which have the oil glands concentrated down the edges.

When brushed against, the glands release a most unpleasant smell. This species should not be confused with *H. hirsutum*, whose leaves are entirely without the oil glands and which emits no unpleasant smell.

H. perforatum. The Common or Perforated St John's wort, native of the copses and shady hedgerows of the British Isles. It is in partial shade that these plants flourish, providing valuable ground cover beneath deciduous trees. It grows 60 cm (2 ft) tall with brown stems and oblong leaves of dark green covered with transparent dots. To this plant genus the French gave the name *mille-pertuis*, 'a thousand perforations'. The petals and anthers are also covered in glandular dots, black in appearance, so that when in bloom the whole plant gives off a most unpleasant smell when handled.

H. prolificum. A native of North America where it inhabits damp situations in partial shade. Unlike most of the species, the stems are round with lance-shaped leaves covered in transparent dots which give off a smell of wet fur.

H. quadrangulum. The Square-stemmed St John's wort, which frequents moist woodlands and ditches and whose leaves are a mass of tiny perforations. The star-like flowers have the stamens bunched together, an attractive characteristic of these plants.

HYSSOPUS (Labiatae—Lavender Family)

A genus of 15 species, native of southern Europe, which had reached England by Tudor times and were used to surround beds of flowering plants and herbs. Hill, in the *Art of Gardening* (1564), wrote, 'It [marjoram] may either be sette with Isope and Time, or with winter savoury and Time, for these endure all the winter thorowe greene'. It was then known as Isope. The poet Spenser wrote of the 'Sharp Isope' as being good to heal wounds, and it was also used for strewing floors. The plant was mentioned so often in the Bible that it became known as the Holy herb, and is indeed named from the Hebrew word *Azob*, 'Holy herb'. There is an item in the fifteenth-century accounts of Adam Vynour, gardener to the Lord Bishop of Ely at his Manor of Holbourne, for 'one quart of ysop seed'.

Species. *Hyssopus aristatus*. It is a dainty aromatic plant making a neat bush only 22.5 cm (9 in) tall and bearing through summer a profusion of tiny bright-blue flower spikes. It is charming when used to edge a shrub border or path or it may even be planted on a rockery in a position of full sun.

H. officinalis. It makes a neat evergreen bush about 60 cm (2 ft) tall and bears bluish-mauve flowers in racemes, which are much frequented by bees. The flowers which are pink, white or blue, possess a rich aromatic fragrance and should be cut when fully open. Though like the lavender, the santolina and the rosemary, the hyssop is a plant to give beauty to the shrub border, it is now rarely seen, though in olden times it was widely grown for flavouring broths and stews. Both its leaves and dried flowers may be used in pot-pourris.

I

IBERIS (Candytuft)
(Cruciferae—Wallflower Family)

It is the annual forms which bear sweetly scented flowers, amongst which are *I. amara* and *I. odorata,* a native of Crete and Greece. Though the plant takes its botanical name from the Iberian Peninsula where it is found, its country name Candytuft is derived from Candia, the ancient name for Crete which has given us the lovely *I. odorata* and *I. umbellata,* though the latter has no scent; the evergreen *I. sempervirens* is also scentless.

A genus of 20 species, many having fleshy leaves whilst the flowers are borne in corymbs and were originally white. Several strains are now obtainable in rose-pink and even scarlet which are varieties of the scentless *I. umbellata.*

The annual candytuft may be given biennial treatment and sown outside in early autumn to bloom in May and June; or seed may be sown in April to continue the display from July onwards.

Species and Varieties. *Iberis amara.* Native to parts of eastern England, it varies in height from the dwarf Little Prince, which bears its white flowers at a height of 15 cm (6 in), to the Giant Hyacinth-flowered which grows 37.5 to 45 cm (15 to 18 in) tall, the flowers being produced in a spike 15 cm (6 in) long and being sweetly scented.

I. odorata. This native of the Mediterranean should be treated as a half-hardy annual and sown in spring. It grows 22.5 to 25 cm (9 to 10 in) tall with toothed leaves, and late in summer bears its powerfully scented flowers of purest white in dense racemes.

IDESIA (Flacourtiaceae—Flacourtia Family)

A genus of a single species, native of Japan where it grows to a large size.

Species. *Idesia polycarpa.* It is also known as *Flacourtia japonica* and *Polycarpa maximowiczii* and was unknown until 1866 when the Russian botanist Maximowicz found it at Yedo and learned that it was native only of the Island of Kiusiu. He named it in honour of the Dutch traveller, Ides, and that is the name by which it is known today.

Its large alternate leaves have strikingly beautiful crimson stalks and are brightest green, downy and glutinous beneath. The flowers are borne in terminal panicles at the end of the branches and are greenish-yellow with orange anthers and have a most delicious perfume which in the warm breezes is wafted far and wide. It blooms in autumn in Britain where it should be confined to the more sheltered and warmer areas. In the East, the female flowers are followed by large yellow cherry-like fruits which are used as dessert.

The Idesia must be one of the loveliest trees in cultivation, with its graceful drooping habit, the bright-green leaves with their crimson stalks and the deliciously scented flowers.

ILEX (Holly) (Aquifoliaceae—Holly Family)

A large genus of about 300 species, distributed throughout northern Europe, North and South America, and represented in Africa, Asia and Australia.

Species. *Ilex aquifolium.* It is native of the

British Isles and northern Europe, and bears in May minute sweetly scented flowers on short axillary stalks; these are followed by brilliant-scarlet berries. It makes a small pyramidal tree with smooth grey bark and has wavy dark-green leaves which are spiny-toothed but are almost without spines near the top of the tree. As many as 60 varieties are known, some with silver or gold margins, and there are some which bear yellow, white or black berries. The flowers may be male, female or bisexual, and are pollinated by insects which seek the nectar secreted at the base of the creamy-white petals.

The white wood has a fine grain and will take a hard polish. It is used for engraving and in cabinet making.

ILLICIUM (Magnoliaceae—Magnolia Family)

A genus of only six species of tender evergreen trees or shrubs, native of the warmer regions of America, and of China, India, and the islands of the Pacific. Its name means 'allurement' from the attractive fragrance and appearance of the trees. The leaves when bruised emit a powerful aromatic odour, due to the volatile oil contained in tiny pellucid vessels which are clearly visible under a microscope. The flowers are borne from the axils of the leaves and also possess a spicy odour. The fruits are most attractive being flat and star-shaped, with eight rayed carpels, similar to starfish in appearance, and they have since earliest times been exported from the Chinese province of Kuang-si. A tree of the Chinese Star anise, *Illicium anisatum*, was planted in Regent's Park, London, in 1870, the first recorded planting in Britain. This tree differs only slightly from the Japanese Star anise, *I. religiosum*. It is, however, now agreed that *I. anisatum* differs from the true Chinese Star anise which is *I. verum*. *I. religiosum* is a Chinese tree which was imported into Japan at an early date and is now naturalized there.

Species and Varieties. *Illicium floridanum.* The Florida aniseed, to be found near the Mississippi; in a sheltered garden it will attain a height of about 2.4 m (8 ft). It has tapering lance-shaped leaves with long stalks, which when bruised or rubbed between the hands leave behind a pronounced aniseed scent. The flowers, which consist of 20 or more petals, are of deepest purple-red and appear during the midsummer months, diffusing a powerful spicy odour. The fruits have 13 carpels and were illustrated in the *American Journal of Pharmacy* in May 1885.

I. griffithii. It is a native of eastern Bengal where it grows in the humid jungles of the Khansia Hills, 1,500 m (5,000 ft) above sea level. The flowers are similar to those of *I. parviflorum* but it is distinguished as a separate species by its strangely beaked carpels which number 15. Griffith found it near Mamloo, Churra, in the Khansia Hills. All parts of the plant are aromatic but do not in any way have the scent of aniseed, being similar to the scent of tarragon, though the fruit has a bitter taste.

I. majus. It is a native of the jungles of Malaya where it grows 9 m (30 ft) in height with leaves 15 cm (6 in) long. Its scented flowers are pink with large fruits of 11 or 13 carpels, the seed being almost black in colour, known as *Bunga lawang* in the bazaars of Singapore.

I. parviflorum. A species native to western Florida (near Lake George) and the hilly regions of Georgia and South Carolina and is distinguished from *I. floridanum* by the smallness of its flowers. The bark and wood have the same scent as sassafras root because of the essential oil Safrol, containing anethol and giving off a scent like cinnamon and bergamot mixed together. *I. parviflorum* grows only 90 cm (3 ft) in height and bears flowers of palest yellow.

I. religiosum. It grows 9 m (30 ft) tall in Japan and has broad leaves but all parts of the tree are fragrant. In Japan it is held in reverence, the natives calling it *Dai ui Kio* and decorating the tombs of the departed with the aromatic branches, whilst they burn the yellow bark in their homes and in Buddhist temples as incense. The Chinese call it *Mang-thsao*, the 'mad herb' for it is said to cause frenzy in humans. Its branches are clothed in smooth poisonous leaves, and during June and July, it bears its fragrant creamy-yellow flowers in dense clusters followed by scented fruits which have eight carpels like the Chinese species. In China and Japan the berries are used in cooking whilst the leaves yield an essential oil consisting of Eugenol and Shikimol and which has the powerful smell of lemon oil and nutmeg.

The Aniseed trees like a well-drained soil yet one containing some peat or leaf-mould to retain summer moisture, and in Britain they must be given a sunny situation, sheltered from cold winds.

INDIGOFERA (Leguminosae—Laburnum Family)

A large genus of deciduous and evergreen shrubs, indigenous to the East and West Indian islands and to parts of India, China and Korea. Several species bear scented flowers. A number are hardy on the western side of the British Isles and North America and they make excellent pot plants, requiring only sufficient warmth to exclude frost. They are amongst the longest-flowering of all shrubs, the long racemes being produced at the leaf axils of the continuously produced shoots. The plant thus bears bloom from June until October, the 15-cm (6-in) racemes of pea-like flowers resembling those of the laburnum, and with several species the scent is similar. They grow from 1.2 to 1.8 m (4 to 6 ft) in height and their beauty is enhanced by the grey acacia-like foliage.

Species. *Indigofera fragrans.* It makes a compact plant 1.2 m (4 ft) tall and bears magenta-purple flowers which smell strongly of vanilla.

I. gerardiana. Native of the Himalayas, it grows 1.2 m (4 ft) tall in the open but twice that height against a warm wall where its elegant foliage and scented racemes of brightest purple present a satisfying picture of great beauty.

I. incarnata alba (syn. *I. decora alba*). It is a native of China and Japan, rarely growing more than 90 cm (3 ft) tall and it makes an ideal pot plant, bearing its vanilla-scented racemes of purest white for twenty weeks or more

INOCARPUS (Leguminosae—Laburnum Family)

A genus of four species, it belongs to the same order as *Cassia fistula* and is native of the islands of Fiji and Tahiti.

Species. *Inocarpus fagiferus.* It grows by the side of streams and is known as the Tahitian chestnut. It is a handsome tree 24 m (80 ft) or more in height with leathery oblong alternative leaves having a conspicuous midrib. The minute white flowers are borne in terminal cymes and diffuse an amazingly powerful scent for so small a blossom. They are followed by edible kidney-shaped fruits which taste exactly like the fruit of the Sweet chestnut.

INULA (Compositae—Daisy Family)

A genus of about 60 species of hardy perennial plants, mostly native of Eastern Europe and the Himalayas. Included are the Elecampane and the Ploughman's spikenard, natives of the British Isles.

Species. *Inula conyza.* It grows on dry banks, and its leaves form a rosette which covers the ground some 30 cm (1 ft) across, destroying the grass beneath. A plant of the British Isles it blooms during July and August, when both the flowers and leaves emit a refreshingly aromatic scent. For its fragrance, it was named Ploughman's spikenard for all parts of the plant are aromatic, especially the roots, which in olden times were burnt upon the fire to scent a room.

I. helenium. It is native of the British Isles and grows more than 1.2 m (4 ft) tall with large leaves, hairy and pointed, like those of Comfrey and Horehound. 'It groweth in meadows that are fat and fruitful', wrote Gerard. Its bloom is like that of a double sunflower, and it is the largest of all British wild flowers.

'Elecampane, the beauteous Helen's flower' was named in honour of Helen of Troy. Like the Lungwort and Horehound it is used for coughs and chest complaints, but with this plant it is the roots that are used. When lifted they smell of ripe bananas, but as they dry take on the scent of violets. At one time they were used as a vegetable and were candied.

The plant, which is readily raised from seed, blooms during late summer and is a most handsome addition for the back of the border. It requires staking and enjoys an open, sunny position. It obtained its botanic name from a starchy property called inulin from which the sugar levulose is obtained.

I. hookeri. It grows about 60 cm (2 ft) tall with lance-shaped leaves, pointed and downy, and it blooms during September and October, a valuable addition to the border at this time. The flowers open to about 7.5 cm (3 in) across and are pale yellow, like *Primula sikkimensis* and with the same sweet, almost violet-like perfume. The flowers have the shaggy appearance as *I. oculus-Christi,* also a valuable border plant, but not scented.

IONOPSIDIUM (Cruciferae—Wallflower Family)

A genus of only two species of annual plants, native of Portugal and parts of North Africa but hardy in the British Isles. It rarely exceeds a height of 5 cm (2 in). Seed should be sown in spring as an edging to a path or in the cracks of paving-stones. It is also a valuable window box or trough garden plant.

Species. *Ionopsidium acaule.* Known as Violet cress, it is a charming little plant, bearing its tiny lilac flowers, tinted with violet, throughout summer. The flowers are borne from the leaf joints and emit a delicious honey-like perfume. It is the only scented species.

IPHEION (Amaryllidaceae—Narcissus Family)

A genus of 25 species, native of Mexico and South America, only one of which, the scented *I. uniflorum,* is in general cultivation. At various times in its history, it has been classed as *Tritelia, Milla, Brodiaea,* etc.

Species. *Ipheion uniflorum.* Native of the Mexican Sierras, it has narrow, rush-like leaves, glaucous and rough to the touch, and it blooms in spring. The flowers, borne singly, open star-shaped, having 3-pointed petals with 3 intervening petals of thick texture, like white satin flushed with lavender, and shaded green on the outside. As would be expected from a bloom of such texture, it diffuses a powerful fragrance.

The bulbs should be planted in a sunny position and in a rich, well-drained, sandy loam. *I. uniflorum* could also be included with those flowers which give off their fragrance at night, for they remain open after dark and on a calm evening scent the garden with their sweet perfume. The blooms appear for several weeks in one long succession.

IRIS (Iridaceae—Iris Family)

A genus of hardy perennials which for convenience may be divided into two main groups, those having a rhizomatous rootstock, and those which grow from a bulb.

Rhizomatous Species and Varieties. They must be considered amongst the most beautiful of all border plants, being entirely at home in the mixed border, but perhaps happier in a border to themselves. The plants require a deeply worked soil and appreciate some lime in their diet, usually given in the form of lime rubble or mortar, whilst they like a soil that is well-drained in winter. They also require a position where the summer sunshine can ripen the rhizomes, essential if they are to bear a full complement of bloom each year.

The Flag iris is an excellent town garden plant, being tolerant of deposits of soot and of a sulphur-laden atmosphere, which in no way harm the sword-like leaves. Usually, however, the plants are confined to a shady corner or to the shrubbery where the sun can rarely reach them and where the soil is devoid of nourishment, so they are never seen in the same glory that they achieve when planted in a specially prepared border to themselves.

The plants should be divided every four years as they quickly exhaust the soil and become overcrowded. The most suitable time is late July, after flowering which commences mid-May. They may also be lifted and divided in October or March, though no bloom can be expected that year. The roots may be divided into sections by cutting with a sharp knife, but each piece must have an 'eye' from which the leaves arise and from which the new plant can develop. Set the pieces 50 cm (2 ft) apart, laying them just below the surface with the fibrous roots downwards and the top of the rhizome exposed to the sun to encourage ripening.

The rhizomatous irises may be divided into three groups:

(i) The Bearded Iris, descended from *I. germanica, I. variegata, I. pallida,*

I. mesopotamica and *I. trojana*. They have a creeping rootstock from which arise dark-green, sword-like leaves 45 cm (1½ ft) long, and an erect scape with several flowers attached at the end. The flowers are like large orchids in shape and colour and have 'fall' petals which are bearded or crested.

(ii) The Beardless Iris. Into this group come the difficult *I. unguicularis*, the winter-flowering iris, and several other species whose large, handsome blooms are free of any beard.

(iii) The Cushion or Oncocyclus Iris. Here the bud appears at the end of a short stolon, whilst the scape bears only a single flower, usually of great size and beauty. The Regelia irises of this section bear more than one flower to a scape. The plants like a well-drained, gritty soil and shallow planting. The flowers are not scented.

BEARDED IRISES. *I. biliottii*. This handsome iris is a native of Asia Minor growing 90 cm (3 ft) tall and with leaves 60 cm (2 ft) in length. The standards are purple-blue with reddish-purple falls, veined with black and with a white beard tipped with gold. The bloom carries a rich fruity perfume.

I. germanica. The Common Flag or German iris is a native of central Europe, and the oldest iris to be given garden cultivation. It is believed to have been grown in the ninth century in the monastery garden of Reichenau by its Abbot, Walfred Strabo. The plant is one of the hardiest and toughest in cultivation, well nigh indestructible but, though by its rugged constitution it has persisted through the years, it received little attention from breeders until the present century. Though the modern flag irises are often classed as being the offspring of *I. germanica*, this species has in fact played little part in their breeding in comparison with the scented *I. pallida*. Under this heading, however, may be listed a number of varieties of outstanding beauty and bearing flowers with the rich perfume of *I. pallida*:

ALINE. An older variety but one of great beauty, being a pure azure-blue self and carrying a more powerful perfume than any other variety, perhaps obtaining its scent from *I. pallida* which bears flowers of similar colouring. 90 cm (3 ft).

BLACK FOREST. One of the darkest of all irises, the large, handsome blooms being purple-black, even to the beard. It is sweetly scented and free-flowering. 60 cm (2 ft).

BLUE SHIMMER. A most handsome iris, bearing a large crisp white flower feathered with blue and sweetly scented. 90 cm (3 ft).

CHRISTABEL. One of the new irises with copper-coloured blooms that is scented. It is an iris of exquisite texture with coppery-purple fall petals and it blooms with freedom. 90 cm (3 ft).

CLEO. Described by its raiser as chartreuse-green in colour, it is a most interesting iris in any company, and in addition it has the scent of orange-blossom. 90 cm (3 ft).

EBONY QUEEN. Like a number of the darker-coloured irises, this one is also deliciously scented. The blue-black flowers have great substance and come into bloom before all others. 90 cm (3 ft).

FASCINATION. A gorgeous iris to plant near those of darkest colouring for its flowers are a lovely dusky lilac-pink with a sweet perfume. 1.2 m (4 ft).

HARIETTE HALLOWAY. A new iris of outstanding form, the ruffled flowers of great substance being a lovely medium blue with a powerful rich perfume. 90 cm (3 ft).

INSPIRATION. Though introduced in 1937 no iris bears a flower of the same rosy-cerise colouring and none has a sweeter fragrance. 1.5 m (3½ ft).

IVORY GLEAM. The huge refined blooms are of solid ivory with touches of gold at the edges to the falls and diffusing a perfume like lily of the valley. 90 cm (3 ft).

LAGOS. Valuable in that, with Coastal Command, it is the latest iris to bloom, its large cream and gold flowers with their soft sweet perfume opening about mid-June to extend the season by several weeks.

MAGGADAN. One of the most unusual and sweetly scented varieties. The standards are slate-blue, the ivory-white falls being flushed with slate. 1.05 m (3½ ft).

MANYUSA. One of the outstanding

pink irises, the flowers with their exquisitely ruffled petals are of soft orchid-pink with a sweet orange perfume. 90 cm (3 ft).

MATTIE GATES. A most attractive variety and, surprisingly, one of the few yellows with a pronounced perfume. The standards are of soft, almost primrose yellow with the falls of brightest gold, blazoned with white. 90 cm (3 ft).

MOONBEAM. With Mattie Gates, the most richly scented of all the yellow irises, the large blooms of clear sulphur-yellow having the scent of the lily of the valley. A variety for the front of the border. 60 cm (2 ft).

RADIANT. This fine iris is a valuable addition to the front of any border, for its bright apricot-orange standards and terracotta falls ensure that it receives the attention it deserves. In addition, it is free-flowering and richly scented. 75 cm (2½ ft).

ROSE VIOLET. A front of the border bicolour with rose-pink standards and violet falls, the whole being a bloom of great substance. Valuable for its lateness of flowering and its rich gardenia scent. 75 cm (2½ ft).

SHOT SILK. The blooms are a lovely chestnut-pink with a gold blaze on the falls. It carries a rich orange perfume. 90 cm (3 ft).

SUNBEAM. A valuable canary-yellow self for the front of a border, bearing flowers of great substance and with a soft, sweet perfume. 60 cm (2 ft).

WHITE CITY. A back-row iris bearing powerfully scented pure-white blooms of great substance. 120 cm (4 ft).

ZWANENBURG. More than half a century old, it still commands attention wherever it is seen. It is one of the earliest to bloom whilst its large flowers are an interesting blend of old gold, silver, bronze and green, with a delicious scent. 60 cm (2ft).

A series of dwarf bearded irises has been introduced from America during the past 25 years. Unfortunately, few of them are scented, but one which carries a pronounced sweet perfume was one of the earliest to be raised, called Mauve Mist. It grows only 20 to 22 cm (8 to 9 in) tall and

bears attractively shaped flowers of a lovely misty lavender-mauve.

I. kashmiriana. A native of Afghanistan, it has sword-like leaves 5 cm (2 in) wide and blooms in June, bearing 3 flowers to each scape. The blooms are creamy-white, with cream fall petals which are beautifully veined with green and have a yellow beard. It is very richly scented of orange.

I. pallida. A flag iris similar to *I. germanica*, which has had a considerable influence on the raising of the modern hybrid varieties. It is native of southern Europe and was introduced into England during Elizabethan times. Gerard mentions that it grew in his garden in Holborn with leaves much broader than any other [iris] and . . . with fair large flowers of a light blue or (as we term it) a watchet colour'. And he adds, 'the flowers do smell exceeding sweete, much like the orange flower'. To some, the perfume is closer to vanilla; to others, it is like civet.

The plant forms a fan of sword-shaped leaves from which arise the flower stems some 90 cm (3 ft) in length; flowering is May to June. The colour of the flowers varies from slaty-lilac through sky-blue to lilac-purple, the falls having a bright-yellow beard and being veined with lilac on a white ground. The flowers really do emit a most penetrating orange perfume.

I. plicata. It grows 90 cm (3 ft) tall, and during June and July bears clusters of showy scented flowers. The standards are white, edged with blue, whilst the falls are also white but veined with lilac at the edges.

I. sambucina. The Elder-scented iris of south-eastern Europe and Asia Minor, bearing tufts of glaucous leaves 37 cm (15 in) long and, in May, purple flowers on a 60-cm (2-ft) stem. The flowers have a yellow standard and beards.

BEARDLESS IRISES. *I. florentina.* The Florentine iris, a native of southern Europe, which forms the heraldic arms of the city of Florence. The flower is white, shaded with violet, whilst the variety *albicans* (now a separate species) is of purest white. The Florentine iris is one of the oldest plants in cultivation. It was introduced into Egypt in 1500 B.C. by Thutmosis III, and on the walls of his temple at Karnak the flowers are depicted exactly as they appear today. Gerard tells us that from its violet-scented root 'sweet waters, sweet powders, and such like are made'. The roots, when dry, possess the fragrance of the violet, and this becomes more pronounced as they wither. In medieval times the roots were powdered (orris-powder), to be placed amongst clothes and linen, and to perfume the hair. Pieces of root when placed upon glowing embers scent a large room and were burnt to clear away the musty smell of a stone floor.

Tieman and Kruger were the first to discover that the odorous principle in orris-root, which gives the same scent as that given off by the violet, is due to a ketone which they named irone. This is freely soluble in alcohol and is used in perfumery. The scent of orris-root is compound, however, and not so pure as that of the violet. Orris-root is one of the chief ingredients of the Italian perfume frangipani, an alcoholic extraction of which is the most enduring of all known perfumes.

I. foetidissima. This is named by countrymen the Stinking iris, Gladdon or Gladwyn, or Roast-beef plant, for the smell of its leaves is thought to resemble that of roast beef. It has not nearly so unpleasant a smell as its reputation has led us to believe, and it is a most handsome plant. It grows 90 cm (3 ft) in height with dark-green, sword-shaped leaves, narrower than those of the yellow water iris, whilst there is a form with leaves striped with white. The flowers, borne in May and June on flattened stems, are purple and are followed in autumn by seed capsules which open when ripe to reveal seeds of brilliant orange-red. The Foetid Gladwyn is native of the British Isles, flourishing by lake and river, and in the garden it enjoys partial shade and a moist soil. The roots emit the same smell of roast beef as do the leaves.

I. graminea. A beardless iris, native of central Europe which grows about 30 cm (1 ft) tall, though the leaves extend above the flower stems. The flowers appear in May with standards of lilac-plum colouring, whilst the fall petals are white, veined with purple-blue. The flowers emit the satisfying scent of ripe plums.

I. pseudacorus. This is the Yellow or Water iris growing by the side of rivers and in marshlands throughout the British

Isles and France, whose king Louis VII took the flower as his blazon during the Crusades and gave it his name, 'flower of Louis'. It is the yellow 'vagabond flag' of Shakespeare's *Antony and Cleopatra* and it became the national symbol of medieval France, in heraldic language: 'Azure powdered with fleurs-de-lis or'. In 1339 when Edward III made claim to the throne of France and began hostilities against Philip VI (Philip of Valois), he took for his arms the three Plantagenet lions and the fleur-de-lis of France.

It is a delightful plant with a scented flower some 7 cm (3 in) across, of a soft golden-yellow. The flowers are produced in succession from May until August amidst sword-like leaves. From the dried rhizomatous roots, a delicately scented essential oil is obtained which at one time was used to adulterate oil of *Acorus calamus.*

I. ruthenica. Native of eastern Europe, Siberia and China, it is a most attractive little iris, at its best in the alpine garden, for it grows no more than 7 to 15 cm (3 to 6 in) tall. It blooms if in a sunny position, before the March winds have ceased to blow cold, the scented flowers, in their perfume like those of *I. reticulata,* appearing amongst a neat tuft of grass-like leaves. The blooms are lilac-purple, the falls being dotted and veined with white but there is some colour variation. Flowering may continue until May.

I. kaempferi. The Japanese water iris, which has the largest flowers of the genus. It grows 60 cm (2 ft) in height with a solid stem and pale-green sword-like leaves, and in its natural habitat grows in moist, peaty soil partly submerged by water. It blooms during June and July, the flowers measuring 15 cm (6 in) across, with standards of pale blue and fall petals of purple-blue, blotched with yellow. The flowers have a sweet, violet fragrance. The Enfield Hybrids strain embrace both single and double forms, whilst *I. laevigata* bears flowers of brilliant violet-blue. There is also a white form of the latter, *alba,* and another, *albo-purpurea,* the flowers being mottled all over with purple and white. Both are sweetly scented.

I. unguicularis (syn. *I. stylosa*). The Winter-flowering iris, it is a beardless Algerian iris which in favourable districts comes into bloom early in the year, and elsewhere during February, continuing until the beginning of April. It is one of the most beautiful of all plants, bearing its gorgeous lilac-blue flowers, streaked with yellow, in long succession amidst tufts of bright-green leaves which terminate above them as if providing the flowers with protection from winter's severest winds.

The plants grow from a thin rhizome which should be planted only just beneath the surface of the soil. They in no way tolerate wet, and should be planted in dry soil, preferably of poor quality, at the foot of a wall facing south. They benefit from the protection provided by the overhanging eaves of a house, whilst plenty of lime rubble and drainage material should be incorporated at planting time.

I. unguicularis is always at its best in the winter following a long dry summer and autumn to ripen the rhizomes, after which the blooms appear in profusion, diffusing their fragrance, like that of the double primrose Marie Crousse, on the bleakest of days.

CUSHION OR ONCOCYCLUS IRISES.

I. barnumae. An Oncocyclus iris from the hills of Kurdistan, with a slender, rhizomatous rootstock, and linear leaves. The flowers are dull wine-purple, with a beard of yellow on the standards, which emit the delicious, sweet, lemony scent of lily of the valley.

Bulbous Species and Varieties. The bulbous irises may be divided into three main sub-sections: the Reticulata group, the Xiphium group, and the Juno group. There are species in each section which bear scented flowers amongst the most deliciously fragrant of those having a violet perfume.

RETICULATA GROUP.

The bulbs require planting 7 cm (3 in) deep in a well-drained soil containing some lime rubble, and in a sunny, sheltered position. They are quite hardy in the British Isles, but come early into bloom and the flowers do not appreciate cold winds. As with almost all members of the iris family, the bulbs require an abundance of summer sunshine in which to ripen. The bulbs should, therefore, be planted on a sunny bank or beneath a wall in full sun where,

on a calm day, the gorgeously coloured flowers will emit a perfume equal to that given off by a bed of Princess of Wales violets. Half a dozen bulbs planted to a pot and brought into bloom indoors will, during February, scent a large room. They are perhaps the loveliest and most satisfying of all indoor bulbs and all flowers of the group emit the violet perfume, the same scent that is present in the root of *I. florentina,* orris-root.

Iris bakeriana. Native of Iraq and Persia, it is the first of this section to bloom. Indoors it will open its flowers early in the year, followed by those outdoors which bloom towards the end of February. The standards are translucent ultramarine, shot with purple, whilst the falls of deepest violet terminate in a snow-white blotch, dotted with black and to a point of almost purple-black. The flowers are slightly smaller than those of *I. reticulata,* but grow to a similar height of 15 cm (6 in) and, if anything, carry a more powerful perfume.

I. danfordiae. A native of the Taurus Mountains of Turkey, it comes into bloom almost at the same time as *I. bakeriana,* bearing its beautiful golden flowers speckled with brown on a stem only 7 cm (3 in) tall, so they appear almost to sit on the soil. After flowering, the bulb dies back, but forms new bulbils from the base which may take a year or more to grow to flowering size. The perfume of the flowers is softly sweet.

I. histrioides. Native of Persia and Iraq, it is a superb plant of vigorous constitution and, like *I. danfordiae* which it follows into bloom, it bears an almost stemless flower. The form *major,* introduced by the Dutch firm of Van Tubergen, is the finest, for the blooms of bright ultramarine, spotted with black and crested with gold, appear before the leaves and measure 10 cm (4 in) across. The blooms appear in February, unmindful of the weather and emit a soft, sweet perfume.

I. kolpakowskiana. This native of Turkestan was described by John Weathers, in his *Practical Guide to Garden Plants* as flowering in March and being fragrant, but it seems unlikely that the plant is now in cultivation. The standards are lilac-mauve; the lance-shaped falls are a combination of bright purple and yellow.

I. reticulata. It grows wild about the hillsides of southern Russia and as far south and east as Persia. It is one of the most precious jewels of the winter garden, completely hardy in the British Isles and coming into bloom during the first days of March. It is known as the 'netted' iris, so called for the net-like markings of the bulbs, and it bears flowers of deep velvety purple-red with an orange splash on the falls. Once established, it spreads rapidly by seeding and by bulblets, making a display of enormous richness when the spring sun shines down on the blooms which have a pronounced violet perfume.

There are a number of lovely varieties, bearing their flowers on 15-cm (6-in) stems of which Cantab, is most arresting with its flowers of brilliant Cambridge blue. Harmony and Joyce, deep pansy-blue with gold or orange blotches on the falls, are equally fine but it is the reddish-purple flowering varieties that are most fragrant. Of these, Violet Beauty and Wentworth, purple-blue, are outstanding both as to colour and perfume whilst Springtime with mid-blue standards and falls of violet-blue chequered with white, and Clairette, with pale-blue standards and violet fall petals, are delightfully attractive and deliciously scented. Royal Blue and J. S. Dijt, with its flowers of reddish-purple, are also violet scented.

I. vartani. This species blossomed in the hilly pastures around Nazareth when Christ walked the earth, and there it still grows, bearing at Christmastime flowers of lavender-grey on a short, slender stem and diffusing the scent of almonds. It is rarely found in Britain, but its white form, *alba*, is sometimes to be seen in alpine houses or about a sunny rock garden and it is equally fragrant.

XIPHIUM GROUP. The group takes its name from *I. xiphium*, the Spanish iris which, together with each of the other species, is native of the Iberian Peninsula and of north-western Africa.

Neither the English irises, developed from *I. xiphioides*, nor the Dutch irises which have *I. tingitana* and *I. xiphium* for parents, bear scented flowers, but the Spanish Irises, in bloom about a fortnight later, which are varieties of *I. xiphium* and possibly *I. juncea*, are sweetly scented.

They should be planted 10 cm (4 in) apart and 7 cm (3 in) deep in October and will bloom the following June, bearing their flowers on stems 60 cm (2 ft) in length.

I. juncea. A native of north-western Africa and southern Spain, it has narrow, rush-like leaves and in July bears its golden-yellow, scented flowers with their fiddle-shaped falls, on a 30 cm (12 in) stem. It is rare in cultivation, but may have passed on its intense perfume to the Spanish irises.

I. xiphium. Widely dispersed about Spain and Portugal and along the coast of North Africa, its flowers are usually deep purple or occasionally golden-yellow, some 10 to 12 cm (4 to 5 in) across and borne on a 60-cm (2-ft) stem. They have some fragrance but not so pronounced as in *I. juncea.* A number of its varieties, however, have a sweet violet fragrance which is especially noticeable in King of the Blues, the finest of all the tall bulbous irises, which bears flowers of deepest blue with a yellow blotch on the falls. Equally strongly scented is Frederika, which provides a charming contrast with its blooms of purest white, blotched with yellow on the falls. It is most sweetly scented. Yellow Pearl, a pale-yellow self, is also scented.

JUNO GROUP. The Juno irises are to be found around the ancient city of Bokhara, from where come the magnificent rugs and carpets, their makers possibly being inspired by the exquisite colourings of these irises which are so exacting in their requirements. They hav fleshy roots which grow from the base of the bulb and are readily damaged in handling and by excessive moisture. They require long hours of sunshine throughout summer to build up a bulb capable of flowering the following year. They are thus the most difficult of all irises to grow well in Britain. Perhaps the easiest is *I. persica* which is also the loveliest and most fragrant.

I. persica. It is the Persian iris and was described in the *Paradisus.* It also has the honour of being the first plant to be featured in the *Botanical Magazine* of 1787. The bulbs are about as large as a bantam's egg, from which arise in March almost stemless flowers some 7 cm (3 in) across. The waved fall petals are bluish-green with a golden keel, in front of which are spots of violet-black. *Purpurea* bears flowers of richest purple, whilst *isaacsonii* has cream-coloured flowers tinted with green and with violet veins. It is characterized by its sickle-like leaves. Each has the pronounced violet perfume of *I. reticulata*.

I. sindjarensis. A Juno iris of the Djebel Sindjar Mountains, with a large bulb and fleshy roots which supply the plant with food and moisture whilst in growth. The leaves are sheathing at the base, and from the axils are borne in March flowers of softest blue with a creamy-white crest and with the scent of vanilla.

ITEA (Saxifragaceae—Rockfoil Family)

A genus of evergreen or deciduous trees or shrubs numbering five or six species which flourish in partial shade and in a sandy soil. They are native of the eastern United States and south-eastern Asia. Propagation is from cuttings of the half-ripened wood which will root readily in a sandy compost.

Species. *Itea ilicifolia.* Native of China and the eastern United States, it has glossy, evergreen serrated leaves which, like those of the Escallonia, are resinous. It makes a compact shrub 2.1 to 2.4 m (7 to 8 ft) in height and is hardy in Europe in all but the most exposed gardens. It bears its elegant drooping sprays of catkin-like scented greenish-white flowers during July and August and is altogether a most valuable shrub for a shady garden.

I. virginica. Native of Virginia, it is a most attractive shrub with deep-green serrated leaves which are deciduous but which turn to crimson in autumn before they fall. The tiny white flowers, like those of privet, are sweetly scented and long-lasting and are produced in horizontal sprays from June until September. They are most attractive displayed against the dark foliage.

The plant is valuable for pot culture, flowering in a cool greenhouse in spring.

IXIA (Iridaceae—Iris Family)

Known as the African corn lily, this genus of half-hardy corm-producing plants may be grown outdoors in Britain or in pots, being given the same culture as freesias. Outdoor ixias should be confined to southern England and to the western seaboard of Scotland and Ireland where they should also be given winter protection by covering the corms, after growth dies down, with a peat and sand mixture. They bear their blooms on wiry stems about 45 cm (18 in) long and are ideal for cutting, being long-lasting in water.

Ixias require a light, well-drained soil and an open sunny situation for they open only when the sun shines upon them. The corms are planted in early April, 7.5 cm (3 in) deep and 7.5 cm apart, placing them on a layer of sand to assist drainage. They bloom in June and though the orange, scarlet and pale-blue varieties have little or no perfume, those bearing white and yellow flowers are highly fragrant. The first species reached Britain towards the end of the eighteenth century from the Cape of Good Hope.

Species. *Ixia gigantea alba.* It grows to a height of 50 cm (20 in) and bears flowers of ivory-white enhanced by the blue-black base and carrying a sweet perfume.

I. odorata. Not as tall-growing as *I. gigantea,* its clear primrose-yellow flowers have a pronounced cloying perfume.

IXORA (Rubiaceae—Bedstraw Family)

A genus of 400 species of evergreen shrubs or small trees, native of Indonesia, Madagascar and southern India, including Ceylon, which require conditions of extreme warmth to grow healthily and to flower in the British Isles and northern Europe. A minimum winter temperature of 13°C (55°F) is necessary, and provided the atmosphere of the greenhouse is kept to a high degree of humidity they will withstand a temperature of 39°C (100°F) during summer. Under these conditions, pot plants will remain free-flowering for upwards of twenty years, bearing their flowering trusses in profusion, which they begin to do after only eighteen months in the pots. Those bearing red or orange flowers e.g. *Ixora amboinica* and *I. javanica,* which are pollinated by humming-birds, are scentless, but the white-flowered *I. alba* and *I. odorata* have delicious fragrance. A very peaty compost containing some sand is most suitable, and increase is by cuttings of ripened shoots 7 cm (3 in) long, in spring, in a temperature of about 27°C (80°F).

Species. *Ixora alba.* A native of southern India, it bears pure-white flowers which are most handsome against the dark evergreen foliage, whilst they are sweetly scented.

I. odorata. A native of Madagascar, it bears cream-coloured flowers tinted with pink, which are powerfully fragrant.

J

JAMESIA (Saxifragaceae—Rockfoil Family)

A genus of a single species native of North America where it makes a small erect shrub 1.5 to 1.8 m (5 to 6 ft) tall.

Species. *Jamesia americana.* It is deciduous, its small grey-green leaves being saw-edged, and in May and June bears panicles of white flowers at the end of the shoots. The flowers have a faint but definite honey scent. The plant likes a well-drained soil and a sunny position; it is increased by seed or cuttings taken in summer, using ripened shoots, placed in a sandy compost.

JASMINUM (Oleaceae—Olive Tree Family)

A genus of about 200 species of erect or climbing shrubs with opposite leaves, bearing their flowers from the tips of the branches or in forked cymes. They are mostly native of southern Europe and Asia. The jasmines are amongst the loveliest of all plants for covering a wall or trellis. They do not achieve the same vigour as wistaria and clematis, but with their dark leaves and glossy green stems, the delicate beauty of the flowers and their lilac perfume, together with their hardiness, and ease of cultivation, they stand supreme.

The Arabic name for the plant is *Ysmyn* whilst the Persian is *Jasemin*, and the Chinese, *Yeh-Lsi-Ming*, changing but little in the English language. It is likely that the fragrant White jasmine, *Jasminum officinale*, had reached Britain and northern Europe from Persia and the Near East early in Tudor times. Certainly Gerard and, later, Parkinson and Ben Jonson mention it as a plant in common use for covering arbours.

From the flowers of *J. sambac* and the White jasmine, the perfume known as oil of jasmine is obtained, its perfume being due to the presence of benzoin compounds lightened by a fruit-scented substance. The ancients captured the evanescent odour of the blossoms by means of *enfleurage*, embedding the fresh flowers in fat from which they made odoriferous ointments. Thomas Hanmer in *The Garden Book* (1659) wrote of the Arabian jasmine with: 'white flowers, extraordinary sweet . . . as partaking both of the scent of the Orange and Jasmyn flowers'.

The species of evergreen and deciduous shrubs are all indigenous to the countries of the East from Egypt and Persia to central China, though one, *J. azoricum*, is native of the Azores whilst *J. odoratissimum* is found in its natural state only in Madeira. Many are completely hardy in North America and northern Europe and are successful in ordinary soil whilst, with their small glossy leaves, like those of the privet and other plants of the family, they are tolerant of town garden conditions. They are readily increased from cuttings of half-ripened wood, removed in August and rooted under glass. Any pruning necessary should be done in April after flowering.

Species and Varieties. *Jasminum azoricum.* A twining species, vigorous and evergreen, but in Britain is suitable only for the mildest localities in which it will bloom almost throughout the year. The flowers are white and heavily scented.

J. beesianum. It rarely exceeds a height of 1.8 cm (6 ft) but may be planted against a low wall. It makes a slender plant and blooms during June and July, its small, deep, rosy-red flowers having a powerful spicy scent.

J. humile glabrum. Native of Nepal, it is a plant of vigorous habit growing 2.4 cm (8 ft) in height, and from May until August bears clusters of slightly scented yellow flowers.

J. nudiflorum. Native of northern China where it is called *Ying Ch'un (Welcomer of Spring)*, it is one of the loveliest plants in cultivation with bright-green polished stems which it sends out to a distance of 3.5 to 4.5 m (12 to 15 ft). The leaves are small and narrow, whilst the tubular blooms of bright golden-yellow are most striking against the stems. The plant comes into bloom in November and continues uninterrupted, whatever the weather, until winter has ended, the blooms having a delicate mossy perfume.

J. odoratissimum. Native of Madeira, it is suitable only for the mildest parts of Britain where it will bear its primrose-yellow flowers in threes from the tips of the branches. The flowers have a heavy sweet perfume.

J. officinale. The Common white jasmine of Tudor gardens, which grows wild from Persia to Kashmir and across northern India to Szechwan, a strong-growing twining plant which is evergreen in all but the coldest localities of the British Isles. It is a plant now rarely found though with its deliciously scented blossoms, borne from June until October, it is a charming companion for the Winter jasmine which blooms from early November to late March, and *J. revolutum* which comes into bloom as the Winter jasmine is ending.

J. officinale reaches a height of 3 to 3.5 m (10 to 12 ft), and bears its glistening, white, funnel-shaped flowers in elegant sprays, which are most beautiful against the dark-green leaves. The variety *affine* has larger flowers, tinted with rose, whilst *aureo-variegatum* has cream-coloured variegations on the leaves and bears ivory-white flowers. The perfume of the flowers is amongst the most powerful of all scents, difficult to extract and to imitate. The associated species, *grandiflorum*, is grown in large numbers near Grasse and the scent is extracted by *enfleurage*.

J. polyanthum. A native of India closely related to *J. officinale,* it is evergreen and

suited only to the milder localities of the British Isles where, during summer and autumn, it bears powerfully scented white flowers, flushed with pink on the outside and distinguished by its paniculate inflorescences.

J. revolutum. Native of northern India it is a delightful plant, semi-evergreen in character, and it blooms from May until early November, its sweetly scented yellow flowers having rolled back petals. It attains a height of about 2.4 m (8 ft) and should be confined to western Britain.

J. stephanense. It is a hybrid of *J. beesianum* and *J. officinale affine*, with the latter's vigour, and bearing pink flowers similar to those of *J. beesianum*, with a powerful perfume. It is a deciduous hybrid, hardy in all but the most exposed gardens, and it blooms from June until October.

JONESIA (Leguminosae—Laburnum Family)

A small genus of evergreen plants, indigenous to India and Burma, one of which, *J. asoca*, bears highly scented flowers with which Hindu women decorate their hair on festive occasions. The plants are suitable only for indoor culture in the British Isles and as they require stove conditions and grow into small trees, they require specialist treatment and are thus rarely seen.

Species. *Jonesia asoca.* It is the finest of all the species and is one of the few plants to bear orange-scarlet flowers which are powerfully scented. The leaves are large and glossy whilst the blooms are borne in corymbs similar to those of the hawthorn and are about the same size, being of deep rusty orange-red colouring. They are a superb sight in their native land, diffusing their perfume for miles around.

JUGLANS (Walnut) (Juglandaceae—Walnut Tree Family)

A genus of eight species having resinous bark and leaves. In many an old garden is to be found a walnut tree, planted not for its fruit but for the resinous quality of its pinnate leaves which are believed to keep away flies during summer. The scent of the leaves when bruised is most pleasant, for though resinous it has a sweetness not usually present in other leaves of a similar nature, but resembling that of the Balsam poplars. The leaves of the Common walnut consist of nine oblong leaflets of grey-green tinged with red and the fruits (nuts), familiar to all, are really plums covered with green husks; the fingers are stained black when the husk is removed, to reveal a wrinkled bony shell containing the edible nut which is opened by two valves.

Walnut oil was and still is used as a hair darkener, whilst it was valued by the master painters of old for it dries slowly, thus allowing them ample time to blend their colours.

To ensure pollination two or three trees should be grown near each other and as the roots resent disturbance they should be planted as young as possible. Walnuts require a heavy, moist soil. The trees may come into bearing after ten years but may take longer. With their ornamental and aromatic foliage they may, however, be considered worthy of planting for this alone until the nuts appear.

Species. *Juglans nigra.* The Black walnut of America with downy tapering leaflets and husks like those of the Horse-chestnut.

J. regia. The Common walnut and a native of Persia, it is completely hardy in Britain making a large spreading tree with beautifully silvered bark when young. Parkinson tells us that the walnut was usually confined to planting in a courtyard on account of its enormous spread and the shade that it gave. He mentions that the Dutch botanist, Clusius, reported having seen at a banquet 'a long walnut differing in form and tenderness of shell'. This would be the variety *bartriana* which has larger nuts than the common form.

JUNCUS (Juncaceae—Rush Family)

A genus of 300 species of marshland herbs, distributed over the Near East, developing one leafy shoot each year which is cylindrical, sometimes reduced to a sheath. The flowers, which are pollinated by wind, are borne in terminal heads and are not scented. *Juncus arabicus*, the Arabian rush, however, has pungent stems which release an incense-like perfume when bruised.

Species. *Juncus arabicus* (syn. *J. maritimus*, var. *arabicus*). It is to be found in marshland along the Nile Banks, about the shores of the Red Sea and into the Sudan, making a densely tufted rush growing some 1.2 m (4 ft) tall with pungent stems which release their fragrance when crushed.

J. punctorius. It is found in Sinai, south of the El-Tih desert and in parts of Cape Province, usually near wells or in permanently wet places. It grows 90 cm (3 ft) tall, the flowering stem being the cylindrical stem-like leaf situated half way up. It is hollow inside and emits a delicious balsamic perfume when bruised.

JUNIPERUS (Cupressaceae—Cypress Family)

A genus of about 60 evergreen species with pungent foliage. Pencil-thin of habit, the junipers may be used almost anywhere about the garden, being planted in small groups and taking up little space. Two species especially, *J. communis* and *J. thurifera*, emit a powerful fragrance from the wood and foliage but thrive only in a heavy soil which is well-drained in winter. The fleshy berries (really cones of pea size) are sweet and balsamic, and are used to flavour gin. The wood, when burnt, gives off the same pleasant aroma and in the *Anatomy of Melancholy*, Robert Burton wrote that 'it is in great request with us at Oxford, to sweeten our chambers'. In Scotland, it is used to impart its peculiar flavour to smoked ham.

The tree has attractive red bark which flakes off, like that of the yew, whilst its awl-shaped leaves are borne in whorls of three. Like the fleshy pea-like berries, the foliage is extremely pungent, leaving a pleasingly resinous smell on the hands when pressed. So powerful is the fragrance of all parts of the tree that the early peoples of the Northern Hemisphere offered it up as a sacrifice to their gods, and with branches of the oak which had been struck by lightning, juniper branches were placed outside the home to prevent the entry of witches. So refreshing is the foliage that in Evelyn's time, juniper trees were trained to form an arbour or bower beneath which one could sit and become invigorated by the sweet resinous smell. Spoons and forks were made from its wood, to impart their perfume to the food. The tiny flowers, borne in spring, are also strongly fragrant.

Oil of juniper obtained from the berries consists chiefly of pinene and has the aromatic and pungent smell of the pine woods. An oil is also obtained by the French from the distillation of the wood of *J. macrocarpa*, the Large-berried juniper of the Mediterranean.

Species and Varieties. *Juniperus communis.* The Common juniper of which *J. hibernica,* the Irish juniper, is the best-known variety. It makes a tall, upright tree of columnar habit, its glaucous foliage having a silvery hue and, like the black berries, it is most resinous. The wood is like that of the cypress, being yellow and very fragrant.

J. sabina. Unlike most of the junipers it is a tree of almost bush-like branching habit and suitable to plant at the front of a small group of conifers or in the shrubbery. With its small pointed leaves it makes an efficient hedge, whilst the creeping or prostrate form will cover an unsightly bank and is evergreen. The form *pfitzeriana glauca* has silver-grey foliage whilst *aurea* has foliage as if splashed with gold. When brushed against they give off a powerful pungent smell.

J. thurifera. It is known as the Spanish Frankincense juniper on account of the fragrance of its foliage and wood which may be likened to the sweet-smelling gum known as olibanum, the frankincense of old. It forms a slender pyramid, clothed in pale glaucous green foliage.

J. virginiana. The Red cedar of commerce which is widely distributed throughout the United States. It is a tree of pyramidal habit, the branches bending down low, and from its fragrant wood pencils are made and 'Cedar' oil is extracted. The small branchlets are covered with scaly leaves which are deep green whilst those of the variety *glauca* are blue covered with silver, hence its name of the Silver cedar.

Another lovely form is *Burkii,* Burk's Red cedar, its grey-green foliage turning bronzy-purple in winter, whilst *tripartita* makes a widely spreading bush with attractive awl-shaped leaves of glaucous green.

K

KADSURA (Magnoliaceae—Magnolia Family)

A small genus of climbing shrubs, native of China, Japan and South-east Asia. They are closely related to the Schizandras but are fully evergreen.

Species. *Kadsura japonica.* A native of Japan and Formosa, with small glossy oval leaves which turn crimson in autumn whilst the small ivory-white flowers, borne throughout summer, emit a soft sweet perfume and are followed by scarlet berries.

KYDIA (Malvaceae—Mallow Family)

A genus of three species, named after Colonel Robert Kyd, founder of the Indian Botanic Gardens at Calcutta.

Species. *Kydia calycina.* It makes a small tree and is distributed throughout India and Burma where the bark, abounding in resinous gum, is used to clarify sugar. It has beautiful heart-shaped leaves which have stalks 5 cm (2 in) long, and the flowers are borne in large panicles during September and October. From the large green calyx the reversely heart-shaped greenish-white petals appear and extend well beyond the calyx, whilst the filaments divide into five spreading branches, each carrying three yellow stalkless anthers. The blooms present a picture of remarkable beauty and are delicately scented.

The plants require stove conditions for cultivation and can be propagated by cuttings of semi-ripened shoots in heat, under a hand light.

L

LABURNUM (Leguminosae—Laburnum Family)

A genus of three species, native of southern Europe, with *L. alpinum* native of Scotland. They are small trees with digitately 3-foliolate leaves and bear their flowers in terminal racemes. Of several fine hybrids, none is lovelier than *Laburnum vossii*, its long racemes of golden freesia-scented flowers enhanced by its shining green bark. Its fragrance, in the evening, scents the whole garden and is sweet and refreshing.

The laburnum is one of the most useful of all trees, for it flourishes in partial shade and in poor, shallow limestone soils. Against a background of dark cypress trees the golden wistaria-like racemes produce a most charming effect, like shafts of brilliant sunlight, and their perfume is quite delicious. The tiny individual flowers are like those of the wild vetch and of the broom, the pea and lupin, and indeed they are all members of the same family, bearing long pods of large pea-like seeds which in laburnum are poisonous. Pliny said that bees will not visit the blossom, which is correct.

The laburnum grew in Gerard's Holborn garden where it was known as the Peascod tree, for its seed-pods are shaped like those of the pea. Its wood, like green ebony, was used for making musical instruments and Matthiolus mentions that (with yew) it made the best bows.

Species. *Laburnum alpinum.* Growing 4.5 m (15 ft) in height, it is known as the Scottish laburnum for it was discovered in the Highlands. It bears long, thin racemes and is valuable in that it is late-flowering, being at its best in July, its deeply-yellow flowers borne in drooping clusters.

L. vossii. By far the best of the laburnums and the most fragrant, its enormous racemes remaining colourful for several weeks; young trees are often so covered in bloom that it is difficult to find the foliage. Its perfume may be likened to that of the Sweet pea and the French honeysuckle, of the same family, like sweet vanilla or maybe freesias and more enjoyable than that of any plant in the garden with the possible exception of the rose. The long drooping racemes of golden-yellow are enhanced by the shining green bark of the tree.

L. vulgare. The Common laburnum, native of central and southern Europe and growing to a height of about 7.5 m (25 ft). The leaflets are ovate and lance-shaped, downy beneath, whilst it blooms during May and June, bearing drooping racemes of brilliant yellow, delicately scented. The variety *serotinum* blooms later than the type.

LACHENALIA (Liliaceae—Lily Family)

A large genus of bulbous plants all of which are native of the Cape of Good Hope and known as the Cape cowslips or Leopard lilies on account of their spotted strap-like leaves. It is a rapidly increasing bulbous plant which may be grown outdoors in Britain only in the mildest parts of the South-west. Elsewhere it should be given the protection of a warm greenhouse. The bulbs are planted two or three to a pot in August and placed in a frame or cool greenhouse with little water until growth takes place, when the temperature may be gently raised to 10°C (50°F) by day and 5°C (42°F) at night. A well-drained compost should be provided, enriched with some decayed cow manure.

The blooms are pendulous and tubular,

and are produced a dozen or more to a 30-cm (12-in) stem. They bloom early in spring (though *L. pendula* may be brought into bloom by the year end) and they remain colourful for several weeks, one or two species emitting a most distinctive perfume.

Species. *Lachenalia contaminata.* One of the most beautiful species, bearing spikes of pendulent rosy-pink flowers which emit the almond-like scent of heliotrope.

L. glaucina. Its strap-like leaves are heavily mottled with purple whilst in March it bears tubular flowers a unique shade of electric-bluish-mauve which emit a delicious honey-like perfume.

L. orchioides. Native of the Cape where it is present on mountainous slopes usually in the shade of bushes, it has two spreading strap-shaped leaves, spotted with purple, and on a 22.5-cm (9-in) purple-spotted stem bears in spring, sweetly scented bell-shaped flowers of palest yellow, shaded blue at the base.

L. pustulata. It is found in sand dunes along the western coastline of the Cape Peninsula, its two strap-like leaves having numerous tubercles on the surface. The long, narrow tubular flowers are pale yellow throughout and are sweetly scented. They are borne in a many-flowered raceme on a 30-cm (12-in) stem.

LAELIA (Orchidacea—Orchid Family)

A genus of 75 species, native of Mexico and tropical America, and differing from *Cattleya* only in that there are eight pollen masses instead of four. In their natural state, they cross readily. They require exactly the same cultivation as *Cattleya.*

Species. *Laelia albida.* A species with white flowers, not very large but charming, particularly with their delicate primrose fragrance. The yellow streaks on the lip enhance their beauty. About six flowers are borne on a spike up to 45 cm (1½ ft) tall, from December to February.

L. anceps. Another graceful winter-flowering plant, with the same primrose-like perfume, but with purplish-rose flowers marked yellow in the throat. It is also a Mexican species, and has many varieties.

LAGERSTROEMIA (Lythraceae— Loosestrife Family)

A genus of 50 species of sub-tropical trees or shrubs native of Burma and eastern India, amongst which *L. parviflora* bears panicles of attractively scented flowers of bluish-white.

Species. *Lagerstroemia parviflora.* In the British Isles, it should be confined to a warm greenhouse with a minimum winter temperature of 9°C (48°F), whilst during summer the plants should be frequently syringed. They require a compost of fibrous peat and sand and require copious amounts of moisture in summer. They come into bloom at the end of July when they should be shaded to prolong their beauty and sweet perfume.

LANTANA (Verbenaceae—Vervain Family)

A genus of about 50 species of downy shrubs of erect or semi-climbing habit. The leaves opposite, toothed or wrinkled, whilst the flowers are borne in stalked flat heads with a slender cylindrical corolla tube. The plants are native of tropical America and their flowers possess the spicy lemon perfume associated with the family, though the leaves of certain species emit a disagreeable smell if bruised.

Species. *Lantana camara.* A vigorous species, it makes a bush about 90 cm (3 ft) tall and the same in width, and requires warm greenhouse culture in all but the most favourable parts of the British Isles. It blooms from June until September, throwing its verbena-like heads above the attractive dark-green foliage. The flowers are golden-yellow, changing to a darker shade with age. They are deliciously scented of verbena. From this species and the white-flowered *L. nivea*, a number of named varieties were raised during Victorian times and were in demand for the decoration of conservatories whilst they were also used for summer bedding, given the same cultural treatment as heliotropes and geraniums.

The sweet verbena perfume is present only in varieties bearing white, pink or pale-yellow flowers; those bearing orange flowers, such as *L. bruanta*, possess little or no perfume, an instance of pigment replacing perfume.

The plants require an open soil, enriched with a little decayed manure. To encourage a bushy habit, nip out the tips of their side shoots as they make growth.

LAPEIROUSIA (Iridaceae—Iris Family)

A genus of 60 species of bulbous plants, native of tropical and southern Africa, named in honour of the French navigator La Peyrouse. They grow on mountainous slopes and sandy flats. From a small conical cone, they bear their flowers solitary or in small numbers on a much-branched stem. They require protection from frost and do best in a sandy loam; potting is in February or March, and seed sown when ripe afford an easy method of increase.

Species. *Lapeirousia fistulosa.* From two prostrate basal leaves arises the 30-cm (12-in) stem, bearing a solitary, 6-petalled cream-coloured flower, tinted with purple and with a slender perianth tube. The flowers are produced in summer and have a sweet lily-like perfume.

LARIX (Larch) (Pinaceae—Pine Tree Family)

A small genus of deciduous trees about which Phillips said, 'we have introduced no exotic tree that has so greatly embellished the country in general'. It is native of central Europe from the Swiss Alps to the Caspian Sea and reached Britain early in the seventeenth century. It is hardy in all parts of our island and no tree is more colourful nor more appreciated as it puts forth its tiny buds of golden-green with the first warm days of spring. Several trees planted amongst a group of sombre conifers will cause so bright a patch of colour as to direct the eyes to it from a considerable distance. The larch differs from other conifers in that it bears its needles singly at the ends of the shoots and in clusters further along the stems. The tiny cones appear reddish-green, maturing to brown and are no more than 2.5 cm (1 in) long. Though hardy, the plant enjoys the protection from cold winds afforded by other trees and requires a deep, rich soil.

Species. *Larix europea* (syn. *L. decidua*). It is the European larch which makes a tree some 42 m (140 ft) tall. The young shoots

have a delicate mossy fragrance as the leaves unfold.

LASTREA (Nephrodium) (Filices—Fern Family)

A series of ferns, native of the British Isles, several of which are fragrant.

Species. *Lastrea aemula.* The Hay-scented fern, widely distributed throughout the British Isles. It is evergreen, adapting itself well to pot culture in a cool greenhouse. Its divided fronds are concave and curve upwards and present a crisped appearance from the recurving edges of the segments. It smells strongly of newly mown hay, especially when dry.

L. montana. It was discovered by Nowell and Stansfield in 1860, growing near Lake Gyrionedd, North Wales. It is also to be found on Scottish moorlands and in the Lake District and is known as the Mountain buckler fern. The fronds are pinnate with the midrib terminating in a horn-like projection near the apex of the frond which may be anything from 30 to 60 cm (12 to 24 in) long. When the hand is passed over the fronds, a pleasant odour is emitted likened to newly mown hay. Though of the mountain regions it is a shade lover.

L. rigidum. A British fern of spreading habit with lance-shaped fronds 30 to 60 cm (12 to 24 in) long and arising from the crown of a thick rootstock in spring, withering at the approach of winter. The fronds are divided into toothed pinnules, glandular beneath, which emit an agreeable hay-like smell when touched.

LATHYRUS (Sweet pea) (Leguminosae—Laburnum Family)

A genus of more than 100 species of annual or perennial plants, a number of which have tuberous roots, but only one, *Lathyrus odoratus*, so named by Linnaeus, has perfume.

Species. *Lathyrus odoratus.* It is an annual, discovered in Sicily in 1697 by a monk, Father Cupani, and he described it in his *Hortus Catholicus* of the same year. In 1700 he sent seed to a Dr Uvedale, a schoolmaster at Enfield Grammar School in Middlesex, one of the few people in England at the time to possess a warm greenhouse. The seed produced a weedy-looking plant bearing tiny maroon flowers with a deep-purple standard but it possessed a powerful sweet fragrance. A century later the number of varieties had increased to no more than six, all with inconspicuous flowers, the one exception being the Painted Lady, a reddish-pink and white bicolour with a particularly sweet perfume.

The flower was first called the Sweet pea by the poet Keats. But in spite of Thomas Fairchild's exhortation that 'the sweet-scented pea makes a beautiful plant' (1722) it was so inconspicuous in the garden that it is surprising it persisted for it produced but little bloom on short, weakly stems. It took someone with considerable foresight to consider this flower worthy of development. But in 1870, Henry Eckford, gardener to Dr Sankey at Sandywell in Gloucestershire, began cross-fertilizing sweet peas. Realizing the commercial possibilities, he left his employment to devote his entire time to the raising of new varieties, working in his garden at Wem, Shropshire. So successful was he that at the Bicentenary Sweet Pea Exhibition held at the Crystal Palace in 1900, of the 264 varieties exhibited half had been raised by Henry Eckford. His variety Lady Nina Balfour, described in Robert Bolton's Catalogue of 1908 as being 'pale lavender, shaded grey', was chosen as the most outstanding variety ever raised and was used for the presentation bouquet at the exhibition. The flowers were deliciously scented.

In the same year, in the garden of the Countess Spencer at Althorp Park, Northamptonshire, appeared the first Sweet pea with frilled petals. It was noticed by the head gardener, Silas Cole, who named it after the Countess, and almost overnight Silas Cole and his new Sweet pea earned universal fame. From a single seed-pod came the world's most beautiful flowers which had a perfume transcending all others. But Countess Spencer had one great fault, it did not always breed true to type. Nature, however, has a way of correcting these things for in the following year there appeared in the garden of a Cambridge grocer, W. J. Unwin, a form of Eckford's Prima Donna which also had waved petals and which he named Gladys Unwin, after his eldest daughter. As soon as Unwin realized that it would breed true, he sold his business and set about the raising of the new Sweet peas for the commercial cut-flower markets and quickly achieved success with the introduction of many lovely varieties. His son, Charles Unwin, has told that Prima Donna had been grown for at least eight years before producing its changed form, which it did at almost the same time in three different places, and never did so again, this being one of the greatest enigmas in all horticultural history.

The Sweet pea is a hardy annual but like so many hardy annuals responds better to half-hardy or biennial culture, seed being sown in a cold frame either in August or in March or in gentle heat early in the year, and the plants being moved to their flowering quarters in April; they will then come into bloom in June. The seed should be sown individually in small pots or in boxes spaced 2.5 cm (1 in) apart so that the young plants have space to develop from the moment of germination. When about 10 cm (4 in) high, the growing point should be removed to persuade the plants to develop a more bushy habit.

The Sweet pea requires an open, sunny situation and does not tolerate any degree of shade. It is a plant of climbing habit and requires to be grown up canes or against a trellis or netting about which it will climb by means of tendrils. It may also be grown up twiggy branches when it will make a delightfully scented 'hedge' some 1.8 m (6 ft) tall. If the dead blooms are continually removed before they set seed, the display will continue well into autumn, providing fragrance in the garden and in the home from the cut bloom. The exhibitor will grow the plants under the cordon system, removing the side shoots and tendrils and fastening the main stem to a cane, a system introduced by Tom Jones of Ruabon in 1911. By this method, the plant is able to concentrate its total energies into one main stem with the result that stems 45 cm (18 in) long may be obtained and on each will be 5 or 6 frilly-petalled blooms of exquisite beauty.

But not all Sweet peas are scented. In the quest to produce larger and larger blooms and of more brilliant colourings, scent has tended to become lost. Some varieties, bearing flowers of enormous charm, such as Jupiter, Dinky, Margot, Matador and Welcome, have no perfume. Here again, it is the scarlet and cerise-coloured varieties which have lost their fragrance, the dazzling scarlet variety Welcome being almost devoid of any perfume. No flower perfume is more satisfying than that of the Sweet pea, sweet and vanilla-like though Henry Phillips likened it to 'that of orange flowers with a mixture of the rose'.

Varieties with pronounced scent:

BALLERINA. The blooms are large with outstanding petal texture and are of rich cream with a deep picotee edge of rose.

CREAM GIGANTIC. Raised from Gigantic and introduced by Robert Bolton, the blooms are of similar substance but of a rich shade of cream with pronounced perfume.

CRIMSON EXCELSOIR. The most richly scented crimson, the enormous blooms being a striking crimson-red.

ELIZABETH TAYLOR. An exhibitor's favourite and the best of its colour, being rich deep mauve with an equally rich perfume.

EVENSONG. One of the most beautiful and sweetly scented of all sweet peas, shades of soft blue and lilac merging with delightful results.

GERANIUM PINK. Its name well describes its rich colour whilst its scent is outstanding.

GIGANTIC. Introduced in 1932 when it received the Gold Medal of the National Sweet Pea Society. It also received the Abol Trophy 'for the greatest advancement since the first world war in any one species or strain of plants'. The florets are enormous and the petals so heavily frilled as to give rise to a 'double' effect, whilst no variety has a richer perfume.

JOHN NESS. Raised by the late John Ness, it is an outstanding exhibitor's variety, the flowers which are borne in fours and fives being an attractive clear mid-lavender with a delicious spicy scent.

LEAMINGTON. Raised by Rev. Kenneth College and introduced in 1958, the variety carries a pronounced perfume and has received many honours, including the Award of Merit from the R.H.S. and also from the National Sweet Pea Society. The frilly-petalled flowers are large and a lovely deep, clear lilac with ideal placement.

MABEL GOWER. A long-established favourite since introduced in 1949, the blooms are a most attractive medium blue with a sweet vanilla perfume.

PATIENCE. The large frilled blooms are deepest lilac with outstanding petal texture and a delicious sweet scent.

PHILIP SIMMONS. A glorious variety of richest perfume with large waved blooms of bright salmon-pink edged cream.

PICCADILLY. A variety with outstanding scent, the large frilly blooms being of deep rose-red suffused with salmon.

PIXIE. The most heavily scented of the Unwin-striped sweet peas for which the firm are famous. The deep-cream ground is veined and marbled with salmon-orange.

ROSE FONDANT. Raised by Messrs. Unwin of Histon, it has the richest perfume of any sweet pea of its colour, and is one of the most beautiful. The frilly blooms are soft rose-pink suffused with salmon.

ROSY FRILLS. A picotee of great charm, the huge frilly blooms, the largest since Gigantic, having a white ground and a wide edge of rose-pink with a most delicious perfume.

VOGUE. The blooms are enormous, held on long sturdy stems and are cool lavender-blue with exceptional perfume.

LAURELIA (Monimiaceae—Hedycarya Family)

A genus of evergreen trees, natives of New Zealand and South America (Chile) with aromatic, opposite leaves and bearing their flowers in axillary panicles.

Species. *Laurelia novae-zelandiae.* Known in New Zealand as the Pukatea, it is peculiar both to that country and to South America. It makes a tall upright tree 4 m (15 ft) in height and, like all members of the order, grows best in partial shade, for where exposed to cold winds, the handsome, aromatic leaves will be badly 'burned'. It prefers an acid soil, well-drained, and in which peat has been incorporated. Propagation is by cuttings of the half-ripened wood which should be removed in August and inserted in a sandy compost under glass. The multicoloured wood is used in furniture making and to build boats for it does not easily split.

L. reynvanii. A neat and handsome shrub with dark, holly-like foliage, which in May and June scents the air with the sweet perfume of its sprays of creamy-white flowers, like those of the lily of the valley.

L. serrata (syn. *L. aromatica*). A handsome evergreen tree with pleasantly aromatic, serrated leaves which are of brightest green. A native of Chile, it is known as the Chilean laurel, and will survive a normal winter almost anywhere on the western seaboard of the British Isles.

LAURUS (Lauraceae—Bay Tree Family)

A genus of two species, one, an evergreen tree *L. nobilis*, being native of southern Europe, the other, *L. benzoin*, inhabiting damp woodlands from Canada to Florida. Both have alternate oblong leaves, deliciously fragrant when handled, and bear dioecious flowers in short racemes, with the parts arranged in fours.

Species. *Laurus benzoin.* Native of North America, it is a deciduous shrub growing 3 m (10 ft) tall with elliptic wedge-shaped leaves which yield an oil of lavender-like fragrance, whilst from the bark and twigs an oil smelling of wintergreen is obtained. The flowers are yellow and appear in clusters on the naked branches and are followed by fruit the size of an olive, but red and in clusters. The berries upon distillation yield a spice-scented oil, somewhat resembling camphor.

L. nobilis. Native of southern Europe where in Roman times it was the 'Victor's laurel': the Romans named it *laurus* from *laudis*, to praise, for it was considered worthy of the highest honours. It probably reached Britain in Roman times. Its name Bay is derived from an Anglo-Saxon word meaning a crown or chaplet for its leaves were placed upon the heads of those held in most esteem. The aromatic fragrance of the trees had a reputation for cleansing the air and keeping pestilence away. For this reason it is said that the Emperor Claudius moved his court to Laurentium, celebrated for its bays, to avoid the plague. During Elizabethan times, it was common to strew the floor of manor houses with the leaves. Several placed in a bath of hot water will bring comfort to aching limbs, and with their fragrance to a tired mind.

The Sweet bay is an evergreen tree which in southern Europe attains a height of 15 m (50 ft). The leaves are lance-shaped and deeply veined and release a sweet aromatic scent when bruised. It bears inconspicuous yellow flowers in early summer. It is also a delightful plant for a small tub, and may be clipped into ball-shape. Though hardy in Britain in all but the most exposed places, it is advisable to lift the tubs (or pots) indoors if exposed to cold winds. The fruit, an ovoid fleshy berry surrounded by the persistent base of the perianth, is also aromatic.

LAVANDULA (Lavender) (Labiatae— Lavender Family)

A genus of 20 species (*L. vera* and its varieties being most widely grown) of perennial herbs or shrubs having opposite, entire or toothed leaves and bearing tubular flowers in short spikes. The plants are native of southern Europe, extending from southern France to the eastern Mediterranean and possibly into India.

It is remarkable that the lavender is not more freely planted in the small garden today as it has been in cottage gardens since medieval times; there are several varieties of dwarf habit which at one time were used to make knot gardens. It is of such easy culture, too. Possessing attractive silvery-grey foliage, it remains colourful and aromatic and no plant makes a more attractive evergreen hedge. Used to surround a bed of highly scented crimson-red roses such as Ena Harkness or Chrysler Imperial, or a bed of fragrant pinks, the dwarf lavender remains neat and compact and may be clipped into shape when the plants are young.

Little is known of the lavender's introduction into Britain though it was almost certainly brought over by the Romans, but there is no mention of it growing in England earlier than mid-Elizabethan times, when because of its clean, fresh smell a laundress was then called a 'lavendre'. Langham in the *Garden of Health* (1579) said, 'Boil it in water, wet thy shirt in it and dry it again and wear it'. Shakespeare associated it with peppermint and marjoram as in *A Winter's Tale* and called it 'hot lavender', whilst Parkinson described its fragrance similarly, as 'piercing the senses . . . to comfort and dry up the moisture of a cold brain'.

The strength and quality of its perfume depend upon where it is growing. Like most shrubby herbs, lavender prefers a light, sandy soil. Soil of a chalky nature suits it most of all, bringing out its fragrance to the full. It also likes plenty of sunshine which is essential where it is grown for oil extraction. It requires neither manure nor much humus in the soil at planting time, though a little hop manure may be forked around the plants in autumn. The more robust varieties should be planted between 0.9 to 1.2 m. (3 to 4 ft) apart, slightly closer together for a hedge. For a dwarf hedge, plant the compact lavenders about 37.5 cm (15 in) apart, for the plants grow as wide as they grow tall. The spikes should be removed just before reaching maturity, before the bloom begins to fade. This is generally towards the end of July. Where growing commercially for oil extraction it is advisable to leave the spikes on the plants for another fortnight or until the bloom has entirely faded. Almost the whole of the stem is removed, the spikes being severed with a sharp knife or with scissors and placed on pieces of canvas. The lengths of canvas are then placed on large trays or on shelves in a dry, airy room away from the direct rays of the sun, and they will dry in about two weeks. The blooms may then be rubbed away from the stems between the two hands, and it will greatly facilitate the rubbing if the spikes have all been placed in the same direction. When growing for oil extraction, the spikes should be removed to the stills intact and immediately after cutting.

The dried blooms may be used in potpourris but are most often made up into small muslin bags to be placed amongst clothes. After removing the bloom do not discard the stems for they may be made up into bundles and, if lighted, the sticks will burn slowly like incense. The Rev. Henry Ellacombe has told in his *Plant Lore of Shakespeare* of how the air would be fragrant for miles around when the growers of Mitcham were burning the old bushes which had passed their best, for all green parts of the lavender are fragrant.

Species and Varieties. *Lavandula atriplicifolia.* A rare form to be found with *L. multifida* in parts of the Arabian desert. It has linear-oblong leaves and forms a dense spike of purple-blue.

L. dentata. It is closely related to *L. stoechas* but is found as far east as Malta and Sicily, its narrow leaves being attractively toothed whilst its flower spikes are small and of deepest lavender.

L. multifida. A rare species native only of a part of the Arabian desert. It makes a small bush and bears a dense, thick spike of lavender-blue on a woolly stem.

L. spica. Known as the Old English lavender of which there are a number of varieties, the most dwarf being *L. nana compacta*, the Munstead lavender, which grows only 60 cm (2 ft) tall with a neat, erect habit. It bears lavender-mauve flowers in a compact spike. Its white counterpart *alba* has pretty silvery-grey foliage, whilst the introduction Baby White bears spikes of purest white above 'frosted' foliage and rarely exceeds a height of 22.5 cm (9 in). *Atropurpurea*, also known as Hidcote Variety, grows 37.5 cm (15 in) tall and bears spikes of richest purple. Twickle Purple is another purple-flowered variety of neat habit whilst *rosea* is most uncommon, bearing spikes of deep pink. Another pink-flowered form is Loddon Pink, a slow-growing variety whilst Folgate Blue makes a pleasing companion with its spikes of purest blue. Both grow 45 cm (18 in) tall.

The most vigorous forms of the Old English lavender are Grappenhall, which bears a loose spike of purple-blue, and Seal Variety which has paler green foliage. Both make a dense bush 0.9 to 1.2 m (3 to 4 ft) in height and are rich in essential oil. On a mature plant as many as a thousand spikes may be counted in a single season. The form *Vera* is less robust, growing 60 cm (2 ft) tall with foliage devoid of the silvery-grey hue. There is also a variety known as Dutch lavender with broader leaves.

L. stoechas. The French lavender, found growing on the Isles of Stoechas near Marseilles which should only be grown in a mild climate. It grows 30 cm (12 in) tall and bears fat short spikes of dark purple in dense heads and it has narrow foliage, densely covered in white hairs. Turner said it was plentiful in West Country gardens and Parkinson wrote, 'we keep it with great care in our gardens', adding, 'It is more tender a great deal than other lavenders'.

LAVENDER: *see* **LAVANDULA**

LAWSONIA (Lythraceae—Loosestrife Family)

A genus of a single species, to be found growing in the Middle East, in northern India and into Burma and China.

Species. *Lawsonia inermis.* From its leaves, henna is obtained which from earliest times was used to stain the body and to colour the hair. It is the camphire of Isaiah: 'My beloved is unto me as a cluster of camphire on the vineyards of Engedi', for the plant was then used to surround vineyards, to give protection from wind. Its tiny white flowers emit a delicious odour, its small branches being woven into chaplets worn around the head and neck of Hindu girls. In Cairo, sprigs of blossom were once sold in the streets with the cry of 'Oh odours of Paradise; Oh flowers of henna'. Thomas Moore wrote of its 'odorous coral branches' and it was one of Milton's 'odorous bushy shrubs' of the Garden of Eden. Planted with the Gallica rose, it is believed to have been used to form fragrant hedges in the Hanging Gardens of Babylon. This ancient city was at one time the chief mart for perfumes in the East, and Herodotus tells us that the people would perfume their whole bodies with the costliest of scents.

LEDUM (Ericaceae—Heather Family)

A genus of ten species of evergreen shrubs which grow 30 to 90 cm (1 to 3 ft) in height, named after the gummy substance secreted by the wood, similar to labdanum. They require a moist peaty soil and being native of Canada and the Rocky Mountains are completely hardy in Britain and northern Europe. They are readily increased by division in autumn.

Species. *Ledum glandulosum.* It has leaves 5 cm (2 in) long, glossy green above, glaucous beneath, which are covered with tiny spots or glands from which a strong resinous scent is given off. The pure-white urn-shaped flowers appear in May, formed in dense clusters at the end of the shoots, and they too have an aromatic perfume.

L. latifolium. A native of Greenland, it is known as the Labrador tea plant for from its leaves an aromatic drink is made. Its oblong leaves are folded back at the edges whilst the underside is a rusty-red colour. The leaves emit a powerful fragrance whilst the small white flowers are also aromatic.

L. minus. It grows only 30 cm (12 in) tall and is a native of Japan, making a rounded bush with narrow leaves, quaintly upturned at the edges and which have a powerful aromatic scent. The tiny white flowers appear in April at the end of the stems.

L. palustre. Native of the Arctic swamplands, its small leaves and stems being covered with rusty down. From its aromatic leaves, the country folk of Scandinavia brew a delicious beer. Its tiny pinky-white flowers are borne at the ends of the shoots early in spring.

LEIOPHYLLUM (Ericaceae—Heather Family)

A genus of a single species, it is a plant similar to the Ledum and native of New Jersey and Atlantic North America.

Species. *Leiophyllum luxifolium.* It is an evergreen of almost prostrate habit and is known as the Sand myrtle. Its box-like leaves are small, shining and of darkest green, and it grows less than 30 cm (12 in) tall. In May it bears small fragrant starry white flowers tinted with pink. The form *prostratum* almost hugs the ground and may be used for ground cover. It has tiny glossy leaves and bears flowers which are smaller than the type and have a delicate perfume. It enjoys a sandy soil, well enriched with peat to maintain summer moisture, and is readily increased from layers in autumn.

LEONURUS (Labiatae—Lavender Family)

A small genus of erect perennial plants taking their name from the Greek words *leon*, a lion, and *oura*, tail, from the resemblance of the flowering stems to a lion's tail.

Species. *Leonurus cardiaca.* It is a rare plant of hedges and waste places, usually to be found near farm buildings. It grows 0.9 to 1.2 m (3 to 4 ft) high with palmately 3- to 5-lobed leaves and is a much-branched plant, resembling *Artemisia vulgaris* (Mugwort). The flowers are purple-pink, borne 6 to 12 in characteristic whorls in the axils of the leaves and with prickly calyces. They bloom from July until September. Known to the countryman as Motherwort, the whole plant is deliciously pungent when handled.

LEPTOSPERMUM (Myrtaceae—Myrtle Family)

A genus of about 28 species of silky-haired small trees or shrubs, native of Australia and New Zealand and hardy only in the more favourable parts of Europe though Weathers reported that the hardiest form, *L. scoparium*, has been known to withstand twelve degrees of frost in the gardens of Belvoir Castle, seat of the Duke of Rutland. The plants require a sandy soil, made more retentive of moisture by the inclusion of peat or leaf-mould, and they grow better in sight of the sea.

Species. *Leptospermum ericoides.* It is found in both islands of New Zealand where it blooms from November to January. In the valleys it assumes tree-like proportions, but upon the windswept hills becomes almost prostrate. It is known as the Heath-like Manuka from the resemblance of its leaves to the heathers, whilst its white flowers are like those of the hawthorn but with a delicate sweet perfume. The wood when burned gives off a delicious aroma.

L. scoparium. In its native lands it is known by the Maori name, Manuka, and from its aromatic leaves Captain Cook brewed a most pleasant tea which proved to be a valuable protection against scurvy. So famous did the plant become that it was known as the New Zealand Tea plant, well known to Capt. Bligh of the *Bounty*.

The shrub, growing 90 cm (3 ft) tall, is the Antipodean counterpart of the heather of the Northern Hemisphere and gives off a pleasant and fragrant odour when rubbed between the hands. In Britain, it bears masses of reddish-purple flowers during January, February and March whenever the weather is mild, and like the leaves possess an aromatic fragrance when handled.

Several forms are an improvement on the type, one of the best being *Chapmanii*, discovered in 1895 by Judge Chapman growing on the hills above Dunedin, its rose-pink flowers being deliciously scented. Another is *Nichollsii* which bears crimson-coloured flowers though perhaps the finest of all is *Keatleyi*, discovered by Captain Keatley in 1917 growing at the most northerly point of New Zealand and which bears very large flowers of carmine-rose with a rich scent. The flowers are nearly 5 cm (2 in) across with the five petals set well apart to reveal the maroon calyx at the base of the corolla. This is the best form of all for winter flowering in the milder parts of Britain, remaining colourful almost throughout the winter.

LEUCADENDRON (Proteaceae—Protea Family)

A small genus of 73 species of trees or shrubs, native to South Africa, few of which bear scented flowers. The flowers are usually ivory-white, hence the plant's name from the Greek *leukos*, white and *dendron*, a tree. The plants have alternate leaves, those surrounding the flowers differing in colour from the other leaves.

Species. *Leucadendron argenteum.* So named because its bark is pale green and its leaves are covered in silver hairs. Its flowers are golden-yellow in colour and are borne in rounded heads. They bloom during September and October and have a pleasant sweet perfume. It is a most handsome tree when in bloom, reaching 6 to 9 m (20 to 30 ft) tall. In Britain it is best grown in a cool greenhouse, with a compost containing plenty of peat and sand. Imported seeds are used for propagation, or well-ripened cuttings in summer will root in gentle heat.

LEUCHTENBERGIA (Cactaceae— Cactus Family)

A genus of a single species, native of Mexico.

Species. *Leuchtenbergia principis.* It stores moisture in its large fleshy roots and has spirally arranged tubercles about 10 cm (4 in) long. From the uppermost aeroles appear flattened spines and from the tips of the tubercles are borne the flowers, measuring 10 cm (4 in) across and remaining fresh for at least seven days. They are yellow, shaded brown on the outside, and are powerfully scented.

LEUCOCORYNE (Alliaceae—Onion Family)

A genus of five species, native of the Chilean Andes and taking its name from *leukos*, white and *koryne*, a club, referring to the anthers. They have small ovoid tunicated bulbs like those of the freesia, whilst all except *L. ixioides ordorata* emit the garlic-like smell of the family. Only one is in general cultivation and, in bloom early in spring, requires protection from frost in gardens of Britain and northern Europe.

Species. *Leucocoryne ixioides ordorata.* Found on grassy mountainous slopes at the foot of the Chilean Andes, it has two rush-like leaves from between which arises a wand-like stem bearing 8 to 9 salver-shaped flowers of cobalt-blue with a white star-like centre. They carry the delicious fruity scent of ripe plums.

Plant the corms outdoors in October 10 cm (4 in) deep and 10 cm (4 in) apart and cover with cloches where frosts are experienced. Or plant in deep boxes in a cool greenhouse. Like freesias, they do not tolerate forcing or humid conditions, being almost hardy and native of the rarefied atmosphere of the lower Andes ranges.

LEUCOJUM (Amaryllidaceae—Narcissus Family)

A genus of nine species of bulbous plants which bear their flowers in umbels on a hollow scape. One species, *L. aestivum*, is naturalized in parts of Britain, chiefly along the banks of the River Loddon in Berkshire where it is known as the Loddon lily. Unfortunately it has no perfume, though it is a delightful plant for a damp situation.

They are mostly plants of southern Europe, stretching from Portugal and Spain across the South of France to Italy and as far as Greece. One bears a fragrant flower, the lovely *Leucojum vernum*, the Winter snowflake of central Europe, which in Britain is the most difficult species to manage.

Species. *Leucojum vernum.* From its round, pale-green bulbs arise three or four strap-like leaves some 15 to 20 cm (6 to 8 in) long, and in March it bears its solitary snow-white drooping bells at the end of hollow stems. The flowers have a powerful scent, likened by some to that of the hawthorn; by others, to that of the violet, hence its name of 'White violet', and it takes its botanical name from the Greek for this, *leucoion*. So powerful is its perfume that Gerard classed it with the 'gillyflowers', naming it the Bulbed Stock Gillyflower for its perfume was at the time likened to that of the stock.

The flower resembles the snowdrop but the bloom opens like a crinoline with the petals pointed and strikingly tipped with green. Growing only 15 cm (6 in) tall, it is quite at home in the alpine garden and does especially well in small pots in the unheated greenhouse, the bulbs being planted early in September and taken indoors at the end of November when rooted.

If naturalizing in short grass, a light well-drained soil is essential to success, and to encourage drainage it is advisable to plant on a layer of sand in October.

LEUCORCHIS (Orchidaceae—Orchid Family)

A small genus of leafy plants with the flowers sessile and spurred and borne in a dense spike.

Species. *Leucorchis albida.* Known as the Small White orchid, it is common to the grassy hills of the lowlands of Scotland and is also found in parts of Derbyshire and Yorkshire but is rare further south. It is prevalent across northern Europe to Siberia and Japan and is also to be found across North America from Alaska to Newfoundland. It rarely exceeds a height of 15 cm (6 in) with a 7.5-cm (3-in) flower spike composed of 30 or more blooms of short spurred hooded white flowers, tinted with green. They emit a powerfully sweet perfume, most pronounced at night to attract the night moths for pollination.

LEUCOTHOE (Ericaceae—Heather Family)

One of a group of heath-like plants which have never been satisfactorily classified. *L. catesbaei* is sometimes listed as *Andromeda catesbaei*, whilst *Andromeda floribunda* is now *Pieris floribunda*. For all that, the Leucothoes are valuable dwarf shrubs and are evergreen. They enjoy a peaty soil with ample supplies of moisture about the roots. They are increased by layers or by root division in autumn.

Species. *Leucothoe acuminata*. It is a pretty North American shrub growing 45 cm (18 in) tall with shining leathery lance-shaped leaves, and in June its slender arching stems are wreathed in sweetly scented drooping bells of purest white.

L. catesbaei. It was one of Miss Gertrude Jekyll's favourite plants in her wild garden and it is one of the best plants to set out between rhododendrons and azaleas for it forms a compact bush 60 cm (2 ft) in height with pointed lance-shaped leaves and it blooms in March. The flowers are pure white, in shape like those of the lily of the valley and as generously fragrant.

L. davisiae. A pretty Californian shrub growing 0.9 to 1.2 m (3 to 4 ft) high with bright-green leaves. It blooms in May, bearing its white bell-shaped flowers in erect clusters and they are sweetly scented.

LEYCESTERIA (Caprifoliaceae—Honeysuckle Family)

A genus of six species, native of the western Himalayas and China.

Species. *Leycesteria formosa*. It is a handsome deciduous shrub of the lower Himalayas, N. China and Formosa.

It is readily propagated from seed and is happiest in partial shade where it is protected from cold winds. It grows to a height of 1.8 m (6 ft) with interesting hollow, cane-like stems or richest green and pointed lance-shaped leaves. It is a handsome plant when in bloom during August and September for its tubular white flowers, delicately scented and borne at the end of the shoots, are backed by crimson bracts.

LIATRIS (Snakeroot) (Compositae—Daisy Family)

A genus of 16 species of hardy perennials, native of North America, which are unusual in that they open their flowers from top to bottom of the spike. The plant obtained its country name snakeroot from the tuberous snake-like roots which are best planted and divided in early springtime. All species bloom during September when the border is beginning to lack colour and bear stiff cylindrical spikes of intense violet-purple blooms which are more than 37.5 cm (15 in) in length and which remain colourful for several weeks.

Species. *Liatris odoratissima*. It grows 0.9 to 1.2 m (3 to 4 ft) high and bears bright-purple flowers and thick fleshy spoon-shaped leaves which, when bruised, emit a rich vanilla-like perfume so that it is known as the Vanilla plant.

LIBOCEDRUS (Pinaceae—Pine Tree Family)

A genus of five species, native of New Caledonia and New Zealand, South America, western North America and South-east Asia, yielding valuable timber, for which purpose they have been introduced into North America.

Species. *Libocedrus chilensis* (syn. *Thuja chilensis*). The Chilean cedar, native of the Chilean Andes, it requires a sheltered garden in Great Britain, but will withstand several degrees of frost. It attains a height of 6 m (20 ft) and has drooping branches of glaucous green, and cones which are also drooping. All parts of the tree are strongly fragrant, especially the wood which when burnt smells of incense.

L. decurrens. Growing at heights ranging from 1,200 to 2,700 m (4 to 9,000 ft), it is known as the Incense cedar from the powerful, incense-like fragrance of the wood and foliage. It is a tree of columnar form and makes a magnificent specimen with its dark-green foliage borne in plaited branchlets, whilst the variety *Aureovariegata* has variegated green and golden foliage. The cones are olive-brown, about 2 cm (1 in) long, and are borne at the ends of the branchlets.

It does best in a position sheltered from strong winds with a deep soil containing plenty of rotted leaf-mould, peat, or similar material. Increase is by cuttings in light sandy soil in autumn under a cold frame, or by seed sown in early spring under glass.

LIGUSTICUM (Umbelliferae—Parsley Family)

A small genus of aromatic plants distributed through the northern temperate regions of Europe and extending south to Egypt, Persia and Afghanistan.

Species. *Ligusticum ajowan.* A small tender annual, commonly known as the Bishop's weed and native to Egypt, Persia, Afghanistan and Bengal. It is a plant of upright habit, growing 37.5 cm (15 in) tall, the stems having few leaves which are divided into numerous filiform segments. The tiny white flowers are borne in umbels and are followed by strongly ribbed fruits covered with small blunt tubercles. When dry and rubbed in the hands, the seeds yield a powerful thyme-like odour, much valued for culinary purposes whilst the distilled water is used as an aid to cholera. The seeds yield an aromatic volatile oil identical with Thymol.

L. scoticum (Lovage). Scotland appears in its botanic name for this now rare herb at one time grew in abundance along the Northumberland coastline and as far north as Tantallon and Dunbar, also in the Shetland Islands. In these parts it was known as Sea parsley for its large glossy succulent leaves, borne on long stems, have a pronounced parsley flavour and aroma, also its yellow flowers. Miss Sinclair Rohde described its scent as that 'of parsley, angelica and pear skin'. On the Continent, the seed was used (instead of pepper) to flavour soups, stews and meats on account of its sharp, hot taste which Parkinson says is 'comforting and warming'. During Parkinson's day, its stems were candied, and were also blanched and stewed, like celery. Thomas Hill (1577) wrote that 'this herb for its sweete savour is used in baths' and Dr Johnson recommended the root as a cure for rheumatism.

Lovage is a perennial plant, best propagated from seed which should be sown as soon as ripe. It quickly attains a height of 0.9 to 1.2 m (3 to 4 ft) and ac-cording to Hill 'it grows well in shade and by running water'.

LILIUM (Liliaceae—Lily Family)

A large genus of flowering plants growing from a (usually) scaly bulb. On an erect leafy stem branched at the end, it bears one or more drooping or erect flowers in racemes. The flowers consist of six segments, the three inner petals being larger and broader than the three outer petals. The lily is widely distributed throughout the northern temperate regions from Oregon in the west, across North Africa and Europe to China and Japan, usually growing where they are exposed to a severe winter with little rain, followed by a long period of sunshine.

No plant is more steeped in history. As a flower it has no rival except the rose. The ancient world consecrated the White lily to Juno from whose milk it was thought to have come forth. This was the White lily of the East, *L. candidum*, the Madonna lily, so named for its purity and sweet perfume. It is depicted more than any other flower in the paintings of the masters, and is also most mentioned by the poets to whom if typified all that was good and beautiful.

At one time so popular in gardens, during the nineteenth century, the lily gave way to the dahlia and other exotic stove plants for summer bedding. It was the introduction to England in 1862 of *Lilium auratum* that began a new interest in the lily which has continued ever since, with the Madonna lily still retaining its popularity for it remains the only pure-white species ever introduced and it seems to grow well anywhere.

Lilies may be divided into several groups each of which demand different cultural conditions. Some are lime tolerant and some, mostly from China and Japan, will not grow where lime is present. Several species, including *L. auratum* prefer an acid, peaty soil. Most Eastern lilies are stem-rooting and require yearly top dressing, while most European species form their roots from the base of the bulb. Some prefer partial shade whilst others enjoy an open, sunny situation. Again, not all lilies are pleasantly scented. Mrs Constable Maxwell in her delightful *Lilies in their Homes* suggests that the European species of the *L. carniolicum* group, the lilies which grew in Elizabethan gardens, smell of decaying vegetable matter. These are: *L. carniolicum, I. albanicum, L. pomponium, L. heldrichii,* and *L. pyrenaicum.* In addition, *L. bulbiferum* and *L. martagon* are scentless. Only the Madonna lily, in Elizabethan gardens, possessed perfume in a pleasant degree and from the 90 or more species grown today, no more than 20 to 30 bear flowers which may be described as being sweetly scented.

Of the scented lilies, all bear flowers that are white (or nearly so, most having yellow markings), pale yellow, or purple. The brilliant-scarlet and the orange-flowered species do not bear scented flowers, only *L. chalcedonicum* having any claim to possessing perfume which to some is unpleasant and to others resembles the smell of dying orange-blossom or of orange peel. Almost all the fragrant lilies grow at an altitude of between 1,500 to 1,800 m (5 to 6,000 ft), at the lower extremity of the snow line. Here the bulbs are ensured of a winter covering of snow to give protection from extreme cold, and are safe from excessive damp when the snow begins to melt. One or two species grow in low-lying ground but they are the exception rather than the rule.

Lilium candidum, L. chalcedonicum, L. longiflorum, L. hansonii and *L. henryi* and its hybrids of the Aurelian group flourish in a limestone soil, whilst *L. auratum, L. parryi* and *L. rubescens* grow well in peaty soil.

With the exception of *L. candidum,* and *L. kelloggii,* the fragrant lilies are stem-rooting and should be planted 15 to 20 cm (6 to 8 in) deep in a light soil. *L. candidum* and *L. kelloggii* should be planted with no more than 5 cm (2 in) of soil above the bulb, less if the ground is heavy and it is advisable to plant on the side.

Species and Varieties. *Lilium amabile.* Native of Korea, it is of Martagon type. requiring a gritty well-drained soil and partial shade, though it is lime tolerant. It blooms in July, bearing 2 to 6 reflexed scarlet flowers to a 1.2-m (4-ft) stem. The flowers are spotted with black and possess a powerful oriental perfume.

L. auratum. With the Madonna lily it must rank as the most handsome of all the lilies, growing 1.8 to 2.4 m (6 to 8 ft) in height and bearing at the end of the stems upwards of thirty enormous blooms of white, edged with gold and spotted with crimson. The blooms open in mid-August and if protected from wind will scent the air for almost eight weeks. Planting depth depends upon the nature of the soil: if light and peaty 20 to 22.5 cm (8 to 9 in) is not too deep but if heavy, half that depth is sufficient. Frequent top dressing with peat or leaf-mould will ensure the long life of the plants. An open, sunny position should be provided.

L. auratum is found wild only in Japan, mostly in Honshu Island, and is usually seen in bloom on mountainous slopes about 1,500 m (5,000 ft) above sea level and often in sight of the sea. The first bulbs to reach Britain were sent by John Veitch and the flowers were exhibited by his firm at the Royal Horticultural Society Show in July 1862.

The variety *Platyphyllum* is superior even to the type, having larger flowers which are more profusely spotted. It is usually in bloom about 1 August and is more amenable to adverse conditions. The flowers have the same penetrating spicy perfume as those of the type.

L. bakerianum. Native of Burma and south-western China, it is a lily of exquisite form, its greenish-white bell-shaped flowers having reflexed petals to reveal markings of purple in the throat, and it is powerfully scented. Plant the bulbs 10 cm (4 in) deep in March in a gritty compost and cover with a cloche in November to protect the bulbs from excess winter moisture.

L. brownii. Its home is believed to be the mountains of the Chinese province of Kwangsi, and it was flowered in England for the first time in 1835 by F. E. Brown of Slough and named after him. It is more likely to be a variety of *L. brownii viridulum* rather than the other way round, for the latter form is more widely dispersed over the whole of China as far south as north-eastern Burma where it grows at altitudes of about 1,500 m (5,000 ft). It enjoys a well-drained loamy soil and an open sunny situation.

L. brownii grows 0.9 to 1.2 m (3 to 4 ft) tall and has flowers of ivory-white, shaded on the outside with rosy-purple and tinted with green. The flowers appear in July, sometimes single and never more than five on one stem. They have a soft sweet fragrance which is more pronounced in the variety *viridulum* which at one time was known as a separate species called *Lilium odorum* on account of its unique perfume. It bears flowers of creamy-white, the petals having a central strike of purple.

Another form, *australe*, found mostly on the hills around Hong Kong is equally fragrant. It has narrower leaves and bears its flowers, usually one, two or three on a 1.2-m (4-ft) stem. The petals are white with a purple stripe down the centre and flushed purple on the outside. They emit a powerful honey perfume, almost musk-like when the air is calm.

L. candidum. It is unusual amongst lilies in that (with *L. catesbaei* and *L. iridollae*) it forms its leaves as soon as the flower stem has died down in autumn. It is then that the bulbs should be moved if necessary. That the plant flourished in cottage gardens of old was owing to its liking for a rich soil and the company of other plants to afford shade to the roots during the heat of summer. It bears its glistening white trumpets early in June and July on 1.2- to 1.5-m (4- to 5-ft) stems, usually between twelve and twenty blooms to each stem. The scent of the flowers in the warmth of the midsummer sun is of heather honey.

The variety *salonikae* is even whiter than the type for its pollen is of palest ivory whilst the perfume if anything is more pronounced.

From seed of this variety and of other forms of *L. candidum* sent to him by the late Abbé Souillet of Gennes on the Loire, Mr Jan de Graaff, in Oregon, raised the wonderful Cascade Hybrids which are sweetly scented.

L. cernuum. It is one of two species bearing scented flowers which are native to Korea. It grows no more than 45 cm (18 in) tall and bears a nodding flower of Turk's-cap shape of rosy-mauve spotted with crimson-purple. Though stem-rooting, it should be planted no more than 10 cm (4 in) deep in a well-drained soil. It blooms with the Madonna lily with which it makes a delightful companion and is sweetly scented. The variety *candidum* bears white flowers spotted with purple which are even more powerfully scented.

L. chalcedonicum. It grew in gardens in Tudor times together with the Madonna lily, bearing its Turk's-cap blooms of sealing-wax red. Its home is Mount Olympus and western Turkey and it is one of the few European lilies with perfume though to some this is far from pleasant. *L. chalcedonicum* has a slight orange perfume which is pleasant as the blooms are just opening but becomes less so as they age. This lily is lime-tolerant but requires a well-drained soil and an open, sunny situation. Like *L. candidum*, the scaly bulbs should be planted on their side.

L. cordatum. See *Cardiocrinum cordatum.*

L. duchartrei. It was discovered by the French missionary Father David in Szechwan (along with *L. davidii*) in 1869 growing in alpine meadows at an altitude of nearly 3,000 m (10,000 ft). From 1 to 10 or more flowers are borne on a stem which may reach a height of 0.9 to 1.2 m (3 to 4 ft) and they appear in July. The blooms are ivory-white with purple markings towards the petal edges and with projecting anthers. They emit a pleasant spicy perfume.

This lily grows well in partial shade and in a soil containing plenty of leaf-mould.

L. formosanum. It is to be found only in Formosa growing some 1,500 m (5,000 ft) above the sea, in open grassland. It is a most handsome species, flowering in September when five or six funnel-shaped blooms appear on a 1.5- to 1.8-m (5- to 6-ft) stem. The flowers are glistening white, streaked with purple on the outside, and diffusing a delicious sweet perfume.

L. fresnense. Native of northern California, it closely resembles *L. pardalinum*, bearing on a 1.2-m (4-ft) stem orange-yellow flowers of Martagon type which are sweetly scented. Though requiring a position of full sun, it should be given a humus-laden soil, retentive of summer moisture.

L. hansonii. It was discovered in its natural habitat only in 1916 on Dagelet Island, off South Korea, growing about 1,050 m (3,500 ft) above the sea, though bulbs had reached Britain and the U.S.A. some sixty years earlier, sent from Japanese gardens. The almost star-like flowers appear late in June on 1.2-m (4-ft) stems; they are of deepest yellow with almost an orange flush and with a slight but sweet perfume, losing fragrance with the increase of pigment in the blooms. This lily is hardy and easy to grow but prefers a position of partial shade.

L. henryii. Like *L. hansonii,* it is an easy lily to manage and is valuable in that like *L. langkongense,* it blooms in August, thus bridging the gap between the midsummer and autumn-flowering species. It forms a graceful arching stem 2.4 m (8 ft) in height on which it may bear up to 60 nodding Turk's-cap flowers of a warm apricot-yellow and enhanced by the bright glossy foliage. They have a pleasant sweet perfume.

Native of the Yangtse Regions of China, it is a lime lover and does not tolerate acid soil conditions.

L. A. Havemeyer is a lovely hybrid raised in New Jersey, its apricot-buff flowers having a delicious perfume, whilst the Aurelian Hybrids, raised by Mr Jan de Graaff in Oregon, are amongst the finest of all lilies, most outstanding being the chartreuse-green Limelight with its outstanding perfume.

L. iridollae. One of the few scented lilies growing in the U.S.A. away from the west coast. A small colony was discovered in a damp, peaty meadow in Alabama during the 1950s. It forms its leaves in autumn and they remain green through winter. It grows to a height of 0.9 to 1.2 m (3 to 4 ft) and the Turk's-cap blooms are a lovely golden-buff with a soft sweet fragrance.

L. kelloggii. It is from the Pacific Coast of America and is one of the few pink lilies to bear scented blooms. The Turk's-cap flowers are borne in July and are a warm rose-pink which darkens with age, and they emit a soft honey-like scent. As many as a dozen blooms appear together on a 90-cm (3-ft) stem. It requires a well-drained peaty soil and an open situation. The bulbs should be planted 5 cm (2 in) deep.

L. lankongense. Found in the Chinese province of Yunnan, it is pink-flowering and with *L. kelloggii* is a welcome addition to the lily border. It too flowers in late July and early August when the rose-pink flowers, purple on the outside and spotted with crimson, appear on stems 60 to 90 cm (2 to 3 ft) tall. This lily prefers a moist peaty soil and some shade, and in these conditions its flowers will retain their colour and delicate fragrance for several weeks.

L. leucanthum. It is native of the Chinese province of Szechwan, and in Britain it is doubtful if any bulbs have survived E. M. Wilson's introduction. It is a species of great beauty, bearing funnels of milky whiteness, tinted with green and purple on the outside. The blooms which are said to have a honeysuckle fragrance, appear on a 90-cm (3-ft) stem.

The variety *centifolium* has a more widely expanded tube flushed with gold on the inside. In Britain, it requires a warm garden in the South-west as it is somewhat tender but where established it will bear a dozen or more blooms on a stem 1.8 to 2.4 m (6 to 8 ft) tall; in the words of Mrs Alice Constable Maxwell, 'they have a delicate scent resembling a gardenia'.

L. longiflorum. It is the Easter lily, so called because indoor bloom is usually available at Eastertime. It is also the Bermuda lily for it was introduced to the island in 1882 and quickly became established as a commercial cut flower. The species is found wild only in the Ryukyu Archipelago south of Japan, growing almost in the sea between the coral reefs. The variety *giganteum,* mostly grown commercially, is found only on the Island of Okinawa. In Britain, it should be confined to the most sheltered gardens of the South-west, otherwise it should be grown under glass for it is easily managed in pots indoors and will bloom from autumn until Easter. To retain the dazzling whiteness of the blooms, nursery growers remove the anthers before they shed their pollen. The flowers are borne on 60-cm (2-ft) stems and diffuse a gentle jasmine-like perfume which is especially pronounced under glass.

In America, a variety called Croft is widely grown as a pot plant for house decoration during summer.

L. monadelphum. Native of the Caucasus, it enjoys a chalky soil like the Madonna lily and others of the same regions, all of which are of easy culture and do well in the British Isles. They have the same flowering period coming into bloom early in June before most other lilies. *L. monadelphum* bears 20 or more blooms on each 1.5-m (5-ft) stem and are of richest yellow with a soft sweet perfume.

which is in no way overpowering as in so many lilies.

L. martagon. The Martagon or Turk's-cap lily of southern Europe and Asia, which from the small yellow bulbs produces its flowers on 60-cm (2-ft) stems. The drooping flowers with their recurved segments appear in May and June as many as 30 at a time in erect racemes. They are dull purple, spotted with crimson, whilst there is also a white form, *album*, which bears more than 40 waxy white flowers to each stem. The flowers are most fragrant at night and rely on the Night hawk-moth for their pollination.

L. nepalense. Native of Nepal and the Himalayas, it should be grown under glass in all but the most favourably situated gardens of the British Isles and northern Europe where it will bloom in June, its funnel-shaped flowers of lime-green being splashed with purple in the throat. They smell strongly of indole. As the flower stems travel underground before turning upwards, the bulbs should be planted in a box rather than a pot.

L. nobilissimum. Its natual habitat is a small island south of Japan and it should be grown under glass in the British Isles and northern Europe. It is stem-rooting and bears 1 to 3 drooping funnel-shaped flowers on a 50-cm (20-in) stem. The flowers are brilliant white and sweetly scented and are enhanced by the glossy dark-green leaves. They appear in June.

L. papilliferum. A native of Yunnan and though discovered by Father Delavay in 1888, it flowered for the first time in Britain when exhibited at Chelsea in 1949. It is found in alpine meadows some 3,000 m (10,000 ft) above sea-level where it grows only 37.5 cm (15 in) tall and so is suitable for the front of the border. It bears its flowers of deepest purple in July and they have a delicious spicy fragrance.

L. parryi. It grows wild in Arizona and southern California and inhabits boggy ground. It may be established in the garden in low-lying ground enriched with peat and is worth some effort with its culture for it is a lily of outstanding beauty bearing funnel-like flowers of brilliant yellow with protruding brown anthers. The blooms, which appear before the end of May, have exquisite perfume and as many as a dozen open together on a 1.2-m (4-ft) stem.

L. philippinense. It is found wild only in the Island of Luzon, the largest of the Philippines, where it grows at an altitude of between 1,500 to 2,100 m (5 to 7,000 ft) in limestone formations. It grows nearer to the tropics than any other species and in Britain should be confined to those gardens most favourably placed. It bears a trumpet-shaped flower of great beauty, the large open funnel being ice-white, streaked with red on the outside, and borne on a 60-cm (2-ft) stem. The flowers have a delicate sweet perfume.

L. polyphillum. Its home is Afghanistan and Kashmir and it is the connecting link between the lilies of eastern Europe and those of western China. It grows in woodlands at an altitude of 1,800 to 3,600 m (6 to 12,000 ft) in soil containing plenty of moisture-holding humus but which is well-drained during the rainy season. Six to a dozen blooms of blush-white streaked with purple on the inside appear in August on a 90-cm (3-ft) stem and they are attractively scented.

L. primulinum, var. *ochraceum.* It is distinguished from *L. primulinum* by the deep-purple patch in the throat of the white flowers. A native of Yunnan, it bears a most striking flower with the green-tipped petals folding back. It has the scent of a freshly peeled orange. Four to six blooms are borne in July on a 60-cm (2-ft) stem and they increase by tiny bulbs which form on the stems beneath the ground. Though tolerant of cold conditions, the plants may not survive long periods of wet weather when they are dormant.

L. pumilum (syn. *L. tenuifolium*). It grows wild in northern China and Mongolia. As would be imagined, it is completely hardy and with its smooth, almost scaleless bulbs, is tolerant of all soil conditions, but it requires an open, sunny position. It has grass-like leaves and produces its Turk's-cap flowers on 45-cm (18-in) stems. As many as a dozen blooms of glistening red may appear on one stem, and at the front of a border several bulbs present a striking picture in the company of the variety Golden Gleam. The blooms have a soft orange-like perfume.

L. regale. It was found by E. H. Wilson in 1903, on the borders of Tibet and

Szechwan, growing in valleys about 1,200 to 1,500 m (4 to 5,000 ft) above sea level, where it is protected from the worst of the Himalayan weather. From June until the end of August, it scents the air around with the rich honeysuckle perfume of its brilliant-white funnels, arranged in a dozen or more around the end of the 1.8-m (6-ft) stems. The blooms are shaded with gold in the throat and may be flushed with wine on the outside. *L. regale* is tolerant of all soil conditions as long as drainage is adequate. If the plant has a fault it is a susceptibility to late spring frosts and so should not be given a position where the early morning sun may cause damage to the frosted stems. For this reason, it is advisable to plant the bulbs between shrubs of low habit.

L. rubellum. It grows wild on the Japanese island of Honshu at altitudes of around 1,500 m (5,000 ft), the funnel-shaped flowers appearing in twos and fours on a 60-cm (2-ft) stem. It is difficult to establish in Britain for it requires plenty of summer moisture but cold, dry conditions in winter, which it enjoys on the lower mountainous regions of Honshu. The flowers with their folded-back petals are satin-pink, shaded deeper pink on the outside. They appear early in June and diffuse a rich, sweet scent.

L. rubescens. It grows wild amongst the Redwood trees of Oregon and northern California where it is known as the Redwood lily. Autumn planting is recommended for British gardens and, like *L. candidum,* it should have no more than 5 cm (2 in) of soil above it.

The blooms appear in July, on a stem 0.9 to 1.5 m (3 to 5 ft) in height, as many as 30 to a single stem being usual, and the narrow trumpets are held erect. The flowers, which have a powerful but pleasant scent, are pale lilac-pink, spotted with purple.

L. sargentiae. It was discovered by E. H. Wilson growing near *L. regale* on the borders of Szechwan and is equally outstanding, coming into bloom mid-July as the Regal lily is finishing. It is similar in all respects to *L. regale,* bearing on a 1.2- to 1.5-m (4- to 5-ft) stem, 1 to 12 (usually 6) flowers of icy-white with a pale-yellow throat and flushed with purple on the outside. It has the same delicious perfume.

Like *L. regale,* the same precautions against late frosts should be taken.

L. speciosum. It is one of the more tender Japanese lilies and does better under glass in Britain where for long it has been grown commercially. Outdoors, in a sheltered border facing south, it blooms in September and October but under glass may be brought into bloom almost the whole year round, the pendent trumpets being blush-white, spotted with crimson-purple. About 12 appear on a 90-cm (3-ft) stem and in pots scent the home for several weeks with their sweet honey perfume. The white form, *album,* is equally scented, likewise the more vigorous *magnificum* which is the most suitable variety for outdoor planting.

L. sulphureum. It was found by Mr Boxhall in 1888 on the hills of northern Burma and in a slightly different form in Yunnan by Father Delavay in the same year, growing at an altitude of about 1,500 m (5,000 ft). It is a most handsome lily, flowering in September and October, and so should be given a warm, sunny situation where it can send up its 1.8- to 2.1-m (6- to 7-ft) stems and bear its large creamy-yellow trumpets in the warmth of the autumn sunshine. It is a valuable lily to plant where late spring frosts prove troublesome for it does not start into growth until early summer. But winter moisture may cause trouble and, like all lilies, the bulbs should be planted on a layer of sand or ashes. The blooms emit a heavy oriental perfume exceeded only by that of *L. auratum.* This lily has been widely used with *L. henryi* and *L. sargentiae* in raising the now famous American hybrids.

L. taliense. Native of Yunnan where it grows about the limestone mountains some 3,000 m (10,000 ft) above Lake Tali, discovered there by Father Delavay in 1883. Like all the lilies of western China, the white Turk's-cap blooms, heavily spotted with purple, are deliciously scented and are enhanced in beauty by the dark-green leaves. It does well in a limestone soil but should be frequently top-dressed with humus for it grows to 3 m (10 ft) and is a gross feeder.

L testaceum. It is believed to be a natural hybrid of *L. candidum* and *L chalcedonicum* and is known as the

Nankeen lily. It blooms in July, bearing 8 or 10 Turk's-cap flowers on a 1.2- to 1.5-m (4- to 5-ft) stem. Like L candidum, it should be planted with only 5 cm (2 in) of soil above it and it does well in a chalky soil. The flowers are golden-apricot with delicious perfume and the petals turn back to reveal the scarlet anthers. It should be planted in autumn.

L. wallichianum. It is native of Nepal where it grows on grassy hillsides at an altitude of about 1,200 to 1,500 m (4 to 5,000 ft). It is a lover of limestone formations and an open situation where it will reproduce itself with freedom by means of underground bulblets. First discovered in 1802, it was re-discovered in 1820 by the Danish botanist, Wallich, after whom the lily is named. The flower, with its long slender tube of greenish-white formed singly at the end of the 1.2- to 1.5-m (4- to 5-ft) stem, possesses outstanding perfume, penetrating and spicy, whilst the bloom is one of the largest of all the species. The bulb should be planted 15 cm (6 in) deep early in spring and it will bloom early in August.

L. wardii. It was discovered in the Himalayas by Captain Kingdon-Ward as recently as 1924 and, like Wallich's lily, increases by its bulblets formed on the underground stems. It is an attractive lily bearing in August upwards of 30 rose-pink flowers on a stem 0.9 to 1.2 m (3 to 4 ft) tall and it is perhaps the most sweetly perfumed of all the Eastern lilies.

L. washingtonianum. It grows wild on Mount Shasta in northern California at an altitude of about 1,500 m (5,000 ft), in the company of trees and shrubs and where the bulbs are beneath a thick layer of snow throughout winter. It requires dry conditions whilst the bulbs are resting and a well-drained soil, and in Britain, where the species is rarely seen, the bulbs often suffer from excess winter moisture.

It blooms in June, with L candidum, the white flowers with their sweet perfume turning purple as they age. They are borne on a 1.5-m (5-ft) stem and usually from 6 to 12 blooms appear on the same stem. Their perfume has been likened to that of Mrs Sinkins pink, being sweet and spicy and in no way overpowering.

LILY OF THE VALLEY: *see* **CONVALLARIA**

LIME: *see* **TILIA**

LIMNANTHEMUM (Floating Heart) (Gentianaceae—Gentian Family)

A small genus of floating water plants also know as *Nymphoides*, native of the British Isles and northern Europe, one species of which bears scented flowers.

Species. *Limnanthemum nymphaeoides* (syn. *Nymphoides peltata*). It is a pretty aquatic plant, native of the British Isles, its glossy green leaves which float on the surface being heart-shaped. Just above the leaves are borne in July bright golden-yellow flowers which have attractive frilled petals, and which give off a delicate almond-like perfume.

It does best in shallow water, and will grow almost too well if the soil is fairly fertile. Increase by seed or by cuttings.

LIMNANTHES (Limnanthaceae— Limnanthes Family)

A genus of 10 species of annual plants, native of North America and closely related to *Geranium*.

Species. *Limnanthes douglasii* (Meadow Foam). It is of spreading habit and though a native of California, is hardy in the British Isles. Growing only 15 cm (6 in) tall, it is a delightful edging plant and seed may be sown in autumn where it is to bloom in spring, or in March to flower from June until the frosts. The flowers, which measure about 2.5 cm (1 in) across, are white with golden markings at the centre and streaked with grey, and they diffuse a gentle sweet perfume most pronounced on a warm, calm day.

LIMNOPHILA (Scrophulariaceae— Foxglove Family)

A genus of 30 species, native of tropical Africa, India, South-east Asia, northern Australia and islands of the Pacific. They are aquatic plants, in Sanskrit called *Ambu-ja*, water-born. They are one of the few plants of the Foxglove family to bear scented flowers.

Species. *Limnophila gratianoides*. It is

native of India and Malaya where it is found about snake-infested swamplands and is known to the native people as *Amragandhaka* 'with an odour of mangoes'. The odour is fresh and agreeable, said by some to be camphor-like with lemony undertones, by others to have a balsam-like scent. The plant is used for medicinal purposes by the Hindus and is described by Dymock in his *Pharmacographia Indica.*

LINDERA (Lauraceae—Bay Laurel Family)

A small genus of evergreen shrubs, native of North America and Japan. Named in honour of the Swedish botanist Linder.

Species. *Lindera benzoin.* Native of North America, it is a deciduous shrub growing 3 m (10 ft) tall with elliptic wedge-shaped leaves which yield an oil of lavender-like fragrance, whilst from the bark and twigs an oil smelling of wintergreen is obtained. The flowers are yellow and appear in clusters on the naked branches and are followed by fruits the size of an olive, but red and in clusters. The berries, upon distillation, yield a spice-scented oil resembling camphor.

L. sericea. A low shrub, indigenous to Japan where it is known as *Kuro-maji* by reason of the black colouring of its bark. From the bark and wood, a dark yellow essential oil is distilled which gives off a rich balsamic odour, and is used in perfumery as Kuro-maji oil, composed upon distillation of Limorene, Dipentene, Terpineol and Carvol.

Another variety of this shrub is known as *Spiro-maji* by reason of its grey bark which has a most agreeable odour when handled.

LINDLEYA (Rosaceae—Rose Family)

A genus of only one species.

Species. *Lindleya mespiloides.* It is a native of Mexico growing 6 m (20 ft) tall with leathery evergreen leaves, and in July and August bears small sweetly scented pure-white flowers at the tips of the shoots. It does best in a well-drained soil containing limestone and should be given a position sheltered from cold winds where it should prove hardy in all but the most exposed gardens of the British Isles.

LINDSAEA (Lindsaeaceae—Lindsaea Family)

A genus of about 200 species of small tropical ferns, native of Ceylon, Java, the Philippines, Tasmania and tropical South America and named after John Lindsay, the English cryptogamic botanist. They are mostly to be found in damp woodlands.

Species. *Lindsaea cultrata.* Native of Guyana, it is a pretty, distinct, evergreen stove fern so named because the frond is shaped like the coulter of a plough. The pinnate fronds are about 15 cm (6 in) long and of palest green with the sweet odour of the Sweet Vernal grass, which it retains when dry.

LINNAEA (Caprifoliaceae—Honeysuckle Family)

A genus of a single species.

Species. *Linnaea borealis.* Known as the Twin flower, it is native to northern Britain and northern Europe (Scandinavia), and it is a pretty trailing plant of shrubby evergreen habit. It bears in June and July, twin bell-shaped drooping flowers which are flesh-coloured and have an evening fragrance like that of the honeysuckle. The plant requires a moist, peaty soil hence its liking for pine forests. It is propagated by division of the roots in spring. It is honoured with the name of the great Swedish botanist, Linnaeus.

LIPARIA (Leguminosae—Laburnum Family)

A small genus of shrubby plants, native to South Africa where they are occasionally found on lower mountainous slopes. They are named from the Greek, *liparos*, meaning brilliant.

Species. *Liparia sphaerica.* In its native country it is called Nodding Head or Geelkoppie. It is a low-growing bush of woody habit and bears early in summer, in round nodding heads, fragrant orange pea-like flowers. The leaves are small, elliptical and stiff, and give off a pungent incense-like smell when pressed, though as they are sharply pointed they must be handled with care.

LIQUIDAMBAR (Hamamelidaceae— Witch Hazel Family)

A genus of six species of balsam-bearing deciduous trees with 5-lobed maple-like leaves which take on brilliant colourings in autumn. Native of North America and western Asia, they require a moist loam to grow successfully. The trees yield a fragrant balsam known as storax; and a valuable wood, satin walnut (satinwood).

Species. *Liquidambar orientalis.* A slow-growing bush rather than a tree but it eventually attains a height of 6 m (20 ft). It is native of the Levant, and the resinous gum it exudes is now the storax used in perfumery having replaced the true *Styrax officinalis,* a Levantine shrub which is now rarely to be found. The balsamic fragrance is present to some extent in the foliage and is noticeable when the leaves are pressed in the hand. The bark is burnt in the homes of eastern peoples, to counteract unpleasant smells due to poor sanitation.

Liquid storax gives greater permanence to the odours of flowers extracted by maceration. It is also used in the imitation of other scents as an alternative to vanilla, ambergris and benzoin, or to complement them.

L. styraciflora. Known as the Sweet gum, it is now one of the sources of balsam-like resins used in perfumery. It is a handsome North American tree eventually reaching a height of 12 to 15 m (40 to 50 ft) and in spring it bears small greenish-yellow flowers. The beautiful palmately lobed leaves take on shades of crimson and gold in autumn and emit a balsam-like fragrance when they fall, which is retained until they have become quite withered.

The tree was first mentioned in a book by the Spanish botanist Hernandez, published in 1650, in which he describes the fragrant gum exuded through the bark like 'liquid amber', hence the name given to the genus. The first plant to reach Britain was planted in Bishop Compton's grounds at Fulham Palace in 1681.

LITSEA (Lauraceae—Bay Tree Family)

A small genus of shrubs or trees, native to the North Island of New Zealand, the shining leaves pale brown when young, usually alternate; the flowers borne in axillary umbels of four or five.

Species. *Litsea calicaris.* Found from North Cape to Rotorua, it is known to the Maoris as *Mangeao.* It is a shining tree 12 m (40 ft) tall with smooth bark and shining aromatic leaves 7.5 to 10 cm (3 to 4 in) long. The flowers, borne 4 or 5 to an umbel, are delicately fragrant and are cream-coloured. They appear during September and October and are followed by shining red oblong berries.

LOBIVIA (Cactaceae—Cactus Family)

A genus of about 70 species of globular plants with spiny ribs. Almost all are to be found on the borders of Argentina and Bolivia. They flower by day, the blooms retaining their freshness for a week or more. They enjoy shade when in bloom and a compost made up of leaf-mould, decayed manure and lime rubble in equal parts. Keep the roots dry in winter. Almost all bear scentless flowers.

Species. *Lobivia chrysantha.* Found at high altitudes, it is a grey-green plant almost like a tiny ball, with 13 acute ribs, and has areoles with wool. The reddish spines are awl-shaped. The flowers possess extreme beauty and are golden-yellow shaded crimson in the throat and have delicious perfume like lily of the valley.

LOMATIA (Proteaceae—Protea Family)

A small genus of half-hardy plants, native of Chile and parts of Australia and evergreen, being closely related to the Grevilleas and growing well in partial shade.

Species. *Lomatia ferruginea.* A native of Chile, it requires a warm, sheltered garden preferably near the coast, and will attain a height of 7.5 m (25 ft). It has rusty-green, pinnate leaves and bears yellowish-white flowers touched with red, in shape like those of the honeysuckle and with a soft honey perfume. It blooms in May.

L. fraxinifolia. A native of Australia, it is a handsome shrub growing 1.8 m (6 ft) tall with crimson bark and ash-like leaves which are cool grey. The strangely shaped flowers are creamy-white, and are borne during June and July. They have a delicate sweet perfume.

L. longifolia. It is hardy in Britain south of a line from the Mersey to the Trent and in western Scotland where it attains a height of 1.8 to 2.1 m (6 to 7 ft). It has beautiful oak-like foliage and in July and August bears tubular flowers of chalky white which possess a powerful fragrance.

L. obliqua. A native of Chile, and of the same hardiness as *L. longifolia.* It makes a bushy shrub some 1.8 to 2.4 m (6 to 8 ft) in height with broad leathery leaves and in May and June it bears sweetly scented flowers of purest white.

LONICERA (Honeysuckle)
(Caprifoliaceae—Honeysuckle Family)

A genus of 80 or more species of climbing or erect shrubs, evergreen and deciduous and named in honour of Adam Lonicer, a Frankfurt physician. Many bear extremely fragrant flowers. Both those of climbing form and those of bushy habit are happy in partial shade as long as they receive some sunshine and have proved themselves tolerant of a lime-laden soil.

Propagation is from shoots of the ripened wood removed in August and inserted in a sandy compost under a frame light, or the outer shoots may be rooted by layering. The deciduous species may be maintained in a healthy condition by the regular thinning of the old wood in autumn.

Species. *Lonicera albertii.* A deciduous shrub growing 90 cm (3 ft) in height and native to Turkestan. It has smooth, slender branches and willow-shaped leaves of a glaucous hue. In June appear its rosy-mauve flowers at the axils of the leaves and they have the delicious honey scent of the genus.

L. americana. Possibly the finest of all the climbing honeysuckles, it is a semi-evergreen North American hybrid, having the fragrant *L. caprifolium* and *L. estrusca* for its parents. It is a plant of vigorous habit, attaining a height of 9 m (30 ft) or more, and when established provides a magnificent display during July and August, being most free-flowering. The flowers are creamy-white, tinted with purple on the outside, and they have a rich spicy perfume.

L. angustifolia. It is a handsome deciduous shrub of the Himalayas, growing 1.5 to 1.8 m (5 to 6 ft) in height with graceful slender branches and narrow lance-shaped leaves. From the axil of the leaves appear, in April, pairs of small tubular flowers of primrose yellow with a pink flush, which have a soft 'honeysuckle' perfume. The flowers are followed by bright scarlet berries.

L. caprifolium. It is distinguished from *L. periclymenum* in having the upper leaves united at their bases. The flowers are creamy-white, borne in whorled heads, and have an extended corolla tube so that they are fertilized entirely by night-flying Lepidoptera and are mostly scented at night-time when their perfume penetrates far and wide.

L. etrusca. Native of the Mediterranean countries, it is a tall-growing more or less evergreen climber, producing in May, June and July, large clusters of fragrant, creamy-yellow flowers, but it does not bloom until several years old.

L. fragrantissima. A hardy Chinese semi-evergreen plant, fully evergreen where sheltered from cold winds and making a dense bush 2.7 to 3 m (9 to 10 ft) tall and the same across. It has handsome pale-brown wood and opposite leaves, oval, but terminating at a point. From the axils arise the short flower stalks, each supporting twin creamy-white flowers which droop down and emit a powerful penetrating perfume. The flowers are produced back to back and appear from mid-December until early April. Their scent is the most penetrating and delicious of winter-flowering plants. The plants grow best in a well-drained loamy soil and may be propagated by layering in August or by cuttings of half ripened wood inserted into sandy soil under glass.

L. heckrottii. A hybrid which has another hybrid, *L. americana,* for one of its parents, and its yellow flowers flushed with purple have a similar scent. It is a deciduous shrub and blooms from June until September.

L. hispida. It is a hardy deciduous shrub of the Himalayas, growing 60 to 90 cm (2 to 3 ft) in height with hairy stems and bright-green leaves. It comes into bloom in May, its short tubular flowers of creamy-yellow having a sweet perfume.

L. japonica. It is the evergreen Japanese honeysuckle, a fast-growing climber of slender habit, with hairy leaves. It bears its powerfully scented cream and pink-tinted flowers at the axils of the leaves and blooms between July and September. The variety *Halliana* bears white flowers which change to yellow with age, and which also have a pronounced lemon-like perfume, whilst *repens* has all parts, including its flowers, tinted with purple.

L. myrtillus. Also of the Himalayas, it greatly resembles *L. hispida,* growing 0.9 to 1.2 m (3 to 4 ft) tall with small oval leaves from the axils of which are produced in May deliciously scented flowers of creamy-white which are shaped like tiny pitchers.

L. periclymenum. Native of the British Isles and Europe, it is a climbing perennial with ovate leaves and creamy-yellow flowers shaded red on the outside and with delicious perfume, especially at eventide. In bloom from July until September, the flowers are followed by crimson berries.

William Turner, Dean of Wells, in his *Names of Herbs* (1548) wrote, 'periclymenon is named in English, woodbynde and in some places, honeysuccles'.

L. purpusii. It is a hybrid of *L. fragrantissima* and *L. standishii,* both Chinese species closely related to one another. It makes a dense twiggy bush with brown wood which enhances the cream-coloured flowers. It blooms during the first three months of the year, the flowers appearing back to back on the bare twigs and they emit a rich heavy perfume, especially pronounced when the day is calm.

L. setifera. Native of northern China, it is a small erect shrub with its stems covered in bristly hairs, and during March and April the branches are clothed in clusters of small pinkish white tubular flowers which are powerfully scented.

L. syringantha. Possibly the loveliest of the bush honeysuckles, it is a deciduous species from northern China and makes a pretty arching shrub 1.2 m (4 ft) in height. It flowers in May and from the axils of the attractive grey-green leaves are borne lilac-pink flowers which have a delicate sweet perfume.

L. thibetica. In habit it greatly resembles *L. syringantha* from which it may be distinguished by its leaves which in this species are downy on the underside, whilst the flowers are a delicate lilac-pink with a delicious scent, especially in the evening.

L. webbiana. It is a native of British Columbia and grows 1.2 m (4 ft) in height with lance-shaped leaves, and in May appear the richly scented flowers of citron-yellow which are covered with protective hairs.

LOROPETALUM (Hamamelidaceae— Witch Hazel Family)

A genus of three species, native of the Himalayas and western China.

Species. *Loropetalum chinense.* It is a valuable addition to the sheltered winter shrub border for it is evergreen, and comes into bloom in autumn, continuing through the winter. At the end of the branches appear 6 or 8 witch-hazel flowers, but of purest white with the familiar, twisted, petals; they emit a delicate sweet perfume. It is best grown in the South-west of Britain, otherwise does well in a cool greenhouse. Increase by cuttings placed in a frame in summer or autumn.

LOTUS: see NELUMBIUM

LOTUS (Trefoil) (Leguminosae— Laburnum Family)

A genus of mostly perennial plants, native of southern Europe and northern Africa, one of which bears flowers of pronounced perfume.

Species. *Lotus corniculatus.* The Bird's-foot trefoil, so called for the seed-pods are the shape of a bird's foot. It is one of 90 or so species and grows in open pastureland from western Europe to Afghanistan. It is a most attractive perennial plant with its trifoliate leaves and its flowers of bright yellow, borne from July until September and turning to rich orange as they age. The flower-heads are composed of as many as 10 pea-like blossoms which by an intricate process of nature are able to pollinate themselves, yet are powerfully scented. The plant is also known as *Lotus odorata* for its tiny flowers have the same vanilla-like perfume of all the family. There is a double-flowered variety which is an attractive rock garden plant and is of similar fragrance, whilst the variety *major*, of more upright habit, grows along the eastern Mediterranean coastal regions and also bears scented flowers.

LOVAGE: *see* LIGUSTICUM

LUCULIA (Rubiaceae—Bedstraw Family)

A small genus of winter-flowering shrubs from South-east Asia which in Britain require the protection of glass unless in a sheltered garden in the South-west.

Species. *Luculia grandifolia.* Introduced from Bhutan during the twentieth century, where it was discovered at a height of 2,100 to 2,400 m (7 to 8,000 ft). It is the hardiest of the species, its large glossy leaves turning crimson in autumn, and they are followed by large trusses of fragrant snow-white flowers whenever the winter sun is shining.

L. gratissima. The most tender species which makes a most attractive indoor plant for winter flowering, its trusses of sweetly scented flowers being a lovely apple-blossom pink.

L. pinceana. It is a semi-evergreen growing 1.5 m (5 ft) in height and it blooms early in the year, its sweetly scented flowers being of soft porcelain-pink colouring.

L. standishii. It is deciduous and one of the loveliest of the winter-flowering shrubs for it has yellow wood which when young is covered with tiny bristles. The flowers appear in the New Year, borne in pairs on short stems which curve upwards, and being almost white, with widely protruding stamens, have the appearance of night moths. They emit the delicate scent of incense inhaled at a distance.

LUPINUS (Lupin) (Leguminosae— Laburnum Family)

A genus of 80 or more species closely related to the Laburnum and Gorse, and which in the perennial form are better known than perhaps any other garden plants, with their attractive palmate leaves and huge spikes of brilliantly coloured flowers which have a not unpleasant peppery smell. The shrubby Tree lupins, however, have the smell of clover whilst the same sweet penetrating scent as in the Sweet pea and Laburnum, to some the most satisfying of all flower scents, is to be found in the annual forms *L. luteus* and *L. densiflorus* (syn. *L. menziesii*). They are raised by sowing the large seeds in the open ground in April when they will bloom from July until September. They grow 60 cm (2 ft) tall and are extremely colourful in the border, bearing yellow flowers, similar to those of the Tree lupin. It is interesting that none of the blue-flowered annual forms carry any scent. Included in this group are *L. succulentus, L. hartwegii, L. hirsutus, L. mutabilis.*

Species and Varieties. *Lupinus arboreus.* Native of California, it makes a multi-branched shrub with attractive lanceolate-linear leaves of pale green and covered with a soft silvery down. It comes into bloom in June, bearing racemes of yellow laburnum-like flowers in great profusion, and they carry the fragrance of White clover. The variety Snow Queen bears spires of purest white, whilst Golden Spire is an improved form of the type and is attractively scented.

L. densiflorus (syn. *L. menziesii* and *L. sulphureus superbus*). It is a Californian plant of outstanding beauty which makes a spreading multibranched plant and bears its sulphur-yellow flowers in dense whorls at a height of about 60 cm (2 ft).

L. luteus. Native of southern Europe it is also known as *L. odoratus* on account of its outstanding fragrance. The fan-shaped leaves are composed of 7 to 9 leaflets whilst the flower spikes are neat and compact. The variety Romulus is an improvement on the species, its lemon-yellow flowers having a most delicious vanilla-like perfume. *L. luteus* is a native of south-eastern Europe where it is widely used as a soil improver.

LUZURIAGA (Liliaceae—Lily Family)

A genus of two or three species of bush-like form and requiring a sheltered situation and an acid, peaty soil. Being natives of Chile, they should be confined to the more temperate parts.

Species. *Luzuriaga radicans.* It is an evergreen of dwarf bushy habit, growing from 30 to 60 cm (1 to 2 ft) in height with slender stems and stalkless lance-shaped leaves. The flowers, which appear in June, are pure white and when open measure 5 cm (2 in) across with a striking cone-shaped centre of golden-yellow anthers. The flowers have an incense-like perfume.

LYCOPSIS (Boraginaceae— Forget-me-not Family)

A small genus of annual plants.

Species. *Lycopsis variegata.* It is to be found on waste ground near the coast of the eastern Mediterranean. It grows 37.5 cm (15 in) high and has oblong leaves that are hairy on the spine, and from March until June bears its funnel-shaped flowers variegated white, pink and purple in clusters at the end of the branches. They are more sweetly scented than those of any other plants of this almost scentless family.

LYCORIS (Amaryllidaceae—Narcissus Family)

A genus of 10 species, native to China and Japan, with tunicated bulbs. They require similar conditions to the Belladonna-lily to which they are closely related. The hardiest and best species is *Lycoris squamigera* which forms a single mature bulb, capable of producing 4 or 5 scapes each with a large truss of sweetly scented flowers. The plants require an open sunny situation and shallow planting, where the bulbs can ripen well and which will enable them to bear a profusion of flowers the following year.

Here again, only those species bearing a bloom almost free of pigmentation are scented, those bearing brilliant-scarlet flowers, e.g. *L. radiata* and *L. sanguinea,* being entirely devoid of perfume, *L. incarnata* and *L. squamigera,* which both bear flowers in soft pastel shades of pink, carry a delicious spicy scent.

Species. *Lycoris incarnata.* A native of central China, it is one of the hardiest species and bears pale-pink flowers that are sweetly scented. It blooms late in August, after the leaves have died down and bears 8 or 10 funnel-shaped flowers in a large umbel.

L. squamigera. A strikingly beautiful Japanese species which comes into bloom about ten days before *L. incarnata,* as soon as the strap-like leaves, some 30 cm (12 in) long, have withered. The blooms are a most attractive lilac-pink, very sweetly scented, and are borne 8 or 10 to an umbel on a stem about 90 cm (3 ft) tall. Several stems appearing at one time from the same bulb make up a magnificent display and drench the garden with their fragrance. It is one of the outstanding plants of the garden and worthy of a little care in its cultivation.

When grown in the greenhouse, the bulbs are potted in autumn between September and December, thereafter repotted each year as soon as they have flowered. Once the flowers have died down the bulbs should be kept dry; the temperature in winter should not fall below 13°C (55°F.). Offsets are used for propagation.

LYONIA (Ericaceae—Heather Family)

A genus of eight species of evergreen or deciduous shrubs bearing racemes of sweetly scented white flowers.

Species. *Lyonia paniculata.* It is native of North America and grows 1.8 to 2.4 m (6 to 8 ft) in height with downy stems and pointed lance-shaped leaves. The tiny white flowers are produced in June in round clusters and they have a soft honey-like perfume. The plant requires a well-drained soil, preferably of a sandy nature and enriched with peat or leaf-mould.

LYONOTHAMNUS (Rosaceae—Rose Family)

A genus of a single species, native only of four small islands off the coast of southern California.

Species. *Lyonothamnus floribundus.* It resembles the sweet-fern *(Comptonia)* in the form and scent of its foliage. A plant of rapid growth, it will make a small tree 3 m (10 ft) tall within 3 years where it is able to grow without check almost the whole year round. Known as the Catalina ironwood, it is a most handsome plant with crimson bark which peels off. Its pinnate fern-like leaves, like those of sweet-fern, when bruised or in a gentle breeze on a warm day release their pine-like scent for a considerable distance. The variety *asplenifolius* has the most attractive foliage. In spring, it bears large clusters of tiny white flowers which contrast strikingly with the crimson bark.

LYSICHITUM (Araceae—Arum Lily Family)

A small genus of handsome but evil-smelling plants confined to North and South America.

Species. *Lysichitum americanum.* A native of North America where, on account of the unpleasant smell it emits, it is known as the Skunk cabbage. Yet it is a handsome plant bearing bronze-purple spathes marbled with green. Its smell is said to be a combination of skunk, carrion and garlic, and attracts flies and midges in such great numbers that spiders weave their webs from plant to plant and enjoy a continuous feast. The huge sulphur-yellow spathes and leaves make it a most handsome plant for the waterside in spite of its obnoxious smell.

L. camtschatense. A handsome Aroid of the swamplands of South America, it is stemless, producing huge oblong leaves often 45 to 50 cm (18 to 20 in) in length and marked like those of the Dieffen-bachia, to which it is closely related. The spathe rises 30 cm (12 in) in height with the spadix some 10 cm (4 in) long. The plant emits an unpleasant animal smell but has not the fetid smell of the other Aroids as the plant does not rely on insects for pollination. The 'flowers' fertilize each other.

M

MAACKIA (Leguminosae—Laburnum Family)

A genus of 10 species of small trees or shrubs, native of South-east Asia and noted for their yellow wood which is used for carving.

Species. *Maackia amurensis.* Known as the Chinese yellow-wood, it is native of the Amur Valley, and in the British Isles and northern Europe should be confined to a warm, sheltered garden where it will reach a height of 3 m (10 ft) in a well-drained sandy soil. Its leaves are composed of 4 pairs of oblong leaflets and it blooms in August, the small greenish-white flowers, borne in their long racemes, having a powerful vanilla-like perfume.

MACROTOMIA (Boraginaceae— Forget-me-not Family)

A genus of six species, native of the eastern Mediterranean and Himalayas.

Species. *Macrotomia cephalotes.* It is closely allied to *Arnebia echoiodes,* the Prophet flower, but is now rarely to be seen. Clarence Elliott has told of how the plant was discovered in the Taurus Mountains by E. K. Balls during a plant-collecting expedition in 1934 and he considered it the most beautiful plant he had ever found.

It makes a spreading plant of perennial habit and it bears, throughout summer, large flower-heads of deep golden-yellow which emit a sweet honey-like perfume.

MAGNOLIA (Magnoliaceae—Magnolia Family)

A genus of 70 species of evergreen or deciduous trees or shrubs, native of tropical Asia and America and also represented in the eastern U.S.A. The leaves are entire, the flowers solitary with a spathe-like bract and 6 to 12 petals. The carpels numerous and borne on a conical receptacle. Hans Hallier regarded the Magnoliaceae as being most representative of the Angiosperms.

M. grandiflora, the evergreen Laurel-leaf magnolia, is a native of Florida where the trees reach up to a height of 30 m (100 ft). It blooms from early July throughout summer, and the flowers, as Henry Phillips wrote, 'perfume the air for a considerable distance around with the most agreeable odour which at one moment reminds us of the jasmine or lily of the valley, the next of the violet mixed with the apricot'; the magnolia growing in the grounds of The Priory, Ryde, in the Isle of Wight, apparently 'often wafted its fragrance for more than a mile in distance, which must make it the most powerfully scented of all flowers and which gave the plant the name of Lily tree'.

M. grandiflora was not mentioned by Philip Miller in the first edition of the *Gardener's and Florist's Dictionary* published in 1724, for the first plant to be grown in England appeared in the Exmouth garden of Sir John Colliton in Devon shortly afterwards. In 1800, the Marquess of Blandford planted twenty-two of them at White Knights, near Reading, which have reached a height of 9 m (30 ft) and are perhaps the finest in the British Isles.

Species and Varieties. The magnolias are placed into groups according to their flowering time.

GROUP I. *Magnolia denudata*. A native of central China and originally named *M. conspicua*, it is known as the Yulan magnolia and is a deciduous species, its large white globe-shaped flowers, suffused with purple on the outside, appearing first towards the end of March and deliciously scented. It has the additional value in that it blooms at an early age. *M. soulangeana* is believed to be a hybrid from this species. It is fertilized by bees.

M. lennei. A hybrid of *M. denudata*, it is the last of the early magnolias to bloom as the first flowers appear at the beginning of May, but they come again in early autumn. They are globe-shaped, the largest of the magnolias and a lovely rosy-purple with a violet-like perfume. This magnolia also blooms when young, before reaching 90 cm (3 ft) in height.

M. liliflora. Native of China, it is one of the parents of *M. soulangeana* and is one of the best of all the early-flowering magnolias. It is slow-growing and rarely exceeds a height of 3 to 3.6 m (10 to 12 ft) but comes into bloom when only about 0.9 m (3 ft) tall, its elegant goblets of glistening white on the inside being shaded with crimson on the outside, and they are deliciously scented.

M. salicifolia. The Willow-leaf magnolia of Japan which grows 6 m (20 ft) or more in height with narrow leaves of palest green, glaucous on the underside. Its star-like flowers also have narrow petals and are of purest white, like driven snow and with a rich fruity perfume. The blooms are at their best during April and May.

M. soulangeana. It comes into bloom before the leaves appear, early in April, its large white flowers being tinted with purple at the base. There is a pure-white form, *alba*, whilst *amabilis* bears large cream-coloured flowers. The variety *nigra* bears flowers the colour of a Black Hamburgh grape and about three weeks later than the others of this group. Plenty of peat should be packed around the roots at planting time.

M. stellata, the Star magnolia. It is the first to open its flowers, usually before the end of March and before the leaves appear. The blooms are star-shaped, each with as many as 15 narrow petals and with a delicate, sweet perfume. It makes a small twiggy spreading bush rather than a tree

and may be planted in the smallest of gardens whilst it comes into bloom when only two years old.

GROUP II. *M. acuminata*. Known as the Cucumber tree, it is a native of North America where it grows to a height of 12 m (40 ft) or more and has tapering leaves 30 cm (12 in) long. It is a hardy, deciduous tree flowering during June and July, the flowers being glaucous green, tinted with yellow, and they have a delicate perfume. The variety *cardata* is a better plant for the garden as it comes into bloom at an early age.

M. fraseri (syn. *M. auriculata*). A deciduous tree of the southern United States with spongy wood. The spoon-shaped leaves are 30 cm (12 in) long, glaucous on the underside. The erect flowers, 10 cm (4 in) across, appear in June and are creamy-white, very sweetly scented.

M. hypoleuca (syn. *M. obsovata*). A native of Japan where it grows to a height of 15 m (50 ft) and more with broad dark-green leaves. Its flowers, borne during June and July, are like huge goblets of creamy-yellow with a mass of scarlet stamens at the centre and they are powerfully scented.

M. macrophylla. A handsome tree of North America with smooth white bark and with leaves of great size, being up to 90 cm (3 ft) long and 30 cm (12 in) across. The bell-shaped flowers are white, blotched with purple at the base of the petals and are sweetly scented. Like *M. hypoleuca*, the tree should be confined to the warmer parts of Britain and it will not bloom until it has reached maturity.

M. parviflora (syn. *M. sieboldii*). Native to Japan it is the most dwarf of all magnolias, rarely exceeding 0.9 to 1.2 m (3 to 4 ft). It has oval, more rounded leaves than the other species and is deciduous. The white flowers, smaller than all others, are tinted with rose and are cup-shaped. They appear towards the end of May and continue until late July when the evergreen magnolias come into bloom.

M. sinensis. Native of western China, it grows to a height of about 3.6 m (12 ft), with large oval leaves of brilliant green amongst which it bears goblets of purest white, the purity being accentuated by the crimson stamens, and they have a perfume as exotic as the whitest lilies. It is in bloom during May and June.

M. tripetala. The Umbrella tree of the eastern United States, so called because of the widely spread leaves at the branch tips. It blooms early May and into June, its chalky-white flowers with their purple stamens having so strong a scent as to be unpleasantly overpowering when the air is calm. But it is a lovely species, the flowers being followed by large rose-red fruits.

M. watsonii. A native of Japan, it makes a neat, compact tree and bears its large white goblets at an early age; they have a refreshing lemon perfume, thought by some to be the loveliest of all magnolia scents.

M. wilsonii. It is the last of the deciduous species to bloom, the white cup-shaped flowers appearing towards the end of June. It contradicts the preferences of most magnolias for it prefers shade and seems to be the only magnolia to grow well on chalk.

GROUP III. *M. grandiflora.* The Laurel magnolia of the southern United States, it has long oval leaves like those of the laurel and with unusual rust-red markings on the under-surface. It produces its flowers during July and August and is at its best in Britain when trained against a warm wall for it is the most tender of the American species. The large creamy-white blooms possess a more powerful perfume than almost any other flower. In its native land, it grows to more than 30 m (100 ft) in height and spreads out to almost 15 m (50 ft) but in Britain it rarely exceeds 12 m (40 ft) in height.

An outstanding form is Exmouth Variety also known as *elliptica*, which comes into bloom when only a young plant. Its large cream-coloured flowers have a refreshing lemon scent which will perfume a room when growing outside an open window. It is hardier than *M. grandiflora.* There is also a form *obovata*, known in Carolina as the Big laurel, whilst Goliath, with waved petals and bearing enormous blooms of creamy-white with a delicious perfume, is also outstanding.

It relies on the Rose-beetle, *Cetonia ausata,* for its fertilization. They find shelter beneath the inner petals of the half-open flowers where they devour the honey secreted between the stigmas. Here they remain until the petals fall, then laden with pollen fly to other flowers. Self-fertilization is impossible as stigmas and anthers mature at different times.

M. glauca. A semi-evergreen, native of the eastern United States where it is known as the Sweet bay or Swamp laurel for it grows on swampy ground, usually close to the sea. It is also known as the Swamp Sassafras, for the properties of its bark are similar to those of the Sassafras. It is also the Beaver tree for the animals construct their dwellings with the bark. It grows to a height of 4.5 m (15 ft) and has leathery leaves of blue-green. In July and August it bears cup-shaped flowers of creamy white which change to apricot with age, the petals being retained for three weeks and they have a delicious aromatic fruity scent, likened to that of the lily of the valley but more aromatic.

M. longifolia is a variety of *M. glauca* and in the southern United States is known as the Evergreen swamp magnolia. It makes a most handsome tree 6 to 9 m (20 to 30 ft) in height, its elliptical leaves being glaucous on the underside whilst the pure-white 12-petalled flowers emit a delicious perfume.

MAHONIA (Berberidaceae—Berberry Family)

A genus of 70 species, native of western China, Japan and North America and differing from Berberis in the compound leaves and spineless stems. Growing well in all soils and in full sun or partial shade, the mahonias are planted in deciduous woodlands and for game coverts, and may be used to cover an unsightly bank. In the shrubbery they provide valuable winter colour from their foliage, flowers and fruits. Plant October to March, and if the plants become leggy cut them well back in May; new growth will appear from the base. The plants are easily increased by layers, suckers, seeds or cuttings.

Species. *Mahonia aquifolium.* Native of North America and naturalized in woodlands in the British Isles, it makes a low, spreading shrub 90 cm (3 ft) tall and the same across, with glossy, dark-green leaves which turn crimson in winter. In March and April, it bears its golden-yellow flowers in dense racemes, and they are delicately scented. They are followed by large blue-black fruits, hence its name of Oregon Grape.

M. bealei. It is to be distinguished from *M. japonica,* for it has broader leaflets which are placed closer together on the stems whilst its golden, sweetly scented flowers are held in erect racemes. It was discovered by Robert Fortune 'in the green-tea country of Bwuy-chow', and was named in honour of his friend, William Beale of Shanghai, in whose garden Fortune kept many of his discoveries.

M. fremontii fasciculata. It forms a tall, open shrub with short grey leaves, and during February and March bears clusters of refreshingly fragrant golden flowers along the whole length of the stem.

M. haematocarpa. Like *M. aquifolium* it is also native of the western United States where it reaches a height of 2.4 m (8 ft) or more. Its evergreen leaves are divided into 5 or 6 leaflets, and are of an attractive grey-green colouring. It comes into bloom in May, just as *M. aquifolium* is finishing, its long, elegant racemes of fragrant pale yellow being followed by brilliant-red fruits.

M. japonica. Native of Japan, it is a plant of extreme hardiness and toughness, growing 1.2 to 1.5 m (4 to 5 ft) tall. It is an evergreen, with glossy, spiny leaves or leaflets, and throughout late winter and spring it bears its lemon-yellow flowers in terminal clusters or spikes which radiate from the base of the leaf shoots. The flowers are most attractive, being bell-shaped and drooping and with a delicious perfume.

The form *hyemalis* has leaves 45 cm (1½ ft) long and bears a larger flower spike, similar to the lily of the valley and almost as fragrant. It comes into bloom early in December, before the type, and continues throughout the winter. The plants appreciate a moist soil and a position of partial shade. Indeed, they are excellent for planting beneath mature, deciduous trees which give protection to the winter flowers.

M. lomariifolia. It is a valuable ever-green for it blooms during autumn and early winter. In Britain, it will survive a severe winter only if given the protection of other shrubs. Forming a single stem, it is almost tree-like in habit, the huge leaves having 15 pairs of leaflets, whilst the fragrant, golden-yellow flower spikes are borne in upright terminal clusters.

M. napaulensis. Native of Nepal, it is evergreen and reaches a height of 2.1 to 2.4 m (7 to 8 ft), and from October until April bears bright golden-yellow flowers on long, slender sprays, which have a sweet delicate fragrance. The flowers are replaced by sloe-black fruits.

M. repens. Also from the Oregon region of the United States, it grows 37.5 cm (15 in) tall, its leaves divided into two or three pairs of spiny leaflets. In April it bears short racemes of golden-yellow followed by powdered blue-black fruits.

MAIANTHEMUM (Liliaceae—Lily Family)

A genus of a single species.

Species. *Maianthemum bifolia.* The Twin-leaf lily of the valley, to be found in the northern temperate regions of Europe and America. From a creeping rootstock it sends up its heart-shaped leaves in pairs. The small greenish-white sweetly scented flowers appear in May, in erect racemes and are unusual in that they have only 4 free oblong segments and 4 stamens.

MALALEUCA (Myrtaceae—Myrtle Family)

A genus of handsome trees, native of South-east Asia and with fragrant leaves which yield Essence of Niaouli.

Species. *Malaleuca viridifolia.* Native of the Straits Settlements, it has elliptical leaves which, when fresh, yield on distillation with water about 2.5 per cent of a pale-yellow oil, the odour of which recalls that of cajuput. Its composition contains eucalyptol, 'citrene', and a terpineol.

MALUS (Rosaceae—Rose Family)

Previously classified under *Pyrus,* a genus of about 50 species of deciduous trees with alternate simple or pinnate stalked leaves and bearing their flowers in terminal cymes. They are followed by brightly coloured edible fruits. No plant was held in greater esteem during medieval times than the Crab-apple from which the orchard apple was evolved. The fruit was made into a delicious conserve and, especially at Christmastime, was roasted to serve with ale. Shakespeare makes several references to the custom of placing roasted crabs in bowls of punch or ale.

With their brilliantly coloured, polished fruits of crimson and gold, and flowering in early summer, the crab-apples are amongst the best of small garden trees, being of compact habit and most of upright growth. Few are fragrant, but the following species bear scented blossom.

Species and Varieties. *Malus angustifolia.* A handsome small tree, native of the eastern United States with ovate leaves and bearing in spring, salmon-pink flowers which have the violet perfume.

Malus coronaria. The Sweet-scented crab, native of North America. It makes a pretty tree 6 m (20 ft) tall with ovate, toothed leaves and in May bears blush-white flowers which are sweetly scented and which are followed by large green fruits. The variety Charlotte bears double flowers of an attractive candy floss pink which are violet scented.

M. hupehensis. It makes a vigorous branching tree 4.5 m (15 ft) tall and is a useful wind-break. In May, every branch is clothed in sweetly scented snow-white blossom which is followed by red cherry-like fruits.

M. sylvestris. The Crab or Wild apple, a native of the British Isles growing about 6 m (20 ft) tall with rounded leaves and bearing flowers in terminal cymes. From the Wild apple, crossed with numerous introductions from the Continent which began to reach Britain during Roman times, the modern orchard apples have been evolved. These are apples used in cider-making, for culinary purposes and for dessert. All have blossom with some degree of perfume but in a number of varieties this is more pronounced than in others.

The apples with most sweetly scented blossom are those which require most assistance with their pollination. The self-fertile and early-flowering Beauty of Bath is almost devoid of perfume but in Bramley Seedling, Cox's Orange, Annie

Elizabeth and Lane's Prince Albert, the perfume is pronounced. Each of these apples requires one or more pollinating varieties to set fruit and their perfume would appear to be provided by nature to call the pollinating insects to them after they have visited blossom of other varieties in bloom at the same time.

MALVA (Malvaceae—Mallow Family)

A genus of 16 species of annual or perennial herbs which flourish in almost any soil and bloom from June until September. They usually grow in wayside hedgerows though the Marsh mallow is a plant of low-lying pastureland. The genus *Malva* was named by Linnaeus from a Greek word meaning 'soft' which refers to the emollient qualities of stem and leaf.

Species. *Malva moschata.* The native Musk mallow which grows to a height of 60 to 90 cm (2 to 3 ft), its dark-green leaves which smell of musk when bruised being divided into 5 large segments, like a fern, and distinguishing it from other native mallows. It blooms during July and August, its flowers of mallow-pink being borne in terminal clusters. There is also a white form, *alba*. The flowers are followed by a ring of seeds, which have the appearance of a small cheese, hence its country name of 'bread and cheese'.

MAMMILLARIA (Cactaceae—Cactus Family)

A genus of about 300 species, mostly native of Mexico, which usually bear their flowers in a circle at the top of the plant. These are followed by small red fruits. In certain species there is a water-like juice, sometimes green in colour, or milk-like. Most species are of easy cultivation, forming large clumps with the leaves (tubercles) merging into the stem. Nectar glands are present. Most bear orange or red flowers and few have any scent.

Species. *Mammillaria camptotricha.* Like many of the genus, it soon makes a large clump composed of numerous offsets which grow about 7.5 cm (3 in) tall, with rounded spines. The small white flowers with their long thread-like petals have the unmistakable honey scent of lime blossom.

A compost consisting of John Innes potting compost with 1/6 part added of broken brick and chippings is suitable. Increase is by seed, or offsets.

MANDEVILLA (Apocynaceae—Periwinkle Family)

A genus of more than 100 species of twining plants, native of tropical South America.

Species. *Mandevilla suaveolens.* A graceful twining plant with small deciduous leaves, it bears throughout summer long racemes of large pure-white tubular flowers which emit a heavy exotic perfume. It is known as the Chile jasmine though it is mostly found in the country around Buenos Aires, and is one of the finest of all climbing plants for a warm, sheltered garden. Its blooms are like small white petunias, measuring 5 to 7.5 cm (2 to 3 in) across, as white as the lily and with a similar perfume.

It is a most desirable plant for decorating the roof of a cool greenhouse or garden room, requiring a minimum winter temperature of no more than 7°C (45°F), and being deciduous it does not deprive other plants of light in winter. When planting, plenty of peat should be packed around its roots which must be spread well out and covered with only 7.5 to 10 cm (3 to 4 in) of compost. The plant is seen to best advantage when growing at the end of a sun room with its shoots trained over wires extending over the roof from which its flowers will hang in clusters scenting the room for weeks during spring and summer. It is a plant of rapid growth and of graceful habit, its handsome dark-green foliage being an additional attraction.

MARIGOLD: see CALENDULA

MARJORAM: see ORIGANUM

MARRUBIUM (Labiatae—Lavender Family)

A genus of seven or eight species of perennial downy herbs, one of which, *M. vulgare*, is native of the British Isles.

Species. *Marrubium vulgare.* It is known as the White horehound and from earliest times has been grown for its medicinal properties, being in constant demand for cough mixtures. The plant grows 60 cm (2 ft) high and is to be found on waste ground, its wrinkled woolly leaves giving it a frosted appearance. When growing, the leaves have a pronounced musky smell which they lose when dry. The small white flowers appear in dense whorls at the leaf axils and are much visited by bees.

MARSDENIA (Asclepiadaceae—Stephanotis Family)

Named after William Marsden, the eighteenth-century orientalist, the genus is closely related to *Stephanotis* and its flowers are as powerfully scented. It is a plant of sub-tropical areas but is most widely represented in Australia which has 14 species, *M. suaveolens* being the most common. The plants are of twining habit, bearing their flowers in axillary inflorescences.

Species. *Marsdenia suaveolens.* It has dark-green lanceolate leaves and bears small greenish-white flowers in axillary umbels. They possess an almost overpowering scent for indole is present as in stephanotis and narcissus.

MARTYNIA (Martinyaceae—Martynia Family)

A genus of a single species which in the British Isles should be raised in gentle heat and, when hardened, planted out in June. Native of Mexico, the plant is covered with down and has long heart-shaped leaves, whilst the gloxinia-like flowers are borne in short terminal racemes, followed by curiously shaped fruits. The hard-coated seed should be steeped in warm water for 24 hours before sowing.

Species. *Martynia fragrans.* It grows 60 cm (2 ft) tall and comes into bloom before the end of June. It has hairy heart-shaped leaves and bears flowers of a striking crimson-purple with contrasting yellow streaks in the throat, and they exhale a powerful vanilla-like odour. The bloom is followed by fruits 10 cm (4 in) long which curve upwards like horns, hence its popular name of Unicorn plant.

MASSONIA (Liliaceae—Lily Family)

A genus of 45 species of small bulbous plants, native of South Africa and named in honour of Frank Masson, a botanist who travelled widely there towards the end of the eighteenth century. The pure-white flowers are borne in clusters between twin opposite leaves, the flower stem being absent or almost so. Not entirely hardy, they are best grown under glass in the British Isles and northern Europe, in a frame or cool greenhouse. Plant 5 or 6 bulbs to a 15-cm (6-in) pot in September. They will bloom late in spring and early summer.

Species. *Massonia amygdalina.* Native of Natal, it is known as the Almond-scented massonia for its white star-like flowers, tipped with green, have the powerful almond-like scent of heliotrope. It has short oval leaves and the flowers bloom during April and May.

MATRICARIA (Compositae—Daisy Family)

A genus of small annual plants growing about dry wastelands and cornfields, several of which have fruit-scented foliage when handled. Known as the Mayweeds, they have leaves divided into narrow segments. The flowers are borne singly or in corymbs.

Species. *Matricaria recutita* (syn. *M. chamomilla*). The Scented mayweed, it is a pungently aromatic annual with bipinnate leaves cut into fern-like segments and growing about 30 cm (12 in) tall. The white daisy-like flowers are borne in corymbs, the ray-florets becoming reflexed immediately after fertilization. It blooms during July and August.

M. suaveolens (syn. *M. matricarioides*). It is known as the Apple-mayweed for its dark-green 2- to 3-pinnate leaves, finely divided into thread-like segments, release the appealing odour of ripe apples when handled or when warmed by the sun. The flowers are composed of greenish-yellow disc florets with sepal-like bracts.

MATTHIOLA (Stock)
(Cruciferae—Wallflower Family)

A genus of about 50 species of branching annual or biennial herbs amongst which is *M. bicornis*, the Night-scented stock: also the Spring-flowering Brompton stocks, and the Summer-flowering Ten-week stocks. Each bears a flower with an exotic penetrating clove perfume which is more pronounced than in any other flower. Like the wallflower, it has a rich Eastern quality about its scent, being heavy and exciting. Henry Phillips evokes the quality of the stock's perfume: 'Though less graceful than the rose, and not so superb as the lily, its splendour is more durable, its fragrance of longer continuance'. Indeed it is and no other plant, except perhaps the wallflower, is able to convey so readily its warm aromatic perfume when warmed by the sun.

The garden stocks are descended from a single species, *M. incana* and its variety *M. annua*, annual (or biennial) plants which are native of southern Europe. Known as the Hoary stock, *M. incana* may be native to the British Isles for in Sussex and elsewhere it grows on the face of chalky cliffs where it has been established for centuries. Both forms were common in Elizabethan gardens and were described by Lyte in his *New Herbal* (1578) as 'Stock Gillofers'. Gerard said that they were 'greatly esteemed for the beautie of their flowers and pleasant sweet perfume'. In Gerard's time, only the white stock was grown, and also the violet or purple from which the flower took its name of Dame's violet or Purple gillyflower, to distinguish it from the Wall and Clove gillyflowers. Dr Turner in his *Herbal* (1568) called it the 'Stock Gelouer' for the purpose of distinction. By the end of the sixteenth century, stocks bearing double flowers were common and all the familiar stock colours including rose, red and 'carnation' (flesh).

Stocks may be divided into four main groups, one for each season of the year.

BROMPTON STOCKS. First come the spring-flowering or Brompton stocks, developed at the Brompton Road Nurseries of Messrs London Wise (who laid out the gardens at Blenheim Palace) early in the eighteenth century. The plants are true biennials, obtainable in white, purple, crimson and rose, and should be sown early in July removing the dark-green seedlings (as with all stocks) as these will give only single flowers. The seedlings should be transplanted in August and they may either be set out in their flowering quarters in October or wintered under a frame and planted out in March. Or they may be grown in pots to bloom under glass early in the year. Lavender Lady and the crimson Queen Astrid are out-standing varieties.

SUMMER-FLOWERING OR TEN-WEEK STOCKS. They are so called because they may be brought into bloom within 10 weeks of sowing the seed in gentle heat early in March. Hansen's 100% Double is a recommended strain for bedding, making branched plants only 22.5 cm (9 in) tall and obtainable in all the stock shades including apple-blossom pink, light blue and yellow.

The Excelsior Mammoth strain in a similar colour range, including 'blood-red, grows 60 cm (2 ft) tall, the large densely packed spikes having a most majestic appearance in the border whilst they are valuable for cutting so that their delicious clove scent may be enjoyed indoors.

AUTUMN-FLOWERING STOCKS. These are the Intermediate or East Lothian stocks. They should also be sown in March for they take several weeks longer to come into bloom than the Ten-week type. They are at their best during the autumn and until the arrival of the November frosts. The Kelvedon strain in all the rich stock colours is outstanding.

WINTER-FLOWERING STOCKS. They are the finest of all stocks, known as the Winter Beauty or Beauty of Nice strain. The seed should be sown in July for winter flowering under glass. Making plants of vigorous branching habit, they grow 45 to 50 cm (18 to 20 in) tall and produce their large dense spikes throughout winter under glass. Amongst the finest varieties are Mont Blanc (white); Queen Alexandra (rosy-lilac); Crimson King and Salmon King. Under glass in a temperature of 10°C (50°F) the perfume of the flowers is almost overpowering.

Species. *Matthiola bicornis* (syn. *M. tristis*). The Night-scented stock, it is native of southern Europe, from Spain to Greece. It is a hardy biennial though is usually treated as a hardy annual. Seed is sown where it is to bloom, in March or April as an edging to a border or path, or in small circles to the front of a border. If the seed is sown thinly, it will not be necessary to thin the plants later. Of slender habit, it grows 22.5 cm (19 in) tall and bears tiny insignificant flowers varying in colour from white to brown; at nightfall they emit so powerful a fragrance that their presence may be detected from many yards away. It is not necessary to stoop to inhale their perfume as with so many flowers, for it fills the garden when the air is heavy and the night is calm and one wonders at the ability of these tiny dingy-looking flowers to store by day so much perfume which is released only when the temperature falls in the evening.

Phillips has told that 'for many ages, the flower has been a favourite with German ladies and is much cultivated in that country in pots for the apartments, hence it obtained the name of Dame's Violet'. It was also called *Nacht Violen*. The plant was grown in England in Elizabethan times and may have been familiar both to Spenser and to Shakespeare. Later, it came to be grown like the mignonette, in pots to be placed on balconies of town houses where its perfume on the summer evenings would penetrate indoors through the open windows and diffuse itself about the home as well as the streets.

M. elliptica. A native of Egypt where it makes a low shrub amongst the stones of mountainous regions. It has elliptic leaves and bears large pure-white flowers which carry the familiar clove-like perfume of the family.

M. odoratissima (syn. *Hesperis odoratissima*). Native of the Caucasus and Tiflis on the Black Sea, it is an erect shrub growing 45 cm (18 in) tall with toothed leaves covered with down. It is also found in Afghanistan and in western Tibet, growing in rocky formations at a height of 3,000 to 3,600 m (10 to 12,000 ft). The flowers are large, of a dingy cream colour, turning purple-brown with age but diffusing at night a delicious clove-like perfume.

M. sinuata. It is native of the sandy coastline of Cornwall and Pembrokeshire and southern Europe, and is the *Cheiranthus tricuspidatus* of Hudson's *Flora Anglica*. To the Cornishman it is known as the Great Sea stock. An herbaceous plant growing 60 cm (2 ft) tall with an erect branched stem, the leaves are oblong and downy whilst the dingy reddish-purple flowers are sweetly scented at night.

MAURITIA (Palmaceae—Palm Tree Family)

A large genus of South American palms of the tribe Hepidocaryeae and known as the Fan palms. A number bear powerfully scented flowers to attract insects for the pollination of the female flowers.

Species. *Mauritia carnana.* It is the amazingly scented Fan palm of the Rio Negro, the white flowers of a single tree having been likened to the scent from an acre of mignonette and causing dizziness if inhaled at close range. The flowers are borne in dense inflorescences from a leafy crown.

MAXILLARIA (Orchidaceae—Orchid Family)

A genus of more than 300 species, native of tropical America and the West Indies. They are epiphytic and vary considerably in their habit of growth, some of them having one large leaf only, or two strap-shaped leathery leaves, and others having rhizomes with the pseudo-bulbs set on them at intervals. They are not often seen, although attractive and usually very fragrant. They do best grown in pots, or pans for the rhizomatous species, with a mixture of three parts sphagnum-moss and one part peat, and plenty of drainage material. A warm humid atmosphere with shade, is necessary, and a winter minimum of about 10°C (50°F). Increase is by division when the plants are large enough.

Species. *Maxillaria grandiflora.* A Peruvian species with white flowers, whose lip is purple and yellow. They are fragrant and appear in spring and early summer. It is a handsome orchid and its flowers are large.

M. nigrescens. The plum-red colouring of this winter-flowering species from New Granada is attractive of itself, and the fragrance of ripe melons that the flowers emit is unusual and adds to its desirability. The flowers are carried in clusters on drooping or erect stems.

M. picta. Although this is a small orchid, growing only a few inches high, it is one of the most easily grown. The fragrant yellow and white flowers are borne singly from January to April, somewhat dwarfed by the leaves which may be 30 cm (1 ft) long.

M. sanderiana. A very handsome species,

from Ecuador, it has white petals and sepals, and a purplish-red lip. The fleshy flowers are fragrant and long-lasting, about 15 cm (6 in) across. It flowers between August and October, and is best grown in a basket.

M. venusta. From Venezuela, this is a very pretty orchid, mostly waxy white, with a yellow, red-spotted lip and strongly scented. The flowers are large, up to 15 cm (6 in) across.

MAZUS (Scrophulariaceae—Foxglove Family)

A small genus of dwarf herbs, native of South-east Asia, Australia and New Zealand, and bearing scented flowers which is rare in this large family.

Species. *Mazus radicans.* It frequents damp low-lying places where it bears its white flowers throughout summer. The upper lip is bi-lobed, the lower lip being tri-lobed with a band of yellow hairs leading to the honey cavity and acting as a guide-line for bees. The flowers are powerfully scented.

MEDEOLA (Liliaceae—Lily Family)

A genus of a single species, native of North America.

Species. *Medeola virginiana.* It takes its name from Medea, the sorceress, for its supposed medicinal qualities. It grows in moist woodlands extending from Nova Scotia to Florida and is known as Cucumber Root for its short rhizomatous rootstock has a pleasant refreshing smell of cucumber. It flourishes in partial shade and may be grown with Trillium and Polygonatum (Solomon's seal) for it enjoys a damp soil containing peat or leaf-mould.

It forms a rootstock 5 to 7.5 cm (2 to 3 in) long, and a slender, erect, unbranched stem 30 to 45 cm (12 to 18 in) tall covered in down and with a whorl of leaves at the middle. The leaves are 5 to 7.5 cm (2 to 3 in) long and 2.5 cm (1 in) wide, narrowing at the base, whilst the small flowers are yellow and are borne in an umbel of 3 to 9 during June. They are scentless and are followed by dark-blue berries.

MEDICAGO (Leguminosae—Laburnum Family)

A genus of shrubby plants known as the Trefoils, one of which, *M. arborea*, the Moon trefoil of southern Europe which is especially prominent in Greece, bears flowers with the well-loved vanilla or sweet-pea scent of the family. The plant requires a sunny situation and a light loamy soil.

Species. *Medicago arborea.* It is the tallest-growing of all the trefoils, sometimes reaching a height of 3 m (10 ft) with evergreen trifoliate leaves and bearing continuously from May until September racemes of laburnum-like flowers of deepest yellow. The plant is enhanced by its hairy grey stems whilst the blooms are followed by circled snail-like seed-pods.

MEDICOSMA (Rutaceae—Rue Family)

A genus of a single species, native of eastern Australia.

Species. *Medicosma cunninghamii.* It is an evergreen shrub and has leaves which release the resinous smell of turpentine when pressed, whilst the white flowers have the scent of orange-blossom.

MELALEUCA (Myrtaceae—Myrtle Family)

A genus of 100 species of entirely Australian evergreen trees or shrubs represented mostly in Western and South Australia but found in most parts. Those bearing white flowers, in cylindrical spikes, are fragrant whilst the leaves are covered with pellucid dots which are oil-bearing glands.

Species. *Melaleuca linarifolia.* It is found mostly on the coast of Queensland and New South Wales, in swamplands where it forms a tree 6 m (20 ft) in height, its slender branches covered with white, papery bark, and it has narrow flax-like leaves, hence its name of the Flax-leaf Paper-bark. The white flowers, borne in pairs, are really bundles of fluffy stamens and give the tree a most attractive appearance. From the fresh leaves, the pale-yellow oil of cajuput is obtained.

Cool greenhouse cultivation is required in Britain, though it may be grown out of doors in the South-west in a sheltered spot. Cuttings are used for propagation.

MELANDRIUM (Caryophyllaceae—Pink Family)

A genus of about 100 species, native of the northern temperate regions, and of tropical Africa and South America.

Species. *Melandrium album* (syn. *Lychnis alba, L. vespertina*). Its scent is so unmistakably like that of the pink and carnation family, being sweet and clove-like, that the plants were grouped together by the Elizabethan poet Michael Drayton, in the *Polyolbion* as being suitable for a pot-pourri:

> Sweet William, sops-in-wine, the campion; and to these
> Some lavender they put, with rosemary and bays,
> Sweet marjoram, with her like sweet basil rare for smell . . .

The White campion blooms from May until September, its pure-white flowers, 2.5 cm (1 in) across, being spicily scented on a calm, damp evening. It grows 60 cm (2 ft) in height, and is a handsome perennial plant, the icy whiteness of the flowers being enhanced by the large ribbed calyx and long tapering leaves which are sticky to the touch. It is propagated either from cuttings or by division of the roots in autumn. *M. alba* is native of the British Isles and central Europe.

MELIA (Meliaceae—Mahogany Family)

A genus of several sub-tropical trees, native of India, Malaya and south-western China where they are used for their timber which smells strongly of musk. A number of species at one time classified under *Melia* are now allocated to the genus *Guarea*.

Species. *Melia azedarach.* It is known in southern Asia as the Bead tree for its pea-sized seeds are heavily musk-scented and are used to make rosary beads. It is the hardiest of the genus, being native of the lower Himalayan regions, Malaya and western China, where it grows to a height of 18 m (60 ft). In the British Isles it will reach 7.5 to 9 m (25 to 30 ft) and may be grown south of the Thames against a high wall, to protect it from cold winds.

It is a handsome deciduous tree, with compound leaves amongst which it bears in summer clusters of small pale lilac-pink flowers which emit a delicate sweet perfume.

Plant in March, into a soil containing plenty of humus-forming materials, and to maintain its shape prune lightly at this time of year, cutting back straggling shoots.

MELIANTHUS (Sapindaceae—Horse-Chestnut Family)

A genus of only four species, natives of South Africa and known as the Honey flowers. One only is suitable for gardens of the British Isles and it has honey scented flowers much frequented by bees. Though requiring a warm, sunny position and a well-drained sandy soil, the plants are so readily raised from seed (like the Tree lupin) that they may be grown in any coastal garden even if cut down by frost.

Species. *Melianthus major.* It is an unusually beautiful plant growing 1.5 to 1.8 m (5 to 6 ft) tall, its glaucous leaves being divided into 4 to 6 leaflets. In June it bears its strange brownish-white flowers in long spikes, like those of the Horse-chestnut, and they have a powerful fragrance.

MELICOPE (Rutaceae—Rue Family)

A genus of about 70 species, chiefly native of Australia and New Zealand, and which are adapted for self-pollination. They are small trees or shrubs with simple or ternate leaves covered in pellucid dots.

Species. *Melicope ternata.* In its native habitat, New Zealand, it makes a small tree some 4.5 m (15 ft) in height and is evergreen, bearing shining yellowish-green leaves. In the British Isles and northern Europe, it may lose its leaves in a cold winter and is best grown in the milder climate of the west. Its pretty trifoliate leaves when bruised release the pungent orange scent associated with the family and in June it bears faintly scented inflorescences of greenish-white. Known as *Wharangi,* the resinous gum was at one time chewed by natives.

MELILOTUS (Leguminosae—Laburnum Family)

A small genus of coumarin-smelling herbs bearing white or yellow flowers in narrow racemes. They grow in fields and about dry ditches, and are annual or biennial plants which release their pleasant smell as they become dry.

Species. *Melilotus albus.* It is biennial, native of the eastern Mediterranean, especially of the Nile Delta, and is perhaps a variety of *M. officinalis.* It is a stiff tall-growing plant bearing small white flowers in elongated racemes. Known as Bokhara clover, it has long been grown in Britain by bee keepers and has become naturalized in places. The whole plant gives off a sweet fragrance when dry.

M. officinalis. It is a plant of the wastelands and hedgerows of the British Isles, growing 60 cm (2 ft) tall and is known as the Tall melilot. The yellow flowers are borne in inflorescences during July and August and contain large amounts of nectar. The trifoliate leaves begin to release their sweet aromatic fragrance as they become dried by the August sunshine and when the plant appears almost dead.

M. sulcatus. It is native of the Mediterranean coastal strip extending from El-Sollum to Rafah and is the only species with deeply laciniate stipules. It bears its pale-yellow flowers in racemes of about 20 blooms and is an annual.

MELIOSMA (Meliosmaceae—Meliosma Family)

A genus of 100 species of hardy and half-hardy trees and shrubs, native of China and Japan and growing to a height of 6 to 21 m (20 to 70 ft). They have handsome ribbed foliage and in summer bear large panicles of greenish-white flowers which emit a hawthorn-like perfume, but without the fishy undertones of the real hawthorn. The plants require a sunny situation and a deep loamy soil.

Species. *Meliosma beaniana.* From northern Burma and south-western China, it has large pinnate leaves composed of 5 to 13 leaflets. Described by E. M. Wilson as the most handsome of the genus, it is also the most vigorous, bearing in May and June panicles of scented creamy-white flowers.

M. cuneifolia. An excellent tree for a small garden on the western side of Britain for it rarely exceeds a height of 7.5 m (25 ft). It has simple cuneate foliage and from the leaf axils bears, in June and July, dense pyramidal panicles of creamy-white flowers scented like sweet aniseed.

M. myriantha. Native of southern Japan and Korea, it is too tender for all but the most sheltered gardens of the British Isles where it will make a tree about 5.4 m (18 ft) tall. In July it bears panicles of small primrose-yellow flowers which diffuse a delicious vanilla-like scent.

M. veitchiorum. Native of south-western China and Burma, it grows about 10.5 m (35 ft) tall with large pinnate leaves 30 cm (12 in) long, and bearing panicles of small greenish-white flowers at least 45 cm (18 in) in length and smelling of honeysuckle.

M. piperella. A native, like so many of the labiates of south-eastern Europe, it is similar to *M. corsica* in its bushy habit, making a tiny mound of dark green, and during July and August bears clusters of pale-pink flowers. Growing about 10 cm (4 in) tall, the whole plant is splendidly aromatic.

M. varia. It makes a compact shrub about 22.5 cm (9 in) tall and has narrow bronze-tinted leaves like those of the Common thyme with the same pungent aromatic scent.

MELISSA (Balm) (Labiatae—Lavender Family)

A small genus of herbs, differing from *Calamintha* only in the curved corolla tube and represented in the British Isles by a single species.

Species. *Melissa officinalis.* It is an erect hairy plant of the hedgerows of South-west England with wrinkled crenate leaves, and during July and August bears white flowers at the leaf axils and in 1-sided whorls. During Elizabethan times, the stems were used to weave into garlands, and for its sweet fragrance the plant was included amongst Tusser's 'herbs for strewing'. The fresh leaves were placed in the bath to refresh and comfort the body. As Gerard said, 'it driveth away melancholy and sadness'. In ancient times, its leaves were used with angelica root, nutmegs and lemon peel to make an in-vigorating wash known as Carmelite Water for it was made by the nuns of that religious order.

MELITTIS (Labiatae—Lavender Family)

A genus of one species.

Species. *Melittis melissophyllum.* It is known as the Bastard balm. It is a handsome perennial native of the British Isles, with a creeping rootstock, and occasionally grows about the margins of woodlands in the South-west. It grows 37.5 to 45 cm (15 to 18 in) tall and has hairy stems and large serrated leaves. It bears its flowers during May and June. They are creamy white, spotted with pink on the lower lip: the form *grandiflora* having a red middle lobe to the lip. They have a pleasing sweet honey-like scent attractive to bees but the oblong serrated leaves only become sweetly fragrant as they dry—like wood-ruff. The plant grows well in partial shade and is a delightful addition to the shrub-bery.

MENTHA (Labiatae—Lavender Family)

A genus of 25 species of the northern temperate regions and with several in South Africa and Australasia, all of which release a pungent smell when pressed.

Since earliest times, mints have been used in all manner of ways. The monk Walfred Strabo, in *The Little Garden*, written during Charlemagne's time, said 'mint I grow in abundance. How many there are. I might as well try to count the sparks from Vulcan's furnace'. In Italy, mint is *Erba Santa Maria*, because at one time it was used to strew the floor of churches. Mint was mentioned in St Matthew's Gospel and Shakespeare coupled it with the other powerfully scented labiates, lavender and marjoram, in *The Winter's Tale*. Culpeper suggested applying hot rose petals and mint leaves to the head as a cure for sleeplessness. Bees will never desert a new hive if it is first rubbed with mint.

There are mints for culinary and medicinal purposes, and other fragrant mints suitable for adding to a warm bath to bring about relaxation of the muscles and for making sweetmeats. For the past two centuries, Mitcham in Surrey has been the centre of the peppermint industry in Britain, and Wayne County in the U.S.A.

Mints like a moist soil containing some decayed manure and they do best in partial shade, unlike most other herbs in this respect. The roots, which are sold by the bushel where planting on a large scale, should be planted in autumn or spring, allowing 30 cm (12 in) between each.

Species and Varieties. *Mentha aquatica.* It is the Water or Bergamot mint, found growing wild on the banks of streams and in meadowland, and its pungent fragrance of bergamot is extremely refreshing. It is a compact, small-leaf plant, and is sometimes called the Orange mint and also Wild peppermint, though it is quite a different species.

M. arvensis. It is the Corn mint which possesses a very strong, almost oppressive mint fragrance. It is able to prevent milk from curdling to a greater degree than any of the mints and in olden times was grown almost entirely for this purpose. The variety *M. arvensis piperascens*, the Japanese mint, is the form from which menthol is extracted for which reason it is widely grown in Japan. The Japanese, and English people in Georgian times, generally carried the dried and pulverized leaves in small silver boxes, a pinch being inhaled whenever required. Both forms are hardy in Britain, though they appreciate rather drier conditions than other mints. Corn mint generally grows about the hedgerows of cornfields, hence its name.

M. citrata. It possesses a most attractive fragrance like citrus or lemon. It has deep-green and yellow variegated leaves which when pressed release a fragrance similar to that of *Pelargonium crispum variegatum.* In medieval times it was likened to the perfume of the orange, the leaves being mixed with orange juice to make a conserve.

A delicious drink may be made by bruising together the leaves of *M. citrata* and some lemon juice. Boil with a cup of sugar and a pint of water and, when cool, add pineapple or orange juice and serve with ice.

There are other forms, one possessing almost a pineapple scent and giving its name to the mint; another having the perfume of Eau de Cologne. They should be in every garden for their attractive fragrance.

M. cordifolia. It has large leaves which possess a spearmint flavour or freshness, making it pleasing when used for mint sauce. The connoisseur will make mint sauce by carefully blending two or three of these mints to suit the palate, a blending of the Apple mint and Spearmint being most delicious.

M. gentilis. The Ginger mint which has bright-green and yellow variegated leaves which smell strongly of ginger when pressed. Dried and kept in a screw-top jar to preserve the strength, they will provide a warming drink (with boiling water) on a cold day and bring relief to pains in the stomach.

M. piperita. The peppermint, its leaves having short stalks, whilst the flower spikes are long. The black-stemmed variety has a larger peppermint content and is usually cultivated for extraction to make peppermint sweets. It is also valuable for making a tea by pouring boiling water on the stems and leaves, to be drunk as a relief for indigestion. There is an attractive wrinkled-leaf form which is even stronger, and a white variety, so called because the stems are pale green as distinct from the black form. It is not quite so hardy nor does it contain such a strong peppermint content, yielding about 25 lb of oil per acre as against 30 lb from the black variety.

M. pulegium. It was so named by Pliny for it was used to rid houses of fleas. In Aelfric's *Vocabulary* there is a reference to *Pollegia* which may be taken to mean Pliny's *M. pulegium,* later Puliall-Royal, because it was used in royal households, then Pennyroyal.

It grows close to water or about damp ground. Gerard mentions that it was to be found 'at Mile End, London' where it was sold in the streets especially to sailors to sweeten drinking water whilst at sea, and to make a refreshing bath 'to comfort the nerves and sinews'. It was also worn around the head to prevent giddiness and was used in posies given by lovers to denote true love. A strong infusion applied to the face will keep away gnats in summer.

Since earliest times, pennyroyal has been used for all manner of ills. Culpeper tells us that when boiled with honey and salt and rubbed on to the gums it helps toothache, and Pliny, who spoke of it more highly than of any plant, said it was a great help for a headache. This was confirmed by Matthiolus, who also recommended it for jaundice and to clear the eyesight.

M. requienii. It forms a thick mat of green peppermint-scented leaves studded with tiny mauve flowers known as the Corsican thyme or Spanish mint.

This creeping mint will grow rampant between stones and may also be used on a dry bank, or may be planted with chamomile and thyme to make a fragrant 'lawn'; like those plants, the more it is trodden upon the faster it grows. Its fragrance when trodden upon is highly refreshing, and unlike the other mints it flourishes under dry conditions, growing in any soil and even in partial shade. Though the plants will withstand clipping, this is not necessary where growing between crazy paving.

M. rotundifolia. It is the Round-leaf or Apple mint, the best form of which is Bowles Variety. It is also known as Monk's herb. It is a deliciously flavoured mint and is not troubled by rust in the same way as the Lamb mint which came to be used in medieval times as a help to digesting the often tough meats. Its leaves and shoots are very pale green, by which it is distinguishable from other mints.

M. sativa. The Marsh Whorled mint which frequents wet places in the British Isles where it may attain a height of 1.2 to 1.5 m (4 to 5 ft). It is a most distinctive species with leaves like those of *M. sylvestris.* It is to be distinguished from the Hairy mint in that the flower bracts are leafy.

M. spicata viridis. Spearmint, also the Lamb or Pea mint of which there are two forms, *angustifolia* with narrow leaves, and *crispa* with curled leaves. It is interesting in that after distillation there is left behind a thick, brown resinous substance which is entirely free of any minty smell.

M. sylvestris. It is the Hairy mint, also known as the White Woolly mint, to be found in damp, shady places, generally by a stream running through deciduous woodlands. The Hairy or Woolly mint also makes excellent sauce, for it possesses a highly distinctive flavour and is a most handsome plant. It may be grown to the

front of the border along with *Stachys lanata* and *Cineraria maritima* for its silvery foliage.

MENTZELIA (Loasaceae—Loasa Family)

A genus of about 70 species of annual or perennial plants, native of the warmer parts of America and named in honour of the seventeenth-century German botanist, Mentzel. Only one or two species are known to European gardeners for the plants require half-hardy treatment. But they produce flowers of the utmost beauty and are of easy culture. From a sowing made in gentle heat in February, several annuals will be ready for their flowering quarters by mid-May and begin to bloom early in July. Where difficulty is experienced with transplanting, seed may be sown in April where the plants are to bloom.

Species. *Mentzelia cerasiformis.* (syn. *Nuttalia cerasiformis*). It is a pretty Californian deciduous suckering shrub growing 1.8 to 2.4 m (6 to 8 ft) tall and forming a dense thicket. It has oblong green leaves and in February, before the leaves appear, bears drooping racemes of greenish-white flowers with a delicious almond-like perfume which on a calm day will pervade the air for a distance. The flowers are followed by large purple plum-like fruits which rarely ripen in Europe.

M. lindleyi (syn. *Bartonia aurea*). A Californian annual growing 37.5 to 4.5 cm (15 to 18 in) tall with striking toothed leaves nearly 15 cm (6 in) long. The symmetrical golden-yellow blooms, orange at the base, are enhanced by a boss of protruding stamens which gives the flower the appearance of *Hypericum* (St John's Wort) but they do not open in dull weather. When the sun is on them, the flowers take on an exquisite beauty and emit a soft honey-like fragrance.

M. ornata (syn. *Bartonia decapetala*). A pretty annual which is native of the State of Missouri. It grows to a height of 60 cm (2 ft) and has hairy, deeply cut leaves and sweetly scented white flowers which open in the evening.

MERCURIALIS (Dog's Mercury) (Euphorbiaceae—Euphorbia Family)

Of the same family as the genus

Euphorbia, plants of the arid wastes of the United States and South Africa, *Mercurialis* is a genus of seven species of which one is native to the British Isles. It is known as Dog's Mercury and is an evil-smelling plant.

Species. *Mercurialis perennis.* It is to be found in dense woodlands for it enjoys the shade, spreading by underground stems and growing to a height of about 60 cm (2 ft). The leaves are oval and of darkest green and the male and female flowers appear on different plants. The leaves contain trimethylamine, present in the Cotoneaster and Hawthorn and in the early stages of putrefaction, and when bruised they give off the smell of decaying fish; in the words of Culpeper, 'somewhat strong and virulent' and with no trace of sweetness as in the hawthorn flower.

MERENDERA (Liliaceae—Lily Family)

A genus of 10 species, native of Spain and south-eastern Europe, extending to Persia, Afghanistan and into northern India. Their name is the Spanish for *Colchicum* to which they are closely related, but they differ in the absence of any perianth tube. Like *Colchicum,* they form a swollen corm or bulb but have narrower leaves. In the warmer parts of the British Isles and northern Europe, they may be grown outdoors on the rock garden or planted to the front of a shrubbery or on a grassy bank; they are also delightful plants for the alpine house or cold frame. One, *M. trigyna,* bears scented flowers.

Species. *Merendera trigyna* (syn. *M. caucasica*). Native of the Caucasus and the Middle East, it has narrow leaves which appear with the flowers in April and May. The flowers are white or palest lilac, tinted with rose and have narrow twisted petals. They are sweetly scented.

MESPILODAPHNE (Lauraceae—Bay Tree Family)

A small genus of aromatic trees, native of the tropical forests of Brazil and called *Pao* by the Portuguese.

Species. *Mespilodaphne pretiosa.* Its inner bark has the most pleasant odour of all the Sassafras trees, resembling cinnamon but mixed with orange. By distillation, it yields 1.16 per cent essential oil with an odour likened to bergamot and with a pungent, aromatic taste. The alternate leaves are oblong and leathery and covered with oil glands which may be seen with the naked eye. The flowers are also citrus-scented.

MEUM (Umbelliferae—Parsley Family)

A genus of only one species.

Species. *Meum catharrarticum.* Known to the countryman as Spignel. All parts of the plant are aromatic, especially the roots which have the scent and flavour of Melilot and were at one time eaten as a vegetable.

It is an elegant perennial native of the British Isles growing 30 to 45 cm (12 to 18 in) in height with leaves which are attractively divided into fern-like leaflets. For its foliage, the plant may be used in the garden to provide a pleasing background to other plants with less attractive foliage. The white or purple flowers are borne in umbels during summer.

MICHELIA (Magnoliaceae—Magnolia Family)

A genus of 50 species, native of tropical Asia and closely related to *Magnolia. M. champaca* yields the celebrated perfume of the East.

Species. *Michelia champaca.* Native of the lowlands of central India where it makes a small evergreen shrub and bears multitudes of lemon-yellow flowers, like tiny magnolia blooms and with a delicious perfume. The flowers yield the champac perfume of commerce, and with them Hindu girls decorate their hair.

MICROMELUM (Rutaceae—Rue Family)

A genus of 10 species of small trees or shrubs, native to India, all parts of which are fragrant.

Species. *Micromelum interriginum.* It is a plant of shrubby habit with leaves that have a resinous scent and it bears small greenish-white flowers which have the scent of orange. These are followed by orange-coloured berries which, when bruised, emit a powerful aromatic scent.

MICROMERIA (Labiatae—Lavender Family)

A large genus of herbs or undershrubs of compact habit. They have small entire leaves and bear tiny white or purple flowers in whorls. All parts of the plant are fragrant when crushed and like all the labiates (except mint), they require a dry, sandy soil and an open, sunny situation for them to be long-living and to bring out the fullness of their scent.

The micromerias are readily increased by cuttings of the half-ripened shoots and rooted around the ' side of a pot, like thyme.

Species. *Micromeria biflora*. It is native of southern Egypt and the Sudan. It has small dark-green leaves and bears its pure-white flowers in dainty whorls. The whole plant is powerfully aromatic when crushed.

M. cordata. Native of Corsica and southern Europe, it makes a tiny rounded shrub, growing no more than 10 cm (4 in) tall with silvery-green thumb-like leaves and in summer bears pale-pink flowers to give it a heather-like appearance. All parts of the plant are deliciously aromatic when pressed, similar in smell to that given off by the lemon-scented thyme. It is a most refreshing scent when the day is warm.

M. douglasii. It is a trailing plant, the *herba buena* of California which the late Clarence Elliott has told was used by John Fothergill, 'mine host' at the Sign of the Three Swans at Market Harborough, when dispensing cooling drinks. It is a valuable plant to trail about a rockery or over paving stones for the prostrate stems take root at the leaf axils whenever they come in contact with the soil. The leaves pressed between the fingers will release a most refreshing lemony scent, resembling verbena and having the same reviving qualities as several of the mints and thymes.

M. myrtifolia. A native of Egypt and Asia Minor, it has ovate or oblong leaves and bears its attractive pink flowers in long whorls. It has outstanding scent.

M. piperella. A native, like so many of the labiates, of south-eastern Europe, it is similar to *M. corsica* in its bushy habit, making a tiny mound of dark green, and during July and August bears clusters of pale-pink flowers. Growing about 10 cm (4 in) tall, the whole plant is splendidly aromatic.

M. sinaica. Native of Sinai, it makes a branched shrublet, the stems being covered in a small number of ovate-oblong leaves. The mauve flowers are borne in lax whorls. The plant is aromatic.

MICROTIS (Orchidaceae—Orchis Family)

A genus of 10 species of erect, slender herbs, native to Malaysia, Australasia and Polynesia. They have sheathing leaves and bear their greenish-white flowers in a thick spike.

Species. *Microtis porrifolia*. Known as the Leek-leaf or Onion-leaf orchis, it is native to Australia and New Zealand where it blooms from October until January. It has a solitary, tubular leaf and as many as 80 tiny flowers crowded into a spike. They have a powerful if sickly scent.

MIMOSA: *see* ACACIA

MIRABILIS (Nyctaginaceae—Four o'clock Family)

A genus of 60 species, native of tropical America, the flowers opening at night to release a heavy perfume.

Species. *Mirabilis jalapa*. The 'Marvel of Peru', a tender, tuberous-rooted perennial which, if treated as a half-hardy annual in Britain and northern Europe will bloom in August from a sowing made under glass early in March. The plants require a sunny position and a rich soil and should be planted 30 cm (12 in) apart. The plants are tuberous rooted and are best grown in small pots so that the roots are not disturbed when planting out after hardening, early in June. The plants, with their dark foliage and funnel-shaped blooms striped rose-pink, yellow or white, make rapid growth and will come into bloom within two months, attaining a height of 90 cm (3 ft).

M. longiflora. It is one of the most exotic of garden plants, growing to a height of 60 cm (2 ft) and bearing, during August and September, narrow tubular flowers of lilac-pink or white which often measure 15 cm (6 in) in length. The blooms open as the air begins to cool in the evening when they emit the rich, heavy fragrance of orange-blossom. It should be given the same culture as *M. jalapa*.

MITCHELLA (Rubiaceae—Bedstraw Family)

A genus of two smooth or downy herbs or shrubs with funnel-shaped flowers, bearded in the throat and borne in pairs with united ovaries.

Species. *Mitchella repens.* It is altogether a delightful little plant, a native of North America, with tiny crimson leaves which, like those of the closely related woodruff, have the smell of hay when dry. The white flowers, tinted with purple, are funnel-shaped and have a pleasant sweet fragrance of their own which is especially noticeable towards evening. It is readily increased by division in spring or from cuttings, and does best in a peaty soil; it will grow in shade.

MOCK ORANGE: *see* PHILADELPHUS

MOHRIA (Mohriaceae—Mohria Family)

A genus of three species, native to tropical and southern Africa and appreciated for the heavy scent of their foliage.

Species. *Mohria thurifraga.* Native of South Africa. *Thurifraga* means frankincense, which denotes the incense-like fragrance given off by the leaves when handled. It is a most attractive fern, arising from a creeping rootstock, the barren fronds being 15 cm (6 in) long, the erect fertile fronds about 22.5 cm (9 in) long.

MOLUCELLA (Labiatae—Lavender Family)

A small genus of annual plants, quite commonly grown in the nineteenth century but rarely seen today. The plants are native of Syria and the Near East and require half-hardy treatment; sow in gentle heat in the new year and transplant to their flowering quarters in May. They require a sandy soil and an open situation.

Species. *Molucella laevis.* It is a curious plant, known as Bells of Ireland for it grows 45 cm (18 in) tall with small round long-stalked leaves, whilst the white bell-shaped flowers are borne at 5-cm (2-in) intervals all the way up the stem. The bells are grouped around the stem and point in all directions. They have greenish-white netted calyces which when dry are retained for a considerable time. Thus besides the plant's decorative value in the garden, the dried flower stems will retain their beauty indoors until Christmas. When just opening the flowers, if slightly bruised, emit the pleasing scent of balm.

MONARDA (Bergamot) (Labiatae—Lavender Family)

A genus of six or seven species of perennial plants, native of the deciduous woodlands of North America, which will grow well in all soils and in partial shade or full sun. Their leaves, stems and roots carry a delicious aromatic orange-like perfume when crushed and are much used in perfumery and in pot-pourris; also to make Oswego tea by an infusion of the leaves in hot water. Both the leaves and the flowers which are borne in whorls at the ends of the shoots may be eaten in salads.

Species. *Monarda didyma.* It bears its red, pink or purple flowers in whorls in candelabra fashion, on 90-cm (3-ft) stems and blooms from early July until mid-September. It is easily raised from seed whilst the named varieties are increased by root division. The genus is named in honour of Dr Nicholas Monardes of Seville who published his *Herbal* in 1569, but the plant obtained the name Bergamot because of the likeness of its perfume to the Bergamot orange. The plant, which was first mentioned by Parkinson in his *Paradisus*, likes a cool, moist soil.

There are a number of excellent varieties of *Monarda didyma*, all of which grow about 90 cm (3 ft) tall, every part of the plant being aromatic.

ADAM. The blooms, borne in whorls, are an attractive shade of cerise.

BLUE STOCKING. The large refined blooms are of deep violet colouring and are the nearest to a 'blue' bergamot.

CAMBRIDGE SCARLET. A handsome plant with flowers of brilliant red and bright green foliage.

MONODORA (Anonaceae—Anona Family)

A genus of 20 species, native of western Africa, the Congo and Madagascar, from where the seeds of *M. myristica* are thought to have been introduced into Jamaica at an early date, possibly by slaves.

Species. *Monodora myristica.* It is the Jamaica nutmeg tree, believed at one time to be the only species. In Jamaica, it makes a small tree of about 6 m (20 ft) but reaches 18 m (60 ft) in the Congo. The flowers, which are borne at the axils of the leaves, are large, richly scented and of extreme beauty. The 3 spreading outer petals of golden yellow spotted with purple have attractively waved edges whilst the 3 inner petals are heart-shaped and erect, white and downy on the outside, smooth and pale yellow with crimson spots on the inside.

The fruit is large and brilliant yellow, varying in size from an orange to a melon and containing numerous seeds tightly packed together. The seeds contain an aromatic oil which has the odour and taste of nutmegs.

MONTBRETIA: *see* CROCOSMIA.

MOREA (Iridaceae—Iris Family)

The iris of the Southern Hemisphere; it is a genus of South African plants named after the English botanist Robert Moore. The leaves are long and narrow, whilst the flowers are borne in terminal clusters. The 3 spreading outer petals resemble in shape the blades of a ship's propeller whilst there are 3 small inner 'blades'. The flowers are distinguished from iris in that the petals are united into a tube, whilst with a number of species there is a blotch of brilliant blue at the base of the outer petals. They grow about sandy mountainous slopes fully exposed to the sunlight. Almost all the moreas bear scented flowers but in several species the scent is more pronounced than in others. They form a globular corm covered with a fibrous tunic and bristly hairs.

Species. *Morea ciliata.* It bears its pale-mauve flowers on short 15 cm (6 in) stems which are almost enclosed in the basal sheath of twin leaves. The flowers are powerfully scented.

M. odorata. A rare form bearing pure-white flowers on 60 cm (2 ft) stems, their beauty accentuated by the long bright-green leaves. In their native land, the flowers open in December and always at 3 p.m., remaining open at night to be pollinated by moths.

M. papilionaceae. The flowers are reddish-brown or brownish-yellow with a yellow blotch at the base of each segment and with the outer segments shorter than in other species. They are borne on 15-cm (6-in) stems.

M. ramosissima. Native of the Cape where it is prominent at Newlands and on Table Mountain. The corms have thick spiny fibres and numerous basal leaves which bear cormlets in the axils. The flowers are dull yellow, borne on 60-cm (2-ft) stems and remain colourful for many weeks. It is one of the hardiest species and the most fragrant (with *M. odorata*).

M. spathulata (syn. *M. spathacea*). Though native of the Transvaal, it is almost hardy in the British Isles and has been known to withstand several degrees of frost. It has leaves 1.2 to 1.5 m (4 to 5 ft) long whilst its flowers, borne in May and June, in August and September in its native land, appear on 60-cm (2-ft) stems. They are brilliant yellow with a 'claw' at the base and have a sweet perfume.

MORISIA (Cruciferae—Wallflower Family)

A genus of a single species.

Species. *Morisia hypogaea.* It is a perennial, native of Sardinia, and grows no more than 7.5 cm (3 in) tall with shiny green toothed leaves which form a tuft on top of the soil. The flowers are a clear daffodil-yellow, about 2.5 cm (1 in) across, and almost sit on the leaves. With their attractive wedge-shaped petals, they appear in profusion during May and emit a pervading scent of hawthorn but with rather sweeter undertones.

The plant requires a sandy loam near the base of the rockery where it will receive moisture in summer. Propagation is by division of the roots in spring or from seed. In their native land, the peduncles bend over when the seed is ripe and bury the capsule in the soil.

MURRAYA (Rutaceae—Rue Family)

A genus of 12 species of trees or shrubs native of China, India, Java and Polynesia, and which in the British Isles and North America are grown as stove plants, requiring a minimum winter temperature of 18°C (65°F). They have dark-green pinnate leaves and bear their flowers in terminal corymbs.

Species. *Murraya exotica* (syn. *Marsana buxifolia*). It is a favourite garden plant with the Chinese and Indonesians where it is known as the Chinese Box tree. It makes a large shrub or small tree 3 m (10 ft) in height with deep-green shining pinnate leaves. The pure-white flowers, most striking against the foliage, are borne in crowded terminal corymbs and are exquisitely scented. They are followed by succulent fruits the size of a pea, the skin of which is covered with small resinous glands, like an orange. The leaves are used in curries.

M. koenigii. It is native of Indonesia and makes a small tree with glossy dark-green leaves which have a powerful curry-like smell and which are used for flavouring, whilst both the bark and root have a similar fragrance.

M. paniculata. Native of the East Indies where it makes a spreading tree 6 m (20 ft) tall, with ovate leaves. Its pure-white flowers, borne in terminal and axillary panicles, diffuse over a wide area the un-mistakable scent of jasmine, whilst its leaves are pleasantly aromatic.

MUSCARI (Liliaceae—Lily Family)

A genus of 50 species, bearing their flowers in dense terminal racemes on leafless scapes. They are widely distributed throughout southern and central eastern Europe, and western Asia. They are perhaps the most free-flowering of all bulbous plants and of easy culture in al-most all soils. Flowering in the British Isles and North America from the end of March until late June, they are most attractive when planted with large trumpet daffodils, with white or yellow primroses and polyanthus. The flower-heads are made up of numerous small bells, like tiny heads or blue-black grapes, hence their name of Grape hyacinths. Many of the species have a delectable perfume. They grow well in a sunny situation and in a dry, well-drained soil.

Their botanical name is derived from the Musk hyacinth, *Hyacinthus* (or *Mus-cari*) *moschatum*, for its dingy yellowish-purple blooms have the true musk per-fume, so pronounced indoors that half a dozen bulbs in bloom in a small pot will scent a large room for several weeks.

Species. *Muscari ambrosiacum.* Native of Asia Minor and closely allied to the Musk hyacinth. It is well named for its distinctly coloured flowers possess an ambrosia-like perfume. It is unlike any other species, the upper bells being of soft lilac colouring with the lower bells creamy-white, whilst each has an attractive bronze rim at the mouth.

M. armeniacum. Native of Asia Minor, it is a species which will excel almost anywhere, seeding and multiplying at a rapid rate and scenting the air around with its sweet honey perfume. It is at its love-liest during May, bearing dense racemes of azure-blue on 22.5-cm (9-in) stems.

Several modern varieties are even more attractive, each with a sweeter perfume. Perhaps the finest is Blue Spike, bearing double flowers of a lovely mid-blue, whilst Cantab bears flowers of Cambridge blue and is the most dwarf of all. For brilliance of colour and size of its spike, Early Giant is outstanding, superb with *Fosteriana* tulips, whilst Heavenly Blue, of sweetest perfume, is grown in larger numbers than any muscari.

M. botryoides. Native of southern Europe, it is a charming little plant for the alpine garden, known as the Italian grape hyacinth and bearing its tiny spikes of pale blue on 15-cm (6-in) stems during April and May. The pure-white form, *album*, is a suitable companion and carries the same fragrance as the type, a scent which Parkinson described as being 'strong ... like unto starch when it is made new and hot'. He gave to the white variety the enchanting name of Pearls of Spain for it originally came from the south-eastern part of that country. Ruskin wrote of it in more romantic mood as 'if a cluster of grapes and a hive of honey had been distilled and pressed together in one small boss of celled and beaded blue', a more accurate description of its perfume which resembles the honey-musk scent of buddleia.

M. comosum. Louise Wilder, the American writer, has described the species, a native of Asia Minor, as a quaint monstrosity, an apt description of its amazing flower-heads. It is an interesting plant, bearing its flowers in May on a 30-cm (12-in) stem. The lower flowers of greenish-purple and brown are fertilized by the upper filaments of brilliant blue, whilst the whole plant presents a plumelike effect making it excellent for indoor decoration. In the form *M. comosum monstrosum,* all the flowers are sterile. Gerard called it the 'fair haired hyacinth', a quaint description of its twisted filaments, whilst it was also known as the Tassel hyacinth. The flowers of both forms have a pleasing perfume which is more pronounced in *M. comosum.*

M. commutatum. Native of south-eastern Europe and Palestine where it grows on dry hills. The 15-cm (6-in) flower stem arises from linear grooved leaves. The 'grapes' are purple-black, formed in dense oval heads, and have outstanding fragrance.

M. moschatum. Like most of the scented muscari, the Musk hyacinth is a native of Asia Minor but is completely hardy in the British Isles. Its flowers carry the now rare musk perfume, which is sweet and penetrating and which compensates for the uninteresting flowers. The purple 'grapes' turn grey then take on a yellowish-brown colour as they age. It blooms in April and should be planted near an open window through which its perfume may enter on a calm, sunny day. *M. moschatum major* is a more vigorous form and is more powerfully scented.

M. racemosum. It is a rare plant, long naturalized in eastern counties of England, with slender prostrate leaves from which arises a 22.5-cm (9-in) scape bearing a cylindrical raceme of dark-blue flowers which John Weathers described as deliciously plum-scented. The colour of the flowers is accentuated by a thin rim of white.

MYOPORUM (Myoporaceae— Myoporum Family)

A genus of 32 species of trees (or shrubs) yielding valuable timber, native of Mauritius, New Guinea, Australia and New Zealand. It takes its name from the Greek denoting glandular leaves, the most prominent in this respect being *M. latum.*

Species. *Myoporum latum.* An evergreen New Zealand shrub or small tree which has leaves similar to those of veronica (hebe), conspicuously covered with pellucid glands which emit a resinous smell when pressed. The flowers, which are white, spotted with purple, are borne at the leaf axils and are also fragrant. Known as Ngaio in New Zealand, it is usually found at the coast and requires the protection of a sheltered garden to survive an average winter in the British Isles and North America. The black buds are covered in a fragrant gummy substance. A decoction of the leaves was used by the Maoris to give protection from mosquitoes.

MYOSOTIS (Boraginaceae— Forget-me-not Family)

A genus of about 50 hairy annual or perennial herbs with alternate leaves in shape like the ear of a mouse, and bearing flowers, rarely scented, in crosier-like cymes. They are native of Europe, Africa (high ground) and New Zealand.

Species. *Myosotis alpestris* (syn. *M. rupicola*). It is a delightful scree plant, in bloom during April and May. It forms a tiny rounded tuft only 7.5 cm (3 in) high with dark-green hairy leaves, whilst its tiny flowers of brilliant blue have a clear yellow eye. As the daylight begins to fade, the flowers become deliciously fragrant though it is difficult to detect any perfume at all during daylight. It is a perennial, occasionally found in the North of England growing about high rocky formations at elevations of 900 to 1,200 m (3 to 4,000 ft), and it enjoys a well-drained gritty soil.

M. macrantha. Native of New Zealand where it is to be found in the Mount Cook district, and it is a most distinctive variety. It grows 45 cm (18 in) tall and bears hanging funnel-shaped blooms of pale yellow which in the evening diffuse a soft sweet perfume.

MYRICA (Myricaceae—Sweet Gale Family)

A genus of 30 species, closely allied to *Comptonia*, the myricas enjoy a sandy well-drained soil and an open situation but are of such easy culture that they will grow almost anywhere and indeed, are to be found almost throughout the world.

Species. *Myrica californica.* The most vigorous of the myricas, in California it attains a height of 9 m (30 ft). It is evergreen, its bright-green leaves with their serrated edges being covered in wax like the berries. The greenish flowers are followed by pale-purple berries which are also coated in a deposit of wax with a balsamic odour.

M. cordifolia. This is a South African species and produces the largest berry of all. It grows well in a moist sandy soil for it prefers its roots to be cool and moist. The attractive leaves are heart-shaped.

M. caroliniensis. The Carolina bayberry, which makes a bushy plant 1.8 to 2.4 m (6 to 8 ft) in height and is semi-evergreen with large oval leaves which are deliciously lemon-scented, whilst its grey berries are covered in white wax.

M. cerifera. A native of Canada and the northern United States, it is known as the Candleberry for from its berries candles were made. It makes a plant 1.5 to 2.4 m (5 to 8 ft) in height with numerous branches which have attractive grey bark. It has shining lance-shaped leaves and it blooms in May, the flowers being followed by small black berries which are covered in a crust of white wax.

The wax is obtained by scalding the berries with boiling water and immersing them for a few minutes. The liquid is then poured off into a wide bowl and the wax is at once skimmed off. The berries are then boiled to extract the wax from the pulp which is again skimmed off, the wax being purified by straining through muslin. It is then made into wax cakes or candles and is allowed to solidify. The wax burns with a clear white flame and gives off a delicious balsamic perfume.

M. gale. The Sweet gale or Bog myrtle, occasionally to be found about the bogs and heathlands of Exmoor, in Scotland and elsewhere in Britain. It grows 90 cm (3 ft) tall with narrow lance-shaped leaves, downy beneath, which emit a delicious sweet perfume when touched. The wood is also scented. The brownish-green flowers are borne in early summer and are followed by an abundance of small berries which when treated with hot water yield what is known as myrtle wax, a resinous substance which emits a powerful balsamic perfume. Candles made from this wax diffuse a delightful odour when burnt.

MYRISTICA (Myristiceae— Myristica Family)

A genus of about 120 trees or shrubs confined to the tropics. In India they are mostly found on the Khasi Hills. In tropical America and the Malayan Archipelago grow several species, of which *Myristica fragrans* (syn. *M. officinalis, M. moschata, M. aromatica*), the best known, is the Nutmeg tree. In the British Isles and northern Europe a stove greenhouse is required, and a compost containing plenty of peat and leaf-mould. Increase is by ripe cuttings in a sandy compost with a little heat.

Species. *Myristica argentea.* First noticed in New Guinea in 1666, and the fruit was then introduced into Europe. The trees are characterized by the large, evergreen leaves having a silvery appearance on the underside, hence its name. The 'nutmegs' differ from true nutmegs in their long, narrow shape whilst their flavour is not so delicate as with the fruits of *M. fragrans.*

From the fruits, 'oil of nutmeg' or 'balsam of nutmeg' is obtained by crushing them between iron plates under hydraulic pressure, when the yield will be about 25 per cent of oil. When cool, it sets into 'cakes' with a most agreeable balsamic odour which is also present in the essential oil of the leaves. The same odour is obtained from the essential oil of the leaves of *Eucalyptus alba.*

M. fragrans. An evergreen tree growing 9 m (30 ft) high, usually with a lofty, undivided trunk; the leaves shining, deep green and aromatic. The small, fragrant, white flowers cluster in the axils of the leaves and are followed by fruits which are pear-shaped, golden-yellow in colour, and with a longitudinal groove on one side (like a peach) which, when ripe, bursts into two parts. The seed is covered by a red fleshy part known as the aril which is dried and sold as mace, whilst the seed itself has a thick, hard, outer shell enclosing the nutmeg which is wrinkled, due to the pressure of the aril.

The tree grows wild on the islands of Geram and Amboina, in the western peninsula of New Guinea, but not further westwards though it was at some time introduced to Java and Singapore, Bourbon and Zanzibar, and to several West Indian islands. It is most luxurious in the Banda Isles, especially the isles of Lontar, Pulo Ai and Pulo Nera, the 'Nutmeg Isles', where the trees flourish in the volcanic soil, deep shade and excessive humidity, a mature female tree yielding about 2,000 lb of round nuts. In the Moluccas, a tree will remain productive for upwards of 80 years and it bears fruit the whole year round. The leaves yield on distillation a colourless limpid oil with a refined nutmeg-like odour and taste. Oil of mace is also colourless and extremely fragrant. The principal constituent is a hydrocarbon, macene, which is distinguished from oil of turpentine in that it does not form a crystalline hydrate on being mixed with alcohol and nitric acid.

M. horsfieldii. A tall tree with light-brown leaves, this species has flowers which are strongly scented of violets, in closely packed round heads. The fruit is egg-shaped, brownish, with a fleshy aril. The tree is a native of Ceylon.

MYROXYLON (Leguminosae—Laburnum Family)

A genus of two species, native of South America and yielding aromatic resins known as Balsam of Peru and Balsam of Tolu. The trees have leaves containing pellucid dots which release an aromatic scent when pressed, whilst the balsam is obtained from the bark which, when cut, has an odour like that of cinnamon.

Species. *Myroxylon pereirea* (syn. *M. balsamum*). The Balsam of Tolu, yielding a resin which is soluble in alcohol and gives permanence to other perfumes. It is a small tree with flowers like those of the laburnum, and it is native of Mexico and El Salvador. The balsam is so mobile that if solidified pieces are placed in a jar in a warm room, they will soon form a treacle-like mass. The principal constituents are cinnamic acid and benzyl cinnamate, both having the scent of cinnamon.

M. peruiferum. Native of El Salvador (not Peru) where it is present in dense forests near the coast, the strip of land where it abounds being known as the Balsam Coast. It yields the Balsam of Peru, a resin in which is also present a liquid oil (Cinnamein) and cinnamic acid. It was at one time widely used for its healing qualities and in the manufacture of toilet soaps.

It is a handsome tree, growing to 15 m (50 ft) in pyramidal form, and all parts are fragrant, even the calyx of the small white flowers. This actually yields the finest balsam but is rarely collected as the flowers are so short-lived. Instead, it is obtained from the trunk of the tree by natives, with an expertise which comes only after long practice. About 1.8 m (6 ft) from the base of the trunk, incisions are made in the bark in such a way that four strips, each 5 cm (2 in) wide, are left intact as it is upon these that the future vitality of the tree depends. Between the strips the bark is beaten with the back of an axe, then cuts made with a knife. At once the balsam begins to flow and is set alight. This causes it to run more quickly when the flame is extinguished after about an hour. Then cotton rags are stuffed into the incisions and when saturated they are placed in earthenware jars and boiling water is poured over them. The resin is collected once a week from November until the end of April, and the average weight of balsam collected from each tree during that time will be about 4 lb. When treated with hot water, the resin rises to the surface and is collected, and it has the appearance of dark-brown treacle.

With careful handling, a tree can be expected to yield for 30 years before being rested for 5 years, after which 'tapping' can be resumed. At the height of the season, so powerful is the scent of balsam that it is noticeable more than a mile out to sea.

MYRTILLOCACTUS (Cactaceae—Cactus Family)

A genus of five species, native of Mexico, Guatemala and California where they make large multibranched shrubs 3 to 3.6 m (10 to 12 ft) tall with smooth, stiff 6- to 8-angled stems. The flowers are borne several from one areole but do not appear until the plant is many years old. The small blue fruits are edible and are sold in the markets of Mexico.

The plants are best grown in large pots in a sunny sheltered garden and in a compost composed of leaf-mould, grit and lime rubble. They may be left outdoors throughout the year in southern Europe but in the British Isles should be removed to a frost-free place during winter.

Species. *Myrtillocactus eichlamii.* It has thick dark-green 6-angled stems and large areoles with 6 radial spines. The purple flower buds open green on the outside, white inside and they have a soft sweet perfume.

M. geometrizans. It grows 60 cm (2 ft) tall, the stems with their 6-angled ribs being about 2.5 cm (1 in) thick and of blue-green colouring. The areoles are spaced 1 in apart over the entire stem and from each a white flower is borne which measures 1 in across. It is sweetly scented.

MYRTUS (Myrtaceae—Myrtle Family)

A genus of 60 species of small trees or shrubs, native of sub-tropical America, with the Common myrtle native also of, or long naturalized in, Mediterranean regions. Of all flowering trees, none was more highly revered in ancient times. After the lily and the rose, the myrtle was the most important flower of the Virgin, representing love, kindness, virginity and chastity. In ancient Greece and Rome, it was the symbol of youth, beauty and marriage. Pliny said that the most powerfully scented myrtles grew in Egypt and that their gum resembled myrrh in its perfume, hence their botanical name. The Common myrtle is said to have been introduced into England in 1585 by Sir Thomas Carew from Spain, and the first myrtle (and also the orange) grew in the grounds of his home at Beddington.

An essential oil and perfumed water known as *eau d'ange* was made from myrtle flowers. In countries bordering the Mediterranean, the berries (fruits) which have an aromatic taste are eaten fresh when ripe, or are dried and used for flavouring food. The leaves retain their fragrance when dry whilst the wood, too, is highly scented. Oil of myrtle was in demand as a cure for bronchitis, depending on the strength of cineol, a body identical with pure eucalyptol which is now more widely used. The rapid passage of the scented oil through the system was first observed by Linarix in 1878 when he noticed that it perfumed the urine with a powerful violet-like smell within 15 minutes of its consumption.

Species. *Myrtus communis.* The Common myrtle of southern Europe and northern Africa, with glossy box-like leaves of darkest green and bearing in July purewhite flowers with protruding golden stamens. It is the myrtle of the ancient Greeks and Romans, every part of the tree being fragrant whilst the fresh flowers which have a sweet taste are used in salads and to make a toilet water known as *eau d'ange.* There is a pretty small-leaved form known as Jenny Reitenbach which blooms in great profusion.

M. lechleriana. A species introduced into the British Isles by the Slieve Donard Nursery, Co. Down. Its bright-green leaves have red stalks and it blooms in May, its white sweetly scented flowers being followed by black fruits. It makes a dense bush well furnished to the base.

M. luma. Native of Chile, it is the most robust myrtle, attaining a height of 7.5 m (25 ft) and in the British Isles it is the hardiest. Its stem bark is cinnamon-coloured and peels off to reveal a white under-surface, whilst its leaves are purple-tinted. Its fragrant white flowers are borne in great profusion.

M. obcordata. Endemic to New Zealand, it grows to a height of about 3 m (10 ft) with stems of almost rush-like form and small leaves and flowers which are pleasantly scented.

N

NARCISSUS (Amaryllidaceae—Narcissus Family)

A large genus of bulbous plants bearing their flowers in clusters or singly at the end of a scape. They are amongst the most richly scented of all flowers, in some cases being so powerful as to bring on headaches and dizziness to those who inhale them. The wild daffodil is a flower beloved of the poets: *N. pseudo-narcissus,* our native Lent lily, flowers in copses and fields throughout England during the cold bleak days of early spring. The flower has a soft mossy perfume, almost primrose-like, and imperceptible in a single bloom but quite substantial in a group. The Lent lily grew in profusion in the fields around London during Elizabethan times, and bunches were sold in the streets. Lyte called it the Yellow Crow-bell or Bastard narcissus for, contrary to modern custom, it was the short-cupped forms that were known as daffodils; however, the name was used by the early English poets to describe our native Lent lily.

Strew me the ground with daffodown-
dillies,
And cowslips and kingcups, and loved
lilies,

wrote Edmund Spenser and the same name was used by Gerard in the *Herball,* in which he recorded a dozen different forms including the short-cupped Tazetta, 'the narcisse good in scent' of the *19th Idyle* of Theocritus. This is one of the powerfully scented Mediterranean species growing wild from the Pyrenees to Greece. The Tazetta form was used to decorate the tombs of the ancient Egyptians, and is the narcissus we know today as the 'polyanthus' or bunch-flowered narcissus, of which the varieties Geranium, Cragford

and Cheerfulness are amongst the best-known, having a more powerful perfume than any other narcissi with the possible exception of the jonquils and the poet's narcissus, *N. poeticus.* Pliny said the plant was named 'narcissus' from *narce,* 'dullness of sense', from which is derived the word narcotic, and Sophocles said that the departed, 'dulled with death, should be crowned with a dulling flower'. Hence, the use of narcissus flowers as funeral wreaths by the Egyptians. Of their powerful perfume Burbidge has written that in a closed room it is 'extremely disagreeable, if not injurious to delicate persons'.

The form of *N. poeticus* known as *N. majalis* was being cultivated in Britain in early Tudor times and possibly before, and by the early eighteenth century had become naturalized in parts of South-east England. Likewise the tiny *N. asturiensis* (syn. *N. minimus*), the Spanish daffodil, the smallest of all and the first to bloom, which is illustrated in the *Paradisus.* For the size of its bloom, it must be one of the most richly scented of all flowers, its perfume being most noticeable when indoors in pots.

Species and Varieties. *Narcissus biflorus.* A native of southern Europe, it is a natural hybrid of *N. poeticus* and *N. tazetta* and in habit is similar to the former. Twin flowers are borne on a scape and have a pure-white perianth and a pale-yellow corona, fringed at the edge. This pretty form had become naturalized in part of England and Ireland at an early date. The Elizabethans knew it as the Primrose Peerless daffodil. It was described by Gerard, and Parkinson said that it had 'a sweet but stuffing scent' like that of its parents.

N. calcicola. It grows wild only in Portugal, near Lisbon, and is similar to *N. juncifolius* but bears somewhat larger blooms of deepest yellow and on a 15- to 17.5-cm (6- to 7-in) stem. The flowers possess outstanding perfume.

N. canaliculatus. Its home is Sicily and it is one of the sweetest plants in the world, both in appearance and with its ravishing perfume which will scent the alpine house during late winter. It is a Tazetta in miniature, growing only 15 to 17.5 cm (6 to 7 in) tall with a white reflexed perianth about 2.5 cm (1 in) across and a cup of orange-yellow. Two, three or four blooms appear on each stem above erect blue-green foliage and it blooms outdoors early in spring.

N. cernuus. Also known as *N. moschatus* from its musky fragrance, it is a sub-species of the Lent lily and is believed to have been found in the Pyrenees though this is not certain. It grows about 17.5 cm (7 in) tall and the blooms are white, flushed with sulphur-yellow. The flowers, which appear in March, have attractively twisted perianth segments. It prefers a damper situation than most of the Spanish species and enjoys the partial shade of a copse.

N. gracilis. Found growing wild only in the Bordeaux region of France, it is possibly a hybrid of *N. juncifolius* (the rush-leaf daffodil of the nearby Pyrenees) and *N. tazetta* for it has the unusual foliage of the former and the heavy perfume of the latter. Three or five blooms of palest yellow appear on each 30 cm (12 in) stem and their perfume is carried afar on a warm June day for this is the latest of all narcissi to bloom, often colourful when the first of the roses come into bloom.

N. jonquilla. This, the sweet-scented single jonquil grows in north-western Africa, Spain and Portugal. It bears 4 or 6 cup-shaped flowers of brilliant golden-yellow on a 25-cm (10-in) stem. The blooms, which are almost intoxicatingly scented, have an undertone of orange in their perfume. The double form *flore pleno*, known as Queen Anne's jonquil, is even more powerfully scented.

A number of lovely varieties classified under Division VII of the genus *Narcissus* have the heavy perfume of the species:

BABY MOON. It is the latest of the jonquils to come into bloom, well into April when it bears 3 or 4 flowers of buttercup-yellow to each 22.5-cm (9-in) stem. It is free-flowering and dainty when in small vases and just a few sprays will scent a large room.

BOBBYSOXER. Like Baby Moon, once established it will increase rapidly. It grows only 15 to 17.5 cm (6 to 7 in) tall, the perfectly rounded flower having a golden perianth and a wide cup of deepest orange. It has a delicious perfume.

CHÉRIE. It is fine to naturalize for it grows 37.5 cm (15 in) tall and bears 2 or 3 flowers on each stem with a perianth of ivory-white and a cup of palest shell-pink, heavily scented.

MOUNTJOY. It has the Campernelle jonquil for one parent and is a delightful plant bearing sweetly scented flowers of clear golden-yellow with overlapping perianth petals on a 60-cm (2-ft) stem.

NIRVANA. One of the most exquisite of the jonquils, the blooms having an overlapping perianth of purest white and a short crown of creamy white with a delicious perfume.

PENCREBAR. Named after the West Country garden in which it was found. It is an early dwarf plant in the true jonquil style with 2 or 3 blooms appearing on one stem, its golden-yellow flowers being double.

SWEETNESS. A truly gorgeous jonquil of exquisite perfume, the golden perianths having pointed petals and a large globular crown.

TREVITHIAN. A superb jonquil for cutting or for forcing in bowls for its pale lemon-yellow flowers, borne 2 or 3 to a stem, are long-lasting and richly scented.

N. juncifolius. A delightful native of northern Portugal and the Pyrenees, flowering in April. It has thin cylindrical leaves, hence its name of the rush-leaf daffodil. Always tidy, for its leaves wither away soon after flowering, it bears tiny cups of deepest yellow in twos and threes on a 10-cm (4-in) stem and is pleasantly scented. Lintie is a delightful hybrid, its flat yellow crown being edged with orange and it is ravishingly scented.

N. minimus (syn. *N. asturiensis*). It is

most attractively depicted in the painting by Jan Baers, *Flowers and Lizards,* in which the tiny golden flower with its twisted petals and frilled trumpet can be clearly seen. This painting was executed in Utrecht in 1629, the year Parkinson published his *Paradisus.*

N. minor. This tiny bicolour trumpet daffodil and its even smaller form, *minimus,* are remarkable for the powerful scent given off by such small flowers: *minor* grows only 15 cm (6 in) tall and has a trumpet less than 2.5 cm (1 in) long, whilst *minimus* is only half the size. A native of Portugal, *minor* blooms in February and is indeed a treasure with its twisted perianth petals and a trumpet which is beautifully waved.

N. odorus. It is known as the Campernelle jonquil and grows wild in Spain and across southern Europe to the Adriatic. Possibly a hybrid between the jonquil and the Lent lily, it has been growing in English gardens since early Tudor times. It has rush-like foliage and bears clusters of bright-yellow flowers on 22.5-cm (9-in) stems. The flowers are so richly scented that they embalm the air for yards around. The variety *regulosus* is slightly more robust with a larger flower whilst Orange Queen bears flowers of deepest orange which are not as fragrant. *Regulosus plenus* bears a double bloom which if anything is even more heavily scented than the type.

N. pseudo-narcissus. It includes the Lent lily and the larger form known as *N. bicolor* for both are bicoloured daffodils from which are descended the modern bicolours. They bloom in March and are suitable only for naturalizing for which they are admirable, remaining long in bloom, and they have the sweet, woodland perfume of the primrose.

N. rupicola. Closely related to *N. juncifolius* and growing in much the same parts of Spain and Portugal. The foliage is 3-sided and grows upright whilst the blooms are of brightest yellow with a 6-lobed corolla and are held on 7.5- to 10-cm (3- to 4-in) stems. They are more powerfully scented than in almost any species. Where happily established, the plant will seed itself in profusion.

N. tenuior. Found along the shores of the Mediterranean where it is known as the Silver jonquil, it is a perfect treasure of

jonquil type. Several flowers appear on a 30-cm (12-in) stem and have a cream perianth and sulphur-yellow cup and they emit a delicious perfume.

N. triandrus concolor. This is the only really scented form of the Angel's Tears daffodil, found by the late Peter Barr in northern Spain where it grows in mountainous regions. The white form *albus* is without scent but *concolor,* with its reflexed perianth and globular corona of primrose yellow, is sweetly scented. It has rush-like foliage and blooms in April.

GARDEN HYBRIDS. Whilst almost all daffodils have the damp, mossy fragrance of the woodlands, pronounced scent is present in only a small number of the trumpet forms, the heavy intoxicating narcissus scent being present in the Tazetta and Poeticus groups and in the Jonquils (see under *N. jonquilla*).

Class IIb. Large-cupped Narcissi:

LOUISE DE COLIGNY. One of the most attractive narcissi ever introduced with a large white perianth of overlapping petals and a charming trumpet-shaped crown of a unique shade of soft pink with an apricot flush. The perfume is sweet and penetrating.

Class IIIc. Small-cupped Narcissi:

POLAR ICE. Very late into bloom, it is a charming variety and aptly named. The perianth is snow-white with a small flat crown of ice-white, shaded green at the centre and with a most delightful soft sweet perfume.

Class IV. Double Narcissi:

ALBUS PLENUS ODORATUS. The Double White *poeticus* which like all the double whites blooms in May later than most other daffodils. The blooms, with their overlapping petals, are like white gardenias and have a glorious perfume.

FALAISE. Raised from a Poeticus and the well-known double, Mary Copeland, it is a double of striking contrasts, with bright orange-red centre petals and outer petals of purest white. The blooms possess the exotic perfume of the Poeticus group.

SANTA CLAUS. A magnificent variety and like Falaise, it would appear to have a Poeticus in its parentage for the huge double blooms are of the same glistening white and with the same intoxicating perfume. It is the last of the daffodils to bloom, the buds not opening until mid-May. The broad petals overlap to the edge, giving it the appearance of a white gardenia.

SNOWBALL. Another double of extreme beauty and most likely of Poeticus parentage. The blooms are gardenia-like and symmetrical with overlapping perianth petals and a tightly formed centre so that the bloom retains its form for many days. It has the powerful Poeticus perfume.

SWANSDOWN. A double with a Poeticus in its parentage. The enormous milk-white blooms are of great substance with broad circular overlapping outer petals and a centre of feather pure-white petals. The bloom has a soft sweet orange-blossom perfume.

Class VIII. The Tazetta Narcissi:

The bunch-flowered narcissus N. tazetta grows wild in Spain and along the French Riviera, through the Near East and Kashmir, and across central China to Japan where they grow in low-lying meadowland. It is rather less hardy in the British Isles than other species, and its varieties with the exception of the hybrids Geranium, Cragford and Bridal Crown should be given a warm, sunny corner and shelter from cold winds. In a mild winter in Cornwall and the Channel Islands, they will bloom from December until March when they will begin to bloom in less favourable districts. Narcissi of the Tazetta section are amongst the most powerfully scented of all flowers. The bulbs may be grown indoors in bowls of stones in water when they will bloom to perfection early in the year.

BRIDAL CROWN. It is a double 'sport' of the Poetaz L'Innocence, bearing in clusters three or four snow-white flowers of exquisite perfume.

CHEERFULNESS. It is a flower of extreme beauty and sweet fragrance with a creamy-white perianth and fully double centre of palest yellow. Several blooms appear together on a single stem. There is a yellow form bearing flowers of a pleasing shade of buttery yellow.

CHAGFORD. One of the finest of all narcissi, the sparkling white of its perianth made more pronounced by its scarlet crown. Its scent may be overpowering in a warm room.

EARLY SPLENDOUR. Like all the Tazettas, it grows 45 cm (18 in) tall and bears as many as 6 or 8 blooms on a single stem, their glistening white perianth being accentuated by the orange cup.

GERANIUM. A Poetaz hybrid which bears 5 or 6 flowers to each stem. The broad white perianth petals overlap and provide a striking contrast to the cup of brilliant scarlet. It is unsurpassed amongst all flowers for its perfume.

GRAND SOLEIL D'OR. Grown in the manner of Paper White, it is most showy, 4 or 5 golden-yellow flowers appearing on each stem.

LAURENS KOSTER. An old variety, bearing 5 or 6 fragrant flowers on a tall, graceful stem with a creamy-white perianth and orange cup.

PAPER WHITE. Narcissus papyraceous, but it is always known by its trade name. Away from Cornwall and the Scilly Isles it is grown only indoors, usually in bowls of moist pebbles, and will bloom early in the year. Five or six starry white flowers of exquisite perfume are borne on each stem.

SILVER CHIMES. A variety of outstanding beauty, with stiff olive-green foliage and a sturdy stem carrying 9 or 10 dangling flowers of creamy-white with an exotic fragrance. One of the last of the bunch-flowered narcissi to bloom, it does well indoors in bowls and in the garden.

Class IX. The Poet's Narcissus and Hybrids:

These are descended from N. poeticus which grows wild along the shores of the Mediterranean from Spain to Greece. The white, solitary flowers, with their tiny red corona measure about 5 cm (2 in) across and appear in April. The double form, albus plenus odoratus, was described under Class IV.

N. poeticus recurvus. The old Pheasant

Eye narcissus which was not introduced into Britain until after Waterloo and which gets its name from the tiny red corona filled with yellow stamens which resembles the colourings of a pheasant's eye. It is one of the last to bloom and is suitable only for naturalizing.

ACTAEA. Probably the best Poeticus, it has a large perianth of ice-white and a large 'eye' margined with crimson-red. It reaches a height of 60 cm (2 ft) and is an outstanding cut flower variety with a powerful perfume.

QUEEN OF NARCISSI. It bears a bloom of fine texture with a large white perianth and a bright-yellow 'eye' edged with red. The flowers carry a pleasant, sweet perfume.

NARRISIA (Cactaceae—Cactus Family)

A genus of 19 species, native of tropical South America, the West Indies and Cuba, several of which are well known in cultivation. The stems grow tall and slender and have long spines whilst the large flowers are borne near the top of the stems formed the previous year. The Narrisias like a compost composed of equal parts gravel, loam and lime rubble, a calcareous soil being essential to their well-being. Provide a sunny situation with a minimum winter temperature of 10°C (50°F) and give plenty of moisture during summer.

Species. *Narrisia regelli.* Native of Jamaica and eastern Argentina, it makes a thin straggling plant 2 m (6 to 7 ft) tall and has grey areoles and short spines. The flowers are borne singly and are large, the outer petals pink, the inner white, and they are powerfully scented, like jonquil. The flowers appear early in summer and again in autumn.

NELUMBIUM (Lotus)
(Nymphaeaceae—Water-lily Family)

A small genus of aquatic plants represented by *N. speciosum*, the Sacred Pink lotus of the Buddhists, distributed throughout the sub-tropical areas of Asia and Africa, and by *N. lutea*, the Water Chinkapin of North America. They are distinguished from the Nymphaeas in that their flower stems rise above the water. In northern Europe, they need greenhouse protection to be a success.

Species and Varieties. *Nelumbium lutea.* A native of the U.S.A. it is similar to *N. speciosum* except that the colour of its flowers is deep yellow and they are not quite so fragrant as those of the Asian lotus. No mention was made of this species until the discovery of America when it was found that the roots were eaten by the Indians (as potatoes).

N. speciosum. It is the Sacred lotus of India and Tibet, the flower on which Buddha sits, and has been cultivated since the beginning of time; its pale-pink flowers were copied to form the head-dress for the sphinxes, emblem of the generative power of the ancient Egyptians. The flowers are like large tea roses and with the same sweet fruity perfume as the hybrid tea rose Tahiti. The seeds were much in demand for food by the inhabitants of Tibet and Kashmir, and Herodotus (484 B.C.) wrote that 'the root is fit for food and is sweet and of the size of an apple'. The plant was introduced into America by E. D. Sturtevant of New Jersey in 1876. Dr Conard, in his *Monograph of the Water Lily* (1905), speaks of its hardiness there but says the roots need to be covered in winter.

The variety *album grandiflorum,* developed in Japan, bears enormous flowers of ice-white with delicious scent, whilst *Pekinense rubrum,* a Chinese variety, bears large globular blooms of rich amaranth-red with outstanding scent.

Of the Chinese lotus, the eleventh-century writer Chan Tun said. 'Since the opening days of the T'ang Dynasty (A.D. 600), it has been fashionable to admire the peony, but my favourite is the water lily ... How modestly it reposes on the clear pool, an emblem of purity and truth. Symmetrically perfect, its subtle perfume is wafted far and wide ...'.

NEMESIA (Scrophulariaceae—Foxglove Family)

A genus of about 20 species and, as with almost all members of the family, few possess perfume, though they make up for this by the brilliance of their colouring. A native of South Africa, where few native flowers are scented, a species was introduced into Britain towards the end of the nineteenth century. This was *N. strumosa,* a plant growing 30 to 37.5 cm

(12 to 15 in) tall, which bears trusses of brilliant pure orange flowers from June until September. From this plant the brilliantly coloured bedding strains were evolved, plants without rival for summer display when massed together in open beds. They are however entirely lacking in perfume.

Species. *Nemesia floribunda.* A species which has been entirely neglected in the breeding programme, it bears sweetly scented flowers in handsome trusses at a height of less than 30 cm (12 in). The blooms, as would be imagined, are of white and pale yellow and are produced over a long period. It is altogether a delightful plant for the summer flower garden but it is doubtful if seed can now be obtained.

NEOTTIA (Orchidaceae—Orchid Family)

A small genus of orchidaceous plants which are devoid of chlorophyll and have to obtain all their nourishment from decayed matter in the soil. They are without leaves whilst the flowers are usually brown or pinkish-brown. They are mostly confined to the dense forests of western China and the lower Himalaya regions, though one species, *N. nidus-avis*, is common in the British Isles where it is mostly confined to southern England.

Species. *Neottia nidus-avis.* It is the Bird's-nest orchid, so called from the dense mass of thick roots it forms. It is to be found growing from damp decayed leaves in woodlands where the sun rarely penetrates and it blooms in June, bearing its dingy brownish-yellow flowers on a 37.5-cm (15-in) stem. The lower flowers emit a most unpleasant smell and are pollinated by insects, though the upper flowers, which open later and are self-pollinated, are quite pleasantly scented.

NEPETA (Labiatae—Lavender Family)

A genus of annual but mostly perennial herbs with aromatic foliage. For edging the herbaceous border or for planting in sun-baked corners, the catmints are most attractive plants with mauve flowers and blue-grey foliage which gives them a misty charm, whilst the plants have the appearance of a lavender hedge when viewed from a distance. Cats enjoy the plants, either to chew the leaves which act as a tonic or to roll about them in the heat of summer, which seems to refresh them.

Before tea reached Britain from China, an aromatic beverage was made by infusing catmint leaves in boiling water and was drunk with milk and sugar. The liquid was also used by countrymen for applying to bruises, in particular to 'black eyes'.

The nepetas prefer a moist soil and an open situation. Though they bloom for five or six weeks of midsummer, the cool, grey foliage remains pleasing for many weeks and should not be removed until early spring, providing protection for the plants during winter. Plant in spring either by root division or from cuttings rooted in a cold frame in summer. The leaves when dried make a pleasing addition to pot-pourri or scented bags.

Species. *Nepeta catara.* A plant native of the British Isles, Gerard's *Herba Cattaria*, so called because 'the smell is pleasant unto cats'. It is found by ditches and damp places and grows 90 cm (3 ft) tall with attractive heart-shaped leaves which release a resinous quality when handled. The flowers are white and borne in whorls.

N. mussinii. Native of the Caucasus, it grows 60 cm (2 ft) tall with broad heart-shaped leaves, toothed and wrinkled and hoary on the underside, and in June and July it bears masses of purple-blue flowers which are enhanced by the blue-grey foliage.

The form now most widely planted is *N. faassenii*, a hybrid of *N. mussinii* which erroneously takes its name. It grows only 30 cm (12 in). tall with neat blue-grey leaves and it bears whorls of lavender-blue flowers from May until August. The foliage is pungently scented.

N. nervosa. It has attractive grey heart-shaped leaves and bears its violet-blue flowers from July until September in dense cylindrical spikes. It is of compact habit, rarely exceeding 30 cm (12 in) tall.

N. septemcrenata. It is found only south of the El-Tih Desert where it makes a slender plant 60 cm (2 ft) tall with woody branches at the base. Its small leaves are heart-shaped and serrated, like those of *N. catara*, and are highly pungent when bruised.

N. spicata. Native of the Himalayas, it makes a bushy plant 30 cm (12 in) tall and has broad heart-shaped leaves which are deeply toothed. The flowers appear in September and are purple with a white lip and are borne in spikes 7.5 to 10 cm (3 to 4 in) long.

NERIUM (Apocynaceae—Periwinkle Family)

A genus of mostly tropical shrubs of which *N. oleander,* the Oleander, bears scented flowers, which is rare in this almost scentless family. All contain poisonous milky juices, used by the natives of central Africa to make poison for darts and arrows. The plants are also fatal to cattle, if consumed.

Species. *Nereum oleander.* It is a tall shrub with stiff, erect branches and is to be found in southern Europe, North Africa and Persia, usually growing close to water for it likes to have its roots in moisture. It has narrow pointed grey-green leaves which are evergreen and bears its flowers, like those of the wild rose of England's hedgerows, in terminal clusters. They are of pale-pink colouring with a soft sweet perfume.

The plant requires the protection of a warm greenhouse in the British Isles, except in the very mildest parts and makes a delightful pot plant. The variety *album* bears white flowers which are also scented.

NICOTIANA (Solanaceae—Nightshade Family)

A genus of about 30 species of usually hairy shrubs or plants with large undivided leaves and bearing tubular flowers in terminal panicles. The flowers are either white, green or crimson, and are borne in continuous succession from July until September.

Nicotiana tabacum is the tobacco of commerce, so well known for the fragrance of its leaves when dried. It is named after Jean Nicot, ambassador to Portugal in 1560, who planted it in the garden of the embassy in Lisbon for the valuable qualities of its dried leaves which were in demand for inhaling as snuff. Most gardens of the Iberian Peninsula at one time grew a few plants of *N. tabacum* for its

curative powers. The first cigars are believed to have been made about 1540 by Demetrio Pela, and by late Elizabethan times the tobacconist was as firmly established in the City of London as the herbalist. Gerard tells us that 'the dry leaves are used to be taken in a pipe and set on fire and sucked into the stomach and thrust forth again at the nostrils . . . '.

Species. *Nicotiana affinis.* The Tobacco plant grows 0.9 to 1.2 m (3 to 4 ft) in height with glaucous ovate leaves some 15 cm (6 in) long, and through late summer and autumn bears its starry white flowers, green on the outside, which open and emit a sweet perfume in the evening. The blooms remain closed by day but those of Dwarf White Bedder, which are similar in all respects but are borne on stems only 45 cm (18 in) tall, remain open and are fragrant by day as well as at night. The Tobacco plants are half-hardy annuals raised from seed sown in gentle heat early in the year and planted out, when hardened, early in June.

N. suaveolens. It is an annual plant, a native of Australia and so should be given half-hardy culture. Growing to a height of 45 to 50 cm (18 to 20 in) it comes into bloom towards the end of July, bearing numerous large white flowers to each stem and at night it is as richly fragrant as the other nicotianas.

N. sylvestris. The Woodland Tobacco, like *N. affinis,* is a perennial, but being a native of the Argentine must be given half-hardy culture in Britain. It will reach a height of 1.8 m (6 ft) and more from the time the seed is sown under glass in February till it comes into bloom towards the end of August. The stems carry generous panicles of drooping, tubular flowers which are of purest white and have the same sweet scent as freesias. It is a handsome plant in all respects for the lower leaves measure as much as 60 cm (2 ft) in length. It requires a rich soil containing leaf-mould and does best in partial shade.

NIGELLA (Ranunculaceae—Buttercup Family)

A genus of 20 species of annuals, native to the Mediterranean regions and central Asia.

Species. *Nigella sativa.* It is a member of the almost scentless Buttercup Family and has been a familiar cottage garden flower since Elizabethan times. Though the flowers have no perfume, the seeds have been used to flavour bread and cakes since the time of the Pharaohs. They were consumed by Egyptian women in the belief that they would bring plumpness to the breasts whilst they were used finely ground to remove lice from the hair; the seed was used in England during Tudor times for this purpose. The deliciously aromatic seeds were also used to place in sweet bags and, when warmed in a muslin bag, were used for inhaling or for hanging near a fire, when the room would be made refreshingly fragrant; the seeds would be changed every third week. In France and Italy, the seed is used to impart its nutmeg flavour to cheese. Indeed, *N. sativa* was in early times known as the Nutmeg-plant for its seeds so resembled this spice, and apothecaries extracted an oil which was used as a substitution for the expensive spikenard oil.

It is an annual plant of the Mediterranean regions and grows 45 cm (18 in) tall with hairy stems and leaves which are divided like those of the fennel. The pale-blue flowers are borne in July and August. It is believed that this plant is the 'fitches' of Isaiah. It differs but slightly from *N. damascena,* the true Love-in-a-mist of our gardens, which does not have scented seeds.

NOLINA (Liliaceae—Lily Family)

A genus of stately, yucca-like plants native of Mexico. They form straight stems, with evergreen leaves which exist as a tuft at the top, and they are long and narrow, recurving and drooping in graceful style. They completely hide the stem and may reach almost to the base, often being 2.4 m (8 ft) or more in length.

As would be expected, the plants require a position of full sun and a minimum night temperature of 10°C (50°F). During summer, the plants in their pots may be stood outside in a wind-protected position, and they will benefit from a regular syringeing of the foliage and copious amounts of moisture at the roots. Propagation is by seed, cuttings or offsets.

Species. *Nolina longifolia.* A magnificent species, attaining a height of 3 m (10 ft), with leaves of the same length, and bearing multitudes of snow-white flowers of sweetest fragrance.

N. recurvata. Grows about 2.4 m (8 ft) tall with elegantly recurving leaves of deep glossy green of tough texture, whilst its scented, pure-white flowers are borne in profusion.

NOTHOLIRION (Liliaceae—Lily Family)

A genus of six species closely related to *Lilium* and *Fritillaria,* but now accepted as a distinct genus. Only one species, *Notholirion thomsonianum,* bears flowers with any degree of scent, and fortunately it is the species most successful in the British Isles and northern Europe. They are all native of Afghanistan, the Himalayas and western China.

Species. *Notholirion thomsonianum.* A native of Afghanistan and being tall-growing requires a sheltered corner, and in Britain a position with some shade. It begins to form its leaves early in the year and blooms in April and May, bearing its funnel-shaped bells of lilac-pink, flushed with crimson on the inside, on 1.2 m (4 ft) stems. The flowers, borne horizontally and 30 or more on a stem, have the pleasing perfume of lily of the valley. After flowering the plant dies, but its offsets or seeds from the blooms may be used for increase.

NOTHOSCORDUM (Alliaceae—Onion Family)

A genus of 35 species of North American plants, closely related to the lily family and having tunicated bulbs and flat, linear leaves. Plant 10 to 12 cm (4 to 5 in) deep, in a well-drained soil and in an open, sunny situation. Increase by seed or offsets.

Species. *Nothoscordum fragrans.* It attains a height of 60 cm (2 ft) or more, and bears a dozen or so flowers in each umbel. The bell-shaped blooms consist of united segments of glistening white, each segment being keeled outside with lilac. The flowers have a rich, sweet lily-like perfume, and are produced in May and June. It is thought by some authorities that this species is in fact *N. inodorum,* but two quite separate plants are described under these names by John Weathers in his book on bulbs written in the early 1800s.

NUPHAR (Nymphaeaceae—Water-lily Family)

A genus of 25 species of north temperate regions, differing from *Nymphaea* in that the seeds have no aril. They are released when the pericarp decays.

Species. *Nuphar lutea.* It frequents ponds and lakes and slow-running water throughout England and Wales, but is rare in Scotland. The leaves are ovate and float on the surface. The yellow flowers are small, about 7.5 cm (3 in) across, and from their brandy-like smell, the plant is known to countrymen as 'brandy bottle'. The unique smell is due to a combination of acetic acid and ethyl alcohol to form ethylacetate. It blooms from July to September.

NYCTANTHES (Verbenaceae—Vervain Family)

A genus of two species of shrubby trees, native of India and the Indonesian Islands and known as the Indian jasmine.

Species. *Nyctanthes arbor-tristis.* It is common throughout India and is a deciduous tree, bearing a profusion of white star-like flowers which open at night, diffusing a honeysuckle fragrance far and wide. After pollination by moths, the petals fall at sunrise and are collected for pot-pourris for they retain their perfume for a considerable time.

N. sambac. A small deciduous tree with star-like flowers which the native women use to decorate their hair. Carl Thunberg, the nineteenth-century Swedish explorer, related that the women of Batavia would tie up their jet-black hair into a large knot on the crown of the head and adorn it with a circle of sweet-scented flowers of this tree. Each evening, dozens of the wreaths would be made up and sold in the towns for the women to wear, diffusing the scent of orange flowers for the whole night and 'enhancing, if possible, the society of the fair sex'.

NYCTOCEREUS (Cactaceae—Cactus Family)

A genus of seven species of night-flowering plants, native of Mexico and the central United States. They are plants of trailing habit which bear their flowers at the end of long, straggling stems.

Species. *Nyctocereus grandiflora* (syn. *Cereus grandiflora*). Native of Mexico, it blooms only at night when it bears one of the largest flowers known. The inside is straw-yellow, the outside chocolate-brown. It often measures 30 cm (12 in) in diameter, and emits a powerful vanilla-like perfume, but blooms for only one night as after fertilization it withers and dies.

N. serpentinus. Native of Mexico, it has pale-green stems made up of 10 to 12 flat ribs and with 12 spines on the areoles. Each spine is half an inch long and is rose-pink at first, later turning white. The flowers measure 15 cm (6 in) across and are white, green on the outside, with a powerful musk-like scent. They are followed by red edible fruits.

NYMPHAEA (Nymphaeaceae—Water-lily Family)

A genus of 50 species present in the British Isles, South-east Asia and the tropical marshes of the Amazon. The common white water-lily, *Nymphaea alba,* which floats upon the surface of the water, is the only species native to the British Isles. Nymphaeas should be planted in spring, in water which is 35 to 45 cm (14 to 18 in) deep. A greater depth of water will check growth and retard flowering. To prevent the water from clouding and becoming stagnant with the spread of algae, oxygenating plants such as *Callitriche verna* and *Lagorosiphon* should be planted with the lilies.

Species and Varieties. *Nymphaea alba.* Native of the British Isles, it bears a flower about 15 cm (6 in) across, with yellow stamens, which open only in sunshine. They bloom during July and August, and have a soft delicate scent.

N. albida. The largest of all water-lilies, the globular flowers with their wax-like petals being as white as driven snow, and with an exotic, heavy fragrance. The flowers are enhanced by the bottle-green leaves. It is a Marliacea hybrid, originating in the garden of Monsieur Marliac, the 'Father of the water-lily'.

N. capensis zanzibariensis. The Royal Purple water-lily of Africa, which can be grown in a small tub indoors. Its dark-green leaves are blotched with brown, whilst its star-like flowers of richest blue have conspicuous golden anthers and a powerful perfume. The form Jupiter, deepest purple-blue, is equally fine and strongly scented.

N. caroliniana. Native of North America, the large globular flowers are a delicate salmon-pink with a soft, sweet perfume. The variety *nivea* bears large flowers of purest white, and *rosea*, flowers of bright rose-pink with golden stamens. Both are pleasantly scented. Likewise the hybrid varieties.

N. carnea. A most free-flowering form, its flesh-tinted flowers having the same vanilla like perfume as *Laburnum vossii.* It is a Marliacea hybrid.

N. chromatella. This hybrid has enormous flowers of clearest primrose-yellow, which have a rich, sweet, almond-like perfume. The blooms are borne from May until the end of autumn. The leaves when young are attractively mottled with brown. It is also a Marliacea hybrid.

N. froebelii. One of the best water-lilies for tub cultivation for a verandah or roof garden. It requires only 25 to 30 cm (10 to 12 in) of water and bears its scented, wine-red flowers with greatest freedom.

N. fulva. The leaves are blotched with brown and crimson, whilst the creamy-yellow flowers are lined with red against which the golden stamens shine like torches. The blooms have a soft, delicate perfume. This is a Laydekeri hybrid.

N. gladstoniana. One of the most beautiful of all hybrid varieties, the huge, white peony-like blooms, with touches of green on the sepals, possess outstanding perfume.

N. lilacea. Like all those of the Laydekeri group, the flowers are small and dainty, measuring about 7 cm (3 in) across, and in this case they are a lovely lilac-rose with a delicate tea-rose scent.

N. Murillo. This variety has large, star-shaped flowers, rose-red on the inside, white on the outside, and sweetly scented.

N. odorata. This attractive North American species, introduced in 1786, resembles *N. alba* in almost every respect but its scent. It comes into bloom before the end of June, and from the fleshy rootstocks arise heart-shaped leaves 22 to 25 cm (9 to 10 in) across, and deliciously scented white flowers, tinted with rose. The flowers open early morning to some 15 cm (6 in) across, when they are most fragrant, for by afternoon they have closed again.

The varieties of *N. odorata* are numerous, but none has a more powerful perfume than *gigantea,* nor is there one of greater beauty, its enormous petals of ice-white having the same sweet perfume as *Paeonia* Duchesse de Nemours, and much of its beauty. The form *minor,* found in shallow swamps in many North American states, bears small, star-like flowers with golden anthers and are deliciously scented. *N. o. sulphurea grandiflora* is golden-yellow, of a similar size to the white variety, and equally strongly scented.

The variety Rose Arey is one of the most beautiful of all the water-lilies, the pointed petals giving the flowers a star-like appearance, whilst they are of deep rose-pink with a pronounced sweet perfume. Equally fine is Helen Fowler, with small, dark-green leaves and bearing flowers of richest pink with golden anthers. It has a sweet perfume. Another heavily scented pink is W. B. Shaw, its blooms being of a lovely soft shell pink.

N. pygmaea helvola. A most elegant little water-lily, native of northern Asia, and it is the smallest of all the species, its heart-shaped leaves being only 10 cm (4 in) across, whilst the charming little white flowers measure only 5 to 7 cm (2 to 3 in) across. The strength of their perfume is, however, remarkable, being noticeable at a considerable distance, whilst the flowers are produced with a freedom unknown amongst the other species and from June until September. It requires no more than a 15-cm (6-in) depth of water.

N. stellata coerulea. The Blue lotus of the Nile, requiring the protection of a greenhouse in northern Europe, it more nearly resembles *nelumbo* in that its flowers, of soft sky-blue, stand several inches above the water. They have a hyacinth-like scent.

N. tuberosa. A native of the north-eastern United States, its circular leaves often measure as much as 45 cm (1½ ft) across, whilst its flowers, as white as driven snow, are almost half that size in diameter. They have attractively waved petals and a fruity perfume, like that of ripe apples. More strongly fragrant is the variety *rosea*, which is an exquisite shell-pink, whilst *richardsonii* bears fragrant double flowers of purest white, which are held above the surface of the water.

N. virginale. It is early into bloom (April) and continues until mid-October, its pure-white petals being of exquisite shape and delicious perfume.

NYMPHOIDES:
see **LIMNANTHEMUM.**

O

OCHROCARPUS (Mammea)
(Guttiferae—St John's Wort Family)

A small genus of tall trees, native of tropical America and the West Indies, Madagascar and islands of the Pacific, the fruit being used in making liqueurs whilst the timber has many uses.

Species. *Ochrocarpus odoratus* (syn. *Mammea excelsa*, and at least 12 others). It makes a tree 18 to 21 m (60 to 70 ft) tall, the close-grained wood being used in building; the Fijians once used the sap for dyeing the hair orange. The tiny white flowers diffuse a powerful sweet perfume.

OCOTEA (Lauraceae—Bay Tree Family)

A genus of 300 to 400 species of tall trees, native of the tropical forests of South America, which provide the valuable Greenheart timber of commerce and aromatic oils from the bark. The leaves are alternate, oblong or elliptical.

Species. *Ocotea cymbarum* (syn. *Ocotea amara*). Found in the woods along the banks of the Orinoco and in the ancient forests of the Rio Negro in Brazil where it reaches a height of 30 m (100 ft) or more. Its bark, known as Orinoco sassafras, is brown and extremely aromatic. From incisions in the trunk, an oil known as *Acéite de Sassafras* is obtained and contains safrol.

The branches of the tree are smooth with oblong-lanceolate leaves, shining above, netted on the underside. The white, sweetly scented flowers are followed by large fruits (drupes). The cup of the fruit is large with a double edge.

O. bullata. It forms a small tree with smooth bark and is evergreen, the upper surface of the leaves as if polished, and they are resinous when handled. The flowers are white and are borne in terminal inflorescences. The fruit is partially enclosed by the fleshy receptacle. The wood releases a pleasant rose perfume when cut or burnt.

N. puchury. Native of the tropical forests of Brazil and from its cotyledons are obtained the seeds known as Puchury beans or Sassafras nuts for they have the familiar aroma of sassafras bark, similar to nutmeg. The cup of the fruit is large and spongy, and in the early months of the year the fruit falls from the cup to the ground where it is collected and cleaned of flesh and pericarp and dried.

The leaves are oblong, tapering to a point and are leathery, releasing a powerful aroma when handled.

OCYMUM (Basil) (Labiatae—Lavender Family)

A genus of several aromatic species native to the East Indies, tropical Africa and the Near East. *O. basilicum,* the Sweet basil, is an annual plant which is only half-hardy in the British Isles. The seed is sown in gentle heat or under cloches in April. There are three distinct forms, one possessing a mint aroma and with purple stems; *pilosum* has a lemon scent, whilst another smells of peppermint. The leaves are used in salads, with discretion, and impart a pleasant aromatic taste. In a dry summer the plant, which grows 60 cm (2 ft) tall, will form plenty of leaf which may be removed in September and dried and used for winter stuffings and in potpourris. *O. basilicum,* native of Persia, reached England early in our history. It was known to Michael Drayton, the

Elizabethan poet who describes two maidens making chaplets; one of them gathers flowers just for their beauty, whilst the other picks hers for their fragrance:

> With Basil then I will begin,
> Whose scent is wondrous pleasing.

The plant figures in the lovely lines by Shelley:

> Madonna, wherefore hast thou sent to me
> Sweet basil and mignonette?
> Embleming love and health which never yet
> In the same wreath might be.

Shelley's reference to 'sweet basil and mignonette' is interesting for the perfumers of France consider the essential oil of the Sweet basil to have such a distinct smell of mignonette that the two are mixed together, for mignonette yields little essential oil.

Species. *Ocymum basilicum.* It has smooth oblong leaves, acutely serrated, which yield about 1.5 per cent essential oil; this when crystallized becomes Basil Camphor.

Of the Bush basil, *Ocymum minimum*, a form of Sweet basil discovered in Chile and which grows 15 cm (6 in) tall (also an annual), Parkinson said it was 'used to make sweet washing water and . . . sometimes it is put into nosegays . . . to procure a cheerful and merry heart'. Tusser included both in his herbs for strewing. The Bush basil forms a round bushy head with leaves no larger than those of the thyme and is an admirable plant for a window-box or pot.

Another form is *O. anisatum* or *O. basilicum citratum* which is planted about the gardens of Hindu temples throughout India. It grows 60 cm (2 ft) tall with downy leaves and it bears greenish-pink flowers the whole year. It has a delicious lemony aroma.

O. canum. It is native of Madagascar, China and Brazil and is the most potently scented of all the basils. It makes a shrubby upright plant 30 cm (12 in) tall and has leaves which narrow at both ends.

O. crispum. It is native of the Nagasaki district of Japan with purple-green leaves, serrated at the edges and about 2.5 cm (1 in) long, a decoction of which is used to increase the red colouring of radishes. The whole plant is pleasantly aromatic.

O. gratissimum. Native of Persia and eastern India, the whole plant emits a powerful lemon odour whilst the leaves also have a citrus taste. In the East, it is planted in temple gardens where it may grow to a height of 1.8 m (6 ft) or more whilst the drooping leaves are 15 cm (6 in) long. The pale-yellow flowers are borne in terminal racemes. It is perennial.

O. menthaefolium. Present in southern Egypt and in the Sudan, it is a low-growing under-shrub with pubescent branches and serrated leaves which release a powerful mint aroma when handled. The pale-pink flowers are borne in racemes.

O. sanctum. Native of all parts of India, inhabiting dry places. It is known as *Tulasi* and for its fragrance is venerated by the Hindus, hence its Western name of the Holy basil. It is a short-stemmed woody perennial with purple hairy stems and downy leaves 3.5 cm (1½ in) long. It is not hardy in the British Isles and northern Europe.

ODONTOGLOSSUM (Orchidaceae— Orchid Family)

A genus of more than 300 species, native of tropical America, Mexico and Jamaica, where they inhabit high mountainous regions. In cultivation they require similar conditions, a cool, well-ventilated house and limited supplies of moisture. A temperature of 10°C (50 °F) is suitable, but in such a temperature transpiration of moisture is slow and care must be taken to allow the plants time to utilize any moisture in the compost and in the house.

Pot in September when the plants begin to grow, and use a small pot, just large enough to take the roots. Half fill the pots with drainage materials and fill up with a compost composed of 3 parts sphagnum-moss and 1 part peat, to which a small amount of coarse sand has been added. The plants should be raised slightly above the rim of the pot.

Species. *Odontoglossum citrosum.* An extremely beautiful orchid, with drooping spikes of rounded white flowers, with a rose-pink lip, produced in May. They are strongly scented of roses. The species needs rather warmer conditions than most orchids.

O. edwardii. From the Andes, the purple to rose-pink flowers of this species have the fragrance of violets and are about 2 cm (1 in) wide, in a many-flowered spike. It grows to a height of about 0.9 to 1.2 m (3 to 4 ft).

O. gloriosum. This Colombian species is summer flowering, with the delicious scent of hawthorn without the fishy undertones. The yellow or sometimes greenish flowers with reddish-brown spots, are produced on a fairly long inflorescence.

O. odoratum. The scent of hawthorn emitted by the flowers of this species is unexpected but nonetheless welcome. Its flowers are borne in spring, and are lomg-lived; they are mostly deep yellow with dark-brown to red spots. The many-flowered inflorescence is handsome, and may grow to more than 90 cm (3 ft) tall.

O. pulchellum. As its name suggests, this is a pretty orchid, its ice-white flowers having a yellow crest. The vanilla fragrance enhances its attraction and its flowers have the peculiarity of being borne on the spike in such a way as to appear upside down.

OENANTHE (Umbelliferae—Parsley Family)

A small genus of aquatic plants which take their name from the Greek words *oinos*, wine, and *anthos*, flower, because of the unmistakable wine-like aroma given off by its flowers, like the aroma of matured port and most pronounced in *O. fistulosa.*

Species. *Oenanthe fistulosa.* The common water dropwort, a fleshy fibrous-rooted plant of perennial habit and frequenting ditches and marshes of the British Isles and northern Europe. It has hollow stems and 2 to 3 pinnate leaves and it bears its creamy-white flowers in umbels during July and August.

OENOTHERA   (Onagraceae—Evening Primrose Family)

A genus of 80 species, native of North America and the West Indies, their nectar being secreted at the end of long tubes.

Species. *Oenothera biennis.* The Evening primrose is a biennial form and the most familiar to British gardeners, being powerfully fragrant at night and visited by moths. The flowers sleep by day, the hooks of the tapering sepals clasping each other so that the bloom cannot open. Then as twilight descends, the bloom is seen to discard its protective hood and opens in all its fragrant loveliness.

The plant comes into bloom at a height of 1.2 m (4 ft) but by the end of summer has reached 1.8 m (6 ft) or more with downy, lance-shaped leaves, and it has one of the longest flowering seasons of all plants, blooming from June until October. The blooms, which measure 7.5 cm (3 in) across, are a lovely clear primrose-yellow and emit a delicious sweet perfume. The flowers soon die but others take their place in endless succession. The plants are readily raised from seed sown in July where they are to bloom, and from then on they will seed themselves.

It is believed that *O. biennis* reached Europe in 1619, seed being sent over from Virginia to Padua, and it must have reached Britain a year or so later for Parkinson (1629) makes mention of it as the 'tree primrose'.

O. californica. The Californian primrose is a native of California and fully perennial, growing about 60 cm (2 ft) in height and bearing throughout summer single flowers with yellow centres and varying from white to blush. Opening at night, they emit a strongly sweet scent. The plants are propagated by root division in the autumn.

O. drummondii. The Texas primrose, native of the state of Texas, is a biennial which grows less than 60 cm (2 ft) tall. It has attractive grey leaves which are beautifully waved and from June until October bears pale-yellow flowers, fragrant at night.

O. caespitosa eximia. A handsome dwarf perennial native of the Rocky Mountains. It grows less than 30 cm (12 in) tall and in midsummer bears its large single chalices of purest white with their long slender calyx tubes. The blooms carry a delicious fragrance at night-time, a perfume of lemon and tuberose.

O. tetraptera. A half-hardy Mexican annual growing 22 to 25 cm (9 to 10 in) high and bearing during July and August, large single flowers of white, delicately tinted with pink and which in the evening emit a more powerful scent than any of the family, only to die as the sun begins to rise. Seed should be sown in April where the plants are to bloom.

O. triloba. A North American annual growing only 15 cm (6 in) tall. It has toothed leaves and an unusually long flowering season, being in bloom from May until September. It bears its cups of pale yellow which open only in the evening when they emit a rich penetrating scent.

OLEARIA (Compositae—Daisy Family)

A genus of pretty evergreen shrubs, all of which bear white flowers and are natives of Tasmania and New Zealand. They are however hardy in all coastal districts of the British Isles where they are most tolerant of salt-laden winds and dry conditions. They require a sandy soil to which some humus has been added for they are heavier feeders than most coastal plants.

They may be readily increased from cuttings taken in August and inserted in a sandy compost in a frame; they will have rooted by spring and may then be planted out.

Species. *Olearia albida.* The hardiest species, with glossy grey-green leaves, downy beneath, and in July and August it bears clusters of delicately scented greyish-white flowers. It makes an upright bush 1.5 to 1.8 m (5 to 6 ft) tall.

O. argophylia (syn. *Eurybia argophylia*). Known as the Silver-leaved Musk tree, it is native of Tasmania but also grows in parts of South Australia and in New Zealand where it attains a height of 7.5 m (25 ft) with a girth of some 90 cm (3 ft). It bears large flower-heads, like those of the perennial aster, but it is for its silvery leaves that it is most loved for they release a powerful musk-like odour.

The plant was at one time to be seen in greenhouses in the British Isles where it may be grown as a shrub. It requires a minimum winter temperature of 13°C (55°F).

O. gunniana. Native of Tasmania and less hardy than the others, it makes a compact bush 0.9 to 1.2 m (3 to 4 ft) tall with narrow, oval, grey-green leaves, and in May and June is covered in clusters of greyish-mauve flowers which have a slight musky perfume.

O. haastii. Native of New Zealand, it is one of the hardiest, growing well anywhere, even in the smoke-laden atmosphere of an inland town. It grows 1.2 to 1.8 m (4 to 6 ft) tall, making a rounded bush with glossy grey box-like leaves, and its tiny white flowers have a scent similar to the hawthorn.

O. ilicifolia. It has holly-like leaves, glossy green and toothed, and in June bears clusters of small daisy-like flowers which have a bright-yellow centre and a strong musky perfume.

O. insignis. A lovely New Zealand species with thick rounded leaves which are glossy above and beneath are like brown felt. The flowers are larger than any of the species and are purest white with a pungent smell.

O. macrodonta. The most robust of all the Daisy bushes, making an upright bush 2.4 m (8 ft) tall with attractive holly-like leaves of grey-green, silver on the underside. In June it bears large white honey-scented flowers in profusion whilst the leaves emit a powerful musk scent when bruised.

O. moschata. Native of New Zealand, it is the most compact of the Daisy bushes growing only 60 cm (2 ft) tall, its small silvery-grey leaves smelling strongly of musk which is also present in the small white flowers.

O. myrsinoides. From Tasmania, it makes a rounded bush 0.9 to 1.2 m (3 to 4 ft) tall with finely toothed leaves of glossy green, and in August bears elegant sprays of pure-white flowers which have a resinous smell.

O. odorata. Native of New Zealand, it makes a loose shrub of medium size with obovate leaves, and in June and July bears, on long wiry stems, insignificant flowers which are, however, powerfully and sweetly scented.

O. paniculata. It makes a large upright shrub with bright-green leaves and is used in its native New Zealand for planting coastal hedges. Though the flowers have little beauty, they are deliciously scented during November and December there.

ONCIDIUM (Orchidaceae—Orchid Family)

A genus of about 750 species, native of tropical America and the West Indies. In cultivation, they require a greenhouse heated to 18°C (65°F) and a moist, humid atmosphere. They will grow on a block of wood with sphagnum-moss and peat in which to root; also in a basket suspended from the roof. The flowers are produced on long stems and continue to appear over a prolonged period, but to preserve the plant so that it does not flower to death each spike should be removed after bearing 5 or 6 blooms. Increase is by division of the plants when sufficiently large.

Species. *Oncidium cavendishianum.* Not an easy plant to cultivate, but worth the challenge. The fragrant yellow, red-spotted flowers appear on spikes 60 to 90 cm (2 to 3 ft) tall in winter and early spring. It is one of the rhizomatous kinds, without pseudo-bulbs.

O. cheirophorum. A bright-yellow flower, a very sweet scent, and ease of cultivation make this a desirable orchid. Autumn and winter are its flowering times. It is a graceful species, growing to only about 15 cm (6 in) high, and carries its many small flowers in arching spikes.

O. incurvum. For a Mexican plant, the delicate fragrance of lilac emitted by the flowers is unusual and adds to its charm; the many-flowered tall spikes are attractive with their small, light-pink and white flowers, produced in autumn and winter. It will grow happily in a cool house, unlike most of the species.

O. olivaceum (syn. *O. cucullatum*). As the name suggests the flowers may be olive-green with a purplish-rose lip, but are also reddish-brown. A violet fragrance typifies this species, which is low-growing, with 45-cm (1½-ft) spikes of flowers in spring. It can be exceedingly variable in colour.

O. ornithorynchum. Easily grown, the rosy-lilac small flowers of this species are carried on tall arching spikes from October to January. The strong fragrance of the flowers is of heliotrope, pervading the atmosphere for some considerable distance.

O. stramineum. Small white flowers, spotted with red, on an arch of drooping spikes characterize this species, and its primrose perfume adds to its elegance. It is a species without pseudo-bulbs.

O. tigratum. This yellow-flowered kind has its petals, sepals and lip banded with brown, and the fragrance is of vanilla, but only in the evening. It is floriferous and grows to about 90 cm (3 ft) tall.

ONCOBA (Flacourtiaceae—Flacourtia Family)

A small genus of evergreen trees, native of South Africa and to be found as far north as Tanzania.

Species. *Oncoba spinosa.* It has thick leathery leaves arranged alternately in two rows whilst the bi-sexual flowers appear in terminal inflorescences and are large, greenish-white, resembling the Dog rose and likewise covered in thorns. The flowers emit a delicious sweet perfume whilst the fruits, called Kei-apples, like horny golf balls, were once used by the native people as snuff containers.

ONONIS (Restharrow) (Leguminosae—Laburnum Family)

A small genus of perennial plants of almost prostrate habit and taking its country name from its ability to bring to almost complete rest the horse-drawn plough or harrow, for it forms a dense mat with its creeping runners. A plant of the Mediterranean shores, it may have been introduced into Britain by the Romans, and has become an obnoxious weed.

Species. *Ononis repens.* A form of *O. spinosa* which has adapted to different conditions. Though much despised by ploughmen of old, it is a handsome plant with small hairy leaves and bearing throughout summer pea-like flowers of brightest pink, whilst the whole plant emits a delicious resinous odour when trodden upon. It is a plant of dry hilly pastures and sandy shores, and where established proves difficult to eradicate.

O. spinosa (syn. *O. procumbens*). Known as the Erect Restharrow, it is a perennial plant frequenting waste places of the British Isles. An erect-growing plant it does not form runners and is not so resinous as *O. repens* though it is pleasantly scented.

ONOSMA (Golden Drop)
(Boraginaceae—Forget-me-not Family)

A genus of about 70 species of hairy annual, biennial or perennial plants, mostly native of the Caucasus, Siberia and the Himalayas for their densely haired foliage enables them to withstand the coldest conditions. However, in the moist climate of the British Isles this hairiness tends to hold winter moisture, and in a winter of excessive dampness the leaves of the perennial forms may decay and also the crowns. Yet *Onosma tauricum* is one of the most beautiful of all alpine plants, bearing bloom of exceptional beauty with a delicious perfume, and it blooms from early June until the frosts come. Once planted in a gritty well-drained soil to which a little peat or leaf-mould has been added it will require no further attention for many years.

Species. *Onosma tauricum*. It reached Britain from the Caucasus in 1800 and in spite of its great beauty and powerful honey scent remains comparatively unknown, yet those who grow it would most certainly include it in the dozen best of all alpine plants. It is fully perennial. It loves a position that is well drained and open to the sunshine. John Wood of Kirkstall, in his book *Hardy Perennials* published in 1884, suggested growing it in a small bed with dwarf hardy fuchsias and blue linums, for they all bloom at the same time and require similar conditions. It is also lovely with the later-flowering *O. pubescens*.

The blooms are bright golden-yellow, like huge 'golden tear drops', pear shaped and tubular, and arranged in branched heads on 22.5-cm (9-in) stems. The leaves are evergreen, long and narrow, and are covered in short hairs which give the plant a grey appearance. The flowers appear in continuous succession for about five months and all the time diffuse their heavenly honey perfume.

Pot-grown plants should be obtained for otherwise they may be slow to become established as they resent root disturbance.

ORCHIS (Orchidaceae—Orchid Family)

A genus of tuberous-rooted plants with sheathing leaves and bearing hooded sessile flowers with a 3-lobed lip and a short spur in which the nectar is readily accessible. Several species are native to the British Isles and are noted for the unpleasant fur-like smell of their flowers.

Species. *Orchis coriophora*. Like a number of its genus, its flowers have a most unpleasant smell, hence its name of Bug orchid. In the sub-species *fragrans* however, which has a smaller flower, the unpleasant fur-like smell is replaced by a pleasant perfume which to some is almost vanilla-like and to others musk-like. The pleasant undertone in this flower is the connecting link between the animal and musk-scented groups, so similar though the first is unpleasant and the other pleasing.

O. coriophora sends up a slender stem to a height of 37.5 to 45 cm (15 to 18 in) and is densely packed with hooded flowers of purple-brown, marked with green and with a 3-lobed purple lip. The spur is short and as would be expected from its odour the flower is pollinated by flies and beetles.

O. mascula. The Early Purple orchid, native of the deciduous woodlands of the British Isles and which comes into bloom in April, before the primrose has finished flowering. It is Matthew Arnold's '... purple orchid with spotted leaves', the blunt-ended leaves, usually 2 or 4 in number, being spotted with purple, brown or black.

The plant loves moisture and grows also in ditches and in damp meadowland where it bears its loose spike of brightest purple which shades almost to white at the centre. Unfortunately, the beauty of the flowers belies their odour, quite pleasant from a distance but with a fur-like smell near to which is especially pronounced at nightfall and as the flowers begin to fade after pollination has been performed by bees. In Sussex the plant is known as Ram's-horns, from the appearance of twin leaves formed at the base and bending over like the horns of a ram.

The plant is widely distributed throughout northern Europe and was a familiar sight of the Warwickshire countryside during Shakespeare's time. In *Hamlet*, he includes it with the most common wild flowers which formed the nosegay of the crazed Ophelia:

There with fantastic garlands did she
  come
Of Crow-flowers, nettles, daisies, and
  long purples
That liberal shepherds give a grosser
  name
But our cold maid's do Dead Men's
  fingers call them.

O. mascula was known by as many country
names as the Cuckoo-pint, 'Long Purples'
being that most commonly used. From the
roots, a beverage known as 'salop' was
made and until the arrival of coffee into
Britain, city 'salop' houses were a favourite
meeting place where the drink could be
enjoyed. It is an excellent tonic, prepared
like arrowroot for those suffering from
dysentery. 'Dead-men's Fingers' it was also
called from the long tuberous roots, white
and thick like human fingers drained of
blood.

O. morio. The Green-veined orchid,
native of all parts of Europe from the
Mediterranean northwards to Scandinavia
and Russia. In the British Isles it grows
mostly in southern England and in the
Counties of Mayo and Roscommon in
Eire. The large flowers are usually lilac or
pink in colour, with the lateral sepals
which form the hood, being veined with
green. It blooms during May and emits a
powerful scent which is not particularly
pleasant. It relies on bees for its pollination. As so often is the case, flowers which
are white or palest lilac emit a more
pleasant perfume.

O. provincialis. The Provence orchid, a
native of France where it grows up to 60
cm (2 ft) in height with purple-spotted
leaves and bearing in a loose spike, flowers
of chrome-yellow with a purple-spotted lip
which has the appearance of decaying
meat and on which the pollinating flies lay
their eggs. As would be expected, the
flowers give off an unpleasant smell which
to some resembles decaying animal matter.

O. simia. The Monkey orchid, to be
found in parts of southern Europe and
North Africa, in the Caucasus and in one
or two small localities in England, chiefly
in Berkshire and Oxfordshire where it occurs by the side of woodlands. From two
broad basal leaves the spike arises to a
height of 15 cm (12 in) and it is unusual in
that the top flowers open first. The hood is

white, often spotted with purple or pink,
whilst the crimson lip is long and narrow,
and at its base is a blunt spur which contains no nectar though sugar is available to
the short-tongued insects. These are attracted by its smell, likened to that of
badly saved hay.

O. tridentata. Native of the Mediterranean coastal regions, it is a striking
plant, its tiny flowers making a round
ball-like head, like the Drumstick primula.
The hood is small and the lip 3-lobed with
the central lobe toothed, hence its name of
the Toothed orchid. The spur is long and
is pollinated by hawk-moths, hence the
odour of the flowers which are usually
lilac, pink or white, is sweet and pleasant,
especially at night.

O. ustulata. The Burnt or Dwarf orchids
which grows less than 15 cm (6 in) tall and
is found in upland calcareous pastures of
South-eastern England. It blooms in May
and June, numerous small flowers forming
a dense oblong spike, deep crimson at first,
turning paler with age until it is almost
white. The flowers with their long spur
diffuse a powerful sweet almond-like scent
which attracts day moths and butterflies;
Godfrey, however, reported having seen
bluebottles on the flowers, which may have
been there for pollination.

ORIGANUM (MARJORAM)
(Labiatae—Lavender Family)
A genus of about 25 species of
somewhat tender herbs of neat shrubby
habit, likened to the upright thymes and
native of the Near and Far East.

Species. *Origanum herecleoticum.* The
Winter marjoram, a tender plant in all but
the most sheltered gardens of northern
Europe. Miss Sinclair Rohde has written
that 'few aromatic plants have such an
exquisite scent, sweeter yet spicier than
lavender, with just a trace of heliotrope'. It
grows only 22.5 cm (9 in) tall and is a
woody shrublet, native of the Mediterranean coastline.

O. majorana. Native of the Mediterranean countries it takes its name
Origanum from the Greek words meaning
'joy of the mountains'. It was grown in
England during Tudor times, in spite of its
tenderness, for Tusser mentions it amongst
herbs for strewing and Gerard says 'it is a

low shrubbie plant, of a whitish colour and of marvellous sweet smell . . . the stalks are slender . . . about which grow forth little leaves soft and hoarie. The flowers grow at the top [and are] of a white colour. The whole plant and everie part thereof is of a most pleasant taste and aromatic smell'. Until the twentieth century, its fragrance was appreciated above all others except for that of the rose, lavender and rosemary. Its fragrance most nearly resembles that of thyme, though it is somewhat sweeter with balsamic undertones.

According to Parkinson it was highly thought of by the ladies of the time 'to put in nosegays' and 'also to use in sweete pouders, sweete bags, and sweete washing waters'. It was the 'knotted' marjoram, commonly used for making the knot gardens of Tudor times but it was called knotted not for this reason but because the tiny buds appear first like knots of dark-brown hair.

Sweet marjoram has many culinary uses. Isaac Walton suggested its use, together with thyme and winter savory, to dress a pike. An infusion makes an appetizing tea whilst before the introduction of hops it was used by brewers to impart its aromatic clove-like flavour to various beers. The dried leaves made moist with hot water and placed in a muslin bag were said to bring instant relief when used as a fermentation for rheumatic parts whilst the essential oil, secreted in ample quantities by the stems and leaves, was used to allay toothache. The plants also yield a deposit of crystalline matter known as Stearoptene, similar to camphor and used in the same way.

Sweet marjoram is best raised from seed sown in a warm greenhouse early in spring. The leaves should be gathered in September just before fully ripened, 'when the sap is full in the top of them' as one old writer put it.

O. onites. The Pot marjoram, so called because as it is tender it was grown indoors in pots during winter and planted out in May. It is a perennial under-shrub, native of the Mediterranean with ovate stalkless leaves and it grows 30 cm (12 in) tall. In the garden, it blooms late in summer, its fragrant white flowers being beloved of bees and butterflies.

O. maru. A rare species of the eastern Mediterranean growing 30 cm (12 in) tall with sessile hairy leaves which emit a powerful mint-like smell when pressed. The white flowers are borne in cylindrical heads. The form *aegyptiacum* is a familiar Egyptian plant with less hairy (and less grey) leaves than the type but equally aromatic.

O. vulgare. Native to Britain it grows on downlands for it prefers a chalky soil. It will reach a height of 60 cm (2 ft) and bears spikes of small purple-pink flowers. Both the flowers and leaves have a sweet yet slightly peppery smell, and it was said that 'a hot infusion would sweat out the most severe cold'. The oil obtained by distillation is an excellent embrocation.

The Wild marjoram was in earlier times known as Origanum and Lyte in his *Herbal* called it 'a noble and odoriferous plant'. Culpeper says it 'groweth plentifully on the borders of cornfields' and that it has small dark-green leaves, very like those of Sweet marjoram, but hardier. This was a correct observation for, indeed, the plant is hardier and only in the South is the Sweet marjoram *(O. majorana)* able to survive a severe winter.

ORIXA (Rutaceae—Rue Family)
A genus of a single species.

Species. *Orixa japonica.* It is a deciduous shrub, native of Japan and grows about 1.8 m (6 ft) tall though with a larger spread. The male and female greenish-white flowers which appear in May are borne on separate plants but it is the leaves which have scented attractions, being covered in pellucid dots which release an orange-like pungency when pressed. In addition, they are of brightest lime-green, turning almost white in autumn to give contrast to the reds and golds of the season.

ORNITHOGALUM (Liliaceae—Lily Family)
A genus of about 100 species, several of which became naturalized in the British Isles following their introduction in Tudor times. Of the genus, only three species have any perfume and these include the two finest, *O. arabicum* and *O. nutans*, both requiring somewhat different culture than the other species.

Species. *Ornithogalum arabicum.* It is Parkinson's Great Star-flower of Arabia which he mentioned has very broad leaves like those of the hyacinth, and of the flowers he said 'the smell whereof is pretty sweet and weak'. It is the outstanding species of the genus and reached England during the early sixteenth century from Palestine or Arabia, home of many of the Ornithogalums, including *O. umbellatum,* the scentless Star of Bethlehem. *O. arabicum* requires some protection, or in northern Europe it should be lifted in autumn, wintered in a box of sand and replanted in March when it will send up a stem nearly 60 cm (2 ft) in length and in June will bear a large head composed of 12 or more starry white flowers which have a jet-black ovary at the centre. It requires a position of full sun and a well-drained soil and may be left undisturbed in the more favourably placed gardens. Like all the species, the flowers remain fresh for a considerable time both in the garden and when cut and placed in water.

O. nutans. It is a most handsome species, unlike any other in that it enjoys the partial shade of woodlands where it will increase rapidly. Six to eight flowers are borne on a spike 45 cm (18 in) tall and they are a most unusual shade of grey-green edged with white, the narrow petals reflexing to provide a star-like appearance. They emit a soft moss-like perfume, usually associated with woodland plants.

O. suaveolens. A native of South Africa, where it blooms during November and December when the leaves have died back. The flowers are yellow with a broad stripe of green and are borne 4 to 10 in a loose inflorescence. They emit a sweet perfume.

OROBANCHE (Orobanchaceae— Broomrape Family)

A genus of about 100 species of succulent plants which are either parasitical on the roots of other plants or saprophytes, living on decayed vegetable matter. They have no leaves, these being replaced by fleshy scales. The flowers are borne in large spikes or racemes. The genus is confined to the temperate regions of the Old World, one of which, *O. caryophyllacea,* is native of the British Isles and bears scented flowers.

Species. *Orobanche caryophyllacea.* The Clove-scented broomrape, it is parasitic of the Goose-grass and other species of *Galium,* known to countrymen as the Bedstraws. The flowers are a brownish-purple colour with hairy stamens and are supported on stems which are almost devoid of colouring matter. The blooms, which appear in June, emit the powerful scent of cloves, in warm weather quite as pronounced as in the carnation and pink. It is a perennial and is mostly to be found in parts of Kent.

ORONTIUM (Araceae—Arum Lily Family)

A genus of only one species.

Species. *Orontium aquaticum.* It is a North American water plant known as the Golden Club, from the yellow club-shaped spadix. From this, a most unpleasant animal smell is emitted. The plant bears long-stemmed elliptic leaves which lie flat on the surface of the water, and in May and June the yellow spadix appears. The plants greatly resemble water-lilies and, when planting them in boggy ground or by the side of a pond, the rhizomes should be placed beneath at least 15 cm (6 in) of water.

ORTHOPENTHEA (Orchidaceae— Orchid Family)

A small genus of South African flowering plants, present in mountainous clefts above Simonstown and bearing 2 to 8 horizontal hooded flowers in a flat raceme. At one time grouped with *Disa,* they are now (as with *Monadenia*) a separate genus.

Species. *Orthopenthea rosea.* It has spreading ovate leaves, dark green above, purple on the underside, whilst the sweetly scented flowers are borne in a slender curving spike of 6 to 8 blooms. They are white, lightly flushed with mauve-pink. The petals have lobes which protrude to the base of the pouch whilst the lip has lobes near the base.

OSCULARIA (Aizoaceae—Aizoon Family)

A genus of five species of succulent plants, native of South Africa and closely related to *Cactus.* They are shrubby plants of straggling growth and take their name from the Latin *osculum*, a mouth, from the resemblance of the toothed leaves, turned up at the margins, to a human mouth.

Species. *Oscularia caulescens.* Native of Cape Province where it is a popular house plant, it has small succulent leaves about 2.5 cm (1 in) long with small 'teeth' along the edges. The pale-pink flowers which measure half an inch across are sweetly scented. In South Africa, the plant is used for bedding schemes.

O. deltoides (syn. *O. muricata*). In every way it is a delightful plant with multi-branched crimson stems and triangular leaves which turn inwards at the margins, along which are small red 'teeth'. The flowers appear in spring and are palest pink with the heliotrope scent of almonds.

OSMANTHUS (Oleaceae—Olive Family)

A genus comprising seven or eight species of evergreen shrubs of which a number flower during the autumn when there is little colour in the garden, whilst those which are most hardy are winter-flowering and are amongst the most powerfully scented of all plants. They are happiest in a position of partial shade and require a well-drained soil, preferably of a sandy nature but one containing leaf-mould or humus to retain summer moisture.

Species. *Osmanthus aquifolium* (syn. *O. ilicifolius*). It is an erect-growing holly-like shrub, worthy of a place in the garden for its many lovely leaf colours whilst it bears small white flowers during autumn and winter which have a powerful fragrance. The form *aureus* has leaves margined with yellow whilst *latifolius variegatus* has leaves which are beautifully marked with silver. For contrast, *purpurascens* has purple-tinted foliage.

O. delavayi. It is a native of China where it was discovered by a Jesuit missionary, the Abbé Delavaye. It delights in a shady situation and a moist soil and is one of the most exquisite of all shrubs, growing as wide as it grows tall and sending up its graceful arching stems to a height of 1.5 to 1.8 m (5 to 6 ft). The stems are furnished with small pointed leaves of glossy green and from the axils are borne dainty tubular flowers of purest white which have the sweet fragrance of the daphnes, scenting the April days and nights.

O. forrestii. Native of China, it has long lance-shaped evergreen leaves which are sharply toothed, and from the axils are borne creamy-white tubes which have a delicate sweet fragrance. It blooms during April and May.

O. fortunei. A natural Japanese hybrid brought into Britain by Robert Fortune. It is a most valuable shrub, flowering from autumn until the year end, the powerfully fragrant pure-white flowers presenting a picture of great beauty amongst the bright-green holly-like foliage.

O. fragrans. It is a handsome Chinese shrub which in a sheltered garden will attain a height of 2.4 to 3 m (8 to 10 ft), with pointed lance-shaped leaves of shining green, and it blooms throughout summer, its yellowish-white flowers having the heavy perfume of the Orient. In the East, the leaves and flowers are used to flavour tea, imparting a pleasant aromatic perfume.

OSMAREA (Oleaceae—Olive Family)

Variety. *Osmarea burkwoodii.* A hybrid variety, it is the result of a cross between *Osmanthus delavayi* and *Phillyrea decora* and combines the finer qualities of both parents. It is evergreen, growing 1.5 to 1.8 m (5 to 6 ft) in height and always remains neat and tidy. It has small pointed leaves of glossy green and at the leaf axils bears densely packed clusters of creamy-white flowers which have a sweet, penetrating perfume. It comes into bloom early in April before the plants take on their green array.

OSMITES (Compositae—Daisy Family)

A small genus of woody herbaceous plants, native of South Africa, and which take their name from the Greek *osme*, scent, for the plants have a sweet resinous scent about them, like *Tagetes*. Low-growing, they are to be found about rocky formations but where they do not lack moisture.

Species. *Osmites dentata.* A compact, woody plant, bearing its flowers in terminal heads. The obovate leaves are sharply toothed.

OSMITOPSIS (Compositae—Daisy Family)

A genus of a single species.

Species. *Osmitopsis astericoides.* It differs from *Osmites* only in that the flowers are without pappus. It is a tall-growing shrub with hairy lanceolate leaves which have the same powerful resinous scent as *Osmites*. It frequents swampy meadowlands in Cape Province.

OSTEOMELES (Rosaceae—Rose Family)

A small genus of shrubby plants with leathery evergreen leaves and bearing pure-white flowers in corymbose clusters, like the hawthorn. Native of western China and South-east Asia they like a dry, sunny situation and are tender in all but the most sheltered gardens.

Species. *Osteomeles anthyllidifolia.* A beautiful shrub growing 1.5 to 1.8 m (5 to 6 ft) tall with strangely twisted wood of deep violet colouring. The leaves consist of 10 pairs of small oval leaflets, downy in texture, and in June, at the ends of the shoots, the pure-white hawthorn-like flowers are borne in loose clusters. They have a delicate scent and are followed by green fruits which turn grape-black when ripe.

OSYRIS (Santalaceae—Sandalwood Family)

A small genus of a small family of Eastern plants, mostly of shrubby habit and frequenting sandy wastelands. Throughout the East, they are famed for the incense-like fragrance of their wood when burned. Sandalwood is also used to make a sweet ointment called *urgujja*, composed also of sweet aloes, attar of roses, and essence of jasmine. Sandalwood is also one of the most common ingredients in Chinese perfumery, and with the wood of Juniper it is much used in funereal rites in the East.

Species. *Osyris alba.* It is native of the Mediterranean regions, extending from the Middle East, across India and into China. It is a plant of slender habit growing about 90 cm (3 ft) tall with upright stems of shining green and with small evergreen leaves. At the ends of the branches are borne, early in summer, sweet honey-scented flowers of ivory-white and these are followed by small red fruits.

OXALIS (Oxalidaceae—Oxalis Family)

A genus of about 800 species of annual or perennial plants, mostly native of South America and to a lesser extent of South Africa, with the scentless *O. acetosella* (Wood sorrel) native of the British Isles. They have either tuberous roots or a fleshy rootstock, and though most are perennial they die back completely during winter. The 5-petal flowers with their funnel-shaped corolla are mostly pollinated by bees and are not fragrant. Where the petals form a narrow tube, pollination is by butterflies and the flowers are scented, the most obvious example being *O. enneaphylla.*

Species. *Oxalis enneaphylla.* It was collected by the late Clarence Elliott in the Falkland Isles and increases from a ring of tiny fleshy bulbs found just below soil level. From the bulbs in spring arise blue-grey clover-like leaves and just above them, on 1.5-cm (3-in) stems, appear the blooms in May. They are like tiny waxed trumpets of frosted white, about 2.5 cm (1 in) across and have a delicious almond-like perfume. Clarence Elliott also collected a shell-pink form of great beauty, *rosea*, which is equally scented and recalls in his book *Rock Garden Plants* that at a Chelsea Show he gave a flower to Lily Langtry: 'she seemed to revel in its delicate waxy beauty, and its fragrance', and apparently the celebrated actress then popped it into her mouth and ate it! It is altogether a delightful little plant which should be found a place in every alpine garden, whilst it does well in pans in the alpine house.

OXYDENDRON (Ericaceae—Heather Family)

A genus of a single species.

Species. *Oxydendron arboreum* (syn. *Andromeda arborea*). Native of the eastern U.S.A. it is a deciduous tree growing 9 to 12 m (30 to 40 ft) tall. There is a splendid specimen in the Royal Horticultural Society gardens at Wisley, in England. It has pointed lance-shaped leaves and in midsummer bears one-sided racemes of pure-white sweet-scented flowers. The leaves are especially handsome, taking on rich purple-crimson colourings before they fall.

OXYTROPIS (Leguminosae—Laburnum Family)

A genus of about 300 species of branched under-shrubs, native of the northern temperate zones of the world.

Species. *Oxytropis foetida*. Native to southern France, it makes a dense low bush 1.2 to 1.5 m (4 to 5 ft) in height with numerous pairs of smooth lance-shaped leaflets which are sticky to the touch and give off a most unpleasant smell of decaying fish when handled. The creamy-white flowers with purple-tinted wings and keels are borne in July and are without the unpleasant smell.

P

PACHYSANDRA (Buxaceae—Box Tree Family)

A genus of dwarf shrubby evergreens, native of China, Japan and the southern United States, one of which, *P. terminalis,* bears sweetly scented flowers. None exceeds 30 cm (12 in) in height and all grow well in semi-shade and in a moist soil.

Species. *Pachysandra terminalis.* It is a native of Japan and is useful for planting beneath mature trees and to cover bare spaces. It forms a dense carpet of glossy green and from it arise, in February and March, spikes of small greenish-white flowers which diffuse a pleasant sweet fragrance.

PAEONIA (Ranunculaceae—Buttercup Family)

A genus of herbaceous or shrubby plants of which the species *P. moutan* and *P. lutea* are representative of the latter type and are known as the shrubby or Tree peonies. They have been growing in the Imperial Gardens of Peking since the fourth century, and with *P. lactiflora* (the herbaceous peony) are amongst the oldest plants still to be found in the garden of today. During the Sung dynasty (960-1279), the Moutan peony was honoured as the King of Flowers *(Hua Wong)* whilst *P. lactiflora,* known as *Shaoyao,* was mentioned in a Chinese *Book of Odes* of the fifth century B.C.

Species and Varieties. *Paeonia moutan* (syn. *P. suffruticosa*). The first mention of it was made by the poet Hsieh Kang-lo of the Tsin dynasty (265-420) who told of it growing amongst the bamboo groves of Chekiang Province but the plant first became prominent during the Sung dynasty when Loyang, in Honan Province, was the centre of its culture and there the double flowering varieties first appeared. There is a treatise on the Moutan peony of Loyang written in 1066 by the scholar Ouyang Hsiu in which he tells that people would bring cuttings (shoots) of different varieties from the hills around Loyang to sell to the townsmen for grafting, and that this operation was carried out by a man whose services were in great demand by the wealthy. It is mentioned that the grafting of buds must be done before the ninth day of the ninth month and details of the method of grafting are given.

In another gardening book of the time, methods of soil treatment with chemicals are given so that the colour of the flowers could be changed. For instance if the soil about the roots was drenched in a solution obtained from the root of *Lithospermum officinale,* the peony blooms would open deep purple.

By the end of the thirteenth century there appeared Chiu Chuans' celebrated *Classified Arrangement of the Varieties of the Moutan Peony.* In modern times the centre of Moutan culture has been transferred to neighbouring Shantung Province, whilst there are also large Moutan plantations near Shanghai.

Plants first reached Britain at the end of the eighteenth century. A Chinese manuscript of the early years of that century describes plants growing in the Province of Shensi with flowers of richest red and scenting the air with their perfume. In its native land *P. moutan* shows a wide variation in the colours of its flowers, not all of which are scented whilst some have a richer scent than others. They bloom in April and May in the British Isles, before the herbaceous peonies, and with their elegant foliage they are amongst the most handsome of shrubs both in outline and in colour. They grow between 1.2 to 1.8 m (4 to 6 ft) tall, and as wide, the hard-wooded shrubs being deciduous but coming early into leaf. So enormous are the blooms that it may be desirable to provide support for the branches whilst the plants are in bloom.

Like most deciduous shrubs the Tree peonies contribute little beauty to the border during the winter months. For this reason they should be planted with evergreens which will not only help to hide the rather severe outlines of the plants whilst leafless, but will more importantly provide the peonies with valuable protection from cold winds when producing new shoots in early spring. To provide the plants with no cover in this respect has more than anything in the past contributed to disappointment in growing the Tree peony, for it comes into life several weeks before the herbaceous peonies begin to send up their new shoots, and at a time when cold winds and frost often prove troublesome to all but the hardiest of plants. In addition to evergreens it is also advisable to plant with the Tree peonies a number of deciduous flowering shrubs which also come early into growth, for they too will provide protection at this time. At the same time it is important not to obscure the great beauty of the plants when in bloom.

These aristocratic shrubs should also be planted in a position where the early morning springtime sun is unable to reach them, for if the new shoots become frosted they will be badly damaged should a warm sun shine directly upon them. It is essential that the shoots are allowed to thaw gradually and without the assistance of the direct rays of the sun. It is therefore important that they should not face due east. The herbaceous peony is hardier in this respect, and only rarely will the shoots be damaged through the sun's rays coming into contact with them whilst frosted. Rather they will suffer from exposure to cold winds and the plants should be protected in this respect.

No amount of cold will harm the Tree peony whilst it is dormant. In its native land it is often subjected to a temperature of more than 40°F below zero and seems to bloom more profusely in temperatures which alternate between extremes. It is only when the plant begins to make new growth that there is danger that the shoots might be damaged, the result being that there would be little bloom that year. A position away from the east and clear of a frost hollow together with protection from cold winds will ensure success with this lovely shrub.

Scented varieties include:

FLORA. The blooms are large and pure white, the petals deeply fringed.

FRAGRANS MAXIMA. A very old variety and the most fragrant, the large blooms being a unique salmon-orange, perfume usually being absent in flowers of this colour.

KIMPAI. The large semi-double blooms are a lovely creamy-white with a soft, sweet perfume.

KOKUHO. A glorious variety, the large fully double blooms being of blackest maroon and with a spicy perfume.

P. lactiflora (syn. *P. alliflora*). Though *P. officinalis rubra*, the old double red scentless peony has been grown in gardens since earliest times, it was not until *P. lactiflora* reached Europe that varieties with any degree of perfume came to be raised. Though it had been grown in Chinese gardens since almost the beginning of time, the first plants did not reach Britain, by way of France, until the turn of the nineteenth century.

In China, *P. lactiflora* is always known as *Shaoyao*, 'Charming and beautiful'. It grows wild in Mongolia and around Yangchow where, during the Sung dynasty it grew in profusion in the gardens of both rich and poor. Mostly, however, it grows in the northern provinces and in Siberia for it does not take kindly to hot, humid conditions.

P. mlokosewitschii. The only other species bearing scented flowers. It is native of the Caucasus and bears large single cup-shaped flowers of citron-yellow with a sweet perfume. It has been used by hybridizers to impart its yellow colouring and also its perfume to modern hybrid varieties.

The French breeders, Crousse, Calot

and Lemoine were the first to introduce a number of fine scented varieties which, in their size and beauty of form and delicious perfume, were to rival the rose in popularity. To the cottager, they were known as 'peony roses' and because of their hardiness and durability (some of the finest peony borders are more than fifty years old) came to be widely planted in Britain and Europe. The plants require a deep rich soil containing plenty of decayed manure, and are quite happy in partial shade. Plant in November when they are dormant, and for best results use a two-year-old root containing 2 to 3 'eyes'. They will take a year to become established and before they come into bloom early in June. Plant 60 cm (2 ft) apart for they make bushy plants about 90 cm (3 ft) tall, the blooms being enhanced by the dark-green leaves which take on brilliant autumnal colourings before they die down. This is the time to lift and divide and replant, taking care not to plant too deeply no more than 5 cm (2 in) below soil level —and not to damage the 'eyes'.

Scented varieties include:

ALEX FLEMING. It bears large double blooms of a lovely rose pink, like a Prima Ballerina rose and with a similar scent.

BARONESS SCHROEDER. Introduced in 1888, it has never been surpassed. Its enormous globular blooms of blush-white produced with freedom having a glorious perfume.

DUCHESSE DE NEMOURS. It flowers longer than any variety, its large double blooms of sulphur-white having the soft, sweet perfume of Pond's face cream.

EDITH CAVELL. Free-flowering and early, its large creamy-yellow blooms are richly scented.

JAMES KELWAY. Selected by the Peony Society of Great Britain as the best variety yet raised, the huge milky-white blooms are produced on 90-cm (3-ft) stems and are heavily scented.

KELWAY'S GLORIOUS. The Peony Society of America's selection as the finest peony, the glistening white flowers of perfect form having the scent of a hybrid tea rose.

KELWAY'S ROSEMARY. Raised by the famous Langport firm, the rose-pink blooms have a silvered appearance and the spicy perfume of rosemary.

MADAME CALOT. A glorious variety, early to bloom, its creamy-white blooms tinted pink being heavily scented.

MARIE CROUSSE. A most reliable variety bearing large globular blooms of rich shrimp-pink which carry a delicious spicy perfume.

PHILIPPE RIVOIRE. The best of all red peonies, the large blooms are crimson-black and carry the pronounced perfume of a tea rose.

SARAH BERNHARDT. One of the loveliest, the large globular blooms are apple-blossom pink, shaded with silver at the edges, and are powerfully scented.

PAGIANTHA (Apocynaceae—Periwinkle Family)

A genus of 20 species of small trees or shrubs, native of Fiji and of other Pacific islands.

Species. *Pagiantha thurstonii.* Known in Fiji as *Tabua* from its original name of *Tabernaemontana.* It is a common small tree with leaves lacking stipules and bearing large white fragrant flowers followed by large yellow fruits.

PALIURUS (Rhamnaceae—Buckthorn Family)

A genus of erect shrubs armed with spines, of which the best known and only scented species is *P. aculeatus* or *P. spina-Christi* for it is believed to be the plant from which Christ's Crown of Thorns was taken. The plants are to be found from the Near East to Japan.

Species. *Paliurus aculeatus.* Native of the coastal regions of the Mediterranean, it grows about 1.8 m (6 ft) in height and in the British Isles requires a dry, sandy soil and a warm garden, flourishing along the coastal areas of the South-west. It has small leaves which are deciduous and at the base of each are two angry-looking spines, one pointing up and the other downwards. As the wood is pliable it is more than possible that this was the plant used to make Christ's Crown of Thorns. The small greenish-yellow flowers are borne from June until August, appearing at the leaf axils, and they have a slight perfume. The red fruits appear to be crowned with a halo or broad rim.

PAMIANTHE (Amaryllidaceae— Narcissus Family)

A genus of but a single species.

Species. *Pamianthe peruviàna.* It was introduced into Britain from the valleys of Peru by Major Pam and named after him. It is distinguished from *Pancratium* and *Hymenocallis* only by its winged seeds and is one of the most beautiful bulbous plants in cultivation, requiring warm greenhouse culture in Britain. It will come into bloom early in March: four flowers appear at the end of a 60-cm (2-ft) stem and have a long green perianth tube and a bell-shaped corona with pointed segments of white with green markings. It is one of the most powerfully scented of all flowers and in a warm greenhouse a single plant can be almost overpowering with the scent of the tuberose.

PANCRATIUM (Amaryllidaceae— Narcissus Family)

A genus of a dozen species of bulbous plants with strap-like leaves and closely related to *Hymenocallis*. It is, however, later flowering, coming into bloom towards the end of July. Whereas *Hymenocallis* is native of South America and the West Indies, the Pancratium is to be found along the sandy shores of the Mediterranean, extending from the Canary Islands to Greece. The bulbs are large and should be grown in a sandy soil at the base of a wall facing south for in the British Isles they need the maximum amount of sunshine to ripen and without it will not bloom well.

Species. *Pancratium canariense.* Native only of the Canary Islands, it is less hardy than *P. illyricum* and in the British Isles it is advisable to cover the bulbs with a cloche during winter. It is a most handsome plant with glaucous strap-like leaves and it bears in September as many as a dozen white lily-like blooms on a 60-cm (2-ft) stem. The scent is nothing like so powerful as that of the other species, being soft and almost primrose-like, resembling the perfume of the Lent lily.

P. illyricum. The large pear-shaped bulbs, covered with brown scales, have a long tapering neck and should be planted nearly 30 cm (12 in) deep. The handsome leaves are covered with a glaucous 'bloom' above which appear, on a 45-cm (18-in) stem, umbels of as many as a dozen large, star-like flowers of purest white and richly scented.

P. maritimum. It has large rounded bulbs covered with brownish-red scales and from them arise glaucous leaves which remain evergreen. To the ancient Greeks it was known as the Sea lily for it has a long perianth tube and cup of purest white and has the exotic lily scent. As many as 6 to 8 flowers appear late in summer on a 30-cm (12-in) stem.

PANDANUS (Pandanaceae—Screw Pine Family)

A genus of 600 or more strong-growing plants of the sub-tropical coastal regions of the Eastern Hemisphere, extending from Madagascar and Mauritius across southern India to the East Indies, where they are known as Screw pines from the screw-form in which the leaves take as they arise from the main stem. Propagation is from suckers produced at the base of the stem. The leaves have spiked edges and taper to a point whilst the flowers of several are powerfully scented. The plants require a minimum winter temperature of 15°C (60°F).

Species. *Pandanus odoratissimus.* It is the *Pandang* of India and the Far East, a tropical tree of coastal areas bearing spiked leaves and white flowers from which is distilled the richest and most powerful of all perfumes, much used by the Hindu women for toilet purposes. Dr Roxburgh writing in the nineteenth century said that it is the male flowers which yield the most powerful perfume though both male and female are present on the same plant, the former appearing above the latter in a dense cylindrical spike.

PAPAVER (Poppy) (Papaveraceae— Poppy Family)

A genus of about 100 species of almost scentless plants though one, the Alpine poppy, native of the European alpine regions, has a slight musky perfume about it. Almost all the family are self-pollinating, and though they are visited by Diptera in search of pollen the flowers do depend upon them for fertilization.

Species. *Papaver alpinum.* It grows 10 to 12.5 cm (4 to 5 in) tall and, though perennial, so readily grows from seed that like the Iceland poppy it is usually treated as an annual or biennial. It is an attractive plant with glaucous hairy leaves finely cut, whilst the flowers are also covered in hairs and are borne throughout summer in shades of yellow, pink, salmon and white. The plants require an open position and ordinary soil.

PARADISIA (Liliaceae—Lily Family)

A genus of but a single species, *P. liliastrum,* St Bruno's lily, an alpine or border plant of great merit, named after the founder of the Carthusian Order. Parkinson (1629) said that it grew in his garden, having been introduced early in the seventeenth century from the lower alpine meadows of central Europe.

Species. *Paradisia liliastrum.* It has a fleshy rootstock like the alstroemeria and hemerocallis, and like them should be given an open situation and a well-drained soil enriched with a little decayed manure.

Spring is the most suitable time for dividing the roots which should be planted 15 cm (6 in) deep and 30 cm (12 in) apart. The plant grows about 45 cm (18 in) tall with tufts of leaves channelled on the upper surface and it bears its blooms in one-sided racemes during May and June. The blooms are white and funnel-shaped, about 5 cm (2 in) long, and each of the spoon-shaped segments is tipped with green. The flowers are amongst the most sweetly scented of all.

This is a valuable plant for the wild garden provided it is given a position where the sun may reach it.

PARIS (Herb Paris) (Liliaceae—Lily Family)

A small genus of perennials, chiefly distributed throughout temperate Europe and Asia and named from the Latin *par,* equal, on account of the equal number of all its parts.

Species. *Paris quadrifolia.* The only British species, it is a most unusual plant, habiting the damp woodlands of the British Isles and North America. It has a creeping rootstock and bears large deep-green leaves, netted with veins, in a whorl of four and at a height of 30 cm (12 in) above the ground. It blooms in May, the solitary flower, about 5 cm (2 in) across, having 4 green outer segments or sepals and 4 thread-like yellow petals. The blooms are pollinated by flies and midges and in order to attract them emit a most unpleasant smell of decaying meat. The blue-black 4-side fruit which follows the flower is most handsome, but like all parts of the plant is extremely poisonous. The plant is of the Trilliaceae tribe which includes the Wood lily.

PARSLEY: *see* PETROSELINUM

PARSONSIA (Apocynaceae—Periwinkle Family)

A small genus of climbing plants, mostly native of New Zealand and unlike most of the family, bearing scented flowers.

Species. *Parsonsia capsularis.* It is unlike all others of the family, being of climbing habit with long, narrow leaves, reddish-brown and leathery to the touch. It bears its white (or occasionally red) flowers in small panicles and they are like those of the jasmine with the anthers protruding beyond the corolla. In New Zealand they bloom in November and December and have a scent similar to jasmine.

P. heterophylla. The long slender stems are of pencil thickness and are glossy, whilst the broad leathery leaves have lobed margins. The flowers are pure white with the anthers contained within the corolla and they emit a delicate perfume.

PASANIA (Lythocarpus) (Fagaceae—Beech Family)

A rare genus of about 300 species of large trees distributed throughout Malaya and islands of South-east Asia. The leaves are arranged in spiral fashion and in most species the upper catkins are androgynous, i.e. the female flowers are borne at the base of the catkins, the male above them and arranged in 3- to 7-flowered cymes. The catkins, as in several of the catkin bearing plants, are held erect and have a strong, unpleasant smell which attracts midges for their pollination though some are pollinated by the wind.

PASSIFLORA (Passion Flower) (Passifloraceae—Passion Flower Family)

A large genus of climbing plants mostly native of South America, only one or two of which may be grown outdoors in the British Isles and then only in the most favourable districts where they should be grown against a sunny wall. Elsewhere they make excellent plants for a warm greenhouse or conservatory. They were so named by the early Spanish missionaries to South America for the parts of the flower were representative of the Crucifixion. The three stigmas represent the three nails of the Cross; the five anthers represent the five wounds. The ten petals represent the ten apostles, and the corona the Crown of Thorns. A number of species bear scented flowers and, in their native country, edible fruits known as passion fruits. They are vigorous climbers and will attain a height of 9 m (30 ft) or more in Britain, *P. caerulea* being the finest and most successful species.

Species and Varieties. *Passiflora caerulea.* Native of Brazil, it enjoys a rich, well-drained loam containing some peat. It blooms from June until October, bearing its flowers in long succession though they last only for about 48 hours. They measure 10 cm (4 in) across and must be amongst the most beautiful of all flowers with petals of palest blue and purple styles, whilst the filaments of the corona appear as two perfect circles and are purple at the base, white in the centre, and blue at the tips. The flowers are delicately scented. The variety Constance Elliott bears flowers of ivory-white and is more fragrant.

P. edulis. Native of Peru, it is more tender than *P. coerulea* but is of similar vigorous habit and bears white or mauve-tinted flowers which are heliotrope scented.

PAULOWNIA (Scrophulariaceae— Foxglove Family)

A small genus of three or four trees native of China and Japan which come into bloom early in May and which require a sheltered position in full sun. They are amongst the most exquisite of all ornamental trees, growing 15 m (50 ft) in height in their native country but only 6 m (20 ft) or so in colder parts.

Species. *Paulownia fargesii.* The finest of the genus, it makes a tree 6 to 9 m (20 to 30 ft) in height with a large rounded head, and comes into bloom at an early age. It is deciduous with huge leaves often 45 cm (18 in) broad, and it bears its flowers in erect panicles. In shape the flowers resemble those of the foxglove, tubular in form and purple, speckled in the throat with deeper purple and with a yellow mark. They emit a delicious warm Eastern fragrance which is unusual in flowers of this family.

P. tomentosa (syn. *P. imperialis*). Native of Japan, it makes a tall tree with a large rounded head but is more difficult to establish than *P. fargesii.* It blooms in May, the flowers being of darkest purple with reddish spots in the throat and with a delicate sweet fragrance.

PAVETTA (Rubiaceae—Bedstraw Family)

A small genus of evergreen tropical trees or shrubs native of South Africa, the Isle of Bourbon and India, with mildly scented flowers but with powerfully scented roots used for medicinal purposes. Several species have handsome foliage. They are not widely grown away from their native lands as they require a minimum winter temperature of 18°C (65°F).

Species. *Pavetta bourbonica.* It is one of the most beautiful of all evergreen stove plants with leaves 30 cm (12 in) long, bright green and shining with a distinct midrib of crimson-red. Both the leaves and roots are strongly aromatic.

P. caffra. A native of Cape Province, it is the most free-flowering of the pavettas, bearing pretty white flowers in small bunches; they are sweetly scented and well adapted for cutting.

P. indica. A native of India; all parts of the plant are aromatic.

PECTIS (Compositae—Daisy Family)

A little-known genus of about 30 species, only one of which has garden value and is scented. It is a half-hardy annual, easily raised from seed sown in the open ground in April; it will come into bloom in July and continue until the frosts. A native of California, it requires a well-drained sandy soil and an open, sunny situation.

Species. *Pectis angustifolia.* It grows less than 15 cm (6 in) tall and is similar to the tagetes in that its foliage has an aromatic fragrance whilst its small yellow daisy-like flowers are also spicily scented.

PELARGONIUM
(Geraniaceae—Geranium Family)

A genus of smooth or downy perennial herbs or under-shrubs with opposite leaves toothed, lobed or cut; petals five, united at the base and slightly perigynous. The genus numbers more than 170 species, almost all being native of South Africa and especially of Cape Province. Amongst them are the Zonal pelargoniums, so much used for summer bedding during the Victorian era which saw the introduction of the glasshouse, for in the British Isles the plants require winter protection in all but the mildest parts. The leaves carry an unmistakable odour, likened to that given off by chlorine gas, an acrid pungent smell, whilst the ivy-leaved species and varieties are with but a single exception entirely without odour. Neither is there any perfume in the flowers, nor in those of the Regal and Zonal pelargoniums. Several species, however, do bear scented flowers though they are rare in cultivation today and have never been widely employed in hybridizing.

But amongst the most fascinating of all plants are those grouped under the heading of Scented-leaved geraniums or, more correctly, pelargoniums, which were discovered at the Cape by English travellers and navigators early in the seventeenth century. Plants first reached London in 1632, during the reign of Charles I, but remained in obscurity for almost two centuries; they were then grown in the newly erected glasshouses of the wealthy, and from there reached the cottage window. They must be considered amongst the best of all plants for window culture, always green, whilst the many different leaf forms and their equally varying scents provide continual interest. From the leaf of *P. capitatum*, an 'otto of roses' is made and sold in Algerian bazaars, some of it at one time finding its way into the rose stills of Bulgaria. The downy leaves of *P. tomentosum* described by Miss Gertrude Jekyll as being 'as thick as a fairy's blanket' and which she used for making a delicious 'peppermint' jelly, have a powerful minty odour, whilst the leaves of *P. clorinda* smell strongly of eucalyptus. And there are others smelling of apple and incense, of nutmeg and pine, of orange and lemon and many in-between scents.

The Victorians loved these plants, placing them by the side of stairways and passages so that their long clothes would brush against them and create a most delicious perfume which would reach to all parts of the house. They would remain indoors until early June when they would be placed outdoors along a path for a similar purpose and where the plants would be invigorated by the sunshine and rain, to be taken indoors again before the arrival of the first frosts of autumn. A few leaves judiciously removed and carefully dried make an excellent addition to a pot-pourri and may be placed between linen to impart one of the many aromatic perfumes. Several leaves placed beneath the pillow will encourage sleep. When the leaves are required to release their scent on the plant only the lightest touch is necessary and in this way they will not be damaged.

Species and Varieties of the Scented-leaved Geranium *Pelargonium abrotanifolium.* So named for its resemblance to *Artemisia abrotanum* (Southernwood) for it has deeply divided leaves which when pressed release the same pungent incense-like fragrance.

P. asperum. Of compact habit, the leaves are deeply cut, of oak-leaf shape, and are oily to the touch, appearing as if covered with specks of gold. When pressed they release an oily resinous smell which to some resembles sage, whilst the cyclamen-purple flowers are also pungent.

P. Attar of Roses. It makes a tiny plant with dainty leaves which smell strongly of roses.

P. canescens. It has attractive grey leaves smelling of incense when pressed and bears white flowers veined with orchid purple.

P. capitatum. One of the most common

species in its native South Africa, it makes an erect woody plant, the leaves and stems being covered in short glandular hairs. The leaves are wrinkled and 3- to 5- lobed, deeply toothed at the margins, and when pressed yield the rose perfume. The pale-pink flowers veined with purple are borne in dense heads almost throughout the year.

P. Catford Belle. It is one of the most charming of all pelargoniums, making a tiny bushy plant 15 to 22.5 cm (6 to 8 in) tall with leaves like those of *P. crispum*, with a lemony odour and bearing large purple flowers blotched Indian lake. It blooms almost the whole year.

P. citriodorum. Its small leaves resemble those of *P. crispum* and they carry the same powerful lemon perfume. The mauve flowers have purple markings on the upper petals.

P. clorinda. The leaves are scented of eucalyptus with an undertone of rose whilst its flowers are the equal of the Show Pelargoniums, being of deepest orange-pink.

P. crispum minor. One of the most beautiful pot plants in existence with a spire-like habit, resembling a cypress tree, with small leaves, crisped at the edges and smelling strongly of lemon-scented verbena. The variety *variegatum* (in the U.S.A. known as Variegated Prince Rupert) is even more attractive for its leaves are grey-green edged with gold. They bear tiny pale-lavender flowers. When removing the leaves, care should be taken not to disturb the balance of the plant.

P. denticulatum. It has elegantly toothed leaves which have the unmistakable smell of balsam.

P. filicifolium. One of the finest of the fern-leaf forms, the plants showing a greater resemblance to a fern than to a geranium. In Messrs Cannells' catalogue of 1910 it is suggested that it is 'well adapted for bouquets and button-holes', though this would appear doubtful with its powerful resinous smell.

P. fragrans. A delightful species of shapely growth with small silver-grey leaves smelling deliciously of pine (to the author, of featherfew) and bearing small white flowers, feathered with purple.

P. grossularioides. The Gooseberry-leaf geranium which in its native haunts is one

of the few species to be found in damp places. It makes a small angular shrub covered in hairs whilst its wrinkled leaves 3- to 5- lobed and cordate at the base release the scent of roses when bruised. The flowers are a pleasing pastel mauve, veined with purple.

P. Joy Lucille. A hybrid which has the deeply serrated leaves of one parent *P. denticulatum* and the soft down and peppermint scent of the other parent, *P. tomentosum*.

P. Lady Plymouth. A most distinct plant, the deeply serrated leaves being variegated with cream and pale green and richly rose scented.

P. Lady Scarborough. From its habit and crinkled leaves like those of parsley, it would appear to be a variety of *P. crispum* and it emits the same lemon odour.

P. Moore's Victory. Its leaves, like those of the oak, have the aroma of cayenne pepper whilst its scarlet flowers equal those of *P. clorinda* in size, far exceeding those of any other scented-leaf variety.

P. nervosum. It is listed in Sweet's *Geraniaceae 1820* and described as having lime-scented foliage, the small leaves of darkest green being sharply toothed. It bears lavender flowers marked with purple.

P. odoratissimum. A very rare species with soft velvety leaves smelling of ripe apples and bearing numerous small white flowers.

P. Prince of Orange. One of the loveliest of all 'the scenteds', a *P. citriodorum* hybrid of dainty, compact habit its tiny deep-green leaves, with their serrated edges, smelling refreshingly of orange.

P. Purple Unique. It has large handsome petunia-purple flowers, almost as large as those of *P. clorinda*, whilst its handsome leaves have the pleasing odour of absinthe.

P. quercifolium. The Oak-leaf geranium, with dark leaves like those of the oak and with a warm pungent smell, reminding one of incense. It bears flowers of mallow-purple. The variety Fair Helen is probably the prettiest of the group for it is of more compact habit with neater leaves, whilst its flowers are of orchid-mauve colouring. Another is Royal Oak which makes a handsome plant, its dark leaves, blotched with brown being tacky and pungent.

P. radula rosea. One of the varieties

known to Stuart gardeners, its rough leaves with narrow straight lobes having the scent of roses whilst its compact habit makes it most suitable for a window-box.

P. tomentosum. Its large spreading leaves and its long footstalks are thickly covered with hairs as a means of protection against the strong sunlight and moisture evaporation. Both leaves and stalks smell strongly of peppermint.

Species with Scented Flowers. *P. triste.* It was introduced into England from South Africa in 1632 by John Tradescant, gardener to Charles I, and is unlike any other geranium, being tuberous-rooted with beautiful carrot-like foliage. It was named 'the sad' geranium for its sombre looking flowers of browny-yellow and green which appear in July. The leaves have a resinous scent whilst the flowers, especially at nightfall, smell deliciously sweet. A single plant will scent a large room or greenhouse and is one more example of a flower of sombre colouring being endowed with sweet perfume as compensation. In its native land, the flowers are visited by moths.

P. gibbosum. It is a rare climbing form and is known as the Gouty pelargonium for it has noticeable swellings at the stem joints. The leaves are heavily indented whilst the greenish-yellow flowers are pleasingly scented, especially in the evening. A hybrid, *apifolium,* of similar habit, has purple-brown flowers, green at the edges, and is even more powerfully scented.

PELTARIA (Cruciferae—Wallflower Family)

A genus of seven species, native of eastern Europe and across the Middle East to central Asia.

Species. *Peltaria alliacea.* One of a small genus of perennial herbs, native of eastern Europe and growing 30 cm (12 in) high. The cordate leaves when bruised give off a powerful smell of garlic which is difficult to remove from the hands. The flowers, which appear in June, are white and borne in corymbs. They are followed by large flat seed-pods. The plant grows in ordinary well-drained soil and is readily increased by root division in spring.

PENIOCEREUS (Cactaceae—Cactus Family)

A genus of two species, native of Arizona and Mexico, with long fleshy roots of considerable weight and size. The flowers open at night and close up during daylight but open again on the following evening. They enjoy a semi-shaded position in cultivation and a porous soil made up of gravel and leaf-mould, together with a small amount of decayed manure. They require a winter temperature of not less than 10°C (50°F) and a dry atmosphere, also almost no moisture at their roots at this time.

Species. *Peniocereus greggii* (syn. *Cereus greggii).* It forms a long fleshy root 60 cm (2 ft) in diameter and has erect stems of blackish-green with 4 or 5 ribs covered in woolly areoles and short spines. The flowers are white, borne along the sides and open for 2 nights. They are powerfully scented.

PERESKIA (Cactaceae—Cactus Family)

A genus of 19 species, native of tropical America and the West Indies and rare in cultivation. They are woody plants with glossy dark-green leaves, in certain species resembling those of camellia, and in no way resemble the cactus. They grow well in sandy soil and withstand long periods of drought. They require a winter temperature of not less than 10°C (50°F) and a position of full sunlight with plenty of moisture during summer. They are readily increased by cuttings taken early in summer and rooted under glass.

Species. *Pereskia aculeata.* It is present in Florida, Mexico and in the West Indies where it makes a large shrub-like plant of semi-climbing habit. The areoles have hooked spines, the leaves being elliptical and pointed with a prominent midrib. The flowers are white (pink or red with most species) and are borne in large clusters. They have a powerful lily-like scent.

PERGULARIA (Asclepiadaceae— Stephanotis Family)

A genus of twining shrubs, native of India, China, Madagascar, Indonesia and Mauritius, with broad cordate leaves and bearing cymes of highly scented greenish-yellow flowers. Their name is derived from *pergula,* an arbour or pergola, for the plants are well adapted to train up and over rafters.

Species. *Pergularia odoratissima.* Native of Java and Sumatra, it was introduced into India by the English to whom it was known as the 'West Coast creeper'. The plant is a vigorous climber with heart-shaped leaves, downy on the veins, and it bears panicles of greenish-yellow flowers, in size like those of the primrose and downy inside the corolla.

The form *minor* has rounded leaves and bears a smaller bloom of similar colouring and of exquisite perfume.

P. sanguinolenta. Native of Sierra Leone, the plant contains a blood-red juice, used to adulterate the 'Dragon's blood' of commerce. The leaves are ovate and glabrous whilst the pale-yellow flowers are borne in large cymes and are sweetly scented.

PERIPLOCA (Asclepiadaceae— Stephanotis Family)

A small genus of climbing plants, native of south-eastern Europe and the Canary Islands, the Near East and western Asia, one of which, *P. graeca,* bears attractively scented flowers.

Species. *Periploca graeca.* It grows in the Canary Islands, across southern Europe and North Africa and as far east as the borders of China. It is a deciduous plant of vigorous habit, attaining a height of 12 m (40 ft) or more and is known as the Silk vine. It is valuable for covering a pergola or trellis. It blooms in July and August, the flowers produced in clusters and purple-brown on the inside, yellowish-green on the outside, and powerfully scented.

PERISTERIA (Orchidaceae—Orchid Family)

A small genus of epiphytic, sometimes terrestrial, orchids from tropical America, one of which, *Peristeria elata,* is the na-tional flower of Panama, where it is known as *El Espirito Santa,* the Holy Ghost plant, or the Dove orchid. They are rarely seen in orchid collections, although attractive. They do best in the warm part of an in-termediate house, and require a mixture of sphagnum-moss, osmunda fibre and fibrous loam. They require a definite rest-ing period after growth has been completed.

Species. *Peristeria eleata.* The cup-shaped flowers of this rather large plant are fleshy and white, the inner column and lip being of similar shape, but very much smaller. They are carried on a spike up to 1.5 m (5 ft) tall and are heavily scented, appearing between July and September.

PEROWSKIA (Labiatae—Lavender Family)

A small genus of handsome sage-like sub-shrubs, native of south-eastern Europe, with deeply cut or toothed leaves.

Species. *Perowskia abrotanifolius.* It makes a bushy plant 0.9 to 1.2 m (3 to 4 ft) tall with aromatic grey-green leaves, and in August and September bears spikes of lavender-blue flowers.

P. antriplicifolia. Known as the Russian sage, it is native of the Crimea, Afghanis-tan and Tibet. In a well-drained soil and in a position sheltered from cold winds, it will attain a height of 1.5 m (5 ft). It is a sub-shrub with aromatic silver-grey leaves, above which it bears elegant spikes of palest blue during August and September.

A hybrid of the two best known species, Blue Haze is a most attractive plant with deeply cut grey-green leaves, pungent when pressed and bearing, late in summer, long spikes of lavender-blue flowers.

PERSEA (Lauraceae—Bay Tree Family)

A genus of about 150 species, native of the tropics, several of which have aromatic leaves and bear edible fruit.

Species. *Persea gratissima.* Native of the southern United States, it makes a small spreading tree with elliptic leaves which when crushed yield the sweet, resinous scent of those of the Bay. The creamy-white flowers are borne in clusters and are followed by large pear-shaped fruits of aromatic scent and delicious flavour, known as the Avocado or Alligator pear. In northern Europe, it requires stove house conditions, and can be propagated by cuttings of ripened wood in May, in heat, or by seed.

PETROCALLIS (Cruciferae—Wallflower Family)

A genus of two species, one native of the Pyrenees, the other of northern Iran.

Species. *Petrocallis pyrenaica* (syn. *Draba pyrenaica).* Native of the mountainous regions of southern Europe, it forms a tiny hummock 5 cm (2 in) tall and is a most valuable plant for a sink or trough garden. It has tiny 3-lobed leaves and comes into bloom early in April, its pale-lilac flowers, lightly veined with purple, emitting a sweet, honey-like perfume, especially pronounced when the day is warm. It is readily raised from seed or is propagated by division of the roots in spring.

PETROSELINUM (Parsley)
(Umbelliferae— Parsley Family)

A genus of five European species of annual or perennial plants.

Species. *Petroselinum sativum.* As with most of the Umbelliferae, the seeds are aromatic and are used both in medicine and in cooking, but it is the leaves which are in most demand, being used in large quantities as a garnish and in sauces; bright-green and fern-like, they are amongst the most attractive of all foliage. It is a perennial plant though it is often treated as biennial, and a pinch of seed should be sown in July each year to maintain a succession of healthy foliage. There is an old country saying that the seed of parsley 'goes nine times to the devil' before germinating and it does seem to take longer to germinate than most other seed.

The plant reached England during the Middle Ages and it is mentioned in the earliest known work of gardening in English, written early in the fifteenth century by Master John, gardener, which is in the library of Trinity College, Cambridge. The plant was much appreciated by Henry VIII who, it is said, enjoyed parsley sauce above all others. Turner, writing in the *Herbal* of 1548, said that he had seen it 'nowhere but in gardens', thus indicating that it is not a native plant. Parkinson tells of first seeing it about the year 1600, growing in the garden of the Venetian Ambassador in Bishopsgate where Shakespeare may also have seen it, for in *Taming of the Shrew* he writes of 'Parsley to stuff a rabbit'.

An infusion of the leaves or seeds in water is an excellent remedy for indigestion and for disorders of the kidneys.

For garnishing, the best form is the Dwarf Green which makes a plant of compact habit with extremely dark-green leaves which are densely curled. The leaves being succulent are not easily dried and require a well-ventilated room which receives long hours of sunlight. Only when the leaves are quite crisp can they be rubbed down for storing in jars for winter use, though usually there will be fresh leaves available throughout the year.

PETTERIA (Leguminosae—Laburnum Family)

The only species of the genus which previously had in turn been classed with *Cytisus* and *Laburnum*.

Species. *Petteria ramentacea.* It is an attractive Dalmatian shrub growing 1.8 m (6 ft) in height and the same across with leaves like those of the laburnum. It blooms during April and May and often into June, bearing its golden-yellow flowers in terminal racemes, and they have the delicious vanilla fragrance of the family. The plant enjoys a well-drained sandy soil and does well near the coast.

PETUNIA (Solanaceae—Nightshade Family)

A genus of about 12 species of often downy or clammy annuals or perennials with entire leaves and bearing funnel-shaped flowers. Only one species is scented and has passed on this quality to modern bedding petunias of which the purple and white varieties release most perfume.

Species. *Petunia violacea* (syn. *Nierembergia phoenicea*). It is a half-hardy South American perennial and one of the parents of the popular bedding petunias. It was introduced into Britain in 1831, its purple tubular blooms diffusing a delicious vanilla-like fragrance especially at night. It grows 22.5 cm (9 in) tall and blooms during July and August. It is not sufficiently hardy to withstand outdoor winter temperatures in the British Isles and northern Europe and should be grown under glass. Bedding petunias are planted out early in June and bloom until late October. They are treated as annual plants.

PEUCEDANUM (Dill) (Umbelliferae—Parsley Family)

A small genus of plants, grown for the carminative properties of its scented seed.

Species. *Peucedanum grande.* It is indigenous to the hills of north-western India, its fruit being known as *Dúkú* in the Hindu vernacular. In Royle's *Materia Medica,* Falconer describes *Dúkú* as a fruit (seed) resembling *Asafoetida.* It may attain a height of 1.8 m (6 ft) or more and is perennial with a large parsnip-like root and long-petioled bipinnate leaves and a round, smooth stem. The fruit is large, reddish-yellow in colour with a powerful lemon odour when dry, and yielding upon distillation a pale-yellow essential oil with a similar scent.

P. graveolens. It is distinguished from other Umbelliferae by the absence of any involucre to the umbel and by its flattened fruit. It is indigenous to central and southern Europe, also Egypt and Abyssinia, and is similar to fennel in that it grows 90 cm (3 ft) high with attractive feathery foliage which has a spicy taste and smell when handled, whilst it bears yellow flowers. The tripinnate leaves have fringe-like segments and broad sheaths. The plant has been esteemed since earliest times, receiving its name from the Norse word *dilla,* to lull, for its seeds were used to lull young children to sleep in the same way that today it is used in sedative mixtures. The leaves were at one time used to flavour salads and sauces to serve with fish in the same way as those of fennel. In ancient times the plant grew in every cottage garden, for it was believed to have powers to safeguard the home against witchcraft. The leaves, with their spicy smell and taste, may be included with new potatoes and with peas, but as the flavour is strong they should be used sparingly. Joseph Cooper, cook to Charles I, gave a recipe for pickling dill and cucumbers.

Seed is sown in March, in a well-drained soil and in a sunny situation. If the fruit (seed) is to be saved, the plants are cut towards the end of summer and stored in a dry room for several days before the seed is removed. From it, a fragrant essential oil is obtained upon distillation, containing 30 per cent carvol, identical with the carvol of carraway.

PHACELIA (Hydrophyllaceae—Nemophila Family)

A genus of some 200 species usually having hairy or downy foliage and large toothed leaves. Mostly natives of California, they require an open, sunny situation but they are completely hardy and are usually sown in March where they are to bloom. The flowers are much visited by bees though only one species bears flowers with any degree of perfume.

Species. *Phacelia ciliata.* A little-known species, it grows only 30 cm (12 in) tall and may be used to edge a scented border. Seed should be sown early in September or in spring, to bloom from early June until October. It is worthy of planting for its free-flowering qualities but, in addition, its lovely lavender-blue flowers carry the sweet almond-like scent of heliotrope.

PHALERIA (Thymeleaceae—Mezereon Family)

A genus of 20 species of small trees or shrubs, native of South-east Asia, Ceylon and Pacific islands.

Species. *Phaleria glabra.* It is native of several of the Fijian Islands and forms a small straggling tree 3 m (10 ft) tall with oblong leaves 10 to 20 cm (4 to 8 in) long and 5 to 10 cm (2 to 4 in) wide. It bears tiny white flowers in a dense inflorescence and they have a powerful lily-like scent. The flowers are followed by small crimson fruits. Stove house conditions are required in northern Europe, and a compost containing much peat and sand. Seeds or cuttings in heat, in spring, are used for increase.

PHELLODENDRON (Rutaceae—Rue Family)

A small genus of quick-growing trees whose deciduous leaves have the same pungent orange-like fragrance as the Rue. They usually give a good account of themselves in a shallow chalky soil and are worthy of a place in the garden if only for the brilliant autumnal colouring of their foliage.

Species. *Phellodendron amurense.* The Amur cork-tree, a native of Manchuria where it attains a height of 12 to 15 m (40 to 50 ft) but only about half that height in Britain. It is quite hardy and is a tree of graceful outline, being most adaptable to a small garden. It has handsome aromatic pinnate leaves 37.5 cm (15 in) long, divided into 7 or 11 leaflets, and turning clear golden-yellow before they fall.

P. chinense. It attains a height of about 9 m (30 ft) and has handsome aromatic leaves divided into 9 leaflets, which, like those of *P. amurense,* turn brilliant gold before they fall.

P. sachalinense. A native of Korea and northern China, it is hardier than any species and will quickly reach a height of 6 to 7.5 m (20 to 25 ft). Like the other species, the leaves are divided into 9 or 11 leaflets which are pleasantly aromatic and which turn to golden-yellow in autumn.

PHILADELPHUS (Mock Orange)
(Saxifragaceae—Rockfoil Family)

A genus of 12 or more species of deciduous shrubs, closely related to *Deutzia* and *Hydrangea.* They take their name of Mock Orange from the likeness of their beautiful white flowers to those of the citrus and they have a more powerful perfume than almost any other flower. They are plants of the easiest culture with cane-like growth, the newly formed green wood turning to golden brown as it ages (ripens). With certain species, the scent is so strong as to be almost unpleasant, especially when cut and placed in a warm room when the blossom may bring about a severe headache. The perfume tends to remain with us for some time after leaving the flowers as if our sense of smell had become saturated. The hybrid varieties are less strongly scented and should be grown, in preference to the species, when planting close to the home.

The Greeks named the shrub after Ptolemy Philadelphus, King of Egypt and with its hollow stems when the pith is removed, it was, like the lilac, given the name *Syringa* from the Greek *syrinx,* a flute, thus giving rise to some confusion though botanically the lilac is the true *Syringa.* The fresh blossoms were at one time used for making tea and it is on record that Captain Cook's sailors used the young shoots, which are also scented, as a substitute for tea, the infusion being aromatic and fragrant.

Linnaeus said that *P. coronarius* was a native of the countryside around Verona, but this is doubtful, South-eastern Europe or the Near East being its more likely habitat. The plant had reached England at an early date for Gerard mentions that it grew in considerable numbers in his garden and it was the earliest species to reach this country. Others followed but at a much later date, coming mostly from China, Japan and Mexico, and in 1883 Lemoine introduced the first hybrid by crossing *P. coronaria* with the equally hardy *P. microphyllus* previously introduced from America and whose blossoms have the refreshing scent of ripe pineapples.

Hybrids descended from the European *P. coronaria* are hardy in all parts of the British Isles and grow well in any type of soil but especially do they flourish in a loamy soil over a limestone formation. They mostly bloom in July, when lilac has finished. Propagation is from suckers, by layering or from cuttings of the half-ripened wood removed in August.

Species and Varieties. *Philadelphus argyrocalyx.* A beautiful and graceful shrub growing 2.4 to 3 m (8 to 10 ft) high and bearing large fragrant flowers of creamy-white which have enlarged pubescent calyces.

P. burfordensis. A hybrid, possibly of the Virginalis group, growing to a height of 3.6 m (12 ft) or more, its large cup-shaped flowers having a conspicuous bunch of stamens at the centre and they are deliciously fragrant.

P. californicus. Native of the western United States, it is a vigorous shrub, reaching a height of 3 to 3.6 m (10 to 12 ft), its single white flowers being produced in clusters of as many as 20 or more and they have a powerful scent.

P. coronarius. It is the European Mock Orange, attaining a height of 3 m (10 ft) or so and it comes into bloom in May, being the earliest species. The creamy-white flowers are borne in racemes, each bloom measuring 2.5 cm (1 in) across and with a powerful orange scent. There is a form, *aureus,* with golden leaves.

P. coulteri. It is somewhat hardier than *P. mexicanus* but should be given protection in the more exposed parts of Britain. It has slender drooping branches and lance-shaped leaves, and early in summer it bears single solitary white cup-shaped flowers which have a purple blotch at the base of the petals.

P. delavayi. A most handsome early-flowering species with grey-green leaves and it bears its sweet orange-scented flowers of ivory whiteness in sprays of 12 or more.

P. grandiflorus. This handsome species is a native of the southern United States and grows 3 m (10 ft) high with ovate leaves, attractively toothed, whilst it bears enormous flowers 10 cm (4 in) across which have a bunch of golden stamens at the centre and are powerfully scented.

P. lemoinei. The original hybrid which has given its name to a group of hybrid varieties. It is a most handsome plant when in bloom, the orange-scented flowers of purest white being borne in clusters of 5 or 6 on numerous small side shoots. So profuse are they that the plants, which grow 3 to 3.6 m (10 to 12 ft) in height, are completely covered in blossom.

Hybrids of the *P. lemoinei* group:

BOULE D'ARGENT. It forms a compact plant, its sweetly scented blooms of purest white appearing in dense clusters.

COUPE D'ARGENT. A plant of exquisite beauty, its large fragrant flowers being almost square in form and produced at intervals along the branches.

ERECTUS. It grows 1.8 m (6 ft) in height and is of erect habit with smaller leaves than usual and bearing its small richly scented flowers in great profusion.

INNOCENCE. The single flowers are creamy-white with a delicious perfume and appear with freedom.

MANTEAU D'HERMINE. It makes a compact plant rarely exceeding 1.2 m (4 ft) in height and bears double blooms of creamy-white with a rich pineapple perfume.

VALLEDA. Its flowers are larger than any of the group, measuring nearly 5 cm (2 in) across, and have attractively waved edges and a rich sweet perfume.

P. mexicanus. A Mexican shrub of exquisite beauty but which in Britain is hardy only in the South-west. It has long tapering leaves whilst its pure-white circular flowers are more than 5 cm (2 in) across with a conspicuous cluster of golden-tipped stamens at the centre, and they have a sweet, refined perfume.

P. microphyllus. It forms a dense twiggy bush growing no more than 1.2 m (4 ft) in height with myrtle-like leaves, hairy on the underside, and it comes into bloom before the end of May, bearing numerous sprays of purest white which have the smell of ripe pineapples.

P. pekinensis brachybotrys. A handsome Chinese species bearing large creamy-white flowers in short sprays along the entire length of stem. Those who prefer their Mock Oranges with a more delicate perfume should give this species pride of place.

P. pubescens. The most vigorous species, growing to a height of almost 6 m (20 ft) and laden during June and July with large richly scented flowers of ivory whiteness.

Its hybrid *Insignis* has a similar vigour and is the last to bloom, remaining colourful until the first days of August, bearing its pure-white cup-shaped flowers in clusters of 20 or more.

P. satsumanus. It is an erect Japanese shrub of slender habit with narrow leaves and bearing, in racemes of mostly 5 small white flowers which, like *P. pekinensis,* have a soft delicate perfume, never oppressive.

P. virginalis. It is a hybrid, covering itself with multitudes of snow-white flowers which are fully double and powerfully scented.

Hybrids of the *P. virginalis* group, bearing double blooms:

BOUQUET BLANC. An extremely lovely variety bearing its orange-scented snow-white blossoms in crowded clusters.

GLACIER. It grows 1.8 to 2.4 m (6 to 8 ft) tall, its milky-white flowers having attractively frilled petals and a rich spicy fragrance.

PHILLYREA (Oleaceae—Olive Family)

A genus of four species, native of Asia Minor, and evergreen, delighting in a deep loamy soil and partial shade. Like the closely related *Osmanthus,* they make neat, compact plants and are valuable for the small garden where their handsome leathery foliage and fragrant flowers in May are always appreciated. They should be given protection in the more exposed gardens. Propagation is from cuttings of the ripened wood, removed in August and inserted in a sandy compost under glass.

Species. *Phillyrea angustifolia.* From the eastern Mediterranean regions, it makes a compact but multibranched shrub 1.5 to 1.8 m (5 to 6 ft) in height, with narrow lance-shaped leaves of darkest green. In April and May it bears clusters of small creamy-white flowers which have an intense penetrating perfume, especially pronounced in dull, moist weather. It is a plant of Elizabethan gardens and Gerard said that it grew in the garden of the Earl of Essex at Barn Elmes and in his own garden in Holborn.

P. decora. Native of Asia Minor, though Gerard said it grew about the mountainous regions of Montpelier in France and that he planted it also in the garden of the Earl of Essex and in his own. It is the hardiest of the genus, reaching a height of 2.4 to 2.7 m (8 to 9 ft), and is a most valuable shrub for partial shade, especially for a coastal garden. It grows wide and dense with lance-shaped leaves almost 15 cm (6 in) long, and in May and intermittently through summer and autumn bears from the axils creamy-white flowers with a sweet perfume. The flowers are followed in autumn by purple fruits, oval in shape, like damsons. This plant, crossed with *Osmanthus delavayi,* gave birth to the fragrant *Osmarea burkwoodii.*

P. latifolia. It is a plant of greater vigour than the others, eventually reaching a height of 6 m (20 ft) or more with large leathery serrated leaves, lobed at the base, and in May it bears clusters of pure-white flowers with a rich fruity perfume.

P. media. The form *buxifolia* has round box-like leaves which give the plant its name of Jasmine box. It is a beautiful plant, growing 3 m (10 ft) tall, the variety *pendula* having graceful drooping branches; from the leaf axils, it bears clusters of pure-white jasmine-like flowers and with the same sweet fragrance.

PHILODENDRON (Araceae—Arum Family)

A genus of about 270 species, mostly climbing or epiphytic and native of tropical America and the West Indies. They form both clasping and aerial roots which grow downwards, reaching into the soil. The handsome glossy leaves, oval or arrow-shaped, have swollen petioles which retain moisture for the plant to live on. Many make strikingly beautiful house plants and do well in a dark room. In their native lands, starchy foods are obtained from the roots and are highly nutritious. One species bears scented flowers.

Species. *Philodendron fragrantissimum.* Native of the tropical forests of Guyana, it has handsome peltate leaves and bears its pure-white flowers in a terminal spike. It is powerfully scented. It requires a temperature of $20°C$ ($68°F$) to bloom to advantage, and plenty of moisture when coming into new growth in spring. Plant the tubers 2.5 cm (1 in) deep in a compost made up of fibrous loam, leaf-mould and sand, and increase moisture supplies as the new leaves are formed. After flowering dry off the plants in autumn and winter in a frost-free room, starting the plants into growth again in spring.

PHLOMIS (Labiatae—Lavender Family)

A genus of some 50 woolly or hairy shrubs or perennial herbs suitable for planting in borders or the shrubbery. The flowers, of yellow, purple or white and with a hairy hood, are borne in dense whorls. The plants flourish in ordinary soil and are completely hardy. They are usually propagated by cuttings of the half-ripened shoots or from seed.

Species. *Phlomis fruticosa.* It is the Jerusalem sage and is native of the Levant. It makes a handsome shrub 0.9 to 1.2 m (3 to 4 ft) tall with wrinkled oblong leaves, woolly beneath, and it blooms during June and July, bearing about 20 golden-yellow flowers in a whorl at the top of the shoots. The leaves when bruised emit an aromatic sage-like perfume.

PHLOX (Polemoniaceae—Phlox Family)

A genus of about 30 species which, with the exception of *P. drummondii,* the popular annual, are plants of perennial habit. The phlox is one of the few flowers whose scent to some is most disagreeable whilst to others it has a special quality. Certainly as the flowers begin to lose their freshness their smell is most unpleasant but, when first showing colour, their fragrance may perhaps be described as wholesome. It is rather like that of the older antirrhinums, best described as a 'cottage garden' smell with just a touch of the refreshing new-mown hay scent of the Sweet alyssum. The many lovely phlox hybrids with which we are most familiar, and which are so valuable in the border in that they bloom during late summer, certainly have some scent but it is nothing like so sweet as that of the species *P. maculata* and *P. paniculata* from which they have descended. Both have purple flowers and it would seem to be one more example of pigment in the orange and scarlet shades displacing the perfume to be found in the original purple flowers. It is of interest that those hybrid phlox bearing flowers of purple, mauve and white, are more pleasantly scented than others.

The phlox is a hardy and accommodating plant but requires a cool, moist soil, one which has been deeply worked and enriched, and it does appreciate a little shade. Planting should take place in November for the plants often suffer from dry conditions if moved in spring.

Species and Varieties. *Phlox alyssifolia.* It is native of the limestone outcrops and prairielands of Nebraska, Montana and northern Dakota, and requires perfect drainage and an open, sunny situation. It is a plant of creeping habit, forming a large cushion 0.9 to 1.2 m (3 to 4 ft) across and growing less than 7.5 cm (3 in tall). It begins to bloom in May and remains colourful for more than a month, bearing bright lavender-pink flowers about 2.5 cm (1 in) across and which have a brilliant glow in the early summer sunshine. They are also pleasantly scented, like the flowers of Sweet alyssum but with greater sweetness, it being the most sweetly scented of all the species of phlox. In cultivation, it requires a soil containing ample supplies of lime which is best provided in the form of mortar or lime rubble.

Phlox maculata. Native of Pennsylvania and Iowa, it has erect stems which reach about 60 cm (2 ft) in height and lance-shaped leaves, and it comes into bloom in July, bearing its sweetly scented purple flowers in pyramidal panicles. The variety *suaveolens* bears flowers of purest white from which the white hybrids are descended and is one of the most sweetly scented of all the phloxes.

P. paniculata. Possibly the most showy species for it grows 1.2 m (4 ft) tall and is known as the Autumn-flowering phlox, a characteristic it has passed on to the modern *P. decussata* hybrids. The flowers vary in colour from mauve-purple to white and are borne in large conical panicles which emit a deliciously sweet perfume.

Hybrids of *P. decussata which are scented:*

FRAU BUCHNER. It received an Award of Merit as long ago as 1910 and for its huge scented trusses of purest white has never been surpassed.

IVER. It grows 60 cm (2 ft) tall, bearing enormous trusses of lilac-mauve enhanced by the dark foliage.

JACQUELINE MAILLIE. The huge trusses are a lovely ivory-cream and sweetly scented. Forms a pleasing contrast to the violet varieties.

LITTLE LOVELY. A 1964 introduction bearing huge refined trusses of deep purple with a striking white contrasting 'eye' and some perfume.

PHOENIX (Palmae—Palm Tree Family)

A genus of 17 species of trees native to northern Africa and extending to Southeast Asia, the columnar stems being covered with the old leaf bases.

Species. *Phoenix dactylifera.* The Date palm, native of the dry sub-tropical regions, extending from the Canary Islands across the Sahara and Arabian Desert to South-east Asia. It forms a slender tree and is one of the tallest-growing of all trees, often attaining a height of 30 m (100 ft) or more, the leaves forming a crown or 'head' at the top. The leaves measure up to 60 cm (2 ft) in length and arise from a fibrous sheath. Both sexes of flowers appear on different trees but only the males are scented. They are creamy-white and are borne in large panicles at first in sheathing spathes. The flowers have a cup-like calyx and 3 thick perianth segments and 6 stamens. They are followed by highly nutritious fruits, some 5 cm (2 in) long and yellowish-brown in colour, which are soft and sticky from the high sugar content. Commercial growers assist pollination by placing a bunch of the male flowers amongst the females.

PHOTINIA (Rosaceae—Rose Family)

A genus of 20 or more species of evergreen trees and shrubs with leathery serrated leaves. They require a rich loamy soil and grow well in partial shade but they do require some protection from cold winds in the more exposed gardens. They are attractive trained against a sunny wall.

Species. *Photinia arbutifolia* (syn. *Heteromeles arbutifolia*). A native of California where it is known as the Californian maybush. It makes a handsome tree 3.6 to 4.5 m (12 to 15 ft) tall, with large lance-shaped leaves which have conspicuous red stems. It blooms in May, at the same time as the hawthorn to which it is closely related, the scented white flowers appearing in long elegant panicles and followed by scarlet berries in autumn.

P. serrulata. The evergreen Chinese hawthorn which makes a tree 4.5 m (15 ft) tall with leathery laurel-like leaves, and from May until July bears small white hawthorn-like flowers in flat corymbs and with a delicate scent.

P. villosa. It makes a dainty tree 3 m (10 ft) tall with bronze leaves which are not evergreen but which turn rich orange-red in autumn before they fall. The white hawthorn-like flowers, of similar fragrance, are produced in May and June and are followed by scarlet berries. This species does not grow well in a chalk-laden soil.

PHUOPSIS (Rubiaceae—Bedstraw Family)

A genus of a single species.

Species. *Phuopsis stylosa.* It is native of the Caucasus and Near East. It has a rootstock which travels far by underground runners and may prove difficult to eradicate but it is a handsome plant for the rock garden, growing 25 cm (10 in) tall and bearing in early summer bright-pink tubular flowers

amongst pale-green leaves. The whole plant emits an unpleasant smell of wet fox fur which can be detected from afar when the weather is warm, like that of the Crown Imperial (*Fritillaria imperialis*).

PHYLICA (Rhamnaceae—Buckthorn Family)

A genus of 150 heath-like shrubs, native of South Africa and Madagascar.

Species. *Phylica superba.* Naturalized in Australia, it is a beautiful small shrub, like a helichrysum, clothed in silvered grey-green leaves and bearing in dense inflorescences tiny greenish-white flowers which open in September and which emit a fragrance similar to that of the Meadowsweet. The plant requires a sunny situation and a sandy soil.

PICEA (Spruce) (Pinaceae—Pine Tree Family)

Mostly native of the Northern Hemisphere, they are hardy but less accommodating as to soil than the pines and rarely give a good account in a shallow soil or one of a chalky nature. Most have resinous attractions.

Species and Varieties. *Picea breweriana.* Brewer's Weeping spruce, a most beautiful tree sending out its slender resinous branches to a great distance. It is native of Oregon and is hardy in the British Isles.

P. excelsa (syn. *P. abies*). The Norway spruce native to Norway, 'where', Gerard wrote, 'I have seen the goodliest trees in the world of this kind'. It makes a pyramidal tree and along its branches which droop in graceful curves are produced at regular intervals small spear-shaped leaves of brightest green. Its cylindrical cones measure up to 1.5 cm (6 in) in length. Spenser called it 'the fir that weepeth'. The foliage has a delicious musky smell, known to those who bring in the Christmas tree each year.

P. glauca. Known as the White spruce for the leaves are almost white, due to a covering of resinous wax. The cones, produced in large numbers, and the needles give off a characteristic strong, resinous smell when crushed. Native of North America, it is extremely hardy and may be used in the most exposed districts but it is slow-growing.

P. orientalis. The Oriental spruce, native of Japan, which makes a densely branched pyramidal tree readily distinguished by its flossy dark-green leaves. There is a golden form, *aureo-spicata.*

P. pungens. The Colorado spruce, of conical habit whilst its orange-brown bark emits a powerful pungent smell. By the side of water it is a fast-growing tree with grey-green foliage and bearing cones of apple-green. The form *glauca,* the American Blue spruce, makes a smaller tree and has blue-grey foliage.

P. schrenkiana. Schrenks Spruce, native of central Asia, bearing hairy shoots and extremely resinous buds. The sage-green leaves are sharply pointed, the cones long and cylindrical. It makes a medium-sized tree and does well in limestone soils.

PIERIS (Ericaceae—Heather Family)

A genus of 10 species, native of Japan and the United States, requiring similar conditions as the Leucothoe and increased by layering in autumn.

Species. *Pieris floribunda* (syn. *Andromeda floribunda*). It is the Arctic heather. It was originally named after Andromeda, daughter of the Ethiopian king Cepheus, a girl of unrivalled charms. It is usually to be found about swamplands and in Britain it will tolerate a severe winter. It makes a compact bush 90 cm (3 ft) high with smooth leathery leaves, and in March bears graceful spikes of bell-shaped flowers of purest whiteness and with a powerful fragrance.

P. japonica. It is a handsome Japanese species, also growing 90 cm (3 ft) tall. It has narrow dark-green foliage and in April and May bears long drooping panicles, up to 13 cm (6 in) long, of pure-white flowers which are delicately scented.

P. mariana. It is a handsome deciduous shrub growing 90 cm (3 ft) tall and is a native of Maryland. It is said that its leaves are poisonous to animals and it should be planted with care but it is a beautiful plant when in leaf and blossom, known as the Lily-of-the-valley Plant, and in April and May bears drooping clusters of fragrant urn-shaped flowers of purest white.

P. nitida. Of the United States, it is evergreen with shining oblong leaves and in March bears clusters of sweetly scented white and purple flowers. As with the other species, the flowers are produced for at least three months and come into bloom as soon as the sun gathers strength.

PIMELEA (Thymeleaceae—Mezereon Family)

A genus of 80 species, native of the Philippine Islands, New Guinea, Australia and New Zealand, one in particular having scented attractions.

Species. *Pimelea longifolia.* A comparatively rare but delightful little shrublet with attractive small but long glossy grey foliage, and in May bears corymbs of silky white flowers which emit the same jonquil-like perfume of the Daphne. The flowers are followed by white berries.

A native of New Zealand, especially North Island where it is known as the New Zealand daphne and to the Maoris as *Taranga.* It grows best in a well-drained loamy soil and in a position of full sunlight.

P. virgata. Common to both islands of New Zealand, it is known as the Twiggy pimelea and makes a small, erect shrub, densely twiggy. The tiny narrow leaves are covered in hairs whilst the scented flowers are borne in small terminal heads.

PIMENTA (Myrtaceae—Myrtle Family)

A genus of evergreen trees, native of tropical South America, the West Indies and Cuba, the aromatic odour of the berries resembling a mixture of cinnamon, cloves and nutmeg, hence its name of Allspice or Pimento. It grows 9 to 12 m (30 to 40 ft) tall with a slender trunk covered with grey aromatic bark. All parts of the plant are scented.

Species. *Pimenta officinalis.* It grows about 9 m (30 ft) tall with opposite leaves, stalked and about 15 cm (6 in) long, shaped like those of the laurel, deep green with a prominent midrib and glandular dots on the underside which release an aromatic perfume when bruised.

The greenish-white flowers are produced in panicles at the ends of the branches, almost covering the tree during the summer months and releasing their perfume over a considerable distance in the breezes.

The fruit is a shining succulent berry, dark purple when ripe and containing two flat pea-size seeds surrounded by sweet pulp, but as the fruits lose their aromatic property as they become ripe, they are marketed when green. They are gathered by hand and dried on mats on wooden floors, being turned each day until quite dry which is denoted by the rattling of the seeds

Pimento berries yield on distillation about 4 per cent of volatile oil composed mostly of Eugenol, similar in all respects to oil of cloves. The leaves yield 1 per cent of oil.

PIMPINELLA (Anise) (Umbelliferae— Parsley Family)

A genus of annual or biennial plants with pinnate leaves and native of southern Europe and northern Africa extending into western Asia.

Species. *Pimpinella anisum.* It is a native of Egypt and Asia Minor and grows about 30 cm (12 in) tall, bearing in umbels pretty white flowers. It is a half-hardy annual requiring a sunny situation, the seed being sown where the plants are to bloom. The seed (Anise) is used in cough mixtures and to flavour liqueurs (e.g. Absinthe) and confectionery, whilst the leaves add interest to a salad, and may be taken with meats to help the digestion. In northern India where the plant grows wild, it is customary to distil oil from the leaves and where cultivated, the plants are heavily manured to obtain as luxuriant a growth as possible.

Oil of anise is used in several compound perfumes such as Eau de Cologne. It is a yellow syrup-like liquid from which is obtained Anise Camphor or Anethol.

PINUS (Pinaceae—Pine Tree Family)

A genus of 80 to 100 resinous evergreen trees of the northern temperate regions. Since earliest times the young pine cones were used to flavour wine and ale. Loudon said that in Tuscany the cones were to be seen floating in the wine vats. The cones were called pin-nuts or pine-apples and until the introduction of pineapples to the country, *P. sylvestris* was known as the 'pine-apple' tree. Gerard called the cones Pyn Appels, for the seeds from the cones

are sweet and juicy. those obtained from the Nut pine, *P. sabiniana,* of the Californian Sierras being much prized by the Indians for food.

During Tudor times, the dry cones were strung together and hung up about the home for their refreshing scent, and were also placed amongst clothes. Parkinson said that the seeds 'whilst they are fresh and newly taken out, are used by apothecaries, comfitmakers and cookes ... with them a cunning cook can make divers kech-choses for his master's table'.

From earliest times, the Scots pine was held in greater esteem than almost any other tree. From its bark, pitch, tar and turpentine were extracted and the trees were afforded the greatest care for as soon as they begin to die back and lose their bark, the resin ceases to flow and they have no further value. The timber, too, was useful for making boats for it was long-lasting in 'water.

Species and Varieties. *P. insignis* (syn. *P. rodiata*). The Monterey pine, which may not be completely hardy in the exposed north but is the finest of all the pines with brilliant-green foliage, strangely twisted, and with long, smooth orange cones as if polished.

P. nigra. The Austrian pine which has grey bark whilst its cones are set horizontally in pairs. Like the Scots pine, the needle-like leaves are also borne in pairs.

Another form, the Corsican pine which reached Britain about 1750, is deep-rooting and extremely hardy and is to be found growing around the summit of Mount Etna. It has attractively twisted glaucous leaves smaller than those of the Austrian pine and small brown cones.

P. pinaster. It is known as the Cluster pine for its cones are borne in clusters or groups of a dozen or more, being 15 cm (6 in) long and a lovely purple-brown. The leaves too are borne in groups, though in pairs, and are nearly 20 cm (8 in) long. The tree is valuable as a wind-break and is so widely planted around Bordeaux for this purpose and also for its resin that in Europe it is known as the Bordeaux pine. The tree is reputed to have been introduced by Gerard in the latter years of Elizabeth's reign.

P. pinea. The Stone pine, growing about

the rocky Mediterranean coast and in the hills around Florence and other northern Italian towns. The short trunks with their red bark are deeply fissured whilst the trees form a multibranched head. The brown oval cones are 15 cm (6 in) long and are as if polished, making them the most beautiful of all cones. The kernels are edible.

P. strobus. The Weymouth pine, introduced to Britain in 1705 by Lord Weymouth from North America and planted on his Wiltshire estates. It is a handsome tree, the soft-green leaves, borne in groups of five, being striped with silver whilst the smooth cones, which hang down, often measure 20 cm (8 in) in length and are so resinous that the resin is exuded from the tips. They may be used to tell accurately the weather, by the opening and closing of the scales.

P. sylvestris. Phillips in *Sylva Florifera* writes: 'The air that is impregnated with the exhalations of these trees is reckoned very wholesome . . . and the fresh cones boiled in whey and beer brewed with the tender hops of the branches are accounted good in inveterate scurvies'. Pliny refers to the resin secreted from the reddish bark and this is also mentioned by Turner in his *Names of Plants* (1548). This resinous secretion was collected and used to make torches, hence the tree was also known as the Scots fir, from the Anglo-Saxon *fyre,* fire. It makes a tall tree and does well in all soils.

PIPER (Piperaceae—Pepper Family)
A genus of about 700 species distributed throughout tropical South America and in several islands of the South Pacific. The plants are mostly shrubs with simple heart-shaped or elliptical leaves with conspicuous nerves. The flowers are borne in terminal spikes and are mostly wind pollinated.

Species. *Piper methysticum.* Native of the Fiji Islands where the lateral roots and thick underground stems are dried and powdered to make an aromatic beverage called *yaqona.* It is a robust shrub growing 3 m (10 ft) tall and with heart-shaped leaves tinted with purple.

P. nigrum. It is a small shrub with opposite leaves, aromatic when pressed owing to the oil-containing cells. The flowers, borne from the axil of the bracts, are bi-sexual and are arranged in spikes 5 to 7.5 cm (2 to 3 in) long. From the large seeds, the pepper of commerce is obtained.

PIPTANTHUS (Leguminosae—Laburnum Family)
A genus of eight species of evergreen trees or shrubs, native of the Himalayas and China.

Species. *Piptanthus nepalensis.* The Evergreen laburnum, native of the Himalayas (Nepal). It is half hardy and is suitable for planting only in coastal gardens of the South-west of the British Isles and on the west coast of Scotland. It requires a sandy soil, preferably containing some humus and a position of full sun.

It grows 3 to 3.6 m (10 to 12 ft) in height with 3-foliate leaves of an attractive soft green and it blooms during April and May, bearing its large golden-yellow flowers in short racemes at the ends of the branches. The flowers have the delicious vanilla-like perfume of the closely related laburnum.

PISTACIA (Anacardiaceae—Cashew Family)
A genus of five or six evergreen or deciduous trees or shrubs abounding in resinous juices. They are mostly native of the Canary Islands and islands and countries of the Mediterranean. In the British Isles it requires a warm, sheltered garden and a rich sandy well-drained soil. Even so, it may not survive a hard winter.

Species. *Pistacia lentiscus.* The Mastic tree of the Island of Chios from which is obtained the drug Mastic used in medicine and in making varnishes. From the resinous gum, a sweetmeat called *masticha* is made and the liqueur *Mastiche.* It reaches a height of 6 m (20 ft) or more with pinnate leaves and it bears in spring at the leaf axils scented flowers of palest green resembling catkins.

P. terebinthus. The Turpentine tree of Cyprus and of Gilead. It is a deciduous tree which reaches a height of 9 m (30 ft), its leaves resembling those of the ash and enhanced with a beautiful red hue when young, like those of the walnut. They are resinous. From the wood and red bark, a resinous gum is obtained by making incisions in the trunk. From it, Cyprus turpentine is obtained. Theophrastus wrote that the Terebinth tree yielded the best of all resins.

The variety *vera,* which yields the pistachio nut, is native of Asia Minor and is mostly cultivated in Syria, Turkey and Greece.

PITTOSPORUM (Pittosporaceae— Pittosporum Family)

A genus of 12 or more species, native of Tasmania, New Zealand, China and Japan, several of which may be grown in the milder parts of the British Isles. They are evergreen shrubs of upright habit, with smooth pale-green leaves which have attractively waved petals. The elegant branches are much in demand by florists for 'mixing' and large quantities are sent to the wholesale markets each year from the South-west where the plants are used as hedges. But they should be grown close to the sea, where the salt-laden atmosphere will give protection from frost.

The plants should be set out towards the end of April when the weather is warm and when the usual showery weather will enable them to make a good start in life. The plants will eventually reach a height of 3 m (10 ft) but are usually kept to half that height by the regular cutting of the shoots which are removed in lengths of 45 to 50 cm (18 to 20 in) for the florist trade. Though the plants require a sandy, well-drained soil, they do need moisture about their roots in summer, and into the soil should be incorporated humus in any available form, especially seaweed upon which the plants seem to thrive. The plants are increased by means of the half-ripened shoots which are removed in August and inserted in a sandy compost under glass, an old-fashioned bell jar or a frame being suitable.

Species and Varieties. *Pittosporum cornifolium.* From New Zealand, it could almost be included with winter-flowering plants for its first blooms appear before the end of March, and are of darkest purple, scenting the air with their distinct musk perfume. The plant grows 1.8 to 2.1 m (6 to 7 ft) tall with bronzy leaves, in shape like those of the Dogwood.

P. crassifolium. A New Zealand species with thick leathery green leaves, downy on the underside. It blooms in May but only rarely; when it does, its purple flowers have the sweet scent of the daphnes.

P. dallii. A New Zealand species of most handsome appearance. It makes a plant of tree-like proportions 3.6 to 4.5 m (12 to 15 ft) in height, the dark-green leaves being displayed to full effect by the contrasting grey bark and stems and the large white flowers which are sweetly scented. A plant in full bloom in June presents a delightful cool effect but it is of tender habit and requires a warm, sheltered situation.

P. heterophyllum. A native of China, it is a plant of somewhat loose habit growing 1.8 m (6 ft) tall with small crinkled leaves and in June bears tiny flowers of palest yellow which have a delicious aromatic perfume.

P. tenuifolium (syn. *P. mayi).* It is a New Zealand plant and the species most widely grown by florists for its attractive foliage. Its pale-green glossy leaves, attractively waved at the edges, are borne along polished black stems. The variety Silver Queen has soft grey leaves margined with silvery white, and Tricolour has grey leaves suffused with red and silver. It may be used as a sea-coast hedge in favourable districts and clipped like a privet hedge. This should be done in April but then, the deliciously scented dark-purple flowers, borne at the leaf axils in May, will be mostly lost. To enjoy the flowers, clipping should be done only in alternate years.

P. tobira (syn. *P. chinense).* A native of China and Japan, and the most vigorous of the species, it reaches a height of 6 m (20 ft) where it is happy, though usually seen at about half that height. It has also the largest leaves, like those of the laurel, dark green and glossy, whilst in May and June it bears clusters of dainty creamy-white flowers in terminal panicles which scent the air with their heavy orange-like fragrance to a considerable distance.

P. undulatum. A glabrous tree, common in eastern Australia, with lanceolate or oblong leaves and wavy margin (hence its name). The flowers are white (or purple) and are borne in dense terminal clusters. The petals are erect, united near the base. The fruit is a capsule, opening by valves to reveal sticky red angular seeds. The flowers are powerfully scented at night and rely on night moths for their pollination. The flowers are followed by small orange-shaped fruits, hence its Australian name of Mock Orange.

PLAGIANTHUS (Malvaceae—Mallow Family)

A genus of deciduous shrubs or climbing plants, none of which are of sufficient hardiness to withstand any degree of frost for they are native of the tropical forests of South America and of China and Japan. They are also present in New Zealand and Tasmania. One or two species only of this predominantly scentless family which is fertilized by humming-birds have scented flowers. Several species may be grown in warm, sheltered gardens of northern Europe, preferably near the coast, and in a well-drained sandy soil enriched with decayed manure. Owing to the presence of an inner ribbon-like bark (used in rope making) it is known as Ribbon-wood.

Species. *Plagianthus divaricatus.* A plant of salt marshes, it grows 1.8 m (6 ft) in height, with birch-like branches, and is deciduous, with small round leaves serrated at the edges. In June it bears tiny creamy-white tubular flowers which have a powerful honey perfume.

P. pulchellus. It is native of South America and climbs to a height of 3.6 to 4.3 m (12 to 15 ft). It has heart-shaped leaves and bell-shaped flowers of purple-blue which emit a sweet aniseed perfume, like that of hawthorn blossom but without the fishy undertones.

PLANTAGO (Plantain) (Plantaginaceae—Plantain Family)

A genus of about 200 species, five of which are native to the British Isles. They are perennial plants, weeds of grassland and coastal wastelands, with broad leaves deeply ribbed and bearing their flower spikes from the axils of the leaves. In bloom throughout the summer, they are self-pollinated by wind, pollination being assured in that the stamens and stigmas ripen at different times. One species in particular has scented flowers.

Species. *Plantago media.* Native of the British Isles and northern Europe where it grows on waste ground, it produces its leaves in rosette formation above which it bears flower spikes of purple-blue, 2.5 to 5 cm (1 to 2 in) long and sweetly scented. It is mentioned in John Gent's *New England's Rarities Discovered* (1672) as being one of the plants introduced into America (with the dandelion) and which would survive climatic conditions.

PLATANTHERA (Orchidaceae—Orchid Family)

A genus of orchids with tapering tubers, the stem arising from two sheath-like leaves. The sessile flowers are hooded and the lip spurred.

Species. *Plantanthera bifolia.* The Lesser Butterfly orchid, it is a perennial plant native of the British Isles and the Mediterranean shores of southern Europe. It blooms in July and August, bearing open spikes of long spurred white flowers tinted with green which diffuse a most seductive perfume at night, likened to that of some tropical epiphytes calling the long-tongued Night Hawk-moth for their pollination. From between two glossy leaves, a slender stem arises to a height of about 30 cm (12 in). The flowers have spreading sepals (like a butterfly) and a slender spur. Gerard said the species grew on Hampstead Heath and 'at a village called Highgate, near London'. It enjoys an open situation and is usually found in damp pastures.

P. chlorantha. Native of the British Isles (and of the Mediterranean coastal regions) where it inhabits the edges of damp copses and woodlands, it is known as the Greater Butterfly orchid and bears its flowers in a loose spike which arises from two basal leaves. The flowers are greenish-white with the sepals widely spreading and with a small slender spur. The flowers diffuse a heavy musk-like perfume.

Like *P. bifolia* it is an accommodating plant, growing well in shade and in any type of soil.

PLATYSTEMON (Papaveraceae—Poppy Family)

A small genus to be found only in Pacific North America where it is known as the Californian poppy.

Species. *Platystemon californicus.* A hardy annual, growing 30 cm (12 in) tall with narrow leaves, and it blooms from June until August. The flowers are pale yellow, held on elongated stalks and consist of 3 sepals, 6 petals and several whorls of stamens. They have a delicate sweet perfume.

Plants may be raised from seed sown in September or early in spring where they are to bloom.

PLECTRANTHUS (Labiatae—Lavender Family)

A genus of about 250 species, native to India, Australia and South-east Asia with aromatic foliage. They require cool greenhouse cultivation in northern Europe and can be increased by cuttings taken in spring and placed in a gently heated frame.

Species. *Plectranthus aromaticus.* A tender perennial labiate of the Moluccas, which is cultivated in gardens throughout India and the East for the refreshing scent of its foliage. It has a succulent stem and grows 60 cm (2 ft) tall, with thick fleshy leaves 7 cm (3 in) long and the same in width, with hairs on the upper surface surmounted by a globular, transparent gland, like a tiny dew-drop. On the under surface, the hairs are so dense as to give rise to a frosted appearance. It is from the hair glands that the resinous perfume is released. The flowers are violet-blue, with a broad upper lip and the lower one long and projecting. They are not scented.

PLEIOSPILOS (Aizoaceae—Aizoon Family)

A genus of 38 species, native to Cape Province and having the appearance of fragments of stone less than 1 cm ($\frac{1}{4}$ in) thick. It takes its name from the Greek *pleios*, full, and *spilos*, dots, for the 'stones' are covered with reddish-brown dots.

Species. *Pleiospilos simulans.* Two pairs of leaves are formed, one above the other and at right angles each pair being 7.5 cm (3 in) long. They are reddish-yellow, dotted with red and resemble pieces of chipped sandstone. The flowers measure 7.5 cm (3 in) across and are yellow, borne on short stems, and they have a heavy jonquil-like perfume.

PLUMBAGO (Plumbaginaceae—Plumbago Family)

A genus comprising 10 species of mostly perennial plants, only one, a climber, bearing scented flowers.

Species. *Plumbago capensis.* It is a native of South Africa and is one of the few true blue-flowering plants to emit a powerful scent. It is a tender perennial which, in all but the most sheltered parts of the British Isles, should be given greenhouse or sun room protection. Readily raised from seed, it will quickly climb over wires suspended across a glass roof, bearing throughout summer masses of fragrant flowers of azure-blue, enhanced by the attractive pale-green foliage. The plant will continue to make healthy growth if all dead wood is removed in spring and if given an occasional feed with dilute liquid manure in summer.

By confining its roots in a small pot, the plant will remain dwarf and bushy and will make a pleasing house plant.

PLUMERIA (Apocynaceae—Periwinkle Family)

A small genus of ornamental trees or shrubs, native of the tropical regions of Mexico and Guiana and the islands of the West Indies. It was named by Tournefort after the Franciscan monk and French botanist, Charles Plumier (1664–1706). The plants have alternate fleshy leaves which grow in tufts at the end of the branches and from which grow upright clusters of funnel-shaped blooms; these distil at night an almost overpowering perfume likened to that made up by the Italian nobleman Frangipani and his family during the Renaissance, from which the plants take their name in commerce.

Species. *Plumeria acutifolia.* It is native of Mexico, Guatemala and the West Indies; though widely distributed in China, Burma and Cambodia, it is not indigenous to these countries but is so common because it was planted near every shrine and temple by Mohammedans and Buddhists alike. Not only is it held in reverence for the delicious scent of its blossom but because it blooms throughout the year, letting fall its creamy-white petals upon the graves of the departed, and they retain their perfume long after they have settled on the ground. The Pagoda tree, as it is called, is also held in regard as a symbol of immortality for it will continue to bloom even if removed from the ground.

P. acutifolia makes a crooked tree some 6 m (20 ft) tall with knotty branches and has grey bark covered with scales, which when cut yields a white viscid juice. The leaves are about 30 cm (12 in) long and taper at both ends with the veins running parallel with the midrib to the leaf edge. The flowers are borne in upright clusters of 12 to 20 and are funnel-shaped with 5 spreading petals of waxy-white, tinted with pink on the outside and with a conspicuous yellow throat.

P. alba. Native of Puerto Rico and Martinique, it is the White frangipani; in Sanskrit, *Kananakaravira.* It grows about 4.5 m (15 ft) tall and has brittle leaves 30 cm (12 in) long which curl inwards at the margins. The flowers are pure white, the corolla having a long incurved tube and oblong oblique segments, and possess the fragrance of jasmine.

Jacquin in his *Stirpium Americanarum Historia,* mentions a scentless form of *P. alba* which grows only 2.4 m. (8 ft) tall and is rarely seen.

P. bicolor. It is native of Peru and is the most vigorous species, attaining a height of 12 m (40 ft), the long lanceolate leaves having flat edges and downy on the underside. The flowers are white with a yellow throat and green tube and are borne in panicles throughout the year. Their scent is like that of the jonquil or tuberose, being especially pronounced at night.

P. pudica. Native of central South America, it makes a sparse shrub 1.5 m (5 ft) tall and has flat oblong leaves. It blooms for about 10 weeks, the flowers being pale yellow and considered by many to have a more pleasing perfume than any other flower.

P. purpurea. It is widely planted in gardens in Peru where it makes a tree 6 m (20 ft) tall with oblong ovate leaves. The flowers are borne in terminal cymes, and are reddish-purple with a yellow hairy throat and are smaller than those of other species. They have the scent of white jasmine and are used by women of Peru to decorate their hair in the evening.

P. incarnata, bearing pale-pink flowers of sweet perfume is a variety of *P. purpurea.*

P. rubra. It is the true Frangipani and is less vigorous than the Pagoda tree, rarely exceeding a height of 5.4 m (18 ft). It is native of Mexico, Ecuador, Jamaica and Martinique where it is known as Red Jasmine, the women adorning themselves with the reddish flowers which they also place amongst linen and clothes for the flowers retain their perfume long after they are dry.

The leaves are oblong, acute and with long downy peduncles. The flowers are borne in erect clusters and are held on red stalks. The petals are oval and crimson-red, yellow at the centre, and emit a delicious jasmine-like perfume which is less heavy than that of the Pagoda tree and which the Indian people call Sambac.

PODALYRIA (Leguminosae—Laburnum Family)

A genus of 25 species of shrubs, native of South Africa and named after Podalyrius, son of Aesculapius. They inhabit the hillsides where they grow 1.2 to 1.5 m (4 to 5 ft) tall, the young branches and leaves being covered in silky hairs to give a silvery appearance. The flowers are pink or white, and have a standard which is broad and notched.

Species. *Podalyria calyptrata.* It forms a dense robust shrub which in its native land blooms from early July until September. The leaves are obovate, pubescent on both sides, whilst the flowers are pink or blush-white and are borne on short axillary branchlets. The standard is broader than it is long. The flowers have the delicious sweet-pea scent of the family. They can be grown in a cool greenhouse in Britain in a sandy compost, and increased by seed; cuttings will also root if placed under a hand light with heat.

PODOCARPUS (Podocarpaceae— Podocarpus Family)

A large genus of evergreen trees closely allied to the Yew but native of South-east Asia, South Africa, Australasia and the Chilean Andes. *P. andinus* bears large edible fragrant fruits, in shape like a grape and in which the seed is covered by a fleshy pulp.

Species. *Podocarpus andinus* (syn. *Prumnopitys elegans*). It is a graceful tree, native of the Chilean Andes where it grows to 15 m (50 ft) in height and is furnished with bright brown-barked branches which sweep to the ground. The leaves are borne in two rows and are deep green above, glaucous on the underside. From its large fragrant fruits, it is known as the Plumfruited yew for it resembles the English yew although its foliage is of brighter hue. It is also resinous whereas the Yew is not and it is said that its fruit is edible whereas that of the Yew is poisonous. The tree grows well in a sandy loam to which some peat has been incorporated.

POGOSTEMON (Labiatae—Lavender Family)

A genus of 40 species of perennial herbs, native to India and South-east Asia, which is believed to have originated in Bengal.

Species. *Pogostemon heyneanus* (syn. *P. patchouli*). An Indian labiate, in appearance much like Balm, from which the perfume known as patchouli is made. To some people it has an agreeable scent, but to others it is most disagreeable. Patchouli reached Britain in 1850, on shawls made in India. It has a smell resembling goats in adulterated form but the otto, mixed with otto of rose and dissolved in rectified spirit, produces a pleasing perfume. It was used to scent linen, whilst in the East the leaves are dried and powdered and placed in muslin bags to be used amongst clothes and linen. The leaves were also used in pot-pourris. One hundredweight of leaves will produce about 1 kg (28 oz) of otto, dark brown in colour, and resembling that of santalwood. Its odour equals in strength that obtained from roses and is the most powerful of any derived from the botanic kingdom.

Cultivation in northern Europe requires the use of a warm or stove house, with a peaty compost. Spring cuttings of semi-hardwood will root in a close frame.

POLIANTHES (Amaryllidaceae—Narcissus Family)

A genus of a single species, native of Mexico and possibly the most powerfully scented of all flowers.

Species. *Polianthes tuberosa.* It is Shelley's 'sweet tuberose, the sweetest flower for scent that blows'. Its perfume is almost intoxicating, especially where grown under glass in gentle heat when it is heavy and sickly almost to the point of unpleasantness. It is not suitable for wintering outside in the British Isles but will flower in the garden in August if potted early in spring and planted out early June. The tuberous roots (bulbs) may be lifted towards the end of September and stored in boxes of sand or peat, like dahlias, to be potted and grown on indoors until ready for planting out again when ground frosts are no longer troublesome.

From the tubers arise linear leaves of brightest green, spotted on the underside with purple, and the flower spikes reach a height of nearly 90 cm (3 ft), with a terminal raceme of pure-white funnel-shaped flowers, wax-like and opening flat like stars. The double variety the Pearl has greater beauty and even more pronounced fragrance than the single form.

The compost should be a fibrous loam, enriched with decayed manure and some silver sand, whilst the plants require copious amounts of moisture when starting into growth.

POLYGONATUM (Liliaceae—Lily Family)

A genus of 50 or more species of herbaceous plants with fleshy creeping rootstocks and with linear verticillate leaves, produced in the form of a ladder, hence the name Ladder-to-heaven given by countrymen to the Common Solomon's seal. There is a general belief that the name 'seal' was given to the plant because of the markings of the fleshy stems which, when cut transversely, show the impression of Solomon's seal, but much more credible is the theory of Dioscorides that the roots of the plant when dried and pounded and laid on wounds of the flesh, healed (or sealed) them in the quickest possible time. A medical author of Elizabeth I's time wrote that 'the roots of Solomon's Seal, stamped whilst fresh and green and applied, taketh away in one night, any bruise, black or blew spots gotten by falls or woman's wilfulness in stumbling upon their hasty husband's fists'. From the ancient name Solomon's heal, it became with the passing of time, Solomon's seal.

Only one species has any degree of perfume, *P. odoratum*, whose fragrant flowers have been described by Miss Sinclair Rohde as having 'a curious rich "thick" smell, quite unlike that of any other English Flower'; it is indeed heavy, like the scent of the tuberose, but more agreeable.

Species. *Polygonatum odoratum.* Native of the British Isles it is the Angular Solomon's seal, so called on account of its angular stems. Its white sweetly scented flowers are borne 1 or 2 to a stem, during June and July. It grows well in semi-shade.

PONCIRUS (Rutaceae—Rue Family)

A genus of a single species.

Species. *Poncirus trifoliata.* It is the Japanese Bitter Orange, native of China and Japan, also known as *Aegle septaria* or *Citrus trifoliata.* It is a wonderful plant for a hedge in the more favourable areas and does particularly well close to the sea. It makes a thick bush some 1.8 to 2.1 m (6 to 7 ft) high and is armed with sturdy spines. It has bright-green stems and in April and May bears large white flowers, like orange-blossom, which appear at the axils of the spines before the leaves. They are deliciously scented. To ensure a display of bloom each year, the plants should be clipped into shape shortly after flowering and they should not be touched for another year.

The plants require a position of full sun and grow well in a chalk-laden soil. In the more favourable districts they will bear small orange-like fruits when established, and though they are too bitter to eat raw they make a delicious conserve and wine, for which purpose they are much in demand in China and Japan.

POPPY: *see* PAPAVER

POPULUS (Salicaceae—Willow Family)

A genus of 35 species distributed throughout northern Europe and America, several of which have scented foliage and fragrant resin covering the buds.

Of the Black poplar Matthiolus wrote: 'the young buds are much used by women to beautify their hair, brushing them with fresh butter and straining them after they have been kept for some time in the sun. The ointment called Populin is singularly good for ... inflammations of any part of the body'. The tall-growing Lombardy is a variety of the Black poplar, known in Britain from earliest times and of which Culpeper wrote in his *Herbal* of 1653: 'The clammy buds hereof, before they spread into leaves are gathered to make Unguantum Populneum ...' The old herbalists extolled the virtues of the leaves of the Black poplar as a suitable cure for gout and Henry Phillips has written that 'the buds of both the White and Black Poplar have an agreeable perfume early in spring and when pressed between the fingers yield a balsamic resinous substance which extracted by spirits of wine smells like storax'.

The Balsam poplars of North America and Siberia are even more powerfully fragrant and should be in every garden where space permits for they make pyramidal trees of slender, branching habit and may be clipped or pruned to keep them within bounds. In Siberia, a medicated wine is made from the buds of the Balsam poplar, whilst game birds feeding on the buds during winter acquire a unique flavour much appreciated by epicures. With the Balsam poplars may be planted the variety of White poplar known as Aurora, its young leaves being creamy-white tinted with salmon, a good contrast with the dark narrow foliage of the Balsam poplar though it is not scented.

Species and Varieties. *Populus alba.* The White poplar. it forms a widely branched tree with maple-shaped leaves, grey-green in colour and with glistening white down on the underside. It grows well in shallow soils when the buds will be most resinous whilst it is especially valuable for an exposed coastal garden.

P. balsamifera (syn. *P. tacamahaca*). Known as the Tacamahac or Balsam poplar, it has given its name to a resin extracted from the tree which was first introduced into Britain in 1692. The smooth leaves taper to a point and have hairy footstalks, and they have the pleasing fragrance of balsam. The buds release the same pungent scent when held over a light and are covered with a resin which is so sticky that it may have to be removed from the hands with turpentine. The delicious scent will be wafted about the garden on a warm summer day.

P. candicans. The Ontario poplar or Balm of Gilead which makes a broad-headed tree with leaves larger than those of the Balsam poplar but having the same balsam-like odour which is especially pronounced as they unfold.

P. nigra. The Black Italian poplar with greenish-white foliage, downy when young and retaining the resinous scent observed in the buds. Growing to a height of 15 m (50 ft), it lives to a great age, trees still standing known to be more than 600 years old. The form *betulifolia,* the Manchester poplar, is a pleasing bushy-headed variety which does well in a town garden. An oil of pleasant balsamic odour is obtained by aqueous distillation of the leaf-buds.

P. simonii fastigiata. A slender-growing Chinese species attaining a height of 12 m (40 ft) in Britain. It has attractive red-dish-brown twigs and small leaves of brightest green which emit a powerful smell of balsam as they unfold.

P. trichocarpa. It makes a tall pyramidal tree and has dark, narrow foliage smelling strongly of balsam. It is valuable to use as a hedge or screen for it comes early into leaf and retains its leaves longer than any deciduous tree. A hybrid of *P. angulata cordata* and *P. trichocarpa, P. generosa* raised at Kew in 1912 is one of the fastest-growing of all trees, a growth of 1.5 to 3 m (5 to 10 ft) in a season being not unusual. It makes a tall pyramid-shaped tree, its buds covered in scented resin and opening to large leaves which are some 30 cm (12 in) long and turn gold when about to fall.

POSOQUERIA (Rubiaceae—Bedstraw Family)

A small genus of tropical evergreen plants of shrubby habit and indigenous to Guyana. They bear handsome bell-shaped flowers, similar to those of the stephanotis and with an equally delicious perfume. Away from their native haunts, the plants require a winter temperature of about 15°C (60°F) at night and tolerate con-siderably higher temperatures during summer but must have ample moisture at the roots. They grow well in fibrous peat to which sand has been incorporated and to encourage a bushy habit, the shoots should be pinched back when 7.5 to 10 cm (3 to 4 in) long.

Species. *Posoqueria fragrans* (syn. *Griffithia fragrans).* The large bell-shaped flowers are of purest white, enhanced by the glossy leaves, and at night they diffuse the powerful fragrance of the tuberose. The abundant honey to be found at the base of the tube can be reached only by nocturnal Hawk-moths which have a proboscis 37.5 cm (15 in) long. Fritz Müller observed that the 5 exserted anthers of the flower are united into a knob directed downwards and containing pollen which escaped from the anthers before the opening of the flower. The stamens have considerable tension which is released in an upwards and sideways direction when the moth enters the flowers, covering its proboscis with pollen.

POTERIUM (Burnet) (Rosaceae—Rose Family)

A genus of erect perennial herbs with pinnate leaves and flowers borne in long peduncled cymes. It was widely planted in 'walks' during Elizabethan times, to be trodden upon, with chamomile and thyme. Culpeper says that Burnet was to be found 'near London, by St Pancras Church and . . . in the middle of a field by Paddington'. Turner in his *Herbal* describes it as having 'two little leives like unto the winges of birdes . . . setteth out when she intendeth to flie', a charming description for indeed the small, serrated leaves are borne about 12 to a stem directly opposite each other, exactly like the wings of a bird. They have a pleasant, sweet smell when trodden upon, likened by Parkinson to that of Balm. His reference is to *P. polygamum,* for the Salad burnet, *P. sanguisorba,* releases little or no perfume when trodden upon; instead, its leaves like those of the Borage have a mild cucumber flavour when used in salads. Both Culpeper and Parkinson said that they were used for flavouring claret, giving it a pleasant 'quick' taste, 'to make the heart merry'. From its use, Pliny said the plant obtained its Latin name *poterium,* a drinking cup.

Species. *Poterium officinale (*syn. *Sanguisorba officinalis).* The Great burnet, it is like *P. polygamum* taller-growing with pinnate leaves and leaflets which are distinctly stalked. It bears in July and August cylindrical flowers of purple-brown.

*P. polygamum (*syn. *P. muricatum).* Its leaves have a stronger scent and flavour than the Salad burnet and perfume the air for a great distance when trodden upon, though they do not possess so pleasant a taste. It is taller-growing than *P. sanguisorba* and if not grazed will reach a height of nearly 90 cm (3 ft). Treading will, however, keep it low.

P. sanguisorba. The Salad burnet, rarely exceeding 30 cm (12 in) in height, the young leaves borne in about 10 pairs and coarsely serrated, imparting a cool cucumber-like flavour to salads and drinks.

PRESILIA (Labiatae—Lavender Family)

A genus of a single species.

Species. *Presilia cervina.* Native of southwestern Europe, it is happiest in a moist soil and so may be planted by the waterside. It is a plant of almost prostrate habit, with aromatic foliage and bears dense whorls of lavender-blue flowers on 30-cm (1 ft) stems, in June and July. It was once considered to be part of the *Mentha* genus, and is increased by division.

PRIMULA (Primulaceae—Primrose Family)

A genus of more than 500 species mostly confined to the Northern Hemisphere where they grow in valleys and upon hilly ground. The long tube of the flowers adapts them for pollination by bees and butterflies. Many species and varieties are amongst the most richly coloured of all flowers with outstanding perfume. They require cool conditions for their culture.

Species and Varieties. *Primula anisodora.* A candelabra primula of great beauty. A native of Yunnan, it requires a damp soil and partial shade. It forms large tufts of glabrous leaves and bears its purple-black flowers in tiers, on scapes 37.5 cm (15 in) tall. The flowers emit a cowslip-like fragrance.

P. alpicola. Discovered by Capt. Kingdon-Ward in Tibet in 1932, it requires similar conditions as *P. involucrata,* plenty of summer moisture but good drainage during winter and some shade from the heat of the summer sun. With its large leaves it is more suited to the woodland garden where it is delightful planted in groups of three or four. In summer, its sweetly-scented flowers of palest yellow are borne in umbels at the end of scapes about 37.5 cm (15 in) long.

The variety Luna bears flowers of pale moonlight-yellow whilst *alba* bears ivory-white flowers. Both are scented and like the type are covered in farina.

P. apoclita. Native of the alpine meadows of Tibet and Yunnan, it forms tiny rosettes from which arise on a 15-cm (6-in) stem covered in yellow farina, small heads of violet-purple flowers which are as richly scented as *P. pubescens.* The plants resemble *P. denticulata* in that they die back during winter. It requires a well-drained, sandy soil enriched with peat but even with the best of care the plant is usually short-lived.

P. auricula. It is one of the loveliest of alpine plants but is rarely seen in gardens. It grows from the Pyrenees to the Alps and the Carpathians, usually with its roots between the rocks, cool and moist, but with its head in the sunlight, exactly the same conditions required by the garden auriculas of which it is the parent. It forms a stout trunk and carrot-like rootstock from which grow the hairy roots. The leaves are round and leathery and above them it bears in spring on 10-cm (4-in) stems sweetly scented flowers of bright golden-yellow. All parts of the plant are covered with farina, like flour, a characteristic it has passed on to many of the derivative Show and Border auriculas (though not the Alpines), whilst it has given all of them its sweet honey perfume.

SHOW AURICULA. With their mealy stems and leaves and the paste-like centre of the flowers, the deliciously scented Show auriculas are usually grown in pots and flowered under glass. They are divided into three groups: (*a*) the Edged varieties, (*b*) the Self colours, and (*c*) the Fancies. Each has a paste centre which should be protected from rain as the blooms expand, but it must be remembered that all are plants descended from species of the Austrian Alps and have the same hardy qualities, though by continually being confined to pots they may have lost some vigour.

Whilst all plants grouped as the Show auriculas have the unique paste centre, not all have the interesting edging or outer zone colour which may be green, grey or white and which is made up of thousands of minute hairs; these, when seen through a microscope, are structurally identical with those to be found on the mealy leaves of the Border auricula. It is the result of mutation, that portion of the petals having been replaced by leaf structures. The degree of mealiness determines the colour of the edging. All the 'Edged' auriculas are really green in colour but the density of the hairs changes the colour either to grey or white. At the end of each hair is a tiny globe from which scented wax or resin is secreted, the denser the concentration the whiter the appearance. Sir Roland Biffen has shown that the hairs may be of various sizes, those at the centre being extremely small and so concentrated as to give a paste-like appearance. With the Border auriculas, the hairs are less dense and give a delightful frosted effect as also with the grey and white-edged Show varieties, all parts of which are covered with meal, whereas in the green-edged varieties the foliage of flower stems is entirely devoid of meal. It is of interest that the amount of meal determines the size of the bloom: the green-edged, free of meal, bear the largest blooms; next in size are the grey, and the white the smallest.

Both the Edged and Show varieties possess the same paste centre which distinguishes the Show auriculas from the white-centred Alpines and is present in no other flower. The body colour of the bloom may be black, dark brown, crimson or dark violet, so dark in colour as to be indistinguishable from black.

The colouring of the Selfs may be divided into two groups, those which follow the parent *P. auricula* and produce yellow flowers, varying in intensity from palest primrose to golden-bronze;. and those derived from *P. hirsuta,* which range from mid-blue to crimson-black. This is owing to the presence of a pigment known as hirsutin which is of a rose-pink colour but changes to crimson if in contact with acid and to mid-blue if treated with an alkali. Varying degrees of acidity and

alkalinity in the cell sap brought about a variation on pigment colouring. In the Shows the colouring is uniform whereas in the Alpines it is not, though both are free from meal.

In the Fancies, the green edging often continues to the paste centre and the flower is entirely free of any ground colour. With others, there may be a scarlet or yellow ground colour. Thus, the Fancies fall somewhere between the green-edged and Selfs. They have now, however, completely disappeared.

a) Edged Varieties.

Green-edged. BROCKENHURST. One of the late Mr C. Haysom's best introductions. It forms a truss of 6 or 7 'pips' which open together. Each has 6 nicely rounded petals with an edging of brilliant green.

GREEN WOODPECKER. It may be expected to open 7 pips to a truss and each bloom has 9 petals to give them a circular appearance. With its round tube, dense paste and wide green edging, this variety would attain perfection except for the odd petal to be pointed.

LANGDOWN. Raised by the late C. Haysom, it forms a large truss with the blooms having dense paste and black body colour with dark-green edging and beautifully rounded petals.

Grey-edged. LOVEBIRD. The best of James Douglas's 'greys' and though the blooms are smaller than in most greys, the paste, body colour and edging are evenly defined.

SHERFIELD. A Cyril Haysom introduction with a beautifully defined tube whilst the bloom is so densely mealed as to come almost into the white-edged category.

GEORGE LIGHTBODY. Introduced in 1857, it is considered by many auricula fanciers to be the finest variety ever raised. It remained supreme on the show bench for 100 years, winning Premier Award at the Northern Auricula Society's Show in 1957. With its smooth paste, jet-black ground colour and beautifully mealed edging, it achieved perfection in the Show auricula.

White-edged. DOROTHY MIDGELEY.Raised by Mr J. W. Midgeley, the 'pip' is large with the 7 petals overlapping to provide a beautifully rounded bloom with the truss numbering 5 to 8 pips.

WILVERLEY. One of the easiest of the Shows to manage, with a perfectly rounded tube, dense paste and black body colour, whilst the heavily mealed petals are nicely rounded.

b) Self Colours

ALICE HAYSOM. The tube is of brilliant gold and is perfectly round with vivid scarlet ground colouring.

HARRISON WEIR. Raised by the late James Douglas at Edenside, it has remained the premier scarlet Self for 70 years. The paste is smooth and clearly defined.

MARY WINN. Raised by Mr Tom Shepherd, it bears a beautifully rounded 'pip' with the paste smooth and regular and with ground colouring of deep primrose-yellow, like its parent, the well named Daffodil.

ALPINE AURICULA. James Douglas, in a lecture given to the members of the Royal Horticultural Society in 1934 said 'The Alpine auricula, devoid as it is of even a suspicion of farina on foliage of flower (when compared with the Show auricula), conveys an appealing sense of distinction'. Perhaps this distinct and beautiful old garden plant really owed its origin to *Primula pubescens* and not to *P. auricula* as generally supposed. It would appear that the Alpine auricula is the result of crossing *P. hirsuta* back to *P. pubescens*, itself a cross between *P. auricula* and *P. hirsuta*, which, though a hybrid, is very fertile; for though the honey perfume of *P. auricula* has been retained, the plants are entirely free from farina (meal) and have taken on the sumptuous shades of blue and crimson to be obtained in varieties of *P. pubescens*.

A natural hybrid, *P. pubescens* was found growing near Innsbruck by the Austrian botanist Kerner, in 1875, and this confirms the description of the plant given three centuries earlier by Clusius, Court botanist to the Emperor Maximilian II, in his *Rariorum Plantarum Historia*, both as to its habit and the fact that it grew wild on certain mountains of the Austrian Alps. Two forms were grown by Clusius in 1575, *P. auricula* and *P. pubescens*, and possibly also *P. hirsuta* which was to be found in the same district. The plant we now know as *P. auricula* was called *Sanicula alpina* by Clusius. This later became *Auricula ursi*, or Bear's Ear from the shape of the leaf and its mealy (hairy) covering. As with *P. pubescens*, the Alpine auriculas may be divided into two groups, those having a white centre and those having one of yellow or gold.

The Mountain cowslips or Bear's Ears first reached England about 1575, brought by the Huguenot refugees fleeing from the massacres in France, and understandably the plants quickly became popular. They had become so widely grown by the end of the century that John Gerard gave a detailed and lengthy account of them in his *Herbal* (1597); thirty years later Parkinson described 21 varieties, and whereas the illustrations in his *Paradisus* showed plants with 12 or more pips (blooms) to a truss, those illustrated in the *Herbal* had shown them with less than half that number, so there had been considerable progress in their breeding. By 1659, Sir Thomas Hanmer, an ardent supporter of Charles I, had 40 varieties growing in his garden in Wales, for the Alpine auricula was and is still a vigorous hardy plant, happiest under cold conditions. It has remained neglected only because it is usually considered to require the same conditions as the Show auriculas which with their paste-like centre need to be brought into bloom under glass, to protect the 'paste' from being washed on to the ground colour by heavy rain. Both the Show and Alpine auriculas are as completely hardy as the hybrids known as the Border auriculas for they are all plants of the Austrian Alps where bitterly cold conditions are experienced. When the Alpine auricula took on the amazing structural change of its petals, about 1750, it came to be grown in pots and was regrouped as the Show auricula. So remarkable were these plants that those which had not taken on this structural change, the pure Alpines, or 'pures' as they were called, quickly became neglected. But for the interest taken in the Alpines by Charles Turner, introducer of Cox's Orange Pippin, in the years 1850-70, they would almost certainly have passed out of cultivation. The House of Douglas took over from where Turner left off, raising many magnificent new varieties and in general improving the alpines as to size and quality of bloom. They remain amongst the most beautiful of all flowers, with petals thick and velvety and with those rich colourings only to be seen in velvet material. Like all scented flowers with thick petals, the perfume they release is more pronounced and more lasting than that of other flowers. In this case, it is the same honeysuckle fragrance as the *P. pubescens* hybrids and the old Border auriculas.

The Alpines may be used in the rock garden but they should be given a position behind a stone, preferably facing north, where they will be protected from the midday sun. They should also be used at the base of the rockery as they are moisture lovers. They are perhaps more easily managed if planted to the front of the border for they grow 22.5 cm (9 in) tall. They require a well-nourished soil containing peat or leaf-mould and should never be allowed to lack moisture.

They are readily propagated by removing the offsets after flowering, or in autumn or spring, but as the plants form a woody, carrot-like rootstock, they should be handled with greater care than most plants.

The blooms have a yellow 'eye' or tube around which is a wide centre or circle of either white or gold; then comes the deep ground colour which shades out to the circular edge of the petals, to present a picture of symmetrical beauty and in addition they have a deliciously sweet honeysuckle perfume, which becomes almost overpowering when the plants are growing in pots in a shaded greenhouse. They bloom during April and May and often into June.

a) Gold-Centred Varieties.

BASUTO. A most striking variety, the large refined blooms being of rich crimson-maroon shading to wine.

BOOKHAM BEAUTY. The beautifully formed blooms make up a large rounded truss and are a striking shade of deep orange-rust, shading to pure orange.

BOOKHAM FIREFLY. Though introduced in 1913, it still remains an exhibitor's favourite for its clear and finely proportioned centre whilst the deep glowing crimson shades out to maroon.

CAROLINA. A plant of vigorous constitution, the colour is deep crimson shading to apricot-bronze.

CICERO. It makes a large truss and is of robust habit. The rich velvety maroon ground colour shades out to crimson-red.

CLOTH OF GOLD. It is a vigorous grower and bears a truss of great beauty. The rich old-gold ground colour shades to pure golden-yellow.

DORIS PARKER. It makes a large truss of medium-sized blooms of exhibition form with ground colour of deepest crimson shading to flame.

DOWNTON. Raised by the late C. G. Haysom, it is in every way a superb variety of ideal exhibition form, with the crimson ground colour shading to buff.

FRANK FAULKNER. Named after its raiser, it is a recent introduction of perfect exhibition form and with blooms of velvet-like texture. The crimson ground colour shades to maroon.

GOLDEN GLEAM. One of the best of the gold-centred Alpines with sturdy footstalks and well-placed 'pips'. The rich golden-yellow ground shades out to mahogany bronze.

KINGCUP. Raised by the late C. G. Haysom, it is an exhibitor's favourite with large well-formed 'pips' of crimson-maroon shading out to medium brown.

LADY DAMASK. A beginner's Alpine, easy to propagate and to manage. The well-shaped blooms make up a large truss and are of deep maroon shading to pale red.

MIDAS. It makes a large truss and is of unique colouring, the ground colour being almost that of medium-brown ale, shading out to golden-bronze.

PRINCE JOHN. One of the best, the centre being larger than in most varieties, whilst the ground colour is of deepest maroon with almost complete lack of shading.

SPARKLE. A magnificent House of Douglas introduction, both tube and centre being almost perfect, whilst the body colour is of rich golden-bronze, shading to pure gold.

b) White- or Cream-centred Varieties.

ARGUS. It was raised by the late J. J. Keen at Southampton (where the late C. G. Haysom had his nursery) as long ago as 1895, and still earns more awards on the show-bench than any other variety. It forms a large truss with the body colour of rich plum-red shading to pale crimson-red.

BLUE BONNET. Of sturdy constitution, it is easy to grow and to propagate. The pure-white centre is clearly defined whilst the ground colour is deep violet-blue shading to mid-blue.

BOOKHAM GLORY. Carrying the well-known House of Douglas prefix, it forms a truss of exhibition quality with the royal-purple body colour shading to pale mauve.

GORDON DOUGLAS. The hardiest, best-known and most easily managed of all Alpine auriculas. It is also the most fragrant with its creamy-white centre and ground colour of violet-blue.

JOY. Raised by Mr Percy Johnson at Altrincham, it is the premier Alpine in its section, the rich velvety crimson ground colour being so delicately shaded that it has the appearance of a Show self.

KATHLEEN. A House of Douglas introduction, the 'pips' are large with as many as 12 forming the truss. The colour is rich purple-blue shading to paler blue and with a powerful fragrance.

LADY DARESBURY. One of the best Alpines of its section ever raised, introduced by Mr C. Faulkner of Hale in Cheshire in 1950. The 'pips' are of exquisite form and make up a large truss whilst the colour is deep wine-red shading to pale cerise.

LUCRECE. A variety of sturdy habit, forming a large well-shaped truss. The centre is large and clearly defined whilst the ground colour is an unusual shade of plum-purple shading to purple-blue.

MRS HEARN. An auricula that should be in every garden if only for its almost overpowering honeysuckle perfume. The centre is pale cream whilst the

body colour is blue-grey, shading to pure Cambridge blue.

PINK LADY. Different in that its blooms are an attractive wine-pink, shading to soft rose-pink, and they make up an effective truss.

SEARCHLIGHT. A variety of considerable beauty with a clearly defined cream centre, with a body colour of purple-plum shading to purple-blue.

SPRING MORNING. A variety of vigorous habit, it makes a well-shaped truss with the body colour an attractive rose-pink shading to deep rose-red.

BORDER AURICULA. A race of plants descended from *Primula auricula* and *P. pubescens* and differing from the Alpine auriculas in that their foliage and bloom are covered with farina; they are known as hardy Border auriculas. With them, however, must be included several which are entirely free from farina but which, with their vigorous coarse habit, cannot be classed with the more refined Alpines. They are plants of great antiquity and with their hardy constitution, freedom of flowering, rich 'old master' colouring and exotic fragrance, are amongst the loveliest of all plants ever to reach this country. They bloom from mid-April until mid-June, and so powerful is their scent that quite a small bed of mixed plants is almost overpowering when the early summer sun shines down upon them. They are plants which, like the honeysuckle their perfume so much resembles, give off their richest scent only when warm.

Since their introduction in about 1575, these lovely auriculas have come to be cherished in garden of cottage and manor alike. They grow in the gardens of lovely Hardwick Hall in Derbyshire, which was built the very year of their introduction, and they may well have been growing there since tha. time. Auriculas also grow in the tiny garden of Shakespeare's boyhood home in Stratford-upon-Avon. They are flowers beloved by one and all and they have been with us for more than four centuries. Never having been grown in pots under glass, the old Border auriculas have never lost their vigour, and as long as they have a sunny situation and a soil which does not readily dry out during summer they will prove adaptable to almost every garden, quickly growing into large vigorous clumps above which they bear, on 22.5-cm (9-in) stems, irregular heads of large velvety blooms. This irregularity adds to their old-world charm. There is nothing stiff about them and when cut and placed in small vases indoors, they will remain fresh for days and scent the house with their warm sweet honey fragrance. They are lovely planted with the scented Darwin and Cottage tulips for they bloom at the same time, and with their grey-green leaves, serrated at the edges, they will provide pleasing ground cover in addition to their richly coloured flowers, equal to the tulips in intensity. The following varieties, of unknown origin but mostly of *P. auricula* influence, have been handed down through the centuries and are still fortunately with us for safe-keeping. They should be planted in the spring or in autumn.

ADAM LORD. A variety of sturdy habit with serrated foliage which forms into numerous rosettes about which in large trusses appear the navy-blue flowers with their creamy-white centre.

AMETHYST. It forms a large truss of bright wine-purple flowers with a clearly defined white centre and is densely covered in farina.

BLUE MIST. Now rare but an outstanding variety and so well named for the medium-sized blooms are of pure sky-blue with the farina providing a silvery, mist-like sheen.

BLUE VELVET. Of vigorous habit, it forms a symmetrical head of purple-blue flowers with a clearly defined creamy-white centre and emits a rich honey perfume.

BROADWELL GOLD. A superb variety found by Mr Joe Elliott in a Cotswold cottage garden but it is now rare. It bears large blooms of brilliant golden-yellow with beautifully waved petals and they diffuse a musk-like fragrance. All parts of the plant are covered with farina.

CRAIG NORDIE. The flowers are burgundy-red with a golden centre and are almost free of farina, whilst the foliage is grey-green.

GOLDEN QUEEN. It forms a large truss of pale sulphur-yellow flowers with a white centre which carry a rich sweet perfume.

LINNET. An old favourite which now seems to have been lost. It is late into bloom and is well named for the blooms are a combination of green, brown and mustard.

McWATT'S BLUE. Raised by the late Dr McWatt in Scotland, the rich mid-blue flowers with their white centre carry a delicious sweet perfume. The foliage is heavily mealed.

MRS NICHOLLS. A most attractive variety, the pale-yellow blooms have a golden centre around which is a circle of white. The blooms have a pronounced musky perfume.

OLD IRISH BLUE. A most beautiful auricula, with serrated foliage above which it bears large trusses of rich mid-blue. The flowers have a white centre and the perfume is outstanding.

OLD PURPLE DUSTY MILLER. Also known as Blue Dusty Miller but the flowers are really of purple colouring, with pronounced perfume, and are held on 30-cm (12-in) stems. All parts of the plant are heavily mealed.

OLD RED DUSTY MILLER. Of great antiquity, it is so heavily mealed as to appear as if covered in flour. The flower-heads are not large but the colour is unique, being of crimson-brown, wallflower colour, and with a heavy perfume.

OLD SUFFOLK BRONZE. A most interesting variety, quite free from farina, it makes a plant of robust habit and over a period of at least ten weeks bears large trusses of flowers 2.5 cm (1 in) in diameter, and in shades of gold, bronze and buff. The scent is almost intoxicating and can be detected for a considerable distance. The plant was obtained by the author from a garden in Suffolk where it has been growing for centuries.

OLD YELLOW DUSTY MILLER. The powerfully scented blooms are deep golden-yellow whilst all parts are covered in farina.

OSBORNE GREEN. It is interesting in that it appears to contain something of the green-edged Show auriculas for the large coarse flowers are deep purple in colour with a white centre whilst the petals are tipped with green. Like the Old Suffolk Bronze, the bloom is free from meal.

P. carniolica. Native of a tiny area of the Maritime Alps, it is a plant of beauty and interest, closely related to *P. auricula* but requiring almost total shade from the direct rays of the sun. Here, in a moist soil enriched with leaf-mould, it will bear its sweetly scented flowers of pure shell-pink on 15-cm (6-in) stems and they are enhanced by the dark-green glossy leaves. All parts are devoid of farina, which gives the plant a brilliance unknown in any other primula.

P. chionantha. A member of the Nivalis group and the easiest to manage. Discovered by George Forrest in the alpine meadows of Yunnan, it prefers a moist situation. The long narrow leaves are covered in farina and from them arise umbels of creamy-white flowers on stems 60 cm (2 ft) tall. The flowers are sweetly scented.

P. florindae. The Giant primula of Sikkim, discovered by Kingdon-Ward in 1922. It is at its loveliest planted in the bog garden or by the side of water where it will bear clusters of pale-yellow bell-shaped flowers 1.2 to 1.5 cm (4 to 5 ft) tall. The heart-shaped leaves are held on stems 30 cm (12 in) long, so that it is in every way a giant. The flowers are sweetly scented.

P. glutinosa. It grows in damp pockets of decaying vegetable matter in the Austrian Alps and is a difficult primula to cultivate in the garden. It likes to have its roots always moist and its head in the sun. The large purple-blue flowers, borne in May on 7.5-cm (3-in) stems, have a delicious perfume. The leaves, borne in rosettes, are sticky to the touch.

P. hyacinthina. It was discovered by Kingdon-Ward as recently as 1935-6 and in the British Isles tends to be of biennial habit, seeding itself each year after a springtime display of great beauty. It forms neat rosettes of farinose leaves some 15 cm (6 in) long and bears its violet-blue flowers on 30-cm (12-in) stems which are covered in meal. The plant was so named for the rich hyacinth-like perfume of the flowers which are also of hyacinth-blue colouring.

P. involucrata. It is a most beautiful little plant, in bloom throughout the spring. It received an Award of Merit as long ago as 1897 and has retained its popularity ever since. Its dark glossy leaves stand erect and from them arise umbels of glossy white flowers which have a conspicuous golden centre and the delicious sweet honey perfume which is characteristic of the alpine primroses. In the alpine garden it should be given a position where it will receive as much moisture as possible. In spring, it should almost be completely immersed in water and can never receive too much at this time of the year.

P. kewensis. It was raised at Kew and has *P. sinensis*, the Chinese primula, for one parent. In the original form, the stems and leaves are covered in farina whilst the flowers, in shape like those of the oxlip, are of primrose-yellow colouring with a soft, sweet perfume. The variety Real Gold has brilliant-green foliage free from farina and it bears flowers of brilliant gold in an umbel at the top of the scape.

The plant is not hardy in the British Isles but requires the minimum of winter warmth, a temperature of 5°C (42°F) being sufficient to maintain growth. From a sowing of seed made in a frame or unheated greenhouse in April, plants may be brought into bloom before the winter and they will continue to bloom for many weeks, diffusing a delicate perfume in a warm room of the house.

P. luteola. This handsome species is a native of the alpine meadows of the Caucasus, enjoying moisture about its roots but not liking bog conditions. It requires a well-drained soil enriched with leaf-mould and some drainage materials in which moisture will be retained in summer yet will drain away during times of excess. Under such conditions it will present few difficulties in its culture and will bloom early in June when most members of the family have finished flowering.

The blooms, of palest yellow, are borne in circular heads on a 30- to 37.5-cm (12- to 15-in) scape. The plant will quickly form a large clump of lush green leaves some 22.5 to 25 cm (9 to 10 in) long, toothed and tapering like those of *Primula denticulata*. Though the flowers have a slight primrose perfume, it is the leaves which are most fragrant, smelling of ripened apples, cool and satisfying when the days are warm and most pronounced when covered with evening dew.

P. nutans. Native of the woods of Yunnan, it is a difficult plant to place in the garden and is equally difficult to maintain for it is believed to be monocarpic, dying after it has flowered once. It may be grown in the alpine garden or in an orchard, but it requires a well-drained soil or else crown rot will set in during winter. It is best grown in a sand and peat mixture and will survive the winter better if covered with a sheet of glass. For all its fickleness, it is a glorious plant, bearing in July umbels of dangling bells of lavender-blue which are held above neat hairy rosettes. The blooms have a rich sweet perfume.

P. palinuri. Once established, it is a vigorous grower, increasing by means of underground stolons. It requires a rich but well-drained soil and a place where it may receive the maximum of winter sunshine; it will then come into bloom before the end of February, bearing its drooping golden-yellow flowers on a stem 90 cm (3 ft) tall. The blooms are sweetly scented.

P. pubescens. A delightful natural hybrid thought to have *P. auricula* and the scentless *P. hirsuta* for its parents, the former passing on its sweet honey scent whilst the latter has contributed to the large range of rich, velvety colours of the group. Varieties include:

ALBA. A very old form of *P. pubescens,* preferring a cool northerly situation. It will form large, spreading tufts of glossy dark-green leaves above which it bears rounded heads of sweetly scented flowers which are as white as driven snow.

BLAIRSIDE YELLOW. It is a tiny hybrid of *P. auricula,* making rosettes of bright-green leaves with serrated edges above which it bears, on 5-cm (2-in) stems, highly scented flowers of golden-yellow. It is a delightful plant for a trough or sink garden.

BLUE WAVE. Raised at Inshriach Nurseries, it is one of the most exquisite plants of the alpine garden, the blooms being of brightest sky-blue with waved petals and with a large creamy-white centre, whilst their perfume resembles that of warm honeysuckle. Unfortunately it is now rarely to be found.

CHRISTINE. Raised at the Inshriach Nurseries, it is a delightful plant bearing, in profusion, large rounded heads a lovely shade of old rose with a delicious perfume.

COMMODORE. A seedling from Faldenside, it is the earliest to bloom and a beauty, the flowers being of mahogany-red with a yellow centre.

FALDENSIDE. A charming form, raised in Scotland by Dr Boyd of *Saxifraga boydii* fame. The flower-heads are large with attractively waved petals and are of brightest crimson. The scent of the blooms is not so pronounced as in the purple forms.

FREEDOM. It appears to have *P. marginata* blood and is a variety of great beauty, bearing richly scented flowers of bright pansy-purple.

GNOME. A delightful little plant, the last to bloom and well-worth waiting for. The bright crimson-scarlet blooms have a conspicuous golden centre.

ILENE. It remains longer in bloom than any variety, the violet-coloured flowers having a clearly defined white centre.

KINGSCOTE. With Gnome, the latest to bloom and the most outstandingly lovely variety, bearing large heads of glowing cerise flushed with salmon-orange and with a large golden centre. It has a delicious scent.

LADYBIRD. It was raised by Clarence Elliott, the Old Red Dusty Miller border auricula being one of the parents, and the large velvety crimson flowers show a similar 'dusting' which is also present on the leaves. A truly superb plant of dainty habit.

MARLENE. It is the most compact of all the hybrid varieties, growing less than 7.5 cm (3 in) tall and bearing small, dainty heads of deep violet-purple.

MRS J. DOUGLAS. It is a plant of vigorous habit and is free-flowering, the blooms of bright petunia-purple having a large white centre.

MRS J. H. WILSON. A magnificent variety and the most free-flowering of all. The blooms are bright lilac-mauve with a large white centre, and they diffuse a powerful honey perfume.

RUBY. Raised by the late James Douglas, the blooms are brilliant ruby-red with a clearly defined white centre.

RUFUS. A plant of great charm, easy and vigorous, with richly scented flowers of brilliant terracotta with a biscuit-brown eye.

THE CARDINAL. It has now become extremely rare but it is a superb form bearing large trusses of brilliant blood-red with a golden centre.

THE GENERAL. An old and magnificent form bearing large heads of velvet-red, flushed with orange. The plant is of compact habit and most free-flowering.

WHITE PEARL. Of dwarf, compact habit, it bears few but large heads of deliciously scented white flowers flushed with shell-pink.

P. reidii. It was discovered in a damp crevasse 3,900 m (13,000 ft) above sea-level in the Tibetan Himalayas and is a most difficult plant to grow away from its natural environment, for it requires a well-drained soil in winter but ample moisture during summer, the reverse of the usual conditions. It forms rosettes of oblong leaves from which arises, on a 10-cm (4-in) stem, an umbel of pure-white sweetly scented flowers. All parts of the plant are covered in meal.

P. sikkimensis. Native to the countries of Sikkim, Burma and Tibet, it is one of the best of all plants for the woodland garden, revelling in a moist soil and partial shade. It forms a neat tuft of oblong leaves from which arises, on a 90-cm (3-ft) stem, an umbel of dangling bells of moonlight-yellow which are sweetly scented. It blooms in June and is known as the Sikkim cowslip.

P. sinoplantaginea. A delightful little plant of the Nivalis section, requiring a soil that remains damp during summer but is well-drained in winter. It should also be given protection from the heat of the summer sun. It is worthy of a little care in providing its requirements for it will more than repay one with the beauty of its sweetly scented purple flowers which appear during May and June on 15-cm (6-in) stems.

P. veris. The cowslip, one of the loveliest flowers of the British Isles where it grows in meadows situated along the banks of rivers and streams, and it blooms during April and May. It has deeply channelled ovate leaves formed at the crown like those of the primrose, the grooves directing every drop of moisture to the roots. The flowers are borne in umbels of 6 to 8 and they have a bell-shaped calyx and a funnel-shaped corolla of deepest yellow with a small red spot at the base of each petal. When in bud, they stand erect, then as they open, the flowers become pendulous awaiting fertilization and diffuse a sweet fragrance about the countryside. After pollination has taken place they again stand erect and remain in this position whilst ripening the seed.

The perfume of the flower is unlike all other flower scents, being likened by some to the breath of a cow which is represented in Saxon vernacular by the word 'cuslippe'. To others, the smell is similar to the sweet, milky breath of a tiny child.

P. viscosa. It is a charming little plant closely related to P. villosa from which it is distinguished only by the height of its scape which is about 15 cm (6 in) high, twice as much as in P. villosa. It is native of the Swiss Alps and has narrow leaves which are sticky to the feel and it bears its fragrant rosy-purple flowers in small umbels.

The form cynoglossifolia is distinguished from the type only by its smaller leaves whilst its flowers are also scented.

P. vulgaris (syn. P. acaulis). The primrose, a plant of the British Isles and, with the violet, the most beloved of all, mentioned by almost every poet from the time of Chaucer to the present day. It is a plant of extreme hardiness and durability with obovate leaves, deeply channelled and hairy on the underside. It blooms, where protected from cold winds, from the first days of the year and reaches a crescendo of bloom during March and April. The pale yellowish-green flowers are about 2.5 cm (1 in) across and are held on hairy pink stalks about 7.5 cm (3 in) long. The calyx has 5 longitudinal plaits. The blooms have the characteristic fragrance of a mossy bank or of deciduous woodlands and this is where the plants prefer to grow, in partial shade and with their roots always comfortably moist.

Chaucer in The Miller's Tale mentioned the 'Prime-role' and this was the manner in which the name was spelt until the end of the sixteenth century when Shakespeare so often wrote of the flower, usually referring to its pale, ethereal quality. The first writer to mention the primrose as a garden plant was Tabernaemontanus who wrote of the double yellow primrose in 1500. It was the double form of our single native primrose known later as the Double Sulphur and which may have appeared with the Double White at about the same time. Indeed, natural 'sports' in yellow and white are quite common and in *Country Life* magazine of 27 June 1975 appeared a photograph of double whites growing in a wood in Kent. Gerard made special mention of the Double White *(alba plena)* in his *Herbal* of 1597, and in his *Catalogue of Plants* published in 1599 he listed both the single and the double green primrose. Writing thirty years later, Parkinson gave a full description of double primroses which were then popular garden plants. He described the flowers as being 'very thick and double and of the same sweet scent [as the common single field primrose]', but very few of the double primroses have any degree of perfume; the old Double White and Double Yellow and Quaker's Bonnet, believed to be a sport of *P. rubra* and amongst the loveliest plants of the garden, are entirely devoid of any scent. Being natural sports they remain, however, amongst the most vigorous of the doubles.

SCENTED DOUBLE PRIMROSES. BON ACCORD CERISE. Raised in Aberdeen early this century together with several others, and they take their name from the motto of the City of Aberdeen. They are what is known as 'bunch' primroses, some flowers being borne on footstalks after the manner of the native primrose, whilst others on the same plant are borne on short polyanthus stems. All are in cultivation and several bear scented flowers, Bon Accord Cerise having the powerful sweet honeysuckle perfume of the auriculas. The blooms are of 2.5-cm (1-in) diameter, of rosette shape with rounded petals, and have the appearance of a small carnation, the colour being clear cerise-pink.

CRATHES CRIMSON. It was found in the grounds of Crathes Castle in Aberdeenshire but would appear to be the long-lost Bon Accord Brightness, being of the same shape and having the yellow shading at the base of the petals as in all the Bon Accords. The neat, rounded button-like flowers are of pale crimson-red with a glorious scent.

MARIE CROUSSE. It was introduced from France in about 1850 and it remains one of the most satisfying plants of the garden. It is a strong grower and blooms in profusion, increasing each year. The foliage is dull green, and it bears on short polyanthus stems, 2.5-cm (1-in) blooms, fully double and a lovely shade of Parma violet, splashed and edged with white. They have a powerful honeysuckle perfume. It received the Award of Merit from the Royal Horticultural Society in 1882.

RED PADDY. It is the *P. rubra plena* of old Irish gardens, possibly a sport of *P. rubra* (syn. *P. altaica*) the so-called 'red' primrose of Eastern Europe. It bears the same neat, flat and symmetrical flower as the Bon Accords and is of similar colouring to Bon Accord Brightness or Crathes Crimson, and it would seem that they had a common ancestor for they have the same sweet perfume. The rosy-red blooms have an attractive wire edge of silver.

THE SINGLE PRIMROSE. In 1900, a plant was introduced into the British Isles from the Caucasus where it is known as the Caucasian primrose, and it was to bring added interest to the primrose as a spring-flowering garden plant. It was called *Primula juliae* and is of the same section of Primulaceae, the Vernales group, as the native yellow *P. vulgaris*. Apart from its extreme hardiness and its earliness to bloom, it had small glossy leaves and its flowers were purple-blue, flushed with crimson with a conspicuous yellow eye. It remained in obscurity in the garden of St John's College, Oxford, until after the First World War when it was taken up by breeders and from it was raised *Primula wanda,* bearing flowers of claret colouring but alas, like its parent, without a trace of perfume.

It is not generally realized that the primroses of Europe bear either flowers of reddish-purple or pale mauve, the yellow-flowering primrose of the British Isles being the exception. Besides *P. juliae, P. rubra* (syn. *P. altaica*) with its pale-mauve flowers and delightfully waved petals has also been widely used for breeding but, here again, it has almost no perfume.

The following single primroses, all bearing white flowers, are the only scented derivatives of *P. juliae*:

CRADDOCK WHITE. Of compact habit, it has bronzy-green foliage and bears large white flowers with a golden eye and with a soft, sweet perfume.

QUEEN OF THE WHITES. A plant of compact habit, it bears large white flowers above small pale-green leaves and is softly scented.

SNOW-WHITE. It forms a low tufted plant studded with icy-white flowers which are delicately scented.

JACK-IN-GREEN PRIMROSES. The flowers are backed by a Tudor ruff of small green leaves, slightly larger than the flowers and which persists long after the flowers are dead. One variety, Eldorado, has the primrose perfume, the blooms being large and of brilliant golden-yellow. Almost certainly a derivative of *P. vulgaris*.

THE HOSE-IN-HOSE PRIMROSE. Gerard called them Two-in-Hose and Parkinson, Hose-in-Hose. He wrote, 'they remind one of the breeches men do wear'. They were also known as Duplex or Cup-and-saucer primroses for one bloom is to be seen growing out of another in the manner of hose worn by Elizabethan gentlemen, one stocking pulled up to the thighs with another turned down immediately below the knees. The botanical explanation of this delightful effect is that the lower bloom is really a petaloid calyx.

Almost all the Hose-in-hose are derivatives of the Common primrose (with but one or two exceptions) and so all diffuse a sweet mossy perfume, more pronounced than the scent of *P. vulgaris* for there are two blooms instead of one. The Hose-in-hose form of *P. juliae* Wanda is entirely without perfume, but the following varieties are scented:

BRIMSTONE. Of semi-polyanthus form, the large bell-shaped blooms are borne on 10-cm (4-in) stems and are a lovely clear sulphur-yellow.

CANARY BIRD. The flowers, borne one

inside the other, are of bright canary-yellow.

COY COLLEEN. A Hose-in-hose of greatest beauty, one bloom fitting almost inside the other and they are of clearest pink with a sweet mossy fragrance.

GOLD LACED HOSE. The Hose-in-hose form of polyanthus habit, the dark crimson-black flowers being held on 15- to 20- cm (6- to 8-in) stems, each bloom clearly edged with gold. The fragrance is even more pronounced than in the single form.

IRISH MOLLY. Also known as Lady Molly, it is a hose of true primrose form and bears large mauve-pink blooms which are delicately scented.

LADY DORA. A delightful old Irish form bearing small, dainty blooms of brilliant golden-yellow with the scent of honeysuckle.

LADY LETTICE. It comes early into bloom, covering itself in a fairy-like mass of dancing apricot-coloured blooms, flushed with salmon and pink, and with a delicious sweet perfume.

THE POLYANTHUS (*P. veris* × *P. vulgaris* × *P. vulgaris rubra*). The date of its introduction was about 1640 and it would seem to be the result of a natural crossing of the Hybrid oxlip with John Tradescant's Turkey-purple primrose obtained from the Caucasus. John Rea, a nurseryman of Bewdley, was the first to describe it in 1665: 'The red cowslip or oxlip, bearing many flowers on one stalk, in fashion like those of the field but of several red colours; some bigger than oxlips . . .' This 'large red oxlip' may then have become crossed with the native yellow primrose to give something like the red polyanthus of modern times. In 1687, in his *Directions for the Gardener* at Sayes Court, Kent, John Evelyn made mention of the polyanthus and its uses for spring bedding. In 1728, John Thomson, in his poem *The Seasons*, wrote of 'the polyanthus of unnumbered dyes', and three years later Philip Miller, Curator of the Physic Garden in Chelsea, described the plant as 'having large red flowers'. Twenty years later, the blooms took on the striking gold lacing or edging to be found in several varieties of *P. pubescens*, similar to the gold centre of the Alpine auriculas, whilst the flowers now carried the rich honeysuckle perfume of *P. auricula*. Ten years later, Rev. William Hanbury said there grew in his garden at Church Langton in Leicestershire more than a thousand varieties of the Gold Laced polyanthus and 'nearly that number of auriculas'. By 1780, Abercrombie wrote that the polyanthus had become 'one of the most noted prize [show] flowers amongst florists for the brilliant gold leaf colouring of the centre and petal edges, against a ground colour of deepest red, caught the imagination of all. By 1860, several hundred varieties were in cultivation, yet within twenty years the greatest of all show winners, Pearson's Alexander, along with almost every other named variety, had completely vanished though there has been a revival of this beautiful plant in recent years.

It is not generally realized that it was not until Miss Gertrude Jekyll found a yellow polyanthus in her garden at Munstead in 1880 that this colour first appeared in the plant.

Two of the finest named polyanthuses, Barrowby Gem and Hunter's Moon, have both the scent of honeysuckle. Miss Sinclair Rohde has told that Barrowby Gem was raised in Scotland in the 1930s by a Mrs McColl and selected from more than 200 seedlings. It comes into bloom in February, its large flattish head being composed of numerous deep yellowish-green flowers. Hunter's Moon is equally fragrant and is a lovely shade of golden apricot. Of all the hybrid strains of polyanthus, the one noted for the fragrance of its flowers is Hansen's F2 hybrid strain, raised in Lincolnshire, the scent of the enormous flower-heads being noticeable almost a mile away from the trial beds.

The polyanthus is readily raised from seed sown in boxes of John Innes compost in April, the seedlings being set out in beds of well-manured soil when large enough to handle. Plant into their flowering quarters in November, 30 cm (12 in) apart, and plant scented winter-flowering pansies or fragrant Cottage tulips between them.

PRINTZIA (Compositae—Daisy Family)

A small genus of South African plants named in honour of Professor H. C. Printz and prominent on dry slopes from Table Mountain to Muizenberg. Both surfaces of the leaves are covered with pellucid dots which release a lemony resinous perfume when bruised.

Species. *Printzia aromatica*. A low-growing shrub with linear leaves and bearing mauve-pink flowers in heads. All parts of the plant are densely covered in hairs and are extremely aromatic.

P. pyrifolia. A low-growing multi-branched shrub with broad oblong leaves, woolly on the underside and bearing purple flowers in dense heads. All parts of the plant, including the fruit, have a pleasing scent.

PROSTANTHERA (Labiatae—Lavender Family)

A genus of 50 evergreen Australian shrubs mostly found in New South Wales. Several require greenhouse treatment in the British Isles and northern Europe with a minimum winter temperature of 10°C (50°F), though they may be expected to survive a moderately severe winter if grown in the most favourable areas and given the protection of a sunny wall. They do not grow well in chalk. Besides the minty aroma given off by their foliage, several species bear attractively scented flowers.

Species. *Prostanthera lasianthos*. It makes a neat bush with small oval leaves scented of mint and during summer bears flowers of petunia-purple which have a spicy perfume.

P. rotundifolia. The Australian Mint-bush, which grows 1.8 to 2.4 m (6 to 8 ft) tall in its native land and against a warm wall in the British Isles. It is one of the few spring-flowering shrubs to bear purple flowers which are scented, like the leaves. The shoots should be pinched back after flowering but it will bloom only where the wood is hardened by the sun.

PRUNUS (Rosaceae—Rose Family)

A genus of 60 or more species of evergreen or deciduous trees or shrubs distributed throughout the northern temperate regions and bearing their flowers solitary or in corymbs. Their fruit is a 1-seeded drupe. No trees of the garden provide a display of greater beauty in spring and early summer than members of the large Prunus family (which includes the Flowering peach, the Almond, the Plum and the Laurels), several of which bear their blossom before the leaves. A number of the family, such as *P. pissardi* and *P. blireiana*, have attractive copper-coloured foliage and are valuable trees for providing coloured foliage to the small garden, but their flowers have no scent. The flowering cherries differ from the Almonds in the fleshy mesocarp and smooth stone; it is deeply furrowed in the almond.

The Bird cherry, *Prunus padus,* bears slightly fragrant flowers with the perfume more pronounced in the double form, *P. padus plena.* This is the tree that Gerard said grew wild in the woods of Kent and in Westmorland, whilst in Lancashire it was to be found 'almost in every hedge'. It bears its white racemes during May and is so hardy that it could well be planted as a wind-break in the most exposed garden.

Like all the Prunus family, the Ornamental cherries enjoy a chalk-laden soil and where this is not available the trees should have some lime rubble packed around the roots at planting time. All are trees of extreme hardiness, being native of the mountainous regions of Japan, and quite apart from their exquisite flowers, no group of trees are more varied.

Species and Varieties. *Prunus angustifolius.* The Chickasaw plum of the U.S.A., it makes a fine tree 5.4 (18 ft) tall, of handsome outline. In April its large, frothy blush-white blossoms appear just before the leaves and are held on attractive red stems. They have a refreshing fruity scent.

P. emaginata. The Japanese *Amanogawa,* meaning Milky Way. It grows tall and upright, like a Lombardy poplar, attaining a height of 9 m (30ft) in a chalky soil. Its almost perpendicular branches are clothed with double flowers of apple-blossom pink and they diffuse a soft honey scent.

A new variety, Spire, of similar habit, bears single flowers of purest white and delicately perfumed.

P. hokusai. It makes a broad, spreading tree almost like Kanzan and blooms during April. It has bronze foliage and bears deliciously scented double pink flowers, held on long stalks.

P. ilicifolia. The Californian Cherry laurel which in the more exposed parts requires some shelter. It grows 1.2 to 1.5 m (4 to 5 ft) in height with sharply toothed evergreen leaves like those of the holly and it blooms in spring, its tiny white sweetly scented flowers being borne in graceful nodding racemes.

P. invesii. Raised at Messrs Hillier's Nurseries from seed of *C. yedoensis.* It will grace any lawn with its dainty weeping habit, its sweetly scented flowers of purest white providing a cascade of beauty during March and April.

P. koyima (Mount Fuji). A mature tree in full bloom with its outstretched lower branches and cone-shaped outline presents one of the most spectacular sights of the garden in May. The flowers are glistening white, borne in pendent clusters and have a delicate sweet perfume.

P. lannesiana affinis (Jo-nioi). A suitable small garden variety, making a plant of compact, bushy but upright habit, its single milk-white blooms which appear in mid-April, having a delicious almond perfume.

P. laurocerasus. The Common laurel and a native of south-eastern Europe. It grows 2.4 to 3.6 m (8 to 12 ft) in height with evergreen lance-shaped leaves. The form *rotundiflora* is the one most widely grown, having rounded leaves of darkest green.

The small dull white flowers are borne in May and are powerfully fragrant. So insignificant are the flowers that it is almost impossible to see them from any distance and it is truly amazing that they are able to diffuse so much scent. The blooms are followed by large sloe-back berries which are most attractive against the glossy foliage.

P. lusitanica. The Portugal laurel, growing up to 6 m (20 ft) in height with dull-green myrtle-like leaves with attractive serrated edges. Its sweetly scented white flowers appear in June in drooping racemes and these are followed by oval fruits of bright sealing-wax red.

P. luteo pleno (Ukon). Known as the Yellow cherry for its flowers are pale primrose-yellow and, appearing early in May against a background of pale bronze-green foliage, present a picture of delicious coolness. The flowers have the same mossy woodland perfume as the primrose.

P. mume. Though known as the

Japanese apricot, it is of Chinese origin, growing in the mountainous valleys of southern Shensi, and is known as *Mei Hua*. It comes into bloom in March before the leaves appear and makes a compact little tree with long pointed leaves, serrated at the edges and downy on the underside. The flowers are white and are borne in pairs. They possess a sweet perfume. There is also a red-flowered form which is not scented. The trees have since earliest times been widely planted in temple gardens and some are known to be at least a thousand years old. The tree remains one of the most important of all Chinese fruiting trees, the apricots being eaten raw or made into conserves.

P. reynvaani. A laurel of recent introduction, it is a plant of neat, upright habit growing 0.9 to 1.2 m (3 to 4 ft) tall with large evergreen holly-like leaves and in May it bears spikes of sweetly scented creamy-white flowers.

P. wadai. A hybrid, raised by Mr K. Wada of Yokohama from the scentless *P. subhirtella*, the winter-flowering cherry, as one parent, it makes a small twiggy tree and early in spring bears small pale-pink flowers with the scent of ripe peaches.

P. yedoensis. It makes a large spreading tree of weeping habit, suitable to plant as a centre-piece for a lawn, and beneath its branches scented flowering bulbs may be planted. It is one of the earliest of the cherries to bloom, the large clusters of pale-pink blossom appearing in March and they emit the delicate scent of almonds.

PSIDIUM (Myrtaceae—Myrtle Family)

An extensive but exclusively tropical genus of about 50 species consisting of trees and shrubs with opposite, entire, feather-veined leaves and bearing large, white flowers, produced either singly at the axil of the leaves or in pairs on axillary stalks. The flowers have an egg-shaped calyx with 4 or 5 free petals and numerous stamens. All are deliciously scented. They are native of sub-tropical South America and the West Indies, India and Ceylon, Indo-China and Indonesia.

Species. *Psidium arach* (syn. *P. guineense*). Native of Guyana, it is widely cultivated in the West Indies where it is known as

Guyana guava. It grows about 3 m (10 ft) tall and all parts are scented, especially the berry which is dull yellow, reddish-brown inside, about the size of a cherry, and of exquisite aromatic (nutmeg) taste.

P. fluviatile. Known as the Riverside guava, for it grows only along the banks of rivers in its native island of Cayenne. It grows 1.8 m (6 ft) tall, the oval leaves being full of pellucid dots which contain a resinous gum. When pressed, they release a balsamic scent.

P. grandiflorum. Found in the province of St Paul, Brazil, where it inhabits mountainsides, making a bush less than 60 cm (2 ft) tall. The leaves which are 7 cm (3 in) long, are covered with down and give off the smell of balm when bruised.

P. guajava. Though indigenous only to Mexico, the plant is now naturalized throughout most countries of South America and India, where it is in commercial cultivation for its fruit, the guava. There are two varieties, *pyriferum* and *pomiferum*, which are more widely dispersed; the former makes a tree 6 m (20 ft) tall and grows in the West Indies, whilst *pomiferum*, also to be found in the islands and throughout South America, makes a tree-like shrub only half that height. It has aromatic foliage and scented flowers.

P. guaviroba (syn. *Campomanesia guaviroba*). Native of the Brazilian province of St Paul, where it inhabits low-lying meadows, and is known as *Guaviroba de Campo*. It makes a bush 1.8 m (6ft) tall, and bears aromatic fruits the size of peas. The flowers and leaves when crushed are fragrant.

The variety *aromaticum* was first mentioned by Aublet in his *Histoire des Plantes de la Guiane Française,* and is native only of Guyana and Cayenne, where it makes a small shrub 1.2 to 1.8 m (4 to 6 ft) tall. The leaves, when crushed, give off the delicious scent of balm, whilst the creamy-white flowers have a balsamic fragrance. The fruit is the same size as a cherry.

P. montanum. Found only in the mountainous areas of Jamaica, where it attains a height of 30 m (100 ft) or more with large oblong leaves quite glabrous. The small kidney-shaped fruits, when dry, have exactly the smell of almond blossom, hence its local name of *Amandron*.

P. polycarpon. Native of Trinidad, where

it grows 1.2 to 1.5 m (4 to 5 ft) tall, and bears its flowers in threes, followed by edible fruits the size of a small plum and delicious in taste.

P. rufum. A rare species found in mountainous fields only in the Brazilian province of Minas Geraes, where it grows 1.2 to 1.5 m (4 to 5 ft) tall, its twiggy, tetragonal branches being covered in scented red hairs. The scented leaves are 10 cm (4 in) long.

PSORALEA (Leguminosae—Laburnum Family)

A genus of shrubs or herbs covered with resinous dots on the leaves and sepals. The leaves are usually trifoliate, the pea-like flowers blue. They are plants of the Mediterranean and of Cape Province, growing on sand dunes and mountainous slopes, and they bloom during October and November.

Species. *Psoralea aculeata.* An erect shrub, densely leafy and extremely aromatic and bearing solitary flowers at the end of the branchlets. The standards and wings are blue, the keel white.

P. bituminosa. It grows on dry banks and by the side of roads close to the Mediterranean shores of North Africa and is a plant of clove-like form with hairy trifoliate leaves, grey-green in colour. It bears its violet flower-heads on 15-cm (6-in) stems during early summer and has a most attractive appearance, whilst when trodden upon the whole plant gives off a refreshing pine-tar smell, hence its name of Pitch trefoil.

P. fruticans (syn. *P. bracteata*). A small, decumbent shrub with pubescent branchlets with trifoliate leaves and bearing its flowers in a dense head with conspicuous bracts. The standard is purple-blue, the keel white, tipped with blue and vanilla-scented, whilst the foliage and bracts have a resinous smell when handled.

P. pinnata. Usually found with *P. aculeata* on mountainous slopes but not on dunes. It is a hairy shrub, densely foliaged at the end of the branchlets, the leaves being aromatic when bruised. The flowers of pale blue and white are borne in axillary clusters at the end of the branchlets and have a vanilla perfume.

PSYCHOTRIA (Rubiaceae—Bedstraw Family)

A large genus of more than 700 species of small trees or shrubs, native of the warmer parts of South-east Asia and the Pacific islands. The flowers of several species are scented and are followed by bright orange or red fruits.

Species. *Psychotria eumorphanthus* (syn. *Eumorphanthus fragrans*). Native of Fiji, it is a vigorous shrub, reaching a height of 3.6 m (12 ft) with elliptic leaves 22.5 cm (9 in) long. It bears white flowers in an 8- to 10-flowered terminal inflorescence and they are strongly scented. They are followed by crimson fruits.

P. fragrans (syn. *Calycodendron fragrans*). A small upright tree with 7.5-cm (3-in) leaves, it was discovered on Mount Naitaradamu in 1927 by Dr Gillespie. Its flowers are white, borne in a many-flowered inflorescence and they are sweetly scented.

PTELEA (Rutaceae—Rue Family)

A genus of two species, native of the United States and Mexico.

Species. *Ptelea polyadenia.* One of a small genus of aromatic shrubs or small trees, numbered amongst which is the Hop tree, *P. trifoliata,* its yellow flowers having a powerful honeysuckle perfume. *P. polyadenia,* like the hop tree, has trifoliate leaves which have the same aromatic orange-like smell of the Rue when pressed. A native of New Mexico, it is hardy in the British Isles but only when growing in a sandy loam and where not exposed to cold winds.

P. trifoliata. The Hop tree, so called because its sweetly scented greenish-yellow flowers have a scent similar to the flowers of the hop, whilst the leaves, when bruised, also give off a suggestion of hops. A native of North America where it is known as the Swamp dogwood, it is a slow-growing tree which eventually attains a height of about 3.6 m (12 ft). The variety *aurea* has attractive yellow foliage, whilst the bark, like the leaves and flowers, is also aromatic. It flourishes in ordinary loam and is completely hardy in the British Isles and northern Europe, flowering during May and June. The blooms are small, borne in hop-like clusters and have the powerful scent of honeysuckle.

PTEROCARPUS (Leguminosae— Laburnum Family)

A genus of 100 species of flowering trees, native of tropical Africa, India and Burma, the Malayan Archipelago and South-east Asia, which bear sweetly scented flowers and exude a sweet-scented gum. *P. santalinus* is famed for the fragrance of its wood.

Species. *Pterocarpus echinatus.* It is present in Senegal and Angola and is known as the Kino tree which grows to 24 m (80 ft) in height. There, the flowers appear in February and March when the trees are devoid of foliage. They are pale yellow, borne in racemes like the laburnum and have a similar scent, resembling vanilla to some but to others, that of the cowslip. The seeds are winged.

P. indicus. Known as the Burma-coast Padank to distinguish it from the true Padank of Burma, *P. macrocarpus.* It grows to a height of about 15 m (50 ft), forming a dense head of dark-green foliage. The handsome leaves 25 cm (10 in) long and divided into 8 or 10 broad, oval deep-green leaflets, are arranged alternately and almost overlapping.

About 1st June, the whole tree comes alight with its long racemes of tiny orange-rust coloured bells which appear from the joints of the twiggy branches, diffusing a most delicious vanilla-like perfume. The flower consists of an erect petal between two wing petals of deepest orange and with two paler keel petals. The 10 stamens appear as two bunches of five with yellow anthers. The flowers appear in flushes at fortnightly intervals until the end of July, and the fruit pods form in January.

The tree is widely planted by roadsides in Malaya and Burma and is also to be found in the streets of Bombay and Calcutta. In the gardens of the East, it is planted for the shade it gives as well as for the beauty and fragrance of its flowers, but it flourishes only in an area of excessive warmth and of high rainfall.

P. santalinus. Native of the islands of the Indian Archipelago, it will grow to 9 m (30 ft) tall but more often to only about 3 m (10 ft) high. The pale-yellow flowers are scentless, but since earliest times the wood has been appreciated for its delightful scent and has been used in India and China for burning as incense and for making wooden statues and boxes. Insects will not attack it. The wood is also used for making musical instruments and, finely powdered, for dusting clothes to keep away pests and to provide the clothes with lasting perfume.

PTEROCARYA (Juglandaceae—Walnut Tree Family)

A genus of four species of ornamental trees, native of eastern Asia and the Caucasus, with large aromatic pinnate leaves divided into numerous narrow leaflets, the greenish flowers borne in drooping catkins or spikes.

Species. *Pterocarya fraxinifolia.* A native of the Caucasus, it grows to a height of 9 m (30 ft) and enjoys a cool, moist soil. The enormous leaves, measuring up to 50 cm (20 in) long, resemble those of the Walnut; they are composed of 15 oblong leaflets, are sweetly resinous, and turn to a clear pale yellow in autumn. The tree has deeply furrowed bark which is aromatic, whilst the long drooping catkins of palest green add to its charms.

P. rhoifolia. Native of Japan where it grows at an elevation of 1,200 m (4,000 ft) above sea-level and where it reaches a height of 24 m (80 ft). The handsome aromatic leaves are 30 cm (12 in) long with a central midrib to which the leaflets are attached. In its native land the flowers are borne in catkins 25 cm (10 in) long.

P. stenoptera. A Chinese species of enormous vigour, making several feet of growth in a season. It has large pinnate leaves, resinous to the touch, and leaf stalks that are winged, which distinguishes it from the others. The round drupes are of more than 2.5 (1 in) diameter.

PTEROCEPHALUS (Dipsacaceae— Teasel Family)

A genus of 25 species, native of the Near East, southern Europe and tropical Africa, few having scented attractions.

Species. *Pterocephalus perennis* (syn. *Scabiosa pterocephalus*). It is native only of

Mount Parnassus and the Balkans and is a delightful plant for the alpine garden, growing 7.5 to 10 cm (3 to 4 in) tall and making a mat of woody stems. Its short grey-green leaves have serrated edges and are deeply channelled and it blooms during July and August. The flowers, lilac-pink in colour, resemble those of the scabious (to which it is closely related) and are held on 7.5-cm (3-in) stems. Like the scabious the plant requires an open sunny position and a well-drained, sandy soil. The whole plant diffuses an unusual fruity scent when warmed by the sun.

PTEROSTYRAX (Styraceae—Storax Family)

A genus of seven species, native of Burma, Malaya, South-east Asia and Japan.

Species. *Pterostyrax lispidum.* A small deciduous tree, native of south-eastern China and Japan growing about 4.5 m (15 ft) tall. Though liking a sunny situation, it is quite hardy and is a most attractive tree with large toothed leaves. In June and July, it bears 22.5-cm (9-in) panicles of pure-white flowers which are sweetly scented. In addition to the beauty of its flowers and leaves, it has most attractive seed vessels in autumn.

PUERARIA (Leguminosae—Laburnum Family)

A genus of 35 species, native to the Himalayas, South-east Asia and Japan.

Species. *Pueraria thumbergiana.* The Kadzu vine of central China, it is a climbing plant of rapid growth, quickly covering a wall 6 m (20 ft) in height, and is quite hardy in sheltered gardens of Britain, though in the more exposed parts it may be cut down in a severe winter. Little harm, however, will be done for in spring the plant will form new growth from the base. The handsome violet flowers are borne in long elegant racemes during July and August and have the sweet vanilla scent of the family.

PUTORIA (Rubiaceae—Bedstraw Family)

A genus of three species, to be found in rocky limestone formations about the eastern shores of the Mediterranean.

Species. *Putoria calabrica.* A dwarf plant with tiny, lance-shaped leaves which emit a somewhat unpleasant smell of animal fur when crushed, yet which take on more attractive tones as they dry, for coumarin is present. The reddish-purple tubular flowers are borne in terminal clusters from April to September, and are enhanced by the red stamens which protrude to the mouth of the tube. They are scentless. The plant does best in a sunny position, preferably in the rock garden. Seeds or cuttings taken in late summer are used for increase.

PYROLA (Ericaceae—Heather Family)

An interesting genus of about 15 species of stolon-bearing perennials which take their name from *pyrus,* a pear, for their leaves are similar in appearance to those of the fruit. Several species are native to the British Isles where they grow in damp, peaty soils usually in the filtered sunlight of pine woods. They are useful plants for the alpine garden provided they are given an acid soil and a position of partial shade. Or they may be planted about the roots of mature conifer trees between sphagnum-moss.

Species. *Pyrola elliptica.* It is a native of North America and is rare in Britain. It will grow 15 cm (6 in) tall and forms a spreading tuft of leathery, wedge-shaped leaves. It bears its attractive little white bells during July and August in one-sided racemes and they have a delicate sweet perfume.

P. minor. The Lesser wintergreen which is to be found in woodlands and in damp places of the British Isles where the soil is of a peaty nature. It bears its white flowers, attractively tinted with pink, during June and July and they are borne in pendulous inflorescences. They have a soft almond scent, not so pronounced as in the Larger wintergreen.

P. rotundifolia. The Larger wintergreen, a native of the British Isles. Its rounded leaves which appear in almost rosette form are attractively crenulated. The plant takes its name from the evergreen nature of its foliage. It is the Gaultheria (of the same family) which yields the wintergreen of commerce. It is one of Britain's rarest and loveliest plants, to be found on heathland

and in woods, growing in a well-drained soil containing peat or leaf-mould, and it will often form large colonies. The pure-white nodding bells, very like those of lily of the valley, are borne on 25-cm (10-in) stems well above the foliage, on an erect scape. They have a delicious almond-like fragrance. It blooms from May until September and, because it has no nectar, its downward curving style bends up at the end to enable pollination to take place. It is readily raised from seed which resembles brown dust.

P. secunda. It is a native of the British Isles though a rare plant, with small ovate leaves, and it blooms in July, bearing its fragrant greenish-white flowers in one-sided scapes.

R

RAFFLESIA (Rafflesiaceae—Rafflesia Family)

A genus of 12 species, native of the tropical forests of western Malaysia with flowers of obnoxious smell.

Species. *Rafflesia arnoldii.* It is one of the most repulsive of the world's flowers for they measure 90 cm (3 ft) across and are of crimson-red blotched with yellowish-brown, and they give off a smell of decaying flesh which can be detected a mile away. The plant is parasitic on vines, piercing the roots to obtain their sustenance. The flowers, which are pollinated by carrion flies, may weigh up to 6.3 kg (14 lb). In spite of the stench and evil appearance, the juices are much in demand by native women to relieve the pains of childbirth.

RANDIA (Chinchonaceae—Chinchona Family)

A large genus of tropical evergreens closely allied to *Gardenia.* The main difference is the 2-celled ovary, surmounted by a disc, whilst the tube of the corolla is shorter than in the gardenia.

Species. *Randia armata* (syn. *Gardenia armata*). It is native of Martinique and St Lucia and makes a thorny tree-like shrub 3 m (10 ft) tall with the thorns appearing in fours at the top of the branchlets. With them appear the flowers, also in fours, and they are large, pure white and powerfully fragrant.

R. capitata. A native of Mexico, it makes a spreading shrub 1.2 to 1.5 m (4 to 5 ft) tall, armed with stiff, short thorns, and as in *R. armata,* four appear together at the top of each branchlet. The pure-white flowers appear 6 to 8 in a capitate fascicle at the tops of the branchlets and have the perfume of freesias.

R. exaltata. Native of the Andaman Islands where it grows in swampy ground, making a slender tree 15 m (50 ft) tall with pubescent branches. The large white, sweetly scented flowers are borne in axillary cymes and are followed by fruits of 2.5-cm (1-in) diameter.

R. fasciculata (syn. *Webera fasciculata*). Native of the mountains of Nepal and Assam where it grows up to an altitude of 1,200 m (4,000 ft). It makes a spreading bush 1.2 m (4 ft) tall and almost as wide with large thorns. The flowers first open white, turning yellow within 48 hours, and have an exotic lily-like perfume.

R. fragrans (syn. *Randia malabarica, Gardenia fragrans, Posoqueira fragrans, Griffithia fragrans*). An erect shrub, native of southern India and Ceylon, it is not uncommon up to 900 m (3,000 ft). Where growing in a fertile soil the plant is unarmed, but where growing in scrubland it is covered in straight spines. The large creamy-white flowers, borne in short cymes, have the jonquil scent and are followed by fruits of pea size.

R. longiflora. An arboreous shrub, native of Chittagong where it forms quite a large tree with leaves 15 cm (6 in) long and large recurved thorns. The flowers are borne in terminal corymbs of 12 or more and open creamy-white, turning yellow on the second day. They are powerfully fragrant.

R. longispina. To be found wild only on the rocky coast of Penang, it grows 1.5 m (5 ft) tall and is armed with massive thorns often 5 cm (2 in) long. The branches extend outwards and at the ends appear the large flowers of purest white with a sweet perfume.

R. macrophylla. Native of Malacca, Penang and Singapore, it grows 1.2 m (4 ft) tall with leaves up to 30 cm (12 in) long, the largest of all the species; likewise the flowers which measure 12.5 to 15 cm (5 to 6 in) across and are white, spotted with purple in the throat, and are intensely fragrant.

R. nutans (syn. *R. dumetorum*). Native of the shady forests of the East Indies, it makes a small slender shrub with long dependent branches which are pubescent while young and armed with few thorns. The leaves are on short petioles whilst the flowers appear under the thorns and are white with lily-like scent.

R. tetrasperma (syn. *Gardenia densa*). Native of Kashmir, Assam and Sikkim where it occurs up to 2,100 m (7,000 ft). It makes a rigid, woody shrub 1.8 m (6 ft) tall with large elliptic leaves and bears small greenish-white flowers of hyacinth-like fragrance.

R. uliginosa. Inhabiting low-lying land in the East Indies, it makes a sparse thorny bush 1.8 m (6 ft) tall with small glossy leaves, and it bears its flowers at the ends of the branchlets. They are large and pure white with the balsamic scent of hyacinths.

RELHANIA (Compositae—Daisy Family)

A small genus of woody shrubs closely allied to *Helichrysum* and named after the Rev R. Relhan, author of books on botany. Plants are to be found on dry mountainous slopes of South Africa. The leaves are small, the flowers yellow and borne in terminal corymbs. The involucre is composed of several rows of dry bracts.

Species. *Relhania genistaefolia.* A plant of shrubby habit, it grows 90 cm (3 ft) tall with oblong leaves covered in sessile glands from which exudes a resinous, sticky substance which gives the plant its pleasant balsamic perfume.

RESEDA (Resedaceae—Reseda Family)

A genus of about 60 species of annual plants, native of North Africa and the Mediterranean regions, only one of which is fragrant.

Species. *Reseda odorata.* The mignonette with its inconspicuous brownish-yellow flowers, and growing 30 cm (12 in) tall, has been developed from the loose, straggling plant to be found growing amongst rocks in North Africa, especially Egypt, where it is a common weed. Though found in most cottage gardens, it was not until Philip Miller of the Botanic Gardens at Chelsea received seed sent to him by Dr van Royer of Leyden in 1752, that it was first grown in Britain. But during the nineteenth century it was the practice to grow it in pots on balconies and terraces in France, for the flowers would release their fragrance on warm summer days. The fashion was begun by the Empress Josephine when Napoleon sent seed to her during his Egyptian campaign. It was named *mignonette*, 'little darling', by the French.

To bloom indoors, in spring, seed is sown in pots in September in a sunny window. Outdoors, sow thinly in circles of 37.5-cm (15-in) diameter, or as an edging to a path, in April for the plants to bloom from mid-June until the end of the summer. Space the plants 20 cm (8 in) apart and provide a sunny situation.

Some modern varieties with well-developed flowers of deep crimson have lost much of the perfume of the original plant.

RHAPHIOLEPSIS (Rosaceae—Rose Family)

A genus of 15 species, native of Southeast Asia and Japan.

Species. *Rhaphiolepsis japonica* (syn. *R. umbellata*, from the formation of the flower-heads). It is native of Japan and the hardiest of the genus, growing 1.5 to 1.8 m (5 to 6 ft) tall, and is evergreen with leathery leaves of darkest green. Early in summer, it bears honey-scented hawthorn-like flowers in graceful sprays and these are followed by berries, covered in bloom, like black grapes. It is an excellent small garden shrub for a sandy soil containing just a little humus to retain summer moisture, whilst it is most tolerant of sea spray.

RHIPSALIS (Cactaceae—Cactus Family)

A genus of about 60 species of epiphytic plants, native of Paraguay, Uruguay and the West Indies, attaching themselves to tree trunks and rocks of shady ravines. They take their name from the Greek *rhips,* wickerwork, a reference to their intertwining stems. The stems are like strands of coral, hence its name of Coral cactus. Their flowers, freely produced, are mostly borne solitary and remain open both by day and by night for 8 to 10 days.

The plants require shade from strong sunlight and a compost made up of loam, grit, leaf-mould and decayed manure in equal parts. Their roots should be kept almost dry throughout the year but in summer the plants require almost daily overhead syringeing. Several are valuable room plants for they require a winter temperature of only 10°C (50°F).

Species. *Rhipsalis lumbricoides.* Native of the forests of Paraguay, forming long cylindrical stems of finger thickness. The flowers are borne on the side areoles and are creamy white with the powerful scent of orange-blossom.

R. warningiara. It has 3- to 4-angled stem segments and no midrib; its pure-white flowers are borne singly and in clusters, and release a powerful fragrance.

RHODODENDRON (Ericeae—Heather Family)

A genus of more than 600 species, with leathery, lance-shaped, evergreen leaves, which bear their flowers in huge clusters at the end of the branches. They require a peaty soil and partial shade and, where given the conditions they enjoy, an established plantation will present a most magnificent spectacle when in full bloom through spring and early summer. The first to bloom is the scentless *Rhododendron dauricum* from the Arctic wastes of Siberia, which bears its rosy-mauve flowers in February, and they range in colour from purest white through lemon-yellow and biscuit to palest rose and intense crimson-scarlet. Unfortunately, only a small number of species and varieties will find inclusion here for, with but few exceptions, and these are plants of regions of high rainfall, bearing white, pale-yellow or pale-pink blooms, they do not bear scented flowers. Those that do are mostly native of the sub-tropical forests of Sikkim and Burma. There are, however, others which are worthy of a place in the peat garden, if only for their aromatic foliage which is delightfully refreshing, with the piercing scent of incense or of lemons.

Rhododendrons, though in most instances completely hardy, are not happy in a wind-swept situation and appreciate the shelter of a dingle or a hollow in the ground over which deciduous trees cast their shadow and provide protection from the early spring sunshine, which may cause damage to the flowers after frost. Also, they tend to be chiefly surface rooting, and benefit from the shade in summertime. For the same reason, they should be given a yearly mulch of peat or leaf-mould, mixed with a little decayed manure, for they are unable to search out for their food to any great depth. Making use of the humus formed by the decaying leaves which continually fall from nearby trees, the plants will flourish particularly well under woodland conditions, but they love moisture and usually give a better account along the western seaboard of the British Isles than elsewhere.

Species and Varieties. WITH FRAGRANT FLOWERS. *Rhododendron auriculatum.* A native of central China where it was discovered by E. H. Wilson. It is a most beautiful plant when established but, like the exotic creature it is, it does not come into bloom until reaching maturity and a height of about 3 m (10 ft), which it will take at least 10 years to achieve. Its handsome white tubular flowers appear in August in large trusses amidst bottle-green leaves and emit a rich sweet fruity scent, a perfume it has passed on to its equally late-flowering hybrid, Polar Bear, which also bears white flowers, with an attractive green throat.

R. azaleoides. A hybrid of an azalea and rhododendron, being almost identical to *R. fragrans,* and the first recorded hybrid rhododendron. It is semi-evergreen and comes into bloom early in June when no more that 45 cm (1½ ft) tall. The azalea-like flowers are borne in rounded trusses and are extremely attractive, being white with a delicate edge of lilac-mauve, and they possess a sweet fragrance which they diffuse far and wide whenever the days are warm.

R. burmanicum. One of the more tender species, native of South-east Asia, growing in sub-tropical mountainous regions 1,500 to 2,100 m (5 to 7,000 ft) above sea-level.

It requires pot cultivation and winter protection in northern Europe and America, though it may prove to be hardy given woodland conditions. The blooms are a lovely greenish-yellow, with a rich honey-like perfume.

R. campylocarpum. Native of Sikkim, where it was discovered by J. D. Hooker in 1850, it is a twiggy shrub growing up to 1.8 m (6 ft) in height with long, leathery leaves, glossy on the surface, glaucous beneath. The clusters of clear pale-yellow buds open to reveal flowers which are attractively bell-shaped, enhanced by the pale-green leaves. They appear in May and they have a delicate sweet perfume.

R. cinnadrum. A hybrid raised from *R. cinnabarinum roylei* x *R. polyandrum*, a species of the Maddenii series, it makes a compact plant and bears large funnel-shaped flowers of blush-white or palest cream which are perhaps more powerfully scented than those of any rhododendron.

R. cyclium. Valuable in that it is one of the earliest to bloom, in March when the earth is beginning to warm again. It grows up to 1.8 (6 ft) tall, and is of stiff upright habit, with leathery, glossy leaves. Early in spring it bears clusters of blush-white flowers which have the Damask rose perfume.

R. dalhousiae. A rare epiphytic species from the sub-tropical forests of Sikkim where it grows on the trunks of other trees.

It is a beautiful plant, growing 1.8 m (6 ft) tall with crimson stems and downy leaves, and from April until July bears bell-shaped flowers of blush-white which have a powerful lemon scent. This same scent it has passed on to its hybrid (x *R. ciliatum*), Countess of Haddington, which bears large trusses of blush-white flowers but which, like *R. dalhousiae,* is not sufficiently hardy for the more exposed gardens of the British Isles and N. America.

R. decorum. It eventually attains a height of 3 to 3.6 m (10 to 12ft) and is of proved hardiness, bearing sweetly scented flowers of white, sometimes flushed with shell-pink from March to May.

R. discolor. Native of western China, it is a valuable species in that it blooms during July, later than all other rhododendrons with but a single exception, and its white, bell-shaped blooms, flushed with shades of rose and pink, emit a soft, sweet fragrance. It makes a tall bush up to 3.5 m (12 ft) or more in height, and has almost black-green foliage which provides a pleasing contrast to the flower trusses. It is possibly the hardiest of all rhododendrons.

R. discolor has produced a number of sweetly scented hybrids when crossed with *R. loderi* which itself is a hybrid of the scented *R. fortunei.* Outstanding is Albatross which bears enormous trusses of purest white funnel-shaped flowers which are powerfully scented, whilst Solent Queen bears fragrant white flowers flushed with pink at the edge.

R. edgeworthii. One of Hooker's early Sikkim discoveries, it makes a small straggling plant and is suitable only for a sheltered garden or for a cool greenhouse, where during April and May, its small, creamy-white flower trusses will diffuse a powerful sweet perfume. It is one of the few species to have both hairs and scales on its leaves, the under-surface of which have a thick, brown indument. A lovely hybrid, Princess Alice (x *R. ciliatum*), introduced in 1862, bears large white flowers flushed with pink on the outside, and is also sweetly scented.

R. formosum. It is native of the eastern Himalayas and suitable only for a cool greenhouse or a sheltered garden in the South-west of Britain. It makes a small neat shrub some 90 cm (3 ft) in height, with shining, lance-shaped leaves, scaly beneath whilst its scented flowers are white, tinted with rose. It makes a delightful pot plant, flowering in May and June.

A hybrid, *R. fragrantissimum* (x *R. edgeworthii*), also bears white flowers with rose tinting and is forcefully scented.

R. fortunei. A species of the woodlands of central China, it has enormous beauty and extreme hardiness and will attain a height of about 3 m (10 ft). Its long, evergreen leaves are pale green, and about them it bears in May loose clusters of bell-shaped blooms of soft lilac-pink, which diffuse a refreshing fruity perfume. This it has passed on to its offspring, *R.* Calfort which bears large trusses of blush-white blooms which are scented.

R. griffithianum. One of Hooker's earliest introductions from Sikkim, where it grows in the forests, in areas of high rainfall. Of this plant, the late Kingdon-Ward said, 'There is an ethereal quality about its enormous bell-flowers, – their vital milk whiteness, their careless rapture of form, their exquisite, effortless grace as they hang clustered from the leafy shoots, their subtle fragrance – which defies description'. It is, however, hardy in only the mildest parts of western Britain and is extremely slow-growing. Flowering is in May.

R. Lady Alice Fitzwilliam. A hybrid of only half-hardy qualities which, in the British Isles, should be confined either to a cool greenhouse or the most sheltered gardens of the South-west. The large, tubular blooms are ivory-white with a sulphur flush, whilst the lobes are tinted with pink. The flowers have a rich sweet perfume.

R. lindleyi. An epiphyte from the sub-tropical forests of Burma and, like *R. nuttallii,* will prove hardy in the British Isles in only the most sheltered gardens of the western coastline. It grows 3.6 m (12 ft) tall, but may be confined to a pot when grown under glass, and will bloom in April. Its flowers are large and of cool marble whiteness with the soft, sweet fragrance one would expect from flowers of such virginity.

R. loderi. Raised by Sir Giles Loder at Leonardslee, near Horsham, Sussex, it is considered to be the finest hybrid rhododendron ever introduced. It was raised from *R. griffithianum* x *R. fortunei,* and its enormous trusses of creamy-white are as richly perfumed as the parents, a pleasing quality it has passed on to several of its own offspring including Albatross and Avalanche (x *R. calophytum*), which also bears flowers of purest white. When crossed with the variety Pink Shell, *R. loderi* produced Coronation Day, possibly the finest of all pink rhododendrons, which in June bears enormous trusses of shell-pink with a powerful spicy scent.

R. magacalyx. When in bloom it is a plant of exquisite beauty, but is too tender in the British Isles for anywhere but in the cool greenhouse. From the jungles of Burma, it will grow 1.8 m (6 ft) tall under glass and has handsome grey leaves whilst its large, white, tubular flowers appear as if waxed and emit the refreshing scent of nutmeg. It flowers from April to May

R. nuttallii. In its native Bhutan it is epiphytic, to be found growing from the branches of its host tree high up in search of the sun. In Britain, where it is hardy only in the South-west, it makes a tall, leggy tree with large, dark-green leaves 22 cm (9 in) long with scales beneath, and in May bears handsome, trumpet-shaped flowers of creamy-yellow which diffuse a delicious sweet perfume.

R. scottianum. Native of the lower Himalayas, it will reach a height of 3 m (10 ft), but in Britain should be grown only in the most favourably situated gardens. The flowers, which are borne in large trusses, are white flushed with pink on the outside and they have a sweet scent.

WITH FRAGRANT LEAVES. *R. brevistylum.*

This species has foliage which is perhaps more powerfully scented than that of any other plant. It is found 3,000 m (10,000 ft) above sea-level, on the borders of Tibet and Burma, growing up to 3 m (10 ft) tall, and covering itself in clusters of purple-pink flowers, and with scaly brown leaves which release an incense-like fragrance in the rarefied breezes. June and July are its main flowering times.

R. cephalanthum. Native of Tibet, making a compact shrub only 60 cm (2 ft) tall. It has oval leaves of glossy green which have the delicious bay-leaf smell, whilst the pale pink-white, daphne-like flowers are also similarly scented. They appear in April and May.

R. desquamatum (syn. *R. heliolepis*). Native of the Himalayas, it makes a large bushy shrub 4.5 m (15 ft) in height, and nearly the same across, its large glossy leaves being powerfully aromatic. It bears large mauve flowers, with deeper purple markings, in May.

R. glaucophyllum. From Sikkim, it is a dainty little species growing 90 cm (3 ft) tall or more. It prefers an open, sunny situation and its glaucous leaves, dotted with tiny scales, become pleasantly aromatic, giving off a lemon-like scent when pressed or rubbed against. The old-rose, bell-shaped flowers appear in May and are borne in clusters of 6 or more. In every way it is a delightful plant.

R. hippophaeoides. It makes a small bush of slender upright growth, and resembles the Sea buckthorn from which it takes its name. It has small, grey-green leaves which are deliciously aromatic, and in April and May bears clusters of lavender-blue bells which are slightly scented.

R. kotschyi (syn. *R. ferrugineum myrtifolium*). One of the oldest of known forms, it does not exceed a height of 60 cm (2 ft). Thought to be a hybrid of *R. hirsutum*, which requires a moist situation, the Myrtle-leaf rhododendron enjoys similar conditions. It is so named for its leaves resemble those of the myrtle, whilst they give off its sweet refreshing fragrance when bruised. It is one of the best of all rhododendrons for a small garden, for it is of neat habit with bronze-green leaves, and it bears its bell-shaped flowers of soft pink in June and in great profusion.

R. minus (syn. *R. punctatum*). A North American species growing to 1.8 m (6 ft) in height, it has smooth elliptic leaves 7 cm (3 in) long, which on the under-surface are covered in resinous glands. The leaves release a lemon-like scent when handled. The handsome rose-red flowers, spotted inside, appear in April and have no perfume.

R. rubiginosum. This species reaches the dimensions of a small tree on the borders of its native China and Tibet, and is most free-flowering. It bears its rosy-mauve flowers in April and May, whilst its large, glossy leaves are deliciously lemon-scented when handled. Like all the scented-leaf species, it is extremely hardy.

R. saluenense. Native of Nepal, it makes a low shrub 45 cm (1½ ft) tall, and has large, glossy, dark-green leaves which are powerfully aromatic. It bears its deep crimson-purple flowers in April, large and flattened, and borne upright on long stalks, either solitary or in pairs. The flowers are not scented but are borne in such profusion as to almost hide the foliage.

The hybrid Pink Drift is a rock garden shrub of compact habit and bears a profusion of flowers of soft rosy-lavender. It also has the same strongly aromatic foliage of its seed-bearing parent.

R. sargentianum. Discovered by E. H. Wilson in western Szechwan in 1903, it makes a dense shrub 60 cm (2 ft) tall and the same in width. The leaves are strongly aromatic, and are of leathery texture. In May, it bears loose umbels of 5 or 7 pale citron-yellow flowers and in such profusion

that they almost hide the foliage. The tubular corolla is about 2 cm (1 in) in diameter.

AZALEA SERIES. It includes those plants known as Azaleas, though Azalea no longer has botanical status. The plants differ in that the azaleas are mostly deciduous and bear long tubular flowers which rely on their perfume to draw the long-tongued insects for their pollination, whilst the rhododendrons are mostly evergreen, with bell-shaped flowers in which the stamens are exposed as the blooms open, so that perfume is less necessary to ensure their continuation. The characteristic by which a plant with brilliantly coloured flowers has less need of fragrance for pollination than those of paler colouring certainly holds true with the azalea, for the most fragrant are those which bear white, yellow or pale-pink flowers. The brilliantly coloured Mollis azaleas have no scent, whilst only slight perfume is to be detected in the Ghent azaleas. No perfume is noticeable in any of the evergreen species.

Azaleas require similar conditions to the rhododendrons, i.e. a lime-free peaty soil, shelter from cold winds, and partial shade, for the brighter colours will fade if exposed to direct sunlight. They are surface-rooting plants and should not be planted deeply whilst they should never be allowed to lack moisture at the roots, especially during summer. Established plants appreciate a mulch of peat or leaf-mould, and a little decayed manure after flowering. Both the evergreen and deciduous azaleas require similar soil conditions, though the evergreen species are tolerant of more shade.

Azaleas have a tendency to form suckers which should be cut away as they appear, whilst after flowering the heads should be removed to prevent seeding and to ensure the formation of strong ripened shoots to produce buds to flower the following year. For convenience those species which have become known as azaleas are separated from the rhododendrons.

Rhododendron (Azalea) arborescens. A deciduous species, native of Pennsylvania, where it grows nearly 6 m (20 ft) tall. It has blunt-ended leaves, glossy above, glaucous beneath, and early in June it bears sweetly scented white flowers, enhanced by the brilliant-scarlet filaments.

R. *atlanticum.* One of the finest of all species, it is native of North America and forms a dense bush 60 to 90 cm (2 to 3 ft) in height and the same across. Its deliciously fragrant white flowers, with their long slender tubes, are flushed with pink on the outside and open early in May.

R. *canadense* (syn. *Rhodora canadense*). A deciduous plant of North America growing 90 cm (3 ft) in height with grey leaves, and it comes into bloom in April, its purple flowers having a powerful sweet perfume.

R. *canescens.* A North American species which grows 3 m (10 ft) in height, with pink and white tubular flowers which open in June and emit a sweet, honeysuckle-like perfume.

R. *linearifolium.* A deciduous Japanese form, its yellow stems being covered in stiff hairs and furnished with willow-like leaves. The rose-pink flowers with their narrow petals have slight scent, and appear in May.

R. *luteum* (syn. R. *flavum, Azalea pontica*). The Yellow azalea or rhododendron from the Caucasus, which bears its sweetly scented yellow flowers, produced at the end of the shoots, late in June. It reaches a height of 2.4 to 3 m (8 to 10 ft), and is of stiff, upright habit. In autumn, its leaves take on gorgeous autumnal tints of purple, orange, crimson and gold before they fall. It is known as the Honeysuckle azalea from the peculiar shape of the flowers and for their honey-like fragrance. It is a species of extreme hardiness and one of the parents (with R. *nudiflorum*) of the Ghent hybrids which come into bloom when varieties of the Mollis azaleas are almost over. The Ghent hybrids inherit the coloured foliage of R. *luteum,* and there is some scent in the yellow-flowering varieties Nancy Waterer, golden-yellow, and Narcissiflora, double yellow. *Altaclarense* is a lovely hybrid variety bearing orange-yellow flowers of powerful fragrance, whilst Sunbeam bears bright golden-yellow flowers with a perfume equally pronounced.

R. *occidentale.* It grows 3 m (10 ft) tall and is valuable in that it blooms in June and July when all other azaleas have finished flowering. The creamy-white flowers emit a delicate sweet perfume, most pronounced at eventide. It is a native of California and is deciduous.

Several hybrid varieties of R. *occidentale* bear sweetly scented flowers: *Delicatissimum,* pink, opening to cream; *Exquisitum,* cream, flushed with pink; Irene Koster, rose-pink; *Magnificum,* creamy-white, flushed pink.

R. *roseum.* A charming little North American shrub with honeysuckle-shaped flowers of shell-pink, which have a powerful spicy fragrance.

R. *viscosum.* It is, with R. *occidentale,* the last to bloom, opening its white, honeysuckle-shaped flowers early in July, and they are sweetly scented. It is the Swamp honeysuckle of North America which grows 0.9 to 1.2 m (3 to 4 ft) in height, its downy leaves being clammy to the touch. There is a pale-pink form, *rubescens,* which is not quite so richly scented, and a hybrid (x R. *molle*) known as A. *viscosum daviesii* which has attractive grey-green foliage and bears in June sweetly scented flowers of ice-white.

RHUS (Anacardiaceae—Cashew Family)

A genus of 120 species of trees or shrubs abounding in resinous juices. They grow well beneath mature trees, in partial shade where the soil is usually dry.

Species. *Rhus aromatica.* A native of North America, it grows 3 to 3.6 m (10 to 12 ft) tall and has thick, downy leaves which emit a delicious sweet resinous scent when crushed. The leaves appear after the catkin-like flowers in May and these are followed by crimson currant-like fruits.

R. *coriaria.* A native of southern Europe and a rare tree in cultivation It grows 6 m (20 ft) in height with hairy leaves composed of 15 elliptic toothed leaflets which turn a brilliant purple-crimson in autumn. This species furnished the sumach of commerce. The flowers, borne in mid-summer, are greenish-white.

R. *cotinoides.* The Chittam wood of the southern United States where it forms a tree 9 m (30 ft) in height. The large round undivided leaves take on glorious shades of scarlet, purple and yellow in autumn, and when young have an aromatic fragrance when bruised.

R. *trichocarpa.* A native of Japan, it

grows to a height of 6 m (20 ft), its resinous leaves being nearly 60 cm (2 ft) in length whilst taking on brilliant scarlet and orange tints in autumn.

Suitable for the warmest gardens of the British Isles and southern Europe, the sumachs enjoy a dry soil and a sheltered situation.

RIBES (Flowering Currant)
(Grossulariaceae—Gooseberry Family)

This family consists of the genus Currant and Gooseberry, in all some 60 species of spiny or unarmed shrubs. Like those grown commercially for their edible fruit, the flowering ornamental currants have attractive pale-green foliage, 5-lobed and serrated and emitting the familiar musty smell, reminiscent of animal fur when bruised, though the leaves of *R. viburnifolium* have a most pleasant pine-like smell. Few species bear genuinely scented flowers though many have a slight musky smell, similar to but less pronounced than the foliage. Those which are scented are aromatic and clove-like. They thrive in almost any type of soil and are tolerant of some chalk in their diet.

Species. *Ribes fasciculatum.* Native of Japan and Korea, it makes a dense bush some 1.5 m (5 ft) tall and the same across, and it comes into bloom early in April, bearing dainty sprays of creamy-yellow flowers, usually in numbers of 7 or 9, and they have a delicious aromatic perfume. The blooms are followed by small bright-red fruits which persist into winter.

R. guyanum. One of the few evergreen species, it is a native of South America and is hardy only in the most sheltered gardens of the British Isles. It is a handsome plant, growing 1.8 m (6 ft) in height and is valuable in that it blooms late in June when the other species have finished flowering. The pale-yellow flowers are borne in dense racemes and have a soft sweet perfume.

R. laurifolium. Native of northern China, it is evergreen, with leathery pointed leaves like those of the laurel, and in a sheltered garden where the winter sun can reach it, it comes into bloom early in February and continues until April. The flowers, which are greenish-white, are borne in drooping racemes and emit a soft sweet perfume.

R. odoratum (syn. *R. aureum*). A native of North America, it is the Buffalo or Golden currant, also the Clove-scented currant, a delightful plant in every way, from the strikingly beautiful golden foliage to the golden-yellow flowers, borne in sprays of 15 or so from the graceful arching stems. It blooms in April and is deliciously clove-scented. In autumn the foliage takes on the most brilliant autumnal tints whilst the flowers are followed by large yellow fruits to complete a symphony in gold.

R. viburnifolium. One of the few evergreen species of the family, flowering in April, its terracotta blooms presenting a striking picture against the dark-green leaves, especially where growing against a stone wall. It is native of California and, unless it can be given the protection of a warm wall, should be confined to the warm, moist climate of South-west England. It is worthy of a select position and against a wall will attain a height of 2.4 to 2.7 m (8 to 9 ft), always remaining neat and unobtrusive; in addition to the beauty of its flowers, it emits a most refreshing pine-like aroma whenever the leaves are bruised.

ROBINIA (Leguminosae—Laburnum Family)

Amongst the most beautiful of all trees are the 'false' acacias known as the Robinias for it was Jean Robin, nurseryman to the King of France, who introduced the first into Europe during the sixteenth century, obtaining the seed from Canada. This was seed of the tree known as the False Acacia or Locust Tree, its white flowers being delicately fragrant. The Robinias are native of North America and are most suited for planting in dry, exposed situations.

In 1662, John Evelyn said: 'The acacia [robinia] deserves a place among our avenue trees, adorning our walks with its exotic leaves and sweet flowers.' Not all the acacias have fragrant flowers but almost all have grey-green fern-like leaves which are retained in winter. Unfortunately, as Evelyn observed, their wood is brittle and their branches are often broken by the wind, whilst during wet or cold weather and at night, the leaves fold up giving the trees the appearance of being defoliated.

Species and Varieties. *Robinia hartwigii.* A valuable July-flowering shrub or small tree, growing 4.5 m (15 ft) tall and bearing its lilac-pink flowers, slightly fragrant, in dense racemes of 20 or more.

R. luxurians. A small tree of Arizona and New Mexico, growing to a height of 6 m (20 ft), and like *R. dubia* it bears its fragrant pale rose-pink flowers during July and August on short drooping racemes. The young wood and the surface of the young leaves are covered with brown hairs. Like the true False Acacia, it is quite hardy in Britain. *R. lispida,* the beautiful Rose Acacia, is similar in habit, bearing deep rose-red flowers early in summer but unfortunately they have no scent.

R. pseudo-acacia. The False Acacia, a tree of great hardiness and worthy, as Evelyn said, or much wider planting. It is the Common Locust Tree of North America, growing to a height of 15 m (50 ft) or more and in May and June bears pendent clusters of handsome white flowers which have the delicious fragrance of the family, like vanilla. A hybrid variety, *R. dubia,* makes a pretty tree 6 m (20 ft) tall with ovate leaves, and in July and August bears pale rose-pink flowers in drooping racemes. They are sweetly scented and are followed by prickly brown seed-pods.

A variety bearing smaller flowers than the type but which are freely produced and of richer perfume is *coluteoides* whilst another form, *frisia,* usually listed as *Robina aurea,* is perhaps the most brilliantly coloured of all trees, its leaves being of brilliant gold, turning to deep orange in autumn. Its flowers are sweetly fragrant.

ROCHEA (Crassulaceae—Crassula Family)

A genus of four species of sub-shrubs, native of South Africa, with opposite leaves joined at the base, which are stem-clasping with hairy margins.

Species. *Rochea coccinea.* Introduced into Europe in 1700 by Dutch settlers, it was for long a popular pot plant. It has suc-culent leaves and bears brilliant-scarlet flowers with the hyacinth scent, most unusual in flowers of this colouring. The white form *albo-flore* is even more heavily scented.

R. jasminea. A dainty species, so named for the resemblance of its flowers to those of the jasmine, being white and with a soft, jasmine-like perfume.

R. odoratissima. A valuable house plant, it bears sweetly scented yellow flowers and is readily raised from seed sown as soon as harvested.

RODRIQUEZIA (Orchidaceae—Orchid Family)

A genus of about 30 species of epiphytic orchids, with pseudo-bulbs and sometimes also rhizomes, mostly from Brazil, but also from other parts of tropical America. They are easily grown with showy flowers, and require a compost of equal parts of osmunda fibre and sphagnum-moss. Drainage. must be plentiful and good. A warm humid atmosphere is required with a winter night temperature of about 16°C (60°F). Plenty of water is necessary, and they should not be allowed to dry out in winter. Increase is by dividing the plants in late spring.

Species. *Rodriquezia candida.* Somewhat tubular in shape, but with a widely ex-panded mouth, the flowers are ice-white, with a central yellow stripe on the lip. They are produced on arching inflores-cences in spring, each flower being about 5 cm (2 in) long and scented of lemons. It is a native of Brazil.

ROMNEYA (Papaveraceae—Poppy Family)

Named after the Irish astronomer, Romney Robinson, they are best known as the Californian Tree Poppies, being native of California where they grow to a height of 1.8 to 2.4 m (6 to 8 ft) in the warm climate and in a sandy soil enriched with leaf-mould and decayed manure. In the British Isles they require similar conditions though they also grow well in sheltered gardens away from the coast but only where the soil is light and well-drained. They resent disturbance and once planted grow into dense bushes, increasing by underground suckers, though each year after flowering they should be cut down to within 15 cm (6 in) of the base; they will make new growth in spring. A requirement of the plants is an abundance of summer moisture.

Species. *Romneya coulteri.* It grows 1.2 to 1.8 m (4 to 6 ft) tall in Britain and has long grey leaves, serrated and hairy at the edges, and it blooms from July until September, before the autumn-flowering plants come into full bloom but after the full flush of early summer. The flowers, like enormous poppies, are pure white with crinkled petals and with attractive golden anthers, and they emit a sweet exotic perfume.

R. trichocalyx. Hardier than *R. coulteri*, it differs only in this respect and in the hairy calyx. In all other ways it is similar.

RONDELETIA (Rubiaceae—Bedstraw Family)

A genus of 60 species of small trees or shrubs, native of South America and Cuba, the West Indies and Nepal, and named after William Rondelet, famous physician and naturalist. The perfume 'Rondeletia' is obtained from the plant.

Species. *Rondeletia discolor.* Native of New Granada, it makes a dense shrub 1.2 to 1.5 m (4 to 5 ft) tall and bears crimson-red flowers of outstanding fragrance.

R. disperma. A native of Brazil and the Islands of Baru and Tierra Bomba where it grows into a tree 4.5 m (15 ft) tall and is usually found in rocky places. The flowers are purplish-white, deliciously scented, and are borne in axillary racemes.

R. exserta (syn. *Wendlandia exserta*). It is found in the forests of Nepal and Sikkim up to a height of 1,200 m (4,000 ft) where it makes a crooked tree 12 m (40 ft) tall. The ovate leaves are borne opposite and are about 15 cm (6 in) long and 7.5 cm (3 in) wide. It bears pyramidal panicles of powerfully scented flowers of purest white. This tree grows about the ruins of the ancient city of Gour in Bengal, drenching the air with its aromatic perfume.

R. odorata. It makes a dense shrub about 1.8 m (6 ft) tall and is native of Mexico and Havana, where it grows about rocky formations close to the sea. The flowers which are borne in terminal corymbs are the most powerfully scented of all scarlet flowers, whilst the projecting ring of the tube is brilliant orange, providing a most striking picture against the dark evergreen foliage.

ROSA (Rosaceae—Rose Family)

A large family of which the most important is the genus *Rosa*, which contains about 250 distinct species. They are mostly native of the Northern Hemisphere. They are erect climbing or trailing plants, prickly, smooth, silky or glandular-haired, with woody stems, and with alternate, oddly pinnate leaves and serrated leaflets. The flowers are borne solitary or in corymbs.

Probably the most varied of all floral perfumes are those of the rose, none being more appreciated in this respect than the old Shrub roses, whilst many of the wild rose species are equally fragrant. For its perfume, the rose reigns supreme amongst the flowers of the world. In his *Herbal* of 1597 Gerard wrote, '... the rose deserved the chiefest and most principal place amongst all flowers whatsoever, being not only esteemed for its beauty, virtues and fragrant and odoriferous smell but also because it is the honour and ornament of our English sceptre.'

From the beginning of time and until the introduction of the modern bicolours, the rose was esteemed more for its perfume than for its beauty. Homer and Pliny, Ovid and Virgil refer especially to this quality. Apollonius, writer of a treatise on perfumes about the year 200 B.C. said that 'the perfume from roses is most excellent at Phasalis, Naples and Capua', and writing at about the same time Theophrastus said that the best 'perfumes are made from roses, white lilies and violets'. Mattresses were made of scented rose petals for men of rank to lie upon, and it is told that when Saladin entered Jerusalem in 1187, he had the walls of Omar's Mosque washed with rose water. Pliny wrote that the Isle of Albion was so called 'from the white roses with which it abounds' and he also said that in his day meat was always served covered with fragrant rose petals. Usually they were the petals of the Damask rose which gave its name to the Syrian town of Damascus where they grew with freedom. It is the Damask rose whose perfume transcends all other rose scents and the Greek writer, Herodotus, wrote of this rose 'with a scent surpassing all others' which flourished in that part of Macedonia where once existed the gardens of Midas.

Of all flowers, none possess a wider variety of perfumes than the rose species. In a letter to *The Gardening World* of 1885, Charles Curtis suggested that there were at least 17 different perfumes, and with the large amount of interbreeding amongst the modern bedding roses, the number of different perfumes must today number many more. This is an additional factor contributing to the popularity of the rose today, providing interest, especially for those who may have lost their sight, in addition to new and exciting colours.

The wild rose species and the old Shrub roses, being of purer breeding than the modern roses, possess a more refreshing and distinctive perfume, though in certain instances this may not be so pronounced as in a number of modern roses. There is, today, a tendency to neglect the best of the old roses for the modern bedding rose has now become the most useful of all garden plants, remaining in bloom from June until almost the year end, while many of the wild rose species bloom for but a short time. They do, however, possess a beauty of their own, some with grey foliage, others with brilliantly coloured hips in autumn, and where space permits several should be in every garden if only for the distinctive perfume of their flowers.

Species. *Rosa alba.* The rose adopted by the House of York as its symbol, and which Gerard described as bearing 'fair double flowers, of a very sweete smell'. The double form, one imposed upon another, is the symbol of our Royalty to this day.

Possibly a hybrid of the Damask rose and *R. canina*, the native Dog-rose, it is a plant of erect habit, growing from 1.2 to 2.4 m (4 to 8 ft) tall with blue-grey foliage as if it has been powdered, and bearing its flowers during June and July. The blooms are white, cream or pale pink. They require little attention as to their pruning; all that is necessary is to shorten any unduly long shoots to a third of their length

and to remove dead and overcrowded wood. This should be done early in March. The *alba* roses have few thorns, but those they have are large, whilst the sweetly perfumed flowers are followed by large hips.

Rosa alba maxima is the Great Double White or Jacobite rose, growing 1.8 to 2.1 m (6 to 7 ft) and the same across. It blooms in early June, being one of the first roses to flower, its large flat, white blooms, folded at the centre, having 60 petals and being followed by red hips. This rose with its powerful scent is grown in Bulgaria for attar of roses.

Rosa alba semi-plena is the White Rose of York and of similar habit to *R. alba maxima*. The semi-double blooms, with their attractive gold stamens, are strongly fragrant and are borne on arching sprays like orange-blossom.

Varieties of *R. alba*:

BELLE AMOUR. Said to have originated from a convent garden in Germany, it is a magnificent rose, growing 1.5 m (5 ft) tall, and the same across. More free-flowering than any of the *alba* roses, its rounded blooms are semi-double, like those of *R. a. semi-plena* and are a lovely pale salmon-pink, with an exciting and unusual aromatic perfume.

CELESTIAL. The leaves are of deep grey-blue, whilst it grows 1.8 to 2.1 m (6 to 7 ft) tall and about 1.2 m (4 ft) across. It bears a beautifully rounded bloom 10 cm (4 in) across of clearest pink followed by oval hips. Also known as the Celest Rose.

FÉLICITÉ PARMENTIER. A delightful rose growing only 1.2 m (4 ft) tall and 90 cm (3 ft) across. Its cream-coloured buds open to rosette-shaped blooms, like the ranunculus, of palest pink, and they have the rich perfume of honeysuckle.

GREAT MAIDEN'S BLUSH. One of our very oldest roses, it grows about 1.5 m (5 ft) tall and 1.2 m (4 ft) across, with blue-green leaves. Its blooms are double and blush-white, with a deeper pink centre, and carry a strong, sweet perfume. Of this rose, the late Vita Sackville-West (Lady Nicolson) wrote in *The Observer* that it holds its petals longer than any other in the gardens at Sissinghurst Castle, Kent.

JEANNE D'ARC. Growing less than 1.2 m (4 ft) tall and 90 cm (3 ft) across, it has blue-green leaves and bears large rosette-shaped blooms of soft creamy-white.

KOENIGIN VON DANEMARK. Though growing only 1.5 m (5 ft) tall it is of less compact habit than the other *alba* roses. The deep-pink buds open to large quartered blooms of a lovely rose-pink, which have a sweet fragrance.

MME LEGRAS DE ST GERMAIN. Grows 1.8 to 2.1 m (6 to 7 ft) tall and the same across, and is almost thornless, with small pale-green leaves, whilst its large blooms, flat like a saucer, are fully double and white, shaded creamy-yellow at the centre.

MME PLANTIER. It grows 1.5 m (5 ft) tall and makes a dense bush at least 1.5 m (5 ft) thick with pale-green leaves. It is most free-flowering, its creamy-white blooms being of perfectly circular form and fully double.

POMPOM BLANC PARFAIT. It makes a compact bush 1.2 m (4 ft) tall and 60 cm (2 ft) across, with grey-green leaves and bears its pompom-like flowers of blush-white on short laterals from mid-June until the end of July.

ROSE DE RESHT. Said to have reached Britain direct from the Persian city of Resht. It grows 90 cm (3 ft) tall, being the most compact of the *alba* roses and it bears masses of camellia-shaped flowers of ruby-red, veined with purple.

R. *banksiae*. This somewhat tender crimson rose was brought into England in 1807 by William Kerr and named in honour of Lady Banks. It bears double white flowers like cherry-blossom which carry the perfume of the violet. It is thornless and has small evergreen leaves. It may be grown against a sunny wall of a sheltered garden in the South or in a cold greenhouse, for it comes early into bloom long before the end of May, and the buds may be damaged by late frosts. The double yellow (straw-coloured) Banksian rose, *lutea*, was discovered growing on a wall at Nanking in 1827 by a Dr Abel. There is also a single form, *lutescens*, both of which have the unmistakable perfume of the violet, though the single forms do not bloom so well outdoors. Do no prun-ing for it is from the old twiggy wood that the blooms are produced.

R. *bracteata*. The Macartney rose, it was introduced in 1793 by Lord Macartney, and like *R. sempervirens* requires no pruning, for the wood is twiggy and brittle. A valuable wall rose in that it is both evergreen and perpetual-flowering, the large, single, white flowers having golden stamens and a delicious sweet perfume. The variety Mermaid is one of the loveliest of all wall plants, its large, single, yellow flowers being enhanced by the glossy foliage. It is, however, difficult to establish, taking some years to get away, and is best planted from a pot so as not to disturb the roots.

R. *bourboniana*. The natural crossing of the China rose with a Damask, which took place at the Isle de Bourbon about the year 1817, resulted in the Bourbon group of roses which, apart from the Quatre Saisons Damask, were the first roses with the recurrent flowering habit. Their flowers range in colour from white and pink to crimson and purple, the large globular blooms being quartered at the centre and filled with overlapping petals. Their beauty of form, combined with a powerful fragrance, gives distinction to the Bour-bons in any garden, and with their freedom of flowering and ability to remain in bloom from June until the end of autumn, they are amongst the best of all plants for the shrubbery. Certain varieties are of less vigorous habit than others, growing between 1.2 to 1.5 m (4 to 5 ft) tall, and these should be used in the small border, but to be seen at their best they require a warm, sunny situation.

The Bourbons require little pruning, but hybrid varieties which make unduly long shoots should be cut back about half-way; or they may be used to clothe a pillar or low wall facing south or west, where they will remain in bloom until almost the year-end. In March, weak and decayed wood should be cut away and the plants given a mulch. Several of the Bourbons make ex-cellent plants for a hedge, being efficient and colourful for six months of the year.

Varieties marked with an asterisk * give little bloom in autumn; dates of introduc-tion are given where known:

ADAM MESSERICH (1920). One of the most recent of the Bourbons, it makes a dense bush 1.5 m (5 ft) tall and the same in width. Its large, semi-double blooms of warm rose-pink have the fresh perfume of raspberries.

BEAUTÉ SÉDUISANTE. It makes a large bush of myrtle-green, the young shoots being tinted with bronze. Its flowers are like huge water-lilies, incurving and of a beautiful coral-pearl colouring with a sweet perfume.

BOULE DE NEIGE (1867). One of the most outstanding of the shrub roses, making a compact, upright plant 1.8 m (6 ft) tall, but only about 60 cm (2 ft) across, with smooth, dark-green foliage. The blooms are symmetrical and open like camellias, and are snow-white with a delicious perfume.

*BOURBON QUEEN (1835). The first of the Bourbons, but is less recurrent-flowering than the others. Of vigorous, upright habit, it sends out long graceful shoots and may be used to cover a wall. Its blooms are flat but cup-shaped, and are of deepest pink with a powerfully sweet perfume.

CHARLES LAWSON (1853). It makes a tall, upright shrub and may be used to cover a fence or pillar. Of different habit from the others, it bears its blooms in clusters at the end of the shoots. The flowers are quartered and are pink with a deeper reverse.

*COMMANDANT BEAUREPAIRE (1874). Also known as Panachée d'Angers. It is a most exciting rose but, like Bourbon Queen, bears only a very few flowers in autumn, possibly because it blooms so heavily in midsummer. It has pale-green leaves and bears its flowers from every shoot. The flowers are incurved, and striped attractively with all the Bourbon colours, pink, crimson, mauve, purple, maroon and scarlet, and are strongly fragrant.

*GREAT WESTERN (1837). Like Bourbon Queen, it forms little bloom in autumn, but is worthy of a place in any border for its sumptuous full blooms of crimson-purple and maroon which are attractively quartered and followed by red hips in autumn.

HONORINE DE BRABANT (1880). A 'sport' from Commandant Beaurepaire, it makes a dense bush 1.5 m (5 ft) tall and the same in width, with pale-green foliage, and it blooms well in autumn. The flowers are cup-shaped and quartered and are striped lilac-pink and purple.

KATHLEEN HARROP (1920). A sport from Zephirine Drouhin and, like that rose, it is thornless and is in bloom for six months of the year. It grows 1.2 to 1.5 m (4 to 5 ft) tall and bears flowers of a lovely clear pink with a raspberry fragrance.

LA REINE VICTORIA (1872). It grows less than 1.5 m (5 ft) tall and together with its sports, Louise Odier and Mme P. Oger, makes up a trio worthy of planting in every garden. The cup-shaped blooms make a perfect circle and are a lovely rose-pink with an exquisite fragrance.

LOUISE ODIER (1856). A sport from La Reine Victoria, and one of the best of all garden roses, making a compact plant 1.2 to 1.5 m (4 to 5 ft) tall with plenty of dark leathery foliage, and bearing perfectly circular blooms of rose-pink flushed with lilac, which carry a sweet fragrance.

MME ERNEST CALVAT (1888). A sport from Mme I. Pereire, it has the same vigorous habit, growing 2.1 to 2.4 m (7 to 8 ft) tall, and it should be confined to a large border, or will make an excellent hedge, for it has attractive purple-bronze foliage and stems, and blooms well in autumn. The blooms are large and globular and a lovely clear pink.

MME ISAAC PEREIRE (1881). A vigorous grower, attaining a height of 2.1 to 2.4 m (7 to 8 ft), and will reach twice that height against a pillar or wall. Its cup-shaped blooms are enormous and of deep crimson-pink, with a strong raspberry fragrance, and they are produced with freedom in autumn.

MME L. DE BARNY (1868). The first of the Bourbons to bloom, but it has few flowers in autumn. It makes a compact bush 1.2 to 1.5 m (4 to 5 ft) tall and, in July, bears a profusion of large, full flowers of an attractive silver-pink.

MME PIERRE OGER (1878). A sport from La Reine Victoria, and a superb garden plant, always in bloom whatever the weather. The leaves have crinkled edges, whilst the blooms are circular and cup-shaped, with almost transparent petals of creamy-pink which are exquisitely fragrant.

MRS W. PAUL (1890). A Mme I. Pereire seedling, it attains a height of 2.4 to 2.7 m (8 to 9 ft) and is best grown against a pillar which it will clothe with its blush-pink flowers, and it is especially colourful in autumn.

*PRINCE CHARLES. Like Bourbon Queen it bears little autumnal bloom. The flowers are large and flat, and are of deep crimson-maroon, but the fragrance is not pronounced.

SOUVENIR DE JENNY PERNET-DUCHER (1890). A sport of Souvenir de la Malmaison and also known as Pink Souvenir. It grows 1.8 m (6 ft) tall with bright-green foliage, and bears enormous globular blooms of carnation-pink with delicious perfume.

SOUVENIR DE LA MALMAISON (1842). It makes a compact bush 0.9 to 1.2 m (3 to 4 ft) tall and blooms profusely in autumn. The flowers are large, and open flat and quartered and are a lovely flesh-pink. The climbing form appeared 50 years later, and will attain a height of 3 m (10 ft) against a warm wall.

*SOUVENIR DE LA PRINCESSE DE LAMBALLE (1874). Similar in habit to Bourbon Queen, it bears its flowers in clusters, veined in a lovely shade of lilac-pink. It also has very attractive bright-red hips.

SOUVENIR DE ST ANNE (1950). It appeared in a Dublin garden and is a sport from Souvenir de la Malmaison. The semi-double blooms are of the same pink as the flowers of the Dog-rose, enhanced by golden stamens.

VARIEGATA DI BOLOGNA (1909). Tall-growing, it is best grown against a pillar or low sunny wall where it will bloom from midsummer until Christmas. The blooms are globular and quartered, and are magnolia-white, striped with black-crimson. They are extremely fragrant.

ZÉPHIRINE DROUHIN (1873). The most valuable rose of the garden, and it is thornless. It may be used to cover a wall or pillar for it may be trained to a considerable height, whilst it makes a delightful hedge. It may also be planted in the shrub border where it will attain a height of 1.8 m (6 ft). It is one of the first of all roses to bloom, before the end

of May, and is usually last to remain in bloom. The semi-double blooms are a lovely bright silver-pink and have a delicious sweet, penetrating perfume.

R. californica plena. Native only to western America, it greatly resembles *R. coryana* in habit, with its arching stems and fern-like foliage. Its semi-double blooms are a lovely glowing deep pink and have a rich perfume.

R. canina. The Dog-briar or Dog-rose, native to the English hedgerow which, with the Damask rose, produced the White roses. *R. canina* is not a plant for the garden, but is best left to send out its arching sprays amongst hedgerow plants surrounding orchards or fields. Its leaves have a delicious fragrance whilst its single cup-shaped flowers vary from white to a lovely pale pink, and are followed by large, brilliant hips. The variety Abbotswood, found in the garden of the late Harry Ferguson (of tractor fame) bears double flowers of deepest pink, followed by large oval, vermilion hips.

R. cantab (R. nutkana × Red Letter Day). A hybrid of recent introduction, raised by Dr Hurst in Cambridge in 1928. It is a plant of upright habit with rather sparse foliage and bears in June large, fragrant, single flowers of lilac-pink, followed by oval-shaped crimson hips which are retained through winter.

R. cantabrigiensis. Raised by Dr Hurst from *R. hugonis*, it comes into bloom before the end of May. It makes a dense bush 2.1 to 2.4 m (7 to 8 ft) tall and the same in width, its long graceful shoots being clothed in large, clear, primrose-yellow blooms which have a fresh fruity perfume. It obtained an Award of Merit in 1931.

R. centifolia. This is the Old Cabbage-rose, so called because the petals fold over like cabbage leaves. It is also the Rose of Provence, and because the blooms have a hundred petals it was known to the writers of old as the Hundred-leaved rose. It is believed to be a hybrid between *R. alba* and the Autumn Damask and is native to the mountain regions of Greece, Bulgaria and Persia. It is the rose that has its petals or flower leaves folded or lapped over each other so closely that they will not open unless forced with the fingers, and therefore always look as if they are in bud, but when expanded are the largest of all the roses. The Rev. Henry Ellacombe wrote, 'I consider [it] to be still unrivalled . . . It is a delightful rose, delightful to the eye, delightful for its fragrance, and most delightful from its associations'. The huge, sumptuous blooms are borne on short laterals during June and July, whilst the large, rounded leaves have serrated edges, the stems being covered in tiny thorns. Several of the varieties grow only 90 cm (3 ft) tall, and may be planted to the front of a shrubbery whilst a number attain a height of 1.8 m (6 ft) or more. They require the minimum of pruning, only the occasional removal of unduly long shoots and of any dead wood. *R. centifolia* itself grows 1.5 m (5 ft) tall and has huge globular blooms of China pink.

It has made its influence felt on the modern rose, for it was from a white sport of the *R. centifolia* seedling, Souvenir de la Reine d'Angleterre, crossed with Mme Caroline Testout, that the wonderful hybrid perpetual, Frau Karl Druschki, was obtained, and this in turn was a parent of the outstanding white-flowered hybrid tea rose, Marcia Stanhope. Frau Karl Druschki is still the best white-flowered rose ever introduced, but alas, it has not the slightest trace of any perfume. The following varieties of *R. centifolia* are fragrant:

BLANCHEFLEUR (1835). Miss Nancy Lindsay, an authority on shrub roses, has suggested this might be the 'dwarf white Damask rose' of Mary Queen of Scots, as it undoubtedly has much of the Damask in its pedigree. The large, cabbage-like blooms are pure white with a delicious scent. It grows 1.5 m (5 ft) tall and l. 2 (4 ft) wide.

BULLATA (1780). A very old variety growing only 1.2 m (4 ft) tall, it is more renowned for its foliage than its flowers. The leaves are like those of the cos lettuce, jade-green with a bronze lustre, and heavily veined or grooved like a polyanthus leaf. The blooms are a lovely cherry-blossom pink.

CHAPEAU DE NAPOLÉON (1826). So named because of the cockade of green, shaped like Napoleon's hat, around its bud, hence its name of the Crested Cabbage-rose. It grows 1.5 m (5 ft) tall and bears medium-sized, cup-shaped blooms of rose-madder which have a pronounced perfume.

DUC DE FITZJAMES. Of vigorous habit with many prickles and growing 1.8 to 2.1 m (6 to 7 ft) tall, it bears cup-shaped flowers which are an attractive carmine when they open, but fade to lilac-pink, almost the colour of the hybrid perpetual rose Mrs J. Laing.

FANTIN LATOUR. One of the most robust in this group, growing 1.5 to 1.8 m (5 to 6 ft) tall and almost as wide. Its graceful arching branches are covered with large flat blooms of a lovely shell-pink.

GROS CHOUX D'HOLLANDE. It is believed to be the result of a cross with a Damask rose and is the Great Dutch Hundred-leaved rose, well known in the sixteenth century. It makes a bush 1.2 m (4 ft) tall and the same in width, and has small pale-green leaves. The blooms, with their tightly curled petals, are a lovely mushroom-pink and are strongly fragrant.

JUNO (1847). It makes a bush 1.2 m (4 ft) tall and the same across, the large blooms which are attractively quartered being filled with petals of delicate blush colouring and with a sweet perfume. The plant has grey foliage.

LA NOBLESSE (1856). Most valuable in that it blooms until the end of July, the last of all the *centifolia* roses. It has bright-green foliage, grows 1.5 m (5 ft) tall and bears richly scented flowers of warm rose-pink.

OMBRÉE PARFAIT (1823). It grows 90 cm (3 ft) tall and nearly 1.2 m (4 ft) wide, with small, pale-green leaves. Its blooms are also small, opening flat and being of black-maroon.

PARFAIT DE FLANDRES. It grows 1.2 m (4 ft) tall with apple-green leaves, the red buds unfolding to enormous blooms of lilac-pink.

PARVIFOLIA. A rose of great antiquity known as the Burgundy rose, or Rose of St Francis. In growth it resembles a hybrid tea, whilst it bears sweetly scented, flat, pompom-like blooms of a lovely shade of deep pink.

PETITE DE HOLLANDE. One of the most compact of the group, growing only 90 cm (3 ft) tall, and bearing small cup-shaped flowers of purest pink over a long period.

POPE PIUS IX. Growing to 1.2 m (4 ft) tall and the same in width, it has foliage of frosted emerald-green. On the long graceful stems, the large flowers may be described as of iridescent purple, like the bloom on a black grape.

REINE DES CENTFEUILLES (1824). The plant grows wider than it grows tall, its blooms being flat and quartered, and a lovely glowing pink, sweetly perfumed.

ROBERT LE DIABLE. It grows only 1.2 m (4 ft) tall and 90 cm (3 ft) in width, and comes late into bloom but continues late. The bloom is of deep purple, with the outer petals recurving.

ROSE DE MEAUX. It grows no more than 90 cm (3 ft) tall and the same in width, and begins to bloom before the end of May. The foliage is pale green, whilst the pompom-like blooms are less that 5 cm (2 in) across, and are a lovely shade of pink.

ROSE D'HIVER. An enchanting thicket rose growing only 0.9 to 1.2 m (3 to 4 ft) tall, with grey-green leaves and bearing small, spicily fragrant flowers of palest pink over many weeks.

SHARASTENAK. From the mountains of northern Persia, it makes a rounded bush 90 cm (3 ft) tall, and the same in width, with red stems and grey leaves. The blooms are enormous, and are of bright rose-pink with a powerful spicy fragrance.

SOUVENIR DE L'IMPÉRATRICE JOSÉPHINE. Growing only 90 cm (3 ft) high, it has silvery-blue leaves, about which it bears huge cabbage-like blooms of rose-pink veined with carmine. The blooms are strongly fragrant and have an attractive silver sheen.

SPONG (1805). It makes a small rounded bush 90 cm (3 ft) tall and comes early into bloom, its rose-pink, cup-shaped flowers being shaded deeper pink at the centre.

THE BISHOP. It is a plant of slender upright habit and bears its flowers in clusters. In colour they are like those of Robert le Diable, cerise with a bloom like that of the black grape, but they turn grey as they age.

TOUR DE MALAKOFF (1856). It makes a plant 1.5 to 1.8 m (5 to 6 ft) tall and the same in width, and in full bloom resembles the Tree Peony. The very large, very fragrant blooms are crimson-red, splashed and veined violet, and shaded lilac at the petal edges. As the blooms age, they turn almost grey.

UNIQUE BLANCHE (White Provence) (1775). Named for the fact that it blooms for six weeks longer than any in the group. Growing 1.2 m (4 ft) tall, its pink buds open to large fragrant blooms of ivory-white which are strongly perfumed. It was found in 1777, in the garden of a baker at Needham Market in Suffolk.

VILLAGE MAID. This is the popular name for the variegated *centifolia*. It grows 1.8 m (6 ft) tall and covers itself in bloom over a period of just a few weeks. The flowers are of cabbage-like appearance and are ivory-white striped with clear pink.

R. centifolia muscosa. The Moss roses are really mutations of the Rose of Provence, moss-like hairs appearing on the calyx, flower stems and leaves, which also carry a distinctive fragrance. They bloom during midsummer and grow from 1.2 to 1.8 m (4 to 6 ft) tall, the blooms being double and cup-shaped. The Moss roses were extremely popular a century ago, and the famous grower, William Paul of Cheshunt, writing at that time, listed more than 50 varieties. Many were noted for the wonderful rich burgundy colouring of their blooms, though the Common Moss rose bears a large double pink bloom, its leaves and stems being heavily mossed. There is also an attractive white form, *alba*, and many lovely hybrids which are not so densely mossed.

It should be said that interbreeding over the years has produced plants which take on the characteristics of both the Damask and the Gallica roses, though all are here grouped together. The Moss roses made their appearance first in Britain, and were introduced into France in 1785 when plants were taken over from this country by Madame de Genlis, having been given to her by Lord Mansfield. Mme de Latour wrote that, 'when Mme de Genlis returned from London to Paris, she had become very celebrated and the crowds of people who went to her house under pretence of seeing the Moss Rose-trees were attracted thither by that lady's celebrity'. She also said that the Moss rose originally came from Provence, but this must be doubted for if so it would surely have been better known throughout France, whereas de Genlis wrote, 'that the cultivation of this superb flower is not yet known in France'. Another version is that the Moss rose originated in Italy, and in an article published a century ago in *Gardeners Chronicle*, Mr Shailer, whose father sent out the White Bath rose early in the nineteenth century, said that this plant was obtained from a Moss rose which reached this country from Italy early in the eighteenth century. Mr Edward Bunyard, in his *Old Garden Roses,* suggests that the plant had its origin in Holland at about the same time. It would seem that the mossing appeared to act as protection against heat, in the same way that *Pelargonium clorinda* has developed hairs on its stems and leaves.

Moss roses should be pruned quite hard during March, cutting back new wood to about halfway and side shoots to about three buds. The following varieties of *R. centifolia muscosa* have a rich fruity perfume (the year of introduction is given where known; R denotes Recurrent-flowering):

ALFRED DE DALMAS (1855). It makes a small, rounded bush about 1.2 m (4 ft) tall and blooms from late June until early September. The blooms are large and cup-shaped and a lovely pale-pink colour with brown moss.

BLANCHE MOREAU (1880). R. It grows 1.8 m (6 ft) tall and is one of the most beautiful of the Moss roses. The cup-shaped flowers open like camellias and are purest white with striking crimson moss. It has the Quatre Saisons Damask in its parentage, and therefore blooms again in autumn.

CAPT. BASROGER (1890). R. It grows tall with the habit of a Pillar rose, and is best used in this way. The flowers are large and of deep crimson, flushed with purple.

CAPT. JOHN INGRAM (1856). It reaches a height of about 1.2 m (4 ft) with purple-tinted foliage and bears, in mid-summer, large rosette-shaped blooms of velvety purple, surrounded with crimson moss.

CELINA (1855). R. It makes a bushy plant 1.5 m (5 ft) tall, and the same in width, and is also known as the Velvet Moss rose on account of the rich damson colour of its flowers enhanced by the circle of gold stamens and red moss.

COMMON MOSS (1727). The Old Pink Moss rose appeared about the mid-eighteenth century, and is a beautiful plant, the chalice-shaped buds opening to large, globular flowers of clearest pink. The plant grows 1.2 m (4 ft) tall and the same in width.

COMTESSE DE MURINAIS (1843). It reaches a height of 1.8 to 2.1 m (6 to 7 ft), and along its graceful arching stems bears sprays of pearly-white flowers which are attractively quartered.

DUCHESSE DE VERNEUIL (1856). It grows 1.2 m (4 ft) tall and the same in width, with pale-green leaves. Its bright-pink flowers are quartered with a large button eye.

DEUIL DU ROI DE ROME (1820). It grows 1.2 m (4 ft) tall with emerald-green foliage, about which it bears its plum-purple flowers in large clusters.

EUGÉNIE GUINOISSEAU (1864). It grows 1.8 m (6 ft) tall and is one of the best Moss roses with glossy dark-green leaves, whilst the stems have few thorns. The rich cerise-red blooms are shaded with purple.

GABRIELLE NOYELLE (1933). R. A modern Moss of great beauty, bearing flowers of a lovely pale salmon-pink with striking golden shading at the base. It makes a bush 1.2 to 1.5 m (4 to 5 ft) high.

GÉNÉRAL KLÉBER (1856). It makes a rounded bush 1.2 m (4 ft) tall and the same in width. The large pink blooms open flat to reveal the button eye whilst the moss is bronzy-green.

GLOIRE DES MOUSSEUX (1852). It grows less than 1.2 m (4 ft) tall, and bears the largest blooms of all the Moss roses, which are of clearest pink, the buds covered with bright-green moss.

GOLDEN MOSS (1930). R. One of the most recent and attractive of the Moss roses. It is a hybrid and the only Moss to bear yellow flowers. The apricot buds, with their dark-green moss, open to large double blooms of clearest yellow.

HENRI MARTIN (1863). It makes a thick bush 1.5 m (5 ft) tall and bears its heavily massed buds in clusters. The crimson-red blooms contrast well with the green moss.

JAMES MITCHELL (1861). The first Moss to bloom and one of the most free-flowering, bearing its shapely flowers of brightest pink along the entire stems. The moss is brown.

JEANNE DE MONTFORT (1851). R. The tallest of the Moss roses, reaching a height of 2.1 m (7 ft), and bearing large sprays of warm-pink flowers with chocolate-coloured moss.

LA BELLE GITANE (1880). It grows 1.2 m (4 ft) tall with dark-green foliage, about which it bears its large blooms of lilac-mauve which turn purple with age.

LITTLE GEM (1880). Almost of hybrid tea style, growing only 90 cm (3 ft) tall, with tiny leaves and bearing small neat crimson flowers.

LOUIS GIMARD (1877). It makes a neat, compact bush, 0.9 to 1.2 m (3 to 4 ft) tall and has bright-green leaves. The blooms are large and cup-shaped and are crimson-mauve, edged with lilac.

MARÉCHAL DAVOUST (1853). It grows 1.2 m (4 ft) high and bears clusters of cup-shaped blooms of deep carmine-pink, edged with lilac, whilst the moss is crimson-brown.

MME DE LA ROCHE-LAMBERT (1850). It makes a compact plant 1.2 m (4 ft) high and the same in width, and is perhaps the best red Moss. The attractively shaped flowers with their quilled petals are of fuchsia-red, shaded crimson at the centre.

MME LOUIS LÉVÊQUE (1898). R. It makes a neat upright plant 1.2 to 1.5 m (4 to 5 ft) tall with pale-green foliage. Its flowers are large with many petals and are of clear pink.

MONSIEUR PELISSON (1848). It forms a dense bush 0.9 to 1.2 m (3 to 4 ft) tall, its graceful stems being covered with small symmetrical flowers of bright clear pink.

MOSS ROSE OF JAPAN (*Muscosa japonica*). It is believed to have originated in Japan and is an interesting little plant growing less than 90 cm (3 ft) high, with its leaves and stems covered

in bright-green moss. The buds, which are extremely mossed, open to large blooms of orchid-purple which turn lilac-grey with age.

NUITS DE YOUNG (1852). It makes a bush 1.5 m (5 ft) tall but less than 90 cm (3 ft) in width and bears camellia-like blooms of black velvet, enhanced by golden stamens and brown moss.

OEUILLET PANACHÉE (1888). Making a small upright plant with tiny leaves, it bears neat blooms of palest pink, striped crimson, which open flat. Known as the Striped Moss rose.

PRINCESS ADELAIDE (1860). Of upright habit, growing 1.2 m (4 ft) tall, it has oak-green foliage. The reddish buds enveloped in dark-green moss open to large quartered blooms of strawberry-pink.

REINE D'ANJOU (1853). It forms a compact little bush 90 cm (3 ft) tall, with grey-green leaves and lilac-grey moss, the strongly fragrant blooms being a lovely orchid-mauve.

ROBERT LEOPOLD (1942). A beautiful plant growing 1.5 m (5 ft) tall, its golden-apricot buds opening to large double flowers of a lovely salmon-pink with green moss.

SALET (1854). R. Forming a neat plant only 1.2 m (4 ft) tall, it has pale-green foliage and bears cup-shaped flowers of warm glowing pink with crimson moss.

VALIDÉE (1862). Growing 0.9 to 1.2 m (3 to 4 ft) in height, it has apple-green foliage, and bears its multipetalled, camellia-shaped blooms of ruby-red embedded in pale-green moss.

WHITE BATH (1817). The year of its introduction is given by Sacheverell Sitwell in *Old Fashioned Flowers*. It is also known as Shailer's White and is really a white sport from the Common Moss rose. It grows only 90 cm (3 ft) tall, its heavily mossed, pinkish buds opening to blooms of pure white.

WILLIAM LOBB (1885). Also known as the Old Velvet Moss rose, it is not suitable for small gardens as it makes a huge plant 1.8 to 2.1 m (6 to 7 ft) tall and the same in width. The densely mossed crimson buds open to a mixture of purple-lilac and grey, and are strongly fragrant.

R. chinensis. We have seen how the various old Shrub roses played their part in the development of the Bourbon roses, raised from a natural crossing between the Autumn Damask and the China rose, *R. chinensis.* The China roses were, indeed, to play a most important role in the development of the modern rose, for they were more perpetual-flowering than any other roses, in China being in bloom almost the whole year, whilst they have a pleasing tea fragrance.

The Pink China Monthly rose, which later became known as Parson's Pink China, was first found growing in the Custom House garden at Canton and reached England in 1750. Thirty years later, the Dutch East India Company introduced the rose into Holland, but it was to play no part in the evolution of the rose until early in the nineteenth century, when it was re-introduced into Britain by Sir Joseph Banks, Director of Kew Gardens; it was recorded as flowering in the garden of a Mr Parsons at Rickmansworth. It was from this rose that the Noisettes and later the Tea roses were raised.

Early in the nineteenth century, a dwarf red form, *R. chinensis semperflorens,* reached Britain, introduced by Gilbert Slater of Leytonstone who gave his name to the rose. The rose eventually reached Italy where, crossed with *R. gallica,* it became the parent of the Portland roses which were long-flowering and had the exquisite fragrance and red colouring of *R. gallica.* When crossed with the Autumn Damask, the Hybrid Perpetuals were born. Being of vigorous habit they are best grown in the shrubbery or border devoted to shrub roses. They have the large, sumptuous blooms and rich colourings of the Damasks and Gallicas, and carry a sweet perfume; though not as perpetual-flowering as the modern Hybrid teas, they are too lovely to be allowed to pass out of cultivation. The Hybrid Perpetual, when crossed with the Tea rose, produced the Hybrid tea, the first being the richly fragrant La France, introduced in 1869.

Varieties of the Hybrid Perpetual (the date of introduction is given where known):

BARON GIRAUD DE L'AIN (1897). It makes a large dense bush, but is not so perpetual-flowering as the others. The enormous crimson blooms are of cup and saucer shape and have a rich clove scent.

BARONNE PRÉVOST (1842). It makes a low, compact bush and bears attractively quartered blooms of shell-pink, which have the sweet Damask perfume.

EMPEREUR DU MAROC (1858). It is one of the oldest Hybrid Perpetuals still to be obtained and it is one of the most compact, making a small bush 0.9 to 1.2 m (3 to 4 ft) tall. Its blooms open flat and are quartered, being of a deep crimson-red colour, most sweetly perfumed.

GENERAL JACQUEMINOT (1853). The first rose which bore crimson flowers without a trace of purple. The large, cup-shaped flowers have a powerful fragrance.

GEORG ARENDS (1910). It has Frau Karl Druschki and La France for its parents and so may be classed as a Hybrid Perpetual Tea rose, with the vigorous habit of Frau Karl Druschki and the rich, sweet perfume of La France. The blooms are a lovely shade of pink.

HUGH DICKSON (1904). It attains a height of 2.1 to 2.4 m (7 to 8 ft), and is best grown against a wall or fence. Its enormous, bright-crimson flowers have a delicious perfume.

MRS JOHN LAING (1887). It should still be planted in every garden, for it will grow in any soil and in the most exposed places, its large globular blooms of deep pink, shaded lilac, having a glorious sweet scent.

REINE DES VIOLETTES (1860). It makes a large bushy plant, but does not flourish unless well cultivated, of which it is worthy, for its huge quartered blooms are a vivid lilac-purple colour, unique amongst roses.

VICK'S CAPRICE (1897). It makes a small, compact bush, but blooms with freedom. Its soft-pink globular blooms are striped and spotted with red, and are deliciously scented.

R. cinnamonea plena. This, the dainty Cinnamon rose, was well known to Tudor gardeners, and was called the Rose de Mai, because it comes into bloom during that month. It makes a neat bush of Hybrid tea size, 'four cubits high', Gerard said, and has small dark leaves, 'like unto those of Eglantine', which give off a pungent, incense-like smell. The fully double flowers of rosette form are quite charming and are a lovely delicate pink. Of this rose, Henry Phillips in his *Sylva Florifera* (Vol. II) wrote: 'It is a favourite with our fair sex as it may be worn in the bosom longer than any other rose without fading whilst its diminutive size . . . adapts it well to fill the place of a jeweller's broach'.

R. coryana. It is a plant of horizontal rather than of upright growth, which characteristic it obtained from *R. roxburghii,* an elegant rose which appears twice in its parentage. It makes a bush 1.8 m (6 ft) tall but will grow to 3 m (10 ft) wide, with fern-like foliage, and during midsummer bears large, single, deep-pink flowers which have a fruity perfume. It makes a most efficient hedge.

R. damascena. Its origin is lost in antiquity. It may be descended from *R. gallica,* the oldest known species, and as it is closely allied to *R. centifolia,* both may have a common ancestor in *R. gallica.* It is possibly the most famous of all the old Shrub roses, frequently mentioned by Shakespeare ('sweet as Damask roses'), for none excels it for fragrance. From the Damask rose, the town of Damascus has taken its name, and it is believed that the plant first reached Britain with early Crusaders.

The Greek historian, Herodotus, mentions the Damask rose as having 60 petals and surpassing all other roses in its fragrance. It must have been the Rose of Paestum mentioned by Ovid, and again by Virgil in the *Georgics,* where he alludes to its unusual quality of blooming twice in the same year. In France, for this reason, it was known as the Quatre Saisons rose, and in Spain as the Alexandria rose, as it was thought to have been brought by travellers returning from the Egyptian port. For this reason it is, with but one or two exceptions, the only rose grown for attar of roses in Bulgaria, Turkey, Persia and India, where the species grows naturally, being particularly prevalent in the Kazanlik valley of Bulgaria. *R. damascena* is depicted on the walls of the Palace of Knossos in Crete of about 2,000 B.C.,

whilst the Autumn Damask, *R. damascena bifera,* which may have been the result of a chance crossing with the China rose, was known to the Romans at Pompeii. It was a seedling of this rose, obtained from a crossing with *R. gallica,* which when crossed with the China rose, in Italy, gave rise to the Portland rose from which came the Hybrid Perpetuals and later the Hybrid teas, which possess the repeat-flowering habit of the Autumn Damask and the China rose, and the rich crimson colouring of the Gallica rose. The ordinary Damask rose flowers but once a year. The autumn-flowering Damask also produced the Bourbon rose from a chance crossing with the China rose. The Bourbon later came to be crossed with the Portland rose, to produce the Hybrid Perpetual. The Damask roses should be pruned in March, thinning out weak and dead wood and tipping back the unripened wood of any unduly long shoots. The Autumn Damask, *R. damascena bifera,* the Quatre Saisons rose, makes a more compact bush 1.2 m (4 ft) tall and bears its fragrant pink flowers intermittently until the end of autumn.

Varieties of *R. damascena*:

BLUSH DAMASK. Sometimes called the Blush Gallica, it was known to Henry VII, and is similar to Kazanlik, attaining a height of 1.8 m (6 ft) and making an excellent hedge. It comes into bloom early in June, the ball-like flowers being a lovely clear pink, flushed with mauve at the centre. Parkinson described the flowers as 'deep blush . . . with pale yellow threads at the centre'.

CELSIANA. It grows 1.5 (5 ft) tall with attractive grey-green foliage and bears, with great freedom, large semi-double blooms of fresh pale pink which open flat to reveal a central golden boss. It is powerfully fragrant.

CHÂTEAU GALLAIRD. A Damask with an interesting history, for it was discovered growing on the walls of Richard the Lionheart's castle in Normandy. It has emerald-green foliage, and bears large sweetly perfumed flowers of fuchsia-pink which turn lavender with age.

CORALIE. It grows only 1 m (40 in) tall with dainty grey leaves, and bears its semi-double, cup-shaped, pink blooms with greatest freedom.

GLOIRE DE GUILAN. Growing 1.2 m (4 ft) tall, it is used for attar of roses at Guilan and Mazanderan, and was introduced to Great Britain from Persia as recently as 1949 by Miss Nancy Lindsay. It has apple-green leaves and bears powerfully scented flowers of pale pink.

HEBE'S LIP. Also known as Reine Blanche, it grows 1.2 m (4 ft) tall with oak-green foliage. Its creamy-white single flowers have an edge or lip of crimson-purple and a central boss of golden stamens. The flowers are followed by good hips.

ISPAHAN. Grows 1.2 to 1.5 m (4 to 5 ft) tall and the same across, and it is almost thornless. It blooms through June and July, the double blooms of warm rose-pink having an incurving centre like a chrysanthemum.

LA TOUR D'AUVERGNE. It grows 0.9 to 1.2 m (3 to 4 ft) tall with densely prickled wood, and bears its flat multi-petalled blooms of bright pink over several weeks.

LEDA. Known as the Painted Damask, it is ideal for a small garden for it makes a compact bush 90 cm (3 ft) tall and the same in width. It has dark leaves and bears masses of white blooms, strikingly tipped with crimson, to give them a picotee appearance.

MADAME HARDY. Raised by M. Hardy in the Luxembourg Gardens in 1832, it grows 1.5 m (5 ft) tall and the same across and has dark foliage. It bears exquisite, circular, cup-shaped blooms of purest white. The petals are attractively folded, whilst the blooms have a button eye of jade-green.

MARIE LOUISE. It grows 1.2 m (4 ft) tall and bears in great profusion its large, flat blooms of mauve-pink which have the attractive incurving centre of the rose Ispahan.

MME ZOTHMANS. It grows only 90 cm (3 ft) tall, and makes a neat, rounded bush, bearing dainty reflexed blooms of blush-white with a large button eye.

OMAR KHAYYAM. Originally raised from seed brought from the rose growing on the grave of Omar Khayyam at Naishapur. The wood has many thorns and grey leaves, the blooms being large and quartered, and a lovely clear pink.

QUATRE SAISONS. One of the oldest of living plants and the only Damask, with its white Moss counterpart, to be perpetual-flowering. It makes a compact, rounded bush 1.2 m (4 ft) high and bears double pink flowers which are sweetly fragrant.

QUATRE SAISONS BLANC MOUSSEUX. A white-flowering Damask Moss rose of similar habit to the Autumn Damask, with stems, leaves and buds covered in moss; it is perpetual-flowering.

ST NICHOLAS. Discovered in a garden in Yorkshire of that name, it grows 1.2 m (4 ft) tall and the same in width, and bears cup-shaped flowers of clearest pink and striking golden stamens.

VILLE DE BRUXELLES. Produces long, arching branches 1.2 to 1.5 m (4 to 5 ft) high, with pale-green foliage on which it bears large flat flowers of warm pink.

YORK AND LANCASTER. The blooms have differently coloured petals of white and rose-pink, but are not borne with any great freedom. It makes a vigorous, upright bush 2.4 m (8 ft) tall.

R. davidii. An outstanding wild rose from central China, it grows to a height of nearly 3 m (10 ft) and may be trained against a wall. It is valuable in that it blooms, like St Mark's rose, in late July and early August, its flowers being of a deep clear pink colour with the delicious spicy fragrance of certain peonies. The blooms are followed by long scarlet hips.

R. dupontii (*R. gallica* × *R. moschata*). A hybrid Musk rose named after the Empress Josephine's gardener, it is one of the best of all Shrub roses. It makes a dense bush 1.8 m (6 ft) tall, and the same in width, with attractive grey foliage, whilst during midsummer it bears clusters of mother-of-pearl coloured flowers, shaded gold at the centre, which have the fragrance of ripe bananas.

R. ecae. Native of Afghanistan, it is a most interesting rose, making a dense erect bush 1.2 m (4 ft) tall, and the same across with tiny leaflets of outstanding beauty. It comes into bloom in May, when an established plant will be smothered in tiny golden blooms like those of the buttercup and which, like the leaves, have an unusual incense-like perfume.

R. eglanteria (syn. *R. rubiginosa*). The Sweet-briar, or Eglantine, native to Great Britain, with its aromatic foliage and slightly scented, clear-pink flowers, which are followed by oval hips of brilliant scarlet. It grows 2.4 to 2.7 m (8 to 9 ft) tall, its arching stems being covered with strong thorns so that it makes a valuable outer hedge. It blooms in June and retains its hips well into winter.

The Sweet-briar, with the Musk rose of the Himalayas (*R. moschata*), is the only rose to give off its perfume from a distance.

'Sweet is the Eglantine ... ' wrote the poet Spenser, and those who have enjoyed the refreshing fragrance of its leaves after a shower, or when the air is still and heavy before a storm, will have experienced one of the most refreshing of all perfumes to which so many other poets have alluded.

The Eglantine may be used as a hedge as Parkinson suggested in the *Paradisus*: 'Sweet Brier and Whitethorn inter-laced together and roses of one, two or three sorts, placed here and there amongst them'. A delightful suggestion, for which the Hybrid musks and the old Shrub roses are ideal. Perhaps the finest of all roses to grow with the Sweet-briars and White-thorn is the Bourbon Zéphirine Drouhin, which remains in bloom from early June until the frosts of winter.

There are a number of lovely hybrid varieties, all with scented foliage—in Gerard's words, 'with leaves glittering, of a beautiful green colour, of smell most pleasant'. Those marked with an asterisk are known as the Penzance Briars.

*AMY ROBSART (1894). The large, semi-double blooms are of deep rose, followed by scarlet hips.

*FLORA McIVOR (1894). The white blooms have a pink flush.

JANET'S PRIDE. Introduced in 1892 but was grown before then as Clementine and was originally thought to be a chance hybrid found in a Cheshire hedgerow. It is of similar habit to the species, but the flowers are of deeper pink with an attractive white centre.

*JEANNIE DEANS (1895). Possibly the best of the Penzance Briars, the blooms being semi-double and of brilliant scarlet.

*JULIA MANNERING (1895). The pearl-white blooms have pink veins.

LA BELLE DISTINGUÉE. The Double Scarlet Sweet-briar, or Red-flowered eglantine, a plant with its origin lost in the past. It makes a compact bush 1.2 to 1.5 m (4 to 5 ft) tall and the same across, being of upright habit and bearing small, flat, multipetalled flowers of crimson-red followed by scarlet hips.

*LADY PENZANCE (*R. rubiginosa* × *R. foetida bicolor*). Introduced in 1894, the bright-yellow, single blooms are flushed with copper, and have the strong heady scent of *R. foetida*.

*LORD PENZANCE (*R. rubiginosa* × Harison's Yellow) (1894). The blooms are of buff-yellow with a slight rose flush.

*LUCY ASHTON (1895). The white blooms have an attractive pink edge.

*LUCY BERTRUM (1894). The blooms are bright crimson with a white eye and followed by scarlet hips.

MANNING'S BLUSH. Similar in habit to the Double Scarlet, it has dark foliage and bears tiny double flowers of blush-pink.

*MINNA. The blooms are salmon-pink with a white centre.

The Penzance Briars are roses of shrubby habit, raised by Lord Penzance during the late nineteenth century, by crossing *R. rubiginosa* with *R. foetida* and a number of Hybrid Perpetuals and Bourbon roses. The Rev. Foster-Melliar in his *Book of the Rose* writes that the object was to raise a series of roses with blooms of Hybrid Perpetual form and in addition having fragrant foliage, but though the Penzance Hybrids have aromatic foliage, the mostly single flowers, though often of intense colouring, have little scent and in form are much removed from the Hybrid Perpetuals.

Apart from the varieties Lord Penzance and Lady Penzance, the result of crossing the Sweet-briar with *R. foetida,* both of which are of compact habit, the other Penzance Hybrids have the same vigorous habit as *R. rubiginosa* and are suitable for a hedge. Though flowering only in mid-summer, they are useful plants to grow against a pillar, the fragrance of the foliage being a welcome addition to the beauty of the blossom.

R. *farreri persetosa*. Known as the Threepenny-bit rose, on account of the size of its flowers which are the smallest of all roses but are borne in profusion along the hairy, arching stems. It grows to a height of 2.4 m (8 ft) or more. The flowers, which are sweetly scented, are a lovely salmon-pink followed by tiny orange hips. It is one of the few roses to grow well in shade.

R. *fedtschenkoana*. It increases by underground suckers and will make a dense thicket when established. For a hedge it is one of the finest of all the Shrub roses for it has grey foliage tinted with purple and is perpetual-flowering, the large white flowers having attractive golden stamens. The blooms, which have the powerful scent of R. *foetida,* are followed by crimson hips, but it blooms so late that in September the hips appear with the blooms.

R. *filipes* Kiftsgate. One of the most vigorous of all roses, for it will cover a wall (or bank) 9 m (30 ft) high and the same in width, the twiggy branches supporting each other. In midsummer, it covers itself with a mass of blooms 5 cm (2 in) across, which are white as snow and possess a powerful, incense-like perfume.

R. *foetida*. Also R. *lutea,* native to Asia Minor and parts of the Middle East. It makes a plant 1.2 m (4 ft) tall and the same across, with small, bright, glossy green foliage and mahogany stems. Its brilliant-yellow blooms are single, with an almost overpowering fragrance, so strong as to be unpleasant when inhaled at short range.

R. *foetida bicolor* (syn. R. *lutea bicolor,* R. *l. punicea*). This is the famous Austrian Copper, the Capucine rose of France, and the only wild rose to bear a bicoloured bloom which is of vivid scarlet-orange with a golden reverse. It is a sport from R. *foetida* and is similar in all other respects. This rose was known in England during Tudor times and is the original of the wonderful modern bicolours.

R. *foetida persiana*. The famous double form of R. *foetida,* the Persian Yellow rose which Parkinson (1629) said had been 'brought to England from Constantinople by one, Nicholas Lete', but had 'perished quickly'. It was reintroduced to Great Britain in 1838 by Sir Henry Willcock and 40 years later was used by Pernet-Ducher at Lyons to pollinate a number of Hybrid Perpetuals. His first success was the raising of Soleil d'Or, which was the first of a new race of roses called after him, the Pernetianas. The Pernetianas were the first yellow roses of strong constitution.

R. *forrestiana*. From western China, it grows to a height of 1.8 m (6 ft), and during midsummer bears large, scented, single carmine-pink flowers, followed by large red hips which are held in green bracts.

R. *gallica*. It is the oldest of all roses, the form *officinalis* being known since early days as the Apothecary's rose, for in medieval times it was widely grown for its medicinal qualities, especially around the town of Provins near Paris. Hence it became known as the Provins rose, as distinct from the Provence rose, which is R. *centifolia*. It was also known as the French rose or the Rose of Gaul, whilst botanically it used to be R. *provincialis*. This was the rose used to adorn the shields of Persian warriors at least 1,000 B.C. and was well known to the Romans, being introduced by them into Britain. It was the rose taken as its symbol by the House of Lancaster.

The Gallica roses are remarkable for their compact, upright habit (which they have passed on to the modern Hybrid tea rose), for their numerous petals, and for their tendency to produce striped or variegated flowers. The formation of the flower is very regular. The Gallica roses brought to the modern dwarf rose, the Portland and later the Hybrid Perpetuals, the deep crimson colouring such as is to be found in the Portland rose Pergolese, introduced a century ago, and in the Hybrid Perpetuals Eugene Furst and Fisher Holmes which followed shortly afterwards. It was not until the yellow roses were used to cross with the crimson Hybrid Perpetuals that the brilliant, purple-free, scarlet roses appeared, to be followed by the bicolours and more recently the hot orange shades. *Rosa gallica officinalis*, the Apothecary's rose, so called because the thickly textured petals are able to retain their spicy fragrance when dried, began it all. The semi-double blooms of rich velvety crimson are enhanced by their golden stamens and are followed by attractive hips.

Gallicas are lovely roses for a small garden, and are amongst the easiest of all to grow for they do well in all soils and are completely hardy. They do well in coastal gardens, too, in sandy soil. The plants should be pruned in March, thinning out the overcrowded wood and shortening the shoots to about a quarter of their length.

The plants have no thorns in the accepted sense, but have numerous hairs, whilst the leaves are pointed and serrated. The blooms of a number of the Gallicas are spotted and marbled, whilst the same marbling is also to be found on the foliage of several. They make upright, bushy plants between 0.9 to 1.2 m (3 to 4 ft) tall, and are summer-flowering only. Thomas Rivers in *The Rose Amateur's Guide* (1840), wrote that to obtain bloom at its best, the buds should be thinned early in June and the plants liberally fed during June and July. The blooms are not so fragrant as the Damask and Bourbons but several carry a spicy perfume.

Varieties of *R. gallica* (the date of introduction is given where known):

AGATHE INCARNATA (1750). Rivers mentions that the 'Agathe' roses were given a separate classification in France for they had thorns and downy foliage, like the Damask. Their flowers also have quilled petals and in this case are of soft, pale pink. They also have the Damask scent.

ALAIN BLANCHARD (1839). This variety has thorns, and bears single, cup-shaped flowers of crimson, mottled with purple and enhanced by golden stamens. There is a sport (Panachée) in which the blooms are striped and not spotted.

ANAIS SEGALES (1837). This also has plenty of prickles and bears lilac-pink flowers which have attractively rolled petals.

ANTONIA D'ARMOIS. Grows less than 90 cm (3 ft) tall and was known two centuries ago. Valuable in that it only begins to bloom when the others are finishing. The flowers are small and a lovely shade of palest pink.

ASSEMBLAGE DES BEAUTÉS (1750). With the Moss rose Henri Martin, it is the only one of the old Shrub roses whose blooms are of pure crimson-red without the familiar purple-maroon colouring. They are ball-shaped and produced with freedom.

BELLE DE CRÉCY. The best of all the Gallicas and the most strongly scented. It is a thornless rose growing to 90 cm (3 ft) with bottle-green foliage. Its honey-scented blooms, flat with a button eye, are a unique shade of violet-pink.

BELLE ISIS (1845). It makes a small, neat plant growing to 90 cm (3 ft), and bears cup-shaped blooms of a lovely flesh-pink colour.

CAMAIEUX (1830). Grows little more than 60 cm (2 ft) tall and the same in width, and bears pretty, small, cup-shaped blooms of crimson-maroon, striped with white. Later, the blooms turn to purple-lavender.

CARDINAL DE RICHELIEU (1840). Whilst it is the most vigorous of the Gallicas, growing 1.5 to 1.8 m (5 to 6 ft) tall and 1.2 m (4 ft) wide, it is also one of the best, bearing orb-like blooms of wine-red, lustred with indigo.

CHARLES DE MILLS. Also called Bizarre Triomphant, it bears enormous, ball-like flowers of all shades of cerise, crimson, maroon and purple, which are of velvety appearance. It grows 90 cm (3 ft) tall.

CRAMOISIE PICOTÉE, (1852). It has dainty foliage and bears small, rosette-shaped blooms of light red, edged with crimson and spotted reddish-brown, and they are produced with freedom.

D'AGUESSEAU (1823). Makes a robust plant about 1.5 m (5 ft) tall and the same across. The large cup-shaped blooms are vivid crimson and are attractively quartered.

DUC DE GUICHE. This forms a dense bush 1.2 m (4 ft) tall and bears beautifully symmetrical blooms of crimson-maroon, flushed with purple, which open flat.

DUC D'ORLÉANS. A thick, sturdy bush bearing large-cupped flowers of Parma violet, spotted with white; they are extremely fragrant.

DUCHESSE D'ANGOULÊME (1836). A charming little plant growing only 1 m (40 in) high, and bearing dainty, rosette-like blooms of malmaison-pink. Possibly the result of a chance crossing with a China rose.

DUCHESSE DE BUCCLEUGH (1846). Forms a thick, bushy plant and is useful for a low hedge. It comes late into bloom and should be planted with Duchesse de Montebello, which blooms early and is of similar height. The large blooms are quartered and are a lovely bright strawberry-pink.

DUCHESSE DE MONTEBELLO. The first of the Gallicas to bloom, and it also has interesting grey foliage which enhances its attractive cup-shaped blooms of blush-pink with their pronounced spice scent. One authority who is familiar with all of the old Shrub roses considers that, taking everything into consideration, this would be his choice as the finest of all Shrub roses.

DU MAÎTRE D'ECOLE. Makes a compact plant, and along its gracefully arching stems bears large flat blooms of lilac-pink lustred with bronze.

GEORGES VIBERT (1853). Forms a neat, upright bush with dark-green foliage. The blooms open flat and are quartered with quilled petals which are striped pink and crimson-lake.

GLOIRE DE FRANCE. Forms a low, straggling bush and blooms with great freedom. The large reflexed flowers open purple-crimson, fading to lilac-mauve.

HENRI FOUCQUIER (1810). Forming a low, spreading bush, it has few thorns and bears large, circular flowers of a lovely soft mauve-pink.

JENNY DUVAL. One of the old 'blue' roses, the large full blooms being of deep violet-purple shaded slate-grey at the centre, and fading to pale lilac, with a delicious scent. It grows 0.9 to 1.2 m (3 to 4 ft) tall.

LA NATIONALE TRICOLORE. To give it the correct name. Of compact habit, the blooms are cup-shaped, of crimson-red, shaded purple and striped white at the centre.

LA PLUS BELLE DES PONCTUÉES. It grows 1.5 m (5 ft) tall and is one of the most robust of the Gallicas. Its scented, semi-double blooms of bright pink are spotted with white and followed by large hips.

MARCEL BOURGOUIN. Makes a small compact plant less than 1 m (40 in) high, and bears large flat blooms of purple-maroon with golden stamens.

NANETTE. It grows less than 90 cm (3 ft) tall, and is of upright habit, bearing small mauve-pink flowers which are striped with crimson-purple, and have a green eye.

PERLE DES PANACHÉES (1845). Like Marcel Bourgouin in habit, the dainty, semi-double, cup-shaped blooms are white, striped and flaked with crimson, and strongly scented.

PETITE ORLÉANNAISE. Grows 1.5 to 1.8 m (5 to 6 ft) tall with small leaves, and flowers which open flat and are a lovely shade of clear pink.

POMPOM PANACHÉE. This makes a tiny plant and covers itself with flowers of great charm which open flat and are creamy-white, striped with pink.

PRÉSIDENT DE SÈZE. Grows 1.2 m (4 ft) tall and bears large quartered blooms of deepest pink with a plum-coloured centre, shading to dove-mauve with age.

ROSA MUNDI. Also known as *R. gallica versicolor*, it makes a dense bush 1.2 m (4 ft) tall, and the same in width. It was named after Rosamond Clifford, mistress of Henry II. Redouté rightly names it 'Fair Rosamond's Rose'. Said to be a sport from *R. gallica officinalis*, it is the best of all the striped roses, its blush-white flowers being striped and flaked with crimson, pink and purple.

ROSE DES MAURES. The Moorish rose from Côte des Maures, which grows 90 cm (3 ft) tall, and bears masses of flowers of reflexed form and of rich mulberry-red.

SISSINGHURST CASTLE. A very old rose re-discovered in the grounds of Sissinghurst Castle by the late Vita Sackville-West. It is almost thornless and makes a neat plant 90 cm (3 ft) tall and the same in width. The blooms are flat, and are a rich plum-purple colour with yellow stamens.

SURPASSE TOUT. One of the few old shrub roses to bear flowers of crimson-red which are devoid of the purple shadings. It makes a dense plant 1.2 m (4 ft) tall and the same in width and may be planted with Rosa Mundi for a hedge.

TUSCANY. The Old Velvet rose, very much like *R. gallica officinalis* as to habit and the colour of its blooms, which open flat and are of rich velvet maroon with golden stamens.

R. glutinosa. A native of southern Europe and related to our native Eglantine, it makes a small bushy plant 60 cm (2 ft) tall and the same in width, its small, clear, pink flowers, like those of *R. rubiginosa,* being followed by large crimson hips. But it is for the scent of its foliage that it should be grown, for the hairy glands on both sides of the leaves emit a refreshing, pine-like perfume.

R. helenae. Native of central China, it is best grown as a low hedge, when the shoots will provide support for each other. The cream-coloured flowers, borne in midsummer, carry a strong spicy fragrance, and are followed by small red hips in autumn. The variety Patricia Macoun is perhaps better, for it is of more upright habit, is extremely hardy and bears its double flowers in dense clusters. The flowers carry a rich fruity perfume and are followed by orange hips.

R hibernica. Believed to be a hybrid of *R. canina* and *R. spinosissima,* it is often to be found growing wild in parts of Ireland. It makes a compact shrub 1.2 m (4 ft) tall with red wood, whilst in June it bears fragrant single flowers of a lovely creamy-pink.

R. hillieri. Said to have *R. moyesii* for one parent, and its orange-red bottle-shaped hips would seem to confirm this. It makes a vigorous plant 3 m (10 ft) tall and the same in width, and during midsummer bears single, maroon-coloured flowers which have a fresh raspberry perfume.

R. hugonis. From central China, it makes a large bush 2.1 to 2.4 m (7 to 8 ft) tall and the same in width, and has at-•tractive, acacia-like foliage. It bears its single, sweetly scented, pale-yellow blooms in May, followed by small blackish-red hips.

R. laevigata. A naturalized American rose and in the United States has become known as the Cherokee rose. It has attractive glossy foliage and bears a large, single, white bloom with a clove-like fragrance. In Britain it should be given a sunny wall. *R. anemonoides* (syn. *R. sinica Anemone*) which bears large, single blooms of a lovely soft pink and has similar narrow leaves, is believed to be a hybrid; its flowers are strongly scented. It, too, does best against a warm wall, although it is hardier than its parent. It is valuable in that it is one of the first of all roses to bloom, before the end of May. A hybrid Silver Moon, the result of crossing *R. laevigata* with *R. wichuraiana,* is a plant of hardier constitution still. It is a vigorous climber with plenty of healthy glossy foliage, and bears large, single, creamy-yellow flowers which carry the refreshing scent of ripe apples.

R. longicuspis. Like all the Himalayan species, it is a rose of vigorous habit, attaining a height of 9 m (30 ft) and it comes into bloom late in summer, when it covers itself in small white flowers which at a distance smell exactly of ripe bananas. Similar is Francis Lester, its white blossoms, also smelling of bananas, being attractively edged with pink, and enhanced by the bottle-green leaves.

R. macrantha. Believed to be the result of a natural crossing between *R. gallica* and *R. canina* which took place in France early in the nineteenth century. It is a rose of trailing habit and is valuable for ground cover. It bears its fruity, fragrant, blush-pink blooms in midsummer on long arching stems, followed by large red hips. The form Daisy Hill is similar in habit, but the blooms are semi-double and have rich scent, whilst the hybrid Harry Maas is a plant of more upright habit and is excellent for a hedge. It bears flowers of brilliant crimson but they have little perfume.

The hybrid Lady Curzon, obtained by crossing *R. macrantha* with *R. rugosa rubra,* makes a bushy plant 2.4 m (8 ft) tall and the same across, the elegant arching stems being smothered in scented, pale-pink flowers during June and July.

R. moschata. The Musk rose, native of the Middle East and of northern India, Spain and North Africa. It is a climbing plant of vigorous habit, sending up its arching stems to a height of 6 m (20 ft) and more. The flowers, almost the colour of the cream of Jersey cows, are borne during July and August, and they emit a delicate musk-like perfume.

The plant was introduced into Britain during the reign of Henry VIII, and may have been known to Shakespeare for it would almost surely have been growing in the gardens of the Bishops of Ely in Holborn, near to Shakespeare's lodgings in Silver Street, and Gerard said that it grew in his garden nearby. 'The flowers grow on the tops of the branches, of a white colour, and pleasant sweet smell like that of Musk', he wrote. He also confirmed that it flowered in autumn. This must have been the same rose which Francis Bacon described in his essay *Of Gardens* for, as the Rev. Ellacombe so rightly says, 'the plant has the peculiarity that unlike any other rose, it gives out its scent of its own accord and unsought, and chiefly in the evening, so that if the window of a bedroom near which this rose is trained, is left open, the scent will soon be perceived in the room'. This did not escape the notice of Bacon. '. . . That which above all others yields the sweetest smell in the air is the violet, . . . next to that is the musk rose'.

From *R. moschata*, the Rev. Joseph Pemberton raised a number of outstanding Hybrid Musk roses between 1913 and 1929, though, earlier, the German grower Peter Lambert had raised Aglaia by crossing *R. multiflora* with the Noisette Rêve d'Or, which had *R. moschata* for a parent. From Aglaia, Lambert raised Trier, said to be the first Hybrid Musk which bore single yellow blooms flushed with pink. Using the fragrant Trier as the seed-bearing parent, the Rev. Pemberton succeeded in raising a perpetual-flowering rose which he named Moonlight, one of the finest roses ever introduced. Its dark-red wood and deep-green leaves provide a striking contrast to the pure-white flowers with their golden stamens, which are produced freely in autumn and which carry the delicious musk perfume. Like all the Hybrid Musks, the plant will attain a height of 1.5 to 1.8 m (5 to 6 ft), and will grow 1.2 to 1.5 m (4 to 5 ft) wide, so that it is ideal for a hedge.

Daybreak, with its coppery-yellow blooms, followed, again having Trier for a parent, and its flowers have the distinct fragrance of Sweet peas, as do those of the vigorous pink-flowering Vanity. Amongst the last to be introduced of the Pemberton Musks were Felicia and Penelope, both magnificent roses and both having Ophelia for one parent, which passed on the exquisite shape of its flowers to them. They may be trained against wires to form a hedge and require but little pruning. Coming into bloom early in summer, they continue to bear their large trusses until the end of autumn and their scent will permeate a large garden. Felicia bears flowers of a lovely salmon-pink, whilst those of Penelope are creamy-pink, followed by coral-pink hips. This rose also has attractive grey foliage.

A Hybrid Musk rose of great beauty is La Mortola, a recent introduction of similar vigour, but it should be given the same sort of warm garden as it enjoys in its native Riviera. It has grey-green leaves, and bears large, white flowers with golden stamens; it is strongly scented.

The form *R. moschata autumnalis*, which blooms only in early autumn, is an interesting rose for a sheltered garden. It will attain a height of 3 to 3.6 m (10 to 12 ft) and bears small sprays of creamy-white flowers which possess the musk perfume.

Una is another with the delicious musk scent and having *R. moschata* for a parent. Of vigorous habit, it has buff-coloured flowers which are followed by green hips. Early in the nineteenth century, *R. moschata* was used by John Champney, a retired rice grower of South Carolina, to cross with *R. chinensis*. The result was a rose of climbing habit which he named Champney's Pink Cluster, and it has the perpetual-flowering qualities of the China rose. The double pink blooms, borne singly and in clusters, possess a strong clove perfume, especially rich on a calm evening. It was from seedlings of this rose that the Noisette climbers were raised by Philippe Noisette, a Frenchman living in America who, knowing that he had something of value, sent seedlings to his brother in Paris. The French breeders were quick to realize their commercial possibilities; crossed with Yellow China roses, a number of valuable seedlings bearing yellow flowers and possessing a sweet tea-like perfume resulted.

Amongst these roses was one named Gloire de Dijon, introduced in 1853, plants of which still grow against many walls in England. Its multipetalled blooms more nearly resemble the Bourbon roses, whilst its deep buff-yellow colouring and pronounced perfume make it an outstanding rose. In his *Book about Roses,* Rev. Reynolds Hole, Dean of Rochester, has this to say, 'It is what cricketers call an all-rounder . . . good in every point for wall, arcade, pillar, standard, dwarf, en masse or as a single tree'. It should still be grown in every garden today.

Another wonderful Noisette climber is Jeune Desprez which has the same flat, many-petalled flower as Gloire de Dijon with an equally delightful scent, resembling apricots, and the plant is of similar colour. Nor must the charming Madame Alfred Carrière be forgotten for, like the Noisettes previously mentioned, it is quite hardy and may also be grown as a large, dense bush. It is recurrent-flowering, its lovely, round, cup-shaped blooms being creamy-white with a rich fruity perfume. Aimée Vibert is also lovely. Grown against a southerly wall, unpruned, it will be almost evergreen whilst it will come into bloom before the Darwin tulips have finished. The blooms are pure white and carry a rich 'heady' perfume, almost overpowering on a calm day.

R. multibracteata. It makes a vigorous, bushy plant 2.4 m (8 ft) tall and the same in width, its arching stems being covered with dainty grey leaves and tiny, raspberry scented rose-pink flowers during July and August. The blooms, which are partially covered by grey-green bracts, are followed by small, red, bottle-shaped heps. From this rose Tantau raised Floradora from which the Americans obtained the first of the so-called Grandifloras, Queen Elizabeth and Montezuma. The foliage has a sharp, fruity scent.

R. multiflora. With its dense, sturdy habit, this is an excellent plant to use for an impenetrable hedge. It blooms in midsummer, bearing its clusters of small white flowers, often 100 or more in one cluster, on dainty, trailing shoots. The blooms possess a delicious sweet, fruity perfume. The wood is smooth, but the leaves are covered with hairs on each side.

Rosa multiflora and *R. moschata* have been frequently crossed together, and some very lovely plants have resulted. Outstanding is The Garland, introduced in 1835. It is less vigorous than its parents and bears clusters of double white flowers on short erect stems and they have a strong orange perfume. Another is Madame D'Arblay, of similar habit and bearing pretty, blush-white flowers which carry the distinct fragrance of musk.

Rosa multiflora gentiliana is another excellent variety. Native to western China, it will quickly cover an arch or pillar and will also make a thick hedge, retaining its bottle-green leaves until the year end. In midsummer it bears clusters of cream-or pinkish-coloured flowers having the powerful fragrance of orange-blossom.

A most distinctive rose in every way is *R. multiflora* Veilchenblau, the Blue Rambler, which grows 4.5 m (15 ft) tall and bears lilac flowers which carry the same delicious orange perfume. Bearing flowers of the same rich scent is the variety Goldfinch, rarely to be found in any garden, but an outstanding plant in every way with its pale-green foliage and bearing clusters of creamy-yellow flowers over a long period.

R. oxyodon. Also known as *R. haemotodes* and one of the best wild roses. It is similar to *R. pendulina*, being thornless, and with crimson-purple wood. It has grey foliage and bears fragrant, single pink flowers from June until October, and these are followed by large, crimson, bottle-shaped hips. In some years it continues to produce its flowers with the hips.

R. paulii. Raised by Mr George Paul, the result of crossing *R. arvensis* with *R. rugosa*, it is a plant of low, rambling habit and will quickly hide an unsightly bank. It grows only 1.5 m (5 ft) in height, but more than 3.6 m (12 ft) across, completely covering the ground. During midsummer its arching stems are clothed with single blooms of purest white, which have the rich clove fragrance of pinks. There is a form, *rosea,* similar in every way except that its single blooms are a warm shade of pink; it has the same clove perfume.

R. polliniana (syn. *R. richardii, R. sancta*). The result of crossing *R. arvensis* with a Gallica rose, the Abyssinian rose grows twice as wide, 2.4 m (8 ft) and more, as it grows tall. During midsummer its branches are covered with blush-white blooms with golden stamens and they have the strong musky scent of *R. arvensis.* A good rose to cover a bank.

R. primula. ·In all respects it is very like *R. ecea,* and is from the same part of the world. It makes a dense bush 1.5 m (5 ft) tall, with twiggy growth, and in May bears masses of tiny, single, primrose-yellow flowers which have the strong smell of incense, hence its common name of the Incense rose. Those who have grown it in an enclosed garden will know of its delights on calm damp days. To inhale its rich perfume leaves one completely refreshed.

R. roxburghii (syn. *R. microphylla*). It is the Briar rose of Japan, or the Sweet Chestnut rose, on account of its spiky hips which resemble the burrs of the Sweet chestnut. It is a most interesting rose, making a compact bush 1.2 m (4 ft) tall and the same across, whose stems are greyish to light brown in colour. The rosette-like blooms, which appear in August and which have several rows of small petals, open flat and are a lovely glowing pink with a fruity perfume. The blooms are followed by the yellow spiky hips, which smell of ripe pineapples.

R. rugosa rubra. This is the Japanese or Ramanas rose, native to Japan, China and Korea, which was introduced to Britain at the end of the eighteenth century by Lee, a nurseryman of Hammersmith. It is possibly the hardiest of all the rose species, being almost indestructible, and is especially valuable for planting in light, sandy soil. It is troubled neither by black spot nor by mildew. Growing about 1.8 m (6 ft) tall and the same in width, increasing by suckers, and with wood which is covered with large thorns, it is a most valuable rose for a field hedge. In addition, it has a continuous flowering habit, the large single, magenta-pink flowers, with their clove perfume, being followed by tomato-red hips which are used throughout the world to make a syrup with the highest vitamin C content of all fruits. *R. r. alba* is a most attractive form, for the blush-white buds open to reveal large saucer-shaped blooms of purest white which are accentuated by the dark-green foliage. There are a number of attractive varieties and hybrids:

AGNES. Raised in Canada by Saunders, of rambler rose fame, by crossing *R. rugosa* with the Persian Yellow rose, and introduced in 1900, it grows 1.8 to 2.1 m (6 to 7 ft) tall and 1.2 m (4 ft) across with plenty of small leaves, and bears pompom-shaped flowers of rich, tiger-yellow, flushed with amber, which are strongly fragrant. One of the best of the modern Shrub roses.

BELLE POITEVINE. Raised by Georges Bruant in 1894 and makes a compact bush 1.5 m (5 ft) tall and the same across. The blooms are a lovely sidalcea pink, opening flat with cream-coloured stamens and are followed by red hips.

BLANC DOUBLE DE COUBERT. It appeared in 1892, the blooms being double and pure white, and though produced with great freedom in midsummer, it is not so perpetual-flowering as the other forms.

CONRAD F. MEYER. Raised in Germany by Muller and introduced in 1899 by crossing *R. rugosa* with a seedling from crossing the famous Gloire de Dijon with Duc de Rohan. It grows 2.1 to 2.4 m (7 to 8 ft) tall and may be grown against a wall or trained along wires to form a hedge. It has plenty of rich foliage and bears, during summer and again in autumn, Hybrid tea-like blooms of a glorious silvery-pink, deliciously scented. Nova Zembla is a white-flowered sport but otherwise is similar.

DELICATA. It was raised in the United States and is one of the most compact of all the Rugosas, growing less than 1.2 m (4 ft) tall. The semi-double flowers are an attractive lilac-rose.

DR ECKENER. Raised by Berger and introduced in 1930, it forms a dense shrub up to 3 m (10 ft) tall and the same across, which is too large and too prickly for the modern garden. The blooms are of Hybrid tea shape and are pale yellow, flushed with pink, and very fragrant.

FIMBRIATA. Raised in 1890 by crossing *R. rugosa* with Mme A. Carrière, a Noisette rose, it grows 1.2 m (4 ft) tall and the same across, and bears pale-pink flowers with attractively serrated petals, like those of a Pink, hence its other name of Phoebe's Frilled Pink.

FRU DAGMAR HASTRUP. An outstanding plant which grows 1.5 m (5 ft) tall and the same across, with very dark foliage, which bears large, single blooms of clear shell-pink followed by attractive crimson hips. As it is perpetual-flowering, the combination of flowers and hips are most beautiful.

HANSA. It is similar to Roserie de l'Hay, but its large double, crimson-purple flowers have not quite the same velvety texture as that variety; but, growing only 1.2 to 1.5 m (4 to 5 ft) tall, it may be recommended for a small garden.

MAX GRAF. The result of crossing *R. rugosa* with *R. wichuraiana,* in 1919, it is the most prostrate rose, almost creeping over the ground. It has plenty of glossy foliage and, in summer only, bears clusters of single, bright-pink flowers which smell of ripened apples.

MRS ANTHONY WATERER. Introduced by Waterer in 1898 by crossing *R. rugosa* with General Jacqueminot. It is of similar habit to Delicata, but bears large, semi-double blooms of crimson-purple which are strongly fragrant.

NEW CENTURY. Raised by Van Fleet in the United States and introduced in 1900, the result of crossing the white Rugosa with Clothilde Soupert. It makes a dense compact bush 1.5 m (5 ft) tall and the same across. The blooms are double, and are lilac-pink, opening flat to reveal attractive cream stamens.

PARFUM DE L'HAY. Introduced by Gravereaux in 1902, and said to be the result of a cross with General Jacqueminot. It grows less than 1.2 m (4 ft) tall and bears neat, double blooms of a lovely cherry-red, which possess a strong perfume.

ROSERIE DE L'HAY. Raised by Cochet-Cochet and introduced in 1901, it is one of the finest of all the Shrub roses and certainly the best of the Rugosas. It grows 1.8 to 2.1 m (6 to 7 ft) and about 1.5 m (5 ft) across and does best against a wall. It begins to bloom early in summer and continues until autumn, its Hybrid tea-like crimson buds opening to large, double blooms of crimson-purple, enhanced by the dark-green foliage to give the plant a truly sumptuous appearance. It has a delicious perfume.

RUSKIN. Raised by Van Fleet and introduced in 1928 by crossing *R. rugosa* with the Hybrid Perpetual Victor Hugo. Though growing only 1.5 m (5 ft) tall it makes a dense bush up to 3 m (10 ft) thick, and bears its Hybrid Perpetual-shaped blooms of bright crimson in midsummer, and again in autumn.

SARAH VAN FLEET. Introduced by Van Fleet in 1926, it makes an upright, bushy plant 1.8 to 2.1 m (6 to 7 ft) tall, and is perhaps the most free-flowering of all the Rugosas. Its Hybrid tea-shaped buds open to flat, semi-double blooms of rose-pink which have a strong clove perfume.

SCABROSA. Of unknown origin, it makes a compact bush 1.5 m (5 ft) tall and the same across with large bottle-green leaves, whilst it bears the largest blooms of all the Rugosas, often measuring 15 cm (6 in) across and being of intense crimson-purple, followed by the longest hips of all roses.

SCHNEEZWERG. Raised by Lambert in 1912, it is an interesting plant, the result of crossing *R. rugosa* with a white dwarf Polyantha rose. Snow Dwarf, as it is also known, grows 1.5 m (5 ft) tall and the same across, and has the small neat leaves of a Polyantha; it bears beautiful flat blooms of purest white with golden stamens. It is in flower through summer and autumn, the blooms having a rich fruity perfume.

SOUVENIR DE PHILÉMON COCHET. A sport from Blanc Double de Coubert which appeared in 1899, the blooms being of similar whiteness but more double, whilst it makes a plant only 1.2 m (4 ft) tall and the same across.

STELLA POLARIS. Raised by Jenson and introduced in 1900, it may be said to be an improved *alba,* the habit being more compact, whilst the large, single, white flowers possess a silvery sheen and are followed by enormous orange hips.

R. sempervirens. The first roses of rambling habit were those of the *sempervirens* type, introduced into Britain in 1629. They will quickly clothe an archway or trellis, and though making a dense mass of twiggy growth they require little or no pruning. Probably the best-known is Félicité et Perpetué, raised by Louis-Philippe's gardener at the Château of Neuilly in 1827. Its flowers possess a sweet perfume, but it became widely planted for another reason—its ability to retain its handsome glossy foliage for at least nine months of the year, though it flowered only in July. Another, whose flowers possess a delicate sweet perfume, is Adelaide d'Orléans, named after the youngest daughter of the Duc d'Orléans and also raised at Neuilly. Its creamy-pink flowers are borne in loose corymbs. Equally fine is Flora, bearing large globular blooms of deep pink, but they possess only slight perfume.

One of the best of the *sempervirens* ramblers is Princess Louise, blooming late in the season, its clusters of red-tinted buds opening to double blooms of creamy-white, which have a rich fruity perfume.

R. sericea. This species has acacia-like foliage and makes a dense bush 2.7 to 3 m (9 to 10 ft) tall and the same in width, and is the only rose whose blooms have less than the usual 5 petals, for they have only 4. They are usually white, but occasionally pink or yellow, borne along the previous year's wood. They are followed by orange hips. It blooms in May. Other forms are Heather Muir, which bears its scented pure-white blooms over a longer period and Hidcote Gold, brought from Yunnan by Major Johnson for his Hidcote garden. The clear primrose-yellow blooms appear at the end of May. The large crimson thorns are conspicuous with the species and its varieties.

R. setigera. The Prairie rose of Canada and the United States. It is of rambling habit and is valuable to use as ground cover. It bears its fragrant, single warm-pink blooms in trusses of a dozen or more and in August, thus extending the season.

R. setipoda. Native of China, it is one of the finest of Shrub roses, making an upright bush 2.4 m (8 ft) tall. Its shell-pink flowers have the aroma of ripe apples; the leaves, the fragrance of the Sweet-briar, whilst the stems have the aromatic perfume of the pine-tree. In addition, it forms large, orange, bottle-shaped hips which are covered with hairs.

R. sinowilsonii. A rose of less hardy constitution which has most attractive foliage, the leaves being long and pointed, and coloured purple on the underside. The single white flowers are sweetly scented, but a hybrid, Wedding Day, bears cream-coloured flowers with pointed petals which emit the heavy scent of orange-blossom. This plant is hardier than the species.

R. soulieana. Native to the Himalayas, it makes a dense bush-like, semi-evergreen plant, its pure-white flowers with their yellow stamens smelling strongly of ripe bananas. This is the greyest-leaved rose, a pleasing quality inherited by its hybrid Kew Rambler which, in addition, has grey stems and bears the same white flowers, with a banana scent. Both plants bear orange-coloured hips.

R. spinosissima. The Burnet or Scots rose which, like *R. rugosa,* increases by suckers and is adaptable to a dry, sandy soil. During Tudor times it was known as *R. pimpinellifolia* but this was later changed to *R. spinosissima* to denote its thorny characteristics which make it suitable for an outer hedge. Gerard said that it was named the Burnet rose, for its leaves 'are set upon a middle rib like those of burnet'. He also mentioned that the rose grew 'in a pasture as you go from a village hard by London, called Knightsbridge unto Fulham, a village nearby'. It grows 1.2 m (4 ft) tall, and comes into bloom before the end of May. The flowers are single and creamy-white followed by large, round, black hips. It blooms only in spring and early summer. From original plantings in the nursery of Robert Brown at Perth, *R. spinosissima* achieved great popularity in Scotland towards mid-nineteenth century, hence it became known as the Scots briar, but in England it earned little favour. It is valuable in that it flowers before the summer-flowering roses come into bloom, and it is extremely hardy. The blooms have a delicious fruity perfume.

The variety *R. s. altaica* is from the Altai Mountains of Siberia, where it is to be found growing with the lovely mauve *Primula altaica.* It is larger, and has more graceful branches than the species, along which it bears large, single blooms of creamy-yellow followed by shiny black hips. It has been widely used for breeding. *R. s. andrewsii* makes a compact plant only 90 cm (3 ft) tall and is possibly the best of all the pink-flowered Burnet roses. The semi-double, cup-shaped blooms are of clear shell-pink with golden stamens.

The following are some of the more attractive varieties and hybrids:

FALKLAND. Reputed to have been found growing in the grounds of the Royal Palace of Falkland in Scotland, it is a beautiful little rose growing 0.9 to

1.2 m (3 to 4 ft) tall and the same across, with grey foliage and semi-double blooms of clear warm pink, followed by crimson hips.

MRS COLVILLE. Thought to be the result of a cross with R. pendulina on account of its long crimson hips. It grows 90 cm (3 ft) tall, and bears plum-coloured blooms which have a striking white zone round the stamens.

OLD SCOTTISH DOUBLE YELLOW. Also known as William's Double Yellow, for it was raised by John Williams (of Worcester) of William's Bon Chrétien pear frame, by crossing the species with R. foetida. The result is a neat branching plant, growing 1.2 m (4 ft) tall and bearing fully double yellow flowers with striking green stamens. It has the heavy perfume of R. foetida.

STANWELL PERPETUAL. The only perpetual-flowering Burnet rose, and is probably the result of a chance crossing with the Autumn Damask, but its parentage is unknown. It was found in a garden near London and was introduced to commerce by Lee of Hammersmith about 1838. All who know it fall in love with it, for it makes a bush 1.5 to 1.8 m (5 to 6 ft) high and the same across, with graceful arching stems and neat grey leaves. Its blooms are blush-white and they have a delightful sweet perfume.

WILLIAM III. It is the most dwarf of the Burnets growing only 60 cm (2 ft) tall, its dainty branches being smothered with tiny grey leaves, whilst it bears dainty, rosette-like blooms of plum-purple with golden stamens followed by black hips.

R. stellata. The Gooseberry-leaf rose of America. It makes a little thicket of pale-green stems with golden prickles, and with leaves similar to those of the gooseberry. The hips are also like gooseberries, being round and amber-coloured. The single blooms of carmine-pink, with their central boss of cream stamens, are produced late in summer and have an unusual perfume. It requires a sheltered garden to flourish. R. s. mirifica is known as the Sacramento rose for it grows wild only in the Sacramento Mountains. Some authorities consider it a species in its own right, the main difference being that it has few

stamens, and glandular stems. The hips are dull red.

R. sweginzowii. From northern China, it grows to a height of 3 m (10 ft) and the same across, its graceful arching stems being covered with enormous red thorns, and with large, single pink flowers sweetly fragrant, followed by bottle-shaped scarlet hips.

R. villosa (syn. R. pomifera). The Apple rose, native to Europe, the double-flowered (duplex) variety of which is most suitable for the garden. Wolley Dod's Rose makes a thick bush 1.8 m (6 ft) tall and the same in width with the grey-green foliage which has the aroma of ripe apples. It bears its double blooms of clear rose-pink in midsummer, and these are followed by crimson hips.

R. virginiana. First discovered in the State of Virginia, America, it is a valuable rose for ground cover, for it spreads by means of suckers. The glossy foliage of summer takes on the rich tints of autumn, and it has beautiful mahogany-red wood. The single, rosy-pink flowers appear from May to August, being followed by scarlet hips. The form alba is similar in all respects, except that the wood is pale green and the blooms are pure white, and more fragrant than the pink form.

Rosa virginiana plena (syn. R. rapa), or the St Mark's rose, is valuable in that it blooms in late July and early August, its tight little buds resembling those of the modern Floribunda Allgold, but instead of being golden they are a beautiful clear, deep pink. It makes a dense little bush growing 1.2 to 1.5 m (4 to 5 ft) in height and 1.5 m (5 ft) wide, increasing by means of suckers, and is excellent for a hedge. The blooms have a fruity perfume.

R. wadei. The result of crossing R. rugosa with R. moyesii, it makes a prostrate plant only 30 cm (1 ft) tall, with yellow-green leaves, and bears small, single flowers of delicate pink which are sweetly scented.

R. wardii. Introduced from Tibet by Kingdon-Ward, it makes a bushy plant 1.8 m (6 ft) tall and the same across, and is thornless with pale-green stems. The blooms are single and of purest white with a boss of golden stamens. They possess a delicate perfume.

R. wichuraiana. Shirley Hibberd in The

Amateur's Rose Book, which so many rose lovers have valued since its publication in 1874, makes no mention of this Japanese species and its many hybrids, but who amongst gardeners has not at some time or other grown Dorothy Perkins, the result of a cross between *R. wichuraiana* and the Hybrid Perpetual, Madame Luizet? *R. wichuraiana* is, in fact, a plant of quite recent introduction and was first taken up by the American firm of Jackson & Perkins during the late nineteenth century. Dorothy Perkins appeared in 1900, being one of the first of the Wichuraiana ramblers, with a habit of sending out a succession of new shoots from the base upon which, on short laterals, the flower clusters are borne the following year.

Dorothy Perkins, however, was not the first Wichuraiana rambler. This honour belongs to May Queen, one of the best roses ever raised for covering a northerly wall. Yet how often is it seen today? It is a strong grower with plenty of shiny disease-resistant foliage, whilst it bears early in summer masses of large pink flowers which have the refreshing apple scent of the species.

With Dorothy Perkins appeared Alberic Barbier, a most valuable rambler in that its foliage is almost evergreen. It bears its large, double, creamy-white blooms early in summer and so is a fitting companion to the later-flowering Sanders' White which is otherwise similar in all respects. Nor must the lovely François Juranville be forgotten, for with its red stems and double blooms of glowing pink and gold, it is a most exquisite rose where used for covering an arch or low wall. Albertine is another and, like the other Wichuraianas, makes an appealing weeping standard rose. Its copper-coloured buds open to large flowers of salmon-pink. Paul Transon is another of great beauty with glossy leaves, the orange buds opening to salmon-pink flowers which have the same scent of ripe apples.

In France, *R. wichuraiana* Alexandre Girault is given pride of place over all rambler roses. It has healthy foliage and bears reddish-crimson flowers, flat and quartered and sweetly apple-scented. Also bearing flat quartered flowers is another French rose, Auguste Gervais, whose flowers are of shades of copper, yellow and salmon, and richly scented.

Another outstanding Wichuraiana rambler was introduced by Dr Van Fleet in 1910, and he named it after himself. Its blush-pink flowers were larger than those of any rambler previously introduced, and it became a great favourite for covering rustic woodwork or trellis. But it was not until twenty years later that it achieved its greatest fame when it produced the sport The New Dawn. This was without doubt the most important rambler rose ever to appear. Though its delicately scented flowers were of similar colour to the parent, revealing the influence of the Hybrid Perpetual Souvenir de Président Carnot which figures in the parentage of Dr Van Fleet, it was for its recurrent or perpetual-flowering habit that it achieved world-wide fame; except for the somewhat intermittent flowering of *R. bracteata,* it was the first rambling rose to bloom again in autumn. This is made possible by the eye immediately below the flower truss 'breaking' to produce new growth upon which a second crop of flowers are borne in August and September.

Since 1930, a number of seedlings have appeared from The New Dawn, all having the same repeat-flowering habit and all being sweetly scented. Amongst them is White Dawn, one of the best of all the white-flowered rambler roses, and Miss Liberty, which bears sweetly scented crimson flowers.

For its extreme hardiness, in addition to its outstanding quality of bloom and repeat-flowering habit, The New Dawn has, in post-war years, been used by a number of American breeders to raise a new race of climbing roses which have been named perpetual-flowering Pillar roses. By crossing New Dawn with Mercedes Gallart, the late Mr Gene Boerner of the firm of Jackson & Perkins introduced the lovely rose Aloha. Bearing large, rose-salmon, Hybrid tea-like flowers, and being of perpetual-flowering habit, it will cover a pillar 2.7 to 3 m (9 to 10 ft) tall with its long canes, and reveals more of the climbing habit than that of the old rambler roses which rambled rather than climbed. Another seedling from The New Dawn has been named Coral Dawn, whilst Coral Satin is the result of a cross between The New Dawn and the floribunda Fashion.

Parade and Pink Cloud are other Pillar roses introduced by Jackson & Perkins, and both are richly scented. These roses do not possess quite the same vigour as the Wichuraiana ramblers and climbing sports and so are best grown against a support extending 1.8 to 2.1 m (6 to 7 ft) above the ground or they may be used to cover a low wall.

Included amongst these large-flowering Pillar roses and requiring much the same cultivation are the roses descended from Turner's Crimson Rambler. William Paul of Cheshunt used this remarkable rose in raising his excellent Carmine Pillar which, when crossed with Pernet Ducher's Soleil d'Or, produced the famous Scarlet Climber or Paul's Scarlet, as it is affectionately known to so many gardeners. In the same year (1915) Paul crossed the Hybrid Perpetual, Frau Karl Druschki, with the famous Noisette, Marechal Niel, and raised the hardy Paul's Lemon Pillar. Both these roses raised by William Paul have been widely planted to this day but, though the flowers are fragrant, they are not repeat-flowering and it would now appear that for this reason they are likely to be replaced by those of perpetual-flowering habit.

In 1950, the French hybridizer Charles Mallerin used Paul's Scarlet to raise the rambler rose Record, which bears vivid scarlet flowers, but it is also only summer-flowering and it was not until he used The New Dawn that he obtained the wonderful Danse du Feu (in America well named Spectacular), an orangey-red Pillar rose of great hardiness which blooms from June until December but alas, its flowers possess little perfume.

Besides their use in the weeping standard form, the Wichuraiana roses may be planted to cover a bank or an unsightly rubbish tip, which may be done by pegging down the shoots and allowing them to trail along the ground. No pruning will be necessary when grown in this way.

CLIMBING ROSES. Almost all the Hybrid tea roses have produced a climbing form and many bear deliciously scented flowers. Others of value for covering a wall, and which may not now be available in the dwarf form, have outstanding perfume.

ALISTER STELLA GRAY. A charming little rose to cover a low wall. It is perpetual-flowering and bears dainty clusters of tiny creamy-yellow blooms which have a delicious sweet scent.

ALLEN'S FRAGRANT PILLAR. One of the very best of the short climbers or Pillar roses and should be more widely planted, for its large double blooms are of brightest scarlet and carry a rich musky perfume, unusual in flowers of this colour.

CHÂTEAU DE CLOS VOUGEOT. A beautiful, recurrent-flowering climber bearing the old-fashioned flat roses with short petals which are almost black and have a particularly sweet perfume.

CLIMBING OPHELIA. It is quite delightful in every way and must not be allowed to pass from cultivation, for it is repeat-flowering, its dainty blooms of flesh-pink having the fresh sweet fragrance of verbena.

COUNTESS OF STRADBROKE. Raised in Australia, it is an excellent Pillar or wall rose and is quite hardy. It has plenty of glossy foliage and bears very large blooms of deepest crimson which are strongly fragrant.

CRAMOISIE SUPÉRIEURE. Really a Hybrid China rose introduced in 1832 and, though of slender habit, it remains in bloom in a sheltered garden almost the whole year. The dainty, blood-red blooms possess a delicious sweet perfume.

CUPID. Introduced in 1914, it is a delightful climbing rose, bearing large, single blooms of a lovely peach-pink which have a pleasingly sweet perfume. The blooms are followed by large orange hips.

DREAM GIRL. It does not grow more than 1.8 to 2.1 m (6 to 7 ft) tall but flowers throughout summer, the flat double blooms of salmon-pink having the distinct clove fragrance.

DR NICHOLAS. The pink colouring of its blooms may be traced back to its parent, George Arends, and to its grandparent, La France, the blooms having the same fullness and the same sweet fragrance. It is repeat-flowering, too, an excellent Pillar rose, yet is rarely to be seen and, though introduced as recently as 1940, may not now be obtainable.

FRITZ NOBIS. Short-growing, rarely exceeding 1.8 m (6 ft) in height, it blooms only during June, but its bright-pink flowers carry a distinctive violet perfume.

GRUSS AN TEPLITZ. It is continuously in bloom, its cupped crimson flowers being held on graceful arching sprays and it may be grown either as a bush or Pillar rose. The blooms have a distinctive raspberry fragrance, unlike that of any other climbing rose. It makes a most attractive hedge when planted with the equally fragrant Hybrid Musk rose Felicia.

GUINÉE. Raised by Mallerin in France and introduced in 1937, it has crimson foliage and bears with great freedom dark velvety red flowers, darker even than those of its parent Souvenir de Claudius Denoyel, and quite free from any purple colouring. As would be expected, the blooms possess the powerful fragrance of so many roses of this colour. Like Mermaid it does best when pot grown, and planted out from the pot.

HAMBURGER PHOENIX. A Kordesii climber introduced in 1955, it is perpetual-flowering, with rich dark glossy foliage, the large, semi-double blooms of crimson-scarlet being richly fragrant and followed by scarlet hips.

MME A. CARRIÈRE. Nearly a century old, it remains one of the finest of all roses to cover a cold sunless wall which it will quickly do, being extremely hardy. It has plenty of glossy foliage, whilst its pure-white flowers possess the true musk perfume.

MME GRÉGOIRE STAECHELIN. Raised in Spain by Pedro Dot, it blooms only once, in early summer, but presents a remarkable picture when in flower, the long, pointed, carmine buds opening to deep carmine-pink flowers which possess the familiar 'old rose' perfume.

PAUL LEDE. The only time I have seen this fine old rose was on a cottage wall in Somerset where its flat, short-petalled flowers of creamy-apricot revealed much of the Noisettes, likewise their perfume. It was a glorious picture in full bloom.

REINE MARIE HENRIETTE. Appearing in 1878, it was one of the first climbing Hybrid teas. It has attractive coppery foliage and bears enormous double flowers of an unusual shade of bright cherry with a rich fruity perfume.

RUTH ALEXANDER. Introduced in 1938, it is of vigorous habit, repeat-flowering and bears large semi-double flowers of apricot-yellow which have the delicate fragrance of apricots.

SÉNATEUR AMIC. The result of a cross between *R. gigantea* with the Hybrid tea rose, General MacArthur. It should be given a sunny sheltered wall where, during midsummer, it will bear a profusion of semi-double flowers of familiar General MacArthur purplish-red colour, which have similar perfume.

SOUVENIR DE CLAUDIUS DENOYEL. Introduced in 1920, it has been sadly neglected, and rose lovers have missed much, for it bears enormous cup-shaped blooms of glowing scarlet which have an exquisite sweet perfume.

R. willmottiae. It grows 1.5 to 1.8 m (5 to 6 ft) tall and is of graceful horizontal habit, growing almost twice as wide as it grows tall. It has attractive fern-like foliage which makes a pleasing foil for the small lilac-pink flowers which are sweetly scented. Hadden's Variety, introduced in 1948, is more attractive, for it has grey foliage, and bears reddish-purple flowers which have a richer fragrance. The species has stiletto-like thorns an inch in length.

R. wintoniensis. The result of crossing *R. moyesii* with *R. setipoda*, it makes a large vigorous bush with brilliant cerise-pink flowers whilst its foliage has the refreshing scent of pine woods.

R. xanthina. From Korea, it is one of the earliest of all roses to flower, the double blooms of brilliant yellow with their rich, oily, clove-like fragrance, appearing before the end of May. It makes a bushy plant 1.8 m (6 ft) tall and the same in width, with attractive grey stems and small foliage.

HYBRID TEA ROSES. The petals of the most highly scented roses have, on their surface, tiny perfume glands which are invisible to the naked eye, but which may readily be seen under a strong microscope. This is particularly so in the case of Wendy Cussons, Ena Harkness, Crimson Glory and Fragrant Cloud.

In 1925, the Mrs Clay Challenge Vase was inaugurated, to be awarded to the raiser of the best new scented rose in any one year, and open only to British hybridists. The winners of the award up to 1965 (when it was replaced by the Henry Edland Memorial Medal were:

For a number of years Mr James Gamble has been taking careful note of the fragrance of roses and in the 1957 Annual of the Royal National Rose Society, he discloses in a special table the results of his work. Out of more than 3,500 Hybrid tea roses which he tested for

Year	Raiser	Variety
1925	S. McGredy & Son	Arthur Cook
1926	A. Dickson & Sons	Dame Edith Helen
1927	A. Dickson & Sons	Flamingo
1928	S. McGredy & Son	Portadown Fragrance
1929	Not Awarded	
1930	A. Dickson & Sons	Barbara Richards
1931	S. McGredy & Son	William Orr
1932	B. R. Cant & Son	Memory
1933	Not Awarded	
1934	A. Dickson & Son	Leading Lady
1935	Bees Ltd	Lady Frost
1936	S. McGredy & Son	Hector Deane
1937	S. McGredy & Son	Viscountess Charlemont
1938	Not Awarded	
1939	A. Dickson & Sons	Dr Chandler
1940-44	Not Awarded	
1945	R. Harkness & Co.	Red Ensign
1946	R. Harkness & Co.	Ena Harkness
1947	Not Awarded	
1948	Wheatcroft Bros.	Charles Mallerin
1949-52	Not Awarded	
1953	S. McGredy & Son	Bridal Robe
1954-56	Not Awarded	
1957	A. Dickson & Sons	Silver Lining
1958	E. B. Le Grice	My Choice
1959	Bertram Park	June Park
1960	Not Awarded	
1961	Herbert Robinson	Westminster
1962	C. Gregory & Sons	Wendy Cussons
1963	S. McGredy & Son	Elizabeth of Glamis
1964	S. McGredy & Son	Lady Seton
1965	A. Dickson & Sons	Scented Air

Winners of the Henry Edland Memorial Medal, open to rose breeders everywhere are:

Year	Raiser	Variety
1966	M. Tantau	Charm of Paris
1967	Mondiel Roses	Princess Paola
1968	M. Tantau	Duke of Windsor
1969	J. Cocker & Son	Alec's Red
1970	No Award	
1971	Experimental Station, Melle	Lily of Gerlache
1972	A. Dickson & Sons	Mala Rubinstein

fragrance, approximately 25 per cent had no fragrance and 20 per cent were very fragrant, the rest being of varying degrees of fragrance. It is, therefore, far from the truth to say of the modern rose that it possesses no perfume, for though only about one in ten possesses scent which is comparable with the roses of older times, at least half of the modern Hybrid tea roses may be said to possess a marked degree of fragrance.

Hybrid tea roses with pronounced perfume (the date of introduction is given where known):

AIDA (1960). With its compact habit, this is an excellent bedding rose, deliciously scented, like Wendy Cussons, which it resembles in colour and in perfume but is more free-flowering.

ALEC'S RED (1970) (Fragrant Cloud × Dame de Coeur). Raised by Mr A. Cocker in Aberdeenshire, it is one of the finest red roses ever introduced, with healthy dark-green foliage and bearing through summer and autumn an abundance of rich-red flowers with exquisite perfume.

ARDELLE (1954) (Mrs C. Lamplough × Peace). With 72 petals, its bloom is one of the largest of all roses, and of a lovely Jersey-cream colour with exquisite fragrance. The blooms may 'ball' and refuse to open in dull, wet weather.

BLUE MOON (1964) (Unbenamito Simling × Sterling Silver). It is a plant of bushy, vigorous habit with plenty of dark-green, glossy foliage against which its shapely blooms of icy-blue appear in delightful blend, and are enhanced by their cool, lemon-like perfume.

BOBBY CHARLTON. A 1974 introduction and a favourite with exhibitors for it has high-centred blooms with reflexed petals of deep pink with a silver reverse. It has outstanding fragrance.

BOND STREET (1965) (Radar × Queen Elizabeth). It has the vigorous upright habit of its parents and will attain a height of 1.5 m (5 ft). It bears its pink flowers in trusses and they have more than 70 petals. The scent is rich and penetrating.

CHANTRÉ (1958) (Luis Brinas × Spek's Yellow × Antheor). A beautiful rose but like its parent, Antheor, it tends to be less hardy than other roses. The lovely apricot-orange blooms are borne on long stems and possess the rich and unique perfume of ripe apricots.

CHARLES MALLERIN (1947) (Glory of Rome × Congo). The blooms have 40 petals and are of darkest crimson with a black sheen; they possess a rich fruity perfume. Not a strong grower but outstanding where it can be grown well.

CHARM OF PARIS (1966) (Prima Ballerina × Montezuma). Of similar breeding to Fragrant Cloud with a perfume of almost equal intensity, though it never achieved any degree of popularity. It bears a full-petalled flower of a lovely shell-pink with a silver reverse, which is enhanced by the dark-green glossy foliage.

CHRYSLER IMPERIAL (1952) (Charlotte Armstrong × Mirandy). One of the best crimson roses, the deep, bright-crimson blooms being borne with freedom above dark leathery foliage. They are tolerant of adverse weather and emit a rich fruity perfume.

CRIMSON GLORY (1935) (Catherine Kordes' seedling × W. E. Chaplin). Since its introduction, it has remained a favourite for bedding in spite of a tendency to mildew. The habit is dwarf and bushy, the large well-shaped blooms being of deep velvety crimson with the rich damask fragrance. It has been widely used in breeding for its perfume.

DIORAMA (1965) (Peace × Beauté). An outstanding rose combining the finest qualities of its parents. Of vigorous habit with plenty of glossy foliage, the blooms with their high centres open to nearly 12 cm (5 in) across and are of apricot-yellow flushed with pink. They have a soft perfume.

DUKE OF WINDSOR (1968) (Prima Ballerina × Seedling). With its compact habit and dark-green healthy foliage, it is an ideal bedding rose, the flowers being of a luminous orange and, rare with this colour, deliciously scented.

ENA HARKNESS (1954) (Crimson Glory × Southport). With two parents bearing such richly coloured bloom and being so fragrant, it is not to be wondered at that their offspring should bear bloom of at least equal beauty and perfume. Its deep crimson-scarlet blooms with their attractively rolled petals make it an exhibitor's favourite. It comes early into bloom and continues almost until the year-end, untroubled by adverse weather.

ERNEST H. MORSE (1964). A magnificent rose of unknown parentage and making a shapely, upright bush with plenty of deep-green foliage. The blooms are large, with 30 petals, and are borne with freedom. They are of bright turkey-red with pronounced perfume.

EVE ALLEN (1964) (Karl Herbst × Gay Crusader). A rose of great beauty and sweetest perfume. It makes a compact bush, well-furnished with deep-green foliage, and bears large shapely blooms of cherry-red with a gold reverse which last well on the plant and when in water.

FRAGRANT CLOUD (1964) (Seedling × Prima Ballerina). One of the most beautiful of all roses, the blooms being a lovely soft coral-red with the same exquisite fragrance as Prima Ballerina. It makes a bushy plant and is an ideal bedding rose.

FRANCINE (1961) One of the outstanding roses of the Royal National Rose Society Summer Show in 1962, and also in the garden that year, but it does not like wet conditions. The blooms are deep crimson-red with a silver reverse, and have a fragrance resembling a mixture of violets and red ink. Of ideal bedding habit.

GAIL BORDEN (1956) (M. H. Verschuren × Viktoria Adelheid). A rose which should be in every garden, for its performance was outstanding during the cold, wet summers of the early 1960s. The high-centred blooms have more than 50 petals and are of pale gold, shaded inside with pink and salmon, whilst they carry a rich sweet perfume.

GENERAL D. MACARTHUR. Though introduced in 1905, it is still widely planted for bedding, for in spite of its rather thin foliage, it makes a plant of low-spreading habit and blooms in long succession from June until October. The medium-size blooms of magenta-crimson possess a pronounced perfume and are tolerant of adverse weather.

GERTRUDE GREGORY (1956). A sport from Lady Bleper and possessing all its excellent bedding qualities of compact habit with bottle-green foliage, it bears its medium-sized blooms of purest yellow, which do not fade, from June until November whatever the weather, and they are sweetly perfumed.

HENRY FORD (1954) (Pink Dawn × The Doctor). A wonderful rose in Britain, bearing blooms of unfading pink which carry the same delicious verbena perfume as The Doctor but it is a plant of much greater vigour.

ISOBEL DE ORTIZ (1962) (Peace × Perfecta). Of vigorous habit with plenty of dark glossy foliage, the attractively shaped blooms with 52 petals are of deep pink with a silver reverse and measure 15 cm (6 in) across when open, the petals reflexing in a most pleasing way. The blooms possess a sweet perfume.

JOSEPHINE BRUCE (1952) (Crimson Glory × Madge Whipp). Of excellent bedding habit with plenty of light-green foliage, the blooms are the darkest crimson of all roses, with a black sheen, and are borne in trusses rather than individually. The fragrance is outstanding.

JUNE PARK (1958) (Peace × Crimson Glory). It is not often that two such highly perfumed roses as this and Wendy Cussons are introduced in the same year. June Park received the Clay Vase and a Gold Medal from the Royal National Rose Society in 1959, for its large deep rose-pink blooms possess outstanding fragrance.

JUST JOEY (1971) (Fragrant Cloud × Dr Verhage). Raised by Cants of Colchester, it is a vigorous grower with plenty of glossy dark-green foliage and richly scented flowers of coppery orange with the unique frilled petals of Dr Verhage.

LADY SETON (1964) (Ma Perkins × Mischief). A Hybrid tea with the freedom of flowering and exquisite scent of Ma Perkins. The shapely blooms have 45 petals and are of clear glowing pink. Awarded the Clay Vase for 1964.

LILY OF GERLACHE (1971) (Perfecta × Prima Ballerina). Raised in Belgium, it bears a full shapely bloom of exhibition quality, of cherry red with exquisite perfume.

MALA RUBINSTEIN (1971) (Sea Pearl × Fragrant Cloud). Of vigorous upright habit with plenty of matt green foliage, the freely produced flowers are of a lovely coral pink with a deeper reverse and outstanding perfume.

MME LAPERRIÈRE (1952) (Crimson Glory × Seedling). It makes a plant of low, spreading habit and bears flowers of darkest crimson which are extravagantly fragrant.

MY CHOICE (1958) (Wellworth × Ena Harkness). The deep-yellow buds, splashed vermilion, open to reveal a bloom with most attractive blendings of gold, pink, salmon and orange. It has a pronounced perfume and earned the Clay Vase and Gold Medal of the Royal National Rose Society for 1958.

OPHELIA (1912). Its parentage is unknown but it is the queen of all scented roses, being the grandparent of Sensation from which the most fragrant of the modern roses are descended. Its pale, flesh-pink blooms carried on long straight stems make it ideal for cutting for which it is still planted under glass.

PERSONALITY (1960) (Peace × Sutter's Gold). It has the jonquil-like perfume of Sutter's Gold, whilst the high-centred, golden-yellow blooms are shaded with red and pink. Altogether an outstanding rose but which has been little grown.

PRIMA BALLERINA (1958). An outstanding rose of unknown parentage, which gives an excellent account of itself everywhere and even in a cold, wet summer. The medium-sized blooms are borne with freedom through summer and autumn, and are of purest rose-pink, whilst the foliage is dark and leathery. One of the most deliciously scented of all roses and in the best half dozen of modern Hybrid teas.

RED DEVIL (1965) (Silver Lining × Prima Ballerina). As to be expected from its parentage, the blooms have outstanding perfume. It makes a vigorous plant with plenty of pale-green glossy foliage and bears large, high-centred blooms of richest scarlet-red. An exhibitor's favourite.

ROSE GAUJARD (1958) (Peace × Opera seedling). It is an outstanding garden rose of compact habit, with plenty of dark leathery foliage and bearing high-centred blooms of bicolouring, the cherry-red flowers being shaded with white on the outside. They carry a pleasing 'tea' perfume.

RUBAIYAT (1946) (McGredy's Scarlet × Mrs Sam McGredy) × (an unknown seedling × Sir B. McFarland). A fine rose, rose-red in colour, its elegant buds opening to reveal a high centre. The blooms have the powerful Damask fragrance.

SCENTED AIR (1965) (Spartan seedling × Queen Elizabeth). It makes a vigorous, upright bush well clothed in deep-green foliage. The shapely blooms, produced with freedom, are of deep salmon-pink with a delicious fruity perfume. Awarded the Clay Vase for 1965.

SHOT SILK (1924). It remains so good a bedding rose that it is still widely planted. Of compact habit, the bloom is freely produced through summer and autumn and is of bright carmine-pink, flushed with salmon and orange. It is perhaps the most sweetly scented of all roses.

SIGNORA (1936) (Julien Potin × Sensation). Of very vigorous habit and bearing blooms of outstanding fragrance, both of which characteristics it has passed to its many offspring, e.g. Tahiti, Sutter's Gold, Symphony. The large shapely blooms are made up of many colours including orange, red and pink. Will not bloom well in a cold, wet summer, but has proved most valuable in breeding scented roses.

SILVER LINING (1957) (Karl Herbst × Eden Rose seedling). It won the Clay Vase for fragrance in 1957 and a Gold Medal of the Royal National Rose Society in 1958, but it does not bloom well in a wet summer. The blooms, with their attractive reflexed petals are of pale Bengal rose, enhanced by deep-green foliage.

STELLA (1959). An outstanding rose, upright in habit, and with plenty of dark-green foliage. The blooms have 36 petals and open to 15 cm (6 in) across, the colour being carmine-pink shading to white at the centre and they have a soft sweet perfume.

STERLING SILVER (1957) (Seedling ×

Peace). It is not a strong grower but the blooms, of chalice form, are most attractive, being a lovely silvery-mauve with a most distinctive sweet perfume. They remain fresh in water for longer than any rose. With Shot Silk, the sweetest-scented of all roses.

SUMMER SUNSHINE (1962). It is the most free-flowering of all yellow Hybrid teas, the medium-size blooms borne on long stems being produced with Floribunda freedom and they have the refreshing wild rose perfume.

SUTTER'S GOLD (1950) (Charlotte Armstrong × Signora). With Tahiti, one of the most fragrant of all roses with the scent of jonquils. Of upright habit with glossy but sparse foliage, the long elegant buds of orange are shaded with gold. A good rose for cutting.

SUZON LOTTHE (1951). An outstanding rose, it makes vigorous cane growth with plenty of glossy foliage and bears one of the largest of all rose blooms with 80 petals. The high-centred bloom, of perfect symmetry, is of cream overlaid pearl-pink deepening at the margins, and it has a powerful fragrance.

TAHITI (1947) (Peace × Signora). One of the most robust and beautiful of all roses and one of the most richly fragrant. It will attain a height of 1.8 m (6 ft) in a season and has thick stems and dark foliage. The blooms are camellia-shaped with frilled petals and are of shades of pale pink, ivory and gold, appearing from July until Christmas and carrying the unmistakable perfume of sweet ripe apples.

TROICA (1973). One of the most outstanding of modern roses with lots of dark-green glossy foliage and a compact habit. The blooms are in soft-orange and chrome-yellow shades and possess outstanding perfume.

TRULY YOURS (1971) (Miss Ireland × Stella). Raised by Mr Herbert Robinson of Hinckley, it is a strong grower with large glossy leaves and bears full blooms of rich coral-salmon shaded with orange and with exceptional perfume.

WENDY CUSSONS (1959) (Independence × Eden Rose). Very early to bloom, it is a fine multi-purpose rose, good for garden display and for exhibition without a fault. It has dark-green glossy foliage and bears masses of rosy-red blooms which have a luminous sheen and take their Damask perfume from Eden Rose.

WHISKEY MAC (1967). It makes a spreading plant with bronzy-green foliage and bears masses of chrome-yellow and orange blooms which are heavily scented though they open quickly in warm weather and soon fade.

FLORIBUNDA ROSES. Until the introduction of a number of new Floribundas in recent years, there was never much perfume in this class of rose, which probably arises from the fact that the Polyantha roses contain only two sets of seven chromosomes, compared to the four sets of seven to be found in the Hybrid teas. Now that the Hybrid tea is having a greater influence on the raising of new Floribundas than in the past, we may expect to have more fragrant varieties. This is indeed borne out by the introduction of Daily Sketch in 1960, which had Grand Gala for a parent; of Elizabeth of Glamis (1964), raised from the scented Crimson Glory, and of Pink Parfait which was raised from a cross between First Love and Pinocchio, the former having Charlotte Armstrong for one parent, so that Crimson Glory also figures in its parentage. This rose is of similar breeding to the fragrant Fashion.

Not only are the flowers of the modern Floribundas of more pronounced Hybrid tea form, but they now carry much of the Hybrid tea perfume. This should increase in the years ahead as the Hybrid tea influence becomes greater, and this must add to the attraction of the hardy and free-flowering Floribundas.

The first scented Floribunda, Fashion, was obtained from a crossing of Pinocchio and Crimson Glory, the former having Kordes' Shrub rose, Eva, for one parent, and the fragrant Geheimrat Duisberg, a yellow Hybrid tea rose, for the second parent. This rose was later named Golden Rapture and bore flowers of pronounced perfume.

To take the fragrant Floribunda a stage further, de Ruiter in Holland used the strongly scented Sutter's Gold (which had Signora for a parent) with an unnamed seedling and obtained Pepe, a Floribunda bearing Hybrid tea-like blooms and the same fruity scent as Signora. It was introduced in 1961. De Ruiter made use of Geheimrat Duisberg (Golden Rapture) to raise the lovely pink Floribunda Sweet Repose, which carries the sweetest perfume of all Floribundas, and which blooms freely whatever the weather.

Another fragrant Floribunda is Woburn Abbey, raised by crossing the scented Fashion with Masquerade. Here, scent is present on both sides, for one of the parents of Masquerade was Holiday, a fragrant Floribunda which had Pinocchio for a parent—also a parent of Fashion. Masquerade has been able to continue the perfume sequence in Rumba, raised by Svend Poulsen and which, with its dwarf, compact habit is an ideal bedding rose for a small garden. For a Floribunda it has quite a pronounced wild rose perfume. By following this same line breeding, it would appear that there may be more fragrant Floribundas to come in the immediate future, but no rose has had a greater influence in this respect than the Hybrid tea, Crimson Glory and this will be apparent in studying the parentage of the highly scented Elizabeth of Glamis.

Elizabeth of Glamis won the Clay Vase for the best new scented rose of 1963, the first time the award had been made to a Floribunda, and the variety had the further honour of winning the President's Trophy of the Royal National Rose Society for the best new rose of the year. It has for its parents those two outstanding Floribundas, Spartan and Highlight, neither of them fragrant but which on each side had Crimson Glory for a grandparent. The pronounced scent of Elizabeth of Glamis was therefore only to be expected, and in the years ahead the influence of this great rose in the breeding of scented Floribundas must surely be outstanding.

The following Floribunda rose varieties possess outstanding perfume: the most fragrant ones are marked with an asterisk.

Amberlight	Cavalcade
Arthur Bell	Chinatown
Bonny Maid	*Circus
*Border Coral	Daily Sketch
Cafe	Dearest
Capriole	*Elizabeth of Glamis
Elysium	*Pepe
Fashion	Pink Parfait
Faust	Polka
Golden Fleece	Rosemary Gandy
Jiminy Cricket	Rumba
Kimono	*Scented Air
Lavender Lassie	Spartan
Lilac Charm	*Sweet Repose
Ma Perkins	Vogue
Marie Elizabeth	*Woburn Abbey
Orange Sensation	

The fragrant varieties include:

ARTHUR BELL (1965) (Clare Grammerstorf × Piccadilly). An outstanding scented Floribunda bearing masses of Hybrid tea-like blooms of brilliant golden-yellow which are heavily scented, but which tend to fade in warm weather.

BONNY MAID (1952). Of ideal bedding habit, the semi-double blooms, in contrasting shades of light and deep pink, are borne in large clusters above bronzy-green foliage, and are pleasingly fragrant.

BORDER CORAL (1958) (Signal Red × Fashion). May be said to be a more vigorous Fashion, bearing a bloom of deeper coral colouring with pronounced clove perfume, whilst the flowers have the same Hybrid tea form, but in miniature. Of excellent bedding habit, it blooms until the frosts and has no faults.

CIRCUS (1955) (Pinocchio × Fandango). One of the best of all Floribundas, with plenty of glossy foliage and most free-flowering in the dullest weather. It bears clusters of miniature Hybrid tea-like flowers from June until November, the golden blooms, shaded with pink and red, possessing a delicious clove perfume.

DAILY SKETCH (1960) (Ma Perkins × Grand Gala). A plum and silver bicolour, like its parent Grand Gala but whereas Grand Gala does not bloom well in adverse weather, Daily Sketch is untroubled by the wet and cold. It makes a bushy plant with bronzy-green foliage and bears Hybrid tea-like blooms of sweet perfume.

DEAREST (1960) (Unnamed seedling × Spartan). Its bushy habit, glossy foliage and double blooms of rose-pink flushed with salmon, coiled at the centre and with a spicy scent, contribute to its popularity.

DOMINATOR (1961) (New Yorker × Sweet Repose). Very similar to its parent, Sweet Repose, in habit, colour of bloom (deep pink) and pronounced scent. It has a similar freedom of flowering.

ELIZABETH OF GLAMIS (Spartan × Highlight). A 1964 introduction of outstanding merit with the fragrance of its grandparents, Crimson Glory, but with an undertone of cinnamon. The blooms are a lovely salmon-pink. The only rose to receive the Royal National Rose Society's President's Trophy for the best new rose of the year and also the Clay Vase for the best new scented rose. It makes a plant of ideal bedding habit and blooms well in adverse weather.

FASHION (1947) (Pinocchio × Crimson Glory). The first Floribunda with pronounced perfume, and the first of its colour; it was also the first Floribunda with flowers of Hybrid tea form, the blooms of 24 petals being of glowing salmon and produced with freedom on a short, bushy plant.

FAUST (1956) (Masquerade × Spek's Yellow). Awarded the President's Trophy for the best new rose of 1956 but it is not so good for bedding as Circus for it grows tall, nor does it bloom as well in wet weather and in autumn. Even so, it is a good rose, its Hybrid tea-like blooms being of deep yellow which take on pink shadings as they age.

GOLDEN FLEECE (1956) (Diamond Jubilee × Yellow Sweetheart). It is one of the ten best of all Floribundas, obtaining its long and free-flowering qualities and the unusual buff-yellow colouring of its blooms from Diamond Jubilee. Its flowers have attractively waved petals and the fresh fruity perfume of raspberries.

JIMINY CRICKET (1955) (Goldilocks × Geranium Red). An outstanding rose for it bears its medium-sized blooms, which are an exquisite shade of coral-rose with an orange flush, from June until November and is untroubled by wet weather. It makes a plant of ideal bedding habit. Received the All America Award in 1955.

KIMONO (1962) (Cocorico × Frau Anny Beaufays). A plant of bushy habit with coppery-bronze foliage and bearing flat rounded blooms made up of 42 small petals, quartered like those of the old roses, which are a lovely shell-pink with a most pleasing sweet perfume.

LAVENDER LASSIE (1959) (Parentage unknown). It makes a bushy, branching plant with light-green foliage and bears a rosette-shaped bloom having more petals (65) than any other Floribunda. The colour is lilac-pink with pronounced fragrance.

LILAC CHARM (1961) (Parentage unknown). A beautiful and interesting rose of dwarf, bushy habit and bearing single flowers of perfect symmetry which are a lovely lilac-mauve, enhanced by the crimson filaments of the anthers. It has the fresh fruity perfume of the wild rose and blooms well in adverse weather.

MAGENTA (1955) (Lavender Pinocchio × unnamed seedling). It is a rose with all the charm of the old Shrub roses, bearing flat quartered blooms of deep magenta-mauve which carry the delicious musk perfume.

MA PERKINS (1952) (Red Radiance × Fashion). No rose bears bloom of such an ethereal shade of pink, like that of mother-of-pearl, the beautiful cup-shaped blooms of 30 petals being borne in large trusses through summer and autumn and having true wild rose perfume.

MANY SUMMERS (1975). Named by the people of Woolston to commemorate the marriage of Princess Anne and Captain Mark Phillips, the hybrid-tea shaped blooms are of rich coppery orange and sweetly scented.

ORANGE SENSATION (1960) (Parentage unknown). Well named, for it is one of the best of all Floribundas, being of compact habit with dark foliage, whilst its blooms of 24 petals open to 7 cm (3 in) across and are of brilliant orange-scarlet, shading to gold at the base. They have a pronounced fragrance, unusual in a rose of its colour.

PEPE (1961) (Amor × Sutter's Gold). An outstanding Floribunda of bushy habit with dark-green foliage and great freedom of flowering. The blooms are large with 30 petals, opening to nearly 10 cm (4 in) across and being a lovely combination of pink and gold with a silver reverse. They are sweetly scented.

ROSEMARY ROSE (1955) (Gruss an Teplitz × unnamed seedling). It heralded a new type of flower, resembling a zinnia or the rose Gloire de Dijon, being large and circular with numerous small petals of strawberry-red and a pleasing perfume. The foliage is dark green, the young leaves having a pronounced dark-red colour.

SWEET REPOSE (1956) (Geheimrat Duisberg × an unnamed Polyantha seedling). After all the vivid, blatant scarlet and orange roses, it is always a pleasure to return to this beauty, so aptly named. It is delightfully fragrant and free-flowering and is of ideal bedding form. The Hybrid tea-like blooms of 28 petals are borne in trusses from June until October, and are pink and gold bicoloured, tinged with carmine.

MINIATURE ROSES. M'Intosh, gardener to the King of the Belgians, in his book The Flower Garden (1829), wrote that the pigmy or miniature roses had previously reached this country from Mauritius. They are dwarf China roses or Lawrence roses, named after Miss Molly Lawrence whose book on roses, published in 1799, was the first important work to be devoted entirely to our national flower. In Britain, the miniatures made but little impact, though they were widely grown in window-boxes by the French aristocracy. It was not until the end of the Second World War when we became a nation of flat-dwellers and small gardeners, that the miniature rose achieved any degree of popularity; at the same time it became popular with collectors in America.

The fairy roses are most charming, growing between 15 cm (6 in) and 45 cm (18 in) tall and possessing extreme hardiness. The first of them, R. roulettii, named in honour of Dr Roulet who found it growing at Onnens in Switzerland, has no perfume, nor does R. peon, a seedling which has been widely used by the Dutch breeder, de Vink, to raise many lovely varieties, but there are several fairy roses which do have scented flowers.

The miniature roses require a deep soil, otherwise the roots will dry out during warm weather, but they require little pruning. After flowering, remove all dead blooms and shorten any unduly long shoots. They are best planted from small pots so as not to disturb the roots and so may be planted at almost any time of the year. The plants must never be allowed to lack moisture. They may be increased from cuttings, taken of the ripened wood in August and inserted around the side of a pot. If covered with a polythene bag to conserve moisture in the compost, they will take root in several weeks when they should be moved to individual pots. Varieties:

BABY BETSY McCALL. It was raised in the United States and, growing 20 to 22 cm (8 to 9 in) tall, is a replica in miniature of the popular Floribunda Betsy McCall. Its blooms, no larger than a thimble, are of pearly-pink and of perfect Hybrid tea form with a sweet perfume.

BABY BUNTING. A de Vink variety, raised by crossing R. peon with the first of the Polyantha roses, Ellen Poulsen. The double magenta-coloured blooms are borne on 22-cm (9-in) stems and have a pleasing fragrance.

BIT O' SUNSHINE. It makes a bushy plant 22 cm (9 in) tall with bright-green foliage and bears fragrant, semi-double blooms of bright yellow.

BOBOLINK. A most attractive plant growing 20 to 22 cm. (8 to 9 in) tall, and bearing large Hybrid tea-like blooms of bright rose-pink which have a delicious sweet perfume.

CENTENNIAL MISS. Raised in the United States, it grows less than 15 cm (6 in) tall. The multipetalled blooms open flat like an old Shrub rose in miniature, and they are of two shades of rosy-mauve with a delicate scent.

FROSTY. The whitest of the fairy roses, growing only 15 cm (6 in) tall with thornless stems, the double pompom-shaped flowers having the fragrance of honeysuckle.

JACKIE. In America it is known as a 'sub-zero hybrid' on account of its extreme hardiness. It bears sweetly fragrant yellow flowers of miniature Hybrid tea form.

LITTLE BUCKAROO. It makes a compact bush 25 to 30 cm (10 to 12 in) tall with ample glossy foliage, and bears tiny double blooms of crimson-red with a white centre, which are sweetly scented.

PINK HEATHER. A most enchanting rose bearing clusters of tiny pompom-like flowers of a lovely shade of heather-pink and delicately scented.

SWEET FAIRY. Was selected for the 'Top Twenty' roses of every type for 1960 in the United States. It grows only 15 cm (6 in) high, making a tiny rounded bush on which it bears its flat, rosette-shaped flowers of a lovely bright lilac-pink with the sweetest perfume.

ROSMARINUS (Labiatae—Lavender Family)

A genus of one species.

Species. *Rosmarinus officinalis.* It bears flowers like tiny white orchids. Of several varieties, Jessop's Variety is of more upright habit and bears lavender-coloured flowers. Another, *R. officinalis prostratus*, almost hugs the ground, though it is not so hardy and should be given a place in full sun where it is sheltered by other herbs of shrubby habit. It grows only 22.5 cm (9 in) tall and in early summer bears bright lavender-coloured flowers. There is also a most attractive pink-flowered form, *roseus*, whilst McConnell's Blue is of semi-prostrate habit and bears flowers of brilliant blue. But perhaps the best form of all is the rare Corsican Blue which grows 3 ft tall and has highly aromatic foliage. Its flowers are of rich porcelain-blue.

The plant is believed to have been introduced into England by Queen Philippa, wife of Edward III, in whose memory Queen's College, Oxford, was founded. Here rosemary still figures in the bringing in of the Boar's Head each Christmastime, to commemorate the founder of the College. A copy of a manuscript in the library at Trinity College, Cambridge, sent to Philippa by her mother, the Countess of Hainault, describes the value of rosemary in numerous ways. It was said to 'gladden the spirits' of all who crushed its fragrant leaves, and its pungent smell, quite unlike that of any other plant, does seem to act in the same way as smelling salts, especially during a period of hot dry weather which brings out its fragrance as strongly as when growing in its native haunts round the shores of the Mediterranean. In fact, rosemary is always at its best in the dry, sandy soil and salt-laden atmosphere of the seashore, from which it has been called the 'dew of the sea' from the Latin, *ros marinus*. But it loves a wall more than most plants and especially a walled East Coast garden where the climate is dry.

'As for rosemary,' wrote the learned Sir Thomas More, 'I let it run over my garden walls not only because the bees love it, but because it is the herb sacred to remembrance, to love and to friendship'. Both in France and in England at the time, it was customary to decorate the bodies of the dead with rosemary as it will remain fresh and fragrant longer than any other herb and because it was a herb of perpetual remembrance—hence the saying, 'keeping the memory green'. William Langham, in *The Garden of Health,* said 'carry powder of the flower about thee to make thee merry, glad, gracious and well-beloved of all men', and Bancke in his *Herbal* of 1525 advised one 'to smell of it oft, and it shall keep thee youngly'.

Rosemary seeds were placed in muslin bags and hung about a bedroom because they were thought to bring on sound sleep. And Thomas Newton, in *A Butler's Recipe Book,* suggested distilling the seed or the flowers, when the water 'drunk morning and evening, first and last, will make the breath very sweet'. It was also used to rub into the hair to promote its growth, and clothes and linen were washed in its water. The principal ingredient of Eau de Cologne, rosemary water, was once believed to be the 'elixir of life', a cure for all ailments.

ROWAN: *see* SORBUS

RUBUS (Bramble) (Rosaceae—Rose Family)

A genus of some 250 species of mostly prickly climbing or under-shrubs, useful for covering unsightly walls or banks but more valuable for use as ground cover beneath mature trees. They will flourish in the poorest of soils, producing a mass of slender purple-red stems which are often as colourful as the flowers and leaves. Propagation is by layering the tips of the shoots or they are readily raised from seed. A number of the species bear flowers with the scent of the Sweet-briar of the same family, another example of plants of the same family and of the same latitude having a similar perfume.

Species. *Rubus australis.* It is native of New Zealand with large shiny green leaves, toothed at the margins whilst the stems are covered in large prickles. The flowers are pink or white, borne early in summer and have a sweet perfume. They are followed by yellow fruits of outstanding flavour.

R. deliciosus. One of the few thornless species, it is a delightful plant for covering a bank or low wall, also to use for ground cover for it grows well anywhere. Native of the Rocky Mountains, it was so named from the delicious perfume of its large paper-white flowers which resemble those of the scentless Dog-rose and open in May. It has also attractive vine-like leaves and bears large fruits of outstanding flavour.

A hybrid, raised by Captain Collingwood Ingram, is a most delightful plant, bearing enormous glistening white flowers all along the arching stems and enhanced by a central boss of golden stamens. They have a delicate sweet fragrance.

R. odoratus. Suitable for planting beneath trees where it will make a rambling shrub. It is native of North America and has handsome palmate foliage. It follows *R. deliciosus* into bloom, its large rosy-purple flowers appearing towards the end of June and continuing until the end of summer. It is not the blooms that are fragrant but the glandular hairs which cover the stems and they have a powerful resinous scent, likened to that of cedarwood, being similar to that of the Sweet-briar.

The form *albus* has snow-white blossoms whilst a hybrid, *R. fraseri,* is a most handsome shade-loving shrub, bearing large rose-pink flowers from July to September, and they have the same pervading scent as the parent, *R. odoratus,* due to the resinous brown hairs.

RUTA (Rutaceae—Rue Family)

A genus of 60 species and one of a large family of more than 600 species of trees and shrubs, many of which bear flowers which carry the fragrance of oranges, whilst the foliage has the pungent smell of orange peel. Included in the family is the Citrus group which includes the orange itself and *Choisya ternata,* the Mexican orange-blossom, and, though bitter to taste, there is in the foliage of the Common rue a distinct orange pungency which makes it one of the most pleasant of all herbs to inhale when bruised.

The mechanism by which the rue releases its scent is remarkable. The essential oil is contained in a cavity immediately beneath the surface of the leaf above which is a thin layer of cells pierced by a narrow cavity in the middle. The cells swell up and bend inwards, pressing on the essential oil beneath, which is driven to the surface of the leaf and there released.

Because of its extreme bitterness to taste, Rue was always the herb of repentance or Herb of Grace.

For you there's Rosemary and Rue; ...
Grace and remembrance be to you both.

said Perdita in *A Winter's Tale*; and in *Hamlet,* Ophelia said:

There's Rue for you; and here's some for me:
we may call it Herb o' Grace o' Sundays:
O, you must wear your Rue with a difference.

Species. *Ruta chalepensis.* It is not so pleasantly scented as the Common rue for its foliage releases a somewhat fetid smell, like wet fur but with slightly sweeter undertones. The attractive leaves are cut into wedge-shaped leaflets whilst the yellow flowers are edged with hairs. It is a plant of the Mediterranean regions, to be found growing from old limestone walls or cliffs.

R. graveolens. The Common rue which is readily distinguished from the former by the smooth petal edges of its yellow flowers and by the pleasant orange-like fragrance of the leaves. It is a perennial, growing about 60 cm (2 ft) tall, its serrated leaves being almost blue-green in colour. In Jackman's Variety, the foliage is almost true blue.

S

SABAL (Palmae—Palm Family)

A genus of 25 species of palms varying considerably in height from dwarf to about 24 m (80 ft). They are native to the tropics, of the West Indies and America, and are handsome trees, making good pot plants. They require warm greenhouse conditions and a well-drained compost containing plenty of coarse sand. Increase is by seed, or by suckers, which need careful treatment after potting. The deeply cut, fan-shaped leaves of these palms make them most attractive.

Species. *Sabal umbraculifera.* The Thatch palm of Jamaica, this makes a tall tree 18 to 24 m (60 to 80 ft) tall, with leaves as much as 1.8 m (6 ft) across. The inconspicuous flowers have a pleasing fragrance.

SAGE: *see* SALVIA

SALIX (Salicaceae—Willow Family)

A genus of 500 species of trees and shrubs mostly of the northern temperate regions, amongst which are included the White and Weeping willows. The name *salix* is from the Celtic words 'sal' and 'lis', near water, whilst willow is derived from an Anglo-Saxon word 'withig' meaning 'to plait', for the twigs had all manner of uses: they were sought after for thatching; for making hurdles to enclose stock, to provide a wind-break, to make baskets and ropes, and even to use for feeding cattle. The bark was spun into thread to make clothes.

Species. *Salix aurita.* The Eared sallow, a plant of short, bushy habit with downy stems of silvery-green and wrinkled leaves. The flowers with their golden stamens ap-

pear in April before the leaves and emit the scent of white jasmine when inhaled close to.

S. pentandra. The Bay-leaved willow which blooms during early summer, a tree preferring drier ground. Its leaves are lance-shaped, some 7.5 to 10 cm (3 to 4 in) long and taper to a sharp point, like those of the Bay and they have a similar sweet, aromatic fragrance, a scent which they retain when dry and so may be used in pot-pourris. The scent, resembling that of oil of wintergreen is due to salicyl aldehyde which in the willow has a pleasant aromatic odour. It also occurs in the sap of the Meadowsweet and, strangely, in the larvae of *Chrysomela populi*, which lives on willows. From small openings in its body, salicyl aldehyde may be pressed out in oily drops.

S. triandra. It is known as the Almond willow for its smooth. flaking bark, dark brown in colour has the smell of almonds. It makes a tall shrub rather than a tree and has dark-green lanceolate leaves. It bears its bright-yellow catkins on leafy stalks.

SALSOLA (Chenopodiaceae—Beetroot Family)

A genus of herbs or shrubs closely related to *Chenopodium*, with leaves that are cylindrical, fleshy and densely hairy, the flowers usually borne in terminal spikes. They have no scented attractions, but one species, *S. baryosma*, has leaves of unpleasant smell.

Species. *Salsola baryosma* (syn. *Salsola foetida*). A small shrub with pale-green leaves, absent on the flowering branches, and bearing yellow-green flowers which emit a most unpleasant smell of decaying fish. It is pollinated by dung-flies and midges.

SALVIA (Labiatae—Lavender Family)

A genus of about 500 species of herbs or sub-shrubs, mostly native of southern Europe but with several to be found in tropical South America and in North America. The leaves are toothed or pinnately cut; the flowers borne in spikes, racemes or panicles.

Mostly of shrubby habit and with most attractive foliage, the sages are delightful plants to include in the shrub border, though it is in the kitchen garden where they are more frequently to be found. Indeed, the ancients gave pride of place amongst all aromatic plants to *Salvia officinalis* (Common sage), and in the ninth century, Walfred Strabo wrote, 'Amongst my herbs, sage holds the place of honour; of good scent it is and full of virtue for many ills'. Sage is reputed to give long life to those who use it, hence its name of *Salvia* (Salvation). It has been used through the years for curing all manner of complaints. Sage cordial, made from the Red-leaf variety, is most valuable for a sore throat, whilst an infusion (an ounce of dried leaves to a pint of boiling water), taken when cold, is an excellent help to the digestion and for those who suffer from anaemia. It may also be used as a hair tonic, and prevents hair falling out better than any other preparation, whilst it will darken greying hair. A little of an infusion of sage water should be massaged into the scalp every day upon rising and, if a little brilliantine is used occasionally, to prevent the hair from becoming too dry, the hair will quickly respond to this treatment.

Since earliest times, sage had been used in stuffings for the richer meats and game, for which purpose more dried sage is sold today than any other herb. But it is important to obtain a broad-leaf strain to use for stuffing though for medicinal purposes the narrow-leaf form is more desirable. There is also a variegated form and one with red-tinted leaves.

Species. *Salvia argentea.* Known as the Silver clary, it is a handsome biennial plant growing 90 cm (3 ft) tall with hairy stems and large oval leaves, formed in rosette fashion and covering almost a square yard of ground. The leaves are woolly to the touch and covered in silver hairs but do not possess the same distinctive pungency as those of *S. officinalis*. The plant will enjoy a longer life if the white flower spike is removed as soon as it forms.

S. azurea. Native of North America, it grows up to 1.2 m (4 ft) tall and has smooth grey-green lance-shaped leaves which are pleasantly pungent. It blooms in July and August bearing deep-blue flowers in long slender spikes.

S. candalabrum (syn. *S. grahami*). A native of Mexico, it is not hardy in northern Europe unless given winter protection, but it is a beautiful plant growing 1.2 m (4 ft) tall with long lance-shaped leaves which are wrinkled and hairy and upon the surface the oily glands are readily observed. In July it forms long white panicles veined with purple, the lower lip of the flowers being of deep violet. The whole plant is very aromatic.

S. officinalis (Common sage). It forms a low, spreading bush with grey-green leaves and is evergreen. The stems are woolly and white whilst the leaves are wrinkled and emit a unique pungent aroma when pressed. There is a form *aurea* which bears yellow flowers instead of purple.

S. glutinosa. Native of the eastern Mediterranean, it is a handsome and interesting plant growing 60 to 90 cm (2 to 3 ft) high, and during summer the whole plant becomes covered in a 'tacky' substance, like a fragrant gum. In July it bears pale-primrose flowers which are attractively stencilled with black and they appear luminous at night. Plant it where not exposed to cold winds.

S. rutilans. It is known as the Pineapple-scented sage and is a plant to include in every garden, whether in the shrubbery, border or herb garden, for its delicious scent likened by Sarbe to that of the orange but nearer that of the pineapple. The dried leaves are delicious in a stuffing. It makes a bushy plant 60 cm (2 ft) tall and bearing throughout summer, in addition to its scented foliage, panicles of crimson-red flowers.

S. sclarea (syn. *S. horminoides*). Native of southern Europe, it is a biennial species and from earliest times, a diffusion of its seeds or its handsome aromatic leaves has been used to aid tired and inflamed eyes, hence its name 'Clear-eyes', later shortened into Clary. The plant grows 0.9 to 1.2 m (3 to 4 ft) tall with clammy hairy stems, the ovate leaves measuring 22.5 cm (9 in) in length. They are wrinkled and so covered in hairs as to give a hoary or frosted appearance. In Tudor times, the leaves were dipped in batter and fried to be served with meat or in omelettes. The dried leaves were also used in scent bags and pot-pourris and from them an oil is extracted for use in perfumery. When pressed, the leaves release the deliciously pungent and refreshing smell of fresh grapefruit, and in Europe they were added to fruit jellies. The large spikes of pale-mauve flowers with their pink bracts adds to the beauty of the plant whilst the flowers are much visited by bees.

S. *virgata*. Native of south-eastern Europe, it grows only 30 cm (12 in) tall with rough ovate leaves, aromatic when pressed, and in August and September bears elegant spikes of deep-blue flowers enhanced by the purple-brown colour of the calyx.

SAMBUCUS (Elder) (Caprifoliaceae—Honeysuckle Family)

A genus of 40 species, distributed in most parts of the world. The flowers of S. *nigra* have a sweet, almost overpowering smell, not exactly pleasant when inhaled near to for it has fishy undertones, but from a distance its musky scent is appealing. It is of the same family as the deliciously fragrant *Viburnum fragrans*. Our native Black elder was in ancient times known as the Bore tree for the branches could easily be made hollow. For this reason the tree came to be widely used to make musical instruments, including the sambuk (sackbut), hence its botanical name, also the dulcimer and pipe mentioned in Daniel.

Spenser wrote of the 'bitter elder', the reference being to S. *ebulus* and no tree was held in less esteem during Elizabethan times. Its reputation arose partly because, as Biron says in *Love's Labours Lost*, 'Judas was hanged on an Elder'. Sir John Mandeville who in 1356 wrote a detailed account of his travels which was most likely known to Shakespeare, stated that he had been shown the original 'tree of eldre that Judas henge himself upon'.

But not everything thought about the elder was bad and through the centuries its crimson-black berries have been used to make a delicious elderberry wine. In Germany the tree is more appreciated than in Britain, being named after Hulda, the goddess of love to whom the tree was held sacred.

Species. *Sambucus canadensis.* The finest form of the Elder, it grows to a height of 3.6 m (12 ft) in damp soil and has large pinnate leaves, whilst its enormous heads of white flowers appear in July and August when so many trees have finished flowering. The flowers are also more pleasantly scented than those of the native Elder, having a muscatel smell.

S. *ebulus.* Called Dane's Blood or Dane's elder for it was introduced to Britain by the Danes. Like S. *canadensis*, it blooms in July and August, its white flowers being tipped with pink, but the whole plant emits a most unpleasant fur-like smell when bruised or knocked against. Especially does the bark smell of stale perspiration.

S. *nigra.* The Common elder, also the Black elder, a tree native to the British Isles which will attain a height of 6 m (20 ft) or more. Its leaves are divided into four pairs of lance-shaped leaflets and it comes into bloom in June, its creamy-white flowers borne in flat-topped cymes, pleasant to behold and to smell, for when the air is calm and the flowers are warmed by the sun the musk-like perfume reaches far and wide.

S. *racemosa.* Known as the Hart's elder and unusual in that its berries are not black but brilliant scarlet. It flowers in May. The form *plumosa aurea* has attractive feathery leaves, golden in colour. Its flowers have a sweet smell, free from any fishy undertones.

SANTALUM (Santalaceae—Sandalwood Family)

A genus of parasitic trees, native of India, Malaysia and eastern Polynesia, the roots of which are scented.

Species. *Santalum album.* A parasitic tree native of Malaya, south-eastern India and the island of Timor where it grows in dense forests. It attaches its roots to those of other trees and, will eventually attain a height of 12 m (40 ft) or more though it is one of the slowest growing of all trees. The opposite leaves are oval, terminating to a point whilst the flowers are composed of 4 stamens only which arise from the calyx. The yellow wood is highly scented and is used to make chests and cabinets whilst the essential oil obtained from it by distillation is used in perfumery. In the religious ceremonies of the Chinese and Hindus, the wood is much offered by way of incense and such has been the demand through the centuries that the Santalum is now extinct in China and large quantities of the wood are obtained annually from Timor.

One hundredweight of wood, usually in chippings, will yield about 30 oz of otto which has a remarkable density. It enters into the composition of many perfumes as 'sandal'. It is almost colourless and assimilates well with rose perfume, thus it is often used to adulterate otto of roses.

As the wood is repellent to insects and is highly scented, it is used to makes chests in which to keep clothes and bedding.

S. yasi. Native of the Fiji Islands where it is known as Yasi or Fiji Sandalwood. Its presence was discovered early in the nineteenth century when large numbers of trees were felled and exported to China and Japan to be used in religious observances, very high prices being paid for them. Its aromatic oil was also used to scent coconut oil and so valuable was the wood in so many ways that, like the cedars of Lebanon, few trees were allowed to remain. The few that are still standing are covered by a government protection order.

S. yasi makes a small tree and was at one time common on the rocky slopes of the Bua and Lekuta coasts of Yanua Levu. All parts of the tree are scented, especially the wood when burnt as incense.

SANTOLINA (Compositae—Daisy Family)

A genus of 10 species of ornate plants, native of the Mediterranean regions. The Cotton or French lavender, Santolina incana, which is in no way related to the true lavender is a most interesting plant. It has beautifully serrated silvery-grey leaves which are retained through winter and make it a valuable plant for a low hedge. It grows almost 60 cm (2 ft) tall, though there are more dwarf forms, but may be clipped in spring and maintained at a height of no more than 30 to 37.5 cm (12 to 15 in). Its leaves are pleasantly pungent and may be used to keep away moths from clothes, for which purpose it is best dried and mixed with lavender flowers and the leaves of Southernwood, hence its French name of Garde-robe. It reached England during Tudor times and it was still rare at the beginning of the seventeenth century, for Parkinson wrote: 'the rarity and novelty of this herb being for the most part in the gardens of great persons doth cause it to be of greater regard'.

To make a hedge, the plants should be set out 45 cm (18 in) apart in autumn and they will be quite happy in ordinary soil provided it is well drained. The cuttings, removed with a heel, strike readily in a sandy soil in the open and if inserted during midsummer will have become well rooted in time for transplanting before winter. The plant bears masses of bright-yellow daisy-like flowers which will be lost if the plants are clipped later than early April. In the less exposed areas the plants may be clipped in autumn.

Species and Varieties. Santolina incana. It grows to a height of 60 cm (2 ft) with small fleshy leaves covered with silvery hairs and in July bears rounded heads of yellow flowers of unpleasant smell.

The form S. incana nana is more compact, attaining a height of no more than 37.5 cm (15 in) whilst its foliage is more pungent than the type.

Finer still is the variety Weston which grows less than 30 cm (12 in) tall but 37.5 to 45 cm (15 to 18 in) across. The stems are made up of numerous tiny 'lamb's tails' or 'catkins' which are brightly silvered and which possess a strong pungent scent.

S. neapolitana. It grows to a height of 0.9 to 1.2 m (3 to 4 ft) with finely cut silvered foliage which is most aromatic, and in July bears lime-green flowers which have the scent of perspiration.

S. serratifolia. A hybrid between S. incana and S. neapolitana, it more closely resembles the latter, having finely cut feathery foliage as if dusted with silver, but its rich golden flowers have not the same unpleasant smell of the parent species.

SAPONARIA (Soapwort) (Caryophyllaceae—Pink Family)

It is a genus of about 30 species of annual and perennial plants closely related to *Silene* and mostly natives of central Europe. One, the Common soapwort, is possibly native to Britain where it is to be found occasionally about ditches and hedgerows, and it is slightly scented.

Species. *Saponaria officinalis.* The two garden forms are the double pink (*rosea plena*) and double white (*alba plena*), both of which grow 60 cm (2 ft) tall and bloom during July. The leaves are smooth and glaucous and when crushed and rubbed in the hands form a lather-like soap, hence its botanical name.

The flowers measure 2.5 cm (1 in) across, the pink variety resembling a flesh-pink carnation, whilst the double white variety is equally lovely. Both are sweetly scented with an undertone of clove present also in the wild form which bears flowers of pale lilac-pink or white.

SARCOCHILUS (Orchidaceae—Orchid Family)

A genus of 10 species of epiphytic plants distributed throughout eastern India and Australia, especially Queensland and New South Wales. They have short stems and flaccid dark-green leaves, and bear their flowers from the axils of the leaves. Cultivation requirements are varied, and depend on the habitat of the individual species.

Species. *Sarcochilus olivaceus.* Inhabits the brush forests of Queensland and New South Wales, where it blooms early in summer. It has dark-green leaves, from the axils of which it bears 3 to 10 flowers in a drooping inflorescence. The flowers have narrow segments, olive-green in colour, the labellum being marked with red. They have a soft, sweet jasmine-like perfume.

It requires a compost mixture of sphagnum-moss and osmunda fibre, and a temperature of not less than 16°C (60°F) during winter, with a humid atmosphere.

SARCOCOCCUS (Buxaceae—Box Family)

A genus of about 20 species dwarf evergreen winter-flowering shrubs with glossy foliage, which grow well in any soil and in partial shade. Their distribution is from the Himalayas, to southern China and throughout South-east Asia.

Species. *Sarcococcus hookeriana.* Native of the western Himalayas, it makes an upright shrub 0.9 to 1.2 m (3 to 4 ft) in height and it is evergreen with small oval leaves from the axils of which appear in January flowers of creamy-white which have a heavy sweet scent; they are followed by sloe-black fruits. The Chinese form, *digyna*, is more compact in habit.

S. humilis. From western China, it makes a dense little bush with small oval evergreen leaves and from the axils are borne, in February, tiny fragrant flowers which are followed by jet-black fruits.

S. ruscifolia. It is native of central China and makes a neat, upright shrub bearing from the leaf axils both male and female flowers which appear early in the year and they have a rich fruity scent.

S. salignus. From the Himalayas, it has narrow willow-like leaves and flourishes in shade, producing its creamy-white scented flowers in February, followed by purple fruits.

SARCOPHYTE (Balanophoraceae— Balanophora Family)

A genus of about 12 species of parasitic plants, native of tropical Africa and extending south into Cape Province. The tiny flowers are borne on short stems, crowded together in a cylindrical head whilst the plant is entirely leafless.

Species. *Sarcophyte sanguinea.* It fastens itself to the roots of trees by means of suckers and bears its flowers on a short stem from a sheath-like protuberance which occurs above the soil. The minute flowers are crowded together in a short spike and are reddish-purple in colour with the offensive smell of decaying fish. Pollination is by midges and flies. This family is closely related to the Aristolochiales, parasitic plants devoid of chlorophyll and having the same evil smell to attract flies for their pollination.

SASSAFRAS (Lauraceae—Bay Tree Family)

A genus of a single species, named by Linnaeus *Laurus sassafras* but now considered a separate genus.

Species. *Sassafras officinale.* It is native to California but extends north into Canada and south to Missouri. In the north, it makes a tree 4.5 m (15 ft) tall but may reach 30 m (100 ft) in the south with many cylindrical branches. It has deeply furrowed bark of greyish-brown which is highly aromatic, more so than the wood, and the root bark is the most pleasant of all. From the the young shoots with their yellow bark, a beer is brewed.

The external bark of the roots is spongy, dull grey in colour whilst the inner bark is reddish-brown and rich in essential oil with a most pleasant odour. It is the inner bark that is used in commerce. It is of a brilliant cinnamon colour and when examined under a microscope is seen to contain a large number of oil cells. Those roots dug when the sap is down contain the highest percentage of oil, 1,000 lb of root chips yielding one gallon of oil under steam pressure. Upon distillation, the crude oil is composed of 90 per cent safrol and is palest yellow, becoming red with age. Safrol has a pleasant aromatic odour and is an extremely stable compound. It is present in the oil of *Cinamomum camphora* and in many other members of the family Magnoliaceae.

The tree bears greenish-yellow unisexual flowers in drooping racemes which appear with the leaves and immediately beneath them. They have a spicy perfume.

The fruit is an oval drupe the size of a pea, of deep-blue colour, supported erect on a red peduncle nearly 5 cm (2 in) long. From it, oil used in perfumery is extracted.

SATUREIA (Labiatae—Lavender Family)

A genus of about 30 species, distributed throughout the warmer regions of the world. Winter savory was included by Tusser in the 21 plants for strewing for its pungency rivalled that of lavender and fennel. It is said that the leaves, rubbed on wasp stings, provide immediate relief. Winter savory is a delightful little plant which will retain its leaves (which turn bronze) and its aromatic fragrance, likened to that of Sweet marjoram, under a covering of snow and ice. The flowers, though insignificant, are a valuable source of nectar.

Species. *Satureia douglasii.* Native of northern California and named after Robert Douglas, the botanist, it is an evergreen of almost prostrate habit to be found about the edges to fields and woodlands, being especially prominent about San Francisco Bay. When crushed, its oval leaves release the pungent smell of nutmeg. Its white or pale-pink flowers, borne at the axils of the leaves, are not scented.

S. hortensis. It is a half-hardy annual and is known as the Summer savory though is now rarely grown in Britain; on the Continent it is widely used to make stuffing for veal and pork sausages. Parkinson tells us that it was 'boiled with peas to make pottage'. The leaves may be finely chopped to sprinkle over vegetable dishes in the same way as parsley and thyme, and in this way it will add interest to scrambled eggs. It is raised from seed sown in shallow drills in March and likes a sandy soil and full sun; it will grow about 50 cm (20 in) high and the same distance across. The shoots are cut in June and again late in summer to prevent the plants from becoming woody.

S. montana. The Winter savory and a perennial form, propagated from cuttings or from pieces of the root. The leaves, which are small, are dried and mixed with other herbs and possess the refreshing pungency of thyme. Thomas Hill in *The Art of Gardening* (1563) wrote that mazes or knots are sometimes 'sette with Isope and Thyme or with Winter Savory and Thyme, for these endure all the winter through greene'. The fresh leaves, boiled with broad beans, greatly improve the flavour.

SATYRIUM (Orchidaceae—Orchid Family)

A large genus of tuberous plants known as the South African ground orchids and they are common in sand dunes near the coast and on mountainous slopes. From twin basal leaves arises a stem 30 to 60 cm (1 to 2 ft) in height at the end of which are numerous flowers, the sepals and petals alike and joined at the base with spreading side sepals, the lip hooded and 2-spurred. It is of interest that *S. corriifolium* which bears flowers of orange-scarlet is scentless whilst *S. candidum* which bears pure-white flowers is sweetly perfumed.

Species. *Satyrium bicorne.* The two basal leaves which cover the ground have purple stems whilst the flowers, borne in a long elegant spike, are of a dull green, spotted with brown. Common on heathlands of the Cape Peninsula, the flowers diffuse a powerful clove-like perfume, especially pronounced at eventide.

S. candidum. Its two basal leaves lie flat on the ground, and on a 30 cm (12 in) stem its sweetly scented flowers of purest white (sometimes tinted with mauve), with their long slender spurs, are borne in a dense spike.

S. emarcidum. It has an almost circular basal leaf which has become dried up by the time the plant blooms in September. The flowers are dull greenish-yellow with a lip of chocolate-brown and a long slender spur and are borne in spikes of 6 or 8.

S. ligulatum. Unlike the others of the genus, it inhabits marshy ground and has broad lanceolate leaves above which it bears white flowers with the tips of the petals and lip turning a milk-chocolate colour when fully open. They are powerfully scented.

S. marginatum. It is to be found in semi-shaded valleys where it blooms in October, its small creamy-white flowers, borne in a long spike, having the same spicy scent as *S. bicorne.*

S. ochroleucum. Occasionally to be found in damp clefts amongst rocks, it has twin basal leaves, oval and fleshy, from between which arises the ochre-yellow flower spike. The lip is recurved at the margins, the spur being long and slender. It emits a powerful clove-like scent.

S. odorum. Common about shady places at the Cape, it has spreading basal leaves and bears its flowers of pale green and purple in a lax spike. They have the distinctive clove carnation scent.

S. striatum. Rare on sandy ground at the Cape where it blooms in September, it has fleshy ovate leaves and bears its small creamy-white flowers, striped with brown in a compact spike of 2 to 8. The sepals and petals have glandular basal hairs and the flower is sweetly scented.

SAURURUS (Saururacae—Saururus Family)

A small genus of aquatic herbs, native of North America and the Philippine Isles and suitable to plant in the bog garden or by the side of lakes and ponds or in swamplands. It is readily increased by root division in spring.

Species. *Saururus cernuus.* Native of North America where it is known as the Swamp lily or Lizard's Tail from the fluffy curved flower spike. It grows 60 cm (2 ft) tall with heart-shaped leaves which taper to a point and it blooms from June until the end of August, bearing its fragrant white flowers in a dense spike. In its native land, the roots were at one time boiled for the extraction was considered valuable to heal flesh wounds.

SAUSSUREA (Compositae—Daisy Family)

A genus of 400 or more species or annual and perennial plants, mostly native to temperate Asia. Very few have scented attractions.

Species. *Saussurea alpina.* It is the only European species, to be found about high ground from the Swiss alpine regions to the Caucasus and, unusual in the Composites, its purple daisy-like flowers are sweetly scented.

S. lappa (syn. *Aplotaxus lappa, Auchlondia costus*). From the dried root, costus, a favourite perfume of the East, is obtained. It has something of the mossy smell of the violet when fresh but tends to develop a fur-like aroma with age, becoming goat-like and most unpleasant the longer it is kept. Like the Valerian, it is a plant of the higher Himalayas.

SAXIFRAGA (Rockfoil)
(Saxifragaceae—Rockfoil Family)

A genus of about 360 species of mostly perennial alpine plants, few of which have flowers which are scented. They are distributed throughout the northern temperate regions and the Andes.

Species. *Saxifraga atlantica.* It is a member of the Nephrophyllum group, most of which are annual or biennial plants and bear solitary white flowers. The plants are native of the Atlantic coastline of southern Spain and northern Africa and usually grow about moist rocky limestone formations.

It is a rockfoil of almost prostrate habit with pale-green leaves which have crenate edges, and during April and May it bears large white flowers, sometimes as many as 5 or 7 to a stem, which emit a sweet perfume, especially during damp humid weather.

S. cotyledon. A perennial saxifrage of the European Alps, a plant to grace a crevice in a wall or for planting between rock formations. Forming rosettes or silvery grey-green tongue-shaped leaves 7.5 cm (3 in) long, it blooms during May and June, sending up its sprays of white flowers, veined with pink to a height of 60 cm (2 ft). The bright-red stems are an added attraction whilst the flowers are deliciously scented. After flowering, the rosette dies back to be replaced the following year by at least one or two younger rosettes so that the flowering sequence is maintained.

The variety Southside Seedling is a perennial rockfoil of outstanding beauty, sending forth its sprays of small white flowers, spotted and marked with crimson, to a height of 45 cm (18 in), and they are also sweetly scented.

SCABIOSA (Dipsacaceae—Scabious Family)

A genus of about 100 species of annual and perennial plants, native of the temperate regions of Europe and Asia. Few are scented.

Species. *Scabiosa atropurpurea.* The Sweet scabious of southern Europe, also known as the Pincushion flower and, on account of its sombre purple colouring, as the Mourning Bride. It is a plant of open fields and requires an open, sunny position in the garden. It does well in ordinary soil but especially of a chalky nature. It is a hardy annual, bearing its flowers on almost leafless stems 90 cm (3 ft) tall so that it is excellent for cutting, lasting ten days in water without dropping its petals.

If seed is sown in shallow drills or about the border in August, the plants will survive the winter and begin to bloom in July. A second sowing may be made in April to bloom from early August until October. Thin to 30 cm (12 in) apart.

King of the Blacks, with its purple-black flowers, and Azure Fairy, pale blue, are the most sweetly scented.

SCAEVOLA (Goodeniaceae—Goodenia Family)

A large genus of herbs or shrubs, native of Australia and islands of the Pacific. inhabiting coastal areas where they bloom almost throughout the year.

Species. *Scaevola suaveolens.* It is known as the Sweet-scented Fan flower and is an almost prostrate shrub with spathulate succulent leaves which enable it to survive long periods of drought. It bears sweetly scented flowers of pale blue (occasionally red) with 5 spreading petals split to the base. They are followed by large succulent fruits.

SCHINUS (Anacardiaceae—Cashew Family)

A genus of evergreen trees or shrubs. native of Peru and suitable for growing only in the western parts of the British Isles where they will grow to a height of about 4.5 m (15 ft). One, *S. molle,* bears red peppercorn-like fruits whilst the oily leaves also smell and taste of pepper when crushed, hence its name of Pepper Tree.

Species. *Schinus molle.* It has attractively pointed pinnate leaves of palest green and it bears, in June, clusters of small slightly scented yellowish-green flowers followed by brilliant-red fruits which hang in dense clusters. From the trees, a purgative known as American mastic is obtained.

SCHIZANDRA (Magnoliaceae— Magnolia Family)

A genus of six climbing shrubs native of central China, with scented flowers and aromatic leaves with pellucid dots. The plants require a warm sheltered wall to be successful and a rich loamy soil containing some peat. Flowers of *S. glaucescens* which are brilliant orange in colour have no scent.

Species. *Schizandra chinensis.* It will eventually attain a height of 6 m (20 ft) and is deciduous with long elliptical leaves. Through spring and summer it bears clusters of pale-pink flowers which are sweetly scented. The flowers are followed by scarlet berries which are retained on the plant all winter.

S. propinqua sinensis. Native of the eastern Himalayas, it is the hardiest species and is semi-evergreen with leaves of bottle-green. It bears its golden-yellow flowers during autumn and they have an aromatic perfume.

SCHIZOPETALON (Cruciferae— Wallflower Family)

A genus of eight species, native of Chile, one having scented flowers.

Species. *Schizopetalon walkeri.* It is a native of Chile and iş one of a genus of five species of half-hardy annuals whose foliage is covered with down which gives it a most attractive grey appearance. It blooms at a height of 45 to 50 cm (18 to 20 in) and bears its flowers from early June until the frosts appear. The flowers are fringed and are of purest white, borne in long racemes and they emit a delicious almond-like scent.

Seed should be sown in April where the plants are to bloom as they do not transplant well.

SCILLA (Liliaceae—Lily Family)

A large genus of bulbous plants, almost all of which bear scented flowers, resembling the powerful balsamic perfume of the hyacinth. 'The Starry Jacinths', Parkinson named them. The scillas are distributed throughout Europe, northern Africa and Asia, as far north as Siberia, those of dwarf habit, the squills, growing in the open mountainous regions whilst the campanulate species, amongst which is included the native Bluebell, *Scilla nutans* (now classified under *Endymion*), grow in the shade of leafy woodlands and in low-lying meadows. They require similar conditions in the garden as in their natural habitat. All are plants of extreme hardiness, increasing rapidly from seed and by offsets of the bulbs. They should be planted in October, 7.5 cm (3 in) deep.

Species. *Scilla bifolia.* It grew in Gerard's garden in Holborn during the time of Elizabeth I though it is not a native plant, being common to the mountainous regions of southern Europe. The brilliant-blue flowers, in Gerard's words 'consisting of six little leaves spread abroad like a star' are about 2.5 cm (1 in) across and borne on 15-cm (6-in) stems, usually in sixes. They appear early in April from two bronzy-green leaves.

An ideal subject for the alpine garden or for pans indoors, for the flowers have a delicate perfume which is not nearly so pronounced as in *S. sibirica.*

S. hyacinthoides. Native of coniferous woodlands of southern Europe, it makes a large bulb 5 cm (2 in) through. The leaves grow 45 cm (18 in) long and are broad and glossy whilst the scented flowers are lilac-blue and borne in a dense raceme during July and August, on a 37.5-cm (15-in) scape.

S. italica. A native of Italy and of parts of southern France, it blooms in May and June, bearing on a 22.5-cm (9-in) stem a conical head of brilliant-blue flowers which are pleasantly scented.

S. odorata. A native of Spain and Portugal, it is the most sweetly scented of all the scillas. It is in bloom during June when its sky-blue bell-shaped flowers, borne on 20-cm (8-in) stems, emit a sweet penetrating perfume over a considerable distance.

S. pratensis. It is native only of parts of the Adriatic coastline and bears in May a spike of lilac bell-shaped flowers which have a soft, sweet perfume. It grows 30 cm (12 in) tall.

S. sibirica. The Siberian squill, native of the northern shores of Russia and of Siberia, did not reach Britain until about 1800. For massing beneath trees, it is one of the finest bulbous plants in cultivation, bearing its spikes of dangling flowers of electric-blue on 10-cm (4-in) stems in long succession from early March until early May. It is always in demand by bees which search for its blue pollen. There is a pure-white form *alba*, whilst the variety Spring Beauty is more beautiful than either form, growing to twice the height and bearing flowers twice the size. They are of deep delphinium-blue and are deliciously scented whilst the blue-grey pollen is much sought after by bees. It is delightful with *Primula denticulata,* Inshriach Carmine or Stormont Red, for it is in bloom at the same time.

S. verna. Native of the British Isles where it is prominent on turfy slopes near the coast of Northumberland and south-eastern Scotland and also Cornwall. It is a delightful little plant, flowering in April, and is known as the Spring-flowering squill. From the strap-like leaves which grow 15 cm (6 in) long arises the leafless scape at the end of which is a corymbose cluster of bright-blue star-shaped flowers with lanceolate bracts. They are sweetly scented.

SECURIDACA (Polygalaceae—Polygala Family)

A genus of 80 species of climbing plants, native of the tropics of the Old and New World, excluding Australasia.

Species. *Securidaca violacea.* Native of the open heathlands of the Congo and tropical Africa where it makes a plant of tree-like proportions 9 m (30 ft) tall. The bark is furrowed and light grey in colour, like the Ash, and the alternate oval leaves are held on short hairy stalks. The flowers which are borne in short racemes at the ends of the twiggy branchlets are of deep purple-violet, in colour like the Sweet violet and with the same perfume hence its name of 'Violet tree'. The wood is used for fuel and gives off a similar violet-like fragrance when burnt. When the tree is cut, it fills the air around with the delicious perfume of its wood.

SEDUM (Stonecrop) (Crassulaceae—Stonecrop Family)

A genus of about 600 species of pros-trate succulent herbs, many native of Mexico, which may be grown over the stones of the alpine garden and about old walls, for with their succulent leaves they are adapted for survival under dry, sun-baked conditions. Few are scented for like *S. acer* the flowers are self-pollinating. There are one or two exceptions.

Species. *Sedum populifolium.* A native of Siberia, it is deciduous with attractive heart-shaped leaves like those of the Poplar. It is one of the few Sedums to bear white flowers (most bear pink or yellow flowers) and they have the aniseed scent of hawthorn blossom without the fishy undertones.

S. rhodiola (syn. *S. rosea, Rhodiola rosea*). It is a plant of the British Isles chiefly to be found on sea cliffs in the North of England and in Ireland, with fleshy stems 15 to 30 cm (6 to 12 in) long and glaucous leaves, toothed at the apex. It is one of the longest of all plants to remain in bloom, being colourful from May until September, bearing pretty purple flowers, pollinated by bees and without perfume. Its rhizome-like roots, however, smell strongly of roses when dry and may be used to distil rose-water. From this characteristic, the plant received its old name of Rose-root.

S. spectabile. It is known as the 'Ice Plant' and grows 45 cm (18 in) tall, spreading to more than 60 cm (2 ft) across with fleshy glaucous pale-green leaves, and in autumn bearing large flat heads of pale-pink flowers measuring 15 cm (6 in) across. The variety Autumn Joy bears flowers of deep rose-pink whilst Meteor is even redder. All the flowers have the honey-like smell of the buddleia and they are also visited by late summer butterflies.

SELENIA (Cruciferae—Wallflower Family)

A genus of only two species of rare an-nuals half hardy in the British Isles and northern Europe, both of which are native of the United States.

Species. *Selenia aurea.* It grows 22.5 cm (9 in) tall and is raised from seed sown in gentle heat in March. Plant out 15 to 20 cm (6 to 8 in) apart towards the end of May. It has oblong leaves about 5 cm (2 in) long and comes into bloom early in July, its sweetly-scented yellow flowers appearing in terminal racemes and lasting for several weeks. The flowers are enhanced by the green sepals.

SELENICEREUS (Cactaceae—Cactus Family)

A genus of about 25 species, present in northern Mexico, the West Indies, Cuba and Haiti, flowering at night and taking their name from the Greek *selene,* the moon. They are plants of trailing or climbing habit with aerial roots, and areoles with needle-like spines. The flowers are large with a long tube and are amongst the most powerfully scented of all. They appear early in June in their native habitat, after their winter rest.

When growing indoors the plants require a compost made up of sterilized loam, leaf-mould and grit in equal parts, into which is incorporated some lime rubble. Provide a winter temperature of not less than 10°C (50°F) and keep the roots dry until the plant begins to grow again in spring. Overhead syringeing in summer is beneficial.

Propagate by cuttings taken in summer and rooted in a sandy compost.

Species. *Selenicereus boeckmannii.* Native of Cuba, it has long pale-green stems and areoles covered with grey wool. The flowers are large with narrow sepals and pure-white lanceolate petals. They are borne with freedom and are sweetly scented.

S. coniflorus. It is found only in eastern Mexico where it makes a trailing plant 6 m (20 ft) in length with glaucous green stems. The flower buds are covered with white hairs which are also present on the ovary and tube. The broad white petals are arranged in 4 rows and, when open, give the flower a lily-like appearance, though the outer petals begin to recurve as soon as the bloom is fully open. Its perfume is unique in that when the flower is inhaled near to it appears scentless, but the further one is from the plant the more powerful does the perfume become. Not until one is several yards away is the perfume lost.

S. grandiflorus (syn. *Nyctocereus grandiflorus*). Known as Queen of the Night, it is one of the wonders of nature. It has dull-green 5- to 8-ribbed stems, and at the tips a tuft of brown hairs. The flowers, which open only at night and last but for a single night, are amongst the most beautiful of nature, measuring 30 cm (12 in) across, and are purest white, surrounded by rayed petals of brightest gold. They have a rich vanilla-like perfume which is given off at intervals of about half an hour, released in 'puffs' of delicious odour. The flowers begin to open about 6 p.m. and, shortly after, the first odour is released after a spasmodic movement of the calyx. Again, after a 30-

minute interval, the plant goes through another spasm as the flower expands, accompanied by another release of scent. These 'puffs' of scent are given off at regular intervals until midnight, after which the strength of the scent becomes less pronounced and the intervals of release become less frequent until, by dawn, the flower has withered and died, its fertilization completed by night-flying Lepidoptera.

The variety *mexicanus,* native of Mexico, has long slender 5-ribbed stems covered with clusters of white spines and bears large cup-shaped flowers with the vanilla scent of the type.

S. hallensis. Native of Colombia, it forms long trailing stems of palest green and bears its large broad, cup-shaped flowers in June. The tube and outer sepals are red; the petals, arranged in 3 rows, being purest white. Throughout the night its flowers emit the powerful vanilla scent.

S. hamatus. Native of southern Mexico, its stems eventually reach out to 9 m (30 ft) or more and will grow 1.8 m (6 ft) in a season. They are glossy green. Whilst the flowers appear only in ones and twos together, they are borne from June until October. The broad pure-white petals, formed in 3 rows, make up a large globular flower with many white stamens. The scent is powerful and penetrating and is carnation-like.

S. kunthianus. It is present in Honduras and is a plant of more compact habit with 7- to 10- ribbed stems. The ovary and tube are covered in pink hairs whilst the pure-white flowers emit the powerful vanilla perfume of the genus.

S. nelsonii. It grows in southern Mexico and has long purple stems and areoles with needle-like pale-yellow spines. The flowers appear at the top of the stems and have a long tube and long elegant petals of purest white. They are powerfully scented.

S. parasisiacus. Found on the island of Haiti, it has long dull-green stems and yellow spines. The wide cup-shaped flowers are yellowish-white with greenish stamens and they open at night, emitting the powerful vanilla perfume.

S. vaupelii. Native of Haiti, it forms a much-branched plant with slender grey-green stems and areoles with grey wool which also covers the flower buds. The pure-white flowers have slightly incurving petals, almost erect, and white stamens. It is most free-flowering, the blooms releasing the vanilla scent but with greater subtlety.

SELINUM (Umbelliferae—Parsley Family)

A genus of a single species.

Species. *Selinum carifolium.* It is known as the Cambridgeshire Parsley for it is to be found only in that county and the smell of its foliage resembles that of the parsley, hence its botanical name, from the Greek *selinan*, parsley. As it closely resembles *Peucedanum* it is also known as the False Milk Parsley.

It is an attractive perennial plant growing 0.9 to 1.2 m (3 to 4 ft) tall with an angular furrowed stem and dark-green leaves, grey on the underside and divided into finely serrated leaflets. The flowers are borne in August, in large flat-topped umbels, bracts being absent.

SERJANIA (Sapindaceae—Horse-Chestnut Family)

A genus of evergreen trees or shrubs of tropical South America. *S. angustifolia* is suitable for growing indoors in pots, in a minimum winter temperature of 13°C (55°F). They are mostly plants of loose, elegant habit and the wiry stems may be trained on canes in an outwards direction or they may be suspended from the roof of a warm greenhouse and the stems allowed to trail over the side of the pot.

Species. *Serjania angustifolia* (syn. *Paullinia angustifolia*). Native of Mauritius and the East Indies, it is a thornless evergreen with shining dark-green leaves and bearing pure-white citrus-scented flowers in short racemes.

SETIECHINOPSIS (Cactaceae—Cactus Family)

A genus of four species, native of the Argentine and Brazil and known as *Flor de la oración.* They are plants of columnar habit but rarely exceed 10 to 12.5 cm (4 to 5 in) tall and they open their white flowers at night.

Species. *Setiechinopsis mirabilis.* Native of the Argentine, it bears columnar shoots of 2.5-cm (1-in) diameter with 11 ribs covered in black spines. The flowers which are borne at the tops of the shoots, measure 7.5 cm (3 in) across and have a jonquil-like scent.

SHOREA (Dipterocarpaceae—Dipterocarpus Family)

A genus of about 180 species of tall trees, grown for their timber and native of Ceylon, Burma and South-east Asia.

Species. *Shorea oblongifolia.* From incisions made in its bark, an aromatic resin (dammar) used in varnishes is obtained. Its white flowers, borne in panicles, are powerfully scented.

SHORTIA (Diapensiaceae—Diapensia Family)

A genus of two species of smooth perennial herbs with long-stalked, heart-shaped leaves, toothed or serrated, and nodding, bell-shaped flowers borne singly.

Species. *Shortia galacifolia.* A low, tufted plant, native of the mountainous regions of North Carolina. The leaves arise from the root and are almost round with crenate edges. During winter they take on crimson colourings. The funnel-shaped flowers measure 2.5 cm (1 in) across, and appear in March. They are white, shaded with pink, and like a number of alpine flowers, emit a soft, almond-like scent.

They are most attractive little plants, preferring some shade, and a cool soil containing plenty of peat or leaf-mould, which does not become waterlogged. They can be increased by division, but the divided plants must be replanted very carefully, as they resent disturbance. Seed can also be used, but is difficult to obtain.

SILAUS (Umbelliferae—Parsley Family)

A genus of a single species.

Species. *Silaus flavescens.* It is known as the Sulphurwort for the whole plant when bruised emits a most unpleasant smell of sulphuretted hydrogen which is difficult to remove from the hands and, if eaten by cattle, will impart its smell to milk and butter. It is a plant of the British Isles.

inhabiting low-lying meadows and is found chiefly in Norfolk. Growing 60 cm (2 ft) tall, it has 3-pinnate leaves and bears umbels of dull-yellow flowers followed by dark-brown fruits.

SILENE (Caryophyllaceae—Pink Family)

A genus of more than 500 species of annual or perennial plants, with erect stems and bearing its flowers in a one-sided spike forming a terminal cluster. Only those that open their blooms in the evening are fragrant, and are pollinated by night moths.

Species. *Silene noctiflora* (syn. *Lychnis dioica*). The Night-scented catchfly is a hardy annual, growing best in a dry, sandy soil. The lance-shaped leaves are 10 cm (4 in) long, and it bears its flowers on stems 37 cm (15 in) long. The blooms, which open at night or as soon as the temperature falls below 8°C (47°F), are of palest yellow on the outside, shaded rose-pink within, and are deliciously fragrant in the evening.

S. nutans. The Nottingham catchfly is a sticky, hairy perennial, and was so named for at one time it was common about the rocky formation on which stands Nottingham Castle. It also grows about the cliffs and rocks of Kent and Sussex, and in the Channel Islands. It blooms during May and June, and from a tuft of lance-shaped leaves, a flower stem 60 cm (2 ft) in length arises, at the end of which are drooping flowers of white or blush-pink which open at night and emit a powerful fragrance. The blooms remain fragrant for three nights; on each of the first two, 5 stamens ripen, and the styles protrude on the third night.

S. venosa. The Bladder campion is a native of the British Isles, and is so called because of the inflated, bladder-like calyx. It is a perennial, growing 60 cm (2 ft) high, and bears its drooping white flowers from June until August, emitting a pleasing, sweet fragrance in the evening.

SILPHIUM (Compositae—Daisy Family)

A genus of 15 species of North American perennials where they are known as the Resin plants for they exude an aromatic resin from the crushed leaves and stems. They grow between 1.2 to 3 m (4 to 10 ft) tall with alternate or opposite leaves which are toothed or lobed and they bear yellow flowers in corymbose panicles.

Species. *Silphium perfoliatum.* A square-stemmed plant which grows 3 m (10 ft) tall and has entire ovate leaves 30 cm (12 in) long, united at the base to form a cup, hence its name of Cup plant. Its large golden daisies are borne in July.

SISON (Umbelliferae—Parsley Family)

A genus of two species, native of Europe.

Species. *Sison amomum.* The Stone parsley, differing from *Carum segetum* (Corn parsley) in having less divided leaves. It is a slender-branched biennial growing 90 cm (3 ft) high with pinnate (or bipinnate) leaves and narrow leaflets. The cream-coloured flowers are borne in few-rayed umbels and are extremely small. It flowers in August and September, the whole plant giving off the rather unusual smell of petrol.

SISYRINCHIUM (Iridaceae—Iris Family)

A genus of about 100 species of perennial plants native of North and South America, with a short woody rootstock like that of the Flag iris from which grow masses of fibrous roots. The species have rush-like leaves some 22.5 cm (9 in) long from which arise the pretty bell-shaped flowers. Nearly all are of pale-blue colouring, hence their name of Blue-eyed Grass and, as would be expected, they have no perfume, whilst those bearing white flowers, are exceptionally fragrant. There is no better example than this of blue flowers having no scent whilst those without colour have been endowed with pronounced fragrance.

The plants grow well in the alpine garden, being especially suited to the alpine lawn. They are also splendid subjects to plant with the snowflakes and snowdrops in the wild garden and they are propagated in the same way, by division of the roots in spring or after flowering in July.

Species. *Sisyrinchium filifolium.* It is a most lovely plant, introduced into Britain by the late Clarence Elliott in 1910 from the Falkland Islands, From erect, rush-like leaves arises the flower stem, at the end of which dangle 2 or 3 bell-shaped flowers, like snowdrops, which are held to the stem by a fine thread. The blooms open from a spathe and are of glistening white with purple lines, and they diffuse a most exotic heavy perfume. They are at their best during May and June and are known in the Falkland Islands as Pale Maidens.

S. odoratissimum. Clarence Elliott has told of how he discovered this plant in 1928 on Elizabeth Island in the Straits of Magellan, also in Tierra del Fuego. It is a plant for the wild garden rather than the rockery for its leaves reach up to a height of 45 cm (18 in) with the flower stems a similar height. From the terminal spathes come several small trumpet-shaped flowers rather less than 5 cm (2 in) long and there are two forms or varieties. One bears flowers of clear primrose-yellow whilst the other is creamy white veined with purple. Both emit a powerful rich penetrating scent and remain in bloom for several weeks of early summer.

The plants prefer a rich moist soil containing some peat or leaf-mould. Though native of the warmer parts, they are completely hardy in Britain.

SKIMMIA (Rutaceae—Rue Family)

A genus of six or seven species of evergreen shrubs with spotted, leathery leaves and flourishing in partial shade and in a moist lime-free soil, enriched with leaf-mould or peat. The skimmias are excellent plants for a town garden, being unharmed by deposits of soot, and tolerant of a sulphur-laden atmosphere. They are readily increased by layering and by cuttings which should be removed with a heel and inserted in a sandy compost to root.

As the skimmias bear male and female flowers on separate plants, it is necessary to plant several of both if berries are required, and they are one of the chief attractions of the plant.

Species. *Skimmia fortunei.* Also *S. reevesiana*, it is a charming Chinese species growing 0.9 to 1.2 m (3 to 4 ft) tall with glossy laurel-like leaves 10 cm (4 in) long which are of deepest green. The small greenish-white flowers have a powerful scent and distinguish this plant from *S. japonica* in that they have both stamens and pistil. It is an evergreen, flowering in April and May. The blooms are replaced by crimson berries.

S. japonica. A Japanese shrub of great beauty, forming a densely domed shrub 1.2 m (4 ft) in height with bright mid-green leaves 10 to 12.5 cm (4 to 5 in) long which are pleasantly aromatic. The blooms appear in clusters in April and are white with a sweet perfume, the scent being especially pronounced, like lily of the valley, in the variety *fragrans*. The female flowers are replaced by attractive fruits of coral-pink.

S. laureola. Native of the Himalayas, it grows 1.2 m (4 ft) in height with long leaves of deep green, narrowing at each end and yellow on the underside. The small yellow flowers are oppressively scented, giving a somewhat unpleasant smell near to though agreeable at a distance, whilst the foliage is strongly aromatic when crushed. The plant is not as hardy as the other species and should be confined to gardens in the south and west where it will appreciate warmth and shade.

S. rogersi. Possibly a hybrid of *S. fortunei* and *S. japonica*, it grows 1.2 m (4 ft) in height with greenish-purple wood and lance-shaped leaves, recurving at the edges. The greenish-white flowers, borne in April, have a sweet perfume.

SMILACINA (Liliaceae—Lily Family)

A small genus of herbaceous perennials with thick, knotted rootstocks and bearing tiny flowers on short pedicles, like those of the Solomon's seal, hence its country name of the False Solomon's seal. The plants enjoy similar conditions, partial shade and a cool, leafy soil.

Species. *Smilacina racemosa.* A North American plant growing to a height of 90 cm (3 ft) and useful in the border in that it blooms before the end of May when few other plants will be in bloom. The handsome lance-shaped leaves are pale green and downy on the underside, enhanced by the dense panicles of creamy-white which have a gentle sweet perfume.

S. stellata. Native of north-western America, it grows 60 cm (2 ft) in height with stem-clasping leaves and in May bears dense racemes of starry-white powerfully scented flowers from which it takes its name of the Star-flowered lily of the valley.

SMILAX (Liliaceae—Lily Family)

A genus of trailing evergreen plants to be found in temperate regions throughout the world. The stems are provided with tendrils with which the plant pulls itself upwards and so may be used in the manner of ivy, to cover old walls and tree stumps. Several bear flowers which have a most unpleasant smell but *S. aspera* bears sweetly scented flowers. Where berries are required, plant both male and female varieties.

Species. *Smilax aspera.* Known as the Prickly ivy, it is an evergreen species, native of the Mediterranean shores of southern Europe. Its densely prickled stems reach up to a height of 3 m (10 ft) with lance-shaped leaves which in the variety *maculata* are attractively spotted with white. The fleshy-white flowers appear in July and have the heavy, sweet perfume of the family, and these are followed by scarlet berries. As near as possible, the same conditions should be provided as they enjoy in their native lands, a sunny situation and a well-drained sandy soil.

S. herbacea. It is a North American species of semi-climbing habit, and from the obnoxious smell of its flowers, like the smell of decaying flesh, it is known as the Carrion flower. Unlike many of the species of the genus, the plant has no prickles and bears attractive heart-shaped leaves, joined to the main stem by a long footstalk.

SMYRNIUM (Umbelliferae—Parsley Family)

A small genus of erect smooth plants, native of the British Isles and also of southern Europe and the Near East, *S. olusatrum* taking its country name of Alexanders from Alexandria, where it abounds, whilst its botanical name is from the Greek *smurna,* myrrh. It is the seeds which have a myrrh-like scent, being almost black in colour and highly aromatic.

Species. *Smyrnium olusatrum* It is a biennial plant growing 0.9 to 1.2 m (3 to 4 ft) high with leaves of brilliant green and bearing its yellowish-green flowers during May and June. It is a sea-loving plant, like celery, and at one time the young shoots were used in the kitchen, boiled and served with white sauce. During Culpeper's time, the seed was sold in apothecaries' shops as a substitute for parsley seed, then a scarce commodity. 'It is grown in every garden in Europe' wrote Culpeper, yet today it is almost unknown to gardeners and is equally rare about the countryside.

The seeds are usually ready to harvest during August.

SNAPDRAGON: *see* ANTIRRHINUM

SNAPHALIUM (Compositae—Daisy Family)

A small genus of annual or perennial plants, native of South Africa and which take their name from *gnaphalion,* the Greek for a downy plant. The leaves are woolly on the underside and on the upper surface are covered in sticky glands which release an aromatic fragrance when pressed. The flowers have no scent.

Species. *Snaphalium undulatum.* It is an erect woody perennial with linear leaves as described. The flowers are dried for indoor decoration and are everlasting but are without perfume.

SOLANDRA (Solanaceae—Nightshade Family)

A small genus of climbing plants of Mexico and tropical South America which produce bell-like flowers of outstanding beauty. They require a minimum winter temperature of 13°C (55°F) and in northern Europe should be confined to a warm greenhouse in an open situation for the plants require abundant sunshine. Propagation is by seed or from cuttings of the ripened wood.

Species. *Solandra grandiflora.* It is a strong-growing deciduous plant which will quickly cover the roof of a greenhouse if trained over the wires. It will be more free-flowering if the roots are restricted and so should be confined to a large pot. After flowering in summer, water should be given sparingly until growth recommences in March.

It has bright-green fleshy leaves and bears sweetly scented chalice-like flowers of creamy-white, marked with chocolate-brown inside the tube which may be 15 cm (6 in) long and 1.5 cm (3 in) across, giving the appearance of a giant convolvulus. It is also known as the Sweet-scented Chalice vine. Its scent is powerful and sweet, like that of honeysuckle.

S. nitida. Native of Mexico, it reached the Fiji Islands and other Pacific islands early in history. A climbing plant, requiring similar culture to *S. grandiflora,* it is known as Cup of Gold for its large golden yellow flowers are cup-shaped and emit a deliciously lily-like perfume.

SOAPWORT: *see* **SAPONARIA**

SOLIDAGO (Compositae—Daisy Family)
A genus of about 80 species of tall-growing perennials, known as the Golden-rods, most of which are natives of North America. Though delightful border plants of great hardiness and able to tolerate almost any soil condition, the sprays of mimosa-like flowers possess no perfume though one or two species have scented leaves from which oil is extracted.

Species. *Solidago odora.* The most important species, known as the Sweet Scented Golden-rod, it is a hardy perennial growing 1.2 m (4 ft) tall. From the leaves a powerfully scented essential oil is obtained whose smell is compared to a mixture of aniseed and sassafras. It is used in perfumery, especially for scenting soaps.

SORBARIA (Rosaceae—Rose Family)
A small genus which is now separated from *Spiraea,* distinguished by the pinnate leaves. The plants flourish under ordinary soil and climatic conditions, losing their leaves during winter. They are of shrubby habit, the wood of several of the species being an attractive reddish-brown colour whilst they add character to the shrub border during late summer with their handsome foliage and dense white plumes.

Species. *Sorbaria sorbifolia stellipila* (syn. *Spiraea sorbifolia*). It is a pretty Asiatic shrub growing 1.2 to 1.5 m (4 to 5 ft) in height, its erect suckering stems forming a dense thicket. The leaves are downy on the underside to give the plant a grey-green appearance, whilst in July and August it bears its creamy-white flowers in large-clustered panicles which are generous with their sweet perfume whatever the weather. The flowers hold their fragrance for a considerable time.

SORBUS (Rowan) (Rosaceae—Rose Family)
The bloom of the rowans greatly resembles the hawthorn and cotoneaster and has a similar sweet but fishy fragrance, though it is less unpleasant. The rowans (or Mountain ash) are valuable garden trees with their fernlike, pinnate foliage which takes on glorious shades of crimson and scarlet in autumn when the white flowers have turned to clusters of scarlet berries. Rather remarkably, though they are found growing high up on rocky ground, the rowans dislike limestone and in such a soil cotoneasters should be planted instead.

Like all members of the family, the trees attain a height of 6 m (20 ft) or more and bear their creamy-white flowers in dense cymes during May and June, followed by scarlet (or yellow) fruits in autumn. Pollination is by flies and midges.

Species and Varieties. *Sorbus asplenifolia.* Known as the Fernleaf rowan for its leaves are beautifully cut like those of the ferns. The berries are amongst the brightest in the garden being of orange-scarlet and borne in great profusion. It grows 4.5 m (15 ft) tall and flowers in June.

S. essertaneana flava. A valuable landscape tree of spreading habit. The foliage turns deep crimson in autumn whilst the berries are of brilliant yellow.

SOWERBAEA (Liliaceae—Lily Family)
A small genus of tufted herbs with rush-like leaves and native to Australia. They are named after the naturalist J. Sowerby and bear pink or purple flowers in a terminal umbel.

Species. *Sowerbaea juncea.* Of rush-like habit, it is found in the swamplands of Queensland and Victoria where it blooms in spring. It bears its flowers of lilac-mauve in small umbels on 37.5 cm (15 in) stems and they emit a soft vanilla fragrance, hence its name of Vanilla plant. After fertilization, the flowers hang downwards.

SPARTIUM (Leguminosae—Laburnum Family)

A genus of possibly two species, though *S. monospermum* is sometimes included with *Genista*. Free of spines and hardy in the British Isles and North America. Unlike most brooms, they form new growth at the base and will improve by regular clipping. This should be done after flowering to encourage new wood to appear at the base.

Species. *Spartium junceum.* It is the Spanish broom, not to be confused with the Spanish gorse, *Genista hibernica*. It is a plant of slender upright habit with twiggy-rush-like branches and is usually without leaves or spines. The bright-yellow flowers are borne ·in erect clusters from June until September and, like all the brooms, resemble those of the laburnum in shape, a plant of the same family but with a more pronounced fragrance, likened to that of oranges. It grows well in any sunny situation and in a dry, sandy soil and flourishes in town and seaside gardens equally well. The flowers are followed by long, smooth seed-pods.

S. monospermum (syn. *Genista monospermum*). A white-flowered broom to be found growing in Gilead and on Mount Carmel and in the deserts of Sinai and Arabia, where it is one of the few plants to afford shade. The white pea-shaped flowers, borne along the branches, are sweetly scented.

SPATHIPHYLLUM (Araceae—Arum Family)

A genus of 50 species of tropical plants, native of India, Malaya, Madagascar and the Solomon Islands. They are shrubby climbing plants with the habit of the ivy, forming roots along the entire length of stem and they attach themselves to anything they can find to cling to. They are valuable for covering the wall of a garden room, and require quite high temperatures, a compost mixture of peat and sphagnum-moss with plenty of water, and shade.

Species. *Spathiphyllum cannifolium* (syn. *Pothos odoratissima*). Whilst several species are grown for their colourful leaves, borne in spiral fashion and alternating from right to left, *P. odoratissima* also bears creamy-white flowers which are pleasantly vanilla-scented.

SPHAERANTHUS (Compositae—Daisy Family)

A genus of about 40 species of annual or perennial plants, native of Persia and Iraq, northern India and Malaysia.

Species. *Sphaeranthus mollis.* A common Indian annual growing 60 cm (2 ft) tall and bearing yellow daisy-like flowers. The whole plant emits a smell of honey (or musk) which may be detected from a distance.

S. ulmaria. It is known as Queen of the Meadows. The Dutch have named it Reinette, or Little Queen, holding the plant in the highest esteem. Its country name is Bridewort whilst Ben Jonson called it 'Meadows-queen' and 'Meadowsweet'.

It is a plant of perennial habit, growing 0.9 to 1.2 m (3 to 4 ft) in height and to be found by the waterside or in low-lying meadowland or in ditches.

It has wiry furrowed stems, purple in colour with leaves that are acutely lobed and downy on the underside. There is also a variegated leaf form. From the resemblance of the leaves to those of the elm (*ulmus*), the plant was known as the Ulmaria, a name which it still carries. It is usually to be found growing in dense masses and is in bloom from the end of June until September. The tiny white flowers are borne in dense inflorescences and as they yield no nectar, they are endowed with a powerful scent like that of the hawthorn, with fishy undertones, to call the pollinating insects.

The leaves are also scented but more pleasantly so, being aromatic when bruised or trodden upon, for which reason they were used, together with scented rushes to strew the floor of church and manor. Gerard tells us that the leaves 'far excel all other strewing herbs, to deck up houses, to strew in chambers, halls and banqueting houses in summertime: for the smell thereof makes the heart merry and delighteth the senses: neither doth it cause headache or lothsomeness to meat, as some other sweet smelling herbs do'. Parkinson described it as having a 'pretty, sharp scent' and added that 'a leaf or two layd in a cup of wine, will give as quick and fine a relish thereto as Burnet will'.

Like fennel, the distilled water of the leaves was used to strengthen the eyes and to prevent them itching. Both the leaves and flowers make a welcome addition to a pot-pourri, retaining strength for many months, the fragrance of the flowers becoming more and more pleasant with age. The leaves also impart a delicious flavour to soups. It is a delightful plant to grow by the side of a stream or pond, and is propagated by division or the plants are readily raised from seed.

SPIRANTHES (Orchidaceae—Orchid Family)

A genus of hardy orchids growing from a fleshy rootstock and bearing their flowers in daintily twisted spikes. The lip of the flower is not spurred but united to the base of the coloumn. It takes its name from two Greek words, *speira*, a spiral (spire), and *anthos*, flower.

Species. *Spiranthes autumnalis* (syn. *S. spiralis*). It is known as the Autumn Lady's Tresses orchid and is to be found in hilly pastures, usually with a lime subsoil, in the South of England and along the borders of the Mediterranean. It forms a root of 2 or 3 ovoid tubers from which arises a stem 22.5 cm (9 in) high from a tuft of 4 leaves. The flowers appear in August and are white, borne in a twisting spire, and in the evening diffuse a penetrating almond-like perfume like heliotrope.

S. aestivalis. The Summer Lady's Tresses which produces tubers 5 to 7.5 cm (2 to 3 in) long, forming two new tubers every year. The flower stems which grow 15 cm (6 in) tall are of palest green whilst the small white flowers appear in a slender spike of 5 to 20, arranged in a twisted spiral. They appear in July and are heavily scented, especially at night.

S. romanzoffiana. It has thin tuberous roots and from the lateral bud at the base of the previous year's stem, the new stem arises to a height of 30 cm (12 in), the creamy-white flowers, borne in 3 spiral rows, emitting a powerful vanilla-like perfume by day and by night.

SPRUCE: *see* PICEA

STACHYS (Labiatae—Lavender Family)

A genus of 200 or more species of perennial or biennial herbs of which *Stachys palustris*, the Marsh woundwort, *S. sylvestris*, the Hedge woundwort, and *S. arvensis*, the Corn woundwort, are native to the British Isles and emit an offensive smell, described by Mr C. A. Hall in his pocket-book, *British Wild Flowers* as 'an odour of neglected festering sores'. The Downy woundwort, the biennial *S. germanica*, was, with its thick lint-like leaves, used to cover wounds or sores when medicated lint was not available for the leaves are both soft and strongly antiseptic. The foliage of the woundworts has the musky smell of stale lint rather than the stench of festering sores but it is an unpleasant smell.

Species. *Stachys arvensis.* The Corn woundwort which is rare in England and is almost extinct in Scotland and in Ireland. It is a plant of the cornfields, of almost prostrate habit, and it bears tiny flowers of purple-red during July and August. The plant has not nearly so unpleasant a smell as the others.

S. palustris. The Marsh woundwort which has a hollow stem and grows to a height of 90 cm (3 ft) or more with lance-shaped leaves serrated at the edges. During July it comes into bloom, its purple-red flowers forming an elegant spike, the flowers being marked with white. It is not so hairy as the Hedge woundwort, neither does it smell so offensively except when the leaves and stem are bruised, The tuberous roots make a delicious food when boiled, during which they will lose their unpleasant smell.

S. sylvatica. The Hedge woundwort which is common about the hedgerows and woodlands of the British Isles. It grows 90 cm (3 ft) in height with heart-shaped leaves which, like the stems are densely covered with small hairs which give off the unpleasant smell. Apart from this, it is a handsome plant bearing its flowers in whorls to form the spike and it blooms from July until September. The flowers, like small antirrhinums, are crimson-red, the lower lip being marked with white. The plant is readily distinguished from *S. palustris* by its solid stem and extreme hairiness, It has also the most disagreeable odour of all the woundworts.

STACHYURUS (Stachyuraceae— Stachyurus Family)

A genus of 10 species, the sole representative of its family, which attain a height of 3 m (10 ft) or more. The leaves take on rich autumnal tints before they fall.

Species. *Stachyurus chinensis.* Native of central China, it is a deciduous shrub with broad leaves and from the axils bears racemes of yellow flowers which appear in March and which have the delicate scent of jasmine.

S. praecox. It may be rightly classed as a winter-flowering plant for its pale golden-yellow flowers open in February if the weather is mild. The flowers are borne in drooping racemes and have a pleasing vanilla perfume.

STAPELIA (Asclepiadaceae—Stephanotis Family)

A genus of 75 species of tropical and South African plants, named after the Dutch physician von Stapel and noted for the horrible appearance and disgusting smell of their flowers. They tend to be of creeping habit, the leaves being replaced by lobes or scales on the fleshy 4-angled stems, pieces of which root readily in a sandy compost if allowed to dry at the end before inserting. At the extremity of the stems, the flowers are borne, at ground-level if the plant is not pot-grown and the stems allowed to trail over the side. The flower buds open with an audible 'pop' to star-shaped blooms with 5-pointed corolla lobes edged with hairs and rayed from a fleshy central boss. The flowers rely on flies for their pollination and to attract them have a most unpleasant carrion-like odour.

Species. *Stapelia flavirostris.* It is of more upright habit than the other species with narrower corolla lobes which are densely covered with hairs. This hairiness, combined with the stench of decaying flesh,

provides in appearance and smell a substitute for bad meat and attracts the flies which lay their eggs at the centre of the flower. As most of the eggs do not hatch out, it is nature's way of restraining the blow-fly population of the warm Cape Peninsula.

S. gigantea. Native of Rhodesia and the Transvaal, it bears a flower 30 to 35 cm (12 to 14 in) across and is yellow, marked with red lines whilst at the margins are long white hairs. It has a most unpleasant smell.

S. nobilis. The largest of the stapelias, with flowers which often measure 20 cm (8 in) or more across and with a smell in proportion to the size, being almost unbearable when ready for pollination. The whole surface is a dirty purple-red colour and covered in tiny purple hairs which gives the appearance of well-decayed flesh. Like all the stapelias, they begin to bloom early in May indoors and continue until August.

S. variegata. The bloom, which measures 7.5 cm (3 in) across, is covered with spots and markings of yellow and brown which resemble putrified meat whilst the smell is, if anything, more appalling than that of *S. flavirostris.* In their native haunts in Cape Province, there is a tendency for the blooms to change their colour to coincide with that of their surroundings, the yellow changing to dirty pale brown with markings that are almost black. The stench remains the same until the flies have completed their task and the blooms begin to die. Not without good reason is it known as the Carrion flower. The angled grey stems are armed with teeth on the edges.

STAUNTONIA (Lardizabalaceae— Lardizabala Family)

A genus of 15 species of evergreen climbing plants of great vigour, often reaching a height of 6 m (20 ft) or more. They are native of the tropical forests of Burma and Formosa and several have scented flowers.

Species. *Stauntonia hexaphylla.* The large palmate leaves are divided into 5 or 7 leaflets and are of deepest green. The flowers appear in May and are white, tinted with purple, and have a pleasant sweet perfume.

STEPHANOTIS (Asclepiadaceae— Stephanotis Family)

A genus of five twining plants, native of Madagascar.

Species. *Stephanotis floribunda.* A beautiful evergreen which requires a minimum winter temperature of 15°C (60°F). Until the high cost of fuel made its culture almost prohibitive in the British Isles, no plant was more widely grown under glass to supply the florists of Covent Garden Market with bunches of long white salver-shaped flowers of exotic perfume. An established plant when trained over wires to cover the roof of a large glasshouse presents a never-to-be-forgotten sight when in bloom, with its glistening flowers of waxy whiteness against the leathery dark-green leaves and diffusing a scent in which it is possible to remain for only a limited time without being overcome.

During summer, it requires a drier atmosphere than most stove plants but needs copious amounts of moisture at its roots. The plants resent root disturbance and should be given a 30-cm (12-in) pot containing fibrous loam to which a small quantity of peat and coarse sand is added. The shoots must be carefully tied in so as to prevent them from becoming entangled. The plants will begin to bloom in June and continue for several months. Afterwards, the flowering shoots must be shortened back and the roots top-dressed with fresh loam when they will remain vigorous and healthy for many years. In its native land it is known as the Madagascar jasmine and few flowers can equal its wax-like purity and its perfume.

STERNBERGIA (Amaryllidaceae— Narcissus Family)

A small genus of bulbous plants which require a dry, sunny situation and which are amongst the most beautiful of the garden. Of additional value is the fact that they bloom in autumn. Native of the Balkan countries and of the Middle East, they are believed to be the 'lilies of the fields' of biblical times. The loveliest form is *S. lutea* which is completely hardy in Britain but alas, it has no perfume. The one which bears scented flowers is *S.*

colchiciflora, the smallest of them all, and which has the reputation of being more difficult to manage than the other species.

Species. *Sternbergia colchiciflora.* The tiny pale-yellow tubes, like tiny crocuses and almost stemless, appear from the naked soil in September and the leaves do not appear until spring. The flowers have a delicious sweet perfume.

STEWARTIA (Theaceae—Tea Family)

A genus of eight or nine species of deciduous shrubs, native of North America and Japan, which flourish in a peaty lime-free soil and in a position of partial shade where nearby trees give protection to the young shoots in springtime. Under favourable conditions, the plants will take on tree-like proportions and bear their axillary flowers early in summer.

Species. *Stewartia malacodendron.* A slow-growing shrub attaining a height of 3 m (10 ft) in about 20 years. Native of Florida, with ovate leaves, its flowers are amongst the most beautiful of all, being creamy-white in colour with serrated edges and deep-purple stamens, whilst they emit a heavy seductive perfume. It is rather rare.

S. serrata. A Japanese species which should be planted if only for the magnificent colourings of its foliage in autumn. Growing to about 9 m (30 ft) tall, it comes into bloom in June, its fragrant, creamy-white flowers shaded crimson at the base of the petals, which have attractively serrated edges.

S. sinensis. It is one of the most beautiful of all garden plants, every part of it making its contribution. The bark is shining brown, whilst in autumn the leaves take on rich crimson colourings. In addition to all this loveliness, the large white flowers are more sweetly scented than those of other species. It grows to about the same height as *S. serrata.*

STRANVAESIA (Rosaceae—Rose Family)

A genus of 10 species, native of the Himalayas, China and Formosa.

Species. *Stranvaesia glaucescens.* An evergreen of the temperate valleys of the Himalayas where it attains a height of 6 m (20 ft). It has leathery lance-shaped leaves and in June bears small white flowers which have a sweet fishy hawthorn smell, and these are followed by small orange fruits. It is hardy in all parts of the British Isles and grows well in ordinary soil.

S. salicifolia. Native of western China, it has dark grey-green leaves like those of the Willow. In May and June it bears hawthorn-like flowers with similar perfume, and these are followed by scarlet berries. It grows 3.6 m (12 ft) tall.

STROPHANTHUS (Apocynaceae—Periwinkle Family)

A genus of about 60 mostly climbing plants, native of West Africa and Madagascar. They have poisonous qualities and furnish the drug strophanthin. The flowers with their long twisted petals open blush-white, changing to clear pink, then to cream. Borne in large terminal clusters, they have the appearance of apple-blossom and a pronounced scent.

STRUTHIOLA (Thymeleaceae—Mezereon Family)

A small genus of shrubs, native of South Africa and to be found on the lower slopes of Table Mountain and in the eastern parts of Cape Province where they bloom from November to March. The flowers are borne in the axils of the upper leaves to produce a spike-like inflorescence and give them a local name of Catstails. Like the Daphnes, the flowers have a delicious scent.

Species. Struthiola dodecandra. A dwarf shrub with glabrous stems with linear leaves borne opposite in 4 rows. The flowers are white or pale pink.

S. striata. It is the most common species, making a small multibranched shrub with the stems clothed in hairs. The leaves are borne opposite, in 4 rows and are heather-like, the lower surface having prominent veins. The flowers are white or palest pink with fleshy petals and are heavily scented.

STYLOMECON (Papaveraceae—Poppy Family)

A genus of 41 species of mostly perennial or biennial plants, all of which bear scentless flowers. The sole exception is M.

heterophylla, an annual. They differ from Papaver in that the 4- to 6-rayed stigma is borne on a distinct style. The flowers appear in cymes and have 2 sepals and 4 petals.

Species. Stylomecon heterophylla. A native of southern California, it is the only annual species and the only one bearing fragrant flowers. It is a rare plant which sets few seeds and relies on its perfume to attract pollinating insects, for self-pollination, as occurs with many other members of the family, cannot take place. The plant grows 30 cm (12 in) tall and should be sown where it is to bloom. The flowers are amongst the most brilliant of all, being coppery-orange with a jet-black centre and are nearly 5 cm (2 in) across. When in water, they rival the Iceland poppies for the length of time they remain fresh and they have the sweet refreshing scent of the lily of the valley.

STYRAX (Styracaceae—Storax Family)

A genus of about 130 deciduous trees and shrubs, mostly native of the United States and Japan and closely related to the Halesia, the Snowdrop tree of Japan. They flourish in a well-drained sandy soil enriched with peat or leaf-mould and enjoy partial shade. They are delightful when massed together in large beds. Several species yield a fragrant gum (storax).

Species. Styrax americanum. The American storax of Virginia which grows 1.8 to 2.4 m (6 to 8 ft) in height and has downy leaves. It comes into bloom in June, bearing clusters of nodding white flowers which have a delicate sweet perfume.

S. benzoin. A native of Sumatra, it makes a small tree which yields gum benzoin, a fragrant resinous gum which is obtained from cuts made in the bark. The flowers are white and are sweetly scented.

S. californicum. A native of California, it makes a compact bush about 1.8 m (6 ft) in height with short-stalked leaves, waved at the margins and it flowers in June, the snow-white blossoms with their hoary calyx and corolla being powerfully fragrant.

S. grandiflora. A native of North America, it grows to a height of about 1.8 m (6 ft) and has pointed leaves 15 cm (6 in) long which are downy on the underside. It is one of the earliest of the species to bloom, the long racemes of fragrant white flowers appearing in April.

S. hemsleyana. This native of western China is the most suitable species to grow in gardens of the British Isles and northern Europe where it will require a sheltered situation. It is a deciduous tree growing 6 m (20 ft) tall with spreading branches, clothed with large oval pale-green leaves, downy on the underside, and tapering towards the base. They turn a brilliant golden-yellow in autumn. The pure-white flowers are borne in panicles of 18 to 20 during June and July and are powerfully scented.

S. japonica. A Japanese species much loved by the people for the exquisite scent of its blossom which is in great demand to beautify the hair and bedeck the home. It makes a small tree rather than a shrub and has leaves of shining green. The dangling white bells with their pink-tinted buds appear in June at the end of the numerous small branches.

S. obassia. It makes a tall handsome shrub with reddish branches and is a native of Japan. The toothed leaves are large and oval and in May it comes into bloom, bearing white bell-shaped flowers in long racemes and they have a more powerful scent than all other species. The flowers are enhanced by their golden stamens.

S. officinalis. Native of the Levant where it makes a small tree 2.4 to 3 m (8 to 10 ft) high with oval leaves about 5 cm (2 in) long, hoary on the underside. It bears its fragrant white flowers in July in short racemes. From its bark, the fragrant gum storax is obtained.

S. pulverulentum. A native of the southern United States, it makes a low bush some 60 to 90 cm (2 to 3 ft) in height with small oval leaves scaly on the underside. Like *S. grandiflora,* it blooms in spring, 2 or 3 of the sweetly scented white flowers appearing together in the leaf axils.

SWEET PEA: *see* **LATHYRUS**

SYMPLOCARPUS (Araceae—Arum Family)

A genus of a single species.

Species. *Symplocarpus foetidus.* A native of North America where, on account of the unpleasant smell it emits and also its leaves, it is known as the Skunk cabbage. Yet it is a handsome plant bearing bronze-purple spathes marbled with green. Its smell is said to be a combination of skunk, carrion and garlic, and attracts flies and midges for miles around in such great numbers that spiders weave their webs from plant to plant and enjoy a continuous feast. It should be planted in a damp corner of the garden in partial shade and will bloom during March and April.

SYMPLOCOS (Styracaceae—Storax Family)

A genus of about 350 species of downy trees or shrubs with leathery toothed leaves and bearing their flowers in loose spikes or racemes. They are mostly native of India and South-east Asia, and the United States. The plants require a sheltered garden in the more exposed parts of Europe and the British Isles and preferably the protection of a sunny wall. They enjoy a well-drained peaty soil but ordinary loam will suit them, provided a small quantity of peat is incorporated about their roots at planting time.

Species. *Symplocos crataegoides.* (syn. *S. paniculatus*). It is distributed from the Himalayas through northern China to Japan where it grows to a height of nearly 12 m (40 ft), though making only a low shrub in European gardens. It has lance-shaped leaves some 7.5 cm (3 in) long, serrated at the margin, and in May bears panicles of small white flowers like those of the hawthorn (hence its botanical name) and having a sweet perfume. If two or three are planted together for cross-pollination, the flowers will be followed by brilliant-blue berries in autumn.

S. japonica (syn. *S. lucida*). A native of Japan, it makes a pretty shrub 1.8 m (6 ft) in height with smooth lance-shaped leaves serrated at the edges. In June appear the sweetly scented flowers of palest yellow, borne in short racemes at the axils of the leaves.

S. tinctoria. The Sweet Leaf bush of the southern United States which attains a height of 1.8 to 2.4 m (6 to 8 ft). The sweetly perfumed yellow flowers appear in

April, in clusters of a dozen or so, whilst the thick downy leaves are also sweet to smell and to taste, being much enjoyed by cattle.

SYZYGIUM (Caryophyllaceae—Pink Family)

A genus of 500 or so species, closely related to *Eugenia* and native to Indonesia and South Pacific islands. It now includes the clove. The close-grained timber is in demand for building underwater structures whilst the fruits of several species are edible. The opposite leaves are evergreen and glossy, the flowers being borne in terminal cymes on long footstalks. The fruits are pleasantly scented.

Species. *Syzygium aramaticus.* The species of evergreen tree which provides the cloves of commerce is native only of the Moluccas from where it was introduced to the Island of Mauritius by the French in 1770. From there the clove reached Zanzibar, flourishing in the yellow clay sub-soil and bringing great wealth to the island. But long before, cloves were imported from the East to be used for flavouring. The Swahili word for clove is *garafa,* from the French *giroflier* from which is derived the old word 'gillyflower', used during Elizabethan times to represent all plants whose flowers had the spicy fragrance of the clove.

Shakespeare mentions the custom of sticking cloves into dried oranges and lemons which were usually stuffed with spices, and were known as pomanders. The origin of pomander is most probably derived from the ancient custom of sticking cloves into apples used for baking, a custom still followed in many a country housewife's kitchen.

A mature clove tree attains a height of 12 m (40 ft) and comes into bearing when 5 or 6 years old, continuing for at least 50 years. Cloves are the expanded buds of the tree which at first are a pinkish-yellow colour, becoming deep red as they mature. The 'season' lasts 4 months when the trees are picked over once a month, the stalks and buds being removed together for drying which takes about a week. Red cloves are more valuable than black.

S. corynocarpum. Native of Fiji, it was first recorded in 1838-9 by a United States expedition under the command of Captain Charles Wilkes. It makes a small spreading tree with dark-green leaves and bears panicles of small white flowers which are heavily scented.

S. neurocalyx. It forms a large tree with handsome oblong leaves, leathery to the touch, and bears white, delicately scented flowers followed by deep-purple fruits which are prominently ribbed and have a pleasant aromatic scent.

T

TABERNAEMONTANA (Apocynaceae— Periwinkle Family)

A genus of about 100 species, native of the tropics of the Old World. They are evergreen shrubs and bear gardenia-like flowers whose scent is most pronounced at night.

Species. *Tabernaemontana coronaria.* A hard-wooded evergreen stove plant of India which forms a dense bush of compact habit and has handsome glossy foliage. Away from its native land, it requires a night-time winter temperature of 15°C (60°F) and a compost composed of fibrous peat. It produces its pure-white gardenia-like flowers throughout winter and they are sweetly scented, having a perfume which is in no way overpowering. After flowering has ended in March, pinch back the shoots and give a once-weekly feed with dilute manure water; the plants will then bloom again in July and August, after which they may be rested until flowering begins again in November. The double form *flore pleno* has even greater attractions and is powerfully scented, especially at night, hence its name of Moonbeam.

T. dichotoma. An Indian evergreen bearing powerfully scented pure-white flowers, it is known as Eve's Apple for it bears a fruit like a partially eaten apple.

TAGETES (Compositae—Daisy Family)

A genus of some 20 species, usually classified as French and African marigolds though all are of Mexican origin. The one known as the true Tagetes, *T. signata*, introduced into England in 1825, became popular during Victorian times for bedding, together with the geranium and calceolaria for it grows only 15 to 20 cm (6 to 8 in) tall and bears its golden daisies from June until October. It is delightful where used as an edging with pale-blue lobelia. So colourful is it that it was named after Tages, a god famed for his beauty, whilst its foliage is deliciously pungent.

Closely allied to *T. signata* is *T. patula*, a plant known since Elizabethan times as the French marigold, so called because it is said to have been introduced into England by the Huguenots fleeing from the Massacre of St Bartholomew in 1572. Originally introduced into Spain from Mexico early in the sixteenth century, from where it reached France, the plant was mentioned by Gerard and by Parkinson and may have been known to Shakespeare. It was held in high esteem and was considered with the auricula and ranunculus as a florist's flower for the perfect symmetry and markings of the blooms made it an exhibitor's favourite during Victorian times. Though Parkinson alluded to its disagreeable smell, the modern French hybrids, which make tiny compact bushes 15 to 30 cm (6 to 8 in) tall, have beautifully cut foliage with a refreshingly aromatic smell, whilst the flowers have a similar scent.

T. erecta, the African marigold which had become naturalized on the coast of North Africa by the early sixteenth century, was described by Lyte as having 'a naughtie and unpleasant savor', and until recent years the smell of both the foliage and flowers, similar to that of stale urine, prevented its use as a cut flower. It was not until *T. lucida*, the Sweet-scented marigold came to be introduced into the breeding programme that the disagreeable smell departed and there is now at least one variety, Hawaii, with scented flowers and odourless foliage. The African marigolds are half-hardy and should be raised by sowing the seed in gentle heat in February and planting out 45 cm (18in) apart in May. They grow 60 cm (2 ft) tall and make bushy plants.

Species and Varieties. *Tagetes hybrida* Hawaii. A magnificent garden plant growing about 50 cm (20 in) tall and bearing in profusion enormous globes packed with petals of deepest orange. The flowers are sweetly scented whilst the foliage is free from any trace of smell.

T. lucida. Though really a perennial of Mexican origin, it is usually treated as a half-hardy annual. It grows 45 cm (18 in) tall and bears in clusters large single orange flowers which are amongst the most sweetly scented of all flowers.

T. patula. The French marigold, whose finely divided dark-green leaves have a refreshing pungent smell when pressed. It grows only 15 to 20 cm (6 to 8 in) tall and in Europe is treated as a half-hardy annual. Many varieties are obtainable, bearing either double or single flowers, amongst the best being Sparky which makes a dwarf bushy plant and bears flowers 3 cm (1¼ in) in diameter, coloured orange-red with a golden centre. Yellow Nuggett makes a mound of brilliant gold.

T. signata. The true Tagetes, which has bright-green foliage and covers itself in masses of brilliant golden single flowers. The variety Golden Gem bears bright golden-yellow daisy-like flowers, whilst Lulu and Lemon Gem bear lemon-yellow flowers. The foliage of this plant is perhaps more refreshingly aromatic than of any other plant, the Lemon verbena-like perfume remaining on the fingers for an hour or more after pressing the leaves.

TALAUMA (Magnoliaceae—Magnolia Family)

A genus of 50 trees or shrubs, indigenous to the sub-tropical regions of the Old and the New World and remarkable for their large glossy leaves and flowers of outstanding perfume. They require a peat-laden soil.

Species. *Talauma candallii.* A native of Java where it grows 1.8 m (6 ft) tall with oblong leaves, acuminated at both ends. The flowers are large, 12-petalled and a lovely shade of Jersey cream with a sweet perfume, enhanced by a lemony undertone.

T. lanigera. It is a small tree inhabiting eastern India with large leaves 30 cm (12 in) long and 12.5 cm (5 in) wide. The flowers are also large with 8 petals. They are of purest white, thick and fleshy with a sweet lily-like perfume.

T. plumiera. A native of Martinique where the flowers, which are deliciously scented are used to flavour wine, in the same way that Chaucer flavoured his ale with pinks. It makes a robust tree 24 m (80 ft) tall with round smooth leaves, and at the apex of the branches bears large pure-white flowers composed of 12 thick velvety petals which diffuse an almost overpowering perfume for miles around.

TARAXACUM (Compositae—Daisy Family)

A genus of 25 species, native to Europe and central Asia which are usually classed as obnoxious weeds.

Species. *Taraxacum vulgare.* The dandelion which Shakespeare does not mention once though it was an important plant at the time. The leaves, though having a bitter taste, were used in salads whilst the roots were ground to be made into a drink similar to coffee. Indeed, the plants are grown for this purpose to this day, the roots being roasted and ground to mix into the less expensive coffees for, when dry, they have the distinct fragrance and flavour of coffee. Dandelion coffee is to be recommended to those who find ordinary coffee indigestible.

The roots contain a sticky, milk-like juice containing latex from which rubber is extracted, and in the U.S.S.R. where the latex content is high, dandelions are cultivated for this purpose.

The leaves were boiled with lentils and Evelyn wrote that they were 'sold in most herb shops in London for being a wonderful purifyer of the blood'. But the best way of enjoying the leaves is to dig up a few roots from a field or hedgerow, plant them in a box in soil and cover them to exclude light. The blanched leaves will then be free from bitterness and make a tasty winter salad, or they may be boiled.

Countrymen have long made use of the juice from the stems to remove warts and it is said that the treatment is infallible. Only during summer should the juice be applied when it is most acrid. If a flower is removed with the stem, a drop of the juice should be squeezed out and applied to the wart. This should be repeated each day until the wart has turned black, when it will soon fall away.

Dandelion flowers have an unpleasant odour but they provide bees with nectar secreted at the base of a tubular corolla. At nightfall the flower-heads close up, thus protecting the pollen and nectar. The honey is strong in flavour and smell, carrying the odour of the flower. Though visited by bees, self-pollination is possible by the styles curving back and coming into contact with the pollen.

TARCHONANTHUS (Compositae— Daisy Family)

A genus of six species of dioecious trees or shrubs native of South Africa (two in Mexico) with alternate leaves, leathery and hairy on the underside, and bearing their small white flowers in terminal panicles. The genus takes its name from the Greek *touchea*, funeral rites, and *anthos*, flower, for all parts of the tree are fragrant and were used at burial ceremonies.

Species. *Tarchonanthus camphoratus*. A tall shrub or small tree, both the wood and leaves smelling strongly of camphor. The leaves are netted above and are woolly on the underside, whilst the white flowers have a style which is also hairy and with an elongated gland at the base. The wood is used by the natives to make musical instruments.

TECOPHILEA (Amaryllidaceae— Narcissus Family)

A genus of only two species, native of the upper Chilean Andes and which must be numbered amongst the greatest beauties of the flower world. The corms, like the bulbs of *Iris reticulata*, are covered with a reticulated tunic and from them appear early in spring crocus-like flowers on 7.5-cm (3-in) stems. Probably the finest display is to be seen at Walpole's Gardens, Mount Usher, Co. Wicklow, where

hundreds grow and bloom at the foot of a wall facing south and are annually top-dressed in winter with decayed sheep manure. The Tecophileas bloom early in the year and are dependent on the weather for their display. Thus where the garden is exposed, it may be advisable to grow them in pans under glass when they will come into bloom early in March and will scent a large greenhouse with their violet-like perfume.

Species. *Tecophilea cyanocrocus*. It bears glossy bright-green leaves 7.5 cm (3 in) long, above which it bears its crocus-like flowers of rich, gentian blue. The variety Leichtlinii bears blue flowers which are white in the throat whilst *violacea* bears flowers of rich purple-blue.

T. violiflora. This species is now rare and is less hardy than the more exquisite *T. cyanocrocus*, and possesses but little perfume. It may now be extinct in cultivation.

TEMUS (Magnoliaceae—Magnolia Family)

A small genus of evergreen trees or shrubs closely allied to *Magnolia* and native of South America, especially Chile, with alternate leaves, the flowers flesh-coloured with 18 petals and a 3-cleft calyx.

Species. *Temus moschata*. Native of Chile, it is an evergreen shrub growing 4.5 m (15 ft) tall with alternate leaves 5 cm (2 in) long crowded on the twiggy branches. They are oval and smooth and of a shining bright green which when handled release the aromatic fragrance of nutmeg. In its native land it is known as the Musk-scented temus. The flowers are flesh or blush-coloured with narrow petals and they are sweetly scented.

TERMINALIA (Combretaceae— Combretum Family)

A large genus of tropical (mostly Indian) trees which are rich in tannin whilst the ripened fruits are an important article of commerce known as myrobalan.

Species. *Terminalia sericea*. Native of South Africa and India, it makes a small tree and flowers in December, bearing hanging racemes of greenish-white blossoms which are sweetly scented. The narrow leaves are enhanced by the silvery hairs on the underside which from afar gives the tree a silver-like appearance.

TETRACLINIS (Cupressaceae—Cypress Tree Family)

A genus of a single species native of North Africa.

Species. *Tetraclinis articulata.* It abounds along the Mediterranean coastline reaching a height of 9 m (30 ft) with drooping branches of flattened leaves and globular cones. It is known as the Arar tree and grows well in a sandy soil. Its wood is scented, like cedarwood, and is readily worked by hand and for this reason it was used in the construction of the ninth-century cathedral of Cordova. Like the closely related Cypress-pines of Australia, and especially *C. intratropica,* it is able to withstand the ravages of white ants better than any other timber and in this respect is followed by *Eucalyptus corymbosa,* the Bloodwood of Western Australia which is also ant-resisting.

The Arar yields the Thyine wood of Revelation, one of the most highly prized commodities of the ancient world. Cicero had a table made of it, and for cabinet making it was 'worth its weight in gold'. It had a high polish and a lemon scent so that the Romans called it Citronwood. From it is obtained a transparent resin known as sandarach, still used for making varnish. It is sold in the form of pale-yellow grains which were burnt as incense on Greek and Roman altars.

TEUCRIUM (Labiatae—Lavender Family)

A genus of 300 perennial herbs of shrubby habit present in most warm parts of the world.

Species. *Teucrium chamaedrys.* Tusser included the Germander amongst his 'strewing herbs' whilst, with its dainty upright habit, it was widely grown during Tudor times for 'knot' gardens. It is perennial, growing 15 to 20 cm (6 to 8 in) tall, with shining green, deeply toothed leaves, and it bears its rosy-pink flowers from July until September. It is a pleasing rockery plant and does well planted in the wall of an old ruin, where its evergreen leaves and short pink spikes are most pleasing against the stone. The leaves have a pungent, aromatic smell, most pronounced when trodden upon, hence its value for strewing. Culpeper wrote of its virtues in restoring the spirits: 'It is good against a continual headache, melancholy, drowsiness and dullness of the spirits'.

T. marum. The Cat Thyme, of the same family as Catmint (*Nepeta mussinii*), is so called because its pungent leaves, in shape like those of the thyme, are enjoyed by cats which love to roll on it and nibble at the leaves.

A native of Europe, it is a shrub growing 30 to 37.5 cm (12 to 15 in) tall with short lance-shaped leaves, downy above and woolly beneath, which gives a silvery appearance. Like the Catmint, the flowers of reddish-purple are borne in pairs in the axils of the leaves.

T. polium. It is a curious little procumbent herb growing only 7.5 cm (3 in) tall, its tiny narrow leaves being densely covered with soft white down, likewise the stems and they have a pleasant aromatic scent. It bears small flowers of white or yellow throughout summer.

T. pyrenaicum. Its grey notched leaves are covered with down and are very aromatic, whilst through summer it bears hooded flowers of purple and white in dense terminal clusters.

T. subspinosum. It makes a tiny grey spiny shrublet no more than 10 cm (4 in) tall whilst its leaves are refreshingly aromatic. It bears mauve-pink flowers during July and August.

THALICTRUM (Ranunculaceae—Buttercup Family)

A genus of some 50 species of perennial herbs which flourish in a moist soil. They are characterized by their attractive fern-like foliage and extreme hardiness.

Species. *Thalictrum foetidum.* The Stinking Meadow rue, it is to be found throughout Europe and Asia, growing in low-lying meadowland and it rarely exceeds a height of 30 cm (12 in). It bears its small red nodding flowers during midsummer and it has heart-shaped leaflets covered with a sticky substance which emits a most unpleasant smell of decayed fish when touched.

THELYPTERIS (Thelypteridaceae— Thelypteris Family)

A small genus of delicate dwarf ferns usually to be found in damp woodlands and by the side of streams, chiefly in northern England and Ireland.

Species. *Thelypteris oreopteris.* A handsome short tufted fern, its pale-green leaves, about 45 cm (18 in) long, release a refreshing lemon scent when bruised. The fronds taper to a point whilst the leaflets are covered in small hairs. The spore cases are near the leaf margins.

THISTLE: *see* CARDUUS

THRYPTOMENE (Myrtaceae—Myrtle Family)

A genus of about 20 species, native of Western Australia and Tasmania, of small heath-like shrubs with opposite leaves and bearing 1, 2 or 3 flowers in leafy racemes.

Species. *Thryptomene micrantha.* It forms a shrub 1.5 to 1.8 m (5 to 6 ft) tall with slender spreading branches and with narrow obovate leaves, blunt at the apex with the oil glands most noticeable and releasing a pungent smell when pressed. It is native only of Tasmania, being common on the eastern side.

THUNBERGIA (Thunbergiaceae— Thunbergia Family)

A genus of tropical stove plants, native of East Africa, India, the islands of the Malayan Archipelago, and the West Indies. The blue-flowered *T. chrysops* and *T. laurifolia* are not scented and it is the white-flowered *T. fragrans* that has the most scent. They are plants of vigorous climbing habit and need a large greenhouse in which to do themselves justice. Under such conditions, their pendent branches and handsome flowers are seen to advantage. They require a 40-cm (16-in) pot containing a compost of fibrous loam and peat in equal parts. At the beginning of the year begin cutting out any weak shoots before tying in the rest quite loosely. They will bloom throughout summer and well into autumn, obtaining great benefit from an occasional watering with liquid manure.

Species. *Thunbergia fragrans.* Native of the Madras district of India, it will quickly attain a height of 6 m (20 ft) and bears its clusters of fragrant white flowers throughout several weeks of summer.

THUYA (Cupressaceae—Cypress Tree Family)

The name is derived from the verb *thyo*, to perfume, because of the sweet pungent smoke given off by the trees when burned, whilst the foliage has the scent of ripe apples. It is native of North America, Japan and the Near East, and may have reached England during early Elizabethan times. Gerard reported that it grew in his garden in Holborn but on account of its sombre foliage it was, with the closely related cypress, usually planted in churchyards. It was known as *Arbor vitae*, the Tree of Life, to the ancients, and is mentioned in Genesis, and may have been so called because it is evergreen or because of the great durability of its wood, which is almost indestructible. Sweeping brushes (besoms) were made from the branches and left their characteristic resinous scent throughout the home. The essential oil was much in demand at the time of the plague for it was said to protect against the disease. The leaves when bruised with honey were used to cure sores of the skin. It grows well in any well-drained loamy soil.

Species and Varieties. *Thuya chilensis.* Native of the Andes, the Incense cedar requires a sheltered garden in Great Britain but will withstand several degrees of frost. It will attain a height of 6 m (20 ft) and has drooping branches of glaucous-green, and cones which are also drooping. All parts of the tree are strongly fragrant, especially the wood when burnt, smelling of incense.

T. occidentalis. The American Arbor Vitae, usually growing along the low-lying rocky valleys by the side of lakes and streams where its flat spreading branches, covered with tiny leaves like the scales of fishes, provide a most picturesque sight. The plant is valuable as a screen for its large branches almost sweep the ground. It will also withstand clipping.

There are a number of lovely varieties.

Rosenthali makes a tall narrow tree and has bright olive-green foliage which provides a happy contrast to the dark green of the species, whilst Rheingold makes a broad pyramid of gold in summer, changing to a lovely old gold in winter. Also fine is *aureospicata* which makes an erect tree, its dark-green branches being tipped with gold.

T. plicata. The Western Red cedar so called because of its red wood. The foliage is darkest green whilst that of the form *semperaurescens* is darkest bronze tipped with gold. *Atrovirens* has foliage of an intense deep green and Zebrina of dark green alternating with bands of gold.

T. gigantea (syn. *T. libbi*). Native of north-western America, it makes a graceful pyramidal tree, often reaching a height of 45 m (150 ft) and is usually to be found in swampy woodlands below 1,500 m (5,000 ft). The leaves, borne in alternate opposite pairs, appear on slender branchlets. The cones are small and ovoid, tapering at both ends. It will withstand clipping and may be planted as an evergreen hedge when it will diffuse the refreshing smell of ripe apples about the garden.

THYMOPHYLLA (Compositae—Daisy Family)

A genus of 25 species, native of North America and Mexico, few of which have scented attractions.

Species. *Thymophylla aurea.* Native of the eastern United States where it is known as the Dahlborg daisy, it is a hardy annual growing only 15 cm (6 in) tall and is a valuable plant for a window-box or for summer bedding. The variety Golden Fleece remains in bloom from June until September, presenting a sheet of golden beauty, whilst the foliage and flowers emit a pleasant aromatic odour.

THYMUS (Labiatae—Lavender Family)

A genus of perhaps 400 species, native of warm Europe and Asia. They may be divided into two main groups, (a) the prostrate or creeping thymes and (b) those of upright bushy habit, like miniature shrubs. The former are members of the *T. serpyllum* (serpent-like) group, the latter of the *T. citriodorus* and *T. nitidus* groups,

valued for their culinary qualities.

Francis Bacon wrote of 'those flowers which perfume the air most delightfully ... being trodden upon and crushed, Burnet, Wild Thyme and Water Mint'. But not only are they plants for the fragrant 'lawn'; they may be used about a rockery or trough garden and planted between crazy paving stones. All the thymes have aromatic foliage, each one possessing a different aroma, like the mints but more pungent.

In an Anglo-Saxon work of the tenth century, *serpulum* is mentioned and in the *Promptorium parvulorum* of 1440, the plant is referred to as *Sepillum piretrum*. The herb first appears in the Latin form *timum* in the Catholic *Anglicum*, since when the name has been used for the plant. The poet Spenser wrote of 'the bees alluring Tyme' and possibly owing to the great activity of bees about the flowers, the plant became an emblem of activity and valour in the days of chivalry. Ingram in his *Flora Symbolica* wrote that ladies 'embroidered their knightly lover's scarves with the figure of a bee hovering about a sprig of thyme' whilst 'to smell of thyme' was an expression of praise. In *Britannia's Pastorals*, William Browne wrote: 'Some from the fens bring reeds, wild thyme from downs', and this is where wild thyme is usually found, in full sun and where the soil is dry and well drained.

Species and Varieties. *Thymus azoricus.* Native of the Azores, it is a delightful plant for crazy paving or for a low wall for it makes a dense mat of brightest green which releases a powerful orange scent when bruised.

T. capitatus. It grows in rocky places around the southern Mediterranean shores and has thick white stems and short, linear leaves turned up at the margins. It is powerfully pungent when handled.

. *T. carnosus.* Native of the Mediterranean region, it is one of the upright thymes though forming a compact plant. It possesses a powerful aromatic fragrance.

T. citriodorus. It is the lemon-scented thyme which releases a perfume which is extremely refreshing. It is a variety of *T. serpyllum* and makes a small-leaved bushy plant growing 22.5 cm (9 in) tall. *T. citriodorus* Silver Queen, is perhaps the best form, its leaves showing silver colouring, whilst there is also a gold-leaf form *aureus*, its leaves taking on the warm golden colouring during winter.

T. coccineus minus is a more dwarf form than the type. Of trailing habit, it bears rich pink flowers and grows only half an inch tall. Almost as prostrate is Annie Hall, which forms mats of fleshy-pink flowers, whilst Pink Chintz is of similar habit and bears dense mats of a beautiful shade of salmon-pink. Bressingham Pink is valuable in that it comes early into bloom, whilst Russetting has rosy-red flowers and very dark foliage.

T. comosus. It is a hairy shrublet growing 7.5 cm (3 in) tall and bearing in July and August lilac-pink flowers. The foliage releases the smell of turpentine when handled.

T. decussatus. It is native only of the Lybian Desert and Sinai where it grows 7.5 cm (3 in) tall. It has linear leaves with margins which turn upwards whilst its tiny purple-pink flowers appear in small heads.

T. doeffleri. It makes a tiny hummock 5 cm (2 in) tall with grey foliage which is powerfully pine-scented, and bears rose-pink flowers.

T. fragrantissimus. It has attractive grey leaves which have the refreshing smell of oranges.

T. herba-barona. It is the Seed-cake thyme, re-discovered in Corsica by Mr Clarence Elliott. In his book, *Rock Garden Plants,* he describes its discovery when he was amazed at the caraway seed fragrance the plant emitted. It should be planted in light loam on a warm bank or sunny slope, and bears rose-coloured flowers.

T. mastichina. It grows 22.5 cm (9 in) tall, making a woody shrublet with powerfully scented foliage and bearing snow-white flowers.

T. membranaceus. One of the finest of all the creeping thymes, making a neat rounded hummock and bearing large heads of tubular white flowers and with leaves which are powerfully aromatic. It was found in Spain by Mr Ashton Lofthouse.

T. micans. It is a plant of almost prostrate habit and has golden heath-like foliage which when trodden upon releases a refreshing pine-like aroma.

T. nitidus. Native of Sicily it is grey-leaved with the same well-known pungency as the Black or English thyme, *T. vulgaris.* The form *albus* makes a tiny hummock with white flowers.

T. pulegioides (syn. *T. ovatus*). It is an infrequent inhabiter of the downlands of south-east England and is of upright growth. Unlike *T. serpyllum*, it has not a creeping rootstock. The stems are square and hairy but the oval aromatic leaves are hairless. The small pink flower-heads are borne during July and August.

T. serpyllum. A native British downland plant of prostrate habit with tiny lance-shaped leaves and bearing rose-purple flowers from June until August. The lovely white form, *T. serpyllum albus,* has leaves of paler green than the others. Gerard described its flowers as being 'as white as snow'. Another form is *T. serpyllum lanuginosus* which has silvered hairy leaves.

T. vulgaris. The Common thyme, a plant noted for its culinary value, which grows 22.5 cm (9 in) tall, with narrow grey-green leaves which release a pungent aroma when bruised.

TILIA (Lime) (Tiliaceae—Linden Tree Family)

A genus of eight species of ornamental trees, native of North America, the British Isles, northern and eastern Europe, the handsome heart-shaped leaves having serrated edges. In England, it was always quite rare. Dr Turner (1560) mentioned its growing in Essex 'in a part within two miles of Colchester', whilst Gerard (1597) wrote that 'it groweth in some woods in Northamptonshire; also near Colchester'. Though a native tree, Evelyn complained of having to import young trees from Holland. Grinling Gibbons worked with superb artistry on lime wood at Petworth House and at Lyme Park in Cheshire, the wood being chosen by the master carvers of the time because of its softness, its delicate green colouring and because it is untroubled by worm.

The lime, or linden as it is called in Holland and in Germany, is one of the most suitable trees for town planting and it may also be clipped to make a pleasing walk or 'alley' to a house. Almost all insects visit the flowers for the honey is secreted in the hollow sepals and is accessible to insects with a short proboscis as well as to others.

Species and Varieties. *Tilia coronallina.* The red-twigged lime which, apart from its scented flowers, provides attractive winter colour from its twigs.

T. euchlara. A beautiful tree of pendulous growth, with bright-green leaves and yellow twigs and bearing greenish-white flowers which are strongly scented.

T. fomentosum. A valuable small garden tree, it is known as the Silver lime for its heart-shaped leaves on the undersides appear as if they have been painted with silver, whilst the yellow flowers are especially fragrant.

TODDALIA (Rutaceae—Rue Family)
A genus of a single species.

Species. *Toddalia aculeata.* In its native Nilgiri Hills, it is known as the Wild Orange and is a small evergreen tree armed with prickles and bearing flowers of purest white which diffuse their citrus-like perfume over a wide area. An essential oil, Toddelia, obtained from its leaves has the scent of basil, somewhat citrus-like and resembling the odour of all other members of the family.

TORREYA (Taxaceae—Yew Tree Family)
A genus of six species, native of eastern Asia, California and Florida. So powerfully smelling is it that it is known as the Foetid Yew for it resembles the yew with its linear leaves arranged in spiral fashion, though the leaves are stiffer and more sharply pointed. It is a valuable tree to plant in a chalky soil.

Species. *Torreya californica.* From the aromatic nutmeg-shaped fruits, the seeds being covered with a hard, bony shell, it is known as the Californian Nutmeg. It is a most beautiful tree of pyramidal habit with leaves of polished green whilst the lower branches sweep the ground, like the yew. The leaves have a powerful resinous smell.

T. taxifolia. Native of the swamplands of Florida, it is so strongly resinous as to be unpleasant near to and it is known as the Stinking Cedar, But it is a handsome

tree, growing up to 15 m (50 ft) tall with widely spreading branches composed of dark-green linear leaves.

TOVARIA (Tovariaceae—Tovaria Family)
A genus of a single species.

Species. *Tovaria pendula.* It is native of Mexico and Jamaica and is a plant of shrubby habit with alternate trifoliolate leaves which when on the plant smell of celery and, when dry, of newly mown hay, due to the presence of coumarin. The white flowers, borne in loose pendulous racemes, have no perfume. The flowers are followed by small green berries.

TRACHELIUM (Campanulaceae—Harebell Family)
Known as the Throatwort, it is a genus of five species, one of which, the best-known *T. coeruleum,* bears slightly scented flowers. Natives of southern Europe, the plants are able to survive the winter in Britain only in the more favourably placed gardens though they frequently survive if given protection of a warm wall. Though perennial, they are best treated as half-hardy annuals or biennials if the garden is exposed; sow the seed under glass in September or early in the year and grow on the seedlings in small pots to be planted out in May. They will come into bloom early July.

Species. *Trachelium coeruleum.* It is a hairy perennial of bushy habit, and growing 30 to 37.5 cm (12 to 15 in) tall it is a most attractive plant to use with pink geraniums for summer bedding or to plant towards the front of the border. It has deeply toothed leaves and bears its flowers in dense panicles. The blooms are salver-shaped, with a long narrow tube from which the bees obtain nectar, and they are of deep violet-blue with a soft, sweet perfume; this is more pronounced in the white form, *album,* which provides a delightful contrast.

TRACHELOSPERMUM (Apocynaceae—Periwinkle Family)
A small genus of evergreen climbing plants introduced in 1846 which has proved hardy in Britain south of the Thames and in sheltered gardens of the

West. Like most of the evergreen climbers, they bloom in late summer and early autumn and they grow best in a well-drained loam to which has been added some peat.

Species and Varieties. *Trachelospermum asiaticum.* Against a warm wall it will attain a height of 4.5 m (15 ft) and is a plant of neatest habit with leaves like those of the periwinkle. It begins to bloom in July, its creamy-white flowers appearing in loose sprays at the end of the shoots and they have a sweet refreshing perfume.

T. jasminoides. A beautiful slender Japanese climbing plant known as the Cape Jasmine. It bears salver-shaped flowers like those of the jasmine and, like that plant, sends out roots from the leaf nodes and the ends of the stems wherever in contact with the ground. The leaves are darkest green and glossy whilst the flowers are of purest white like wax with the petals turned back like the jasmine and deliciously scented. The form *variegatum* has leaves splashed with cream.

T. majus. It is hardier and more vigorous than the other species and has also the longest leaves. It will clothe a large wall quite quickly, clinging to the mortar like the ivy, the leaves often taking on a crimson hue in winter. The white flowers, which appear only when the plant is established, have a soft perfume but are not so fragrant as the other species.

TRICHOCEREUS (Cactaceae—Cactus Family)

A genus of about 30 species, native of the warmer parts of North and South America. They form an erect stem with numerous ribs thickly studded with spiny areoles. The white funnel-shaped flowers are nocturnal and are amongst the most handsome of all cactus blooms. They require a compost made up of gravel or coarse sand, leaf-mould and decayed manure in equal parts and into which is incorporated some mortar. Provide a sunny situation and a minimum winter temperature of 10°C (50°F). Give plenty of moisture in summer, little or none in winter.

Species. *Trichocereus bridgesii.* Native of Bolivia where it makes such vigorous

growth as to be planted as a field hedge. It grows up to 2 m (6 to 7 ft) high, its branching stems being covered in long spines. The handsome flowers appear at the top of the stems and have greenish outer petals and pure-white inner petals. They scent the air around with jasmine and, though opening at night, last well into the following day.

T. candicans. It is rare in northern Argentina where it forms a dense plant, branching from the base and growing 1 m (3 to 4 ft) tall. The stems are covered in long yellow spines whilst the flowers are borne at the sides towards the top. They are funnel-shaped and purest white with a powerfully sweet scent.

T. pachanoi. Native of Ecuador and Peru, it forms a stem up to 6 m (20 ft) high from which appear numerous vertical branches, often spineless. The flowers are borne at the ends of the stems and are pure white with a jasmine-like scent.

T. schickendantzii. Native of northern Argentina, it has glossy green stems 60 cm (2 ft) high with 16 ribs clothed in yellow areoles. The flowers, borne at the top of the stems, are large, of purest white and sweetly scented.

T. strigosus. Native of western Argentina, it has grey-green stems 1 m (3 to 4 ft) tall and dark-red spines, becoming grey with age. The flowers are large, of satiny white with the scent of magnolias.

TRICHOPILIA (Orchidaceae—Orchid Family)

A small genus of epiphytic, rhizomatous orchids from tropical America often the mountainous regions. They are beautiful plants, requiring warm house temperatures, and not less than 13°C (55°F) in winter. Pans are the best containers with a compost of two parts osmunda fibre and one part sphagnum-moss. Good drainage is most important and a humid atmosphere except when flowering. Increase is by division of large plants.

Species. *Trichophilia fragrans.* A most attractive orchid, the white flowers are borne 2 to 4 on a partially erect spike in winter. The perfume of narcissus which it emits is only produced in the evening; during the day it is almost completely scentless.

T. suavis. From Costa Rica, this

hawthorn-scented orchid flowers in spring, on short spikes. The flowers may be about 10 cm (4 in) across and are creamy white, spotted with rose-pink; the lip is frilled and has spots of dark rose. It is often considered the most handsome species.

TRIGONELLA (Fenugreek)
(Leguminosae—Laburnum Family)

A genus of annual herbs, native of the eastern Mediterranean, which release a smell of new-mown hay as they become dry. The genus takes its name from the Latin *foenum graecum*, Greek hay, for in southern Europe the plant was grown especially to provide its sweet scent to hay of inferior quality. The leaves are trifoliate with dentate leaflets.

Species. *Trigonella arabica.* It is common to sandy wastes of the eastern Mediterranean and grows 45 cm (18 in) tall. It bears cream-coloured flowers with a violet heel whilst the leaves have a high coumarin content. The seed-pods are bristly at the margins.

T. purpurascens. Known as the Bird's-foot fenugreek, it is a plant of prostrate habit with leaves similar to those of the Restharrow. The small pea-like flowers are borne in short racemes and are of pinkish-white. Found in sandy ground but not common in Britain, it is an annual plant, in bloom during July and August. When dry, the whole plant takes on the sweet hay-like scent of woodruff.

T. stellata. It is to be found in all desert lands of Egypt and the Near East where it grows 45 cm (18 in) tall with long petioled leaves. The flowers appear at the axils of the leaves and are followed by small pods grouped into star-like shapes. The leaves are powerfully scented when dry.

TRILLIUM (Liliaceae—Lily Family)

A genus of about 40 species of herbaceous perennials, the Wood lilies are mostly native of the woodlands of North America with one or two appearing in northern Asia. A sweet scent is present in several, though *T. erectum* and one or two other species are known for their smell of decaying meat. It is of interest that *T. erectum* has flowers of purple-red, whilst the sweetly scented species bear white flowers. The plants, so named from the arrangement of their leaves and flowers in threes, enjoy a moist peaty soil and some shade. They are increased by a spreading tuberous rootstock.

Species. *Trillium cernuum.* Native of the moist deciduous woodlands of Newfoundland and extending south to North Carolina, the leaves are long, tapering to a point, whilst the white (or pale-pink) flowers are almost hidden by the foliage, hence its name of 'bashful Ben'. The flowers are sweetly scented.

T. erectum (syn. *foetidum*). It is native of the woodlands of North America where it is known as 'birthroot'. It grows to a height of about 30 cm (12 in) with rhomboid leaves which taper abruptly to a point and, like those of Herb Paris to which it is closely related, are borne in whorls, and are arranged in threes. The solitary flowers appear in May and there are 3 outer petals, 3 inner petals and 3 stigmas, the inner petals being purple. The flower is purple-brown, in appearance like decaying meat and is pollinated by flies. It gives off the highly unpleasant smell of putrefied flesh. The white-flowered form *blandum* is not nearly so offensive, indeed, it seems to have lost most of its smell.

T. luteum. It is found only in the Indian Reserve of North Carolina and is a most distinctive plant with purple-mottled leaves and bearing greenish-yellow flowers (large for the genus) which appear in the centre of a whorl and which have a refreshing lemon-like fragrance.

T. sessile. Native of the eastern U.S.A., it has sessile, ovate dark-green leaves mottled with white, and it bears sweetly scented white flowers which snugly fit into the dark-green whorl.

TRIPHASIA (Rutaceae—Rue Family)

A genus of two species, native of tropical Asia, and present in the Philippine and Fiji Islands. They are small spiny shrubs and grow on arid ground.

Species. *Triphasia trifolia.* A small shrub with branches covered in angry-looking spines and leaves covered in pellucid dots which release a resinous scent when pressed. The small white flowers have the scent of orange-blossom and these are followed by round lemon-scented berries which the native people use to make a delicious preserve.

TRIPTERYGIUM (Celastraceae—Celastrus Family)

A small genus of deciduous climbing plants, native of Burma south-western China, Korea and Japan, and introduced into the British Isles by Robert Forrest. They are closely related to *Celastrus,* differing only in their winged seed-vessels. In Britain, they should be confined to a sunny wall in the west where they should prove completely hardy and happy in any well-drained soil.

Species. *Tripterygium forrestii.* It was discovered by Forrest on the borders of Burma and western China and grows 2.4 to 3 m (8 to 10 ft) tall. In summer it bears clusters of tiny creamy-white flowers which diffuse a soft, sweet perfume and they are followed by conspicuous purple seed-vessels.

T. rebelii. It is native of Japan and Korea and grows 6 m (20 ft) tall with large leaves. It bears softly scented cream-coloured flowers in June and July which are followed by pale-green winged fruits.

TRITELIA (Liliaceae—Lily Family)

A genus of 16 species known as the Spring Star flowers and closely related to the Californian *Brodiaea* which are scentless.

Species. *Tritelia uniflora.* It is native of the Mexican Sierras and has narrow rush-like leaves, glaucous and rough to the touch, and it blooms in spring. The flowers, borne singly, open star-shaped, having 3 pointed petals with 3 intervening petals of thick texture, like white satin flushed with lavender and shaded green on the outside. As would be expected from a bloom of such texture, it diffuses a powerful fragrance.

The bulbs should be planted in a sunny position and in a rich well-drained, sandy loam. *T. uniflora* could also be included with flowers which give off their fragrance at night for they remain open after dark and on a calm evening scent the garden with their sweet perfume. The blooms appear for several weeks in one long succession.

TROPAEOLUM (Tropaeolaceae—Nasturtium Family)

A genus of 34 species of climbing or erect annuals or perennials, native of Mexico and noted for the brilliant colourings of their flowers.

Species. *Tropaeolum majus.* The first species to reach England was *T. majus,* a climbing plant bearing bright-yellow flowers streaked with red. Seed of this plant was received in Spain by Dr Monardes and distributed throughout Europe, reaching Gerard from the French king's gardener about 1595. By Parkinson's time, it had become one of the most popular plants of the garden. He called it 'the yellow Larkspur' for it had pointed petals and spurred flowers. Parkinson mentions its 'fine small scent, very pleasing, which being placed in the middle of some carnations or gilloflowers...make a delicate tussiemussie...'. Soon after Parkinson's death it was, surprisingly, lost and was not re-introduced until the end of the seventeenth century.

Apart from *T. majus,* no nasturtium possessed perfume until the double-flowered Golden Gleam was discovered in a garden in California in 1929. It would appear to be a *T. majus* hybrid for its bloom, though larger, was of similar colouring whilst it possessed much the same sweet perfume. Its immediate popularity was fantastic, and from 1931 when it received a Royal Horticultural Society Award of Merit many tons of seed have been sold annually.

No plant grows better in poor soil nor is there one so hardy and accommodating. It will grow virtually anywhere and comes up each year from self-sown seed. The seeds are delicious when pickled and used with fish whilst the leaves may be included in salads in place of watercress. From a March sowing, a few seeds will transform an unsightly dry sunny bank into a sheet of fragrant colour.

Hybrid varieties of *T. majus:*

GLEAM HYBRIDS. Deliciously scented and of gorgeous colourings, the plants grow 30 cm (12 in) tall and are semi-trailing. Scent is especially pronounced in the Golden and Primrose Gleams.

CHERRY ROSE. One more addition to

the semi-double scented varieties. The plants grow only 22.5 cm (9 in) tall, remaining neat and compact, and through summer and autumn bear scented flowers of a new shade of cherry-red.

DELIGHTFUL. The plant remains neat and tidy like Cherry Rose whilst the sweetly scented flowers are a unique salmon-cerise.

FIERY FESTIVAL. Raised by Messrs Hursts, it is a superb plant, retaining its compact habit throughout summer and bearing masses of luminous scarlet flowers, the colour of Paul Crampel geranium and with a surprisingly powerful scent. The blooms are enhanced by the dark-green foliage.

TSUGA (Pinaceae—Pine Tree Family)

A genus of 14 species, native to the Himalayas, North America and Japan, they are handsome yew-like trees with horizontal branches and drooping branchlets. They require a moist, deep soil to grow well, and are hardy in all parts of the British Isles and northern Europe. *T. canadensis* was called Hemlock spruce by the early American settlers as the needles emit the unpleasant smell of the native British hemlock when crushed.

Species and Varieties. *Tsuga brunoniana* (syn. *T. dumosa*). Native of the eastern Himalayas, it emits so powerful a balsamic scent that it is known as the Fragrant fir. It grows to 24 m (80 ft) in height with drooping brittle branches and has leaves which are flat and borne in 2 rows, glossy above, powdery silver below. The cones solitary, sessile, are borne at the ends of the branches.

T. canadensis. The Eastern hemlock, it is to be found near the north-eastern seaboard of America and Canada on dry exposed ridges. It is readily distinguished by its trunk which is often forked quite low down, but it forms a big tree, growing wide and bushy rather than tall, with a trunk up to 1.2 m (4 ft) in diameter. It has dark foliage and cones which are borne on short stems. The form *albo-spica* is extremely lovely for the tips of the shoots are silvered. The long, ascending feathery branches are divided into small twigs.

TULBAGHIA (Liliaceae—Lily Family)

A genus of 26 species, closely related to *Allium* (onion) and native of tropical and southern Africa.

Species. *Tulbaghia alliaceae.* In its native South Africa it is known as the Wild Garlic (*Wilde-knoflok*) for the whole plant has a powerful aroma of garlic. It is to be found on sandy flats and has fleshy tuberous roots and erect narrow leaves which appear after the flowers. The flowers are yellowish-brown, often spotted with red and borne in a small umbel. They have an unpleasant smell and are pollinated by flies.

TULIPA (Liliaceae—Lily Family)

A genus of about 100 species of brilliantly coloured bulbous plants readily recognized from their brown-skinned bulbs. The large-flowered Dutch hybrids are amongst the most widely planted of all bulbs for late spring and early summer flowering, for they bridge the gap between spring and summer, and no flower is more gay. It is not usually realized that a number of the large-flowered hybrids are deliciously scented, and will augment the spring-flowering stocks and wallflowers both as to their scent and beauty, whilst a number of the dainty species, so suitable for pots indoors and for the alpine garden, will diffuse their sweet fragrance whenever the sun shines upon them.

Native of Persia, the tulip takes its name from the Eastern head-dress known as a *tolipan* or turban, which the flower so much resembles in form and colour. It was from Turkey that both seeds and bulbs were sent to the Emperor Ferdinand I of Germany by Auger Busbec. This was in 1554, and in 1559 the German botanist, Conrad Gesner, wrote of first seeing the flower in the garden of John Harwart at Augsburg; but it was not until about 20 years later that the tulip reached England. In his *History of Plants* which Turner dedicated to Elizabeth I, no mention is made of the tulip, but in 1582 Richard Hakluyt wrote: 'Within these four years there have been brought into England from Vienna in Austria, divers kinds of flowers called Tulipas'. Gerard also confirms the date of introduction as 1577-8. This was the common tulip, *Tulipa gesneriana* (named after Conrad Gesner), and now widely distributed in the wild state throughout southern Europe. From the sweetly scented scarlet flowers, the most fragrant of the Cottage tulips are descended. Writing of the plant in 1559, Gesner said '. . . it was like a red lily with a pleasant smell, soothing and delicate'. Note that the fact of the flowers being fragrant was given great prominence: in the sixteenth century this was the most important quality of any flower. For this reason, tulips were in demand for evening wear by ladies of the French aristocracy during the seventeenth century. But so magnificent is the colouring of the modern bedding tulip that there is a tendency to select a particular variety entirely for its colour, when its most endearing quality may be absent. Scent in tulips is present in all colours; it is one of the few flowers where perfume in the scarlet-flowering varieties is as pronounced as in those oearing white or pale-yellow blooms, though it is most pronounced in those bearing double flowers, as is the case with so many plants.

The earliest forms to capture the imagination of florists were striped and streaked in the most amazing fashion, and were divided into groups known as Bizarres, Bybloemens and Edgers. This was due to a virus disease which caused the self-coloured forms to 'break' into stripes and feathering. These forms could be propagated only vegetatively and so the bulbs always commanded a high price, yet so great was the demand that in 1796 the catalogue of Maddock, a London nurseryman, contained nearly 700 varieties, and Hogg writing in 1823 said that 'a moderate collection of choice tulips could not be purchased for a sum less than £1,000'.

One of the earliest tulips still obtainable is Keiserskroon, a single tulip, but it has no scent. The double tulip appeared first in 1581 in Vienna and was recorded, in Hakluyt's words, 'by an excellent man called Carolus Clusius'. In the double Murillo tulips, scent is most pronounced, also in the Breeder tulips, the lily-of-the-valley perfume being most noticeable in the golden-yellow and bronze Cherbourg. Indeed, its perfume is so delicious as to make this variety worthy of planting solely

for this quality. Several flowers near an open window will, on a calm day, scent a large room.

Almost every known species of the tulip is to be found in its natural state in countries bordering the Black Sea and the southern shores of the Mediterranean, and in Persia to the south. In Rumania and Bulgaria, in that part of the U.S.S.R. around the Sea of Azov, and in the Caucasus and Turkey, appear most of the scented species, including *T. suaveolens,* from which was evolved the scarlet single tulip which is also scented.

Completely perennial, the taller-growing species may be naturalized in grass, whilst the more dwarf forms may be used in the alpine garden. The taller-growing Cottage and Darwin tulips, usually planted in beds, may also be naturalized and will prove quite long-lasting if the flower-heads are removed as soon as they fade. Delightful together, planted against a background of cypresses, are the almond-scented Mrs Moon of palest yellow colouring, and the violet-blue Demeter which has the perfume of dried cloves. Or plant a bed of the white, honey-scented Schoonoord with the primrose Marie Crousse for an edging, for its double purple flowers have a similar perfume.

Species and Varieties. *Tulipa aucheriana.* Native of the rocky mountainous regions of northern Persia, it is one of the most attractive and exquisitely scented of all the tulip species. It should be grown in pans in the alpine house so that its qualities may be fully appreciated. It will then come into bloom in March, its flowers of soft mauve-pink flushed with orange and resembling water-lilies, with their pointed petals, being held on 7-cm (3-in) stems. The flowers open flat, like stars, and diffuse a rich sweet perfume.

T. celsiana (syn. *T. persica*). The handsome Persian tulip, its deep-green leaves being edged with crimson, whilst it bears on 10- to 15-cm (4- to 6-in) branched stems several scented, star-like flowers of brilliant yellow, shaded with bronze on the outside, which are deliciously scented. It blooms in June, being one of the latest species.

T. gesneriana. Distributed throughout south-eastern Europe and Asia Minor, it has broad, ovate lance-shaped glaucous leaves. In May and June it bears on 22-cm (9-in) stems brilliant-scarlet flowers with a striking black centre, and they are sweetly scented.

T. primulina. Native of the mountains of eastern Algeria, it is closely related to *T. sylvestris* which inhabits the lower regions of the same area, and extends north into the British Isles. It has smooth, pale-green leaves and in April bears bell-shaped flowers of primrose-yellow, tinted red on the outside. They emit the lily-of-the-valley perfume.

T. saxatilis. It grows wild close to the seashore of Crete, with broad leaves of bright shining green, unlike those of·any other tulip. It blooms in April, bearing several flowers of clearest lilac to each 22-cm (9-in) stem, and they have a delicate sweet primrose perfume.

T. suaveolens. A native of south-eastern Europe, it is believed to be the parent of the scented red (crimson) Duc van Tol tulips, which bear their flowers on 7- to 10-cm (3- to 4-in) stems, and which at one time were forced in large numbers for bowls at Christmas-time. *T. sauaveolens* is of similar habit, its sweetly scented, bright-scarlet blooms, edged with gold, appearing on a 15-cm (6-in) stem; outdoors in the alpine garden, they appear early in April.

T. sylvestris. Found in low-lying ground from North Africa through Europe and in Britain and Scandinavia. It is probably the French tulip of Gerard's *Herball.* Chalk pits and low-lying waste land are its native habitat, and once established it is difficult to eradicate, increasing by underground stolons. It bears two or three flowers to a stem some 45 cm (1½ ft) tall and has a more graceful appearance than any other tulip. The flowers appear in mid-April and are of richest yellow, shaded with green on the outside, and with a most pronounced perfume, even more noticeable in the Algerian form *T. fragrans* (it is, however, not so hardy).

SINGLE EARLY TULIPS. Ideal for pot cultivation, and outdoors they will bloom in April. Several of the scarlet varieties descended from *T. suaveolens* bear scented flowers.

BELLONA. A most beautiful tulip, bearing huge globes of buttery-yellow, shaded with orange, and with the scent of orange-blossom.

DOCTOR PLESMAN. A most showy tulip, the globular blooms being of ox-blood red throughout, and with the lily-of-the-valley perfume.

FRED MOORE. One of the finest tulips ever raised, the large globular blooms are of terracotta colouring, flushed with orange-scarlet, and have a honey perfume.

GENERAL DE WET. A sport of Prince of Austria which had *T. suaveolens* in its parentage, hence the delicious perfume of the fiery orange blooms which defy all the laws of nature. It grows 30 cm (1 ft) tall and may be brought into bloom indoors by Christmas.

PRINCE CARNIVAL. Also a sport of Prince of Austria, its flowers of scarlet and gold possess outstanding perfume.

PRINCE OF AUSTRIA. Unsurpassed for forcing, its orange-scarlet blooms scented like orange-blossom have enormous substance.

VERMILION BRILLIANT. A sport from Prince of Austria, the dazzling scarlet blooms are long-lasting and sweetly scented.

DOUBLE EARLY TULIPS. Like the Single Early tulips, they may be grown in pots of five or six bulbs indoors or are long-lasting and early flowering in outdoor beds. Deliciously honey-scented is the old Murillo and its several sports.

MARQUETTE. A lovely Murillo sport, the huge globular blooms being of richest crimson-red, providing a striking contrast to the white Schoonoord.

MME TESTOUT. One of the most attractive of the Murillo sports, the blooms of satin-pink have a striking golden base.

MURILLO. The multipetalled blooms are large and are white-flushed and shaded with rose-pink.

SCHOONOORD. A beautiful white Murillo sport. with lily-like scent.

TEA ROSE. It bears a bloom of exquisite charm, being of primrose-yellow flushed with salmon in which the honey scent is most pronounced.

BREEDER TULIPS. These are early summer flowering and of enormous size, whilst the colours include shades of copper, orange and bronze, to provide a display of great richness. They grow about 75 cm (2½ ft) tall, and in addition to their beauty one or two have pronounced perfume.

CHERBOURG. The large, globular blooms are of orange-yellow, shaded with bronze and flushed with purple, and have the refreshing sweet scent of lily of the valley.

MOROCCAN BEAUTY. One of the finest of all May-flowering tulips, the huge blooms are of Moroccan-red over a gold base, and shaded bronze inside. The blooms have an almost lily-like perfume.

PRINCE OF ORANGE. An old variety bearing large orange blooms of outstanding fragrance.

DARWIN TULIPS. A race of tulips imported into Holland from northern France in 1889, but their origin is unknown. They are the latest of all to bloom, continuing until almost the end of June. Only one or two are scented.

DEMETER. It is the first of the Darwins to bloom, its deep violet-blue flowers, held on 75-cm (2½-ft) stems having a distinct clove perfume.

PHILIPPE DE COMMINES. An older variety but its purple-maroon flowers stand out in any company and are sweetly scented.

WHITE VICTORY. The large, refined flowers are purest white with the scent of white jasmine.

COTTAGE TULIPS. They were discovered in an old English cottage garden and flower in early May. They grow rather less than 60 cm (2 ft) in height, and are ideal for bedding or for naturalizing. Several bear scented blooms.

GRENADIER. The large, orange-scarlet blooms have a striking golden base and a delicious perfume to make it one of the finest of all tulips.

MRS MOON. An old favourite of distinct form, the long flowers of clear canary-yellow having pointed reflexed petals and an unmistakable almond perfume.

LILY-FLOWERED TULIPS. Unsurpassed for elegance and charm, with their pointed reflexed petals. They grow 60 cm (2 ft) tall, and flower in early May. Several have pronounced scent.

ELLEN WILLMOTT. Its honey perfume is most noticeable whilst the long slender flowers with their reflexing petals are most elegant.

LA MERVEILLE. One of the most exquisite and sweetly scented of all tulips, the flowers with their pointed petals being of scarlet-orange, flushed with rose at the margins.

PARROT TULIPS. They are sports of all the various sections and have heavily laciniated petals and an unusual brilliance of colouring. They are May flowering and several bear scented blooms.

BLACK PARROT. A sport of Philippe de Commines, bearing large, glossy, maroon-black flowers of delicious perfume.

ORANGE FAVOURITE. Probably the most striking tulip in existence, the orange-scarlet blooms being tinged with old rose and with featherings of apple-green on the outside. It is scented of white jasmine.

ORANGE PARROT. A sport of the scented Breeder tulip, Prince of Orange, and equally sweetly scented. It is the last of the Parrots to bloom, the glowing mahogany-orange blooms being marked with old gold.

U

ULEX (Leguminosae—Laburnum Family)

A genus of 10 or more species of sharply spined shrubs, the leaves being replaced by spines with age. They bear flowers of golden-yellow.

Species. *Ulex europaeus.* The European gorse, native to the British Isles and northern Europe, which is to be found on heaths and wastelands where it grows 0.6 to 1.2 m (2 to 4 ft) high and forms a shrub-like plant of dense growth. It blooms in profusion during February, March and April, but bears at least some bloom at almost all times of the year. The scent is similar to that released by the laburnum, a smell of vanilla with undertones of orange or pineapple, being one of the most refreshing of all flower scents, greatly resembling that of the Sweet pea. To obtain a profusion of flowers, the plants should be grown in poor dry soils and a really sunny position. Propagation is by seed, or by cuttings taken in August.

U. minor (syn. *U. nanus*). Growing to 30 or 60 cm (1 or 2 ft) high, this species flowers later in the year, from July to October. It likes similar conditions to *U. europaeus*, and makes a good plant for a dry sunny bank.

UMBELLULARIA (Lauraceae—Bay Laurel Family)

A genus of a single species.

Species. *Umbellularia californica.* It is known as the Californian bay tree; also *Oreodaphne californica*, Balm of Heaven and Mountain laurel. In its native state it will attain a height of 30 m (100 ft) in mountainous ravines. It has dark-green lance-shaped leaves which emit a powerful, camphor smell when bruised, so, powerful that it has been known to bring about dizziness. Dr Palmer, in the *American Journal of Pharmacy* for December 1878, said that 'by rubbing the hands and face for a short time with the leaves, a severe headache will be produced . . .' At a meeting of the Philadelphia College of Pharmacy held in 1875, Dr Heaney stated that all parts of the tree abounded in volatile oil which he named oreodaphnol when oxygenated and which produced the same effects as described by Dr Palmer.

The tree is hardy in the British Isles only south of the Thames and in favourable districts in western Scotland and southern Ireland, where it may attain a height of about 6 m (20 ft) in a sheltered, sunny situation and in a well-drained sandy soil.

V

VACCINIUM (Vacciniaceae—Cranberry Family)

A genus of about 100 or more species which flourish in a moist, peaty soil and in partial shade. The genus was given the name by Virgil, to denote a small plant bearing black berries for the genus includes the Bilberry, Huckleberry and Cranberry. The one bearing flowers of especially pronounced fragrance is *V. leucobotrys*, the tallest of the species, which blooms during autumn.

Species. *Vaccinium leucobotrys*. It is a native of China and is an evergreen with narrow leaves of deepest green, and will reach a height of 1.5 to 1.8 m (5 to 6 ft). It is a shade-lover and requires ample moisture about its roots. From August until late October, it bears pure-white flowers, set with bracts and which have a delicious sweet myrtle-like perfume; on a calm evening, it will scent the air for some distance. It is propagated by layering and by cuttings, removed in August and inserted in a sandy compost in a closed frame.

VALERIANA (Valerianaceae—Valerian Family)

A genus of some 300 species, the plants containing valeric acid, also present in perspiration, hence the unpleasant smell given off by the flowers and leaves of *V. officinalis* though from the roots of the Himalayan species, *V. jatamansi* (syn. *Nardostachys jatamansi*), spikenard is obtained. Their habitat extends from Britain across central Europe to the Himalayas and as far east as Sikkim, growing at anything up to 5,000 m (16,000 ft) above sea-level.

Species. *Valeriana celtica*. The Celtic nard is a perennial of the Swiss alpine regions (the country of the Celts) and was described by Dioscorides as being one of the three commercial 'nards'. It is of similar appearance to the true Spikenard though the sweetly scented roots are black and were at one time highly prized by the peoples of the Near East for aromatizing their baths; the roots were exported to Egypt and India. The essential oil has a powerful odour, resembling chamomile and patchouli.

V. dioscoridis. Native of Lycia, it is believed to be the *Valeriana Phu* of Dioscorides and is the most aromatic of all the valerians. The root consists of several fleshy tubers (like *V. tuberosa*, the Spanish nard) from which an erect stem arises to a height of 60 cm (2 ft) with lanceolate leaves and bearing flesh-coloured flowers in cymes. The whole plant, especially the root, is strongly aromatic.

V. jatamansi (syn. *Nardostachys jatamansi*). It is one of the most remarkable of all plants, for long, hidden in secrecy, for few know that it supplied the costly spikenard of Biblical times. It is the Mountain or Indian nard of Dioscorides to be found wild only in the remote valleys of the Himalayas from Kumaon to Sikkim, at a height of between 3,600 to 5,000 m (12 to 16,000 ft), and it has proved completely hardy in the British Isles. Its remoteness accounts for its rarity and only small quantities reached Arabia and Palestine, conveyed across northern India and Afghanistan into Persia and to the eastern shores of the Mediterranean. It was considered so precious by the Romans that Horace promised Virgil a *cadus* (equivalent to 50 bottles) of wine for a small onyx-box of spikenard.

It is an erect perennial herb with elongated spathulate leaves and bearing its flowers in small cymes. The woody rootstock is covered with fibres from the petioles of withered leaves and this is the part from which the drug spikenard is obtained. i.e. the hairy portion of the stem just above the root. It comes from the Himalayas as thick as a little finger, grey in colour, and is surrounded by the hairs (fibres), like the tail of a sable. The odour is 'heavy', like patchouli, and its taste is bitter and aromatic. Even when green (recently dug up), this portion of the plant is fragrant but its scent becomes more pronounced as it dries as with many roots.

V. officinalis. It is known as the Cat's valerian for cats appear to enjoy the smell of its leaves and roll about the foliage as they do about the Catmints. It is a plant which is native to the British Isles and is found in damp pastures and in damp, shady situations. It is a handsome plant, growing 90 cm (3 ft) tall with pinnately cut glaucous leaves and bearing in July and August pale-pink or white flowers in 3-forked corymbs; they have the rancid smell of stale perspiration as they begin to fade.

V. saliunca (syn. *V. supina*). A perennial to be found just beneath the snow-line of the higher alpine regions of northern Italy, it has spathulate leaves and bears in corymbs small white flowers tinted with pink which are, unusual in the genus, deliciously scented. Believed to be the *Saliunca* of Virgil, the plant grows about 10 cm (4 in) high and its root has the same sweet odour of the flowers.

V. saxatilis. A hardy perennial to be found in the Swiss Alps and in the alpine regions of Austria and northern Italy. The plant grows 15 cm (6 in) tall with shining leaves and bears corymbs of small white flowers. The root is dark grey and very sweetly scented.

VANDA (Orchidaceae—Orchid Family)

A genus of 60 species of sub-tropical plants mostl, to be found in the rain forests of eastern Asia, where they perch on the uppermost branches of trees, in search of sunshine and moisture; this is the position they should be given under cultivation. They may be grown in teak cylinders, or baskets with a base of charcoal and crocks, and topped with sphagnum-moss and osmunda fibre to form a rooting medium. Suspend from the roof of a greenhouse in a temperature of 18°C (65°F) and keep constantly moist by syringeing daily. Rooted stems can be taken off and potted in spring.

Species. *Vanda coerulea.* The Blue orchid, first seen by Dr Griffith in the Khasi Hills of Assam in 1849. It grows only near the village of Larnac, on oak trees, at an elevation of about 1,200 m (4,000 ft). The trees are small and gnarled so that the orchids have full exposure to the wind and rain, and here they bear their pale-blue tassellated flowers, about 10 cm (4 in) across, in panicles of between 4 and 20 blooms, diffusing a sweet perfume over the surrounding countryside.

V. tricolor. The whitish sepals and petals of this species are spotted with deep purple, and the lip is rose-purple. Flowers are produced in spikes of between 3 and 10 on stems 0.45 to 1.5 m ($1\frac{1}{2}$ to 5 ft) tall, in autumn and winter. It has a pervading perfume, strongly reminiscent of the English wallflower. The variety *suavin* has larger flowers with brown-purple spots, and a more deeply coloured lip. The fragrance of the variety is quite different, of cloves, and it is sometimes considered as a species.

VANILLA (Orchidaceae—Orchid Family)

A genus of 90 species of epiphytic plants native of the tropics.

Species. *Vanilla planifolia.* A perennial climbing herb of the tropical forests of South America, Mexico, and the islands of Indonesia and Madagascar. In the natural state, the plants pull themselves to the top of large trees by aerial roots in their search for sunlight, but where grown commercially their climbing is restricted. In their natural surroundings, their rootstock is as woody as the vine. The leaves are thick and fleshy and up to 22.5 cm (9 in) long whilst the greenish-yellow flowers are borne in dense inflorescences and are followed by pods 20 cm (8 in) long. From the unripened fruits (vanilla beans) and pods, vanilla extract is obtained by a process of fermentation and is much used in perfumery and in cooking to impart its particular flavour and perfume. The odoriferous principle is vanillin and the finest vanilla comes from Mexico and has a scent of greater purity than obtained from any other source.

Johnson stated that 'the fragrance of vanilla acts upon the system as a stimulant, exhilarating the mental functions, and increasing the energy of the system'. The pods were first seen in England in the late sixteenth century when John Morgan, an apothecary, showed one to Queen Elizabeth, saying that he knew not what it was except that 'it had been brought from abroad by Spanish merchants' who had found it in South America. The pods resemble runner beans and are imported in bundles of 50 or more. To obtain the perfume, they are sliced and placed in a gallon of alcohol when, after 4 to 5 weeks the scent will have been extracted. The tincture is drained off and is included in 'bouquets', also for flavouring foods. The early perfumers usually included vanilla as a complement to extract of Tonquin. Later, François Coty used it in his ever popular L'Aimant perfume, one of the all-time classic perfumes. Vanilla extract combined with that of orange-blossom will give an imitation essence of Sweet pea.

In the wild, a vanilla plant will grow as thick as a man's thigh but, when grown commercially, the offsets are continually removed and replanted. A plant will, in its fourth year, bear pods suitable for export and will continue to do so in ever-increasing quantities until 50 or more years old. The pods are gathered in autumn, just before fully ripe, and excess moisture is dried off before being exported when the outside will be covered in needle-like crystals of vanillin, a condition known to the trade as 'frosted'.

Vanillin, the synthetic which is now obtained from coal tar, was discovered in 1875 by Tiemann and Rieman who originally obtained it from fir sap or resin.

VAVAEA (Meliaceae—Mahogany Family)

A genus of about 20 species of hardwood trees, native of the islands of South-east Asia and the Pacific.

Species. *Vavaea amicorum.* It is native of the Pacific islands where it grows 12m (40 ft) tall and is to be found to an altitude of 900 m (3,000 ft), its white or pale-yellow flowers being powerfully scented; they are followed by black fruits.

VERBENA (Vervain) (Verbenaceae— Vervain Family)

A genus of about 80 species of mostly perennial plants, natives of sub-tropical America, which in Britain and northern Europe are usually treated as half-hardy annuals. The seed is sown in gentle heat early in the year and the plants set out early in June after hardening. With their attractively toothed leaves and bearing clusters of richly coloured flowers from July until October, they grow from 22.5 to 30 cm (9 to 12 in) tall and with their semi-trailing habit are delightful plants for a window-box or hanging basket as well as for massing in small beds. The colouring of the flowers is enhanced by their contrasting white eye whilst they possess a soft, sweet perfume rather like heliotrope, which they obtained from the night-scented *V. teucrioides,* a plant of semi-trailing habit which bears flowers of purest white. The scarlet *V. chamaedrifolia* also figures in the parentage of the garden hybrids but it is lacking in perfume as would be expected, likewise those hybrid varieties of similar colouring.

Species and Hybrids. *Verbena hybrida grandiflora.* The plant grows 30 cm (12 in) tall with large flower-heads which are obtainable in a number of brilliant colours. The verbena perfume is most pronounced in the pure white, Snow Queen, and in the pastel shades which have a fragrance sweet and clove-like which is unsurpassed by and unlike that of any other flower.

V. tenuisecta. It is the Moss verbena, a charming plant growing 22.5 to 25 cm (9 to 10 in) tall with attractive fern-like foliage and bearing dainty flowers of lilac-pink. For contrast, *alba* has pure-white flowers with a sweet perfume.

V. teucrioides. A native of Brazil, it is a somewhat tender plant growing 60 cm (2 ft) tall and should be treated as a half-hardy annual. It has hairy stems whilst the pinkish-white flowers, fragrant at night, are borne in terminal hairy heads during July and August.

VERONICA (Hebe) (Scrophulariaceae— Foxglove Family)

A genus of nearly 200 species varying in habit from the trailing *V. spicata,* a native plant, to *V. kirkii* which grows 3 m (10 ft) in height. Named in honour of St Veronica, most of the shrubby species are native of New Zealand and are evergreen and, though amongst the most beautiful of all plants for a coastal garden, few bear scented flowers.

There is however one species whose wood and foliage are strongly aromatic and which may be planted to the front of a shrub border or on the rockery where its leaves may be within reach to bruise.

Species. *Veronica cupressoides* (syn. *Hebe cupressoides*). It is a pretty shrub, hardy around the western coastline of England and Scotland where it makes a dainty rounded plant 45 cm (18 in) tall, its small bright-green leaves being pressed against the stems so that the whole plant resembles the cypress. It is evergreen and late in summer bears tiny violet flowers at the ends of the slender branches. No perfume is apparent in the flowers but the whole plant has the aromatic fragrance of the cedar, the rich pungent smell of a cigar box, especially pronounced in an Indian summer.

V. Midsummer Beauty. A hybrid and one of the few veronicas bearing flowers with any degree of scent. It makes a plant 90 cm (3 ft) tall and is conspicuous by the crimson-brown underside of the leaves. The lavender-mauve flowers appear in slender spikes in July and August and are sweetly scented.

VERVAIN: *see* VERBENA

VETIVERIA (Gramineae—Grass Family)

A genus of 10 species, native of tropical India, Africa and South-east Asia, and closely related to *Andropogon.*

Species. *Vetiveria zizanioides* (syn. *Andropogon muricatus*). Native of India and from its violet-scented rhizomatous root known as vetivert or kus-kus, the perfume known as Mousseline is made; the name is derived from Indian muslin with its peculiar odour as at one time it was treated with the perfume before being sent to the European markets.

In India and the East, sun-blinds are made from the roots, and when watered in the sun release the pleasing scent of violets. The roots are also used to weave into baskets which release a sweet perfume when damp.

VIBURNUM (Caprifoliaceae— Honeysuckle Family)

A genus of 120 or more species of evergreen or deciduous shrubs and trees which must be considered amongst the most beautiful of the garden. They may be divided into four groups, the fragrant winter-flowering species which are deciduous; the spring-flowering species which are also fragrant; the midsummer-flowering *V. opulus* and *V. tomentosum,* which are deciduous and have no perfume; and the summer-flowering evergreen species which bear sweetly scented flowers and which are amongst the loveliest of all plants for a shaded garden. The evergreen viburnums like a cool, moist soil, one containing plenty of leaf-mould or some other humus. They flourish in a chalk-laden soil which seems to bring out the clove-like scent of the flowers to the full.

Mr Donald Egolf, cytogeneticist at the U.S. National Arboretum, writing in the *American Horticultural Magazine* (Vol. 41, No. 3) mentions the scent of the foliage of several species, e.g. *V. sieboldii, V. cassinoides, V. dentatum* and *V. lantana,* as it falls early in autumn. 'When the leaves are crushed', he writes, 'the odour is most prevalent. Normally, the pungent odour is not observed, but on rainy or humid days it can become obnoxious ... probably due to increased decomposition and less air circulation.... The odour is seldom detectable for more than a few days of the year.'

Species and Varieties. *Viburnum bitchivense.* It is a handsome native of Japan resembling *V. carlesii* though it is of taller, or more loose habit, and comes later into bloom, It is deciduous, flowering during April and May, bearing sweetly scented pinkish-white flowers in loose heads.

V. × bodnantense. Raised by Charles Puddle at the Bodnant Gardens, North Wales, it is a hybrid of *V. fragrans* and *V. grandiflorum.* It is deciduous, growing 2.4 to 2.7 m (8 to 9 ft) tall and bears rounded clusters of fragrant pink flowers on leafless stems from November until April.

Dawn, another Bodnant hybrid of *V. fragrans,* grows tall and angular with bronzy tinted foliage and during a mild winter bears clusters of fragrant pink flowers at the end of the branches.

The cultivatar Deben, raised by R. C. Notcutt Ltd., of Woodbridge, is outstanding, being of vigorous habit with flowers of palest pink which measure 2.5 cm (1 in) across and which appear from December until April, diffusing their rich perfume about the garden.

V. buddleifolium. It has long pointed leaves, grey on the underside, like those of the Buddleia, and in May forms clusters or heads of small white flowers, followed by crimson-black berries. The plant is semi-evergreen, growing 2.1 to 2.4 m (7 to 8 ft) in height.

V. × burkwoodii. It has *V. carlesii* for a parent and is a compact but multi-branched shrub growing 1.2 to 1.5 m (4 to 5 ft) in height, its semi-evergreen leaves being glossy and ribbed, and it comes into bloom at an early age bearing its pure-white flowers in rounded clusters at the end of every stem, and they are most deliciously scented, drenching the May garden with their exotic perfume. The older leaves turn brilliant orange before they fall.

V. × carlcephalum. A hybrid of vigorous habit having *V. carlesii* for a parent, it makes a dense deciduous bush which grows as wide as it grows tall, and at the end of the shoots appear in April large heads of creamy-white, often measuring 15 cm (6 in) or more across and which are powerfully clove-scented.

V. carlesii. Native of several islands off western Korea, where it was found by William Carles in 1885, it is not as vigorous as the other viburnums nor is it so free-flowering, but it has an additional attraction in that its handsome grey foliage turns a brilliant crimson in autumn before it falls. It is then followed by white flowers,

borne in terminal cymes which have the clove scent of pinks whilst their long tubes resemble those of the Bouvardia.

Several lovely hybrid varieties raised in Ireland have a more vigorous habit than their parents, *V. carlesii* and *V. burkwoodii,* and come into bloom at a height of less than 90 cm (3 ft). Aurora is known as the Pink viburnum for its blooms are an attractive shade of shell-pink which does not fade whilst the flower retains its form. Diana is similar, but possibly better than either is Charis which has a vigour and freedom from pest attack which *V. carlesii* never possessed. Its rose-pink buds, formed the previous autumn, open to flowers of purest white and borne in dense clusters. Fulbrook and Anne Russell, both bearing larger, more refined flowers than the parents, are others which are attractively scented. All carry the aromatic clove perfume of the parent. They may be propagated from leaves inserted into sandy compost under glass.

V. cylindricum. An interesting Chinese species growing 3 m (10 ft) in height but which retains its neat shape throughout its life. It has handsome grey leaves, long and pointed and with wavy edges which are sticky to the touch, and in July it bears cylindrical white flowers which have striking purple anthers and they are sweetly scented.

V. davidii. A native of China, it is an evergreen with oblong pointed leaves 15 cm (6 in) long which are so deeply ribbed as to give the appearance of being held together in sections of four. The small scented flowers, borne in terminal cymes, are of purest white, males on one plant, females on another, and so as to have its exquisite berries of shining turquoise-blue it is necessary to plant both sexes.

V. erubescens. Native of the Himalayas and central China, it grows 3 to 3.6 m (10 to 12 ft) tall and should receive some protection from cold winds; it will then amply reward one with its handsome foliage and drooping panicles of deliciously scented pinkish-white flowers, borne in July and August. The leaves have crimson petioles which contrast with the brilliant green.

V. foetidum. An evergreen native of Kashmir, it is one of the less well known viburnums for it is less free-flowering. The blooms appear between October and March, each twig carrying a pure-white posy of waxy-white scented blossoms borne in a cluster 5 cm (2 in) long. The scent is delicious from a distance, but overpowering when inhaled near-to. It is, however, from the unpleasant odour of its foliage when crushed that its name is derived.

V. fragrans (syn. *V. farreri*). Introduced into Britain from China in 1914 by Reginald Farrer who discovered it in the hills to the south of Shihor, it is a deciduous shrub of upright habit with chocolate-brown wood and lance-shaped leaves of richest green. Discovered at an altitude of 1,500 m (5,000 ft) it is perfectly hardy and is a strong grower. It will eventually reach a height of 3 m (10 ft) and, when established, the bush is studded from November through winter with tiny pinkish-white flowers borne on short spurs in panicles and which diffuse a sweet and cloying perfume of heliotrope. However, unlike the Witch hazel and the Wintersweet, it is not suitable for cutting as the flowers soon fall. In the open they are followed by sparkling red fruits which hang like rubies from the branches. The plant needs pruning like an apple or pear tree, shortening the branches each year of the newly formed wood, otherwise it will bear little blossom.

V. henryi. A Chinese species growing 3 m (10 ft) in height with large evergreen leaves which are oblong and glossy. In June, it bears wide heads of purest white flowers which have a sweet fragrance, and these are followed by enormous bunches of crimson fruits which later turn jet-black.

V. japonicum. A native of Japan and suitable only for a warm garden, it resembles *V. davidii* with its large glossy ribbed leaves of brilliant green, and in May and June bears large flat heads of white flowers which have a jonquil-like perfume. The flowers are followed by scarlet berries.

V. × juddii. Raised in 1920 by William Judd, chief propagator at the Arnold Arboretum, it begins to bear its neat heads of blush-white flowers towards the end of March, and so may justifiably be included with the winter-flowering forms. Like *V. carlesii*, which appears in its parentage, it is slow-growing, making a bushy plant well clothed in grey-green foliage, whilst the flowers carry the same carnation-like perfume as *V. carlesii*.

V. odoratissimum. Native of Malaya, it is evergreen and in the British Isles and northern Europe requires a warm sheltered garden where it will grow into a large majestic bush with handsome glossy leaves. Late in summer it bears its sweetly scented pure-white flowers in generous panicles.

VICTORIA (Nymphaeaceae—Water-lily Family)

A genus of two species, the first of which was discovered in the waters of the Mamore River, a tributary of the Amazon, in 1800 by the German botanist Haenke. It was named *Victoria regia* by Dr Lindley of Kew in honour of the British queen.

Species. *Victoria regia*. It is known as the Queen's Water-lily and reached Britain in 1837. Being native of the Amazon it requires warm greenhouse culture, a minimum temperature of 27°C (82°F). A plant may be seen at the Royal Botanic Gardens at Kew, but it is not for the small greenhouse for its leaves are of the height of an average man in diameter and are kept afloat by an upturned edge some 30 cm (12 in) high which prevents their being submerged. On the underside, the leaves are armed with spines. The blooms are also large, being about double the size of those of *N. odorata grandiflora* and with a powerful heavy perfume. It begins to flower early in August, each flower opening on two consecutive nights. On the first it is pure white with a delicious fruity perfume, like ripe plums; on the second night the pink inner petals appear when the bloom begins to lose its scent. In its native land it is pollinated by large beetles, attracted by its fruity scent. During the flowering season, a single plant may be expected to produce between 30 to 40 flowers and they are pollinated by the insect transferring the pollen from a flower which opens on its second night to that of a flower opening on its first night.

VIOLA (Violaceae—Violet Family)

Included in this genus of about 400 species of annual or perennial herbs are many which must be numbered amongst the most delightful of all plants to be found growing wild and in the garden. Plants of this family are mostly of the temperate regions of the Northern Hemisphere, growing across North America and northern Europe from the British Isles (16 species) to the Urals, inhabiting countries with a cool climate, for with but one or two exceptions they are intolerant of hot, dry conditions. Even where growing under cold conditions the plants will seek the coolness and moisture of the hedgerows and woodlands and crevices between rocks, for they must have moisture in abundance at their roots in addition to cool conditions during summer.

Many of the species of Viola are of tufted or creeping habit, the dainty flowers being held above the foliage on thin wiry stems. The flowers are hermaphrodite, with 5 sepals, elongated into a spur. Petals and stamens are also 5 in number. In their native haunts the plants remain comparatively inconspicuous, requiring careful search and for this reason are all the more appreciated. They also possess the charming habit of blooming at the most unexpected times, generally when there is little other bloom in the countryside and garden. The flowers are cleistogamic, i.e. the first to appear do not set seed. Seed is set by the smaller blooms which appear later and are apetalous. They are not scented and are self-pollinating, whilst the plants bury their own seed-capsules. The earlier flowers are visited by insects, drawn by the sweet perfume in their search for nectar which is stored in the spur formed by the front or lower petal.

Most important of all the species is *Viola odorata*, the Sweet violet, which long before the birth of Christ was in cultivation, one might even say in commercial cultivation, for the blooms were used by the ancient Greeks for sweetening purposes, and the plant was so highly regarded that it became the symbol of ancient Athens. In France a vast quantity of blooms are grown each year, as it has been from earliest times, not only for sale as posy bunches, but for the perfume industry, and the violet has always been held in reverence there. It was cultivated during medieval times in England, as the blooms were cooked with food for sweetening as

an alternative to honey. Both meat and game were sweetened, and the violet was much in demand for this purpose. In the library of Trinity College, Cambridge, is a fifteenth-century treatise on gardening written in rhyme by one, 'Mayster Jon, Gardener', in which several flowers then in cultivation are mentioned:

Peruynke, violet, cowslyppe and lyly ...
Holyhocks, coryawnder, pyony.

All were used either for flavouring or for medicinal purposes.

Species and Varieties. *Viola blanda.* Native of North America, it has a creeping rootstock and heart-shaped leaves, slightly downy. The flowers are white with the side petals veined with purple and with a short spur. They have a soft sweet perfume.

V. cornuta. Known as the Alpine or Horned violet of the Pyrenees, it was introduced into England in 1776 and was used in the breeding of the garden viola and the violettas. A fibrous rooted plant of short, tufted habit with heart-shaped toothed leaves, it blooms from May until August, the pale-blue flowers having a long, awl-shaped spur. There is also a white form, *alba*, and both bear sweetly scented flowers especially in the evening when they are visited for their pollination by nocturnal Lepidoptera.

Using the tufted *V. cornuta* as the seed-bearing parent and by crossing this with a pansy called Blue King, Dr Stuart of Chairnside, Berwickshire, obtained a strain of rayless violas which he called Violettas. The plants have the same tufty habit as *V. cornuta*, yet the blooms are larger, being longer in shape, quite rayless and possessing a delicious fragrance, like that of vanilla.

In *Pansies and Violas*, published in 1892 by Messrs Dobbie and Co., appeared in Dr Stuart's own words a short account of his hybridizing, which is worth quoting. 'In 1874, I took pollen from pansy, Blue King, a bedding variety then in fashion, and applied it to *V. cornuta*. There was a podful of seed which produced twelve plants and which were all blue in colour, but with a good tufted habit. I then took pollen from a pink pansy and fertilised the flowers of the first cross. The seed from this cross gave more variety of colour and the same tufted habit [of *V. cornuta*]. The best were sent to the R.H.S. for trials at Chiswick. After being in the ground for some time, I received a letter from a member of the Floral Committee inquiring how they had been raised as they were all different in habit from all other violas sent for trial. I heard no more until the autumn of 1875 and was surprised when informed that I had received six First Class Certificates.

'It was, however, ten years before I succeeded in finding a really rayless viola. In Queen Victoria's Jubilee Year whilst walking round a seed bed, I found what I had for long been seeking—a pure white rayless self. It was a warm night and the perfume from the blooms attracted my attention. The plant was pulled to pieces and every bit propagated.'

A box of bloom was sent to William Robinson, editor of *The Garden*, who at once recognized a new strain. It was given the name of Violetta and quickly became a favourite in the cottage garden. It was Robinson who wrote in *The English Flower Garden*, 'No family has given our gardens anything more precious'. Almost a century later, the same may be said of it and yet it is known to few gardeners.

D. B. Crane continued with violettas where Dr Stuart had left off towards the end of the century, and amongst his finest introductions were Diana, with its lovely clear primrose-yellow blooms; Eileen, pale blue with a gold eye; and the blue and white Winifred Phillips. Though more long-flowering than any of the pansies and violas, and being of more perennial habit, it is surprising that these charming plants have never become as popular as the ordinary bedding violas. They come into bloom in April, with the primroses, and continue until the frosts, the dainty flowers hovering like butterflies about the neat dark-green foliage. On a year-old plant, as many as 56 blooms have been counted at one time. Also, with their fibrous roots and tufted habit, the plants present no difficulty in their propagation, being lifted and divided in March like any other herbaceous plant, whilst they are extremely long-lasting. Above all is their delicious vanilla perfume, like that of *Laburnum alpinum*, but richer, almost like sweet peas.

Varieties of Violetta:

ADMIRATION. The larger than usual flowers are a rich shade of purple-violet.

BABY GRANDE. The oval-shaped blooms are an attractive pale crimson-pink colour.

BLUE CARPET. The small blooms are a brilliant blue.

BUTTERCUP. One of the loveliest of all the violettas, the oval blooms being a rich butter-yellow.

COMPACTUM. One of the best, the pale-lavender blooms having a conspicuous yellow eye.

DAWN. Lovely for planting with Iden Gem or Jersey Gem, for the blooms are a pale primrose-yellow.

DUCHESS. A lovely variety, the cream-coloured blooms being margined with lavender-blue.

GERTRUDE JEKYLL. Now rarely seen, but a lovely bicolour with the upper petals pale primrose, and the lower ones golden-yellow.

HEATHER BELL. An outstanding variety bearing a bloom of rich mauve-pink.

IDEN GEM. The very dark blue flowers are held on long stems.

JERSEY GEM. Also known as Blue Gem. The dainty flowers are of a deep aniline blue colour.

LA GRANDEUR. The blooms, which are rather larger than usual, are a lovely shade of mid-blue.

LITTLE DAVID. The cream-coloured blooms held well above the foliage possess the rich fragrance of freesias.

LORNA. A beautiful variety, the bloom being a lovely shade of deep lavender-blue.

LYRIC. An original variety, the pale-lilac blooms being attractively marbled with lavender-mauve.

MAUVE QUEEN. The flowers are a reddish-violet borne in profusion.

MRS GRIMSHAW. A recent introduction, bearing blooms of a lovely shade of rose-pink.

PAPILIO. The blooms are of violet-blue shading to white at the edges.

PERFECTION. The dainty blooms are a delicate clear sky-blue.

PRINCESS MAY. The blooms are a unique shade of bluish white.

QUEEN OF THE YEAR. A beautiful

variety bearing small blooms of a lovely shade of China blue.

TOM TIT. Of more recent introduction; the blooms are a clear purple-blue, held well above the foliage.

TOTTIE. The pale-mauve blooms are heavily striped with a deeper shade of mauve.

VIOLETTA. The original hybrid and still obtainable. The blooms are white suffused yellow on the lower petals, and are produced over a long period.

V. odorata. The Sweet violet, it is distributed from the British Isles, across northern and southern Europe to the Himalayas and northern Asia. It has a short rootstock with long runners, whilst the leaves are heart-shaped at the base with glandular stipules. The flowers are borne from January to June, depending upon the locality and are violet-blue, white or purple, the side petals with or without a tuft of hair, whilst the spur is short. Propagation is by division of the crown or by detaching the 'runners'. They should be grown in a rich soil, in partial shade, and April is the most suitable time to make a planting.

Amongst the most sweetly scented single varieties are: Coeur d'Alsace, rose-pink; John Raddenbury, China blue; Luxonne, navy-blue; Princess of Wales, violet-blue. And in double varieties, the most highly perfumed are Countess of Shaftesbury, blue with a rose-pink centre; Lady Campbell, lavender-blue; Mrs J. J. Astor, rose-pink.

V. suavis. Known as the Russian violet, it is of similar habit to *V. odorata,* increasing from rooted stolons. It has downy heart-shaped leaves and it flowers from March until May. The dainty blossoms are palest blue, at the base, and are very sweetly scented.

VIRGILIA (Leguminosae—Laburnum Family)

A small genus of tall deciduous trees, native of South Africa and named in honour of Virgil, the poet. Like *Podalyria,* all parts of the tree are covered in silky pubescence. Inhabiting hillsides and woodlands, they bloom almost throughout the year, the pink flowers being deliciously scented.

Species. *Virgilia oroboides* (syn. *V. capensis*). It forms a dense twiggy tree with leaves composed of 6 to 20 pairs of oblong leaflets, covered in silky hairs. The pink flowers are borne in dense inflorescences and they have a prominent beaked keel. They have the Sweet pea-like scent of the family.

VITEX (Verbenaceae—Vervain Family)

A genus of smooth, hairy or downy shrubs or trees with deciduous palmate leaves, downy on the underside. Of some 60 species, only one, *Vitex agnus-castus,* has attained garden stature but several species native of India and Ceylon have valuable scented properties.

Species. *Vitex agnus-castus.* It was known as the Chaste Tree for its seeds were, during earliest times, taken to prevent sexual desire in the human male. It is to be found close to the sea around the Mediterranean where it will attain a height of 3.6 to 4.5 m (12 to 15 ft) but reaches only about 3 m (10 ft) in the British Isles where it should be given the protection of a warm wall and should be planted only in gardens enjoying a favourable climate. The handsome leaves are composed of 5 to 7 tapering leaflets and it blooms in August and September, forming spikes of pale-lilac flowers, deliciously scented and appearing at the end of the branches. It will ripen its fruits only in its natural surroundings and they are fleshy and crimson-red in colour, whilst the seeds have a pungent lemony perfume when dry.

V. incisa. It is a native of India, growing to a height of about 3 m (10 ft) and is less hardy than *V. agnus-castus.* It has the same palm-shaped leaves and bears spikes of deep-purple flowers which have a most pronounced musk-like perfume.

V. trifolia. A variable shrub of India and Ceylon, the branches and the leaves being covered in white down. When growing close to the sea, it is trifoliate with short petioles. Inland, the leaf petioles are longer and the whole plant takes on a more delicate appearance. The odour of the leaves, which contain an essential oil and a resin, is similar to that of the Sweet gale whilst the black berries which follow the blue flowers are also aromatic.

VITIS (Ornamental Vine)
(Vitaceae—Vine Family)

A genus of more than 200 species of ornamental climbing plants amongst which are included the self-clinging Ampelopsis. All are noted for the brilliant autumnal tints of their leaves which they take on before they fall. Making rapid growth and being completely hardy the ornamental vines are valuable for growing against a trellis for all bear edible purple-black fruits after flowering in summer. The flowers of several species are attractively scented of mignonette. The plants grow best in a rich, moist soil.

Species. *Vitis aestivalis.* Known as the North American Summer Grape, it has heart-shaped leaves, woolly on the underside, and it bears sweetly scented creamy-white flowers during May and June which are followed in autumn by small black grapes.

V. cordifolia. A vigorous North American climber, it is known as the Winter Grape or Frost Berry for the blue-black fruits which follow the sweetly scented flowers are hard and acidy until they have been frosted. It is most successful where lime rubble has been incorporated in the soil.

V. labrusca. The Plum or Fox Grape of North America which has round lobed leaves, rusty on the underside. The flowers have the characteristic mignonette scent and are followed by large purple-black grapes which have a musky aroma when eaten.

V. riparia. The Riverbank Grape of North America, it has broadly lobed leaves and bears flowers which are powerfully scented of mignonette followed by blue-black berries.

V. vinifera. The Grape vine, common in all temperate regions of the world since earliest times for seeds have been found in the tombs of ancient Egypt, and from the juice of the fruit wine has been made by civilized people everywhere. It is a deciduous woody plant which climbs by tendrils. It has 3 to 5 lobed leaves almost 15 cm (6 in) wide and 15 cm long and bears racemes of small greenish-white flowers opposite the leaf stalks. They are intensely fragrant whilst the berries (grapes) yield wines of rich bouquet.

V. vulpina. A handsome North American species with shiny dark-green leaves and sweetly scented white flowers, whilst the purple fruits have a powerful musky flavour.

W

WALLFLOWER: *see* **CHEIRANTHUS**

WATSONIA (Iridaceae—Iris Family)

A genus of corm-bearing plants, native of South Africa where they are known as the Southern Bugle lilies and were named in honour of Dr Watson, an apothecary of England. Distinguished from *Gladiolus* only by the division of their stigmas, they are found on mountainous slopes and few have scented flowers for they mostly bear scarlet flowers, pollinated by birds. In the British Isles and northern Europe, in all but the most sheltered gardens, the corms need lifting each autumn and replanting in April. They should be given a sandy soil and an open, sunny position. But as they resent disturbance, a better method is to plant the corms in pans to be wintered under glass and planted in beds (in the pans) just as beginning to make new growth.

Species. *Watsonia marginata*. To be found on mountainous slopes of south-western Cape Province, it is the finest form and the most fragrant. In its native haunts, it will attain a height of 1.5 m (5 ft) and has large basal leaves with brownish-yellow margins. The flowers are borne in dense spikes and are of pale magenta-mauve with a sweet perfume.

WEBERA (Chinchonaceae—Chinchona Family)

Closely related to *Rondeletia*, the Weberas are to be found about the hills of the Deccan Peninsula, in Assam and the Malayan Archipelago, growing like the rondeletias, usually about rocky formations and attaining tree-like proportions.

Species. *Webera fragrans* (syn. *Rondeletia lucida*). It is the most vigorous of the species, native of Singapore and Borneo where it will attain a height of 15 to 18 m (50 to 60 ft). The pale-brown leaves are about 15 cm (6 in) long, narrowing at the petiole, and it bears white flowers of exotic perfume.

W. odorata. It is native of the hills of Assam and of Penang where it makes a dense shrub, 1.5 m (5 ft) tall and has leaves 20 to 22.5 cm (8 to 9 in) long. The flowers are large, of purest white, and are borne in large panicles. They are powerfully fragrant.

WEIGELA (Caprifoliaceae—Honeysuckle Family)

A genus of handsome flowering shrubs known from the shape of the flowers as the Bush Honeysuckles. Like all members of the family they are tolerant of lime but prefer a deep loam for they are moisture lovers. They are also tolerant of partial shade and grow well in a town garden. They are amongst the easiest and most satisfactory of all shrubs but only few bear scented blossom and these are species and varieties bearing white or cream-coloured flowers. Those bearing flowers of carmine-pink and crimson-red are devoid of scent. Propagation is from cuttings of the half-ripened wood or by layering, and the vigour and shape of the plants are maintained by cutting out some of the old wood each year in the autumn.

Species and Varieties. *Weigela hortensis nivea*. A native of Japan, growing 1.5 m (5 ft) in height with broad pointed leaves of palest green.

It closely follows *W. praecox* into bloom,

continuing to flower until the garden hybrids bloom in July. The large white flowers have a soft sweet perfume.

Hybrid varieties of *W. hortensis nivea:*

BUISSON FLEUR. It resembles *W. praecox* in almost all respects except its flowering time though it is the earliest of the hybrids to bloom. The soft rose-pink blossoms have a broad yellow stripe and a honeysuckle perfume.

MONT BLANC. A beautiful variety, coming into bloom towards the end of June, its large pure-white flowers having a powerful honey fragrance.

W. praecox. The earliest of the weigelas to flower, coming into bloom early in May, its pale rose-pink flowers having attractive yellow markings in the throat and diffusing the familiar rich honey-scent of most of the family. A native of Korea, it grows 1.5 to 1.8 m (5 to 6 ft) tall and the same across, and is deciduous.

WILMATTEA (Cactaceae—Cactus Family)

A genus of a single species.

Species. *Wilmattea irridiflora.* It is native of the tropical forests of Guatemala. An epiphytic plant, it climbs to a distance of 6 to 9 m (20 to 30 ft) and has dark-green slender stems. The flowers are nocturnal and are small, with a short tube and reddish-green outer petals and narrower inner petals of purest white. They are sweetly scented.

WISTARIA (Leguminosae—Laburnum Family)

A genus of 10 species, it was introduced into Britain from China in 1816 by Captain Wellbank as *Glycine sinensis* and first flowered in the garden of Charles Turner, near Godstone in Surrey. Later, the plant was renamed by the botanist Nuttall in honour of the American botanist, Charles Wistar. It was known as the Grape-flower vine, being a high-climbing deciduous shrub of considerable hardiness, flourishing in all soil types anywhere in the British Isles. The pea-like flowers are borne in drooping terminal recemes, like the laburnum and have a similar perfume.

Wistarias enjoy a deeply worked soil of well-drained loam and they should be given a sunny position, preferably facing west. They may be grown against a wall both upwards and horizontally so that a large wall will be entirely covered.

To bring the plants to the fullness of their beauty it is necessary to keep them well watered and syringed throughout their first summer, after planting from pots in April, otherwise if the weather is dry they may have difficulty in breaking into growth, and whilst it is usual to allow the new stems to run on without restriction to cover the wall as quickly as possible, this is a mistake for unless encouraged to form spurs, the plant will bear no blossom. During summer, the new shoots should be pinched back to the third leaf and it is from the axils of the leaves that the racemes form. Winter pruning should consist of cutting back all shoots to within 7.5 cm (3 in) of the old wood. This is done in February, before the plant begins to grow again. The shoots should be entwined or fastened against stout wires or against a trellis firmly fixed to the wall for a mature plant in full leaf will be extremely heavy to support.

Species and Varieties. *Wistaria floribunda.* It is a native of Japan, bearing short racemes of violet-blue. The form *macrobotys,* previously known as *W. multijunga,* is finer in all respects, bearing its lilac and blue flowers in racemes 90 cm (3 ft) in length and with a powerful vanilla scent, whilst *alba* also bears long elegant racemes with a delicious perfume.

W. macrostachya. It is native of the U.S.A. and is a species of vigorous habit with pinnate leaves divided into 9 leaflets, and in May and June bears crowded racemes of soft lilac-blue of ten 30 cm (12 in) long. The flowers have a delicate perfume.

W. sinensis. This is the finest form, bearing drooping racemes often up to 30 cm (12 in) long and of a lovely clear mauve colour. Whilst *W. floribunda* may be more free-flowering, no wistaria can equal the perfumed flowers of *W. sinensis,* the Chinese wistaria, which have a pleasant vanilla scent. The white form *alba* was the first wistaria introduced and though now rarely to be seen, is even more beautiful and more heavily scented. The flowers are produced in May and June, shortly after the appearance of the foliage, bronzy-green when young.

W. venusta. A native of Japan, it too has delicately scented flowers which are larger than those of *W. sinensis* and are of purest white, appearing during May and June. There is also a variety, *violacea,* which bears scented purple flowers and which provides a striking contrast to the white form.

X

XIMENIA (Oleaceae—Olive Tree Family)
A genus of 4 or 5 species named in honour of Ximenes, a Spanish monk who published four important books on the flora of South America. The small trees are covered in spines and the leaves are alternate, ovate or lanceolate, with the flowers borne in short racemes.

Species. *Ximenia aegyptiaca* (syn. *Balanites aegyptiaca*). It is a native of Egypt and parts of tropical eastern Africa whilst a sub-species has been found on the plains of Deccan where it grows 6 m (20 ft) tall and is armed with spines. Pliny said that it was one of the ingredients of the celebrated spikenard ointment, though which part contributed he did not say. Both the wood and the flowers are deliciously scented.

X. americana. It is to be found in India, Ceylon and Malaya, and in tropical Africa and America where it makes a small tree 4.5 m (15 ft) tall with spreading branches covered in red bark, and often ending in a spine. The greenish-white flowers, yellow on the inside, are borne in axillary racemes and are powerfully scented. The wood is also fragrant, like sandalwood for which it is used as a substitute in western India.

X. elliptica. Native of Fiji and of other South Sea Islands, the branches being completely without spines. The leaves are elliptical whilst the flowers are produced in great quantity and are followed by large round orange fruits which have the odour and taste of bitter almonds.

X. inermis. Native only of Jamaica, it is also free of spines whilst the small greenish-yellow flowers possess a penetrating perfume.

Y

YUCCA (Agavaceae—Agave Family)

Native of the southern United States and Mexico where it is known as the Palm Lily, the yuccas are perennial plants, bearing at the top of a tall woody stem sharply pointed sword-like leaves, whilst the large drooping bell-shaped flowers of greenish white are borne in racemes. They are scented most heavily at night when fully open, and are pollinated by the moth *Pronuba yuccasella*. The female first collects the pollen from one flower then lays her eggs in another, in the ovary of the flower through a hole drilled in the side. After each egg has been laid, the moth collects pollen from the anthers and with her tongue presses it into the stigma opening. In this ingenious way, development of larva and seed are complementary. The young insect eats its way out of the pericarp and falls to the ground where it winters in its cocoon, emerging as a moth just when the yuccas are in bloom again in June.

Yuccas flourish in a rich loamy soil and will survive a winter in the British Isles and central Europe if given shelter from cold winds and if planted in a mild locality, and they will remain pleasantly green throughout the year. They are increased by dividing the basal tufts in autumn.

Species. *Yucca aloifolia.* Native of the West Indies and of North Carolina, it sends up its slender stems to a height of about 4.5 m (15 ft), its long glaucous-tinted leaves having a white edge. Its snow-white flowers are borne in huge panicles often 60 m (2 ft) in length and are powerfully fragrant at night. The form *purpurea* has purple-tinted foliage.

Y. angustifolia. Native of Missouri, it produces multitudes of sharply pointed leaves 60 cm (2 ft) in length, and early in summer bears its greenish-white flowers in 30 cm (12 in) racemes at the end of a 90 cm (3 ft) scape.

Y. glauca. A North American species and the hardiest. It bears tufts of sword-like leaves 45 cm (18 in) long, which are edged with brown and above which are borne the white bell-shaped flowers in dense panicles 60 to 90 cm (2 to 3 ft) long. The scent of the flowers is most pronounced at night.

Y. gloriosa. Native of the southern United States, it grows to a height of 1.8 (6 ft) or more with branched stems. The 60 to 90 cm (2 to 3 ft) leaves of glaucous green appear in rosettes and are retained through winter, whilst the greenish-white bell-shaped flowers are borne in panicles often 1.5 m (5 ft) in length.

Z

ZALUZIANSKYA (Nycterinia)
(Scrophulariaceae—Foxglove Family)

A genus of 35 species, native of South Africa and known as the Night Phloxes. They were named after Adam Zaluzianskya, a famous physician of Prague in the early seventeenth century.

Species. *Zaluzianskya capensis.* The Night Phlox, an annual which should be given the usual half-hardy treatment in Britain. The plants, which grow to a height 30 cm (12 in) come into bloom early in July, the phlox-like flowers being white, shaded with purple-brown on the reverse side, and at night emit a delicious scent.

Z. villosa. It requires similar culture to *Z. capensis* and grows to a height of 22.5 to 25 cm (9 to 10 in). Though its white flowers, with their orange centre, remain open by day, only at night do they emit their deliciously aromatic fragrance. The flowering time is July and August.

ZANTHOXYLUM (Rutaceae—Rue Family)

A genus of about 80 species, mostly native of North America, which are smooth or downy trees or shrubs, with or without spines. The leaves are alternate, usually 3-foliate. The flowers are borne in axillary cymes. The species described below are hardy and easily grown.

Species. *Zanthoxylum americanum.* Native of north-eastern America, where it is known as the Toothache Tree, for a distillation of the dried bark will cure an aching tooth. It is a small, deciduous tree, growing 6 m (20 ft) tall, its stems being covered in stiff spines. The alternate leaves are up to 20 cm (8 in) long, and emit a delicious, resinous, orange-like perfume when bruised. The small, pale-yellow flowers, borne in clusters from the leaf axils, are also fragrant, likewise the black fleshy fruits and the shiny oblong seeds.

Z. piperitum. The Pepper Tree of Japan where its aromatic seeds are used as a substitute for pepper. It makes a low tree 2.7 to 3 m (9 to 10 ft) tall, and it bears green flowers followed by red fruits early in summer. The glossy leaves are amongst the most powerfully aromatic of all leaves when crushed, leaving behind a pungent smell on the hands.

Z. simulans. A tall Chinese shrub or small tree, growing to a height of 3 to 3.6 m (10 to 12 ft), and has prickly branches and glossy compound leaves which are strongly aromatic. The small white flowers are followed by brilliant-scarlet fruits in autumn.

ZATARIA (Labiatae—Lavender Family)

A genus of a single species.

Species. *Zataria scabra.* It is a small shrubby plant found only on the hills near Muscat in Arabia. It is similar in appearance to thyme, with rounded leaves, leathery to the touch and being no more than 0.5 cm ($\frac{1}{4}$ in) long. When magnified the leaves are seen to have a moss-like surface, thickly pitted all over, and in each pit is a granule of red, resinous oil. The flowers are borne in knotted clusters upon a slender spike and the whole plant diffuses a delicious lemon-like fragrance in the warmth of the Arabian sun. An infusion of the dried leaves forms a pleasant aromatic stimulant which is much in demand in the East.

ZELKOVA (Ulmaceae—Elm Family)

A genus of several species of hardy deciduous trees to be seen in few gardens of the British Isles, though magnificent specimens of *Z. crenata* grow at Kew and at Oxford.

Species. *Zelkova crenata.* It makes a large tree up to 30 m (100 ft) in height and is a native of the Caucasus. It is closely related to our native elm and is indeed known as the Siberian elm and has the same toothed and veined leaves, oval in shape. In May it bears its powerfully fragrant flowers of greenish-white in clusters at the upper leaf axils and their scent may be enjoyed to a considerable distance, like that of the lime-tree in bloom, a heavy sweet scent similar to the flowers of the Hop.

ZENOBIA (Ericaceae—Heather Family)

Native of the southern United States, it is a genus of a single species.

Species. *Zenobia speciosus.* It is a glaucous shrub growing 0.9 to 1.2 m (3 to 4 ft) tall and blooming early in summer, when several planted together present a delightful picture. Propagation is by layering in autumn. It is deciduous with long leathery leaves. The drooping white urn-shaped flowers, like those of the lily of the valley, have a delicious honey-like scent. The form *pulverulenta* is perhaps superior to the type. It has rounded glaucous leaves and bears large heads composed of tiny pure-white urns which have a more pronounced honey perfume.

ZEPHYRANTHES (Amaryllidaceae—Narcissus Family)

A genus of bulbous plants with narrow leaves, the Zephyr flowers are native of the West Indies and of Cuba, though *Zephyranthes atamasco*, the Atamasco lily, is to be found in the swampy woodlands of Florida and the damp pasturelands of Virginia, but it has no perfume. Some 34 species make up the genus, but few have scent, and equally few are hardy in British gardens. The hardiest and best form is *Z. candida* but here again, it has no perfume. Increase is by offset, planted between August and November, or by seed.

Species. *Zephyranthes tubispatha.* This native of the West Indies (Jamaica) and of Cuba is a most handsome plant, and the only one of the genus to bloom in summer, the others flowering in autumn. It will flourish in a sunny border if given the protection of ashes or sand during winter, or it makes a most appealing pot plant in the cool greenhouse. The solitary flowers are borne from April to June on a hollow scape about 22 cm (9 in) long, and issuing from a spathe-like bract. The flowers are funnel-shaped and pure white with a soft, sweet fragrance. One bulb is put in a 15-cm (6-in) pot, 5 cm (2 in) deep, with little water until growth starts. The compost should be well drained. After flowering no water is given until the plant is repotted in the autumn.

ZINGIBER (Ginger) (Zingiberaceae—Ginger Family)

A genus of tropical plants, the product ginger having been a favourite commodity of the Romans who introduced it into Britain and it was a common ingredient in Anglo-Saxon recipes. Russell in his *Book of Nurture* mentioned several kinds and it was then widely grown in England under hot-bed cultivation. Gerard reported that he tried to grow it, but without success. The rhizome-like roots were known as a 'race'.

Species. *Zingiber officinalis.* Well known for the pungency of its roots, it is a plant of the tropics and is a particularly valuable crop in Jamaica, China, and in Queensland. The roots take almost twelve months to develop from the time they are planted in March, an average yield being some 4,000 lb per acre. The rhizomes are washed and scraped and allowed to dry in the open, the resulting product being known as white ginger. The roots are covered in numerous projecting fibres embedded in a mealy tissue which give it a horny appearance. The best Jamaican ginger cuts white inside and will yield about 1.5 per cent of essential oil which, like the root itself, has a powerful aromatic smell and taste which often 'catches' the breath when inhaled. Essence of ginger is a valuable product of aerated waters.

ZIZIPHORA (Labiatae—Lavender Family)

A small genus of almost prostrate woody plants, native of south-eastern Europe and the Near East. Possibly the 'wild thyme' of the Greeks. They are half-hardy and do best in a well-drained soil. Increase is by cuttings.

Species. *Ziziphora mariana* (syn. *Cunila mariana*). Known in the United States as the Common dittany, and is especially prolific in the hills around New York, where it grows about 30 cm (1 ft) tall, and has small, narrow, thyme-like leaves. Like the thyme, the plant bears small, tubular, lilac flowers.

Z. serpyllacea. It is native of the Caucasus and of south-eastern Europe, resembling *Thymus serpyllum* in its habit. The leaves have a sweeter scent than those of *Z. tenuior,* for which it is known as the Sweet-scented ziziphora.

Z. tenuior. A plant native of Persia and Afghanistan, where it is sold in the markets as *Rang*. It is a small shrubby plant resembling thyme and grows 5 to 7 cm (2 to 3 in) tall. The woody stems branch from the ground and are square, being thickly studded with opposite, linear leaves which have prominent veins on each side of the midrib. They bear purple flowers in short spikes. The entire plant gives off a refreshing peppermint odour, and has a similar taste when the leaves are diffused.

ZYLOPIA (Anonaceae—Anona Family)

A genus of some 40 species of trees or shrubs indigenous to Brazil and the warmer parts of South America and the West Indies, whilst several species are native of West Africa, Ceylon and Malaya. It takes its name from two Greek words meaning 'bitter wood', whilst several species are remarkable for the aromatic properties of their fruit and seed.

Species. *Zylopia ferruginea.* Native of Malacca and the Malayan Peninsula, it grows 1.8 m (6 ft) tall with leaves 15 cm (6 in) long, glabrous and shining on the upper side, glaucous beneath with a rust-like pubescence on the veins. The pale-yellow pendulous flowers are sweetly scented and are followed by aromatic seeds.

Z. frutescens. Native of Brazil and Guyana where the seeds, full of a fragrant oil, are much in demand by natives for all purposes. It grows 1.8 m (6 ft) tall, the oblong-lanceolate leaves having a silky undersurface. The leaves, wood and seeds are sweetly aromatic, much like the juniper, whilst the flowers are deliciously scented too.

Z. glabra. It is native of Barbados and Jamaica where it makes a tree 12 m (40 ft) tall with large smooth oblong leaves and it has many uses. The wood yields a bitter tonic whilst it is used to make furniture for no insects will attack it, though carpenters who work the wood are troubled by a bitter taste in the mouth and throat. The seeds are also bitter but with an agreeable flavour, like that of orange seeds, and they are much sought after by wild pigeons: they impart their particular aroma to the birds' flesh, making them a great delicacy in restaurants.

APPENDIX A

Trees and Shrubs
with Scented Flowers

Plant	Family	Scent	Habitat
Abelia chinensis	Caprifoliaceae	Vanilla	C. China
Abelia floribunda	Caprifoliaceae	Soft	Mexico
Abelia serrata	Caprifoliaceae	Spicy	C. China
Abelia triflora	Caprifoliaceae	Vanilla	W. China
Acacia drummondii	Leguminosae	Sweet	Australasia
Acacia baileyana	Leguminosae	Violet	Australasia
Acacia dealbata	Leguminosae	Violet	Australasia
Acacia farnesiana	Leguminosae	Violet	Australasia
Acacia armata	Leguminosae	Sweet	Australasia
Acacia longifolia	Leguminosae	Violet	Australasia
Aesculus flava	Sapindaceae	Slight	N. America
Aesculus hippocastanum	Sapindaceae	Honey	S. Europe
Aesculus parviflora	Sapindaceae	Honey	S. Europe
Aglaia odorata	Meliaceae	Vanilla	W. China, Malaya
Amoora decandra	Meliaceae	Vanilla	W. China, Malaya
Araujia albens	Asclepiadaceae	Lily	Brazil
Arbutus andrachne	Ericaceae	Honey	Greece, Crete
Arbutus menziesii	Ericaceae	Honey	California
Arbutus unedo	Ericaceae	Honey	Greece, Turkey
Aromadendron elegans	Magnoliaceae	Clove	Java
Bignonia chelonoides	Bignoniaceae	Sweet	India
Bignonia quadrilocularis	Bignoniaceae	Sweet	India
Bignonia suaveolens	Bignoniaceae	Sweet	India
Bignonia suberosa	Bignoniaceae	Sweet	Burma. Malaya
Bignonia xylocarpa	Bignoniaceae	Sweet	India
Boldoa fragrans	Nyctaginaceae	Aromatic	Chile
Boronia megastigma	Rutaceae	Verbena	Australia
Boronia pinnata	Rutaceae	Balsamic	Australia
Boronia serrulata	Rutaceae	Lemon	Australia
Boswellia serrata	Burseraceae	Lemon	Arabia
Bouvardia candidissima	Rubiaceae	Sweet	Mexico
Bouvardia flava	Rubiaceae	Primrose	Mexico
Bouvardia jasminiflora	Rubiaceae	Heavy	Mexico
Brachyglottis rangiora	Compositae	Heavy	New Zealand
Brachyglottis repanda	Compositae	Mignonette	New Zealand
Cassia corymbosa	Leguminosae	Vanilla	Argentine
Cassia fistulosa	Leguminosae	Vanilla	Syria
Castanea sativa	Fagaceae	Hawthorn	S.E. Europe
Castanopsis delavayi	Fagaceae	Hawthorn	S.E. Asia

Plant	Family	Scent	Habitat
Catalpa bignonioides	Bignoniaceae	Sweet	N. America
Catalpa kaempferi	Bignoniaceae	Sweet	Japan
Citrus aurantium	Rutaceae	Sweet	S. Europe
Citrus bigarradia	Rutaceae	Orange	S. Europe
Citrus ichangense	Rutaceae	Heavy	S.W. China
Citrus japonica	Rutaceae	Heavy	Japan
Citrus limon	Rutaceae	Heavy	S. Europe
Citrus limonia mayeri	Rutaceae	Jonquil	China
Citrus maxima	Rutaceae	Sweet	S. Europe
Citrus medica	Rutaceae	Orange	S. China
Citrus nobilis	Rutaceae	Pineapple	S. China
Citrus taitensis	Rutaceae	Orange	S. China
Citrus trifoliata	Rutaceae	Orange	Japan
Cladrastis amurensis	Leguminosae	Vanilla	N. China
Cladrastis tinctoria	Leguminosae	Vanilla	N. China
Cordyline australis	Liliaceae	Sweet	New Zealand
Crataegus carrierri	Rosaceae	Balsamic	N. America
Crataegus crus-galli	Rosaceae	Sweet/Fishy	N. America
Crataegus flava	Rosaceae	Sweet	N. America
Crataegus orientalis	Rosaceae	Sweet	Levant
Crataegus oxyacantha	Rosaceae	Balsamic/Fishy	British Isles
Cupia corymbosa	Chinchonaceae	Seductive	Ceylon
Cupia cymosa	Chinchonaceae	Sweet	Borneo
Cupia scandens	Chinchonaceae	Lily-like	Silpet
Cupia thyrsoides	Chinchonaceae	Sweet	Deccan Peninsula
Datura suaveolens	Solanaceae	Lily	Mexico
Dipelta floribunda	Caprifoliaceae	Honey	W. China
Dipelta yunnanensis	Caprifoliaceae	Honey	Yunnan
Drimys winteri	Magnoliaceae	Jasmine	S. America
Ehretia dicksonii	Boraginaceae	Spicy	China, Korea
Ehretia thyrsiflora	Boraginaceae	Sweet	China, Korea
Elaegnus angustifolia	Elaeagnaceae	Orange	S.E. Europe
Eleagnus argentea	Elaeagnaceae	Orange	N. America
Franklinia altamana	Theaceae	Sweet	N. America
Fraxinus ornus	Oleaceae	Sweet	Lebanon
Galipea cusparia	Rutaceae	Balsamic	Venezuela
Gardenia arborea	Rubiaceae	Orange	East Indies
Gardenia calyculata	Rubiaceae	Sweet	S. India
Gardenia carinata	Rubiaceae	Sweet	Penang
Gardenia citriodora	Rubiaceae	Orange	Natal
Gardenia clusloefolia	Rubiaceae	Hyacinth	Bahamas
Gardenia coronaria	Rubiaceae	Balsam	Chittagong
Gardenia devoniana	Rubiaceae	Jasmine	Sierra Leone
Gardenia grandiflora	Rubiaceae	Orange	Indo-China
Gardenia gummifera	Rubiaceae	Balsam	Ceylon
Gardenia jasminoides	Rubiaceae	Jasmine	China
Gardenia latifolia	Rubiaceae	Orange	East Indies
Gardenia lucida	Rubiaceae	Sweet	Luzon
Gardenia montana	Rubiaceae	Spicy	E. Indies
Gardenia radicans	Rubiaceae	Jonquil	S.E. China
Gardenia rothmannia	Rubiaceae	Exotic	Cape Province
Gardenia stanleyana	Rubiaceae	Jonquil	Sierra Leone

Plant	Family	Scent	Habitat
Gardenia thunbergii	Rubiaceae	Orange	Manilla
Gardenia tomentosa	Rubiaceae	Sweet	Java
Gleditschia macrantha	Leguminosae	Vanilla	China
Gleditschia sinensis	Leguminosae	Vanilla	China
Gleditschia triacanthos	Leguminosae	Sweet	N. America
Halesia carolina	Styracaceae	Sweet	N. America
Halesia hispida	Styracaceae	Slight	Japan
Halesia monticola	Styracaceae	Sweet	N. America
Halesia tetraptera	Styracaceae	Slight	N. America
Helichrysum antennarium	Compositae	Hawthorn	Australia
Helichrysum elatum	Compositae	Sweet	New South Wales
Helichrysum italicum	Compositae	Hawthorn	Australasia
Hopea odorata	Dipterocarpaceae	Jasmine	Chittagong
Idesia polycarpa	Flacourtiaceae	Lily	Isle of Kiusiu
Jonesia asoca	Leguminosae	Vanilla	India, Burma
Laburnum alpinum	Leguminosae	Vanilla	Scotland
Laburnum vossii	Leguminosae	Freesia	Hybrid
Leycesteria formosa	Caprifoliaceae	Sweet	Himalayas
Lindleya mespiloides	Rosaceae	Sweet	Mexico
Lonicera angustifolia	Caprifoliaceae	Honey	Himalayas
Lonicera spinosa	Caprifoliaceae	Sweet	Turkestan
Lonicera syringantha	Caprifoliaceae	Honey	N. China
Lonicera webbiana	Caprifoliaceae	Honey	Colombia
Malaleuca riridifolia	Myrtaceae	Sweet	S.E. Asia
Malus coronaria	Rosaceae	Sweet	N. America
Malus hupehensis	Rosaceae	Sweet	N. America
Mauritia carnara	Palmaceae	Mignonette	S. America
Melia azedarach	Meliaceae	Sweet	Himalayas
Meliosma beaniana	Sabiaceae	Hawthorn	S.W. China, Burma
Meliosma cuneifolia	Sabiaceae	Aniseed	Burma
Meliosma myriantha	Sabiaceae	Honey	S. Japan, Korea
Meliosma veitchiorum	Sabiaceae	Honeysuckle	S.W. China, Burma
Michelia champaca	Magnoliaceae	Lily	C. India
Monodora myristica	Anonaceae	Jasmine	Zaire
Murrya exotica	Rutaceae	Jonquil	China, India
Murrya paniculata	Rutaceae	Jasmine	Indonesia
Myrtus communis	Myrtaceae	Sweet	Mediterranean
Myrtus lechleriana	Myrtaceae	Sweet	Chile
Myrtus luma	Myrtaceae	Sweet	Chile
Myrtus obcordata	Myrtaceae	Sweet	New Zealand
Ocotea amara	Lauraceae	Sassafras	Brazil
Olearia albida	Compositae	Soft	Tasmania, New Zealand
Olearia gunni	Compositae	Musky	Tasmania
Olearia haastii	Compositae	Hawthorn	New Zealand
Olearia ilicifolia	Compositae	Musky	Tasmania, New Zealand
Olearia insignis	Compositae	Pungent	New Zealand
Olearia macrodonta	Compositae	Honey	Tasmania, New Zealand
Olearia moschata	Compositae	Musky	New Zealand
Olearia myrsinoides	Compositae	Resinous	Tasmania
Osyris alba	Santalaceae	Honey	Middle East, China
Pandanus odoratissimus	Pandanaceae	Lily	India, East Indies
Pasania	Fagaceae	Hawthorn	S.E. Asia

Plant	Family	Scent	Habitat
Pavetta caffra	Rubiaceae	Orange	South Africa
Paulownia fragesii	Scrophulariaceae	Sweet	China
Paulownia tomentosa	Scrophulariaceae	Sweet	Japan
Petteria ramentacea	Leguminosae	Vanilla	S.E. Europe
Photinia arbutifolia	Rosaceae	Hawthorn	N. America
Photinia surrulata	Rosaceae	Sweet	China
Photinia villosa	Rosaceae	Hawthorn	N. America
Plumeria acutifolia	Apocynaceae	Vanilla	C. America, China
Plumeria alba	Apocynaceae	Jasmine	Puerto Rico
Plumeria pudica	Apocynaceae	Vanilla	C. America
Plumeria purpurea	Apocynaceae	Jasmine	Peru
Plumeria rubra	Apocynaceae	Jasmine	C. America
Prunus angustifolius	Rosaceae	Fruity	N. America
Prunus emarginata	Rosaceae	Honey	Japan
Prunus ilicifolia	Rosaceae	Sweet	California
Prunus ivensii	Rosaceae	Sweet	Hybrid
Prunus koyima	Rosaceae	Sweet	Japan
Prunus lannesiana	Rosaceae	Almond	Japan
Prunus laurocerasus	Rosaceae	Lily	S.E. Europe
Prunus lusitanica	Rosaceae	Sweet	Portugal
Prunus luteo pleno	Rosaceae	Mossy	N. America
Prunus mume	Rosaceae	Sweet	China
Prunus yedoensis	Rosaceae	Almond	Japan
Psidium guaviroba aromaticum	Myrtaceae	Balsam	Guyana
Ptelea trifoliata	Rutaceae	Hops	N. America
Pterocarpus erinaceus	Leguminosae	Cowslip	Angola
Pterostyrax lispidum	Styracaceae	Sweet	S.E. China, Japan
Randia armata	Chinchonaceae	Hyacinth	Martinique
Randia capitata	Chinchonaceae	Freesias	Mexico
Randia exaltata	Chinchonaceae	Hyacinth	Andaman Isles
Randia fasciculata	Chinchonaceae	Hyacinth	Nepal
Randia fragrans	Chinchonaceae	Jonquil	Ceylon
Randia longiflora	Chinchonaceae	Hyacinth	India
Randia macrophylla	Chinchonaceae	Hyacinth	Malacca
Randia nutans	Chinchonaceae	Hyacinth	East Indies
Randia tetrasperma	Chinchonaceae	Hyacinth	Kashmir
Randia uliginosa	Chinchonaceae	Hyacinth	East Indies
Raphiolepsis ovata	Rosaceae	Honey	Japan
Robinia hartwigii	Leguminosae	Slight	N. America
Robinia luxurians	Leguminosae	Jonquil	N. America
Robinia pseudo-acacia	Leguminosae	Vanilla	N. America
Rondeletia discolor	Rubiaceae	Sweet	New Granada
Rondeletia disperma	Rubiaceae	Sweet	Brazil
Rondeletia exerta	Rubiaceae	Aromatic	Nepal
Rondeletia odorata	Rubiaceae	Orange	Mexico, Havana
Sambucus canadensis	Caprifoliaceae	Muscatel	N. America
Sambucus ebulus	Caprifoliaceae	Fur-like	Denmark
Sambucus nigra	Caprifoliaceae	Musk	British Isles
Sambucus racemosa	Caprifoliaceae	Sweet	N. America
Sassafras officinale	Lauraceae	Sassafras	USA, Canada
Schinus molle	Anacardiaceae	Slight	Peru

Plant	Family	Scent	Habitat
Sorbus asplenifolia	Rosaceae	Hawthorn	British Isles
Sorbus essertaneana	Rosaceae	Hawthorn	British Isles
Stranvaesia glaucescens	Rosaceae	Hawthorn	W. China
Stranvaesia salicifolia	Rosaceae	Hawthorn	W. China
Talauma candallii	Magnoliaceae	Sweet	Java
Talauma lanigera	Magnoliaceae	Lily	E. India
Talauma plumiera	Magnoliaceae	Lily	Martinique
Temus moschata	Magnoliaceae	Musk	Chile
Tilia corallina	Tiliaceae	Honey	N. America, Europe
Tilia euchlara	Tiliaceae	Sweet	N. America, Europe
Tilia fomentosum	Tiliaceae	Honey	N. America, Europe
Viburnum bitchivense	Caprifoliaceae	Sweet	Japan
Viburnum bodnantense	Caprifoliaceae	Sweet	Hybrid
Viburnum buddleifolium	Caprifoliaceae	Honey	C. China
Viburnum burkwoodii	Caprifoliaceae	Sweet	Hybrid
Viburnum carlcephalum	Caprifoliaceae	Clove	Hybrid
Viburnum carlesii	Caprifoliaceae	Clove	W. Korea
Viburnum cylindricum	Caprifoliaceae	Sweet	China
Viburnum davidii	Caprifoliaceae	Sweet	China
Viburnum erubescens	Caprifoliaceae	Sweet	Himalayas, C. China
Viburnum foetidum	Caprifoliaceae	Jonquil	Kashmir
Viburnum fragrans	Caprifoliaceae	Heliotrope	W. China
Viburnum henryi	Caprifoliaceae	Sweet	China
Viburnum japonicum	Caprifoliaceae	Jonquil	Japan
Viburnum juddii	Caprifoliaceae	Clove	Hybrid
Vitex agnus-castus	Verbenaceae	Sweet	Mediterranean
Vitex incisa	Verbenaceae	Musk	India
Webera fragrans	Chinchonaceae	Exotic	Singapore, Borneo
Webera odorata	Chinchonaceae	Seductive	Assam, Penang
Weigela hortensis nivea	Caprifoliaceae	Honey	Japan
Weigela praecox	Caprifoliaceae	Honey	Korea
Ximenia americana	Oleaceae	Sandalwood	Ceylon, Malaya
Ximenia inermis	Oleaceae	Piercing	Jamaica
Zelkova crenata	Urticaceae	Sweet	Caucasus

APPENDIX B

Trees and Shrubs
with Scented Leaves

Plant	Family	Scent	Habitat
Abies amorika	Pinaceae	Resinous	C. Europe
Abies balsamea	Pinaceae	Balsam	N. America
Abies bracteata	Pinaceae	Resinous	California
Abies grandis	Pinaceae	Orange	N. America
Amyris punctata	Lauraceae	Sassafras	Chittagong
Artemisia abrotanum	Compositae	Lemon	S. Europe
Artemisia absinthium	Compositae	Pungent	N. Europe
Artemisia argentea	Compositae	Aromatic	Madeira
Artemisia dracunculus	Compositae	Aromatic	W. Asia
Atherosperma moschata	Athero-spermataceae	Nutmeg	Chile
Barosma crenulata	Rutaceae	Musk	S. Africa
Barosma serratifolia	Rutaceae	Musk	S. Africa
Betula lenta	Betulaceae	Balsamic	E. USA
Boldoa fragrans	Nyctaginaceae	Resinous	Chile
Boswellia serrata	Burseraceae	Lemon	Arabia
Brachyglottis rangiora	Compositae	Balsamic	N. Zealand
Bupleurum fruticosum	Umbelliferae	Pungent	Spain
Buxus sempervirens	Buxaceae	Pungent	British Isles
Buxus suffruticosa	Buxaceae	Pungent	British Isles
Buxus elegantissima	Buxaceae	Pungent	British Isles
Callitris quadrivalis	Cupressaceae	Cedarwood	Australasia
Calycanthus floridus	Calycanthaceae	Apples	USA
Camphorosma monspeliaca	Chenopodiaceae	Camphor	S. Europe
Canella alba	Canellaceae	Musk	Florida/Cuba
Carya alba	Juglandaceae	Resinous	E. USA
Carya armara	Juglandaceae	Resinous	E. USA
Carya tomentosa	Juglandaceae	Resinous	E. USA
Cedrus atlantica	Pinaceae	Resinous	N. Africa
Cedrus deodara	Pinaceae	Resinous	Himalayas
Cedrus libani	Pinaceae	Resinous	Syria, Lebanon
Chamaecyparis lawsoniana	Cupressaceae	Pungent	California
Cinnamomum glanduliferum	Lauraceae	Cinnamon	S.E. China
Cinnamomum zeylonicum	Lauraceae	Cinnamon	Ceylon
Comptonia asplenifolia	Myricaceae	Cinnamon	N. America
Comptonia paniculata	Myricaceae	Cinnamon	N. America
Cunninghamia lanceolata	Taxodiaceae	Resinous	China
Cupressus arizonica	Cupressaceae	Resinous	N. America
Cupressus leylandii	Cupressaceae	Resinous	Hybrid

Plant	Family	Scent	Habitat
Cupressus nootkatensis	Cupressaceae	Resinous	N. America
Cupressus sempervirens	Cupressaceae	Resinous	C. Europe
Doryphora sassafras	Athero-spermataceae	Balsamic	Australia
Drimys aromatica	Magnoliaceae	Resinous	Tasmania
Drimys winteri	Magnoliaceae	Resinous	S. America
Escallonia illunita	Saxifragaceae	Pungent	Chile
Escallonia viscosa	Saxifragaceae	Pungent	Chile
Eucalyptus alba	Myrtaceae	Balsamic	Australia
Eucalyptus cneorifolia	Myrtaceae	Eucalyptus	Australia
Eucalyptus coccifera	Myrtaceae	Eucalyptus	Australia
Eucalyptus dumosa	Myrtaceae	Eucalyptus	Australia
Eucalyptus globosus	Myrtaceae	Balsamic	Australia
Eurybia argophylla	Compositae	Musk	Tasmania
Galipea aromatica	Rutaceae	Resinous	Guyana
Galipea cusparia	Rutaceae	Orange	Venezuela
Galipea ossana	Rutaceae	Orange	Cuba
Gardenia arborea	Rubiaceae	Aromatic	East Indies
Gaultheria cuneata	Ericaceae	Wintergreen	N. America
Gaultheria fragrantissima	Ericaceae	Camphor	N. India
Gaultheria nummulariodes	Ericaceae	Cedar	N. India
Gaultheria procumbens	Ericaceae	Wintergreen	N. America
Gaultheria trichophylla	Ericaceae	Aromatic	Himalayas
Gaylussaca baccata	Vacciniaceae	Resinous	N. America
Illicium floridanum	Magnoliaceae	Aniseed	Florida
Illicium griffithii	Magnoliaceae	Tarragon	E. Bengal
Illicium majus	Magnoliaceae	Nutmeg	Malaya
Illicium parviflorum	Magnoliaceae	Bergamot	Florida
Illicium religiosum	Magnoliaceae	Nutmeg	Japan
Juglans cinerea	Juglandaceae	Resinous	N. America
Juglans nigra	Juglandaceae	Resinous	N. America
Juglans regia	Juglandaceae	Resinous	Persia
Juniperus cannarti	Cupressaceae	Resinous	S. Europe
Juniperus communis	Cupressaceae	Resinous	Ireland
Juniperus sabina	Cupressaceae	Resinous	S. Europe
Juniperus thurifera	Cupressaceae	Incense	S. Europe
Juniperus virginiana	Cupressaceae	Incense	N. America
Larix europea	Pinaceae	Mossy	N. Europe
Larix leptolepsis	Pinaceae	Mossy	N. America
Laurelia novae-zelandiae	Monimiaceae	Aromatic	New Zealand
Laurelia sempervirens	Monimiaceae	Aromatic	Chile
Laurelia serrata	Monimiaceae	Aromatic	Chile
Laurus benzoin	Lauraceae	Wintergreen	N. America
Laurus nobilis	Lauraceae	Bay	S. Europe
Ledum glandulosum	Ericaceae	Resinous	N. America
Ledum latifolium	Ericaceae	Resinous	Greenland
Ledum minus	Ericaceae	Resinous	Japan
Ledum palustre	Ericaceae	Resinous	Arctic zone
Leptospermum ericoides	Myrtaceae	Aromatic	New Zealand
Leptospermum scoparium	Myrtaceae	Aromatic	New Zealand
Libocedrus decurrens	Cupressaceae	Incense	Hybrid
Lindera benzoin	Lauraceae	Lavender	N. America

Plant	Family	Scent	Habitat
Lippia citriodora	Verbenaceae	Lemon	Chile
Liquidambar orientalis	Hamamelidaceae	Balsamic	Levant
Liquidambar styraciflua	Hamamelidaceae	Balsamic	N. America
Magnolia salicifolia	Magnoliaceae	Lemon	Japan
Mespilodaphne pretiosa	Lauraceae	Cinnamon	Brazil
Myoporum latum	Myoporaceae	Resinous	New Zealand
Myrica californica	Myricaceae	Balsam	N. America
Myrica caroliniensis	Myricaceae	Lemon	N. America
Myrica gale	Myricaceae	Resinous	British Isles
Myrica cerifera	Myricaceae	Resinous	Canada
Myristica fragrans	Myristicaceae	Nutmeg	Indonesia
Nectandra cymbarum	Lauraceae	Aromatic	Brazil
Nectandra puchury major	Lauraceae	Aromatic	Brazil
Ocotea amara	Lauraceae	Balsamic	Brazil
Olearia macrodonta	Compositae	Musk	Australasia
Olearia moschata	Compositae	Musk	New Zealand
Olearia solandri	Compositae	Musk	New Zealand
Osmites dentata	Compositae	Aromatic	S. Africa
Osmitopsis astericoides	Compositae	Aromatic	S. Africa
Phellodendron amurense	Rutaceae	Musky-orange	Manchuria
Phellodendron chinense	Rutaceae	Musky-orange	China
Phellodendron sachalinense	Rutaceae	Musky-orange	Korea
Picea breweriana	Pinaceae	Resinous	N. America
Picea excelsa	Pinaceae	Musky	Norway
Picea glauca	Pinaceae	Resinous	N. America
Picea orientalis	Pinaceae	Resinous	Japan
Picea pungens	Pinaceae	Resinous	N. America
Picea sitchensis	Pinaceae	Resinous	N. America
Pinus insignis	Pinaceae	Resinous	S. Europe
Pinus montana	Pinaceae	Resinous	C. Europe
Pinus nigra	Pinaceae	Resinous	Corsica
Pinus pinaster	Pinaceae	Resinous	S. Europe
Pinus pinea	Pinaceae	Resinous	S. Europe
Pinus strobus	Pinaceae	Resinous	N. America
Pinus sylvestris	Pinaceae	Resinous	British Isles
Pittosporum eugenioides	Pittosporaceae	Lemon	New Zealand
Podocarpus andinus	Podocarpaceae	Resinous	Chile
Populus alba	Salicaceae	Resinous	C. Europe, British Isles
Populus balsamifera	Salicaceae	Balsamic	N. America
Populus candicans	Salicaceae	Balsamic	N. America
Populus nigra	Salicaceae	Balsamic	S. Europe, British Isles
Populus simonii fastigiata	Salicaceae	Balsamic	C. China
Populus trichocarpa	Salicaceae	Balsamic	C. China, N. America
Primula luteola	Primulaceae	Apple	Caucasus
Ptelea polyadenia	Rutaceae	Musky-orange	S. America
Ptelea trifoliata	Rutaceae	Hops	N. America
Pterocarya fraxinifolia	Juglandaceae	Resinous	Caucasus
Pterocarya japonica	Juglandaceae	Resinous	Japan
Pterocarya stenoptera	Juglandaceae	Resinous	China
Relhania genistaefolia	Compositae	Resinous	S. Africa
Rhododendron cephalanthum	Ericaceae	Bay	Tibet
Rhododendron desquamatum	Ericaceae	Aromatic	Tibet

Plant	Family	Scent	Habitat
Rhododendron glaucophyllum	Ericaceae	Aromatic	Sikkim
Rhododendron hippophaeoides	Ericaceae	Aromatic	Sikkim
Rhododendron kotschyi	Ericaceae	Sweet	Sikkim
Rhododendron rubiginosum	Ericaceae	Lemon	Sikkim
Rhododendron saluenense	Ericaceae	Aromatic	Nepal
Rhododendron sargentianum	Ericaceae	Aromatic	Burma
Rhus aromatica	Anacardiaceae	Aromatic	N. America
Rhus coriaria	Anacardiaceae	Aromatic	S. Europe
Rhus cotinoides	Anacardiaceae	Aromatic	USA
Rhus trichocarpa	Anacardiaceae	Resinous	Japan
Salix pentandra	Salicaceae	Aromatic	N. temperate zone
Santolina incana	Compositae	Pungent	S. Europe
Santolina neapolitana	Compositae	Pungent	S. Europe
Santolina serratifolia	Compositae	Pungent	S. Europe
Sassafras officinale	Lauraceae	Balsamic	N. America
Schizandra chinensis	Magnoliaceae	Aromatic	S.E. China
Schizandra propinqua sinensis	Magnoliaceae	Aromatic	Himalayas
Symplocos tinctoria	Styracaceae	Sweet	S. USA
Tarchonanthus camphoratus	Compositae	Camphor	S. Africa
Temus moschata	Magnoliaceae	Nutmeg/Musk	Chile
Thuya chilensis	Cupressaceae	Apples	Chile
Thuya occidentalis	Cupressaceae	Resinous	N. America
Thuya plicata	Cupressaceae	Resinous	N. America
Torreya californica	Taxaceae	Resinous	USA
Torreya taxifolia	Taxaceae	Resinous	USA
Tsuga canadensis	Pinaceae	Unpleasant	N. America
Umbellularia californica	Lauraceae	Camphor	N. America
Vaccinium hispidulum	Vacciniaceae	Aromatic	N. America
Zanthoxylum americanum	Rutaceae	Aromatic	N. America
Zanthoxylum piperitum	Rutaceae	Pepper	Japan
Zanthoxylum simulans	Rutaceae	Aromatic	China

APPENDIX C

Trees and Shrubs
with Aromatic Bark

Plant	Family	Scent	Habitat
Atherosperma moschata	Athero-spermataceae	Musk	Chile
Baeckea camphorosma	Myrtaceae	Camphor	Australia
Beilschmiedia obtusifolia	Lauraceae	Balsamic	Australia
Betula alba	Betulaceae	Balsamic	N. Europe
Betula lenta	Betulaceae	Wintergreen	E. USA
Bigonia chelanoides	Bignoniaceae	Slight	India
Boldoa fragrans	Nyctaginaceae	Sweet Gale	Chile
Boronia megastigma	Rutaceae	Lemon	W. Australia
Calycanthus floridus	Calycanthaceae	Cinnamon	USA
Camphorosma monspeliaca	Chenopodiaceae	Camphor	S. Europe
Canella alba	Canellaceae	Cinnamon	Florida, Cuba
Carya alba	Juglandaceae	Resinous	E. USA
Carya armara	Juglandaceae	Resinous	E. USA
Carya microcarpa	Juglandaceae	Resinous	E. USA
Carya tomentosa	Juglandaceae	Resinous	E. USA
Chloranthus inconspicuus	Chloranthaceae	Aromatic	China, Japan
Chloranthus officinalis	Chloranthaceae	Aromatic	Java
Chloranthus elatior	Chloranthaceae	Aromatic	China, Korea
Chloranthus serratus	Chloranthaceae	Aromatic	Japan
Cinnamodendron axillare	Canellaceae	Cinnamon	Brazil
Cinnamodendron corticosum	Canellaceae	Cinnamon	Jamaica
Cinnamomum glanduliferum	Lauraceae	Cinnamon	S.E. China
Cinnamomum zeylonicum	Lauraceae	Cinnamon	Ceylon
Clerodendron inerme	Verbenaceae	Apple	India, Ceylon
Coleonema album	Rutaceae	Orange	S. Africa
Croton eleutheria	Euphorbiaceae	Balsamic	Bahamas
Davidia involucrata	Davidiaceae	Incense	China
Dicypellium caryophyllatum	Lauraceae	Clove	Guyana
Doryphora sassafras	Athero-spermataceae	Balsamic	Australia
Drimys aromatica	Magnoliaceae	Aromatic	Tasmania
Drimys winteri	Magnoliaceae	Aromatic	S. America
Dryobalanops aromatica	Dipterocarpaceae	Camphor	China
Eriostemon buxifolius	Rutaceae	Resinous	New South Wales
Eriostemon myoporoides	Rutaceae	Resinous	New South Wales
Eriostemon neriifolius	Rutaceae	Resinous	New South Wales
Eucalyptus globosus	Myrtaceae	Balsamic	Australia
Evodia hortensis	Rutaceae	Orange	India

Plant	Family	Scent	Habitat
Evodia drupacea	Rutaceae	Orange	India
Galipea aromatica	Rutaceae	Resinous	Guyana
Galipea cusparia	Rutaceae	Orange	Venezuela
Galipea ossana	Rutaceae	Orange	Cuba
Gardenia arborea	Rubiaceae	Aromatic	East Indies
Gardenia corinata	Rubiaceae	Resinous	Penang
Gardenia latifolia	Rubiaceae	Balsam	East Indies
Gardenia rothmannia	Rubiaceae	Spice	Cape Province
Gardenia tomentosa	Rubiaceae	Resinous	Java
Geonoma pumila	Palmaceae	Violet	Brazil
Guarea trichilioides	Meliaceae	Musk	Caribbean
Hopea odorata	Dipterocarpaceae	Resinous	Chittagong
Illicium parviflorum	Magnoliaceae	Cinnamon	S.E. USA
Illicium religiosum	Magnoliaceae	Cinnamon	Japan
Juglans regia	Juglandaceae	Resinous	S.E. Europe
Juglans cinerea	Juglandaceae	Resinous	N. America
Limnophila gratioloides	Scrophulariaceae	Camphor/Lemon	India
Lindera benzoin	Lauraceae	Wintergreen	N. America
Lindera sericea	Lauraceae	Balsamic	Japan
Liquidambar orientalis	Hamamelidaceae	Resinous	Turkey
Liquidambar styraciflua	Hamamelidaceae	Balsamic	N. America
Litsea calicaris	Lauraceae	Aromatic	New Zealand
Magnolia soulangeana	Magnoliaceae	Lemon	Hybrid
Magnolia glauca	Magnoliaceae	Sassafras	USA
Melia azedarach	Meliaceae	Musk	India, China
Melicope ternata	Rutaceae	Orange	New Zealand
Mespilodaphne pretiosa	Lauraceae	Bergamot	Brazil
Nectandra cymbarum	Lauraceae	Aromatic	Brazil
Nectandra puchury major	Lauraceae	Aromatic	Brazil
Oenanthe fistulosa	Umbelliferae	Wine	N. Europe
Pavetta bourbonica	Rubiaceae	Aromatic	Isle of Bourbon
Pavetta indica	Rubiaceae	Aromatic	India
Pistacia lentiscus	Anacardiaceae	Benzoin	Chios
Pistacia terebinthus	Anacardiaceae	Turpentine	Cyprus
Pittosporum eugenioides	Pittosporaceae	Lemon	New Zealand
Prostanthera lasianthos	Labiatae	Mint	Australia
Prostanthera rotundifolia	Labiatae	Mint	Australia
Psidium arach	Myrtaceae	Balm	Guyana
Psidium fluviatile	Myrtaceae	Balm	Cayenne
Psidium grandiflorum	Myrtaceae	Balm	Brazil
Psidium guaviroba aromaticum	Myrtaceae	Balm	Guyana
Pterocarya fraxinifolia	Juglandaceae	Resinous	Caucasus
Pterocarya japonica	Juglandaceae	Resinous	Japan
Pterocarya stenoptera	Juglandaceae	Resinous	S.E. China
Sassafras officinale	Lauraceae	Aromatic	E. USA, Canada
Styrax officinalis	Styracaceae	Incense-like	S. Europe
Vitrex trifolia	Verbenaceae	Resinous	India
Ximenia americana	Oleaceae	Sandalwood	Ceylon, Malaya
Ximenia elliptica	Oleaceae	Rosemary	Fiji

APPENDIX D

Shrubs bearing Scented Flowers
for an Acid Soil

Plant	Family	Scent	Habitat
Azalea (Rhododendron) arborescens	Ericaceae	Sweet	N. America
Azalea atlanticum	Ericaceae	Lily	N. America
Azalea canadense	Ericaceae	Sweet	N. America
Azalea canescens	Ericaceae	Honeysuckle	N. America
Azalea linearifolium	Ericaceae	Slight	Japan
Azalea luteum	Ericaceae	Sweet	Caucasus
Azalea occidentale	Ericaceae	Sweet	California
Azalea roseum	Ericaceae	Spicy	N. America
Azalea viscosum	Ericaceae	Sweet	N. America
Bruckenthalia spiculifolia	Ericaceae	Honey	N. America, S.E. Europe
Calycanthus floridus	Calycanthaceae	Ripe apples	N. America
Calycanthus glaucus	Calycanthaceae	Slight	N. America
Calycanthus laevigatus	Calycanthaceae	Slight	N. America
Cephalanthus occidentalis	Rubiaceae	Hay-like	N. America
Clethra acuminata	Clethraceae	Cloying	S. USA
Clethra alnifolia	Clethraceae	Sweet	E. USA
Clethra arborea	Clethraceae	Lily of Valley	Madeira
Clethra canescens	Clethraceae	Lily of Valley	China
Clethra delavayi	Clethraceae	Lily of Valley	W. China
Clethra fargesii	Clethraceae	Lily of Valley	C. China
Comptonia paniculata	Myricaceae	Lily	N. America
Comptonia tomentosa	Myricaceae	Lily	N. America
Cyathodes colensii	Epacridaceae	Sweet	New Zealand
Diapensia lapponica	Diapensiaceae	Soft	Lapland
Enkianthus campanulatus	Ericaceae	Sweet	Japan
Enkianthus perulatus	Ericaceae	Jonquil	Japan
Epigaea asiatica	Ericaceae	Sweet	Japan
Epigaea repens	Ericaceae	Spicy	N. America
Erica arborea	Ericaceae	Honey	S. Europe
Erica bowieana	Ericaceae	Sweet	S. Europe
Erica denticulata	Ericaceae	Honeysuckle	S. Africa
Erica fragrans	Ericaceae	Honey	S. Europe
Erica mediterranea	Ericaceae	Sweet	S. Europe, S. Ireland
Erica odorata	Ericaceae	Honeysuckle	S. Europe
Erica veitchii	Ericaceae	Sweet	Hybrid
Eucryphia glutinosa	Eucryphiaceae	Soft	Chile
Eucryphia lucida	Eucryphiaceae	Honey	Tasmania
Gaultheria cuneata	Ericaceae	Aromatic	N. America

Plant	Family	Scent	Habitat
Gaultheria forrestii	Ericaceae	Aromatic	N. China
Gaultheria fragrantissima	Ericaceae	Lily of Valley	N. India
Gaultheria nummulariodes	Ericaceae	Aromatic	N. India
Gaultheria procumbens	Ericaceae	Aromatic	N. America
Gordonia alatamaha	Theaceae	Vanilla	N. America
Gordonia chrysandra	Theaceae	Freesia	S.E. China
Gordonia lasianthus	Theaceae	Sweet	S. USA
Halesia carolina	Styracaceae	Sweet	N. America
Hermannia fragrans	Sterculiaceae	Sweet	S. Africa
Ledum glandulosum	Ericaceae	Aromatic	N. America
Ledum latifolium	Ericaceae	Aromatic	Greenland
Leiophyllum buxifolium	Ericaceae	Sweet	New Jersey
Leucothoe acuminata	Ericaceae	Sweet	N. America
Leucothoe catesbaei	Ericaceae	Lily of Valley	N. America
Leucothoe davisiae	Ericaceae	Sweet	N. America
Luzuriaga radicans	Ericaceae	Incense-like	Chile
Lyonia paniculata	Ericaceae	Honey	N. America
Magnolia acuminata	Magnoliaceae	Sweet	N. America
Magnolia denudata	Magnoliaceae	Sweet	China
Magnolia fraseri	Magnoliaceae	Sweet	S. USA
Magnolia grandiflora	Magnoliaceae	Lemon	Mexico
Magnolia glauca	Magnoliaceae	Fruity	USA
Magnolia hypoleuca	Magnoliaceae	Heavy	Japan
Magnolia lennei	Magnoliaceae	Violet	Hybrid
Magnolia longifolia	Magnoliaceae	Violet	S. USA
Magnolia macrophylla	Magnoliaceae	Sweet	S. USA
Magnolia parviflora	Magnoliaceae	Fruity	Japan
Magnolia salicifolia	Magnoliaceae	Fruity	Japan
Magnolia sinensis	Magnoliaceae	Exotic	W. China
Magnolia soulangeana	Magnoliaceae	Heavy	Hybrid
Magnolia stellata	Magnoliaceae	Sweet	Japan
Magnolia tripetala	Magnoliaceae	Unpleasant	N. America
Magnolia watsonii	Magnoliaceae	Lemon	Japan
Magnolia wilsonii	Magnoliaceae	Freesia	Hybrid
Mahonia aquifolium	Berberidaceae	Very sweet	N. America
Mahonia haematocarpa	Berberidaceae	Very sweet	N. America
Mahonia japonica	Berberidaceae	Lily of Valley	China, Japan
Mahonia repens	Berberidaceae	Very sweet	N. America
Oxydendron arboreum	Ericaceae	Sweet ·	E. USA
Pieris floribunda	Ericaceae	Sweet	E. USA
Pieris japonica	Ericaceae	Soft	Japan
Pieris mariana	Ericaceae	Aromatic	E. USA
Pieris nitida	Ericaceae	Sweet	E. USA
Rhododendron auriculatum	Ericaceae	Fruity	C. China
Rhododendron azaleoides	Ericaceae	Very sweet	Hybrid
Rhododendron campylocarpum	Ericaceae	Sweet	Sikkim
Rhododendron cyclium	Ericaceae	Damask rose	Sikkim
Rhododendron dalhousiae	Ericaceae	Lemon	Sikkim
Rhododendron decorum	Ericaceae	Sweet	Sikkim
Rhododendron discolor	Ericaceae	Sweet	W. China
Rhododendron edgeworthii	Ericaceae	Sweet	Sikkim
Rhododendron formosum	Ericaceae	Sweet	Formosa

Plant	Family	Scent	Habitat
Rhododendron griffithianum	Ericaceae	Soft	Sikkim
Rhododendron Lady Alice Fitzwilliam	Ericaceae	Sweet	Hybrid
Rhododendron lindleyi	Ericaceae	Sweet	Burma
Rhododendron loderi	Ericaceae	Lily	Hybrid
Rhododendron megacalyx	Ericaceae	Nutmeg	Burma
Rhododendron scottianum	Ericaceae	Sweet	Himalayas
Stewartia malacodendron	Theaceae	Heavy	Florida
Stewartia serrata	Theaceae	Sweet	Japan
Stewartia sinensis	Theaceae	Sweet	Japan
Styrax americanum	Styracaceae	Sweet	S. USA
Styrax californicum	Styracaceae	Jonquil	W. USA
Styrax grandiflora	Styracaceae	Jonquil	N. America
Styrax japonica	Styracaceae	Sweet	Japan
Styrax obassia	Styracaceae	Sweet	Japan
Styrax pulverulentum	Styracaceae	Sweet	S. USA
Symplocos crataegoides	Styracaceae	Sweet	Himalayas
Symplocos japonica	Styracaceae	Sweet	Japan
Symplocos tinctoria	Styracaceae	Sweet	S. USA
Vaccinium leucobotrys	Vacciniaceae	Myrtle-like	China
Zenobia speciosus	Ericaceae	Honey	S. USA

APPENDIX E

Shrubs bearing Scented Flowers
for a Chalky or Limestone Soil

Plant	Family	Scent	Habitat
Abelia chinensis	Caprifoliaceae	Vanilla	China
Abelia triflora	Caprifoliaceae	Vanilla	W. China
Ceanothus incanus	Rhamnaceae	Orange	California
Ceanothus,			
Gloire de Versailles	Rhamnaceae	Sweet	Hybrid
Daphne alpina	Thymeleaceae	Spicy	C. Europe
Daphne arbuscula	Thymeleaceae	Spicy	C. Europe
Daphne aurantiaca	Thymeleaceae	Spicy	China
Daphne caucasica	Thymeleaceae	Spicy	Caucasus
Daphne cneorum	Thymeleaceae	Sweet	S. Europe
Daphne Somerset	Thymeleaceae	Sweet	Hybrid
Daphne collina	Thymeleaceae	Sweet	S. Italy
Daphne gnidium	Thymeleaceae	Sweet	S. Europe
Daphne oleoides	Thymeleaceae	Spicy	Himalayas
Daphne petraea	Thymeleaceae	Spicy	C. Europe
Daphne retusa	Thymeleaceae	Heavy	W. China
Daphne striata	Thymeleaceae	Heavy	C. Europe
Dipelta floribunda	Caprifoliaceae	Honey	W. China
Dipelta yunnanensis	Caprifoliaceae	Honey	W. China
Leycesteria formosa	Caprifoliaceae	Sweet	Himalayas
Ligustrum compactum	Oleaceae	Hawthorn	Japan
Ligustrum japonicum	Oleaceae	Lilac	Japan
Ligustrum ovalifolium	Oleaceae	Hawthorn	Japan
Ligustrum sinense	Oleaceae	Lilac	China
Ligustrum vulgare	Oleaceae	Lilac	British Isles
Lomatia ferruginea	Proteaceae	Honey	Chile
Lomatia fraxinifolia	Proteaceae	Sweet	Australia
Lomatia longifolia	Proteaceae	Vanilla	Chile
Lomatia obliqua	Proteaceae	Sweet	Chile
Lonicera angustifolia	Caprifoliaceae	Honey	Himalayas
Lonicera hispida	Caprifoliaceae	Honey	Himalayas
Lonicera myrtillus	Caprifoliaceae	Honey	Himalayas
Lonicera spinosa	Caprifoliaceae	Honey	Turkestan
Lonicera syringantha	Caprifoliaceae	Honey	N. China
Lonicera thibetica	Caprifoliaceae	Honey	N. China
Lonicera webbiana	Caprifoliaceae	Honey	Canada
Osmanthus aquifolium	Oleaceae	Vanilla	Japan
Osmanthus delavayi	Oleaceae	Daphne	China
Osmanthus forrestii	Oleaceae	Sweet	China

Plant	Family	Scent	Habitat
Osmanthus fragrans	Oleaceae	Heavy	China
Osmarea burkwoodii	Oleaceae	Sweet	Hybrid
Philadelphus argyrocalyx	Saxifragaceae	Jonquil	S.E. Europe
Philadelphus burfordensis	Saxifragaceae	Jonquil	S.E. Europe
Philadelphus californicus	Saxifragaceae	Jonquil	California
Philadelphus coronarius	Saxifragaceae	Jonquil	S. Europe
Philadelphus coulteri	Saxifragaceae	Jonquil	S. Europe
Philadelphus delavayi	Saxifragaceae	Jonquil	S. E. Europe
Philadelphus grandiflorus	Saxifragaceae	Jonquil	S. USA
Philadelphus lemoinei	Saxifragaceae	Jonquil	Hybrid
Philadelphus mexicanus	Saxifragaceae	Jonquil	Mexico
Philadelphus microphyllus	Saxifragaceae	Jonquil	Mexico
Philadelphus pekinensis	Saxifragaceae	Sweet	W. China
Philadelphus pubescens	Saxifragaceae	Sweet	W. China
Philadelphus satsumanus	Saxifragaceae	Sweet	Japan
Philadelphus virginalis	Saxifragaceae	Jonquil	Hybrid
Phillyrea angustifolia	Oleaceae	Piercing	S.E. Europe
Phillyrea decora	Oleaceae	Sweet	Asia Minor
Phillyrea latifolia	Oleaceae	Fruity	Asia Minor
Phillyrea media	Oleaceae	Jasmine	S. E. Europe
Pimelea longiflora	Thymeleaceae	Jonquil	New Zealand
Poncirus trifoliata	Rutaceae	Orange	China
Prunus angustifolius	Rosaceae	Fruity	USA
Prunus emarginata	Rosaceae	Honey	Japan
Prunus ilicifolia	Rosaceae	Sweet	W. USA
Prunus koyima	Rosaceae	Sweet	Japan
Prunus laurocerasus	Rosaceae	Almond	S.E. Europe
Prunus lusitanica	Rosaceae	Sweet	Portugal
Prunus mume	Rosaceae	Sweet	Japan
Prunus yedoensis	Rosaceae	Almond	Japan
Ribes fasciculatum	Grossulariaceae	Aromatic	Japan
Ribes guyanum	Grossulariaceae	Sweet	S. America
Ribes odoratum	Grossulariaceae	Clove	N. America
Romneya coulteri	Papaveraceae	Heavy	California
Skimmia fortunei	Rutaceae	Lily	China
Skimmia japonica	Rutaceae	Sweet	Japan
Skimmia laureola	Rutaceae	Heavy	Himalayas
Skimmia rogersi	Rutaceae	Sweet	Hybrid
Syringa amurensis	Oleaceae	Sweet	N. China
Syringa chinensis	Oleaceae	Sweet	Hybrid
Syringa henryi	Oleaceae	Sweet	Hybrid
Syringa josiflexa	Oleaceae	Sweet	Hybrid
Syringa josikaea	Oleaceae	Clove	Hungary
Syringa julianae	Oleaceae	Sweet	Hungary
Syringa meyeri	Oleaceae	Sweet	China
Syringa microphylla	Oleaceae	Sweet	bm. China
Syringa pekinensis	Oleaceae	Slight	N. China
Syringa persica	Oleaceae	Sweet	Persia
Syringa pinnatifolia	Oleaceae	Sweet	N. China
Syringa pubescens	Oleaceae	Jonquil	N. China
Syringa swegenzowii	Oleaceae	Sweet	N. China
Syringa villosa	Oleaceae	Jonquil	N. China

Plant	Family	Scent	Habitat
Syringa vulgaris	Oleaceae	Jonquil	S.E. Europe
Syringa wilsonii	Oleaceae	Jonquil	W. China
Syringa wolfii	Oleaceae	Spicy	N.E. China
Syringa yunnanensis	Oleaceae	Sweet	W. China
Viburnum bitchivense	Caprifoliaceae	Sweet	Japan
Viburnum bodnantense	Caprifoliaceae	Sweet	Hybrid
Viburnum buddleifolium	Caprifoliaceae	Honey	Japan
Viburnum burkwoodii	Caprifoliaceae	Cloying	Himalayas
Viburnum carlcephalum	Caprifoliaceae	Clove	Hybrid
Viburnum carlesii	Caprifoliaceae	Clove	Korea
Viburnum cylindricum	Caprifoliaceae	Sweet	China
Viburnum davidii	Caprifoliaceae	Sweet	China
Viburnum erubescens	Caprifoliaceae	Sweet	Himalayas
Viburnum foetidum	Caprifoliaceae	Jonquil	Korea
Viburnum fragrans	Caprifoliaceae	Heliotrope	W. China
Viburnum henryi	Caprifoliaceae	Sweet	China
Viburnum japonicum	Caprifoliaceae	Jonquil	Japan
Viburnum juddii	Caprifoliaceae	Clove	Hybrid
Weigela nivea	Caprifoliaceae	Honey	Japan
Weigela praecox	Caprifoliaceae	Honey	Korea

APPENDIX F

Shrubs bearing Scented Flowers for a Sandy Soil

Plant	Family	Scent	Habitat
Adenocarpus decorticans	Leguminosae	Sweet	Spain
Brachyglottis rangiora	Compositae	Heavy	New Zealand
Brachyglottis repanda	Compositae	Mignonette	New Zealand
Buddleia alternifolia	Buddeiaceae	Heliotrope	S.W. China
Buddleia auriculata	Buddleiaceae	Honey	S. Africa
Buddleia caryopteridifolia	Buddleiaceae	Honey	Himalayas
Buddleia crispa	Buddleiaceae	Honey	Himalayas
Buddleia davidii	Buddleiaceae	Honey	Himalayas
Buddleia fallowiana	Buddleiaceae	Honey	W. China
Buddleia forrestii	Buddleiaceae	Honey	S. China
Buddleia globosa	Buddleiaceae	Honey	Chile
Calophaca volgarica	Leguminosae	Vanilla	Siberia
Caranga aurantiaca	Leguminosae	Sweet	Siberia
Caranga boisii	Leguminosae	Sweet	Tibet
Caranga chamlagu	Leguminosae	Treacle	N. China
Carmichaelia australis	Leguminosae	Orange	New Zealand
Carmichaelia petriei	Leguminosae	Laburnum	New Zealand
Carpenteria californica	Saxifragaceae	Sweet	W. USA
Clerodendron bungei	Verbenaceae	Sweet	China
Clerodendron fargesii	Verbenaceae	Sweet	China
Clerodendron trichotomum	Verbenaceae	Balsamic	China
Colletia armata	Rhamnaceae	Almond	Uruguay
Colletia cruciata	Rhamnaceae	Sweet	Uruguay
Coronilla emerus	Leguminosae	Sweet	S. Europe
Coronilla glauca	Leguminosae	Sweet	S. Europe
Cytisus battandieri	Leguminosae	Pineapple	Morocco
Desfontainea spinosa	Loganiaceae	Honey	Chile
Deutzia campanulata	Saxifragaceae	Soft	China
Deutzia compacta	Saxifragaceae	Sweet	China
Deutzia corymbosa	Saxifragaceae	Hawthorn	Himalayas
Deutzia elegantissima	Saxifragaceae	Sweet	Hybrid
Deutzia magnifica	Saxifragaceae	Soft	Hybrid
Deutzia parviflora	Saxifragaceae	Honey	China
Deutzia sieboldiana	Saxifragaceae	Vanilla	Japan
Deutzia staminea	Saxifragaceae	Hawthorn	Himalayas
Deutzia vilmoreana	Saxifragaceae	Honey	China
Dorycnium hirpitum	Leguminosae	Vanilla	S. Europe
Dorycnium suffruticosum	Leguminosae	Slight	S. Europe
Elaeagnus argentea	Elaeagnaceae	Orange	N. America

Plant	Family	Scent	Habitat
Elaeagnus glabra	Elaeagnaceae	Pungent	Japan
Elaeagnus longipes	Elaeagnaceae	Lilac	Japan
Elaeagnus macrophylla	Elaeagnaceae	Daphne	China
Elaeagnus pungens	Elaeagnaceae	Pungent	Japan
Elaeagnus umbellata	Elaeagnaceae	Pungent	S.E. Asia
Escallonia illinita	Saxifragaceae	Pungent	Chile
Escallonia macrantha	Saxifragaceae	Pungent	Chile
Escallonia pterocladon	Saxifragaceae	Resinous	Chile
Escallonia virgata	Saxifragaceae	Sweet	Chile
Fothergilla gardenii	Hamamelidaceae	Very Sweet	N. America
Fothergilla monticola	Hamamelidaceae	Sweet	N. America
Genista hispanica	Leguminosae	Pineapple	S. Europe
Halimodendron argenteum	Leguminosae	Almond	Siberia
Hedysarum multijugum	Leguminosae	Soft	Mongolia
Itea ilicifolia	Saxifragaceae	Sweet	China
Itea virginica	Saxifragaceae	Sweet	S. USA
Lupinus arboreus	Leguminosae	Clover	California
Melianthus major	Sapindaceae	Honey	S. Africa
Olearia albida	Compositae	Soft	New Zealand
Olearia gunni	Compositae	Musky	New Zealand
Olearia haastii	Compositae	Hawthorn	New Zealand
Olearia ilicifolia	Compositae	Musky	New Zealand
Olearia insignis	Compositae	Pungent	New Zealand
Olearia macrodonta	Compositae	Honey	New Zealand
Olearia moschata	Compositae	Musky	New Zealand
Olearia myrsinoides	Compositae	Resinous	Tasmania
Osteomeles anthyllidifolia	Rosaceae	Soft	W. China
Paliurus aculeatus	Rhamnaceae	Slight	E. Mediterranean
Petteria ramentacea	Leguminosae	Vanilla	S.E. Europe
Phylica superba	Rhamnaceae	Meadowsweet	Australia
Piptanthus nepalensis	Leguminosae	Vanilla	Nepal
Pittosporum cornifolium	Pittosporaceae	Musk	New Zealand
Pittosporum crassifolium	Pittosporaceae	Daphne-like	New Zealand
Pittosporum dalli	Pittosporaceae	Sweet	New Zealand
Pittosporum heterophyllum	Pittosporaceae	Aromatic	China
Pittosporum tenuifolium	Pittosporaceae	Lily	New Zealand
Pittosporum tobira	Pittosporaceae	Orange-like	China
Plagianthus divaricatus	Malvaceae	Honey	S. America
Plagianthus pulchellus	Malvaceae	Aniseed	S. America
Rhaphiolepsis japonica	Rosaceae	Honey	Japan
Spartium junceum	Leguminosae	Orange	Spain
Ulex europaeus	Leguminosae	Vanilla	N. Europe
Ulex minor	Leguminosae	Vanilla	British Isles
Veronica cupressoides	Scrophulariaceae	Cedar	New Zealand

APPENDIX G

Herbaceous Plants with Scented Flowers

Plant	Family	Scent	Habitat
Achillea ageratum	Compositae	Pungent	N. Europe
Achillea argentea	Compositae	Pungent	N. Europe
Achillea eupatorium	Compositae	Aromatic	Caucasus
Achillea millefolium	Compositae	Aromatic	N. Europe
Achillea rupestris	Compositae	Aromatic	N. Europe
Achillea taygetea	Compositae	Aromatic	S. Europe
Adenophora fischeri	Campanulaceae	Sweet	Siberia
Alstroemeria ligtu	Amaryllidaceae	Mignonette	Peru
Androsace pubescens	Primulaceae	Honey	Alps
Androsace villosa	Primulaceae	Honey	Pyrenees
Anthemis cupaniana	Compositae	Soft	Caucasus
Anthemis nobilis	Compositae	Aromatic	N. Europe
Alegia fragrans	Ranunculaceae	Clove	Himalayas
Aquilegia glauca	Ranunculaceae	Sweet	Himalayas
Aquilegia viridiflora	Ranunculaceae	Daphne-like	Siberia
Aruncus sylvester	Rosaceae	Meadowsweet	N. Eur., N. Amer.
Asphodelinetea	Liliaceae	Sweet	S. Europe
Asphodelus cerasiferus	Liliaceae	Sweet	S. Europe
Asphodelus fistulosus	Liliaceae	Sweet	S. Europe
Baptisia alba	Leguminosae	Slight	N. America
Baptisia leucophaea	Leguminosae	Slight	N. America
Chrysanthemum haradjanii	Compositae	Aromatic	W. China
Chrysanthemum indicum	Compositae	Lemon	China, Japan
Chrysanthemum parthenium	Compositae	Aromatic	N. Europe
Chrysanthemum poterifolium	Compositae	Aromatic	Himalayas
Cimicifuga americana	Ranunculaceae	Sweet	N. America
Delphinium brunonianum	Ranunculaceae	Musk	Himalayas
Dimopotheca barberiae	Compositae	Ripe apples	S. Africa
Echinops sphaerocephalus	Compositae	Clove	S. Europe
Epilobium hirsutum (Hybrids)	Onagraceae	Apple	N. Hemisphere
Eremurus elwesii	Liliaceae	Lily	E. Europe
Eremurus kaufmannianus	Liliaceae	Lily	E. Europe
Eremurus olgae	Liliaceae	Lily	E. Europe
Erysimum alpinum	Cruciferae	Cinnamon	Norway
Erysimum linifolium	Cruciferae	Violet	Spain
Erysimum pulchellum	Cruciferae	Soft	China
Erysimum pumilum	Cruciferae	Violet	Pyrenees
Filipendula hexapetala	Rosaceae	Meadowsweet	British Isles

Plant	Family	Scent	Habitat
Filipendula kamtschatica	Rosaceae	Sweet	E. Europe
Geranium robertianum	Geraniaceae	Foxy	British Isles
Hedysarum coronarium	Leguminosae	Clover	Italy
Helenium nudiflorum	Compositae	Sweet	N. America
Hemerocallis citrina	Liliaceae	Honeysuckle	Japan
Hemerocallis dumartieri	Liliaceae	Sweet	Siberia
Hemerocallis flava	Liliaceae	Honeysuckle	Siberia
Hemerocallis minor	Liliaceae	Honeysuckle	Siberia
Hosta plantaginea	Liliaceae	Lily-like	Japan
Inula hookeri	Compositae	Violet-like	Himalayas
Iris biliottii	Iridaceae	Fruity	Asia Minor
Iris graminea	Iridaceae	Ripe plums	C. Europe
Iris pallida	Iridaceae	Vanilla	S. Europe
Iris plicata	Iridaceae	Sweet	S. Europe
Macrotomia cephalotes	Boraginaceae	Honey	Taurus Mts.
Morisia hypogaea	Cruciferae	Hawthorn	Sardinia
Onosma tauricum	Boraginaceae	Honey	Caucasus
Paeonia lactiflora	Ranunculaceae	Sweet	Siberia, Mongolia
Paeonia mlokosewitschii	Ranunculaceae	Sweet	Caucasus
Paeonia moutan	Ranunculaceae	Soft	China
Papaver alpinum	Papaveraceae	Musky	N. Europe
Paradisea liliastrum	Liliaceae	Sweet	C. Europe
Phlox maculata	Polemoniaceae	Sweet	E. USA
Phlox paniculata	Polemoniaceae	Sweet	N. America
Pimelea longifolia	Thymeleaceae	Jonquil	New Zealand
Preslia cervina	Labiatae	Aromatic	W. Europe
Silphium perfoliatum	Compositae	Resinous	N. America
Smilacina racemosa	Liliaceae	Sweet	N. America
Smilacina stellata	Liliaceae	Lily	N. America
Tanacetum balsamita	Compositae	Mint	S. Europe
Tanacetum vulgare	Compositae	Aromatic	N. Europe
Trachelium caeruleum	Campanulaceae	Sweet	S. Europe
Trillium cernuum	Liliaceae	Sweet	E. USA
Trillium luteum	Liliaceae	Lemon	E. USA
Trillium sessile	Liliaceae	Sweet	E. USA

APPENDIX H

Herbaceous Plants with Scented Leaves

Plant	Family	Scent	Habitat
Achillea ageratum	Compositae	Pungent	Greece
Achillea argentea	Compositae	Pungent	Caucasus
Achillea eupatorium	Compositae	Pungent	Caucasus
Achillea millefolium	Compositae	Musky	British Isles
Achillea rupestris	Compositae	Pungent	Italy
Acorus calamus	Araceae	Orange	British Isles
Agrimonia eupatoria	Rosaceae	Sweet-briar	British Isles
Agrimonia odorata '	Rosaceae	Sweet-briar	British Isles
Ajuga chamaepitys	Labiatae	Pine	British Isles
Anthemis cotula	Compositae	Unpleasant	British Isles
Anthemis cupaniana	Compositae	Aromatic	Caucasus
Anthemis nobilis	Compositae	Aromatic	British Isles
Anthemis tinctoria	Compositae	Aromatic	British Isles
Artemisia abrotanum	Compositae	Lemon	S. Europe
Artemisia absinthinum	Compositae	Pungent	British Isles
Artemisia argentea	Compositae	Aromatic	Madeira
Artemisia chamaemelifolia	Compositae	Aromatic	S. Europe
Artemisia dracunculus	Compositae	Aniseed	N. Asia
Artemisia maritima	Compositae	Aromatic	British Isles
Artemisia odoratissimum	Compositae	Aromatic	S. Europe
Asperula odorata	Rubiaceae	Hay-like	British Isles
Calamintha ascendens	Labiatae	Minty	British Isles
Calamintha nepeta	Labiatae	Minty	British Isles
Chrysanthemum balsamita	Compositae	Balsamic	British Isles
Chrysanthemum haradjanii	Compositae	Aromatic	Caucasus
Chrysanthemum parthenium	Compositae	Aromatic	N. Europe
Chrysanthemum poterifolium	Compositae	Aromatic	N. Europe
Clinopodium vulgare	Labiatae	Aromatic	British Isles
Erodium moschatum	Geraniaceae	Musky	British Isles
Filipendula ulmaria	Rosaceae	Aromatic	British Isles
Geranium macrorrhizum	Geraniaceae	Aromatic	British Isles
Geranium robertianum	Geraniaceae	Pungent	British Isles
Glechoma lederacea	Labiate	Aromatic	British Isles
Hypericum androsaemum	Guttiferae	Aromatic	British Isles
Hypericum elodes	Guttiferae	Resinous	British Isles
Hypericum perforatum	Guttiferae	Goat-like	British Isles
Hyssopus aristatus	Labiatae	Pungent	S. Europe
Lamium album	Labiatae	Aromatic	British Isles
Lamium galeobdolon	Labiatae	Aromatic	British Isles

Plant	Family	Scent	Habitat
Lavandula atriplicifolia	Labiatae	Pungent	Arabia
Lavandula dentata	Labiatae	Pungent	Malta
Lavandula multifida	Labiatae	Pungent	Arabia
Lavandula spica	Labiatae	Pungent	S. Europe
Lavandula stoechas	Labiatae	Pungent	S. Europe
Ledum glandulosum	Ericaceae	Aromatic	Colombia
Ledum latifolium	Ericaceae	Aromatic	Greenland
Ledum minus	Ericaceae	Aromatic	Japan
Ledum palustre	Ericaceae	Aromatic	Arctic
Malva moschata	Malvaceae	Musky	British Isles
Matricaria recutita	Compositae	Aromatic	British Isles
Matricaria suaveolens	Compositae	Pineapple	British Isles
Melissa officinalis	Labiatae	Lemon	British Isles
Melittis melissophyllum	Labiatae	Aromatic	British Isles
Mentha aquatica	Labiatae	Bergamot	British Isles
Mentha arvensis	Labiatae	Acrid	British Isles
Mentha citrata	Labiatae	Lemon	British Isles
Mentha piperita	Labiatae	Peppermint	British Isles
Mentha pulegium	Labiatae	Mint	British Isles
Mentha requienii	Labiatae	Mint	British Isles
Mentha rotundifolia	Labiatae	Mint	British Isles
Mentha spicata	Labiatae	Mint	British Isles
Monarda didyma	Labiatae	Bergamot	N. America
Nepeta catara	Labiatae	Pungent	British Isles
Nepeta mussinii	Labiatae	Pungent	Caucasus
Nepeta nervosa	Labiatae	Pungent	Caucasus
Nepeta septemcrenata	Labiatae	Pungent	Egypt
Nepeta spicata	Labiatae	Aromatic	Himalayas
Ocymum basilicum	Labiatae	Mignonette	S. Europe
Ocymum canum	Labiatae	Pungent	Madagascar
Ocymum crispum	Labiatae	Aromatic	Japan
Origanum heracleoticum	Labiatae	Lavender	S. Europe
Origanum marjorana	Labiatae	Sweet	S. Europe
Origanum onites	Labiatae	Aromatic	S. Europe
Origanum syriacum	Labiatae	Minty	S.E. Europe
Origanum vulgare	Labiatae	Peppery	British Isles
Poterium sanguisorba	Rosaceae	Cucumber	British Isles
Rosmarinus officinalis	Labiatae	Pungent	S. Europe
Ruta graveolens	Rutaceae	Orange	S. Europe
Salvia argentea	Labiatae	Pungent	S. Europe
Salvia azurea	Labiatae	Pungent	N. America
Salvia candalabrum	Labiatae	Aromatic	Mexico
Salvia nutilans	Labiatae	Pineapple	S. Europe
Salvia officinalis	Labiatae	Pungent	S. Europe
Salvia pratensis	Labiatae	Aromatic	British Isles
Salvia sclarea	Labiatae	Musky	British Isles
Salvia virgata	Labiatae	Pungent	S. Europe
Santolina chamaecyparissus	Compositae	Pungent	S. Europe
Satureia hortensis	Labiatae	Aromatic	S. Europe
Satureia montana	Labiatae	Aromatic	S. Europe
Tanacetum vulgaris	Compositae	Aromatic	S. Europe
Teucrium chamaedrys	Labiatae	Aromatic	British Isles

Plant	Family	Scent	Habitat
Thymus azoricus	Labiatae	Orange	Azores
Thymus capitatus	Labiatae	Pungent	S. Europe
Thymus carnosus	Labiatae	Aromatic	S. Europe
Thymus citriodorus	Labiatae	Lemon	S. Europe
Thymus comosus	Labiatae	Turpentine	S. Europe
Thymus decussatus	Labiatae	Pungent	Libya
Thymus doeffleri	Labiatae	Pine	S. Europe
Thymus fragrantissimus	Labiatae	Orange	S. Europe
Thymus herba-barona	Labiatae	Caraway	Corsica
Thymus mastichina	Labiatae	Pungent	Corsica
Thymus membranacous	Labiatae	Pungent	Spain
Thymus micans	Labiatae	Pine	Spain
Thymus nitidus	Labiatae	Pungent	Sicily
Thymus pulegioides	Labiatae	Aromatic	British Isles
Thymus serpyllum	Labiatae	Aromatic	British Isles
Thymus vulgaris	Labiatae	Pungent	S. Europe

APPENDIX I

Annual and Biennial Plants
with Scented Flowers or *Leaves

Plant	Family	Scent	Habitat
Abronia arenaria	Nyctaginaceae	Honeysuckle	California
Abronia umbellata	Nyctaginaceae	Honey	California
Alyssum maritimum	Cruciferae	Hay-like	S. Europe
Antirrhinum hybrids	Scrophulariaceae	Sweet	British Isles
Calendula officinalis	Compositae	Pungent	S. Europe
*Cannabis sativa	Cannabinaceae	Resinous	India
Celsia cretica	Scrophulariaceae	Pineapple	Crete
Centaurea moschata	Gentianaceae	Musk	S.E. Europe
Centaurea suaveolens	Gentianaceae	Lily	Levant
Cerinthe minor	Boraginaceae	Honey	S.E. Europe
Cheiranthus cheiri	Cruciferae	Balsamic	C. Europe
Cuphea lanceolata	Lythraceae	Incense-like	Mexico
Dracocephalum moldavica	Labiatae	Lemon	Siberia
Eritrichium nothofulvum	Boraginaceae	Honeysuckle	S.E. Europe
Erysimum suffruticosum	Cruciferae	Sweet	N. America
Exacum affine	Gentianaceae	Pungent	Socotra
Fagophyrum esculentum	Polygonaceae	Honey	C. Europe
Iberis amara	Cruciferae	Sweet	British Isles
Iberis odorata	Cruciferae	Sweet	S. Europe
Ionopsidium acaule	Cruciferae	Honey	Portugal
Lathyrus odoratus	Leguminosae	Vanilla	Sicily
Limnanthes douglasii	Limnanthaceae	Sweet	California
Lupinus densiflorus	Leguminosae	Sweet pea	California
Lupinus luteus	Leguminosae	Vanilla	S.E. Europe
Lycopsis variegata	Boraginaceae	Soft	S.E. Europe
Martynia fragrans	Pedalinae	Vanilla	Brazil
Martynia proboscidea	Pedalinae	Sweet	Brazil
Matthiola bicornis	Cruciferae	Clove	S. Europe
Matthiola odoratissima	Cruciferae	Clove	Caucasus. Abyssinia
Matthiola sinuata	Cruciferae	Clove	British Isles
Mentzelia lindleyi	Loasaceae	Honey	USA
Mentzelia ornata	Loasaceae	Sweet	USA
Molucella laevis	Labiatae	Balm	Syria
Nemesia floribunda	Scrophulariaceae	Sweet	S. Africa
Oenothera tetraptera	Onagraceae	Sweet	Mexico
Pectis angustifolia	Compositae	Spicy	California
Phacelia ciliata	Hydrophyllaceae	Heliotrope	California
Reseda odorata	Resedaceae	Mignonette	Egypt
Saxifraga atlantica	Saxifragaceae	Sweet	Spain

Plant	Family	Scent	Habitat
Scabiosa atropurpurea	Dipsaceae	Sweet	Italy
Schizopetalon walkeri	Cruciferae	Almond	Chile
Selenia aurea	Cruciferae	Sweet	USA
Tagetes lucida	Compositae	Sweet	Mexico
Thymophylla aurea	Compositae	Aromatic	USA
Tropaeolum minus	Tropaeolaceae	Sweet	USA
Verbena tenuisecta	Verbenaceae	Heliotrope	S. USA
Verbena teucrioides	Verbenaceae	Heliotrope	Brazil

APPENDIX J

Bulbs and Corms
with Scented Flowers

Plant	Family	Scent	Habitat
Acidanthera bicolor	Iridaceae	Violet	Abyssinia
Albuca nelsonii	Liliaceae	Lily	Natal
Allium moly	Liliaceae	Sweet	S. Europe
Allium neapolitanum	Liliaceae	Violet	Italy
Allium triquetrum	Liliaceae	Sweet	S. Europe
Allium ursinum	Liliaceae	Sulphur	S. Europe
Amaryllis belladonna	Amaryllidaceae	Lily	S. Africa
Babiana bainsii	Iridaceae	Mossy	S. Africa
Babiana disticha	Iridaceae	Soft	S. Africa
Babiana plicata	Iridaceae	Soft	S. Africa
Babiana sambucina	Iridaceae	Muscat	S. Africa
Babiana stricta	Iridaceae	Mossy	S. Africa
Calochortus pulchellus	Liliaceae	Sweet	N.W. America
Calochortus uniflorus	Liliaceae	Sweet	N.W. America
Cardiocrinum cathayanum	Liliaceae	Freesia	S.W. China
Cardiocrinum cordatum	Liliaceae	Lily	Japan
Cardiocrinum giganteum	Liliaceae	Lily	Nepal
Chlidanthus fragrans	Amaryllidaceae	Lily	Peru
Crinum asiaticum	Amaryllidaceae	Lily-like	S. Africa
Crinum bulbispurmum	Amaryllidaceae	Sweet	Transvaal
Crinum moorei	Amaryllidaceae	Sweet	Natal
Crocus chrysanthus	Iridaceae	Primrose	Balkans
Crocus imperati	Iridaceae	Primrose	Naples
Crocus laevigatus	Iridaceae	Sweet	Balkans
Crocus longiflorus	Iridaceae	Honeysuckle	Sicily, Malta
Crocus sativus	Iridaceae	Sweet	Spain to Kashmir
Crocus suaveolens	Iridaceae	Violet	Italy
Crocus versicolor	Iridaceae	Sweet	S. France
Cyclamen cilicium	Primulaceae	Vanilla	Lebanon
Cyclamen europeum	Primulaceae	Musk	W. Europe
Cyclamen libanoticum	Primulaceae	Vanilla	Lebanon
Cyclamen neapolitanum	Primulaceae	Sweet	W. Europe
Cyclamen repandum	Primulaceae	Sweet	S. Italy
Cyrtanthus cooperi	Amaryllidaceae	Sweet	S. Africa
Cyrtanthus odorus	Amaryllidaceae	Lily	S. Africa
Endymion hispanicus	Liliaceae	Balsamic	Spain
Endymion non-scriptus	Liliaceae	Balsamic	N. Europe
Eranthis, Guinea Gold	Ranunculaceae	Sweet	S. Africa
Eucharis candida	Amaryllidaceae	Lily	Colombia

Plant	Family	Scent	Habitat
Eucharis grandiflora	Amaryllidaceae	Lily	Colombia
Eucomis autumnalis	Liliaceae	Mossy	S. Africa
Eucomis comosa	Liliaceae	Sweet	S. Africa
Freesia refracta	Iridaceae	Violet	S. Africa
Fritillaria citrina	Liliaceae	Mossy	Asia Minor
Fritillaria camchaticensis	Liliaceae	Sweet	Siberia, Alaska
Galanthus ikariae	Amaryllidaceae	Mossy	Isle of Nikaria
Galanthus latifolius	Amaryllidaceae	Cucumber	Caucasus
Galanthus nivalis	Amaryllidaceae	Sweet	C. Europe
Galtonia candicans	Liliaceae	Soft	S. Africa
Gladiolus alatus	Iridaceae	Sweet	S. Africa
Gladiolus carinatus	Iridaceae	Violet	S. Africa
Gladiolus caryophyllaceus	Iridaceae	Clove	S. Africa
Gladiolus gracilis	Iridaceae	Violet	S. Africa
Gladiolus grandis	Iridaceae	Clove	S. Africa
Gladiolus recurvus	Iridaceae	Violet	S. Africa
Gladiolus orchidiflorus	Iridaceae	Sweet	S. Africa
Gladiolus tristis	Iridaceae	Clove	Natal
Hyacinthus amethystinus	Liliaceae	Balsamic	Spain
Hyacinthus azureus	Liliaceae	Balsamic	E. Europe
Hyacinthus dalmaticus	Liliaceae	Balsamic	Jugoslavia
Hyacinthus orientalis	Liliaceae	Balsamic	Persia
Hyacinthus romanus	Liliaceae	Incense-like	S. Europe
Hymenocallis amancaes	Amaryllidaceae	Sweet	Peru
Hymenocallis harrisiana	Amaryllidaceae	Sweet	Mexico
Hymenocallis narcissiflora	Amaryllidaceae	Sweet	Peru
Hymenocallis rotata	Amaryllidaceae	Jonquil	Florida
Hymenocallis speciosa	Amaryllidaceae	Sweet	West Indies
Iris bakeriana	Iridaceae	Violet	Persia, Iraq
Iris danfordiae	Iridaceae	Sweet	Taurus Mts.
Iris histrioides	Iridaceae	Sweet	Persia, Iraq
Iris juncea	Iridaceae	Sweet	Spain, N. Africa
Iris kolpakowskiana	Iridaceae	Sweet	Turkestan
Iris persica	Iridaceae	Almond	Persia, Iraq
Iris reticulata	Iridaceae	Violet	Turkestan
Iris vartani	Iridaceae	Almond	Israel
Iris xiphium	Iridaceae	Fruity	Spain, Portugal
Ixia gigantea alba	Iridaceae	Sweet	S. Africa
Ixia odorata	Iridaceae	Sweet	S. Africa
Lachenalia contaminata	Liliaceae	Heliotrope	S. Africa
Lachenalia glaucina	Liliaceae	Sweet	S. Africa
Leucocoryne odorata	Liliaceae	Lily	Chile
Leucojum vernum	Amaryllidaceae	Violet	S. Europe
Lilium auratum	Liliaceae	Sweet	Japan
Lilium brownii, var. *viridulum*	Liliaceae	Soft	S.W. China
Lilium candidum	Liliaceae	Sweet	S.E. Europe
Lilium cernuum	Liliaceae	Soft	Korea
Lilium chalcedonicum	Liliaceae	Orange	S.E. Europe
Lilium duchartrei	Liliaceae	Soft	S.W. China
Lilium formosanum	Liliaceae	Sweet	Formosa
Lilium hansonii	Liliaceae	Sweet	S. Korea

Plant	Family	Scent	Habitat
Lilium henryii	Liliaceae	Sweet	C. China
Lilium iridallae	Liliaceae	Sweet	Alabama, USA
Lilium kelloggii	Liliaceae	Honey	W. USA
Lilium lankongense	Liliaceae	Soft	Yunnan
Lilium leucanthum	Liliaceae	Sweet	S.W. China
Lilium longiflorum	Liliaceae	Sweet	Ryukyu Archipelago
Lilium monadelphum	Liliaceae	Sweet	S.E. Europe
Lilium papilliferum	Liliaceae	Cloying	Yunnan
Lilium parryi	Liliaceae	Lily of Valley	W. USA
Lilium philippinense	Liliaceae	Sweet	Luzon
Lilium polyphillum	Liliaceae	Sweet	Afghanistan
Lilium primulinum, var. ochraceum	Liliaceae	Orange	Yunnan
Lilium pumilum	Liliaceae	Orange	N. China, Siberia
Lilium regale	Liliaceae	Jonquil	S.W. China
Lilium rubellum	Liliaceae	Sweet	Japan
Lilium rubescens	Liliaceae	Heavy	W. USA
Lilium sargentiae	Liliaceae	Sweet	S.W. China
Lilium speciosum	Liliaceae	Sweet	Japan
Lilium sulphureum	Liliaceae	Sweet	Burma
Lilium taliense	Liliaceae	Sweet	Yunnan
Lilium testaceum	Liliaceae	Sweet	China
Lilium wallichianum	Liliaceae	Sweet	Nepal
Lilium wardii	Liliaceae	Lily of Valley	Nepal
Lilium washingtonianum	Liliaceae	Sweet	W. USA
Lycoris incarnata	Amaryllidaceae	Sweet	China
Lycoris squamigera	Amaryllidaceae	Sweet	Japan
Muscari ambrosiacum	Liliaceae	Musk	Asia Minor
Muscari armeniacum	Liliaceae	Honey	Asia Minor
Muscari botryoides	Liliaceae	Starch	S. Europe
Muscari comosum	Liliaceae	Sweet	Asia Minor
Muscari moschatum	Liliaceae	Musk	Asia Minor
Muscari racemosum	Liliaceae	Plum	England
Narcissus asturiensis	Amaryllidaceae	Lily	Portugal
Narcissus biflorus	Amaryllidaceae	Sweet	S. Europe
Narcissus calcicola	Amaryllidaceae	Sweet	Portugal
Narcissus canaliculatus	Amaryllidaceae	Sweet	Sicily
Narcissus cernuus	Amaryllidaceae	Musky	N. Spain
Narcissus gracilis	Amaryllidaceae	Honey	France
Narcissus jonquilla	Amaryllidaceae	Jonquil	N.W. Africa, Spain
Narcissus juncifolius	Amaryllidaceae	Sweet	Portugal, Spain
Narcissus minor	Amaryllidaceae	Jonquil	Portugal
Narcissus odorus	Amaryllidaceae	Sweet	S. Europe
Narcissus poeticus	Amaryllidaceae	Sweet	S. Europe
Narcissus pseudo-narcissus	Amaryllidaceae	Mossy	Europe
Narcissus rupicola	Amaryllidaceae	Sweet	Portugal, Spain
Narcissus tazetta	Amaryllidaceae	Sweet	Spain to Kashmir
Narcissus tenuior	Amaryllidaceae	Sweet	S. Europe
Narcissus triandrus concolor	Amaryllidaceae	Sweet	N. Spain
Notholirion thomsonianum	Lilaceae	Lily	Afghanistan
Nothoscordum fragrans	Alliaceae	Sweet	N. America
Pamianthe peruviana	Amaryllidaceae	Sweet	Peru

Plant	Family	Scent	Habitat
Pancratium canariense	Amaryllidaceae	Lily	Canary Islands
Pancratium illyricum	Amaryllidaceae	Lily	S. Europe
Pancratium maritimum	Amaryllidaceae	Lily	S. Europe
Polianthes tuberosa	Amaryllidaceae	Balsamic	Mexico
Scilla bifolia	Liliaceae	Soft	S. Europe
Scilla sibirica	Liliaceae	Balsamic	Siberia
Sternbergia colchiciflora	Amaryllidaceae	Sweet	Balkans
Techophilea cyanocrocus	Amaryllidaceae	Sweet	Chile
Techophilea violiflora	Amaryllidaceae	Slight	Chile
Trillium sessile	Liliaceae	Sweet	W. USA
Tritelia uniflora	Liliaceae	Sweet	Mexico
Tulipa gesneriana	Liliaceae	Sweet	S.E. Europe
Tulipa persica	Liliaceae	Sweet	Persia
Tulipa primulina	Liliaceae	Sweet	Algeria
Tulipa saxatilis	Liliaceae	Primrose	Crete
Tulipa suaveolens	Liliaceae	Lily	S.E. Europe
Tulipa sylvestris	Liliaceae	Sweet	W. Europe
Zephyranthes tubispatha	Amaryllidaceae	Sweet	West Indies

APPENDIX K

Scented Plants
of Climbing and Trailing Habit

Plant	Family	Scent	Habitat
Abobra tenuifolia	Cucurbitaceae	Lily	S. America
Abronia arenaria	Nyctaginaceae	Honeysuckle	California
Abronia fragrans	Nyctaginaceae	Vanilla	California
Abronia umbellata	Nyctaginaceae	Honey	California
Actinidia arguta	Actinidiaceae	Sweet	Japan
Actinidia chinensis	Actinidiaceae	Sweet	China
Actinidia coriacea	Actinidiaceae	Soft	Japan
Actinidia kolomikta	Actinidiaceae	Soft	China
Actinidia melanandra	Actinidiaceae	Soft	China
Actinidia polygama	Actinidiaceae	Honeysuckle	Japan
Akebia lobata	Lardizabalaceae	Soft	China, Japan
Akebia quinata	Lardizabalaceae	Sweet	China, Japan
Apios tuberosa	Leguminosae	Violet	N. America
Artabotrys odoratissima	Anonaceae	Ripe apples	Tropics
Beaumontia grandiflora	Apocynaceae	Lily	Burma, W. China
Billardiera longiflora	Pittosporaceae	Lily of Valley	Tasmania
Bougainvillea glabra	Nyctaginaceae	Lily	Brazil
Centrosema grandiflora	Leguminosae	Vanilla	S. America
Clematis cirrhosa	Ranunculaceae	Sweet	Spain
Clematis Duchess of Edinburgh	Ranunculaceae	Soft	Hybrid
Clematis eriostemon	Ranunculaceae	Sweet	Hybrid
Clematis flammula	Ranunculaceae	Almond	Spain
Clematis fortunei	Ranunculaceae	Almond	Japan
Clematis jouiniana	Ranunculaceae	Sweet	Japan
Clematis montana	Ranunculaceae	Soft	Himalayas
Clematis orientalis	Ranunculaceae	Cowslip	India
Clematis paniculata	Ranunculaceae	Hawthorn	Japan
Clematis pavoliniana	Ranunculaceae	Sweet	China
Clematis rehderiana	Ranunculaceae	Cowslip	China
Clematis uncinata	Ranunculaceae	Sweet	China
Clematoclethra integrifolia	Actinidiaceae	Spicy	W. China
Clerodendron fragrans	Verbenaceae	Clove	China
Clerodendron phlomoides	Verbenaceae	Sweet	India
Cupia truncata	Chinchonaceae	Jonquil	Penang
Decumaria barbara	Hydrangeaceae	Sweet	E. USA
Decumaria sinensis	Hydrangeaceae	Honey	China
Ercilla volubilis	Phytolacaceae	Sweet	Chile
Gelsemium sempervirens	Loganiaceae	Honey	USA

Plant	Family	Scent	Habitat
Holboellia latifolia	Lardizabalaceae	Exotic	Himalayas
Hoya bella	Asclepiadaceae	Honey	Malacca
Hoya carnosa	Asclepiadaceae	Honey	India, China
Hoya globulosa	Asclepiadaceae	Honey	N. India
Humulus japonicus	Cannabinaceae	Soft	Japan
Humulus lupulus	Cannabinaceae	Soft	N. Europe
Jasminum azoricum	Oleaceae	Heavy	Azores
Jasminum humile glabrum	Oleaceae	Sweet	Nepal
Jasminum nudiflorum	Oleaceae	Sweet	China
Jasminum odoratissimum	Oleaceae	Lily	Canary Islands
Jasminum officinale	Oleaceae	Jasmine	Persia
Jasminum polyanthum	Oleaceae	Lily	India
Jasminum stephanense	Oleaceae	Lily	Hybrid
Kadsura japonica	Magnoliaceae	Sweet	Formosa
Lonicera americana	Caprifoliaceae	Spicy	Hybrid
Lonicera caprifolium	Caprifoliaceae	Honey	S. Europe
Lonicera etrusca	Caprifoliaceae	Cloying	S. Europe
Lonicera heckrotii	Caprifoliaceae	Spicy	Hybrid
Lonicera japonica	Caprifoliaceae	Gardenia	Japan
Lonicera periclymenum	Caprifoliaceae	Honey	British Isles
Mandevilla suaveolens	Apocynaceae	Lily	Chile
Marsdenia suaveolens	Asclepiadaceae	Stephanotis	Australia
Passiflora caerulea	Passifloraceae	Soft	Brazil
Passiflora edulis	Passifloraceae	Heliotrope	Peru
Pergularia odoratissima	Asclepiadaceae	Lily	Java, Sumatra
Pergularia sanguinolenta	Asclepiadaceae	Sweet	Sierra Leone
Periploca graeca	Asclepiadaceae	Lily	S.E. Europe
Plumbago capensis	Plumbaginaceae	Heliotrope	S. Africa
Pueraria thunbergiana	Leguminosae	Vanilla	C. China
Rubus deliciosus	Rosaceae	Sweet-briar	N. America
Schizandra chinensis	Magnoliaceae	Sweet	N. China
Schizandra propinqua	Magnoliaceae	Aromatic	Himalayas
Smilax aspera	Liliaceae	Sweet	S.E. Europe
Stauntonia hexaphylla	Lardizabalaceae	Sweet	Burma
Stephanotis floribunda	Asclepiadaceae	Exotic	Madagascar
Thunbergia fragrans	Thunbergiaceae	Violet	Madras
Trachelospermum asiaticum	Apocynaceae	Sweet	S.E. Asia
Trachelospermum jasminoides	Apocynaceae	Sweet	Japan
Trachelospermum majus	Apocynaceae	Soft	Japan
Tripterygium forrestii	Celastraceae	Sweet	Burma, W. China
Tripterygium regelii	Celastraceae	Soft	Japan
Vitis aestivalis	Vitaceae	Sweet	N. America
Vitis cordifolia	Vitaceae	Sweet	N. America
Vitis labrusca	Vitaceae	Mignonette	N. America
Vitis riparia	Vitaceae	Mignonette	N. America
Vitis vulpina	Vitaceae	Sweet	N. America
Wistaria floribunda	Leguminosae	Vanilla	Japan
Wistaria macrostachya	Leguminosae	Soft	USA
Wistaria sinensis	Leguminosae	Vanilla	China
Wistaria venusta	Leguminosae	Soft	Japan

APPENDIX L

Winter-flowering plants
with Scented Flowers

Plant	Family	Scent	Habitat
Abelia chinensis	Caprifoliaceae	Vanilla	China
Abelia floribunda	Caprifoliaceae	Soft	Mexico
Abelia serrata	Caprifoliaceae	Spicy	China
Abelia triflora	Caprifoliaceae	Vanilla	Himalayas
Abeliophyllum distichum	Oleaceae	Sweet	Korea
Arbutus hybrida	Ericaceae	Sweet	Hybrid
Camellia sasanqua	Theaceae	Sweet	Japan
Chimonanthus fragrans	Calycanthaceae	Violet	C. China
Coronilla glauca	Leguminosae	Sweet	S. Europe
Corylopsis himalayana	Hamamelidaceae	Primrose	Himalayas
Corylopsis pauciflora	Hamamelidaceae	Almond	Himalayas
Corylopsis spicata	Hamamelidaceae	Cowslip	Japan
Corylopsis willmottiae	Hamamelidaceae	Cowslip	W. China
Corylopsis wilsonii	Hamamelidaceae	Primrose	W. China
Daphne collina	Thymeleaceae	Sweet	S. Italy
Daphne laureola	Thymeleaceae	Unpleasant	British Isles
Daphne mezereum	Thymeleaceae	Violet	British Isles
Daphne odora	Thymeleaceae	Spicy	W. China
Daphne pontica	Thymeleaceae	Sweet	E. Europe
Dirca palustris	Thymeleaceae	Sweet	N. America
Edgeworthia papyrifera	Thymeleaceae	Clove	Japan
Eriobotyra japonica	Rosaceae	Exotic	Japan
Eupatorium weinmannianum	Compositae	Soft	Mexico
Forsythia giraldiana	Oleaceae	Vanilla	Yunnan
Forsythia ovata	Oleaceae	Vanilla	Korea
Fothergilla gardeni	Hamamelidaceae	Sweet	N.E. America
Gordonia alatamaha	Theaceae	Vanilla	S. USA
Hamamelis japonica	Hamamelidaceae	Soft	Japan
Hamamelis mollis	Hamamelidaceae	Very sweet	Japan
Lonicera fragrantissima	Caprifoliaceae	Honey	China
Lonicera purpurii	Caprifoliaceae	Honey	China
Loropetalum chinense	Hamamelidaceae	Sweet	China
Luculia grandifolia	Rubiaceae	Incense	Bhutan
Luculia gratissima	Rubiaceae	Sweet	S.W. China
Luculia pinceana	Rubiaceae	Sweet	S.W. China
Luculia standishii	Rubiaceae	Incense	Burma
Mahonia bealei	Berberidaceae	Sweet	China
Mahonia fremantii fasciculata	Berberidaceae	Very sweet	China

Plant	Family	Scent	Habitat
Mahonia haematocarpa	Berberidaceae	Freesia	W. USA
Mahonia japonica	Berberidaceae	Lily of Valley	Japan
Mahonia lomariifolia	Berberidaceae	Sweet	Japan
Mahonia napaulensis	Berberidaceae	Sweet	Nepal
Mahonia repens	Berberidaceae	Soft	W. USA
Mentzelia cerasiformis	Loasaceae	Almond	California
Osmanthus fortunei	Oleaceae	Lily	Japan
Sarcococcus hookeriana	Buxaceae	Sweet	Himalayas
Sarcococcus humilis	Buxaceae	Sweet	W. China
Sarcococcus ruscifolia	Buxaceae	Fruity	China
Sarcococcus salignus	Buxaceae	Spicy	Himalayas
Spiraea pubescens	Rosaceae	Sweet	Magnolia
Stachyurus chinensis	Stachyuraceae	Jasmine	China
Stachyurus praecox	Stachyuraceae	Vanilla	China
Viburnum bodnantense	Caprifoliaceae	Sweet	Hybrid
Viburnum carlesii	Caprifoliaceae	Clove	Korea
Viburnum foetidum	Caprifoliaceae	Jonquil	N. Europe
Viburnum fragrans	Caprifoliaceae	Heliotrope	N. Europe
Viburnum juddii	Caprifoliaceae	Clove	Hybrid

APPENDIX M

Night-Scented Flowering Plants

Plant	Family	Scent	Habitat
Abronia fragrans	Nyctaginaceae	Vanilla	California
Abronia umbellata	Nyctaginaceae	Honey	California
Calonyction aculeatum	Convolvulaceae	Lily	S. America
Cestrum parqui	Solanaceae	Heavy	Chile
Datura ceratocaula	Solanaceae	Heavy	Cuba
Datura chlorantha	Solanaceae	Sweet	India
Datura fastuosa	Solanaceae	Lily	Egypt
Datura metel	Solanaceae	Exotic	Egypt
Datura meteloides	Solanaceae	Soft	Egypt
Datura suaveolens	Solanaceae	Lily	Mexico
Erinus selaginoides	Scrophulariaceae	Heavy	S. America
Gladiolus tristis	Iridaceae	Clove	S. Africa
Hebenstreitia comosa	Scrophulariaceae	Lily-like	S. Africa
Heliotropium convolvulaceum	Boraginaceae	Spicy	New Mexico
Hesperantha buchrii	Iridaceae	Clove	S. Africa
Hesperantha stanfordiae	Iridaceae	Lily-like	S. Africa
Hesperis fragrans	Cruciferae	Clove	Siberia
Hesperis matronalis	Cruciferae	Clove	S. Europe
Hesperis tristis	Cruciferae	Violet	S. Europe
Hesperis violacea	Cruciferae	Sweet	Asia Minor
Linnaea borealis	Caprifoliaceae	Honeysuckle	N. Europe
Mentzelia ornata	Loasaceae	Sweet	Missouri
Mirabilis longiflora	Nyctaginaceae	Orange	Mexico
Mirabilis jalapa	Nyctaginaceae	Heavy	Peru
Myosotis alpestris	Boraginaceae	Sweet	British Isles
Myosotis macrantha	Boraginaceae	Soft	New Zealand
Nicotiana affinis	Solanaceae	Sweet	S. America
Nicotiana suaveolens	Solanaceae	Sweet	Australia
Nicotiana sylvestris	Solanaceae	Freesias	Argentine
Oenothera biennis	Onagrariaceae	Sweet	Virginia
Oenothera californica	Onagrariaceae	Sweet	California
Oenothera drummondii	Onagrariaceae	Vanilla	Texas
Oenothera eximia	Onagrariaceae	Lemon	N. America
Oenothera tetraptera	Onagrariaceae	Vanilla	Mexico
Oenothera triloba	Onagrariaceae	Violet	N. America
Petunia violacea	Solanaceae	Vanilla	S. America
Silene noctiflora	Caryophyllaceae	Carnation	British Isles
Silene nutans	Caryophyllaceae	Carnation	British Isles
Sisyrinchium odoratissimum	Iridaceae	Exotic	S. America

Plant	Family	Scent	Habitat
Verbena teucrioides	Verbenaceae	Sweet	Brazil
Zaluzianskya capensis	Scrophulariaceae	Sweet	S. Africa
Zaluzianskya villosa	Scrophulariaceae	Aromatic	S. Africa

APPENDIX N

Scented Aquatic Plants

Plant	Family	Scent	Habitat
Aponogeton angustifolius	Aponogetonaceae	Almond	S. Africa
Aponogeton distachyus	Aponogetonaceae	Hawthorn	S. Africa
Nelumbium lutea	Nymphaeaceae	Brandy	USA
Nelumbium speciosum	Nymphaeaceae	Tea Rose	India
Nymphaea caroliniana	Nymphaeaceae	Sweet	N. America
Nymphaea froebelii	Nymphaeaceae	Lily	N. America
Nymphaea gladstoniana	Nymphaeaceae	Sweet	N. America
Nymphaea odorata	Nymphaeaceae	Sweet	N. America
Nymphaea stellata coerulea	Nymphaeaceae	Hyacinth	N. America
Nymphaea virginale	Nymphaeaceae	Sweet	Egypt
Nymphaea zanzibariensis	Nymphaeaceae	Lily	Tropical Africa

APPENDIX O

Plants with Scented Fruits

Plant	Family	Scent	Habitat
Atherosperma moschata	Athero-spermataceae	Nutmeg	Chile
Caryophyllus aromaticus	Caryophyllaceae	Clove	Moluccas
Drimys winteri	Magnoliaceae	Aromatic	S. America
Gaultheria shallon	Ericaceae	Aromatic	N. America
Helianthus annuus	Compositae	Turpentine	Peru
Illicium floridanum	Magnoliaceae	Aniseed	Florida
Illicium griffithii	Magnoliaceae	Bitter	E. Bengal
Illicium majus	Magnoliaceae	Aromatic	Malaya
Illicium religiosum	Magnoliaceae	Incense	Japan
Juniperum species	Cupressaceae	Balsamic	N. Hemisphere
Laurus nobilis	Lauraceae	Aromatic	S. Europe
Ligusticum ajowan	Umbelliferae	Thyme	Persia, Afghanistan
Monodora myristica	Anonaceae	Nutmeg	Africa, Jamaica
Myrica californica	Myricaceae	Balsamic	California
Myrica cerifera	Myricaceae	Resinous	N. USA
Myristica argentea	Myristicaceae	Balsamic	Tropics
Myristica fragrans	Myristicaceae	Nutmeg	Indonesia
Podocarpus andinus	Podocarpaceae	Fragrant	S.E. Asia, Australasia
Psidium arach	Myrtaceae	Nutmeg	Guyana
Psidium guaviroba	Myrtaceae	Aromatic	Brazil
Psidium montanum	Myrtaceae	Almonds	Jamaica
Sassafras officinale	Lauraceae	Aromatic	USA, Canada
Vitex agnus-castus	Verbenaceae	Lemon	S. Europe
Ximenia elliptica	Oleaceae	Almonds	Fiji
Zanthoxylum americanum	Rutaceae	Resinous	N.E. America
Zanthoxylum piperitum	Rutaceae	Aromatic	Japan

APPENDIX P

Plants with Scented Roots

Plant	Family	Scent	Habitat
Acorus calamus	Araceae	Camphor	British Isles
Agrimonia eupatoria	Rosaceae	Fruit	British Isles
Agrimonia odorata	Rosaceae	Resinous	British Isles
Allium cepa	Liliaceae	Onion	Asia
Allium sativum	Liliaceae	Onion	S. Europe
Allium ursinum	Liliaceae	Sulphur	British Isles
Alpinia officinarum	Zingiberaceae	Ginger	China
Alpinia sessilis	Zingiberaceae	Aromatic	Bengal
Anthriscus cerefolium	Umbelliferae	Aniseed	N. Hemisphere
Aplotaxus lappa	Compositae	Violet	Himalayas
Apium graveolens	Umbelliferae	Celery	N. Hemisphere
Asarum canadense	Aristolochiaceae	Ginger	N. America
Calycanthus floridus	Calycanthaceae	Camphor	America
Carum carvi	Umbelliferae	Pårsnip	N. Hemisphere
Curcuma rubescens	Zingiberaceae	Aromatic	Bengal
Curcuma viridiflora	Zingiberaceae	Camphor	Sumatra
Curcuma zedoaria	Zingiberaceae	Camphor	S.E. Asia
Curcuma zerumbet	Zingiberaceae	Camphor	E. India
Daucus carota	Umbelliferae	Sweet	N. Hemisphere
Dryobalanops aromatica	Dipterocarpaceae	Camphor	Borneo, China
Eryngium maritimum	Umbelliferae	Parsnip	British Isles
Geum rivale	Rosaceae	Beer	N. Hemisphere
Geum urbanum	Rosaceae	Clove	N. Hemisphere
Glycyrrhiza glabra	Leguminosae	Liquorice	Spain
Hedychium spicatum	Zingiberaceae	Violet	Punjab, Nepal
Inula helenium	Compositae	Violet	British Isles
Inula odora	Compositae	Aromatic	British Isles
Iris florentina	Iridaceae	Violet	S. Europe
Iris pallida	Iridaceae	Violet	British Isles
Laurus sassafras	Lauraceae	Cinnamon	USA
Meum athamanticum	Umbelliferae	Hay-like	British Isles
Pavetta bourbonica	Rubiaceae	Aromatic	Isle of Bourbon
Pavetta idica	Rubiaceae	Aromatic	India
Peucedanum sativum	Umbelliferae	Pungent	N. Hemisphere
Sassafras officinale	Lauraceae	Cinnamon	USA, Canada
Sedum roseum	Crassulaceae	Rose	British Isles
Taraxacum officinale	Compositae	Coffee	N. Hemisphere
Valeriana celtica	Valerianaceae	Camomile	Swiss Alps
Valeriana dioscoridis	Valerianaceae	Aromatic	Balkans

Plant	Family	Scent	Habitat
Valeriana jatamansi	Valerianaceae	Patchouli	Sikkim
Valeriana saxatilis	Valerianaceae	Sweet	Swiss Alps
Valeriana spica	Valerianaceae	Patchouli	Himalayas
Vetiveria zizanioides	Gramineae	Violet	India
Zingiber officinalis	Zingiberaceae	Ginger	Tropics

APPENDIX Q

Trees and Shrubs with Scented Wood

Plant	Family	Scent	Habitat
Betula lenta	Betulaceae	Russian leather	N. America
Boswellia serrata	Burseraceae	Lemon	Yemen, India
Camphorosma monspeliaca	Chenopodiaceae	Camphor	S. Europe
Doryphora sassafras	Athero-spermataceae	Balsam	Australia
Dryobalanops aromatica	Dipterocarpaceae	Camphor	Borneo, Japan
Juniperus thurifera	Cupressaceae	Olibanum	S. Europe
Juniperus virginiana	Cupressaceae	Violets	N. America
Myrica gale	Myricaceae	Lemon	British Isles
Tarchononthus camphoratus	Compositae	Camphor	S. Africa
Veronica cupressoides	Scrophulariaceae	Violet	New Zealand
Ximenia americana	Oleaceae	Sandalwood	India, Tropics
Ximenia aegyptiaca	Oleaceae	Sandalwood	Egypt, E. Africa
Ximenia elliptica	Oleaceae	Rosemary	Fiji

APPENDIX R

Trees and Shrubs
with Scented Gums

Plant	Family	Scent	Habitat
Abies grandis	Pinaceae	Balsamic	N. America
Amyris punctata	Lauraceae	Lemon	Asia Minor
Boswellia serrata	Burseraceae	Lemon	Yemen, India
Canarium commune	Burseraceae	Fennel	Philippines
Canarium edule	Burseraceae	Verbena	Philippines
Canarium mulleri	Burseraceae	Lemon	Philippines
Cistus aquilari	Cistaceae	Balsamic	S.E. Europe
Cistus creticus	Cistaceae	Balsamic	S.E. Europe
Cistus cyprius	Cistaceae	Balsamic	Cyprus
Cistus monspeliensis	Cistaceae	Balsamic	S. Europe
Cistus ladaniferus	Cistaceae	Balsamic	Portugal
Cistus laurifolius	Cistaceae	Balsamic	S.W. Europe
Cistus parviflorus	Cistaceae	Balsamic	Crete
Cistus populifolius	Cistaceae	Balsamic	S.W. Europe
Cistus skanbergii	Cistaceae	Cedarwood	S.W. Europe
Cistus villosus	Cistaceae	Balsamic	S.W. Europe
Commiphora myrrha	Burseraceae	Balsamic	Arabia, W. India
Dryobalanops aromatica	Dipterocarpaceae	Camphor	Borneo, Japan
Gardenia arborea	Rubiaceae	Balsamic	East Indies
Gardenia gummifera	Rubiaceae	Balsamic	Ceylon
Gardenia lucinda	Rubiaceae	Balsamic	Luzon
Pistacia lentiscus	Anacardiaceae	Benzoin	Chios
Pistacia terebinthus	Anacardiaceae	Turpentine	Cyprus
Pittosporum tenuifolium	Pittosporaceae	Violet	New Zealand

APPENDIX S

Scented Cacti and Succulents

Plant	Family	Scent	Habitat
Astrophytum myriostigma	Cactaceae	Violet-like	Mexico
Crassula coccinea	Crassulaceae	Pear-drop	S. Africa
Crassula jasminea	Crassulaceae	Jasmine	S. Africa
Crassula lactea	Crassulaceae	Slight	S. Africa
Echinocereus luteus	Cactaceae	Sweet	Mexico
Echinopsis eyriesii	Cactaceae	Vanilla	Brazil
Echinopsis viliana	Cactaceae	Jonquil	C. America
Glottiphyllum fragrans	Aizoaceae	Vanilla-like	S. Africa
Mammillaria camptotricha	Cactaceae	Honey	Mexico
Narrisia regelii	Cactaceae	Jonquil	S. America, W. Indies
Nyctocereus serpentinus	Cactaceae	Musk	Mexico
Selenicereus grandiflorus	Cactaceae	Vanilla	Mexico, West Indies

APPENDIX T

Plants bearing Flowers or Leaves* of Unpleasant Smell

Plant	Family	Scent	Habitat
Aethusa cynapium	Umbelliferae	Hemlock	British Isles
*Ajuga chamaepitys	Labiatae	Fur-like	British Isles
Amorphophallus titanum	Araceae	Fetid	Sumatra
*Anagyris foetida	Leguminosae	Rancid	S. Europe
*Anthemis cotula	Compositae	Fur-like	N. Europe
Asarum canadense	Aristolochiaceae	Fetid	N. America
Aristolochia clematitis	Aristolochiaceae	Fetid	N. Europe
Aristolochia elegans	Aristolochiaceae	Putrid	Brazil
Aristolochia sipho	Aristolochiaceae	Manure	N. America
Arum crititum	Araceae	Nauseating	Corsica
Arum maculatum	Araceae	Urinous	British Isles
*Ballota nigra	Labiatae	Perspiration	N. Europe
Ceropegia sandersoni	Asclepiadaceae	Putrid	S. Africa
*Chenopodium vulvularia	Chenopodiaceae	Fetid	British Isles
Chrysanthemum leucanthemum	Compositae	Perspiration	British Isles
*Cimicifuga elata	Ranunculaceae	Fetid	N. Hemisphere
Cimicifuga foetida	Ranunculaceae	Putrid	N. Europe
Codonopsis ovata	Campanulaceae	Fur-like	Himalayas
*Conium maculatum	Umbelliferae	Nauseating	N. Europe
Cotoneaster acuminata	Rosaceae	Fetid	Himalayas
Cotoneaster bacillaris	Rosaceae	Fetid	Himalayas
Cotoneaster cornubia	Rosaceae	Sickly	Hybrid
Cotoneaster frigida	Rosaceae	Fetid	Himalayas
Cotoneaster watereri	Rosaceae	Fishy	Hybrid
Dracunculus vulgaris	Araceae	Fetid	S. Europe
*Erysimum alliaria	Cruciferae	Garlic	British Isles
Ferula communis	Umbelliferae	Rancid	S. Europe
Ferula glauca	Umbelliferae	Fetid	S. Europe
Fritillaria imperialis	Liliaceae	Foxy	Persia
*Helleborus foetidus	Ranunculaceae	Putrid	British Isles
Hyoscyamus niger	Solanaceae	Fishy	N. Europe
Lysichitum americanum	Araceae	Skunk	N. America
Lysichitum camtschatense	Araceae	Animal	S. America
*Mercurialis perennis	Euphorbiaceae	Fetid	British Isles
*Oxytropis foetida	Compositae	Fetid	S. France
Paris quadrifolia	Liliaceae	Putrid	British Isles
*Peltaria alliacea	Cruciferae	Garlic	S.E. Europe
Primula viscosa	Primulaceae	Fetid	Pyrenees

Plant	Family	Scent	Habitat
Rafflesia arnoldii	Rafflesiaceae	Putrid	Malaya
Sambucus ebulus	Caprifoliaceae	Fur-like	British Isles
Silaus flavescens	Umbelliferae	Sulphur	British Isles
Sison amomum	Umbelliferae	Petrol	British Isles
*Smilax herbacea	Liliaceae	Putrid	N. America
*Stachys arvensis	Labiatae	Stale lint	British Isles
*Stachys palustris	Labiatae	Stale lint	British Isles
*Stachys sylvatica	Labiatae	Stale lint	British Isles
Stapelia flavirostris	Asclepiadaceae	Putrid	S. Africa
Stapelia nobilis	Asclepiadaceae	Putrid	S. Africa
Stapelia variegata	Asclepiadaceae	Putrid	S. Africa
*Thalictrum foetidum	Ranunculaceae	Putrid	N. Hemisphere
Trillium erectum	Liliaceae	Putrid	N. America

Bibliography

Title	Author	Year and publisher
Aromatics and the Soul	McKenzie	1890 Heinemann
Book of Perfumes, The	Rimmel	1863 Chapman & Hall
British Flora, The	Bentham & Hooker	1886 Reeve & Co.
Classification of Flowering Plants	Rendle	1925 C.U.P.
Dictionary of Flowering Plants and Ferns	Willis	1897 C.U.P.
English Flower Garden, The	Robinson	1883 John Murray
Fertilisation of Flowers, The	H. Muller	1883 Macmillan
Flora of the British Isles	Clapham, Tutin & Warburg	1953 C.U.P.
Flora of the Cape Peninsula	Adamson & Salter	1950 Juta & Co.
Flora Odorata	Mott	1843 Orr & Co.
Flowers of the Field	Johns	1908 Routledge
Herbal Simples	Fernie	1896 John Wright
Herbs for Health & Beauty	Genders	1975 Robert Hale
History of Scent, A	Genders	1972 Hamish Hamilton
Mystery and Lure of Perfume	Thompson	1927 John Lane
Odorographia	Sawyer	1890 Gurney & Jackson
Piesse's Art of Perfumery	Piesse	1880 Piesse & Lubin
Plants of the Bible	Moldenke	1952 Ronald Press
Plants of New Zealand	Laing & Blackwell	1907 Whitcombe & Tombs
Scented Garden, The	Rohde	1931 Medici Society
Scent of Flowers & Leaves, The	Hampton	1925 Dulau
Scented Wild Flowers of Britain, The	Genders	1971 Collins
Students Flora of Egypt	Tackholm	1956 Anglo-Egyptian Books
Sweet Scented Flowers and Leaves	McDonald	1895 Sampson Low

Index